MCSE
Windows® XP Professional

FOR
DUMMIES®

by Glenn Weadock

Hungry Minds™

Best-Selling Books • Digital Downloads • e-Books • Answer Networks • e-Newsletters • Branded Web Sites • e-Learning

New York, NY ◆ Cleveland, OH ◆ Indianapolis, IN

MCSE Windows® XP Professional For Dummies®

Published by
Hungry Minds, Inc.
909 Third Avenue
New York, NY 10022
www.hungryminds.com
www.dummies.com

Library of Congress Control Number: 2001099318

ISBN: 0-7645-1631-0

Printed in the United States of America

10 9 8 7 6 5 4 3 2 1

1B/QW/QS/QS/IN

Distributed in the United States by Hungry Minds, Inc.

Distributed by CDG Books Canada Inc. for Canada; by Transworld Publishers Limited in the United Kingdom; by IDG Norge Books for Norway; by IDG Sweden Books for Sweden; by IDG Books Australia Publishing Corporation Pty. Ltd. for Australia and New Zealand; by TransQuest Publishers Pte Ltd. for Singapore, Malaysia, Thailand, Indonesia, and Hong Kong; by Gotop Information Inc. for Taiwan; by ICG Muse, Inc. for Japan; by Intersoft for South Africa; by Eyrolles for France; by International Thomson Publishing for Germany, Austria and Switzerland; by Distribuidora Cuspide for Argentina; by LR International for Brazil; by Galileo Libros for Chile; by Ediciones ZETA S.C.R. Ltda. for Peru; by WS Computer Publishing Corporation, Inc., for the Philippines; by Contemporanea de Ediciones for Venezuela; by Express Computer Distributors for the Caribbean and West Indies; by Micronesia Media Distributor, Inc. for Micronesia; by Chips Computadoras S.A. de C.V. for Mexico; by Editorial Norma de Panama S.A. for Panama; by American Bookshops for Finland.

For general information on Hungry Minds' products and services please contact our Customer Care Department within the U.S. at 800-762-2974, outside the U.S. at 317-572-3993 or fax 317-572-4002.

For sales inquiries and reseller information, including discounts, premium and bulk quantity sales, and foreign-language translations, please contact our Customer Care Department at 800-434-3422, fax 317-572-4002, or write to Hungry Minds, Inc., Attn: Customer Care Department, 10475 Crosspoint Boulevard, Indianapolis, IN 46256.

For information on licensing foreign or domestic rights, please contact our Sub-Rights Customer Care Department at 212-884-5000.

For information on using Hungry Minds' products and services in the classroom or for ordering examination copies, please contact our Educational Sales Department at 800-434-2086 or fax 317-572-4005.

For press review copies, author interviews, or other publicity information, please contact our Public Relations Department at 317-572-3168 or fax 317-572-4168.

For authorization to photocopy items for corporate, personal, or educational use, please contact Copyright Clearance Center, 222 Rosewood Drive, Danvers, MA 01923, or fax 978-750-4470.

Hungry Minds is a trademark of Hungry Minds, Inc.

About the Author

Glenn Weadock is president of Independent Software, Inc., a consulting firm he founded in 1982 after graduating from Stanford University's engineering school. One of the country's most popular technical trainers, Glenn has taught Windows to thousands of students in the United States, United Kingdom, and Canada in more than 190 seminars since 1988. He has written many intensive two-day seminars, including The Windows 2000 Registry and Supporting and Troubleshooting Windows 2000, and has written and presented several computer videos.

Glenn is the author of fourteen computer books, including *MCSE Windows 2000 Professional For Dummies, MCSE Windows 2000 Network Infrastructure For Dummies, Small Business Networking For Dummies* and *Look & Learn Dreamweaver 4*. He is a member of the Association for Computing Machinery and the American Society for Training and Development. He served as an expert witness in the Microsoft antitrust trial and was actually on CNN for about two seconds.

Dedication

To my brother Jeff.

Author's Acknowledgments

Thanks to Emily, Carina, and Cecily for supporting an author's life; to my literary agent, Mike Snell; at Hungry Minds, to everyone who contributed time and effort to this project, especially Jill Byus Schorr, Paul Levesque, and Andy Cummings; to my technical editor, Jim Kelly; to Jeff Durham for his work on the CD; and to Megan Kahn at Waggener-Edstrom, for assistance with research materials.

Publisher's Acknowledgments

We're proud of this book; please send us your comments through our Hungry Minds Online Registration Form located at www.dummies.com.

Some of the people who helped bring this book to market include the following:

Acquisitions, Editorial, and Media Development

Project Editor: Paul Levesque

Acquisitions Editor: Jill Byus Schorr

Copy Editor: Nicole Laux

Technical Editor: Jim Kelly

Editorial Manager: Constance Carlisle

Permissions Editor: Laura Moss

Media Development Specialist: Megan Decraene

Media Development Manager: Laura VanWinkle

Media Development Supervisor: Richard Graves

Editorial Assistant: Amanda Foxworth

Production

Project Coordinator: Dale White

Layout and Graphics: Joyce Haughey, Jackie Nicholas, Julie Trippetti, Jeremey Unger, Erin Zeltner

Proofreaders: Laura Albert, Andy Hollandbeck, Angel Perez, Marianne Santy, TECHBOOKS Production Services

Indexer: TECHBOOKS Production Services

General and Administrative

Hungry Minds Technology Publishing Group: Richard Swadley, Senior Vice President and Publisher; Mary Bednarek, Vice President and Publisher, Networking; Joseph Wikert, Vice President and Publisher, Web Development Group; Mary C. Corder, Editorial Director, Dummies Technology; Andy Cummings, Publishing Director, Dummies Technology; Barry Pruett, Publishing Director, Visual/Graphic Design

Hungry Minds Manufacturing: Ivor Parker, Vice President, Manufacturing

Hungry Minds Marketing: John Helmus, Assistant Vice President, Director of Marketing

Hungry Minds Production for Branded Press: Debbie Stailey, Production Director

Hungry Minds Sales: Michael Violano, Vice President, International Sales and Sub Rights

Contents at a Glance

Cartoons at a Glance

By Rich Tennant

"You know, this was a situation question on my Windows XP exam, but I always thought it was just hypothetical."

page 9

"I couldn't get this 'job skills' program to work on my PC, so I replaced the mother-board, upgraded the BIOS and wrote a program that links it to my personal database. It told me I wasn't technically inclined and should pursue a career in sales."

page 223

"We sort of have our own way of mentally preparing our people to take the Windows XP exam."

page 45

"Remember — I want the bleeding file server surrounded by flaming workstations with the word 'Motherboard' scrolling underneath."

page 337

"Sales on the Web site are down. I figure the servers chi is blocked, so we're fudgin' around the Feng Shui in the computer room, and if that doesn't work, Ronnie's got a cure that should do it."

page 393

"It appears a server in Atlanta is about to go down, there's printer backup in Baltimore and an accountant in Chicago is about to make level 3 of the game, 'Tomb Pirate'."

page 407

Before installing Windows XP, Dwayne prepares to partition the hard drive.

page 145

Cartoon Information:
Fax: 978-546-7747
E-Mail: richtennant@the5thwave.com
World Wide Web: www.the5thwave.com

Table of Contents

Introduction

●●●

*Y*ou hold in your hands a quick, no-nonsense guide to passing the Windows XP Professional MCP/MCSE test. This introduction covers the book's purpose, style, and organization, and describes the icons I use to guide you through the text.

About This Book

One of the many ways in which the computer industry shows its relative youth is the lack of an organized system of credentials for technical professionals. This situation makes life needlessly difficult for managers and job seekers alike. Managers have a hard time qualifying job applicants, and applicants have a hard time explaining just what it is that they know without getting overly technical.

Manager: So, Andy, tell me, what are your areas of computer knowledge?

Applicant (hesitating): Well, I'm mainly into TCP/IP, DHCP, DNS, HTML, DHTML, XML, and C++. That is, recently.

Manager (confused): I see. Well, well, that all sounds fine. But do you know anything about networking, Web design, or programming?

For businesses looking to hire technical consultants, the problems are similar. As the computer business grows exponentially in importance with each passing year, the need for some system of credentials has increased dramatically. In typical fashion, the computer industry has utterly failed to get together on a single, industry-wide certification program for software expertise, so the larger individual vendors (most notably Microsoft, Novell, and Cisco) offer their own programs.

Many certifications now exist for computer professionals, such as the Certified NetWare Engineer (CNE) from Novell and the A+ designation for hardware technicians. As Microsoft has increased its dominance on the desktop and has made inroads in the server market, the MCSE (Microsoft Certified Systems Engineer) certification has grown in importance, making it the most desired professional certification in today's PC industry.

"Installing, Configuring, and Administering Microsoft Windows XP Professional," that is, Exam #70-270, is one of the core exams in the Windows XP/2000 track that computer professionals can pursue towards obtaining MCSE certification. Exam #70-270 also conveys the somewhat less exalted certification of MCP, or Microsoft Certified Professional. For those who want to put three letters after their names instead of four and if you already use Windows XP at home or at work, this is the test to take.

Whatever your particular goal, *MCSE Windows XP Professional For Dummies* is the only book you need to pass the test.

What this book is

This book's goal is simply to help you pass the Windows XP Professional certification test while investing as little study time as possible. (Time is of the essence; pass this test, and you've got six more to go to get your MCSE.) As a result, this book isn't as chatty as other *For Dummies* books you may have read. The style is get-to-the-point. Although I do throw in the occasional zinger or chuckle to enliven the (we may as well admit it) often-dry material, the jokes stay out of your way.

Also because of the time factor, I personally don't like the approach in which you first read a 1500-page tome covering the material (much of it irrelevant) in excruciating detail, then also buy and read and learn by rote a 200-page collection of bullet items to use for "cramming" right before the exam. That approach is inefficient if your primary goal is to get certified, although book publishers love it because they get to sell twice as many books.

MCSE Windows XP Professional For Dummies does three things:

- ✔ It gives you enough technical explanation so that you can understand the various key technology concepts.
- ✔ It gives you enough sample questions in each chapter so that you can assess your own readiness and identify areas that need more work.
- ✔ It lets you do some "cramming" right before the test by providing practice tests in print and hundreds of sample questions on the enclosed CD.

Feel free to consult other books to supplement this one if you want to increase your odds still further, or if you need to know more about Windows XP Professional than the exam covers. But if your goal is to pass the exam in the minimum time and with minimum effort, this book is designed to be your primary resource.

Most of you know by now that the *For Dummies* series has grown beyond introducing computer basics to rank novices. Titles like the one you now have in front of you are clearly designed for a professional readership. How can that make sense? Simple. The hallmarks of the *For Dummies* book series are clear writing, good organization, lighthearted irreverence, respect for the reader, and value for the dollar. Those are important attributes for a test-prep book.

I've added to the mix the same commitment to accuracy that gained my earlier books, *MCSE Windows 2000 Professional For Dummies*, *MCSE Windows 2000 Network Infrastructure For Dummies*, and *MCSE Windows 98 For Dummies*, wide recognition as the most error-free books available on those exams. I built a test network of four PCs running various versions of Windows, including Windows XP Professional, Windows 2000 Professional, and Windows 2000 Server, so that I could test everything in this book against reality.

So, your friends may rib you about buying one of these yellow-and-black titles, but let me encourage you to zing them back when you get your MCSE many weeks (and dollars) before they do.

I've tried to make this the book about the Windows XP Professional test that I'd want if I were preparing to take it. I hope you'll tell me how you like this book, and how I can make it better for the next edition. You can reach me through my company's Web site, which is at www.i-sw.com.

What this book isn't

First off, this book isn't a "preview" based on someone's guess about what the test will look like (or on beta software code). This book is based on Microsoft's published objectives list and on multiple takings of the exam by yours truly. Also, it is based on "golden code" — I'm writing this on a PC running the commercial version of Windows XP Professional. This fact means that the publisher and I aren't putting out the first book to market on this particular subject, but we won't rush a product like this out the door unless we're confident that it's as relevant and accurate as it needs to be.

This book also isn't an encyclopedia of Windows XP Professional information. It only contains stuff that I think you'll need to know on the exam. Therefore, this book is not, or at least should not be, your last stop on the way to Windows XP mastery. Passing the test is the first milestone en route to Windows XP guru-hood, not the last. You'll need to read other materials, work (and experiment) with the product, and converse with other Windows XP experts (for example, on public Internet newsgroups) to gain true practical expertise. This book isn't a rehash of a text on the Windows NT 4.0 Workstation exam. Windows XP is similar to Windows NT 4.0 Workstation in many ways, but Windows XP has lots of new stuff in it, including a healthy dollop of Windows Me technology. I wrote this book from the ground up to be 100 percent specific to Windows XP.

Finally, this book is not a guarantee. If you read it carefully, you should pass the first time you take the test. If you don't, you may not. I can't control whether you study this book earnestly and seriously, or out of the corner of your eye while you're watching *Attack of the Killer Mutant Ninja Hamsters*. I *can* try to do a good job presenting the material you'll need to know in a clear and concise way, and that's been my goal.

Who you are

MCSE Windows XP Professional For Dummies is for actual or aspiring computer professionals. I don't make a lot of assumptions in these pages about you or your business, but the few assumptions I do make are as follows:

- ✔ You have some prior experience with computers, and you've logged some hours in the air flying Windows Me, 98, or NT 4.0.

- ✔ You have better things to do than to read a thousand-page epic on the Windows XP certification test.

- ✔ You want to pass the certification test on the first try.

- ✔ You haven't bought *MCSE Windows 2000 Professional For Dummies,* which covers a lot of the same ground as this book. If you take the Windows 2000 Professional exam, there's no reason to take the Windows XP Professional exam also.

- ✔ You'd like to pick up some tips in the course of studying for the exam that you'll actually be able to use in real life, after you get a cool job with the help of your MCP or MCSE status.

If this sounds like you, read on!

Who I am

The value of any book depends on the experience of the author, so you should want to know just who the heck is writing this book. I've run a computer consulting business, Independent Software, Inc., since 1982, and I've been a seminar developer and instructor since 1988. As a consultant, I normally work with large organizations on rolling out and supporting Windows technologies, although for a change of pace I provided consulting services and testimony in the Microsoft antitrust trial for about a year. My seminars target the professional technical market, and have included intensive two-day courses on Windows 3.0, 3.1, 95, 98, 2000, and (now) XP.

An MCSE myself, I've taken more Microsoft exams than I care to remember. I've received MCP status for all versions of Windows since 3.1, and I've also passed various weird limited-time Microsoft tests, such as "Windows 95 Migration Specialist." In addition, I've been a Windows 2000 and Windows XP beta tester.

I've written a few other books on Windows before this one. *Windows 2000 Registry For Dummies*, *Windows 98 Registry For Dummies*, and *Windows 95 Registry For Dummies* make the inscrutable Registry database at least moderately scrutable. And you may be interested in *MCSE Windows 2000 Network Infrastructure For Dummies*, which covers another core exam.

How This Book Is Organized

Microsoft publishes a list of *objectives*, or *skills*, for each test in the MCSE series. (See www.microsoft.com/trainingandservices/default.asp and navigate to the MCSE program pages. I'd provide a direct link, but it changes too often!) I've designed this book to follow that list. (In a few cases, I've juggled topics so they fit where they make a bit more sense, and in other cases, I've added material that doesn't appear on the objective list but that shows up on the exam.)

As with most *For Dummies* books, you can dip in and out of specific chapters according to where you are in your studies and what level of knowledge you already have about particular subjects. You can certainly read this book cover to cover, but each chapter is designed to give you all the information you need on a specific topic and not leave you hanging if you haven't read the entire book up to that point.

Part I: The Backdrop

In Part I, I answer the following burning questions: 1) What's the Windows XP Professional test all about? and 2) What are the basics of Windows XP Professional that you must know to profitably study the rest of the book? I recommend that everyone read Chapter 1. If you already have a fair amount of hands-on experience with Windows XP Professional, skim Chapter 2, and if you see anything that looks new or unfamiliar, read it.

Part II: Planning, Installation, and Basic Configuration

Part II is where you should start if you have to take the test tomorrow and you plan to read all night to get ready. (Not the recommended strategy, by the way.) Chapter 3 deals with file systems: FAT, FAT32, and NTFS. Chapter 4 covers the actual installation, automation options, uninstall procedures, and dual-boot setups. Chapter 5 covers language, localization, and desktop setup issues. Chapter 6 deals with networking protocols, with a decided emphasis on TCP/IP.

Part III: Installing and Configuring Hardware

Windows XP Professional brings many new hardware-related features to the table (oops, I mean "desktop"), so Part III looks at them in the detail you'll need. Chapter 7 deals with disks, tapes, and printers. Chapter 8 covers displays and other input/output devices. Chapter 9 focuses on portable computing hardware, including power management and wireless communications.

Part IV: Configuring and Managing Resource Access

In Part IV, I walk you through the essentials of using Windows XP to control resource access in a network. Chapter 10 covers resource access on the local machine, exploring concepts of users and groups. Chapter 11 explores the various access restrictions that you can apply to shared folders and NTFS disks, and shows how to share and monitor resources. Chapter 12 examines the core concepts of "IntelliMirror" the Registry, user profiles, offline folders, and the Windows Installer service. And Chapter 13 covers resource access via the special case of Dial-Up Networking.

Part V: Tuning and Troubleshooting Windows XP

Part V shows you, in Chapter 14, how to monitor Windows XP's performance using the built-in tools — and how to optimize that performance. Chapter 15 covers the key troubleshooting techniques you'll need to correct the more common Windows XP problems, and discusses the various methods for recovering a Windows XP system that has become damaged.

Part VI: The Part of Tens

The Part of Tens is a standard feature of *For Dummies* books, and this one is no different. Chapter 16 offers ten test-taking tips that have nothing to do with Windows XP but everything to do with passing the exam.

Part VII: Appendixes

The first appendix is a practice test that you can take shortly before the actual exam, to refresh the main points, fill in any gaps in your knowledge, and get you comfortable with the probable format of the actual test questions. The last is a description of the software goodies on the enclosed CD-ROM.

Chapter Structure

You may be familiar with other books in the *For Dummies* series, but the MCSE books share some design features that don't appear in non-MCSE titles. You'll appreciate their usefulness as you work your way through the chapters, but here's a capsule description of those features.

Page One

The first page of each chapter presents the exam objectives that I cover in the chapter, along with a brief two- or three-paragraph introduction to the subject matter. If you're in a major hurry, you can use each chapter's first page to focus your attention on the subjects you know least well, and skip chapters covering material you already know.

Quick Assessment

Immediately after the first page is a quick assessment test covering the exam objectives for that chapter. If you get every question right, you may not even need to read the chapter; you should jump to the end and take the "Prep Test." If you miss a few of the quick assessment questions, which is the more normal scenario, you can flag the chapter sections that you should focus on with particular zeal. Little "sticky notes" appear next to the quick assessment questions to help you match the questions with their associated objectives.

Labs, tables, and graphics

Throughout the main part of each chapter are various labs, tables, and graphics to help you study. *Labs* are simply sequences of numbered steps that you can perform on an actual Windows XP PC (assuming you have access to one) in order to grasp a subject more fully. *Tables* are columnar lists of information that would be awkward if presented in paragraph form. *Graphics* are either screen snapshots of actual Windows XP systems or line drawings that illustrate specific points. These features aren't unique to MCSE books, but they are used a bit more heavily here than in other titles.

Prep Test

Each chapter of exam material ends with a "prep test" that is designed to look and feel like a chunk of the actual exam. Of course, there's no guarantee that the prep test questions will actually appear on the test, but they're great for double-checking that you really understand the chapter material. They also have value in preparing you for the format of questions that Microsoft likes to use in the real test.

Icons Used in This Book

Several graphical icons highlight certain kinds of material:

Use this icon to avoid a *gotcha* — a common trap or pitfall, either in test-taking technique or in understanding some aspect of Windows XP.

These are tips to save you time when preparing for, or actually taking, the certification exam.

This icon points out a bit of knowledge that's worth committing to your long-term memory because it's likely to appear in the test.

Short suggestions, hints, and bits of useful information appear next to this icon.

Add this fact to your vocabulary . . . or else!

That's it for this Introduction. Stand up, stretch, pour yourself a cup of tea, and come back when you're ready to start prepping for a successful exam.

Part I
The Backdrop

The 5th Wave   By Rich Tennant

"You know, this was a situation question on my Windows XP exam, but I always thought it was just hypothetical."

In this part . . .

You may have never taken a Microsoft certification exam before. You may have never studied Windows XP Professional in detail before. In either case, this part's for you. This part may also be for you if you could use a refresher on exam procedure or on Windows XP itself.

Every Dummies book is what editors like to call a "non-linear" read; that is, you can dip in and out of different sections as needed, when needed (sort of a literary salad bar). This part is a little bit of an exception. You really should read it, or at least skim over it, before diving into the rest of the book.

Chapter 1 goes over the look and feel of MCSE exams so you have a good sense of what to expect when you walk into that testing room. This chapter also presents Microsoft's objective map for exam #70-270, cross-referenced to chapters in this book. Chapter 2 is a technology primer that outlines key features of the operating system.

Chapter 1

The Windows XP Professional Test

....

In This Chapter

▶ Finding out how the Windows XP Professional test fits into the Microsoft certification scheme

▶ Getting familiar with testing procedures

▶ Understanding the test's style and format

▶ Discovering the list of skills Microsoft says you need to know to pass the test

▶ Picking up a few hints about test taking

....

Microsoft Exam #70-270, which has the catchy name *Installing, Configuring, and Administering Microsoft Windows XP Professional*, helps fulfill certification requirements for the following credentials:

✔ Microsoft Certified Professional

✔ Microsoft Certified Trainer

✔ Microsoft Certified System Engineer

You can read a lot more detail on these (and other) Microsoft certification programs at www.microsoft.com. For now, just know that by passing this test, you not only gain the right to add the MCP certification to your résumé, you also pass a core requirement of the MCSE certification's Windows XP/2000 track.

 You must take either Exam #70-270 (the one this book's about) or 70-210 (the analogous test for Windows 2000 Professional) to achieve Windows XP/2000 MCSE status, and the Windows 95, 98, and NT Workstation exams don't count for anything toward your Windows XP/2000 MCSE. This is a change from the NT track, which permitted a choice: You could take a test on Windows 95, Windows 98, or NT Workstation 4.0 to fulfill the workstation exam requirement. That isn't true for the Windows XP/2000 track.

Is the Windows XP Professional exam the only one you want to take? If an MCP is good enough for your needs, 99 percent of this book remains relevant for you despite the "MCSE" in the title. Your MCP designation will remain in force longer into the future if you achieve it with the Windows XP Professional exam as opposed to the Windows 98 or Windows NT 4.0 Workstation exams.

If you aspire to MCSE certification, taking the Windows XP exam as your first test makes sense.

- ✔ You may already know Windows XP as a user, so you won't have to start from scratch to know it as a technician.
- ✔ You don't have to know much about some challenging Windows XP/2000 Server topics, such as Active Directory, to pass the Windows XP Professional exam.

Having said that, I'm here to tell you that the Windows XP Professional test is significantly harder than the Windows 98 test, and that one was no piece of cake! So don't take it lightly, even if you do take it first.

About the Exam

When it comes to MCSE exams, you have to master *both* the style and substance aspects of the tests if you hope to pass them. This section lays out the key points in both categories, but first, a few words on procedure.

Procedure

You should know about a few formalities and procedural issues before diving into the exam.

Signing up

Microsoft exams are delivered by two organizations: Sylvan Prometric and Virtual University Enterprises (VUE). The usual procedure is to get in touch with one of these organizations (by phone or Web site) at least one day in advance of the test, make payment arrangements (credit cards are okay), and set up a time and a place. Here's some contact information:

- ✔ **Sylvan Prometric** (www.prometric.com, www.2test.com): 800-755-EXAM (from the U.S. and Canada), 410-843-8000 (from anywhere)
- ✔ **NCS Virtual University Enterprises (VUE)** (www.vue.com/ms): 888-837-8616 (from the U.S. and Canada), 952-995-8800 (from anywhere)

Two things can save you trouble when you take the exam:

- ✔ Provide a zip code or postal code and let the customer representative find the testing location nearest you. The shorter the drive, the fresher you'll be when you walk into the testing center.
- ✔ Call the testing center directly for detailed directions.

Plan to arrive about 15 minutes before test time. At Sylvan Prometric centers, you must normally present two forms of identification, at least one with a photograph on it. You also have to sign a form and a sign-in sheet, which takes a few minutes. However, if you're late, don't fret; depending on how busy the testing center is, you may still be able to slide on in and take your test.

After you sign in, you receive a few sheets of scratch paper and a couple of pencils, and the proctor asks to see your forearms and palms to make sure you haven't made a body part into a human cheat sheet with a Rapidograph technical pen.

Okay, nobody really asks to see your skin. And anyway, scribbling on your epidermis or hiding papers down your pants wouldn't help you because most test sites have TV cameras watching your every move. Don't be offended by this; video monitoring is a good way to ensure that someone else doesn't gain an unfair advantage over you by cheating. And by the way, at the end of the exam you'll have to turn in any paper you take in with you.

Agree or go home

As your session at the testing center starts, you have to agree to a statement written by Microsoft that says things like "I agree not to use my belt-buckle spy camera to make screen shots of this test, which I will then sell on the Internet for big bucks." As an honest, upright citizen, you will most likely click the Agree button and move on. (If you want to actually read the agreement, doing so takes no time off the actual exam clock.)

Easy questions that (alas) don't count

You're likely to see a timed questionnaire before the graded test questions. Your answers provide various marketing data to Microsoft. The meter isn't really running while you fill out this questionnaire because the 15 minutes don't count against the 90 minutes you have for the "real" test. So, you can take your time, but I recommend that you blast through the questionnaire quickly without paying a lot of attention. Save your brain cells for the questions that count.

My personal opinion is that if Microsoft wants marketing data, they should pay you, not the other way around. I normally check box "A" on every answer.

Call for comments

At the end of your exam, after you click the Finish button, you have an opportunity to comment on the test. I always feel that this part is premature; I'd like to know whether I passed before telling Microsoft whether its test is excellent or no darned good. However, you can use this time to talk about specific questions you thought were misleading, unfair, or just plain wrong.

If you do feel strongly about some aspect of the test, then by all means, let your feelings be known. Otherwise, skip this part. You may need to get out of the testing center as quickly as possible, for reasons I explain in a minute.

Signing off

At the end of the test, you find out whether you passed. The two bars at the top of the page indicate the required score and your score.

On some tests, the report breaks down your performance by category, so you can spend a little time reviewing where you did well and where you could have done better. That information may be useful as you study for other exams, if you're en route to your MCSE, or if you need to take the Windows XP test again to pass. If the report doesn't break down your performance by category, and if you failed, then you need to read the next section, "Rerun readiness."

After the test, you can click Exit or Print another report. (One report prints automatically.) Printing one or two extra reports as file copies is a good idea; you can give one to your boss, keep one for your own file, frame another, and so on. You'll most likely have to get the printouts from an administrator after you leave the test center.

Rerun readiness

If you have to take the exam again, increase your odds of success by

1. Leaving the testing center.

2. Heading for the nearest desk and chair.

3. Whipping out a pen and notebook (or notebook computer).

4. Writing down as much as you can remember about the questions you just faced — especially the tough ones.

Do this while the material is still fresh in your mind. You're not likely to see all the same questions again next time, but you're likely to see some of them, and if you make some post-mortem notes, you can focus your study time and increase your odds of passing next time. My technical editor on this book suggests you make a special effort to write down the questions you KNOW you got wrong, and the answers you chose, because the tougher questions tend to appear on retakes.

Style

Knowing something about an exam's design can help get you comfortable with the format in advance, so here are a few words on what you can expect to see after you sign in at the test center.

Microsoft is free to modify the exam format whenever and however it wants. As I write this, the two styles that Microsoft uses are

- ✓ "Classic" multiple choice
- ✓ Adaptive

This section discusses both. Don't make the assumption that the exam is one style or the other, despite what you may see on various MCSE-related Web sites. Microsoft is known to change a test's style midway through its life cycle.

Choose from multiples

The "classic" MCSE test is a closed-book, multiple-choice exam (no bringing your well-worn copy of this book, and no essay questions such as "Describe the probable impact of Windows XP on world history, in 500 words or less"). Computers are well suited for grading multiple-choice tests, and it *is* nice to get your grade right away.

Just because the exam is multiple choice doesn't mean that you can ignore the question format. A common pitfall is giving only one answer when the question calls for multiple answers.

You can usually tell by the graphical element next to the answers:

- ✓ If they're circles (radio buttons), only one answer is right.
- ✓ If they're squares (check boxes), maybe more than one answer is right.

Be very aware whether the question calls for the best answer, two answers, three answers, "all that apply," or whatever the case may be. I recommend marking questions that expect more than one answer for later review (see "Skipping to success" later in this chapter) because of their inherent trickiness. (Bear in mind that if your test is the adaptive type, you can't mark questions for review. See the section "Adapting to adaptive tests" later in this chapter.)

Some of the questions are pretty long, and they sometimes give you more information than you really need. I'm in favor of reading through these long paragraphs once and only once, noting the key facts (and maybe even drawing a picture) on your scratch paper. This way, you won't have to read those long spiels multiple times.

A graphic example

Some of the questions involve a graphical screen, either as part of the question (the screen is called an *exhibit*) or as the way to provide the answer (the screen is called a *simulation*).

When a graphic is an exhibit, don't skip over it! You can click a button at the question's main screen to show the exhibit, but overlooking the button is possible. Most often, the test question exhibits show a simplified network diagram illustrating the hypothetical setup you're being quizzed about.

Consider looking at the exhibit before even reading the question. That way, you already have a mental picture of the question's premise. You can look at the exhibit as often as you want.

When a graphic is the vehicle for *providing* an answer, it's normally a screen shot of a dialog box or property sheet. The cursor turns into a riflesight icon, and you must point and click at the check box(es) or radio button(s) in the dialog box to answer the question. (The inclusion of such dialog boxes and property sheets on the test is one reason I include plenty of screen shots in this book.)

Although no one who can talk about it really knows how accurate you have to be for your answer to register with the test engine, take your time and click right in the middle of the check box or radio button.

No point losing points for poor pointing.

You may also see questions in which you must click one or more computer icons in a network diagram to convey your answer. I've taken some MCSE tests that even ask you to drag-and-drop little graphical boxes saying things like "Application Server" and "Router" onto specific computers in a network diagram. Don't be surprised to see one or two of these drag-and-drop questions on the test.

So, although most of the exam questions and answers don't involve pictures, know how to deal with those that do. By the time you take the test, Microsoft may cook up some other clever graphical exam elements, but at least you'll be aware of the ones in this section, if you encounter them.

Skipping to success

In the classical multiple-choice test style, you can skip any questions you don't immediately understand, and come back to them later. That's actually a good practice. Because your grade in a classical-style test depends solely on the percentage of questions you answer correctly, you need to make sure that you answer as many questions as you can. An unanswered question may as well be wrong; you only get points for questions you answer, and answer correctly.

So, if a question stumps you, or even makes you feel mildly uncertain, go ahead and make your best guess, but "mark" the question for later review by clicking the Mark button on the test screen. Then move on to the next question. After you're done with the first pass through all the questions, you get a review screen that shows the questions you've marked. A click of the mouse takes you back to ponder further on those knotty problems. You may run out of time before you can study all the questions you marked, but at least you're not missing the opportunity to score on questions that you can quickly answer correctly.

If your test uses the classic style, *use every last minute you have coming to you.* You may very well finish in less than the allotted 90 minutes, especially if you've done a great job preparing by studying this book carefully. So apply these rules:

- Take the time to go back and review questions that you marked, especially those asking for multiple answers.

- Look for keywords in the test questions that may offer a clue that you missed on first glance.

- Draw diagrams.

- For questions that you don't understand well, use the process of elimination to improve your odds.

Adapting to adaptive tests

Adaptive, or "hybrid" tests, have two parts:

- A regular, what-percent-did-you-get-right part
- An adaptive part

Unfortunately, you don't necessarily know where the dividing line is between the two parts, so you may have to treat the whole test as if it is adaptive, unless Microsoft gives you some clues in the testing instructions.

Okay — so what does "adaptive" mean? An *adaptive* exam's grades are based on the hardest question you can answer on the subject matter of the test. You encounter a series of questions of increasing difficulty. Each question depends on the previous answer: If you got the previous answer correct, then you get a harder question, but if you got it wrong, then you get an easier question. The questions "adapt" to your answers.

Pace yourself by using the on-screen clock. Adaptive tests don't have as many questions, so you can allow yourself more time per question than on a classic-style test. However, you typically don't know in advance how many questions you'll receive. What I usually do is take the average of the maximum and minimum number of questions (the test tells you this information) and calculate the approximate amount of time I should spend per question using that number.

You don't have the luxury of marking and reviewing questions on an adaptive exam: You have one shot at each question. So the test-taking style is very different indeed from the "classic" test in which your grade depends solely on the percentage of questions you answer correctly. Here are two suggestions for taking an adaptive test:

   ✔ Go slowly and carefully.

   ✔ Do your best on each question, skipping none of them.

Substance

This section deals in more detail with exam content. First, I present the formal Microsoft test objectives, then I offer a few subjective comments.

Testing by objectives

When the "real" part of the test begins, you deal with exam questions designed to test your knowledge in a wide variety of areas. Microsoft publishes objectives, or "skill areas," for each MCP exam on its Web site under `www.microsoft.com/mcp`. (These objectives appear elsewhere, too, sometimes in somewhat different form, as in the *Microsoft Windows XP Professional MCSE Training Kit,* which you don't need to buy now that you have this book.) In the following sections, I provide Microsoft's objective list for the Windows XP Professional exam at this writing, along with a cross-reference to the relevant chapter in this book.

This book's organization doesn't match the organization of the objective list for the good reason that the objective list's organization is (in my humble opinion) a confusing mess. I've rearranged the flow of subjects for easier learning. For example, what do you do when you set up a new PC? You typically choose a file system, install the operating system, install the networking software, and get all your hardware working. Later, you set up users and groups, define access permissions, set up user profiles, and the like. Typically, the last things you do are to optimize the performance of your system and troubleshoot anything that isn't working. That's the organization of this book.

The formal list is subject to change at any time, so you may want to see whether Microsoft has added or removed topics by checking the Web site. However, don't take the list of objectives as gospel. Some exam questions don't relate to the stated objectives, and, conversely, any given exam may not cover every stated objective. If I spend some time on a subject that doesn't explicitly appear in the objective list at the start of the chapter, you can assume that I saw one or more exam questions covering that subject!

Installing Windows XP Professional

✔ Perform an attended installation of Windows XP Professional. (See Chapter 4.)

✔ Perform an unattended installation of Windows XP Professional. Methods include using Remote Installation Services (RIS), using the System Preparation Tool, and creating unattended answer files by using Setup Manager. (See Chapter 4.)

✔ Upgrade from a previous version of Windows to Windows XP Professional. Methods include preparing a computer to meet upgrade requirements and migrating existing user environments to a new installation. (See Chapter 4.)

✔ Perform post-installation updates and product activation. (See Chapter 4.)

✔ Troubleshoot failed installations. (See Chapter 15.)

Implementing and Conducting Administration of Resources

✔ Monitor, manage, and troubleshoot access to files and folders. Methods include configuring, managing, and troubleshooting file compression. (See Chapter 3.)

✔ Monitor, manage, and troubleshoot access to files and folders. Methods include controlling access to files and folders by using permissions and optimizing access to files and folders. (See Chapter 11.)

✔ Manage and troubleshoot access to shared folders. Methods include creating and removing shared folders, controlling access to shared folders by using permissions, and managing and troubleshooting Web server resources. (See Chapter 11.)

✔ Connect to local and network print devices. Methods include managing printers and print jobs, controlling access to printers by using permissions, connecting to an Internet printer, and connecting to a local print device. (See Chapter 7.)

✔ Configure and manage file systems. Methods include converting from one file system to another file system, and configuring NTFS, FAT32, or FAT file systems. (See Chapter 3.)

✔ Manage and troubleshoot the use and synchronization of offline files. (See Chapter 12.)

✔ Configure and troubleshoot fax support. (See Chapter 7.)

Implementing, Managing, Monitoring, and Troubleshooting Hardware Devices and Drivers

✔ Implement, manage, and troubleshoot disk devices. Methods include installing, configuring, and managing DVD and CD-ROM devices; monitoring and configuring disks; monitoring, configuring, and troubleshooting volumes; and monitoring and configuring removable media, such as tape devices. (See Chapter 7.)

- ✔ Implement, manage, and troubleshoot display devices. Methods include configuring multiple-display support and installing, configuring, and troubleshooting a video adapter. (See Chapter 8.)

- ✔ Configure Advanced Configuration Power Interface (ACPI). (See Chapter 9.)

- ✔ Implement, manage, and troubleshoot input and output (I/O) devices. Methods include monitoring, configuring, and troubleshooting I/O devices, such as printers, scanners, multimedia devices, mouse, keyboard, and smart card reader; monitoring, configuring, and troubleshooting multimedia hardware, such as cameras; installing, configuring, and managing modems; installing, configuring, and managing USB devices; and installing, configuring, and managing handheld devices. (See Chapter 8.)

- ✔ Implement, manage, and troubleshoot input and output (I/O) devices. Methods include installing, configuring, and managing Infrared Data Association (IrDA) devices, and installing, configuring, and managing wireless devices. (See Chapter 9, where I put all the topics of interest mainly to mobile users.)

- ✔ Manage and troubleshoot drivers and driver signing. (See Chapter 15.)

- ✔ Monitor and configure multiprocessor computers. (See Chapter 14.)

Monitoring and Optimizing System Performance and Reliability

- ✔ Monitor, optimize, and troubleshoot performance of the Windows XP Professional desktop. Methods include optimizing and troubleshooting memory performance; optimizing and troubleshooting processor utilization; optimizing and troubleshooting disk performance; optimizing and troubleshooting application performance; and configuring, managing, and troubleshooting Scheduled Tasks. (See Chapter 14.)

- ✔ Manage, monitor, and optimize system performance for mobile users. (See Chapter 9.)

- ✔ Restore and back up the operating system, system state data, and user data. Methods include recovering system state data and user data by using Windows Backup; troubleshooting system restoration by starting in safe mode; and recovering system state data and user data by using the Recovery Console. (See Chapter 15.)

Configuring and Troubleshooting the Desktop Environment

- ✔ Configure and manage user profiles. (See Chapter 12.)

- ✔ Configure support for multiple languages or multiple locations. Methods include enabling multiple-language support; configuring multiple-language support for users; configuring local settings; and configuring Windows XP Professional for multiple locations. (See Chapter 5.)

- ✔ Manage applications by using Windows Installer packages. (See Chapter 12.)
- ✔ Configure and troubleshoot desktop settings. (See Chapter 5.)
- ✔ Configure and troubleshoot accessibility services. (See Chapter 5.)

Implementing, Managing, and Troubleshooting Network Protocols and Services

- ✔ Configure and troubleshoot the TCP/IP protocol. (See Chapter 6.)
- ✔ Connect to computers by using dial-up networking. Methods include connecting to computers by using a virtual private network (VPN) connection; creating a dial-up connection to connect to a remote access server; connecting to the Internet by using dial-up networking; and configuring and troubleshooting Internet Connection Sharing. (See Chapter 13.)
- ✔ Connect to resources using Internet Explorer. (See Chapter 11.)
- ✔ Configure, manage, and implement Internet Information Services (IIS). (See Chapter 11.)
- ✔ Configure, manage, and troubleshoot remote desktop and remote assistance. (See Chapter 13.)
- ✔ Configure, manage, and troubleshoot an Internet Connection Firewall. (See Chapter 13.)

Implementing, Monitoring, and Troubleshooting Security

- ✔ Configure, manage, and troubleshoot Encrypting File System (EFS). (See Chapter 3.)
- ✔ Configure, manage, and troubleshoot local security policy. (See Chapter 11.)
- ✔ Configure, manage, and troubleshoot local user and group accounts. Methods include configuring, managing, and troubleshooting auditing; configuring, managing, and troubleshooting account settings; configuring, managing, and troubleshooting account policy; configuring and troubleshooting local users and groups; configuring, managing, and troubleshooting user and group rights; and troubleshooting cache credentials. (See Chapter 10.)
- ✔ Configure, manage, and troubleshoot a security configuration. (See Chapter 11.)
- ✔ Configure, manage, and troubleshoot Internet Explorer security settings. (See Chapter 11.)

Hints that may help

Here are a few tips to smooth your way to Microsoft certification:

✔ Although the formal list of objectives is incredibly wide ranging, expect a heavy focus on features that are new since Windows NT 4.0 Workstation. For example, you can bet the exam includes questions on Plug and Play, power management, personalized menus, Active Directory, dynamic disks, file protection, encryption, safe mode boot, recovery console, management consoles, and so on.

I try to highlight such features in each chapter to help you focus on them.

✔ Know Windows XP/2000 Server features before taking the Windows XP Professional test. You don't have to know how to set up DHCP, DNS, WINS, and Active Directory on the server to pass Exam #70-270, but you should have an understanding of those technologies because Windows 2000 Server and Windows XP Server implement them. Microsoft always throws in a fair dose of networking material in its workstation operating system exams.

✔ Most people learn best by doing. Therefore, if at all possible, set yourself up a little test network consisting of at least one Windows XP Professional PC and one Windows 2000 or Windows XP Server PC. You can use an old and slow "leftover" computer for the server PC if you're just using it for educational purposes. (Don't go slower than a Pentium II/266 with 64MB of RAM.)

✔ After you pass the test, reward yourself! Buy that CD you've been wanting, go to the movies, pick up some real French champagne — do whatever you do for fun.

From a psychological standpoint, rewarding yourself for passing each test gives you positive reinforcement for the next test. But that's not why you should do it. Good work deserves celebration. When I finish this book, for example, I plan to buy a brand new, bright red Audi A6 Quattro. (Assuming, of course, that I can convince my publisher that covering the down payment would be a great way to reward a hardworking author.)

Chapter 2

Fundamentals of Windows XP

● ●

In This Chapter

▶ Getting to know the members of the Windows family tree

▶ Mastering the basics of the Windows XP architecture (non-PhD version)

▶ Finding out what sets Windows XP apart from Windows NT Workstation 4.0

● ●

*N*one of the material in this chapter is on the exam. However, all the material in this chapter is on the exam.

What I mean is this: You need a good basic understanding of the Windows XP history and architecture to deal with some of the detailed questions that presume such an understanding. For example, you may encounter a question that asks about the relative merits of Windows XP versus Windows NT Workstation or Windows 98 when it comes to installing Plug and Play hardware. (XP and 98 support Plug and Play, but NT doesn't.) For another example, you may be expected to understand what the HAL is. (It's the *Hardware Abstraction Layer,* a key component of the Windows XP Professional operating system that determines, among other things, power management and Plug and Play capabilities.)

My suggestion is that you get comfortable with this information before you move on to the detailed chapters. I keep it brief and avoid arcane topics that probably won't surface on the exam.

When you're comfortable with the information that I present in this chapter, you're ready to move on to specific exam preparation in the remainder of the book.

Windows Operating Systems

This section explains where Windows XP falls within the Windows product family. In a nutshell, Windows XP combines many of the benefits of both the Windows 9x/Me product line and the Windows NT 4.0/2000 product line, but it is more closely associated to NT/2000 in its inner workings.

The Windows 3.x clan

Windows 3.x (that is, Windows 3.0, Windows 3.1, Windows for Workgroups 3.1, and Windows for Workgroups 3.11) is still in use worldwide. Microsoft describes all Windows 3.x products as operating *environments* rather than operating *systems* because Windows 3.x doesn't entirely replace MS-DOS. Windows 3.x is 16-bit software, and application programs written for Windows 3.x are (with rare exceptions) also 16-bit software.

Windows 3.1 brought the PC user the following key elements:

- A graphical user interface using drop-down menus, dialog boxes, program icons and groups, and (to some extent) a drag-and-drop metaphor
- A platform for applications that can use more memory than 640K
- A vehicle for running multiple applications simultaneously (*cooperative multitasking*) and for rapidly switching between applications loaded in memory (*task switching*)
- An environment where all programs use a single set of print and screen drivers
- A structure for exchanging data more easily between programs

Windows for Workgroups 3.1 introduced peer networking. Its successor, Version 3.11, was a much more stable and versatile network client than its predecessors.

Windows 3.x and DOS machines use the old 8.3 file-naming convention, and therefore can't see the full name of a shared folder on a Windows XP PC if that folder's share name exceeds the 8.3 limit.

The Windows 9x clan

Windows 95 and its successors, Windows 98 and Windows Me, bring 32-bit capabilities to the Intel-and-compatible PC, along with a heavily revised user interface. Windows 9x (as the exam may refer to versions Me, 98, and 95 collectively) focuses on compatibility, whereas Windows NT and Windows 2000 focus on security and reliability.

Design goals

The nine key goals of the Windows 9x design team tell you nearly all you need to know about where Windows 9x fits. The goals are:

✔ **Compatibility:** If you have an old DOS device driver that loads in CONFIG.SYS or AUTOEXEC.BAT, chances are excellent that you can use that device with Windows 9*x*. Need to run an old 16-bit Windows 3.1 application? It probably runs fine under Windows 9*x*, too.

✔ **Performance:** Windows 9*x* was designed to perform well under low memory conditions, so its designers had to forego the extra layers of memory protection that make NT, 2000, and XP more reliable.

✔ **Robustness:** Windows 9*x* is more reliable than Windows 3.*x* (fewer crashes and lockups), and less reliable than NT, 2000, or XP.

✔ **Better setup and configuration:** Windows 9*x* autodetects a wide variety of hardware during setup, in large part thanks to the Plug and Play standard. You can install Windows 9*x* from a network server as well as from a CD-ROM, and the Batch Setup tool helps you script LAN-based installations. As for configuring the software, Windows 9*x* control panels use the Registry database for most system settings, centralizing such settings but adding to system complexity.

✔ **Better user interface:** The Start button, taskbar, and property sheet made their debut in Windows 95, along with dozens of other user interface (UI) changes and a new emphasis on the right mouse button. Windows 98 makes few changes to the core UI of Windows 95 although the Web View of folders and Active Desktop add a new Internet look.

✔ **Protected mode design:** Nearly everything in Windows 9*x* runs in the Intel processor's "protected mode," which affords better reliability, as opposed to the "real mode" that DOS software uses.

✔ **Support for 32-bit applications:** Windows 9*x* can run 32-bit applications, conferring upon them goodies such as a private memory space, preemptive multitasking, and multithreaded execution. However, Windows 9*x* does not use 32-bit software through and through; many modules are still 16-bit code.

✔ **Better client and workgroup functionality:** Windows 9*x* contains the peer-to-peer networking capabilities introduced by Windows for Workgroups, adding peer services for Novell networks, too. Microsoft also provides better support for multiple concurrent networks, 32-bit network components at every level, a more modular design, and better speed.

✔ **Better mobile computing support:** From Dial-Up Networking to Direct Cable Connection and Briefcase, Windows 9*x* makes life easier on road warriors who need to connect to office or public networks.

Versions

Table 2-1 lays out the genealogy of the Windows 9x/Me product line. (You can check the version number for all Windows 9*x* products by right-clicking the My Computer icon, choosing Properties, and looking at the version on the General tab.) Note especially that Windows Me is essentially an evolution of

Windows 98, bringing various minor advances (improved TCP/IP stack, home networking wizard, Movie Maker application, system restore facility) to the 9*x* product line.

Table 2-1	Windows 9x/Me Versions
Version	*Distinguishing Features*
4.00.950	Original Windows 95 product
4.00.950a	Windows 95 with Service Pack 1, which corrected mostly minor bugs
4.00.950B, 4.00.950C	OSR2, or OEM Service Release 2 Windows 95 variant that added the FAT32 file system and (with "C") USB support
4.10.1998	Windows 98, mainly a bug fix release with some handy new utilities and native support for USB
4.10.2222A	Windows 98 Second Edition, more bug fixes and Internet Connection Sharing
4.90.3000	Windows Me, basically "Windows 98 Third Edition"

The Windows NT/2000/XP clan

Windows NT, 2000, and XP can all function as workstation operating systems or as server operating systems. In either situation, Microsoft recommends these products for situations in which security and reliability take precedence over maximum hardware and software compatibility. Having said that, I must add that Windows XP does improve over Windows 2000 in the compatibility area.

Reliability and security

Reliability in the NT platform is achieved through various architectural characteristics, including the following:

- No support for 16-bit device drivers: 16-bit drivers and Windows 9*x*-style VXDs (virtual device drivers) are a major source of Windows 9*x* and 3.*x* crashes.

- Total hardware protection (software is never allowed to communicate directly with a device) via a *Hardware Abstraction Layer,* or HAL.

- Restricted list of approved hardware devices compared to Windows 9*x* (see HCL.TXT in the SUPPORT directory of the Windows XP CD-ROM for the Hardware Compatibility List, or www.microsoft.com/hcl for the updated online version).

Windows XP, 2000, and NT have their own self-contained security system (users, passwords, permissions, rights, and so on). This is in sharp contrast to Windows 9x/Me, which offer only relatively weak share-level security or which can leverage the security capabilities of NT or NetWare.

The price of progress

Microsoft has said for a long time that the NT product line is its long-term, strategic platform. Nevertheless, Windows 2000 and XP haven't made Windows 9x/Me obsolete. The main reason is that for many customers, a move to Windows 2000/XP means abandoning some older software and hardware. In order to provide enhanced reliability and security, the NT/2000/XP product line sacrifices compatibility with some legacy devices and programs. Windows XP, 2000, and NT operating systems don't support DOS-style device drivers, and they don't support all 16-bit Windows programs. However, Windows XP is notably more compatible with existing hardware and software than Windows 2000 — with the large exception of XP's much higher minimum hardware requirements.

Here's a quick check for legacy issues:

✔ If an exam question refers to 16-bit software, remember that Windows 98/Me provides a greater likelihood of compatibility than Windows XP or Windows 2000.

✔ If a question refers to "real-mode device drivers," or "legacy device drivers," know that Windows 2000/XP doesn't support them at all. They're the kind of device drivers that load via CONFIG.SYS or AUTOEXEC.BAT.

What NT and 2000/XP have in common

You should understand the basic differences between the NT/2000 products and the Windows 9x products. Here are some of the key common features of NT/2000/XP:

✔ Full 32-bit operating system.

✔ High reliability. All applications and the operating system itself run in protected memory areas.

✔ Preemptive multitasking for all applications, providing generally better performance running 32-bit software. Windows 9x uses the less sophisticated *cooperative multitasking* for 16-bit applications.

✔ Support for symmetrical multiprocessing; that is, multiple CPUs in the same box. Windows 2000/XP Professional supports machines having one processor or two processors. Windows XP Home Edition only supports one CPU. Server versions of Windows 2000 support more.

- ✔ High-performance file system (NTFS) with transaction logging and file-level security. Windows 9*x* only offers folder-level security.

- ✔ Incompatible with real-mode device drivers and with software that tries to "speak" directly to hardware devices.

What's New about XP?

What's new with Windows XP? That's a hugely important question because the exam tends to focus on these new features.

Windows 2000/XP flavors

Starting with Windows 2000, the various products are as follows:

- ✔ Windows 2000 Professional (the successor to Windows NT Workstation)
- ✔ The Windows 2000 Server family, which is available in three flavors:
  - • Windows 2000 Server (the basic package)
  - • Windows 2000 Advanced Server (successor to Windows NT Server, Enterprise Edition)
  - • Windows 2000 Datacenter Server

Windows XP debuts in two versions, Professional and Home. (MCSE exam 70-270 covers the Professional product.) Windows 2000 never existed in a "home" edition. Server versions, expected to parallel the versions of Windows 2000 Server listed above, are slated for 2002 under the family name "Windows 2002 Server," continuing Microsoft's pattern of confusing anyone trying to understand its naming system.

Here, in a nutshell, is what Windows XP Professional has that Windows XP Home Edition does not:

- ✔ Two-way Symmetric MultiProcessing (SMP)
- ✔ Domain logon (that is, you can't use Home Edition in a corporate client/server environment)
- ✔ Support for roaming user profiles
- ✔ Remote Desktop, a remote terminal capability similar to Terminal Services
- ✔ Offline files and folders, a way to work with network data when disconnected from the network
- ✔ Encrypting File System (EFS), a way to secure stored data
- ✔ Internet Information Server 5.1 (IIS), Microsoft's Web server product

Windows 2000/XP represents a combination of the Windows 9*x* and NT product lines in the following ways:

- ✔ Tight security is available but you don't have to use all the security features.

- ✔ Compatibility with DOS and DOS games is almost as good as 9*x*/Me, with XP better than 2000 in this regard.

- ✔ Reliability is very good but ease of use is equal to that of Windows 9*x*/Me.

- ✔ Workgroup networking and client/server networking are both supported.

- ✔ Works on more hardware than NT4 (largely thanks to Plug and Play), with XP notably better than 2000 here.

Windows XP is more nearly "Windows NT 5.1" than it is "Windows 99," but the new operating system borrows much from the 9*x*/Me platforms, such as Plug and Play and broader software and hardware compatibility.

The remainder of this section compares Windows XP Professional to Windows NT 4.0 Workstation. The new goodies break out into the following categories:

- ✔ Active Directory
- ✔ Active Desktop and Internet software
- ✔ Security
- ✔ Usability
- ✔ Hardware
- ✔ Deployment and Activation
- ✔ Management
- ✔ Remote Support
- ✔ Digital Media

I cover each category in the following sections.

Active Directory

One of the most important new features of Windows XP/2000, at least for network users, is *Active Directory* (AD). AD is supposed to act like a master Rolodex for your whole network: It contains details on all network resources, from users and groups to printers and programs. Actually, because AD also handles access control, it's a bit more like a security guard holding a master Rolodex. AD uses constructs to organize the network, including the following, which you should recognize as AD structures but whose specific definitions you don't need to know for exam #70-270:

- Forests
- Trees
- Domains
- Organizational units
- Groups

The Active Directory model simplifies the earlier Windows NT 4.0 networking model in some ways:

- **All domain controllers are peers.**

  The concept of primary and backup domain controllers is gone.

- **Trust relationships are transitive.**

  That is, if domain A trusts domain B and B trusts C, then A trusts C. This simplifies network design and administration.

- **A single database contains the entire network directory, instead of a collection of databases.**

  The network directory data moves out of the Registry and into a more extensible, scalable, and speedy structure.

 Many of the benefits of Windows XP/2000 are possible only when a combination of Windows 2000 Servers and Windows XP/2000 Professional clients interact in the context of Active Directory.

Other exams in the Windows XP/2000 track zero in on AD, but you can bet you'll see some related material on Exam #70-270.

Active Desktop and Internet software

Windows XP/2000 includes the Internet Explorer Web browser (version 6 with XP, version 5 with 2000) with the operating system and also provides a "Web view" option for folders and for the desktop itself. The Web view feature enables users to specify an HTML file, with whatever objects you want to include (ActiveX, Java, and so on), to appear as the desktop or folder background. The Web objects occupy a layer underneath the typical desktop and folder icons.

Web view also allows you to specify that:

- Selectable objects should appear underlined, as they do on a Web page.
- Moving a cursor over an object highlights it.

✔ Single-clicking (instead of double-clicking) a highlighted object activates it.

✔ Thumbnails of selected data files appear in a separate pane.

Active Desktop enables you to plop an entire Web page onto the desktop as well, in which case you can tell Windows XP/2000 how often you'd like it to be updated. Active Desktop also includes a number of enhancements not related in any functional way to Internet technologies, such as new support for drag-and-drop operations on the taskbar.

Unlike Windows 2000 Professional, Windows XP Professional silently turns on Active Desktop whenever you place "Web content" (such as a JPG file) onto the desktop.

The "single Explorer" aspect of Windows XP/2000 means that you can

✔ Invoke a Web-browsing window from a Windows Explorer screen by typing the URL (Uniform Resource Locator) into the address bar.

✔ Switch between the local view and the browser view by using the Back and Forward buttons.

Most of the menu bar buttons change between the two views, which is why I put "single Explorer" in quotes when introducing this list.

Microsoft has brought Internet technology into the help system, too, by making HTML documents the starting point instead of RTF (Rich Text Format) documents. HTML Help

✔ Functions like the Windows 98 help engine

✔ Lets application vendors add graphics more easily

Windows XP/2000 Professional comes with a variety of other Internet-related software, such as

✔ Outlook Express

✔ NetMeeting

✔ MSN Explorer (XP only, not 2000)

✔ Internet Information Server (IIS)

✔ Indexing Service (This is an IIS feature (off by default) that accelerates local drive searches)

Security

Windows XP/2000 updates and expands security options as follows:

- ✔ **The Kerberos security protocol replaces the older, slower NTLM mechanism for LAN communications.**

  Kerberos is the big news in Windows XP/2000 security.

- ✔ **Encryption joins the NTFS file system.**

  Users can encrypt data files so that no one else can open or modify those files (Professional edition only).

- ✔ **The TCP/IP protocol that underlies Internet applications is improved.**

- ✔ **Communication is more secure with new support for**

  - IPsec (secure IP)
  - L2TP (Layer 2 Tunneling Protocol)

- ✔ **The default access control restrictions for the file system and the Registry are stricter for Windows 2000 than for Windows NT Workstation 4.0.**

- ✔ **A** *regular* **user account in NT may need to be upgraded to a** *power* **user account in Windows XP/2000 to perform the same tasks and run the same applications.**

- ✔ **Windows XP/2000 supports hardware-based authentication devices, such as "smart cards."**

  These are common in the military and are becoming popular in the corporate world.

Usability

Windows XP makes a number of strides forward (and a couple backward) compared to the NT 4.0 platform when it comes to usability.

Dialog boxes

Various dialog boxes have been refined in Windows XP and 2000, such as the Open, Save As, Logon, and Shut Down dialog boxes. These improvements are generally of the incremental, evolutionary nature. If you see any dialog boxes on the exam, you should find the changes intuitive and easy to grasp.

New wizards

The Network Connection Wizard is the most important new one in Windows XP and 2000 Professional (Windows 2000 Server has lots and lots of new wizards).

New to Microspeak? A *wizard* is a guided sequence of steps that helps the user accomplish a common task.

AutoComplete and MRU lists

Many Windows XP dialog boxes automatically complete fields as the user begins typing them.

AutoComplete creates convenience for some and security holes for others. The Most Recently Used (MRU) lists have grown very long indeed, including even individual fields on Web site forms, and Microsoft has not provided a mechanism for clearing them all. Where the security and privacy of user computing aren't important, AutoComplete and the proliferation of MRU lists save users time while going about daily tasks.

Personalized menus

After a period of time, Windows XP begins hiding menu selections that users have not chosen. The Start menu and its cascading submenus show only recently used choices, hiding others beneath a chevron character that, if clicked, shows (after a delay) all the menu options.

Organizations must weigh the potential convenience of disappearing menu options against the potential confusion and delays it can introduce. Personalized menus may be easily disabled via a dialog box, policy setting, or Registry setting.

"Windows" dressing

Windows XP Professional adds the following user interface changes to the previous list:

- *Visual Styles* that govern the interface's "look and feel"
- Wider use of the "Web View" pane in Explorer windows for file-type-specific actions
- A more minimalist desktop by default, which omits the usual My Computer and other icons
- A *fast user switching* capability for rapidly changing between logged-on accounts
- Support for ClearType, a resolution-enhancing technology for LCDs
- A revamped, two-part Start menu
- A control panel that presents functions in groups of related tasks

Hardware

The big news when it comes to hardware support is in

- Power management
- Plug and Play
- Device and bus support
- Driver signing

Power management

Windows XP manages PC power much differently than Windows NT 4.0 does. In fact, power management is tied very closely to Plug and Play. Two acronyms come into play here:

- **APM,** or Advanced Power Management, is an older standard that was less than rigorous and therefore inconsistently implemented. Most PCs built before 1999 use APM if they offer any power management features at all.
- **ACPI,** or Advanced Configuration and Power Interface, is a newer standard that's more completely defined. Windows XP much prefers ACPI to APM. ACPI is a better-defined standard that gives more control to the operating system and less to the BIOS.

On ACPI machines, Windows XP's better power management makes it a viable, and even convenient, operating system for notebook computers that meet Windows XP's hardware requirements — something that could never truly be said about Windows NT 4.0 Workstation. Standby and hibernate modes are both supported.

Plug and Play

Windows XP builds on the Plug and Play support in Windows 98 and Windows 2000. It puts to shame the limited add-in Plug and Play support that you could retrofit to Windows NT Workstation 4.0. Windows XP does a very good job of detecting and configuring most Plug and Play hardware.

Modems and COM ports are unhappy exceptions — you must usually detect these devices manually, via the Phone and Modem Options control panel or the Add New Hardware Wizard.

Improvements include

- Eliminating resource assignment spreadsheets, which were required by Windows NT 4.0
- Reducing the likelihood that the operating system won't be able to boot because of hardware problems

PCs designed to the ACPI specification work *much* better with Plug and Play.

New devices and buses

Windows XP supports a variety of relatively new devices and buses, including:

- **Universal Serial Bus (USB)**

  A single daisy-chained cable to connect keyboards, speakers, scanners, mice, monitors, and other devices to a PC port. The port only uses one interrupt. Windows XP supports USB 2.0 ports and devices, which offer much higher transfer rates than the previous version.

- **FireWire (IEEE 1394)**

  Transfer rates are high enough to handle consumer electronic devices, such as camcorders and VCRs.

- **Wireless Networking (IEEE 802.11 or Wi-Fi)**

  The operating system now includes built-in support for wireless networking (but not the personal-area network Bluetooth protocol).

- **DVD**

  The standard read-only flavor is supported although neither Windows XP nor Windows 2000 comes with a DVD decoder. DVDs can hold video, audio, and computer data on the same disc.

- **Digital scanners and cameras**

  Digital scanners and cameras get their own control panel icon.

- **Multiple displays**

  Graphics professionals and power users can connect extra monitors to make larger continuous desktops.

  The feature is limited to AGP and PCI adapters. Even then, not all models work.

With respect to disk drive management, Windows XP Professional brings three new items to the table:

- The space-saving FAT32 file system introduced in Windows 95 OSR2 comes with Windows XP, along with a one-way conversion utility.

  - Windows XP supports FAT32 on any partition, including the boot partition.

  - FAT32 lets you create much larger disk partitions than FAT16 but remains less secure and reliable than NTFS.

- Windows XP introduces yet another update of *NTFS,* the NT File System. This is the recommended file system for Windows XP. It provides

  - File-and-folder security

  - Extensible volumes

  - Support for multiple-disk stripe sets

- Encryption (but not simultaneously with compression)
- Compression (but not simultaneously with encryption)

✔ Windows XP now includes a basic *disk defragmenter* that's improved over the Windows 2000 version in that the XP version can be scheduled and scripted.

Driver signing

Windows XP provides a new level of authentication called *driver signing*. Microsoft brands a *digital signature* into the core operating system files and drivers that it ships with Windows XP and 2000.

✔ Windows XP can tell when a program installation tries to replace one of those core files with a version not "signed" by Microsoft.

✔ Administrators can control whether any given PC can accept unsigned drivers.

The *Windows File Protection* background program watches system files and replaces them if necessary with "known good" versions from a special "hip pocket" folder named DLLCACHE.

Deployment and Activation

Windows XP makes several changes to installation and deployment, including the controversial Windows Product Activation.

Interactive installations

The Windows XP installation process is improved in some ways over that for Windows NT 4.0 and Windows 9*x*, and regresses in other ways.

Here are some positive aspects of the new installation procedure:

✔ Fewer reboots

✔ Better (although not perfect) "clumping" of question-and-answer screens

✔ "Dynamic Update" feature letting you update Setup with the latest fixes and drivers at install time

✔ Better overall hardware detection than Windows NT 4.0

✔ More wizards to ease setup chores (especially valuable in Server)

On the minus side, customers have less choice about which accessories, applets, and options should be installed:

- The familiar "typical," "custom," and "minimal" installation options are gone.

- Users not on a corporate license must activate the product (more on this in the section "Product Activation").

- The only area in which an interactive user can choose components to install is in the networking area.

Automated installations

Microsoft offers two options for automated deployment of the Windows XP operating system:

- **Remote Installation Service (RIS)**

  With RIS, a server can install Windows XP onto a PC that doesn't even have an operating system on it. RIS was available for Windows 2000 Professional, but with XP it supports server installations as well as workstation installations, and has new operating system repair capabilities.

- **SysPrep**

  Use this with disk-cloning software such as Ghost or Drive Image. SysPrep helps create the master image, and your cloning software duplicates it.

The usual scripted installation options using "answer files" are still available, too.

New migration paths

You can upgrade a Windows 98, 98 SE, or Me system to Windows XP Professional. That's a positive step in that a direct upgrade path from the 9x platform to Windows NT 4.0 never existed. Because of the greater similarities between NT-family operating systems, the upgrade path to XP from Windows NT 4.0 or Windows 2000 Professional is likely to be smoother.

Product Activation

A new (and controversial) requirement for users of the retail Windows XP Professional product is product activation. This is a step in which your PC sends the product key to Microsoft, along with a hashed code that reflects details of the PC's hardware configuration, via the Internet or a phone call to Microsoft. Microsoft then supplies a return code that activates your product. Failing activation, the operating system locks up after 30 days.

The acronym for this anti-piracy feature is WPA, for Windows Product Activation. Chapter 4 deals with WPA in more detail.

Management

Microsoft says that it's focusing on TCO (Total Cost of Ownership) these days, and administrators may be able to reduce TCO with certain new Windows XP Professional features. Note that many of these features don't apply to Windows XP Home Edition, which doesn't support domain-style networking.

Group Policy

Policies are a mechanism for implementing and controlling the various other types of Windows XP security, not a new type of security themselves. Policies can be

- Local only
- Network-based only (using Active Directory)
- Both local and network-based

Think of policies as the "rules of the house" that set forth all the security restrictions (both machine-specific and user- and group-specific) that you've chosen to implement.

After an administrator sets policies, policies automatically modify the Registry (applying security, user-interface consistency, or both) at

- Boot time
- Logon time
- Periodic refresh intervals

Technically, Windows XP policies work differently on

- Standalone machines
- Computers in a solely Windows XP and 2000 network
- Computers in mixed-mode networks with Windows NT 4.0 clients

Winning the award for most awkward name for a software utility, Microsoft calls the Windows XP/2000 implementation of policies *Group Policy*:

- The Local Group Policy utility runs on local workstations.
- The Group Policy property sheets are included in the various Active Directory administrative tools on a Windows 2000 server.

Automatic IP Addressing

Automatic IP Addressing allows Windows XP Professional PCs to assign themselves IP addresses if no address server exists on the network. (Windows 2000 and 98 also offer this capability.) That's handy for computers on purely private networks; that is, networks that don't need to connect to the public Internet.

Microsoft Management Console

Windows XP uses a new kind of control panel in addition to the older *.CPL files. This new variation is called *Microsoft Management Console,* or *MMC* for short. Microsoft used MMCs in a few products (such as its Internet server software) before Windows XP and even before Windows 2000, and it seems to be the way the company is moving.

MMC is a little like a standard car chassis within which software developers can put whatever engine they want. The framework has some consistent elements, but the contents of any given MMC window may vary greatly. One nice feature of MMC is that it enables administrators to build their own customized consoles with whatever snap-ins they find most useful.

Windows Update

Windows 98's Windows Update migrates intact to Windows XP. This feature allows a user to connect to a Microsoft Web site that downloads ActiveX controls to the PC. Those programs then scan the software environment, consult a central Microsoft server, and present recommended downloads to the user, even organizing them by priority (critical, nice-to-have, and so on).

With users free to run Windows Update at random times and free to choose whichever updates they deem appropriate, administrators, technicians, and troubleshooters can't know in advance just what updates any given PC may contain. You can disable Windows Update through the Group Policy tool, which I discuss in Chapter 11.

Windows Installer

The new Windows Installer model attempts to bring some order to the chaos of application installation. Some key elements of Windows Installer technology include the following:

- Organized "package" file format that lists application actions in a structured and organized manner
- One-click installation repair capability
- Full uninstall capability (including Registry entries)

Remote Support

Windows XP expands on the remote-administration capabilities of Windows 2000 Professional, which added the ability to "point" certain administrative tools (such as the System Monitor program or either Registry editor) to remote computers. In Windows XP, two new capabilities should make life easier for corporate help desks and software tech support staff:

- *Remote Assistance,* which lets you convey to someone else the necessary credentials to administer or even take over your PC over a local or WAN link, and

- *Remote Desktop,* basically a repackaging of Terminal Services functionality, in which a user at one machine can connect to another machine and take over that second machine via remote control. The second machine may be running a workstation or server version of Windows XP/2000.

Note that certain administrative support actions can be taken via Remote Assistance without necessitating use of Remote Desktop. Remote Registry editing is one example.

Digital Media

Windows XP includes a number of features that debuted in Windows Me, including the Windows Movie Maker applet, which enables you to create digital videos from analog or digital sources and then perform some simple editing chores. Also, the new operating system comes with an updated version of Windows Media Player that Microsoft has renamed "Media Player for Windows XP" and that the company isn't making available as an upgrade for users of other Windows versions. This utility is notably Microsoft-centric and omits format support for some popular multimedia file types, such as QuickTime, RealPlayer, and so on.

Windows XP makes certain activities automatic that were available manually in the past. Connect a digital camera, and the Camera and Scanner Wizard appears, for example. In other areas, Windows XP facilitates functionality that was formerly either awkward or not present without add-on software; an example here is archiving files to CD-R or CD-RW devices.

Understanding the Windows XP/2000 Architecture

This section presents a very concise overview of the Windows XP/2000 architecture for those of you unfamiliar with Windows NT 4.0. (The underlying architecture is very similar between all three operating systems.)

The three "multi's" — multitasking, multithreading, and multiprocessing

The following list clarifies three key Windows XP architectural concepts:

✔ *Multitasking* runs multiple programs at the same time.

Actually, the computer seems to be doing multiple things at once but is really slicing up CPU (Central Processing Unit) time into tiny amounts and distributing it to multiple activities.

Windows 9*x*, NT, 2000, and XP use a clever system called *preemptive* multitasking.

- The operating system figures out in advance how much CPU time each program gets when its turn comes around (that job is handled by the scheduler).

- The operating system can jump in and suspend a piggish application instead of waiting for it to yield control.

✔ Windows 3.*x* can multitask, but only in a fairly unsophisticated manner known as *cooperative* multitasking. In that model, programs are expected to be good citizens, periodically yielding control of the computer to other programs. Windows 3.*x* has no way of "giving the hook" to a program that's hogging the stage.

✔ *Multithreading* means that a single program can create (or *spawn*) several threads of execution that proceed simultaneously. For example, a word processor may spawn a spell-check task in a separate, independent thread, while another thread performs document repagination at the same time. Windows 9*x*, NT, 2000, and XP support multithreading.

✔ *Multiprocessing* means that the operating system can use more than one CPU.

Windows XP/2000 and NT support multiprocessing, but Windows 9*x* does not.

- Windows 2000 Professional supports machines having one or two CPUs.

- Windows XP Professional, ditto.

- Windows XP Home Edition supports only one CPU.

- Windows 2000 Server supports as many as four CPUs (more with vendor-specific support). Windows 2000 Advanced Server supports as many as 8, and Datacenter Server as many as 32.

✔ The type of multiprocessing supported by Windows XP/2000 is *symmetric* (the acronym is SMP); each CPU is the same and has access to the same memory. Many operating system tasks still run only on the first CPU in a multi-CPU system.

User mode and kernel mode

Any given program or thread in Windows XP/2000 runs in *user mode* or *kernel mode*.

✔ **User mode is safer, slower, and further removed from the underlying hardware**. Applications run in user mode.

✔ **Kernel mode is riskier, faster, and closer to the hardware.** Core operating system functions run in kernel mode, such as

- Memory management
- File system management
- Device driver management

Virtual memory

Every loaded 32-bit program in a Windows XP/2000 environment thinks that it has access to a 4GB address space, half of which it can use for its own code, and half of which is reserved for operating system code (the API). However, Windows XP/2000 and all Windows applications can only use a maximum of 4GB physical memory on the entire PC. (Windows XP, 64-Bit Edition isn't subject to this limit, but the exam isn't likely to cover the 64-Bit Edition product.) The way in which Windows lets multiple programs think that they can each see the entire 4GB is through *memory mapping*.

At any given moment, Program X isn't using its entire 4GB memory space, so Windows can present to Program X only the memory that it's using at that moment. Think of an analogy: Most banks couldn't pay all depositors their entire balance at the same moment, but they could give each depositor a portion of his or her balance over the span of a typical day. So, in a sense, your bank accounts are virtual money. No wonder people still hide cash in coffee cans or under the mattress.

Even after parceling out physical memory on an as-needed basis in this elaborate shell game of memory mapping, sometimes physical memory (RAM) becomes exhausted. (That's likely to occur faster with Windows XP than with Windows NT 4.0, partly because Windows XP needs more RAM to hold all the extra Internet and other software that loads at startup.) When an application demands more memory than Windows can find in physical RAM, Windows XP grabs a chunk of disk space to use as *virtual memory,* also known as the *pagefile.* Disks are much slower than RAM, but the principle is that a system that runs slowly is better than one that stops entirely.

Windows XP manages the swap file size automatically, shrinking and expanding it as needed, in the default configuration.

You have a couple of options to maximize performance:

- ✔ Specify a higher minimum pagefile size yourself to reduce Windows XP overhead (processor and disk time spent expanding the pagefile to meet demand).
- ✔ Place the pagefile on your fastest local hard drive for better speed.

Dynamic Link Libraries

Dynamic Link Libraries, or *DLLs,* are files that (typically) contain program code. A program or the Windows XP operating system itself can load a DLL into memory on an as-needed basis. The DLL concept enables you to run programs with less RAM than would be required if all programs loaded every bit of code they needed, every time they started.

Much of Windows XP itself is in the form of DLLs, and most Windows applications use DLLs, too. Many Windows programs call upon DLLs in Windows to accomplish certain tasks; such DLLs go by the name of *system DLLs.*

The DLL model has presented some problems in the past. Microsoft often updates and modifies system DLL files between version releases of Windows. Application software developers sometimes "redistribute" specific versions of system DLLs, under license from Microsoft, so that the application knows that the PC is using a recent-enough version of the system DLLs for the application to work correctly. However, sometimes application installation routines overwrite newer DLLs with older ones, which can cause other applications that need the newer DLLs to break. Conversely, other times, a newer DLL may not work with an older program that needs an older version of that DLL. So both newer *and* older DLLs can create problems.

The new System File Checker utility (SFC), Windows File Protection, Driver Signing, and the Windows Installer model have features designed to reduce DLL problems. Make sure that you understand their purposes!

Hardware abstraction

The layer of Windows XP that communicates directly with the PC's hardware is called the *HAL,* or Hardware Abstraction Layer. Windows XP chooses an appropriate HAL for a given PC during the early stages of the installation program, based on factors such as

- CPU type
- Number of CPUs
- Power management support in the BIOS

The HAL design, which "abstracts" the underlying hardware from the rest of the Windows XP operating system, allows Windows XP to run on non-Intel processors. However, for various economic and political reasons, Windows XP's ability to run on non-Intel processors is much less of a factor than it might have been. Therefore:

You probably won't see any exam questions on non-Intel processors.

You can't change the HAL without reinstalling Windows XP. (The only exception: If you add a second CPU, you can change the HAL by updating the computer's "driver" in the System control panel's Device Manager.)

If you're not comfortable with the information that I present in this chapter, before continuing, you may want to spend a little time with the Windows XP help system, targeting the areas that seem a little fuzzy.

32-bit and 64-bit Windows

Windows XP Professional and Windows XP Home Edition are both 32-bit products, but Microsoft has developed in parallel 64-bit operating systems with nearly identical feature sets (the 64-bit products exclude some bundled applications and capabilities). Microsoft dubs these operating systems "Windows XP 64-bit Edition," "Windows 2002 Server 64-bit Edition," and "Windows 2002 Advanced Server 64-bit Edition."

These 64-bit products target the high-end market in their respective client and server categories and will only run on 64-bit processors such as Intel's Itanium. They offer a larger memory model (16TB, or terabytes, where 1TB = 1024GB) and improved precision for numerical calculations. Customers will not have an upgrade path from the 32-bit products to the much more expensive 64-bit products. The 64-bit products will be able to run 32-bit applications via a compatibility layer although Microsoft isn't recommending this approach for the server family.

Part II
Planning, Installation, and Basic Configuration

"We sort of have our own way of mentally preparing our people to take the Windows XP exam."

In this part . . .

Somebody once said that computer software can't be considered truly user-friendly until setting up a PC becomes as simple as setting up a toaster. If Windows XP Professional is a toaster, it's a nuclear-powered one with ten-thousand moving parts! Setting up Windows XP correctly is no simple task, and this beefy part covers the initial work you're likely to do when setting up Windows XP Professional — whether for one user or for an entire worldwide corporation. The focus here is on software setup; Part III deals with hardware.

Chapter 3 covers choosing and using the file system, no simple task because Windows XP lets you choose from three options. Chapter 4 runs through a typical interactive installation and also discusses automated installation options, a favorite exam topic. Chapter 5 covers user environment settings, such as language, locale, and accessibility options. Chapter 6 looks at setting up network cards and lower-level networking software pieces.

Chapter 3

Planning the File System

● ●

Exam Objectives

▶ Choosing between FAT16, FAT32, and NTFS file systems

▶ Discovering compression and encryption capabilities

▶ Getting a handle on dynamic disks

▶ Converting from one file system to another

● ●

*W*indows XP supports more file systems than any other Microsoft operating system, and each file system has its own set of features and foibles. Choosing the appropriate file system for a given situation is an important part of using Windows XP successfully, and it's also an important part of the certification exam. (Other aspects of managing disks appear in Chapter 7.)

Quick Assessment

Configure
file systems
by using
NTFS, FAT32,
or FAT

1 Microsoft recommends the use of _____ on PCs that will dual-boot with an earlier version of Windows.

2 NTFS version _____ in Windows XP is the new version of the NTFS file system in Windows NT Workstation 4.0.

3 The FAT32 file system allows Windows XP to use partitions up to 2 _____ in size.

4 NTFS gives administrators greater control over access permissions by providing _____ and _____ security.

5 To convert an NTFS partition to FAT32, use the command _____.

Convert
from one file
system to
another file
system

6 If you move a compressed file to a different folder on the same disk, and that folder is uncompressed, the moved file is _____ (compressed or uncompressed).

7 If you compress a folder on an NTFS partition, you cannot also _____ that folder.

Configure,
manage,
and
troubleshoot
file
compression

8 The control panel that lets you make compressed files visible is the _____ control panel.

Encrypt data
on a hard
disk by using
Encrypting
File System
(EFS)

9 The Encrypting File System uses public and private _____.

10 An encrypted file stays encrypted as long as it stays on an _____.

Answers

1 *FAT or FAT32.* See the sections "FAT" and "FAT32" for details.

2 *Five.* Windows NT uses NTFS 4. The "NTFS" section explains the differences.

3 *Terabytes.* (Good name for a lady crocodile.) See "FAT32" for more.

4 *File, folder.* (Also acceptable is "file, directory.") Miss this one? Read the "NTFS" section.

5 *No such command exists.* Trick question (you may as well see them here first!). See the "Converting from One File System to Another" section if this one eluded you.

6 *Compressed.* The section "Copying and moving" lays out these sorts of rules.

7 *Encrypt.* See "Setting compression on files or folders" if you missed this one.

8 *Folder options.* This one's new since NT 4.0. See "Setting compression on files or folders."

9 *Keys.* The "Encryption" section elaborates.

10 *NTFS disk.* Again, the "Encryption" section has the details.

File System Choices

The file system determines how the operating system organizes disk space. Which file system you choose has implications for security, speed, efficiency, reliability, recoverability, and compatibility. You must choose a file system before you format a disk partition (on a regular, "basic" disk) or volume (on a "dynamic" disk — see the section "Basic versus dynamic disks" later in this chapter).

Microsoft's operating systems have presented a variety of file systems, most of which are incompatible with each other, as shown in Table 3-1.

Table 3-1 Windows Versions and File System Support			
Operating System Version	*FAT?*	*FAT32?*	*NTFS?*
Windows 95 (original release and OSR1)	Y	N	N
Windows 95 (OSR2 and higher)	Y	Y	N
Windows 98 and Me	Y	Y	N
Windows NT 4.0	Y	N	Y
Windows 2000	Y	Y	Y

Windows XP gives you three choices for a hard disk file system: FAT16 (or plain old FAT as it's sometimes called), FAT32, and NTFS — more specifically, NTFS Version 5. (Windows XP supports other file systems for other types of devices: CDFS, or Compact Disc File System, for CD drives, and UDF, or Universal Disk Format, for DVD drives.)

You're allowed to choose different file systems for different partitions or volumes on the same computer. For example, on a dual-boot computer, you may want to use FAT for the C drive (so that you can boot to Windows 98 or Windows XP), FAT32 for the D drive (which would contain Windows 98 or Me), and NTFS for the E drive (which would contain Windows XP). Note also that, in this example, the logical drives C, D, and E could all reside on a single physical disk. (A "logical drive" is just a chunk of disk space that the user refers to with a single drive letter.)

Lab 3-1 shows you how to see which file system is in use for a given logical drive.

Lab 3-1   Checking the File System in Use

1. **Double-click the My Computer icon on the desktop, if present, or choose My Computer from the Start menu.**

2. **Right-click the icon for the logical drive that you want to check.**

3. **Choose Properties.**

   The General tab of the computer property sheet appears.

4. **Look at the third line down.**

   It should say "File system: FAT," "File system: FAT32," or "File system: NTFS."

The method that I outline in Lab 3-1 works for Windows 2000, NT 4.0, and Windows 9x, also. Another method that's unique to Windows XP/2000 is to run the Disk Management console plug-in, as I detail in Lab 3-2.

Lab 3-2   Running the Disk Management Utility

1. **Right-click the My Computer icon, on the desktop (if present) or on the Start menu.**

2. **Choose Manage.**

3. **Click the Disk Management icon in the left window pane.**

   You can see the file systems listed in the diagram in the right window pane. For those of you familiar with Windows NT Workstation 4.0, you've just discovered the Windows XP version of the NT Disk Administrator utility.

If an exam question asks whether DOS, Windows 3.x, or Windows 9x can "see" a FAT32 or NTFS partition over a network — for example, when connecting as a client to a Windows XP PC that is sharing its files as a server — the answer is yes. The Windows XP PC "serves up" FAT32 and NTFS disks in a way that disguises, or abstracts, their underlying file system.

FAT

FAT, generally also known as FAT16, is the most compatible file system in the PC world. It works with DOS, Windows 3.x, Windows 9x, Windows NT, Windows 2000, and Windows XP. (If the exam refers to *FAT12,* that's the version used to format diskettes, or any volumes smaller than 16MB.)

The Windows XP setup program uses FAT to format the system partition if *both*

✔ NTFS isn't chosen

✔ And the disk is less than or equal to 2GB in size

However, FAT has limitations that are more serious as disk drives (and the operating systems, applications, and data files that those drives contain) become larger:

✔ A FAT partition can be no larger than 4GB (gigabytes) on Windows XP, 2000, and NT 4.0. That means, in turn, that a drive letter (such as C or D) can't be larger than 4GB because a logical drive must reside on no more than one partition.

✔ Windows 95, 98, and Me only let you set up 2GB FAT partitions.

✔ If you create a FAT partition that's larger than 2GB in Windows XP, 2000, or NT 4.0, some application compatibility problems may arise because of the 64K cluster size that such partitions require. (A *cluster* is the smallest chunk of disk space that the operating system can allocate; check cluster size with CHKDSK and look for the "allocation unit" value.)

✔ With larger hard drives, the FAT cluster also must become larger. Otherwise, too many clusters would exist for the file allocation table to track. (Remember, FAT is a 16-bit structure with limited size.) Larger clusters, in turn, waste more disk space, especially with lots of small files.

Microsoft recommends FAT only in dual-boot systems or where you need compatibility with a DOS boot diskette.

FAT32

Microsoft's update of the FAT16 file system is FAT32, which made its debut in Windows 95 OSR2 and which uses 32-bit structures.

The Windows XP installation program will automatically use FAT32 to format a hard drive if you say "no" to NTFS and if the disk to be formatted is larger than 2GB. Windows XP also uses FAT32 to format DVD-RAM discs.

FAT32 brings the following advantages:

✔ A FAT32 partition can theoretically be 2TB (terabytes) in size, where 1TB = 1,024GB.

That's a lot of space, which explains why Microsoft refers to FAT32 as "large disk support" when you run the FDISK partitioning program. If you're upgrading from a Windows 98 machine, Windows XP will use FAT32 partitions of larger than 32GB if they already exist (Windows 98 can create a 128GB FAT32 partition, and Windows Me can create a 2TB FAT32 partition!). However, Windows XP doesn't let you create a *new* FAT32 partition larger than 32GB. Even so, that's still much larger than the FAT16 limitation of 4GB.

✔ FAT32 can be used on a PC set up to dual-boot between Windows XP and Windows 98.

✔ Because FAT32 is a 32-bit structure that can therefore handle larger data sets, the cluster size can stay low — 4KB on drives up to 8GB in size (see Table 3-2).

Smaller clusters mean less wasted space. Conversion to FAT32 can increase the free space on disk by as much as 25 percent.

✔ The 4KB cluster size that FAT32 uses on disks up to 8GB in size matches up more neatly with the Windows XP memory management scheme.

Many applications can load into memory more rapidly from a FAT32 partition.

Table 3-2	Common Cluster Sizes under FAT16 and FAT32	
Size of Partition	*Cluster Size, FAT16*	*Cluster Size, FAT32*
257MB to 511MB	8KB	4KB
512MB to 1023MB	16KB	4KB
1024MB to 2GB	32KB	4KB
2GB to 4GB	64KB (XP/2000/NT only)	4KB
4GB to 8GB	Not available	4KB
8GB to 16GB	Not available	8KB
16GB to 32GB	Not available	16KB

FAT32 has limitations that may make it inappropriate in some cases:

- ✔ FAT32 doesn't work on disks smaller than 512MB in size.

- ✔ Without third-party software, FAT32 isn't readable by MS-DOS, Windows 3.*x*, or Windows NT running on the same PC.

  That rules out FAT32 on the C drive for systems that must dual-boot to one or more of those operating systems.

- ✔ FAT32 may create problems for older disk utilities designed for FAT16. Not many of these utilities are around anymore, but it's something to double-check.

- ✔ Some older applications may be able to "see" only 2GB per drive letter, even on a FAT32 system.

FAT32 partitions don't permit compression, but that's usually not too big a deal because FAT32 partitions are more space efficient than FAT16 partitions to begin with.

Windows XP supports FAT32 on any partition, including the system partition (that is, the one from which the computer boots). As with FAT, Microsoft recommends FAT32 only for PCs that must dual-boot with older Windows versions.

NTFS

NTFS (NT File System) is Microsoft's recommended file system for Windows XP hard drives if you aren't setting up a dual-boot system.

The suggested minimum size for an NTFS disk is 10MB. NTFS can't be used on floppies.

NTFS basics

NTFS isn't nearly as compatible with other operating systems as FAT16 is; in fact, NTFS only works with Windows NT and Windows XP/2000. Heck, it's not even completely compatible between NT and XP/2000, as I explain later in this section. However, the goodies that you get with NTFS include the following:

- ✔ **Extra security:** With NTFS, you can control access at the folder level and at the file level. (Microsoft therefore often calls NTFS access control "file- and folder-level security." You also see the terms *file security* and *directory security* in this context.) I call NTFS access control "extra" security because it is in addition to the access controls that you can set when you share a folder (*share security*).

- ✔ **More flexible compression:** You can specify particular files or folders to compress. With FAT16, you must compress an entire drive, all or nothing.

- ✔ **Better performance on large drives:** FAT disks slow down on large drives; NTFS disks slow down too, but not as much.

- ✔ **Larger disk sizes:** Microsoft recommends NTFS for disk sizes up to 2TB using basic volumes. (*Dynamic* volumes, which are only compatible with XP and 2000, permit NTFS volumes of up to 16TB with 4K clusters, and 256TB with 64K clusters! See "Basic versus dynamic disks" later in this chapter.) Microsoft strongly advises using NTFS rather than FAT32 for partitions larger than 32GB.

- ✔ **Larger file sizes:** The maximum size of a file on a FAT disk is 2GB; on a FAT32 disk, 4GB; and on an NTFS disk, 16TB (for practical purposes, the size of the disk).

New NTFS perks

The Windows XP version of NTFS is nearly identical to Windows 2000's but is definitely not identical to the Windows NT Workstation 4.0 version. Windows XP and 2000 use NTFS 5 while NT uses NTFS 4. The new version supports the following additional features:

- ✔ **Quotas:** Administrators can limit the amount of disk space used by a given user on a given partition or volume. I examine disk quotas in detail in Chapter 7.

  This feature is a bigger deal for Windows 2000 Server, but you can still use it on Windows XP Professional.

- ✔ **Encryption:** For additional security, users can encrypt files that are then off-limits to anyone who logs onto the machine with a different account.

- ✔ **Change journal:** The operating system tracks all changes (that is, filename, time of change, and type of change, but not the actual changed data) made to the file system in the change journal.

  Again, this feature is more important for the server product line, but services and applications on the XP Professional product can use it, too. The feature is off by default.

- ✔ **Mount points:** A *mount point* lets you map an entire physical disk onto a folder on another disk.

  For example, if you add a second hard drive (one that you would normally designate D) to a PC, you can assign that new drive to the folder `C:\Newdata`. The user will never need to use the D drive letter or modify backup jobs that specify the folder on the C drive. In Chapter 7, I explain how to use mount points.

✔ **Sparse files:** A sparse file is a file with lots of "air" in it, like a spreadsheet with data in cells A1 and Z100 but nothing in between. NTFS 5 lets application developers specify files as sparse, so the sparse files can occupy much less disk space than they would (for example) under FAT or FAT32.

On a dual-boot machine, NT can't "see" an NTFS 5 partition unless you've updated the PC to run NT Service Pack 4 or higher. Service Pack 4 installs an updated NTFS.SYS file system driver that can understand NTFS 5 partitions. (However, the new features that NTFS 5 makes possible, such as disk quotas, are inoperable when you boot to Windows NT Workstation 4.0.) Therefore, the following tip is worth remembering:

If you plan to install Windows XP onto a machine presently running Windows NT Workstation 4.0, and you plan to make that machine dual-boot, upgrade to Service Pack 4 or higher before you install Windows XP. Windows XP automatically converts any NTFS 4 partitions that it finds to NTFS 5.

Focus on NTFS 5

In this section, I take a closer look at some of the new goodies Microsoft built into NTFS Version 5, namely, compression, encryption, and dynamic disks. These are very likely subjects for exam questions!

Compression

Compression enables you to reduce the amount of space on disk that a file or folder occupies. NTFS compression is *transparent;* that is, after you've designated a file as compressed, you don't need to expand it manually before you can use it again. NTFS automatically handles that, as well as the recompression after you've edited and saved the file. Any Windows or DOS program that can run under Windows XP can work with compressed files. If you designate a *folder* as being compressed, then when you create a new file inside that folder or copy an existing file into that folder, NTFS automatically compresses the file.

The compression technology built into NTFS 5 is more sophisticated than that available in earlier Windows operating systems. With NTFS compression, you can specify a drive, a folder, or a file within a folder. With Windows 98 and DoubleSpace compression, you had to specify an entire drive to be compressed.

Setting compression on files or folders

Compressing a file or folder is simple, as shown by Lab 3-3. The lab assumes that your system drive is formatted with the NTFS file system.

Lab 3-3	Compressing a Folder

1. **Log on as an administrator to the local PC.**

   You must have Write permission for any file or folder that you want to compress.

2. **Right-click the My Computer icon on the desktop or Start menu, and choose Explore.**

3. **Expand the tree in the left window pane to display (for example) the** `C:\Program Files\NetMeeting` **folder.**

   If your Windows XP system uses a different drive letter, substitute it for C.

4. **Right-click the NetMeeting folder in the left window pane and choose Properties.**

5. **Click the Advanced button in the Accessories Properties dialog box.**

   You should see the Advanced Attributes dialog box, as shown in Figure 3-1.

6. **Click the box labeled Compress Contents to Save Disk Space.**

   Note that you can't select this option simultaneously with the check box that says Encrypt Contents to Secure Data. (Go ahead and try.)

7. **Click OK and then click OK again (to close two dialog boxes).**

8. **In the Confirm Attribute Changes dialog box (see Figure 3-2), check the box labeled Apply Changes to This Folder, Subfolders, and Files.**

   This action means that Windows XP will compress everything inside the NetMeeting folder. If you check the other box, then you designate the folder as being compressed without designating any of its contents as being compressed. That's perfectly legal, and if you did so, from that point forward, any file that you copy into the NetMeeting folder is automatically compressed.

Figure 3-1:
The
Advanced
Attributes
dialog box.

Note also that you get this same option when you "uncompress" a folder.

9. Click OK.

The NetMeeting folder and its contents are now compressed.

Figure 3-2:
The Confirm
Attribute
Changes
dialog box.

Viewing compressed files and folders

Most of us find it handy to have a visual cue to indicate whether a given file or folder is compressed. Windows XP gives you the option to specify that you'd like the user interface to show compressed files and folders in a different color than uncompressed ones. Lab 3-4 takes you through the simple procedure, again assuming that your C drive uses NTFS.

Lab 3-4	Seeing the Difference between Compressed and Uncompressed Files

1. Choose Start⇨Control Panel and double-click Folder Options.

2. Click the View tab.

3. **Check the box that says Show Encrypted or Compressed NTFS Files In Color.**

4. **Click OK.**

   Now, glance at `C:\WINDOWS\SYSTEM32\DLLCACHE`. It should appear in an alternate color, indicating (in this case) that the folder's contents are compressed.

Copying and moving

What happens to a compressed file when you copy or move it? The rules aren't intuitively obvious, and they make perfect fodder for exam designers. So here we go, easier rules first:

- ✔ *Copying* or *moving* a compressed file to a FAT disk or to a diskette: The file is uncompressed in its new location.

  This makes sense when you remember that compression is an NTFS-only feature.

- ✔ *Copying* or *moving* a compressed file from one NTFS volume to another: The file inherits the compression status of the destination folder.

- ✔ *Copying* a compressed file within an NTFS volume: The file inherits the compression status of the destination folder.

- ✔ *Moving* a compressed file or folder within an NTFS volume: The file or folder keeps its compression status, regardless of the status of the destination folder.

Compression tips

Here are a few tips to remember:

- ✔ Don't compress if you don't need it. Even if you need it, consider alternatives (such as adding a hard drive). Compression may be transparent after you've set it up, but it does incur some system overhead.

- ✔ Don't compress files with formats that tend to be space efficient to begin with, such as JPG, GIF, ZIP, DLL, and EXE files. You don't realize any appreciable space savings and you increase system overhead.

- ✔ Don't compress volatile files that change often (again, because of system overhead). For example, compression is generally a bad idea for active database files.

Encryption

Windows XP's NTFS 5 brings encryption to the file system, a feature unavailable in all previous Windows versions except 2000. (The acronym — you *knew* there had to be an acronym, didn't you? — is EFS, for Encrypted File System.) *Encryption* simply means "scrambling" data in such a way that only someone with a software key can unscramble it.

EFS is a *public key encryption* method, meaning that a public key is used to encrypt a file, and a private key is used to decrypt it. Windows XP handles the public and private keys automatically, behind the scenes; the encryption keys actually reside on the disk as part of the encrypted file's header.

Unless you log on with the correct user name and password, you can't access encrypted files, even if you yank out the hard drive and put it into a different computer.

How to do it

The procedure for encrypting a folder is very similar to the procedure for compressing a folder (refer to Lab 3-3). The only difference is Step 6, wherein you should check the Encrypt Contents to Secure Data box. After you encrypt a folder, you can only have access to that folder and its contents when you log on with the same user account and password that you used when you encrypted the folder originally.

Decrypting a file or folder is a piece o' cake. Log on with the correct user account, view the file or folder's property sheet, click Advanced, and clear the Encrypt Contents to Secure Data check box.

You can encrypt and decrypt files from the command line, too, using the CIPHER command (/E to encrypt, /D to decrypt).

Core facts

Here are some core facts about encryption that you must know for the test:

- ✔ It's available only with the NTFS file system.
- ✔ It doesn't work with system files. You can't encrypt PAGEFILE.SYS, for example.
- ✔ It's incompatible with compression.

    A file or folder may be compressed or encrypted, but not both at the same time.

✔ Unlike in Windows 2000, encrypted files appear in an alternate color (green by default) if the Show Encrypted or Compressed NTFS Files in Color check box is selected in the Folder Options control panel.

✔ When you encrypt a folder, you encrypt all the files in that folder; the folder itself isn't really encrypted.

✔ A file stays encrypted if you rename it, move it, copy it, or back it up, as long as the file stays on an NTFS disk. You can back up an encrypted file to a non-NTFS disk by using the included Backup program, and as long as you restore it to an NTFS disk, the file stays encrypted.

✔ Someone other than an encrypted file's owner gets an "access denied" error when attempting to open the file.

✔ In a nice advance since Windows 2000, you can now share access to a file you've encrypted via the Details tab of the Advanced Attributes dialog box.

✔ You can see who has encrypted a file by clicking the Details button on the Advanced Attributes dialog box.

✔ You can't share an encrypted folder. (That falls into the "painfully obvious" category, but I have to be thorough here.)

✔ Encryption, like compression, is transparent. That is, you don't have to explicitly descramble a file before you edit it and rescramble it when you're done.

Secure security

As long as applications create temporary or backup files within the same folder as the original data file, you're protected because encryption works on a folder basis. That is, if you open up LOVELETTER.DOC in C:\Personal\Letters, which is an encrypted folder, and your word processor creates an *autosave* temporary file named ~LOVELETTER.DOC in the same folder, the temporary file is encrypted, just like the original file.

To go one better, Microsoft makes sure that the encryption keys never show up in the pagefile. You wouldn't want someone sifting through PAGEFILE.SYS in the middle of the night and discovering how to decrypt your encrypted files.

In a network environment, administrators can use Windows XP *policies* to control the use of encryption. For example, an administrator could disable EFS for a domain or for an organizational unit within a domain. I explore the concept of policies in painful detail in Chapter 11.

The safety net

If a user forgets his or her account password, and you just know that's going to happen at some point, the *recovery agent* has a private key that will unlock an encrypted file.

By default, the recovery agent is the administrator of the local PC, or (if the PC is on a network) the domain administrator who first logged on to the first domain controller in the domain.

The recommended practice is to copy (for example, by using Backup) the encrypted file to the recovery agent's PC, where the recovery agent can decrypt the file simply by clearing the Encrypt Contents to Secure Data check box on the file's property sheet.

Basic versus dynamic disks

Windows XP supports two kinds of disk organization:

- *Basic disks,* which use partitions in much the same way as Windows NT Workstation 4.0 or Windows Me/98/95.

- *Dynamic disks,* which are unique to Windows XP and 2000. The default behavior is for Windows XP to set up your disks as basic disks, unless you're upgrading a Windows NT Workstation 4.0 machine that uses advanced disk management features. Check out Chapter 7 for the details.

  You need to use a dynamic disk if you want to create

  - *Striped volumes* (a single drive letter with multiple physical disks running a high-speed configuration)

  - *Spanned volumes* (a single drive letter with multiple physical disks running a normal-speed configuration)

  - *Very large volumes* (greater than 2TB)

For now, just know that you can use dynamic disks with any of the three Windows XP file systems, but certain features (such as extending a volume) are only available if you use NTFS.

Converting from One File System to Another

So you chose file system A, and now you realize you should have chosen file system B. What can you do?

- ✔ If you're installing Windows XP, the setup program asks you if you'd like to convert an existing FAT16 or FAT32 drive to NTFS. The default answer is No on Windows XP Professional (but Yes on Windows 2000 Server).

- ✔ If you're past the installation phase, you can use a supplied program to convert from FAT or FAT32 to NTFS, but not in the reverse direction.

From FAT or FAT32 to NTFS

The conversion utility typically lives in C:\WINDOWS\SYSTEM32 and is named CONVERT.EXE. This tool converts your disk while keeping all the files on the disk intact, unlike a format operation. (Still, you're well advised to make a backup of the drive before conversion, anyway, just in case.) The syntax is

```
CONVERT.EXE <driveletter>: /fs:ntfs [/v] [/cvtarea:filename]
            [/nosecurity]
```

where *<driveletter>* is the letter of the drive you want to convert.

- ✔ The */v* qualifier is optional (hence the square brackets, which you would not actually type) and means "run the utility in verbose mode," that is, with status messages

- ✔ The */cvtarea* qualifier tells Windows to create an unfragmented root directory file to contain the Master File Table (MFT), so that the MFT doesn't become fragmented in the future; this is an improvement over Windows 2000. By the way, you have to use the FSUTIL FILE CREATENEW command to actually create the file, before you use the CONVERT command with the */cvtarea* qualifier.

- ✔ The */nosecurity* qualifier tells Windows not to apply default NTFS permissions to the converted volume, which is now the default behavior of CONVERT.EXE (again, a change from Windows 2000).

Note that you can't convert the current drive. If you have only a C drive on a given PC, CONVERT.EXE advises you that it will perform the conversion at the next restart.

From NTFS to FAT or FAT32

You can go through the looking glass, but not back again. The CONVERT.EXE utility doesn't let you change an NTFS disk back to FAT16 or FAT32. If you need to perform this operation, you must perform a backup, reformat, and restore cycle. (Or go out and get a copy of PowerQuest Partition Magic, which won't be on the test but which I highly recommend for real life.)

Prep Test

1 You're setting up a PC to dual-boot between Windows 98 and Windows XP Professional. You want the most efficient possible use of disk space. You also want to see all partitions from each operating system. Which file system is best for the system partition?

A ○ NTFS

B ○ FAT

C ○ FAT16

D ○ FAT32

E ○ FAT64

2 You've encrypted a file SECRETS.DOC on your Windows XP Professional PC's C drive, which uses NTFS. The D drive on your system uses FAT32. You need to call the file something less obvious, so you rename it MISCINFO.DOC. To back it up for safekeeping, you copy MISCINFO.DOC with your other data files from drive C to drive D. One day, your C drive is corrupt, so you reformat it and reinstall the operating system. You then copy all the data files from D back to C, including MISCINFO.DOC. Which of the following statements are true? (Choose all that apply.)

A ❑ MISCINFO.DOC is still encrypted because you restored it to an NTFS disk.

B ❑ MISCINFO.DOC is no longer encrypted because you lose encryption the moment you rename a file.

C ❑ MISCINFO.DOC is no longer encrypted because you lose encryption the moment you copy a file to a FAT32 disk.

D ❑ MISCINFO.DOC is still encrypted because FAT32 supports the encryption attribute.

3 You've encrypted a file MCSE.TXT on your Windows XP Professional PC's C drive, which uses NTFS. A different user (named Friedrich) logs onto your PC. Which of the following statements are true? (Choose all that apply.)

A ❑ Friedrich can see the encrypted file in Windows Explorer, but he can't open it.

B ❑ Friedrich can see the encrypted file in Windows Explorer, but he can't edit it.

C ❑ Friedrich can see the encrypted file in Windows Explorer, but he can't delete it.

D ❑ Friedrich can see the encrypted file in Windows Explorer, but he can't rename it.

E ❑ Friedrich can't see the encrypted file in Windows Explorer.

4 Mary, an employee at the corporation whose Windows XP workstations you manage, comes to you with a special request. She needs to maximize the performance of her Windows XP Professional computer for playing back digital video. She has the fastest video card available, as well as the fastest processor (256MB of RAM) and two fast hard drives. What step could you suggest to Mary to improve file I/O performance? (Choose the best answer.)

A ○ Convert her hard drives to basic disks and combine them into a spanned volume.

B ○ Convert her hard drives to basic disks and combine them into a striped volume.

C ○ Convert her hard drives to dynamic disks and combine them into a spanned volume.

D ○ Convert her hard drives to dynamic disks and combine them into a striped volume.

5 You compress a file named HUGE.XLS that resides on your Windows XP Professional system in the folder C:\DATA. You move the file to the uncompressed folder D:\WORKFILS. Both C and D are formatted to use the NTFS file system. Which of the following statements are correct? (Choose all that apply.)

A ❑ The file D:\WORKFILS\HUGE.XLS is uncompressed.

B ❑ The file D:\WORKFILS\HUGE.XLS is compressed.

C ❑ When you move the file, Windows XP asks you whether it should be compressed in its new location.

D ❑ You can't move compressed files between disks without uncompressing them first.

6 You're asked to set up a Windows NT 4.0 Workstation PC running NTFS for dual-booting with Windows XP Professional. Which NT Service Pack level is the minimum required for such a system?

A ○ 3
B ○ 4
C ○ 5
D ○ 6

7 Angelina wants to install Windows XP Professional. She deals with data files as large as 3GB per file, but which will never exceed that value. Which file systems could you advise under Windows XP?

A ○ FAT
B ○ FAT32
C ○ NTFS Version 4
D ○ NTFS Version 5

8 You've set up a dual-boot PC that runs both Windows NT Workstation 4.0 and Windows XP. You set up disk quotas under Windows XP, but you notice that users can exceed those quotas when working under NT. Why? (Choose the best answer.)

A ○ Windows NT and Windows XP use a different Registry.

B ○ Windows NT can't use features specific to NTFS Version 5.

C ○ Windows NT can't use features specific to NTFS Version 4.

D ○ A default policy setting in Windows XP limits quotas to users with Windows XP accounts.

9 You want to convert a FAT32 disk (presently drive C) to NTFS. What is the correct syntax for the CONVERT command?

A ○ CONVERT.EXE C: /FS:NTFS

B ○ CONVERT.EXE C: /FS:FAT32

C ○ CONVERT.EXE C: FAT32

D ○ CONVERT.EXE C: NTFS

Answers

1 **D.** Both FAT and FAT32 are supported by both operating systems, but FAT32 uses less disk space and is therefore the better choice here. NTFS is out because Windows 98 can't see NTFS partitions, and FAT64 doesn't exist. *Review "FAT32".*

2 **C.** Renaming a file doesn't change its encryption status, but the file must remain on an NTFS disk. The copy made onto drive D therefore is unencrypted, and it's this copy that's later restored to drive C. (If you use a backup program instead of a copy operation, you can maintain the file's encryption status as long as you restore the file to an NTFS disk.) *Review "Encryption."*

3 **A, B, C,** and **D.** Users can see files that other users have encrypted, but that's it — they can't open, edit, delete, or rename them. If you think about it, it has to be this way: A Recovery Agent can't recover a file if he can't even find it in Windows Explorer. *Review "Encryption."*

4 **D.** Striping is the fastest disk setup in Windows XP Professional. You have to have dynamic disks in order to support striping, so A and B are out. Spanned volumes don't do a thing for speed. *Review "Basic versus dynamic disks."*

5 **A.** When you copy or move a compressed file to a folder on another NTFS volume, the file inherits the compression status of the destination folder. *Memorize this and other compression rules in "Copying and moving."*

6 **B.** Service Pack 4 is the minimum level necessary to ensure that you can boot to Windows NT 4.0 and still see NTFS disks after Windows XP automatically upgrades them to NTFS Version 5. *Review "New NTFS perks."*

7 **B** and **D.** The maximum size of a file on a FAT disk is 2GB; on a FAT32 disk, 4GB; and on an NTFS disk, 16TB. For all practical purposes, file size is limited only by the size of the disk. Windows XP and 2000 use NTFS Version 5; Windows NT 4.0 uses NTFS Version 4. *Review "NTFS basics."*

8 **B.** Just because an NT system can "see" an NTFS Version 5 disk doesn't mean that NT 4.0 can use the features that NTFS Version 5 and Windows XP make possible. *Review "New NTFS perks."*

9 **A.** The CONVERT program doesn't need to be told whether the present disk is FAT or FAT32; it can figure that out on its own. *Review "From FAT or FAT32 to NTFS."*

Chapter 4

Installing Windows XP Professional

***

Exam Objectives

▶ Performing an attended installation of Windows XP Professional

▶ Installing Windows XP Professional by using Remote Installation Services (RIS)

▶ Installing Windows XP Professional by using the System Preparation Tool

▶ Creating unattended answer files by using Setup Manager to automate the installation of Windows XP Professional

▶ Preparing a computer to meet upgrade requirements

▶ Migrating existing user environments to a new installation

***

*I*nstalling Windows NT Workstation was never a piece of cake, and Microsoft knew that it had to do significantly better on the installation procedure if it wanted to make the NT-family platform less user-hostile. Fortunately, you'll have much more hair left on your head after installing Windows XP than after installing NT — or even 2000.

In addition to installing Windows XP Professional interactively, Microsoft provides three separate methods for installing the software in an automated fashion. In this chapter, I cover what you must know about all the various methods, starting with the one-user, one-machine, interactive install.

Quick Assessment

1 To install Windows XP onto a Windows 3.1 PC, run the program _____.

Attended installation of Windows XP Professional

2 To ensure networking components install correctly in a domain environment, verify that a _____ and a _____ are available at install time.

3 Two server operating systems that can run RIS are _____ and _____.

Using Remote Installation Services (RIS)

4 The network services that must be available in a RIS environment are _____, _____, and _____.

5 When a user starts a PC for the first time after it has been configured using SysPrep, the _____ executes one time only.

Using the System Preparation Tool

6 The default name for an answer file is _____.

7 The batch file that Setup Manager creates to run setup with an answer file is named _____.

Using Setup Manager to automate the installation

8 Update packs usually consist of _____ files.

Preparing a computer to meet upgrade requirements

9 To perform a quick software and hardware compatibility check, run WINNT32.EXE with the _____ qualifier.

Migrating existing user environments

10 (True/False) Windows XP is just like Windows NT 4.0 in that you must reapply service packs after making major configuration changes.

Answers

1 *WINNT.EXE.* Use WINNT32.EXE for Windows Me, 98, NT, or 2000, as I explain in the section "Which setup?"

2 *Domain controller, DNS server.* See the "Network choices" section for more.

3 *Windows 2000 Server, Windows 2000 Advanced Server.* When Windows 2002 Server comes out, that'd be correct too. See "Method three: RIS" in this chapter.

4 *DNS, DHCP, Active Directory.* See "Method three: RIS" for more on this remote installation method.

5 *Mini-Setup Wizard.* The "Using SysPrep" section explains.

6 *UNATTEND.TXT.* However, you can use other names. The "Scripting basics" section goes into detail.

7 *UNATTEND.BAT.* If you missed #6, you probably missed this one too. "Implementing the scripted setup" contains more info.

8 *DLL.* See "Upgrade packs" for more.

9 */CHECKUPGRADEONLY.* If you didn't know this one, read "Prepping for installation" in this chapter.

10 *False.* Praise be! See "Installing Upgrade Packs and Service Packs."

Installing Windows XP Interactively

In this section, I deal with the one-on-one installation scenario: one person sitting in front of one PC installing one copy of Windows XP Professional.

I realize that you may not have a test machine available, but if you do, use it. The fastest way to understand the Windows XP installation process is to run through it two or three times on a test PC.

Minimum hardware requirements

The minimum hardware requirements that Microsoft publishes for its operating systems are always an entertaining subject for debate.

For the exam, know the company line about minimum and recommended hardware requirements:

- **CPU:** Pentium 233 MHz minimum, Pentium II 300 MHz or higher recommended
- **RAM:** 64MB minimum, 128MB or more recommended
- **Disk:** 2GB partition with 650MB free space minimum, 2GB free space recommended
- **CD or DVD:** Required for CD installations; any speed minimum, 12X or faster recommended
- **Display:** VGA minimum, SVGA recommended
- **Input:** Keyboard, mouse, or other pointing device minimum (recommended is the same)

For real life, realize that the minimum practical requirements for CPU, RAM, and disk depend greatly on the particular services and applications you intend to run.

In every situation, Windows XP requires substantially more hardware horsepower than Windows Me and 9*x*, and moderately more horsepower than Windows NT 4.0 and 2000.

Prepping for installation

Here are a few pre-installation checks that you should perform:

✔ Verify that you're running the most recent functional BIOS. Windows XP decides which Hardware Abstraction Layer (HAL) to install partly on the basis of the BIOS type and version that it detects at install time.

✔ Verify that all hardware is on Microsoft's Hardware Compatibility List (HCL). You can check the HCL.TXT file on the CD in the SUPPORT folder, or consult the Microsoft Web site (www.microsoft.com/hcl) among other places. In general, hardware that works in NT 4 or Windows 2000 should work with Windows XP but may need new drivers.

✔ If you're upgrading a Windows NT 4.0, Windows Me, Windows XP (Home Edition), Windows 2000 or Windows 98 machine, you can run WINNT32.EXE with the **/CHECKUPGRADEONLY** qualifier to see a report of potential upgrade problems (see Figure 4-1).

You can perform a compatibility check without performing an actual upgrade when running a scripted installation over Windows Me or 98. Include the line **ReportOnly=Yes** in the [Win9xUpg] section of UNATTEND.TXT. Windows writes the compatibility report as a text file to the root of the system drive by default, but you can change the location with the **SaveReportTo** option. That's handy if you want to specify a network location where you can collect all the reports for review. Use a parameter such as *%computername%* in the filename that you specify with SaveReportTo in order to save each file under a different name. See "Method one: Scripting" later in this chapter.

✔ Run a virus scanner on your system and correct any reported problems.

If your system has a BIOS-based virus scanner, disable it for the installation, or be prepared to click Continue when the scanner asks you if it's okay to modify the boot record.

✔ If you're upgrading a Windows XP (Home Edition), Me, or 98 machine, check Device Manager for any conflicts (red X's) or alerts (yellow !'s). Correct these if possible.

✔ If you're upgrading a Windows NT 4.0 machine, check the System, Application, and Security event logs for errors or warnings. Deal with these before proceeding.

✔ If you're upgrading a Windows NT 4.0 machine, make sure that you've installed Service Pack 6 (or higher) before you upgrade.

✔ In an upgrade scenario, record system resource assignments (IRQs, DMA channels, base I/O addresses, upper-memory addresses). You can use a tool such as MSINFO to print or save such data to disk.

Network choices

You should also figure out some network choices ahead of time.

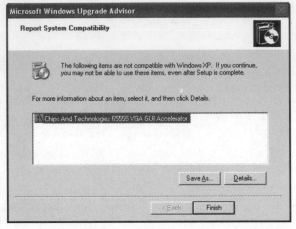

Figure 4-1:
The
upgrade
check
reports
on any
potential
upgrade
problems.

If a Microsoft *network domain* (the usual choice in the corporate environment)
is the environment, bear in mind the following:

- ✔ You must know the *domain name,* such as `corphq.i-sw.com`.

- ✔ You must provide for a *computer account* in the domain.

  Do so by defining it ahead of time (domain administrators can do this)
  or by specifying an account at setup time that has administrative rights
  on the domain and can, therefore, create the computer account as part
  of the setup process.

- ✔ A *domain controller* and a *DNS server* should be up and running and
  connected to the workstation PC during the Windows XP Professional
  installation. If this condition doesn't apply, then you can specify
  "workgroup" at install time and join the domain after running setup;
  it's just more convenient to get it all done at once.

If you're joining a *workgroup* environment, you need the workgroup name,
which can be the name of an existing workgroup or the name of a new one.

Which setup?

In addition, you should determine which version of the setup program you
should run, as follows:

- ✔ Run WINNT.EXE if you're performing a clean installation on a PC running
  DOS or Windows 3.*x*.

- ✔ Run WINNT32.EXE if you're performing a clean installation or an
  upgrade on a PC running Windows 98, Me, NT, or Windows XP
  (Home Edition).

Clean or dirty?

Finally, resolve whether to perform an upgrade or a "clean install" (Microspeak).

A *clean* installation doesn't necessarily mean that the existing hard drive is wiped clean; it means, at minimum, that Windows XP installs into a fresh folder or partition. These are your options:

- ✔ Choose a clean installation if you have an existing operating system with which you'd like to dual boot; if you want to make sure that you've removed all traces of a previous operating system; if you'd like to reformat a partition with NTFS 5; if you're using Windows 95, Windows 3.*x*, or DOS; or if your PC doesn't have an operating system on it already.

  This route entails reinstalling applications and making any customizations that differ from a "stock" operating system installation.

- ✔ Choose an upgrade installation if you have an existing operating system with which you don't want to dual-boot, and you want to retain the Registry settings that allow you to run existing applications, as well as retain the applications themselves.

If you decide to perform a clean installation *and* wipe the disk, you must provide for Windows XP's setup program to start somehow. That is, you must provide a path to display a command prompt from which to run WINNT.EXE or WINNT32.EXE. Choose one of these methods:

- ✔ Create a DOS or Windows 9*x* boot diskette with the appropriate device drivers for your CD-ROM or network share.

- ✔ Boot from the setup CD-ROM, but only if the PC supports the "El Torito" bootable CD standard. (You may have to enable CD-based booting in the BIOS, then press a key at restart when the BIOS prompts you to boot from the CD.)

- ✔ Create a set of boot diskettes by downloading the necessary files from the Microsoft Web site (the MAKEBOOT program in the BOOTDISK folder of the Windows 2000 Professional CD is not included with Windows XP Professional).

- ✔ Install a network card with remote-boot capability. (You may also have to set the PC's BIOS to boot from the network in this case.)

Installation phases

The typical installation procedure has four distinct stages: (1) collecting information, (2) dynamic update, (3) preparing installation, and (4) installing Windows. The following sections take a closer look.

Stage 1: Collecting information

You can start the installation several ways. For example, you can boot from the CD-ROM to do a clean install (if your PC supports the El Torito specification), or you can run WINNT or WINNT32 from the CD or from a network distribution point to do a clean install or an upgrade install.

Here are the key steps in Stage 1, with notes on which you'd do in an upgrade scenario and which you'd do in a clean install (say, by booting from CD):

1. Setup loads a bare-bones version of Windows XP into memory (clean), or the Welcome to Windows XP screen appears and you choose Install Windows XP (upgrade).

   If you're booting from the Windows XP CD, you have to press the F6 key to install a SCSI or RAID driver necessary for Windows to see your hard drive. Windows XP can normally detect SCSI hard drives on the PCI bus, but it won't detect an ISA bus device.

2. Choose the type of installation, upgrade or clean, if you already have an operating system installed. (You don't get this option if you're booting from CD because that method only permits a clean install.)

3. You review and accept the licensing agreement.

4. In a boot-from-CD scenario, you create an installation partition or specify an existing partition for the installation. You don't get this choice in an upgrade installation; Windows XP will use the partition that already hosts your operating system.

   You can delete partitions here, too. No more FDISK!

5. If you create a new partition, you must pick a file system so that Windows XP can format it.

6. Enter the product key (for example, from the back of the retail CD).

Stage 2: Dynamic Update

If you have a working Internet connection and are upgrading a previous version of Windows, then Dynamic Update connects you to Microsoft after the initial data collection phase, and downloads the following items:

- Critical updates to existing device drivers
- Updates or fixes to files used during Setup (such as WINNT32.EXE)

The download is a silent procedure as far as I've tested it; that is, you're not advised whether anything is actually downloading or not, and you don't get a report. When Dynamic Update is finished, you move to the "Preparing installation" phase.

Stage 3: Preparing installation

Here's what happens in Stage 3:

1. You get a system compatibility report (for example, listing any unsupported device drivers).

2. Windows XP copies some files to your hard drive.

3. The system restarts. In an upgrade scenario, you can press F6 to supply a third-party SCSI or RAID driver.

4. Setup copies a lot of files over to your hard drive.

Stage 4: Installing Windows

Here's what happens during Stage 4:

1. Windows performs hardware detection for both Plug and Play and legacy devices.

2. If you're not upgrading from a previous version of Windows, you must supply

    - Language information
    - Locale
    - Keyboard layout
    - Name
    - Organization
    - Computer name

    If you're upgrading, the setup program asks you for this stuff before Stage 1.

The computer name (also known as NetBIOS name) must contain no more than 15 characters. It must also be unique among other computer names, domain names, and workgroup names! Also note that on a Windows XP network, the computer name appears in Active Directory as an object; unlike Windows 9x, computers in Windows XP and 2000 have their own security accounts.

3. You supply a password for the Administrator account.

4. You specify dialing information (area code, how to get an outside line, tone versus pulse dialing) if your PC has a modem.

5. You set the date and time and time zone.

6. Windows XP tries to autodetect your network card.

7. Windows XP copies a bunch of network-related files to your PC.

8. You must tell Windows XP whether you want typical network settings (defined as: Client for Microsoft Networks + File and Printer Sharing + TCP/IP) or custom settings.

   FYI, I always recommend going with the typical settings and customizing things after setup completes.

9. If you're not upgrading, Windows XP asks you to join a workgroup or join a domain. (If you are upgrading, Windows XP uses your existing settings for these options.) You may have to provide a password for an account with domain administration rights in order to create a computer account if one doesn't already exist for you. Also, you see errors if a domain controller and DNS server aren't available at this time.

10. Windows XP configures your network setup amidst much clicking and whirring.

11. Various file copy and installation steps occur, typically including COM+, games, accessories, and Indexing Service, among others.

12. Windows performs Start menu initialization, component registration, saving settings, and removing any temporary files used.

13. The PC restarts.

14. If your computer isn't a member of a domain, your screen supports 800x600 mode, and you didn't set up a computer account, then you'll see the Windows Welcome screen, which prompts you to activate the installation (see "Product Activation" later in this chapter), optionally register with Microsoft, and run Internet Connection Wizard.

Upgrading from Windows 9x

You'll need to know a few specific points regarding the upgrade process from Windows 98/Me, as follows:

- Windows XP makes a mandatory backup of the Windows 9x system, creating a 300MB file. After a certain amount of time following the upgrade, Windows XP asks the user if she wants to delete the backup.

- A user can uninstall Windows XP and revert to the Windows 9x system if Windows XP isn't working for some reason.

- Users do _not_ get an uninstall option for an upgrade from Windows 2000 Professional. (Don't ask me why.)

Product Activation

The final step of the setup process is a new one: _Windows Product Activation,_ also known as WPA. Microsoft is hoping to deter license abuse by requiring that each copy of Windows XP Professional sold at retail be *activated,* through an interactive session with Microsoft, within 30 days of installation.

What happens during activation is that Windows XP combines your unique product key with a hardware ID that is derived from your computer's hardware configuration. The result is an *installation ID.* When you connect to Microsoft, over the Net or by phone, you provide Microsoft with the installation ID. Microsoft checks to make sure that you haven't already used your product key with another computer; if not, then you get a *confirmation ID* that activates your system. Henceforth, Windows XP checks your installation ID against the installed hardware, and if it detects a difference, you'll have to perform activation again.

WPA will not be required for customers with volume licenses. Only retail customers and small businesses will have to mess with it.

The problem, of course, is that people often upgrade their PC hardware. It remains to be seen how Microsoft will handle legitimate requests to reactivate Windows XP on upgraded machines; all Microsoft is saying on their public Web site at this writing is that "If the hardware is substantially different, then reactivation is required." The exam will omit consideration of such potential frustrations, so I won't waste time here explaining all the reasons why WPA is a really bad idea.

Notes on dual-boot systems

Microsoft has generally not supported dual-boot systems in the past. The company has changed its position regarding dual-booting Windows XP, however. You can bet that the exam has a couple of dual-boot questions on it, so here's the lowdown. (You can get more information at www.microsoft.com/windows/multiboot.asp.)

Dual-boot pros and cons

Advantages of dual-boot systems include:

- ✔ Reduced costs for research and test-bench environments
- ✔ Handy for support technicians who must support multiple operating systems
- ✔ Excellent teaching tool
- ✔ Ability to compare performance on identical hardware

Disadvantages include:

- ✔ Far more complex software setup
- ✔ More complex maintenance and troubleshooting
- ✔ Potential file system incompatibilities
- ✔ Potential application incompatibilities
- ✔ Larger hard drive space requirements

Operating systems

In the absence of third-party partitioning and multiboot software, Microsoft supports Windows XP dual-booting with any of the following operating systems:

- ✔ Windows 2000
- ✔ Windows NT 4.0 (preferably with Service Pack 4 or higher for NTFS 5 compatibility)
- ✔ Windows 95 (all versions)
- ✔ Windows 98 (all versions)
- ✔ Windows Me
- ✔ Windows for Workgroups 3.11
- ✔ Windows 3.1
- ✔ DOS
- ✔ OS/2

If you use Microsoft software without any additional utilities, the general rule is to install operating systems in order from oldest to newest. That is, if you want to create a dual-boot machine with Windows 98 and Windows XP, install the operating systems in that order. In that scenario, you would specify a different folder for Windows XP, and you would dedicate a separate disk partition to Windows XP. (Microsoft is very big on using separate partitions in dual-boot systems, the only exception being if you're dual-booting between different versions of Windows XP, such as Professional and Home.)

When installing Windows XP to multiboot with NT, you won't be able to use features of Windows XP's version of NTFS from NT. That is, if you encrypt files from Windows XP and then boot to NT 4.0, you won't be able to access those files because NT 4.0 doesn't understand about encryption.

Partitioning considerations

Here are a couple of rules for creating partitions:

- If you have more than two operating systems you want to boot to, and you can't install each operating system onto its own partition, the next best thing is to install Windows XP on its own partition, while leaving other operating systems (Windows 9x, 3.x, DOS) on their own "group" partition.

- Each partition must be large enough to meet the minimum hardware requirements published for that particular operating system.

File system considerations

Here are the rules for deciding on file systems on a multiboot machine:

- If you want to dual-boot with DOS, Windows 3.x, or Windows 95 (original version through OSR1), and you want those operating systems to be able to see the Windows XP partition, use the FAT file system for Windows XP and for the primary partition.

- If you want to dual-boot with Windows 95 (OSR2 and higher) or Windows 98, and you want those operating systems to be able to see the Windows XP partition, use the FAT or FAT32 file system for Windows XP and for the primary partition. (FAT32 uses less disk space but is incompatible with DOS and Windows 3.x.)

- On a dual-boot machine with Windows 9x, you may configure a Windows XP partition as NTFS, but the primary (boot) partition must be FAT or (in the case of Windows 95 OSR2+ and Windows 98) FAT32.

Procedural notes

A few points to bear in mind when setting up a dual-boot system:

- During the installation, say "no" to the upgrade question and choose a clean install instead.

- At each boot after the installation finishes, you can select "Windows XP Professional" or "Windows." (The exact wording resides in BOOT.INI.) The second option runs your earlier version of Windows.

- If you need to correct drive letter mismatches, for example a CD-ROM drive that is E: under Windows 98 but F: under Windows XP, then boot to Windows XP, right-click the My Computer icon (on the desktop or on the Start menu), and choose Manage. Then use the Disk Management snap-in to change the drive letter so that it matches the other operating system.

Automating the Windows XP Installation

Up to this point, this chapter has dealt with an interactive installation, but that type isn't the norm in most organizations — users have too many opportunities to take a wrong turn! In this section, I show you the three primary methods that Microsoft provides for automating the Windows XP installation: scripting, cloning, and Remote Installation Service (RIS).

A fourth method, using System Management Server or SMS, is available for rolling out Windows XP, but only to PCs that are already connected to the network and running an existing operating system. This method provides centralized control and scheduling flexibility. You're unlikely to see SMS questions on the test, so don't worry about learning more than the contents of this paragraph.

Method one: Scripting

This method involves running the setup program from a central network server (or, alternatively, from a custom-built CD) under control of a script.

When to use scripting

This method works well in situations where you have a hodgepodge of PC makes, models, and components. The setup program can still autodetect PC hardware and make adjustments for the fact (for example) that Carina has a 3Com network card while Cecily has a Madge network card.

The customized script that you create to guide the setup program doesn't mandate that everyone's initial Registry look identical — that doesn't work, for example, with the two different network cards. The script mandates only that certain settings, such as the time zone and standard networking language, are identical on each PC.

Scripting basics

With any version of Windows, the setup program asks you a number of questions. The *answer file* in Windows XP is a text-format script that behaves like a virtual user, automatically answering each of the setup program's questions as they come up. Because the answers come from a file instead of an interactive user, the installation is termed *unattended,* hence the typical name of the answer file: UNATTEND.TXT. Figure 4-2 shows an example.

Typical answer file parameters include the following items:

- Product (Windows XP Professional, Windows 2000 Server)
- Automation level (from "Fully Automated" to "Provide Defaults")
- Default user data and computer names (may use UDF file to feed)
- Network settings (workgroup, domain, and so on)

✔ Custom wallpaper

✔ Run Once commands

✔ CMDLINES.TXT

✔ Code pages

✔ Regional options

✔ Time zone

✔ Telephony details

Figure 4-2:
A fairly brief
and simple
answer file.

Microsoft provides a compiled help document (DEPLOY.CHM, located in
the DEPLOY.CAB file on the Windows XP CD's \SUPPORT\TOOLS folder)
explaining all the details of creating an answer file. I recommend you read
this file if you have access to it; the exam is likely to include one or two very
nitpicky questions covering possible UNATTEND.TXT settings. Happily, the
company also provides a friendly, graphical utility called *Setup Manager*
(SETUPMGR.EXE, now in version 3.0) that does a pretty good job of building
an answer file for you, along with a batch file demonstrating how to run setup
with the answer file (see Figure 4-3). The DEPLOY.CHM file is handy to know
about in case you want to fine-tune your answer file by hand.

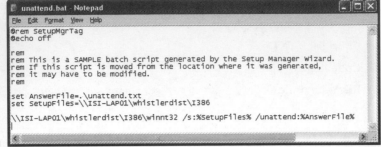

Figure 4-3:
An auto-
generated
batch file to
run setup
with the
answer file.

```
unattend.bat - Notepad
File  Edit  Format  View  Help
@rem SetupMgrTag
@echo off

rem
rem This is a SAMPLE batch script generated by the Setup Manager wizard.
rem If this script is moved from the location where it was generated,
rem it may have to be modified.
rem

set AnswerFile=.\unattend.txt
set SetupFiles=\\ISI-LAP01\whistlerdist\I386

\\ISI-LAP01\whistlerdist\I386\winnt32 /s:%SetupFiles% /unattend:%AnswerFile%
```

Installing Setup Manager

Windows XP doesn't automatically install Setup Manager, so you have to install it yourself. The tool lives in a cabinet file named DEPLOY.CAB on the Windows XP CD in the \SUPPORT\TOOLS folder. Follow these steps to install Setup Manager:

1. **Put the Windows XP CD-ROM into the drive.**

2. **Open Windows Explorer.**

3. **Create a new folder for the Setup Manager program.**

4. **Double-click the CD file \SUPPORT\TOOLS\DEPLOY.CAB.**

   Windows XP automatically opens up compressed CAB, or *cabinet,* files within the Explorer window. You don't have to extract the files one by one, as you do with some other Windows versions.

5. **Drag and drop all the contents of DEPLOY.CAB into the folder you created in Step 3.**

6. **Right-click and drag SETUPMGR.EXE onto the desktop and choose Create Shortcut Here. Alternatively or additionally, you can drag and drop this file to a position on your Start menu.**

After you install Setup Manager, running it is a matter of double-clicking the icon you created, or selecting the Start menu option you made. You then see the manager's main screen.

Setting script options via Run Once

As you go through the various screens in Setup Manager, you provide the answers to as many setup questions as you want. These screens are mostly self-explanatory until you come to the name Run Once screen. (To see the Run Once screen, you must click yes when asked if you want to specify additional settings after you've created the basic answer file.)

The commands that you enter here run automatically the first time a user logs onto Windows XP after setup has finished. You can include here, for example, a command such as **REGEDIT CUSTOM.REG** if you want to merge the contents of CUSTOM.REG into the user's Registry. (The commands that you enter in Setup Manager's Run Once screen appear in the [GUIRunOnce] section of UNATTEND.TXT.)

Because the Run Once commands execute after the first user logon, any user-related settings affect the current user rather than the default user. Also, the Run Once commands are subject to any permissions restrictions that may apply to the logged-on user. If you want to perform actions that are not restricted by any potential permissions issues, you should use the CMDLINES.TXT file instead, which I discuss later in this section.

Creating the distribution point

An essential step in creating a network-based setup procedure is to install a complete copy of the Windows XP source files onto a server, called a *distribution server,* from which a new user can install Windows XP across the network onto the workstation. (The server "distributes" Windows XP to the network users.)

Setup Manager offers to create a distribution point for you as its final act, saving you the trouble of manually copying the necessary files to your network server. Creating a distribution point is also necessary if you want to run a CMDLINES.TXT file (see next section), which won't run from a CD-ROM even if you burn your own.

If you want to include your own custom help files, application files, drivers, utilities, or any other sort of files in the Windows XP distribution folder, Setup Manager lets you do that in the Additional Files or Folders window toward the end of the procedure. Those additional files go into the folder named OEM in recognition of the fact that Original Equipment Manufacturers (*OEMs*) make heavy use of this feature; see Figure 4-4. (The OEM folder is also used for custom *HALs,* or *Hardware Abstraction Layers,* and for hardware-specific SCSI drivers.)

You can use Setup Manager to create an answer file that you can use *without* a distribution point. For example, you can distribute the answer file on diskette and have users install Windows XP from the Microsoft-supplied CD. If you take this approach, the answer file must have the name WINNT.SIF, the PC must support booting from the CD via the "El Torito" specification, and you must include in the answer file a [Data] section with options set up as described in DEPLOY.CHM.

Creating CMDLINES.TXT

After you tell Setup Manager where you want your distribution point to be, and after you answer a few more questions, you get to the Additional Commands screen. Any additional commands that you type into this window ultimately go into the text file CMDLINES.TXT, which Setup Manager places into the OEM folder of your distribution point.

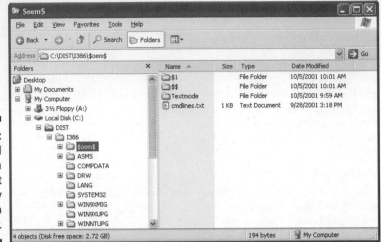

Figure 4-4:
A typical
distribution
point
created by
Setup
Manager.

The simple CMDLINES.TXT file has a section labeled *[Commands]* under which
appear the commands you created in the Additional Commands screen. As
with the Run Once section, these commands can include instructions to load
REG files of your own devising. And if you want to get fancy, they can also
include VBScript or JavaScript programs that you create.

Unlike the Run Once commands, commands in CMDLINES.TXT execute at the
end of the setup procedure but *before* the user logs on to Windows XP for the
first time. These commands basically run with system privileges, so they
aren't subject to any user-specific access control restrictions. Furthermore,
CMDLINES.TXT runs whether the user is performing an upgrade from a
previous version of Windows, or from a fresh install. However, because no
user is logged on, no access to protected network resources is available.

Implementing the scripted setup

Your final step is to include the setup command file (typically
UNATTEND.BAT) in a network logon script. Here's a typical procedure:

1. **Set up a special user account (for example, UPGRADE) for the user
   who wants to install Windows XP to log on to.**

2. **Define appropriate security for the UPGRADE account (no changing
   passwords, rights to the server with Windows XP on it, and so on).**

3. **Create a logon script and associate it with the UPGRADE user.**

When a user wants to install Windows XP, she can log on to the UPGRADE
account and answer only the questions that you left for users to decide on
their own (if any).

Method two: Cloning

If you're lucky enough to work in a network where everyone has pretty much the same hardware, you may want to consider disk cloning as an alternative to a scripted, network-based setup. Microsoft provides the *SysPrep* utility for this situation. (This utility actually made its debut late in the life cycle of Windows NT 4.0 Workstation.)

You use SysPrep in conjunction with a third-party image replication tool, such as a hard drive duplicating machine, or a program such as Ghost or Drive Image.

Cloning basics

Disk *cloning* normally means that you crank out carbon-copy hard drives that include not only Windows XP but also any desired Windows XP applications.

This technique works only if all the PCs have the same basic hardware (Hardware Abstraction Layer, power management, hard disk controller, and number of processors); because of Windows XP's Plug and Play detection capabilities, other hardware can vary. That is, Windows XP can autodetect devices such as network cards and display adapters after the main installation is finished.

If your network PCs are all very similar, disk cloning may be faster and easier than setting up a network-based setup with a custom script. Cloning a hard drive over a network can take as little as ten minutes.

Using SysPrep

To clone Windows XP by using SysPrep, follow these steps:

1. **Create a test PC with Windows XP installed just the way you want it.**

   Don't specify a domain or an administrative password.

2. **Install whatever applications you need and customize them, too.**

3. **Clean up the event logs and any other application install log files that you don't need to duplicate.**

4. **Put the files SYSPREP.EXE, SETUPCL.EXE (which generates new security IDs), and (optionally) the answer file SYSPREP.INF (which has the same structure as UNATTEND.TXT) into the folder** %SystemDrive%\SYSPREP.

   (%SystemDrive% is shorthand for the drive letter of the system drive, usually C but not always.) The files reside in DEPLOY.CAB on the Windows XP CD's \SUPPORT\TOOLS folder. Windows XP deletes the

SYSPREP folder after the Mini-Setup Wizard runs on the user's cloned machine. The SYSPREP.INF file provides predefined answers to the Mini-Setup Wizard. If you'd rather use the Out Of Box Experience (also known as OOBE or Windows Welcome) method that Microsoft introduced with Windows Me, you can do that too: Instead of SYSPREP.INF, the file that drives the OOBE Wizard is OOBEINFO.INI.

5. **Add a CMDLINES.TXT file, if desired, to the SYSPREP folder to run post-Setup commands; for example, to install software applications after Windows XP has already been installed.**

6. **Run SYSPREP.EXE with the** -reboot **qualifier to make sure it runs as desired.**

7. **Run SYSPREP.EXE again, this time without the** -reboot **qualifier, and shut down the machine.**

8. **Image the disk with a hardware or software duplicator (such as Ghost) and (depending on your choice) install cloned disks into the target PCs or run the image copying program across the network.**

When a cloned PC is first started, if you specify the Mini-Setup Wizard instead of the Out Of Box Experience, then depending on whether you used SYSPREP.INF and on the options included in that answer file, the wizard asks the user to specify the following:

- Agreement with the license (as if you have a choice!)
- Regional options
- User and company name
- Computer name and administrator password
- Network settings
- Time zone

Although the more typical use for SysPrep is to clone identical hard drives, you can also use it to create a custom installation CD-ROM.

The exam is likely to ask you about SysPrep's so-called *factory mode*, which you invoke with SYSPREP.EXE using the qualifier **-factory**. This mode lets you install new or updated drivers that the original image didn't include. When you reboot after running SysPrep in factory mode, the PC doesn't start OOBE or the Mini-Setup Wizard. Instead, it processes its own private answer file, a text file named WINBOM.INI (the "BOM" means "Bill of Materials"), which has various sections. One section is *[PnPDrivers]*, where you can specify new or updated drivers. When you're done with factory mode, run SysPrep with the **reseal** qualifier to prepare the PC for delivery.

Method three: RIS

You can set up a Windows 2002 or 2000 Server with Remote Installation Service (RIS), which enables you to install Windows XP onto PCs that don't even have an existing operating system on their hard drives. Such PCs can boot to a special diskette that the network administrator provides, or the PCs may have a network card with remote-boot capabilities (compatibility with the *Pre-Boot eXecution Environment,* or *PXE,* remote-boot standard is presumed). The network card uses DHCP to find a RIS server from which to download the operating system files.

Using RIS places a fair amount of traffic onto the network and requires a server optimized for file-intensive tasks.

RIS requirements

Here's what you must know about requirements for a RIS installation:

- ✔ RIS does *not* ship with Windows XP Professional.

  The software comes with all server versions of Windows 2000 and 2002 and requires that operating system. (This rules out RIS for sites that don't run Windows 2000 or 2002 Server.)

- ✔ The new version of RIS lets you deploy any version of the Windows 2000 and XP family except Windows 2000 Datacenter Server.

- ✔ Clients must have a PXE-capable BIOS (version .99c or greater), a PXE-capable network card, or a regular PCI-bus network card that's on the list of those supported by the Remote Boot Disk Generator program, RBDG.

- ✔ The user account you intend to use for installation must have the right to log on as a batch job.

  Assign this via Active Directory utilities on the server.

- ✔ The server running RIS can be a member server or a domain.

- ✔ DNS must be running on some network server for Windows XP to find Active Directory and workstation computer accounts.

- ✔ DHCP must be running on some network server so that PCs with bootable network cards can receive an IP address.

  If you're using RIS with routers that don't support the relaying of DHCP/BOOTP messages, then you must have *either* a DHCP server or a DHCP *relay agent* (which can be a Windows NT 4.0 server or a Windows 2000 or 2002 server) running on the same subnet as the client PC.

- ✔ The RIS software must reside on a shared NTFS volume on a drive other than the drive from which Windows 2002 or 2000 Server runs.

Installing and configuring RIS

The procedure for installing RIS onto a Windows 2000 Server machine probably won't be on Exam #70-270, so I'll keep this brief. On the server, open the Control Panel, run Add/Remove Programs, click Add/Remove Windows Components, and select Remote Installation Services.

After your server reboots, follow the prompts to configure RIS. You specify (among other things) a folder on an NTFS volume where the Windows XP Professional installation files should reside. Make sure at least 300MB is available at this location. The wizard copies all the files for you.

On the client side, you can set up computers to boot from the network if the BIOS or network adapters support PXE. Set the BIOS to use the network card as the primary boot device.

If neither the BIOS nor the network card supports PXE, create a boot diskette using the *Remote Boot Disk Generator* (RBFG.EXE, and yes, the F is for Floppy and it should be D for Disk). RBFG comes with the RIS software. The exam is likely to test your knowledge of this program's name.

If you want to get fancy, you can use RIS to set up a client PC, modify that client PC so that it looks exactly the way you want all other PCs to look (for example, by installing user applications), then run RIPREP.EXE (the *Remote Installation Preparation Wizard*) to copy the files from the client up to the RIS server. As with SysPrep, the client PC that you set up to be the master image must use the same HAL as the PCs onto which you intend to install Windows XP. Another caution: After you copy the files to the RIS server, you can't change the installation image.

Installing Upgrade Packs and Service Packs

Service packs upgrade the operating system; *upgrade* packs upgrade applications. Here are a few words of wisdom on each subject.

Upgrade packs

Upgrade packs are collections of files (usually one or more DLLs) that update applications for better compatibility with Windows XP. For example, an upgrade pack DLL may contain information about moving configuration settings from one part of the Registry to another. You normally use an upgrade pack when upgrading an earlier version of Windows to Windows XP, as opposed to performing a clean install.

Upgrade packs are available from the application vendor rather than from Microsoft, although Microsoft provides information for designing them via the Software Development Kit (SDK). Follow the vendor's guidelines for installation; Windows XP processes the upgrade packs during the graphical mode of setup. You can see examples on the Windows XP CD under \I386\ WIN9XMIG.

Service packs

One of the welcome changes from Windows NT 4.0 is the *slipstreaming* of service packs. This term means that you can apply a Windows XP service pack to your network-based distribution server, and all future installations from that server incorporate the service pack updates and changes. That is, installers or users don't need to install Windows XP Professional first and then apply the service pack in a separate step. When you apply a service pack to a distribution server, subsequent installations are called "integrated installations." Note that you cannot undo such a service pack application!

The command for applying a service pack to a master image is **UPDATE. EXE -S:<distpath>**, where *<distpath>* is the path to your existing distribution image. You'd run UPDATE.EXE from the I386 folder on your service pack CD. So, for example, if your service pack CD is on drive D: and your network distribution point is K:\WINXP, the command you'd run would be as follows:

```
D:\I386\UPDATE\UPDATE.EXE -S:K:\WINXP
```

Another nice improvement is that you no longer have to reinstall Windows components (such as network protocols) after applying a service pack, a requirement that often reared its ugly head in NT 4.

The command for applying a service pack to an individual Windows XP Professional workstation is simply **UPDATE.EXE.** If you run it from a script or batch file, you'd normally use the -U and -Q qualifiers to run the install in unattended, quiet mode.

Third and last, in the "old days" with NT 4, you had to reapply service packs after changing the configuration of operating system services. For example, if you added the file and printer sharing service, you'd have to reapply the service pack. Windows XP is smart enough to ask for the proper files when you make a configuration change, removing the need to perform a service pack reinstall. Three cheers for these three changes.

Prep Test

1 What are ways of checking a PC's hardware and software compatibility before upgrading to Windows XP Professional? (Choose all that apply.)

A ❑ Run WINNT32.EXE /CHECKUPGRADE.

B ❑ Run WINNT32.EXE /CHECKUPGRADEONLY.

C ❑ Download and run CHKUPGRD.EXE from Microsoft's Web site.

D ❑ Download and run UPGRDCHK.EXE from Microsoft's Web site.

E ❑ For Windows 98 systems, add the line ReportOnly=Yes to the [Win9xUpg] section of UNATTEND.TXT.

2 You decide to automate your Windows XP deployment by using SysPrep. Which file do you need to create in order to avoid users having to answer questions during the Mini-Setup Wizard?

A ○ UNATTEND.TXT

B ○ ANSWER.TXT

C ○ SYSPREP.INF

D ○ SYSPREP.TXT

E ○ OOBEINFO.INI

3 You use Remote Installation Service (RIS) to deploy Windows XP Professional. However, many of the PCs aren't PXE-compliant at the BIOS level or the network adapter card level. What program do you use to create a boot diskette for these PCs?

A ○ MAKEBOOT.EXE

B ○ RIPREP.EXE

C ○ RBFG.EXE

D ○ RBDG.EXE

4 You create an unattended installation script with Setup Manager. Users will install Windows XP Professional from their CD-ROM drives by using the Microsoft-supplied Windows XP CD. You will distribute the answer file on diskette as UNATTEND.TXT. All the user PCs support booting from the CD by using the El Torito specification. During a test, the setup program doesn't seem to use the UNATTEND.TXT file on the diskette, and the program asks the user for answers to all the setup questions interactively. What must you do to fix this problem? (Choose all that apply.)

A ❑ Rename the file WINNT.INF.

B ❑ Rename the file WINNT.SIF.

C ❑ Create a folder named OEM on the hard drive and create a batch file on the diskette that copies UNATTEND.TXT to that folder.

D ❑ Make sure the answer file contains a [Data] section containing the required keys.

5 You have set up a Windows 2002 Server as a RIS server for automating the deployment of Windows XP. However, when you boot a PXE-enabled PC, it can't seem to find the RIS server. What are the possible reasons for this problem? (Choose all that apply.)

A ❑ No DHCP server exists on the subnet, and the router isn't configured to forward DHCP or BOOTP packets.

B ❑ A DHCP server exists on the subnet, but it's down.

C ❑ You must boot PXE-enabled PCs from a diskette created by RBFG.EXE.

D ❑ The PXE BIOS is too old.

E ❑ The BIOS isn't set to boot from the network.

6 What file automatically generates security IDs on cloned machines?

A ○ SETUPCL.EXE

B ○ SYSPREP.EXE

C ○ SID.EXE

D ○ SYSPREP.DLL

7 Which of the following commands runs before the user logs on to Windows XP Professional for the first time after a fresh installation? (Choose all that apply.)

A ❑ Run Once

B ❑ Run Twice

C ❑ CMDLINES.BAT

D ❑ CMDLINES.TXT

E ❑ CMDLINE.TXT

8 You are creating a dual-boot PC with Windows 98. Microsoft recommends that you install Windows XP Professional into its own:

A ○ Folder

B ○ Partition

C ○ Physical drive

D ○ Directory

9 What is the minimum amount of RAM specified by Microsoft for a successful Windows XP Professional installation?

A ○ 16MB

B ○ 32MB

C ○ 64MB

D ○ 128MB

10 **What is the name of the answer file for SysPrep's factory mode?**

A ○ SYSPREP.INF

B ○ OOBEINFO.INI

C ○ OOBEINFO.TXT

D ○ WINBOM.INI

Answers

1 **B, C,** and **E.** Memorize the syntax because this is a likely candidate for an exam question. *Review "Prepping for Installation."*

2 **C.** This file is optional. If you use it, put it in the folder %SystemDrive%\ SYSPREP, or on a diskette. As for E, note that OOBEINFO.INI works with the Out Of Box Experience, not the Mini-Setup Wizard. *Review "Using SysPrep."*

3 **C.** It stands for Remote Boot Floppy Generator — if you can remember that, you're in good shape. *Review "Installing and configuring RIS."*

4 **B** and **D.** If you meet these requirements, the setup program automatically uses the answer file on the diskette. You might use this method, for example, to upgrade a bunch of notebook computers not connected to any network. *Review "Creating the distribution point."*

5 **A, B, D,** and **E.** PXE uses DHCP to obtain an IP address for itself and for the RIS server. *Review "RIS requirements."*

6 **A.** This file also activates the Mini-Setup Wizard. *Review "Using SysPrep."*

7 **D.** The Run Once commands execute *after* the user logs on and within the user's security context. (No Run Twice commands exist.) *Review "Creating CMDLINES.TXT."*

8 **B.** To be more specific, unless you're dual booting with Windows XP Home Edition, Microsoft recommends installing every operating system on a multiple-boot machine into its own partition; failing that, install Windows XP onto its own partition, and all other operating systems into a second partition. *Review "Partitioning considerations."*

9 **C.** It'll run with 64MB, but "walk" would be a better word. A far cry from Windows 95's minimum requirement of 4MB! *Review "Minimum hardware requirements."*

10 **D.** Factory mode doesn't activate either the Mini-Setup Wizard or the Out Of Box Experience, and it has its own private answer file. *Review "Using SysPrep."*

Chapter 5

Configuring the User Environment

***

Exam Objectives

▶ Enable multiple language support

▶ Configure multiple language support for users

▶ Configure local settings

▶ Configure Windows XP Professional for multiple locations

▶ Configure and troubleshoot desktop settings

▶ Configure and troubleshoot accessibility services

***

*W*indows XP Professional supports multiple languages, multiple locations, and a wide variety of user-specific and machine-specific desktop settings. You control these settings through the old, familiar "Control Panel" and through the new (and possibly less familiar) Microsoft Management Consoles. This chapter looks at language, locale, and accessibility settings in detail, and presents some general points on control panel and management console technology

Quick Assessment

Enable multiple language support

1 Adding language support to Windows XP requires access to _____.

2 The two technologies for displaying foreign-language documents are _____ and _____.

Configure multiple language support for users

3 You configure additional language groups by using the _____ control panel.

4 The system locale defines the code page that Windows XP will use for _____ applications.

Configure local settings

5 The four tabs that define a given PC's standards and format settings are _____, _____, _____, and _____.

Configure Windows XP Professional for multiple locations

6 If you want to change the default locale, use the Languages tab of the Regional and Language Options control panel and click _____.

7 The quickest way to switch locales is to use the _____.

Configure and troubleshoot desktop settings

8 The two types of tools that you normally use to change desktop settings are _____ and _____.

Configure and troubleshoot accessibility services

9 The control panel that lets you set up accessibility options is called the _____ control panel.

10 The accessibility feature that would let you type Ctrl, Alt, and Del in succession, instead of simultaneously, is called _____.

Answers

1   *The Windows XP CD or the network installation point.* Didn't know this one? See "Implementing multiple language support" in this chapter.

2   *Code pages and Unicode.* See the sections "What's a code page?" and "What's Unicode?" for more.

3   *Regional Options.* The "Implementing multiple language support" section goes into details.

4   *Non-Unicode.* Again, see the "Implementing multiple language support" section.

5   *Numbers, Currency, Time, and Date.* The "Locales" section explains.

6   *Details.* For more, see "Locales" in this chapter.

7   *Language bar.* Ditto.

8   *Control panels and management consoles.* Miss this one? Check out the section titled (appropriately) "Control Panels and Management Consoles."

9   *Accessibility Options.* Okay, you deserve a gimme from time to time. See the "Accessibility" section.

10   *StickyKeys.* The "Accessibility" section has more on this.

Language Support

Windows XP Professional can support multiple languages via the Control Panel's Regional Options icon. With multiple language support installed, you can create documents in a foreign language, as well as read documents created in that language.

What's a code page?

You have to understand code pages before you can grasp the mechanics of multiple language support. A *code page* is typically a table of characters in which each character corresponds to a single byte. Because a byte has a minimum value of 0 and a maximum value of 255, a code page can contain a maximum of 256 characters. That's not enough to contain all the possible characters in all possible languages, so computer systems use different code pages for different languages.

Some code pages support only a single language; others can support multiple languages. Furthermore, for some languages, such as Chinese and Japanese, 256 characters aren't enough, hence the existence of *double-byte code pages* to handle those special situations.

In a system based on code pages, a program needs to know two pieces of information to properly display and print a character: the byte value of the character within the code page, and which code page to use (expressed as a number — for example, "Latin 1" is code page 1252). You can see the potential problem when a user running a PC with a specific code page creates a document and sends it to a user running a different code page: The document is likely to look like gibberish.

What's Unicode?

Unicode is an international-standard character set that has extra characters above and beyond those that appear in the ASCII (American Standard Code for Information Interchange) character set. Unlike ASCII, which uses a single-byte code, Unicode uses a double-byte character code, which makes code pages irrelevant. Every character in every language can be defined by a single double-byte value. Therefore, all a program needs to know to properly display a Unicode character is the double-byte value of that character.

Windows XP supports Unicode Version 2.0, which permits roughly 40,000 unique characters. Windows NT 4.0 also supports Unicode, but Windows 98 does not. (Office 97, Internet Explorer 4.0 and above, and SQL Server 7.0 and above support Unicode although they don't require a Unicode operating system.) Over time, Unicode will continue to phase in and code pages will continue to phase out.

Implementing multiple language support

So, how do you add multiple language support in Windows XP? The procedure centers on the Regional and Language Options control panel (see Figure 5-1). (If you aren't familiar with code pages or Unicode, please read the preceding sections before you read this one.)

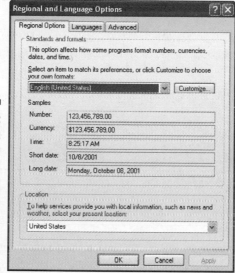

Figure 5-1:
Add multiple language support in the Regional and Language Options control panel.

Lab 5-1 shows you how to add support for a new language.

Lab 5-1	Adding a New Language

1. **Log on as the local PC's Administrator.**

   You must have administrative rights to add language support. Also note that the ability to add language support may be restricted by group policies; this lab assumes that it is not.

2. **Choose Start⇨Control Panel.**

3. **Double-click the Regional and Language Options icon.**

   The Regional Options tab of the Regional and Language Options property sheet appears.

4. **Click the Languages tab.**

5. **Click the Details button.**

   The Text Services and Input Languages property sheet appears (see Figure 5-2). The default language choice appears at the top of the property sheet, under "Default input language."

Figure 5-2: Here's where you can add additional languages.

6. **Click the Add button.**

7. **In the Add Input Language dialog box, choose the Input language.**

   You would choose a language in which you need to compose or read documents. If you don't see the one you need, then you may need to go back to the Languages tab and check one of the boxes under "Supplemental language support."

   If you compose a document that depends on a supplemental language group that you've added, anyone else to whom you send that document must have the same language group support installed on his or her computer.

8. **In the Add Input Language dialog box, choose the keyboard layout (if different from the default).**

9. **Click the OK button to close the Text Services and Input Languages dialog box.**

10. **Click OK to close the Regional and Language Options control panel.**

So what actually happens when you choose to add support for an alternative language? Basically, three things:

- ✔ The operating system loads the necessary *code page translation tables*.
- ✔ Windows XP sets a default *keyboard layout* for that language. (Many languages have alternative keyboard layouts, which you can set in the Add Input Language dialog box.)
- ✔ Windows XP modifies the list of allowable locales.

Now, what's that "Default input language" field on the Text Services and Input Languages dialog box? That lets you specify the language support (that is, the code page and associated font sets) that Windows XP uses by default for any applications that don't include Unicode support.

In Windows 2000, Microsoft used to call the default input language the *system locale*, so don't be surprised if you see that terminology on the exam.

Locales

Windows NT 4.0, Windows 2000, and Windows XP all support the concept of a *locale*, or *input language*, while Windows 98 does not. What does the locale setting do?

In a nutshell, it's a convenient way to set the other Regional Options choices all at one time (that is, the ones on the Number, Currency, Time, and Date tabs). These tabbed property sheets define how Windows XP displays (and, for example in spreadsheet or database applications, sorts) numbers, currency, time values, and date values. Sure, you could change each of these individually. But chances are that in a given locale, you're going to want the most common settings for users in that locale. After you set the locale, you probably don't need to fiddle with the Number, Currency, Time, and Date tabs because they'll be set as you would want them.

Some Windows XP, 2000, and NT 4.0 applications check the locale setting to determine the behavior of specific features (such as a spell checker, for example). Windows 98 applications typically don't do this.

The locales that are available on any given machine are determined by which languages are installed on that machine. Most languages are installed by default in XP, unlike Windows 2000. However, you must perform a separate step to install support for Chinese, Japanese, and Korean as well as for Arabic and other complex script and right-to-left languages. Open the Regional and Language Options control panel, click the Languages tab, and check the boxes under Supplemental Language Support, as follows:

- Check the Install Files for Complex Script and Right-to-Left Languages box if you want to add support for Arabic, Armenian, Georgian, Hebrew, Indic languages, Thai, and Vietnamese.

- Check the Install Files for East Asian Languages box if you want to add support for Chinese, Japanese, and Korean.

The Settings tab (it's the only tab!) of the Text Services and Input Languages dialog box lets you change the default locale. If you want to add *nondefault* locales that you can switch to by using a special hotkey combination (or the locale icon that appears automatically in the System Tray part of your taskbar), you must use the Add button on that dialog box. The Installed Services list shows the locales and keyboard layouts currently installed.

When you add a locale via the Text Services And Input Languages dialog box, you can use the same dialog box to perform other actions, such as

- Defining *hotkeys* to switch from one locale to another (click the Key Settings button)

- Controlling whether Windows puts an icon on the taskbar to make changing locales easier, and how that icon behaves in terms of labels and transparency (click the Language Bar button)

Number formats

The Numbers tab of the Customize Regional Options property sheet gives you fine control over how Windows XP displays and sorts numbers. Some of the options you can control include:

- Decimal point character
- Number of digits to display after decimal point
- *Digit grouping* character (for example, the comma in 1,000)
- Negative number indicator
- Displaying a leading zero in decimal numbers

Currency formats

The big news here, and the point to remember for the test, is that Windows XP supports the *Euro,* the European currency standard.

The Currency tab of the Customize Regional Options property sheet also lets you change the decimal point character and the digital grouping character, as in the Numbers tab.

Time and date formats

The Time tab lets you set the time format, the time separator symbol, and the AM and PM symbols. The Date dialog box lets you set the date format (short and long versions) and date separator. The Date tab also lets you change how Windows XP interprets two-digit dates. The default is to assume a year between 1930 and 2029; that is, "30" would mean "1930" and "29" would mean "2029."

Make a note that if you use the Offline Files feature of Windows XP — in which Windows makes a copy of a network file on your hard disk so that you can work with it away from the network — the computer time and date are critical! Windows uses the time and date stamp when synchronizing offline files, for example, after you've been away on a trip. If your PC's time and date (which you set in the Date and Time control panel) don't match up with your network servers' settings, synchronization isn't reliable.

Troubleshooting Languages and Locales

If you're having problems with a PC that has multiple languages and/or locales installed, here are a few troubleshooting tips:

- ✔ If you're having trouble with a single application, check to see if it supports Unicode. If it doesn't, you may need to change the "default input language" (the language that Windows XP uses for non-Unicode applications)

- ✔ If you're moving documents between two PCs, make sure both have the same language groups added via the Regional and Language Options control panel.

- ✔ Try learning the language in which the document you're reading was written. (Windows XP can't help you there! Maybe Windows 2020. . . .)

Accessibility

Windows XP includes some accessibility features that make it friendlier to a wider variety of users. The Accessibility Options control panel has five tabs: Keyboard, Sound, Display, Mouse, and General. (Unlike most control panels, the General tab doesn't appear first; the Keyboard tab does.)

Keyboard

Here are the various accessibility settings you can control on the Keyboard tab:

- **StickyKeys:** Lets you type a multikey combination (the most famous example being Ctrl+Alt+Del, the "three-finger salute") one key at a time, instead of all keys simultaneously.

  The keys that become sticky are Ctrl, Alt, Shift, and the Windows logo key. By default, you can toggle StickyKeys on or off by tapping the Shift key five times in succession; the Settings button offers various other customizations.

- **FilterKeys:** Lets you customize how Windows XP deals with quick keystrokes and repeated keystrokes.

  Some users may tap keys involuntarily and unintentionally; the Settings button lets you specify a minimum time that a user holds a key down before Windows recognizes it as a bona fide keystroke. You can also specify key repeat delay and repeat rate settings that override those on the Keyboard control panel.

- **ToggleKeys:** Lets you instruct Windows XP to make sounds when the user types the CapsLock, NumLock, and ScrollLock keys.

  A high tone sounds when one of these keys turns on, and a low tone sounds when it turns off.

Sound

The Sound tab lets you instruct Windows XP to provide some visual cues for those who cannot hear system sounds easily or at all:

- **SoundSentry:** An on/off check box that lets you tell Windows XP to "flash" a part of the screen (which you can select via the Settings button) whenever Windows or a Windows program plays a sound.

- **ShowSounds:** Another on/off check box that signals applications to display captions for any sounds they may generate. Application developers must write their programs to support this feature for it to work.

Display

The Display tab's Use High Contrast check box lets you instruct Windows XP to override the color scheme on the Display control panel and use a high-contrast color scheme, which is more easily viewable by those with vision limitations. The Settings button gives you a few options for customizing the display's appearance (white-on-black, black-on-white, regular size, large size, or a custom color scheme).

Mouse

The MouseKeys feature lets the user operate the mouse with the numeric keypad. The Settings button lets you control speed and whether to use the Ctrl and Shift keys to modify acceleration.

General

Here are the features that you control via the General tab:

- ✔ **Automatic reset:** Deactivates accessibility features automatically after a specified number of minutes ranging from 5 to 30. You can turn the features back on by using their shortcuts (such as pressing Shift 5 times to activate StickyKeys).

  Automatic reset is handy in a multiuser situation, such as a kiosk application.

- ✔ **Feature switch notification:** This helps ensure against accidental feature deactivation or activation.

- ✔ **SerialKey:** This setting lets Windows XP use a serial port for an alternative keyboard device.

- ✔ **Administrative options:** You can set the accessibility options so that they apply only to the currently logged-on user or to all users of the machine automatically at logon time.

Accessibility Accessories

If you think that the only Windows XP accessibility options are in the Accessibility control panel, well, that would be reasonable (I assumed it myself!) but wrong. Microsoft put some new tools on the Accessories branch of the All Programs menu, including the following:

- ✔ **Magnifier:** This utility helps people with poor vision see the screen by placing a magnified view of the present cursor location at the top of the display (or wherever you want it to appear). You can set the zoom level, window size (drag the border), window placement, tracking options (cursor, keyboard, or both), and color scheme.

✔ **Narrator:** This program provides voice feedback for vision-impaired users. You can control whether Narrator relates typed keystrokes; announces screen events (new windows and menus); and moves the mouse pointer to follow the active screen item. You can also control the Narrator's voice (speed, volume, and pitch). Don't rely on Narrator to work in programs other than Windows XP's desktop and control panels, WordPad, Notepad, and Internet Explorer. I was also unable to get it to sound like Charlize Theron, but maybe in Service Pack 1. . . .

✔ **On-Screen Keyboard:** This utility displays a keyboard image on your screen and lets you "type" using a mouse, joystick, or other device. You can enable a click sound on the Settings menu, where you can also select a typing mode: *click* (in which you click keys on the virtual keyboard), *scan* (in which the keyboard display cycles through rows and keys until you select the key you want with a joystick or other device), and *hover* (in which Windows selects a key after you hover the cursor over it for a preset duration).

✔ **Accessibility Wizard:** This wizard steps you through a series of windows that help you select accessibility options. It's handy in that you don't have to slog through the control panel and every individual accessibility accessory.

✔ **Utility Manager:** An administrator can run this utility to specify which accessibility accessories should start automatically with Windows. (How this differs from simply putting programs into the Startup group, I'm not sure.) You can also see which accessibility accessories are running; again, the taskbar works fine for that purpose.

Control Panels and Management Consoles

Well beyond language, locale, and accessibility settings, you can use *control panels* and *management consoles* to tailor many other aspects of the user environment.

Although I examine specific control panel and management console settings throughout the book as appropriate, a few words are in order here to introduce these two technologies.

Control panels and new views

The control panels that appear when you choose Start⇨Control Panel look and work much like their predecessors in earlier versions of Windows. These icons, and the underlying software code that determines their appearance and actions, live in files with the extension *.CPL. The files typically reside in the C:\WINDOWS\SYSTEM32 folder.

Control panels provide a relatively safe, user-friendly way to modify Windows XP settings and preferences. Most control panels offer context-sensitive and field-level help via the ? button on the title bar. Many include data entry filters to help prevent users from keying in inappropriate or badly formatted data.

Some control panels modify settings that apply to all users of the machine, while others modify settings that apply only to the currently logged-on user.

Note especially the following new and modified control panels:

- ✔ **Folder Options:** Lets you modify the behavior of specific file types and is also accessible from Windows Explorer via the Tools⇨Folder Options command.

- ✔ **User Accounts:** Lets you manage local user accounts and profiles.

- ✔ **Scanners and Cameras:** Controls these digital devices.

- ✔ **Network Connections:** Redesigned, Network Connections now combines local network settings and dial-up connection settings.

- ✔ **Sounds and Audio Devices:** Likewise, combines settings that formerly occupied separate control panels.

- ✔ **Speech:** A new control panel, although Windows still doesn't handle speech recognition just yet.

- ✔ **Taskbar and Start menu:** Formerly off the Settings submenu, this is now a control panel as it always should have been.

While nearly all the control panels in Windows XP Professional modify the Registry, that is, the computer's central database of configuration data, the boot options that appear on the System control panel's Advanced tab (click the Settings button under Startup and Recovery) modify the BOOT.INI file at the root of the system partition (usually C) rather than the Registry. Furthermore, on Windows 2000 Server, some control panels and management consoles modify the Active Directory database rather than the Registry. And on Windows XP machines running Internet Information Server (IIS), management consoles can also modify an IIS-only configuration database that Microsoft calls the *metabase*.

You can control which control panels users can and cannot see by using *policies* (see Chapter 11 for details). You can also exercise such control (although less elegantly) by moving, deleting, or renaming the various *.CPL files.

Microsoft Management Console (MMC)

A new kind of control panel, the *Microsoft Management Console (MMC)*, appears in Windows 2000 and XP. You can reach most of the management consoles on your computer by choosing Start➪Control Panel and selecting the Administrative Tools folder (see Figure 5-3). The preconfigured MMC consoles that appear are easily distinguishable from traditional control panel files by the presence of a shortcut arrow on the icon. These shortcuts point to *.MSC files on disk, which run the MMC host program MMC.EXE.

Figure 5-3: You can find most management consoles in the Administrative Tools folder.

All these preconfigured consoles share the same basic window layout and certain menus. In fact, the idea behind MMC is to provide a somewhat standardized structure for hosting administrative tools. Microsoft supplies a number of such tools, but third parties can write their own, too. In other words, MMC.EXE provides the frame, and the tool designer (be it Microsoft or someone else) provides the painting.

If you select one of the Administrative Tools shortcuts (for example, "Computer Management"), you see a typical management console layout (see Figure 5-4). (You can also see this console by right-clicking the desktop's or Start menu's My Computer icon and selecting Manage.)

The left window is a hierarchical, Explorer-like "console tree" showing the individual *snap-ins* (which are programs that actually do useful work within that particular console). Examples of snap-ins are Device Manager and Event Viewer. (And no, they don't actually make a sound when you add them to a console.)

Microsoft distinguishes between *standalone* snap-ins and *extension* snap-ins. The latter work only as helpers in the context of one or more standalone snap-ins. Some snap-ins can function either way.

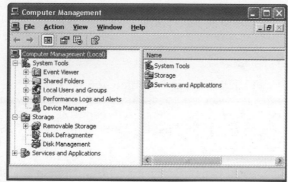

Figure 5-4:
A typical
MMC
console.

The right window is the "details pane" showing the contents of the active snap-in that's highlighted in the console tree. The menu bar of every console contains the Action and View menus, but the choices beneath these menus can and do vary widely. In most MMC consoles, you can generally avoid menus completely by right-clicking the object on which you want to perform an action.

The level of standardization that MMC provides is minimal, and MMC windows are inherently no more user-friendly than tabbed property sheets. However, one significant benefit for technical folks is that you can put together your own MMC consoles with any combination of snap-ins. That's something you can't do with the traditional control panel files, and it's sure to come in handy for those who have to spend a lot of time configuring or managing Windows XP systems.

If you want to experiment with making your own "mission control" MMC consoles, choose Start⇨Run, type **MMC**, and press Enter. When the Microsoft Management Console is up and running, choose File⇨Add/Remove Snap-In, click Add, and select the snap-ins you want. When you're done, save your custom console.

Some important snap-ins don't appear in any supplied consoles — you have to build a custom console in order to use them! These include the Group Policy editor, the Security Templates tool, and the Security Configuration and Analysis tool. Most of the MSC files on your system live in the C:\WINDOWS\ SYSTEM32 folder.

If you use the Administrative Tools often, you may want to put them on your Programs menu. To do so, choose Start⇨Control Panel⇨Taskbar & Start menu, click the Start menu tab, click the Customize button, click the Advanced tab, scroll down the Start menu Items list to System Administrative Tools, and check the Display On The All Programs Menu radio button. And while you're there, check the Display As A Menu Item button under Control Panel as well; this lets you navigate to a specific control panel from the Start menu.

Connecting to Resources with Internet Explorer

Another part of the user environment that Microsoft continues to emphasize is the Internet Explorer browser. Microsoft touts use of the browser window for nontraditional tasks, such as browsing local resources, and the exam expects you to know how to use Internet Explorer to open data files and run programs on the local disk.

✔ To open a data file, you can open the IE window, choose File➪Open, click Browse, and navigate to the file.

✔ Another way to open a data file is to type the file's URL into the address bar. You can use an "informal" URL like **c:\boot.ini**, or a more formal URL like **file://c:\boot.ini**. (If you omit the *c:* part of the file path, it will be assumed.)

✔ To run a program, type its URL into the address bar. Again, you can use an informal path like **c:\myprog.exe**, or a formal one, like **file://c:\ myprog.exe**.

If you install IIS (that's *Internet Information Server,* the Microsoft Web server product that comes with Windows XP Professional but that you must install separately), then you may want to access one or more Web sites that you create on your PC. You can use the *file://* URL as just discussed, but you can also use the *http://* URL with the name of your site.

Speaking of opening files within the browser, Internet Explorer 6 adds a "media bar" to the more familiar bars (search, favorites, history, and so on). This feature lets you play a variety of media files on both local and remote hosts from within the browser. Its advantage is that it starts more rapidly than Windows Media Player, which also comes with Windows XP Professional. Display this "lightweight" media bar by clicking its icon on the IE toolbar.

Prep Test

1 A user in your office has a disability that makes it hard for him to make the "three-finger salute" by holding down Ctrl, Alt, and Del at the same time. How could you ease his computing sessions? (Choose the best answer.)

A ○ Choose Start⇨Control Panel⇨Keyboard. Click the Accessibility tab and check StickyKeys.

B ○ Choose Start⇨Control Panel⇨Keyboard. Set the repeat rate to the lowest value.

C ○ Choose Start⇨Control Panel⇨Keyboard. Set the delay period to the lowest value.

D ○ Choose Start⇨Control Panel⇨Accessibility Options. Click the Use StickyKeys check box.

E ○ Choose Start⇨Control Panel⇨Accessibility Options. Click the Use FilterKeys check box.

2 You're teaching some PC troubleshooters at your organization how to get familiar with Windows XP Professional. One of them asks you how you can tell an MMC console icon from an old-style Control Panel icon. Which of the following answers are correct? (Choose all that apply.)

A ❑ MMC icons all have a shortcut arrow on them; old-style Control Panel icons don't.

B ❑ The property sheet for old-style Control Panel icons points to CPL files, while for MMC icons it points to MSC files.

C ❑ The only way you can tell is to run the icon. All MMC consoles have a dual-pane window and an Action and View menu.

D ❑ Look at the location. The Control Panel folder itself only contains control panels; the Administrative Tools folder only contains MMC consoles.

3 As your company's Windows support guru, you get a call from an employee who's working in your Kuwait office. He received a PC shipped from the U.S. with all U.S. settings. What steps would you advise that he take to configure his PC for Kuwait? (Choose all that apply.)

A ❑ Add Arabic language support by clicking the Install Files for Complex Script and Right-to-Left Languages check box on the Languages tab of the Regional and Language Options control panel.

B ❑ Add Arabic language support by clicking the Arabic check box on the Language tab of the Regional and Language Options control panel.

C ❑ Specify Kuwait as a locale via the Languages tab of the Regional and Language Options control panel.

D ❑ Set the proper choices for Kuwait by modifying the Currency, Date, Time, and Numbers tabs of the Regional and Language Options control panel.

4 **What entities can Windows XP control panels and management consoles modify? (Choose all that apply.)**

A ❑ The Registry

B ❑ INI files

C ❑ The Master Boot Record

D ❑ Active Directory

5 **What's the name that Microsoft uses to describe console snap-ins that only function as subsidiary nodes to one other specific snap-in, as opposed to standalone snap-ins that can function without any other snap-in present? (Choose the best answer.)**

A ○ Ancillary

B ○ Auxiliary

C ○ Extension

D ○ Subordinate

6 **A code page can contain a maximum of how many characters?**

A ○ 64

B ○ 128

C ○ 256

D ○ 512

7 **Name one Microsoft Management Console snap-in that you must add yourself to a custom console because it doesn't come with any prebuilt consoles in Windows XP Professional.**

A ○ System Configuration and Analysis

B ○ Security Analysis

C ○ Security Configuration and Analysis

D ○ Security Configuration

E ○ System Template Security Policy Configuration Analysis

8 **Where do most console files make their home?**

A ❑ `C:\WINDOWS\SYSTEM32`

B ❑ `%systemroot%\SYSTEM32`

C ❑ `C:\WINDOWS`

D ❑ `C:\WINNT\CONSOLE`

Answers

1 **D.** The StickyKeys feature in the Accessibility Options control panel enables the user to press Ctrl, Alt, and Del in sequence instead of all at once. *Review "Keyboard."*

2 **A** and **D.** Remember also for the exam that MMC.EXE is the executable file for consoles, but each console has the extension MSC (not MMC). *Review "Microsoft Management Console (MMC)."*

3 **A** and **C.** Choice A by itself isn't enough; you need to add the language support, and then specify a locale. Remember that locales include settings for currency, number, date, and time formats, so you don't have to set those individually. *Review "Locales."*

4 **A, B,** and **D.** The System control panel can modify BOOT.INI, which contains (among other things) details about the operating system boot menu. Most control panels on the Professional product modify the Registry; many consoles on the Server product modify the Active Directory database. *Review "Control Panels."*

5 **C.** Just another term you should memorize. *Review "Microsoft Management Console (MMC)."*

6 **C.** Code pages use one byte, or eight bits, per character. Two raised to the eighth power is 256. Unicode uses two bytes per character. *Review "What's a code page?"*

7 **C.** The exam expects you to know this one, as well as the Security Templates console; Chapter 11 takes a closer look at these two. *Review "Microsoft Management Console (MMC)."*

8 **A** and **B.** This is a bit of a trick question for two reasons. The question doesn't tell you how many choices to select, so you must pay attention to whether the answers use circles or squares. (The exams seem to be getting a bit friendlier in this regard, and recent ones I've taken actually warn you if you choose the wrong number of answers, but don't count on such a safety net!) Second, the question expects you to know that the variable %systemroot% normally is the same as C:\WINDOWS. You should also know the variable %systemdrive%, which is normally C. *Review "Microsoft Management Console (MMC)."*

Chapter 6

Configuring Network Components and Protocols

● ●

Exam Objectives

▶ Configure and troubleshoot the TCP/IP protocol

● ●

*O*ne of the best things any test prep book can do is clue you in to which areas carry greater weight on the exam than others. Therefore, verily I say unto you, networking is a *huge* topic on the Windows XP Professional exam. This chapter deals with a single network-related objective, but it's much more important than many other objectives on Microsoft's list. It also happens to be more complex than most of the other topics this book covers.

This chapter takes a look at getting Windows XP Professional ready for network participation, from installing a network card driver to configuring the protocols necessary to run Microsoft and Novell networks. (Yep, even though the exam objectives don't mention Novell, you should know a few basic facts about it.) Think of this material as "network plumbing." Other chapters (10 and 13) deal with other, higher-level aspects of networking. The dishwasher doesn't work if the pipes are misrouted, so it makes sense to look at the plumbing issues first.

Quick Assessment

Configure and troubleshoot the TCP/IP protocol

1 Plug and Play network adapters automatically show up in the _____ folder.

2 Settings that are specific to a particular make and model of network adapter appear on the _____ tab of the adapter's configuration sheet.

3 The Microsoft adapter driver standard that permits multiple network protocols to work with a single network adapter is called _____.

4 The command line utility you'd use to renew an IP address lease is called _____.

5 The network feature that automatically assigns Windows XP IP addresses without a DHCP server present is called _____.

6 The subnet mask divides out the _____ ID part of the IP address from the _____ ID part.

7 If you can see local computers but not remote ones, you have probably misconfigured the _____.

8 You can use WINIPCFG in Windows 98 to examine IP settings. In Windows XP, you use _____.

9 The part of TCP/IP that guarantees delivery is _____.

10 The name of Microsoft's implementation of Novell's IPX/SPX protocol is _____.

Answers

1 *Network Connections.* See "Installing a network adapter" if you missed this question.

2 *Advanced.* "Configuring and troubleshooting a network adapter" has more.

3 *NDIS.* No points if you said "Network Device Interface Specification" because nobody likes a show-off. See "Installing a network adapter" for this tidbit.

4 *IPCONFIG.* See "Troubleshooting TCP/IP" for details.

5 *Automatic Private IP Addressing.* The "DHCP" section holds forth on this new-to-the-NT-platform feature.

6 *Network, host.* See "The IP address and subnet mask" if this is Greek to you (and you're not Greek).

7 *Default gateway.* See "The default gateway" in this chapter for details.

8 *IPCONFIG.* Windows XP doesn't get the pretty user interface of the Windows 98 tool, but the information is the same. See "Troubleshooting TCP/IP."

9 *TCP.* The IP part assembles and delivers packets. See "TCP/IP."

10 *NWLink.* No, this isn't really a TCP/IP question, but the exam may deal with NetWare protocols, even though Microsoft's objective list doesn't. See "NWLink, or 'IPX/SPX/NetBIOS-compatible transport protocol.'"

Network Layers

Years ago, when vendors other than IBM got into the computer networking act, the industry realized the importance of defining a standard interface between different layers of the network *stack* (the software levels through which data travels, on both sending and receiving machines). Thus was born the famous seven-layer OSI (Open Systems Interconnect) model.

The OSI model

In case you see a question on the OSI model on the exam, the layers from top to bottom are

- Application (7)
- Presentation (6)
- Session (5)
- Transport (4)
- Network (3)
- Datalink (2)
- Physical (1)

The interfaces between each layer are published and standardized, so that you can use, say, a transport protocol from one vendor with a network card driver from another vendor, if both vendors follow the model.

For the exam, you probably won't need to know exactly what each layer does, but I suggest that you remember the layer order. Use a memory aid. The phrases "**P**lease **D**o **N**ot **T**hrow **S**ausage **P**izza **A**way" (bottom to top) or "**A**ll **P**eople **S**eem **T**o **N**eed **D**ata **P**rocessing" (top to bottom) can jog your memory by providing the first letter of each layer.

Microsoft modules

Microsoft designed Windows XP in a modular fashion, including the networking bits, which correlate fairly closely to the OSI model. Some of the OSI layers are fixed in Windows XP, such as the Win32 network API (Application Program Interface) that programmers use when writing applications. Some other OSI layers combine to form a single software component that you can add, replace, or delete in Windows XP. The end result is that in Windows XP, user-installable networking modules fall into the following four categories:

✔ **Adapter:** The network interface card (NIC) adapter requires a software device driver so that the upper layers of network software can communicate across the physical medium (copper cable, fiber optic cable, and so on). You must have at least one adapter to participate in a network.

✔ **Protocol:** The "network language," or transport protocol, defines how Windows XP packages information. Two computers must speak the same protocol to communicate across a network. You must have at least one protocol to participate in a network.

✔ **Client:** The network client allows Windows XP to communicate with specific network operating systems, such as Windows 2000 Server and Novell NetWare. You must have at least one client to participate in a network.

✔ **Service:** Network services provide specialized capabilities, such as resource sharing (File and Printer Sharing for Microsoft Networks). You don't necessarily have to have any services loaded to participate in a network, but services are necessary to perform certain network functions.

You can see evidence of this four-level structure when you right-click a local area connection in the Network Connections folder and choose Properties, displaying a screen like what you see in Figure 6-1.

✔ The adapter for the specific LAN connection appears at the top in its own little area.

✔ Clients, protocols, and services are in the main list of "connection items."

Figure 6-1:
The LAN
link's
property
sheet.

This layout differs from that in Windows 9x, where all adapter drivers appear in the same list with all the other connection items, in the Network control panel.

The fact that these four modular pieces are separately installable means that you can mix and match pieces to some extent. For example, a single adapter can support two protocols; you can run two or more clients over a single protocol; you can run a specific client over one protocol, or over a different one; and so on. You can also get modules from manufacturers other than Microsoft. The freedom to mix and match components provides flexibility, but it also begets a certain amount of complexity for the system designer.

Network Adapters

Network adapters, also known as network interface cards or NICs, typically plug into a bus slot of the PC on one end and into a network cable on the other end. Windows XP comes with a wide variety of network adapter *drivers*, the software components that allow Windows to communicate with the devices. Windows XP supports traditional Ethernet and Fast Ethernet NICs, as well as newer wireless and HPNA (Home Phoneline Network Adapter) devices. You can have as many NICs as your hardware can support.

Installing a network adapter

You can install a network adapter driver two ways:

- ✔ If it's Plug and Play compatible, pop it into a bus slot and start the computer. Windows XP may ask for the installation CD-ROM or for a third-party diskette. An icon automatically appears for the network card in the Network Connections folder.

- ✔ If it's not Plug and Play, run the Add New Hardware Wizard from the control panel and follow the prompts to select the adapter's make and model.

NDIS (Network Device Interface Specification) Version 5.0 is Microsoft's preferred adapter driver type. It permits several different protocols and networks to run on a single adapter, and it supports Plug and Play hardware detection.

Configuring and troubleshooting a network adapter

You can configure network adapter properties in two places:

⊮ Device Manager tab of the System control panel

⊮ Configure button in the network connection's property sheet

You generally won't need to change the resource settings that Windows XP assigns automatically (see Figure 6-2), and indeed you may not be *able* to change them depending on your PC and network card. But check the Resources tab for any reports of a conflict with another device's interrupt or memory requirements.

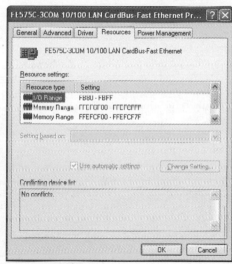

Figure 6-2:
The resources this NIC uses can't be changed here.

The Advanced tab's appearance varies from one network adapter to the next (see Figure 6-3).

You may find settings to

⊮ Use a twisted-pair connection (possibly abbreviated *TPE*, for Twisted-Pair Ethernet) or a coaxial cable connection (possibly appearing as *BNC*, for British Naval Connector) on a combo card. These connection choices sometimes go by the name "transceiver type" in the dialog box.

✔ Select a regular Ethernet plug or a Fast Ethernet plug.

✔ Choose full- or half-duplex communications. (Generally, full-duplex is for switches, half-duplex is for hubs.)

✔ Offload error-checking calculations to the network card (usually a good idea as it frees up the main CPU for other chores).

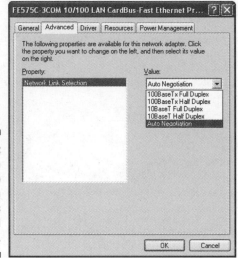

Figure 6-3:
Settings on
this tab
depend on
the NIC's
make and
model.

Installing and configuring a network adapter is usually no big deal. The next section looks at the next higher network layer, the transport protocol, which (unfortunately) can get a *lot* more complicated.

Network Protocols

The *protocol,* or, more properly, *transport protocol,* describes how network clients and servers package information for delivery and unpackage it upon receipt. The protocol communicates downward with the adapter driver, and upward with both client and service software. Protocol setup ranges from fairly simple (IPX) to pretty darned complicated (TCP/IP).

Two computers must "speak" the same protocol to communicate across a network.

Windows XP supports two main protocols, which are in common use for general purpose networking:

- IPX/SPX
- TCP/IP

Note that XP drops support for *NetBEUI*, *DLC* (Data Link Control), and *AppleTalk,* although Windows 2000 still supports all three. In a pinch, you can install NetBEUI from the Windows XP CD, but Microsoft doesn't support it anymore.

The operating system also supports some secondary protocols, which are less common or provide a specialized networking function:

- 802.1 and 802.11, wireless networking protocols
- Network Monitor Driver (a pseudo-protocol that enables statistical reporting on the user's network interface)

You can install all of them via the local area network connection's property sheet by clicking the Install button and choosing Protocol, as shown in Figure 6-4. Note that when you install a protocol for one network adapter, that protocol becomes available for all other network adapters, too.

Although the published objective list only mentions TCP/IP, I'll bet a deep-dish pizza that the exam you take has at least one question on one other protocol.

Old hands at Windows should note that in Windows XP, you activate network protocols on a *per-connection basis*, by opening the Network Connections folder, right-clicking the connection of interest, and choosing Properties. For example, if you have two network cards in one PC, you can run TCP/IP on one card and IPX on the other. In previous versions of Windows, you configured all connections in one big catchall control panel window that could get pretty confusing.

NWLink, or "IPX/SPX/NetBIOS-compatible transport protocol"

Novell developed the IPX/SPX protocol (Internet Packet eXchange/Sequenced Packet eXchange) for its popular NetWare network.

Figure 6-4:
Installing a
network
protocol.

You can use this network protocol in two ways:

✓ Microsoft workstations communicating with NetWare servers

✓ Microsoft-only environment (but you give up the benefits of Active Directory, which requires TCP/IP)

NWLink basics

Microsoft's version of IPX/SPX goes by the name "IPX/SPX/NetBIOS-compatible transport protocol" or *NWLink* for short. NWLink is a workalike for Novell's network protocol in all key respects:

✓ NWLink is routable, so you can use it in large networks.

✓ For computer addressing purposes, this protocol uses a unique identifier (the "MAC address" where MAC = Media Access Layer) that is burned into a chip on the network interface card.

✓ This protocol is relatively easy to manage, because NIC manufacturers worry about ensuring unique MAC addresses on every adapter.

✓ IPX/SPX grew out of the PC DOS environment, which means support for other platforms (notably, UNIX) isn't strong.

NWLink and related components

If you install the *Client Service for NetWare* (which lets you access NetWare 2.*x*, 3.*x*, or 4.*x* servers), Windows XP installs NWLink automatically. However, you can use NWLink in all-Microsoft networks, too, so don't be fooled.

Client Service for NetWare doesn't support NetWare 5.*x* servers running IP.

The Client Service for NetWare supports NDS (NetWare Directory Services) without additional components. NDS is software for NetWare versions 4.*x* and above that organizes network resources into a single, hierarchical structure.

This method is an advance over the "bindery" method in NetWare 3.*x*, because the bindery is a server-centric database of users and groups. In other words, if you want to use a resource on a bindery-based server other than the bindery-based server you're logged onto already, you must log on to the other server. When a user logs on to an NDS "tree," however, all the network resources that that user has rights to access are available, regardless of where those resources live. Microsoft Active Directory is a direct response to the success of NDS in large organizations.

When you configure Client Service for NetWare (and, oddly, you must do that via the CSNW control panel; the client's Properties button in the Network Connections folder doesn't work), you can set either a *preferred server* (for bindery-based networks) or a *default tree and context* (for NDS-based networks). But you shouldn't set both. The "context" is the tree location of the user's NetWare user object. And that's about all you need to know about that; you shouldn't have to know any details about the NDS structure or about Novell's NDS object naming conventions for the Windows XP Professional exam.

If you only need to connect to client/server applications (such as SQL Server) running on a NetWare server, NWLink is all you need. You don't have to have the Client Service for NetWare, unless you also need connectivity to NetWare file and print services.

If the exam refers to a network component named File and Print Services for NetWare (FPSN), that animal only works with Windows 2000 or 2002 Server. It lets NetWare clients access file and print services on a server machine. Many test takers confuse FPSN with the Client Service for NetWare, which runs on Windows XP Professional.

Configuring NWLink

Configuring NWLink is pretty simple. This section covers the three variables you can set: internal network number, frame type, and network number. Set these via the property sheet for the protocol, as listed on the General tab of the connection's property sheet (see Figure 6-5).

Internal network number

This eight-digit number is for internal routing. You normally don't need to use it unless you're running Windows 2002 or 2000 Server and either File and Print Service for NetWare or IPX routing. The default value is 00000000.

Frame type

One of the more common reasons for a failure to connect in an NWLink network is a frame type mismatch.

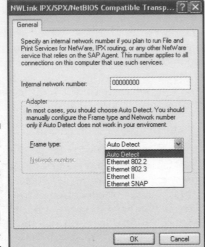

Figure 6-5: NWLink properties for a specific LAN connection.

Don't worry about the details of what a frame type is. Just know that it affects how Windows packages network data, and must match the frame type that your server uses for you to connect to that server.

The default setting of "Auto Detect" means that Windows XP tries to sense the correct frame type at the time you install NWLink. However, if it can't, then on an Ethernet network, it defaults to 802.2, the frame type used by NetWare 3.12 and above. (The 802.3 frame type is an older version in less common use today, despite the newer number.) You can manually set the frame type and not worry about whether Windows XP's autodetection will work properly or not.

Network number

Computers on an NWLink network segment must all have the same network number to see each other. Usually, Windows XP's autodetection capability works fine and you don't need to modify this value. (Good thing because to change it, you must use a Registry editor.) In fact, if you enable autodetection for the frame type, you can't manually enter a network number — the field appears grayed out in the dialog box.

TCP/IP

Configuring TCP/IP is simple and fun, and I'm wealthier than Bill Gates. The subject receives its own major section (following this one) because TCP/IP can be complex to configure and because Exam #70-270 (to say nothing of the other exams) focuses on it. But first, a brief introduction is in order.

TCP/IP is the protocol of choice in organizations large and small. Why, if it's so complicated?

- ✔ PCs can connect to the Internet without adding another protocol, because TCP/IP is the native protocol of the Net.

- ✔ TCP/IP is routable and works well over wide-area networks.

- ✔ TCP/IP runs on lots of operating systems: Mac, UNIX, and so on.

- ✔ TCP/IP isn't a proprietary, closed standard, but rather, a set of standards developed with public funds and not controlled by any single computer company.

TCP/IP is actually two network protocols: TCP, or Transmission Control Protocol, guarantees delivery and handles errors while IP, or Internet Protocol, packages and delivers data packets.

Focus on TCP/IP

This rather long section presents the details you should know about TCP/IP, which the exam covers fairly aggressively. If this is new territory for you, don't expect to absorb this stuff in a single read; it may take two or three.

The IP address and subnet mask

In the TCP/IP scheme of things, computers find each other by means of *IP addresses:* unique numbers having four numeric parts (called *octets*) separated by periods (like 127.0.0.1). Actually, it's more correct to say *network cards* find each other because two or more network cards in the same computer may have their own IP addresses, subnet masks, and default gateways (a situation known as "multihoming").

You can assign a specific, *static* IP address to a network card via the Internet Protocol (TCP/IP) Properties sheet's Use The Following IP Address radio button and related fields (see Figure 6-6). You might do that, for example, if other computers on the network need to know your computer's IP address ahead of time. Such might be the case when you're playing a multiuser Internet game in which other players need to know your PC's IP address. Another time you'd use a static IP address is when you're configuring a Windows 2002 or 2000 Server machine that workstations may be configured to find at a specific, constant IP address — for example, a server running the DNS or WINS service. (I discuss DNS and WINS a bit later in this chapter.)

The more normal situation (and the default setup) for Windows XP Professional is to have Windows go fetch an IP address from another computer on the network whose job is to provide such dynamic addresses on demand. Such a computer is called a *DHCP server* (see "DHCP, WINS, and DNS" later in this section).

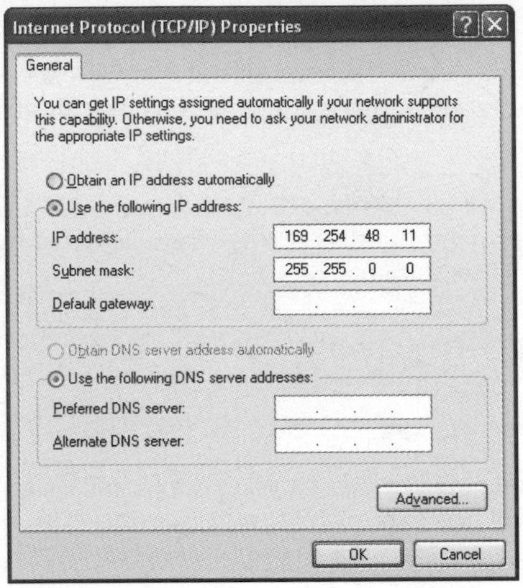

Internet Protocol (TCP/IP) Properties ? X

General

You can get IP settings assigned automatically if your network supports this capability. Otherwise, you need to ask your network administrator for the appropriate IP settings.

○ Obtain an IP address automatically
⦿ Use the following IP address:

IP address: 169 . 254 . 48 . 11
Subnet mask: 255 . 255 . 0 . 0
Default gateway:

○ Obtain DNS server address automatically
⦿ Use the following DNS server addresses:

Preferred DNS server:
Alternate DNS server:

Advanced...

OK   Cancel

Figure 6-6:
This connection uses a static IP address instead of a dynamic one.

Windows XP adds yet a third option, which is to try to fetch an address from a DHCP server, but to use a specific "alternate configuration" (with a static IP address or an automatic Windows-assigned address) if no such DHCP server is around. Use the Alternate Configuration tab (viewable by clicking the Advanced button of the Internet Protocol (TCP/IP) Properties sheet) to configure this option.

The *subnet mask* is another four-number number, but it has a very specific function. Wrapped up in the four octets of an IP address are actually two addresses: the network ID and the computer or "host" ID (kind of like a street name and a house number in a physical mail address). However, the dividing line between where the network ID ends and where the host ID begins is a flexible one; that is, it can change from one network to the next.

In order to figure out what exact part of any given IP address is the network ID and what part is the host ID, it's necessary to look at a second number that defines where the dividing line is for this particular IP address. That second number is — you guessed it — the subnet mask. TCP/IP uses the subnet mask to figure out, for example, whether a particular IP address is on the local network or on a remote network.

An example of a subnet mask is 255.255.255.0.

The bare minimum configuration information that a Windows XP Pro PC must have to participate in a TCP/IP network are

- ✔ IP address
- ✔ Subnet mask

If a PC's IP address and subnet mask are correctly configured, then the PC should be able to connect to a server on the local network.

You probably won't have to know the details of different classes of IP addresses, or how to interpret a particular subnet mask, for the Windows XP Professional exam.

The default gateway

If you want to connect to other networks, then you must configure TCP/IP to look for a *gateway* — a computer that links your network with another one (such as the public Internet). In this context, a gateway is simply a *router*, if you're already familiar with that term.

You can specify a default gateway on the General tab of the TCP/IP protocol's properties sheet, and you can specify additional gateways by clicking that properties sheet's Advanced button and entering the gateway IP addresses on the IP Settings tab (see Figure 6-7). The default gateway is the one your computer will use to connect to other networks unless the default gateway isn't available, in which case Windows XP tries to use a gateway that appears on the supplemental list.

You're likely to see more than one exam question expecting you to know that on a routed network, the proper default gateway for a client workstation is the IP address of the router's network port nearest that workstation — that is, on the same subnet as the workstation.

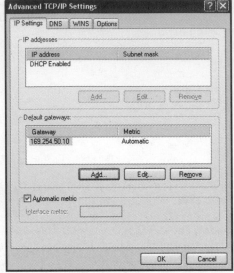

Figure 6-7:
You can
enter one or
more extra
gateway
addresses
here.

If you have a DHCP server on your network and you choose the Obtain An IP
Address Automatically radio button (refer to Figure 6-6), then the DHCP
server assigns your Windows XP PC a default gateway upon logon. If you
specify a static IP address for the default gateway, the static address for the
gateway takes precedence over the address that the DHCP server would
assign.

Windows XP Professional only uses one default gateway at a time, so if you're
connected to your company LAN and you dial up an ISP via a modem,
Windows switches from the default gateway you've defined for your LAN to
the default gateway specified by the ISP. That means that as long as you're
connected to the dial-up account, you won't be able to see computers on
your company LAN that are on a different subnet.

DHCP, WINS, and DNS

Hold out your bowl because here comes the alphabet soup. The programs in
this section all have one overarching goal: to make managing IP addresses
more automatic.

DHCP

DHCP (Dynamic Host Configuration Protocol) is a service that assigns, or "leases," a computer an IP address from a range of IP addresses when that computer logs on to the network. Actually, DHCP also typically assigns a subnet mask, a default gateway address, and a DNS server address. DHCP can run on a Windows 2002 and 2000 Server, but it can also run on an NT server, a NetWare 4.11 or 5.0+ server, or a UNIX computer. The DHCP service does *not* run on Windows XP Professional or Windows 2000 Professional, although those machines can be DHCP clients. (A special case is when you set up Windows XP to use Internet Connection Sharing, in which case it runs a very limited version of DHCP, but still not the full-blown and configurable DHCP service that the server products use.)

DHCP sure beats running around from machine to machine keying in fixed, or static, IP addresses and subnet masks in the TCP/IP control panel. Activate a Windows XP Professional machine as a DHCP client by clicking the Obtain An IP Address Automatically option on the General tab of the TCP/IP properties sheet. That's it!

You can see the currently assigned IP address for your computer, and lease details for that address, by running the command-line program IPCONFIG (use the qualifier /ALL for the most complete display). You can also see a subset of address information by clicking the connection icon in the Network Connections folder and looking at the Details display at the bottom of the left window pane.

If you've set the automatic option, but no DHCP server is available, Windows XP uses a new feature called *Automatic Private IP Addressing (APIPA)*. This feature makes the PC assign itself an IP address with a predefined format (169.254.x.x and a subnet mask of 255.255.0.0, which you should probably memorize for the exam).

The only way to turn APIPA off is to hack the Registry, but you don't need to know the specific key for the exam.

Windows XP PCs that have assigned themselves an IP address via Automatic Private IP Addressing can usually only communicate with other Windows XP, 2000, or 98 PCs on the same subnet that have done the same.

If no DHCP server exists on a subnet, Windows XP Professional machines can still use DHCP in two cases: If a router on the subnet supports DHCP forwarding (also called *DHCP/BOOTP forwarding*), or if a server (Windows 2002, 2000, or NT 4) on the subnet runs a service called *DHCP Relay Agent*. A machine running DHCP Relay Agent knows the IP address of the remote DHCP server, and can shuttle DHCP messages back and forth from subnet to subnet. You may see this tidbit crop up in exam questions having to do with Remote Installation Service (RIS), which only works if clients can "see" a DHCP server in one fashion or another.

WINS

In the Windows NT networking scheme, every Windows computer has a *NetBIOS name*, or "computer name," which identifies it on a Microsoft-based network. In order for a network user to find your PC anywhere on a TCP/IP network by specifying your PC's NetBIOS name, the TCP/IP protocol must consult a lookup directory somewhere that correlates the NetBIOS name with an IP address.

That lookup is exactly what a *WINS (Windows Internet Naming Service)* server does. You set it up on the WINS tab of the Advanced TCP/IP Settings sheet (see Figure 6-8), which by the way you can configure differently for each different network adapter in the PC, if you have more than one. WINS is another program that can run on a Windows 2002, 2000, or NT Server in a TCP/IP network.

Figure 6-8:
You can let DHCP provide WINS information, or specify it yourself.

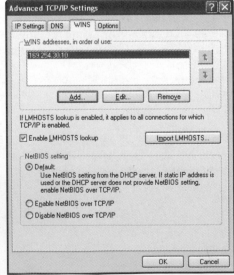

There are two ways to set the address of a WINS server:

- ✔ Click the Default radio button.

  Windows XP gets the address of a WINS server from the DHCP server.

- ✔ Click the Enable NetBIOS Over TCP/IP radio button and type the WINS server's IP address(es) yourself.

Without WINS, you can still browse the local subnetwork by using NetBIOS names, but you can't connect to Windows PCs on a remote subnetwork. The exam may include a question describing a situation where a user can see other PCs on the local subnet but can't find PCs on other subnets by using their NetBIOS names. The answer will probably reflect the likelihood that the user's WINS configuration isn't correct, or the WINS server is down, or NetBIOS over TCP/IP has been disabled on the client.

It's possible that the exam will ask you about LMHOSTS (refer to the related check box in Figure 6-8). This text file lives on the local PC and correlates NetBIOS names with IP addresses. Because administrators must maintain LMHOSTS manually every time an IP address change or a computer name change occurs on the network, LMHOSTS is an awful pain. Just remember that with WINS, you don't need LMHOSTS anymore. In fact, with DNS, one day you won't need WINS anymore, either, as I explain in the following section.

DNS

Yet another way of accessing computers on a TCP/IP network is by domain name (also called *host name*). You're already familiar with domain names such as www.dummies.com. A TCP/IP network doesn't have to use domain names, but doing so is often very convenient; for example, in a company-wide intranet. Here again, some facility must exist for domain names to be matched up with IP addresses. The typical facility is a DNS server, where DNS is short for Domain Naming Service (or, sometimes, Domain Naming System). Windows XP and 2000 networks rely heavily on DNS, not least for the new Active Directory service.

The DNS service itself only runs on Windows 2002 or 2000 Server, but you must know how to configure a Windows XP Professional machine to locate a DNS server on the network. The usual approach is to leave the Obtain DNS Server Address Automatically radio button selected on the TCP/IP properties sheet (refer to Figure 6-6) for the connection of interest. (This method uses DHCP to get the DNS server address or addresses — see earlier in this chapter.) Otherwise, you can click Use The Following DNS Server Addresses and type in a main and alternate IP address for the DNS server(s) on your network.

Troubleshooting TCP/IP

The more settings that exist for a given computer feature, the greater the likelihood that something won't work. Client configuration problems are rare under NWLink but as common as Bill Gates haircut jokes under TCP/IP. Following is my five-step program for troubleshooting TCP/IP connections, which illustrates the use of two utilities you may well see on the exam: *IPCONFIG* and *PING*.

1. **Make sure that the TCP/IP protocol has initialized itself on your computer. Open a command prompt with Start⇨Run⇨CMD, and then type** IPCONFIG /ALL | MORE.

   You should see a display something like what you see in Figure 6-9 if the protocol is running, including your IP address, subnet mask, and other details. If the subnet mask is 0.0.0.0, then your computer has a duplicate IP address!

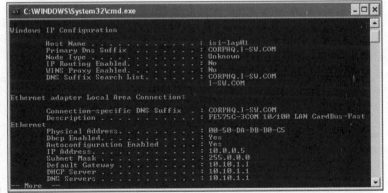

Figure 6-9: Windows XP offers IPCONFIG as a text command.

Note also that IPCONFIG /ALL shows you a "physical address" that looks like 00-10-5A-CE-02-D6. That's the *MAC (Media Access Control) address*, a unique sequence burned into the network card's silicon. TCP/IP correlates a computer's IP address to the MAC address using *ARP*, or *Address Resolution Protocol*. Use the MAC address when you must to refer to a specific physical device that may have a variable IP address.

2. **While still at the command prompt, type** PING 127.0.0.1 **to confirm that TCP/IP is bound to your network adapter.**

   The IP address 127.0.0.1 is known as the *loopback address*. A successful result is a "reply from" message repeated four times. If this step fails, then your TCP drivers may be corrupt or your network card may not be working.

3. **Ping the default gateway.**

   If you get a successful result here (again, four happy reply messages), then your computer can "see" other computers on the same subnet and (specifically) the gateway computer or router that is your link to computers on other subnets.

4. **To ensure that your computer can see computers on the other side of the router, ping a computer on a remote subnet.**

5. **To ensure that name resolution is working properly, ping a computer on a remote subnet using its host name.**

   If you can ping a computer by IP address but not by host name, then your problem has to do with name resolution (DNS or WINS) instead of physical connectivity. For example, if PING gives you an "unknown host" error, make sure that your DNS server addresses are correct on the TCP/IP property sheet (if configured locally) or on the DHCP server (if assigned automatically by DHCP).

The IPCONFIG tool has other uses, too, which you'd do well to memorize:

- ✔ You can force a network client to update the registration of that client's DNS name with a DNS server by opening a command prompt and typing **IPCONFIG /REGISTERDNS**.

- ✔ If a client PC is resolving domain names incorrectly — for example it can't find a remote host by its host name but can find it by its IP address — you can flush and reset the DNS cache on the client PC with **IPCONFIG /FLUSHDNS**.

- ✔ Release an IP address lease by executing the command **IPCONFIG /RELEASE** at a command prompt window at the client computer. For example, if you're getting ready to move a PC to a different subnet, you should release its lease because the present IP address and subnet mask won't work at the new location.

- ✔ You can force a network client to manually renew its IP address lease by executing the **IPCONFIG /RENEW** command. In fact, after you run **IPCONFIG /RELEASE**, the client can't communicate anymore using TCP/IP until it restarts or you run **IPCONFIG /RENEW**.

Other TCP/IP troubleshooting utilities include *NBTSTAT*, useful for NetBIOS name resolution troubleshooting, and *TRACERT* (trace route), handy for chasing down router problems. Here's some introductory information on these command-line tools, and you may want to experiment with them if you have access to a networked Windows XP machine:

✔ The **nbtstat -n** command lets you check out the local NetBIOS name table, which should contain a name resembling the computer name that appears on the Computer Name tab of the System control panel. You can force TCP/IP to reload NetBIOS name entries in the LMHOSTS file by typing **nbtstat -R** at a command prompt. You can see all the other quali-fiers for this command by typing **nbtstat /?** and be aware that they *are* case-sensitive.

✔ The **tracert** command traces the path from one machine to another, through any intervening routers, for up to 30 hops. This command-line utility can help you discover if a router has gone down. You can also use the commands **route print** or **netstat -r** to display the routing table, although exam 70-270 isn't likely to quiz you about the nuances of TCP/IP routing.

Bound for Glory

A *binding* is simply a rather unusual word for an active connection between network layers. View bindings by opening the Network Connections folder and choosing Advanced➪Advanced Settings (see Figure 6-10). As usual, you've got to be an Administrator to make any changes here.

Figure 6-10: Control active network bindings here.

The check boxes indicate which network protocols, services, and clients you can use at this moment on the selected connection. You may very well want to modify these settings. For example, if you use your adapter solely for communicating on a NetWare network running NWLink, you would clear the TCP/IP check box. (You may have TCP/IP installed for use with a modem, but you configure that connection by using a different icon in the Network Connections folder.)

Remember these two rules of the Adapters and Bindings tab:

✔ Disable unused adapter bindings for better speed and security and for a somewhat smaller memory footprint.

Perform this task by clearing the related check boxes.

✔ Position protocols in the order that you're likely to use them, by using the up and down arrows to the right of the dialog box.

This improves performance over the long run because Windows doesn't waste as much time trying to establish connections with inappropriate protocols.

Prep Test

1 James can't access computers at a remote office, although he can access computers in the local office just fine. When you go to James' computer and ping the default gateway as specified in James' Network Connections folder, you get an error message instead of the normal "reply from" messages.

Which of the following explanations are possible? (Choose all that apply.)

A ❑ The router whose address appears in the default gateway field on James' machine has a problem.

B ❑ The router address specified in the default gateway field on James' machine is incorrect.

C ❑ James has an invalid subnet mask setting.

D ❑ James has an invalid DHCP setting.

E ❑ The primary domain controller for the network is down.

2 You're setting up a small, 10-computer workgroup network (all running Windows XP) that will not need Internet connectivity or a connection to your corporate WAN. The workgroup is to be managed by the users and therefore should be as simple and easy to configure and maintain as possible. Which network protocol would be a good choice for this situation? (Choose the best answer.)

A ○ DNS

B ○ NetBIOS

C ○ NetBEUI

D ○ IPX/SPX

E ○ TCP/IP

3 In order for computers on the same physical TCP/IP network (subnet) to communicate with each other, they must have the same what? (Choose all that apply.)

A ❑ Network ID

B ❑ Host ID

C ❑ Subnet mask

D ❑ Workgroup name

4 You set up a subnet of 20 computers running TCP/IP and Windows XP Professional, and 1 computer running Windows 2000 Server. A router connects the subnet to other subnets in your company. However, the router does not support DHCP/BOOTP forwarding, and you have no DHCP server on your subnet, although two DHCP servers exist on the other side of the router. How could you configure the network so that the Windows XP Professional machines can use DHCP? (Choose all that apply.)

A ❏ Load and activate the DHCP service on the Windows 2000 Server machine on your local subnet.

B ❏ Load and activate the DHCP service on a relatively lightly used Windows XP Professional machine on your local subnet.

C ❏ Load and activate the DHCP Relay Agent on the Windows 2000 Server machine on your local subnet.

D ❏ Load and activate the DHCP Relay Agent on a relatively lightly used Windows XP Professional machine on your local subnet.

5 NWLink is required by which of the following network services? (Choose all that apply.)

A ❏ Client Service for NetWare

B ❏ Novell Client for Windows NT/2000

C ❏ Gateway Service for NetWare

D ❏ IPX/SPX

6 Which IP address is known as the loopback address?

A ○ 10.0.0.1

B ○ 10.1.1.1

C ○ 169.254.0.1

D ○ 127.0.0.1

7 What does PING stand for?

A ○ Pretty Important Network Gizmo

B ○ Packet InterNet Groper

C ○ Packet Internet Notification Genie

D ○ It's not an acronym; it's the sound a submarine's radar makes.

8 A Windows XP Professional machine has the "Obtain DNS Server Address Automatically" radio button selected. What service does this workstation actually use to obtain one or more DNS server addresses? (Choose the best answer.)

A ○ APIPA

B ○ Broadcast

C ○ WINS

D ○ DHCP

9 You are a local PC tech support person for a large company. A user in your office named Vicky complains of poor performance when accessing network resources. You call the corporate guru, who tells you to install the Network Monitor Driver on Vicky's machine. How do you do this? (Choose the best answer.)

A ○ On Vicky's computer, open Network and Dial-Up Connections, right-click the Local Area Connection icon, choose Properties, click the Install button, and choose Protocol.

B ○ On Vicky's computer, open Network and Dial-Up Connections, right-click the Local Area Connection icon, choose Properties, click the Install button, and choose Service.

C ○ On Vicky's computer, open Network and Dial-Up Connections, right-click the Local Area Connection icon, choose Properties, and check the box labeled "Network Monitor Driver."

D ○ Run the Add/Remove Programs Wizard and choose Windows Components.

10 James (from Question #1) calls back. You fixed his system so that he can communicate with remote computers as long as he specifies their IP addresses. However, he can't communicate with them by specifying their NetBIOS names. What should you do? (Choose the best answer.)

A ○ Tell James to go away because he's being a pest.

B ○ Check out the address setting for James' DNS server.

C ○ Check out the address setting for James' WINS server.

D ○ Check out the address setting for James' default gateway.

Answers

1 **A** and **B.** If James had an invalid subnet mask, or an invalid DHCP setting, he couldn't see local computers. If the domain controller were down, James wouldn't be able to log on to the network. *See "The default gateway."*

2 **D.** Okay, this is a bit of a trick question. NetBEUI would be a good choice, but Microsoft doesn't support it with Windows XP Professional. Choices A and B aren't protocols in the sense that the question implies. Choice E wouldn't make sense here, despite the advance that Automatic Private IP Addressing makes in terms of ease of use for small TCP/IP networks; IPX is still simpler to set up. *See "NWLink, or 'IPX/SPX/NetBIOS-compatible transport protocol.'"*

3 **A** and **C.** Because the same network ID is required, the same subnet mask is also required; two computers cannot have the same network ID without also having the same subnet mask because the subnet mask determines how many bits are in the network ID. The workgroup name answer is wrong because the computers may not even be in a workgroup — they may be in a domain, in which case the computers would not have workgroup names configured. *See "The IP address and subnet mask."*

4 **A** and **C.** The exam expects you to know that you can use the DHCP service or the DHCP Relay Agent service on a subnet to permit Windows XP Professional machines to access DHCP. The exam also expects you to know that these services require a member of the Windows 2000 Server family. No, these aren't strictly workstation topics, so be aware that the exam expects a fair knowledge of server technology! *Take a look at "DHCP, WINS, and DNS."*

5 **A** and **C.** Novell's client software comes with Novell's own implementation of IPX/SPX and also supports TCP/IP access to NetWare 5 servers. Remember for the exam that CSNW runs on Windows XP Professional, while GSNW runs on Windows 2000 Server. *See "NWLink, or 'IPX/SPX/NetBIOS-compatible transport protocol.'"*

6 **D.** You would use this address (memorize it) with the PING command in order to verify that TCP/IP is properly installed and bound to your network adapter. *Review "Troubleshooting TCP/IP."*

7 **B.** Yes, this is the gag question, but the answer is correct. My favorite computer industry acronym of all time, however, remains APL, which stands for A Programming Language. I swear.

8 **D.** The DHCP service can provide DNS server addresses in addition to IP addresses, subnet masks, and default gateway addresses. *Check out "DHCP, WINS, and DNS."*

9 **A.** The Network Monitor Driver allows a Windows 2000 Server machine running Network Monitor to gather performance data about Vicky's network connection. *See "Network Protocols."*

10 **C.** WINS, or Windows Internet Name Service, is responsible for matching up NetBIOS names with IP addresses on a routed network. *Review "DHCP, WINS, and DNS."*

Part III
Installing and Configuring Hardware

The 5th Wave   By Rich Tennant

Before installing Windows XP, Dwayne prepares to partition the hard drive.

In this part . . .

A huge part of any operating system's day-to-day responsibilities is acting as intermediary between user and hardware. This part breaks out hardware into three groups. Chapter 7 deals with disks, tapes, and printers. Chapter 8 covers displays and other input/output devices. Chapter 9 concentrates on portable computing hardware, including important discussions on Plug and Play and power management — two features that set Windows XP apart from Windows NT.

Chapter 7

Installing and Configuring Disks, Tapes, and Printers

Exam Objectives

▶ Monitor and configure disks

▶ Monitor, configure, and troubleshoot volumes

▶ Install, configure, and manage DVD and CD-ROM devices

▶ Monitor and configure removable media, such as tape devices

▶ Manage printers and print jobs

▶ Connect to a local print device

▶ Connect to an Internet printer

▶ Configure and troubleshoot fax support

1 f you have a CPU, some RAM, a keyboard, and a display, you can do some computing. However, if you want to *keep* your work from one session to another, or share it with others, then disks, tapes, printers, and faxes come in mighty handy. Ergo, almost all PCs have some form of magnetic storage and printout capability.

In this chapter, I discuss how Windows XP Professional deals with storage devices of the magnetic and paper variety. As usual, I cover all bases, but you would be smart to focus especially closely on the "new and cool" topics — such as dynamic disks and Internet printing. Hint, hint, nudge, nudge. In Chapter 8, I look at how Windows XP supports other, less universal hardware, such as multiple displays and USB devices.

Quick Assessment

Monitoring and configuring disks

1 Nearly all your disk configuration activity can be performed with the _____ console snap-in.

Monitoring, configuring, and troubleshooting volumes

2 If you want to monitor disk usage by user, activate the _____ feature.

3 How many partitions can you create on a dynamic disk?

Installing, configuring, and managing DVD and CD-ROM devices

4 For the best possible disk performance, create a _____ volume.

5 If Windows XP doesn't play movies with a given DVD drive, you should _____.

Monitoring and configuring removable media

6 A removable cartridge disk can contain a maximum of _____ partition(s).

Managing printers and print jobs

7 In Microspeak, the software interface between the operating system and a physical print device is called a _____.

Connecting to a local print device

8 You can create a printer _____ so that a single logical printer connects to multiple physical print devices.

9 You can tell that a specific printer is the default printer because its icon features a _____.

Connecting to an Internet printer

10 You can connect to a TCP/IP network printer by using the printer's _____ or its _____.

Answers

1   *Disk Management.* "Hard Drives, Partitions, and Volumes" refers to this utility, which supersedes the NT 4.0 Disk Administrator tool.

2   *Quota.* See "Setting quotas" for the details.

3   *None.* Mildly tricky, sorry. Dynamic disks use volumes instead of partitions. See "Hard Drives, Partitions, and Volumes" for this and other wisdom.

4   *Striped.* No points if you said "fast." The "Creating dynamic volumes" section has the lowdown.

5   *Get a decoder.* Windows XP doesn't come with one. The "Optical Disks" section elaborates.

6   *One.* The "Removable Media" section has more.

7   *Printer.* If you missed this one (and most do), "A bit of terminology" is the section to read.

8   *Pool.* See "Pooling" in this chapter for how to set this up.

9   *Check mark.* See "Installing a new printer" for more.

10 *IP address, DNS name.* The "Finding a printer" section explains.

Hard Drives, Partitions, and Volumes

Organizing disk drives is a central function of any operating system and a sure subject for exam questions. Windows XP supports two kinds of disk organization:

- ✔ *Basic disks*, which use *partitions* (which Microsoft also calls *basic volumes*) to organize the disk into storage units in much the same way that Windows NT Workstation 4.0, Windows 98, and MS-DOS do.

- ✔ *Dynamic disks*, which use *dynamic volumes* to organize the disk and which are unique to Windows XP and 2000.

Use partitions with basic disks. Use volumes with dynamic disks.

Dynamic disks use a special database, called the *Logical Disk Manager* (LDM) database, that lives on the disk's last megabyte of space. Windows replicates the LDM database onto each disk in a dynamic disk group. Because only Windows XP and 2000 know how to access and interpret the LDM, dynamic disks work only with those operating systems.

A single physical disk must be basic or dynamic. On a PC with multiple disks, however, basic disks can cohabitate with dynamic disks.

Windows XP sets up disks as basic disks by default. You can upgrade a basic disk to a dynamic disk with the Disk Management utility (see Lab 7-1 later in this chapter). You might perform such an upgrade if you want to create a *striped volume* (for better speed) or a *spanned volume* (for better use of space).

If you're upgrading a Windows NT 4.0 system to Windows XP Professional, and that NT system uses a mirror set, stripe set, or stripe set with parity (all of which are multidisk sets that NT permits), Microsoft suggests you back up and delete the multidisk set before upgrading to XP because XP can't see NT multidisk sets. If desired, you can re-establish a multidisk set by converting basic to dynamic disks after you perform the operating system upgrade, and restore from your backups. In the special case of an NT system with a mirrored system volume or boot volume, you can break the mirror set before performing the upgrade, but you don't have to do a backup and restore.

You can use dynamic disks with any of the three Windows XP file systems, but certain features, such as extending a volume, are available only if you use NTFS. (If you don't know what the heck NTFS is, please read Chapter 3.)

No matter whether you use basic or dynamic disks, Windows XP Professional does *not* provide any form of fault tolerance for disks in any configuration. Sadly, you don't get mirroring, duplexing, or RAID unless you use Windows 2002 Server or Windows 2000 Server, or unless you buy a third-party hardware solution that provides such features independently from the operating system.

Configuring hard drives

The actions that you can take to configure hard drives are

- Partition a basic disk
- Extend a partition
- Promote a basic disk to a dynamic disk
- Create dynamic volumes
- Extend dynamic volumes
- Set quotas
- Set mount points

The following sections examine each action in turn.

Partitioning a basic disk

Those of you who are familiar with partitioning disks in earlier versions of Windows will see no earth-shattering differences with Windows XP Professional, but do take note that, as with Windows 2000, you can use either Windows XP setup (during installation) or the Disk Management snap-in (after installation) to partition disks. Windows XP adds a new command-line utility, DISKPART, which you can use from a script or batch file to create extra partitions when rolling out Windows XP in a scripted or cloned installation. (You can forget about FDISK, praise be.)

Creating a partition in Disk Management (DISKMGMT.MSC) is simplicity itself:

- On a primary partition, right-click an area of unallocated space in the graphical display and choose New Partition.
- On an extended partition, right-click an area of free space and choose New Logical Drive.

Know the following two key terms for the exam. These may be the same, but they don't have to be; the boot partition could live on a second primary partition, for example, or on a logical drive on an extended partition.

- The *system partition* is the partition containing hardware-specific files and the one from which Windows XP starts the boot process.
- The *boot partition* is the partition containing the operating system files themselves (usually, the WINDOWS folder).

The terminology is perverse:

- ✔ The computer *boots* from the *system* partition.
- ✔ The operating *system* is on the *boot* partition.

Here are the basic rules of partitioning:

- ✔ Any basic disk must have at least one partition.
- ✔ Partitions come in two types:
  - • Primary: You can set this as the active system partition.
  - • Extended: Cannot be the active system partition, but can contain multiple logical drives, each of which you format separately.
- ✔ A hard disk may have no more than one extended partition.
- ✔ A hard disk may have no more than four partitions total. These can be three primary plus one extended, or four primary.
- ✔ Microsoft recommends using a separate partition for each operating system in a multiple-boot setup.
- ✔ You must create a primary partition first, then (if desired) an extended partition, and then any logical drives on the extended partition.

Extending a partition

A handy advance that Microsoft has made since Windows 2000 is the ability to extend a partition on a basic disk. Here are the facts to remember for the test:

- ✔ Two new command-line utilities let you extend a partition: FSUTIL and DISKPART, both of which use the EXTEND qualifier.
- ✔ You can only extend a partition if it uses NTFS.
- ✔ You can extend any partition, even the boot or system partition, without restarting the PC.
- ✔ The partition to be extended must have a contiguous chunk of unallocated space immediately after it.
- ✔ You cannot span multiple disks when you extend a partition; it must stay on the same disk.

Promoting a basic disk to a dynamic disk

Windows XP sets up your disks as basic disks by default. So, usually, when you want to set up a dynamic disk, you'll be upgrading, or *promoting*, a basic disk. You can promote a basic disk to a dynamic disk without losing data, but watch out: Going in the reverse direction (*reverting* to a basic disk) wipes out all the data on the disk!

Promoting a basic disk to a dynamic disk is simple, as Lab 7-1 explains. You can also use the new command-line tool DISKPART to promote a disk, which would be handy, for example, if you wanted to promote disks as part of a scripted Windows XP upgrade deployment.

Lab 7-1	Promoting a Basic Disk to a Dynamic Disk

1. **Back up the disk that you want to promote.**

   You may not need this backup, but better safe than sorry.

2. **Log on as Administrator or the equivalent.**

3. **Right-click My Computer and choose Manage.**

   The Computer Management console appears.

4. **Click the Disk Management icon in the tree pane (on the left; see Figure 7-1).**

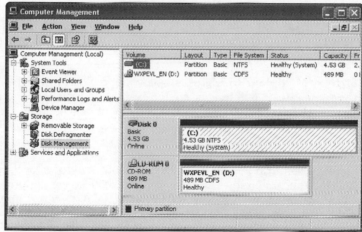

Figure 7-1: The Disk Management snap-in offers a tree view (upper right) or a graphical view (lower right).

5. **In the lower-right window frame, right-click the box containing the disk icon and the words "Disk 0" or "Disk 1" or whatever number it may be.**

   Don't right-click any of the partition boxes that appear to the right.

6. **Select the Convert To Dynamic Disk menu option.**

   You won't see this option on removable disk devices because such devices can only be basic disks in Windows XP Professional.

7. **Confirm your choice of which disk to promote by checking the correct box next to the disk name.**

Windows then displays various warning messages that you should read but (if you're like me) probably won't.

8. **Finish with the upgrade wizard and reboot.**

The option to upgrade a basic disk to a dynamic disk may appear on a portable PC, but Microsoft doesn't support Windows XP dynamic disks on portable computers. The reason is simple: Dynamic disks only convey benefits when you have more than one hard drive in a computer, and most notebook PCs have only one hard drive. Also, if a notebook PC uses one hard drive internally, and a second hard drive in a docking station, the two drives' LDM databases could easily get out of sync. FYI, Windows XP doesn't support dynamic disks on removable (such as Zip) or detachable (for example, USB) drives, either.

Creating dynamic volumes

Windows XP Professional supports three kinds of volumes on dynamic disks:

- **Simple:** One disk, one volume.

- **Spanned:** Multiple (2 to 32) disks, one volume. Windows fills the first disk completely before moving to the second, and so on. Efficient use of space (no *slack* at the end of a disk).

- **Striped:** Multiple (2 to 32) disks, one volume. Windows fills each disk at the same rate, in 64K blocks, so, for example, a 2-disk striped volume that's half full consists of 2 disks, each of which is half full. Fastest performance (multiple physical disks working concurrently equals better speed).

Don't let the exam trip you up if it asks you about Windows XP Professional and fault tolerance: Windows 2002 Server and 2000 Server support mirrored and RAID-5 volumes, but Windows XP Professional does not support these two additional types. Spanned and striped volumes are not fault-tolerant: If you lose one disk in the set to hardware failure, you lose the whole volume.

To create a volume on a dynamic disk, first make sure that the disk is dynamic (see the previous section if necessary). Then, in the Disk Management window (lower-right pane), right-click in the unallocated space area and then choose the New Volume menu option. (If you choose only a single unallocated space area, you'll create a simple volume. If you want to create a spanned or striped volume, select unallocated areas from multiple disks before right-clicking one of them, and choose spanned or striped in the Select Volume Type window.) Give the volume a size, assign it a drive letter, and specify how you want Windows XP to format the volume.

Extending dynamic volumes

You can extend a simple volume to include unallocated space on the same physical disk without restarting the PC, if the simple volume uses NTFS. The result is a larger simple volume.

You can extend a simple volume to include unallocated space on *another* physical disk, thereby creating a *spanned volume*. You can do this with a FAT volume as well as with an NTFS volume, but after you create a spanned FAT volume, you can't extend it further.

You can't extend a striped volume, the system volume, or the boot volume.

Follow this procedure to extend a volume in the Disk Management snap-in:

1. **Right-click the volume that you want to extend.**

2. **Choose the Extend Volume menu option.**

3. **Follow the wizard prompts.**

Setting quotas

Disk *quotas* are a new feature of NTFS 5 (you can't use quotas on non-NTFS disks). This feature enables you to limit the amount of disk space that any user on the system can use on a given volume. (Windows determines usage based on *ownership*; when a user saves a new file or copies a file, the user takes ownership of that file.) You can set different limits for specific users, and you can set different limits for different drive letters or volumes. So this feature is fairly flexible.

Although the disk quotas feature is (as you'd expect) more important on the Server product than on Windows XP Professional, you may see it crop up on Exam #70-270 anyway, so here are the basics in a nutshell:

✔ Disk quotas are off by default.

Turn them on by right-clicking a drive icon in My Computer or Explorer, choosing Properties, clicking the Quota tab, and checking the box labeled Enable Quota Management (see Figure 7-2). You must do this separately for each logical drive or volume on the system.

✔ You must be an Administrator to set up and configure quotas.

✔ To use quotas for enforcement rather than mere usage monitoring, check the Deny Disk Space to Users Exceeding Quota Limit box, as shown in Figure 7-2. A user who is about to create or take ownership of a file that would put her over the limit receives an Out of Disk Space error message from Windows XP.

✔ Quotas permit two threshold settings:

- *Warning* level, at which point Windows creates an entry in the system event log.

- Higher *limit* level, at which point Windows denies disk space to the user.

  Decimal values are okay for both.

✔ When you activate quotas, the values you specify for warning and limit levels apply to new users only. To set quotas for existing users, click the Quota Entries button and choose New Quota Entry from the Quota menu. Choose a local or domain user account and set the warning and limit values.

✔ To limit the event logging that the quota system performs, clear one or both of the check boxes that say Log Event When a User Exceeds Their Quota Limit and Log Event When a User Exceeds Their Warning Level. (Yes, it's bad grammar, but most programmers no write can.)

Figure 7-2:
The traffic light icon is red if quotas are off, green if on, and yellow if Windows is rebuilding data.

The initial values for the warning and limit levels are 1KB! Don't forget to change KB to MB in a real-world situation.

Quotas don't look at the compressed value of files; they look at the uncompressed value. So it's possible for a user to own 40MB of actual space but still trigger a 50MB quota limit. (This is quotas Version 1.0, remember!)

If a user on a dual-boot system gets an error from Windows XP when trying to save or create a file, but is able to save or create that file with no error when working from Windows NT on the same machine, suspect a quota violation. NT doesn't know about quotas and therefore can't enforce them, which is why the user's operation succeeds from the NT side.

Setting mount points

When you're going through the wizard screens in order to create a new volume, you have the option to select a check box (on the Assign Drive Letter or Path window) that says Mount This Volume At An Empty Folder That Supports Drive Paths. What this means is that you can create a new volume that maps to an existing folder on an NTFS disk. That is, you can add a 4GB hard drive that the user sees as a very large 4GB folder living under an existing drive letter.

If a user is running out of room on drive C, you can add a second physical drive but map it in its entirety to a folder on drive C. This way, the user doesn't have to worry about keeping track of a second drive letter. ("D colon? What's that? Part of D intestine?") Magically, drive C has a new folder with 4GB of free space. You've just discovered the wonder of *mount points*, a type of "reparse point" that's new to NTFS Version 5.

If the exam asks you how to add disk capacity when you're already maxed out on drive letters, mount points should figure into the correct answer.

Monitoring hard drives

You can check various details of a local hard drive by using the Disk Management snap-in to the Computer Management console:

1. **In the lower-right window frame, right-click the box containing the disk icon and the words "Disk 0" or "Disk 1" or whatever number it may be.**

   Don't right-click any of the partition boxes that appear to the right.

2. **Choose Properties, and you see a window like what you see in Figure 7-3.**

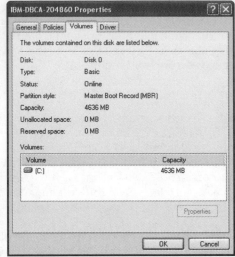

Figure 7-3:
Monitoring
drive
details.

Again in Disk Management, if you right-click a *partition* on a basic disk (as opposed to the disk itself) and choose Properties, you see some or all of the following tabs:

- General
- Tools
- Hardware
- Sharing
- Security (on an NTFS partition)
- Quota (on an NTFS partition)

Right-click a volume on a dynamic disk and you see the same tabs as when you right-click a partition on a basic disk.

You can use the Disk Management snap-in remotely, to manage other PCs, as long as you log on with an account that has administrative privileges both on your PC and on the remote PC, and both computers are within the same domain or at least within trusted domains. You can redirect the management console (COMPMGMT.MSC) by right-clicking the computer icon and choosing Connect To Another Computer. Alternatively, you can create a custom Microsoft Management Console containing the Disk Management snap-in, and point that snap-in to the remote computer when you add it to the console.

Finally, you can monitor disk space use on a user-by-user basis by *enabling* disk quotas but not *enforcing* them. That is, on the Quota tab of the disk property sheet, check the Enable Quota Management box, but uncheck the Deny Disk Space to Users Exceeding Quota Limit box. This way, when you click the Quota Entries button, you can view space usage by user name without having any impact on users' ability to create new files. For convenience, you can set warning and limit levels that trigger system event logging and that affect the icons that appear in the Quota Entries list, but these settings don't have any effect on users. (For more information, see the "Setting quotas" section earlier in this chapter.)

Optical Disks

Windows XP Professional supports CD-ROM and DVD optical storage devices. Some (but not all) writeable optical devices, such as CD-RW drives, can also work with Windows XP Professional depending on the availability of Windows XP device drivers.

CD-ROM

Windows XP either works with a given make and model CD-ROM drive, or it doesn't. The famous Microsoft Hardware Compatibility List (HCL) is the guide here.

 If you need to install Windows XP Professional and your PC's CD-ROM drive isn't on the HCL and doesn't work, Microsoft recommends that you choose an alternative method of installation (such as using a network distribution server) or install a different model CD-ROM drive.

 If the exam mentions *El Torito*, it's not referring to a brand of tortilla chip. It's referring to a specification that lets a computer boot from the CD-ROM drive. You may have to set the option in the PC's BIOS setup. Booting from the Windows XP Professional CD is handy for installation and system recovery purposes (beats the heck out of using diskettes to start the computer).

One advance since Windows 2000 is the ability to burn a writeable CD (CD-R or CD-RW) by just dragging and dropping files onto the CD drive's icon in the user interface, or by selecting the files in My Computer or Explorer and copying in the usual way (for example, with the context menu's Copy command). However, you must format the CD before trying to copy to it.

If audio CDs aren't working, check the CD-ROM drive's property sheet via Device Manager (in the System control panel). You may need to clear the Enable Digital CD Audio For This CD-ROM Device check box to ensure analog playback of audio content.

DVD

So what does DVD stand for? No one seems to know, and the exam doesn't ask. These devices can store 133 minutes of digital video/audio data in the MPEG-2 format; they can also store 4.7GB of data per layer, with up to two layers per side for a total of four layers. DVD drives also let you play regular CD audio discs and read CD-ROMs. Standard CD-ROM drives, however, can't read DVD discs.

You need a *DVD decoder* (which can be hardware- or software-based) to play DVD movies. If you upgraded from Windows 98 or Me and you had a software DVD decoder, you'll need to install an updated one for XP. Windows XP Professional can play DVD movies via Windows Media Player after a decoder is installed; open Windows Media Player and choose Tools⇨Options, and then click Formats and check DVD Video under File Types.

The world of DVD is one of many competing standards, including the read-only variant DVD-ROM and the writeable variants DVD-RAM, DVD-RW, and DVD+RW. Out of the box, Windows XP Professional supports DVD in read-only mode for both multimedia and data using the UDF (Universal Disk Format), and supports the DVD-RAM variant in read-write mode with the FAT16 and FAT32 file formats.

Removable Media

Although Microsoft lists configuring and monitoring removable media as a test objective, the exam isn't likely to cover this material in any depth. Tape backup is much more relevant in connection with Windows 2000 and 2002 Server, and very few Windows XP Professional PCs have tape drives, much less robotic tape library devices.

Regardless, here are a few basics you may need to know about Windows XP removable media:

- Removable storage disks, such as Zip or Jaz disks, are basic disks containing one primary partition only.

- You can manage removable media to some extent via the Removable Storage snap-in from the Computer Management console. However, most of your interaction with tape drives will be through an application such as Microsoft Backup.

✔ Windows XP doesn't support backing up directly to CD-R or CD-RW drives. You have to back up to a file, then copy that file to the writeable CD. The reason has to do with the physical requirements of writing to a CD in a continuous stream.

✔ A removable storage *library* is a device, such as a robotic tape changer or a standalone tape drive unit.

✔ A *media pool* is a group of removable media that Windows XP or a Windows application manages the same way. For example, a backup program could create one media pool for incremental backups and another (using a higher capacity media type) for full backups. (By the way, an *incremental* backup is a backup of all files that have been created or changed since the last full or incremental backup. A *differential* backup, on the other hand, is a backup of all files that have been created or changed since the last full backup.)

A freshly formatted tape cartridge that Windows XP has never seen before is in an "unrecognized" media pool. You must use the Removable Storage snap-in to drag and drop the tape to a free media pool before you can use it.

Many tape drives are not Plug and Play-compatible and you'll therefore need to install them with the Add New Hardware Wizard. Running the wizard requires administrative privileges.

In Chapter 15, I discuss the Microsoft Backup program in more detail.

Configuring Printing

Printing in Windows XP isn't radically different from printing in Windows NT 4.0 or Windows 2000, so if you feel very comfortable with how printing works in those older operating systems, you can skim this section lightly. It provides the basics that the exam expects you to know.

This section looks at configuring printing. The section that follows looks at using a preconfigured printer. You have to know how to do both!

A bit of terminology

You should have some understanding of Microspeak when it comes to answering printer questions on the exam. Here are the terms to know:

✔ A **printer** isn't a printer, it's a software construct representing the interface between the operating system and the physical print device. Microsoft sometimes uses the term **virtual printer** to mean the same thing.

✔ A **print device** is what you'd refer to as a "printer" in normal speech: a physical printing machine. It can be connected locally, via a parallel, serial, infrared, or USB port, or remotely, across a network cable (in the case of *net-direct* printers having their own network interface card). Microsoft is starting to use the term **physical printer** as a synonym for "print device."

✔ A **printer port** is the software interface to such a hardware port, not a hardware port to which a print device is attached.

This distinction is a bit fine, but it may clarify things if you consider that some computers permit printing via an infrared link that appears to the operating system as a COM port. In that case, the COM port is the "printer port" even though the actual hardware isn't a typical serial interface at all.

✔ A **print server** is a computer that manages print requests for a shared printer.

A print server may manage a locally connected print device or a network-connected print device; the physical location doesn't matter. What does matter is that the print server receives print requests from clients, queues such requests, converts documents into printer-specific code via the printer driver, and transmits the code to the physical print device. Printers in Active Directory require an associated print server.

✔ A **printer pool** is a single "printer" that can send documents to multiple ports and multiple identical print devices. The ports can be local or net-worked. Windows XP finds the first available print device for any given document.

✔ A **printer driver** is the software that describes to Windows XP the features and commands of a particular model of print device.

Installing a new printer

Installing a printer follows a very similar sequence of steps, whether the printer connects directly to your PC or to the network. The procedure centers on the Add Printer Wizard in the Printers and Faxes control panel.

You must be logged on as Administrator to install a printer by launching the wizard manually. You must be logged on as at least a Power User to install a local printer at all.

If Windows XP detects your printer automatically, as it typically will if the printer is local and connects via a USB or FireWire port, then Windows launches the wizard itself. When you launch the Add Printer Wizard yourself, the general procedure is as detailed in Lab 7-2.

If you connect a printer to a parallel or serial port, Windows XP probably won't detect it right away. Restart the operating system with the printer turned on, or run the Add Printer Wizard as described in this lab, to detect the new printer.

Lab 7-2   Installing a Printer with the Add Printer Wizard

1. **Specify whether the printer is directly attached to your PC or connected to the network.**

   If the printer is directly attached, you can let Windows XP try to auto-detect it, or you can skip autodetection and provide the manufacturer and model information yourself. Most modern print devices support the Plug and Play standard, and Windows XP typically recognizes them automatically and prompts to install the necessary driver. Plug and Play doesn't work over the network wire, however, so autodetection isn't an option in this case.

   You have to click the Local Printer radio button even if you're setting up your PC to be a print server for a network-attached printer. Seems counterintuitive, but if you click Network Printer, you can only search for printers that already have print servers created for them; you can't create a new print server on the local PC.

2. **Specify the printer port (see Figure 7-4).**

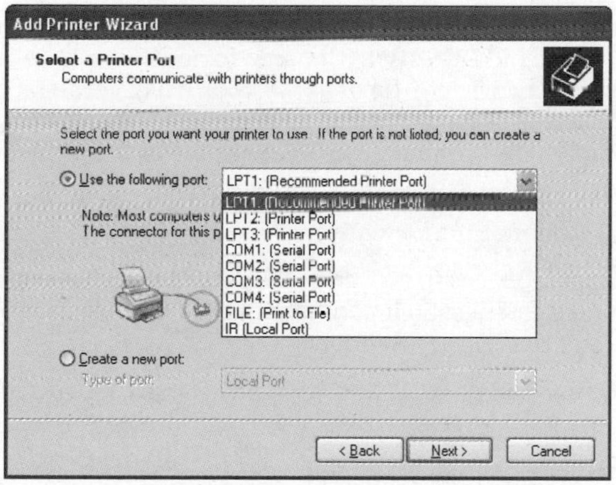

Figure 7-4:
Specifying a local or network port for your new printer.

A direct-attached printer typically connects to a serial (COM:) or parallel (LPT:) port, although FILE: is an option if you want to create print files that you'll send out (for example, to a printing service bureau) for hard copy output. A network-attached printer generally requires you to click the Create a New Port radio button and specify a port type. For example,

"Standard TCP/IP Port" would normally be your choice for a TCP/IP printer, and you would then be prompted to specify an IP address or DNS name for the printer.

Hewlett-Packard net-direct printers (which use the trade name "Jet-Direct") often use the DLC (Data Link Control) protocol for communications. Windows XP doesn't provide this protocol anymore, so your only recourse would be to replace the net-direct card with a newer one that supports TCP/IP.

3. **Specify manufacturer and model.**

   Skip this step if Windows XP correctly autodetects your printer.

4. **Give the printer a name.**

   You can use a name that's different from (and more descriptive than) the device driver name. Just remember that 31 characters is a safe maximum length. The name you assign here appears with the printer's icon in the Printers folder.

5. **Choose whether the printer should be the default printer for Windows applications.**

   You see this choice only if you have at least one printer already defined. The default printer appears in the user interface with a black check mark on its icon.

6. **Give the printer a share name, if you plan to share it.**

   The *share name* defaults to the printer name you assigned in Step 4, chopped off to the old DOS-style 8.3 name format. That's because other people on your network may be using DOS or early versions of Windows that get confused with longer resource names. When network users browse a list of shared printers, the share name is what they see.

7. **If you gave the printer a share name in Step 6, you can enter optional Location and Comment information.**

   This information appears in an Active Directory network when users perform printer searches. So it can help users find the right printer if the share name isn't descriptive enough.

8. **Print an optional test page. When it asks if the page printed correctly, choose Yes, or No to have a wizard walk you through troubleshooting.**

9. **View and confirm a summary of your choices.**

   If everything's correct, click the Finish button, and Windows XP installs the required files (it may prompt you for the installation CD-ROM or the location of the installation files on the network). The wizard will also share the printer for you. If any of the information on the summary screen is wrong, you can go back and make changes until it's all correct.

As the Add Printer Wizard enables you to share a printer with others, a word is in order here about using Windows XP Professional as a print server. This operating system makes a limited print server (although it does support UNIX clients).

You would use Windows 2002 or 2000 Server instead if any of the following conditions apply:

✔ The print server must support more than ten simultaneous clients.

✔ The print server must support Macintosh computers. (The Server product includes Services for Macintosh.)

✔ The print server must support NetWare users.

Configuring a new printer

After you install the printer, you can configure it by setting options in the printer's property sheet. This section looks at a few of the common ones.

Copy printer icons from the Printers and Faxes folder onto the desktop. Users can then quickly print files by dragging and dropping them onto the printer icons.

If you share a printer with the Add Printer Wizard, Windows XP installs printer drivers for Windows NT and Windows Me/9x clients so that those operating systems can automatically download the necessary driver when the user first prints to the shared printer.

Bidirectional local printing

Windows XP supports *bidirectional* parallel printing (U.S. standard *IEEE-1284*) because of its faster speed and because the printer can "tell" the computer about configuration details and operating conditions (such as "toner low"). For the exam, know these requirements for bidirectional printing:

✔ **An IEEE-1284-compatible parallel port on the printer:** These usually go by the name ECP (Extended Capabilities Port) or EPP (Enhanced Parallel Port).

✔ **An IEEE-1284-compatible parallel port on the PC, activated in the BIOS setup:** Some BIOS models still default to the old, slow "compatible" mode for the parallel port.

✔ **An IEEE-1284-compatible parallel cable:** These aren't the same as the older, Centronics-standard parallel cables.

✔ **Bidirectional printing enabled on the printer driver's property sheet:** The Enable Bidirectional Printing check box is on the Ports tab.

Spooling

By default, Windows XP spools print jobs to disk (normally, to the folder C:\WINDOWS\SYSTEM32\SPOOL\PRINTERS) before submitting them to the physical local printer. Spooling brings several benefits:

- ✔ The ability to create a print queue of documents that can be managed
- ✔ The ability to resubmit a job that doesn't print without restarting the application that created it
- ✔ Deferred printing — for example, with an undocked notebook PC
- ✔ A quicker return-to-application time for the user

Windows XP gives you some control over spooling options in the printer's Advanced properties sheet, shown in Figure 7-5. Get there by right-clicking the printer icon in the Printers and Faxes folder, choosing Properties, and clicking the Advanced tab.

Figure 7-5: You can configure spool settings for each printer individually.

You can bet that you'll see a question on these spool options on the exam, so here are the salient facts about each option:

- ✔ Spool Print Jobs So Program Finishes Printing Faster is the same as saying "turn on spooling."
- ✔ Start Printing After Last Page Is Spooled provides the quickest return-to-application time, but requires enough disk space to hold the entire print job and doesn't necessarily get you your physical printout in the shortest time.

✔ Start Printing Immediately provides a slower return-to-application time, but requires less disk space.

✔ Print Directly To The Printer is the same as saying "turn off spooling." For a local printer, you can use this option for troubleshooting. I've found that, in rare cases, documents don't print correctly using spooling. Further, disabling spooling removes one variable (the disk drive) from the printing equation.

Spooling carries an implicit hardware requirement for adequate disk space. Windows XP must be able to create a disk image of a print document before it can actually send that document to the print device. Without lots of megabytes at the ready, spooling may fail, and print jobs can stop before they start.

Pooling

You can create a *pool* of printers wherein two or more identical physical printers correspond to a single logical printer in the operating system. (Actually, the physical print devices don't need to be identical, but they must use the same printer driver.) Windows XP automatically routes documents to the first available device in the pool.

Simply check the Enable Printer Pooling box on the Ports tab of the printers' property sheets, then (in the same dialog box) check each of the ports that connects to a printer that you want to be in the pool.

Redirecting

If you find that you need to redirect documents to a different printer — for example, due to a printer hardware glitch — Windows XP provides a method, which I describe in Lab 7-3.

Lab 7-3	Redirecting Documents from a Stuck Printer

1. Choose Start⇨Control Panel⇨Printers and Faxes to open the Printers and Faxes folder.

2. Right-click the stuck printer and choose Properties.

3. Click the Ports tab.

4. If a working printer of the same type exists on a different local port on the *same print* server, click the port's check box and click OK. Otherwise, if a working printer of the same type exists on a *different* print server, proceed to Step 5.

5. Click the Add Port button.

6. Click Local Port in the Printer Ports dialog box.

7. Click the New Port button in the Printer Ports dialog box.

8. **In the Port Name dialog box, specify the working printer with UNC notation.**

That is, use the form *printservername**printersharename*.

If a printer fails, you don't want to lose queued documents, and if another print server has a compatible printer, add a local port on the stuck print server.

Adding drivers

If you share a printer that already exists on a Windows XP PC, as opposed to sharing the printer when you create it (see "Installing a new printer" earlier in this chapter), you have to add drivers to your PC for any non-Windows XP operating system that may print to the printer. The procedure is mercifully easy: Click the Sharing tab of the printer's property sheet and click the Additional Drivers button.

Windows NT, 2000, and XP clients check the print server for driver updates before they print each document. That's handy because when you update a driver on the PC that acts as print server, you don't have to run around updating all the client PCs as well. Note, however, that Windows 9*x* clients do not perform this check and therefore do require manual driver updates.

Playing with priorities

Unlike Windows 9*x*, the NT platform (including Windows XP) lets you assign a priority to a printer. Just right-click the printer icon, choose Properties, click the Advanced tab, and pick a number from 1 (low) to 99 (high).

Priority 1 is the lowest priority, 99 is the highest. I used to have a terrible time keeping this rule straight; just remember, "high number, high priority."

You can use printer priorities in a tricky way to make sure that one user or group's print jobs always receive preferential treatment. (This bit of wizardry *always* seems to be on the MCSE tests.) Suppose, for example, that you have a single physical print device but two users who print to it. In order to give user A's print jobs priority over user B's, you can create two Windows XP virtual printers with different names, each of which points to the same physical print device. Give one printer a high priority, the other a low one. Then configure user A's computer to print to "Serf" and user B's computer to print to "Lord." (You can enforce these settings using access permissions on the printer objects. With a large number of users, you'd assign access permissions to groups instead of individual users.) Their documents go to the same device, but Windows XP prioritizes them differently. You could also use the same trick to differentiate different kinds of documents, instead of different users or groups.

Using a Printer

This last section deals with some common actions that users perform in the course of printing documents: finding a printer, managing print jobs, and printing offline.

Finding a printer

First things first: You must find a printer before you can print to it. Finding locally attached printers is easy — they appear by default in the drop-down list box in the Print dialog box of most Windows applications. Finding network printers is almost as easy in Windows XP. Simply run the Add Printer Wizard, click the Network Printer radio button in the Local or Network Printer dialog box, click Next, and you see a dialog box like what's shown in Figure 7-6. (If you're not running an Active Directory network with Windows XP Server, you won't see the option to Find a Printer In the Directory.)

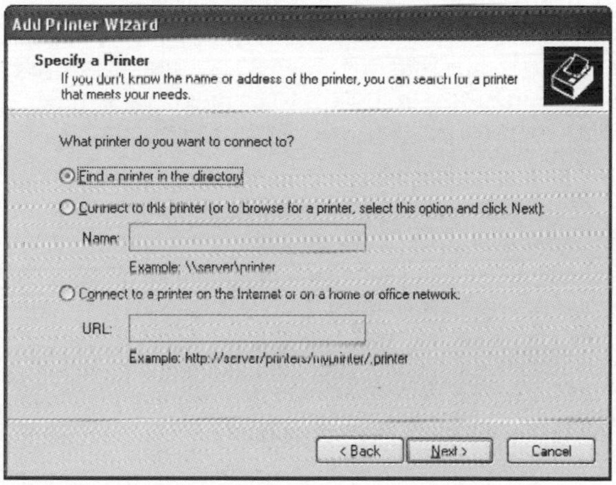

Figure 7-6:
You can find a network printer three main ways.

Here are your options:

- On an Active Directory network, you can click Find a Printer in the Directory. Clicking Next takes you to a dialog box where you can search based on printer name, location, comment, or printer capability (such as color).

- You can click Connect to This Printer and specify a printer name (such as the UNC, or Universal Naming Convention, name — format *printserver**printername*), or leave the name field blank and click Next to browse the network (Active Directory or otherwise) to view all printer names.

✔ You can click the Connect to a Printer on the Internet or on a Home or Office Network button to find a TCP/IP printer by URL (Uniform Resource Locator).

Many applications will also support Windows XP's new Print dialog box, which includes a handy Find Printer button just below the Preferences button.

Managing print jobs

Some of the routine chores associated with managing your print jobs are as follows:

✔ To pause printing, right-click the Printer icon in the Printers folder and select Pause Printing.

✔ Resume printing with the same procedure, which toggles the Pause Printing setting off.

✔ To cancel all documents, right-click the Printer icon and select Cancel All Documents.

✔ To pause one or more specific documents, double-click the Printer icon, right-click the document(s) you want to pause (you can use the Shift or Ctrl keys to choose multiple documents), and choose Pause.

✔ To resume one or more specific documents, double-click the Printer icon, right-click the document(s) you want to resume, and choose Resume. (Note that this procedure doesn't work like the pause/resume procedure for the entire printer, which is a toggle setting. Hey, if the user interface were consistent, it wouldn't be Windows.)

✔ To cancel one or more specific documents, select them as in the previous item, right-click, and choose Cancel.

✔ If you want to start a document print job over from the beginning, select one or more documents, right-click, and choose Restart.

✔ To schedule a document to print at a later time (as, for example, when the printer isn't busy), right-click the document in the printer's window and choose Properties. You can then set the "Only From" time to the earliest time you want the job to start printing (see Figure 7-7).

✔ To change the priority of a document, right-click the document, choose Properties, and change the priority setting by using the graphical slider control. Priority 1 is the lowest, and 99 is the highest, just as with printers.

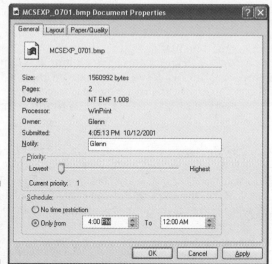

Figure 7-7:
Setting a
print job's
time slot.

Generally, you can print, pause, resume, cancel, and restart document print jobs that you own (that is, that you submitted with a Print command); another way to put this is that the Everyone group has the *Print* permission. To modify jobs submitted by other users, you need the *Manage Documents* permission for that printer. To have full administrative control of the printer — pause it, stop it, start it, share it, change its properties — you need the *Manage Printers* permission for that printer. By default, Administrators and Power Users have all three printer permissions: Print, Manage Documents, and Manage Printers. They can change printer permissions via the printer's property sheet, Security tab.

Printing offline

Users can *defer* printing in Windows XP, meaning that they create the spool file from their application program, but physically print the document later — for example, when they return to the office and dock their notebooks. Windows XP handles deferred printing automatically with notebook PCs, but a user can set it manually with the Printers and Faxes folder command File➪Use Printer Offline.

Another way to defer printing is by selecting File as the port, instead of a parallel or serial port, on the printer's property sheet. If you do this, Windows XP creates print files with the suffix *.PRN. You can then print the document on your printer, or on someone else's printer (as long as it's the same model), by copying the PRN file to the printer port.

Printing to fax devices

Normally, you print to a fax modem just as you would print to a physical print device. Fax devices appear in the Printers and Faxes folder. If Windows XP doesn't show your fax modem, the Fax service may not be installed. Click the Set Up Faxing task in the left pane of the Printers and Faxes folder, or choose File⇨Set Up Faxing. You'll need the setup CD (or access to the setup files over a network).

After you install the Fax service, you'll see a Fax icon in the Printers and Faxes folder. Double-click it to run the Fax Configuration Wizard, where you specify user information and whether you want to automatically receive faxes (the default is no). After you run the wizard, double-clicking the Fax icon opens the Fax Console, where you can see incoming and outgoing jobs.

To set up a fax modem for automatic reception, right-click the Fax icon and choose Properties. Click the Devices tab, choose the fax modem if you have more than one, and click the Properties button. Finally, click the Receive tab and check the Enable Device To Receive box. (Could Microsoft have made this any more tedious? I doubt it!)

Set up fax cover pages by opening the Fax Console (double-click the Fax icon) and choose Tools⇨Sender Information. If you have personal cover pages defined, select one with Tools⇨Personal Cover Pages.

Configure page size, image quality, and orientation (portrait vs. landscape) by right-clicking the Fax icon in the Printers and Faxes folder and choosing Printing Preferences.

The Tracking tab of the Fax icon's property sheet controls the automatic opening of the Fax Monitor window when a fax arrives; the display of a taskbar icon; notification of progress of sent and received faxes; notification by sound; and success and failure notifications.

e PC's
al and
hat
d you

for a large cookie manufacturer. You get a
nable to save new documents to his My
lder redirection to point My Documents to
No one else in Dino's office is experiencing
able to save new files to his My
out difficulty. What would be a likely course
(Choose the best answer.)

e printer.
e printer.

sk with a larger one.

it to an empty folder on Dino's main hard

Which of
h

Dino.

nage-
l printer

s to different users who share the same
You create two different logical printers, A
sical port. Then, you modify the access con-
change each printer's priority settings.

dd Printer

dd Printer

n order to make Printer A the highest pos-

rinter.

e update
ks offer
nfigured
wer)

lexibility.
erse the

ng for your network PCs. As part of your
disk space usage as a function of time.
s for this purpose.

e
ment. The
e PC run-
nputers,

ta feature so that you can see, via Event
nd when users exceed 100MB? (Choose

gement box for each drive you want to

ows XP
hat factors
pply.)

Jsers Exceeding Quota Limit check box.
age radio button.
adio button.
to activate quotas on existing user

4 A Windows XP Professional computer shares a printer connected to t
parallel port. Users of that printer are running Windows XP Professio
Windows 98. You receive a driver update and you want to make sure
every computer on the network gets the new driver. What steps shou
take? (Choose all that apply.)

A ❑ Update the driver on the computer sharing the printer.

B ❑ Update the driver on all network clients that use the printer.

C ❑ Update the driver on all Windows XP network clients that use th

D ❑ Update the driver on all Windows 98 network clients that use th

5 You receive a brand new printer preconfigured for TCP/IP networking
the following statements must be true in order to use this printer wi
Windows XP Professional? (Choose all that apply.)

A ❑ TCP/IP printers have an icon in the Printers folder for queue ma
ment, but no property sheets for configuration. You configure al
options from the Web browser interface.

B ❑ You can use the printer's DNS name when identifying it in the /
Wizard.

C ❑ You can use the printer's IP address when identifying it in the /
Wizard.

D ❑ You should use DHCP to assign IP configuration details to the ｜

6 Wilma calls you with a Windows XP Professional question. Should s
her notebook PC to a dynamic disk? She has heard that dynamic di:
cool new features. Wilma never uses DOS and her machine is not cc
for dual-booting. How should you answer her? (Choose the best an:

A ○ Yes. Dynamic disks have the greatest feature set and the most

B ○ Yes. Dynamic disks are more flexible, and Wilma can easily rev
setting later if she desires.

C ○ Yes. Dynamic disks offer the best possible performance.

D ○ No. Dynamic disks generally offer no benefit for notebook PCs

7 Betty, your boss, has asked you to configure a network printer for tl
Windows XP Professional network that you manage for your depar
network consists of 14 PCs running Windows XP Professional and c
ning Windows 2000 Server. The network contains no Macintosh co
nor does it contain any NetWare servers.

You must decide whether to share the network printer from a Wind
Professional machine or from the Windows 2000 Server machine. V
should you consider when making that decision? (Choose all that ￼

A ❑ Performance
B ❑ Expected print volume
C ❑ Windows licenses
D ❑ Potential future growth

8 **Which of the following disk fault tolerance features work with Windows XP Professional without requiring any third party software or specialized hardware? (Choose all that apply.)**

A ❑ RAID 0
B ❑ RAID 5
C ❑ Mirroring
D ❑ Duplexing
E ❑ Power backup

9 **Fred is trying to receive a fax on his standalone Windows XP Professional computer, but he's unable to do so. He's tested his modem via the Phone and Modem Options control panel, and it passes diagnostics. You advise him to check the Advanced Options tab of his Fax control panel, but he reports that no such tab exists. What should you do? (Choose all that apply.)**

A ❑ Tell Fred to log off and log back on as an Administrator.
B ❑ Tell Fred to open the Fax Service Management console to enable the receive toggle for his device.
C ❑ Tell Fred to reinstall the modem driver in Add/Remove Hardware.
D ❑ Tell Fred to open the Phone and Modem Options control panel instead of the Fax control panel. When the Advanced Options tab appears, he should click it and then enable the receive toggle for his device.

Answers

1 **D.** The folder redirection means that Dino's My Documents folder actually lives on the SRV01 server machine. Adding local disk space isn't likely to help. Adding disk space to SRV01 isn't likely to solve the problem; apparently, SRV01 has space available, given that other users are able to save their files. *Review "Setting quotas."*

2 **C.** Microsoft loves questions on printer priorities. *Review "Playing with priorities."*

3 **A, B, D,** and **E.** Choice D is the one that's most likely to trip you up, but if you don't set a limit, you can't enter a threshold value to trigger a logged event. The question suggests that merely logging warning events is insufficient because two threshold values must be logged — namely, warnings and limit violations. As long as the Deny Disk Space to Users Exceeding Quota Limit check box is clear, the quota feature cannot prevent a user from exceeding a quota. *Review "Setting quotas."*

4 **A** and **D.** Windows XP clients automatically check the print server for an updated driver before printing. Windows 98 clients do not. You must install the new driver manually on the Windows 98 clients. *Review "Adding drivers."*

5 **B** and **C.** Typically, TCP/IP printers permit configuration both by property sheets and by the browser interface, so A is wrong. Also, the recommended practice is to give network printers fixed, or static, IP addresses. These devices need to be available at all times and therefore do not benefit by leasing an IP address; also, printer configuration and troubleshooting is easier if the IP address is fixed. *Review "Installing a new printer."*

6 **D.** Notebook computers typically have only one hard drive, and the benefits of dynamic disks apply to systems with two or more hard drives. Note that choice B's comment about easy reversibility is incorrect. Choice C may be correct in a multiple-drive system with striping configured. *Review "Promoting a basic disk to a dynamic disk."*

7 **C.** This question is a bit sly because all the choices are normally worth considering. However, in this situation, only one criterion matters: the fact that a Windows XP Professional machine is only licensed to support ten simultaneous users at a time of any shared resource, be it a printer or a folder. *Review "Installing a new printer."*

8 **E.** If you want any of the other four features, you must use Windows 2002 Server or Windows 2000 Server — or buy a third-party hardware and/or software solution. *Review "Creating dynamic volumes."*

9 **A** and **B.** In general, when you know an option exists but a user can't access it, chances are good that the user needs administrative privileges. The default behavior of Windows XP's fax service is to enable sending but not receiving. *Review "Printing to fax devices."*

Chapter 8

Installing and Configuring Displays and I/O Devices

Exam Objectives

▶ Configure multiple-display support

▶ Install, configure, and troubleshoot a video adapter

▶ Monitor, configure, and troubleshoot I/O devices, such as printers, scanners, multimedia devices, mice, keyboards, and smart card readers

▶ Monitor, configure, and troubleshoot multimedia hardware, such as cameras

▶ Install, configure, and manage modems

▶ Install, configure, and manage USB devices

▶ Install, configure, and manage handheld devices

*T*his chapter focuses on hardware that moves data around without necessarily storing it. (Hardware for portable computers gets its due in Chapter 9.) For example, you may display, type, and download many megabytes whose final resting place is your brain (or that of someone else), rather than a magnetic disk or printed page. Windows XP offers generally improved support for *input/output* (I/O) devices, such as keyboards, displays, and modems, that facilitate getting information into or out of the PC. (When people use the term *I/O devices*, they typically aren't referring to disks or printers.)

The exam tends to focus on goodies that are relatively new to the NT architecture, such as multiple displays, the Universal Serial Bus (USB), DVD, multilink connections, and the like. However, you can expect a question or two on "traditional" topics, such as how to configure a single video adapter, just to keep you honest.

Quick Assessment

Configure multiple-display support

1 Adapters for multiple displays must use either the _____ bus or the _____ bus.

2 You have to enable a secondary video adapter by using the Display control panel's _____ tab.

Install, configure, and troubleshoot a video adapter

3 If a game isn't working, you can test DirectX for your display driver by using the program _____.

4 If your new video adapter makes the mouse cursor disappear, try changing the _____ setting.

Monitor, configure, and troubleshoot I/O devices

5 If Device Manager shows a red "stop" icon by a device name, the device was _____.

6 I/O devices are allowed to share the same interrupt on the _____ bus.

Monitor, configure, and troubleshoot multimedia hardware

7 You can change a camera's or scanner's color profile by using the _____ control panel.

Install, configure, and manage modems

8 The name of the log file that Windows XP uses to record modem activity is _____.

Install, configure, and manage USB devices

9 No USB device can be farther than _____ meters from a USB hub.

Install, configure, and manage handheld devices

10 The maximum number of concurrent inbound serial connections is _____.

Answers

1 *PCI, AGP.* See "Multiple display requirements and limitations" if this was news to you.

2 *Settings.* The "Troubleshooting multiple monitors" section has more.

3 *DXDIAG.EXE.* You get half a point if you said "DirectX Diagnostic Tool." See the "DirectX marks the spot" section for details.

4 *Acceleration slider.* See "Configuring single displays" if you missed this one.

5 *Disabled.* Check for a resource conflict. The section "Device Manager errors" has more.

6 *PCI.* The "IRQ sharing" section elaborates. If you said "USB," you get full credit as well, because the USB bus uses a single interrupt for all connected devices.

7 *Scanners and Cameras.* No points if you said "cameras and scanners." See the "Scanners and cameras" section.

8 *<ModemName>LOG.TXT.* This is sort of a trick question because <ModemName> depends on the specific modem. See "Analog modems" for more.

9 *Five.* You get full credit if you said "5." See "Getting on the Universal Serial Bus" if you missed this detail.

10 *One.* You can have up to three concurrent inbound network links, but only one of the same type at the same time. "Holding Hands" has more.

Displays, Single and Multiple

Windows XP Professional configures single displays much as Windows NT 4.0 and Windows 98 do, although DirectX support is new since NT 4.0. In the first two parts of this section, I cover the essentials, which may crop up on the exam. Things get a bit more interesting when I discuss multiple displays, in the third part of this section.

Single display technology

Notable improvements in Windows XP's core display capabilities include support for DirectX, OpenGL 2.1, and better support for Advanced Graphics Port (AGP) adapters.

DirectX marks the spot

The biggest advance that Windows XP Professional brings to single display technology on the NT technology platform is support for *DirectX*, specifically, DirectX 8.1. DirectX is a set of APIs (Application Program Interfaces) that Microsoft designed to provide multimedia and graphics software developers a degree of consistency across different Windows versions, and to alleviate the need for developers to know details about specific hardware playback devices within a given class.

The list of specific APIs is a long one: DirectSound, DirectInput (for joysticks), Direct3D, DirectDraw, DirectAnimation (for vector graphics mainly), DirectShow (formerly ActiveMovie), and so forth. Don't memorize the functions of each API — just be generally aware of their existence.

Test your version of DirectX (it's upgradable) and various DirectX features and functions by using the handy DXDIAG.EXE program in C:\WINDOWS\ SYSTEM32 (see Figure 8-1). The utility offers specific tests for the video-related DirectDraw and Direct3D interfaces.

OpenGL

Silicon Graphics developed the OpenGL language for use with its high performance workstation chips, and Windows XP supports version 2.1 of this language. To see it at work, preview any of the 3D screen savers on the Display control panel's Screen Saver tab.

AGP

Touted as a technological advance, in one sense AGP (Accelerated Graphics Port, also known as Advanced Graphics Port, supported by Windows XP and 2000) is a step backward in computer design to the days of single-purpose expansion slots. You can put anything you want into an AGP slot as long as it's an AGP video adapter. Also, you can't put an AGP video adapter onto a motherboard that doesn't have an AGP port built in.

Theoretically, AGP cards are faster than PCI cards, for at least two reasons: They don't have to deal with traffic on the shared PCI bus, and peak data rates are higher. I've seen some awfully slow AGP systems, so I suspect that here, as in certain other aspects of life, the execution is more important than the theory.

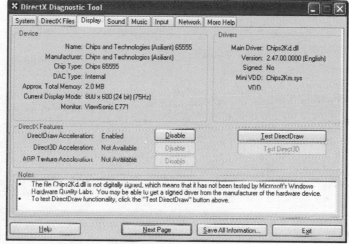

Figure 8-1:
Testing
DirectX with
the DirectX
Diagnostic
Tool.

Configuring single displays

Not much is new compared to earlier versions of Windows when it comes to configuring a single display system. You still set the resolution, color depth, refresh rate (important for eye fatigue), background, colors-and-fonts scheme, and (optionally) temperature or color profile in the Display control panel. The quick way to get there: Right-click any empty space on the desktop and choose Properties.

A handy quick way to set an adapter's color depth and pixel resolution at once, along with the refresh rate, is as follows:

1. Choose the Display control panel.

2. Click the Settings tab.

3. Click the Advanced button.

4. Click the Adapter tab.

5. Click the List All Modes button to display a dialog box that looks like the one in Figure 8-2.

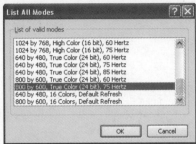

Figure 8-2: Set three display settings in one fell swoop.

Note that if the monitor appears in the Display control panel as "Default Monitor," then either the video adapter or the monitor is not compliant with Plug and Play, and you should install the driver manually. If the monitor appears as "Plug and Play Monitor," then the monitor is compliant, but Windows XP needs a driver from the hardware manufacturer.

The Web tab (included in Windows 2000 and 98), which allowed you to control whether or not your desktop appears as a Web page, and if so, which Web elements you want to be there, has been both changed and moved. The change is that you can't turn off Web view anymore (surprise!). As to the new location, open the Display control panel, choose the Desktop tab, click the Customize Desktop button, and then you can see the Web tab.

You can change the video resolution on the fly (that is, without restarting), but you see a message that doing so can create problems for some programs, so some testing on your part can confirm or deny whether you must, in fact, restart after changing pixel resolution or color depth. Set the default behavior in the General tab of the Advanced Settings property sheet, in the box marked Compatibility.

You may need to know that the *acceleration slider* (which by the way isn't a baseball pitch) can be found on the Display control panel by clicking Settings, Advanced, and Troubleshoot. Back off from full acceleration if you have mouse pointer problems or problems with images getting corrupted (see Figure 8-3). Also, clear the Enable Write Combining check box if you experience display corruption. Leave it checked otherwise, as it improves display performance.

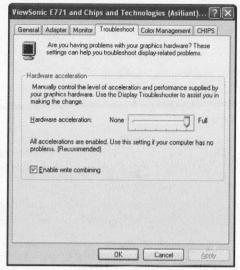

Figure 8-3:
The
acceleration
slider is
handy for
trouble-
shooting
display
problems.

If you're having video problems, one time-honored technique is to boot with the plain old VGA driver and then check your configuration in Device Manager. Windows XP Professional automatically uses the plain VGA driver if it detects a video problem, but who's to say its detection is perfect? You can manually force basic VGA by pressing F8 during the early text-mode stage of the boot process (you have to be fast!), then selecting Enable VGA Mode. Once you get Windows running, change or update the video driver and reboot.

You can also fire up the Windows XP display troubleshooter (part of the help system) by clicking the Troubleshoot button on the Settings tab.

Configuring multiple displays

Microsoft introduced multiple monitor support in Windows 98, and the feature has found its way onto the NT platform in Windows XP and 2000. You can have up to ten monitors running simultaneously. A number of prerequisites and caveats apply, however.

Multiple display requirements and limitations

First, a terminology note. The *POST device* is the video adapter that displays the BIOS messages and memory test during the Power On Self Test. The *primary display adapter* is where Windows XP displays the startup screens, logon dialog box, prompts, pop-up windows, and where applications typically display their main window at startup. The primary display adapter doesn't have to be the same as the POST device. A *secondary display adapter* is any adapter above and beyond the primary one.

Here are the rules and regs for multiple monitor support in Windows XP:

- Both display adapters must connect via a PCI (Peripheral Component Interconnect) or AGP (Accelerated Graphics Port) slot.

- The primary adapter is the only one that enjoys full hardware DirectX acceleration, and the only one that can run DirectX applications in full-screen mode. Ideally, the adapter with the best hardware performance should be the primary adapter.

- For a device to work as a secondary display adapter, it must be on the Microsoft list of acceptable secondary display adapters (see the HCL, or Hardware Compatibility List). Many video cards work as primary adapters, but not as secondary adapters.

- If one of the display adapters is integrated onto the motherboard, that adapter must always be a secondary adapter.

- The BIOS in some PCs automatically disables an on-board video adapter if it detects a plug-in video adapter. You may be able to turn this "feature" off in the BIOS setup, but you may not.

- If one of the display adapters is integrated onto the motherboard, you must install Windows XP before you install the add-in adapter. Setup isn't smart enough to know about multiple displays, and if it sees an on-board display adapter and a plug-in display adapter, it disables the on-board one. Install the add-in adapter by using the Add/Remove Hardware Wizard if Windows XP doesn't detect the adapter automatically.

Troubleshooting multiple monitors

A few tips for shooting multiple-monitor trouble follow:

- If a secondary monitor doesn't seem to be coming up, you probably haven't activated it. (I know, this should be automatic, but it isn't.) Go to the Display control panel's Settings tab, click the number two monitor (or three or four or whatever), and enable the Extend My Windows Desktop onto This Monitor check box. You'll usually need to restart the PC for the change to take effect.

- A modern docked laptop can typically use the internal display for multiple display capability if the docking station supports PCI, but you'll have to use the onboard display adapter as the primary adapter. Also, you won't be able to perform a hot-undock operation.

- You can set the color depth and resolution separately for each monitor.

- You can set the relative positioning of the two (or more) monitors by dragging and dropping the monitor images in the Display control panel's Settings tab.

✔ If your primary monitor isn't the one you want it to be, and both video adapters are plug-in cards, swap their positions in the PCI bus. The PC BIOS activates these cards in order according to their slot number. The BIOS on some PCs lets you override this automatic assignment.

✔ If an application doesn't extend its window to a secondary display, try maximizing the application window.

Modems, Single Link and Multilink

Modem connectivity in Windows XP Professional is considered part of the networking architecture, and therefore to set up and configure modem connections, you use the command Start⇨Control Panel⇨Network Connections.

In this section, I focus on getting the hardware installed and configured. Chapter 13 contains a lot more information about configuring specific connections.

Analog modems

Installing and configuring good old digital-to-analog-to-digital modems (called *analog modems* now for short, as opposed to all-digital devices such as ISDN adapters, which aren't really modems at all) may be the subject of an exam question or two.

Modem driver installation

Windows XP Professional just isn't very good at automatically detecting modems. If the operating system fails to detect a new modem (and in my experience it *always* fails if the modem connects via an external COM port), then you must initiate the driver installation process yourself. Do so by double-clicking the Phone and Modem Options icon in Control Panel and clicking the Modems tab followed by the Add button. Go ahead and let Windows try to autodetect the modem first; if that fails, specify the manufacturer and model yourself. If you don't have an INF file provided by the modem manufacturer, you can install the Standard Modem driver, at the possible expense of some functionality and speed.

If Windows XP Professional can't seem to find your modem to install its driver, you may need to perform a separate step to install a COM port serial driver associated with that modem. You may also consider disabling any unused COM ports, too, as they always tie up system resources (interrupts, and so forth) even if they're not active.

The redesigned Phone and Modem Options control panel replaces two control panels found in Windows NT 4.0, Modems and Telephony.

Connection logging

Modem logging is on by default in Windows XP Professional. You can't turn it off; all you can do is control whether a new log gets created every time a dial-up connection occurs, or the logging info appends to the existing log. Set this via the Telephone and Modem Options control panel, on the Diagnostics tab of the modem's property sheet (see Figure 8-4).

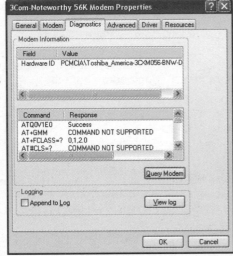

Figure 8-4:
Here you can control logging and view the current log file.

The log file is typically in C:\WINDOWS and has a name that begins with MODEMLOG and ends in .TXT. The precise filename depends on the make and model of your modem.

Modem testing

You can click the Query Modem button on the property sheet's Diagnostics tab to perform a routine communications check. If this check fails, then Windows and your modem aren't on speaking terms, and you may want to check whether you have the correct driver. Also look for a problem icon in Device Manager indicating a resource conflict.

ISDN

Integrated Services Digital Network (ISDN) lines are digital lines, installed by the phone company, that provide better speed than analog modems. An ISDN connection sports two "B" channels for data and voice, each of which can handle 64 kilobits per second, and one 16Kbps "D" channel for control.

Windows XP generally autodetects newly installed ISDN adapters automatically upon restart. Failing that, run the Add/Remove Hardware Wizard and provide the disc supplied by the manufacturer if the wizard doesn't detect the device.

You can configure in Device Manager the type of switch the line connects to, such as AT&T or Northern Telecom. Then, create ISDN network connections by using the Make New Connection Wizard in the Network Connections folder.

Internal ISDN adapters show up in Device Manager under the Network Adapters category. External ones appear in the Modems category.

Multilink setups

Multilink dialing means that you can combine two communications devices to act as a single "virtual" channel. Windows XP Professional supports multilink setups with ISDN and analog modem lines, with the caveat that the server side of the connection must support them, too. That is, if you're connecting to the Internet, for example, your ISP (Internet Service Provider) must support multilink access, and some don't.

You set up multilink connections in the Network Connections folder, on a connection-by-connection basis. Chapter 13 provides the details. It's not necessary to do anything special in Device Manager other than make sure both devices (ISDN adapter, two modems, whatever) are properly installed.

I/O Hardware Configuration Tips

This section contains small bits of wisdom on Device Manager, interrupt sharing, a Plug and Play wrinkle, and mouse configuration.

Device Mangler

Microsoft uses Device Mangler (oops, that's "Manager") for all those hardware configuration details that don't appear in any control panel. The Device Manager display (see Figure 8-5) has been around for a long time in the Windows 9x environment but it's a relatively new (and welcome) addition to the NT platform.

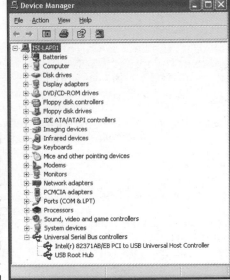

Figure 8-5:
The Device
Manager
window
goes
beyond the
Control
Panel.

Get to the Device Manager in a variety of ways, including:

✔ Choose Start➪Control Panel, choose the System control panel (assuming you're using the "classic" view), click the Hardware tab, and click the Device Manager button.

✔ Right-click My Computer, choose Properties, click the Hardware tab, and click the Device Manager button.

✔ Right-click My Computer, choose Manage, and click the Device Manager icon in the left window.

The general procedure is to expand the tree by clicking the + sign next to the device category of interest. Then, right-click the device you want to configure and choose Properties. What you see at that point varies from device to device.

Device Manager errors

Device Manager communicates errors three ways:

- A yellow exclamation point icon next to a device name means the device's driver is wrong, configured improperly, or missing.

- A red "stop" icon next to a device name means either you or Windows XP has disabled the device.

- A yellow question mark means Windows XP knows that something is there, but doesn't know what it is or which driver to assign it.

In any of these three cases, the device doesn't work right, and you must give its property sheet some attention. For example, the Resources tab of the device's property sheet should list the interrupts, base memory addresses, upper-memory addresses, and (if applicable) Direct Memory Access (DMA) channels that the device is using. You may need to clear the Use Automatic Configuration check box and set one or more of these values manually if you find a conflict reported at the bottom of the Resources tab.

Another place where you can view actual or potential conflicts is the System Information utility. This used to be a snap-in of the Computer Management console, but now you can access it by typing **MSINFO32** in the Run dialog box (see Figure 8-6), or by choosing Start⇨Help and Support and clicking the link labeled Use Tools To View Your Computer Information And Diagnose Problems, and then clicking Advanced System Information in the left window pane.

- The **Conflicts/Sharing** subfolder lists any conflicting resource assignments (however, see the next section "IRQ sharing" before concluding that a shared interrupt is actually a problem).

- The **Forced Hardware** subfolder lists any resource settings that you have made manually via Device Manager, and that therefore Plug and Play may not reconfigure in the future.

The System Information utility can generate reports in custom or text formats. You can also run it remotely by choosing View⇨Remote Computer.

If you install a device driver that creates an error that you detect in Device Manager or System Information, Windows XP now lets you "roll back" to the previously installed driver. Open the device's property sheet, click the Driver tab, and click the Roll Back Driver button. Assuming a previous driver exists, you'll get an "Are you sure?" dialog box and then Windows will revert to the old driver. If no previous driver exists, Windows tells you so, and offers to start the hardware troubleshooter.

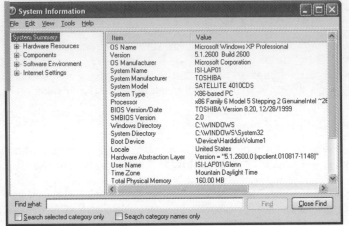

Figure 8-6:
The System
Information
snap-in
contains a
wealth of
detail.

Administrators and Plug and Play

An interesting quirk of Plug and Play is that the procedure for automatically installing a device driver doesn't normally require you to be logged on as an administrator — unless Windows asks you to provide a location for the driver file. If Windows can't find the driver itself, it asks you to find it, but you must have administrative rights on the system to do so. I guess the theory is that you could point to a location containing an untrusted and buggy driver if you didn't have administrative experience. Anyway, you may well see an exam question covering this quirk.

On a related note, all the drivers supplied by Microsoft are in the file DRIVER.CAB in `C:\WINDOWS\DRIVER CACHE\I386`. Every file in this cabinet archive has a Microsoft digital signature. Having all the drivers already on the hard disk is handy because you don't have to go scurrying for the Windows XP setup CD every time you need to install a new device.

IRQ sharing

In the "olden days" of the ISA (Industry Standard Architecture) bus, sharing interrupts (IRQs) was *verboten*. The PCI bus, however, permits multiple devices to share the same interrupt without any major problems. Generally, Windows XP configures such interrupt sharing behind the scenes. In fact, on an ACPI (Advanced Configuration and Power Interface) machine, you can't modify interrupt sharing by using Device Manager. However, you can have a performance problem if two very busy, high-bandwidth devices share the same IRQ. You may need to use setup software from the device manufacturer to manually assign an unused IRQ when Windows wants to assign a shared IRQ.

A mouse tip

Mice generally don't appear on the exam, except in really grungy test facilities (joke), but you may see a question pertaining to the "Snap To Default" feature. Set this via a check box on the Pointer Options tab of the Mouse control panel; it moves the mouse cursor to the default button of (most) dialog boxes, saving wrist wear and tear. The behavior is odd at first but you may grow to like it (I do). Too bad it doesn't work in all dialog boxes.

Getting carded

Smart cards are authentication devices that can provide a higher degree of authentication security than simple username and password schemes. You must have the card (suitably "enrolled" by a system administrator with a public key pair and certificate) and your personal identification number (PIN) to authenticate yourself to the network. The reader devices typically connect via the PC Card bus (what we used to call PCMCIA) or a serial port.

Microsoft makes the following recommendations about smart card readers:

- ✔ If they're not Plug and Play compatible, don't use 'em.
- ✔ If they don't carry the Windows Hardware Quality Labs logo, don't use 'em.
- ✔ Let Windows XP autodetect the reader at startup; supply any third-party device drivers at that time if necessary.

Multimedia Hardware

A few notes are in order here about multimedia hardware, specifically, the Windows Driver Model, DVD, and the Scanners and Cameras control panel. (See "DirectX marks the spot" earlier in this chapter for display-related multimedia issues.)

Windows Driver Model

Windows Driver Model (WDM) is a 32-bit driver model in which Windows XP, NT, and 2000 drivers work with Windows 98 and vice versa. It is supported for USB and FireWire devices, but not all other types of hardware. The idea of WDM is to make life a bit easier on device manufacturers by not making them write a separate device driver for each Windows version.

Multimedia devices in Windows XP Professional typically use the WDM *streaming class driver* for audio and video. This driver permits more than one application to play sound at the same time, and it allows sound output to travel to any relevant device on any system bus. It also lets the operating system handle audio mixing instead of hardware, which is why you now sometimes hear a beep five seconds after you see its related dialog box, for example.

You should generally not expect Windows NT 4.0 drivers to work under Windows XP. The only ones in my experience that do seem to work are the SCSI miniport drivers and a few printer drivers. Display drivers, network card drivers, mouse drivers, and so forth seem to require specific Windows XP support to work properly with the new operating system.

DVD

DVD (short for *Digital Video Disc* or *Digital Versatile Disc*) devices now receive Windows support in the form of a DVD-ROM driver and a DVD-Video player. DVDs can hold video, audio, and computer data content on the same disc, and their capacity can go as high as 17GB. Windows XP supports writeable DVD using the FAT32 file format.

Read-only DVD devices typically use the *Universal Disk Format (UDF)* file system. A UDF disk can be a boot device. UDF also supports Unicode filenames and file-and-folder level access control, much as NTFS does.

DVD drives use the *streaming class* WDM driver (see previous section), which supports both of the compression types found on DVD disks, MPEG-2 and AC-3 (Dolby Digital). In addition to the WDM driver, you typically need a minidriver from the manufacturer to support features specific to the drive make and model.

Scanners and cameras

Windows XP Professional sports a control panel specifically for *Scanners and Cameras*. The new acronym here is WIA, for Windows Image Acquisition, describing both a device driver interface and an application programming interface for imaging devices that use USB, SCSI, FireWire, or COM hardware ports.

✔ Double-click this control panel's Add Device icon to install drivers for a camera or scanner that Plug and Play doesn't find on its own. You may need to specify the port (serial, infrared, and so on) that the device uses.

✔ To modify the color profile that a scanner or camera uses, select the device, click Properties, and click the Color Management tab.

✔ To have Windows XP load one or more pictures from a digital camera, you can simply click the device in the Scanners and Cameras folder. You can then save the image or images (the default location is the My Pictures folder, which now resides at the same hierarchical level as My Documents).

✔ To make a just-scanned document load into a specified application program automatically: Select the device, click Properties, click the Events tab, choose the application, and click Send to This Application.

Windows XP doesn't directly support parallel-port still image devices or those on a network. That's not to say that those devices don't work, but you'll probably need third-party drivers for them.

Getting on the Universal Serial Bus

The *Universal Serial Bus*, or *USB*, is a popular choice for adding low- to medium-speed peripherals to a Windows XP PC. (Windows 98 supports USB natively, and Windows NT 4 never successfully supported USB.)

The data transfer speed of the USB depends on whether it's operating in *isochronous* or *asynchronous* mode. Both modes can't be active simultaneously.

✔ In isochronous mode, data transfers occur at a fixed, guaranteed level of 12 Mbps (megabits per second).

Speakers, modems, and monitors typically use this mode.

✔ In asynchronous mode, data transfers occur at 1.5 Mbps.

Keyboards and mice typically use this mode.

Remember these basic facts about USB for the test, which is highly likely to ask you at least one USB-related question:

✔ USB is an external bus.

You can use a single port (and interrupt) to daisy-chain up to 127 devices, such as mice, keyboards, speakers, and monitors.

✔ You may not exceed five tiers on the USB bus.

- USB is a Plug and Play bus that supports hot swapping (nothing to do with experimental marriages), so you can add and remove devices without powering down the computer.

- Unlike devices on other buses, USB devices typically don't have resource settings that can cause device failure.

- You may have to enable your USB controller in the PC's BIOS for USB devices to work. Windows XP doesn't even show the controller in Device Manager if the BIOS doesn't enable it.

- Bus-powered hubs (as opposed to self-powered hubs with their own power supply) can support a maximum of four downstream ports.

- The bus fails if devices on a bus-powered hub draw too much power. "Too much" is determined by checking the milliamp rating on the root hub's property sheet in Device Manager; look at the Power tab. Generally, self-powered hubs provide 500mA of power per port, and bus-powered hubs provide 100mA per port.

- You can suppress USB error messages on the USB controller's property sheet in the Advanced tab, but as a general rule, you shouldn't.

- Hubs provide device connection points, power management, and device detection services. USB devices can be no more than five meters from the hub to which they connect. The USB host (usually a circuit on the PC's motherboard but may be an add-in adapter) is also called the root hub.

- Don't connect a bus-powered hub to another bus-powered hub.

Older PCs that support USB 1.0 generally don't work well with modern USB peripherals.

If the PC's BIOS enables the USB bus but Windows XP still has problems finding devices on the bus, try removing the bus host controller in Device Manager and rebooting. That lets Windows redetect the controller and every USB device connected to it.

FireWire: USB Plus Caffeine

FireWire, or *IEEE 1394* (which isn't nearly as much fun to say but which you should memorize anyway), is yet another new hardware bus that Windows XP supports. This bus is suitable for high-bandwidth devices, such as digital camcorders and VCRs, video teleconferencing equipment, and so on. FireWire hardware support may be built in to a given PC's system board, or added via an adapter. Windows XP Professional provides the system-level support.

FireWire is a lot like the Universal Serial Bus (Plug and Play, external bus, daisy-chain design, asynchronous and isochronous modes, and so on), but bigger and faster.

- FireWire supports up to 63 devices on a single bus, and you can connect up to 1023 buses together, for a total number of devices that is . . . well, let's just say a lot.

- FireWire supports data transfer rates of 100, 200, and even 400 Mbps (megabits per second), compared to the 12 Mbps maximum for USB. Although you can put devices having different speeds on the same bus, the maximum bus speed is limited by the slowest device.

- FireWire components come in four flavors: devices, splitters, bridges, and repeaters. Don't learn any more detail than this for the exam. Learn a lot more detail if you plan to set up a large net of FireWire components.

Holding Hands

Microsoft is working hard to conquer the handheld device market with its Windows CE operating system. Therefore, don't be surprised if the exam throws out a question on palmtop device connectivity. Here are the basic facts you should know:

- Create an incoming network connection via the Make New Connection Wizard in the Network Connections folder.

- You may set up a total of three incoming connections as long as none of them are the same type. (Typical types are infrared, serial, parallel, and modem.)

- The synchronization software for CE computers, ActiveSync, disables IrTran-P, the infrared image exchange protocol. To use IrTran-P, you must disable ActiveSync, and vice versa.

- To control who may access the computer's incoming connection, right-click the connection's icon in the Network Connections folder, choose Properties, and click the Users tab. Add or remove users as desired.

- To set up a direct connection so that it bypasses the usual authentication requirements, get to the Users tab (see previous bullet) and check Always Allow Directly Connected Devices Such As Palmtop Computers To Connect Without Providing A Password.

Prep Test

1 Thurston comes to you with a PC question. He has just installed Windows XP Professional and he's excited about using the new peripherals and buses that it supports. However, after removing and reinstalling new USB speakers, keyboard, and mouse several times, none of the devices are working properly, even though the USB host controller appears in Device Manager without an exclamation point or a red "X." What would you advise Thurston to try? (Choose two answers.)

A ❑ Disable the USB host controller in Device Manager, and reboot.

B ❑ Consult the PC documentation to find out if the USB hardware version is 1.0.

C ❑ Uninstall the USB host controller in Device Manager, and reboot.

D ❑ Enable the USB host controller in the BIOS.

2 Ginger adds an ISDN adapter to her Windows XP Professional machine. Windows doesn't detect it automatically at the next restart, so she runs the Add/Remove Hardware Wizard. However, she doesn't see a separate category for ISDN adapters. Which category contains this class of device? (Choose two.)

A ❑ Network adapters

B ❑ Modems

C ❑ Multi-Port serial adapters

D ❑ System devices

E ❑ Other devices

3 What file system do DVD devices use under Windows XP Professional? (Choose all that apply.)

A ❑ CDFS

B ❑ FAT32

C ❑ NTFS

D ❑ UDF

E ❑ UDP

4 Mary Ann reports a device failure on her Windows XP Professional PC. Her sound system stopped working when she installed a video capture card. You suspect a device resource conflict. Where could you look to confirm or refute this suspicion? (Choose all that apply.)

A ❑ The MSINFO32 program's Conflicts/Sharing folder.

B ❑ The Computer Management console, Device Manager snap-in, Resources property sheet for the sound card.

C ❑ The Computer Management console, Device Manager snap-in, Resources property sheet for the video capture card.

D ❑ The System control panel, Hardware tab, Device Manager button, Resources property sheet for the sound card.

E ❑ The System control panel, Hardware tab, Device Manager button, Resources property sheet for the video capture card.

5 **As PC technical liaison for your department, you get a call from an employee named Skip who is having problems with intermittent dial-up modem connections. Sometimes he's able to connect to a remote server, other times he's not. You check Skip's connection icon settings and they appear to be in order. So, you decide to take a look at modem log activity. Where do you look? (Choose the best answer.)**

A ○ The Event Viewer

B ○ The file `C:\WINNT\MODEMLOG.TXT`

C ○ The file `C:\MODEMLOG.TXT`

D ○ The file `C:\WINNT\MODEM<modelname>LOG.TXT`

E ○ The file `C:\WINDOWS\MODEM<modelname>LOG.TXT`

6 **You install a new PCI modem into your Windows XP Professional computer. Upon restart, Plug and Play doesn't detect the modem. When you run the Add/Remove Hardware Wizard, Windows XP doesn't detect the modem then, either. What is a likely guess about what you must do first in order to get Windows XP to detect the modem? (Choose the best answer.)**

A ○ Disable IRQ conflict checking.

B ○ Disable IRQ sharing on the PCI bus.

C ○ Add a driver for the integrated serial port.

D ○ Activate the modem in the BIOS.

7 **Your Windows XP Professional PC has an internal SCSI adapter for your hard drive, but the adapter also has an external connection for I/O devices. You connect a scanner to the external connection and add a scanner driver from the manufacturer's CD via the Add/Remove Hardware Wizard. Everything works fine for six months, at which time you update the scanner driver. When you restart the computer and log on, the scanner no longer works. How can you get the scanner working again quickly? (Choose the best answer.)**

A ○ Reboot, press F8, and choose Safe Mode at the text-mode boot menu. Then remove the driver by using Device Manager and reinstall the original driver from the manufacturer's CD.

B ○ Reboot, press F8, and choose Last Known Good Configuration. Then remove the driver by using Device Manager and reinstall the original driver from the manufacturer's CD.

C ○ Open the scanner driver's property sheet in Device Manager and click the Roll Back Driver button.

D ○ Reboot from the Windows XP CD and enter the Recovery Console. Disable the SCSI service with the DISABLE command. Reboot normally and let Windows XP autodetect the scanner.

8 **Windows XP supports the AGP bus for what types of devices?**

A ○ Video adapters

B ○ Network adapters

C ○ Multiport serial adapters

D ○ SCSI host controllers

9 **When installing a Plug and Play device, Windows XP Professional prompts you for the location of the device driver. You provide the drive letter of your CD-ROM drive (the device manufacturer provided the CD). However, the installation fails. What's the likely cause?**

A ○ Your computer supports APM but not ACPI.

B ○ The CD is corrupt.

C ○ You aren't logged on as an Administrator.

D ○ Plug and Play has been disabled by a group policy.

10 **Approximately how many times faster can a FireWire device be than a USB device, in terms of data transfer?**

A ○ 5

B ○ 10

C ○ 33

D ○ 67

Answers

1 **B** and **C.** Merely disabling the controller won't work. Uninstalling it forces Windows XP to re-detect the controller, and all connected peripherals, at the next restart. Choice D is wrong because the controller wouldn't even appear in Device Manager if it were disabled at the BIOS level. *See "Getting on the Universal Serial Bus."*

2 **A** and **B.** Just one of those facts to memorize, I'm afraid. It all depends on how the adapter's manufacturer decided to implement the driver. *See "ISDN."*

3 **B** and **D.** UDF stands for Universal Data Format. UDF has some of the features of NTFS, but it isn't the same animal. UDP stands for User Datagram Protocol, a transport-level network protocol used in TCP/IP networks. FAT32 may be used in Windows XP for writeable DVD-RAM discs. CDFS is the CD-ROM File System. *Check out "DVD."*

4 **A, B, C, D,** and **E.** The Windows operating system is becoming well known for providing several different paths to the same utility. Sometimes that's handy, sometimes it's confusing, but you never know which method the exam expects you to know. So know them all. *Review "Device Manager errors."*

5 **E.** Examples are *MODEMLOG_56K Data Fax Modem PnP.TXT* and *MODEM-LOG_Conexant SoftK56 PCI Modem(M).TXT*. One could make a strong argument that this information really should be in the Event Viewer, so that answer is logical but wrong. The modem logging feature works just like in Windows 98, which doesn't have Event Viewer, so that may explain why Windows XP logs these activities this way. Oh, and by the way, C:\WINNT is the system folder in Windows 2000, not Windows XP! *Take a look at "Analog modems."*

6 **C.** Once you add the port driver, Windows XP can probably access the port and detect the modem's presence. Choices A and B aren't options that Windows XP allows you to perform, and choice D isn't necessary. *See "Analog modems."*

7 **C.** Now, let me say right away that this question presupposes some knowledge from Chapter 15, so if you haven't read that one yet, don't feel too bad about missing this one. The main point here is that Windows XP adds a very handy "Roll Back Driver" button for just such situations. You don't need to reboot before clicking this button, and you don't need to enter Safe Mode. Choice B won't work because you already logged on after reconfiguring the system, a step that overwrites the Last Known Good configuration. *Refer to "Device Manager errors."*

8 **A.** AGP is for video adapters only. *See "Single display technology."*

9 **C.** Only an administrator can install a Plug and Play device for which Windows XP can't automatically find the driver. *See "Administrators and Plug and Play."*

10 **B.** 400 divided by 12 is 33.33. This is one of those questions where it's handy to be able to use the Windows calculator. *Take a look at "FireWire: USB Plus Caffeine."*

Chapter 9

Mobile Computers and Power Management

• •

Exam Objectives

▶ Configure Advanced Configuration Power Interface (ACPI)

▶ Install, configure, and manage Infrared Data Association (IrDA) devices

▶ Install, configure, and manage wireless devices

▶ Manage, monitor, and optimize system performance for mobile users

*W*indows NT Workstation 4.0 was notorious for being less than completely convenient on portable computers. With the world getting more mobile every day, Microsoft wisely added two Windows 9*x* features to the NT platform in Windows XP: power management and Plug and Play. Windows XP provides some evolutionary advances in both areas. This chapter looks at these two technologies as well as a couple other issues of interest to notebook users: wireless devices and performance optimization through hardware profiles. (The topic of offline files and folders, also of interest to mobile computer users, gets its due in Chapter 12, as it's considered part of IntelliMirror.)

Quick Assessment

Configure Advanced Configuration Power Interface (ACPI)

1 You're on an airplane and asked to power down your notebook computer. Would you choose Hibernate or Standby?

2 The power management standard that Windows XP prefers is _____.

3 A group of settings for powering down disks and displays is known as a _____ in Windows XP.

4 You typically connect a UPS to a PC with a _____ cable.

5 Before removing a PC Card, you should tell Windows XP about your intention via the _____ control panel.

Installing, configuring, and managing Infrared Data Association (IrDA) devices

6 If two infrared devices aren't communicating reliably, consider reducing the _____ setting.

7 Most infrared devices need to be within _____ of each other in order to communicate.

Installing, configuring, and managing wireless devices

8 If you want to use a wireless device to connect a computer to a network, use the _____ control panel.

Manage, monitor, and optimize system performance for mobile users

9 Portable computers typically have two hardware profiles, _____ and _____.

10 To create a new hardware profile, use the _____ control panel's Hardware tab.

Answers

1   *Hibernate.* Didn't know this one? See "Power Management."

2   *ACPI.* See the "ACPI" section for more information.

3   *Power scheme.* The "Power Management" section explains.

4   *Serial.* See "Uninterruptible Power Supplies" for details.

5   *Add/Remove Hardware.* The "PC Cards" section includes this and other tips.

6   *Maximum connection speed.* The "Infrared and Wireless Devices" section has more.

7   *One meter.* They also typically need to be pointing at each other. See "Infrared and Wireless Devices" for details.

8   *Network and Dial-Up Connections.* Again, the "Infrared and Wireless Devices" section elaborates.

9   *Docked, undocked.* See "Docking stations" and "Hardware Profiles" for more.

10   *System.* The "Hardware Profiles" section explains.

Power Management

The basic idea behind power management is that the operating system, in cooperation with the BIOS, can power down your display, hard drive, and certain other components after a predefined period of inactivity. The goal is to save battery juice on your mobile computer, extending your work time — or to reduce the part of your electric bill that's attributable to your desktop computer!

All power management functions in Windows XP Professional appear in the Power Options control panel, whose contents can vary depending on the power-saving features of the specific computer. You typically see four or five tabs on this control panel, as follows:

- **Power Schemes** (see Figure 9-1) lets you select from a predefined group of schemes for when to turn off your monitor and hard disk, and when (or whether) to put the computer into standby mode. (Standby mode is a low-power mode that preserves memory contents; it's suitable for stretches when you're not using the PC but you expect to resume doing so in a few minutes.) If you enable Hibernate support (see two bullets down), you can also specify how long a period of inactivity must occur before the PC hibernates. You can change an existing scheme and save it under a new name, as I explain in Lab 9-1.

- **Alarms** lets you specify the threshold battery power and corresponding action for two states: low battery and critical battery.

- **Advanced** (see Figure 9-2) lets you specify whether the Power Management icon appears in your system tray (the sunken area on the taskbar opposite the Start button, which Microsoft has now taken to calling the *notification area*). If you chose a standby mode option on the Power Schemes tab, the Advanced tab also lets you specify whether Windows should prompt you for your password when you bring your PC out of standby mode. On most modern portable computers, you also get to choose whether pushing your PC's power switch truly powers it down or instead puts it into standby mode, does nothing at all, or asks the user what to do. Similar options exist for closing the lid.

- **Hibernate** lets you turn hibernation on or off via the Enable Hibernate Support check box. Hibernation is different from standby. When your PC hibernates, Windows writes the contents of memory to a disk file and then powers off. When you power back on later, Windows retrieves the contents of memory from the disk file, which is usually a lot quicker than a normal boot process. Your programs and even LAN connections come back to life.

Standby = low power but still on; hibernate = off, but ready to restart fast.

✔ **APM** only appears if your PC supports it. See the "APM" section for details.

✔ **UPS** lets you configure a battery backup device (you won't typically see this tab on a laptop). See the "Uninterruptible Power Supplies" section for details.

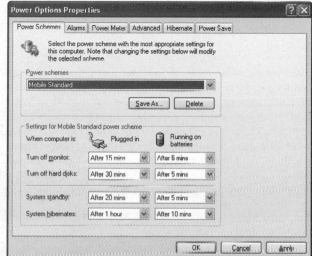

Figure 9-1:
You can use predefined power schemes or define your own.

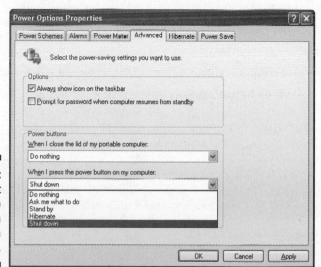

Figure 9-2:
You may not see all these options on any given PC.

You can manually put your computer into hibernation mode by choosing Start⇨Shut Down and choosing Hibernate in the Shut Down Windows dialog box. If your computer supports hibernation fully, you can also specify when to hibernate automatically with the Power Schemes tab of the Power Options control panel. The same holds true for manually and automatically entering Standby mode. Most portable computers let you choose a Power Options setting to force Standby mode or hibernation mode when you close the computer's lid.

You're responsible for saving your work to disk before initiating Standby mode. If your battery dies while your computer is on Standby, and you haven't saved your data files, you could lose some work. If you see an exam question that asks about a course of action that will prevent data loss, think "hibernate" rather than "standby."

On any given PC, some power management features may require activation in the BIOS setup program. The procedure for changing BIOS settings varies, but you usually have to press a function key, or combination of keys, during power-up. The startup text sequence usually clues you in on the details.

Lab 9-1 presents the steps for modifying an existing scheme and saving it under a new name.

Lab 9-1   Changing a Power Management Scheme

1. **Open the Power Management control panel by choosing Start⇨ Control Panel⇨Power Options.**

2. **Choose the scheme Always On by using the drop-down list box on the Power Schemes tab.**

   Note also the aptly named Presentation scheme, which differs from Always On by never turning off the display when the PC is running on AC power. The PC will not enter standby or hibernation mode when using the Presentation scheme.

3. **Change the setting for Turn Off Hard Disks to read After 4 Hours.**

4. **Click the Save As button and provide a name for the new power scheme.**

   If you simply click OK instead of Save As, Windows XP saves the revised settings with the same scheme name.

Windows XP Professional recognizes two different power management standards: APM (Advanced Power Management) and ACPI (Advanced Configuration and Power Interface). The next two sections explore the differences.

APM

Advanced Power Management, or APM, is a pseudo-standard common on pre-1999 machines but getting less common every day. I say "pseudo-standard" because APM doesn't nail down a lot of details, leaving the computer manufacturer to interpret some of its guidelines. That's one of the reasons APM isn't completely satisfactory; another is that APM doesn't let the operating system do much in the way of controlling power usage, leaving that task to the BIOS. To be able to use it, APM must be supported by a given computer's hardware and BIOS for Windows XP Professional.

You can tell whether Windows XP thinks your PC fully supports APM by choosing the Power Options control panel and looking for the APM tab. If it's there, you can make sure APM is enabled by checking the box labeled Enable Advanced Power Management Support. (Windows automatically checks the box and enables APM support if the APM BIOS is known to be compatible, but a given BIOS might be compatible and Windows doesn't know it — hence the opportunity for you to check the box manually.) If the APM tab isn't there, Windows XP doesn't perceive your PC as APM-capable, and you shouldn't try to use APM.

If your APM machine isn't powering down at shutdown, and it used to do so with a previous version of Windows, go to the APM tab of the Power Options control panel, enable APM, and restart.

Three quick facts you may need:

- ✔ Windows XP Professional supports APM version 1.2.

- ✔ You have to be logged on as an Administrator in order to turn APM on or off.

- ✔ You can use the support tool APMSTAT.EXE (installable by running SETUP in the installation CD's \SUPPORT\TOOLS folder) to see whether Windows XP supports the version of APM that your computer uses. (If your PC uses ACPI, which I describe in the next section, then APMSTAT tells you that your inquiry about APM isn't "relevent." Guess somebody turned off his spel chekker.)

ACPI

Advanced Configuration and Power Interface (ACPI) is a newer and more rigorous standard than APM, and the designers of Windows XP Professional wrote the operating system with ACPI in mind. ACPI makes power management (and, incidentally, Plug and Play) work better.

As with APM, the PC must support ACPI in the hardware and the BIOS for Windows XP to use this standard. You can tell whether Windows XP thinks your PC fully supports ACPI by choosing Start⇨Control Panel⇨System⇨ Hardware, clicking the Device Manager tab, and expanding the Computer icon. If the computer's label says:

- ✔ Advanced Configuration and Power Interface (ACPI) PC
- ✔ ACPI Uniprocessor PC
- ✔ ACPI Multiprocessor PC

you have ACPI support. If it says

- ✔ Standard PC
- ✔ MPS Uniprocessor PC
- ✔ MPS Multiprocessor PC

you don't.

If your BIOS setup program lets you switch between these two power management standards, don't try doing so after Windows XP is already installed (unless you want to reinstall the operating system!). Windows XP installs a *Hardware Abstraction Layer*, or *HAL*, based on what power management standard Windows "sees" in the BIOS at installation time. You can't change the HAL to support a different power management standard without reinstalling Windows!

Uninterruptible Power Supplies

You probably don't typically carry an *Uninterruptible Power Supply (UPS)* with your notebook computer as you travel around. However, while I'm on the subject of power management, I might as well give you a brief look at UPS support in Windows XP.

A UPS is a battery backup device that can supply power to your plugged-in notebook or (more likely) desktop computer if AC power fails. For example, I'm writing this in the foothills of the Rocky Mountains, where power glitches occur so frequently that no VCR in the county displays the correct time. Many UPS devices can communicate with your PC via a serial cable. That way, the UPS can let your PC know when AC power has been lost or when the UPS battery is low.

Setup

To set up your UPS, first install it according to the manufacturer's instructions, then click the Select button on the UPS tab of the Power Options control panel. You can specify the vendor, model, and which serial port the UPS attaches to (you may need to use a special cable supplied by the UPS manufacturer).

Configuration

To configure your UPS, click the Configure button on the UPS tab of the Power Options control panel. The options you can set here include:

- Enabling notification messages of power failure, power restoration, low battery condition, and UPS-to-computer communication.

- If you enable notification messages, setting a time after a power failure that Windows XP waits to display a message the first time and how long it waits to display subsequent messages.

- Specifying when Windows issues a *critical alarm* if the UPS didn't issue one automatically because of a low battery. Enter the number of minutes you feel confident the UPS can run your PC. This is a belt-and-suspenders setting just in case the low-battery-sensing feature of the UPS fails.

- Running a program (if any) when a critical alarm occurs. The UPS vendor typically provides such a program.

- Shutting down or (if hibernation is enabled) hibernating after the vendor-supplied program runs.

Infrared and Wireless Devices

Windows XP provides infrared and wireless device support equivalent to that of Windows Me and superior to that of Windows NT Workstation 4.0. With a wireless link, you can transfer files between two computers, print a document from a computer to a printer, or download a file from a digital camera, without an interconnecting cable. (Better have a good clear line of sight, though.)

Heck, you can even create a network link, which you accomplish via the New Connection icon in the Network Connections control panel. The procedure is very similar to creating a Direct Cable Connection link: You specify one machine to be the "host" and the other to be the "guest."

The most common wireless device is the *infrared* link. Infrared light has a wavelength longer than visible red light (and a frequency less than red light). In the personal computer world, nearly all infrared devices adhere to one or more of the various *IrDA (Infrared Data Association)* standards, which lay out as follows:

✔ **IrDA-SIR**, an older device standard, specifies a speed of 115Kbps.

✔ **IrDA-FIR** specifies 4Mbps.

✔ **IrDA-VFIR** specifies 16Mbps.

IrDA-SIR, IrDA-FIR, and IrDA-VFIR are *half-duplex* systems. That is, communication only occurs in one direction at a time.

Other standards you may need to know for the exam are as follows:

✔ **IrTran-P** is an image transfer standard. (By the way, it conflicts with ActiveSync 3.0, the synchronization software for Windows CE. You have to turn off one or the other. Turn off IrTran-P in the Wireless Link control panel via the Image Transfer tab by clearing the Use Wireless Link To Transfer Images From A Digital Camera To Your Computer check box.)

✔ **IrComm** is a cell phone communications link standard.

✔ **IrNET** is a PC-to-PC networking standard.

IrDA-equipped computers and printers have a little red window somewhere on the device that acts as the line-of-sight communications port.

Windows XP normally autodetects built-in infrared devices such as often come with notebook computers, but you may have to run the Add/Remove Hardware Wizard if you're retrofitting an infrared device to a serial port. On some computers, enabling the built-in infrared port requires that a COM port be disabled in the BIOS setup program. After you do that, Windows XP will probably detect the infrared port at the next reboot via Plug and Play. After you install an infrared or other wireless device and Windows XP recognizes it, a new icon (*Wireless Link*) appears in the Control Panel and offers various options for notification and access control (see Figure 9-3). Also, if you run the Add Printer Wizard, a new port (IrLPT) appears in the list of available device ports.

Relevant facts about infrared communications include the following:

✔ Windows XP can support multiple sessions (programs communicating with each other) over a single link, albeit very slowly.

✔ Windows XP can support multiple infrared links, too, but each infrared port can only communicate with one other infrared port at a time.

✔ Most infrared devices need to be within one meter of each other, and with each red window pointing at the other, to communicate.

✔ When two infrared devices are within range and properly positioned, an infrared port icon appears on the taskbar, and a wireless link icon appears on the desktop.

✔ You can copy files from one infrared device to another by dragging and dropping files to the Wireless Link icon, or by running IRFTP.EXE from the Run dialog box, selecting the files, and clicking the Send button.

✔ Lowering the maximum connection rate on the infrared device's property sheet may correct some communication problems.

Figure 9-3:
The
Wireless
Link dialog
box.

In addition to infrared devices, Windows XP Professional adds native support for wireless network adapters that adhere to the IEEE 802.11 and 802.11b standards. (802.11 supports transfer rates of 1 to 2 Mbps while 802.11b supports 11Mbps. Newer and even faster standards are in development.) These devices fall into the category of "wireless LAN" because they have much greater range than infrared connections.

A special icon (Wireless Network Connection) appears automatically in the Network Connections folder when you install an 802.1x wireless network adapter to your PC. You must be logged on as an Administrator to set properties for this connection, and your wireless adapter must adhere to the Wireless Zero Configuration standard, too.

The default settings let Windows XP automatically detect the presence of a wireless network, as evidenced by another PC with an 802.1x adapter (so-called "ad hoc" mode) or a Wireless Access Point that acts as a signal relay station ("infrastructure" mode). The Network icon in the system tray on the taskbar (which Microsoft now calls the "notification area") lets you right-click it to browse, and connect to, any available wireless networks.

Windows XP uses Wireless Electronic Privacy, or WEP, by default as a way to protect wireless communications from eavesdropping. A synonym for WEP is 802.1x authentication.

Plug and Play and Mobile Computers

Plug and Play is a system-wide specification that makes adding, configuring, and removing devices easier and more automatic. This technology is especially important to portable computer users who often disconnect and reconnect different devices to their notebook PCs. Plug and Play's goal is to allow such users to plug and unplug devices as they need to without having to worry about installing or uninstalling device drivers; manually resetting resource assignments (interrupts, memory addresses, and so on); or restarting their computers.

For Plug and Play to work, the specification requires support at all levels: computer hardware, BIOS, bus, operating system (ta-daa), device driver, and device. Windows XP looks at the first two items at setup time and installs the appropriate HAL, or Hardware Abstraction Layer.

As with power management, Windows XP Plug and Play works best with PCs that support the ACPI standard (see the "ACPI" section).

If you need to remove and reinstall a Plug and Play driver (for example, because you chose the wrong driver file when you originally installed the device), here's how: Uninstall the driver by using Device Manager, then restart the system, and let Windows XP Professional autodetect the device again. At that time, you can provide the proper driver files — for example, on a CD from the device's manufacturer.

Plug and Play can normally install devices even if you're not logged on as an Administrator, as long as the computer doesn't have to ask you for the location of a device driver, and as long as the driver is digitally signed by Microsoft. Otherwise, you must be a Power User to be able to install, uninstall, and configure Plug and Play hardware, and you must be an Administrator to install, uninstall, and configure non-Plug and Play hardware. The usual practice is to make portable computer users either Power Users or Administrators.

Installing certain scanners, printers, and ISDN adapters and some PDA software requires you to be logged on as an Administrator. You must also be an Administrator to run the Internet Connection Wizard.

PC Cards

Plug and Play doesn't work equally well for all different computer buses, but it works quite well on mobile computers that use the *PC Card* bus (what we formerly called PCMCIA, an acronym that you still see occasionally). PC Card devices also go by the name *credit-card devices*. Typically, PC Cards are modems, disk drives, and network adapters. PC Cards that use a 32-bit data path often go by the name *CardBus*.

The system level software that controls PC Cards is *card services*.

ACPI machines support dynamic reconfiguration of PC Card devices, meaning that you can plug in and unplug these devices without having to reboot. However, if you're removing an Ethernet, SCSI, or hard disk PC Card, you should "stop" the card before removing it, by using the PC Card icon on the notification area. Windows XP tells you when it's okay to remove the device.

PC Card modems (as well as internal PCI modems) often require you to install a COM port driver first, before you can install the modem driver itself.

Docking stations

Many mobile computer users plug their computers into a *docking station* when they're dropping by the office to collect a paycheck, submit an expense report, or flirt with the boss's [son, daughter] (choose the best answer). The docking station may have a different keyboard, display, network adapter, and so on.

Plug and Play support in Windows XP makes it more likely that the operating system can detect all that different hardware automatically. It also enables the user to connect or disconnect the computer to or from the docking station without powering everything down (*hot-docking*). To hot-dock a system that's powered up, just plug it into its docking station. To hot-undock a system, use the Start⇨Eject PC command, and then disconnect your notebook PC from the docking station.

Windows XP only supports hot-docking and -undocking on ACPI machines.

Don't undock your machine when it's in standby or hibernate mode; you could lock up the machine and lose data.

Hardware Profiles

You probably know that you can log on to Windows XP Professional with different user names, and that you can see different desktop settings, programs, menus, and so forth. These different sets of preferences go by the name *user profiles*.

Similarly, you can set up the operating system so that the computer hardware itself changes, depending on which *hardware profile* you activate at boot time.

Normally, desktop computers don't change hardware configurations frequently (if ever), but many mobile computers often do. For example, your notebook computer may have a drive bay that can hold either a diskette drive or a CD-ROM drive. Or you may want to use your notebook computer on an airplane or train sometimes, and in the office connected to a docking station at other times.

Although you could rely on Plug and Play to redetect all the hardware changes at boot time, doing so can add precious minutes to the startup process. Furthermore, some of your hardware may not be Plug and Play compliant. Finally, if Windows XP tries to detect hardware that Windows expects to see but that *isn't* present, the boot process slows to a crawl while Windows waits the maximum prescribed time for the device to respond before concluding that it's missing.

Windows XP's hardware profiles feature lets you predefine two, three, or any number of discrete hardware configurations to avoid these potential problems. (According to Microsoft, Windows is supposed to create the Docked and Undocked profiles automatically during setup if you use a laptop computer, but my experience is that that doesn't always happen.) Lab 9-2 presents the technique for creating a new hardware profile.

Lab 9-2 Creating a New Hardware Profile

1. **Choose Start⇨Control Panel.**

2. **Double-click the System icon.**

   (I'm presuming you've set the control panel for classic view instead of category view.)

3. **Click the Hardware tab of the System control panel.**

4. **Click the Hardware Profiles button to display the dialog box shown in Figure 9-4.**

   On this portable PC, Windows XP created the "Profile 1 (Current)" profile automatically during setup.

5. **Highlight (that is, click) a profile in the Available Hardware Profiles list.**

6. **Click the Copy button for a new profile based on the existing one.**

7. **Name the new profile in the Copy Profile dialog box and click OK.**

8. **Click OK twice to close all open dialog boxes.**

Figure 9-4:
Create a
new
hardware
profile here.

How does Windows XP choose a hardware configuration at startup? You set the options in the Hardware Profiles dialog box: Either you make Windows wait for you to choose from the list, or you let Windows pick the top profile in the list after a fixed delay period. Change the relative position of any listed profile by selecting it and moving it with the arrow keys.

After you boot to a hardware profile, you can use the System control panel's Device Manager tab to navigate through the *hardware tree* on a device-by-device basis, and specify which hardware configurations any given device should belong to (see Figure 9-5). The Registry stores all hardware profile information.

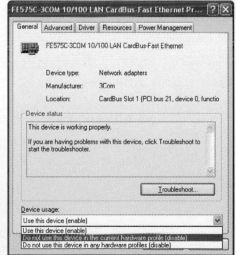

Figure 9-5:
Disable a
device in
the current
profile or in
all profiles.

If you *disable* a device by using Device Manager, the driver remains on the local hard disk and is available for use in other hardware profiles. Disabling a device renders it inactive, prevents the Registry from loading the driver at startup, and frees the resources (interrupt, memory, and so on) that the device was using. However, if you *uninstall* a device, Windows XP deletes the driver files and the device is not available for use in other hardware profiles.

Disable devices in the appropriate hardware profile to save power. For example, if you're on the road, you can create a "road" profile in which you disable the PC Card Ethernet adapter. You won't need it, so why run down your battery feeding it power?

I'll end this discussion with a side note on user profiles. I cover these in Chapter 12 in more detail; suffice it to say here that user profiles contain all your personal preferences and some or all your personal data files. User profiles can follow you around a network, a feature called *roaming profiles*. Microsoft recommends against using roaming user profiles for laptop users who often use dial-up connections to link to the corporate LAN or WAN. The reason is that dial-up connections are slow and get bogged down when the network updates your user profile data. So, improve performance for mobile users by not using roaming profiles, or a related feature called *folder redirection* (which maps folders like My Documents to a network share).

Prep Test

1 You have a portable computer that you've upgraded to Windows XP Professional from Windows 98. You notice that the computer no longer powers down when you execute the Shutdown command. What must you enable with the Power Options control panel in order to fix this problem? (Choose the best answer.)

A ○ APM

B ○ ACPI

C ○ A power scheme

D ○ MPS

E ○ SMP

2 You have a portable computer that runs Windows XP Professional. You spend about half your time at the office and half your time on the road, so your manager authorizes a docking station, which you get a good deal on because it's been discontinued by the manufacturer. You set up a second hardware profile so that Windows XP can take advantage of the docking station's network card and high-res display adapter.

You reboot the computer, go for a cup of coffee, and come back to find that your docked computer doesn't seem to be using the network card. You check the maximum resolution of the display, and the computer isn't using the high-res video card, either. What setting should you change in order to fix this problem? (Choose the best answer.)

A ○ Wait until I select a hardware profile, on the Hardware Profiles property sheet

B ○ Select the first hardware profile listed, on the Hardware Profiles property sheet

C ○ Profile= , in the BOOT.INI file

D ○ StartupProfile, in the Registry

3 You're traveling on a transatlantic flight and need to conserve battery power for your ACPI Windows XP Professional notebook computer. When you get ready to take a nap after the delectable airline meal, what state should you put your notebook computer into in order to minimize the likelihood of lost data? (Choose the best answer.)

A ○ Perform a normal shutdown that powers your PC off.

B ○ Initiate Standby mode.

C ○ Initiate Hibernate mode.

D ○ Initiate ACPI mode.

4 You're a traveling salesperson with a Windows XP Professional notebook computer. While on the road, it's very important for you to be in touch with the home office. So, you travel with two modems, just in case one breaks. Both use the PC Card bus. You install the first one with Plug and Play, and it tests out fine; the installation script puts the modem on COM1. Then you install the second modem into your second PC Card slot. It seems to install fine, but when you try to use it, you get an error message that says "Unable to open port."

Clearly, the two devices aren't happily coexisting on this computer, probably because both are wanting to use COM1. What should you do to correct the problem? (Choose all that apply.)

A ❑ Create two hardware profiles. Uninstall one modem in each profile.

B ❑ Create two hardware profiles. Disable one modem in each profile.

C ❑ Use Device Manager to disable one of the modems.

D ❑ Use Device Manager to uninstall one of the modems.

E ❑ Use Phone and Modem Options to disable one of the modems.

F ❑ Use Phone and Modem Options to uninstall one of the modems.

5 Jim is a member of the Power Users group. He gets a new PC Card network adapter for his notebook computer. During the installation, Plug and Play asks Jim for the location of the appropriate driver for the network adapter. He provides that information, but the driver installation fails. What should Jim do? (Choose the best answer.)

A ○ Run the Add/Remove Hardware Wizard instead of using Plug and Play.

B ○ Run the Scan New Hardware command in Device Manager.

C ○ Log on as Administrator and try again.

D ○ Obtain another copy of the driver media.

6 You want to retrofit an infrared data port to your Windows XP Professional computer. You evaluate various models and review their spec sheets. Which of the following is the most attractive specification? (Choose the best answer.)

A ○ IrLPT

B ○ IrDA-SIR

C ○ IrDA-FIR

D ○ IrDA-XIR

7 You're installing a PC Card modem into a Windows XP notebook and you can't get the modem driver to install. What should you try? (Choose the best answer.)

A ○ Boot to Safe Mode.

B ○ Install a COM port.

C ○ Install the generic PC Card minidriver.

D ○ Disable Plug and Play.

E ○ Log on as a Power User.

8 You're configuring a notebook computer for Standby mode. You want to set the machine so that it prompts for a user name and password when it comes out of Standby. Where do you make this setting? (Choose the best answer.)

A ○ Power Options, Advanced tab

B ○ Power Options, Standby tab

C ○ Power Options, Power Schemes tab

D ○ Local Security Policy console

Answers

1 **A.** APM version 1.2 is supported for Windows XP Professional running on older computers, but it isn't enabled by default if Windows Setup doesn't recognize the specific APM BIOS as being one that's supported. Activate APM on the APM tab of the Power Options control panel. You can't enable or disable ACPI; if Windows XP detects that a machine is ACPI-capable, Windows uses ACPI features automatically. *Review "APM."*

2 **A.** What happened, most likely, is that when you rebooted the PC and left for a caffeine infusion, Windows waited the default number of seconds and chose the first hardware profile in the list, which specifies the undocked configuration. In that case, Windows may not autodetect the hardware in the docking station, especially considering that the station is a bit outdated. Your best bet would be to tell Windows to always wait and let you decide which profile you want at boot time. Choice B isn't flagrantly wrong, but if you spend half your time at the office (docked) and half on the road (undocked), you don't have a clear choice. *Review "Hardware Profiles."*

3 **C.** On most machines, hibernation is the best choice. Performing a normal shutdown takes more time, both to shutdown and to restart, thereby expending more battery power. Regarding choice B, Standby mode is a low-power mode, but Hibernate is a no-power mode, and therefore better for conserving precious battery juice. There's no such thing as ACPI mode (D). By the way, if the plane crew advises you to turn off all electronic devices, you must choose hibernation or a complete shutdown; standby mode is not allowed. *Review "Power Management."*

4 **B** and **C.** You want to disable one of the modems, not uninstall it. If you uninstall a modem, then you'd have to reinstall the driver from CD or diskette if you ever needed it later. You couldn't get the device driver from the Internet because your modem is broken! Either go the hardware profile route, or simply use Device Manager. To switch between the two modems on a regular basis, the profile method is the preferable one. *Review "Hardware Profiles."*

5 **C.** If Plug and Play can't find the right driver, you must log on as an Administrator to install. You run into the same problem if the device driver isn't digitally signed by Microsoft. *Review "Plug and Play and Mobile Computers."*

6 **C.** IrDA-FIR supports much faster data transfers than IrDA-SIR, although 4Mbps is noticeably slower than a regular Ethernet connection (10Mbps). IrLPT is the protocol for an infrared printer port. IrDA-XIR doesn't exist. IrDA-VFIR isn't listed, but it would be the best choice if it was because of to its higher speed of 16Mbps. *Review "Infrared and Wireless Devices."*

7 **B.** This method also works often for non-PC Card modems. Installing the COM (serial) port allows Windows XP to autodetect the modem at the next restart. Make sure that the new COM port doesn't conflict with any built-in devices, such as an external COM1 port or an infrared port. *Review "PC Cards."*

8 **A.** If the option doesn't appear, then your computer doesn't fully support Standby mode. Review "Power Management."

Part IV
Configuring and Managing Resource Access

The 5th Wave   By Rich Tennant

"I couldn't get this 'job skills' program to work on my PC, so I replaced the mother-board, upgraded the BIOS and wrote a program that links it to my personal database. It told me I wasn't technically inclined and should pursue a career in sales."

In this part . . .

Network designers work hard to make important resources shareable, and then they turn right around and work equally hard to make sure only the right people can gain access to those resources. (It's a bit like fertilizing your lawn and then mowing it.) Part IV deals with providing (and restricting) access to files, printers, and other resources for both local and networked users. Microsoft was clearly very focused on this area when building Windows XP, and the company has extended Windows NT's strengths in several key ways.

The local users and groups model that Chapter 10 explores is very similar to Windows NT's architecture, as is the concept of access permissions at both the share level and the file-and-folder level (Chapter 11). Chapter 12 takes the concept of the roaming user to a higher level with a discussion of IntelliMirror and user profiles, while Chapter 13 focuses on dial-up access and the new Remote Assistance and Remote Desktop features.

Chapter 10

Managing Local Users and Groups

● ●

Exam Objectives

▶ Configure and troubleshoot local users and groups

▶ Troubleshoot cache credentials

▶ Configure, manage, and troubleshoot account settings

▶ Configure, manage, and troubleshoot user and group rights

▶ Configure, manage, and troubleshoot auditing

▶ Configure, manage, and troubleshoot account policy

● ●

Microsoft exam-writers' jobs mainly consist of making exams difficult enough that certification continues to mean something. When these anonymous test architects run across a topic as complex and confusing as Windows XP security, you can imagine their cold gray eyes sparkling with malicious glee in the dim half-light of their grim cubicles. You can beat them at their own game, but it's no walk in the park. For example, you may have to read this chapter twice (and Chapter 11 three times).

You can categorize Windows XP security features into pre-logon security (computer accounts), logon security, user and group rights, object permissions (access control), encryption for stored data, encryption for transmitted data, auditing, and policies.

Sometimes you can implement security in these areas with multiple techniques and tools, and sometimes the areas overlap. For example, group membership can determine user rights ("User" versus "Power User"), domain-level policies, or both.

This chapter takes a user-and-group focus and deals with four of the eight features: logon security, rights, auditing, and a subset of policies called account policies. Chapter 11 targets access control and covers permissions, computer accounts, and group policies. Finally, file system encryption gets its due in Chapter 3, and transmission encryption in Chapter 13.

Quick Assessment

Configure and troubleshoot local users and groups

1 Windows XP automatically creates a local user account that is, however, not enabled. Its name is _____.

2 A local user account name has a maximum of _____ meaningful characters.

Troubleshoot cache credentials

3 Cache your Passport name and password by using _____ as the server name.

4 Disable the display of last logged-on user with the _____ administrative tool.

Configure, manage, and troubleshoot account settings

5 For proper security, always _____ the local Administrator account.

Configure, manage, and troubleshoot user and group rights

6 The Windows 2000 built-in group that corresponds most closely to the Users group in Windows NT 4.0 is _____.

7 You can view current user rights assignments by using the _____ administrative tool.

Configure, manage, and troubleshoot auditing

8 To track logon events on a domain, choose the _____ auditing policy.

Configure, manage, and troubleshoot account policy

9 Setting the password history policy is a way of limiting how often users can _____ old passwords.

10 To help foil unauthorized access through repeated logon attempts, set the account _____ policies.

Answers

1   *Guest.* See "Built-in user accounts" for more.

2   *20.* "Creating local user accounts" offers additional details.

3   **.passport.com.* See "Troubleshooting domain accounts" for more.

4   *Local Security Policy.* The "Domains" section explains further.

5   *Rename.* See "Built-in user accounts" for more.

6   *Power users.* "User rights and built-in local groups" has details.

7   *Local security policy.* See "User rights and built-in local groups" for this and related tidbits.

8   *Audit account logon events.* The "Auditing User Activities" section provides this nugget.

9   *Reuse.* See "Sorry, it's company policy" for other password policy settings.

10 *Lockout.* "Sorry, it's company policy" has the details on lockout options.

Windows XP Networking Models

Windows XP supports two basic networking models: workgroups and domains. The exam focuses on domains, but you need to understand the difference between these two models.

Workgroups

In the workgroup, or *peer-to-peer*, networking model, no central database of users, groups, and access permissions exists. (Another way to say this is that no central logon authority exists.) Instead, each PC user has the option to share resources (printers, disks, folders — not individual files) and to control access to those resources by user or group name. In a workgroup, you typically have no "dedicated" server: Any PC can act both as client and as server.

Workgroup networking in Windows XP and 2000 is different from workgroup networking in Windows 9*x*. With 9*x* systems, you assign passwords to shared resources (Microsoft calls this *share-level security*), and you have no database of users and groups. With Windows XP and 2000 systems, you use the local database of users and groups on each PC to assign access permissions.

Some small organizations may have only a single workgroup; larger organizations may have several, broken out by department, office, or project. Workgroup names (set on the Computer Name tab of the System control panel) shouldn't exceed 15 characters, shouldn't contain any spaces, and shouldn't duplicate any existing computer names. (Workgroup names, like computer names, are NetBIOS names and so they have the same format.)

If you use a workgroup, the Computers Near Me folder inside the My Network Places folder shows other computers in the same workgroup.

The workgroup networking model is appropriate for up to ten users, according to Microsoft. Administrative chores, such as making backups, are decentralized (shared resources exist on several PCs instead of just one) and therefore unwieldy beyond a small number of computers. However, you don't need to buy a separate license for Windows 2002 or 2000 Server to set up a Windows XP workgroup. You have all the software you need:

- ✔ A network adapter driver
- ✔ A transport protocol
- ✔ A network client (Client for Microsoft Networks)
- ✔ A sharing service (File and Printer Sharing for Microsoft Networks, which appears simply as "Server" in the Services console of the Administrative Tools folder)

Domains

Domain-based networks are more common than workgroups in the business environment, and they have a number of advantages: better security, centralized administration, and better expandability. In a simple domain-based network, a central server maintains a database of users, groups, and access permissions, and handles network logons. In Windows XP and 2000, that database is called *Active Directory*.

One of the cool features of a domain is that Windows may *replicate* the security database if more than one server is present on the network. In this situation, you can have several servers acting as *domain controllers*, sharing the same database and updating each other automatically when the database changes on one of the machines. Unlike Windows NT 4.0 Server, Windows 2002 Server and Windows 2000 Server don't distinguish between primary and backup domain controllers; all domain controllers have equal standing.

In addition to handling the security database, central servers can also host shared programs, data files, and hardware for use by the client workstations. In fact, a server doesn't have to be a domain controller. If a server is simply sharing one or more resources, but doesn't participate in user authentication, it's called a *member server*.

Windows XP contains all the software elements necessary for accessing a domain-type network:

- A network adapter driver
- A transport protocol
- A network client (Client for Microsoft Networks)

You don't need the sharing service if the Windows XP Professional PC won't be sharing any of its own local resources. However, it's optional, and you can therefore make a Windows XP "client PC" into a "mini-server" by sharing a folder with other domain users. Sometimes a network like this, which uses the domain model but which lets client machines as well as servers share resources, goes by the title of *hybrid* network.

In order to host an Active Directory-based domain-type network — that is, in order to be a domain controller or member server — you must have Windows 2002 Server or Windows 2000 Server.

Creating Local Users

Unlike Windows 98, Windows XP Professional maintains its own *local* database of users and groups. This database lives in the SAM and SECURITY Registry hives of the local computer, and it's entirely separate and distinct from the domain-based Active Directory database (NTDS.DIT) that lives on a Windows 2000 or 2002 Server domain controller. Windows XP Professional uses the local user and group database to help determine who can access resources on the local PC.

In a workgroup environment, no domain-based database exists, meaning that each user must have a local user account on at least one Windows XP Professional machine. Each workgroup user must log on to a local PC. In a domain environment, however, you can log on to Windows XP Pro in one of two ways: you can log on to the local machine (through a local user account), or to the domain (through a domain account). On a PC configured as a domain client, you can choose which entity you want to log onto at the logon dialog box.

When you create a user account in Windows XP Professional through the User Accounts control panel, it's a *local* user account. (You'd create a domain account on a Windows 2000 or 2002 Server machine with the Active Directory Users and Computers console.) Microsoft recommends not creating local user accounts on PCs that participate in a domain, for two reasons: Local users can't gain access to domain resources, and domain administrators can't manage local user accounts.

Built-in user accounts

To get you started, Microsoft sets up Windows XP Professional with built-in local user accounts, only some of which you can view with the User Accounts control panel (see Figure 10-1): Administrator, Guest, and HelpAssistant. You may never need more than that if you're configuring a domain PC because you'd use the domain account for everyday use and the built-in Administrator account to manage or configure the local PC. The HelpAssistant account (shown in Figure 10-2, along with the disabled-by-default Guest account) is related to the Remote Assistance feature, which I discuss in Chapter 13.

Here's what you must know about these accounts:

- The Administrator account is all-powerful. You should log on as Administrator when you need to configure or manage the computer.

- Always rename the Administrator account.

- You can't delete the Administrator account.

- Don't use the Administrator account for everyday work. The risk of unintentionally damaging your system (or of giving a virus unfettered access to it) is too great.

✔ The Guest account is weak and is disabled by default. Microsoft recommends using it for occasional, temporary purposes.

✔ You should probably rename the Guest account if you use it, but at least assign a password to it.

✔ You can't delete the Guest account, either.

When you install software, configure desktop icons, modify the Start menu, and so on, while logged on as a particular user, you don't see those changes when you log on as a different user. Chapter 12 explores the issue of *user profiles* in greater detail.

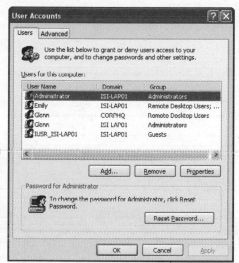

Figure 10-1:
View some, but not all, local accounts here.

Creating local user accounts

The built-in Administrator and Guest accounts may not meet all your needs for local user accounts. For example, if you're setting up a workgroup PC, you probably want an account for that PC's regular user — an account that won't have the unlimited power of the Administrator account, but that has more power than the measly Guest account. (If you're setting up a domain PC, you're probably better off creating domain accounts on a Windows 2002 or 2000 Server machine than creating local user accounts.)

You can create additional local user accounts two ways: by running the User Accounts control panel (if you've enabled the more efficient Classic control panel view, choose Start⇨Control Panel and double-click User Accounts) on a non-domain PC, and by running the computer's management console (right-click My Computer and choose Manage) on a domain or non-domain PC.

Method #1 doesn't work if you have a domain PC: When you click the Add button on the Users tab of the User Accounts control panel, Windows XP prompts you to add a pre-existing domain user. I *told* you Microsoft doesn't want you adding local accounts to a domain PC!

Lab 10-1 goes through the steps for using Method #2.

Lab 10-1   Creating a Local User Account

1. **Right-click My Computer (either on the Start menu or on the desktop) and choose Manage.**

2. **Expand the Local Users and Groups node in the tree pane (to the left) by clicking the + sign next to it.**

3. **Click the Users icon in the tree pane.**

4. **Right-click any blank space in the details pane (to the right) and choose New User (see Figure 10-2).**

Figure 10-2:
The management console's Local Users and Groups snap-in.

5. **Fill in the requested data fields in the New User dialog box (see Figure 10-3).**

   You can specify that the user must change the password at the next logon, placing the user in charge of his or her own password. If you don't specify this, then you can tell Windows that the user may never change the password, and/or that the password never expires.

   Finally, you can disable the account for the time being — for example, if you're setting it up in advance of hiring a new employee, or if you're about to delete an account and you want to verify first that no ill effects will occur.

Figure 10-3:
Creating a
new local
user is easy.

Windows NT 4.0 users, note that the Local Users and Groups snap-in is the successor to NT's User Manager utility.

Here are some tips on creating new local user accounts:

✔ User names must be unique among other user names on the machine and among other user names on the domain (if the PC belongs to a domain) or on the workgroup (if the PC belongs to a workgroup).

✔ Windows only cares about the first 20 characters of the user name.

✔ You can't use the special characters - + [ ] \ | / ; : < > or ?.

✔ The full name and description fields are optional.

✔ Passwords can't be longer than 127 characters, and Microsoft recommends they not be shorter than 8.

✔ Passwords can't use the special characters that are forbidden for user names (see third bullet point).

Fast account switching

A handy feature of Windows XP is the ability to switch to a different user account without having to log off the current account. The procedure is to choose Start⇔Log Off, and then click Switch User. You can have multiple programs and data files open for each logged-on user. Note that this new feature is not available on computers that belong to a domain, only to those that belong to a workgroup or that are standalone workstations.

You can disable or enable fast account switching via the User Accounts control panel's Use Fast User Switching check box.

Deleting user accounts

Lab 10-2 goes through the simple procedure for deleting a user account through the Users and Groups management console snap-in.

Lab 10-2	Deleting a Local User Account

1. **Right-click My Computer and choose Manage.**

2. **Expand the Local Users and Groups node in the tree pane (to the left) by clicking the + sign next to it.**

3. **Click the Users icon in the tree pane.**

4. **Right-click the user's icon in the details pane (to the right) and choose Delete.**

5. **Read the warning message and click the Yes button.**

   The warning message you see reminds you that if you delete a user account, you permanently and irretrievably delete the Security ID (SID) associated with that account, as well as all its various access tokens conveying permissions to shared files, folders, printers, and so on. Which point leads me to an Instant Answer, as follows.

If an employee leaves your organization and you replace him with someone new, and you want the new person to have the same access privileges as the old person, don't delete the old employee's account. Right-click its icon in the Local Users and Groups snap-in and choose Rename to give the account a new name. Then, right-click it again and choose Set Password to give it a new password.

FYI, unique SIDs exist for groups and computers as well as for individual users.

Configuring user accounts

Two aspects of configuring user accounts are likely to receive mention on the test: account policy and group membership.

Sorry, it's company policy

If you ask most Microsoft network administrators to identify the most complex and confusing security feature of Windows operating systems, I'll bet a nickel that most of them respond with a single word: *policies*. From system policies in Windows NT 4.0 and Windows 9*x* to group policy, account policy, security policy, and so on *ad nauseam* in Windows XP, it takes a combination of dogged determination and hundreds of hours playing around with real live networks to fully grasp how Windows policies really work.

Thankfully, you don't have to achieve total policy enlightenment. Partial enlightenment serves you just fine. This section aims to illuminate a small subset of the entire policy population: *account policies*. As you may have guessed, account policies apply to user accounts, which is why I'm talking about them in this chapter.

Account policies can do two things for you:

✔ They can enforce requirements that can increase the security of passwords.

✔ They can help prevent crackers from getting into a system by guessing account names and passwords.

View account policies in the Local Security Policy console (it's in the Administrative Tools control panel folder); see Figure 10-4. Change an account policy by double-clicking it and modifying its value. (If the same policy exists at the domain level, the domain policy overrides the local policy.)

Figure 10-4:
Password
policies are
one of two
types of
account
policy.

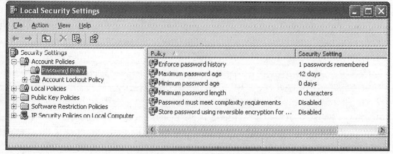

Here's what the password policies mean, in brief:

✔ **Enforce password history:** How many new passwords the user must specify before he or she is allowed to reuse an old one.

✔ **Maximum password age:** This value is in days and the default is 42; a value of 0 means the password doesn't expire.

✔ **Minimum password age:** How many days a user must keep a password before changing it. Zero means you can change a password at any time, which sort of defeats "Enforce password history" if you think about it.

✔ **Minimum password length:** The range is 0 to 14 characters; 0 means no password is required for the account (bad idea, for one reason because the "Run As" service and the Remote Desktop service require non-blank passwords). Windows XP Professional permits passwords up to 127 characters in length, but if you go longer than 14, you won't be able to log on to the network from Windows 9*x* clients.

✔ **Passwords must meet complexity requirements.** This option makes the user include numbers or punctuation marks in the password and forbids including the user's account name or full name (if present).

Note that these policies apply to all local user accounts on the computer. You can't set 'em on an individual-by-individual basis.

I describe the account lockout policies, which help foil evil people who repeatedly try to log on to your PC, in the following list:

- **Account lockout duration:** How many minutes Windows XP locks out a user after the user makes X number of invalid logon attempts. A value of zero means "until an Administrator clears the account."

- **Account lockout threshold:** How many invalid logon attempts trigger the lockout, at which point Windows won't let the user try anymore until the account lockout duration period has passed. The range is 0 to 999.

- **Reset account lockout counter after:** How many minutes to wait after an account lockout before giving the user a "clean slate" to try logging on again. The range is 1 to 99,999 minutes.

Members only

If you use the Computer Management console to create a local user account (Method #2 in the section "Creating local user accounts" earlier in this chapter), you can't assign the new local user account to any local groups until you create it and it appears as a new entry in the Local Users and Groups snap-in. After it does, you can right-click it, choose Properties (see Figure 10-5), and click the Member Of tab to assign the account to one or more groups. If you use the User Accounts control panel, on the other hand (Method #1), the wizard asks you to join the new account to a group during the creation process.

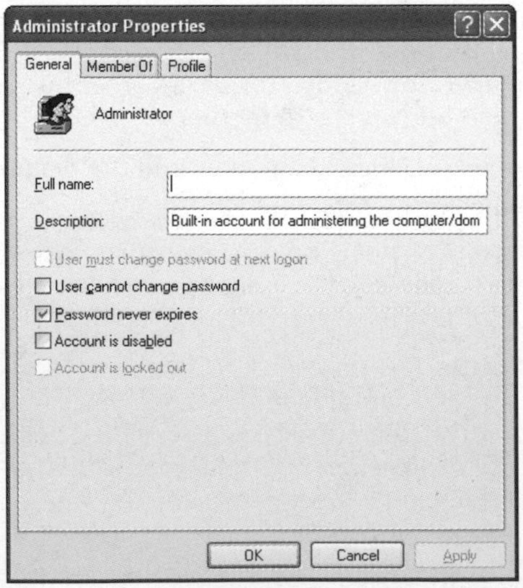

Figure 10-5:
A user's property sheet offers the Member Of tab.

| Administrator Properties | ? X |

General | Member Of | Profile

Administrator

Full name: |

Description: Built-in account for administering the computer/dom

☐ User must change password at next logon
☐ User cannot change password
☑ Password never expires
☐ Account is disabled
☐ Account is locked out

| OK | Cancel | Apply |

Why would you want the local account to belong to a group? And, going back a step, what is a group, anyway? The next section walks you through some group therapy, Windows XP style.

Groups in Windows XP

A Windows XP group is just a defined group of user accounts who share certain security-related settings. So why do you need groups? Why not treat every individual as a unique and special being? The short answer: You work in a corporation, which consists not of unique and special beings, but of replaceable cogs in a giant machine!

Seriously (although for some of you, the previous answer *may* be serious!), the real reason is simply ease of administration. In most organizations, configuring every employee with a unique set of rights and access permissions just isn't necessary. Chances are pretty good that everybody in Bookkeeping does more or less the same thing and needs more or less the same rights and permissions on the network. (And because I'm discussing the network situation here, you can correctly infer that groups are far less useful when you have a standalone PC.) If I'm a network manager, configuring one batch of settings for the Bookkeeping group is a heckuva lot faster (and more secure) than configuring every Tom, Dick, and Harriet individually.

Local and global groups

Just as with user accounts, Windows XP offers two sorts of groups: *local* and *global*. A local group consists of local user accounts. A global group consists of domain user accounts. Here's what you must know about local and global groups:

- ✔ Users can belong to more than one group at a time.

- ✔ Groups can belong to other groups, with limitations (for example, although you can add a global group to a local group, you can't do the reverse).

- ✔ Local groups live on the local PC's security database and are for assigning permissions to resources on the local PC.

- ✔ Global groups live on the domain's security database (Active Directory) and are for assigning permissions to resources on the domain.

- ✔ You can't create local groups on Windows 2000 or 2002 Server domain controllers.

✔ Global groups can belong to local groups, allowing domain users to have rights and permissions at a local PC.

✔ Windows XP Professional can't create or manage global groups; that's a job for Server.

✔ As is the case with local user accounts, and for the same reasons, Microsoft discourages you from creating local groups on a domain PC.

User rights and built-in local groups

As with local users, where Microsoft provides built-in accounts, so it is with local groups, with the exception that there are more of 'em. You see these built-in local groups on Windows XP Professional machines and on Windows 2002 or 2000 servers that aren't domain controllers. These built-in local groups convey sets of rights, or privileges, on the local PC.

What's a *right?* It's an action that a user or group is allowed to do. Changing the desktop, installing a program, backing up the local hard drive, sharing a folder, are all examples of user rights. (For an example of how user rights can affect seemingly unrelated chores, see the sidebar "User rights and Task Scheduler.") So you can think of built-in local groups as offering convenient groupings of user rights that often correspond to different roles of users on the PC.

If you want to see which rights Microsoft has associated with which built-in local groups, open the Local Security Policy console (it's in the Administrative Tools control panel folder) and look under *Local Policies\User Rights Assignment* (see Figure 10-6).

If you have a Windows XP machine available, you should spend a little time getting familiar with the user rights listings (and the Security Options listings, too), but a few rights are worth special mention here:

✔ **Access This Computer From The Network** lists the users and groups that can connect to this computer over the wire.

✔ **Add Workstations To Domain** is a right you can only assign on a domain controller, such as a Windows 2000 Server machine. It conveys the right to add up to 10 PCs to an Active Directory domain, which is a nice way to delegate that task without setting up a bunch of people as domain administrators.

✔ **Allow Logon Through Terminal Services** is a right conveyed by default to Administrators and to members of the Remote Desktop Users group.

✔ **Log On Locally** lists the users and groups that can log on at the computer. You could trim this list, for example, if you wanted a particular group to be able to log on to the domain without being able to log on to the local PC.

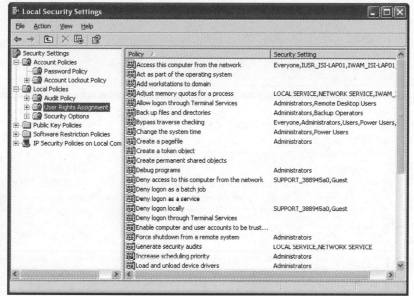

Figure 10-6:
A fine-grained look at user rights.

The distinction between rights and permissions can be subtle. Users and groups have *rights*. Objects (such as NTFS files and folders, Registry keys, and so on) have *permissions*. Chapter 11 deals with object permissions in excruciating detail.

You can change the default rights that accrue to users in different groups by applying security templates (see Chapter 11) with the Security Analysis and Configuration snap-in, or the SECEDIT command-line utility.

Here's a list of the more important built-in local groups and their usual functions:

- ✔ **Administrators:** Includes the built-in local user account, Administrator. Belonging to this group means you can do anything on the computer.

- ✔ **Guests:** Includes the built-in local user account, Guest. Members of Guests can't change their desktop setup, and you normally must grant them explicit rights to do just about anything productive.

- ✔ **Users:** Windows XP also (inconsistently) calls these "Restricted Users" in certain dialog boxes. When you add a local user account, it automatically receives membership in this group.

  - • Membership in this group entitles the user to run "certified" Windows XP applications, but may not provide sufficient rights and access permissions to run some "legacy" Windows NT 4.0 applications.

  - • Users can't share folders (that is, designate them to be shared).

- Users can't install programs for use by other Users.
- Users can't modify system-wide settings, whether in the operating system, the Registry, or applications.
- Users can't create local printers.

The COMPATWS.INF security template (see Chapter 11) relaxes some of the restrictions on the Users group to improve compatibility with Windows NT 4.0 applications. Other options for letting members of Users run older applications include moving Users to the Power Users group and upgrading the applications to Windows XP-compliant versions if available.

- **Power Users:** This group corresponds roughly with the Windows NT 4.0 group "Users" and sometimes appears in the Windows XP user interface as "Standard Users."

  - Members can create local user accounts and offer resources for sharing across the network.

  - They can install applications, as long as the applications don't install operating system services or modify operating system files.

  - They can stop and start system services as long as the services didn't start automatically.

  - They can't modify or delete user accounts that they did not create.

  - They can remove users from the Guests, Users, and Power Users groups.

  - They can't modify membership in the Administrators or Backup Operators groups.

  - They can't take ownership of files.

- **Remote Desktop Users:** Members of this group, which is new in XP, can log on to the local PC from a remote PC. You can add or remove members to this group via the Remote tab of the System control panel. Chapter 13 deals with the Remote Desktop feature in detail.

- **Backup Operators:** Members of this group can back up and restore files on the system, irrespective of file access permissions, which a regular member of the Users group can't do.

All Windows XP and 2000 systems also sport a number of built-in *system groups* whose memberships you cannot change but which reflect how a user achieved access to the PC or network. (The list of system groups increases in a domain environment, to include Domain Administrators and Domain Users.) You shouldn't be quizzed heavily on these for the XP Professional exam, so just be familiar with their fairly self-explanatory names:

> ✔ *Everyone* (which includes the Guest account)
>
> ✔ *Authenticated Users* (that is, authenticated on the local PC or on the domain; the same as the Everyone group, minus anonymous users)
>
> ✔ *Creator/Owner* (such as the user who creates a folder)
>
> ✔ *Network* (someone who gains access to the computer via a network)
>
> ✔ *Interactive* (someone who gains access to the computer by logging on to it interactively)
>
> ✔ *Anonymous Logon* (that is, unauthenticated)
>
> ✔ *Dialup* (someone who gains access to the computer via a dial-up connection)

Creating and deleting local groups

Should you find that the built-in local groups don't meet all your needs, you can create new ones. (Remember that Microsoft suggests you not do this on PCs that participate in a domain-based network.) The procedure is exactly analogous to creating new local user accounts; see Lab 10-3.

User rights and Task Scheduler

The Task Scheduler has come a long way since its early incarnation as System Agent in the Plus! add-on product for Windows 95. In Windows 2000, the scheduler service appears as the Scheduled Tasks folder (odd grammar that!) in the Control Panel. You can define a task, such as backing up your C drive, and schedule it for recurring automatic operation, say at 2 a.m. nightly. You might not suppose so, but using this tool successfully requires an awareness of user and group rights!

When you define a task by using the Add Scheduled Task Wizard, Windows asks you for the name of the user account under whose security context the task should run. That is, you must decide whether you want the task to run as though initiated by the user account named Bob, or Sue, or Administrator. (That user doesn't have to be logged on when time comes

for the task to run, by the way.) If you choose a user who doesn't have sufficient rights to run the scheduled task, the task doesn't run. Whether you're notified of the problem depends on whether you've activated the Notify Me of Missed Tasks toggle on the Task Scheduler's Advanced menu. (If not, then the log file C:\WINDOWS\SCHEDLGU.TXT may give you some clues; you can read it with the View Log command on the Advanced menu.)

Insufficient rights may not be the only reason a scheduled task fails. Someone may have stopped the service by choosing Stop Using Task Scheduler on the Advanced menu; the service doesn't automatically restart. That's probably the cause of a problem in which *no* tasks are running, even ones that don't normally require special rights or permissions. Chapter 14 offers more details on Task Scheduler.

Lab 10-3   Creating a Local Group

1. **Right-click My Computer and choose Manage.**

   The Computer Management console opens.

2. **Expand the Local Users and Groups node.**

3. **Click the Groups icon in the tree pane.**

4. **Right-click in any blank area of the details pane and choose New Group.**

5. **Give your new group a name (up to 256 characters).**

6. **Add users via the Add button. Additions are duly added to the Select Users or Groups property sheet, as shown in Figure 10-7.**

   You can also add users to the group later, through the user's Member Of property sheet or through the group's property sheet in the Local Users and Groups console.

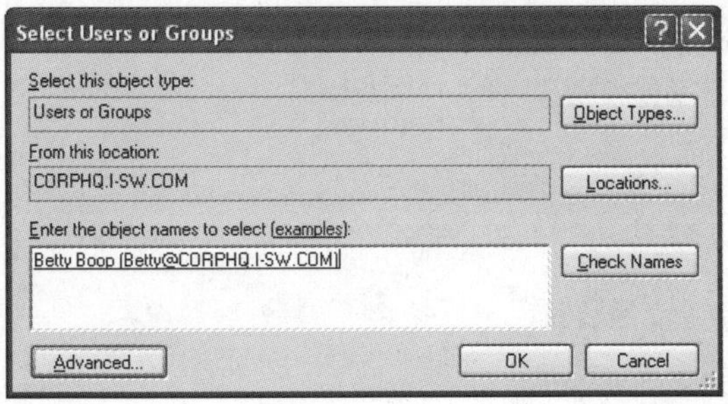

Figure 10-7:
Adding a
user to a
new local
group.

Deleting local groups is a matter of right-clicking and choosing Delete. Note that you don't blow away any user accounts by deleting groups to which those users may belong.

Domain User Accounts

The bulk of this chapter (and the exam) deals with local user accounts, but you also need to know a few facts about domain user accounts. Create these accounts using the Active Directory Users and Computers console, which is present by default on a domain controller, and which you can install onto a Windows XP Professional machine by double-clicking ADMINPAK.MSI on the Server CD. Configure domain accounts by clicking the Users node in the console's tree pane, right-clicking the user account icon in the details pane, and choosing Properties.

Configuring domain accounts

Although the Windows 2002 and 2000 Server exams cover this material in much greater detail, the more common domain user configuration chores include the following:

- **User profile:** As I discuss in more detail in Chapter 12, you can specify the location of a server-based roaming user profile for a domain account, so that the user's documents and settings follow them from PC to PC. Use the Profile tab of the property sheet for this setting.

- **Logon hours:** You can set a schedule for permitted domain logons; use the Account tab of the property sheet.

- **Idle disconnect:** You can kick a user off the network after a predetermined amount of idle time; set this on the Sessions tab.

- **Group membership:** Change the groups to which the domain user belongs in the Member Of tab.

- **Dial-in permission:** Control whether the user has permission to call up remote access servers with the Dial-In tab. You can also set a callback option here for better security; see Chapter 13.

You can also disable accounts, copy them (creating a new user based on an existing user's account), change passwords, move an account to a different organizational unit, delete, and rename accounts — all from the user's property sheet in the Active Directory Users and Computers console.

Troubleshooting domain accounts

The main domain account troubleshooting issue likely to pop up on the exam has to do with *cached credentials*. (Credentials assert a user's identity, and in Windows XP consist of a user name and password.) Two policy settings in the Local Security Policy control panel's Security Options area deal with this issue.

The first has to do with the logon screen, which normally displays the name of the last user to log on to the computer (that is, Windows caches the user name). You can override this behavior to improve security, at the expense of some convenience, by enabling the policy **Interactive Logon: Do Not Display Last User Name In Logon Screen**. (Follow the logic carefully here: If you enable a policy that says "do not do something," then Windows will not do that thing.)

The second issue has to do with the fact that Windows XP Professional users who belong to a domain may occasionally work away from the network — or need to work on the local PC when a domain controller is unavailable. In that case, XP lets the user log on with the domain account, but only a certain number of times, defined by the policy **Interactive Logon: Number Of Previous Logons To Cache**. The default value is 10 logons, the maximum is 50, and a value of 0 disables credential caching.

One other aspect of credential caching doesn't have anything to do with domain accounts but is worth mentioning here. If you open the User Accounts control panel, click the Advanced tab, and then click the Manage Passwords button, you can add passwords for different services and sites (for example, Microsoft Passport) to your local *password cache*. You specify the server name (such as *.passport.com), the user ID, and the password for that server (see Figure 10-8). All such added credentials become part of your user profile.

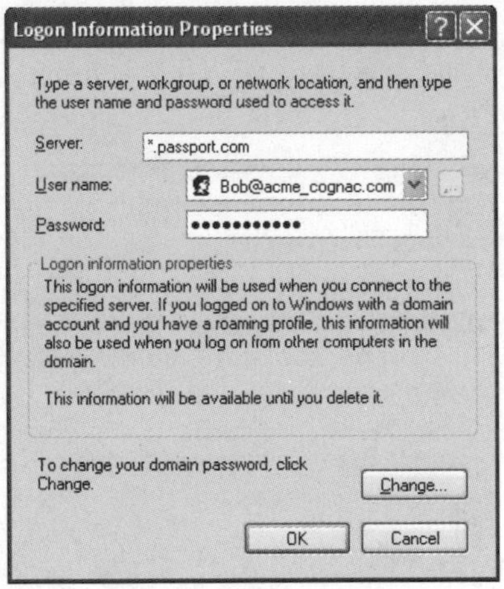

Figure 10-8: Adding a Passport entry to the password credentials cache.

Know the following additional tips for troubleshooting access problems with domain accounts:

- ✔ A new domain account takes time to propagate to all the domain controllers in an organization. If you've just created a new account on one server, other domain controllers can't immediately authenticate the user and permit logon.

- ✔ If a user can't log on to a domain account, ensure that the user has chosen the correct domain from the list box at the logon window, and is not trying to log on to the local PC or a different domain. Also check the log on hours restriction and any security constraints that appear on the Account tab, such as Smart Card Is Required For Interactive Logon.

- ✔ Remote dial-in access is denied by default for a new account. If a domain user can't connect to a remote access server, change the access setting on the Dial-In tab of the account property sheet from Deny to Allow.

> ✔ Domain group policies override local group policies. In Active Directory Users and Computers, right-click the domain, choose Properties, and then click the Group Policy tab to inspect policy settings for the domain that may be countermanding locally set policies. (More on policies in Chapter 11.)

Auditing User Activities

If you're reading this chapter end to end, and you're not confused yet, either your mind is seriously warped or you've been doing this sort of thing for a while in the real world. Windows XP users and groups aren't radically different from Windows NT 4.0 users and groups, after all. Not that this tidbit is much help to those of you who never had the pleasure of wrestling with NT.

In either case, whether you're warped or simply experienced, I have to throw one more iron into the fire before I can be legitimately done with Windows XP users and groups: *auditing*. The good news is that unlike relatively abstract concepts such as user rights, auditing is pretty easy to understand. Chapter 11 explains how to use auditing to monitor user access to files, folders, and the Registry. All I want to do here is mention logon event auditing.

Logon event auditing (see Lab 10-4) means that Windows XP can monitor logons, both successful and unsuccessful, and record them in the Security event log (which you can view with the Event Viewer snap-in to the Computer Management console). This could help you find out if and when Snidely Whiplash is trying to crack his way into a PC by guessing account names and passwords. It may also lead you to inquire why Bertram the bookkeeper is logging on to his system at 3 a.m. when the workday is over at 5 p.m. Incidentally, logon event auditing also lets you know who's connecting to the PC via a network connection.

Lab 10-4   Activating Logon Event Auditing

1. **Choose Start⇨Control Panel.**

2. **Double-click Administrative Tools.**

   I'm assuming you've enabled the more convenient classic view of the control panel here.

3. **Double-click Local Security Policy.**

4. **In the tree pane to the left, expand Local Policies.**

5. **In the tree pane, click Audit Policy.**

   All the various quantities that you can audit now appear in the details pane to the right (see Figure 10-9).

6. **In the details pane, double-click Audit Logon Events.**

   If you're interested in Snidely (see paragraph just before this lab), click Failure; if you're interested in Bertram, click Success; and if you're interested in both, click both.

7. **Click OK and close the Local Security Policy console.**

8. **Restart the machine to make your changes take effect.**

   From this point forward, watch the Security log. Bertram can't see it because he's not an Administrator — at least, he'd better not be!

Figure 10-9:
Categories you can audit appear in the Local Security Settings window.

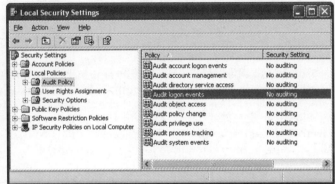

If you double-click Audit Account Logon Events instead of Audit Logon Events in Step 6 of Lab 10-4, Windows XP tracks *domain* logon events (that is, successful or failed attempts to log on to a domain controller). Yeah, I know, you'd never guess that from the names, but that's why an MCSE is such a treasured certification: It demonstrates your ability to memorize all kinds of stuff that should be obvious in the user interface, but isn't.

Prep Test

1 In a pure Windows XP network, what sort of machine authenticates domain users when they log on? (Choose all that apply.)

A ☐ Domain controller

B ☐ Primary domain controller

C ☐ Backup domain controller

D ☐ Primary or backup domain controller, whichever is closer to the user

E ☐ Member server

F ☐ Workstation

2 You receive an anonymous tip that someone who's not an employee but who has a key to your office is trying to log on to your Windows XP domain from your workstation in the middle of the night. You decide to enable auditing so that you can check domain logon attempts in the Security event log (SECEVENT.EVT). Which item and logging option do you choose in the Local Security Policy tool? (Choose the best answer.)

A ○ Audit Account Logon Events. Click Failure.

B ○ Audit Account Logon Events. Click Success.

C ○ Audit Account Logon Events. Do not click Failure or Success.

D ○ Audit Logon Events. Click Failure.

E ○ Audit Logon Events. Click Success.

F ○ Audit Logon Events. Do not click Failure or Success.

3 Vendela is a new employee at Acme Cognac, where you enjoy gainful employment as a PC coordinator. One of your jobs is to set up new user accounts. In Vendela's job, she needs to run three applications, all of which have Microsoft logo certification to run on Windows XP. She needs the ability to modify user-specific application settings for her own account; to shut down her own computer; and to print to shared network printers. Which predefined group should you select for Vendela's new user account? (Choose the best answer.)

A ○ Users

B ○ Power Users

C ○ Guests

D ○ Administrators

E ○ New Users

4 Rebecca is a new employee at Acme Cognac, and you're still a PC coordinator there, by virtue of having successfully answered Question 3. Rebecca needs a domain user account. What Windows XP tool would you use to create such an account? (Choose the best answer.)

A ○ Users and Passwords

B ○ Local Users and Groups

C ○ Active Directory Users and Computers

D ○ Local Users and Passwords

E ○ Domain Users and Groups

F ○ User Manager for Domains

5 You receive a promotion after answering Question 4, and you're now a network administrator at Acme Cognac (motto: "Cheap, but Not Too Bad"). Tyra comes to you complaining that her Windows XP Professional computer isn't allowing her to set the following account password: HEYITSMETYRA!. However, she tried using a different password, 1234PASS, and the system permitted that setting. You advise her that this is a security precaution that you have implemented with a local account policy. Which one? (Choose the best answer.)

A ○ Passwords must not contain user name

B ○ Passwords must contain alpha and numeric characters

C ○ Require alphanumeric passwords

D ○ Passwords must meet complexity requirements

E ○ Maximum password length

F ○ Passwords must not contain special symbols

6 Cindy, an Acme Cognac employee, quits her job as a brandy taster to become a restaurateur. You have no plans to replace her in the next six months as Famke, her boss, assumes Cindy's brandy-tasting responsibilities. Therefore, you delete Cindy's account in the Local Users and Groups utility.

What else do you delete when you delete Cindy's account? (Choose all that apply.)

A ❑ Cindy's SID

B ❑ Cindy's ACLs

C ❑ Cindy's access tokens

D ❑ Cindy's user profile

7 **Which of the following statements is true about Power Users? (Choose all that apply.)**

A ☐ They cannot delete user accounts that they did not originally create.

B ☐ They cannot install applications.

C ☐ They cannot remove users from the Backup Operators group.

D ☐ They can take ownership of files.

E ☐ They can make folders and printers available for sharing.

8 **You set Heather's account lockout threshold to 3, and her account lockout duration to 0. Heather is a terrible typist and one day she misspells her password three times in a row. What must she do next? (Choose the best answer.)**

A ○ Try again. The account lockout duration of 0 means that she can retype her password immediately.

B ○ Wait five minutes and try again. The account lockout duration of 0 means that Windows uses the default value of five minutes.

C ○ Find an administrator. The account lockout duration of 0 means that Heather can't attempt additional logons until her account is cleared.

D ○ Quit Acme Cognac and go to work in TV.

Answers

1 **A.** Windows XP doesn't implement primary and backup domain controllers; all domain controllers are peers. *Review "Windows XP Networking Models."*

2 **A.** Because you suspect someone of trying to access a domain account, you should specify "account logon events" as plain old "logon events" to audit logons to the local PC's security database only. You must choose Success or Failure or both. Typically, if you suspect that someone doesn't already have a valid username, or password and is trying to guess one or the other or both, you audit failed logon attempts. *Review "Auditing User Activities."*

3 **A.** The Users group conveys all the necessary rights. If Vendela needed to run applications written for NT Workstation 4.0, you would consider making her a Power User. As for choice E, no predefined group named New Users exists. *Review "User rights and built-in local groups."*

4 **C.** The Users and Passwords control panel is intended for adding local user accounts, so choice A is out. Ditto for choice B, hence the word "local" in the program's name. Choices D and E don't exist, and choice F harks back to Windows NT Server 4.0. *Review "Creating Local Users."*

5 **D.** Choices A, B, and C don't exist, nor does choice E (although a policy does exist to enforce a minimum password length). Choice F is not a valid policy, and furthermore, the use of special characters, such as the exclamation point, is encouraged as it makes passwords harder to guess. The complexity requirement means that Tyra can't include her user name or any part of her full name in her password. *Review "Sorry, it's company policy."*

6 **A and C.** You delete Cindy's Security ID and, with it, all of her access tokens for accessing shared resources. Access Control Lists, or ACLs, are associated with objects rather than users. As for choice D, deleting an account doesn't automatically delete a user profile, so you may want to run Windows Explorer to remove `C:\Documents and Settings\Cindy`. *Review "Deleting user accounts."*

7 **A, C,** and **E.** Power Users can install applications, as long as the applications don't install system services or modify operating system files. Power Users cannot take ownership of files; only Administrators can do that. *Review "User rights and built-in local groups."*

8 **C.** Maybe Heather could also trim her fingernails a bit. *Review "Sorry, it's company policy."*

Chapter 11

Access Permissions

● ●

Exam Objectives

▶ Control access to files and folders by using permissions

▶ Optimize access to files and folders

▶ Create and remove shared folders

▶ Control access to shared folders by using permissions

▶ Configure, manage, and implement Internet Information Services (IIS)

▶ Manage and troubleshoot Web server resources

▶ Configure, manage, and troubleshoot a security configuration

▶ Configure, manage, and troubleshoot Internet Explorer security settings

▶ Configure, manage, and troubleshoot local security policy

● ●

*F*ollowing on the discussion of users and groups in Chapter 10 (which I strongly suggest you read before this one), this chapter looks at securing Windows XP systems by posting virtual "Authorized Personnel Only" signs all around the operating system. Share permissions, file-and-folder (NTFS) permissions, computer accounts, Web server permissions, and Local Group Policy are the topics of the day here. This chapter also looks briefly at auditing object access in the file system and the Registry.

You can expect three or more exam questions on the material in this chapter, as access permissions are always a prime concern of corporate network managers (and, therefore, exam question authors).

Quick Assessment

Control access to files and folders by using permissions

1 You can control local or network access to specific files on a Windows XP Professional machine by using _____.

2 On an NTFS disk, the one permission that a folder can have, but a file cannot, is _____.

Optimize access to files and folders

3 When using shared folder permissions or NTFS permissions, ease administrative chores by assigning permissions to _____ rather than to _____.

Create and remove shared folders

4 The fastest way to share a folder is to right-click it and choose _____.

5 To share a file on a Windows XP Professional machine with other users over a local area network connection, you must copy the file to a _____.

6 The three shared folder permissions are _____, _____, and _____.

Configure, manage, and implement Internet Information Services (IIS)

7 To use IIS help, you must enable _____.

Manage and troubleshoot Web server resources

8 Internet Information Server allows you to control user access by IP address as well as by _____.

Configure, manage, and troubleshoot a security configuration

9 To refresh a domain security change, use the command _____.

Configure, manage, and trouble-shoot local security policy

10 The pecking order for Group Policy settings, from weakest to strongest, is _____, _____, _____, and _____.

Answers

1   *NTFS permissions.* See the "NTFS Permissions" section if you missed this one.

2   *List folder contents.* The "NTFS Permissions" section has more.

3   *Groups, users.* See "Who can have access" in this chapter.

4   *Sharing.* The section "Sharing a folder" expands on this subject.

5   *Shared folder.* See "Sharing a folder."

6   *Read, change, full control.* The section "Assigning shared folder permissions" has more.

7   *Indexing service.* See the section titled "Installing Internet Information Services (IIS)."

8   *DNS address.* The "Web Server Access Control" section fills in this and other gaps.

9   *GPUPDATE.* See "Policies and the Local Security Policy console" for more.

10   *Local, site, domain, organizational unit.* "Policies and the Local Security Policy console" contains this invaluable nugget.

Access Permissions Overview

Access. The ability to see, read, touch, change, explore, append, copy, destroy. Too little access and you can't do your work; too much, and you can (accidentally or intentionally) prevent other people from doing theirs. As organizations transfuse more and more of their lifeblood information into computer systems, controlling access becomes a hugely important task — one that Windows XP addresses through many features and facilities.

The subject is so large that it can seem overwhelming, so I begin by breaking it down into more manageable chunks. First, consider access control over network links as opposed to access control on the local PC. Second, consider the main steps in configuring access permissions: which, who, and what. The following sections elaborate.

Network access control versus local access control

One way to make access control more understandable is to divide it out into two major categories: access control over a network connection, and access control for users who log on at the local PC. Here are some facts about controlling access:

✔ On a FAT, FAT32, or NTFS disk, you can control access over a network by using *shared folder permissions* or *share permissions*. This control extends to identifying who may use a shared folder and, in a limited way, what they can do with it. This is folder-level access control only.

✔ On an NTFS disk, you can also control access over a network by using *NTFS permissions*, also known as *file-and-folder permissions*. This control extends to identifying who may use a file or folder and, in a detailed way, what they can do with it. You can control access at the folder level or at the file level.

NTFS permissions apply access control for network users and for local users, and for unshared as well as shared folders.

✔ You can control network access to an Internet or intranet server by using the Internet Information Service (IIS) snap-in to the Computer Management console. This control gives you lots of options for restricting access (see the "Web Server Access Control" section later in this chapter).

✔ On a local PC, you can control access by using NTFS permissions (see previous bullet). Shared folder permissions don't work in this case; they only work over a network connection.

✔ On both networked and local PCs, you can control access by using *policies*. See the "Local Group Policy" section later in this chapter.

Configuring access control

Three considerations exist when you configure access permissions for any given resource on a Windows XP PC. Remember them easily by the key words *which*, *who*, and *what*.

Which resources users can access

The first step in configuring access permissions is to specify which resources users can access. *Resources* typically means files, folders, printers, Registry keys, and Web servers (which you can create in Windows XP Professional through the optional IIS component).

- ✔ To share a resource across a network link, you typically right-click the resource and click a command like "Sharing." The main requirement is that you have the File and Printer Sharing for Microsoft Networks service (which appears as simply "Server" in the Services administrative tool) installed for the network connection. Open the Network Connections folder from the Control Panel menu, right-click the icon for your network adapter, and see whether this service appears in the list and is checked as active (see Figure 11-1). If it doesn't appear, install it by clicking the Install button.

- ✔ You can control access at the folder level only when using the shared folders method on a non-NTFS disk. If you want to share a file, put it into a shared folder. If you want to control access to a file, set access privileges for the folder in which it resides.

- ✔ In the absence of a policy setting to the contrary, you can share folders on removable disc devices, such as CD-ROM drives, as well as hard drives.

- ✔ In the case of local resources, the default behavior is for all files, folders, and printers to be accessible to all users. In the case of network resources, the default behavior is just the opposite, and you must explicitly share resources.

Who can have access

Step 2 in configuring access permissions is to specify who you want to have access to the resource. You may want to share a folder and make it available to certain departments but not others.

- ✔ If you're using shared folder permissions and/or NTFS permissions, you can grant access based on user names and group memberships.

- ✔ Generally, using groups is preferable, because it takes less time and effort to administer group-based security.

- ✔ Certain special groups make granting access permission more convenient.

Figure 11-1:
This
network
connection
has the
sharing
service
installed
and
activated.

What users can do with the resource

You can control which resources become shared, and who gets to use those resources. Even that may be insufficient control, however. In many cases, you want to control *what* those users can do with those resources. The third and (usually) final step is to specify what users can do with the resources that you share.

✔ The specific actions vary depending upon the type of resource. For example, the action "query a Registry key" doesn't really mean anything when you're talking about accessing a printer.

✔ You define which actions are allowed and which aren't by checking and unchecking boxes in an *ACL editor* window where ACL means *Access Control List*. The three types of ACL editors you see are for Registry keys, files/folders (on NTFS disks), and printers.

Shared Folder Permissions

Use *shared folders* to give network users access to folders on your PC. Use *shared folder permissions* to control access to folders on your PC.

Shared folders don't restrict what locally logged-on users can do on your PC.

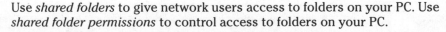

Shared folder permissions are the *only* means available for restricting network user access to a FAT or FAT32 disk. One more reason Microsoft suggests you use NTFS instead.

Sharing a folder

The procedure for sharing a folder is simple. You must be a member of the Administrators or Power Users groups to share folders.

To share folders, you need to install the File and Print Sharing for Microsoft Networks service for at least one network connection in your Network Connections folder.

Open Windows Explorer, right-click the folder you want to share, and choose Sharing and Security from the context menu. In the dialog box shown in Figure 11-2, give the shared folder a share name and (optionally) a comment. You can also reduce the maximum number of simultaneous users from the default maximum of 10. (If you want to share a resource with more than 10 simultaneous users, Microsoft wants you to get Windows 2002 or 2000 Server.)

Figure 11-2:
Sharing a folder.

When you look at the folder in Windows Explorer next time, it will appear with a small hand below it, indicating that it has become a "served" folder.

Shorter share names ensure visibility by downlevel clients. For example, using a maximum of eight characters guarantees that Windows 3.*x* and DOS users can see the share.

Assigning shared folder permissions

Clicking the Permissions button on the Sharing tab brings up the dialog box shown in Figure 11-3, from which you can add and remove groups or users from the permissions list, and change which permissions each group or user has. (You can also add, remove, and change permissions by computer name.)

Figure 11-3: Applying shared folder permissions.

The three sorts of permissions that you can assign for a shared folder are as follows:

- ✔ **Read:** Users can open and read files and file attributes, but not modify them. Users can run programs.

- ✔ **Change:** Users can do everything granted by the Read permission, plus change files and file attributes and delete files and folders.

- ✔ **Full Control:** Users can do everything granted by the Change permission, plus take ownership of files and change permissions.

The default for a newly shared folder is Full Control assigned to the Everyone group. "Everyone" is a predefined group that includes any network user, whether authenticated or not. You cannot use the built-in Authenticated Users group to assign permissions.

Normally, you'd remove Full Control from the Everyone group, then add back the specific groups or users that you want to have access. After you add groups or users, you can modify which of the three permissions each of those groups or users has, by using the Permissions For *<username>* dialog box. For example, in a shared folder that holds programs that users can run, you may want to assign Full Control to the Administrators group only, and Read to the Users group. In a shared folder that contains data, give the Users group the Change permission.

If you plan to combine shared folder permissions with NTFS permissions (see next section), one common practice is to use the default "Full control for Everyone" shared folder permissions and then use the finer-grained NTFS permissions to control access.

NTFS Permissions

NTFS permissions only work on NTFS disks (duh). Further, you can use these permissions to control network access as well as access by local users logged on to the PC hosting the resources. Unlike shared folder permissions, NTFS permissions do not require the presence of the File and Printer Sharing for Microsoft Networks service.

The technique for assigning NTFS permissions is pretty similar to that for assigning shared folder permissions (see previous section), with the exception that you don't have to "share" a folder first. Simply right-click the file or folder you want to apply permissions to, choose Properties, and click the Security tab. (You can now also choose Sharing and Security instead of Properties, although I favor the Properties method because it works the same in Windows 2000 and NT.) You should see something like Figure 11-4.

Figure 11-4:
Applying
NTFS
permissions.

The various sorts of NTFS permissions that you can allow or deny for a file or folder are as follows, roughly in order from least powerful to most powerful:

- ✔ **Read:** Users can open and read files, file attributes, subfolders, and permissions, but not modify them.

- ✔ **Read and Execute:** Read permissions, plus the ability to "traverse" folders you don't have permissions to in order to get to files or folders you do have permissions to.

- ✔ **List Folder Contents:** (Folders only) Pretty self-explanatory.

- ✔ **Write:** Users can modify files and subfolders.

- ✔ **Modify:** The sum of the Read and Execute and Write permissions, plus the ability to delete stuff.

- ✔ **Full Control:** Everything the other permissions allow, plus the ability to change permissions and take ownership of resources.

Permission Conflicts and Inheritance

This section discusses two important nuances of access permissions: conflict resolution and inheritance. (If you haven't read the two previous sections on shared folder permissions and NTFS permissions, please do so first.)

Conflict resolution

Sometimes, permissions that you assign can potentially conflict with each other. For example, you may assign an access permission to one group, but deny it in another group. What about Mary, who belongs to both groups?

Here are the rules for conflict resolution:

- ✔ If Mary belongs to two groups, one of which grants an access permission and the other of which denies it, Mary is denied. *Denials override everything else.* (That's why you should use denials sparingly.) This is true of shared folder permissions and NTFS permissions.

- ✔ If Jill belongs to two groups, one of which grants a shared access permission (such as Read) and the other of which grants an even broader access permission (such as Change), Jill gets the broader permission, which incorporates the narrower permission. In other words, the effective permission is the sum of all the individual permissions. This is true of shared folder permissions and NTFS permissions.

✔ If Tom has an NTFS permission to a file, but has been denied an NTFS permission to the containing folder, then Tom can still access the file, but he has to find it using a complete path name — he can't browse Explorer to find it.

✔ If Jim accesses a file that lives in a folder having shared folder permissions, and furthermore the file lives on an NTFS disk and has NTFS permissions, then Jim needs both the shared folder permission *and* the NTFS permission to access the file. Put another way, when both NTFS and shared folder permissions apply, the effective overall permission is the more restrictive of the two.

The Advanced Security Settings dialog box now has a new tab, "Effective Permissions," that's very helpful when you want to double-check the resultant permissions on a folder when you have multiple groups or multiple access control types (shared folder, NTFS).

Inheritance

When you share a folder that contains other folders, and you assign permissions to the upper-level folder in order to prescribe what users can and can't do with that folder, what permissions does Windows XP associate with the subfolders? Or, with NTFS permissions, when you assign a permission for a folder, does it automatically apply to subfolders?

Here are the rules for permissions inheritance:

✔ The default behavior is for permissions you assign to folders to "propagate downwards" to all contained files and subfolders, including new ones you create later on. This applies for both shared folder permissions and NTFS permissions.

✔ To change the shared folder permissions of a subfolder to be different than its parent, you have to create a separate share name for the subfolder to which you want to grant different access rights. Any such explicit change overrides the inherited rights, in either direction (more rights or fewer rights).

✔ To change the NTFS permissions of a subfolder to be different than its parent, click the Security tab for the subfolder, click the Advanced button, and clear the check box that says Inherit From Parent The Permission Entries That Apply To Child Objects. At that point, you can assign different NTFS permissions, which by default will then flow downward to sub-subfolders and files.

Connecting to Shared Resources

You can connect to shared resources on a Microsoft network in several ways, including the following:

✔ **Mapped drives:** These are network shares that associate with a drive letter. (Create drive mappings by right-clicking a network folder and choosing Map Network Drive. See Figure 11-5.) Creating mapped drives is not the best practice anymore, largely because there are only so many letters in the alphabet. However, many users are accustomed to accessing the network this way — largely because it was the *only* way available in years past.

✔ **Universal Naming Convention (UNC) paths:** These are path names of the format *server**folder**file*, where the *server* part of the name is the computer's legacy (NetBIOS) name.

✔ **My Network Places:** Formerly "Network Neighborhood" (why does Microsoft change these names?), this virtual folder lives on the desktop if you activate the icon via the Display control panel, and lets users connect to any servers on the LAN or WAN — subject to server availability and access restrictions.

 If you can't connect to a shared folder on a remote computer by using a UNC name, your connection's TCP/IP property sheet may not be properly configured to find a WINS server, or no WINS server may be available on the network at that moment. WINS servers let you find a computer on a TCP/IP network by using the NetBIOS computer name.

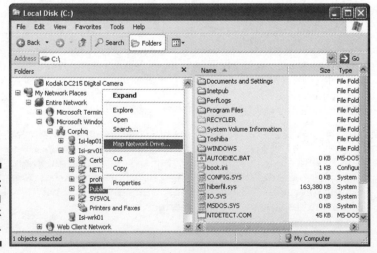

Figure 11-5:
Mapping
a network
drive.

Another type of shared resource is an intranet Web server or a public Internet site, and the exam will expect you to know something about Internet Explorer's security zones. You control these through the Internet Options control panel's Security tab.

You probably won't need to memorize every little detail of Internet security zones. Here are the key points you should try to remember:

✔ A zone is a collection of intranet or Internet sites having the same access control characteristics.

✔ Internet Explorer defines four zones, as follows:

- Local intranet
- Trusted sites
- Internet
- Restricted sites

✔ All sites that you don't explicitly include in one of the other zones fall by default into the Internet zone.

✔ Each zone can have one of four security levels:

- High (excludes potentially damaging content)
- Medium (warns before running potentially damaging content)
- Low (doesn't warn)
- Custom

✔ The default security levels for each zone are:

- Local intranet (medium)
- Trusted sites (low)
- Internet (medium)
- Restricted sites (high)

✔ You can change the security level of a zone, to another of the predefined security levels or to a custom security level.

You can add intranet or Internet sites to the trusted sites, restricted sites, or local intranet categories. Just choose the category by clicking it and then click the Sites button. Type the site's Uniform Resource Locator (URL) in the field labeled "Add this Web site to the zone." (Sites that already live in the specified zone appear in the field labeled "Web sites.")

Web Server Access Control

Windows XP Professional comes with *Internet Information Server (IIS)* Version 5.1, although the software doesn't install with the operating system unless you're upgrading a system with an earlier version of the Microsoft Web server software (that is, an earlier version of IIS, or the even older Personal Web Server or PWS). IIS lets you share resources on your computer with users running Web browsers or FTP utilities.

Installing Internet Information Services (IIS)

Installing IIS is easy, as long as you have the Windows setup files available on CD or network server, but you should heed a few tidbits before you do it:

- ✔ Install IIS onto an NTFS disk for security reasons.

- ✔ Install TCP/IP first, if you haven't already.

- ✔ Don't install IIS onto a PC that's already huffing and puffing under XP's increased processor and memory demands. IIS and its related services are likely to stress out low-end hardware and reduce the performance of foreground applications.

- ✔ Consider setting up a DNS server on your network if you don't already have one. DNS lets users connect to resources via friendly domain names, like *corphq.acme-cognac.com*.

Use the Add/Remove Programs control panel to install IIS. Click the Add/Remove Windows Components button at the left, then check the box labeled Internet Information Services (IIS).

By default, Windows XP installs common files, documentation, FrontPage 2000 server extensions, the IIS snap-in, the SMTP service, and the WWW service. If you also want FTP, or if you want to exclude any of the default components, you have to click the Details tab and deal with the relevant check boxes. Otherwise, click Next, and the wizard does its wizardry, albeit slowly!

After the service is installed, you can begin adding Web pages to your computer, specifically to `C:\INETPUB\WWWROOT`. You should make your home page a file with the name `DEFAULT.HTM`, `DEFAULT.ASP`, or `INDEX.HTM`. (You can change these default settings if you want, but adhering to the traditions usually makes good sense, for support and troubleshooting reasons.)

The IIS help system is separate from the Windows XP help and support system. Access it through your browser by typing **http://localhost/iishelp** into the address bar.

Configuring IIS

You can restrict access to IIS servers by one or more of the following methods, many of which you can reach via the Internet Information Services snap-in to the Computer Management console (part of the default IIS installation):

✔ Don't start all the services. For example, if you don't want FTP, make sure the service is disabled.

✔ Change the service's TCP/IP port. The default port for a Web server is 80, while the default port for an FTP server is 21. Changing these port numbers forces users to append the port number (preceded by a colon) to the URL in order to access the server. If a user doesn't know the port number, then he's not going to gain access.

By the way, another way to open the IIS snap-in is to type **INETMGR** in the Run dialog box. It also shows up in your Administrative Tools folder.

Speaking of ports, you can also restrict access to an IIS server by setting *TCP/IP filtering* via the advanced TCP/IP property sheet for the Local Area Connection. You can set filters so that only specific TCP or UDP ports, or specific IP protocols, are allowed for incoming traffic.

✔ Limit the maximum number of simultaneous connections.

✔ Limit the number of users with operator privileges for the Web server.

✔ Control access to the service's home directory (read, write, browse, and so on). The WWW and FTP services each have their own.

✔ Modify rights associated with the user account that Windows uses for anonymous users, or disable anonymous access entirely.

✔ Grant or deny access for specific IP addresses or address ranges, or for specific DNS addresses.

✔ Enable client certificates for secure authentication.

If you take Microsoft's advice and install IIS onto an NTFS disk, then you have the full range of file-and-folder permissions at your disposal.

Managing IIS

Virtually all management of an IIS Web site occurs through the IIS console in the Administrative Tools folder (and elsewhere, as already noted). Here are some of the tabs in this console and some notes on what they do:

- ✔ **Web Site:** Identify your site with descriptive text, an IP address, and (optionally) a port number that users would have to know if it's different from the default port of 80. Control connection timeouts and logging options here, too.

- ✔ **Home Directory:** Specify where the site's content resides (it can be local, as in the default WWWROOT folder, or remote).

- ✔ **Documents:** Specify the name of the default document that appears when the user navigates to the site root.

- ✔ **Directory Security:** Pay attention to this one: It's where you assign or change the types of access you permit to the Web site. By default, anonymous access is permitted; the account used for such access is **IUSR_<*machinename*>**, which shows up in the Local Users and Groups snap-in of the Computer Management console as the "Internet Guest Account." If you disable anonymous access, then users will have to have a domain account in order to be authenticated to the site.

- ✔ **HTTP Headers:** Here's where you can specify content expiration data for time-sensitive material, and where you can also specify content ratings, so that you can help users shun your site if it contains sex, nudity, violence, or bad language.

- ✔ **Custom Errors:** Here, you can rewrite the error messages that users receive.

- ✔ **Server Extensions:** The main function of this tab is to enable or disable authoring of the Web site via FrontPage.

One tricky point that may arise on the exam is how you connect to one of two or three different Web sites that may be defined on the same PC running IIS *on a single IP address*. The solution is to create *host headers* that allow users (including the user of the PC running IIS) to connect to the different sites using different DNS names. Create host headers by clicking the Advanced button on the IIS console's Web Site tab.

If you want to use IIS help but you get an error message instead, you may need to start the Indexing Service manually. The easiest way to do this is to open the PC's management console (right-click My Computer and choose Manage), expand the Services and Applications node in the left ("tree") pane, right-click Indexing Service, and choose Start.

Sometimes the only way to fix a stubborn IIS problem is to stop and restart the Web site. You can do so within the IIS console by right-clicking the site node in the tree pane and choosing Stop, then going back and choosing Start. In more extreme cases, you can stop and restart the whole IIS service by right-clicking the computer in the tree pane and choosing All Tasks⇨Restart IIS. You can then choose the precise action you want in the ensuing dialog box (for example, whether to stop the service, stop it and restart it, reboot the PC, and so on).

Local Group Policy

The Group Policy feature in Windows XP is, shall we say, a tad bit confusing. However, you have to know about it for the exam — although not in as much detail as for other Windows XP track MCSE tests.

Policies and the Local Security Policy console

If you took my advice and read Chapter 10 before reading this chapter, you've already been introduced to one galaxy of the Group Policy universe, namely, *account policies*. These appear in the Local Security Policy console (in the Administrative Tools control panel folder) and apply to users and groups, which is why I deal with them in Chapter 10.

Another galaxy of settings is in the *local policies* branch of the security settings tree. The general idea is that local policies apply to the machine, rather than to users, although between you and me, this distinction doesn't stand up under critical scrutiny. Local policies consist of *audit policies* (which I discuss later in the "Auditing Object Access" section), *user rights assignment* (which I mention in Chapter 10), and *security options*, a mishmash of access- and security-related settings. Figure 11-6 shows a flock of policies in the security options node.

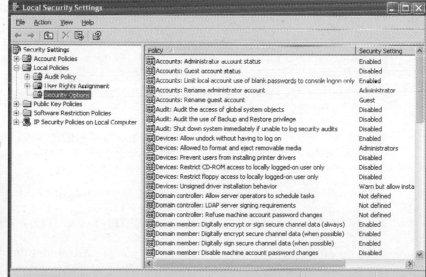

Figure 11-6:
Set security options through the Local Security Policy console.

After you set them, these policies apply to the local computer *assuming it's not participating in an Active Directory network*. If the computer is part of an AD network, any local policies you set through the Local Security Policy console may be overridden by higher-level policies set by a network administrator. The order of precedence, from weakest to strongest, is local; site; domain; and organizational unit. Put differently, if you set a local policy, it goes into effect as long as no contradictory setting for that policy has been made on a Windows 2000 or 2002 Server at a site, domain, or organizational unit level.

The MCSE exams are likely to present a scenario in which a policy change is made on a domain controller, but does not immediately reflect on client computers. Policies refresh, by default, at 90 minute intervals, but you can perform an immediate policy refresh with the GPUPDATE command-line tool. Both computer and user settings are refreshed by default, but you can use the /TARGET qualifier to specify just one or the other. (Note that some policy changes, such as folder redirection, don't occur until you log off and back on, and still other changes require a full restart.)

A few of the access-related policies of interest in the security options node are as follows:

- ✔ Accounts: Guest Account Status (this is either enabled or disabled, disabled being the default)
- ✔ Devices: Prevent Users from Installing Printer Drivers
- ✔ Devices: Restrict CD-ROM Access To Locally Logged-On User Only (and there's another similar policy for floppy drives)
- ✔ Interactive Logon: Do Not Require CTRL-ALT-DEL (for domain members, set at domain level only)
- ✔ Network Security: LAN Manager Authentication Level (this setting can affect your ability to communicate with NT 4.0 servers prior to service pack 4, which don't support NTLMv2 authentication)
- ✔ Recovery Console: Allow Automatic Administrative Logon (bypasses the logon requirement for Recovery Console)

If a policy setting conflicts with a *user right* that you would normally have, for example, by virtue of belonging to a group such as Power Users, the policy setting wins. (See Chapter 10 for more on user rights.)

Policies and the Local Group Policy console

If you were hoping that the Local Security Policy console contained all the policy settings you may need to understand for the exam, you may be right, but you probably aren't. The Local Security Policy console only shows a fairly small subset of the entire policy cornucopia. In order to see the whole banana, you need to create your own custom Microsoft Management Console. Lab 11-1 shows you how.

Lab 11-1   Creating a Group Policy Console

1. **Choose Start⇨Run, type MMC in the dialog box, and click OK.**

   This runs the Microsoft Management Console "host" program, MMC.EXE.

2. **Choose File⇨Add/Remove Snap-In.**

3. **Click the Add button.**

   You should see a list of snap-ins available on your PC, as shown in Figure 11-7.

Figure 11-7:
Build your own custom management console with one or more snap-ins.

4. **Click Group Policy and then click Add.**

5. **In the Select Group Policy Object dialog box, click Finish.**

   For the purposes of viewing and editing policies on the local PC, the local group policy object (default) is the one you want.

6. **Click Close and OK to close the two dialog boxes.**

   You should see something like Figure 11-8. The "Console1" title reflects the fact that you haven't saved your console yet.

7. **Choose File⇨Save and give your new custom console a name ("Local Group Policy" is a good choice).**

   The default save location is the Administrative Tools folder.

To run the new console, choose Start➪All Programs➪Administrative Tools➪Local Group Policy. (I suggest creating a shortcut to the MSC file in the Administrative Tools folder in the Control Panel, too. Unfortunately, Windows doesn't automatically synchronize these two locations.)

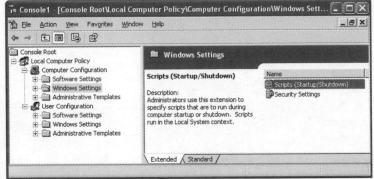

Figure 11-8: A custom console for the Local Group Policy snap-in.

As you expand the nodes in the left window pane, notice that the top-level categories pertain to the machine and to the user, respectively. Windows XP applies machine-specific policies before the network user even logs on; the user-specific policies apply after logon. This setup is a primary reason that computers in a Windows XP/2000 network have their own unique account IDs — Windows must have some way of assigning machine-specific policies to each computer as it connects to the network. This requirement for each computer to have a unique computer account ID is the rationale behind utilities like SysPrep (see Chapter 4).

Note that in each of the two main categories exists a subcategory called "Administrative Templates." These are settings contained in *.ADM files that modify the local Registry. You find a variety of miscellaneous settings under Administrative Templates, and more nodes appear here as you add applications that come with their own *.ADM files.

Just for fun, expand the node *Local Computer Policy\Computer Configuration\ Windows Settings\Security Settings*. Look familiar? If not, open up the Local Security Policy console in your Administrative Tools folder.

Working with Security Templates

Policies aren't the only way to apply security settings in a Windows XP environment. Consider, for example, a small organization with a dozen or so standalone PCs. You don't have a domain-based network, so the advantage that the Group Policy tools confer in terms of easing administration chores doesn't apply to your situation. You need to apply security to the workstations, but you don't look forward to going around from one computer to the next, firing up the Local Group Policy or Local Security Policy consoles, and making a lot of settings one by one.

Security templates are convenient just for such a situation. They're files with the suffix INF that contain a whole slew of security settings which you can apply to a computer in one fell swoop. These settings include account policies, local policies, group membership, registry key security, file system access controls, and configuration of operating system services. Microsoft supplies a number of pre-assembled templates that live in C:\WINDOWS\ SECURITY\TEMPLATES.

Although security templates come in handy when you don't have a domain-based network, you can certainly use them in a network environment, too. For example, you can apply a security template to a Group Policy object (GPO), thereby applying all the individual security settings in the template to a domain or organizational unit. (The command is Import Policy on the context menu of the policy object's Security Settings node.)

Security template snap-ins

Microsoft figures that most Windows XP Professional users won't need to muck around with security templates, so if you want to use them, you have a bit of customizing to do. Lab 11-2 takes you through the process of creating a custom management console containing the two snap-ins that are relevant to security templates: *Security Templates* and *Security Configuration and Analysis*.

Lab 11-2   Building a Security Templates Console

1. Choose Start⇨Run, type MMC in the dialog box, and click OK.

2. Choose File⇨Add/Remove Snap-In.

3. Click the Add button.

4. Click Security Templates and then click Add.

5. Click Security Configuration and Analysis and then click Add.

6. In the Select Group Policy Object dialog box, click Finish.

7. Click Close and OK to close the two dialog boxes.

8. Choose File⇨Save and give your new custom console a name ("Security Templates" is a good choice).

   The default save location is the Administrative Tools folder.

The Security Templates snap-in

The job of the Security Templates snap-in is to add and edit INF security templates (see Figure 11-9). This is a great place to view the settings in an organized, hierarchical structure.

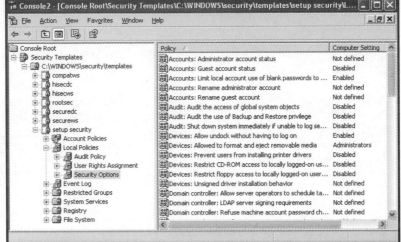

Figure 11-9:
Divine the
meaning of
inscrutable
INF files
here.

You should memorize the meaning of the various predefined templates:

- **SETUP SECURITY** is the default template containing security settings applied during setup. It's for disaster recovery purposes only and shouldn't be applied via Group Policy.

- **COMPATWS** relaxes access controls for the Users group and is therefore well suited for workstations that need compatibility with older applications, such as those written for Windows NT 4.0. Don't apply this template to a domain controller. (Make *sure* you understand this one for the exam!)

- **HISECDC** is for a maximum-security domain controller.

- **HISECWS** is for a maximum-security workstation. Power Users have more restrictions than usual.

- **SECUREDC** is for a high-security domain controller.

- **SECUREWS** is for a high-security workstation.

The Security Configuration and Analysis snap-in

The Security Configuration and Analysis snap-in has two jobs: first, to compare the PC's current configuration against a security template, and second, to apply a template to a local PC (or Group Policy object, in a networked environment).

To compare the PC's current configuration against a security template, right-click the Security Configuration and Analysis node in the console's tree pane and choose Open Database. If this is a new database, Windows prompts you to specify a security template to load into the database. For example, if you want to see how your system stacks up against a secure workstation configuration, you'd choose SECUREWS.

After you open the database, perform the analysis by right-clicking Security Configuration and Analysis and choosing Analyze Computer Now. When the utility finishes its evaluation, it presents a results display. A green check mark by a setting means that your PC's setting matches the one in the database; a red "X" means that your PC is less secure than the setting in the database would make it.

SECEDIT

Microsoft supplies a command-line tool, SECEDIT.EXE, which performs most of the same tasks that the console snap-ins perform, but from a batch file or script — handy if you want to put a SECEDIT command into a system-wide logon script, for example. With SECEDIT, you can create templates, apply templates, and analyze security.

The exam is likely to quiz your knowledge of the various SECEDIT command qualifiers, which include the following:

- ✔ **/analyze** analyzes the current system's security, and uses the /DB and /CFG parameters.
- ✔ **/configure** configures the current system's security, and uses the /DB and /CFG parameters.
- ✔ **/export** exports a template from a security database to an INF template file, and uses the /DB and /CFG parameters.
- ✔ **/DB** *<filename>* specifies the database containing a stored configuration against which the analysis will be made (with the /analyze option) or into which a template will be imported (with the /configure option).
- ✔ **/CFG** *<filename>* specifies the path to the security template that SECEDIT will use to analyze or configure the database specified in /DB.
- ✔ **/validate** *<filename>* checks the syntax of a security template.

Auditing Object Access

Object access auditing means that Windows XP can monitor accesses (both successful and unsuccessful) to files, folders, the Registry, and printers, and record those accesses in the Security event log (which you can view with the

Event Viewer snap-in to the Computer Management console). The details that Windows XP records include the action performed, who performed it, when it occurred, and whether it succeeded or failed.

If you're having some trouble with file corruption, file system performance, Registry errors, or potential cybervandalism, object access auditing may help you figure out who's trying to gain access to what. (For logon auditing, please see Chapter 10's section entitled "Auditing User Activities.")

Activating object access auditing

Auditing is always off by default because of its system overhead. To activate object access auditing on your PC, open the Local Security Policy console (it's in the Administrative Tools folder of Control Panel). In the left pane, under Local Policies, click Audit Policy. All the various quantities that you can audit appear in the right pane. Double-click Audit Object Access (or, alternatively, single-click it and choose Action⇨Security) and choose whether you want to track successful events, unsuccessful ones, or both. (Careful here — file system reads occur frequently, and can easily swamp the event log, creating both disk space and performance problems for your system.) Restart the machine to make your changes take effect.

Auditing *successful* actions is a good way to do some capacity planning and performance analysis. Auditing *failed* actions is a good way to zero in on potential security problems.

Choosing what to audit

Activating object auditing simply turns the feature "on" — you must tell Windows XP which specific objects you want it to audit.

Use Windows Explorer to identify files and folders to audit. Use REGEDIT to identify Registry keys to audit.

File and folder auditing

On an NTFS volume, Windows XP can audit access to files and folders. To tell Windows XP which ones to track, simply open Windows Explorer (for example, by right-clicking My Computer and choosing Explore), right-click the file or folder to audit, and choose Properties. Then, click the Security tab and the Advanced button. Finally, click the Auditing tab to display a dialog box that looks like the one in Figure 11-10.

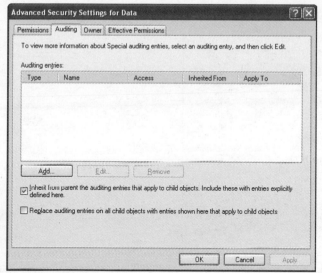

Figure 11-10:
Set auditing
on an NTFS
folder.

Note the two check boxes at the bottom of the Auditing dialog box:

✓ **Inherit from parent the auditing entries that apply to child objects.** The default behavior is for auditing settings to propagate downward in the file structure; that is, if you enable auditing for a folder, you automatically enable auditing for all subfolders contained therein. Clearing this check box defeats this inherited behavior for the selected folder.

✓ **Replace auditing entries on all child objects with entries shown here that apply to child objects.** This clears any pre-existing auditing settings on any subfolders of the current folder and sets them to inherit the settings you make on the folder.

From the Auditing tab, simply click the Add button and specify whose actions you want to audit. You can choose from local users, local groups, domain users, and domain groups. After you choose who, Windows prompts you to choose what, by displaying the ACL editor ("Auditing Entry"), shown in Figure 11-11. Enable the relevant check boxes and click OK, OK, OK.

Registry auditing

Registry auditing is really similar to file-and-folder auditing. Run REGEDIT.EXE and navigate to the Registry key of interest. Right-click it and choose Permissions. Choose the Advanced button and click the Auditing tab, just as in the preceding section. The "who" part works just the same; the "what" part looks a bit different, because Registry accesses don't work exactly like file and folder accesses.

Figure 11-11:
Tell
Windows
what file
system
actions to
track.

Printer auditing

The procedure is similar for setting printer auditing options. Open the printer's property sheet (Start⇨Printers and Faxes, right-click the printer icon, and choose Properties). Then click the Security tab and the Advanced button. Finally, click the Auditing tab.

Prep Test

1 Which of the following types of permissions can you assign to file system directories for local users of a Windows XP Professional computer? The local hard disk is formatted with the FAT32 file system as a basic disk.

    A ○ Shared folder permissions

    B ○ Shared printer permissions

    C ○ File-and-folder permissions

    D ○ Access Control Lists

    E ○ None of the above

2 Alicia comes to you with a suspicion that someone is using her files and damaging them in the process. You decide to enable auditing so that you can confirm or dismiss her suspicion. What tool would you use to designate specific folders for auditing? (Choose the best answer.)

    A ○ Local Group Policy

    B ○ REGEDT32

    C ○ Local Security Policy

    D ○ Windows Explorer

    E ○ Disk Management

3 Robin is an employee at your software company. She has happily run a particular application for a couple of years now as a Windows NT Workstation 4.0 user. You upgrade her system to Windows XP Professional, and her application no longer works. Which of the following security templates might solve Robin's problem? (Choose the best answer.)

    A ○ COMPATWS.INF

    B ○ BASICWS.INF

    C ○ BASICWK.INF

    D ○ SECUREDC.INF

4 You're running Windows XP Professional. You try connecting to a shared folder on another Windows XP Professional computer by creating a desktop shortcut pointing to the shared folder. You use the Universal Naming Convention. You verify that the computer name and folder name you're using are correct, and you also verify that the remote computer is powered on. However, you still can't get the shortcut icon to work. You can successfully PING the remote computer using its IP address. What setting on your system should you check?

    A ○ Capitalization of the UNC path

    B ○ Your PC's DNS server address setting

    C ○ Your PC's WINS server address setting

    D ○ Your PC's NetBIOS name

5 Someone has disabled the Ctrl+Alt+Del requirement for logon on a standalone Windows XP Professional computer. You want to restore that requirement. How would you do so? (Choose all that apply.)

A ❏ Right-click My Computer, choose Manage, click the Local Security Policy node, navigate to Security Settings, and clear the policy named Disable Ctrl+Alt+Del Requirement for Logon.

B ❏ Right-click My Computer, choose Manage, click the Local Security Policy node, navigate to Account Settings, and check the policy named Disable Ctrl+Alt+Del Requirement for Logon.

C ❏ Choose Start➪Run and type **GPEDIT.MSC**. Navigate to the Security Policy node and clear the policy named Interactive Logon: Do Not Require CTRL-ALT-DEL.

D ❏ Open the Administrative Tools folder and double-click Local Security Policy. Navigate to the Security Policy node and clear the policy named Interactive Logon: Do Not Require CTRL-ALT-DEL.

6 Jim has Full Control access to a shared folder on Jill's machine. Jim also belongs to a group for which the Full Control NTFS permission has been denied on that same shared folder. What effective permissions does Jim have on the folder?

A ○ Full Control

B ○ Read

C ○ Modify

D ○ None

7 You decide to restrict access to your Windows XP Web server by excluding all traffic except Web traffic and all protocols except ICMP. What TCP/IP port number would you permit using packet filtering? (Choose the best answer.)

A ○ 21

B ○ 23

C ○ 40

D ○ 60

E ○ 80

8 The NTFS "Modify" permission includes which of the following permissions? (Choose all that apply.)

A ❏ Read

B ❏ Write

C ❏ Execute

D ❏ Take Ownership

Answers

1 **E.** Choice A is wrong because shared folder permissions only work across the network, and the question posits local users. Choice B is wrong because the question asks about file system directories, not printers (read those questions carefully). Choice C, file-and-folder permissions, is another name for NTFS permissions and those aren't available on a FAT32 disk. Access Control Lists are associated with NTFS permissions, ruling out choice D. *Review "Access Permissions Overview."*

2 **D.** Use Windows Explorer. The procedure is to right-click the folder on which you want to enable auditing; choose Properties; and click the Security tab. Then, click Advanced and click the Auditing tab. As for choice B, that program doesn't even exist anymore in Windows XP. *Review "File and folder auditing."*

3 **A.** In fact, that's the reason for the COMPATWS template's existence. It relaxes access controls for the Users group and permits members of that group to run applications designed for Windows NT 4.0. As for choices B and C, careful, these templates come with Windows 2000 but not Windows XP! *Review "The Security Templates snap-in."*

4 **C.** WINS is responsible for mapping the NetBIOS name that you use in a UNC path with the IP address of the remote computer. Therefore, if your computer has an incorrect or missing WINS server address in its TCP/IP property sheet, you can't use NetBIOS names (computer names) to contact machines on a different physical subnet. *Review "Connecting to Shared Resources."*

5 **C and D.** You can't change policy settings from the Computer Management console, logical though that may seem. You can get to the local security policies with GPEDIT.MSC or the Local Security Policy console. *Review "Policies and the Local Group Policy console."*

6 **D.** A denial overrides everything else. A denial on the Full Control permission means Jim can't do jack with Jill's folder. Incidentally, the new "Effective Permissions" tab of the Advanced Security Settings dialog box is a great way to familiarize yourself with these sorts of scenarios. *Review "Permission Conflicts and Inheritance."*

7 **E.** Web traffic uses TCP port 80. *Review "Web Server Access Control."*

8 **A, B,** and **C.** Know your NTFS permissions for the exam. *Review "NTFS Permissions."*

Chapter 12

IntelliMirror and Roaming Access

● ●

Exam Objectives

▶ Configure and manage user profiles

▶ Manage and troubleshoot the use and synchronization of offline files

▶ Manage applications by using Windows Installer packages

● ●

*I*ntelliMirror is a semi-catchy name for the Windows XP version of some technologies that have actually been kicking around on the Windows platform for a few years now. These technologies include *user profiles, offline files,* and the *Add/Remove Programs Wizard* (as enhanced by Windows Installer technology). The common denominator among these technologies, and the reason Microsoft gives them a unifying buzzword, is that they enable users to move from one computer to another with less bother.

The Windows 2002/2000 Server exams address certain aspects of IntelliMirror — specifically, publishing and assigning applications in the Active Directory hierarchy — that the Windows XP Professional exam does not. Even so, the three aspects of IntelliMirror that I address in this chapter are likely candidates for Exam #70-270 because they're new (sort of) and they make users' lives easier (sometimes).

Quick Assessment

Configure and manage user profiles

1 The Registry component of user profiles exists in two files, _____ and _____.

2 Two items not in the Registry that also make up a user's profile are _____ and _____.

3 You can control what parts of a user's profile roam the network by modifying _____.

4 Delete, copy, and change user profiles by using the _____ tab of the System control panel.

Manage and troubleshoot the use and synchronization of offline files

5 When working with an offline file, the file appears to be in the same network _____ and it has the same _____.

6 What does Microsoft call the kind of logoff synchronization in which Windows XP doesn't guarantee that your local copy of offline files is up-to-date? _____

7 (True/False) Windows XP offline files work with Novell servers if they're running NetWare version 4.0 or greater.

8 The default idle time Windows XP waits before starting synchronization is _____ minutes of inactivity.

Install applications by using Windows Installer packages

9 As opposed to INF files, Windows Installer packages use _____ files.

10 The executable program that installs, repairs, and removes Windows Installer packages is _____.

Answers

1 *NTUSER.DAT, USRCLASS.DAT.* If you just got the first one right, don't feel bad; I pick nits when it comes to the Registry. See the "File structure" section.

2 *Network connections, printers, My Documents folder, Start menu shortcuts, Favorites, History.* If you didn't choose two of these, read "User Profiles" in this chapter.

3 *Group policies.* The section "What roams, what doesn't" explains.

4 *Advanced.* Why Microsoft felt the need to move this from its sensible location in Windows 2000 is beyond me. See "Managing profiles" if you missed this answer.

5 *Location, access restrictions.* If you said "location, name" you would also be correct, just less of a show-off. See "The offline concept" for explanations.

6 *Quick.* See the section "Client-side setup."

7 *False.* Offline files don't work with NetWare servers at all; "Offline in practice: A mixed blessing" mentions other limitations.

8 *15.* That's the computer's inactivity, by the way, not yours. See the "Client-side setup" section for this tidbit.

9 *MSI.* Stands for Microsoft Software Installer; see "Windows Installer Service" for more.

10 *MSIEXEC.EXE.* Again, "Windows Installer Service" has this detail plus a few others you should know.

Registry 101

To really understand how user profiles work (and group policies, for that matter), you should understand at least the most basic basics of the Registry. The Registry is the central store of information that Windows XP and Windows XP programs use to track all the software and hardware on the machine, including details about how that software and hardware are configured.

The Registry isn't the brain of Windows XP, but it's a lot like its spine: that is, where most of the nerve endings come together. And, like your spine, the Registry is vitally important. Windows XP can't even roll out of bed without the clues that Microsoft has tucked away inside the Registry. After startup, Windows XP, and the programs you run with it, use the Registry many thousands of times in a typical computing session — to find necessary files, recall user preferences, enforce security restrictions, and perform hundreds of other actions.

If something goes wrong with your Registry, you may not be able to use your computer until you fix it. If something goes wrong with a program you're running, or with Windows XP itself, you may need to use the Registry to repair it. If a hacker knows more about the Registry than you do, you could be at risk for some of the more insidious viruses around, like the "I Love You" bug that kissed tens of millions of PCs in May 2000.

Microsoft is moving away from the concept of having the Registry contain every possible configuration setting. Windows 2002 and 2000 Server use a separate database, *Active Directory*, which maintains information about how the network is organized. Most of the low-level details about network nuts and bolts remain in the Registry, though.

The Windows XP Registry shares many similarities with NT 4.0, which incidentally is why the upgrade path from NT 4.0 or Windows 2000 is much smoother than from Windows Me or 98.

The exam is sure to include one or two questions about the Registry. Also be aware that you'll spend more time mucking about with the Registry in the real world than the exam leads you to believe.

File structure

The Registry appears as a single, unified database when you view it with the new, unified Registry Editor (REGEDIT.EXE), but it doesn't reside in a single file on disk. Most of the Registry's several files live in `C:\WINDOWS\SYSTEM32\CONFIG`, but some live in the profile folders under `C:\Documents and Settings`.

Why not just have one big meaty file with everything in it? Although the "one monster file" design has a certain aesthetic appeal, a few very good reasons exist for separating the Registry into multiple files:

- Different users can create and see different user-specific settings (NTUSER.DAT, USRCLASS.DAT) based on their logon names, but all users on a machine can share the same machine-specific settings.

- On a network, the user-specific settings (NTUSER.DAT, USRCLASS.DAT) can live on a network server and "follow a user around" as he or she logs onto different machines.

- You can maintain a separate group of default settings (the NTUSER.DAT that lives in the `Default User` profile folder) for any new user who logs on, while keeping every existing users' settings intact.

- The security-related parts of the Registry (SECURITY and SAM) can be restricted from view and protected against modification.

- The machine-specific parts of the Registry (HARDWARE, SOFTWARE, SYSTEM) stay with the machine.

- If something goes haywire, you may be able to restore part of the Registry from an earlier backup, instead of restoring all of it. The benefit of such a "surgical restore" is that you may lose less work.

Database structure

When you view or edit the Registry with REGEDIT.EXE, you see a hierarchical database structure in the left window pane, as shown in Figure 12-1. This structure expands before your eyes when you click the little plus signs, just as a directory tree does in Windows Explorer. Also, as in Explorer, the right window pane displays the contents of whatever item you highlight in the left pane.

Figure 12-1: Primary Registry branches, or "root keys."

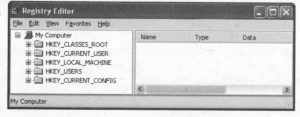

Root keys

The five so-called *root keys* are the top-level organizational structures in the Registry. The display in Figure 12-1 is a little misleading in that of the five root keys, three are aliases, or pointers, to subkeys of the two "real" root keys.

For example, *HKEY_CURRENT_USER* (abbreviated HKCU) contains all the user-specific Registry settings for the currently logged-on user. Saying (and writing) *HKCU* is easier than figuring out the current user's Security ID and specifying a key such as *HKU\S-1-5-21-448539723-842925246-2089417427-500* (where HKU is short for *HKEY_USERS*). Also, Windows 9*x* programs don't know about Security IDs, and therefore need to see *HKCU* to run under Windows XP.

Here's another example. You often spend time in *HKEY_CLASSES_ROOT* (abbreviated *HKCR*) because it contains information about how different file types behave. Saying (and writing) *HKCR* is easier than *HKLM\SOFTWARE\Classes* (where *HKLM* is short for *HKEY_LOCAL_MACHINE*). The two locations contain pretty much the same information, though. Check it out yourself.

HKCR and *HKLM\SOFTWARE\Classes* contain *pretty much* the same information because *HKCR* now contains a merged view of information in *HKLM\SOFTWARE\Classes* and *HKCU\Software\Classes*. Therefore, HKCR is actually an alias for the combination of those two keys, when in prior versions of Windows it was an alias for the *HKLM* key only.

HKCC, HKCR, and *HKCU* just point to other places in *HKLM* and *HKU*. The "core" branches *HKLM* and *HKU* actually contain the entire Registry contents. (For the curious, *HKLM* corresponds to the physical files SAM, SECURITY, SOFTWARE, and SYSTEM, while *HKU* corresponds to the physical files NTUSER.DAT, USRCLASS.DAT, and DEFAULT.)

Keys and values

Beneath the five root keys, you find keys and values.

- ✔ *Keys* are just named containers that can contain other keys, values, or both. The Registry Editor displays keys as folder icons in the left window pane. Sometimes, the exam refers to top-level Registry branches as "keys," and that's technically what they are, so don't be confused.

- ✔ A value is a "leaf" element in the Registry database tree; that is, it can't contain anything else, but rather is an endpoint of a specific Registry path.

A typical value has both a name and some data associated with it. The name and data columns appear in the right pane of the Registry Editor. Values usually take one of three forms, determined by the type of data they contain:

- ✔ A *string* value can contain letters and numbers, and is by far the most commonly encountered value type.

- ✔ A *binary* value is numeric and consists of a series of two-digit, one-byte hexadecimal (that is, base 16) numbers separated by spaces.

- ✔ A *DWORD* value is a four-byte (or "double word") binary value, that appears in REGEDIT as "0x" plus eight hexadecimal bytes with no spaces.

Like the NT and Windows 2000 Registries, the Windows XP Registry also permits *multi-string* values (that basically contain a list of strings) and *expandable-string* values (that use replaceable parameters like *%systemroot%*). However, you don't see these often.

Do not waste time memorizing particular Registry settings. If you can remember the names and primary functions of the five main branches, and if you understand the differences between branches, keys, and values, you're good to go.

A unified editing tool

Windows XP, unlike Windows 2000, provides a single, unified Registry Editor that incorporates the features of the NT tool, REGEDT32, into the more user-friendly REGEDIT, which descends from the Windows 9*x* product line. Specifically, the old REGEDT32's ability to set permissions on Registry keys, and its ability to deal with NT-platform data types such as multi-string values, are now part of the new REGEDIT.

Don't use REGEDIT unless no other way exists for you to make the setting you need. The Windows XP control panels, consoles, and property sheets are always preferable to directly editing the Registry, for two main reasons:

✔ Unbelievably, the Registry Editor still has no "undo" feature.

✔ Changes you make in the Registry Editor take effect immediately, unlike the control panels and property sheets, which let you think about your change (and maybe reverse it!) before clicking OK or Apply.

If you want more information about the Registry and what you can do with it, check out *Windows 2000 Registry For Dummies* by yours truly (published by Hungry Minds, Inc.). As you would expect, given that Windows XP is really "Windows 2000.1," the Windows 2000 Registry is nearly identical to the Windows XP Registry, with the new unified REGEDIT being the major difference between the operating systems.

User Profiles

User profiles in Windows XP still do what they've always done on the Windows 9*x* and NT platforms. They let different users maintain their own individual settings and preferences — desktop icons, Start menu, application settings, network connections, and so on. User profiles make it possible for different users to share the same computer while each keeps his own settings; profiles also enable a user to log on to different computers and still see his usual desktop environment.

You can think of a user profile as containing two big categories of information: Registry stuff and non-Registry stuff.

- **Registry stuff:** This is basically everything in the *HKCU* branch of the Registry (Windows customizations, such as Control Panel settings; Explorer viewing options; printer connections; Dial-Up Networking connections; command prompt window settings; and any user-specific settings for Windows applications).

  Those settings include stuff like whether your word processor checks your spelling as you type, whether you want your spreadsheets to print with gridlines, and so on.

- **Non-Registry stuff:** This is everything in the subfolders under `C:\Documents and Settings\<username>`. (If you upgraded from Windows NT 4.0, your profile folders live in `C:\WINNT\PROFILES`.) You mostly see shortcuts in these folders, but some contain actual data files, most notably the My Documents folder. Non-Registry stuff includes the recently used documents list, user-specific Start menu shortcuts, Internet Explorer cookies, contents of the Network Neighborhood and Printers folders, lists of favorite documents or Web sites, history lists, and so on.

Every time you add a user to a Windows XP system, Windows XP creates these resources:

- Subdirectory under `C:\Documents and Settings`.
- NTUSER.DAT file in the new subdirectory.

  The file is based on the default user information in `C:\Documents and Settings\Default User\NTUSER.DAT`.

- USRCLASS.DAT file.

  The file is buried in `C:\Documents and Settings\<username>\Local Settings\Application Data\Microsoft\Windows`. This file contains any per-user file type association information, such as the fact that Emily wants to run Photoshop rather than Internet Explorer when she opens a JPG file.

The virtual folder *Desktop\My Documents* is actually an alias, pointing to *C:\Documents and Settings\<username>\My Documents* where *<username>* is the name of the currently logged-on user. Therefore, the "My Documents" folder changes if a user logs off the system and logs on again using a different account. Similarly, the virtual folder *Desktop\My Documents\My Pictures* is an alias pointing to *C:\Documents and Settings\<username>\My Documents\My Pictures*. Certain applications from Microsoft and other vendors use this virtual folder as the default save directory for image files.

You should see an "All Users" folder in the main profile folder of your machine. The contents of this folder — usually some Start menu shortcuts and other scattered miscellany — *combine* with the contents of a user's individual profile folders to create the actual user profile. So, for example, the actual Start menu that you see is really the sum of all the shortcuts in `C:\Documents and Settings\<username>\Start Menu`, plus all the "community" shortcuts in `C:\Documents and Settings\All Users\Start Menu`. Only administrators can add, change, or delete contents of the All Users folder.

You may see an exam question scenario in which a PC's Administrator configures the desktop a certain way (Start menu options, desktop shortcuts, and so on), but another user (who may have Administrator privileges but has a different account) logs on later and doesn't see those configured changes. The reason, as you now know, is that each user has a separate profile. You can solve the problem by copying the Administrator's profile into the other user's profile folder via the System control panel's Advanced tab.

Roaming versus local profiles

User profiles have two flavors:

- Local
- Roaming

The test expects you to understand both.

Local profiles

Local profiles are user profiles that live on a particular PC, as opposed to a network location. To clarify, a *local* profile doesn't mean that the user *account* must be on a standalone, non-networked PC. You can have a local profile for a network user account as well as for a standalone user account.

A local profile stays on the local hard drive of a single PC. If you take a local profile for a network user account and then give it a new home so that it lives on the network instead of solely on the local hard drive, it then becomes a "roaming" profile, as I describe in the next section.

With Windows XP, unlike Windows 95/98, you don't have to take a separate step to activate user profiles; the feature is already "on," you just have to create the user accounts and log on with them. Also unlike Windows 9*x*, you can't necessarily just log on with a new user name and have Windows XP create an account for you automatically. You have to create the account ahead of time and then log on.

Which tool you must use and which procedure you must follow to create a local profile depends on your circumstances, as follows:

- ✔ On a machine that's *not* on a network domain, you have two options:
  - Fire up the User Accounts control panel.
  - Run the Computer Management console from the Administrative Tools control panel and select the Local Users and Groups snap-in.

- ✔ On a machine that *is* on a network domain where you want to add a user who's already defined on the domain, you have three choices:
  - Run the User Accounts control panel.
  - Start the Local Users and Groups snap-in to the Computer Management console.
  - Simply log on to Windows XP Professional as that user.

- ✔ On a machine that *is* on a network domain where you want to add a local (non-domain) user, run the User Accounts control panel and use the Advanced tab.

To run the User Accounts control panel or the Computer Management snap-in, you must log on as Administrator. Windows XP cares about security, so only an Administrator can create a new user account.

Roamin' profiles (or, "Caesar, who broke your nose?")

Creating a roaming profile allows a user to log on to any PC on the domain and have a server download his settings to that PC immediately after logon. So the procedure for creating a roaming profile is to create a folder on the server for profile data; point the user's account to that folder; and (optionally) load that folder with customized profile information that Windows XP will download the next time the user logs on at any PC.

Lab 12-1 presents more detailed steps for creating a roaming profile (this example assumes the user's domain account already exists):

Lab 12-1	Creating a Roaming User Profile

1. **Log on to a Windows 2002 or 2000 Server domain controller as Administrator.**

2. **Using Windows Explorer, create a new profiles folder on the server (such as** `C:\PROFILES`**).**

3. **Right-click the new folder, choose Sharing, share the folder as "PROFILES," and give the Everyone group the Full Control permission.**

   Each user's individual profile folder will live beneath the main `C:\PROFILES` folder.

4. **Run the Active Directory Users and Computers plug-in from the Control Panel's Administrative Tools folder.**

5. **Navigate to the user's icon, right-click it, and choose Properties.**

6. **On the Profiles tab, type the path to the user's profile folder, such as** \\server1\profiles\christine.

7. **Optionally, run the System control panel, click User Profiles, and copy a template profile to the user's profile folder to "preload" it.**

On a networked PC with roaming profiles enabled, Windows XP maintains a user-specific copy of NTUSER.DAT under `C:\Documents and Settings\` `<username>` just as it does with local profiles, but Windows XP keeps a copy on the network, too.

Here's what happens on the network:

1. When you log on, Windows XP checks for an NTUSER.DAT file on your local hard drive in `C:\Documents and Settings\<username>`, and it also checks for an NTUSER.DAT file in the user's profile directory on the server.

2. If either copy of NTUSER.DAT is newer than the other, Windows XP updates the older version and then starts up. Ditto with USRCLASS.DAT.

Windows XP performs a similar comparison with all the non-Registry user profile stuff, too, including the My Documents and My Pictures folders. If a file hasn't changed, Windows XP doesn't download it — and that's a good thing, because otherwise network performance would really suffer from all the unnecessary file transfers.

When you log off, Windows XP copies any changed profile settings back to your profile folder on the network, so the latest settings and documents are available next time you log on — wherever you log on.

What roams, what doesn't

By default, the folders History, Local Settings, Temp, and Temporary Internet Files do not "roam" with the user. They typically contain too much stuff; having these files roam would bog down the network. You can specify additional files that you'd like to exclude from the roaming profile. Run the Group Policy utility and modify the Exclude Directories in Roaming Profile policy. You can find it under User Configuration\Administrative Templates\ System\ Logon-Logoff. This policy modifies the text file `C:\Documents and Settings\<username>\NTUSER.INI`.

Mandatory profiles

You can replace the NTUSER.DAT file that resides in the user's network directory with an NTUSER.DAT file that you want to make mandatory and unchangeable.

1. **Create a roaming profile folder as you would normally.**
2. **Copy the NTUSER.DAT file you want to use into that folder.**
3. **Rename it NTUSER.MAN, and you've created a mandatory user profile.**

In the case of NTUSER.MAN, Windows XP never copies an NTUSER.DAT on the user's PC hard drive back to the network location, as it does with regular user profiles. Instead, Windows XP always uses the NTUSER.MAN file. It's as though you've made the file read-only.

If you're planning to use this feature, point a whole group of users to the same roaming profile folder, so you only have to manage one copy of NTUSER.MAN for the entire group. For example, you could make periodic changes to the mandatory profile by modifying the profile settings on a test PC, logging off, logging on again as an Administrator, copying the profile back up to the network location using the Advanced tab on the System control panel, and renaming the file NTUSER.MAN.

Mandatory user profiles don't provide any control over the settings in the other Registry hives. You may be able to use group policies in combination with mandatory user profiles, but doing so creates a security environment that's so complex that not many organizations would want to manage it. So, organizations typically choose group policies to impose restrictions on users, rather than mandatory user profiles. However, if you want to freeze user settings for application programs and if those programs don't come with policy templates that let you use group policies to impose restrictions, then you may need to consider mandatory user profiles.

Managing profiles

On a Windows XP Professional machine, you manage user profiles with the User Accounts control panel that I describe earlier in this chapter, and with the System control panel's User Profiles dialog box (see Figure 12-2). Use the latter to delete a user profile, copy a profile from one location to another (you can't use Windows Explorer for this task), and change the type of profile from local to roaming or vice versa.

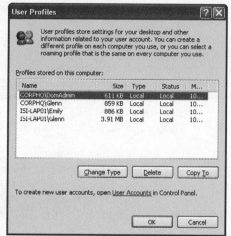

Figure 12-2:
Create,
delete, and
change
profile
types here.

If you want to change a roaming profile back to a nonroaming profile, or (for that matter) vice versa, run the System control panel's Advanced tab, click the Settings button in the User Profiles area, and click the Change Type button to display the Change Profile Type dialog box (see Figure 12-3). If the "roaming profile" choice appears dimmed, as in the figure, then the user account is probably not a domain account — or no profile directory was set up for it.

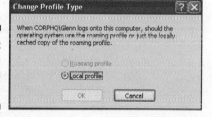

Figure 12-3:
Changing a
profile's
type.

Folder redirection: An alternative to roaming profiles

Roaming user profiles are cool, but they can add a lot of traffic congestion to a busy network. Every time you log on to a particular network computer for the first time, all your roaming profile data flows across the wire. A good way to work around that problem is to use *folder redirection*. Files in redirected folders only travel across the wire if and when the user works with them.

You have to set up folder redirection on a Windows 2002 or 2000 server machine, using the Group Policy tools. The process is pretty easy. You simply choose an organizational structure, such as a domain, and open the Group Policy editor for that structure. (I'm omitting the boring details; they won't be on Exam #70-270.) Then you navigate your way to a policy node named Folder Redirection. There, you can specify that (for example) when any domain user logs on, the user's My Documents folder doesn't live on the workstation hard drive, but rather on a network server — for example, in \\srv01\redirect\ *%username%*, where *%username%* is a variable corresponding to the user's logon name.

You can use folder redirection as a way of providing personal documents to users if you find that roaming profiles put too much traffic on the network.

Folder redirection doesn't let user settings roam the network with the user; for that, you must enable roaming profiles.

Home folders

The *home folder* (or *home directory*, as we called it in Windows NT 4.0) is an alternative to the My Documents folder as a place for users to keep their data files.

Microsoft prefers that you use My Documents, but it continues to provide home folders — mainly for organizations that have used them in the past and are happy with them, or that have decided against roaming profiles for some reason.

Home folders typically live on a network server, where users can get to them from any workstation, although technically home folders can live on client PCs. Microsoft recommends putting them on an NTFS disk for the greater control over access permissions that such disks provide. Microsoft also suggests putting all home folders under one "umbrella" folder, which makes your server's file structure cleaner and easier to manage.

After the home folders are set up on the server, all you have to do at the user's workstation is run the Computer Management console, open Users and Groups, right-click the user name, choose Properties, and (on the Profile tab) point a drive letter with the home folder (see Figure 12-4). Users can then save their data files to that drive letter without worrying about specifying a long and involved network path.

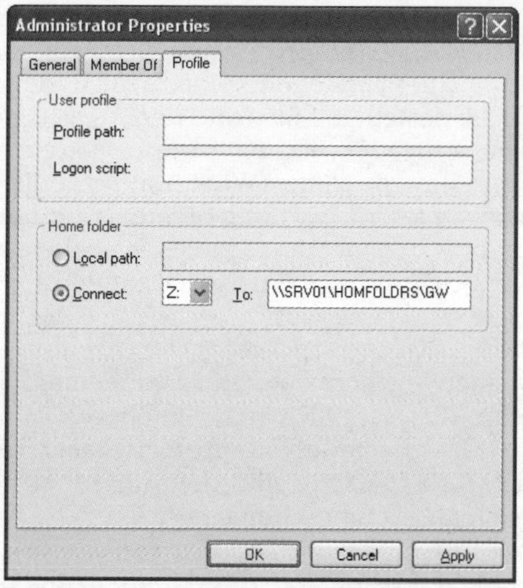

Figure 12-4:
Pointing a
drive letter
at a home
folder on the
server.

Offline Files and Folders

Windows users have been able to "work offline" to some degree for quite a while now — the "Briefcase" concept debuted in Windows 95, as did offline printing — but Windows XP extends the capability and makes it more convenient for network users. (That convenience may not extend to network administrators, who must deal with the extra traffic burden that synchronization can bring!)

The venerable, little-used Briefcase is still present, by the way, and recommended for situations where you use a Zip disk or direct cable connection (parallel or serial) to reconcile notebook files with those on a desktop machine. If you use a network connection to synchronize versions of files that you take away from the office, then Offline Files and Folders is the preferred choice.

The offline concept

Offline files and folders are similar in many ways to roaming user profiles. However, while roaming user profiles let you work with your settings and documents regardless of what PC you log onto, offline files and folders are intended to let you work with your network documents regardless of whether the network's available or not.

The basic concept is that administrators and, optionally, users can designate network files and folders to be *cached* (copied) to the local workstation. Why would users want to do this? If a network connection breaks, the affected user can keep working with the designated files and folders as if the network connection were still present — the view of the network stays the same, file and folder access permissions stay the same. (When the server is down, the user is working with the local copies, or "working offline," whether she knows it or not.) Then, when the network connection again is available, Windows can automatically update, or *synchronize*, the network copies of any changed files and folders.

Savvy network users have effectively performed this same function with critical documents well before Windows XP's arrival by periodically copying server-based files down to their workstations to protect against server unavailability, or to get ready for a road trip with their notebook PCs. Windows XP makes such manual "caching" unnecessary.

The synchronization can work in the opposite direction, too. If a user connects to the network and the network version of a file is newer than the user's local version, then Windows XP can download the network version to the user's PC. Also, if a user or administrator has marked an entire network folder to be made available offline, then any new files that others may have saved to that folder since Joe User last logged off will copy over to Joe's local PC at synchronize time, too (say, his next logon).

Setting up offline files and folders

As the offline files and folders feature involves network machines and local machines, you'd expect to have to do some configuration on servers as well as clients, and you'd be right.

Server-side setup

The first step in setting up offline folders is telling the server that you want them. That's a network administrator's job, and the tiny details are more important for the server exam than for this one. Suffice it to say here that you right-click the shared folder of interest, choose Sharing, click the Caching button, and check the box that reads Allow Caching of Files in This Shared Folder. You can also specify one of three settings: Automatic Caching For Documents (which caches all files in the folder as users open them); Manual Caching For Documents (which lets the user choose which files to make available offline); and Automatic Caching For Programs, for folders containing read-only applications that run from the server.

Client-side setup

On the client side (where you're running Windows XP Professional), you also have to enable the offline files and folders feature. You can do so two ways:

- ✔ Open My Computer and choose Tools⇨Folder Options.

- ✔ Choose Start⇨Control Panel and double-click Folder Options (assuming you've activated the more convenient "classic view" of the control panel).

Either way, click the Offline Files tab to see a screen like the one in Figure 12-5.

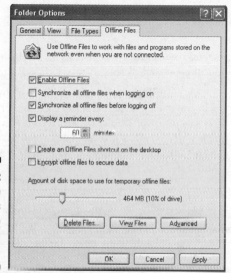

Figure 12-5: The Offline Files tab is one of two places you must visit.

Here are the things you should know about the Offline Files property sheet:

- ✔ Check Enable Offline Files to turn on the feature for the client PC.

- ✔ Checking Synchronize All Offline Files Before Logging Off ensures that when you log off, your locally cached files are completely up-to-date. This is "full" synchronization in Microspeak.

    If you clear this check box, Windows XP makes sure you have all the files you should have offline, but doesn't guarantee that they're the latest versions; this is the "quick" synchronization option.

- ✔ You can also set Windows to synch up your files at logon time, via the Synchronize All Offline Files When Logging On check box. (For maximum synchronization, choose both the logon and logoff check boxes, which you can set independently of each other.)

✔ Display A Reminder turns on the display of a Taskbar balloon when a network server is unavailable and you're working offline.

✔ The Encrypt Offline Files To Secure Data check box is new in Windows XP (you can't encrypt the client-side cache in Windows 2000) and adds a layer of security to locally cached files by applying NTFS encryption to them. Encryption ensures that nobody else who may log on to your PC can see or modify the contents of your offline files.

✔ The disk space slider specifies what percent of the drive you want to permit Windows XP to use for files that your network administrator wants you to have offline, but that you haven't specifically designated to be made available offline. (These are "temporary offline files" in Microsoft lingo.)

✔ The Delete Files button deletes the local, cached copy of offline files, but not the network copy.

✔ The Advanced button lets you designate how Windows XP behaves when different servers become unavailable.

For example, you may want to "go offline" and continue working with locally cached documents in most cases. But if a particular server goes down, you may not want to use in an offline manner the files that it shares — say, highly time-sensitive data such as stock quotes, which could do damage if they aren't current but appear to be so! You can specify normal behavior and a list of exceptions to achieve the desired configuration.

After you've set your preferences using Folder Options, you simply open My Documents or Windows Explorer, find the folder you want to make available offline, right-click it, and choose the menu option "Make Available Offline." If you've never made this folder available offline before, a wizard activates to walk you through the process. A dialog box appears saying "Synchronizing" as Windows caches the network copy to your local disk.

Finally, you can go back at any time and modify your settings with something that Microsoft calls *Synchronization Manager*. Get there one of two ways: Open My Computer or Explorer and choose Tools⇨Synchronize, or choose Start⇨All Programs⇨Accessories⇨Synchronize. From the Items to Synchronize dialog box that appears, you can manually synchronize any offline files or folders, change certain of their synchronization settings by clicking the Properties button, or click Setup to display the Synchronization Settings dialog box shown in Figure 12-6.

Here are a few notes regarding the Synchronization Settings dialog box:

✔ The Logon/Logoff tab lets you control which items synchronize at logon and/or logoff, and whether the user gets prompted before synchronizing. The behavior must be the same for any single network connection (LAN or dial-up).

✔ The On Idle tab lets you specify that Windows should synchronize offline files and folders after a period of inactivity, which you can define. You can also specify the synchronization repeat frequency for continued idle states, and whether to disable synchronization if your machine's running off a battery.

✔ The Scheduled tab lets you add or edit schedules for synchronization events ("sync this network connection every Friday at 1:00 am"). Scheduled jobs appear in the Control Panel's Scheduled Tasks folder.

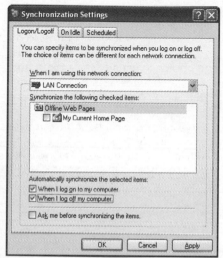

Figure 12-6: Still more synchronization settings.

Offline in practice: A mixed blessing

The first drawback to using offline files and folders is that they can dramatically increase network congestion. I've heard from a few corporate IS managers that the additional traffic from frequent offline file synchronization can bring a busy network to its little silicon knees.

The next drawback has to do with ease of use. The concept is that the offline files and folders feature works transparently. However

✔ Someone has to set up the feature on each network server that shares folders containing files to be cached, as I explain in the previous section.

✔ Cases can often crop up in which the user must resolve a conflict and perform file reconciliation manually.

That last item deserves attention, as it may well appear on the exam. Suppose, for example, that Forsberg has designated a shared network file as cached, and Roy has done so, too. Forsberg undocks his notebook computer, goes on a trip, and makes some changes to the file. Roy undocks his notebook, also goes on a trip, and makes some changes of his own. Forsberg gets back to the office first, and hooks up to the LAN. Windows XP sees that his cached (local) copy is newer than the network copy, so it synchronizes by copying the cached copy to the server. Roy then arrives at the office, docks his notebook, and — sacré Bleu, a dilemma! If Windows XP copies Roy's version to the server, it will overwrite Forsberg's changes. But if it *doesn't* copy Roy's version, then Roy's work never gets put onto the server.

What happens in this situation is that Windows XP asks Roy to decide whether to nuke Forsberg's file, save Roy's file to the server under a different name, or do nothing. The second choice is usually the safest, but someone must then manually merge Forsberg's changes with Roy's to create a properly updated file that reflects both their work. Not exactly transparent.

Clearly, the offline files and folders feature works best if each user has his or her own data area on the server and only makes those files available offline. And yes, such an arrangement defeats the purpose of network file sharing to some extent! So the offline files and folders feature isn't as cool as it seems at first glance. (Learn it anyway.)

One final drawback: The offline files and folders feature only works on Microsoft networks, so Novell shops can't use it.

Windows Installer Service

Microsoft's published exam objectives specify that you be able to install applications onto a Windows XP Professional machine by using the Windows Installer service. Happily, that's about the easiest objective in the entire list! In general, all you need to do is double-click an MSI file — it doesn't get much simpler than that! (MSI files are associated in the Registry with MSIEXEC.EXE.) Alternatively, you can right-click an MSI file and choose Install from the context menu.

Another alternative if you need more control is to invoke the Microsoft Software Installer Executive, or MSIEXEC.EXE, at a command prompt or Run dialog box. For example, if H: is your local CD-ROM drive containing the Windows XP Professional CD, then this command installs the Windows XP Resource Kit Support Tools onto your machine:

```
MSIEXEC /I H:\SUPPORT\TOOLS\SUPTOOLS.MSI
```

You may need to know some of the other MSIEXEC command-line qualifiers, so here are a few besides /I for Install:

- ✔ **/F** means "Fix" and has several variations, which you don't need to memorize. MSIEXEC will need to see the original MSI file to complete this operation, which also goes by the name Repair in the user interface (for example, on the context menu of an MSI file). That may mean that you have to provide the original setup CD-ROM, or make available the network distribution point from which the program was originally installed.

- ✔ **/L** means "Log" and has several variations specifying just what exactly the log file should contain (again, don't memorize 'em). Note that Windows Installer logs significant events to the Application event log by default. You can view this log with Event Viewer.

- ✔ **/P** means "Patch" and modifies an existing administrative image, usually on a server, from which the application installs to client machines.

- ✔ **/X** means "eXtract," or uninstall.

Installing MSI packages from Active Directory gets a bit more complex. For example, using Group Policies, you can specify that a particular application is to be *published* to users, that is, made available to any user who wants it. Such an application appears in the users' Add/Remove Programs control panel. Or, you can specify that the application is to be *assigned* to a particular user or computer, that is, installed onto the client machine in such a way that it can't easily be removed. However, beyond understanding these terms, you don't need to master the intricacies of assigning and publishing applications (at least, not for this exam!).

The impact of Windows Installer on the Add/Remove Programs Wizard is significant for two reasons:

- ✔ The wizard lets users "repair" an installation that may be damaged in some way.

    Select the program from the list, click the Support link, and you usually see the repair option. This option is a graphical front end to the MSIEXEC /F command.

- ✔ The wizard performs a more complete "uninstall" because the MSI file lets the wizard see exactly what needs to be removed — including Registry entries, shortcuts, the whole ball of wax.

    This option is a graphical front end to the MSIEXEC /X command.

Incidentally, the exam may expect you to know that MSIEXEC shows up as a service named "Windows Installer" in the list that you can display via the Services icon in the Administrative Tools folder.

Prep Test

1 **In the lingo of Active Directory and Windows Installer, what does it mean to publish an application to a computer?**

A ○ To make that application available to all users on the computer

B ○ To make that application available to the currently logged-on user on the computer

C ○ To initiate an automatic installation of the application the next time the computer is rebooted

D ○ Nothing

2 **Lloyd is a tech support guy for your nonprofit organization. As such, he hops around from one PC to another on a regular basis. Often, he has to log on to the Windows 2000 Server domain using his own account, so that he can run special tools, such as various troubleshooting tools, consult his own private online documentation, log trouble calls, and so forth. You have configured Lloyd with a roaming user profile.**

Lloyd complains to you that his profile takes a while to download from the network when he logs on at a machine that is not his own. He also tells you that he doesn't really use his Favorites folder when away from his usual PC. How would you modify Lloyd's profile behavior to exclude the Favorites folder from roaming? (Choose the best answer.)

A ○ Modify the list of roaming folders in the Registry.

B ○ Edit the file NTUSER.DAT in Lloyd's profile folder.

C ○ Edit the file NTUSER.INI in Lloyd's profile folder.

D ○ Set Favorites as an exclusion in the Local Group Policy editor.

3 **You set up roaming user profiles, but you find that network performance has become unacceptably slow. What other options does Windows XP Professional give you for providing users with network-based access to documents and settings, without imposing as much of a traffic burden on the network infrastructure? (Choose all that apply.)**

A ❑ Home folders

B ❑ Redirected folders

C ❑ Mandatory profiles

D ❑ Dynamic disks

4 Which of the following filenames contains a mandatory user profile? (Choose one.)

- **A** ○ NTUSERMAN.DAT
- **B** ○ NTUSER.MAN
- **C** ○ USER.MAN
- **D** ○ PROFILE.MAN

5 Bertram calls you for help in troubleshooting user profiles on his machine. When you arrive at his side and take over the keyboard after he logs on, you notice that the `C:\Documents and Settings` folder doesn't exist. Bertram mentions that he upgraded to Windows XP Professional from Windows NT 4.0 Workstation. Where are Bertram's profiles? (Choose the best answer.)

- **A** ○ `C:\WINNT`
- **B** ○ `C:\WINNT\PROFILES`
- **C** ○ `C:\PROFILES`
- **D** ○ `C:\WINNT\SYSTEM32\PROFILES`
- **E** ○ `C:\WINDOWS\PROFILES`

6 You decide to implement offline files on your Windows XP Professional PC. How can you make sure that your locally cached versions are always in full synchronization with the network versions of your offline files? (Choose the best answer.)

- **A** ○ In the Folder Options control panel's Offline Files tab, check the box labeled Synchronize All Offline Files Before Logging Off.
- **B** ○ In the Folder Options control panel's Offline Files tab, check the box labeled Synchronize All Offline Files Before Logging On.
- **C** ○ In the Synchronization Manager's General tab, check the box labeled Synchronize All Offline Files Before Logging Off.
- **D** ○ This setting is only available on a Windows 2002 or 2000 Server PC and must be set by an administrator.

7 You're preparing a master disk image for the cloning and deployment of Windows XP Professional. Your plan is to use the SysPrep utility in combination with a disk cloning utility. When you configure the machine, you do so while logged on as the Administrator. You install applications, configure desktop shortcuts, and tailor the Start menu.

When you perform a small-scale test deployment, you discover that when users log on with their own network accounts, they don't see the tailoring that you performed. What can you do to fix this problem before you deploy Windows XP to the entire department? (Choose the best answer.)

A ○ Using the User Profiles control panel, copy the Administrator's user profile to the Default User profile.

B ○ Using the System control panel, copy the Administrator's user profile to the Default User profile.

C ○ Using the System control panel, copy the Administrator's user profile to the All Users profile.

D ○ Create a home directory on the network server.

8 A software vendor advises you that you must modify the access control list for a specific Registry key in order for that vendor's application to work properly under Windows XP. Which of the following Registry tools should you use to make the modification?

A ○ REGEDT32.EXE

B ○ REGEDIT32.EXE

C ○ REGEDIT.EXE

D ○ REGEDIT.MSC

Answers

1 **D.** Tricky question, this. The statement means nothing because you can't publish an application to a computer; you can only publish applications to users. You can, however, assign applications to computers — or to users, as you choose. *Review "Windows Installer Service."*

2 **D.** Choice C isn't as good an answer, because whenever you have a choice between using a management console or editing a text file (or the Registry) directly, you should use the console for safety and reliability. Note that you'd use the Local Group Policy tool (GPEDIT.MSC) here, rather than a domain-based policy, because you only want to change the behavior for Lloyd's account. *Review "What roams, what doesn't."*

3 **A** and **B.** Both home folders and redirected folders permit users to keep documents on network servers without moving them across the wire unless users need them. Microsoft would prefer that you use folder redirection, which is a component of IntelliMirror, because it's transparent and makes use of the My Documents and My Pictures desktop elements. *Review "Folder redirection: An alternative to roaming profiles"* and *"Home folders."*

4 **B.** One more fact to memorize. *Review "Mandatory profiles."*

5 **B.** Microsoft made a command decision to leave profiles in its Windows NT 4.0 location if a user upgrades to Windows XP Professional from NT. The idea is that one or more applications may expect to see profile data in the old location. *Review "User Profiles."*

6 **A.** If you clear the check box, then you're sure to have all your files on the local disk, but you can't be sure that they're all up-to-date. Choice B is almost valid but the check box isn't worded correctly (sorry, but the exam is nitpicky). *Review "Setting up offline files and folders."*

7 **B.** Choice B is the best answer. But it may not be perfect. For example, the Administrator's profile may contain some programs that others can't execute because of user rights issues. *Review "User Profiles."*

8 **C.** REGEDT32.EXE would be the correct answer for Windows 2000, but not XP! Microsoft finally got around to integrating REGEDT32's features into REGEDIT in Windows XP. The Registry Editor isn't a management console and so doesn't have the suffix MSC. *Review "A unified editing tool."*

Chapter 13

Dial-Up Networking and Remote Access

• •

Exam Objectives

▶ Create a dial-up connection to connect to a remote access server

▶ Connect to computers by using a virtual private network (VPN) connection

▶ Connect to the Internet by using dial-up networking

▶ Configure and troubleshoot Internet Connection Sharing

▶ Configure, manage, and troubleshoot an Internet connection firewall

▶ Configure, manage, and troubleshoot remote desktop and remote assistance

• •

Setting up a dial-up connection was always a bit of a headache in Windows NT Workstation 4.0. Windows 98 handled the task more intuitively, but even there, creating a "DUN connectoid" was still fraught with opportunity for error and confusion. Even the terminology was weird (whoever came up with the word "connectoid"?).

Microsoft has revamped the dial-up networking user interface in Windows XP in an effort to make creating a connection more straightforward. For example, dial-up connections now live in the same folder as LAN and WAN connections, reinforcing the concept that a modem works just like a slow network adapter. The Make New Connection Wizard is significantly more capable, versatile, and (therefore) useful. You can create secure computer-to-computer dial-up links by using the Internet as a communications medium. You can set up a computer so that it shares its Internet connection with other connected computers. Microsoft now provides a basic firewall product, recognizing the popularity of always-on broadband connections. And the Remote Assistance and Remote Desktop features borrow technology from Terminal Server to ease support chores.

Remote network access is a traditional favorite topic of Microsoft workstation exams, so you should probably memorize just about everything in this chapter. As usual, if you can also practice building remote links in real life, so much the better; if not, please read this chapter twice, and when you're done, read it again.

Quick Assessment

Create a dial-up connection to connect to a remote access server

1 If you're creating a link to a remote network and you want to use encryption for the entire communications session, the protocols that you can use are _____, _____, and _____.

2 When you create a link to a remote computer, you can specify whether the link should be available to you only, or to _____.

3 The precise name of the folder where all dial-up connections reside is _____.

Connect to computers by using a virtual private network (VPN) connection

4 Create a VPN connection by choosing the option named "Connect to a _____ network through the Internet."

5 The two communications protocols you can use with VPN links are _____ and _____.

Connect to the Internet by using dial-up networking

6 (True/False) A connection that links to the Internet must have the Client for Microsoft Networks component installed and checked on the connection's Network property sheet.

7 When you choose to "Dial up to the Internet" in the Network Connection Wizard, that wizard hands you off to another program named _____.

Configure and troubleshoot Internet Connection Sharing

8 You should not use Internet Connection Sharing on a network that also has one or more PCs running _____ or _____.

Configure, manage, and troubleshoot an Internet connection firewall

9 (True/False) When setting up a LAN using ICS, activate the firewall on each PC to prevent hacker access.

10 The Remote Desktop Connection program's Windows Installer file name is _____.

Answers

1 *MS-CHAP, MS-CHAPv2, and EAP/TLS.* The section "Security tab" in this chapter helps explain the alphanumeric gobbledygook.

2 *All users of the PC.* The section "Creating a connection" offers this tidbit and many others.

3 *Network and Dial-Up Connections.* This is different from previous Windows versions. See the "Central control" section.

4 *Private.* Or, the "P" in "VPN." See "Setting up a VPN link" in this chapter.

5 *PPTP, L2TP.* If this alphabet soup tastes strange, read "VPN protocols."

6 *False.* The Internet isn't a Microsoft network (at least not yet). See "Networking tab" for more.

7 *Internet Connection Wizard.* Sort of a wizard baton race. "Creating a connection" is worth your inspection.

8 *Windows 2002/2000 domain controller, DNS server, DHCP server, TCP/IP with a static IP address.* If you didn't get two out of these four possibilities, read the "Internet Connection Sharing" section.

9 *False.* You only need to activate the firewall on the ICS machine. See "Internet Connection Firewall."

10 *TSCLIENT.MSI.* This file comes with Windows XP Professional. For more, see "Remote Desktop."

Configuring for Remote Access

This "get ready" section discusses hardware, software, and configuration preparations for remote access with dial-up connections.

Hardware prep

If you're looking to make connections to remote computers, you need some sort of hardware connection to those computers. Configuring your PC for remote access involves one or more of the following:

- A modem and phone line

- An ISDN (Integrated Services Digital Network) adapter and ISDN phone line

- A network interface card (NIC) and connection to a Local Area Network (LAN), DSL adapter, or "cable modem"

- A parallel or serial cable configured for bidirectional communication, or an infrared port (for Direct Cable Connection, a modemless approach)

Software prep

On the software side, the components that you need depend on the kind of system you're connecting to. For example:

- If you need to connect to the Internet with a Web browser, all you need is the TCP/IP protocol. You don't need a networking client, such as the Client for Microsoft Networks. However, you do need a Web browser. Internet Explorer 6 comes with Windows XP, and you can add other browsers to your system as well.

- If you need to connect to a corporate network, then you need a transport protocol (the same as your corporate network uses) plus a networking client.

- If you need to share resources with the computer or computers you're connecting to, then you need the File and Printer Sharing for Microsoft Networks service.

Typically, the Network Connection Wizard handles these details for you when you first create the connection. You may need to make some manual changes, however, if you create a new connection by copying and renaming an existing one.

Configuration prep

You should configure Windows XP properly for your *dialing location* or
locations. You normally perform this task when adding a modem driver via
the Modems control panel or the Add New Hardware Wizard, but you need
to come back to it any time your dialing properties change, or if you want to
add new dialing locations.

To configure dialing location information, open the Phone and Modem
Options control panel and click the Dialing Rules tab. Click on the location of
interest (only one may appear) and click the Edit button. A dialog box similar
to Figure 13-1 appears.

Figure 13-1:
The Edit
Location
box lets you
set dial-out
options.

Here's what you need to remember about dialing rules:

✔ Change dialing rules whenever you move your PC to a new location that
has different ones (for example, a different area code, which you may
find yourself in after a crosstown relocation).

✔ Dialing rules are available to all Windows applications that support
TAPI (Telephony Application Program Interface). Other TAPI-compliant
programs are Outlook Express and MSN (Microsoft Network).

✔ Dialing rules are *global*. That is, if you change the location in the Phone
and Modem Options control panel, the dialing rules change for all dial-up
connections that you may have created.

> ✔ On a location-by-location basis, you can specify whether Windows XP
> needs to dial an area code for local calls (an increasingly common
> situation) via the Area Code Rules tab.
>
> ✔ Also on a location-by-location basis, you can specify calling card
> information via the Calling Card tab.

Network Connections: First Principles

The Network Connections folder lets you connect a Windows XP PC to a
remote computer or to a remote network over a telephone line (be it regular
analog, ISDN, or DSL) or cable, or infrared link.

Central control

In Windows XP, Microsoft decided to lump all connections — local and
remote, regardless of media — into a single folder. Get there by choosing
Start➪All Programs➪Accessories➪Communications➪Network Connections,
or (more quickly) by choosing Start➪Control Panel➪Network Connections,
or (most quickly) by right-clicking My Network Places and choosing
Properties. You see a window that looks something like the one in Figure 13-2;
note the handy new Network Tasks and Details boxes in the left pane.
No more bouncing around between a Dial-Up Networking folder and a
Network control panel, as in Windows 98; all connection settings are here
in one place.

Network Connections is where you configure both inbound and outbound
connections because Windows XP Professional can host incoming sessions
as well as dial out to other networks.

The Network Connections folder, which replaces the Network control panel in
earlier versions of Windows, is very "deep" — that is, it has lots of settings
and options. Thankfully, Microsoft has provided a Create New Connection
Wizard that gets you through most of the initial configuration.

Also, certain aspects of this folder's setup are automatic. For example, you
can't manually create an icon for a LAN connection; Windows XP creates one
for you "automagically," when it detects a network interface card. (Windows XP
does *not* automatically create an icon for a dial-up connection if the operating
system detects a modem, however, for the good reason that a human
being must supply a phone number and sundry other details to create a
dial-up link.)

Figure 13-2:
The
Network
Connections
folder.

Why create a connection?

You would create a Network Connection link in the following situations:

- ✔ Employees need Internet access from the workplace, but your organization doesn't have a constant Internet connection.

- ✔ Employees in your organization travel and need to be able to "dial in" to the LAN at headquarters.

- ✔ Employees in your organization travel and need to be able to connect to the Internet (for example, to check e-mail).

- ✔ Your organization has telecommuters who need to be able to "dial in" to a single PC at the office.

- ✔ You have a notebook PC with no network card, and you need to exchange files with a desktop PC.

- ✔ You're planning to take an MCSE test and you decide to practice with the software. (Smart.)

Connection independence

With some exceptions (such as dialing rules, rules for how Windows "fills in" partial DNS names, and so on), each connection that you create has its own communications settings. That is, one connection can have a different set of

DNS server addresses on its TCP/IP property sheet than another connection. (I know, it sounds obvious, but it didn't work that way in Windows 95!) Generally, if a given setting isn't connection-specific but instead is global, the relevant property sheet advises you of the fact.

Creating a connection

A *connectoid* is Microspeak for a connection icon. You create connectoids by using the Create New Connection Wizard in the Network Connections virtual folder, as Lab 13-1 demonstrates. You can create as many connections as you want; each time you create a new connection, a new connectoid appears in the Network Connections folder.

The procedure for creating a dial-up connection is similar whether you're creating a "regular" dial-up link, a virtual private network link, or a direct cable connection. Lab 13-1 demonstrates the procedure for a plain vanilla modem link and assumes that you've installed a modem.

Lab 13-1 Creating a Connectoid

1. **Right-click My Network Places and choose Properties.**

2. **Click the Create A New Connection link in the left pane.**

   An explanatory screen appears. Note its title, New Connection Wizard. The Make New Connection icon launches the New Connection Wizard (got that?).

3. **Click Next to get past the verbiage.**

   The screen shown in Figure 13-3 appears.

Figure 13-3: You can create just about any kind of connection here.

4. **Click the Connect To The Network At My Workplace button and click Next.**

   If you choose Connect To The Internet, then Windows XP disables File and Printer Sharing (if installed) for security reasons and hands you off to the old *Internet Connection Wizard*, which is largely the same as it was in earlier Windows versions. You can create a new ISP account, move an existing account's settings to this PC, or specify details for a LAN-based Internet connection. Your other option is Set Up An Advanced Connection, which leads you through the various options for setting up incoming connections or for creating a direct PC-to-PC connection using a serial, parallel, or infrared port.

5. **Choose Dial-Up Connection or Virtual Private Network Connection, and click Next.**

6. **If you have more than one dial-up device, choose the one you want for this connection and click Next.**

7. **Type a name for the new connection.**

8. **Enter a phone number to dial and click Next.**

9. **Specify whether you want all users of this PC to have access to the connection, or only you. Click Next.**

   You only see this option if you're logged on as an Administrator.

10. **Click Finish and marvel as Windows creates a new icon in the Network Connections folder. (Click the Add A Shortcut To This Connection To My Desktop first, if you desire that.)**

    After you click Finish, you're not really finished, of course. You probably need to configure your network protocol settings and modem settings, for example. The procedures for doing all of that appear in the next section.

Anatomy of a Connection

The Make New Connection Wizard automates only a fairly small part of the connection creation procedure, leaving a lot of settings for you to configure manually after the wizard has left the scene in a flash of orange smoke. Access these settings by right-clicking your freshly minted "connectoid" and choosing Properties. The ensuing dialog box has five tabs, redesigned somewhat from earlier Windows versions:

✓ **General:** Settable options

✓ **Options:** General settings (Sorry, but these generic names are so lame.)

✓ **Security:** Authentication options

✔ **Networking:** Network modules, bindings, and data required for this link

✔ **Advanced:** Whether, and how, to implement Internet Connection Sharing (ICS)

The following sections elaborate on each tabbed dialog box.

General tab

The General tab (see Figure 13-4) and the Options tab are just two dialog boxes full of settings that Microsoft couldn't figure out how to categorize.

Figure 13-4: The General tab.

You can specify more than one hardware device for the connection. You could use two modems to create a *multilink* connection, by checking both of them in this dialog box. (Other multilink settings, however, live on the Options tab — go figure.) If the two modems should both call the same phone number, click the All Devices Call the Same Numbers check box. Otherwise, clear the check box, and enter the appropriate phone number for each modem by highlighting the modem and filling in the Phone Number fields.

Speaking of the Phone Number area, you can also specify whether the connection should follow your global dialing rules, and whether you want to key in one or more alternate phone numbers in case the first number is busy.

You can modify several modem settings by clicking the Configure button. (Again, in a multilink setup, click the modem of interest first and then click Configure.) The settings that you make sound like the same ones that you set in the Phone and Modem Options control panel, but these settings apply only to the connection icon that you're configuring. That is, they're local rather than global. You can tailor them to the characteristics of the servers you're dialing up. For example, one information service may support error correction, while another may not. These settings include

- ✔ Maximum speed, in bits/second
- ✔ Hardware flow control (on or off)
- ✔ Modem error control (on or off)
- ✔ Modem compression (on or off)
- ✔ Whether to show a terminal window before making connection
- ✔ Modem speaker (on or off)

After you create a connectoid, if you later make a change to the Phone and Modem Options control panel, don't assume that the change automatically propagates to your Network Connection icons. Some changes do, but most don't. Verify the change by checking the icon properties, and make the change there again, if necessary.

Options tab

Whatever miscellany didn't fit on the General tab, Microsoft put on the Options tab (see Figure 13-5). This section runs through the options.

Figure 13-5:
The Options
tab.

qwest Properties

General | Options | Security | Networking | Advanced

Dialing options
☑ Display progress while connecting
☑ Prompt for name and password, certificate, etc.
☐ Include Windows logon domain
☑ Prompt for phone number

Redialing options
Redial attempts: 3
Time between redial attempts: 1 minute
Idle time before hanging up: 20 minutes
☑ Redial if line is dropped

Multiple devices
Dial devices only as needed | Configure...

X.25

OK | Cancel

Prompt for Name and Password, Certificate, etc. is an important setting. If you clear this check box, Windows won't give you the chance to enter a username or password the next time you run it (see Figure 13-6). Windows just assumes the previous settings you used, or pulls your authentication data from a smart card reader if you have one. Check this option if you want to ensure maximum security in case someone steals the PC.

Figure 13-6:
You can set
Windows
XP to
display
this dialog
box or to
bypass it.

Include Windows Logon Domain (refer to Figure 13-5) lets you choose a domain if you're also prompting for username and password. Use this if you're dialing into a Microsoft network and you want users to be able to choose different domains into which to log on. Clear it if you're dialing into an ISP for Internet access.

Prompt for Phone Number (Figure 13-5 again) is mighty handy for notebook users because it lets them choose a different phone number and/or dialing location before making the connection.

Redialing options are self-explanatory so I will not explain them. However, it may be worth knowing that Internet Explorer overrides the connectoid's redial settings with its own redial settings, which you reach via the Internet Options control panel.

If you want Internet Explorer to use the modem to automatically connect you to the Internet, you can make that setting in the Internet control panel's Connection tab. (Outlook Express shares that setting, by the way.)

If you selected multiple devices on the General tab, then you can configure the multilink connection. If you choose Dial Devices Only As Needed, then you can click the Configure button to display the Automatic Dialing And

Hanging Up dialog box (see Figure 13-7) and set your BAP and BACP options. Bandwidth Allocation Protocol (BAP) and Bandwidth Allocation Control Protocol (BACP) let you save cash if you're paying by the minute.

Figure 13-7:
Windows
XP can
dynamically
add or drop
multilink
devices as
needed.

Security tab

The Security tab (see Figure 13-8) lets you specify how Windows XP should handle the authentication, or logon, phase of the connection.

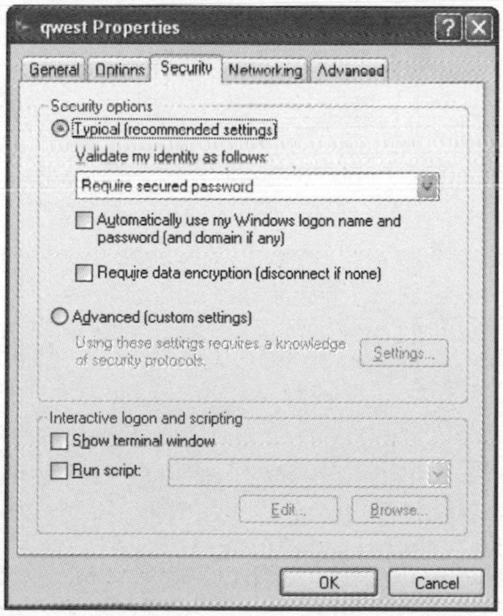

Figure 13-8:
The Security
tab.

If you choose Allow Unsecured Password in the Security options part of the dialog box under Validate My Identity As Follows:, then the other two settings just below the list box appear grayed-out, as they are irrelevant. (Many ISPs require unsecured passwords, rendering this dialog box very simple for those kinds of links.) If you choose Require Secured Password, which only lets you make a connection if the remote computer also supports encrypted passwords, then you can set both of these settings. If you choose Use Smart Card, you can set the data encryption check box only.

✔ The setting Automatically Use My Windows Logon Name and Password (and domain if any) is appropriate if you're dialing into a Microsoft network. Your domain user name and password will authenticate you to the remote server.

✔ The Require Data Encryption (disconnect if none) check box means that if the remote computer supports Data Encryption Standard, or DES, then the entire communications session is encrypted and secure. The protocols that support encryption are MS-CHAP, MS-CHAPv2, and EAP/TLS; see the list following for more on this acronymania.

For organizations with very specific security requirements, the Advanced (Custom Settings) radio button leads to the dialog box in Figure 13-9.

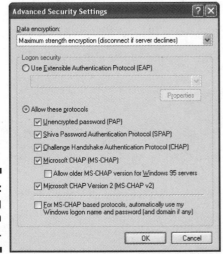

Figure 13-9:
Getting
secure, in
great detail.

The top of the dialog box lets you choose one of four data encryption settings that apply to the entire communications session: require encryption, use it if it's available but don't require it, require maximum-strength encryption, or require that encryption *not* be used.

The Logon Security area throws a lot of alphabet soup at you. Here's what you need to know about logon authentication protocols. It's dry, I know, but you should just memorize all this stuff:

- ✔ **PAP (Password Authentication Protocol)** uses no password encryption and may be required for dialing up non-Windows systems.

- ✔ **MS-CHAP (MicroSoft Challenge-Handshake Authentication Protocol)** works with Windows 9*x* and NT 4. It authenticates the client and uses one-way encryption.

- ✔ **MS-CHAPv2** is another Microsoft protocol; this extension of MS-CHAP authenticates both client and server.

- ✔ **SPAP (Shiva Password Authentication Protocol)** is used for dialing into and out of Shiva (that's a brand name) communication products. It doesn't support data encryption.

- ✔ **EAP (Extensible Authentication Protocol)** is an extension to PPP and evolved to support smart cards and other related devices. With EAP, client and server negotiate an authentication method — such as Transport Level Security (TLS), a smart card authentication standard.

If you're setting up a smart card, when you choose EAP on the Advanced Security Settings dialog box, you must also choose Smart Card Or Other Certificate from the drop-down list; that's the TLS part. Also notice that as soon as you choose EAP, the other options — PAP, SPAP, MS-CHAP, and so on — aren't available. If you see a question that asks you which settings you must make on this dialog box, EAP is all the alphabet soup you need!

Networking tab

After the connection is made, your computer can communicate over the modem in exactly the same ways that it communicates over a NIC: Sending and receiving TCP/IP packets, IPX/SPX packets, and so on. Your network link is just a communications device that connects to a cable — never mind that for a modem, the communications device is slow and the cable is very long. (This method of networking goes by the moniker *remote node*, as opposed to *remote control*, in which keyboard, mouse, and display data travel the phone lines.) Figure 13-10 shows the Networking tab of a dial-up connection's property sheet.

Connection protocols

The first decision you must make is the Type of Dial-Up Server I Am Calling at the top of the Networking tab. This setting is actually something called a *connection protocol*, or *communications protocol*. It's basically an extra network protocol that you need for dial-up lines, but that you don't need for hardwired LAN links.

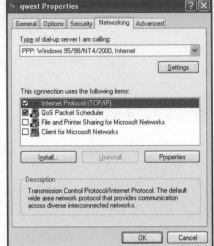

The choice you make for your connection protocol is determined by the kind of computer (server) you're dialing into. Choose one that the server doesn't support, and you won't connect.

✔ **PPP:** Point-to-Point Protocol is the default choice for dial-up connections because it's the most reliable, secure, and efficient connection protocol. Unlike SLIP, PPP supports error checking. It works with NetBEUI, IPX/SPX, and TCP/IP network protocols.

✔ **SLIP:** This is a UNIX server running Serial Line Interface Protocol. SLIP is old, slow, and a bad choice unless you're calling up an old, slow UNIX server that doesn't work with PPP. No error correction, no encrypted passwords, no automatic IP address assignment.

Network bindings and protocol settings

You create and destroy bindings on this tab by checking and clearing check boxes in the central scrolling list (a much simpler way to do it than on the Network control panel of previous Windows versions, by the way). A *binding* is nothing more than an active connection between two different layers of network software: for example, between a network interface adapter (modem) and any installed network protocols (such as TCP/IP), or between a protocol and a service (such as File and Printer Sharing for Microsoft Networks).

One way to improve a connection's logon speed is to uncheck the protocols, clients, and services you know you won't use over a given connection. Rule to live by: Activate only one network protocol for any given connectoid.

You can configure each active (checked) network protocol, service, or client for this specific dial-up connection by clicking the network component in the list and then clicking the Properties button. This is convenient. Some ISPs, for example, may support dynamic IP address assignment via DHCP or some similar mechanism; others may require you to set up a static IP address.

Much of the time, especially with a PPP connection protocol, you'll choose "Obtain an IP address automatically" and "Obtain DNS server address automatically," because most ISPs and TCP/IP hosts provide this information automatically after you connect. However, you have the flexibility to "hardcode" specific IP addresses for your computer, for multiple DNS servers, and for multiple WINS servers, via the Advanced button on the TCP/IP configuration property sheet.

Note that if you're connecting to the Internet to browse the Web, you use domain names, so you don't need a WINS server.

The upper check box on the General tab of the TCP/IP Advanced settings property sheet, Use Default Gateway on Remote Network, tells Windows XP not to use the default gateway you may have configured on your local TCP/IP LAN, if both it and your dial-up connection are live. As with the check box Use IP Header Compression, which improves performance, you normally leave this option checked.

The exam may ask you about protecting the security of a dial-up connection. Disabling the binding to File and Printer Sharing for Microsoft Networks is one way to do that, as you don't want other people on the remote network or computer to see, read, modify, or even delete resources that you've shared on your PC. You would also disable this binding if you wanted to create an incoming connection on a PC that should only act as a gateway to a network, but that should not share any of its own resources to users dialing in.

Advanced tab

Here's where you set up Internet Connection Sharing, which is important enough to warrant its own section — coming up next.

Internet Connection Sharing

If you create an Internet link (see "Creating a connection" earlier in this chapter) and you want to share that link with other computers on the same local area network, you can now do so, with some significant limitations. For example, the Windows XP PC you configure to share an Internet connection must be the only computer on the network that provides an Internet gateway.

Also, you have to have that gateway PC turned on whenever any of the other PCs on the network are connected to the Internet or want to connect to the Internet.

Internet Connection Sharing (ICS) made its debut in Windows 98 Second Edition, and it works similarly in Windows XP and 2000. (You may also see the acronym NAT, for Network Address Translation, used in the context of ICS. NAT is the Windows 2002/2000 Server service that, along with DHCP and DNS, provides ICS-type capabilities for larger networks.)

Here's what you must know for the exam:

- ✔ Enable the feature by checking the Allow Other Network Users To Connect Through This Computer's Internet Connection box on the Advanced tab of the connection's property sheet (see Figure 13-11). You must be an Administrator to do this. Make sure you choose the right connection: It should be the one that links your PC to the Internet, whether that's a dial-up modem or an Ethernet card that connects to a DSL adapter.

- ✔ If your connection isn't an "always-on" type, then you can check Establish A Dial-Up Connection Whenever A Computer On My Network Attempts To Access The Internet, so that your PC calls up the ISP when any networked PC tries to gain access.

- ✔ The ICS feature is for SOHO (Small Office/Home Office) and personal home networking applications.

  Don't use it on networks that have Windows 2002 or 2000 Server domain controllers, DHCP servers, DNS servers, or any computers with static IP addresses. Such networks should use NAT instead of ICS.

- ✔ When you create a shared Internet connection, Windows XP assigns your PC network card a static (that is, unchanging) IP address (192.168.0.1, subnet mask 255.255.255.0), and all present TCP/IP connections between your PC and other network PCs are lost.

- ✔ Other computers on the network that will use the ICS link must be set up to obtain IP addresses automatically on their TCP/IP property sheets.

  The PC you're configuring to connect to the Internet effectively becomes a DHCP server, allocating IP addresses to other PCs on the local network. The range of allocatable addresses is 192.168.0.2 to 192.168.0.254.

- ✔ Those other computers must also configure their Internet Options control panel's Connection tab to never dial a connection; to not automatically detect LAN settings; to not use an automatic configuration script; and to not use a proxy server.

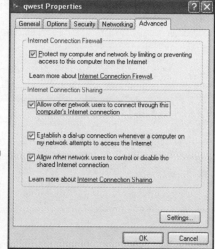

Figure 13-11:
Set up your
ICS server
machine
here.

Internet Connection Firewall

Windows XP adds simple firewall protection automatically for Internet connections that you create with the Make New Connection Wizard or the Home Networking Wizard (the latter borrowed from Windows Me). If you're sharing an Internet connection, the Internet Connection Firewall, or ICF, need only be activated on the PC connection that actually links to the Internet. (ICF works on a per-connection basis.)

What ICF does is conceptually simple. It allows traffic to flow inbound from the public Internet only if that traffic is in response to a message that originated from the local PC (or one of the other PCs using the local PC's Internet connection as a gateway). So, if a user on a PC configured for ICF types a URL in the browser's address bar, ICF will permit traffic to flow back from that public URL to the user because the traffic is in response to a query that originated on the user's PC.

Don't activate ICF on a VPN connection. ICF gets in the way of file sharing. (See "Virtual Private Networking" later in this chapter.)

If you want to modify ICF to forward unsolicited inbound traffic to a Web server on your LAN, you can do so by enabling the HTTP service (port 80) on the ICF computer; just click the Settings button on the Advanced tab of the connection's property sheet and click Add. You'll need to specify the Web server's NetBIOS name or IP address. Another service you may want to add is Remote Desktop (that's port 3389).

Setting the ICF status is an on/off proposition. Use the Advanced tab on the property sheet for the Internet connection to control whether ICF is on or off. Select Protect My Computer and Network by Limiting or Preventing Access to This Computer from the Internet.

Creating Inbound Connections

The Network Connections folder also contains icons for any inbound connections you may want to create. Windows XP supports inbound connections for modem, ISDN, VPN, serial and infrared ports. Lab 13-2 goes through the steps.

Lab 13-2	Creating an Inbound Connection

1. **Log in as Administrator and start the Create a New Connection Wizard as usual. Click Next.**

2. **Choose Set Up an Advanced Connection in the Network Connection Type dialog box, and click Next.**

3. **Choose Accept Incoming Connections, and click Next.**

4. **Choose the device (modem and parallel port are the usual choices) and configure it, if you want, by clicking the Properties button.**

5. **Tell Windows to accept incoming VPN connections, as long as your computer has a unique Internet domain name or IP address.**

6. **Specify who can have access to this inbound connection, and (if you're using an analog or ISDN modem) set** *callback* **options for each user via the Properties button. Click Next.**

   Callback simply means that your computer authenticates the incoming caller, hangs up, and calls him back at a predefined phone number. This method increases security and localizes long distance or other carrier charges.

7. **In the Networking Software dialog box, select the network components that you need for the inbound connection. Click Next.**

   Choose only the minimum components (protocols, services, and clients) necessary to provide the required connectivity.

8. **Name your connection, and you're done.**

Virtual Private Networking

One of the nifty features that Windows XP offers is *Virtual Private Networking*, or *VPN* for short. VPN is a private network link that isn't really private and doesn't use a normal network connection (hence the "virtual"). VPN creates a secure tunnel through an intermediary network, such as the public Internet, through which two computers can communicate privately and securely.

Think of VPN as using the Internet as the communications medium instead of a traditional web of leased lines and Wide Area Network (WAN) carriers. The speed of a VPN is always subject to the speed of the various intervening Internet links, but if that's not a big deal, then a VPN can save a company some money.

VPN protocols

The protocols that VPNs use are *PPTP*, or *Point-to-Point Tunneling Protocol*, and *L2TP*, or *Layer 2 Tunneling Protocol*. Here's what you must know about these communications protocols:

- Both PPTP and L2TP work over dial-up lines, local network links, wide area network links, and public TCP/IP networks such as the Internet.

- PPTP is easier to configure.

- L2TP provides tunneling but not encryption. You would therefore normally use L2TP in combination with *IPsec* (Internet Protocol Security, a set of security protocols to protect the privacy of IP communications). PPTP provides encryption via PPP.

- L2TP in combination with IPsec is more secure.

- L2TP uses header compression for lower overhead; PPTP doesn't.

Setting up a VPN link

You create a VPN link in Windows XP by starting the Make New Connection Wizard in the Network Connections folder. Choose the Connect to the Network at My Workplace option.

Typically, to use the Internet to make a VPN connection, you use one icon to establish the Internet link, and another to establish the VPN tunnel. The first icon may already exist, in which case you should select it and click Automatically Dial This Initial Connection. If you don't need to create an ISP link (for example, because an always-on link already exists), click Do Not Dial the Initial Connection.

Follow the wizard and specify the domain name or IP address of the VPN server. As usual, you can also specify if you want the connection all to yourself or if you prefer to share it with other users of that PC. Name the connection and you're done.

Don't create a VPN link to a remote corporate network if you're also using Internet Connection Sharing on the same PC. If you do, the ICS service will automatically route traffic intended for the public Internet to the corporate intranet instead, and clients will lose Internet connectivity.

When your PC is connected to a corporate intranet over a VPN, you must configure your browser to use a corporate proxy server if you want Internet connectivity. The VPN uses the Internet as a physical transmission medium, but doesn't permit any logical connection to public Internet sites.

Placing a VPN call

Establishing a VPN link via the Internet is easier than it is in Windows 98. Just double-click the connectoid that you created in the previous section. After Windows establishes the link, your PC behaves just as if it were logged on to the private network, rather than to the public Internet.

Remote Desktop

Remote Desktop is a new feature that lets you connect to a PC from a second PC and "take over" the first PC as though you were seated right in front of it. You can think of Remote Desktop as a remote control facility for your computer. Programs run on the first PC, and keyboard, mouse, and display data traverse the remote link. Remote Desktop works over any TCP/IP connection: LAN, WAN, DSL, VPN, ISDN, and so on.

The technology in Remote Desktop isn't new — it's been around ever since Microsoft introduced Windows NT Server, Terminal Server Edition (catchy name eh?) — but Microsoft has repackaged it in a convenient way, hiding many of the gory configuration details. Here are the facts you need to master for exam #70-270:

✔ The remote PC can be running virtually any version of Windows, including 95, 98, Me, NT, and 2000.

✔ The remote PC needs a client software component called *Remote Desktop Connection.* The usual way to install this component is to insert the Windows XP CD, choose Perform Additional Tasks from the main Autorun menu, then choose Set Up Remote Desktop Connection. (Old versions of Windows, such as NT 3.51 and Windows for Workgroups, must install a different client component called Terminal Services Client.)

✔ An administrator on the host PC (running Windows XP Pro) must enable Remote Desktop, which is off by default for security purposes. The System control panel has a Remote tab with a check box labeled Allow Users to Connect Remotely to This Computer.

> ✔ The other thing the administrator on the host PC must do is add users to the Remote Desktop Users local group, by clicking the Add button on the Remote tab of the System control panel.

To connect to the Windows XP machine from a remote PC with the Remote Desktop Connection client installed, just choose Start⇨Programs⇨ Accessories⇨Communications and choose Remote Desktop Connection. Enter the XP machine's computer name or IP address, and click the Connect button. Finally, enter your credentials in the Log On To Windows dialog box. After the connection is made, the XP machine is "locked down" to other users and you have control of it.

Remote Assistance

A close cousin of Remote Desktop (and also based on Terminal Server technology from NT), *Remote Assistance* differs in a few key ways:

> ✔ You (the "Novice") have to send an invitation (via Start⇨Help and Support) to someone else (the "Expert") if you want to give that person remote access to your PC via Remote Assistance. You can send the invitation using the Windows Messenger service or using an e-mail program such as Outlook or Outlook Express.
>
> The invitation requires authentication, either by using a Microsoft Passport account on the public Internet, or by using an Exchange Server account on a private intranet. In either case, both computers must be connected to a common network.

> ✔ For extra security, before actually sending the invitation, you can optionally specify that you want to set a password, which the Expert must know in order to respond to your invitation. Whether you specify a password or not, you must specify an expiration time after which the Expert will not be able to connect to your PC.

> ✔ When you send an invitation, it includes your IP address (and an IP port number if your PC is on a network that uses Internet Connection Sharing to hide individual PCs from the public Internet). If you disconnect from the Internet after sending the invitation and reconnect later, receiving a different IP address, the person to whom you sent the invitation won't be able to connect to your PC.
>
> Note that the act of sending an invitation activates the special built-in HelpAssistant account.

> ✔ After establishing the session, the Expert and the Novice can communicate via chat boxes that appear on each computer. The Expert can see everything that occurs on the Novice's PC.

✔ The Expert can take control of the Novice's desktop, but the Novice must grant permission first. Once the Expert has taken control, the Novice can take it back by pressing Esc.

✔ Unlike Remote Desktop, both PCs participating in a Remote Assistance session must be using Windows XP.

✔ Remote Assistance permits two users to work at the same time, while Remote Desktop only permits one. (That is, if you connect to PC #1 with Remote Desktop, nobody can simultaneously use PC #1 directly.)

Prep Test

1 Bob is setting up his Windows XP Professional machine to access the Internet via a dial-up connection. He goes through the Make New Connection Wizard and answers the questions. When finished, he looks at the connection's networking property sheet to confirm his choices. Which elements should he make sure are present and activated?

A ○ Microsoft TCP/IP

B ○ Client for Microsoft Networks

C ○ File and Printer Sharing for Microsoft Networks

D ○ Microsoft NetBEUI

2 Jeannie has installed an additional network card in her Windows XP Professional computer, for a total of two network cards. She goes to the Network Connections folder to configure her second network card; however, it doesn't appear as an Icon. What should Jeannie do to add the icon to the folder? (Choose the best answer.)

A ○ Open Device Manager and drag the second network card's icon into the Network Connections folder.

B ○ Open My Network Places and drag the second network card's icon into the Network Connections folder.

C ○ Run the Add New Network Adapter Wizard from the Network and Dial-Up Connections folder's Advanced menu.

D ○ Run the Add New Hardware Wizard from the computer's Control Panel.

3 You're configuring a Windows XP Professional machine for a user who needs dial-up access to the corporate LAN. This user has a "smart card" authentication device. On the Advanced Security Settings dialog box for the connection, which items should you select? (Choose all that apply.)

A ❑ MS-CHAP Version 2 (MS-CHAPv2)

B ❑ For MS-CHAP-based protocols, automatically use my Windows logon name and password (and domain if there is one)

C ❑ Unencrypted password (PAP)

D ❑ Use Extensible Authentication Protocol (EAP)

E ❑ Smart Card or other certificate (encryption enabled)

4 You're configuring a Windows XP Professional home machine for a telecommuter who plans to work from home 50 percent of the time. Your company is a government contractor and this employee works with sensitive military information. Therefore, you must provide a secure connection. Your boss tells you to set up a VPN link. Which protocol or protocols would be appropriate?

A ○ IPsec and NWLink

B ○ PPTP and NWLink

C ○ L2TP and IPsec

D ○ PPTP and L2TP

5 You administer a Windows XP network that contains both Professional machines and Server machines in a domain-based network using Active Directory. You consider activating Internet Connection Sharing (ICS) in order to avoid having to run high-speed DSL lines to every user in the Research department, which has its own domain. How should you proceed? (Choose the best answer.)

A ○ Create an Internet connection by using the Create New Connection Wizard, then access the icon's property sheets, click the Sharing tab, and check the Enable Internet Connection Sharing check box.

B ○ Create an Internet connection by using the Create New Connection Wizard, answering "yes" to the question "Do you wish to enable Internet Connection Sharing?".

C ○ Create an Internet connection by using the Create New Connection Wizard, then access the icon's property sheets, click the Advanced tab, and check the Allow Other Network Users to Connect Through This Computer's Internet Connection check box.

D ○ Configure the NAT service on a Windows XP Server computer.

6 You travel frequently and you want to set up your Windows XP Professional notebook computer so that you can dial up your corporate network while you're on the road. What step or steps should you take to increase security, in case your notebook is stolen? (Choose all that apply.)

A ❑ Configure Windows XP for autologon via the User Accounts control panel.

B ❑ Configure Windows XP for interactive logon via the User Accounts control panel.

C ❑ Enable callback security on your corporate communications server.

D ❑ Encrypt important files using EFS.

7 You use your Windows XP Professional machine to dial up two different Internet Service Providers. These two ISPs require you to enter different IP addresses for DNS servers. Assuming that you've already created connection icons for each account, how can you configure them for different DNS server addresses? (Choose the best answer.)

A ○ Open the Network control panel, right-click the connection icon for the first ISP account, click TCP/IP, click Properties, and enter the DNS server address. Repeat for the connection for the second ISP account.

B ○ Create a separate hardware profile for each configuration. Reboot into the first profile, right-click the connection icon for the first ISP account, click TCP/IP, click Properties, and enter the DNS server address. Reboot into the second hardware profile and repeat.

C ○ Open the Network Connections folder, right-click the connection icon for the first ISP account, choose Properties, click Networking, click TCP/IP, click Properties, and enter the DNS server address. Repeat for the connection for the second ISP account.

D ○ You can't take advantage of this action. Windows XP Professional supports just a single DNS configuration for the computer.

8 You configured a dial-up connection to an Internet Service Provider. When you double-click the connection icon, Windows XP Professional seems to dial the remote host and initiate a connection, but it hangs up shortly after you see the dialog box saying "Verifying username and password." After a couple of minutes, you see a dialog box stating "Error 619: The specified port isn't connected." Another user with a notebook computer running Windows 98 can use your phone connection to browse the Web with no problem. What could be the problem? (Choose the best answer.)

A ○ The phone line is noisy.

B ○ Your ISP doesn't support Windows XP.

C ○ Your connection is set up to require an encrypted password.

D ○ Your modem speed setting is too high.

9 You've created a dial-up connection to a private network by using the Create New Connection Wizard. Three other people use your computer. None of them can see the connection that you created. Why? (Choose the best answer.)

A ○ When you ran the wizard, you checked the box that says "Only for myself" in the Connection Availability dialog box.

B ○ The default setting on the connection icon's Sharing property sheet is for new connections to apply to your user profile only.

C ○ You were logged on as an administrator when you created the connection. No non-administrators can see a connection created by an administrator.

D ○ The three other people have poor vision.

10 You set up ICF on a Windows XP Professional machine but you want the ability to access the machine remotely via Remote Desktop. However, that doesn't seem to be working. What should you do to enable access? (Choose the best answer.)

A ○ Disable ICF. The firewall will not permit unsolicited access from outside.

B ○ Add the Remote Desktop service to ICF via the connection's Advanced tab.

C ○ Check the Allow Authenticated Inbound Access box on the Personal Firewall property sheet.

D ○ Install the File and Printer Sharing for Microsoft Networks service.

Answers

1 **A.** All Bob needs to connect is TCP/IP and a Web browser. The browser's included with Windows XP. The Client for Microsoft Networks is needed only if Bob is connecting to a Microsoft network, but just needs to connect to the Internet. File and Printer Sharing isn't needed and is, in fact, good to avoid. Finally, NetBEUI isn't the language of the Internet; TCP/IP is. *Review "Software prep."*

2 **D.** The absence of the card's icon means that Windows XP hasn't automatically detected the card's presence. That could happen with an older card that doesn't support Plug and Play, for example. In order to detect the new hardware, Jeannie must run the Add New Hardware Wizard, at which point the icon appears automatically in the Network Connections folder. *Review "Central control."*

3 **D** and **E.** If you choose D, options A, B, and C aren't available! Note that choice E also goes by the name of Transport Level Security, or TLS. *Review "Security tab."*

4 **C.** The combination of L2TP, which provides tunneling but not encryption, and IPsec, which provides encryption, would create a secure connection capability. *Review "VPN protocols."*

5 **D.** This is the only correct answer because you aren't supposed to enable ICS in a domain environment. The NAT service (Network Address Translation) on Windows 2002/2000 Server provides the same functionality that ICS does on a workgroup network. *Review "Internet Connection Sharing."*

6 **B** and **D.** You don't want automatic logon, because that means a thief doesn't need to know your username and password. You can't use callback security for a traveling user because the user isn't at a predetermined phone number. Encryption is a good idea because if a thief figures out how to log on (say, as Guest) but can't guess your particular username and password, he or she can't open your encrypted files. This last tidbit isn't in this chapter, but it's an example of the sort of cross-topic question you're likely to see on the exam. *Review "Creating Inbound Connections."*

7 **C.** Choice A is wrong because Windows XP doesn't have a Network control panel, it has a "Network Connections" control panel (picky, I know). Choice C works just fine. *Review "Connection independence."*

8 **C.** The most likely cause is that you've set the Security dialog box for your connection to require an encrypted password, but the ISP only supports unencrypted passwords. *Review "Security tab."*

9 **A.** The default selection at this dialog box is "For all users." Choice B is wrong because the Sharing tab is present in Windows 2000, not XP. D could be correct, but the odds are against it. *Review "Creating a connection."*

10 **B.** By adding a service, you're telling ICF that certain types of unsolicited inbound traffic are OK to permit and/or forward. *Review "Internet Connection Firewall."*

Part V
Tuning and Troubleshooting Windows XP

The 5th Wave   By Rich Tennant

"Remember—I want the bleeding file server surrounded by flaming workstations with the word 'Motherboard' scrolling underneath."

In this part . . .

The PC operating system that tunes itself, and fixes itself, isn't quite here yet. (Heck, we still don't even have a file system that automatically defragments itself. Ten years ago, I wouldn't have dreamed we'd still be running defrag utilities in the year 2002! And where are those personal jetpacks and flying cars that we were all supposed to be zipping around the metropolis with, anyway? Someone needs to get busy.)

So, performance tuning and problem-solving remain essential skills for computing professionals and favorite topics for MCSE questions. Chapter 14 looks at how you can make Windows XP go faster, and Chapter 15 looks at how you can make Windows XP go, period, when it decides to stop.

Chapter 14

Performance Optimization

· ·

Exam Objectives

▶ Optimize and troubleshoot processor utilization

▶ Monitor and configure multiprocessor computers

▶ Optimize and troubleshoot memory performance

▶ Optimize and troubleshoot disk performance

▶ Optimize and troubleshoot application performance

▶ Configure, manage, and troubleshoot Scheduled Tasks

· ·

The Microsoft exam objective list combines optimizing and trouble-shooting goals, which often fall into two separate mental buckets in the real world of system management. A typical corporate attitude is that a functioning, trouble-free system is *de rigueur,* and performance optimization is nice to have, assuming any money is leftover.

In fact, a computer component that's running really slowly may be even *worse* than something that's broken outright. The user may not know about the slow performance problem while she'd certainly know about (and fix) the obvious failure. So a big part of being a computer pro is knowing how to use the various stethoscopes and thermometers at your disposal.

The good news is that Windows XP provides some fairly good tools "out of the box" to monitor performance. The exam expects you to be quite familiar with these tools. The bad news is that with this operating system, optimizing and troubleshooting computer performance often involves the injection of cold, hard cash in the form of beefier hardware!

Quick Assessment

Optimize and troubleshoot processor utilization

1 The two common ways to add CPU horsepower are _____ and _____.

2 You could have a processor bottleneck if the queue length is greater than _____.

3 Windows XP Professional supports a maximum of _____ CPUs.

Monitor and configure multi-processor computers

4 After adding a second processor, you may be able to update the computer driver in _____ instead of reinstalling Windows.

5 A *hard page fault* is a situation where the computer must access _____.

Optimize and troubleshoot memory performance

6 The pagefile name is _____.

7 Before you defragment a disk, press the _____ button in Disk Defragmenter.

Optimize and troubleshoot disk performance

8 (True/False) . . .You can schedule Disk Defragmenter to run automatically at specified intervals.

9 The setting for whether foreground applications should get more CPU time is found on the _____ tab of the System control panel.

Optimize and troubleshoot application performance

Configure, manage, and troubleshoot Scheduled Tasks

10 The command-line version of the Task Scheduler is _____.

Answers

1 *Replace the processor with a faster one, add a second processor.* The "Processor Tuning" section explains.

2 *Two.* See "Processor monitoring" for more.

3 *Two.* The Home version only supports one. "Adding a second processor" has details.

4 *Device Manager.* Again, see the section "Adding a second processor."

5 *The disk.* See "Performance console method" for more.

6 *PAGEFILE.SYS.* See the "Location" section.

7 *Analyze.* The disk may not need defragmenting. See the "Defragmenting" section if you missed this one.

8 *True.* This statement is false for Windows 2000 Professional. See "Defragmenting."

9 *Advanced.* The "Foreground/background adjustment" section has more.

10 *AT.EXE.* See "Disk maintenance and Scheduled Tasks" for this and other riveting tidbits.

Monitoring Tools

This first section introduces the performance monitoring tools that come with Windows XP, along with a primer on their operation. In later sections, you can apply this knowledge to specific troubleshooting and optimization areas, such as disk, CPU, and memory.

The very running of a performance monitoring tool has an effect on performance, because the tool has its own CPU, memory, and graphical requirements.

Performance Monitor

The fanciest performance monitoring tool in Windows XP is the Performance console, which you can get to (assuming you've set the control panel for the simpler "classic view" instead of the new, more complex "category view") by choosing Start➪Control Panel, opening Administrative Tools, and then opening the Performance icon. (Alternatively, you can create a desktop shortcut to C:\WINDOWS\SYSTEM32\PERFMON.MSC or just choose Start➪Run and type **PERFMON**.)

The two main snap-ins to this console are *System Monitor* and *Performance Logs and Alerts*. (Note that you can also view Performance Logs and Alerts on the Computer Management console.)

Objects, counters, and instances

In the Performance console's System Monitor snap-in, an *object* is a computer component to measure, and a *counter* is a specific performance measurement. Any given object may have more than one associated counter. For example, in a track meet, a runner would be an object, and that runner's times in the hundred-yard dash and in the mile would be two separate counters for the runner object.

Objects and counters often appear together, separated by a backslash or hyphen. For example, *Runner\100yarddash* would mean the counter "100yarddash" for the object "Runner."

An *instance* identifies which object the Performance console should monitor when more than one such object exists in the system. If, at the track meet, four runners are competing in each race, you will have four instances of the Runner object: Runner(1), Runner(2), Runner(3), and Runner(4). So the counter that reports how quickly Runner 2 performs in the mile race would appear as *Runner(2)\mile*. Note that not all objects in a computer system have multiple instances; memory is an example.

Add counters by right-clicking anywhere in the System Monitor display area and choosing Add Counters, or by clicking the + button on the toolbar. You should see a dialog box similar to the one shown in Figure 14-1. You choose an object first and then a counter. The Explain button opens a window of text that elaborates on the counter you highlight.

Figure 14-1:
Adding a
counter to
an object
in the
Perform-
ance
console's
System
Monitor.

Notice in Figure 14-1 that you can monitor remote computers with System Monitor (see the drop-down list under "Select counters from computer:"), which is very handy for technicians and troubleshooters. Just keep the update frequency as low as you can while still capturing the data you need. Also be aware that your account must have administrative privileges on the machine that you're monitoring.

Views

System Monitor offers a variety of ways to view data, controllable via three toolbar buttons:

- ✔ **Graph:** What we used to call "line graph" in college; the most useful general-purpose view

- ✔ **Histogram:** Ten-dollar term for bar chart

- ✔ **Report:** Text mode only, for those who like decimal places

If you right-click System Monitor in the snap-in tree on the left, or scan the various text menus, you may notice that the Properties option is conspicuously absent. Oops! However, if you click the Properties toolbar button (normally fourth from the right) or type Ctrl+Q, you get a proper Properties window. This property sheet (see Figure 14-2) lets you control the sample frequency (default 1 second), displayed screen elements, and what the histogram and report modes actually show: current data, an average, maximum, minimum. Other tabs let you set color, font, and scaling preferences.

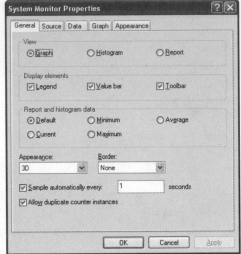

Figure 14-2:
A proper
Properties
sheet.

Performance logs and alerts

If you have a heart problem, the doctor may put you on a heart monitor that tracks cardiac activity for a 24-hour period or longer. That monitoring device may also have an alarm that sounds when the patient's heart rate strays outside safe limits, for example, when watching *Baywatch*.

The Performance console's Performance Logs and Alerts snap-in can generate log files that you can collect over a reasonable time period and then view at your leisure later, using the same System Monitor display that you use to watch real-time data. (Click the View Log Data toolbar icon and specify the log filename on the Source tab.) You can also configure performance alerts that trigger events or messages when certain threshold levels are violated.

Here's what you must know about the Performance Logs and Alerts snap-in:

✔ **Counter logs** let you create disk files that record the state of object counters you specify, at a frequency you specify. The default format is *.BLG, for Binary LoG.

✔ **Trace logs** monitor a particular value continuously, rather than at sampling intervals. You can't trace every object counter that you can run counter logs for.

✔ **Alerts** can specify a minimum or maximum threshold for any counter, and can generate an application log entry, send a message to any computer on the network (see Figure 14-3), start a log file, and/or run any program you specify.

✔ **Create** a new log or alert by selecting the appropriate branch under the Performance Logs and Alerts snap-in in the left window pane, and by right-clicking the right (details) window pane and choosing New Log Settings or New Alert Settings. Give the log or alert a name and set its properties.

✔ All logs go by default to the C:\PERFLOGS folder.

✔ You need to be an Administrator to set logs and alerts.

✔ If you set the sampling frequency or number of counters too high, you can run out of disk space in a major hurry.

✔ You can use the Schedule tab on the property sheets of logs and alerts to set begin and end times, or you can start and stop logs and alerts manually by right-clicking the icon in the details pane and choosing Start or Stop.

Figure 14-3:
An alert message stating that lots of disk paging is going on.

Task Manager

If the Performance console is like a $500 oscilloscope, Task Manager is like a $50 handheld voltmeter. Less complete than the Performance console, but also easier to understand and use, Task Manager comes in handy for taking a quick look at key system performance variables. Activate Task Manager by pressing Ctrl+Alt+Del and clicking the Task Manager button. (I know, it seems like a weird way to get to a program. A faster way is to choose Start⇨Run and type **TASKMGR**.) You should see a screen similar to the one shown in Figure 14-4, with (at minimum) the three tabs Applications, Processes, and Performance, and (if you're networked) Networking.

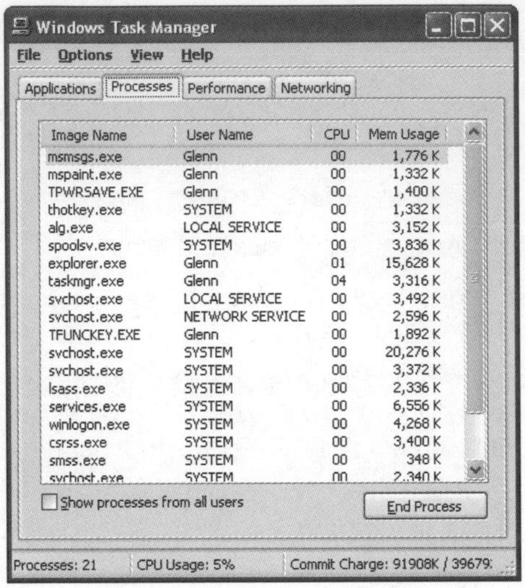

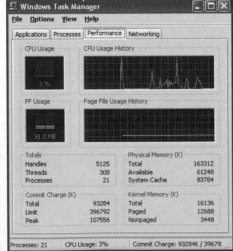

Figure 14-4:
The Task
Manager
Processes
display.

The Applications tab has the simplest display and shows a list of running programs and their status (usually either "running" or "not responding"). The Processes tab shows not only programs but also services and operating system executables, along with CPU and memory usage by process. The Performance tab (see Figure 14-5) shows overall figures for CPU and memory usage, along with rolling line graphs. I'll have more to say about the Performance tab later in this chapter in the section "Determining the right amount of RAM." Finally, the Networking tab shows network card traffic as a percentage of available bandwidth; the scale adjusts automatically.

Figure 14-5:
The Task
Manager
Performance
display.

Network Monitor

Windows 2002 and 2000 Server come with a tool named *Network Monitor*, which permits analysis of frames (network packets) sent and received by using the server's network interface card(s). The BackOffice product Systems Management Server comes with an industrial strength version of Network Monitor that can monitor packet traffic at client workstations as well as servers. Windows XP Professional doesn't come with either version of Network Monitor, but it does come with a Network Monitor driver that permits SMS to watch traffic on a Windows XP Professional PC. Install the Network Monitor driver as you would any network protocol.

Processor Tuning

Processor tuning falls into three categories: monitoring existing CPU usage, adjusting the foreground-to-background CPU time split, and adding a second CPU. The next sections deal with each topic in turn.

Microsoft specifies a Pentium 233 CPU for running Windows XP Professional. As a practical matter, you want a more powerful CPU than that. A Pentium II class processor running at 300 megahertz is a more realistic minimum level. Windows XP is, shall we say, not the most efficient operating system in terms of processor requirements!

Processor monitoring

You can perform some quick-and-dirty CPU monitoring in Task Manager. The Applications and Processes tabs let you see which applications and processes are using the most CPU time while the Performance tab lets you watch total CPU usage via a graphical display. You can keep an eye on the Performance tab while opening and running typical applications on the system to get a sense of whether the CPU may be a bottleneck. You may find that one application in particular is a CPU hog and you may be able to modify its default settings to reduce the performance drain it causes.

If a quick analysis suggests a closer look, then you can collect and analyze more detailed data on CPU usage with the Performance console. Here are some of the counters to watch:

 ✔ **Processor\% Processor Time:** What percent of total time the CPU is busy doing useful work. Periodically pegging out at 100% is okay, but long stretches over 85% indicate a bottleneck (or a misbehaving application).

✔ **Processor\Interrupts\Sec:** How many hardware interrupts the CPU deals with per second. Hardware interrupts come from devices rather than from programs. Microsoft says watch out if you have more than 15 here.

✔ **Processor\% Privileged Time:** What percent of the CPU's busy time (or "non-idle time" as Microsoft puts it) is spent in *privileged mode*, that is, handling operating system and hardware requests (as opposed to *user mode*, which applications typically use). If this value goes up suddenly and dramatically, you may have a failing network card or other device; adapters sometimes flood the CPU with interrupts when they go bad.

✔ **System\Processor Queue Length:** How many threads are waiting around in line to be handled by the CPU (or CPUs, in a two-processor system). Any number greater than two may mean processor bottleneck.

On a multiple-processor system, you can specify which processor you want to measure by making a selection in the instances list of the Add Counters dialog box. You can specify that you want to measure all processors, in aggregate, by choosing the *_Total* instance.

Foreground/background adjustment

You can make a very broad adjustment to modify whether Windows XP pays more CPU attention to the *foreground* program (the application you're running in an open, active window with a highlighted title bar) or pays equal attention to foreground and background programs (background programs being applications and services that are not running in the top window).

Windows XP Professional defaults to the traditional Windows behavior of favoring the foreground program, but you may prefer a more server-like distribution of processor power if you often run background programs (such as backup or printing operations) and if those programs run poorly. To make such a change, follow the steps in Lab 14-1.

Lab 14-1   Adjusting Processor Behavior

1. **Right-click My Computer and choose Properties.**

   The System control panel appears.

2. **Click the Advanced tab.**

3. **Click the Settings button in the Performance area.**

4. **Click the Advanced tab.**

5. **In the Processor Scheduling area, click the Background Services radio button.**

6. **Click OK and click OK again to close the dialog boxes.**

Adding a second processor

Based on monitoring as I discuss earlier in this section, you may find that you need to add processing power to a PC for which the CPU has become a bottleneck. If you run graphics-intensive applications, engineering design software, or scientific analysis programs, then you may be a candidate for CPU turbocharging. You can add processing power two ways: by replacing your CPU with a faster one (assuming the particular PC supports such replacement), or by adding a second CPU to a single-processor machine (again, assuming your PC has the expansion socket available).

Windows XP Professional supports up to two processors in a single PC, using a scheme called *symmetric multiprocessing* or *SMP*. If you install Windows XP onto a PC with two processors, the setup program should automatically detect them and install SMP support. However, if you install Windows XP onto a PC with only one CPU installed and then add a second CPU later, Windows XP doesn't automatically detect the change and make adjustments. Adding a second processor fundamentally changes how Windows XP deals with your hardware, and it's not an action that a mere Plug and Play device detection can handle. For one thing, Windows XP uses a different HAL (Hardware Abstraction Layer) for an SMP machine than for a single-CPU machine.

So, the multiple-CPU upgrade requires one of two actions: You can reinstall Windows XP over itself, or you can update the driver for the Computer object in Device Manager. Lab 14-2 details the second method, which usually works fine and which is a lot faster; if it fails, you must reinstall.

The method that I describe in Lab 14-2 may render your PC unusable if you haven't actually installed a second CPU!

Lab 14-2   Reconfiguring for Multiple Processor Support

1. **Log in as an Administrator.**

2. **Run the System control panel by right-clicking My Computer and choosing Properties.**

3. **Click the Hardware tab.**

4. **Click the Device Manager button.**

5. **Double-click the Computer icon at the top of the tree to expand its contents.**

6. **Right-click your computer model (just under the Computer icon) and choose Update Driver.**

7. **Click Install From A List Or Specific Location (Advanced).**

8. **Click Next.**

9. **Click Don't Choose. I Will Choose The Driver To Install, and click Next.**

10. **Select the new driver in the Model column, based on your best educated guess.**

    For example, you would normally upgrade an "ACPI PC" to an "ACPI Multiprocessor PC."

11. **Click Next, click Next again, and click Finish.**

Before considering a processor upgrade, use Task Manager to make sure you aren't running any unnecessary services on your PC. Check your startup group and system tray for any utilities that may be loading at boot time but that you may not need. Modify the settings of any loaded programs (such as antivirus utilities) and see whether the changes reduce the burden on the CPU. And make sure that you don't have a PCI or ISA card that's flooding the CPU with interrupts in a failure mode.

On a dual-processor PC, you can specify that a particular process run on a particular CPU: Because you're denying Windows some flexibility in managing the load balance between the two CPUs, you should make such a setting permanent only after careful experimentation with System Monitor. Open Task Manager, click the Processes tab, right-click the process of interest, choose Set Affinity, and specify the CPU. (You won't see this option on a single-CPU machine.)

Memory Tuning

Windows XP Professional memory tuning is vital to the performance of your PC. Optimizing memory has two components: tuning RAM and tuning the pagefile.

Determining the right amount of RAM

Windows XP Professional is more of a memory hog than any previous version of Windows. When Windows XP runs out of physical RAM, it uses the disk-based *pagefile*, at a serious performance penalty. (You may see the word *swap file* on the exam; it's synonymous with *pagefile* for all intents and purposes.) So the best action you can take for improved memory performance is to add RAM so that Windows XP doesn't need to use the pagefile much, if at all.

Task Manager method

One quick way to see how much more memory you may need in a given PC is to load the applications you usually run, open some typical size data files in each application; then run Task Manager and click the Performance tab. Look at the graph titled PF Usage. You see that the number shown is the same as the Total Commit Charge in the lower left of the display (making adjustments for units — that is, divide Total Commit Charge [KB] by 1024 to get PF Usage [MB]).

"Commit" memory is the sum of memory used by all the software on the computer: operating system, applications, services, the lot.

Task Manager also shows the Commit Charge Limit (which is RAM plus page-file size), and Commit Charge Peak (maximum commit charge since last reboot).

Diagonally up and to the right of the Commit Charge memory figures is the Physical Memory area. Total Physical Memory is how many kilobytes of RAM the PC has. If you subtract Total Physical Memory from Total Commit Charge, you can see how much more RAM you need at that moment to avoid paging. Taking things one step further, if you subtract Total Physical Memory from Peak Commit Charge, you can see how much more RAM you'd need to avoid paging during the entire computing session since the last reboot.

Now go buy your RAM expansion module, and enjoy a faster PC.

Performance console method

In the Performance console, the two most relevant counters for the Memory object are:

- **Pages/second:** This number is how many "hard" page faults occur, that is, cases when a program needs data that isn't in RAM but resides on disk in the pagefile. Hard page faults slow down the system, so bigger numbers are bad. Frequent peaks over 20 indicate a potential problem.

- **Available Mbytes:** How much physical RAM is available for use by the operating system or programs. If this value falls below 4 on a regular basis, you need more RAM.

Windows XP adds a fairly obscure memory setting that you can tweak if your PC acts primarily as a server. Click the Advanced tab of the System control panel, click the Settings button in the Performance box, and click the Advanced tab again in the Performance Options dialog box. In the Memory Usage box, the Programs radio button is checked by default, meaning that Windows allocates memory for programs preferentially to file caching. Click the System Cache radio button for Windows to allocate more RAM for file caching.

Optimizing the pagefile

If you can't put as much RAM into your system as the previous section indicates, the next best thing is to optimize the pagefile. You can modify the pagefile's size, location, and fragmentation level to improve virtual memory performance. The first two are available to you via the Advanced tab of the System control panel; click the Settings button in the Performance area, click the Advanced tab, and click the Change button in the Virtual Memory area. You'll see a dialog box like that in Figure 14-6.

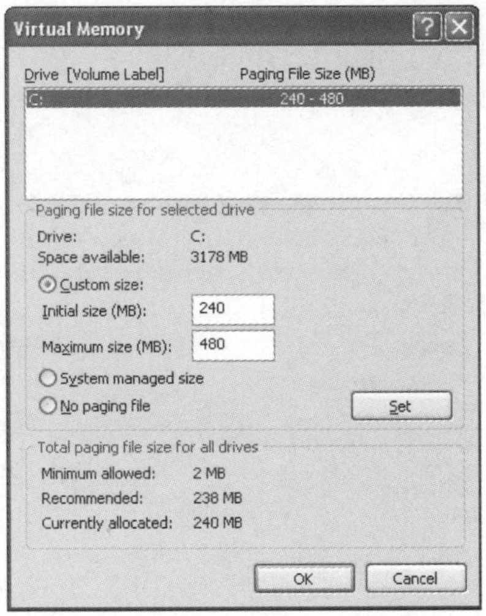

Figure 14-6:
Verify optimum pagefile settings here.

Virtual Memory

Drive [Volume Label]   Paging File Size (MB)
C: 240 - 480

Paging file size for selected drive
Drive: C:
Space available: 3178 MB

⦿ Custom size:
Initial size (MB):   240
Maximum size (MB):   480
○ System managed size
○ No paging file   Set

Total paging file size for all drives
Minimum allowed: 2 MB
Recommended: 238 MB
Currently allocated: 240 MB

OK   Cancel

You must be logged on as an Administrator to change pagefile settings.

Size

By default, the pagefile size is 1.5 times the amount of installed RAM. You may need to increase that if you work with a lot of applications loaded into memory at the same time and get "out of memory" errors. The maximum pagefile size is the sum of available disk space on all local hard drives, but you would usually increase the size in reasonable increments (for example, 32MB) until the error messages go away, so you don't tie up disk space needlessly.

Increasing the pagefile size doesn't generally require a restart, but decreasing it does.

If the preset pagefile size is too small, overall performance is likely to suffer. When Windows must increase pagefile size to meet memory demand, the system practically comes to a halt during the resizing operation.

You can use the Performance console to check pagefile usage. The object is Paging File and the counter is % Usage.

Normally, Windows dynamically increases pagefile size from the Initial Size up to the Maximum Size on the dialog box, depending on system requirements. By setting the Initial Size to be the same as the Maximum Size, you reduce the operating system overhead associated with dynamic size adjustment. This is a good performance tip if you have plenty of disk space.

Location

The default location for the pagefile (PAGEFILE.SYS) is on the root of the boot drive, but you can change that. For example, you could set up the pagefile to live on a second physical hard drive, in order to perform some rudimentary load balancing.

You don't even have to limit yourself to a single pagefile: You can create several of the rascals and put 'em onto different drives. In fact, the more hard drives on which you have pagefile fragments living, the better Windows XP performs.

Fragmentation

Disk Defragmenter doesn't defragment the pagefile in Windows 2000, but it does in Windows XP Professional, so running a defrag operation may help improve paging performance. See the "Defragmenting" section later in this chapter for details on this utility.

Disk Tuning

Hot on the heels of CPU and memory optimization comes disk tuning, which typically involves monitoring, defragmenting, and scheduled periodic cleanup.

Disk performance monitoring

Task Manager isn't much help when it comes to disk performance monitoring, so you should use the Performance console here. (Note that if you want to monitor disks by volume or logical drive letter rather than by physical disk, you no longer need to activate the necessary counters by typing the **DISKPERF –YV** command, as you need to do with Windows 2000.) The values to watch for the PhysicalDisk object include the following:

> ✔ **% Disk Time:** 90 percent or more for extended periods, and your disk is a bottleneck. Adding a hard drive could help, as could replacing the existing one with a faster unit.
>
> ✔ **Current Disk Queue Length:** If this value is over 2 + the number of physical disks, your disk is a bottleneck.
>
> ✔ **Disk Reads/Sec and Disk Writes/Sec:** If the total of reads and writes is up around 40 or so and you have an EIDE disk, consider replacing it with a new Ultra SCSI one.

Adding RAM, if necessary, and optimizing the pagefile can dramatically reduce disk activity. Take those steps before deciding that you need a newer, faster hard drive. (There's a reason I put these topics in a certain order!) Also, you may find that defragmenting your disk can bring the counter values down, too, as I explain in the next section.

Defragmenting

Unlike Windows NT Workstation 4.0, Windows XP Professional comes with a simple disk defragmenter. Defragmenters improve performance by undoing the fragmentation or "chopping up" that operating systems typically perform as they allocate space for files. That is, defragmenters realign all the bits and pieces of a file so that they are adjacent, or *contiguous*, meaning that the disk drive's read/write heads have to do less bouncing around to read or write the file. Whatever file system you use, NTFS, FAT32, or FAT, the Disk Defragmenter utility can consolidate most of the fragmented files. (This utility now defragments the pagefile, unlike the Windows 2000 version, making it even more useful.)

In what can only be explained as an attack of Overly Obsessive Paranoia Syndrome (OOPS), Microsoft programmers decided that you need to be logged on as an Administrator before you can defragment your disks. Having done so, you can access Disk Defragmenter by right-clicking a drive in My Computer, choosing Properties, clicking the Tools tab and then clicking the Defragment Now button. Defragment Now doesn't "defragment now," it just opens the Disk Defragmenter window (see Figure 14-7). (A quicker method is to run CMD and type **DFRG** to activate the DFRG.MSC console.)

The suggested approach is to analyze a disk before defragging it, as Windows XP may advise you that the disk doesn't need optimizing. I recommend that you close all applications before running this utility; open files may not be able to be consolidated. Disk Defragmenter doesn't have any options that you can set.

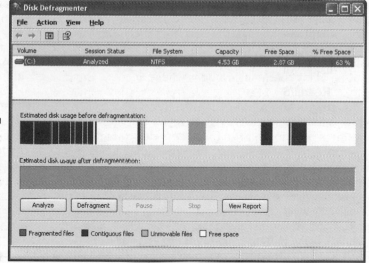

Figure 14-7:
The colored
regions
show
optimized
and
fragmented
areas.

You need to have about 15 percent free disk space for this utility to do its job properly. Therefore, on a really full disk, you may enjoy better performance if you use the Cleanup Wizard (CLEANMGR.EXE) before running Disk Defragmenter.

You can run Disk Defragmenter only on local drives. And you can have only one instance of the program going at a time.

A major improvement in Windows XP is the existence of a command-line equivalent to the graphical Disk Defragmenter console, and that's DEFRAG.EXE. The **-a** qualifier does an analysis, and the **-f** qualifier forces a defrag even if the utility doesn't think you need it. You can now run defrag operations via batch files, scripts, and the Scheduled Tasks tool — which brings us to the next section.

Disk maintenance and Scheduled Tasks

If remembering to defragment your disks once in a while is helpful, having Windows XP automatically defragment them on a regular basis is more helpful. This is as good a time as any to introduce the Scheduled Tasks utility (which is similar to the utility of the same name in Windows 98). Microsoft sometimes calls this utility the Task Scheduler, so don't be confused.

Get to Scheduled Tasks through the Control Panel and run the wizard by double-clicking the Add Scheduled Task icon. You can specify a program to run, a descriptive name for the task, how often the task should run (daily, weekly, monthly, at each reboot, at each logon, or once), when the task should run (time and date), and the name and password (which, by the way, cannot be blank) of the user under whose account the task should run.

This last item is important because many tasks (such as defragmenting a disk) require administrative rights. If you configure several scheduled tasks and a single task doesn't run but others do, you may have a problem with user rights. If you configure several scheduled tasks and none of them run, then you may suspect that the Task Scheduler service itself has been stopped, paused, or never started. (You can manually restart the service by using the Services console in the Administrative Tools folder.)

After you create a scheduled task, you can view its property sheet from the Scheduled Tasks folder to modify it further. For example, the Settings tab (see Figure 14-8) provides additional options for starting and stopping tasks, such as whether to wait for idle time before starting a task and whether to run a task when the computer is using battery power. The scheduled task object is actually a file with the suffix .JOB, and the default location is `C:\WINDOWS\TASKS`.

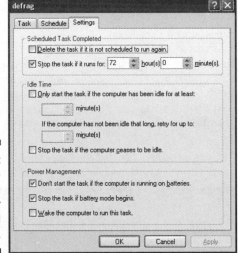

Figure 14-8:
Set con-
figuration
options for
scheduled
tasks here.

You should know for the exam the meaning of the various options on the Scheduled Tasks folder's Advanced menu, as follows:

✔ **Stop Using Task Scheduler:** This one's self-explanatory.

✔ **Pause Task Scheduler:** This one morphs into "Continue Task Scheduler" if you choose it. If the time specified for a task comes and goes while the scheduler is paused, the task doesn't run until its next scheduled time (if any).

✔ **Notify Me of Missed Tasks:** Oddly, the default for this toggle setting is off (cleared). You may see an exam question that expects you to know this fact.

✔ **AT Service Account:** Here, you name the user account for all tasks created with the command-line utility, AT. (See this section's last paragraph for more on AT.)

✔ **View Log:** This command runs Notepad with a log of the utility's actions (the file SCHEDLGU.TXT in C:\WINDOWS).

Use the task scheduler tool to schedule recurring maintenance tasks, such as running the disk defragmenter or the Disk Cleanup Wizard. Scheduled Tasks is also handy for running resource-intensive programs when you don't need the computer, for example at night.

Make sure your PC's system date and time are set correctly via the Date and Time control panel. If this information is inaccurate, any tasks you have scheduled won't run when you expect them to.

You may need to modify the command line to accomplish an automated task. For example, when scheduling the Backup program, you would normally specify a backup job name on the command line so that the program knows what files you want to back up, and where they should go.

A command-line version of the graphical Scheduled Tasks utility is AT.EXE. All tasks that you create by using this program must run under the same user security context, which you set in the Advanced menu of the graphical utility. The graphical utility is more flexible than AT.EXE, in that each task can run in a different user security account context.

Application Tuning

The method for tuning application performance that's likely to be on the exam is the foreground/background split adjustment for CPU time, which I explain in the section "Foreground/background adjustment" earlier in this chapter.

You can set the priority levels of individual processes by using the Task Manager's Processes tab. That's a bit risky, but you can experiment with the technique if you like. Just right-click a process and choose Set Priority, followed by the value you want. The values are, from highest priority to lowest, realtime; high; abovenormal; normal; belownormal; and low. Note that any priority changes you make in Task Manager remain in effect only while the process is running: If you stop and restart the process, it reverts to the default base priority level that its programmer originally coded for it.

One final performance tidbit has to do with display effects. Strangely, Microsoft placed these settings in the System control panel instead of the Display control panel; click the Advanced tab, the Settings button in the Performance box, and have a look at the nine zillion options on the Visual Effects tab (shown in Figure 14-9). If you want maximum performance and don't have a lot of time to tweak individual effects, just click the Adjust For Best Performance radio button.

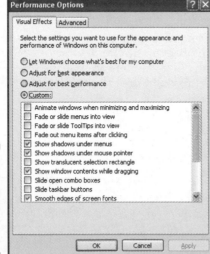

Figure 14-9:
The fewer visual effects, the faster your PC goes.

Prep Test

1 You install Windows XP Professional onto 14 computers using a disk cloning technique. You discover that (unbeknownst to you) the 14 machines have dual Pentium processors. However, the machine you used to make the master disk image only has one CPU. As a result, the cloned systems are not using their second CPUs. You do not want to reclone the operating system onto the 14 computers if you can help it. What can you do? (Choose the best answer.)

A ○ Go to each machine's System control panel. Click the Advanced tab and check the box labeled "Enable SMP."

B ○ Go to each machine's System control panel. Click the Hardware tab and check the box labeled "Enable SMP."

C ○ Go to each machine's System control panel. Click the Hardware tab, open Device Manager, and update the driver for the Computer device to a multiprocessor version.

D ○ Go to each machine and enable multiprocessor support in the BIOS.

E ○ Go to each machine and remove the second CPU.

2 What is the default size of the pagefile? (Choose one answer.)

A ○ 1.0 times installed RAM

B ○ 1.5 times installed RAM

C ○ 2.0 times installed RAM

D ○ 256MB minus installed RAM

3 On a multiprocessor machine, Windows XP's Performance console lets you use System Monitor to track activity on each CPU separately. In this situation, the graph for each CPU's "percent processor time" would correspond to a separate:

A ○ Object

B ○ Counter

C ○ Instance

D ○ Module

4 You set up a Windows XP Professional computer in a small workgroup. You decide to dedicate this particular computer to sharing files for the group, and you put all the shared files onto this machine. You're aware that no more than 10 computers can access these files simultaneously, but that's not a problem because your workgroup consists of 8 computers. You install the File and Printer Sharing service and bind it to the local area connection.

Before you lock away the monitor in a closet, what performance setting or settings should you change from the default value? (Choose all that apply.)

A ❑ Optimize Performance For Background Services, in the Processor Scheduling area of the System control panel

B ❑ System Cache, in the Memory Usage area of the System control panel

C ❑ Optimize Performance For Applications, in the System control panel

D ❑ Optimize Performance For Workgroup Services, in the System control panel

E ❑ Increase the priority of the LSASS.EXE process, in Task Manager

5 While logged on as an Administrator, you set up Scheduled Tasks to run the Backup program every night at 2 a.m. to perform a data folder backup from your C drive to your D drive. For the task's security context, you specify a member of the Users group. The next day, you find that Backup did not execute. Why not?

A ○ You must create the task when logged on as a Backup Operator.

B ○ You must specify a different security context.

C ○ You must use the AT.EXE command to run Backup.

D ○ NTBACKUP doesn't perform disk-to-disk backups.

6 You run System Monitor on a PC whose user is complaining of poor performance. You add counters for Available MBytes and Pages/second for the Memory object. After watching these values while the user performs normal daily tasks, you see that Available MBytes frequently drops below 16 but never drops below 8. The Pages/second graph shows frequent spikes in the range from 5 to 10. What do these monitoring statistics indicate? (Choose the best answer.)

A ○ The user's pagefile is heavily fragmented.

B ○ The user's disk is heavily fragmented.

C ○ The user needs more RAM.

D ○ The user has enough RAM.

E ○ The foreground/background setting needs adjusting.

F ○ The maximum pagefile size is set too low.

7 Bob comes to you with a problem. He has 920MB used on a 1000MB hard drive that is formatted with NTFS. When he runs DFRG.MSC, he receives a warning message. Bob knows he has too many files on his system. Of the following values, which is the smallest amount of additional space that Bob can free up in order to make the error message go away? (Choose the best answer.)

A ○ 120MB

B ○ 100MB

C ○ 80MB

D ○ 60MB

E ○ 40MB

8 In the Task Manager's Performance tab, what's the commit charge limit?

A ○ The current pagefile size

B ○ The minimum pagefile size

C ○ The maximum pagefile size

D ○ The maximum pagefile size plus installed RAM

E ○ The maximum pagefile size minus installed RAM

Answers

1 **C.** By "updating" the driver for the computer itself, you're actually changing the Hardware Abstraction Layer (HAL), which you must do if the multiprocessor machines are to recognize the second processor. *Review "Adding a second processor."*

2 **B.** So, the more RAM you have, the larger your swap file — which doesn't necessarily make sense, so you should remember it! Also remember that too small a swap file hurts system performance. *Review "Optimizing the pagefile."*

3 **C.** The object is "processor," the counter is "% processor time," and the instances are processor #1 and processor #2. *Review "Objects, counters, and instances."*

4 **A** and **B.** This computer won't be running any foreground applications, so a bit more CPU time should go to programs running in the background, such as the Server service (File and Printer Sharing). Choice B is a new setting with Windows XP and gives file caching priority over programs when it comes to allocating RAM. As for choice E, modifying the priority of a process is a temporary setting, not a persistent one. *Review "Foreground/background adjustment."*

5 **B.** The user account that you specify as the task's security context must have appropriate user rights to perform the task — in this case, you should specify a member of the Backup Operators group or a member of the Administrators group. *Review "Disk maintenance and Scheduled Tasks."*

6 **D.** This user probably has enough RAM for the application mix. The general rules are that Available MBytes shouldn't fall below 4 on a regular basis, and Pages/second shouldn't have sustained rates above 20. As for choices A and B, memory counters don't tell you anything about pagefile fragmentation. *Review "Determining the right amount of RAM."*

7 **C.** 920 minus 80 is 840, leaving 16 percent of the drive free; the Disk Defragmenter needs to see 15 percent free in order to perform optimally. *Review "Defragmenting."*

8 **D.** The commit charge limit is effectively the maximum amount of memory, whether RAM-based or pagefile-based, available to the system. *Review "Determining the right amount of RAM."*

Chapter 15

Troubleshooting and Recovering Windows XP Systems

● ●

Exam Objectives

▶ Troubleshoot failed installations

▶ Manage and troubleshoot drivers and driver signing

▶ Recover system state data and user data by using Windows Backup

▶ Troubleshoot system restoration by starting in Safe Mode

▶ Recover system state data and user data by using the Recovery Console

● ●

Anybody could be a Windows XP expert if things always went right. When trouble strikes, the pros rub their hands together with relish (the attitude, not the condiment) while the amateurs bolt for the phone. Your days of bolting are about to be over.

The certification exam expects you to know what to do when Windows XP goes awry, and specifically how to use features brought over from Windows 2000 — signed drivers, safe mode, the new backup program, and recovery console — to resuscitate a dead or dying PC. Windows XP introduces some new recovery tools to the NT/2000 product line, including Automated System Recovery, driver rollback, and System Restore. The exam is likely to hit these topics as well, so I'll do the same.

Quick Assessment

Troubleshoot failed installations

1 If Windows XP Professional is having trouble installing network components, make sure that a _____ and a _____ are online.

2 If the setup program fails during the graphical phase, a good log file to check would be _____.

Manage and troubleshoot drivers and driver signing

3 Probably the most convenient way to update device drivers is via the _____ display.

4 Vendors sometimes provide driver updates in the form of an _____ file which you can right-click and choose Install.

5 The three options for driver signing are _____, _____, and _____.

6 (True/False) To set the driver signing option for all users of the PC, you must log on as Administrator.

Recover system state data and user data by using Windows Backup

7 The set of files that Windows Backup calls the _____ contains by default the Registry and protected system files.

Troubleshoot system restoration by starting in Safe Mode

8 The name of the log file created during a Safe Mode boot is _____.

Recover system state data and user data by using Recovery Console

9 You can install Recovery Console "permanently" by running WINNT32 with the _____ option.

10 (True/False) The Recovery Console commands are the same that you would type in a regular command prompt window.

Answers

1 *Domain controller, DNS server.* See "Setup lockups" for more on installation woes.

2 *SETUPACT.LOG.* The section "The trail of crumbs" lays out log file details.

3 *Device Manager.* The "Driver updating" section has more on the different methods.

4 *INF.* Again, check out "Driver updating."

5 *Ignore, warn, and fail.* The section "Driver signing (not by famous golfers)" elaborates.

6 *True.* You have to be an Administrator to set darned near anything on this operating system. See "Driver signing (not by famous golfers)."

7 *System state.* The section "System state backups" has more.

8 *NTBTLOG.TXT.* See "Safe Mode" for details if you missed this one.

9 */CMDCONS.* The section "Installing Recovery Console onto the hard disk" includes this important detail.

10 *False.* See the section entitled "Recovery Console" for more.

Installation Irritations

Your first introduction to Windows XP system recovery may be an early one if the setup process fails to complete correctly.

Setup lockups

Several situations or conditions can cause the Windows XP setup program to fail at various different points. The following list describes common failure modes along with recommended fixes:

- **Inadequate disk space:** The general rule is that you should have 2GB of free space on the partition (not necessarily disk!) to which you're installing Windows XP Professional.

- **Failure to detect essential hardware:** For example, if the setup program doesn't recognize your CD-ROM drive, you can start an upgrade from Windows 98 but you may not be able to continue it after the first reboot. In such a case, you may need to use a different drive (one that's on the Hardware Compatibility List) or install Windows from a network distribution server.

- **Conflicts with running applications:** If you're upgrading from an earlier version of Windows, you may need to disable any third-party power management, antivirus, disk quota, and networking software before running setup. (Note that this includes BIOS-based antivirus software!)

- **Failure to find server(s):** If you tell setup that you want to join an existing domain, a domain controller and DNS server (they may be the same machine) must be up and connected to the PC where you're installing Windows XP Professional. You also have to get the domain name correct when running the setup program and make sure that the local computer name is unique among other computer names, domain names, and workgroup names.

- **Flaky hardware:** If a disk controller, memory module, or other essential piece of hardware isn't performing up to spec, Windows XP Professional may consistently fail to install. Any newly added hardware is suspect. Consider updating device firmware (such as a SCSI controller's BIOS) before tossing the hardware in the trash bin.

The trail of crumbs

The setup program makes a number of plain-text log files as it goes along, recording the things that go right as well as those that go wrong. You don't have to memorize all of them (the list is quite long). Here are the key ones you should know for the exam (the list assumes you install Windows XP into the default folder `C:\WINDOWS`):

- `C:\WINDOWS\SETUPACT.LOG` is a chronological list of pretty much every action the setup program takes, after its graphical mode begins, and any errors that the program encounters. Microsoft sometimes calls this the "action log."

- `C:\WINDOWS\SETUPERR.LOG`, or simply the "error log," just has the errors in it, along with severity codes.

- `C:\WINDOWS\WINNT32.LOG` records the checking of available disk space and the copying of temporary boot files (for example, from the installation CD-ROM to the hard drive's system partition).

- `C:\WINDOWS\DEBUG\NETSETUP.LOG` covers network connection steps.

- `C:\WINDOWS\SECURITY\LOGS\SCESETUP.LOG` includes details of access control settings on Registry keys and files. (The "SCE" part of the filename stands for Security Configuration Editor.)

- `C:\WINDOWS\SETUPAPI.LOG` includes details on processing of *.INF files, that is, a whole lot of hardware device driver information.

- `C:\WINDOWS\COMSETUP.LOG` includes details on installation of COM+ (Component Object Model) modules.

Most of the log files live in `C:\WINDOWS` but a few live elsewhere. Don't ask me why, just memorize the exceptions.

Application conflicts

Sometimes Windows XP installs okay, but one or more applications that worked under Windows 98, Me, or NT don't work right anymore. Four ideas:

- You may be able to fix such problems with *upgrade packs*, which are typically DLL files that you get from the application supplier.

- You can also experiment with the settings on the EXE file's property sheet, in the Compatibility tab. You can fool the application into thinking that it's running under Windows 95, 98/Me, NT 4.0 SP5, or Windows 2000; you can also force the program to run in a restricted display mode.

✔ The application may expect users to have rights and access permissions that they no longer have because the Windows XP "Users" group is more tightly restricted than in Windows NT 4.0. Try running the application when logged on as a member of the Power Users group. If that's not practical, consider applying the COMPATWS.INF security template.

✔ If the application is consistently crashing, check `C:\Documents and Settings\All Users\Application Data\Microsoft\DrWatson\ DRWTSN32.LOG`. If the log mentions an executable file that's part of your cranky application, e-mail the log to the software manufacturer for analysis and (perhaps) a fix.

Boot Blunders

Separate from setup problems are problems that occur when Windows XP boots. True, these problems may occur immediately after a fresh installation, but they may also crop up at later dates, and they often require different troubleshooting approaches.

A normal boot

To understand abnormal psychology, you first must understand normal psychology. In this sense, (and perhaps this sense only!) dealing with Windows is similar to dealing with humans.

Typical sequence of events

Here's what happens (or should happen) when you turn on your Windows XP Professional PC, in more detail than you ever wanted to know:

1. The Power-On Self Test (POST) runs, under control of BIOS.

2. The Plug and Play BIOS performs enumeration of (that's a fancy way of saying "finds") system board hardware devices.

3. The BIOS finds and runs the Master Boot Record (MBR) program.

4. The MBR finds the boot sector on the active partition and loads the superhidden file NTLDR on the root directory. (*Superhidden* just means that NTLDR has both of the file attributes System and Hidden.)

5. NTLDR throws the CPU into 32-bit mode and loads FAT and NTFS file drivers. (Without these, it couldn't go any further.)

6. NTLDR reads BOOT.INI, also in the root directory, to see whether any other operating systems live on the machine. If so, NTLDR asks the user to pick one, please. If you pick an older operating system, NTLDR then

runs BOOTSECT.DOS, which contains the boot sector from the system before Windows XP was installed onto it. For example, BOOTSECT.DOS might start Windows 98. Note that BOOT.INI also contains details on where the operating system(s) reside (typically C:\WINDOWS for Windows XP).

7. If you choose Windows XP in Step 6, or if that's the only operating system on the PC, then the next program to take the baton is NTDETECT.COM. This program, as its name suggests, performs a good deal of hardware detection (but not for network cards).

8. NTLDR steps back in and presents you with a list of hardware profiles, along with an option to use the Last Known Good Configuration, assuming you've defined more than one hardware profile. If not, you'd have to tap F8 at boot time to see this menu.

9. The kernel load phase is next, displaying the "Starting Windows" text message and progress bar at the bottom of the screen. NTOSKRNL.EXE loads, the Hardware Abstraction Layer (HAL) loads, the control set (essentially a Registry-based list of device drivers, services, and settings) loads, and low-level device drivers load.

10. Kernel initialization follows, displaying the graphical boot progress screen. NTOSKRNL.EXE takes over from NTLDR here, building the HKLM\HARDWARE Registry key, initializing the low-level device drivers, loading more device drivers, and starting services via the Session Manager (SMSS.EXE).

11. The logon dialog box shows up (it's associated with WINLOGON.EXE and LSASS.EXE) and a last set of high-level services starts (such as the Workstation service).

12. Post-logon, Windows creates a new version of the Last Known Good control set based on the current control set.

After putting this list together, I admit feeling a little bit sheepish complaining about how long my system takes to boot.

ARC path nomenclature

In Windows XP, ARC (Advanced RISC Computing) paths in BOOT.INI help NTLDR figure out where the heck the operating system is. Now, I admit I don't like ARC nomenclature. It's obscure and inconsistent and the chances are good that you'll never need it. However, Microsoft loves to put it on the exam, so here are a couple of examples, with explanations following:

```
multi(0)disk(0)rdisk(0)partition(3)
scsi(0)disk(0)rdisk(0)partition(1)
```

✔ In the first of the preceding examples, multi(0) refers to the first disk controller, which can be an IDE type or a SCSI type with SCSI BIOS enabled; disk(0) doesn't mean anything, but the number must be zero if the path uses the "multi" designation instead of "scsi"; rdisk(0) means the first disk on the controller; and partition(3) means the third partition, where the numbering starts with the primary partition and continues with logical drives defined on an extended partition (if present).

✔ In the second example, scsi(0) refers to the first SCSI disk controller whose BIOS is disabled; disk(0) refers to the SCSI ID of the disk drive; rdisk(0) doesn't mean anything; and partition(1) refers to the first partition. Because most SCSI controllers work best with their own BIOS enabled — for example, the BIOS must generally be enabled to boot from a disk on that controller — the SCSI nomenclature has become rather rare. Learn it anyway.

In ARC nomenclature, controllers and disks start counting at zero, but partitions start counting at one. I *told* you I hate this stuff.

If you want to modify BOOT.INI, use the handy new BOOTCFG.EXE command-line tool provided by Microsoft (type **BOOTCFG /?** for a list of qualifiers). If you insist on opening the file in Notepad, though, you must first make it viewable (use the Folder Options control panel to see hidden files and folders) and then turn off the read-only attribute (use the file's property sheet). In real life, you rarely need to modify this file directly; for example, you can change the operating system menu selection delay (the "timeout=xx" line) via the System control panel.

Boot logging

If you want to create a text file listing the events that occur (mainly drivers loading) during a normal boot, press F8 at the "Starting Windows" prompt and choose Enable Boot Logging. The log file is NTBTLOG.TXT and it typically lives in C:\WINDOWS.

Device derailments

One of the common reasons for a boot problem is a device driver problem. A driver may conflict with another device driver, be corrupt or buggy, doesn't let itself be detected by the operating system, point to a device that isn't working right, or tries to work in a way not supported by Windows XP. The following sections cover these situations.

Resource conflicts

You can discover resource conflicts quickly in two ways — by using Device Manager and by using the System Information console (MSINFO32.EXE). You can get to Device Manager quickly by right-clicking the My Computer icon and choosing Manage. Note also that a command-line version of System Information exists, SYSTEMINFO.EXE, although it doesn't provide as much detail as the GUI utility.

Here's how to use these utilities:

✔ Device Manager typically shows devices with resource conflicts by using a yellow-and-black exclamation point.

✔ System Information has a separate category for "Conflicts/Sharing" (see Figure 15-1). Note that it isn't abnormal to see several devices sharing the same interrupt on a PCI-bus computer.

Figure 15-1: System Information combines conflicts and resource sharing data.

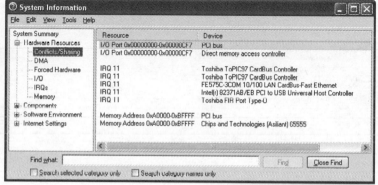

You must use Device Manager to manually correct a resource conflict. Lab 15-1 describes the typical procedure.

Lab 15-1   Correcting a Resource Conflict

1. **Right-click My Computer and choose Manage.**

2. **In the tree pane, click the Device Manager icon under the System Tools node.**

3. **Find the device with a problem in the details pane and double-click it.**

4. **Click the Resources tab.**

5. **Clear the Use Automatic Settings check box, if it lets you.**

   If you can't modify the check box's setting, Windows XP doesn't permit you to configure the device manually. You may be able to use a third-party utility in this case.

6. **Manually set interrupts and memory ranges that don't display a conflict in the Conflicting Devices List window.**

7. **Click OK and close the Computer Management console.**

STOP screens and crash dumps

A "STOP" screen is something you'd really rather not see. It's a fatal error (fatal to Windows XP, at least) indicating that something has gone so horribly awry that Windows XP believes it should shut itself down, before anything on disk gets messed up worse than it already is.

The exam doesn't expect you to know all the different hexadecimal STOP screen codes, so don't memorize them. What you *do* need to know is how to configure Windows XP's behavior in the event of a stop screen.

Click the Advanced tab of the System control panel, and then click the Settings button in the Startup and Recovery box to see the dialog box shown in Figure 15-2. The System Failure box is where you can tell Windows XP how to act if and when it encounters a STOP screen.

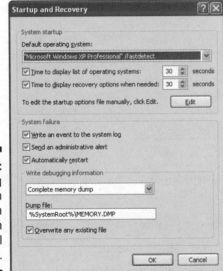

Figure 15-2: Setting crash options in the System control panel.

If you specify that you want to "Write Debugging Information," Windows XP creates a memory dump file (with suffix .DMP) containing the contents of RAM when the crash occurred. You would then typically send this file to Microsoft, or a third-party software vendor, for detailed analysis. You have three choices for a crash dump, in decreasing order of size: complete, kernel, and small.

You must have enough disk space to hold the whole contents of RAM, plus 1MB breathing room, for a complete dump. The kernel dump is smaller but varies in size, and the small dump is about 64K in size.

Note also that you can specify whether Windows should automatically reboot upon encountering a STOP screen. If yes, then you may never get to see the blue STOP screen with its various details. Automatic reboot is a better idea for a server than for a workstation.

The STOP screen isn't the only place you may be able to find clues about a system crash. Check the System event log (under Event Viewer in Management Console), and also check the Dr. Watson utility (open a command window and type **DRWTSN32**). If you want to report errors to Microsoft automatically via the Internet, the Error Reporting button on the Advanced tab of the System control panel lets you do that, too.

Detection woes

A device or driver may not be Plug and Play compatible, meaning that Windows XP cannot automatically load the correct driver for the device. In such situations, use the Control Panel's Add New Hardware Wizard to install the driver. (It should really be called "Add Old Hardware" but we won't quibble.)

USB problems

By far the most common USB snafu is having too many bus-powered devices on the chain. Replace some of the devices with powered versions, or plug in their power supplies if they have them. If the bus comes back to life after you disconnect one or more devices, then current drain may well be the problem.

The second most common USB snafu is that support for USB hasn't been enabled at the BIOS level. In this case, Windows XP doesn't even see the USB host controller in the Device Manager tree.

For more on USB configuration rules, please see Chapter 8.

Multi-display problems

The problems you're likely to run into here usually result from one of three things:

- ✔ The display adapters aren't on the right bus or buses. AGP and PCI are the only ones that work.

- ✔ The BIOS is trying to set your secondary display as the system's primary display. A simple BIOS setting change should fix this one in short order.

- ✔ You're trying to use an adapter for a secondary display when that adapter is only certified by Microsoft for use with a primary display. Check the Hardware Compatibility List (HCL) for details.

Curing and preventing device problems

As seasoned Windows troubleshooters have known for years, many problems find their solution in an updated or patched device driver. In Windows XP Professional, you can update device drivers several different ways, and — even better — you can control whether non-Microsoft drivers can even infiltrate your PC in the first place. XP adds the ability to roll back to a previous device driver, if one exists.

Driver updating

Here are some of the more common ways that you can update a device driver:

- ✔ Double-click a driver in the Device Manager display (get to Device Manager via the System control panel or the Computer Management console), click the Driver tab and then click the Update Driver button. This procedure activates the Hardware Update Wizard, which gives you various choices for hunting new drivers (see Figure 15-3).

- ✔ Open the relevant control panel for the device you want and update the driver from there. For example, choose the Settings tab of the Display control panel, and then click Advanced, Adapter, Properties, Driver, and Update Driver. (As an exercise, try finding the driver update option in the Sounds and Audio Devices control panel.)

- ✔ Choose Windows Update from the Start menu to connect to the Microsoft update Web site, and follow the prompts to update a driver if one's available. This method is really intended primarily for updating Windows XP system files as opposed to device drivers, but you can update select drivers this way. Note that you can't use Netscape or any other non-ActiveX browser to use Windows Update, because it uses an ActiveX control to inventory your machine and recommend updates.

- ✔ Run a vendor-supplied EXE program or INF file (which you would right-click and choose Install).

For the exam, know the difference between Windows Update and Windows Catalog. (They appear next to each other on the All Programs menu.) Windows Update lets users update system files with security patches and bug fixes from the Microsoft Web site. Windows Catalog takes you to a marketing site where Microsoft promotes Windows-compatible products.

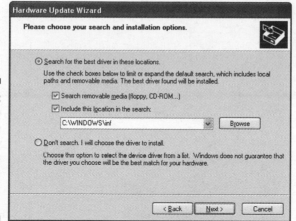

Figure 15-3:
The
Hardware
Update
Wizard lets
you choose
where to
look.

Driver signing (not by famous golfers)

Microsoft brands a *digital signature* into the core operating system files and drivers that it ships with Windows XP, as well as files and drivers released subsequently that have passed testing at Windows Hardware Quality Labs (WHQL). That way, Windows XP can "tell" when a program installation tries to replace one of those core files with a version not "signed" by Microsoft. (Microsoft has stated that all files that appear on the Windows Update Web site will be cryptographically signed, too.)

The Registry contains settings that govern how Windows XP behaves with respect to driver signing. If you want to see the settings in the Local Security Policy utility, look up *Devices: Unsigned driver installation behavior* and *Devices: Unsigned non-driver installation behavior* under *Security Settings\Local Policies\Security Options*.

You can set the behavior options on an individual PC through the System control panel's Hardware tab by clicking the Driver Signing button to display the dialog box shown in Figure 15-4. If you have administrative privileges on the machine, you can make one setting the default for all users who log on to the PC; otherwise, the setting you make is only effective for the currently logged on user, and if you log on later with a different account, the setting may be different. The three behaviors, which activate upon an attempt to install a new driver or software component, are as follows:

- ✔ **Ignore:** Unsigned drivers may load without notification.
- ✔ **Warn:** Unsigned drivers prompt a warning message to the user.
- ✔ **Block:** Unsigned drivers may not install.

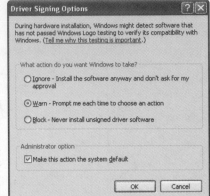

Figure 15-4:
Setting
options for
driver
signing.

If a domain-based policy exists for driver signing, it takes precedence over any setting you may make with the Local Security Policy console.

Drivers aren't the only files that have digital signatures in Windows XP. *System protected files* are the 1,800-plus files for which the Windows File Protection system keeps duplicates in the C:\WINDOWS\SYSTEM32\DLLCACHE folder. The idea is that Windows can restore the original copies from the DLL-CACHE folder if the "live" ones become corrupted, overwritten, or destroyed. Two utilities enable you to explore signed system files: SIGVERIF and SFC.

- **SIGVERIF.EXE,** the Signature Verification tool, lets you quickly scan protected system files and verify that their digital signatures are intact. This utility produces a log file, SIGVERIF.TXT, showing the version, modification date, and signed-or-unsigned status of each file. Using the utility's advanced settings dialog box, you can set the program to scan non-system files in any location you specify.

- **SFC.EXE,** the System File Checker, also lets you check the digital signature of system protected files. It works from a script, batch file, or command prompt. SFC doesn't show you the file details that SIGVERIF does, and it doesn't let you scan non-system files. However, SFC does two things that SIGVERIF doesn't: It repopulates the DLLCACHE folder if it detects system files added since Windows was installed, and it offers to replace any system files that it determines are missing or different from their original versions.

The key parameters for SFC.EXE are as follows:

- **/CACHESIZE** lets you specify the maximum size of the DLL cache.

- **/PURGECACHE** clears the DLL cache, and then repopulates it.

- **/SCANNOW** initiates an immediate scan of system protected files.

> ✔ **/SCANONCE** sets SFC to perform a scan at the next reboot.
>
> ✔ **/SCANBOOT** sets SFC to perform a scan at every reboot.
>
> ✔ **/REVERT** returns the scan setting to the default.

Windows XP Recovery Methods

In times of serious trouble, when you can't even get Windows XP Professional to start properly, you're looking at performing some system recovery. Windows XP offers various degrees of recovery, and this section treats them in the same order I usually recommend trying them: from least destructive (Last Known Good boot) to most destructive (Automated System Recovery).

Last Known Good boot

When you log on successfully to Windows XP Professional, the operating system assumes a "good" boot and writes the control set information to the Registry as the "Last Known Good" control set. (Remember, a control set is a collection of device drivers and their settings.)

Later, if you add a device that interferes with Windows' ability to start normally, you can apply the Last Known Good boot technique, as described in Lab 15-2. Windows XP takes the "LKG" process a bit further than Windows 2000 does by rolling back device drivers to their state at the last known good boot, not just the Registry control set information.

Lab 15-2	Using the Last Known Good Configuration

1. **Restart the system after the failed boot by pressing F8 at the "Starting Windows" text mode prompt.**

   You can also boot while holding down the Ctrl key, if you're worried about tapping the F8 key quickly enough.

2. **At the text mode boot menu, choose Last Known Good Configuration (Your Most Recent Settings That Worked).**

   Doing so instructs Windows to use the last known good control set instead of the current, or default, control set. Because the last known good control set doesn't call the new device driver, it should let you boot normally.

If you suspect a device problem, restart the computer, and forget to choose Last Known Good Configuration, don't log on. The moment you do, the current control set becomes the Last Known Good control set, and you'll have to figure out some other way to exorcise the evil device driver.

Now that Windows XP lets you "roll back" a single device driver via the Roll Back Driver button on the Driver tab of the device's property sheet, you may save time by trying that route instead of Last Known Good, unless you've upgraded multiple device drivers at the same time.

Safe Mode

Windows 9x offers a Safe Mode boot option that doesn't activate the Registry and that loads only a minimal set of device drivers (basic VGA, mouse, keyboard, disk). Safe Mode also disables startup programs and "nonessential" operating system services. Safe Mode has been a boon to troubleshooters, and its absence in NT 4.0 prompted a great deal of pressure from corporate customers for Microsoft to implement something similar in its next operating system.

Depending on your PC's BIOS, USB mice and keyboards may not be available in a Safe Mode boot!

As a result, Windows XP also offers a Safe Mode boot option (press the F8 key at the text-mode boot menu and select Safe Mode, Safe Mode Command Prompt, or Safe Mode with Networking), but it differs from the Windows 9x Safe Mode in some key ways. The most important distinction is that Windows XP Safe Mode activates the Registry, meaning that you can't back up or restore the Registry by using file copy commands in Windows XP Safe Mode.

When you're running in Safe Mode, the words "Safe Mode" appear in all four corners of your display. Windows XP doesn't load network software in the basic Safe Mode, nor does it load any system services beyond the bare necessities. If you need network access, you can choose Safe Mode with Networking, which allows processing of network logon, logon scripts, and Group Policy settings. The Safe Mode with Command Prompt option starts Windows XP with the command-line user interface instead of the graphical user interface.

So what would you actually *do* in Safe Mode? Typically, you'd open up Control Panel and undo whatever setting you recently made which may be causing Windows to start abnormally or hang up at boot time. For example, you could remove a newly installed device driver, or start or stop a system service. Then you'd restart normally and see if everything looks fine. If not, you may have to move to the next recovery option, Recovery Console (coming up soon).

Safe Mode in any of its three flavors automatically creates a boot log named NTBTLOG.TXT in the Windows folder (usually C:\WINDOWS). See the section, "Boot logging" earlier in this chapter.

You may be curious about the boot menu options "Directory Services Restore Mode" and "Debugging Mode." April Fools! These options don't apply to Windows XP Professional, only to the 2002/2000 Server products! (You'd think Windows would know which version of itself was installed on a given PC, but apparently it doesn't, at least not this early in the boot process.)

System Restore

Borrowing a bit of technology from Windows Me, Windows XP offers the *System Restore* feature that lets you "roll back" your system to a previous (and, presumably, functional) state. Windows creates "restore points" automatically and you can create your own manually, too. Use this facility to recover from bad drivers, application installations, or system reconfigurations, but try Last Known Good and Safe Mode first because they're less destructive. The System Restore feature only pertains to operating system files and neither backs up, nor wipes out, your data files.

The System Restore tool lives in the System Tools submenu of the Accessories menu; you can run it directly, too (it's RSTRUI.EXE in C:\ WINDOWS\SYSTEM32\RESTORE). Here's the other stuff you need to know for the exam about System Restore:

✔ System Restore monitors certain operating system and application files and backs them up to hidden archives when those files are changed or updated. The list of files is C:\WINDOWS\SYSTEM32\RESTORE\ FILELIST.XML. Windows compresses the archives on NTFS disks when the system is idle.

✔ A "restore point" consists of a Registry snapshot and any backups of monitored files.

✔ System Restore creates a restore point whenever you install an unsigned device driver, install a logo-compliant application, restore data from backup media, restore using System Restore, or manually create a restore point with the System Restore Wizard.

✔ In addition, System Restore creates a restore point once a day if the computer's left on, and if it has been at least one day since the last restore point if the computer is turned on after being off. (The interval is configurable in Group Policy.)

✔ When System Restore hits 90 percent of its allocated disk space, it starts dumping old data to make room for new.

✔ You have to log on as an Administrator to perform a restore with this utility.

✔ You must be able to boot Windows XP, in normal mode or in Safe Mode, to use this utility.

✔ Most of this program's options are only configurable via the Registry. The exam won't expect you to know individual settings.

✔ System Restore is a major resource hog, requiring at least 200MB of free disk space and putting a burden on your CPU as well, and is one of the reasons for XP's hefty hardware requirements. You could disable it on a slower PC to reduce system overhead, as long as you have a sound backup program in place. You could also reduce the amount of disk space available to System Restore. Both settings live on the System Restore tab of the System control panel.

Recovery Console

Okay, Last Known Good didn't work, and neither did Safe Mode or System Restore. Time to bring out a bigger hammer. Recovery Console is new since Windows NT 4.0. It lets you start Windows XP Professional when Professional won't start otherwise, and it provides a limited number of command-line utilities for repairing a damaged system. (Note that these commands aren't identical to the commands you can type in a "regular" command prompt running under Windows XP Professional in normal operation.) One of the nice aspects of Recovery Console is its capability of working with NTFS drives in a command-line environment.

Recovery Console doesn't start the Registry, so you can copy backed-up Registry files from (for example) C:\WINDOWS\REPAIR to C:\WINDOWS\ SYSTEM32\CONFIG to do a brute-force Registry restore.

Running Recovery Console

Here's the weird part. You run the Recovery Console by starting Windows XP setup. You can do this with the installation CD-ROM, if your PC can boot from the CD (using the "El Torito" specification).

When you get to the Welcome to Setup screen, type **R** to open the Repair Options screen. Then, type **C** to activate the Recovery Console. The computer asks you which Windows XP installation you want to work with (usually there's only one, but the program is too dumb to figure this out, and you must make a selection). Finally, you have to log on with the Administrator password, unless you previously set a security policy to allow Recovery Console to bypass this step automatically. (If the system is so fouled up that it doesn't recognize this password, you're looking at a restore from a previous backup because you can't use Recovery Console.)

Type **help** at the command prompt to see a list of Recovery Console commands. Here are a few you should know:

- ✔ Many viruses infect a hard drive's Master Boot Record, or MBR. You can often clear out such infections by using the Recovery Console's FIXMBR command.

- ✔ LISTSVC lists services.

- ✔ The DISABLE and ENABLE commands let you start and stop system services and device drivers.

- ✔ FDISK lets you do some partitioning work (be careful! this option deletes data!).

- ✔ EXIT ends your Recovery Console session.

- ✔ COPY lets you copy files, but only from and to the hard disk or disks. You can't copy to or from a diskette or Zip drive.

Installing Recovery Console onto the hard disk

If you find yourself doing a lot of Recovery Console work on a particularly troublesome system, you may want to speed up the load time by installing it onto your hard drive as a boot option on the Choose an Operating System menu. Doing so is easy: Just run the setup program WINNT32.EXE with the /CMDCONS qualifier (it stands for "command console"). You can find WINNT32.EXE on the Windows XP Professional CD-ROM, or on the network server from which you installed the operating system.

Don't worry: In spite of the fact that you're running WINNT32, this command doesn't reinstall Windows XP Professional onto your system.

Automated System Recovery (ASR)

A new option for bringing a Windows XP system back to a stable condition is *Automated System Recovery*, or *ASR*. This option is just barely more convenient than reinstalling Windows from scratch and performing a restore from a backup set (see the next section, "Windows Backup"), but it does let you restore a PC to functionality without requiring you to re-enter manually your operating system settings.

ASR is considered a last-resort solution because it formats the system drive as part of the restore process, and may format non-system partitions, too. So you're likely to wipe out any user data on the system, and you'll have to restore that data from a previous backup after you complete the system restore via ASR. Therefore, you'll only use ASR if you've exhausted all other options. (By the way, for those of you familiar with Windows 2000 or NT, ASR more or less replaces the Emergency Recovery Diskette, or ERD, procedure, which is no longer available in XP.)

ASR is an option of the Windows Backup program (which I discuss in more detail in the next section). Create an ASR backup by choosing Start⇨All Programs⇨Accessories⇨System Tools⇨Backup, clicking Next in the Backup Utility Wizard screen, and then choosing Prepare An Automated System Recovery Backup. You'll provide a floppy diskette, which ASR uses to record details of your hard drive's configuration, and a backup medium (such as tape, but not a network drive), to which ASR will make a backup of key system files.

To perform an ASR restore, you must boot from the Windows XP CD-ROM, and then press F5 when you see the message Press F5 To Run Automated System Recovery (ASR). ASR will prompt you for the diskette and for the backup media. When it's finished, you'll have to restore any user data and applications from a separate backup set.

Windows Backup

Sometimes even ASR isn't enough to resuscitate a Windows XP Professional system. In such cases, you can turn to the backup-and-restore program that comes with Windows XP, NTBACKUP.EXE or Microsoft Windows Backup. This program is significantly different from the backup utility included with versions of Windows before 2000. It's actually a scaled-down version of the popular Veritas (formerly Seagate Software) program, Backup Exec.

Advantages

- NTBACKUP can compress files on the fly.

- If you have to use a diskette drive as your target device, NTBACKUP has no trouble creating a multiple-diskette backup to deal with files that are typically too large to fit on one diskette.

- NTBACKUP can also back up to a good variety of target devices, including Zip, Jaz, and writeable optical drives, as well as the more traditional tape drives and network directories. Unlike the Windows NT 4.0 backup program, NTBACKUP can back up to another hard drive (hurrah!).

- NTBACKUP logs its activities (typically in `C:\Documents and Settings\<username>\Local Settings\Application Data\ Microsoft\Windows NT\NTBackup\data`).

- NTBACKUP is able to make a backup of your Registry even though the files are open and "in use." That is, NTBACKUP can copy Registry files even when COPY and XCOPY and drag-and-drop can't.

Disadvantages

NTBACKUP requires Windows XP to be running in order to restore the files. So, if you experience total hard disk failure and you have to replace the drive, you first have to reinstall Windows XP onto the drive before you can run NTBACKUP in order to restore the files you backed up earlier.

If your system is so damaged that you can't boot Windows XP at all, even in "Safe Mode," then you can't run NTBACKUP to restore your system. Here again, you may be faced with a reinstall (and, in extreme cases, a reformat before the reinstall) before you can restore your backup.

Another drawback of NTBACKUP is that you can't save all your backup settings and options to a disk file so that you can run NTBACKUP with a single click. All you can save is the list of files you want to back up. This limitation is all the more limiting in that the command-line version of the program doesn't offer every option that the graphical version does.

Procedure

Lab 15-3 shows the basic steps to running Windows Backup.

Lab 15-3   Running Windows Backup

1. **Choose Start⇨All Programs⇨Accessories⇨System Tools⇨Backup to start running the program.**

   If you've never run the program before, it starts in Wizard mode, but you can choose an Advanced Mode link instead. If you have run the program before and chose to start in Advanced Mode, then you'll see the "Welcome To The Backup Utility Advanced Mode" screen.

2. **Click the Backup tab and design your backup job in the utility's main window.**

   Using the Backup tab is a little more flexible than using the wizard.

3. **Choose which directories or files you want to back up in the two Explorer-like windows that occupy most of the main screen (see Figure 15-5).**

   When you're done choosing files and folders, you can choose Job⇨Save Selections As, which lets you create a disk file such as FILELIST.BKS containing your file selections. You can later load those file selections in one fell swoop by choosing Job⇨Load Selections.

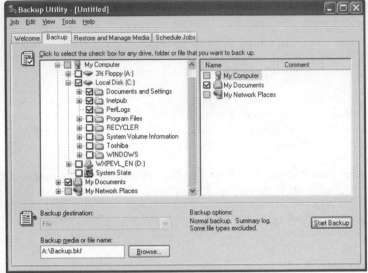

Figure 15-5:
The Backup
tab of
Windows
Backup.

4. **Choose Tools⊅Options to set your preferences for this backup job.**

I always recommend going to the General tab and checking the box labeled Verify Data After The Backup Completes. Microsoft recommends that, too, so it's odd that this check box is cleared by default.

5. **Pick a target device in the lower-left corner of the window.**

6. **Click the Start Backup button in the lower-right corner, set a few final options, and you're done.**

You can't save all those choices along with your file list as you can, for example, with a Windows 98 Backup job file. In NTBACKUP, you have to choose your backup options each time you back up (although you can, at least, save a file list with the Job⊅Save Selections command).

To restore a backup set with this program, you must first install Windows XP Professional (if it isn't already present), and then run NTBACKUP and click the Restore tab. As the saying goes, "installation is the reverse of removal."

Scheduling backups

You can schedule your backups from within the Backup program. When you do so, a new icon appears in your Scheduled Tasks folder. (Microsoft Backup, Scheduled Tasks, and AT.EXE all rely on the *Task Scheduler* service, which normally starts automatically at boot time. You can check the status of this service with the Services control panel.)

The online help for the Scheduled Tasks program lays out the details for specifying the file you want to run (it doesn't have to be Microsoft Windows Backup) and how often you want to run it (every Friday night at 2 a.m., for example). Access the Scheduled Tasks utility by choosing Start➪All Programs➪Accessories➪System Tools➪Scheduled Tasks, or Start➪Control Panel➪Scheduled Tasks. (For more details on Scheduled Tasks, please refer to Chapter 14.)

System state backups

When you use NTBACKUP, you're likely to see the term *system state* in the hierarchical tree listing of things you can back up (or restore). Microsoft defines the system state to include the following specific elements:

- **The Registry:** Actually, you don't quite get all the Registry, but you do get most of it.

- **The boot files:** Specifically, NTLDR and NTDETECT.COM. These are the minimum files that you need to boot Windows XP.

- **The COM+ Class Registration Database:** This has to do with software components that may be accessed over a network.

- **All the system files in the C:\WINDOWS folder:** These files (which have the suffixes DLL, EXE, FON, OCX, SYS, and TTF) amount to more than 200 megabytes. Thankfully, you can exclude them when backing up the system state, at least from NTBACKUP's graphical interface. (You don't have the option to exclude them by using NTBACKUP's command-line interface.)

The only way you can back up the local Registry in Microsoft Windows Backup is to select the System State check box in the directory tree on the main backup window. (Checking the folder C:\WINDOWS\SYSTEM32\CONFIG, or checking the individual files therein, works when you back up a remote Registry but doesn't work when you back up your own Registry. NTBACKUP lets you check them, but it won't back them up. These aren't ordinary files, so ordinary procedures don't apply.)

When you do choose to back up the system state, NTBACKUP gives you the opportunity to exclude the system files in the C:\WINDOWS folder because they occupy so much space (see Figure 15-6).

Figure 15-6:
Backup
normally
wants to
back up
system files
with the
System
State.

Even the system state backup bypasses the multiple possible copies of NTUSER.DAT and USRCLASS.DAT that make up the user-specific Registry files. So, if you want to create a backup job that includes all of these (strongly recommended), go check them as well. These files will live under the `C:\Documents and Settings\<username>` folder, or under the `C:\WINDOWS\ PROFILES\<username>` folder, depending on whether Windows XP is an upgrade of a Windows NT 4.0 system or not.

Prep Test

1 You decide to perform a Registry backup before installing the latest game program from Subconscious Software. First, you check the current Registry size via the System control panel and see that it is about 14 MB. Then, you fire up NTBACKUP and click the System State check box. You choose a Zip drive as your target device. When you make the backup, however, you find that you need three 100 MB Zip disks. Why is the Registry backup so much larger than you anticipated? (Choose the best answer.)

A ○ The System State includes every file on the C drive.

B ○ The System State includes every EXE, DLL, and OCX file on the C drive.

C ○ You didn't click the check box excluding protected files.

D ○ You didn't click the check box excluding the pagefile.

2 You're running Recovery Console in order to stop a service that has rendered your PC unbootable. You don't know the exact name of the service, but you think that you would know it if you saw it. Which two Recovery Console commands would you use? (Choose the best answer.)

A ○ LIST, STOP

B ○ LISTSVC, STOPSVC

C ○ SERVICES, DISABLE

D ○ LISTSVC, DISABLE

E ○ SVCLIST, HALT

3 You install Windows XP Professional as a fresh installation onto a new PC. The installation fails repeatedly. Where is the first place you would look to get more information on what's going wrong? (Choose the best answer.)

A ○ ERROR.LOG

B ○ SETUPERR.LOG

C ○ WINNTERR.LOG

D ○ WINNTERR.DAT

E ○ The Event Log

4 What does the command WINNT32.EXE /CMDCONS do? (Choose the best answer.)

A ○ Installs the Command Console

B ○ Installs Windows XP Professional, with the Recovery Console option on the text mode boot menu

C ○ Installs Windows XP Professional, with the Safe Mode option on the text mode boot menu

D ○ Installs the Recovery Console onto the local hard disk

5 All the PCs in your office come equipped with built-in removable disk devices (100MB Zip drives). Al, a user in Marketing, is having a problem getting Windows XP Professional to start properly. You decide to try booting into Safe Mode, and you're able to get the system running. You have a diagnostic tool (which occupies 35MB) on your server-based home directory, and you want to run that tool next in order to zero in on Al's problem, but you can't seem to access the network. What should you do? (Choose the best answer.)

A ○ Load real-mode network drivers. Then you can copy the diagnostic tool from the network share.

B ○ Reboot and choose Safe Mode With Networking. Then you can copy the diagnostic tool from the network share.

C ○ Reboot and run the Recovery Console. Then you can copy the diagnostic tool from the network share.

D ○ Log on to another computer and copy the diagnostic tool to a Zip disk. Load it onto Al's computer.

6 At which point does Windows XP Professional write the current control set into the Last Known Good control set? (Choose the best answer.)

A ○ When the "Welcome to Windows" screen appears

B ○ When the "Starting Windows" text message appears

C ○ When any user logs on successfully

D ○ When the Startup folder is processed

7 Andrea wants to update a device driver on her system. She downloads a new driver from the device manufacturer's Web site (the manufacturer is not Microsoft). She tries installing the driver, but the process fails. She then logs on to her PC as Administrator, opens her System control panel, and changes the Driver Signing setting from Block to Ignore. Upon attempting to install the driver again, the process fails once more. What could be causing the installation to fail?

A ○ Andrea belongs to a domain that includes a Group Policy that sets driver signing behavior to Block.

B ○ Andrea hasn't run the local Group Policy editor, GPEDIT.MSC, to set the local policy for driver signing to Ignore.

C ○ Andrea needed to set Driver Signing to "Warn" in the System control panel.

D ○ Windows XP Professional doesn't permit third-party device drivers to run in any circumstance.

8 A Windows XP Professional PC isn't booting all the way to the logon prompt. You enable boot logging by pressing the F8 key at startup and choosing the option from the text mode boot menu. Where can you typically find the boot log file? (Choose one answer.)

A ○ C:\WINDOWS\NTBTLOG.TXT

B ○ C:\WINDOWS\SYSTEM32\NTBTLOG.TXT

C ○ C:\WINDOWS\BOOTLOG.TXT

D ○ C:\WINDOWS\SYSTEM32\BOOTLOG.TXT

9 An application is creating fatal crashes and the vendor advises you to submit a complete memory dump. You enable the feature on the System control panel, but after the next crash, you discover that a complete memory dump was not created. What could be the problem? (Choose all that apply.)

A ❑ You didn't have Administrative rights when you enabled the memory dump.

B ❑ You didn't have Backup Operator rights when you enabled the memory dump.

C ❑ Available disk space is less than (RAM + 1MB).

D ❑ Available disk space is less than 64KB.

10 You provide tech support for your company, which has standardized on Windows XP Professional. Christina is an employee who is having trouble with her notebook computer's display after recently installing a driver update. She is about to catch a plane and offers you a bottle of your favorite single malt Scotch if you can fix her notebook before she has to leave for the airport in five minutes. What do you do? (Choose the best answer.)

A ○ Boot to the Recovery Console and run FIXMON.

B ○ Boot to Safe Mode and reinstall the original driver from the Windows XP setup CD.

C ○ Run Device Manager and perform a rollback of the display driver.

D ○ Perform a System Restore operation by using the most recent restore point.

E ○ Tell Christina sorry, you never touch the hard stuff.

Answers

1 **C.** The default behavior of the System State backup is to include all system pro-tected files, that is, system files (mostly DLLs) under *%SystemRoot%*. You must clear the check box that reads Automatically Backup System Protected Files With The System State before making your Registry backup. *Review "System state backups."*

2 **D.** Recovery Console commands are likely subjects for an exam question or two. If you have access to a Windows XP machine, boot to the Recovery Console and type **HELP** to see a list of commands. Type **HELP** followed by a command name to get detailed information on that command. *Review "Running Recovery Console."*

3 **B.** The error log `C:\WINDOWS\SETUPERR.LOG` is probably the best place to start. Because Windows hasn't fully installed, the event logs are not likely to contain any useful information. The SETUPACT.LOG file may also contain some hints. *Review "The trail of crumbs."*

4 **D.** This command lets you run Recovery Console from the hard drive instead of by booting the Windows XP CD. Note that despite the syntax, nothing called a "Command Console" exists. Also note that this command does *not* install the operating system itself. *Review "Installing Recovery Console onto the hard disk."*

5 **B.** The "regular" Safe Mode excludes network support, but you can also choose Safe Mode With Networking, which is easier than choice D, although D would work. *Review "Safe Mode."*

6 **C.** Therefore, if you don't notice a device driver problem until you've restarted and logged on, you can't use the Last Known Good boot option to recover. You would most likely try Safe Mode next in that circumstance. *Review "Last Known Good boot."*

7 **A.** A domain-based policy always overrides a local policy in a Windows XP net-work, so it doesn't matter what Andrea sets on her local PC if her domain policy contradicts the local setting. Choice B is wrong for the additional reason that the System control panel setting is enough to make the behavior change for the local PC, if no domain setting overrides it. *Review "Driver signing (not by famous golfers)."*

8 **A.** Some other versions of Windows use BOOTLOG.TXT and I guess Microsoft wanted to distinguish the NT-platform version of the file. It's a normal ASCII text file that you can view with Notepad. You'd typically search the file for mes-sages saying "Driver not loaded." *Review "Boot logging."*

9 **A** and **C.** Only Administrators can set crash dump options, and a complete memory dump requires enough disk space to contain the entire contents of RAM plus an extra megabyte for safety. *Review "STOP screens and crash dumps."*

10 **C.** You know it's the display driver, and the Roll Back Driver option is the fastest way to revert to a working configuration. Choices B and D would also work, but they would take longer. *Review "Last Known Good boot."*

Part VI
The Part of Tens

The 5th Wave   By Rich Tennant

Meditations, Inc.
BOOKS • SEMINARS • TAPES

"Sales on the Web site are down. I figure the server's chi is blocked, so we're fudgin' around the Feng Shui in the computer room, and if that doesn't work, Ronnie's got a cure that should do it."

In this part . . .

The famous "Part of Tens" is a fixture of the *For Dummies* books, and one of my favorite aspects of the series. (I admit to turning directly to The Part of Tens whenever I buy a new *For Dummies* book. After reading the cartoons, that is.) So here's Chapter 16, with ten valuable test-taking tips to help speed you on your way to certification.

I thought about including one more chapter in this part, but that would mean a total of 17 chapters, and the idea of a computer book having exactly 16 chapters has a sort of nerdy elegance to it. (I also have a family of 4, and we live off highway exit 256. Coincidence, you say? Then explain my 65,536 computer magazine subscriptions!)

Chapter 16

Ten Test-Taking Tips

In This Chapter

▶ Discovering great resources (free and otherwise) to help you prepare

▶ Getting both your brain and body fired up for the exam

▶ Finding out tips on answer changing and checking

▶ Staying cool under pressure

Knowing a few test-preparation tricks can give you a bit of an edge on the exam, so here are ten suggestions that may help rocket you to a passing grade after you've dutifully studied the core material.

Many of the tips and resources in this chapter will help you with other MCSE tests besides the Windows XP Professional exam.

Do Your Homework

The best single bit of advice that I can give you for passing the Windows XP Professional exam is *use the product*. Even if you normally work with Windows Me, 98, or NT 4.0 at work or at home, consider switching to Windows XP Pro for the weeks prior to the MCSE test. Set up a dual-boot machine if you need to; use an alternate PC if one is available. (See Chapter 4 for more information on setting up a dual-boot system.) Whenever you have a few minutes free during the day or night, experiment with the Windows XP control panels, property sheets, and system utilities. If you can practice by using Windows XP in a network environment, so much the better: Map drives, print to printers, configure TCP/IP, and try out Dial-Up Networking. The more you use the software, the easier the exam becomes.

With plenty of hands-on experience and careful study of this book, you have the tools you need to pass the Windows XP Professional test. Of course, you never know when Microsoft will change the content or the format of an exam, and you can count on facing a steady stream of fresh challenges throughout your career. So, far be it for me to discourage you from exploring other

396 Part VI: The Part of Tens

resources that could help fill in your knowledge gaps. Here's a bushelful of
resources that can help you with the book learnin', whether you can wangle
access to a Windows XP machine or not.

Windows XP Professional Resource Kit

Buying the *Resource Kit* for Windows XP (confusingly retitled *Administering
Microsoft Windows XP Professional, Operations Guide*) is a good idea, especially if you plan to use the operating system after you take the exam. You're
not going to read all 1,792 pages cover to cover (at least I hope not), and you
really don't need it to pass the exam. However, for dipping in and out of various technical subjects that you may need to understand more thoroughly,
this hefty tome is a smart addition to your bookshelf.

You'll typically find the best price on Microsoft resource kits at www.
provantage.com, but you may want to check other online bookstores as
well. The list price is an unconscionable US $69.99, but you can usually find it
online at 30–40 percent off. The ISBN number is 0-7356-1485-7.

For those who aren't independently wealthy, you get a subset of the full
Resource Kit product "free" on the Windows XP Professional CD. Install the
Resource Kit tools, which take about 35MB of disk space if you do a complete
install, as follows:

1. **Log on as a member of the Administrators group.**

2. **Run SETUP.EXE from the** \SUPPORT\TOOLS **folder of your setup CD.**

3. **Choose "Typical" if you just want workstation-related tools, or
   "Complete" to install server- and network-management tools.**

The tools install onto your local hard drive, typically C:\Program
Files\Support Tools. The tools appear on the taskbar; simply choose
Start➪All Programs➪Windows Support Tools to find them. Be aware that
although most of the software resides in a cabinet file (SUPPORT.CAB),
merely extracting the files from the cabinet file doesn't perform a complete
installation of the Resource Kit tools.

You can also install the tools from the command prompt. Microsoft has pack-
aged them by using the Windows Installer methodology, so you can use
MSIEXEC.EXE with the appropriate options. For example, if E is your local
CD-ROM drive, you could use a command (such as the following) from the
directory where you want the tools to install:

```
MSIEXEC /I E:\SUPPORT\TOOLS\SUPTOOLS.MSI
```

The Resource Kit Tools consist of three menu choices:

- **Command Prompt** opens a command prompt window in the Support Tools folder. (Note that you can execute command-line utilities from anywhere, because the installation procedure adds the Support Tools folder to the PATH environment variable.)

- **Release Notes** (README.HTM) is an HTML file with the most current details on installing and using the Support Tools.

- **Support Tools Help** (ST.XML) is an XML file detailing functions and command-line qualifiers for the utilities. This module of the new Help and Support Center is your most convenient single point of reference for all the support tools, both GUI and command-line varieties. It provides syntax and (even better) examples.

The Resource Kit Support Tools package contains GUI-mode utilities and command-line utilities. Many of the utilities are holdovers from the Windows NT 4.0 and 2000 Resource Kits, so if you're familiar with those products, you'll see some old friends. However, you cannot "update" Windows NT or Windows 2000 support tools with the Windows XP support tools. The XP programs are (at least mostly) operating system-specific.

Note that some of the support tools pertain to specific environments. For example, Active Directory Administration Tool and Active Directory Replication Monitor are not relevant for an environment that doesn't use AD.

Finally, you should also know that some of the support tools duplicate functions that already exist in the user interface. MEMSNAP.EXE, for example, overlaps with the Windows Task Manager display (press Ctrl+Alt+Del and click the Processes tab).

Hungry Minds, Inc.

Hungry Minds has some great Windows XP and 2000 books at reasonable prices (in contrast to Microsoft Press, which generally offers average books at high prices). The list is evolving as I write this, so check out www. hungryminds.com and www.dummies.com to see the most current listing. One in particular that I can vouch for (warning, shameless plug coming) is my own *MCSE Windows 2000 Network Infrastructure For Dummies*.

Microsoft TechNet

Whether you subscribe to the CD-ROMs (recommended; $295 per year) or simply patronize the Web site (www.microsoft.com/technet), TechNet is a good reference for common problems and their solutions. However, TechNet has expanded considerably beyond its early scope of presenting the Microsoft knowledge base in CD format. Now it includes selected resource kits, service packs, online seminars, white papers, walkthroughs, and client and server utilities.

As I write this, you get a 50 percent discount on your TechNet subscription when you get your MCSE. (That could change though; you used to get a year of TechNet for free.)

Internet search engines

Internet search engines are great for finding Windows XP information; choose "Windows XP" as a search phrase and go wild, or get more specific with a query such as ("Windows XP Professional" and "Plug and Play"). Here are some of the more popular search services:

- All the Web, All the Time (www.alltheweb.com)
- Altavista (www.av.com)
- Excite (www.excite.com)
- Google (www.google.com)
- HotBot (www.hotbot.com)
- Lycos (www.lycos.com)
- Northern Light (www.northernlight.com)
- Yahoo! (www.yahoo.com)

If you do a lot of Internet searching (and who doesn't these days), you may want to check out Copernic 2000, a program that consults many popular search engines in one fell swoop. Point your browser to www.copernic.com to download the software.

Usenet newsgroups

Usenet newsgroups are like Internet bulletin boards. Some contain lots of information about Windows XP. These groups can also be good places to post a question when you can't get an answer anywhere else, or when you just want to read what other Windows XP users are saying. Newsgroups also often post FAQs (Frequently Asked Questions documents) within the newsgroups themselves and on related Web sites: Such FAQs can be good sources of distilled information on specific subjects.

Newsgroups are public. Any sloppy, lazy, uninformed, or even malicious bozo can post to them. Use newsgroups for clues, ideas, and potential problem solutions, but check every tip yourself before you use it or pass it along to others.

Some newsgroups of interest include the following:

- alt.certification.mcse
- comp.os.ms-windows.misc
- microsoft.public.certification.mcse
- microsoft.public.windowsxp.accessibility
- microsoft.public.windowsxp.basics
- microsoft.public.windowsxp.customize
- microsoft.public.windowsxp.games (I won't tell anyone)
- microsoft.public.windowsxp.general
- microsoft.public.windowsxp.hardware
- microsoft.public.windowsxp.help_and_support
- microsoft.public.windowsxp.messenger
- microsoft.public.windowsxp.music
- microsoft.public.windowsxp.network_web
- microsoft.public.windowsxp.newusers
- microsoft.public.windowsxp.perform_maintain
- microsoft.public.windowsxp.photos
- microsoft.public.windowsxp.print_fax
- microsoft.public.windowsxp.security_admin
- microsoft.public.windowsxp.setup_deployment
- microsoft.public.windowsxp.video
- microsoft.public.windowsxp.work_remotely

Software is required to read postings from these newsgroups. Windows XP comes with Outlook Express 6. If you use America Online to access the Internet, you can't use Outlook Express, but you can use AOL's built-in news-reader. Just choose the keyword *newsgroups,* click the Expert Add button, and type in the newsgroup name.

Exam simulations

Some companies make a business of providing exam simulations. The fees for these tests have gone down somewhat in recent years, and you can often download demos from the Web before shelling out cash. Here are a couple to check out:

- ✔ Transcender (www.transcender.com)
- ✔ Self-Test Software (www.stsware.com)

Microsoft Web sites

Microsoft has hundreds of pages on its own Web site that pertain to Windows XP. Here are a few to get you started:

- ✔ www.microsoft.com/trainingandservices
- ✔ www.microsoft.com/windowsxp
- ✔ www.microsoft.com/windowsxp/pro/default.asp
- ✔ www.microsoft.com/windows2000/server/default.asp
- ✔ http://msdn.microsoft.com/default.asp
- ✔ www.microsoft.com/technet/
- ✔ http://support.microsoft.com/support

Third-party exam information sites

Dozens of non-Microsoft sites offer aid and sustenance to the MCP-seeker. Here's a small sample:

- ✔ www.certificationshack.com (that's Certification Shack, not Certifications Hack) is a pretty useful site with details on most Microsoft exams.

✔ www.cramsession.com has some good overview pages for review the day or two before you take the exam, just to make sure you have all the important bases covered.

✔ www.mcsedirectory.com is an MCSE smorgasbord, featuring everything from sample exams to online books. A really useful site.

Magazine Web sites

Here are a few webzine sites that are worth a visit. Most have their own keyword search facilities:

✔ PC World (www.pcworld.com/pcmag)

✔ InfoWorld (www.infoworld.com)

✔ PC Magazine (www.zdnet.com/pcmag)

✔ PC Computing (www.zdnet.com/pccomp)

✔ PC Week (www.zdnet.com/pcweek)

✔ Windows 2000 Magazine (www.winntmag.com)

For ongoing technical education, I recommend a print subscription to Windows 2000 Magazine. Call 800-621-1544 or 970-663-4700, or write P.O. Box 447, Loveland, CO USA 80539-0447.

Leverage Your Biorhythms

Do you experience a lull in alertness in mid-afternoon, anywhere between 1:30 p.m. and 3:30 p.m.? If so, don't schedule the exam to fall during this time period! For most people, midmorning is best.

You know your own body. If you're an evening person rather than a morning person, slate the exam for as late in the day as you can arrange it. The point is to take the test at the time of day when you normally feel productive and energized.

Get Fired Up

When taking the timed exam, you don't have the luxury of breaks, making a phone call or two to interrupt the tedium, or walking around the building in midtest to get the blood flowing. So you put yourself in a good position to sit down for 100 minutes or so and focus like a laser beam the entire time.

What helps you focus? People are different, but here are some suggestions:

- ✔ **Get plenty of sleep the night before:** Don't party hardy on Exam Eve. You know how much sleep you need to be at your peak; for most people, the amount is between seven and eight hours.

- ✔ **Exercise:** The morning of the test, oxygenate your brain. Run, swim, walk, pump iron, or just do some jumping jacks and running in place. For most people, a little exercise improves alertness.

- ✔ **Eat light:** Don't chow down on heavy food before the exam. A full stomach means naptime. Eat a light breakfast or lunch that won't weigh you down. And avoid fast-food burgers, which induce drowsiness.

- ✔ **Drink a caffeinated beverage:** If a mug of java or a can of soda (Mountain Dew has high caffeine content) revs your engine and doesn't violate your religion, go for it. However, keep the quantity low, so that you don't have to waste valuable exam time on an unplanned biological imperative.

- ✔ **Eat cinnamon:** No one knows why, but cinnamon seems to be an energizing spice. A suitably sinful cinnamon roll half an hour before the test may be your tasty ticket to alertness. If that would weigh you down too much, go for a slice of cinnamon toast, or just sprinkle some in your coffee (see previous tip).

One substance you *don't* want swimming through your veins on test day is alcohol. If you're taking an afternoon exam, the lunchtime martini, beer, or glass of wine slows you down. Celebrate after you pass, not before.

Get Warmed Up

Whether you believe that "cramming" is a good idea, warming up shortly before the test seems to help most of the people whom I've talked with about the exam. I always do it. The difference between cramming and warming up is one of degree. You don't want to be exhausted before you start the exam, but you do want to get your brain going so you don't have to shift from first gear into fifth as you enter the testing center.

Spend some time before you go to the test center shifting your mental momentum. You can do this several ways: with the CD-based material in this book, with the sample tests, by running through some of the labs, or simply by flipping through the book looking for points that you highlighted and making sure you understand them.

My advice is to spend between one and two hours on your warm up. Too little time doesn't do you any good; too much makes you tired.

Reread Chapter 1 as part of your warm up. It'll remind you of what to expect regarding the mechanics of the exam.

Kill a Tree

The testing centers I've visited are strangely stingy about the amount of scratch paper they provide. Some just give you a small whiteboard.

If you don't get at least a dozen sheets of paper, ask for more. If you aren't comfortable with the whiteboard, ask for paper. (Bring your own pad just in case. I did that once, and after the administrator looked it over to be sure I hadn't written notes on a tiny sheet tucked up by the adhesive strip, or scratched answers onto the pages with a leadless mechanical pencil, I was allowed to use my pad. Good thing, too; all the center provided was the marker board, which I hate. Why waste time erasing that thing every 20 seconds?)

Your own mini-diagrams can be a great help, especially in the scenario questions that tell a rather long story. The last thing you want between you and a successful exam is a problem as mundane as not having enough paper.

Jump the Gun

Remember that the exam clock doesn't start running until you click the button that displays the first exam question. Here's a clever trick: Write down any charts, mnemonic devices (such as the OSI model), or other memory-joggers (such as the address range of Windows XP's Automatic Private IP Addressing feature) on your scratch paper before starting the exam. Why use up valuable exam time for this sort of thing if you don't have to? True, you may not use all the bits and pieces that you jot down ahead of time, but, on the other hand, it doesn't cost you anything and it can't hurt.

Don't Reinvent Wheels

When I take a nonadaptive multiple-choice certification test, I mark off a half-page on the first sheet of scratch paper to keep track of eliminations: answers I know are wrong on questions I plan to review later. If you study question #19, for example, and you're not quite sure what the answer is but you know it isn't B or C, you mark "19. A B C D" on the scratch paper and cross out the B and C. When you review tough questions after your first pass through the exam, you don't waste time figuring out all over again that B and C aren't correct answers. Putting this "record of eliminations" on the first sheet of your scratch paper means that you don't have to hunt for these notes.

Trust Your Gut

You should certainly review questions that you have doubts about, and check your reasoning twice on every question if you have the time. (In a non-adaptive test, you can mark questions for review as you go along, then go back and study them after you reach the end of the test.) But if you're tempted to change an answer, be sure you have a compelling reason.

Although the exam questions can be tricky on occasion, most of them are fairly straightforward, which means that you should give some extra weight to your first reaction. I've found from taking lots of MCSE assessment tests that my gut instinct is more often right than wrong.

Check the Numbers

The most frustrating missed answers are those in which you click one answer when the question really calls for two or three or "as many as apply." Therefore, I double-check whether the question asks for a single answer or multiple ones. Although I'm aware of this pitfall, I usually catch one or two questions where I didn't pay enough attention and omitted a relevant answer.

Keep Your Head

You certainly want to pass the test on the first try. However, don't get worked up about it. Worry can become a self-fulfilling prophecy: If you agonize over whether you're answering enough questions right instead of answering the questions themselves, you're likely to create cause for worry!

Remind yourself of the following, and you're more likely to succeed:

✔ The exam fee is the equivalent of six pizzas. Even if you have to retake the exam, your $200 investment comes back to you many times as you progress in your career. (If your company is paying, pay the retest fee out of your own pocket if you feel awkward asking the boss again.)

✔ The exam is *not* a measure of how smart you are! It's a measure of how well you know what Microsoft thinks you need to know about Windows XP, how well you take tests, and how sharp you feel on exam day.

✔ Microsoft, the testing center, the test, and this book aren't going anywhere anytime soon. If you don't pass today, you can pass next week, or next month, or whenever you feel ready.

✔ These MCSE tests are designed so that almost nobody gets a perfect score, and darn few people get an "A" (90 percent or above). An MCSE with a 71 percent average in six exams gets the same letters after her name as an MCSE with a 95 percent average.

✔ Rumor has it that even Bill Gates has trouble passing some of the MCSE tests. Of course, he has a more impressive credential: MSCEO.

✔ You have a great advantage over most exam takers by virtue of having read this book. You can feel confident because of that edge.

✔ Don't tell everyone you know that you're taking the exam. The fewer who know you're taking it, the less you'll worry about what others will think of you if you don't pass the first time out.

Part VII

Appendixes

The 5th Wave   By Rich Tennant

"It appears a server in Atlanta is about to go down, there's printer backup in Baltimore and an accountant in Chicago is about to make level 3 of the game, 'Tomb Pirate'."

In this part . . .

The two appendixes (and before you defenders of the English language fire up your e-mail programs to send me a message, let me assure you that it is just as correct to say "appendixes" as it is to say "appendices") in this part can be critically important parts of your successful path to MCSE-dom.

The practice test in Appendix A gives you a very good flavor of the actual exam while also pointing out any knowledge gaps you may have. Finally, the CD-ROM appendix (Appendix B) explains the various goodies on the enclosed disk, which are well worth a chunk of your time.

Appendix A

Practice Exam

• •

Practice Exam Rules

▶ 90 minutes

▶ 50 questions

▶ At least 73 percent to pass

▶ Treat this test as closed-book: Don't look ahead (to the answers) or behind (to the chapters)

• •

*H*ere's a sample exam to help prepare you for the real deal.

The actual passing percentage is 73 percent as I write this, but Microsoft can change it at any time. Also, the passing percentage is likely to change for adaptive versions of the test. If you get 85 percent or better on this sample exam, you should be in very good shape for the real thing. If you get 100 percent, I salute you.

I cover the same topics that the Microsoft exam covers, but it's almost certain that none of the questions in this sample exam appear verbatim on the Microsoft exam. If you understand all the concepts, you don't need to memorize specific questions and answers. If you miss a question, reread the section in the book that covers that topic. The answers guide you to the correct chapter and objective.

The actual exam includes the occasional simulation and graphical exhibit. I dispense with these here; if you can understand the word questions, the graphical simulations and exhibits will actually be easier for you.

Like the actual exam, this practice exam has circles to mark your answer when only one answer can be correct and square boxes when there may be more than one correct answer.

The test questions in this sample exam are different from the ones in the prep tests at the end of each main chapter. Therefore, even if you've gone through each chapter's prep test, this sample exam is worth taking. Good luck!

Prep Test

1 You're a network administrator at a company that has standardized on Windows XP Professional. Bob in Sales comes to you with a complaint: A print job he started never finished. Upon further investigation, you discover that several users have submitted print jobs that never finished. You discover that the printer, connected to the PC named PSERV, has malfunctioned, and you can't restart it. Another identical printer is on the network, but you don't want to have to tell 20 users to resubmit their print jobs to that other printer. What's your best approach to solve this problem?

A ○ Go to the Printers and Faxes folder on the machine sharing the printer, click the printer, and choose File⇨Pause Printing. Then physically move the identical network printer to the PSERV machine. Choose File⇨Pause Printing again to clear the toggle.

B ○ Open the spool folder on the PSERV machine and drag and drop all the spooled files to the icon in the Printers folder for the identical network printer.

C ○ Right-click the stalled printer's icon and choose Properties and then Ports. Choose Add Port, Local Port, New Port, and type the UNC name for the functioning network printer.

D ○ Right-click the stalled printer's icon and choose Properties and then Ports. Choose Redirect Port, Local Port, Network Port, and type the UNC name for the functioning network printer.

2 Gina stores some data files on a Windows 2000 Server. She wants to move those files down to her Windows XP Professional workstation, which she has configured with two drives: a C: drive using FAT32 and a D: drive using NTFS. The data files Gina wants to move reside in an encrypted folder on the server and she wants to maintain their encryption status when she copies them to her workstation. What must she do? (Choose the best answer.)

A ○ Do a backup of the server folder with NTBACKUP.EXE. Restore the folder to her local system, using either the C: or D: drive.

B ○ Copy or move the entire server folder to her C: drive.

C ○ Copy or move the entire server folder to her D: drive.

D ○ Copy or move the entire server folder to either the C: or D: drive, as she prefers.

E ○ Create a new folder on the D: drive, set it to use encryption via the folder's property sheet, and then copy or move the individual files to that new folder.

3 You're installing Windows XP Professional onto a brand new computer that will become a member of a domain having both Windows 2000 and Windows NT servers. Which of the following statements is true regarding the computer name? (Choose all that apply.)

A ❑ It should contain no more than 15 characters.

B ❑ It should be unique among all other NetBIOS computer names in the domain.

C ❑ It should not have the same name as the domain.

D ❑ It should use the 8 + 3 naming convention if it will share resources to Windows 98 clients.

4 You're a software application developer, and you need to set up a dual-boot machine that can run Windows NT Workstation 4.0 and Windows XP Professional. After you install NT onto an NTFS partition, you install Windows XP onto a separate NTFS partition, per Microsoft's advice. You notice immediately after installing Windows XP, however, that you're no longer able to boot to Windows NT! What gives?

A ○ Windows XP automatically upgraded the NT partition to NTFS version 4, and you didn't have Service Pack 3 installed.

B ○ Windows XP automatically upgraded the NT partition to NTFS version 5.1, and you didn't have Service Pack 4 installed.

C ○ You must run the NT Emergency Recovery process and restore the boot sector.

D ○ You must use FAT for the system partition on a dual-boot machine with NT 4.0 and Windows XP.

5 You decide to roll out Windows XP Professional by using RIS (Remote Installation Service). You use RIS to install Windows XP Pro onto the client computer you'll use as a "master" image. Then you install the user applications you want to roll out along with Windows XP Professional.

What utility do you need to run in order to copy the master image to the network server?

A ○ The Remote Installation Preparation wizard

B ○ The Remote Image Replication wizard

C ○ The System Preparation program

D ○ Systems Management Server (SMS)

6 You work for Acme Cognac Inc., which is using RIS to roll out Windows XP Professional. In a test using five PCs, you find that three of them work fine but two do not. You verify that all five PCs can see a DHCP server, a DNS server, and a domain controller. All five PCs use the same network interface card, which is PXE-compliant. What would you check next?

A ○ Verify that the BIOS includes the network card as an allowable boot device.

B ○ Verify that the BIOS specifies the network card as the first boot device.

C ○ Verify that the BIOS supports ACPI.

D ○ Verify that the Hardware Abstraction Layer is identical for all five PCs.

7 You're creating a new user account on a Windows XP Professional PC, and you want to make it a member of one of the built-in local groups. Which of these groups most nearly approximates a standard user account in Windows NT Workstation 4.0?

A ○ Users

B ○ Restricted Users

C ○ Power Users

D ○ Administrators

8 You want to connect to a networked TCP/IP printer on your corporate intranet. Which of the following statements about the Add Printer Wizard is correct? (Choose all that apply.)

A ❑ You can specify the printer by using a Uniform Resource Locator.

B ❑ You can specify the printer by using its share name.

C ❑ You can specify the printer by browsing the network for it.

D ❑ You can specify the printer by using its SID.

9 You install a USB speaker system on your Windows XP Professional computer. It doesn't work, however, even after you restart the computer. You open Device Manager, and you expand every node but you can't find an entry for the USB host controller. What should you do next?

A ○ Enable the USB controller in the BIOS.

B ○ Run the Add New Hardware Wizard.

C ○ Enable the USB controller in the System control panel.

D ○ Reinstall Windows XP with a different HAL.

10 Thelma is an employee of your company. She gets a sweet job offer from an Internet startup and quits your brick-and-mortar business faster than you can say "dot com." Your company hires a replacement, Louise. What's the easiest way for you to disable Thelma's local user account and create a local user account for Louise that has the exact same access rights as Thelma's old account?

A ○ Delete Thelma's account and create Louise's account by using the User Accounts control panel. Recreate any special file and folder access permissions manually by using Windows Explorer.

B ○ In the Local Users and Groups console, copy Thelma's account to create a new account for Louise, and then delete Thelma's account.

C ○ In the Local Users and Groups console, rename Thelma's account to Louise, and then change the account password.

D ○ In the User Accounts control panel, select Thelma's account, type Ctrl+V, and then click anywhere in the user list and type Ctrl+P.

11 You have a small local area network at home, with three PCs running Windows XP Professional, one of which connects to the Internet via an "always-on" DSL link. Every now and then, you need to connect to one of those home PCs (not the one with the DSL connection) from the office. The home PC that connects to the Internet has been automatically set up to use Internet Connection Firewall (ICF). What do you need to do, if anything, to set up your home network so that you can use Remote Desktop to access a home PC from work? (Choose the best answer.)

A ○ Install a different firewall product. ICF doesn't permit forwarding of unsolicited inbound packets.

B ○ Install File and Printer Sharing for Microsoft Networks on the home PC you want to connect to, and share the C: drive. ICF will detect that you've enabled file sharing on that PC and permit the inbound connection.

C ○ On the home PC that connects to the Internet, click the Advanced tab for the DSL connection icon's property sheet and check Allow Remote Administration of This Computer.

D ○ On the home PC that connects to the Internet, click the Advanced tab for the DSL connection icon's property sheet and add Remote Desktop as a service.

E ○ On the home PC that you want to connect to, click the Advanced tab for the LAN connection icon's property sheet and add Remote Desktop as a service.

12 How can you use NTBACKUP.EXE to back up the local Registry? (Choose all correct answers.)

A ○ Check the C:\WINNT\SYSTEM32\REG folder.

B ○ Check the C:\WINNT\SYSTEM32\CONFIG folder.

C ○ Check the System State check box.

D ○ Use the Emergency Repair Diskette Wizard and check the optional check box.

13 You have to use the Registry to troubleshoot a device driver problem. The device manufacturer's tech support person tells you to open windows in REGEDIT for the "two main Registry keys" and minimize the other windows.

Which of the following Registry main keys is merely a pointer to a subkey of one of the other main keys, and therefore not one of the "two main" keys? (Choose all that apply.)

A ❑ HKEY_CLASSES_ROOT

B ❑ HKEY_CURRENT_USER

C ❑ HKEY_LOCAL_MACHINE

D ❑ HKEY_DYN_DATA

14 Carla recently upgraded her Windows NT 4.0 Workstation computer to Windows XP. She discovers that she can now specify a password for her account that's shorter than ten characters, something she wasn't able to do under NT. She comes to you, the PC administrator, to reset her system so that it again requires at least ten characters for the account password. Which of the following actions accomplishes this goal?

A ○ Open the Computer Management console, choose the Local Security Policy snap-in, and set Minimum Password Length under the Password Policy node.

B ○ Open the Administrative tools console, choose the Local Security Policy snap-in, and set Minimum Password Length under the Password Policy node.

C ○ Open the User Accounts control panel, click Carla's account in the list, click the Properties button, choose the Passwords tab, and enter the number 10 in the Minimum Password Length field.

D ○ Open the Computer Management console, choose the Local Users and Groups snap-in, and set Minimum Password Length under the Password Policy node.

15 Mary is an Administrator of her own Windows XP Professional PC. She runs the Local Security Policy console and changes the Maximum Password Age policy from 60 days to 90 days. However, the next time she restarts, she notices that the policy setting has reverted to 60 days. Why? (Choose the best answer.)

A ○ A Group Policy setting that overrides Mary's local setting has been made at the domain level.

B ○ A Group Policy setting that overrides Mary's local setting has been made at the site or domain level.

C ○ A Group Policy setting that overrides Mary's local setting has been made at the site, domain, or organizational unit level.

D ○ Mary forgot to choose File⇨Save to commit her changes to disk.

16 A remote network user is having application problems. Which of the following utilities can you use on your Windows XP Professional PC to diagnose and/or troubleshoot remote computers? (Choose all that apply.)

A ❑ REGEDIT

B ❑ REGEDT32

C ❑ Event Viewer

D ❑ System Monitor

E ❑ Remote Desktop

F ❑ Remote Help Desk

17 You install a new device driver, reboot Windows XP Professional, log on, and discover that the system is no longer working correctly. What should your first system recovery step be? (Choose the best answer.)

A ○ Restart, press F8, and specify Last Known Good Configuration.

B ○ Roll back the driver in Device Manager.

C ○ Restart, press F8, specify Safe Mode, and remove the driver.

D ○ Roll back to the most recent system restore point.

E ○ Boot from the Windows XP CD and choose Recovery Console.

18 Jenna complains that she is unable to access the BUDGET folder on Jim's Windows XP Professional computer from her Windows XP Professional machine. Jim has shared the folder by using shared folder permissions as follows: Read access allowed to the Sales group; Change access allowed to the Managers group; and Full Control access denied to the Staff group. Jenna belongs to both the Sales and Staff groups. What can you do to give her access to the BUDGET folder? (Choose one answer.)

A ○ Make Jenna a member of the Managers group.

B ○ Have Jim add Jenna's individual user account to the BUDGET folder's permission list, with Full Control access allowed.

C ○ Make Jenna a member of the Power Users group.

D ○ Remove Jenna from the Staff group.

19 You're configuring a notebook computer to dial up a private LAN. The notebook computer is equipped with a smart card. Which dial-up security protocol are you most likely to use? (Choose the best answer.)

A ○ MS-CHAP

B ○ MS-CHAPv2

C ○ SPAP

D ○ EAP

E ○ SCSP

F ○ IPsec

20 You're in charge of securing your company's Windows XP network. You decide to study the various settings in the predefined security templates so that you can determine which one is the best fit for your organization. What's the best tool for you to use when studying the settings in the INF template files?

A ○ The Security Templates snap-in

B ○ The Security Configuration and Analysis snap-in

C ○ The Local Security Policy console

D ○ The Local Group Policy console

E ○ The SECEDIT program

21 You're the PC tech support manager for Bridget's Widgets Inc. One of your engineer's Windows XP Professional computers has become unstable in recent weeks. You decide to scan the system areas and make a list of all files that don't have a Microsoft digital signature. Which tool would you use to perform this task?

A ○ SFC

B ○ SYSCONFIG

C ○ SIGVERIFY

D ○ SIGVERIF

E ○ Device Manager

22 You get a complaint from Baxter, who believes that another user of his PC, Frieda, is meddling with Baxter's files. You decide to enable auditing on the file system in order to see if Baxter's claims have merit. Which of the following audit policies should you enable in the Local Security Policy console?

A ○ Audit system events

B ○ Audit account management

C ○ Audit process tracking

D ○ Audit object access

23 Your organization has a TCP/IP network of Windows XP workstations and Windows 2000 Server computers. One of the servers is set up to provide a link to the Internet. Sunny complains that she can connect to any of the local servers on her subnet but not to the public Internet. What's most likely causing this problem? (Choose the best answer.)

A ○ Sunny's PC has an incorrect IP address on the General tab of the TCP/IP property sheet for the LAN connection.

B ○ Sunny's PC has an incorrect IP address for the default gateway on the IP Settings tab of the TCP/IP property sheet.

C ○ No Windows 2000 or 2002 server is running WINS.

D ○ No Windows 2000 or 2002 server is running DHCP.

24 You install Windows XP Professional onto a portable PC that supports the Advanced Control and Power Interface specification. Jonathan, the portable PC's user, takes his computer to a day-long management meeting. When Jonathan comes back to the conference room after lunch, the PC has shut down and Jonathan lost recent changes to the Word document he was using for note taking. How would you reconfigure Jonathan's computer to make such problems less likely in the future? (Choose all that apply.)

A ❑ You can't. If Jonathan is too lazy to shut down his laptop before lunch, he's hopeless.

B ❑ In the Power Options control panel, enable Hibernation, and on the Advanced tab, choose Hibernate under When I Close the Lid of My Portable Computer.

C ❑ In the Power Options control panel, choose the Power Schemes tab and set the computer to hibernate after 30 minutes of inactivity.

D ❑ In the Power Options control panel, choose the Power Schemes tab and set the computer to go into standby mode after 30 minutes of inactivity.

E ❑ In the Power Options control panel, enable Hibernation, and then choose the Alarms tab and set the Critical Battery Alarm action to Hibernate.

25 What's the default file extension for a Windows Installer package?

A ○ MSI

B ○ WMI

C ○ INF

D ○ WSI

26 Bertie is an employee at your company and says his dial-up link to an ISP is too slow. He works in an office that has a spare phone line, and you decide to implement a multilink setup. Which of the following statements are true about multilink connections in Windows XP Professional? (Choose all that apply.)

A ❑ Both modems must be the same speed.

B ❑ You can combine a modem and an ISDN line.

C ❑ The ISP must support multilink connections.

D ❑ Both modems must be internal.

27 You're working on a network-connected Windows XP Professional notebook machine and you've made a particular file on a Windows 2000 Server "available offline." You synchronize files and leave on a trip. While you're away, you make changes to the file, but another user makes changes to the copy on the server machine, too. When you return, and attempt to synchronize with the network, what happens with this file?

A ○ Windows XP detects that both copies have been edited and asks you what you want to do.

B ○ Windows XP detects that both copies have been edited and automatically saves your version to the server but with a different filename.

C ○ Windows XP doesn't detect that both copies have been edited and simply replaces the older file with the newer one. Changes made to the older file are lost.

D ○ You receive an Error 601 from the Synchronization Manager.

28 You need to access the C:\WINDOWS folder of a remote Windows XP Professional computer on your company's local area network. However, the user hasn't shared any folders. What "secret" share name can you use to connect to this folder? (Choose the best answer.)

A ○ ADMIN$

B ○ C$\ADMIN

C ○ C$\WINNT

D ○ WINNT$

29 You need to set up a Virtual Private Network connection over the public Internet. Your boss has asked you to set up your VPN link with the tightest possible security. How should you proceed? (Choose the best answer.)

A ○ Use the L2TP protocol with all the default settings.

B ○ Use the L2TP protocol with IPsec.

C ○ Use the PPTP protocol with IPsec.

D ○ You can't create a VPN connection over the Internet. You can only create VPN links across private networks.

30 Which of the following statements is true about Disk Defragmenter? (Choose all that apply.)

A ❑ It only works with NTFS volumes.

B ❑ It only works with local volumes.

C ❑ Microsoft recommends that you have five percent or more free space on disk before using it.

D ❑ It defragments the Windows page file.

E ❑ You can create a Scheduled Task to automate it.

31 Your boss tells you that he's sick and tired of PCs crashing because of buggy third-party device drivers, and he wants you to make sure that users can't install any unsigned drivers onto their Windows XP Professional machines. The network you manage has 100 PCs and three servers, and all the servers are running Windows 2000 Server (two are domain controllers). What's your best move to meet your boss's demand?

A ○ Set a "block" value for the policy Unsigned Driver Installation Behavior at the domain level.

B ○ Use the Local Security Policy console to set a "block" value for the policy Unsigned Driver Installation Behavior on each local workstation.

C ○ Log on as an administrator and run the System control panel on each local workstation. Choose the Hardware tab and the Driver Signing button. Click Block – Prevent Installation of Unsigned Files and check the Apply Setting as System Default box.

D ○ Do nothing. This is Windows XP Professional's default behavior.

32 When setting up roaming user profiles on Windows XP Professional computers in a network whose servers are running Windows 2000 Server, you decide that you want to limit the profile data that's stored on network servers. Which file on each user's local hard drive contains information about roaming profile exclusions?

A ○ C:\PROFILES\<*username*>\EXCLUSIONS.TXT

B ○ C:\WINDOWS\PROFILES\<*username*>\EXCLUSIONS.DAT

C ○ C:\DOCUMENTS AND SETTINGS\<*username*>\NTUSER.INI

D ○ C:\DOCUMENTS AND SETTINGS\<*username*>\EXCLUSIONS.TXT

33 You receive Service Pack 12 for Windows XP Professional. You want to apply this service pack to your master distribution server so that all subsequent installations of Windows XP Professional from the server will incorporate the service pack. What command should you use?

A ○ UPDATE.EXE -S

B ○ UPDATE.EXE

C ○ UPDATE.EXE /IMG

D ○ PATCH.EXE /IMG

34 To ensure that no one in your organization (Wallace's Window Washers) can encrypt information that may not be retrievable later, Wallace, the president, decrees that the Encrypting File System be disabled for all PCs running Windows XP Professional. He asks you to carry out this directive. The company uses an Active Directory networking model with two domains and a mix of Windows 2000 and Windows NT 4.0 servers. All the clients run Windows XP. Wallace's dog is named Gromit. How should you proceed?

A ○ Run the Local Security Policy on each client PC and disable the Permit Encrypting File System policy.

B ○ Edit the Default Domain Policy on the two domain controllers and disable the Permit Encrypting File System policy.

C ○ Run the Local Security Policy on each client PC and enable the Restrict Encrypting File System to Domain Administrators policy.

D ○ Edit the Default Domain Policy on the two domain controllers and delete the Encrypted Data Recovery Agents policy.

35 You're setting up some PCs for international language support because your company is managing an international research project. You know that Windows XP Professional supports Unicode, an international-standard character set that has extra characters above and beyond those that appear in the ASCII character set. However, one of the applications you run doesn't support Unicode, and menus and dialog boxes don't appear correctly in that application.

How can you change the default language that Windows XP uses for non-Unicode applications on a single Windows XP Professional machine?

A ○ In the Regional Options and Languages control panel, choose the Advanced tab and set the Language for Non-Unicode Programs.

B ○ In the Regional Options and Languages control panel, click the appropriate language in the Language Settings for the System list.

C ○ In the Regional Options and Languages control panel, click the appropriate language in the Language Settings for the System list, and then click the Set as Default button.

D ○ Windows XP doesn't support applications that don't support Unicode.

36 Ralph has shared a folder, RALPHSTUFF, on his NTFS drive with the share permission Full Control to EVERYONE. Later, Ralph sets the NTFS permission, Read & Execute, to the same folder for the group TEMPS. Ralph also removes inherited NTFS permissions for the group EVERYONE, so the only NTFS permissions for RALPHSTUFF apply to the group TEMPS. Francine is a member of TEMPS but also (naturally) a member of EVERYONE, which still has the share permission of Full Control. Can she delete a file in the RALPHSTUFF folder? (Choose the best answer.)

A ○ Yes. The share permission Full Control overrides the NTFS permission Read & Execute.

B ○ No. When NTFS permissions exist, share permissions are ignored.

C ○ Yes. Just because Francine can Read and Execute files at the NTFS permision level doesn't mean she can't delete files at the share permission level.

D ○ No. Francine's effective permissions are the most restrictive combination of share permissions and NTFS permissions.

37 You've just graduated from business school. Your boss asks you to analyze the costs and benefits of using multiple displays as opposed to very large single displays, so you begin gathering facts that may affect the overall cost of multiple display setups. Which of the following statements about Windows XP Professional's multiple display support are correct? (choose all t6hat apply.)

A ❑ You can have a maximum of three simultaneously active displays.

B ❑ All video adapters in a multiple display setup must use the PCI bus.

C ❑ All video adapters in a multiple display setup must use the PCI bus or the AGP bus.

D ❑ Some video cards work as a primary display but not as a secondary display.

E ❑ Some computers automatically disable onboard video circuits when one or more plug-in adapters are detected.

38 You want to test 200 PCs for compatibility with Windows XP Professional before you upgrade them. You have several options for performing this test. Which files could you use? (Choose all that apply.)

A ❑ CHKUPGRD.EXE

B ❑ WINNT32.EXE

C ❑ UNATTEND.TXT

D ❑ APCOMPAT.EXE

39 Which of the following accessibility settings help users who may tap keyboard keys unintentionally and involuntarily? (Choose the best answer.)

A ○ ToggleKeys

B ○ FilterKeys

C ○ StickyKeys

D ○ QuickKeys

40 In order to reduce the hassles of maintaining static IP addresses, you've enabled Automatic Private IP Addressing on a Windows XP Professional work-group. Which of the following is a valid address for a computer in that work-group?

A ○ 169.254.10.10

B ○ 127.0.0.1

C ○ 169.10.10.2

D ○ 255.255.0.0

41 You come to work one morning and discover that your PC won't boot to Windows XP but hangs at the graphical startup splash screen. You think about using the Recovery Console, but you realize that your boss is on vacation and she's the only one with a Windows XP Professional CD. Thankfully, you remember that you installed the Recovery Console from the Windows XP CD onto your computer's hard disk.

Assuming that your CD drive uses letter E, what command did you use to install the Recovery Console onto your hard disk?

A ○ WINNT32.EXE /CMDCONS

B ○ WINNT.EXE /CMDCONS

C ○ CMDCONS.EXE C:

D ○ CONSOLE.EXE E: C:

E ○ RECOVER.EXE /S:E /T:C

42 You have a portable computer that can have a diskette drive or a CD-ROM drive in the internal drive bay, but not both. You need to create two hardware profiles under Windows XP Professional for this situation. How do you begin?

A ○ Run the System control panel. Choose the Hardware tab. Click the Hardware Profiles button. Copy the current profile and give the copy a new name.

B ○ Run the System control panel. Choose the Hardware tab. Click the Hardware Profiles button. Click the New button and give the new profile a name.

C ○ Run the Add New Hardware Wizard. Specify Hardware Profile as the device type to add.

D ○ Right-click the Computer icon in Device Manager. Choose Add Hardware Profile from the context menu.

43 Which of the following security templates provides the strictest security for a Windows XP Professional workstation?

A ○ BASICWK

B ○ HISECWK

C ○ HISECWS

D ○ SECUREWS

E ○ SECUREWK

44 Jennifer, an employee at Acme Cognac, is concerned that she doesn't have enough RAM in her Windows XP Professional computer, which runs a manufacturing program essential to the operation of your plant. You decide to use the Performance Logs and Alerts console snap-in to track page faults per second. However, you can't slow down her computer excessively. Which option would you choose? (Pick the best answer.)

A ○ Alert

B ○ Trace log

C ○ Counter log

D ○ Message

45 Your Windows XP Professional PC isn't properly resolving computer names on your company's network. You suspect that the problem is WINS-related. Which of the following command-line utilities will show you the contents of the current NetBIOS name table? (Choose all that apply.)

A ❑ ipconfig

B ❑ nbtstat n

C ❑ nbtstat -R

D ❑ netstat

46 A user comes to you with performance complaints about his Windows XP Professional computer. He has 64MB of memory and about 75MB of free disk space. What steps would you suggest he take? (Choose all that apply.)

A ❑ Defragment the hard disk.

B ❑ Run the Disk Cleanup Wizard.

C ❑ Set the pagefile to 32MB.

D ❑ Add another 64MB of memory.

47 WINS is the name of a network service that matches up which of the following?

A ○ NetBIOS names with domain names

B ○ Domain names with IP addresses

C ○ IP addresses with workgroup names

D ○ NetBIOS names with IP addresses

48 You set up a single Scheduled Task on your computer to run at 2 a.m. You find out the next day that it didn't execute. What could be possible reasons for this? (Choose all that apply.)

A ❑ Someone has stopped the Task Scheduler service.

B ❑ You didn't specify a proper security context for the task.

C ❑ You didn't log on as Administrator when creating the task.

D ❑ No one was logged on to the PC at 2 a.m.

49 You have a notebook computer that has a PC Card USB host adapter. You use the USB controller when the notebook is at your office in its docking station. However, while you're on the road, you don't use any USB peripherals. How can you reduce the computer's power consumption while on battery power? (Choose the best answer.)

A ○ Run the System control panel, click the Hardware tab, and click the Hardware Profiles button. Double-click the profile corresponding to the undocked state. Go to Device Manager and disable the USB controller.

B ○ Run the System control panel, click the Hardware tab, and click the Hardware Profiles button. Right-click the profile corresponding to the undocked state and choose Properties. In the device list, clear the check box for the USB controller.

C ○ Undock the computer, reboot it, and choose the undocked profile if Windows doesn't select it automatically. Remove the USB controller in Device Manager.

D ○ Undock the computer, reboot it, and choose the undocked profile if Windows doesn't select it automatically. Disable the USB controller in Device Manager.

50 You're using System Monitor to track CPU utilization, specifically, interrupts per second. At what value of sustained interrupt activity do you begin to suspect that a second processor is necessary to optimize system performance?

A ○ 5

B ○ 10

C ○ 15

D ○ 50

Answers

1 **C.** By adding a port to the existing printer definition, you allow Windows to automatically redirect all existing print jobs. Choice A is wrong because you could strain your back moving the printer. Choice B might work, but some of those files may be incomplete (in the process of spooling). Choice D is wrong because no such option exists. *Objective: Manage printers and print jobs (Chapter 7).*

2 **C.** You must keep encrypted files on an NTFS disk to keep them encrypted, so anything involving disk C: is incorrect. It's not necessary to create a new folder, however; you can just copy or move the existing folder. Backing up and restoring with NTBACKUP does preserve encryption as long as you restore to an NTFS disk, but that's a time-consuming approach. *Objective: Monitor and configure disks (Chapter 7).*

3 **A, B,** and **C.** Choice D would be true if it said "Windows 3.1" instead of "Windows 98," but Windows 98 can understand computer names that are longer than the 8 + 3 convention allows. *Objective: Configure, manage, and troubleshoot account settings (Chapter 10).*

4 **B.** Windows XP doesn't ask you about performing the file system upgrade, nor does it check to verify that your currently installed version of NT can handle NTFS 5.1. Choice C isn't correct because it's not just the boot sector that's causing the problem, it's the whole doggoned file system. And choice D just isn't true. *Objective: Configure file systems by using NTFS, FAT32, or FAT (Chapter 3).*

5 **A.** The Remote Installation Preparation Wizard also goes by the name of its executable file, RIPREP.EXE, which resides on the Windows 2002/2000 server where you've installed the RIS service. *Objective: Perform an unattended installation of Windows XP Professional by using Remote Installation Services (RIS) (Chapter 4).*

6 **B.** The network PC gets its own IP address, and that of the RIS server, via DHCP. DNS and Active Directory are necessary for Windows XP to locate the directory service, computer accounts, and the RIS server itself. But those various servers are visible to all five PCs, so the problem must be the BIOS. Microsoft advises setting the network device as the first boot device, not just one in a list of boot devices. *Objective: Perform an unattended installation of Windows XP Professional by using Remote Installation Services (RIS) (Chapter 4).*

7 **C.** The regular Users group in Windows XP is more restrictive than the regular Users group in Windows NT 4.0 Workstation. Applications written for Windows XP or 2000 should work fine with the built-in Users group, but older applications may need users to be members of the built-in Power Users group. *Objective: Implement, configure, manage, and troubleshoot user and group rights (Chapter 10).*

8 **A, B,** and **C.** To browse the network for the printer, leave its name blank in the wizard and click the Next button. You can't find a printer in the wizard by using its security ID. *Objective: Connect to an Internet printer (Chapter 7).*

9 **A.** If the controller doesn't appear in Device Manager, Windows XP isn't seeing the controller, much less the speakers. Because the controller is typically a motherboard device, the best guess is that it isn't enabled in the BIOS, although it's possible that the motherboard has a hardware problem, too. Because USB is a Plug and Play bus, Windows should autodetect it, therefore running the Add New Hardware Wizard would typically not be necessary. *Objective: Install, configure, and manage USB devices (Chapter 8).*

10 **C.** No command exists for copying a user account in the User Accounts control panel or in the Local Users and Groups console (which you access via the control panel's Advanced tab). By renaming the account and immediately choosing a new password, you create a secure account with the same security identifier as the old one — and therefore all the same access permissions, group memberships, and rights. *Objective: Configure and troubleshoot local users and groups (Chapter 10).*

11 **D.** Choice A isn't true. As for B, you don't need File and Printer Sharing in order to make a PC accessible via Remote Desktop, and anyway ICF doesn't automatically detect that service and configure itself to forward incoming unsolicited packets. The option specified by choice C doesn't exist. As for D versus E, ICF is running on the PC that connects to the Internet, not the PC that you want to connect to. *Objective: Configure, manage, and troubleshoot an Internet connection firewall (Chapter 13).*

12 **C.** You can't simply back up the Registry by checking the folder that contains the Registry files (which by the way is C:\WINNT\SYSTEM32\ CONFIG) because the files are in use by the system. The System State backup does back up the Registry, and it lets you specify any target folder. The Emergency Recovery Diskette Wizard is gone as of Windows XP, having been replaced (sort of) by the Automated System Recovery Wizard. *Objective: Recover system state data and user data by using Windows Backup (Chapter 15).*

13 **A** and **B.** In fact, the only two "real" root keys are HKLM and HKU. HKEY_DYN_DATA isn't present in Windows XP. *Objective: Monitor, configure, and troubleshoot I/O devices (Chapter 8).*

14 **B.** The Local Security Policy console in the Administrative Tools folder is what you want; note that the policies you set under the Account Policies node apply to all local user accounts on that computer. You can't get to the account policy settings via the Computer Management console or the User Accounts control panel, although you can set some user-specific password options there, such as whether to prevent a given user from changing his or her password. *Objective: Configure, manage, and troubleshoot account policy (Chapter 10).*

15 **C.** You may also want to remember that the order of precedence for the processing of policies in Windows XP is, from lowest to highest, local — site — domain — organizational unit. Incidentally, no File⇨Save command exists in the Local Security Policy console. *Objective: Configure, manage, and troubleshoot local Group Policy (Chapter 11).*

16 **A, C, D,** and **E.** Using these tools remotely assumes that you and the computer you're trying to administer share at least one network protocol in common. Choices B and F do not exist in Windows XP. *Objective: Optimize and troubleshoot application performance (Chapter 14).*

17 **B.** You can't use Last Known Good Configuration because you already logged on after installing the driver, making the LKG setup a defective setup. Safe Mode would probably work, but it takes a lot longer than simply rolling back the driver in Device Manager. As for choice D, it's unnecessarily draconian and could revert other settings unnecessarily. Choice E is more of a last resort; Safe Mode is much easier and faster. *Objective: Troubleshoot system restoration by starting in Safe Mode (Chapter 15).*

18 **D.** Denials override all other permissions, so the only way to let Jenna into the company budgets is to remove her from the Staff group, which has been denied the Full Control permission. *Objective: Control access to shared folders by using permissions (Chapter 11).*

19 **D.** The Extensible Authentication Protocol is your best bet for smart card authentication; the exam may also refer to EAP/TLS. *Objective: Create a dial-up connection to connect to a remote access server (Chapter 13).*

20 **A.** The Security Templates snap-in (which you must add to a new, custom console of your own devising) presents all the security settings of each available template in a handy hierarchical structure. *Objective: Configure, manage, and troubleshoot a security configuration (Chapter 11).*

21 **D.** Choice A, System File Checker, can detect violations of Windows File Protection and rebuild the DLLCACHE folder, but it doesn't report on digital signatures. Choice B doesn't exist; the System Configuration utility in Windows XP is MSCONFIG, not SYSCONFIG, and it doesn't report on digital signatures, anyway. C is wrong because of spelling. E isn't the best choice because, although Device Manager does show you digital signature information on the Driver tab of device property sheets, it doesn't cover non-driver system files. *Objective: Manage and troubleshoot drivers and driver signing (Chapter 15).*

22 **D.** Object access permits auditing the file system and the Registry. *Objective: Configure, manage, and troubleshoot auditing (Chapter 10).*

23 **B.** If the IP address for the default gateway is wrong or missing, then Sunny's PC has no way to connect to the Internet via the gateway. If her own PC's IP address was wrong or missing, she couldn't see local Windows 2000 servers. WINS doesn't enter into the equation because the gateway is specified in Windows XP using a numeric IP address, not a NetBIOS computer name. And DHCP doesn't have to be running for Sunny to access the Internet. Here's a tip to remember: If Sunny connects to the Internet or other subnets via a router, the default gateway is the IP address of the network port on the router that communicates with her subnet. *Objective: Configure and troubleshoot the TCP/IP protocol (Chapter 6).*

24 **B**, **C**, and **E**. Unlike Standby, Hibernation dumps memory contents to disk, so Hibernate will protect Jonathan's unsaved files. You may want to consider a combination of all three in order to achieve maximum power savings. *Objective: Configure Advanced Configuration Power Interface (Chapter 9).*

25 **A**. It stands for Microsoft Software Installer, never mind that the technology goes by the name of Windows Installer just about everywhere in the Microsoft documentation. The associated executable is MSIEXEC.EXE. *Objective: Install applications by using Windows Installer packages (Chapter 12).*

26 **B** and **C**. The modems can be different speeds, and can be either internal or external devices. *Objective: Install, configure, and manage modems (Chapter 8).*

27 **A**. Then you have the option of deciding whether to overwrite the server-based copy, or save your file to a different name (which you must specify). *Objective: Manage and troubleshoot the synchronization of offline files (Chapter 12).*

28 **A**. This is a so-called "administrative share." The root directory of each hard drive is also shared (as C$, D$, and so on). *Objective: Create and remove shared folders (Chapter 11).*

29 **B**. L2TP with IPsec provides the greatest security level for a VPN connection. You don't have the option of using IPsec with PPTP. *Objective: Connect to computers by using a virtual private network (VPN) connection (Chapter 13).*

30 **B**, **D**, and **E**. Choice A is wrong because the defragger works with all the file systems that Windows XP supports. B is true: You can't run this utility to defragment a server disk, for example. As for choice C, the figure is 15 percent, and both D and E weren't true in Windows 2000 but are true in XP (hurrah!). *Objective: Optimize and troubleshoot disk performance (Chapter 14).*

31 **A**. Generally, the easiest way to assign any network-wide setting is to set a policy at the network level, rather than run around and make each setting at the local workstation. Choice C is the correct procedure for blocking unsigned drivers on a single local PC. Choice D is simply wrong. *Objective: Manage and troubleshoot driver signing (Chapter 15).*

32 **C**. You would actually set the exclusion list by using Group Policies, most likely on a server acting as a domain controller (the specific policy is Exclude Directories In Roaming Profile). Note that on a PC upgraded from Windows NT 4.0 Workstation, user profiles reside under C:\WINNT\ PROFILES\ *<username>*. *Objective: Configure and manage user profiles (Chapter 12).*

33 **A.** You'd follow the -S qualifier with the location of the distribution files. The command is simply UPDATE.EXE to apply the service pack to a standalone PC. *Objective: Perform post-installation updates and product activation (Chapter 4).*

34 **D.** If the Encrypted Data Recovery Agents policy isn't present, EFS won't work on any computer that's a member of the domain. Making a policy change on the domain controller is a whole lot easier than making a change on each workstation, and besides, the policies mentioned in choices A and C do not exist. *Objective: Configure, manage, and troubleshoot Encrypting File System (EFS) (Chapter 3).*

35 **A.** This accurately-named list box setting lets non-Unicode applications display menus and dialog boxes in the language in which they were created. *Objective: Configure multiple-language support for users (Chapter 5).*

36 **D.** You must remember that when both share level permissions and NTFS permissions have been set for the same resource, any restrictions at either level do apply. *Objective: Control access to files and folders by using permissions (Chapter 11).*

37 **C, D,** and **E.** Windows XP actually supports as many as ten simultaneously active displays. Because choice C is true, choice B is not. *Objective: Configure multiple-display support (Chapter 8).*

38 **A, B,** and **C.** Note that the qualifier you'd use with WINNT32.EXE is /CHECKUPGRADEONLY. You could add the line ReportOnly in UNATTEND. TXT to create a log file of compatibility issues without actually installing the operating system. *Objective: Prepare a computer to meet upgrade requirements (Chapter 4).*

39 **B.** No such setting as QuickKeys exists. StickyKeys lets you type key combinations, such as Ctrl+Alt+Del, in sequence instead of all at once. ToggleKeys makes sounds when you hit NumLock, CapsLock, or ScrollLock. *Objective: Configure and troubleshoot accessibility services (Chapter 5).*

40 **A.** The range for APIPA addresses is 169.254.0.1 through 169.254.255.254. Yes, this question is nitpicky. So is the exam. *Objective: Configure and troubleshoot the TCP/IP protocol (Chapter 6).*

41 **A.** The Recovery Console takes five to seven megabytes, but it sure could come in handy in a situation such as this. The PC is apparently booting far enough to get to the splash screen, meaning that you should have the chance to choose Recovery Console from the text menu that appears earlier. *Objective: Recover system state data and user data by using the Recovery Console (Chapter 15).*

42 **A.** You can also specify which profile should be the default and how long Windows XP should wait before it chooses the default profile. *Objective: Manage hardware profiles (Chapter 9).*

43 **C.** You just gotta memorize these. Watch out; the "BASIC" templates are supplied with Windows 2000 — not with XP. *Objective: Configure, manage, and troubleshoot a security configuration (Chapter 11).*

44 **C.** A counter log has less impact on system performance than a continuous trace log, especially if you set the counter interval to a fairly long value. Alerts are for sending messages regarding one-time threshold events. *Objective: Optimize and troubleshoot memory performance (Chapter 14).*

45 **B.** It's not a bad idea to make sure you understand the functions of ipconfig, nbtstat, and tracert. (Be especially careful to learn the ipconfig command qualifiers.) *Objective: Configure and trouble-shoot the TCP/IP protocol (Chapter 6).*

46 **A, B,** and **D.** The system is low on disk space, which means fragmentation is likely to be a problem. The Disk Cleanup Wizard gets rid of unnecessary files and allows the Disk Defragmenter tool to work more effectively. More RAM helps; Windows XP itself typically needs around 80MB before you load any programs or data files. However, setting the pagefile size to a low value (the default is 1.5 times RAM) hurts performance as Windows dynamically resizes the pagefile upward. *Objectives: Optimize and troubleshoot memory performance, optimize and troubleshoot disk performance (Chapter 14).*

47 **D.** Remember also that the NetBIOS name is the same as the computer name. You don't need WINS in a pure Windows XP/2000 network, just for networks that include legacy computers (everything prior to Windows 2000!). *Objective: Configure and troubleshoot the TCP/IP protocol (Chapter 6).*

48 **A** and **B.** You don't have to log on as an Administrator to schedule a task, nor do you have to be logged on when the task is due to execute. You do, however, have to specify a user account that has appropriate rights to execute the program, when you create the task. FYI: If you schedule lots of tasks, and none of them run, the Task Scheduler service is likely stopped. If some run but others don't, you probably have a security issue. *Objective: Configure, manage, and troubleshoot the Task Scheduler (Chapter 14).*

49 **D.** If you removed the device driver, as choice C suggests, you wouldn't have it available in any hardware profile, and you'd have to reinstall the driver next time you used your docking station. *Objective: Manage, monitor, and optimize system performance for mobile users (Chapter 9).*

50 **C.** Also watch out if % processor time is over 85 percent for long stretches of time. You should probably just memorize some of the performance guidelines in Chapter 14. *Objective: Optimize and troubleshoot processor utilization (Chapter 14).*

Appendix B

About the CD

● ●

In This Appendix:

▶ System Requirements

▶ Using the CD with Windows and Mac

▶ What You'll Find on the CD

▶ Troubleshooting

● ●

System Requirements

Make sure that your computer meets the minimum system requirements listed below. If your computer doesn't match up to most of these requirements, you may have problems using the contents of the CD.

- ✔ A PC with a Pentium or faster processor

- ✔ Microsoft Windows 95 or later or Windows NT 4.0 or later.

- ✔ At least 16 MB of total RAM installed on your computer. For best performance, we recommend at least 32 MB of RAM installed.

- ✔ A CD-ROM drive — double-speed (2x) or faster.

- ✔ A sound card for PCs.

- ✔ A monitor capable of displaying at least 256 colors or grayscale.

- ✔ A modem with a speed of at least 14,400 bps.

Using the CD with Microsoft Windows

To install the items from the CD to your hard drive, follow these steps.

1. **Insert the CD into your computer's CD-ROM drive.**

2. **Click Start➪Run.**

3. **In the dialog box that appears, type** D:\HMI.EXE.

Replace *D* with the proper drive letter if your CD-ROM drive uses a different letter. (If you don't know the letter, see how your CD-ROM drive is listed under My Computer.)

4. **Click OK.**

A license agreement window appears.

5. **Read through the license agreement, nod your head, and then click the Accept button if you want to use the CD — after you click Accept, you'll never be bothered by the License Agreement window again.**

The CD interface Welcome screen appears. The interface is a little program that shows you what's on the CD and coordinates installing the programs and running the demos. The interface basically enables you to click a button or two to make things happen.

6. **Click anywhere on the Welcome screen to enter the interface.**

Now you are getting to the action. This next screen lists categories for the software on the CD.

7. **To view the items within a category, just click the category's name.**

A list of programs in the category appears.

8. **For more information about a program, click the program's name.**

Be sure to read the information that appears. Sometimes a program has it's own system requirements or requires you to do a few tricks on your computer before you can install or run the program, and this screen tells you what you might need to do, if necessary.

9. **If you don't want to install the program, click the Back button to return to the previous screen.**

You can always return to the previous screen by clicking the Back button. This feature allows you to browse the different categories and products and decide what you want to install.

10. **To install a program, click the appropriate Install button.**

The CD interface drops to the background while the CD installs the program you chose.

11. **To install other items, repeat Steps 7 – 10.**

12. **When you've finished installing programs, click the Quit button to close the interface.**

You can eject the CD now. Carefully place it back in the plastic jacket of the book for safekeeping.

In order to run some of the programs on this *MCSE Windows XP Professional For Dummies* CD-ROM, you may need to keep the CD inside your CD-ROM drive. This is a good thing. Otherwise, the installed program would have required you to install a very large chunk of the program to your hard drive, which may have kept you from installing other software.

What You'll Find

Shareware programs are fully functional, free, trial versions of copyrighted programs. If you like particular programs, register with their authors for a nominal fee and receive licenses, enhanced versions, and technical support. *Freeware programs* are free, copyrighted games, applications, and utilities. You can copy them to as many PCs as you like — for free — but they offer no technical support. *GNU software* is governed by its own license, which is included inside the folder of the GNU software. There are no restrictions on distribution of GNU software. See the GNU license at the root of the CD for more details. *Trial, demo,* or *evaluation* versions of software are usually limited either by time or functionality (such as not letting you save a project after you create it).

Here's a summary of the software on this CD.

Dummies test prep tools

This CD contains questions related to MCSE Windows XP Professional administration. Most of the questions cover topics that you can expect to be on the test.

The Dummies Test Engine is designed to help you get comfortable with the certification testing situation and pinpoint your strengths and weaknesses on the topic. You can customize the settings. You can choose the number of questions and even decide which objectives you want to focus on.

After you answer the questions, the Dummies Test Engine gives you plenty of feedback. You can find out which questions you answered correctly and incorrectly. Then you can review the questions — all of them, all the ones you missed, all the ones you marked, or a combination of the ones you marked and the ones you missed.

Links Page

I've also created a Links Page, a handy starting place for accessing the huge amounts of information on the Internet about the certification tests. You can find the page at D:\Links.htm.

Commercial demos

W2000 Prof. MCSEprep, from Super Software

This demo, designed to help you prepare for the Windows 2000 Server exam, gives you another 20 practice questions. Get lots more by ordering the software. Learn more by visiting the Web site, www.mcseprep.com.

Self Test Software for MCSE Windows 2000, from Self Test Software

Self Test Software's demo is designed to help you learn more about the Windows 2000 Professional exam by giving you extra practice questions. Learn more by visiting the Web site, www.selftestsoftware.com.

Exam Simulator for exam 70-270, from Specialized Solutions

Learn more by visiting the Web site, www.specializedsolutions.com.

If You've Got Problems (Of the CD Kind)

I tried my best to compile programs that work on most computers with the minimum system requirements. Alas, your computer may differ, and some programs may not work properly for some reason.

The two likeliest problems are that you don't have enough memory (RAM) for the programs you want to use, or you have other programs running that are affecting installation or running of a program. If you get error messages like Not enough memory or Setup cannot continue, try one or more of these methods and then try using the software again:

✔ **Turn off any antivirus software that you have on your computer.** Installers sometimes mimic virus activity and may make your computer incorrectly believe that it is being infected by a virus.

✔ **Close all running programs.** The more programs you're running, the less memory is available to other programs. Installers also typically update files and programs; if you keep other programs running, installation may not work properly.

✔ **In Windows, close the CD interface and run demos or installations directly from Windows Explorer.** The interface itself can tie up system memory, or even conflict with certain kinds of interactive demos. Use Windows Explorer to browse the files on the CD and launch installers or demos.

✔ **Have your local computer store add more RAM to your computer.** This is, admittedly, a drastic and somewhat expensive step. However, adding more memory can really help the speed of your computer and enable more programs to run at the same time.

If you still have trouble installing the items from the CD, please call the Hungry Minds Customer Service phone number: 800-762-2974 (outside the U.S.: 317-572-3342) or e-mail techsupdum@hungryminds.com.

Index

● P ●

• W •

● Z ●

Hungry Minds, Inc.
End-User License Agreement

READ THIS. You should carefully read these terms and conditions before opening the software packet(s) included with this book ("Book"). This is a license agreement ("Agreement") between you and Hungry Minds, Inc. ("HMI"). By opening the accompanying software packet(s), you acknowledge that you have read and accept the following terms and conditions. If you do not agree and do not want to be bound by such terms and conditions, promptly return the Book and the unopened software packet(s) to the place you obtained them for a full refund.

1. **License Grant.** HMI grants to you (either an individual or entity) a nonexclusive license to use one copy of the enclosed software program(s) (collectively, the "Software") solely for your own personal or business purposes on a single computer (whether a standard computer or a workstation component of a multi-user network). The Software is in use on a computer when it is loaded into temporary memory (RAM) or installed into permanent memory (hard disk, CD-ROM, or other storage device). HMI reserves all rights not expressly granted herein.

2. **Ownership.** HMI is the owner of all right, title, and interest, including copyright, in and to the compilation of the Software recorded on the disk(s) or CD-ROM ("Software Media"). Copyright to the individual programs recorded on the Software Media is owned by the author or other authorized copyright owner of each program. Ownership of the Software and all proprietary rights relating thereto remain with HMI and its licensers.

3. **Restrictions On Use and Transfer.**

   (a) You may only (i) make one copy of the Software for backup or archival purposes, or (ii) transfer the Software to a single hard disk, provided that you keep the original for backup or archival purposes. You may not (i) rent or lease the Software, (ii) copy or reproduce the Software through a LAN or other network system or through any computer subscriber system or bulletin-board system, or (iii) modify, adapt, or create derivative works based on the Software.

   (b) You may not reverse engineer, decompile, or disassemble the Software. You may transfer the Software and user documentation on a permanent basis, provided that the transferee agrees to accept the terms and conditions of this Agreement and you retain no copies. If the Software is an update or has been updated, any transfer must include the most recent update and all prior versions.

4. **Restrictions on Use of Individual Programs.** You must follow the individual requirements and restrictions detailed for each individual program in Appendix B of this Book. These limitations are also contained in the individual license agreements recorded on the Software Media. These limitations may include a requirement that after using the program for a specified period of time, the user must pay a registration fee or discontinue use. By opening the Software packet(s), you will be agreeing to abide by the licenses and restrictions for these individual programs that are detailed in Appendix B and on the Software Media. None of the material on this Software Media or listed in this Book may ever be redistributed, in original or modified form, for commercial purposes.

5. **Limited Warranty.**

    (a) HMI warrants that the Software and Software Media are free from defects in materials and workmanship under normal use for a period of sixty (60) days from the date of purchase of this Book. If HMI receives notification within the warranty period of defects in materials or workmanship, HMI will replace the defective Software Media.

    (b) **HMI AND THE AUTHOR OF THE BOOK DISCLAIM ALL OTHER WARRANTIES, EXPRESS OR IMPLIED, INCLUDING WITHOUT LIMITATION IMPLIED WARRANTIES OF MERCHANTABILITY AND FITNESS FOR A PARTICULAR PURPOSE, WITH RESPECT TO THE SOFTWARE, THE PROGRAMS, THE SOURCE CODE CONTAINED THEREIN, AND/OR THE TECHNIQUES DESCRIBED IN THIS BOOK. HMI DOES NOT WARRANT THAT THE FUNCTIONS CONTAINED IN THE SOFTWARE WILL MEET YOUR REQUIRE-MENTS OR THAT THE OPERATION OF THE SOFTWARE WILL BE ERROR FREE.**

    (c) This limited warranty gives you specific legal rights, and you may have other rights that vary from jurisdiction to jurisdiction.

6. **Remedies.**

    (a) HMI's entire liability and your exclusive remedy for defects in materials and workmanship shall be limited to replacement of the Software Media, which may be returned to HMI with a copy of your receipt at the following address: Software Media Fulfillment Department, Attn : *MCSE Windows XP Professional For Dummies*, Hungry Minds, Inc., 10475 Crosspoint Blvd., Indianapolis, IN 46256, or call 1-800-762-2974. Please allow four to six weeks for delivery. This Limited Warranty is void if failure of the Software Media has resulted from accident, abuse, or misapplication. Any replacement Software Media will be warranted for the remainder of the original warranty period or thirty (30) days, whichever is longer.

    (b) In no event shall HMI or the author be liable for any damages whatsoever (including without limitation damages for loss of business profits, business interruption, loss of business information, or any other pecuniary loss) arising from the use of or inability to use the Book or the Software, even if HMI has been advised of the possibility of such damages.

    (c) Because some jurisdictions do not allow the exclusion or limitation of liability for consequential or incidental damages, the above limitation or exclusion may not apply to you.

7. **U.S. Government Restricted Rights.** Use, duplication, or disclosure of the Software for or on behalf of the United States of America, its agencies and/or instrumentalities (the "U.S. Government") is subject to restrictions as stated in paragraph (c)(1)(ii) of the Rights in Technical Data and Computer Software clause of DFARS 252.227-7013, or subparagraphs (c) (1) and (2) of the Commercial Computer Software - Restricted Rights clause at FAR 52.227-19, and in similar clauses in the NASA FAR supplement, as applicable.

8. **General.** This Agreement constitutes the entire understanding of the parties and revokes and supersedes all prior agreements, oral or written, between them and may not be modified or amended except in a writing signed by both parties hereto that specifically refers to this Agreement. This Agreement shall take precedence over any other documents that may be in conflict herewith. If any one or more provisions contained in this Agreement are held by any court or tribunal to be invalid, illegal, or otherwise unenforceable, each and every other provision shall remain in full force and effect.

Photoshop CS6

the missing manual®

The book that should have been in the box®

Photoshop CS6

the missing manual®

The book that should have been in the box®

Kristen —
may the
Creative force,
be with you!
Lesa Snider

Lesa Snider

O'REILLY®

Beijing | Cambridge | Farnham | Köln | Sebastopol | Tokyo

The Missing Credits

About the Author

 **Lesa Snider** is on a mission to teach the world to create—and use!—better graphics. She's an internationally acclaimed speaker; stock photographer and chief evangelist for iStock-photo.com (*www.lesa.in/istockdeal*); as well as the founder of the creative tutorial site PhotoLesa.com. Lesa is the author of many video-training workshops (*www.lesa.in/clvideos*) and the coauthor of *iPhoto '11: The Missing Manual*. She writes a regular column for *Photoshop User, Elements Techniques,* and *Macworld* magazines, and contributes frequently to Design-Tools.com and PlanetPhotoshop.com. Lesa is also a long-time member of the Photoshop World Dream Team of instructors and can be spotted teaching at many other conferences around the globe. She also teaches Advanced Photoshop for the international graphic design school, Sessions.edu. You can connect with her online on Facebook (*www.facebook.com/PhotoLesa*), YouTube (*www.lesa.in/ytvideochannel*), Twitter (@PhotoLesa), and *www.PhotoLesa.com*.

During her free time, you'll find Lesa carving the twisties on her sportbike, dressed up in her Star Trek best at a sci-fi convention, or hanging with fellow Apple Mac enthusiasts. Lesa is a proud member of the BMWMOA, F800 Riders Club, and the Colorado Mac User Group (*www.CoMUG.com*) a.k.a. the Boulder Mac Maniacs. Email: *lesa@photolesa.com*.

About the Creative Team

Dawn Mann (editor) is associate editor for the Missing Manual series. When not working, she hikes, beads, and causes trouble. Email: *dawn@oreilly.com*.

Melanie Yarbrough (production editor) lives in Cambridge, Massachusetts, where she works as a production editor. When not ushering books through production, she's writing and baking whatever she can think up. Email: *myarbrough@oreilly.com*.

Julie Van Keuren (copy editor) quit her newspaper job in 2006 to move to Montana and live the freelancing dream. She and her husband, M.H. (who is living the novel-writing dream), have two sons, Dexter and Michael. Email: *little_media@yahoo.com*.

Ron Strauss (indexer) is a full-time freelance indexer specializing in IT. When not working, he moonlights as a concert violist and alternative medicine health consultant. Email: *rstrauss@mchsi.com*.

Charles Holt (technical reviewer) is an aerodynamic man of random talents. He's created computer games, ghost-written parts of a book about tea, and won a ukulele design contest. He currently works with his wife, Melissa, as an Apple Consultant in beautiful Colorado (*www.PEBMAC.com*), but he dreams of once again snorkeling in Napili Bay.

Shangara Singh (technical reviewer) is the author of the popular exam aids for Photoshop and Lightroom—study guides for people who want to become an Adobe Certified Expert—published by *Examaids.com*. He has also authored a keyword hierarchy for stock photographers (*Keyword-Catalog.com*) and has his own stock photo website: SensaStockImages.com.

■ Acknowledgements

This book is dedicated to my beloved cat of 16 years, Sylvester, who returned to The Realm of Feline Gods during the creation of this edition. His laid-back nature and unconditional love will remain with me always.

I'd like to express galactic thanks to iStockphoto.com for providing most of the imagery you see throughout this book: An image really is worth a thousand words (if you ever need high-quality, affordable graphics, visit *www.lesa.in/istockdeal*). A big hug and thanks to David Pogue who roped me into this project and so graciously wrote the foreword for this book. To Jeff and Scott Kelby for believing in me and nurturing my career in immeasurable ways throughout many years. To Derrick Story for his wisdom and guidance before I got started on this project, and a great big jug of Umbrian vino rosso to Dawn Mann for editing this book and keeping me on track. Her input has made me a better writer and for that I will forever be grateful! To my brilliant tech-editors, Shangara Singh and J. Charles Holt, whose expertise and watchful eyes helped create the best Photoshop book yet.

Special thanks to Jeff Gamet (*www.macobserver.com*) for keeping me sane and helping with the first edition, to Richard Harrington (*www.photoshopforvideo.com*) for his help on the actions chapter, to Taz Tally (*www.taztallyphotography.com*) for helping with the print chapter, to Marcus Conge (*www.digitalmanipulation.com*) and Bert Monroy (*www.bertmonroy.com*) for their help with all things 3-D and vector-related, and to the brilliant Veronica Hanley who helped make the drawing chapter make sense to mere mortals. To Deborah Fox (*www.deborahfoxart.com*) for the beautiful art in the painting chapter, to Tanya and Richard Horie (for their expert advice on the painting chapter and brush customization options), to Karen Nace (*www.karennace.com*) for her HDR and wide-angle photography, and to Tony Corbell (*www.corbellproductions.com*) for his guidance on the plug-ins chapter. And without the determination of Jay Nelson (*www.design-tools.com*) and the expertise of Rod Harlan (*www.dvpa.com*), the new video chapter would not exist.

To my esteemed colleagues—and good friends—Andy Ihnatko, Ben Willmore, Peter Cohen, Kevin Ames, Dave Cross, Larry Becker, Jack Davis, Gary-Paul Prince, Terry White, Dave Moser, Matt Kloskowski, and Eddie Tapp who all expressed how very proud of me they are and who each, in their own special way, convinced me I could survive writing (and subsequently updating) a book of this magnitude.

Last but not least, buckets of appreciation to my friends and neighbors who continually gave their support—or a cocktail!—when I needed it most: Carol Morphew, Elsbeth Diehl, Leslie Raguso, Kathryn Kroll, Ruth Lind, Leslie Fishlock, Melissa Olilla, Erica Gamet, Kirk Aplin, Lorene Romero, and most importantly, Fran Snider, the best mama a girl could have (wish Daddy could've held this book!). To my true love, Jay Nelson, whose respect, support, and caring nature makes me strive to be a better person every single day, and to our beautiful cat, Samantha, who forced me to get out of my pretty purple Aeron chair and play The Laser Pointer Game with her at exactly 5:15 pm each day.

May the creative force be with you all!

— *Lesa Snider*

Introduction

Congratulations on buying one of the most complicated pieces of software ever created. Fortunately, it's also one of the most rewarding. No other program on the market lets you massage, beautify, and transform your images like Photoshop. It's so popular that people use its name as a verb: "Dude, you Photoshopped the *heck* out of her!" You'd be hard-pressed to find a published image that *hasn't* spent some quality time in this program, and those that didn't probably should have.

The bad news is that it's a tough program to learn; you won't become a Photoshop guru overnight. Luckily, you hold in your hot little hands a book that covers the program from a *practical* standpoint, so you'll learn the kinds of techniques you can use every day. It's written in plain English for normal people, so you don't have to be any kind of expert to understand it. You'll also learn just enough theory (where appropriate) to help you understand *why* you're doing what you're doing.

> **NOTE** This book focuses primarily on the standard edition of Photoshop CS6. Adobe also offers Photoshop CS6 Extended, which costs more and offers extra features primarily designed for folks who work in 3D, as well as fields like architecture and medical science.

■ What's New in Photoshop CS6

Adobe has added some amazing new features to Photoshop and incorporated many items that have been on customers' wish lists for years (such as being able to change the blend modes of several layers at once and create dashed and dotted lines). In fact, this is one of the most *feature-packed* upgrades the program has seen in years. Here's an overview:

- **Workspace updates**. No matter *which* version you're upgrading from, the Photoshop workspace now looks completely different thanks to a new charcoal-gray color theme. Adobe also removed the Application bar to give you more screen real estate (the controls that roosted in it are now sprinkled throughout the Tools panel and various menus). Settings for Adjustment layers, layer masks, and 3D items are now consolidated into the new Properties panel, and the whole workspace sports more consistent wording across panels and dialog boxes.

  This new version also sports a new Mercury Graphics Engine that relies much more heavily on your computer's graphics processing unit. This speeds up the live previews of things like Free Transform, Warp Transform, Puppet Warp, Liquify, and Lighting Effects. (The Lighting Effects feature was also redesigned in this version.)

  Several familiar features—such as the Move tool, the Crop tool (which has been *completely* revamped and is now nondestructive) and the Free Transform command—now display an info overlay next to your cursor when you use 'em that shows size, rotation angle, and other useful info (the exact info depends on what you're doing). You also see this handy overlay when you resize a brush cursor by Ctrl-Option-dragging on a Mac (Alt+right-click+dragging on a PC); it displays brush size, hardness, and opacity.

- **Auto Save, Auto Recover, and Background Save**. When a complicated program like Photoshop crashes, it's heartbreaking; depending on when you last saved your document, you could lose *hours* of work. That's why Adobe has added an auto-save feature that automatically saves your file every few minutes (you control the interval) and then *reopens* the last saved version when you restart the program after a crash. Also, saving files now takes place in the background (whether it's an automatic save or you choose File→Save), meaning you don't have to wait until the program is finished saving your document before you perform other edits.

- **64-bit Bridge**. To give you even faster access to files through Bridge (see Chapter 21), Adobe has updated it to run in 64-bit mode. Unfortunately, this means that the Mac version of Photoshop only works in 64-bit mode (the Windows version still works in both 32-bit and 64-bit modes—see the box on page 4). The Mini Bridge panel in CS6 also has a new filmstrip mode that lets you view images in a single row at the bottom of your screen.

- **Video editing**. The Extended version of Photoshop has included video-editing features for a few versions now, but in CS6 you get the full suite of video-editing controls in the *standard* version. This book sports a brand-new chapter (Chapter 20) that shows you how to import, trim, and split clips; create effects using filters, Adjustment layers, and layer styles; and export your finished videos.

- **Content-Aware Patch and Move tools**. With each new version of the program, Adobe includes more tools that use Content-Aware technology. Now the Patch tool takes advantage of it, which makes removing objects from photos easier and more realistic than ever. When you set the Patch tool to use Content-Aware, you can use it on an empty layer thanks to the new Sample All Layers option. There's also a brand-new tool called Content-Aware Move that lets you move an object from one spot in an image to another, as well as *extend* objects beyond their original size (in order to make them taller, wider, and so on).

- **New Fill and Stroke options for Shape layers**. Once you create a Shape layer in CS6, you'll spot a slew of new settings in the Options bar that let you add a fill and/or stroke (even dashed and dotted lines), as well as align paths in a variety of ways. These new settings work like their counterparts in Adobe Illustrator and designers have been begging to have 'em in Photoshop for years.

- **New blur filters**. The new Field Blur, Iris Blur, and Tilt-Shift filters make creating blurry backgrounds easier than ever. Best of all, these filters use a brand-new workspace where you can see the image at its full size, and you get on-image controls that let you easily determine the blur's placement, size, and strength. These filters also include a Bokeh option that you can use to make any specular highlights in your photo sparkle and shine.

- **Adaptive Wide Angle filter**. This new filter makes it a snap to fix the distortion problems that can happen when you shoot with a wide-angle or fish-eye lens. Simply draw a line across the distorted area (a curved horizon that ought to be straight, say) and Photoshop uses the lens profile database that was added to the Lens Correction filter back in CS5 to straighten your image in no time flat.

- **Improved Camera Raw**. The newest version of the Camera Raw plug-in has undergone a substantial overhaul and includes a re-ordered set of sliders, including new ones for Highlights, Shadows, Whites, and Blacks (which replace the Recovery, Fill Light, and Brightness sliders in previous versions). With these changes, Camera Raw should do a much better job of correcting the color and lighting in images while preserving details in the shadows and highlights. (Camera Raw is discussed throughout this book, but the bulk of the coverage lives in Chapter 9.)

- **Painting upgrades**. Adobe keeps on improving the painting experience in Photoshop, and CS6 includes two new brush tips that make digital painting more realistic than ever before. The new Erodible brush tip wears down as you use it (just like real chalk or a graphite pencil), and the new Airbrush tip works *less* like a can of spray paint and *more* like a professional airbrush rig. You'll also find new customization settings in the Brush panel that let you introduce color changes to individual brush marks *within* a brushstroke (look for the Apply Per Tip checkbox in the Color Dynamics settings), tilt and stretch brush marks made by shaped brush tips by rotating and tilting your stylus (see the Brush Projection checkbox in the Transfer settings), and the Texture settings sports new Brightness and Contrast sliders. And with the new Oil Paint filter, you can create a shockingly nice painting from a photo with the flick of a few sliders, no brushstrokes required!

- **Layer filtering**. Layers got a few upgrades, too. For example, you can now make Photoshop hide or show layers in the Layers panel based on criteria that you set with the new buttons at the top of the Layers panel. You can filter layers by kind (Smart Object, Type layer, Shape layer, and so on), name, effects (layer styles), attribute (whether the layer is locked, linked, and so on), and color-coding. You can also change the blend mode of multiple layers at once, duplicate several layers at one time by pressing ⌘-J (Ctrl+J on a PC), and see the Opacity, Fill, and blend mode settings of layers whose visibility is turned off. And once you've highlighted a layer's name to rename it, you can press the Tab key to highlight the *next* layer's name (pressing Shift-Tab moves backward through 'em instead).

- **New character and paragraph styles**. You can now save frequently-used text formatting as character or paragraph styles that you access via new Character Styles and Paragraph Style panels. You'll also spot a brand-new Type menu that includes handy commands to convert text into a shape or path, change font preview size, rasterize Type layers, and so on. This version also includes a Paste Lorem Ipsum command that automatically creates placeholder text.

There are also tons of little changes in Photoshop CS6, too, that are the direct result of Adobe's customer feedback initiative called Just Do It (JDI). For example, the Contact Sheet II and PDF Presentation plug-ins are back (they were removed in CS4); you can apply custom scripts to introduce randomness into patterns made with the

What Does "64-bit" Mean?

The cool phrase in computing circles for the past few years has been "64-bit." While that term may sound pretty geeky, it's actually not that intimidating. 64-bit programs (a.k.a. "applications" or "apps") simply know how to count higher than 32-bit programs.

So what does that mean in practice? 32-bit programs can open and work with files that are up to 4 gigabytes in size—which is already huge. 64-bit programs, on the other hand, can open files that are way bigger than that, as long as your operating system can handle 64-bit apps. (Mac OS X 10.5 [Leopard] and Microsoft Windows Vista [the 64-bit version, anyway] and later are up to the task.) 64-bit programs can also make use of more memory than their 32-bit counterparts, which is crucial when you're working with big honkin' files. For example, the 64-bit version of Photoshop lets you use more than 4 gigs of RAM, which makes it run faster. (You can change how your machine's

memory is allotted by tweaking Photoshop's preferences as described on page 33.)

The bottom line is that, if you work with gigantic files, you'll want to use the 64-bit version of Photoshop. And since most third-party plug-ins (Chapter 19) and filters (Chapter 15) have now been upgraded to work in 64-bit mode, there's little reason to cast a single glance backward. In CS6, the 64-bit version is all you get on a Mac; however, when you install Photoshop on a PC, you get two full versions of the program in two separate folders: one for 32-bit mode and another for 64-bit mode (located in *Program Files\Adobe\Photoshop CS6* and *Program Files [x86]\Adobe\Photoshop CS6*, respectively). Simply quit one program and then launch the other.

You can still share Photoshop files with both Mac and PC folks just like you always have.

Edit→Fill command; you can increase brush size to 5000 pixels; the Eyedropper tool's Sample menu now lets you snatch color from the current layer and any layers below it (you can have it ignore Adjustment layers); Photoshop automatically chooses the best resampling (interpolation) method when you use Free Transform, the Crop tool, or the Image Size dialog box; holding the Shift key while you launch the program disables third-party plug-ins; the Auto button in a Levels and Curves adjustment uses new and improved math; the Color Range command includes a new option for helping you select skin tones; and much, *much* more.

■ About This Book

Adobe has pulled together an amazing amount of information in its online help system (Appendix B), but despite all these efforts, it's geared toward seasoned Photoshop jockeys and assumes a level of skill that you may not have. The explanations are very clipped and to the point, which makes it difficult to get a real feel for the tool or technique you're learning about.

That's where this book comes in. It's intended to make learning Photoshop CS6 tolerable—and even enjoyable—by avoiding technical jargon as much as possible and explaining *why* and *when* you'll want to use (or avoid) certain features of the program. It's a conversational and friendly approach intended to speak to beginners and seasoned pixel pushers alike.

Some of the tutorials in this book refer to files you can download from this book's Missing CD page on the Missing Manuals website (*www.missingmanuals.com/cds*) so you can practice the techniques you're reading about. And throughout the book, you'll find several kinds of sidebar articles. The ones labeled "Up to Speed" help newcomers to Photoshop do things or explain concepts that veterans are probably already familiar with. Those labeled "Power Users' Clinic" cover more advanced topics for the brave of heart.

NOTE Photoshop CS6 functions almost identically on Mac and Windows computers, but the screenshots in this book were all taken on a Mac for the sake of consistency. However, the keyboard shortcuts for the two operating systems are different, so you'll find both included here—Mac shortcuts first, followed by Windows shortcuts in parentheses. In a few instances, the locations of certain folders differ, and in those cases, you get the directions for both operating systems.

About the Outline

This hefty book is divided into six parts, each devoted to the type of things you'll do in Photoshop CS6:

- **Part One: The Basics.** Here's where you'll learn the essential skills you need to know before moving forward. Chapter 1 gives you the lay of the land and teaches you how to work with panels and how to make the Photoshop workspace your own. You'll also find out the many ways of undoing what you've done, which is crucial when you're still learning. Chapter 2 covers how to open and view documents efficiently, and how to set up new documents so you have a solid foundation on which to build your masterpieces.

Chapter 3 dives into the most powerful Photoshop feature of all: layers. You'll learn about the different kinds of layers and how to manage them, the power of layer masks, and how to use layer styles for special effects. Chapter 4 explains how to select part of an image so you can edit just that area. In Chapter 5, you'll dive headfirst into the science of color as you explore channels (Photoshop's way of storing the colors that make up your image) and learn how to use channels to create selections; you'll also pick up some channel-specific editing tips along the way.

> **NOTE** In this book, the word "select" is mainly used to refer to the act of creating actual selections. In most other instances, the word "activate" is used instead, as in "activate the layer" or "activate the Crop tool."

- **Part Two: Editing Images.** Chapter 6 starts off by explaining a variety of ways you can crop images, both in Photoshop and in Camera Raw. The chapter then demystifies resolution once and for all so you'll understand how to resize images without reducing their quality. In Chapter 7, you'll learn how to combine images in a variety of ways, from simple techniques to more complex ones. Chapter 8 covers draining, changing, and adding color, arming you with several techniques for creating gorgeous black-and-white images, delicious duotones, partial-color effects, and more. You'll also learn how to change the color of almost anything.

  Chapter 9 focuses on color-correcting images, beginning with auto fixer-uppers, and then moving on to the wonderfully simple world of Camera Raw and the more complicated realm of Levels and Curves. Chapter 10 is all about retouching images and is packed with practical techniques for slimming and trimming, and explains how to use the Dodge and Burn tools in ways that won't harm your images. This chapter also covers using the various Content-Aware tools to remove objects from images or scoot an object from one spot to another, and using the Puppet Warp command to move just your subject's arms and legs. Chapter 11 covers all kinds of ways to sharpen images to make them look especially crisp.

- **Part Three: The Artistic Side of Photoshop.** This part of the book is all about creativity. Chapter 12 explains the many ways of choosing colors for your documents, and teaches you how to create a painting from scratch. Chapter 13 focuses on using the mighty Pen tool to create complex illustrations and selections, along with how to use Photoshop's shape tools. Chapter 14 teaches you the basics of typography and then moves on to how to create and format text in Photoshop. You'll find out how to outline, texturize, and place text, among other fun stuff. Chapter 15 covers the wide world of filters; you'll come away with at least one practical use for one or more of the filters in each category.

- **Part Four: Printing and the Web.** In Chapter 16, you'll learn about printing images, beginning with why it's so darn hard to make what comes out of your printer match what you see onscreen. You'll learn about the different color modes and how to prepare images for printing, whether you're using an inkjet printer or sending your files to a commercial printing press. Chapter 17 focuses on preparing images for the Web, walks you through the various file formats you can use, explains how to protect your images online, and shows you how to use Bridge to create web galleries. Rounding out the chapter is info on using the Slice tool on a web page design, and step-by-step instructions for creating an animated GIF.

- **Part Five: Photoshop Power.** This part is all about working smarter and faster. It starts with an entire chapter devoted to using actions (Chapter 18), which help you automate tasks you perform regularly. Chapter 19 covers installing and using plug-ins (small programs you can add on to Photoshop) and recommends some of the best on the market today. Chapter 20 teaches you how to edit videos in Photoshop, and Chapter 21 explains how to use both Adobe Bridge and Photoshop's Mini Bridge panel.

- **Part Six: Appendixes.** Appendix A covers installing and uninstalling Photoshop. Appendix B gives you some troubleshooting tips, explains Photoshop's help system, and points you to resources other than this book. Appendix C gives you a tour of the mighty Tools panel. And finally, Appendix D walks you through Photoshop CS6's 200+ menu items. All the appendixes are available on this book's Missing CD page at *www.missingmanuals.com/cds*.

For Photographers

If you're relatively new to digital-image editing or you've always shot film and are taking your first brave steps into the world of digital cameras, you'll be amazed at what you can do in Photoshop, but there's a lot to learn. By breaking Photoshop down into digestible chunks that are most important to *you*, the learning process will feel less overwhelming. (There's no sense in tackling the whole program when you'll only use a quarter of it—if that much.)

The most important thing to remember is to be patient and try not to get frustrated. With time and practice, you *can* master the bits of Photoshop that you need to do your job better. And with the help of this book you'll conquer everything faster than you might think. As you gain confidence, you can start branching out into other parts of the program to broaden your skills. Here's a suggested roadmap for quickly learning the most useful aspects of the program:

1. **Read all of Chapter 1 and Chapter 2 (or at the very least skim them).**

   These two chapters show you where to find all of Photoshop's tools and features and explain how the program is organized. You'll learn how to open, view, and save images, which is vital stuff to know.

2. **If your photos aren't on your computer already, read Chapter 21 about Adobe Bridge.**

Bridge is an amazingly powerful image organizer and browser that can help get your images onto your computer. It takes care of importing, renaming, and even backing up your precious photos.

3. **If you shoot in Raw format (page 57) and need to color-correct your images in a hurry, skip ahead to the section on editing in Camera Raw in Chapter 9 (page 363).**

   This chapter includes an entire section on practical editing techniques you can use in Camera Raw, and a quick reference that points you to where you'll find other Camera-Raw techniques throughout this book.

4. **If you're *not* shooting in Raw and you need to resize your images before editing them, read Chapter 6.**

   This chapter explains resolution and how to resize images without reducing their quality.

5. **Proceed with Chapters 8, 9, and 10 to learn about color effects, color-correcting, and retouching people, respectively.**

6. **When you're ready to sharpen your images, read Chapter 11.**

7. **Finally, when you want to print your photos, read the section on printing with an inkjet printer in Chapter 16 (page 684).**

   This chapter walks you through printing photos and includes advice on how to print borderless images.

That's all you need to get started. When you're ready to dive more fully into Photoshop, pick back up at Chapter 3, which covers layers, and then move on through the book as time permits.

The Very Basics

This book assumes that you know how to use a computer and that, to some extent, you're an expert double-clicker, and menu opener. If not, here's a quick refresher:

To *click* means to move the point of your cursor over an object on your screen and then press the left mouse or trackpad button once. To *right-click* means to press the right mouse button once, which produces a menu of special features called a *shortcut menu*. (If you're on a Mac and have a mouse with only one button, hold down the Control key while you click to simulate right-clicking.) To *double-click* means to press the left button twice, quickly, without moving the cursor between clicks. To *drag* means to click an object and use the mouse to move it while holding down the left mouse button. Most selection buttons onscreen are pretty obvious, but you may not be familiar with *radio buttons*: To choose an option, you click one of these little empty circles that are arranged in a list. If you're comfortable with basic concepts like these, you're ready to get started with this book.

You'll find tons of keyboard shortcuts along the way, and they're huge timesavers. If you see "Press ⌘-S (Ctrl+S on a PC) to save your file," that means to hold down the

⌘ (or Ctrl) key while pressing the S key. Press the first, and keep holding it as you press the other. (This book lists Mac keyboard shortcuts first, followed by Windows shortcuts in parentheses.) Other keyboard shortcuts are so complex that you'll need to use multiple fingers, both hands, and a well-placed elbow.

About→These→Arrows

In *Photoshop CS6: The Missing Manual* (and in all Missing Manuals, for that matter), you'll see arrows sprinkled throughout each chapter in sentences like this: "Choose Filter→Blur→Tilt-Shift." This is a shorthand way of helping you find files, folders, and menu items without having to read through painfully long and boring instructions. For example, the sentence quoted above is a short way of saying: "At the top of the Photoshop window, locate the Filter menu. Click it and, in the list that appears, look for the Blur category. Point to the word Blur without clicking and, in the resulting submenu, click Tilt-Shift" (see Figure I-1).

About MissingManuals.com

On the Missing Manuals website (*www.missingmanuals.com*), you'll find this book's Missing CD page, which includes links to downloadable images mentioned in this book's tutorials, in case you want to practice techniques without using your own photos.

A word about the image files for the tutorials: To make life easier for people with dial-up Internet connections, the file sizes have been kept pretty small. This means you probably won't want to print the results of what you create (you'll end up with a print about the size of a matchbook). But that doesn't really matter because the files are only meant for onscreen use. You'll see notes throughout the book about which practice images are available for any given chapter.

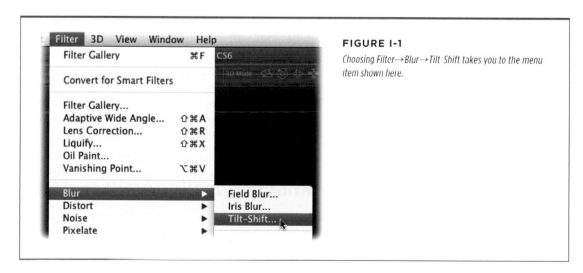

FIGURE I-1

Choosing Filter→Blur→Tilt-Shift takes you to the menu item shown here.

Chances are, you'll either love the Application Frame or hate it. If you're on a computer running Windows, you're used to programs looking and behaving this way. But if you're on a Mac and you're upgrading from an older version of Photoshop (like CS3), this arrangement may feel a little odd; in that case, you can turn off the frame by choosing Window→Application Frame to make Photoshop switch to the floating-window view used in older versions of the program. (PC folks are stuck with the frame.)

Tools panel
Options bar
Document tabs
Panels

Zoom level   More panels   Document window   Drag to resize frame

FIGURE 1-1

You can open several images at the same time; just click a document's tab to summon it front and center for editing. Photoshop stores the tools and adjustments you'll use most in the panels on the left and right sides of the Application Frame; a full introduction to panels starts on page 17. (See page 22 to learn how to make your Tools panel have two columns like the one shown here.)

The upside to using the Application Frame is that all of Photoshop's bits and pieces stay together as you move things around (as long as the panels are still docked). Resizing the frame also resizes the panels and windows so they fit within it.

NOTE Adobe reduced clutter in Photoshop CS6 by removing the Application bar. Introduced in CS4, it housed extras like guides, grids, and rulers, as well as several menus. As you'll learn in the next few pages, those items are now sprinkled throughout the Tools panel and Window menu.

The Almighty Options Bar

Lording over the document window is the Options bar (Figure 1-2, top), which lets you customize the behavior of nearly every item in the Tools panel. This bar automatically changes to include settings related to the tool you're currently using. Unfortunately, the Options bar's labels are fairly cryptic, so it can be hard to figure out what the heck all those settings do. Luckily, you can point your cursor at any setting to see a little yellow pop-up description called a *tooltip* (you don't need to click—just don't move your mouse for a couple seconds).

> **TIP** If the tooltips drive you crazy, you can get rid of 'em by choosing Photoshop→Preferences→Interface [Edit→Preferences→Interface on a PC] and turning off Show Tool Tips.

When you first install Photoshop, the Options bar is perched at the top of the screen, but it doesn't have to stay there. If you'd rather put it somewhere else, grab its left end and drag it wherever you want, as shown in Figure 1-2, middle. If you decide to put it back later (also called *docking*), just drag it to the top of the screen (see Figure 1-2, bottom).

UP TO SPEED

Hiding vs. Quitting

If you need to do some work on your desktop or in another program, you can temporarily *hide* Photoshop, saving you the time and toe-tapping of quitting it and then restarting it again later.

On a Mac, press ⌘-Control-H or click the yellow dot at the top left of the Application Frame. Your workspace disappears, but Photoshop keeps running in the background. To bring it back to the forefront, click its shrunken icon in the Dock. You can also make Photoshop temporarily disappear by pressing ⌘-H; the first time you do, a dialog box appears asking if you'd like to *assign* that keyboard shortcut to make it hide Photoshop instead of hiding text highlighting, guides, and so on. (To change

it back, edit your keyboard shortcuts as explained in the box on page 37, or delete Photoshop's preferences as described in Appendix B, online at *www.missingmanuals.com/cds*.)

On a PC, you can hide (minimize) the program by clicking the _ button in Photoshop's upper right; Windows tucks the program down into your taskbar. To get it back, click its taskbar icon.

If your machine has at least 8 GB of memory (RAM), there's no downside to hiding the program other than a crowded Dock (Mac) or taskbar (PC). However, if you're low on memory and your machine's fan is cranking away, then choose File→Quit to free up memory.

TIP If a tool seems to be misbehaving, it's likely because you changed one of the Options bar's settings and forgot to change it back. These settings are *sticky*: Once you change them, they *stay* that way until you change them back.

FIGURE 1-2

Top: The Options bar is customization central for whatever tool you're currently using. However, it doesn't have to live at the top of the screen; you can undock it by dragging the tiny dotted lines circled here.

Middle: Once you've freed the Options bar, you can drag it anywhere you want by grabbing the dark gray bar on its far left.

Bottom: To redock the Options bar, drag it to the top of your screen. Once you see a thin blue line like the one shown here, release your mouse button. (If you're feeling frisky, you can dock it to the bottom of your screen instead!)

NOTE In Photoshop CS6, the Options bar also includes the workspace menu, which lets you change the way your Photoshop environment is set up. You'll learn all about workspaces on page 21.

Swapping Screen Modes

Photoshop includes three different *screen modes* for your document-viewing plea-sure. Depending on what you're doing, one will suit you better than the others. For example, you can make an image take up your whole screen (with or without the Menu and Options bars), hide Photoshop's panels, and so on (see Figure 1-3). To give each mode a spin, you first need to open an image file: Choose File→Open, navigate to where the image lives, and then click Open.

It's a snap to jump between modes. Just press the F key repeatedly (unless you're in the middle of cropping an image or using the Type tool—if you are, you'll type a bunch of F's) or use the Screen Modes pop-up menu at the bottom of the Tools panel (circled in Figure 1-3, top). These are your choices:

- **Standard Screen Mode** is the view you see when you launch Photoshop for the first time. This mode includes menus, the Application Frame, the Options bar, panels, and document windows. Use this mode when the Application Frame is active and you need to scoot all of Photoshop—windows and all—around on your monitor (except for undocked panels or free-floating windows).

FIGURE 1-3

The many faces of Photoshop: Standard with Application Frame on (top), Full Screen With Menu Bar (bottom left), and Full Screen (bottom right). You can edit Images in any of these modes, though some give you more screen real estate than others. You can also hide or show the Options bar and panels by pressing the Tab key.

The Screen Modes pop-up menu used to live in the Application bar, but in CS6 it moved to the bottom of the Tools panel. (Page 22 tells you how to switch to the two-column Tools panel shown here.)

- **Full Screen Mode With Menu Bar** completely takes over your screen, puts your document in the center on a dark gray canvas or frame, and attaches any open panels to the left and right edges of your screen. This mode is great for day-to-day editing because you can see all of Photoshop's tools and menus without being distracted by the files and folders on your desktop. The dark gray background is also easy on the eyes and a great choice when color-correcting images (a brightly colored desktop can affect your color perception).

> **TIP** You can change Photoshop's canvas color anytime by Control-clicking (right-clicking on a PC) the canvas itself. From the shortcut menu that appears, choose from Default (the dark, charcoal gray you see now), Black, Dark Gray, Medium Gray, or Light Gray. If none of those colors float your boat, you can pick your own by choosing Select Custom Color to open the Color Picker, which is explained on page 491.

- **Full Screen Mode** hides all of Photoshop's menus and panels, centers the document on your screen, and puts it on a black background. (If you've got rulers turned on, they'll still appear, though you can turn 'em off by pressing ⌘-R [Ctrl+R on a PC]). This mode is great for displaying and evaluating your work or for distraction-free editing. And the black background really makes images pop off the screen (though the next section shows you how to change its color).

Changing Photoshop's Appearance

While the new dark gray colors in CS6 are supposed to be easier on the eyes and help you see the colors in images more accurately, you may disagree. You may also want to increase the size of the text labels in the Options bar and panels. Fortunately, you can change several aspects of the program's appearance by choosing Photoshop→Preferences→Interface (Edit→Preferences→Interface on a PC), as Figure 1-4 shows.

> **TIP** You can cycle through Photoshop's color themes by pressing Shift-F1 and Shift-F2 (to go darker and lighter, respectively). If you'd rather not involve the Shift key, you can set things up so you can use the F1 and F2 keys all by themselves; the box on page 37 explains how).

The next section explains how to customize Photoshop's look and feel even *more* by opening, closing, rearranging, and resizing panels. Read on!

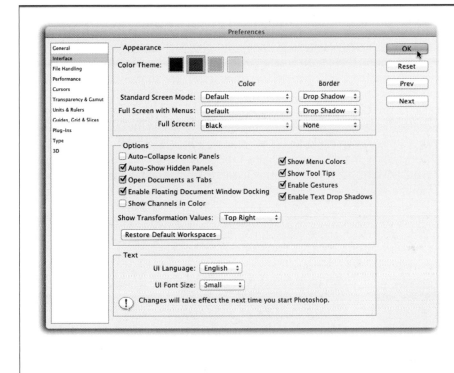

FIGURE 1-4

Not a fan of CS6's dark gray color theme? Use the Appearance settings shown here to pick something lighter (click the light gray square to revert to CS5's color theme). To change Full Screen Mode's background (discussed in the previous section) to something other than black, use the Full Screen pop-up menu.

If the text labels throughout the program having you squinting, you can make 'em bigger with the UI Font Size menu near the bottom of the dialog box. Once you make a selection, you have to choose File→Quit (File→Exit on a PC) and then restart Photoshop to make it take effect.

Working with Panels

The right side of the Application Frame is home to a slew of small windows called *panels* (years ago, they were called *palettes*), which let you work with commonly used features like colors, adjustments, layers, and so on. You're free to organize the panels however you like and position them anywhere you want. Panels can be free floating or *docked* (attached) to the top, bottom, left, or right sides of your screen. And you can link panels together into *groups*, which you can then move around. Each panel also has its very own menu, called (appropriately enough) a *panel menu*, located in its top-right corner; its icon looks like four little lines with a downward-pointing triangle and is labeled in Figure 1-5.

Take a peek on the right side of your screen, and you'll see that Photoshop starts you off with three docked panel groups filled with the goodies it thinks you'll use a lot (there's more on docked panels coming up shortly). The first group includes the Color and Swatches panels; the second group includes Adjustments and Styles;

and the third includes Layers, Channels, and Paths. To work with a panel, activate it by clicking its tab.

Panels are like Silly Putty—they're incredibly flexible. You can collapse, expand, move, and resize them, or even swap 'em for other panels. Here's how:

- **Collapse or expand panels.** If panels are encroaching on your editing space, you can shrink them both horizontally and vertically so they look and behave like buttons. To collapse a panel (or panel group) horizontally so that it becomes a button nestled against the side of another panel or the edge of your screen, click the tiny double arrow in its top-right corner; click this same button again to expand the panel. To collapse a panel vertically against the bottom of the panel above it, as shown in Figure 1-5, double-click the panel's *tab* to make it roll up like a window shade; single-click the tab to roll the panel back down. To adjust a panel's width, point your cursor at its left edge and, when the cursor turns into a double-headed arrow, drag left or right to make the panel bigger or smaller.

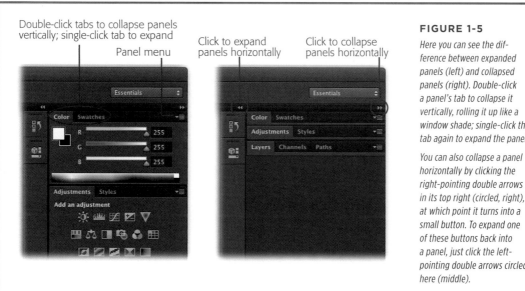

Double-click tabs to collapse panels vertically; single-click tab to expand

Panel menu

Click to expand panels horizontally

Click to collapse panels horizontally

FIGURE 1-5

Here you can see the difference between expanded panels (left) and collapsed panels (right). Double-click a panel's tab to collapse it vertically, rolling it up like a window shade; single-click the tab again to expand the panel.

You can also collapse a panel horizontally by clicking the right-pointing double arrows in its top right (circled, right), at which point it turns into a small button. To expand one of these buttons back into a panel, just click the left-pointing double arrows circled here (middle).

NOTE In Photoshop CS5, you collapsed and expanded panels by double-clicking the dark gray, empty area to the right of a panel's tab (in CS4, you single-clicked the same spot). But in CS6, you *double-click the tab itself* to collapse the panel and then *single-click the tab* to expand the panel. Boy howdy, Photoshop sure keeps you on your toes!

- **Add and modify panel groups.** You can open even *more* panels by opening the Window menu (which lists all of Photoshop's panels) and then clicking the name of the one you want to open. When you do, Photoshop puts the panel in a column to the left of the ones that are already open and adds a tiny button to its right that you can click to collapse it both horizontally and vertically (just click the button again to expand it). If the new panel is part of a group, like the Character and Paragraph panels, the extra panel tags along with it. If it's a panel you expect to use a lot, you can add it to an existing panel group by clicking and dragging the dotted lines above its button into a blank area in the panel group. Figure 1-6 shows this maneuver in action.

FIGURE 1-6

Top: When you open a new panel, Photoshop adds it to a column to the left of your other panels and gives it a handy button that you can click to collapse or expand it. The tiny dotted line above each button is its handle; *click and drag one to re-position the panel in the column, add the panel to a panel group, and so on. If the panel you opened is related to another panel—like the Brush panel and the Brush Presets panel—then both panels will open as a panel group with a single handle (note the two buttons above the circle here).*

Middle: When you're dragging a panel into a panel group, wait until you see a blue line around the inside of the group before you release your mouse button. Here, the Kuler panel is being added to a panel group. (You can see a faint version of the Kuler panel's button where the red arrow is pointing.)

Bottom: When you release your mouse button, the new panel becomes part of the group. To rearrange panels within a group, drag their tabs (circled) left or right.

- **Undock, redock, and close panels.** Straight out of the box, Photoshop docks three sets of panel groups to the right side of your screen (or Application Frame). But you're not stuck with the panels glued to this spot; you can set them free by turning them into *floating* panels. To liberate a panel, grab its tab, pull it out of the group it's in, and then move it anywhere you want (see Figure 1-7). When you let go of your mouse button, the panel appears where you put it—all by itself.

    You can undock a whole panel group in nearly the same way: Click an empty spot in the group's tab area and drag it out of the dock. Once you release your mouse button, you can drag the group around by clicking the same empty spot in the tab area. Or, if the group is collapsed, click the tiny dotted lines at the top of the group, just below the dark gray bar.

    To dock the panel (or panel group) again, drag it back to the right side of your screen.

NOTE In Photoshop CS6, the Timeline panel (formerly called the Animation panel) and Mini Bridge panel are docked to the *bottom* of your workspace, which is now a docking hotspot, too.

To close a panel, click its tab and drag it out of the panel group to a different area of your screen (Figure 1-7); then click the tiny circle in the panel's top-left corner (on a PC, click the X in the panel's top-right corner instead). Don't worry—the panel isn't gone forever; if you want to reopen it, simply choose it from the Windows menu.

FIGURE 1-7

To undock a panel or panel group, click the panel's tab or a free area to the right of the group's tabs and then drag the panel or group somewhere else on your screen. To dock it again, drag it to the right side of your screen—on top of the other panels. When you see a thin blue line appear where you want the panel or group to land, release your mouse button.

TIP If the blue highlight lines are hard to see when you're trying to group or dock panels, try dragging the panels more *slowly*. That way when you drag the panel into a group or dockable area, the blue highlight hangs around a little longer and the panel itself becomes momentarily transparent.

Getting the hang of undocking, redocking, and arranging panels takes a little practice because it's tough to control where the little boogers land. When the panel you're dragging is about to join a docking area (or a different panel group), a thin blue line appears showing you where the panel or group will go.

Customizing Your Workspace

Once you arrange Photoshop's panels just so, you can keep 'em that way by saving your setup as a *workspace* using the Workspace menu at the far right of the Options bar (see Figure 1-8). Straight from the factory, this menu is set to Essentials, which is a good general-use setup that includes panels that most people use regularly. The menu's other options are more specialized: "New in CS6" includes only new features, 3D is designed for working with 3D objects (this is available only in Photoshop Extended), Motion is for video editing (new in Photoshop Standard), Painting is for (you guessed it) painting, Photography is for working with photos, and Typography is for working with text. To swap workspaces, simply click one of these *presets* (built-in settings), and Photoshop rearranges your panels accordingly.

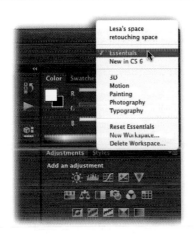

FIGURE 1-8

Most of the built-in workspaces are designed to help you perform specialized tasks. For example, the Painting workspace puts the Brushes and Navigation panels at the top right and groups together the color-related panels you'll undoubtedly use when painting. Take the built-in workspaces for a test drive—they may give you customization ideas you hadn't thought of. If you're familiar with Photoshop but new to this version, try out the "New in CS6" workspace, which highlights all the menu items that include new features—a great way to see the additions at a glance.

TIP   If you don't see the Workspace menu and you've got the Application Frame turned on, position your cursor on the right side of the Photoshop window and, when the cursor turns into a double-headed arrow, click and drag rightward to increase the size of the frame.

To save your own custom workspace, first arrange things the way you want. Next, click the Workspace menu and choose New Workspace. In the resulting dialog box, give your setup a meaningful name and turn on the checkboxes for the customizations you want Photoshop to save. Aside from panel locations, you can have Photoshop save any keyboard shortcut and menu settings you may have changed (see the box on page 37 for more on changing these items)—just be sure to turn on the options for *all* the features you changed or they won't be included in your custom workspace. After you click Save, your custom workspace shows up at the top of the Workspace menu.

If you've created a custom workspace that you'll never use again, you can send it packin'. First, make sure you aren't currently using the workspace you want to delete. Then, choose Delete Workspace from the Workspace menu and, in the resulting dialog box, pick the offending workspace and then click Delete. Photoshop will ask if you're sure, so you have to click Yes to finish it off.

The Tools Panel

The Tools panel (Figure 1-9, left) is the home base for all of Photoshop's editing tools, and it's included in all the built-in workspaces. Until you memorize the tools' keyboard shortcuts, you can't do much without this panel! When you first launch the program, you'll see the Tools panel on the left side of the screen, but you can drag it anywhere you want by clicking the tiny row of vertical dashes near its top (Figure 1-9, right).

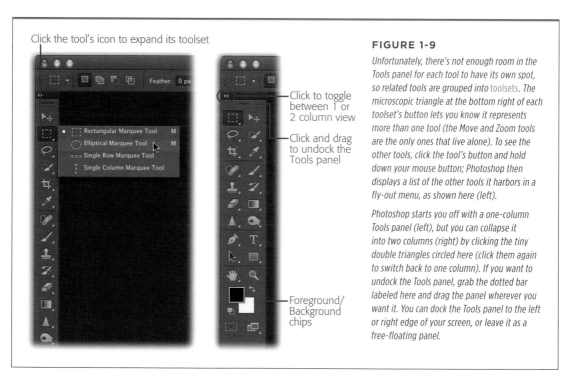

Click the tool's icon to expand its toolset

Click to toggle between 1 or 2 column view

Click and drag to undock the Tools panel

Foreground/
Background
chips

FIGURE 1-9

Unfortunately, there's not enough room in the Tools panel for each tool to have its own spot, so related tools are grouped into toolsets*. The microscopic triangle at the bottom right of each toolset's button lets you know it represents more than one tool (the Move and Zoom tools are the only ones that live alone). To see the other tools, click the tool's button and hold down your mouse button; Photoshop then displays a list of the other tools it harbors in a fly-out menu, as shown here (left).*

Photoshop starts you off with a one-column Tools panel (left), but you can collapse it into two columns (right) by clicking the tiny double triangles circled here (click them again to switch back to one column). If you want to undock the Tools panel, grab the dotted bar labeled here and drag the panel wherever you want it. You can dock the Tools panel to the left or right edge of your screen, or leave it as a free-floating panel.

Once you expand a toolset, you'll see the tools' keyboard shortcuts listed to the right of their names. These shortcuts are great timesavers because they let you switch between tools without moving your hands off the keyboard. To access a tool that's hidden deep within a toolset, add the Shift key to the tool's shortcut key, and you'll cycle through all the tools in that toolset. For example, to select the Elliptical Marquee tool, press Shift-M repeatedly until that tool appears in the Tools panel.

TIP If you need to switch tools *temporarily*—for a quick edit—you can use the spring-loaded tools feature. Just press and hold a tool's keyboard shortcut to switch to that tool and then perform your edit. As soon as you release the key, you'll jump back to the tool you were using before. For example, if you're painting with the Brush and suddenly make an error, press and hold E to switch to the Eraser and fix your mistake. Once you release the E key, you're back to using the Brush tool. Sweet!

You'll learn about the superpowers of each tool throughout this book. For a brief *overview* of each tool, check out Appendix C, which you can download from this book's Missing CD page at *www.missingmanuals.com/cds*. For a quick reminder of what each tool does, point your cursor at its icon for a couple of seconds while keeping your mouse perfectly still; Photoshop displays a handy tooltip that includes the tool's name and keyboard shortcut.

■ FOREGROUND AND BACKGROUND COLOR CHIPS

Photoshop can handle millions of colors, but its tools let you work with only two at a time: a foreground color and a background color. Each of these is visible as a square *color chip* near the bottom of the Tools panel (labeled in Figure 1-9, they're black and white, respectively). Photoshop uses your foreground color when you paint or fill something with color; it's where most of the action is. It uses your background color to do things like set the second color of a *gradient* (a smooth transition from one color to another, or to transparency) and erase parts of a locked Background layer (page 87); this color is also helpful when you're running special effects like the Clouds filter (page 662). To change either color, click its color chip once to open the Color Picker (page 491), which lets you select another color for that particular chip. To swap your foreground and background colors, click the curved, double-headed arrow just above the two chips or press X. To set both color chips to their factory-fresh setting of black and white, click the tiny chips to their upper left or press D. Remember these shortcuts; they're extremely handy when you work with layer masks, which are discussed in Chapter 3.

Common Panels

As mentioned earlier, when you first launch Photoshop, the program uses the Essentials workspace, which includes several useful panels. Here's a quick rundown of why Adobe considers these panels "essential":

- **Color.** In the upper-right part of your screen is the Color panel, which includes your current foreground and background color chips. This panel lets you pick a new color for either chip *without* opening the just-mentioned Color Picker (which means Photoshop won't pop open a big dialog box that hides part of your image). This panel is discussed in detail in Chapter 12.

- **Swatches.** The Swatches panel holds miniature samples of colors, giving you easy access to them for use in painting or colorizing images. This panel also stores a variety of color libraries like the Pantone Matching System (special inks used in professional printing). You'll learn all about the Swatches panel in Chapter 12.

- **Adjustments.** This panel lets you create Adjustment layers. Instead of making color and brightness changes to your original image, you can use Adjustment layers to make these changes on a *separate* layer, giving you all kinds of editing flexibility and keeping your original image out of harm's way. They're explained in detail in Chapter 3, and you'll see 'em used throughout this book.

- **Styles.** *Styles* are special effects created with a variety of layer styles (page 131). For example, if you've created a glass-button look by using several layer styles, you can save the whole lot of 'em as a *single* style so you can apply them all with a single click (instead of adding each style individually). You can also choose from tons of built-in styles; they're all discussed starting on page 135.

- **Layers.** This is the single most important panel in Photoshop. Layers let you work with images as if they were a stack of transparencies, so you can create one image from many. By using layers, you adjust the size and opacity of—and add layer styles to—each item independently. Understanding layers is the *key* to Photoshop success; you'll learn all about them in Chapter 3.

- **Channels.** *Channels* are where Photoshop stores the color information your images are made from. Channels are extremely powerful, and you can use them to edit the individual colors in an image, which is helpful in sharpening images, creating selections (telling Photoshop which part of an image you want to work with), and so on. Chapter 5 has the scoop on channels.

- **Paths.** *Paths* are the outlines you make with the Pen and shape tools. But these aren't your average, run-of-the-mill lines—they're made up of points and paths instead of pixels, so they'll always look perfectly crisp when printed. You can also make them bigger or smaller without losing any quality. You'll learn all about paths in Chapter 13.

- **History.** The History panel is like your very own time machine: It tracks nearly everything you do to your image (the last 20 things, to be exact, though you can change this number using preferences [see page 33]). It appears docked as a button to the left of the Color panel group. The next section explains how to use it to undo what you've done.

- **Properties.** Also docked to the left of the Color panel group, CS6's new Properties panel is a combination of the Adjustments and Masks panels. It gives you one-stop access to all the settings in an Adjustment layer and their preset menus. This panel also lets you create and fine-tune *layer masks*. You'll dive headfirst into masks in Chapter 3, but for now, you can think of them as digital masking tape that lets you hide the contents of a layer.

The Power of Undo

Thankfully, Photoshop is extremely forgiving: It'll let you back out of almost anything you do, which is *muy importante* when you're getting the hang of things.

You've got several ways to retrace your steps, including the lifesaving Undo command. Just choose Edit→Undo or press ⌘-Z (Ctrl+Z on a PC).

Unfortunately, the Undo command lets you undo only the last edit you made. If you need to go back *more* than one step, use the Step Backward command instead: Choose Edit→Step Backward or press Option-⌘-Z (Alt+Ctrl+Z on a PC). Out of the box, this command lets you undo the last 20 things you did, one at a time. If you want to go back even further, you can change that number by digging into Photoshop's preferences, as the next section explains. You can step *forward* through your editing history, too, by choosing Edit→Step Forward or Shift-⌘-Z (Shift+Ctrl+Z on a PC).

NOTE Out of the box, Photoshop lets you undo up to 20 changes, back to the point when you first opened the document you're working on, meaning you can't close a document and then undo changes you made *before* you closed it.

Changing How Far Back You Can Go

If you think you might someday need to go back further than your last 20 steps, you can make Photoshop remember up to *1,000* steps by changing the program's preferences. Here's how:

1. Choose Photoshop→Preferences→Performance (Edit→Preferences→ Performance on a PC).

2. In the Preferences dialog box, look for the History States field (it's in the History & Cache section) and then pick the number of undo steps you want Photoshop to remember.

   You can enter any number between 1 and 1,000 in this field. While increasing the number of history states might help you sleep better, doing so means Photoshop has to keep track of that many more versions of your document, which requires memory and processing power. If you increase this setting and notice that the program is running like molasses, try lowering it.

3. Click OK when you're finished.

Turning Back Time with the History Panel

Whereas the Undo and Step Backward commands let you move back through changes one at a time, the History panel (see Figure 1-10) kicks it up a notch and lets you jump back *several* steps at once. (You can step back through as many history states as you set in Photoshop's preferences.) Using the History panel is much quicker than undoing a long list of changes one by one, and it gives you a nice list of *exactly* what you've done to the image—in chronological order from top to bottom—letting you pinpoint the exact state you want to jump back to. And, as explained in a moment, you can also take snapshots of an image at various points in the editing process to make it easier to jump back to the state you want.

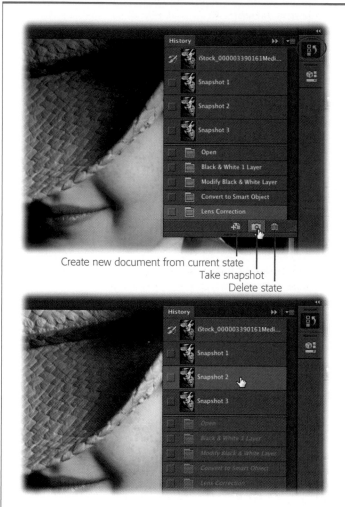

Create new document from current state
Take snapshot
Delete state

FIGURE 1-10

Top: The History panel keeps track of everything you do to your images, beginning with opening them. You can even take snapshots of an image at crucial points during the editing process, like when you convert it to black and white and add a color tint.

Bottom: If you take a snapshot, you can revert to that state later with a single click. For example, if you've given your image a sepia (brown) tint and later changed it to blue, you can easily go back to the sepia version by clicking the snapshot you took of it, as shown here, without having to step back through all the other changes you made. What a timesaver!

After you make a few changes to an image, pop open the History panel by clicking its button (circled in Figure 1-10, top), or by choosing Window→History. When you do, Photoshop opens a list of the last 20 things you've done to the image, including opening it. To jump back in time, click the step you want to go back to, and Photoshop returns the image to the way it looked at that point. If you stepped back further than you meant to, just click a more recent step in the list.

If you'd like the top of the History panel to include thumbnail previews showing what your image looks like each and every time you *save* the document—in addition to the thumbnail you automatically get by *opening* the image—choose History Options from the History panel's menu. In the resulting dialog box, turn on the Automatically Create New Snapshot When Saving checkbox. Clicking one of these saved-state thumbnails is a fast and easy way to jump back to the last saved version of the document.

> **TIP** You can also get back to the last saved version of a document by choosing File→Revert (page 29).

Taking *snapshots* of an image along the way lets you mark key points in the editing process. A snapshot is more than a preview of the image because it also includes all the edits you've made up to that point. Think of snapshots as milestones in your editing work: When you reach a critical point that you may want to return to, take a snapshot so you can easily get back to that particular version of the document. To take a snapshot, click the little camera icon at the bottom of the History panel (labeled in Figure 1-10). Photoshop adds the snapshot to the top of the panel, just below the saved-state thumbnail(s). The snapshots you take appear in the list in the order you took them.

> **NOTE** History states don't hang around forever: As soon as you close the document, they're history (ha!). If you think you'll ever want to return to an earlier version of the document, click the "Create new document from current state" button at the bottom of the History panel. That way, you've got a totally separate document to return to so you don't have to recreate that state.

The History Brush

The History Brush takes the power of the History panel and lets you focus it on specific parts of an image. Instead of sending the *entire* image back in time, you can use this brush to paint edits away *selectively*, revealing the previous state of your choosing. For example, you could darken a portrait with the Burn tool (page 324) and then use the History Brush to undo some of the darkening if you went too far, as shown in Figure 1-11.

> **NOTE** The Art History Brush works similarly, but it adds bizarre, stylized effects as it returns your image to a previous state, as shown in the box on page 533.

FIGURE 1-11

By using the History Brush set to the image's earlier state—see step 4 on this page—you can undo all kinds of effects, including a little over-darkening from using the Burn tool.

You can also reduce the opacity of the History Brush in the Options bar to make the change more gradual.

Here's how to use the History Brush to undo a serious burn you've applied:

1. **Open an image—in this example, a photo of a person—and duplicate the image layer.**

   You'll learn all about opening images in Chapter 2, but, for now, choose File→Open; navigate to where the image lives on your computer, and then click Open. Next, duplicate the layer by pressing ⌘-J (Ctrl+J on a PC).

2. **Activate the Burn tool by pressing Shift-O and then darken part of your image.**

   The Burn tool lives in a toolset, so cycle through those tools by pressing Shift-O a couple of times (its icon looks like a hand making an O shape). Then mouse over to your image and drag across an area that needs darkening. Straight from the factory, this tool darkens images pretty severely, giving you a *lot* to undo with the History Brush.

3. **Grab the History Brush by pressing Y.**

   You'll learn all about brushes and their many options in Chapter 12.

4. **Open the History panel and then click a saved state or snapshot.**

   This is where you pick which version of the image you want to go back to. If you dragged more than once in step 2, you'll see several Burn states listed in the panel. To reduce some of the darkening, but not all of it, choose one of the first few Burn states (or choose the Open state to get rid of *all* the darkening where you painted). Just click within the panel's left-hand column next to a state to pick it, and you'll see the History Brush's icon appear in that column.

5. **Mouse over to your image and drag to paint the areas that are too dark to reveal the lighter version of the image.**

   To make your change more gradual—if, say, you clicked the Open state but you don't want to erase *all* the darkening—just lower the Opacity setting in the Options bar. That way, if you keep painting in the same place, you'll expose more and more of the original image.

You can use the History Brush to easily undo anything you've done; just pick the state you want to revert to in the History panel and then paint away!

Revert Command

If you've taken your image down a path of craziness from which you *can't* rescue it by using Undo or the History panel, you can revert back to its most recent saved state by choosing File→Revert. This command opens the previously saved version of the image, giving you a quick escape route back to square one.

> **NOTE** If you haven't made any changes to your image since it was last saved, you can't choose the Revert option; it's grayed out in the File menu.

■ Tweaking Photoshop's Preferences

As you learned earlier in this chapter, Photoshop is pretty darn customizable. In addition to personalizing the way its tools behave and how your workspace looks, you can make lots of changes using the program's preferences, which control different

POWER USERS' CLINIC

Erasing to History

At some point, you'll realize that the perfect fix for your image is something you zapped 10 steps ago. For example, you may change the color of an object only to decide later that it looked better the way it was. Argh!

Happily, Photoshop's "Erase to History" feature lets you jump back in time and paint away the edits you no longer want. Erasing to history is a handy way to leave *some* changes in place while recovering your original image in other areas.

First, grab the Eraser tool by pressing E and then turn on the "Erase to History" checkbox in the Options bar. Next, in the Layers panel, click the layer you want to edit, and then start

erasing the areas you want to restore to their former glory.

How is erasing to history different from using the History Brush? They both do basically the same thing. The only benefit to using the History Brush instead of "Erase to History" is that the brush lets you use the Option bar's blend mode menu to create different color effects as you erase to the previous state. You'll learn more about blend modes in Part 2 of this book; they control how the colors you add to an image—by painting, darkening, filling, and so on—blend with or cancels out the color that's already there.

aspects of Photoshop and let you turn features on or off, change how tools act, and fine-tune how the program performs.

TIP Tooltips work on preference settings, too! So if you forget what a setting does, just point your cursor at it for a second or two and you'll get a tiny yellow explanation.

To open the Preferences dialog box, choose Photoshop→Preferences→General (Edit→Preferences→General on a PC), or press ⌘-K (Ctrl+K). When you choose a category on the left side of the dialog box, tons of settings related to that category appear on the right. The following pages give you an idea of the kinds of goodies each category contains, and you'll find guidance on tweaking preferences sprinkled throughout this book.

General

The General section of the Preferences dialog box (Figure 1-12) is a sort of catchall for preferences that don't fit anywhere else. Most of these options are either self-explanatory (Beep When Done, for example) or covered elsewhere in this book. A few, however, are worth taking a closer look at.

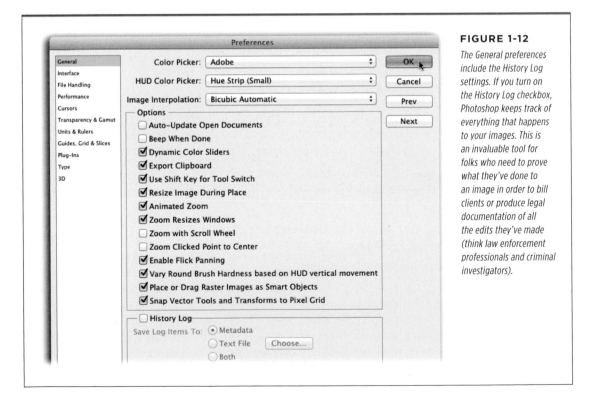

FIGURE 1-12

The General preferences include the History Log settings. If you turn on the History Log checkbox, Photoshop keeps track of everything that happens to your images. This is an invaluable tool for folks who need to prove what they've done to an image in order to bill clients or produce legal documentation of all the edits they've made (think law enforcement professionals and criminal investigators).

Unless you tell it otherwise, Photoshop displays the Adobe Color Picker (see page 491) anytime you choose a color. If you're more comfortable using your operating system's color picker instead, you can select it from the Color Picker pop-up menu. If you download and install third-party color pickers, they show up in this menu, too. However, since the Adobe Color Picker is designed to work with Photoshop and all its built-in options, using another color picker may mean losing quick access to critical features like Color Libraries (page 494).

The HUD Color Picker refers to the on-image color picker you can summon when using a tool that paints, such as the Brush tool. In CS6, the HUD Color Picker is available in new and improved sizes (small, medium, and large), and you can choose among 'em here. (See page 504 for more using the HUD Color Picker.)

The Image Interpolation menu controls the mathematical voodoo Photoshop performs when you resize an image with the Image Size dialog box (page 238) or the Crop tool (page 222). New in CS6 is the Bicubic Automatic option, which tells Photoshop to pick the method that it thinks will work best for your image. Will it always choose wisely? Only you can tell.

Other notable options here involve a couple of cool features called animated zoom and flick-panning (both covered in Chapter 2). If your computer is running at a snail's pace, try disabling one or both features by turning off their checkboxes (both features can *really* tax slower video cards).

The other new options in CS6's General preferences have to do with painting and drawing vectors (Chapters 12 and 13, respectively). For example, "Vary Round Brush Hardness based on HUD vertical movement" means that dragging up or down with your mouse while changing paint color with the on-image color picker (page 504) changes the brush's hardness; if you'd rather have that motion change opacity instead, turn this checkbox off. "Snap Vector Tools and Transforms to Pixel Grid" causes new vector shapes and paths to automatically snap to Photoshop's pixel grid, ensuring precise alignment when you're designing graphics for the Web. Both these settings are turned on right out of the box.

NOTE Deleting Photoshop's preferences file can be a useful troubleshooting technique. (It resets all the preferences to what they were when you first installed the program.) Just choose File→Quit (File→Exit on a PC), and then press and hold Shift-Option-⌘ when you restart Photoshop (Shift+Alt+Ctrl on a PC). Online Appendix B has more about this procedure; head to *www.missingmanuals.com/cds* to download it.

Interface

The Interface preferences control how Photoshop looks on your screen. As you learned on page 16, you can use CS6's new Color Theme swatches at the top of these settings to change Photoshop's colors (click the light gray swatch to resurrect the color theme of CS5). You can squeeze a little more performance out of slower computers by setting the Border pop-up menus near the top of the dialog box to None. That way, Photoshop won't waste any processing power generating pretty drop shadows around your images or around the Photoshop window itself.

If you're familiar with all of Photoshop's tools and don't care to see the little yellow tooltips that appear when you point your cursor at tools and field labels, turn off the Show Tool Tips checkbox. And if you'd like new documents to open in separate windows instead of in new tabs, turn off the "Open Documents as Tabs" checkbox.

NOTE If you use Photoshop on a Mac laptop and you're constantly zooming and rotating your canvas with your trackpad by accident, turn off the Enable Gestures checkbox.

File Handling

These preferences control how Photoshop opens and saves files. If you're a Mac person and you plan on working with images that'll be opened on both Macs and PCs, make sure the Append File Extension pop-up menu is set to Always and that Use Lower Case is turned on. These settings improve the chances that your files will open on *either* type of computer without a hassle. (PC users can leave their File Handling settings alone because file extensions are *automatically* added in Windows.)

New in CS6 is the ability to keep working while Photoshop saves your file in the *background*, meaning you don't have to wait until it's finished to do something else. You'll learn more about this incredible new Auto Recovery feature in Chapter 2, but the File Handling preferences let you control how it works. To have Photoshop save your file more often than every 10 minutes, pick another duration from the Automatically Save Recovery Information Every pop-up menu in the File Saving Options section near the top (your choices are 5, 10, 15, or 30 minutes, or 1 hour).

Straight from the factory, Photoshop is set to display a dialog box each time you save a file that asks if you want to save the image for maximum compatibility with *PSD* and *PSB* files (the native Photoshop format and the format for really big files, respectively; see page 49); doing so improves the chances that your files can be understood by other programs like Adobe InDesign or QuarkXPress. If that pesky dialog box annoys you, change the "Maximize PSD and PSB File Compatibility" pop-up menu to Always and you'll never see the dialog box again (plus you'll have the peace of mind that comes with knowing your images will play nice with other programs). And new in CS6 is the ability to keep Photoshop from automatically compressing these files, which makes it save 'em faster, though the end result will be much bigger file sizes. If speed is more important to you than file size, then turn on "Disable Compression of PSD and PSB Files."

NOTE The Adobe Drive option lets you for organize, track, and store files in a central location that other folks using other programs can then access (this process is called *asset management,* and it replaced the now dead Version Cue). If you didn't use Version Cue, you can forget you ever heard of it. If you *did* use Version Cue, you can download Adobe Drive and then turn this option *on* to access those files once again. Visit *www.adobe.com/products/adobedrive.html* for more info.

Another handy option lies at the very bottom of the dialog box. It lets you change the number of documents Photoshop lists in the Recent files menu (found by choosing File→Open Recent). This field is automatically set to 10, but feel free to change it if you frequently need to reopen the same documents.

Performance

The Performance preferences (Figure 1-13) control how efficiently Photoshop runs on your computer. For example, the amount of memory the program has to work with affects how well it performs. In the Memory Usage section, the Let Photoshop Use field's factory setting tells the program to use up to 60 to 70 percent of your machine's available memory (the exact number may vary). If you're tempted to increase it to 100 percent for better performance, *don't*. Other programs need to use your computer's memory, too, and leaving it set between 60 to 70 percent ensures that all of them get their fair share (after Photoshop takes the biggest chunk, that is).

The History & Cache section on the right lets you change the number of history states that Photoshop remembers, as explained on page 33. You can also let the program set optimal cache levels and tile sizes *for* you; all you have to do is pick the kind of document you work on the most. Your options are "Tall and Thin," "Default," and "Big and Flat"; just click the one that's the closest match to what you regularly use. Here's why this matters. Cache levels controls how much image info is temporarily stored in your computer's memory for things like screen and histogram refreshing (you'll learn about histograms on page 375). The cache tile size is the amount of info Photoshop can store and process at one time (for example, larger tile sizes can speed things up if you work with documents with really large pixel dimensions). See? Now you *appreciate* Photoshop managing these settings for you!

If your computer's hard drive is running low on space, consider adding another drive that Photoshop can use as a *scratch disk*—the place where it stashes the bazillions of temporary files it makes when you're editing images (like various history states). (If you don't have a separate scratch disk, Photoshop stores those temporary files on your computer's hard drive, taking up space you could be using for other documents.) When you add a new internal hard drive or plug in an external drive, that drive appears in the Scratch Disks list shown in Figure 1-13. To give Photoshop the green light to use it, put a checkmark in the disk's "Active?" column, and then drag it upward into the first position. After you do this, Photoshop will be a little zippier because it'll have *two* hard drives reading and writing info instead of one!

NOTE When it comes to Photoshop's scratch disk, speed matters, and faster is better. Since the speed at which the disk spins plays a big role in scratch disk performance, stick with disks rated 7200 RPM (revolutions per minute) or faster. Slower 5400 RPM disks can take a toll on Photoshop's performance, and 4200 RPM drives slow...Photoshop...to...a...crawl.

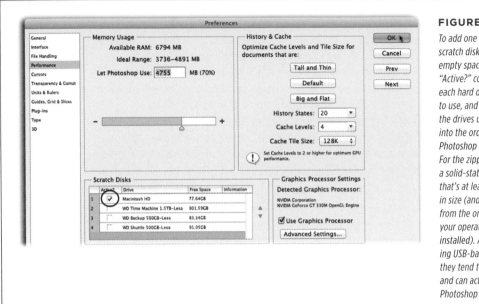

FIGURE 1-13

To add one or more scratch disks, click the empty space in the "Active?" column next to each hard drive you want to use, and then drag the drives up or down into the order you want Photoshop to use them. For the zippiest feel, use a solid-state drive (SSD) that's at least 256 GB in size (and is separate from the one where your operating system is installed). Also, avoid using USB-based drives, as they tend to be sluggish and can actually make Photoshop run slower.

More than ever before, Photoshop CS6 takes advantage of your computer's built-in ability to draw and process graphics. This results in faster and smoother performance when you're resizing images with Free Transform, rotating your canvas temporarily with Rotate View, using the HUD Color Picker—the list goes on and on (you'll learn about *all* these options throughout this book). If you turn off the Use Graphics Processor checkbox at the bottom right, you lose all these superpowers, though you might squeeze a little more performance out of your machine. If you've got a newer machine, be sure to leave this setting turned on. That said, you control *how much* your graphics processor is being tapped by clicking the Advanced Settings button (your choices are Basic, Normal, and Advanced).

Cursors

These preferences control how your cursor looks when you're working with images. There are no right or wrong choices here, so try out the different cursor styles and see what works best for you. Photoshop includes two types of cursors: painting cursors and everything else. When you choose different options, Photoshop shows you a preview of what each cursor looks like. At the bottom of the dialog box is a Brush Preview color swatch that controls the color of the brush preview when you resize your brush by Control-Option-dragging (Alt+right+click-dragging on a PC) left or right. To change the preview's color, click the color swatch, choose a new color from the Color Picker dialog box, and then click OK. (See page 499 to learn how these options affect the Brush tool.)

Transparency and Gamut

The Transparency settings let you fine-tune what a layer looks like when part of it is transparent. Like the cursor settings, these options are purely cosmetic, so feel free to experiment. (You'll learn more about transparency in Chapter 3.) The Gamut Warning option lets you set a highlight color that shows where colors in your image fall outside the safe range for the color mode you're working in or the printer you're using. (Chapter 16 has more about these advanced color issues.)

Units and Rulers

The Units & Rulers preferences (Figure 1-14) let you pick the unit of measurement Photoshop uses. The Rulers pop-up menu, not surprisingly, controls the units displayed in your document's rulers (see page 69); your choices are pixels, inches, centimeters, millimeters, points, picas, and percent. If you work on a lot of documents destined for print, inches or picas are probably your best bet. If you create images primarily for the Web, choose pixels instead. Leave the Type pop-up menu set to points unless you need to work with type measured in pixels or millimeters, which can be handy if you need to align text in a web page layout.

The Column Size settings are handy when you're designing graphics to fit into specific-sized columns in a page-layout program like Adobe InDesign. Just ask the person who's creating the InDesign layout which measurements to use.

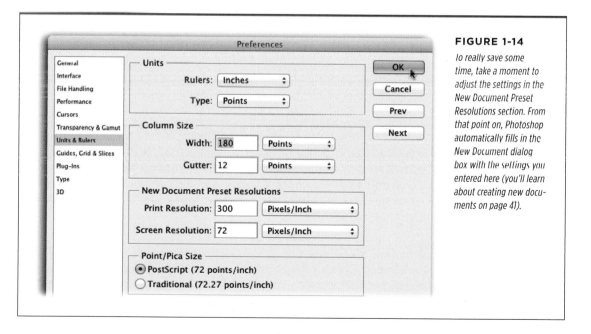

FIGURE 1-14

To really save some time, take a moment to adjust the settings in the New Document Preset Resolutions section. From that point on, Photoshop automatically fills in the New Document dialog box with the settings you entered here (you'll learn about creating new documents on page 41).

Guides, Grid, and Slices

These preferences let you choose the colors for your document guides (page 69), grid (page 71), and slice lines (page 738). You can also set the grid's spacing and the number of subdivisions that appear between each major gridline with the "Gridline every" and Subdivisions fields, respectively.

Plug-ins

You can make Photoshop do even more cool stuff by installing third-party programs called *plug-ins*. There are so many useful plug-ins that this book has an entire chapter devoted to them (Chapter 19). The preferences in this category let you store plug-ins somewhere other than your computer's Photoshop folder, which can help you avoid losing your plug-ins if you have to reinstall Photoshop. Leave both checkboxes in the Extension Panels section turned on so Photoshop can connect to the Internet if a plug-in or panel needs to grab information from a website. For example, the Kuler panel (page 489) lets you use color themes posted on the Web by folks in the Kuler community. If you turn off these checkboxes, Photoshop can't connect to the Internet and you can't use Kuler. To make any changes in this pane take effect, you need to restart Photoshop.

Type

Photoshop has an amazing text engine under its hood (it's even better in CS6), and you'll learn all about it in Chapter 14. The preferences here let you toggle smart quotes (the curly kind) on or off, as well as enable other languages. If you work with Asian characters, turn on the East Asian option in the Choose Text Engine Options section and make sure the Enable Missing Glyph Protection checkbox is also turned on. That way you won't end up with weird symbols or boxes if you try to use a letter or symbol that isn't installed on your machine. And new in CS6, Photoshop can now work with Middle Eastern languages, too. (Any changes you make in the Choose Text Engine Options section take effect only after you restart Photoshop.)

Because seeing a font in its typeface is so handy when you're choosing fonts, Adobe turned on font previews automatically in CS5, and then in CS6 they *removed* the Font Preview Size from preferences altogether. These days you can adjust the preview size by choosing Type→Font Preview Size, where you can pick among six handy options, including none to huge.

> **NOTE** If you have Photoshop CS6 Extended, you'll see one additional preference category: 3D. This book doesn't cover Photoshop's 3D features in depth, though you can learn all about them in *Photoshop 3D for Animators* by Rafiq Elmansy (Focal Press, 2010).

Customizing Keyboard Shortcuts and Menus

Keyboard shortcuts can make the difference between working quickly and working at warp speed. They can drastically reduce the amount of time you spend taking your hands off the keyboard to move your mouse to do things like choose menu items or grab tools. Photoshop has a ton of built-in keyboard shortcuts and menus, but that doesn't mean you're stuck with 'em. You can reassign shortcuts, add new ones, and show or hide menu options. Here's how to add or change keyboard shortcuts:

1. Choose Edit→Keyboard Shortcuts to open the "Keyboard Shortcuts and Menus" dialog box.

2. Choose which type of shortcuts you want to add or change from the Shortcuts For pop-up menu. Your options are Application Menus (like the File and Edit menus), Panel Menus (the menus on the program's various panels), and Tools.

3. In the list below the Shortcuts For menu, pick the shortcut you want to change. (If a list item has a flippy triangle next to it, click the triangle to see all the options nested within that menu item.)

4. Enter a new shortcut in the Shortcut field and then click Accept.

5. To save your new shortcut to Photoshop's *factory* set of shortcuts, click the first hard-disk icon near the top of the dialog box to the right of the Set pop-up menu. Click the Save button in the resulting dialog box, and Photoshop names them Photoshop Defaults (Modified). To create a brand-new set of shortcuts instead, click the *second* hard-disk icon with the little dots underneath it; in the Save dialog box that appears, give your custom shortcut set a meaningful name and then click Save. Creating separate keyboard shortcut sets lets you quickly switch back to Photoshop's factory shortcuts, or switch between sets you've made for specific tasks by using the Set pop-up menu at the top left of the dialog box.

You can also clear an existing keyboard shortcut for something else, such as freeing up the F1 and F2 keys so you can use them to cycle through Photoshop's new color themes. First, make note of which menu the existing shortcut currently lives in (for example, F1 and F2 are in the Edit menu on a Mac and they're in the Edit *and* Help menus on a PC). Next, find the same menu in middle of the "Keyboard Shortcuts and Menus" dialog box, click its flippy triangle to expand the menu, and then click to highlight the shortcut. Finally, click the Delete Shortcut button on the right and consider it free at last.

To help you remember the new shortcuts, Photoshop lets you print a handy chart to tack up on the wall. In the "Keyboard Shortcuts and Menus" dialog box, pick your custom set from the Set pop-up menu and then click Summarize. In the resulting Save dialog box, give the list of shortcuts a name, choose where to save it, and then click Save. Photoshop creates an HTML file that you can open in any Web browser or HTML-savvy software and then print. When you're finished, you can impress your colleagues by telling them that you *reprogrammed* Photoshop to do your bidding; unless they've been in this dialog box themselves, they'll have no idea how easy this stuff is to change.

What if you need to reinstall Photoshop or upgrade to a newer version? CS6's new Migrate Presets feature copies over your keyboard shortcuts so you don't lose 'em (see the Note on page 39).

The "Keyboard Shortcuts and Menus" dialog box also lets you modify the program's menus: If there are commands you rarely use, you can hide 'em to shorten and simplify the menu. Click the Menus tab near the top of the dialog box and then, from the Menu For pop-up menu, choose Application Menus or Panel Menus, depending on which ones you want to tweak. Next, click the little flippy triangle next to each menu's name to see the items it includes. To hide a menu item, click its visibility eye; to show a hidden item, click within its Visibility column. If you suddenly need to access a hidden menu item, choose Show All Menu Items from the very bottom of the affected menu. You can even *colorize* menu items so they're easier to spot. To do that, pick the item you want to highlight, click the word None in the Color column, and then choose a color from the resulting pop-up menu. Click OK and enjoy your new customizations.

Working with Presets

Once you get comfortable in Photoshop, you can customize the behavior of almost every tool in the Tools panel. If you find yourself entering the same settings in the Options bar over and over again for the same tool, then saving those settings can save you time. In fact, Photoshop includes a bunch of built-in tool recipes, called *presets*, such as frequently used crop sizes, colorful gradient sets, patterns, shapes, and brush tips. You can access 'em through the tool's Preset Picker at the far left of the Options bar. Figure 1-15 (top) has the scoop.

The Preset Manager handles loading, saving, and sharing the built-in presets, as well as the ones you create yourself. You can open it by choosing Edit→Presets→Preset Manager. Each group of settings, like a category of brushes, is called a *preset library*. To see a certain preset library, choose it from the Preset Type pop-up menu at the top of the Preset Manager dialog box (Figure 1-15, bottom).

Clicking the little gear icon that's labeled in Figure 1-15 (top) lets you set the category of presets you're viewing to the factory-fresh settings (choose "Reset [name of category] Presets" and then click OK) or load new ones. You can make these adjustments when you're using the tools themselves, but the Preset Manager gives you a bigger preview space, which makes these organizational chores a little more tolerable.

FIGURE 1-15

Top: To access a tool's presets or create new ones, open its Preset Picker at the far left of the Options bar (circled). Click a preset in the list to activate it and then use the tool as you normally would. To save a new preset, enter your custom settings in the Options bar and then click the Create New Preset button labeled here. Give the preset a name in the resulting dialog box, click OK, and it appears in the Preset Picker list. To reset a tool to its factory fresh settings, load additional presets, or access the Preset Manager, click the little gear icon.

Bottom: The Preset Manager gives you access to all the presets for all of Photoshop's tools. Click the gear circled here to open this menu, which lets you change the size of the previews, as well as reset, replace, and otherwise manage presets. To save your eyesight, it's a good idea to set the preview size to Large List so you can actually see what your options are. Changing the preview size here also changes it in the Preset Picker.

NOTE CS6's new Migrate Presets option lets you transfer presets from previous versions of Photoshop (though it can only work with presets from CS3 or newer). The first time you crack open Photoshop CS6, the program kindly asks whether you want to transfer your presets from any older versions that might be hanging around on your machine. If you accept, your goodies are copied over to CS6 (if the older presets have the same name as the newer ones, Photoshop copies only the newer ones). (If you don't encounter the Migrate Presets option when you first launch CS6, it means the installer didn't find any presets to copy over.) If you didn't migrate your presets when you first launched the program, you can do it anytime by choosing Edit→Presets→Migrate Presets, or by resetting your preferences (see the Note on page 31 to learn how).

Sharing Presets

Once you've got your own custom settings for tools, styles, or what have you, feel free to share them with the masses. You can share them with other computers (handy when the whole team needs to use the same color swatches or brushes) and upload them to the Web (for the whole world to download).

In Photoshop CS6, managing and sharing presets is easier than ever before. You've got a couple of ways to import and export these little gems:

- **To share *all* your presets**—including actions, keyboard shortcuts, menu customizations, workspaces, brushes, swatches, gradients, styles, patterns, contours, custom shapes, and tools—choose Edit→Presets→Export/Import Presets. In the resulting dialog box, tell Photoshop which goodies you want to share (say, actions and workspaces) in the Export Presets tab, and then click Export Presets (see Figure 1-16). Photoshop opens the "Choose a Folder" dialog box—just pick a spot that's easy for you to find and then click Open. Photoshop creates a new folder named Exported Presets in the location you picked and dutifully lets you know that it has put your presets there. To *import* presets, click the Import Presets tab and then click the Select Import Folder button at the bottom of the dialog box. In the resulting dialog box, navigate to where the presets live on your hard drive and click Open. Back in the Export/Import Presets dialog box, choose the presets you want to import from the left-hand list (or click the Add All button) and then click Import Presets.

- **To share just a *few* presets** (excluding actions, keyboard shortcuts, menu customizations, and workspaces) create a preset library of your own by opening the Preset Manager and choosing the presets you want to share (Shift-click or ⌘-/Control-click to highlight 'em). Next, click the Save Set button, and in the resulting Save dialog box, give your custom library a name. Unless you pick a different location on your hard drive, Photoshop automatically saves it in the folders where it stores *all* custom settings. When everything looks good, click Save. Once you've saved your custom library, you can email it to folks or upload it to a website for others to download. If you're uploading it to the Web, make sure the file doesn't have any spaces in its name. For example, instead of calling the file "Dragon Scales Brush," name it "DragonScalesBrush."

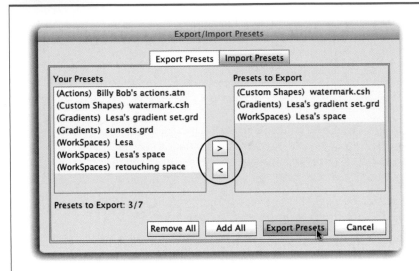

If you're on the receiving end of a preset library, open the Preset Manager (Edit→Presets→Preset Manager) and then click the Load button. Navigate to where the library lives and then click Open. (Alternatively, you can choose Edit→Presets→Export/Import Presets, and then click the Import Presets tab shown in Figure 1-16.) The next time you use a tool that has custom presets, you'll see the new library's options in the tool's Preset picker menu.

To add to the fun, you can also rename individual presets. In the Preset Manager dialog box, choose the relevant library from the Preset Type pop-up menu and then click to activate the soon-to-be-renamed preset. Click the Rename button, type a new moniker in the Name field, and then click OK. To delete a preset library you never use, choose it from the Preset Manager's Preset Type pop-up menu and then click Delete.

TIP If you've managed to mess up one of Photoshop's built-in preset libraries by adding items that don't work the way you want, you can easily restore it: Open the Preset Manager and choose the library you want to reset. Then, click the gear icon that's circled back in Figure 1-15 and choose "Reset [type of preset]" (for example, Brushes). Photoshop asks if you want to replace the current brushes or append (add to) them instead. Click OK to replace the brushes, and you'll be back to the factory-fresh settings.

Opening, Viewing, and Saving Files

Chances are good that If you're holding this book, you're spending a lot of time in Photoshop. So the ability to shave off a minute here and there from routine stuff can really add up. Heck, if you're lucky, you'll save enough time to read a book, ride your bike, or catch an episode of *The Big Bang Theory*.

One way to steal back some of that time is to work more efficiently, and that means learning tricks for the less glamorous stuff like opening, viewing, and saving files. And since you'll be doing these things so often, it's important to form good habits so your documents are set up properly from the get-go. (It would be truly heartbreaking to find the artwork you've spent weeks creating is too small to print, or that you saved the file in such a way that you can't change it later on.) Finally, since a key part of working with images is navigating vast pixel landscapes, this chapter teaches you some handy ways to move around within your images onscreen.

Creating a New Document

Photoshop gives you a variety ways to accomplish most tasks, including creating a new document. Sure, you can choose File→New, but it's faster to press ⌘-N (Ctrl+N on a PC). Either way, you'll be greeted with the New dialog box shown in Figure 2-1.

You'd think naming a document would be simple: Just type something in the Name box and you're done, right? Not quite. Here are a few things to keep in mind:

- If you're working on a Mac, don't start file names with periods. Files whose names start with periods are invisible in Mac OS X (meaning neither you *nor* Photoshop can see them), which makes 'em darn hard to work with.

- If folks need to open your files on both Mac and Windows machines, don't put slashes (/), colons (:), angle brackets (<, >), pipes, (|), asterisks (*), or question marks (?) in the file names, either.

- Leave *file extensions* on the file name (the period and three letters at the end of the name, like .psd, .jpg, and so on). The file extension makes it easier for your computer to tell what *kind* of file it is so it can pick a program that can open it.

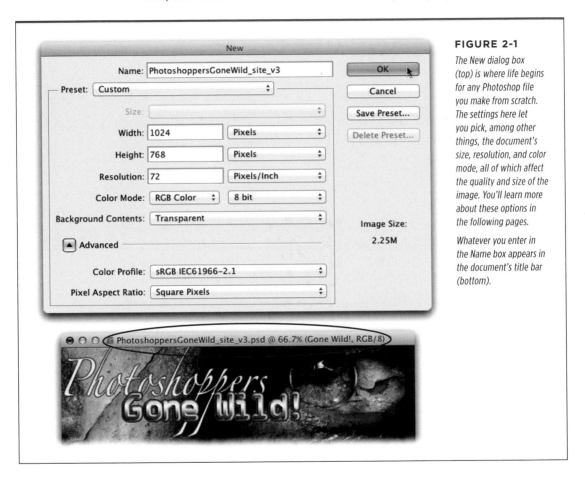

FIGURE 2-1

The New dialog box (top) is where life begins for any Photoshop file you make from scratch. The settings here let you pick, among other things, the document's size, resolution, and color mode, all of which affect the quality and size of the image. You'll learn more about these options in the following pages.

Whatever you enter in the Name box appears in the document's title bar (bottom).

Photoshop's Ready-Made Documents

After you've named your document, you need to pick a size for it. You've got two choices here: Enter the dimensions you'd like in the Width and Height boxes or pick one of Photoshop's canned choices (4"x6" landscape photo, 640x480–pixel web page, and so on) from the Preset and Size menus shown in Figure 2-2.

FIGURE 2-2

Once you choose an option from the Preset menu (which includes different types of paper, electronic formats, and recently used document sizes), Photoshop fills the Size menu and its related fields with the appropriate settings—including Width, Height, Resolution, and Color Mode. Presets are great timesavers, and they can help you avoid mistakes when creating new documents.

TIP Photoshop CS6 includes a bunch of new presets for common devices such as the iPhone and iPad. Choose "Mobile & Devices" from the New dialog box's Preset menu, and you'll see that the resulting Size pop-up menu is three times longer!

The advantage of picking a canned option is that, in addition to filling in the dimensions for you, Photoshop plugs in resolution and color mode settings. You'll learn more about these two options in a minute, but if you're new to the program, these *presets* (document recipes) are a great way to make sure you're starting off with a well-configured document. Besides, the presets can be helpful even if they're not

UP TO SPEED

Stealing Document Settings

Need to create a document that's the same size and resolution as an *existing* document? No problem—just snag the original file's settings and use 'em to make another. You can swipe a document's settings in several ways:

- Open the existing document and press ⌘-N (Ctrl+N on a PC) to open the New dialog box. Click the Preset pop-up menu, which lists the names of all open documents. When you pick the document you want, Photoshop adjusts all the dialog box's settings to match.

- With the existing document open, press ⌘-A (Ctrl+A) to select everything in it and then press ⌘-C (Ctrl+C) to copy the document's contents to your computer's memory (a.k.a. the Clipboard). Next, choose File→New or press ⌘-N (Ctrl+N on a PC) and Photoshop automatically fills

in the document's settings for you. You can also choose Clipboard from the Preset menu shown in Figure 2-1 (top).

- If you want to base your new document on the *last* document you created, press Option-⌘-N (Alt+Ctrl+N) or hold down the Option key (Alt on a PC) while you choose File→New.

- To create a new document that's the same size and resolution as your current selection, create the selection, copy the contents to your computer's memory by pressing ⌘-C (Ctrl+C), and then choose File→New or press ⌘-N (Ctrl+N). Photoshop creates a document that matches your selection's dimensions perfectly. (See Chapter 4 for the full story on selections.)

exactly what you need. For example, if you find one that's the right size but the wrong resolution, just pick it, adjust the resolution, and you're on your way.

> **NOTE** If you copy all or part of an image to your computer's temporary memory (also called the *Clipboard*), Photoshop grabs the copied image's settings for you, making it super simple to match those settings without having to write down the dimensions or resolution. This happens automatically, and it's the same as choosing Clipboard from the Preset menu.

Setting Size and Resolution

In Photoshop, "size" refers to two different things: file size (640 kilobytes or 2.4 megabytes, for example) and dimensions (like 4"x6" or 640x480 pixels). You'll find plenty of advice throughout this book on how to control file size, but this section is about the size of your document's *canvas*.

Photoshop can measure canvas size in pixels, inches, centimeters, millimeters, points, picas, and columns. In the New dialog box, just pick the unit of measurement that's appropriate for your project—or the easiest for you to work with—from the pop-up menus to the right of the Width and Height fields. If you're designing a piece for the Web or for use in presentation software, pixels are your best bet. If you're going to print the image, inches are a common choice. Columns come in handy when you're making an image that has to fit within a specific number of columns in a page-layout program, such as Adobe InDesign or QuarkXPress.

> **NOTE** Photoshop assumes you want to use the same unit (say, inches) to measure width and height, so it automatically changes both fields when you adjust one. If you really *do* need to work with different units, just hold the Shift key while you pick the second unit to make Photoshop leave the other field alone.

The Resolution field controls the number of pixels per inch or per centimeter in your document. High-resolution documents contain more pixels per inch than low-resolution documents of the same size. (You'll learn all about resolution in Chapter 6.)

For now, here's some ready-to-use guidance if you haven't mastered the fine art of resolution just yet: If you're designing an image that will be viewed only onscreen (in a web browser or a slideshow presentation, for example) enter *72* in the Resolution field. If you're going to print the image at home, set the resolution to at least 240 pixels per inch (if it's headed to a professional printer, enter *300* or more instead).

> **TIP** If you don't know the exact size your document needs to be, it's better to make it really big; you can always shrink it down later. See page 236 for more on resizing images.

Once you enter values in the Width, Height, and Resolution fields, Photoshop calculates the document's *file size*—the amount of space it takes up in Photoshop's memory—and displays it in the New dialog box's lower right corner (in Figure 2-1, for example, the file size is 2.25 MB).

Just because you make a document a certain size doesn't mean you can't have artwork in that file that's bigger than the document's dimensions. Photoshop is perfectly fine with objects that extend beyond the document's edges (also called *document boundaries*), but you can't see or print those parts. It may sound odd, but if you paste a photo or a piece of vector art (page 52) that's larger than your document, those extra bits will dangle off the edges (text that you make with the Type tool can dangle off, too). To resize your document so you can see everything—even the stuff that doesn't quite fit—choose Image→Reveal All to make Photoshop modify the document's dimensions so everything fits.

Choosing a Color Mode

The New dialog box's Color Mode field (see Figure 2-1) determines which colors you can use in the document. You'll spend most of your time working in RGB mode (which stands for "red, green, blue"), but you can switch modes whenever you like. (The pop-up menu to the right of the Color Mode field controls the document's *bit depth*, which is explained in the box on page 46.)

Unless you choose a different color mode, Photoshop automatically uses RGB. The Color Mode menu gives you the following options:

- **Bitmap** restricts you to two colors: black and white. (Shades of gray aren't welcome at the Bitmap party.) This mode is useful when you're scanning high-contrast items like black-and-white text documents or creating graphics for handheld devices that don't have color screens.

- **Grayscale** expands on Bitmap mode by adding shades between pure black and pure white. The higher the document's bit depth, the more shades of gray—and so the more details—it can contain. Eight-bit documents include 256 shades of gray; 16-bit documents extend that range to over 65,000; and 32-bit documents crank it up to over 4.2 billion (see the box on page 46 for more on bit depth).

- **RGB Color** is the color mode you'll use the most, and it's also the one your monitor and digital camera use to represent colors. This mode shows colors as a mix of red, green, and blue light, with each having a numeric value between 0 and 255 that describes the brightness of each color present (for example, fire-engine red has an RGB value of 250 for red, 5 for green, and 5 for blue). As with Grayscale mode, the higher a document's bit depth, the more details it can contain. In this mode, you can choose among 8-, 16-, and 32-bit documents. (See Chapter 5 for more on RGB mode.)

- **CMYK Color** simulates the colors used in printing (its name stands for "cyan, magenta, yellow, blacK"). It doesn't have as many colors as RGB because it's limited to the colors a printer—whether it's an inkjet, commercial offset, or digital press—can reproduce with ink and dyes on paper. You'll learn more about CMYK in Chapter 5, and Chapter 16 explains if and when you should switch to CMYK mode.

- **Lab Color** mode, which is based on the way we see color, lets you use all the colors human eyes can detect. It represents how colors *should look* no matter which device they're displayed on, whereas RGB and CMYK modes limit a file's colors to what's visible onscreen or in a printed document, respectively. The downside is that many folks have a hard time learning to create the colors they want in Lab mode. You'll find various techniques involving Lab mode sprinkled throughout Part 2 of this book.

Understanding Bit Depth

You may have heard the terms "8-bit" and "16-bit" tossed around in graphics circles (and neither has anything to do with Photoshop being a 64-bit program, as the box on page 4 explains). When people refer to bits, they're talking about how many colors an image contains. Photoshop's color modes determine whether a document is an 8- or a 16-bit image (other, less common options are 1-bit and 32-bit). Since you'll run into these labels fairly often, it helps to understand more about what these numbers mean.

A *bit* is the smallest unit of measurement that computers use to store information: either a 1 or a 0 (on or off, respectively). Each pixel in an image has a *bit depth*, which controls how much color information that pixel can hold. So an image's bit depth determines how much color info the image contains. The higher the bit depth, the more colors the image can display. And the more colors in your image, the more info (details) you've got to play with in Photoshop.

To understanding bit depth, you need to know a little about *channels*, where Photoshop stores your image's color info (see Chapter 5) on separate layers (Chapter 3). For example, in an RGB image you have three channels: one each for red, green, and blue. If you combine the info contained in each channel, you can figure how many colors are in your image.

With all that in mind, here's a quick tour of your various bit choices in Photoshop:

- In **Bitmap** color mode, your pixels can be only black or white. Images in this mode are called 1-bit images because each pixel can be only one color—black or white (they're also known simply as *bitmap* images).

- An **8-bit image** can hold two values in each bit, which equals 256 possible color values. Why 256? Since each of the eight bits can hold two possible values, you get 256 combinations. (For math fans, it's two to the eighth power, which equals 256). Images in Grayscale mode contain one

channel, so that's 8 bits per channel, equaling 256 colors. Since images in RGB mode contain three channels (one each for red, blue, and green), folks refer to them as 24-bit images (8 bits per channel x 3 = 24), but they're still really just 8-bit images. With 256 combinations for each channel (that's 2^8 x 2^8 x 2^8), you can have over 16 million colors in an RGB image. Since CMYK images have four channels, folks refer to them as 32-bit images (8 bits per channel x 4 = 32), but again, these are *still* 8-bit images. Over 200 combinations per channel and four channels add up to a massive number of possible color values, but since you're dealing with printed ink, your color range in CMYK is dictated by what can actually be reproduced on *paper*, which reduces it to about 55,000 colors.

- **16-bit images** contain 65,536 colors in a single channel and are produced by some high-end digital cameras (*digital single-lens reflex*, or DSLR, cameras) shooting in Raw format and by really good scanners. These files don't look any different from other images on your screen, but they take up twice as much hard drive space. Photographers really like 16-bit images because the extra colors give them more flexibility when they're making Curves and Levels adjustments (Chapter 9), even though the larger file sizes can *really* slow Photoshop down. Also, not all of Photoshop's tools and filters work with 16-bit images.

- **32-bit images**, referred to as *high dynamic range* (HDR), contain more colors than you can shake a stick at. See page 398 for more info.

For the most part, you'll deal with 8-bit images, but if you've got a camera that shoots at higher bit depths, by all means, take a weekend and experiment to see if the difference in quality is worth the sacrifice of hard drive space (and editing speed). And if you're restoring a really old photo, it may be helpful to scan it at a high bit depth so you have a wider range of colors to work with. See the box on page 57 for more scanning tips.

Choosing a Background

The New dialog box's Background Contents pop-up menu lets you choose what's on the Background layer—the only layer you start out with in a new document or when you open a photo. Your choices are White, Background Color (which uses the color that your background color chip is set to [page 23]), and Transparent (which leaves the background completely empty).

What you choose here isn't crucial—if you change your mind, you can fill the Background layer with another color (page 93) or turn off its visibility (page 84). The Transparent option is handy if your document is part of a bigger project where it'll be placed in front of other artwork; when you choose this option, you see a gray-and-white checkerboard pattern, as explained in the box below.

Advanced Options

The Advanced button at the bottom of the New dialog box also reveals a couple of pop-up menus:

- **Color Profile.** A *color profile* is a set of instructions that determine how computer monitors and printers display or print your document's colors. This menu is set to the same profile listed in the Color Settings dialog box (page 676), which, unless you've changed it, is set to "sRGB IEC61966-2.1." Leave this setting alone unless you know you need to use a specific color profile for your project; otherwise, the image's colors may not look the way you expect them to on other computers or when they're printed. You'll learn about color profiles in Chapter 16.

- **Pixel Aspect Ratio.** This setting determines the shape of the pixels by changing their size. This setting gets its name from the term *aspect ratio*—the relationship between an image's width and height. (For example, a widescreen television has an aspect ratio of 16:9.) Out of the box, Photoshop's pixels are square. Although square pixels are fine for photos, printed images, and onscreen use, they look funky and distorted in video, which has a tendency to make everything look short and fat (including people). So if you're using Photoshop to work on a movie, try to find out which video format the filmmakers are using and then choose it here.

FREQUENTLY ASKED QUESTION

Seeing Transparency

Dude, what's up with the gray-and-white checkerboard pattern in my new document? I thought it was supposed to be blank!

When you tell Photoshop to make your Background layer transparent, it fills your new document with a checkerboard pattern. Don't worry: That checkerboard is just what the program uses to *represent* transparency on the Background layer. In other words, the checkered pattern is just a reminder that there aren't any pixels on that layer (or on that particular *part* of a layer).

You can change how the checkerboard pattern looks by choosing Photoshop→Preferences→Transparency & Gamut (Edit→Preferences→Transparency & Gamut on a PC). In the Transparency Settings area, tweak the options to make the squares bigger or smaller or change their colors. If you can't stand seeing the checkered pattern no matter what it looks like, turn it off by setting the Grid Size field to None. When you've got things set the way you want, click OK.

■ SAVING YOUR CUSTOM SETTINGS

If you've gone to the trouble of getting your document's settings just right and you expect to create lots of similar documents, save those settings as a preset. Click the Save Preset button to open the dialog box shown in Figure 2-3, and then type a descriptive name for your new time-saving preset.

FIGURE 2-3

Use these checkboxes to tell Photoshop which settings you want it to remember. When you create a new document using a preset you've created, the program grabs any settings you didn't *include in the preset from the last new document you made. For example, if you turn off the Profile checkbox shown here, your preset doesn't include a color profile, so Photoshop assigns the currently active color profile (from Color Settings—see page 676) to the new document.*

■ Saving Files

After you've put a ton of work into whipping up a lovely creation, don't forget to save it or you'll never see it again. As in any program, be sure to save early and often so your efforts don't go to waste if your computer crashes or the power goes out.

> **TIP** Photoshop CS6 sports a new Auto Recovery feature that automatically saves your documents every 10 minutes (though you can change the time interval; see the box on page 50). Also new in CS6 is the ability to keep working *while* Photoshop saves your file in the background, meaning you don't have to wait until it's finished to do something else.

The simplest method is to choose File→Save or press ⌘-S (Ctrl+S on a PC). If you haven't previously saved the file, Photoshop summons the Save As dialog box so you can pick where to save the file, give it a name, and choose a file format (your options are explained in the next section). If you *have* already saved the file, Photoshop replaces the previously saved version with the *current* version without asking if that's what you want to do. In some situations, that's fine, but it can be disastrous if you wanted to keep more than one version of the image.

You can play it safe by using the Save As dialog box every time you save. It *always* prompts you for a new file name (see Figure 2-4), which is handy when you want to save another version of the document or save it in a different format. Choose File→Save As or press Shift-⌘-S (Shift+Ctrl+S on a PC) to open the dialog box. From the factory, the Format pop-up menu is set to Photoshop, which is perfect because that format (also known as PSD format) keeps all your layers and Smart Objects intact in case you need to go back and change them later. This is the format you want to use while editing images. Then, when you're finished and ready to save the image for use in another program—or for posting on the Web or sending in an email—you can save it in a different file format, as the next section explains.

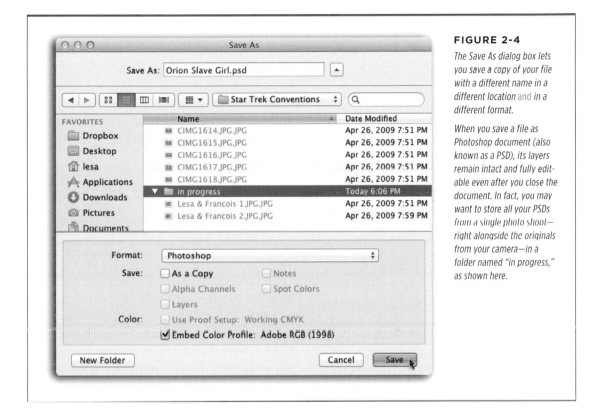

FIGURE 2-4

The Save As dialog box lets you save a copy of your file with a different name in a different location and in a different format.

When you save a file as Photoshop document (also known as a PSD), its layers remain intact and fully editable even after you close the document. In fact, you may want to store all your PSDs from a single photo shoot—right alongside the originals from your camera—in a folder named "in progress," as shown here.

NOTE When you run the Save As command, Photoshop assumes you want to save the document in the original folder from whence it came. To change this behavior, choose Photoshop→Preferences→File Handling (Edit→Preferences→File Handling on a PC) and turn off the "Save As to Original Folder" checkbox.

File Formats

You'll learn more about file formats in Chapters 16 and 17, but here's a quick overview.

If you remember nothing else, remember to save your images as *PSD files* (Photoshop documents) because that's the most flexible format (as explained in the previous section). That said, sometimes you need to save a document in other formats because of where the file is *headed*. For example, Adobe InDesign and recent versions of QuarkXPress (popular page-layout programs) are adept at handling PSD files, but not all programs understand what the heck a PSD file is. In that case, try saving the document as a TIFF file because nearly every image-handling program ever invented can open TIFFs.

NOTE If you need to save a document that's bigger than 2 GB, save it in Large Document Format (.PSB format) instead, which you get past Photoshop's 2-gigabyte limit on PSD files. Photoshop CS6 also supports BIGTIFF format, which lets you circumvent the 4-gigabyte size limit of TIFF format.

Graphics destined for the Web are a different animal because they're specially designed for onscreen viewing and faster downloading. Here's a quick cheat sheet to tide you over until you've got time and energy to make your way to Chapter 17:

- **JPEG** is commonly used for graphics that include a wide range of colors, like photos. It compresses images so they take up less space, but the smaller file size comes at a price: loss of quality.

UP TO SPEED

CS6's Magical Auto Recovery

Every time you lose a Photoshop document to a computer crash, a baby frog dies.

OK, not really, but it sure can ruin an otherwise perfectly good day.

Happily, Photoshop CS6 includes a new Auto Recovery feature that automatically saves all your open Photoshop documents as fully layered PSD files every 10 minutes. (If you've ever used Microsoft Word, you've encountered a similar feature already.) That's right: If the program crashes, the documents pop back open the next time you launch Photoshop.

These back-up, or *recovered*, documents are stored in a folder named PSAutoRecover on your *scratch disk*, the hard drive that's specified in the Performance pane of Photoshop's Preferences (see page 33 for more on scratch disks). The only caveat is that if you run out of hard-drive space on your scratch disk, the back-up documents won't be saved.

These back-up documents are temporary and don't hang around forever (which isn't a big deal if you remember to save your file every so often). They disappear if you do any of the following:

- Choose File→Save in your original document.
- Choose File→Revert in your original document.
- Close your original document without ever saving it first.
- Close a back-up document without saving it first.
- Save a back-up document to another location.

This fabulous, derrière-saving feature is turned on straight from the factory, though all of this automatic saving can take a toll on performance. If you notice that Photoshop feels sluggish—say, if you frequently work with a lot of big documents all open at the same time—you can always turn it off. Choose Photoshop→Preferences→File Handling (Edit→Preferences→File Handling on a PC) and turn off the Automatically Save Recovery Information Every checkbox. You can also change the auto save interval to every 5 minutes by using the pop-up menu to the right of the checkbox (handy if you're doing detailed retouching and your image is changing significantly every few minutes). If you want to leave Auto Recovery on but have it happen *less* frequently (to increase performance), you can set the auto-save interval to 15 minutes, 30 minutes, or an hour.

NOTE Photoshop automatically saves 16-bit JPEGs as 8-bit files. If that sentence is as clear as mud to you, flip back to the box on page 46 to learn more about image bit depth.

- **GIF** is a popular choice for graphics that include a limited number of colors (think cartoon art), have a transparent background, or are animated (page 731).

- **PNG** is the up-and-comer because it offers true transparency and a wide range of colors. It produces a higher-quality image than a JPEG, but it generates larger files.

For more on creating and preparing images for the Web, hop over to Chapter 17. If your image is headed for a professional printer, visit Chapter 16 instead.

◾ Opening an Existing Document

Opening files is simple in most programs, and that holds true in Photoshop, too. But Photoshop gives you a few more options than you'll find elsewhere because it's amazingly versatile at working with a wide range of images. Photoshop knows how to open Adobe Illustrator, Camera Raw (page 57), JPEG, GIF, PNG, TIFF, EPS, and PDF files (page 55), along with Collada DAE, Google Earth 4 KMZ, Scitex CT, Targa, and several other file types most folks have never heard of.

NOTE Photoshop CS6 supports even *more* formats including JPS and PNS (a stereo image pair that's captured by cameras with two lenses or one lens that's split in half to produce 3D images), as well as BIGTIFF (for TIFFs larger than 4 GB). CS6 also allows for more bit depth (think colors) in TIFF files. (For more on bit depth, see the box on page 46).

You can open files in Photoshop in several ways, including the following:

- Double-clicking a file's icon whose format is associated with Photoshop (like JPEG or TIFF), no matter where it's stored on your computer.

- Dragging the file's icon onto the Photoshop Dock icon (the blue square with "Ps" on it) on a Mac. (This trick *doesn't* work in the Windows taskbar.)

- Control-clicking (right-clicking on a PC) the document's icon and, from the resulting shortcut menu, choosing Open With→Adobe Photoshop CS6. (This method works only for files formats that are associated with Photoshop.)

- Launching Photoshop and then choosing File→Open or pressing ⌘-O (Ctrl+O) to rouse the Open dialog box, discussed in the next section.

- Dragging the document's icon into the Photoshop program window.

- Choosing File→"Open as Smart Object" as discussed later in this chapter (page 54).

You can also use Adobe Bridge—or the Mini Bridge panel—to preview and open documents. Head over to Chapter 21 to learn more about Bridge and Mini Bridge.

Raster Images vs. Vector Images

The images you'll work with and create in Photoshop fall into two categories: those made from *pixels* and those made from *paths*. It's important to understand that they have different characteristics and that you need to open them in different ways to *preserve* those characteristics:

- **Raster images** are made from pixels, tiny blocks of color that are the smallest elements of a digital image. The number of pixels in an image depends on the device that captured it (a digital camera or scanner) or the settings you entered when you created the document in Photoshop (page 41). The size of the pixels depends on the image's resolution (see page 237), which specifies the number of pixels in an inch. Usually pixels are so small that you can't see them individually; but, if you zoom in on a raster image, the pixels get bigger and the image starts to look like a bunch of blocks instead of a smooth image. JPEGs, TIFFs, and GIFs are raster images.

- **Vector images** are made up of points and paths that form shapes; these shapes are then filled and stroked (outlined) with color. (In Photoshop CS6, you can create vector images as easily as in drawing programs such as Adobe Illustrator or CorelDraw.) Paths are based on mathematical equations that tell monitors and printers exactly how to draw the image. Because there aren't any pixels involved, you can make vector images as big or small as you want, and they'll still look as smooth and crisp as the original. Photoshop can open vector images, but unless you open them as Smart Objects (discussed later in this chapter), Photoshop will turn them into pixel-based raster images through a process called *rasterizing*.

In the figure below, the upper image is a vector image (the right-hand version shows the paths it's made from) and the bottom image is a raster image. Vectors are handy when you're designing logos and other illustrations that you might need to make bigger at some point. You'll end up working with rasters more often than not because *photos* are raster images and Photoshop is a pixel-based program (as are all image-editing and painting programs). That said, Photoshop CS6 has a slew of tools you can use to draw vectors (see Chapter 13), and it lets you open vector files, as discussed in the next section. And as page 304 explains, you can create amazing artwork by combining raster and vector images.

The Open Dialog Box

When you choose File→Open or press ⌘-O (Ctrl+O on a PC), Photoshop summons the dialog box shown in Figure 2-5. All you need to do from there is navigate to a file on your hard drive and then click the Open button.

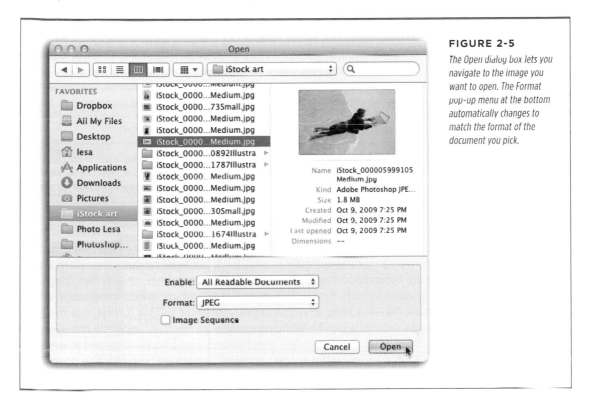

FIGURE 2-5

The Open dialog box lets you navigate to the image you want to open. The Format pop-up menu at the bottom automatically changes to match the format of the document you pick.

NOTE PC users don't get as many options in the Open dialog box as Mac users do. Instead of the Enable pop-up menu, PC folks get a "Files of type" menu, and the Format pop-up menu doesn't appear at all.

In addition to letting you hunt through the murky depths of your hard drive, the dialog box also lets you narrow your search by choosing a format from the Enable pop-up menu. If you pick just the format you want to find, Photoshop will dutifully dim everything else (you can't choose dimmed items), which is handy when you've saved the same image in several different formats—like PSD, JPEG, and TIFF.

TIP To open more than one file, ⌘-click (Ctrl-click) to choose files that aren't next to each other in the list or Shift-click to choose files that are. When you click Open, Photoshop opens each file in a separate tab if you've got the Application Frame turned on (page 11) and you've kept Photoshop's Interface preferences set to "Open Documents as Tabs" (page 31).

You open PDFs the same way you open any file: Choose File→Open, find the PDF you want, and then click the Open button. If someone created the PDF in Photoshop, it opens right up. If someone created it in another program, Photoshop displays the Import PDF dialog box (Figure 2-7) so you can choose which parts of the document you want to import (full pages or just the images) and set the resolution, dimensions, and so on.

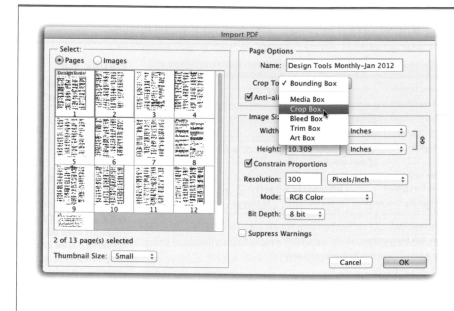

FIGURE 2-7

If you decide to import multiple pages (as shown here), Photoshop creates a new document for each one. If you're lucky and the person who created the document was a PDF pro, she may have included size-specification goodies like crop size, bleed area, trim, and art size (you'll learn about most of these terms in Chapter 16). In that case, you can eliminate some resizing work on imported files by choosing one of the size options from the Crop To pop-up menu (shown here, right).

Working with Scanned Images

The Open dialog box isn't the only way to get images into Photoshop. If you have a scanner that knows how to talk to Photoshop, you can use it to import images straight into the program. But, first, you need to install the scanner's software. Check the owner's manual to learn how to do that, and then read Chapter 19, which covers plug-ins in detail. (*Plug-ins* are applications that expand Photoshop's abilities.) To find your scanner's plug-in, check the manufacturer's website for the most recent version. Once everything is all set, you can start importing scanned documents.

To import an image from a scanner into Photoshop CS6 on a Mac, choose File→Import→"Import from Device," and then pick your scanner from the resulting list. Each scanner has its own software, so there's no standard set of steps to work through—they're all different. Unfortunately, that means you have to read the documentation that came with your scanner to figure out how to import files (the nerve!). Nevertheless, the box on this page has some scanning tips for your reading pleasure.

NOTE The TWAIN plug in, which lets Photoshop communicate with scanners, is an older technology that's no longer being updated. These days, Adobe wants you to use the scanning software that came with your scanner instead. Another option is to use the third-party plug-in VueScan (*www.hamrick.com*). If you go that route, save your image as a TIFF and then open it in Photoshop.

Working with Raw Files

Of all the file formats Photoshop can understand, *Raw* may be the most useful and flexible. Professional-grade digital cameras (and many high-end consumer cameras) use this format. The info in a Raw file is the exact information the camera recorded when it took the picture. (When shooting in JPEG format, the camera itself applies a little noise reduction, sharpening, and color boosting to the image.) Raw files contain the most detailed information you can get from a digital camera, including what's known as *metadata:* info on all the settings the camera used to capture the image, like shutter speed, aperture, and so on. You can edit Raw files using a Photoshop plug-in called *Adobe Camera Raw* (shown in Figure 2-8), which you'll learn more about in Chapter 9.

UP TO SPEED

Scanning 101

Just because all scanning software is different doesn't mean there aren't a few guidelines you can follow to produce good scans. Keep these things in mind the next time you crank open your scanner's lid:

- **Scan at a higher bit depth than you need for the edited image.** Yes, the files will be larger, but they'll contain more color info, which is helpful when you're editing them. (See the box on page 46 for more on bit depth.)

- **Scan at a higher resolution than you need for the finished image so the files include more details.** You can always

lower the resolution later, but you can't increase it...or, rather, you *shouldn't* increase it without knowing the trick (see the box on page 241 for the scoop).

- **If your scanner software lets you adjust the image's color before you import the file into Photoshop, do it.** Making adjustments before you import the image lets you take advantage of all of the info your scanner picked up. (The amount of information the scanner passes along to Photoshop when you import the file is almost *always* less than the amount of info in the original image.)

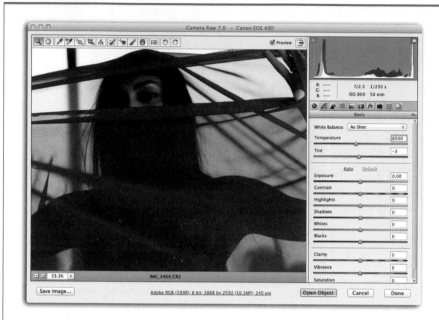

FIGURE 2-8

Adobe Camera Raw (a.k.a. ACR or just Camera Raw), launches automatically when you open a Raw file in Photoshop, Bridge, or the Mini Bridge panel. Camera Raw is one of the most frequently updated plug-ins known to man— good news, because manufacturers release new camera models faster than photographers can buy 'em! If you've got a brand-new camera, you may have to update Camera Raw before you can open your file, which means it's time for a trip to Adobe Updater. To run it, choose Help→Updates (online Appendix A has more on checking for updates). If there's a newer version of Camera Raw, Photoshop lets you know so you can download and install it.

■ OPENING RAW FILES

Opening a Raw file in Photoshop is just like opening any other kind of image except that it opens in the Camera Raw window instead of the main Photoshop window. You can open Raw files by:

- Double-clicking the file's icon. Your computer launches Photoshop (if it wasn't running already) and then opens the Camera Raw window.

- Control-clicking (right-clicking on a PC) the file's icon and then choosing Open With→Photoshop. (Since Camera Raw is a plug-in that runs inside Photoshop and Bridge, it doesn't get listed separately, but your computer knows to open the file in Camera Raw.)

- Using Bridge to pick the file and then choosing File→"Open in Camera Raw" or pressing ⌘-R (Ctrl+R on a PC). You can also Control-click (right-click) the file in Bridge or the Mini Bridge panel and then choose "Open in Camera Raw" from the resulting shortcut menu. (Bridge and Mini Bridge are covered in Chapter 21.)

TIP If you've got a bunch of Raw images that need similar edits (cropping, color-correcting, and so on), you can open them all at once by Shift or ⌘-clicking (Ctrl-clicking on a PC) them in Bridge or the Mini Bridge panel, or by choosing them on your desktop and then double-clicking or dragging them onto the Photoshop icon. When you click the Select All button in the top-left corner of the Camera Raw window, any edits you make from then on affect all your open images. See the box on page 406 for more on editing multiple files.

Duplicating Files

If your client or boss asks you to alter an image and you suspect he'll change his mind later, it's wise to edit a *copy* of the image (or PSD) instead of the original. That way, when he asks you to change everything back, you don't have to sweat bullets hunting for a backup of the original or try to recreate the earlier version. Duplicating files is also handy when you want to experiment with a variety of different effects.

You can duplicate a file by choosing File→Save As and renaming the image, but there's a faster way: Make sure the file you want to copy is in the currently active window (just click its window to activate it), and then choose Image ›Duplicate. In the Duplicate Image dialog box (Figure 2-9), give the file a new name and then click OK. You've just set yourself up to be the office hero.

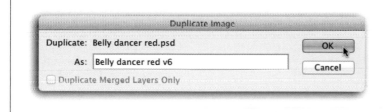

FIGURE 2-9

A duplicate PSD file is exactly the same as the original, including layers, layer styles, and so on. If you need to create a single-layer (flattened) version—for use in a program that doesn't support PSDs, say—turn on the Duplicate Merged Layers Only checkbox. (Page 115 has more about flattening files.)

POWER USERS' CLINIC

Opening Images as a Stack

If you sprang for Photoshop CS6 Extended (see the Note on page 1), you've got a bonus feature called Stacks that lets you open multiple images on separate layers within the same document. It's a *huge* timesaver when you need to combine several images into a collage or several group shots into one perfect image where everyone's eyes are open, when you're editing individual frames of a video, and so on.

To open a group of images as a Stack, choose File→Scripts→ "Load Files into Stack." In the resulting Load Layers dialog box, tell Photoshop where the images are stored on your hard drive and then click OK.

The Load Layers dialog box's Use pop-up menu lets you choose what you want to open: individual images or whole folders of images. If you're combining several shots into one, turn on the "Attempt to Automatically Align Source Images" checkbox. To convert all the layers into a single Smart Object so you can resize the image later, turn on the "Create Smart Object after Loading Layers" checkbox. (For more on using Smart Objects, see page 126.)

■ Changing Your View

Photoshop gives you a variety of ways to look at images. Different views are better for doing different things. For example, you can get rid of the Application Frame (page 11), view images full screen, zoom in and out, or rotate your canvas to view images at an angle. This section teaches you how to do all that and more.

Zooming In and Out

Being able to zoom closely into your image is crucial; it makes fixing imperfections, doing detailed clean-up work, and drawing accurate selections a zillion times easier. One way to zoom is to use the Zoom tool, which looks like a magnifying glass. You can click its icon at the bottom of the Tools panel or simply press Z (see Figure 2-10); then click atop your image, hold down your mouse button, and drag right to zoom in or left to zoom out. Alternatively you can click repeatedly with the Zoom tool to get as up close and personal to those pixels as you want, and then Option-click (Alt-click on a PC) to zoom back out. You can also zoom using your keyboard, which is faster if your hands are already on it: Press ⌘ and the + or – key (Ctrl+plus or Ctrl+minus).

FIGURE 2-10

Top: You can use the Zoom tool to dive into part of your image, though you have to turn off the Scrubby Zoom checkbox in the Options bar first. Then drag with the Zoom tool to draw a box around the pixels you want to look closely at. As soon as you let go of the mouse button, Photoshop zooms in so that the area you selected fills your document window. You can also zoom by typing a percentage into the lower-left corner of the document window (not shown).

Bottom: Zoom in to 501 percent or closer and you'll get this handy pixel-grid view that lets you edit precisely, pixel by pixel. If you're moving items around, this grid makes it easy to see whether pixels are perfectly aligned horizontally and vertically.

> **TIP** To turn off the pixel grid that appears when you're zoomed in to 501 percent or more, choose View→Show→Pixel Grid.

If your computer has a graphics processor that supports *OpenGL* (see the box on page 64), you can hold down your mouse button while the Zoom tool is active to *fly* into your image, zooming to a maximum of 3,200 percent; simply Option-click (Alt-click) and hold down your mouse button to zoom back out. This animated zooming makes you feel like you're flying into and out of the image—and it saves you several mouse clicks along the way.

When the Zoom tool is active, the Options bar gives you the following choices:

- **Resize Windows to Fit.** To have Photoshop resize your document window to accommodate the current magnification level, leave this checkbox turned on.

- **Zoom All Windows.** Turn on this checkbox to use the Zoom tool to zoom in on *all* open windows by the same amount *simultaneously*. This setting is helpful if you've opened a duplicate of an image in order to see what your edits look like at roughly the size the image might print. You can also use the Window→Arrange submenu to do pretty much the same thing. Your options there include these:

    — **Match Zoom.** Zooms all open windows to the same magnification level.

    — **Match Location.** Zooms to the same spot in each window.

    — **Match Rotation.** Rotates each window's canvas to the same angle.

    — **Match All.** Does all of the above.

- **Scrubby Zoom.** This option lets you click and *drag* to zoom. Drag left to zoom out, or right to zoom in.

> **TIP** If you've got a scroll wheel on your mouse, you can use that to zoom, too. Just choose Photoshop→Preferences→General (Edit→Preferences→General on a PC), turn on the "Zoom with Scroll Wheel" checkbox, and then click OK.

- **Actual Pixels.** Click this button to see your image at 100 percent magnification. You can do the same thing by pressing ⌘ 1 (Ctrl 1 on a PC), by double-clicking the Zoom tool in the Tools panel, by entering *100* into the zoom percentage field at the bottom-left corner of the document window, or by choosing View→Actual Pixels. Whew!

POWER USERS' CLINIC

Zooming with Gestures

If you use a Mac with a multitouch trackpad, you've got yet *another* way to zoom even if the Zoom tool isn't active: Use the finger pinch and spread gestures. You can also flick left or right with two fingers to move across the image or twist with your finger and thumb to rotate the canvas.

You can see examples of each of these gestures in the Mouse Preference pane. From the menu, choose System Preferences→Mouse, and then click the Trackpad tab. Pick an item in the action list on the left side of the pane to see that gesture in action.

Zooming with gestures is all well and good...until you accidentally zoom or rotate your canvas by accident. That's why it's helpful to have the ability to turn Photoshop gestures *off*. Choose Photoshop→Preferences→Interface and, in the Options section, turn off Enable Gestures.

If you're using Windows 7 and you've got a touch screen or a graphics tablet (see the box on page 518 for more on the latter), you can use gestures, too, though you don't get the Enable Gestures checkbox described above.

- **Fit Screen.** Clicking this button makes Photoshop resize the active image window to fit the available space on your screen and fit the image inside the document window. (You can also press ⌘-0 (Ctrl+0) or choose View→"Fit on Screen" to do the same thing.) This is incredibly handy when you're using Free Transform (pages 259) on an image that's larger than your document—it's tough to grab bounding-box handles if you can't see 'em!

- **Fill Screen.** This button enlarges your image to the largest possible dimensions within the window. Clicking Fill Screen makes your image a little bigger than it gets when you use Fit Screen because it uses all the available vertical space.

- **Print Size.** When you click this button, Photoshop makes your image the size it'll be when you print it. (You can do the same thing by choosing View→Print Size.) Keep in mind that your monitor's resolution settings can make the print size sample look bigger or smaller than it really will be, so use this feature only as an approximation.

> **TIP** If your image is smaller than the document window (meaning you see a gray border around the edges of the image) or if the document window itself is smaller than the available space in the Application Frame, you can double-click the Hand tool in the Tools panel to make Photoshop enlarge your image so it fills the document window.

Moving Around in an Image

Once you've zoomed in on an image, you can use the Hand tool to move to another area without zooming back out. Grab this tool from the Tools panel or just press and hold the space bar on your keyboard (unless you're typing with the Type tool—then you'll type a bunch of spaces!). When your cursor turns into a hand, hold your mouse button down and then drag to move the image. When you get to the right spot, just let go of your mouse button.

> **TIP** If you press and hold the Shift key while you're using the Hand tool, Photoshop moves *all* your open window content at the same time. (You can do the same thing by turning on the Scroll All Windows checkbox in the Options bar.)

Photoshop CS5 introduced a couple of other ways to move around your document: *flick-panning* and the *birds-eye view* feature. If you've got a computer that can run OpenGL (see the box on page 64), you can use these fast and efficient ways to scoot from one point to another in an image. Here's how they work:

- **Flick-panning** lets you "toss" an image from one side of the document window to the other. Just grab the Hand tool, click your image, and hold down the mouse button. Then, quickly move your mouse in the direction you want to go and then release the button—the image slides along and slowly comes to a stop. You can do the same thing by holding your space bar and then moving your mouse quickly while holding down the mouse button, or while using gestures on a Mac (see the box on page 61).

- **Birds-eye view** lets you zoom out of a *magnified* document quickly to see the whole thing (helpful when you're zoomed in so far that you don't know *where* you are in the image). To use it, just press and hold the H key and then click your image and hold the mouse button down: You'll get an instant aerial view of your image with a box marking the area you're zoomed in on. Let go of your mouse button (and the H key) to zoom back in.

GEM IN THE ROUGH

The Status Bar: Document Info Central

At the bottom of each document window is the *status bar*, shown below, which gives you a quick peek at important info about your document. When you first start using Photoshop, the status bar shows the size of the document; K stands for kilobytes and M for megabytes. (If you don't see any status information, the document's window may be too small. Just drag the lower-right edge of the window to enlarge it.)

Click the little triangle next to the status bar (circled) and you get a menu that lets you control what the bar displays. Here's what you can choose from:

- **Adobe Drive** connects to *Version Cue* servers. Version Cue was Adobe's method of attaching versions and enabling asset management throughout all of its programs. However, Adobe discontinued Version Cue back in Photoshop CS5. For more on Adobe Drive, see the Note on page 32.

- **Document Sizes** displays the image's approximate size for printing (on the left) and its approximate saved size (on the right). This option is selected from the factory.

- **Document Profile** shows the image's color profile (page 674).

- **Document Dimensions** displays the width, height, and resolution of the image.

- In Photoshop CS6 Extended, you can choose **Measurement Scale** to see the scale of pixels compared with other units of measurement. For example, an image from a microscope can measure objects in microns, and each micron can equal a certain number of pixels.

- **Scratch Sizes** tells you how much memory and hard disk space Photoshop is using to display your open documents.

- **Efficiency** lets you know if Photoshop is performing tasks as fast as it possibly can. A number below 100 percent means the program is running slowly because it's relying on scratch-disk space (page 33).

- **Timing** shows how long it took Photoshop to perform the most recent activity.

- **Current Tool** displays the name of the currently active tool.

- **32-bit Exposure** lets you adjust the preview image for 32-bit HDR images (see page 46).

- **Save Progress** displays the world's tiniest status bar, which indicates the progress of Photoshop CS6's new Auto Recovery feature (page 50).

Zoom percentage

Status bar

Getting Oriented with the Navigator Panel

You can think of the Navigator panel as your GPS within Photoshop. If you want to know *exactly* what part of an image you're zoomed in on, it can show you. To open it, choose Window→Navigator. The panel displays a smaller version of your image called a *thumbnail* and marks the area you're zoomed in on with a red box called the *proxy preview*. At the bottom of the panel, the zoom field shows your current magnification level. You can zoom into or out of the image by clicking the zoom buttons at the bottom of the panel (they look like little mountains) or by using the slider nestled between them (see Figure 2-11). To zoom to a specific level, enter a number in the percentage field in the panel's lower left.

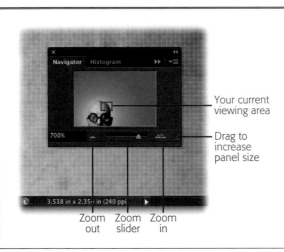

Your current viewing area

Drag to increase panel size

Zoom out   Zoom slider   Zoom in

FIGURE 2-11

As you zoom in on an image, the proxy preview box shrinks because you're looking at a smaller area. You can drag the box around to cruise to another spot in the image.

To make the Navigator panel bigger, drag its bottom-right corner downward. You can change the color of the proxy preview box by choosing Panel Options from the Navigator panel's menu. In the dialog box that appears, click the red color swatch, pick another color from the resulting Color Picker, and then click OK.

UP TO SPEED

Understanding the GPU and OpenGL

You might not know it, but your computer actually has *two* brains: a CPU (central processing unit) for interpreting and executing instructions, and a GPU (graphics processing unit, also called a *video card*) for displaying images and videos.

Newer GPUs take advantage of a technology called *OpenGL* that helps computers draw graphics faster and more efficiently. (To learn more about it, go to *www.opengl.org*.) You can tell whether your GPU uses OpenGL by choosing Photoshop→ Preferences→Performance (Edit→Preferences→Performance on a PC). In the Graphics Processor Settings at the bottom right, check whether the graphics processor listed includes "OpenGL" in its name and whether the Use Graphics Processor checkbox

is turned on (it probably will be). If the checkbox is grayed out (meaning you can't turn it on), then your computer's video card isn't fast enough or doesn't have enough memory to run OpenGL—bummer.

If your computer can't run OpenGL, some Photoshop features will take a long time to run, and others—like flick-panning, canvas rotating, and pixel-grid overlay (Figure 2-10)—won't work at all. Other nifty features in CS6 that require OpenGL include Auto Recovery (page 50), Free Transform→Warp (page 261), Puppet Warp preview (page 448), Liquify (page 428), and Adaptive Wide Angle filters (page 636).

Rotating Your Canvas

If you're an artist, you're gonna love this feature! The Rotate View tool rotates your canvas—without harming any pixels—so you can edit, draw, and paint at a more natural angle (see Figure 2-12). It's like shifting a piece of paper or angling a painting canvas, but it doesn't rotate the actual image—just your *view* of the image. Bear in mind, though, that your computer needs to be able to run OpenGL (page 64) for this feature to work. To use this tool, choose it from within the Hand tool's toolset at the bottom of the Tools panel.

> **NOTE** MacBook, MacBook Air, and MacBook Pro users with multitouch trackpads can rotate the canvas by using the two-finger rotate gesture. See the box on page 61 for more on Mac gestures.

FIGURE 2-12

Grab the Rotate View tool, mouse over to your image, and then drag diagonally up or down to rotate it. When you drag, a compass appears that shows how far from "north" you're rotating the canvas, as shown here. If you're not the dragging kind, you can type a number into the Options bar's Rotation Angle field or spin the little round dial to the field's right. To straighten your canvas back out, click the Reset View button (also in the Options bar). To rotate all open images, turn on the Rotate All Windows checkbox.

This tool is especially handy if you use a graphics tablet (page 518) and you're retouching people (Chapter 10) or using Photoshop's painting tools (Chapter 12).

■ Arranging Open Images

The Application Frame and tabbed-document workspace help you manage several open documents; if you turn off the Application Frame, your documents can get scattered across your screen. However, you can herd those open windows together by using the commands listed under Window→Arrange (see Figure 2-13).

Photoshop CS6 offers a slew of new choices that used to live in the Arrange Documents menu of the now-deceased Application bar:

- **Tile All Vertically** resizes your windows so you can see them all in vertical columns.

- **Tile All Horizontally** does nearly the same thing, but arranges them in horizontal rows.

- **2-up, 3-up Horizontal** resizes two or three windows so they fit one on top of the other in horizontal rows.

- **2-up, 3-up Vertical** resizes two or three windows so they fit side by side in vertical columns.

- **3-up Stacked** resizes three windows side by side with one in a vertical column and two in horizontal rows.

- **4-up, 6-up** resizes four or six windows side by side in a tic tac toe–style grid.

> **NOTE** You can select a 2-up option only if you have two images open, a 3-up option if you have three images open, and so on. If you've got fewer images open, the commands listed above are grayed out.

- **Consolidate All to Tabs** groups your open images in a single, tabbed window (as shown in Figure 2-14, top).

- **Cascade** stacks your windows on top of one another, putting the largest one on the bottom and the smallest on the top.

- **Tile** resizes your windows to identical sizes and arranges them in rows and columns.

- **Float in Window** puts the current document in its own window if it's part of a tabbed group of documents that share the same window.

- **Float All in Windows** splits all tabbed documents out into their own windows and cascades the new windows.

> **TIP** You can Control-click (right-click on a PC) a document's tab to reveal a shortcut menu that lets you close the window, close all windows, create a new document, open an existing one, or reveal where that document lives on your hard drive.

FIGURE 2-13

Use the Window→Arrange commands to create order out of chaos by tiling (top) or cascading (bottom) your windows. (You can't cascade tabbed documents because they're attached—or rather, docked—to the top of the Photoshop window. The fix is to choose Window→Arrange→ "Float All in Windows" first, and then choose Cascade.)

Sadly, the Arrange Documents menu disappeared in CS6 along with the Application bar. Ah, well—Adobe giveth and Adobe taketh away.

UP TO SPEED

Document Size vs. Canvas Space

One thing that's super confusing to Photoshop beginners is the difference between document size (also known as image size) and canvas size. In Photoshop, the *canvas* is the amount of viewable and editable area in a document (it's the same as the document's dimensions) and you can add to or subtract from it anytime. By doing so, you add or subtract pixels from the image, which either increases or decreases the document size.

For example, say you're designing a poster for a chili cook-off and you're experimenting with the design. Instead of limiting your work area to the final size of the poster, you can make the canvas bigger than that (page 253) so you have room to spread out and try different design ideas. Then, once you've nailed down the final design, you can crop (page 222) or trim (page 230) it back down to size.

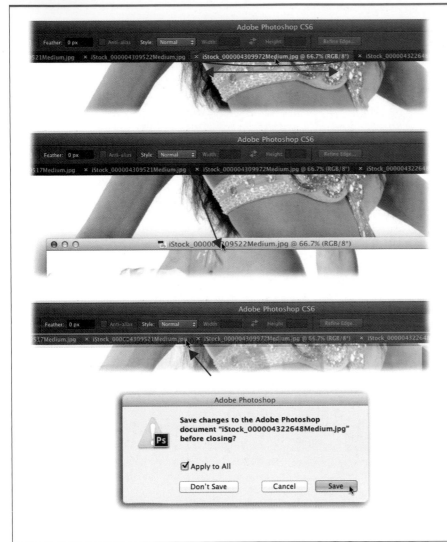

FIGURE 2-14

Photoshop's tabbed document feature is a handy way of organizing open windows. You can slide the tabs left or right to rearrange them (top) or drag a tab out of the tab area to create a floating window (upper middle). To redock a floating window, just drag its tab back into the main tab area (lower middle).

You can close all tabbed documents by choosing File→Close All. If Photoshop sees that you've edited some or all of those images, it asks if you'd like to save each edited image before closing it. To apply your answer to all the documents you're closing, turn on the "Apply to All" checkbox, shown here (bottom). If the Move tool is active, you can Option-click (Shift-click) the tiny X at the far left (far right on a PC) of each document tab to close all open documents, but for unknown reasons you don't get the "Apply to All" option with this method. Weird!

TIP You can cycle through all open documents by using the ⌘-tilde (~) keyboard shortcut (Ctrl+Tab on a PC). To cycle through documents in the reverse order, press Shift-⌘-tilde (Shift+Ctrl+Tab). This is especially handy when you're showing off images in Full Screen mode, as described on page 16.

■ Guides, Grids, and Rulers

Placing all the components of your design in just the right spots can be challenging, and if you're a real stickler for details, close isn't good enough. This section teaches you how to use Photoshop's guides, grids, and rulers to get everything positioned *perfectly*. Adobe calls these little helpers *extras,* and in Photoshop CS6 you access them via the View menu.

Rulers and Guiding Lines

Properly positioning objects on your canvas can be the difference between a basic design and a masterpiece. The quickest way to position and align objects is by drawing a straight line to nestle them against. You can do just that using Photoshop's nonprinting *guides*—vertical and horizontal lines you can place anywhere you want (see Figure 2-15).

FIGURE 2-15

Guides help you position items exactly where you want 'em. Here, the light blue (cyan) guides help make sure all the text is the same width and the edges of the poster are free of clutter. The guides won't show up when you print the image, so you don't have to worry about deleting them.

To add a guide in a certain spot in a document, choose View→New Guide and then enter the position in the resulting dialog box. If you have trouble grabbing a guide to move it, try making the document window bigger than the canvas by dragging any edge of the document window, or its lower-right corner, diagonally. That way, the guides extend beyond the canvas so they don't overlap other elements that you might accidentally grab.

Before you can create guides, you need to turn on Photoshop's rulers. The fastest way to do that is by pressing ⌘-R (Ctrl+R on a PC), but you can also turn them on by choosing View→Rulers. Whichever method you use, the rulers appear on the top and left edges of the image window. (The units on the rulers are controlled by the settings in the Units & Rulers preferences.)

Once you've turned rulers on, you can add a guide by clicking either the horizontal or vertical ruler, and then dragging the guide into your document as shown in Figure 2-15 (you won't see the guide until you start dragging). After that, you can do any of the following:

- **Move the guide** by grabbing the Move tool (see Appendix C, online) from the Tools panel or by pressing V, and then dragging the guide to a new position (your cursor turns into a double-sided arrow like the one circled in Figure 2-15).

- **Snap objects to the guide** by turning on Photoshop's *snap* feature. Snapping makes it super easy to align objects because when they get close to one of your guides, they jump to it as if they were magnetized. You can tell that an object has snapped to the nearest guide because it pops into place. After the object aligns to a guide, you can move it along that line to snap it into place with other guides, too. If you don't want an object aligned with a certain guide, just keep moving it—it'll let go of the guide as soon as you move it far enough. This feature is turned on out of the box, though you can turn it off by choosing View→Snap To→Guides (handy when you can't position an object where you want to because it keeps snapping to align with a guide).

> **NOTE** Straight from the factory objects snap to grids (page 71), layers (Chapter 3), slices (Chapter 17), *and* the edges of your document. You can choose among these items by choosing View→Snap To and then picking the elements you *really* want objects to align with. For example, choosing both Guides and Layers makes the object you're moving snap to guides *and* the edges of objects on other layers.

- **Hide the guide** temporarily by pressing ⌘-; (Ctrl+; on a PC) or by choosing View→Show→Guides.

- **Delete a guide** by dragging it into the ruler area.

- **Delete all guides** by choosing View→Clear Guides.

- **Lock all guides** by choosing View→Lock Guides or pressing Option-⌘; (Alt+Ctrl;)—useful when you don't want to accidentally move a guide.

■ SMART GUIDES

Smart Guides are a little different from regular guides in that they automatically appear onscreen to show the spatial relationship between objects. For example, they pop up when objects are aligned or evenly spaced in your document. As you drag an object, Smart Guides appear whenever the current object is horizontally, vertically, or centrally aligned with other objects on other layers. To turn on Smart Guides, choose View→Show→Smart Guides. You can see 'em in action in on page 103.

■ USING THE DOCUMENT GRID

If you want *lots* of guides without all the work of placing them, you can add a grid to your image instead by choosing View→Show→Grid. Straight from the factory, Photoshop's gridlines are spaced an inch apart with four subdivisions, although you can change that by choosing Photoshop→Preferences→"Guides, Grid & Slices" (Edit→Preferences→"Guides, Grid & Slices" on a PC), as Figure 2-16 explains.

FIGURE 2-16

Photoshop's grid is helpful when you need to align lots of different items, like the text shown here. You can turn it on by pressing ⌘-' (Ctrl+' on a PC).

In the Preferences dialog box, adjust the gridline marks by changing the number in the Gridline Every field, and use the pop-up menu next to it to change the grid's unit of measurement: pixels, inches, centimeters, millimeters, points, picas, or percent. Use the Subdivisions field to control how many lines appear between each gridline—if any.

TIP To turn off *all* of Photoshop's extras—that is, guides, grid, and slices—in one fell swoop, choose View→Extras.

The Ruler Tool

In addition to the rulers you learned about earlier, Photoshop also gives you a virtual tape measure and protractor: the Ruler tool, which lets you measure the distance between two points in a document. Just grab the tool by pressing Shift-I repeatedly (it's hiding in the eyedropper toolset and it looks like a little ruler), and then click and hold your mouse button where you want to start measuring. Drag across the area or object, and you'll see a line appear in your document (see Figure 2-17).

FIGURE 2-17

To measure a perfectly straight horizontal or vertical line, press and hold the Shift key as you drag. When you release your mouse button, Photoshop displays the measurement between the line's start and end points in the Options bar.

When you're using the Ruler tool, the Options bar's measurements get a little confusing. Here's what they mean:

- **X and Y.** These *axes* mark the horizontal and vertical coordinates (respectively) at the start of your ruler line. For example, if you start the line at the 4-inch mark on the horizontal ruler and the 7-inch mark on the vertical ruler, your coordinates are X: 4 and Y: 7.

- **W and H.** Calculates the distance your line has traveled from the X and Y axes.

- **A.** Displays the angle of the line relative to the X axis.

- **L1.** Indicates the length of the line.

- **L2.** You see a number here only if you use a virtual *protractor*. (Thought you left protractors behind in high school, didn't you? Quick refresher: Protractors help you measure angles.) To create a protractor, Option-drag (Alt-drag on a PC) at an angle from the end of your ruler line, or just double-click the line and then drag. This number represents the angle between the two lines.

- **Use Measurement Scale.** Photoshop includes a set of rulers, but it has nothing upon which to *base* the measurements you make with those rulers. For example, a photo of a garden gnome doesn't indicate its actual size; if you measure the width of the gnome in Photoshop, it could be .25 inch or 25 pixels—depending upon the unit of measurement you've picked in Units & Rulers preferences—rather than its real-world size of 6 inches. However, by choosing Image→Analysis→Set Measurement Scale→Custom and then entering the logical (real-world) length of an inch or pixel, you give Photoshop a scale upon which to base its measurements. This new scale is used when you turn on Use Measurement Scale in the Options bar and is available in the Extended version only.

- **Straighten Layer.** To use the Ruler tool to straighten your image, draw a line across an area that should be straight (like the horizon). Then click this button, and Photoshop straightens and crops the image. To make Photoshop straighten the image without cropping it, Option-click (Alt-click on a PC) this button instead. (If you forget to press Option [Alt], you can undo the crop by pressing ⌘-Z [Ctrl+Z].)

NOTE In Photoshop CS6, image straightening is a feature of the Crop tool, too (see page 222 for the scoop). You can also straighten images using Camera Raw, as explained on page 236.

- **Clear.** Any ruler line you draw hangs around until you tell it to go away by clicking this button or drawing another ruler line. But ruler lines don't print even if you forget to clear them, so don't lose any sleep over 'em.

TIP To change the angle of a ruler line, just grab one of its end points and drag it to another spot. To move a ruler line, grab it anywhere *other* than the end points and drag it to another location.

Layers: The Key to Nondestructive Editing

Photoshop gives you two ways to edit files: destructively and nondestructively. *Destructive editing* means you're changing the original image—once you exceed the History panel's limit (page 25), those changes are (gulp) permanent. *Nondestructive editing* means you're not changing the original file and you can go back to it at any time. Folks new to image editing tend to use the first method and experienced pixel-jockeys the second—and you'll likely see a tiny cloud of smugness floating above the latter.

When you're working in Photoshop, you need to keep your documents as flexible as possible. People (even you!) change their minds hourly about what looks good, what they want, and where they want it—all of which is no big deal if you're prepared for that. If not, you'll spend a ton of time *redoing* what you've already done from scratch. To avoid that kind of suffering, you can use *layers*, a set of stackable transparencies that together form a whole image (see Figure 3-1). Layers are your ticket to nondestructive editing.

With layers, you can make all kinds of changes to an image without altering the original. For example, you can use one layer to color-correct your family reunion photo (Chapter 9), another to whiten Aunt Bessie's teeth (page 425), and yet another to add a photo of the Great Pyramid to make the reunion look like it was held in Egypt instead of at the local park (page 275). Using layers also lets you do the following:

- Resize an object independently of everything else in the document, without changing the document's size (page 44).

- Move an object around without moving anything else (page 100).

- Combine several images into one document to make a collage (page 103).

- Hide parts of an image so you can see through to layers below (page 116).

- Change the opacity of a layer to make it more or less see-through (page 97).

- Change the way colors on various layers interact with one another (page 280).

- Fix the color and lighting of a photo (or just parts of it) without harming the original (see Figure 3-28 on page 122).

The best part about using layers is that once you save a document as a PSD file (page 49), you can close it, forget about it, and open it next week to find your layers—and all your changes—intact. Learning to love layers is the key to a successful Photoshop career because they let you edit with maximum flexibility.

In this chapter, you'll learn about the different kinds of layers, when to use them, and how to create them. You'll also find out about the fun and useful features that tag along with layers, like layer styles and layer masks. By the time you're done, you'll be shouting the praises of nondestructive editing from the highest rooftop! (Whether you do it smugly or not is up to you.)

FIGURE 3-1

You can think of layers as a stack of slides. If some parts of the top layer are transparent, you can see through those areas to the layers below.

If you look straight down at the top of the stack for a bird's-eye view, you see a single image even though it's made up of pieces and parts of several different transparencies. This kind of image is called a composite.

◼ Layer Basics

Layers come in many flavors, all of which have their own special purpose:

- **Image layers.** These layers are pixel-based (page 52), and you'll work with them *all* the time. If you open a photo or add a new, empty layer and paint on it (Chapter 12), you've got yourself an Image layer.

- **Type layers.** In Photoshop, text isn't made from pixels, so it gets its own special kind of layer. Anytime you grab the Type tool and start pecking away, Photoshop automatically creates a Type layer. See Chapter 14 for the full story on creating text in Photoshop.

- **Shape layers.** These layers are vector-based (page 52), meaning they're not made from pixels. Not only can you create useful shapes quickly with these babies, but you can also resize 'em without losing quality *and* change their fill color by double-clicking their layer thumbnails or using CS6's new Fill and Stroke settings in the Options bar. Photoshop creates a Shape layer automatically anytime you use a shape tool, unless you change the tool's mode as explained in Chapter 13 (page 537).

- **Fill layers.** When it comes to changing or adding color to an image, these layers are your best friends. They let you fill a layer with a solid color, gradient, or pattern, which comes in handy when you want to create new backgrounds or fill a selection with color. Just like Shape layers, you can double-click a Fill layer's thumbnail to change its color anytime. The next time you're tempted to add an empty layer and fill it with color (page 93), try using one of these layers instead.

- **Adjustment layers.** These ever-so-useful layers let you apply color and brightness changes to all the layers underneath them, but the *changes* actually happen on the Adjustment layer. For example, if you want to change a color image to black and white, you can use a Black & White Adjustment layer (page 312) and the color removal happens on its *own* layer, leaving the original unharmed. These layers don't contain any pixels, just instructions that tell Photoshop what changes you want to make. You can access these handy helpers in the Adjustments panel on the right side of the Photoshop window (if you don't see it, choose Window→Adjustments), via the Adjustment layer menu at the bottom of the Layers panel (it looks like a half-black/half-white circle), or in the Layer menu (choose Layer→New Adjustment layer). There are 15 kinds of Adjustment layers, and you'll learn how to use 'em in Part 2 of this book.

- **Smart Objects.** Adobe refers to this kind of layer as a *container*, though "miracle layer" is a better description. Smart Objects let you work with files that weren't created with Photoshop, like Raw (page 57) and vector files (page 52). The best thing about a Smart Object is that you can swap and resize its content without trashing its quality (as long as you don't exceed the file's original pixel dimensions, unless it's a vector). Flip to page 126 for more info.

- **Video layers.** New in the standard version of CS6 (see the Note on page 1) is the ability to import, edit, and export video (previously, these options were available only in the Extended version). You can use Photoshop to edit and apply custom color effects and filters to individual video frames as easily as you can any other layer type. You'll learn all about editing videos in Chapter 20.

- **3D layers.** In the Extended version of Photoshop, you can import 3D files into their own special layers, which is helpful if you want to create 3D objects or paint them. For a little more on 3D, head to this book's Missing CD page at *www.missingmanuals.com/cds*.

The Layers Panel

No matter what kinds of layers your document contains, the one that's most important to you at any given time is the *active* layer. You can tell which layer is active by peeking at the Layers panel, where Photoshop highlights it in blue, as shown in Figure 3-2. (To open the Layers panel, click its tab in the panel dock on the right side of your screen, or choose Window→Layers.) The next edit you make will affect *only* that layer.

Double-click tab to
collapse vertically

Panel
menu

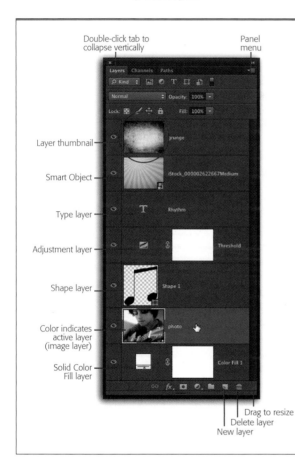

Layer thumbnail

Smart Object

Type layer

Adjustment layer

Shape layer

Color indicates
active layer
(image layer)

Solid Color
Fill layer

Drag to resize
Delete layer
New layer

FIGURE 3-2

In the Layers panel, Photoshop highlights the currently active layer in blue, as shown here (the exact color of blue depends on the color theme you're using [page 16]). Each layer has its own little preview of what the layer contains, called a layer thumbnail *(circled). (To make layer thumbnails bigger so they're easier to see, open the panel menu labeled here and then choose Panel Options. The resulting dialog box includes a list of thumbnail sizes to choose from. Alternatively, in CS6 you can Ctrl-click or right-click the layer thumbnail and choose a size from the resulting shortcut menu.)*

If you're trying to use a tool and Photoshop doesn't seem to be responding, take a peek at the Layers panel and make sure you've got the right layer activated. Nine times out of ten, you'll find that you don't!

Activating Layers

About the easiest thing you'll ever do in Photoshop is activate a layer—just mouse over to the Layers panel and click the layer you want to work on. However, just because this process is easy doesn't mean it's unimportant. As you learned in the last section, whatever you're doing in Photoshop affects only the *currently active layer*.

As your document gets more complex and your Layers panel starts to grow (and it will), it can be hard to figure out which layer each part of the image lives on. If you want, you can make Photoshop *guess* which layer an object is on: Press V to activate the Move tool, head up to the Options bar at the top of your screen, turn on the Auto-Select checkbox, and then choose Layer from the pop-up menu to its right (the other option, Group, is discussed on page 108). After that, when you click an object in the document, Photoshop activates the layer it *thinks* that object is on (it'll do this next time you use the Move tool, too, unless you turn off the Auto-Select option). The program may or may not guess right, and it really works only if your layers don't completely cover each other up. If you've got a document full of isolated objects—ones without backgrounds—on different layers, give this feature a shot. But if you're working on a multilayered collage, forget it. For that reason, you'll probably want to leave Auto-Select turned *off*.

TIP You can have Photoshop narrow down your layer-hunting options by prodding it to give you a list of layers it *thinks* an object is on. Press V to grab the Move tool, Control-click (right-click) an object in your document, and then choose one of the layers from the resulting shortcut menu. This trick only works if the layer's visibility eye is turned on and you click an area that's more than *10* percent opaque (it was 50 percent in previous versions of the program).

■ ACTIVATING MULTIPLE LAYERS

You'd be surprised how often you need to do the same thing to more than one layer. If you want to rearrange a few of them in your layer stack (page 85), move 'em around in your document together (page 100), or resize them simultaneously (page 98), you need to activate them first. Photoshop lets you activate as few or as many as you want, though how you go about it depends on where they live in the Layers panel:

- **All layers.** To activate the whole kit and caboodle, choose Select→All Layers. Choose Deselect→All Layers to (you guessed it) deactivate everything. Keyboard shortcut: ⌘-Shift-A or Ctrl+Alt+A on a PC.

- **Consecutive layers.** To activate layers that are next to each other in the Layers panel, click the first one and then Shift-click the last one; Photoshop automatically activates everything in between (see Figure 3-3, left).

- **Nonconsecutive layers.** To activate layers that *aren't* next to each other, click the first one's name and then ⌘-click (Ctrl-click on a PC) the rest of them (see Figure 3-3, right).

- **Linked layers.** If you've linked any layers together (page 106), you can activate them all by choosing Layer→Select Linked Layers. This command also lives in the Layers panel's menu—the one in its upper right—as well as the shortcut menu you get by Ctrl-clicking (right-clicking on a PC) to the right of the layer thumbnail.

NOTE Activating a layer is *completely* different from loading a layer's contents as a selection. When you load a layer as a selection, you see marching ants running around whatever is on that layer. Activating a layer simply makes that layer active so you can perform other edits. See Chapter 4 for more on selections.

Click in this area to activate a layer

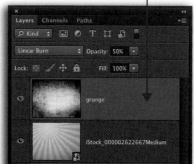

FIGURE 3-3

You can activate consecutive layers (left) or nonconsecutive layers (right). To avoid loading a layer as a selection (page 141) when you're selecting nonconsecutive layers, make sure you ⌘-click (Ctrl-click) the area to the right of the layer thumbnail, as shown here.

■ FILTERING LAYERS

If your list of layers is *really* long, you'll have to scroll through the Layers panel to find the ones you want to activate. However, in CS6 you can make Photoshop *hide* layers based on conditions you specify using the new row of filtering controls at the top of the Layers panel (labeled in Figure 3-4, top). You tell Photoshop which layers you want to view, and it temporarily hides the rest in the Layers panel (though the content of those layers is still visible in your document).

To filter layers, you pick an option from the pop-up menu in the upper left of the Layers panel, and then use the controls to the menu's right to refine your search. Here are your options:

- **Kind.** This is what the pop-up menu is set to unless you change it. This option lets you tell Photoshop what *type* of layers you want to see. Use the buttons to this menu's right to have Photoshop display only the Image, Adjustment, Type, or Shape layers, or Smart Objects. For example, to see only the Type layers—so you can activate 'em all and change their fonts, say—make sure the pop-up menu is set to Kind (it should be unless you've changed it) and then click the T button to its right, and Photoshop hides all the layers in the Layers panel *except* the Type layers (see Figure 3-4, bottom). You can also click more than one button to see more than one kind of layer—like the Type and Shape layers, say.

- **Name.** If you've given your layers meaningful names, choose this option from the pop-up menu and a search field appears to the menu's right. Enter some text (it's not case-sensitive) and Photoshop displays only the layers whose names include what you entered. You don't need to press Return/Enter—Photoshop begins filtering layers as soon as you start typing.

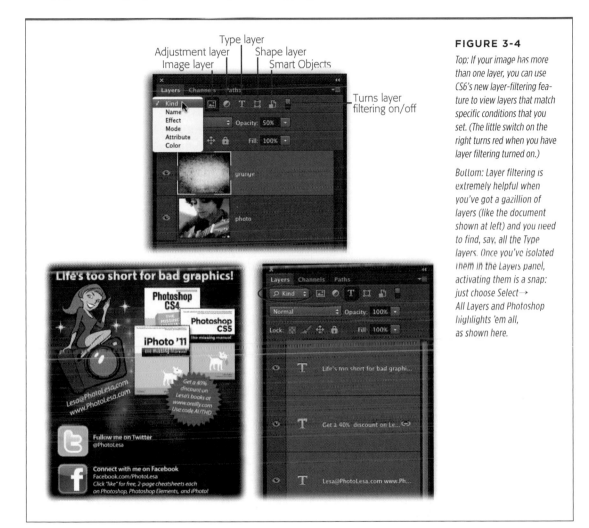

FIGURE 3-4

Top: If your image has more than one layer, you can use CS6's new layer-filtering feature to view layers that match specific conditions that you set. (The little switch on the right turns red when you have layer filtering turned on.)

Bottom: Layer filtering is extremely helpful when you've got a gazillion of layers (like the document shown at left) and you need to find, say, all the Type layers. Once you've isolated them in the Layers panel, activating them is a snap: just choose Select→ All Layers and Photoshop highlights 'em all, as shown here.

TIP   When you choose Select→Find Layers or press Shift-Option-⌘-F (Shift+Alt+Ctrl+F on a PC), Photoshop CS6 automatically sets the filtering pop-up menu to Name and plops a cursor into the text field to its right so you can start typing.

- **Effect.** This option lets you filter layers based on layer styles (page 131). For example, to see all the layers that have a drop shadow, choose this option and then choose Drop Shadow from the pop-up menu that appears to this menu's right.

- **Mode.** To filter layers based on their blend modes (page 280), pick this option and then choose the blend mode you're after from the pop-up menu that appears on the right.

- **Attribute.** When you pick this option, a pop-up menu appears that lets you filter layers based on whether or not they're visible, empty, locked or linked to other layers (page 106), clipped to other layers (page 126), include a pixel- or vector-based layer mask (page 116), include effects (think layer styles [page 131]), or use advanced blending options (page 293).

- **Color.** If you've color-coded your layers (page 105), you can use this option to view layers labeled with a certain color. For example, if you applied a red label to all the layers you used to fix skin imperfections in a portrait, choose this option and then pick Red from the pop-up menu that appears to its right and Photoshop displays only those layers.

After you've filtered the layers so that only the ones you're interested in are visible, you can quickly activate all the visible ones—save for a locked Background layer—by choosing Select→All Layers. You can work with filtered layers just like any other layers: Delete 'em, change their stacking order, and so on. Your filter remains in effect until you turn it off or close the document (Photoshop doesn't save your layer filter settings when you save the document).

When you're ready to see *all* the layers again, *Option*-click (Alt-click on a PC) the little red switch near the top right of the Layers panel; it turns gray to let you know it's turned off. Photoshop reveals all your layers and then sets the filtering controls to their factory settings so you can use 'em again. (If you just click the switch, Photoshop still shows all your layers but it takes several more clicks to use layer filtering again: you have to click the switch *again* to turn it back on and *then* tweak the filtering options to reveal the layers you want. Yuck.)

> **NOTE** In light of the new layer filtering features in Photoshop CS6, Adobe removed the Select→Similar Layers command. Hooray! It's a rare thing when a menu gets *shortened*.

Adding New Layers

Most of the time, Photoshop creates new layers *for* you, like when you copy and paste an image (page 92), create text (page 582), draw a shape (page 550), and so on. But if you want to do something like paint with the Brush tool—to colorize a grayscale image (page 343), say—you need to create a new layer manually. Otherwise, you'll paint right on your original image. Photoshop gives you five ways to create a new layer:

- Click the "Create a new layer" button at the bottom of the Layers panel (it looks like a piece of paper with a folded corner).

- Choose Layer→New→Layer.

- Choose New Layer from the Layers panel's menu.

- Press Shift-⌘-N (Shift+Ctrl+N on a PC).

- Drag a file from your desktop into an open Photoshop document; the item you dragged appears on its own layer in the document—as a Smart Object to boot! (See the Tip on page 54 for more on this feature.)

When you click the "Create a new layer" button, Photoshop creates an empty layer called *Layer 1*, though you can double-click this name in the Layers panel to change it. (If you already have a layer called *Layer 1*, Photoshop names the new one *Layer 2*, and so on.) If you use the menu options or keyboard shortcut instead, the program displays the New Layer dialog box (Figure 3-5) where you can name the layer, color code it (page 105), choose its blend mode (page 280), set its opacity, and use it in a clipping mask (see the box on page 126). Whichever method you use, Photoshop adds the new layer above the one that was active when you added it.

> **TIP** If your fingers are flexible enough, you can create a new layer *and* bypass the New Layer dialog box by pressing Shift-*Option*-⌘-N (Shift+Alt+*Ctrl*+N on a PC). This shortcut is handy if you want new layers and don't care what they're called.

FIGURE 3-5

In the New Layer dialog box (top), you can give your layer a name and a colored label. Color-coding layers makes them easier to spot in a long Layers panel (bottom).

You can double-click a layer's name to rename it, and turn its visibility on or off by clicking the little eye icon to the left of its thumbnail. The new layer's thumbnail shown here is the checkerboard pattern because the layer is empty and transparent. (See the box on page 47 for more on transparency.)

TIP To create a new layer *below* the one that's currently active, ⌘-click (Ctrl-click) the "Create a new layer" button at the bottom of the Layers panel. (If the only layer in your document is the locked Background layer, you've got to double-click it to make it editable before you can add a new layer below it.) This shortcut saves you the extra step of dragging the new layer to a lower position later; over the course of a year, this tip has been known to produce an *entire* vacation day!

Hiding and Showing Layers

The little visibility eye to the left of each layer lets you turn that layer off and on (Figure 3-5, bottom). Photoshop calls this incredibly useful feature *hiding*. Here are some examples of what hiding layers lets you do:

- **See an instant before-and-after preview.** If you've spent some time color correcting (Chapter 9) or retouching people (Chapter 10) on duplicate layers, hiding the layers you used to do that is an easy way to see the effect of your handiwork.

- **Experiment with different looks.** If you're trying out different backgrounds or background colors, you can add them all to your document and then turn them on one at a time to see which one looks best.

- **See what you're doing.** When you're working on a document that has a bunch of layers, some of them may hide an area you need to see or work on. The solution is to hide in-the-way layers while you're working on those parts of the image and then turn 'em back on when you're done.

- **Print certain layers.** Only layers that are visible in your document will print, so if you want to print only parts of an image, hide the other layers first.

To hide a layer, simply click the little eye to the left of its layer thumbnail; to show it again, click the empty square where the eye was. To hide *all* layers except one, Option-click (Alt-click on a PC) the visibility eye of the layer you want to see; to display the other layers again, Option-click (Alt-click) that same layer's visibility eye again. Alternatively, you can Control-click (right-click) a layer's visibility eye (or, if the layer is hidden, the spot where the eye was) and then choose "Show/Hide this layer" or "Show/Hide all other layers" from the shortcut menu. You can also find the Show/Hide Layers command in the Layer menu.

TIP To hide or show several layers, drag up or down over their visibility eyes in the Layers panel while holding down your mouse button.

Restacking Layers

Once you start adding layers, you can change their *stacking order*—the order they're listed in the Layers panel—to control what's visible and what's not. When you think about stacking order, pretend you're peering down at your Layers panel from above: The layer at the very top can hide any layers below it. For example, if you fill a layer with color (page 93) and then place it above another layer containing a photo, the color will completely cover the photo. But if you've merely painted a swish or two with the Brush tool, your brushstrokes will cover just that *part* of the photo.

You can rearrange your layers manually, or make Photoshop do it for you:

- **By dragging.** Click a layer's thumbnail and drag it up or down to change its position as shown in Figure 3-6. (Technically, you can click the layer *anywhere* to grab it, but targeting the thumbnail is a good habit to get into, lest Photoshop think you want to rename the layer instead.) When you get it in the right place, let go of your mouse button.

Shortcuts for Activating and Moving Layers

It's a little-known fact that you can use keyboard shortcuts to activate and move layers. This trick can be a real timesaver since you don't have to lift your hands off the keyboard. It's also helpful when you're creating actions (discussed in Chapter 18). Here's the rather complicated list of shortcuts:

- To activate the layer *below* the current layer (and deactivate the current layer), press Option-[(Alt+[on a PC). To activate the layer *above* the current layer, press Option] (Alt+]). You can also use these two keyboard shortcuts to cycle through all layers.

- To grab a bunch of layers in a row, activate the first layer and then press Shift-Option-[(Shift+Alt+[) to activate the layer below it (while keeping the first layer active), or Shift-Option-] (Shift+Alt+]) to activate the layer above it. This shortcut lets you grab one layer at a time; just keep pressing the [or] key to grab more layers.

- To activate the top layer in the Layers panel, press Option-. (Alt+.)—that's Option or Alt plus the period key. To activate the bottom layer, press Option , (Alt+,)—Option or Alt plus the comma key.

- To activate all the layers between the currently active layer and the top layer, press Shift-Option-. (Shift+Alt+.)—Option or Alt plus Shift and the period key. To activate all the layers between the currently active layer and the bottom layer, press Shift-Option , (Shift+Alt+,)—Option or Alt plus Shift and the comma key.

- To activate every layer *except* the locked Background layer, press ⌘-Option-A (Ctrl+Alt+A). If you've unlocked the Background layer (page 87), it gets activated, too.

- To move the current layer up one slot in your layer stack, press ⌘-] (Ctrl+]). To move it down one slot, press ⌘-[(Ctrl+[).

- To move the current layer to the top of the layer stack, press Shift-⌘-] (Shift+Ctrl+]). To move it to the bottom of the layer stack—but still above the Background layer, if you've got one—press Shift-⌘-[(Shift+Ctrl+[).

Page 100 has more about moving layers around.

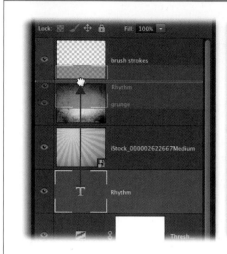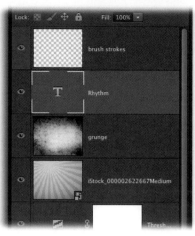

FIGURE 3-6

To rearrange layers, simply drag a layer's thumbnail up or down. When you drag, your cursor turns into a tiny closed fist as shown here (left). As you drag, you see a ghost image of the layer you're dragging, which is helpful visual feedback. When the dividing line between two layers changes so it looks more like a gap (left), let go of your mouse button to make the layer you dragged hop in between them (right).

- **Using the Arrange command.** If you've got one or more layers activated, you can choose Layer→Arrange to move them somewhere else in the layer stack. Depending on the location of the layer(s) in the Layers panel, you can choose from these commands:

    — **Bring to Front** moves the layer(s) all the way to the top of the layer stack. Keyboard shortcut: ⌘-Shift-] (Ctrl+Shift+] on a PC).

    — **Bring Forward** moves the layer(s) up one level. Keyboard shortcut: ⌘-] (Ctrl-]).

    — **Send Backward** sends the layer(s) down one level. Keyboard shortcut: ⌘-[(Ctrl-[).

    — **Send to Back** sends the layer(s) all the way to the bottom of the layer stack (or just above the Background layer, if you've got one). Keyboard shortcut: ⌘-Shift-[(Ctrl-Shift+[).

    — **Reverse.** If you've got two or more layers activated, this command inverts the stacking order of the active layers. You probably won't use this command very often, but give it a try just for fun; it can produce some mildly interesting results. (There's no keyboard shortcut for this one).

> **NOTE** If you've got a long Layers panel, these keyboard shortcuts can save you lots of time.

The only layer you *can't* move around (at least not without giving it some special treatment) is a locked *Background layer*. The Background layer isn't really a layer, although it looks like one. It behaves a little differently from other layers, as the box on page 87 explains, so if you want to move it around it in the Layers panel, you first have to double-click its thumbnail and then rename it—or simply click OK—in the resulting New Layer dialog box. When you do, it becomes a normal, everyday layer that you can position wherever you want.

To *really* understand how layer stacking works, it helps to put theory into practice. Let's say you want to make a photo look like one side of it fades to white and then add some text on top of the white part. To do that, you need to place the photo at the bottom of the layer stack, the white paint layer in the middle, and the text layer on top (see Figure 3-7).

UP TO SPEED

The Background Layer and You

Only a handful of image file formats understand Photoshop's layer system: PSD (Photoshop) and TIFF are the two most popular. Most other image file formats can handle only *flat* images (unlayered files). So if you save a multilayered PSD file as a JPEG, EPS, or PNG file, for example, Photoshop flattens it, smashing all the layers into one. (See page 115 for more on flattening files.)

When you open an image created by a device or program that *doesn't* understand layers, like your digital camera or desktop scanner, Photoshop opens it as a flat image with a single layer named Background. Though a Background layer looks like a regular layer, it's not nearly as flexible as the layers you create in Photoshop. For example, you can paint on it with the Brush tool (page 497), select part of it and then fill the selection with color (page 185), or use any of the retouching tools on it (Chapter 10), but you can't use the Move tool to make it hang off the edges of your document or make any part of it transparent—if you try to use the Eraser tool, nothing happens other than painting with the background color (and you can almost *hear* Photoshop snickering at your efforts). Also, if you make a selection and press Delete (Backspace on a PC) or use the Crop tool to make your canvas bigger (page 228), Photoshop fills that area with the color of your background chip (page 23).

The same thing happens when you create a *new* document in Photoshop: the program opens a more universally compatible flat file containing only a Background layer. You can convert this Background layer into a fully editable and movable layer in a couple of different ways. The easiest way is to double-click the Background layer in the Layers panel and then click OK (you can also give it a new name if you'd like). You can also activate the Background layer in the Layers panel and then choose Layer → New → "Layer from Background," or ⌘-click (right-click) the Background layer and choose "New layer from Background" from the resulting menu.

The only way to create a new document *without* a Background layer is to choose Transparent from the Background Contents pop-up menu (see page 47). Otherwise, you're doomed to double-clicking and renaming the Background layer each time you create a new document.

If you want, you can convert a normal layer into a Background layer by choosing Layer → New → "Background from Layer," but it's tough to think of a reason why you'd want to. If you do this, Photoshop politely moves it to the bottom of the layer stack for you.

Duplicating and Deleting Layers

Duplicating a layer comes in handy when you want to do something destructive like sharpen an image (Chapter 11) or soften Great-Grandma's skin (page 433). By duplicating the image layer first, you can work on a *copy* of the image instead of the original. But duplicating isn't limited to whole layers; you can duplicate just *part* of a layer. That technique comes in handy when you want to whiten teeth or make multiple copies of an object and move it around (like the hippie chicks in Figure 3-8).

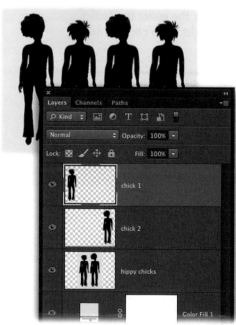

FIGURE 3-8

By selecting each of the silhouettes (top) and then pressing ⌘-J (Ctrl+J on a PC), you can put copies of them onto their own layers (bottom). To move them around in your document, activate one of the new layers, press V to grab the Move tool, and then drag to reposition the selected figure. (Chapter 4 has more on how to make selections.)

Photoshop automatically adds the word "copy" to duplicated layers' names. To keep it from doing that, open the Layers panel's menu, choose Panel Options, and then turn off the "Add 'copy' to Copied Layers and Groups" checkbox at the bottom of the resulting dialog box.

NOTE You can follow along by visiting this book's Missing CD page at *www.missingmanuals.com/cds* and downloading the file *Chicks.jpg*.

You can duplicate a layer in a gazillion ways:

- **Press ⌘-J (Ctrl+J on a PC) or choose Layer→New→"Layer via Copy"** to copy the active layer onto another layer just like it.

TIP In Photoshop CS6, you can duplicate multiple layers at the same time. Just activate the layers by Shift- or ⌘-clicking (Ctrl-clicking) them, and then press ⌘-J (Ctrl+J). Think of this as "jumping" the content onto other layers—it makes the keyboard shortcut easier to remember. (So many shortcuts, so little time to memorize 'em!).

- **Drag the original layer atop the "Create a new layer" button at the bottom of the Layers panel.** When Photoshop highlights the button (which looks like a piece of paper with a folded corner), let go of your mouse button.

- **Option-drag (Alt-drag on a PC) the layer somewhere else in the Layers panel.** Your cursor turns into a double black-and-white arrowhead as soon as you start to drag. When you let go of your mouse button, Photoshop duplicates the layer.

- **Choose Duplicate Layer from the Layers panel's menu or choose Layer→Duplicate Layer.** This method gives you a chance to name the new layer, as well as to send it to a new document. If you choose to send it to a new document, pick an open document from the Destination section's Document pop-up menu or choose New to create a brand-new document (enter a name for the new document in the Name field).

- **Control-click (right-click on a PC) the layer in the Layers panel.** From the resulting shortcut menu, choose Duplicate Layer.

- **To duplicate part of layer, create a selection using any of the tools discussed in Chapter 4 and then press ⌘-J (Ctrl+J)** to move your selection onto its own layer. If you want to *delete* the selected area from the original layer and *duplicate* it onto another layer at the same time, press Shift-⌘-J (Shift+Ctrl+J). You can think of this trick as *cutting* to another layer since you'll have a hole in the original layer where the selection used to be.

Adding layers can *really* increase your document's file size, so it's always a good idea to delete layers you don't need (*especially* if you have a slow computer or very little memory). To delete a layer (save for a locked Background layer), activate it in the Layers panel and then do one of the following:

- **Press Delete (Backspace on a PC).** This is the fastest deletion method in the West.

- **Drag it onto the trash can Control at the bottom of the Layers panel.**

- **Click the trash can icon.** When Photoshop asks if you're *sure* you want to delete the layer, click Yes and then turn on the "Don't show again" checkbox if you don't want to see this confirmation box in the future.

TIP If you delete a layer and then wish you had it back, just use Photoshop's Undo command: Choose Edit→Undo or press ⌘-Z (Ctrl+Z on a PC).

- **Control-click (right-click on a PC) near the layer's name in the Layers panel and choose Delete Layer from the shortcut menu.** (Be sure to click near the layer's *name*—if you click its thumbnail, you won't see Delete Layer in the shortcut menu.) When Photoshop asks if you really want to delete the layer, click Yes to send it packin'.

- **Choose Layer→Delete or open the Layers panel's menu and then choose Delete Layer.** You'll get a confirmation dialog box this way, too, so just smile sweetly, click Yes, and be on your way.

TIP If you've hidden multiple layers (page 84), you can delete 'em all at once by opening the Layers panel's menu and choosing Delete→Hidden Layers (hey, if you're not using 'em, you might as well toss 'em!). Getting rid of extra layers shortens the Layers panel *and* reduces the document's file size.

Copying and Pasting Layers

You can use the regular ol' copy and paste commands to move whole or partial layers between Photoshop documents, too:

- **To copy and paste a whole layer into another document,** choose Select→All (or press ⌘-A [Ctrl+A]) to select everything on the layer and then press ⌘-C (Ctrl+C). Next, click the other document's window and press ⌘-V (Ctrl+V) to add the layer.

- **To copy part of a layer into another document,** create your selection first and then press ⌘-C (Ctrl+C on a PC) to copy it. Then open the other document and press ⌘-V (Ctrl+V); Photoshop pastes those pixels onto a new layer.

Photoshop also includes a Paste Special option in the Edit menu, which is incredibly handy when you're combining images. It's discussed at length on page 270.

TIP When you copy an image from another program and paste it into a Photoshop document, it lands on its very own layer. If the pasted image is *bigger* than your document, you may need to resize the new layer using Free Transform (page 98). Alternatively you can choose Image→Reveal All, and Photoshop resizes the canvas so you can see everything it contains.

Filling a Layer with Color

One of the most common things you'll do with a new layer is fill it with color. If, for example, you've hidden your image's original background with a layer mask (page 113) or added an interesting edge effect (see Figure 12-22 on page 514), you can spice things up by adding a solid-colored background. Photoshop gives you a couple of different ways to tackle this task:

- **Fill an existing layer with color.** After you've created a new layer using one of the methods listed on page 82, choose Edit→Fill. In the resulting Fill dialog box (Figure 3-9), pick a color from the Use pop-up menu and then click OK. You can also fill the active layer with your foreground color by pressing Option-Delete (Alt+Backspace on a PC), or your background color by pressing ⌘-Delete (Ctrl+Delete on a PC).

> **NOTE** If you increase your canvas size (page 253) after you've filled a layer with color, you'll need to refill the layer or it'll be smaller than your document and you'll see the contents of layers below it peeking through. To avoid this extra step, use a Fill layer instead, as discussed in the following bullet point.

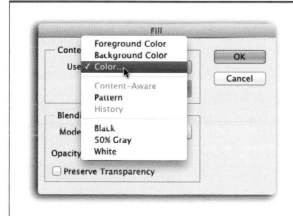

FIGURE 3-9

The Use pop-up menu lets you tell Photoshop to fill a layer with your foreground or background color, or summon the Color Picker by choosing Color.

- **Create a Fill layer.** If you're not sure which color you want to use, choose Layer→New Fill Layer→Solid Color, or click the half-black/half-white circle at the bottom of the Layers panel and choose Solid Color. In the New Layer dialog box that appears, name the layer and then click OK. Photoshop then displays the Color Picker so you can choose a fill color. If you decide to change this color later, double-click the Fill layer's thumbnail, and Photoshop opens the Color Picker so you can choose a new color or *steal* one from your image as shown in Figure 3-10. Fill layers also come with their own layer masks, making it super simple to hide part of the layer if you need to.

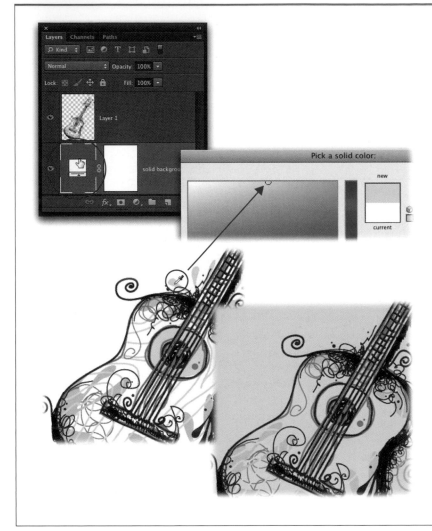

FIGURE 3-10

Top: Dragging your new Fill layer to the bottom of the layer stack creates a solid-colored (in this case, white) background for your image. To change the color, double-click the Fill layer's thumbnail (circled) to pop open the Color Picker.

Bottom: If you want to get super creative, you can snatch color from your image by mousing over to it while the Color Picker is open (your cursor turns into an eyedropper, circled). Click once to grab the color you want, and then click OK to close the Color Picker. And if you want to hide part of the Fill layer (to, say, create a color fade), just paint in the included layer mask (see page 116).

One of the many advantages of using Fill Layers is that, unlike image layers, the *whole* layer gets filled with color even if you enlarge the canvas. In addition to using Fill layers to create solid backgrounds, you can use them to fill a layer with a gradient or a repeating pattern, as shown in Figure 3-11.

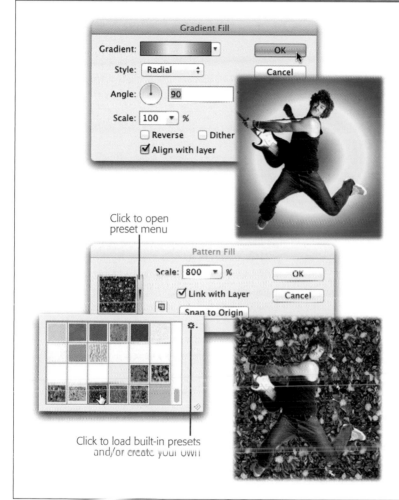

FIGURE 3-11

Fill layers aren't just for adding solid color; you can use them to create a gradient- or pattern-filled background as shown here (top and bottom, respectively). To change the gradient or pattern, just double-click the Fill layer's thumbnail to make Photoshop display the appropriate dialog box—Gradient Fill or Pattern Fill. By adjusting the Scale setting in these dialog boxes, you can make the gradient or pattern bigger or smaller. And the box on page 96 explains how to make your patterns more realistic.

You can also add a Fill layer via the Adjustment layer menu at the bottom of the Layers panel (it looks like a half-black/half-white circle). You'll find Solid Color, Gradient, and Pattern listed at the very top of the resulting menu.

Click to open preset menu

Click to load built-in presets and/or create your own

NOTE Photoshop CS6 includes two new pattern preset categories that you can access in the Pattern Fill dialog box by clicking the down-pointing triangle to open the preset menu (labeled in Figure 3-11, bottom) and then clicking the tiny gear icon in the upper right of the resulting menu. Both new categories—Artists Brushes Canvas and Erodible Textures—are useful when creating paintings from scratch, as described in Chapter 12 on page 505.

Scripted Patterns

One of the problems with Photoshop's pattern fills is their complete lack of randomness in shape, color, and position. Basically, the program just takes an image that's perfectly square and then repeats it in a grid-like pattern, no matter whether the image is one built into the program as a preset or one you load using the preset menu (labeled in Figure 3-11, bottom). But a real brick wall, for example, isn't made from perfectly identical bricks; each brick varies in color, texture, and sometimes size.

That's why Adobe added the ability to apply *scripts* to pattern fills in CS6. You can access these scripts via the Fill dialog box or when you're filling a path (page 564).

To give scripted patterns a spin, create a new layer and then choose Edit→Fill. In the resulting dialog box, from the Use pop-up menu, choose Pattern and then pick a pattern from the Custom Pattern menu. Next, turn on the Scripted Patterns checkbox at the bottom of the dialog box, and then choose from the five built-in scripts: Brick Fill, Cross Weave, Random Fill, Spiral, and Symmetry Fill. Click OK and Photoshop adds a whole lotta randomness to your pattern, as shown here (Spiral is the only one that doesn't introduce random color). For example, the Brick Fill script makes Photoshop offset the pattern every

second row by half of the pattern's width, and introduce a variety of colors based on the original pattern's color (in this case, the gray Sandpaper pattern in the new Erodible Textures preset category). These scripts become even *more* useful if you use 'em on a custom pattern you create yourself, such as one made from the leaf and chili images shown here. For step-by-step instructions, visit this book's Missing CD page at *www .missingmanuals.com/cds* and click the Scripted Patterns link.

You can customize the built-in scripts or (gasp) create your own. They're written in the *JavaScript* programming language (which you can learn all about in *JavaScript & jQuery: The Missing Manual, Second Edition*) and they live in the *Applications\Adobe Photoshop CS6\Presets\Deco* folder on a Mac. On a PC running Photoshop in 32-bit mode, they're in the *C:\Program Files (x86)\Adobe\Adobe Photoshop CS6\ Presets\Deco* folder. On a PC running Photoshop in 64-bit mode, peek in *C:\Program Files\Adobe\Adobe Photoshop CS6 (64 Bit)\Presets\Deco* instead. After you modify a script or add a new one, you have to quit Photoshop and restart it before they'll show up in the Scripted Patterns menu.

Now you've got something new and exciting to try this weekend!

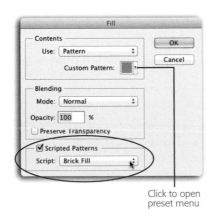

Click to open preset menu

Sandpaper Fill

Sandpaper + Brick Fill

Leaf image + Random Fill

Chili image + Spiral Fill

Tweaking a Layer's Opacity and Fill

All layers begin life at 100 percent opacity, meaning you can't see through them (except where they're empty, as shown in Figure 3-7). To make a layer semitransparent, you can lower its Opacity setting, which is a good way to lessen the strength of a color or lighting adjustment (Chapter 9), the amount of sharpening you applied to a duplicate layer (Chapter 11), and so on. The Opacity setting affects everything on a given layer equally.

The Opacity and Fill settings live near the top of the Layers panel (see Figure 3-12). Unlike Opacity, the Fill setting it *doesn't* affect the whole layer. For example, if you create a Shape layer or a Type layer, lowering its Fill setting will lower only the opacity of the color *inside* the shape or letters, not the opacity of any layer styles or Stroke settings you've added.

FIGURE 3-12

If you lower the opacity of this white fade layer to 75 percent, the white paint becomes partially transparent, letting you see through to the photo layer below, as shown here.

To look like a real Photoshop pro, point your cursor at the word Opacity. When the cursor turns into a little pointing hand—known as a scrubby cursor—like the one shown here, you can drag to the left or right to lower or raise the layer's opacity, respectively (you can even drag the cursor off the Layers panel if you want to). This trick works for any Photoshop setting with similar controls, including the Fill setting, most everything in the Options bar (no matter which tool is active), the options in the Character and Paragraph panels, and more!

TIP In Photoshop CS6, if you've hidden a layer by turning off its visibility eye, you can *still* see its Opacity, Fill, and blend mode settings. Nice!

To change Opacity or Fill, mouse over to the Layers panel, activate the layer you want to tweak, and then do one of the following:

- **Enter a new value in the Opacity or Fill field.** Double-click the current value in either field, enter a new value, and then press Return (Enter on a PC).

- **Use the field's slider.** Click the down arrow to the right of the Opacity or Fill field, and then drag the resulting slider to the left or right to decrease or increase that setting, respectively.

- **Use your keyboard.** Press V to activate the Move tool (think "moVe"), and then change the active layer's Opacity setting by typing *1* for 10 percent, *2* for 20 percent, *3+5* for 35 percent, and so on (type *0* for 100 percent or, new in CS6, 0+0 for 0 percent). If you've got any other tool that works with transparency active *besides* the Move tool (such as the Brush or Healing tools) you'll change the *tool's* opacity setting instead. You can use the same keyboard trick to adjust the Fill setting, too; just hold down the Shift key while you type the numbers.

> **TIP** You can change the opacity and/or fill of multiple layers at once: Just Shift- or ⌘-click (Ctrl-click on a PC) to activate more than one layer and then adjust the Opacity and/or Fill settings.

Resizing and Rotating Layers

To resize the contents of a layer—or many layers—*without* changing the size of your document, you can use the Free Transform tool shown in Figure 3-13. (You'll learn a lot more about this tool in Chapter 6, so consider this a sneak peek.) To resize or rotate a layer, follow these steps:

1. **In the Layers panel, activate the layer(s) you want to adjust (see page 79 for the scoop on activating multiple layers).**

2. **Press ⌘-T (Ctrl+T on a PC) to summon the Free Transform tool.**

    Photoshop puts a box lined with small square handles (called a *bounding box*) around the contents of the active layer(s). If you're resizing a normal layer, the handles are white; if you're resizing a Smart Object (page 126), they're black instead, as shown in Figure 3-13. The difference is purely cosmetic—they work exactly the same.

3. **Drag one of the corner handles toward the center of the layer to make the layer content smaller.**

    Grab any of the white corner handles and drag diagonally inward to decrease the layer content's size. To resize the content proportionately so it doesn't get squished or stretched, hold down the Shift key as you drag.

4. **To rotate the layer(s)**, position your cursor outside the bounding box and then—when the cursor turns into a curved, double-headed arrow—drag up or down in the direction you want to turn the layer(s).

5. **Press Return (Enter on a PC) or double-click inside the bounding box** to let Photoshop know you're done.

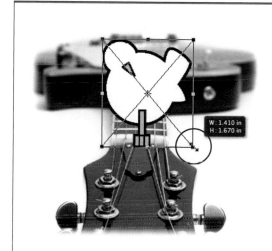

FIGURE 3-13

You can drag any of the bounding box's square handles to resize your object. To adjust all four sides of the box simultaneously, hold down Option (Alt on a PC) as you drag a corner handle. Don't forget to press Return (Enter) when you're finished because Photoshop won't let you do anything else while you've got an active bounding box.

New in CS6, the Free Transform tool shows you a handy heads-up display (HUD) of the object's size (the W and H numbers shown here) when you drag a corner handle. If you click within the bounding box and drag to reposition it, the display changes to show your X and Y coordinates on the document relative to where you started dragging or angle if you're rotating it (the Move tool does the same thing).

W: 1.410 in
H: 1.670 in

> **TIP** To see the Free Transform command's resizing handles whenever the Move tool is active—without actually using the Free Transform command—press V to grab the Move tool and then turn on the Show Transform Controls checkbox in the Options bar. Seeing the handles is handy if you're jumping between layers to resize or rotate objects and don't want to stop and summon Free Transform each time.

Do you risk reducing your image's quality by resizing layers this way? Sure. Anytime you alter pixel size, you change the image's quality a little bit, too, whether it's a single layer or the whole document. But as long as you *decrease* the layer's size, you won't lose much quality (though you don't want to decrease its size *repeatedly*—try to do it once or twice and be done with it). You definitely risk losing quality if you *increase* the size of a pixel-based Image layer, because when pixels get bigger, they also get blockier (though if you increase the size of an object just a *little*, nobody will be the wiser).

That said, if you're working with a Smart Object (page 126), Shape layer (page 550), or Type layer (Chapter 14), you've got no worries. You can resize those babies all day long—larger or smaller, as many times as you want—and you won't affect their quality, which is why you should use those kinds of layers whenever possible. (However, you don't want to enlarge a raster-based Smart Object too much beyond its original dimensions because it could become pixelated and blocky.)

TIP The rest of the transform tools—including Skew, Distort, and so on—work on layers, too. See page 259 for the details.

Moving and Aligning Layers

One of the many advantages of using layers is that you can scoot 'em around independent of everything else in your document. To move a layer, first activate it in the Layers panel, and then press V to grab the Move tool and drag the layer wherever you want. For example, to move the text in Figure 3-12 a bit to the left, press V and drag it to the new spot. To move the layer in a perfectly vertical or horizontal line, hold down the Shift key while you drag. As soon as you start dragging, you'll see a slightly transparent, dark gray border around the item you're dragging—and it moves as you drag. This is extremely helpful when you're moving items that are really small, and thus easy to lose sight of.

NOTE You can also nudge the layer one pixel at a time by pressing the arrows on your keyboard (holding down the Shift key while you press the arrow keys scoots the layer by *10* pixels per keystroke).

If you want to move only *part* of a layer, select that portion first using one of the methods explained in Chapter 4. Then you can grab the Move tool and move just the selected bits.

■ ALIGNING LAYERS

When you need to position layers, Photoshop has several tools that can help you get 'em lined up just right. The program tries to help you align layers by *snapping* the one you're moving to the *boundaries* (content edges) of other layers. As you drag a layer with the Move tool, Photoshop tries to pop the layer into place when you get near another layer's edge. (To make the program stop popping them into place, choose View→Snap.) If you'd like to *see* the boundaries of your layer, press V to activate the Move tool, and then hop up to the Options bar and turn on the Show Transform Controls checkbox (Figure 3-14).

TIP If you're trying to align one layer perfectly with the layer below it, it's a good idea to temporarily lower the top layer's opacity (page 97) so you can actually *see* the layer underneath.

In addition to snapping layers and showing their boundaries, Photoshop offers you the following alignment helpers:

- **Alignment settings.** These settings come in handy if you need to align the edges of more than one layer. You'll see them in the Options bar when the Move tool is active *and* you have more than one layer activated (see Figure 3-14 for details). You can also find them in the Layer→Align submenu (you still need to have more than one layer activated, but you don't have to activate the Move tool). Figure 3-15 shows you what each button does.

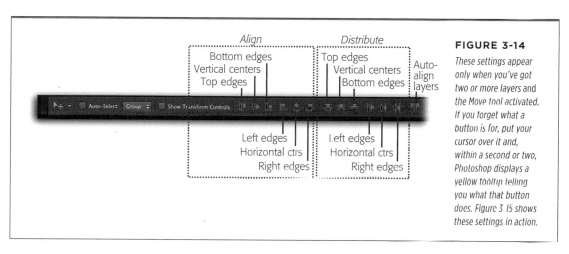

FIGURE 3-14

These settings appear only when you've got two or more layers and the Move tool activated. If you forget what a button is for, put your cursor over it and, within a second or two, Photoshop displays a yellow tooltip telling you what that button does. Figure 3-15 shows these settings in action.

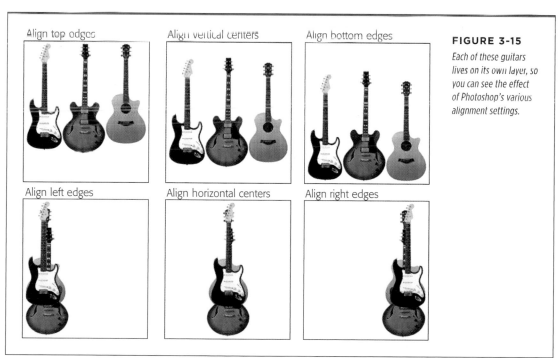

FIGURE 3-15

Each of these guitars lives on its own layer, so you can see the effect of Photoshop's various alignment settings.

- **Distribute settings.** Nestled snugly to the right of the alignment settings are the distribute settings (Figure 3-14). Their mission is to evenly space the contents of the active layers based on each layer's horizontal or vertical center, and you need to have at least *three* layers activated to use them. For example, these options are handy when you're designing buttons for website navigation because you can use them to space the buttons equally.

- **Auto-alignment.** If you choose Edit→Auto-Align Layers or click the Auto-Align Layers button labeled in Figure 3-14, Photoshop does the aligning *for* you by looking at the corners and edges of the objects on the active layers. This command is really handy when you're combining multiple images of the same shot (see page 299), but it doesn't work on Adjustment layers, Smart Objects, or Shape layers.

- **Smart Guides.** Unlike the regular guides you learned about in Chapter 2 (page 69), Smart Guides show up automatically anytime you drag a layer near another layer's edge or center (see Figure 3-16). They're extremely helpful when you're manually aligning layers with the Move tool since they make it easier to position layers precisely in relation to each other. To turn 'em on, choose View→Show→Smart Guides.

WORKAROUND WORKSHOP

When Layers Won't Align

If you try to align the bottoms of two Type layers using the Align Bottom Edges command, you may run into trouble. If there's a *descender* (a letter that goes below the baseline, like the letters *y* and *p*) in one layer but not the other, the two layers won't align properly because their bottoms aren't even. The fix is to replace the troublesome letter(s) temporarily with one that doesn't have a descender and *then* click the Align Bottom Edges button. Once the layers are aligned, you can change the letter(s) back. It's not elegant, but it works.

Photoshop can also do strange things when you're using the alignment commands on layers that have layer masks (page 116). Instead of aligning the layers according to what you've hidden with the mask (which is probably what you're trying to do), Photoshop ignores the mask and tries to align the layers using the *actual* pixel information. In that situation, you may need to turn on Rulers (page 69), create a few guides (also on page 69), and manually align the layers with the Move tool (page 100).

FIGURE 3-16

With *Smart Guides* turned on, Photoshop alerts you with a thin red line anytime you approach the edge or center of another layer so you know that you're about to move past it.

■ MOVING LAYERS BETWEEN DOCUMENTS

In addition to copying and pasting layers from one document to another (as described back on page 92), you can also drag and drop them straight from the Layers panel to another document, as shown in Figure 3-17. When you do that, Photoshop leaves the layer in the original document and places a *copy* in the target document, so you don't have to worry about losing anything from either file. This technique is really helpful if you want to create a collage (Chapter 7), swap backgrounds, or share color corrections across documents. Here are the details:

1. **Open the two documents you want to combine.**

2. **Choose Window→Arrange and choose one of the 2-up display options.**

   To drag a layer from one document to another document that contains *multiple* layers, you have to be able to *see* both documents, as explained in Figure 3-17. Choosing one of the 2-up display options or "Float All in Windows" makes Photoshop rearrange your document windows so you can see 'em both at the same time. (Page 66 has more on display options.)

FIGURE 3-17

Top: To combine two images into one document, first arrange your workspace so that you can see both windows. (The 2-up Vertical arrangement was used here.) Then drag one layer's thumbnail from the Layers panel into the other document.

Bottom: When you release your mouse button, the new layer appears in the other document's Layers panel, as shown here.

You can also drag an image file from your computer's desktop into an open Photoshop document and the object lands on its own layer as a Smart Object. Sweet!

3. **Click the document that contains the layer you want to *move*, and then drag the layer's thumbnail onto the other document.**

   As you drag, your cursor turns into a tiny closed fist, as you can see in Figure 3-17. When Photoshop highlights the inside border of the destination window in light gray, let go of your mouse button to make Photoshop add the layer to that document.

   TIP To center the moved layer perfectly in its new home, hold the Shift key as you drag the layer between documents.

■ EXPORTING LAYERS TO SEPARATE FILES

If you've got a bunch of layers that you want to separate into individual files (with each layer in its own file), choose File→Scripts→"Export Layers to Files." In the resulting dialog box (Figure 3-18), use the Destination field to tell Photoshop where you want it to save the files. In the File Name Prefix box, create a naming scheme (Photoshop uses whatever you enter in this field as the first part of your files' names) and, from the File Type pop-up menu, choose a format. When you're finished, click Run and sit back while Photoshop does all the work.

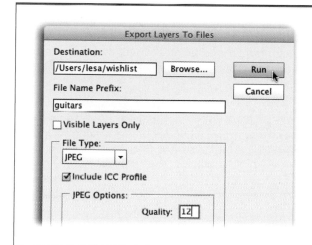

FIGURE 3-18

The Export Layers To Files dialog box lets you choose where to put the new files and what to name them. To exclude any hidden layers, turn on the Visible Layers Only checkbox.

In the File Type pop-up menu, you can choose from BMP, JPEG, PDF, PSD, TARGA, TIFF, PNG-8, and PNG-24 (all of which are discussed on pages 50–58). Each format gives you different options; for example, choosing JPEG lets you pick a quality setting.

Photoshop includes your document's ICC profile in each file unless you turn off the aptly named Include ICC Profile checkbox shown here.

■ Managing Layers

If one thing's for certain in Photoshop, it's that your Layers panel will get long and unwieldy in a hurry. Now that you've seen a smidgen of the increased editing flexibility layers give you (moving, resizing, and so on), you'll want to put *everything* on its own layer—and you *should*. However, learning a wee bit about organizing layers can keep you from spending ages digging through the Layers panel to find the layer you want. This section gives you the lowdown.

Naming and Color Coding Layers

The simplest way to organize layers is to name the darn things something other than Layer 1, Layer 2, and so on. If you didn't name them when you made 'em, you can always double-click a layer's name in the Layers panel and rename it right there (Photoshop highlights the name when you double-click it, so you can just start typing). When you're done, press Return (Enter on a PC).

> **TIP** If you double-click in the Layers panel *near* the layer's name but not directly on it, Photoshop opens the Layer Style dialog box (shown on page 133) instead of highlighting the layer's name. No problem: Just close the dialog box and try again.

Another renaming option in CS6 is to choose Layer→Rename Layer. When you do, Photoshop highlights the name of the active layer; just type some text to rename it. To rename additional layers, press the Tab key to highlight the name of the next layer down, or Shift-Tab to highlight the name of the next layer up. (You can assign a keyboard shortcut to the Rename Layer command, too, by going to Edit→Keyboard Shortcuts; the box on page 37 has the details.)

In addition to giving layers meaningful names, another great way to keep them organized is to color-code them. For example, you could color-code various sections of a poster like the header, footer, body, and so on. As you learned back on page 83, you can assign a color to a layer when you first create it, and in CS6 you can assign a color anytime by activating the layer(s) and then Ctrl-clicking (right-clicking on a PC) the layer(s) and picking a color from the resulting shortcut menu. (To remove color coding, do the same thing but choose No Color from the shortcut menu).

Linking and Locking Layers

Editing layers can be a lot of work, and once you get them just right, you want to make darn sure they stay that way. You can protect yourself from making accidental changes by linking layers together or locking down certain aspects of them. Read on to learn how.

■ LINKING LAYERS

If you need to move something in your image that's made from several layers, it'd be a real pain to move each layer individually and then reconstruct the image. Fortunately, you can *link* layers before you grab the Move tool so that they travel as a single unit; Figure 3-19 shows you how. Linking related layers can help you avoid accidentally misaligning layers with a careless flick of the Move tool. For example, if you've placed some text next to an image, linking the image layer with the Type layer ensures that they stay perfectly aligned.

■ LOCKING 'EM DOWN

You can add a more serious level of protection with *layer locks*, which prevent layers from being edited or moved. At the top of the Layers panel is a row of four buttons that you can use to lock various aspects of layers (Figure 3-20). First activate the layer you want to lock, and then click the appropriate lock button to prevent any changes. Here are your options:

- **Lock transparent pixels.** This protects the layer's transparent pixels so they don't change *even* if you paint across them or run the Edit→Fill command. For example, if you created the faded-color effect shown on page 88, you could apply this lock to change the fade's color without affecting the layer's see-through bits. This lock's button looks like the transparency checkerboard.

- **Lock image pixels.** This won't let you do *anything* to a layer but nudge it around with the Move tool. The button for this lock looks like the Brush tool.

- **Lock position.** If you've carefully positioned a layer and want to make sure it stays put, click this button, which looks like a four-headed arrow. You can still *edit* the layer, you just can't move it.

- **Lock all.** This is your deadbolt: Use it to prevent the layer from being edited *or* moved. You know this lock means business because its button is a padlock.

Link layers

FIGURE 3-19

Once you've got more than one layer activated, you can link them by clicking the tiny chain icon at the bottom of the Layers panel. When you do, the same chain appears to the right of each layer's name (circled) to show that the layers are linked. To unlink them, simply activate a layer and then click the chain icon at the bottom of the Layers panel again. Easy, huh?

The layers shown here are also color-coded with Violet.

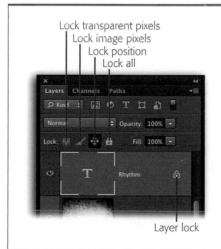

Lock transparent pixels
Lock image pixels
Lock position
Lock all

Layer lock

FIGURE 3-20

Use these buttons to protect your layers from accidental editing or repositioning. No matter which lock you apply, you'll see the padlock icon labeled here to the right of the locked layer's name.

When it comes to layer locks, your keyboard's forward slash key (/) acts like a switch for the last lock you applied. When a locked layer is active, tap this key once to remove that particular lock (press it again to turn that same lock back on). When an unlocked layer is active, tapping this key makes Photoshop apply the "Lock transparent pixels" lock.

Photoshop CS6 also lets you apply locks to multiple layers at the same time. Just activate the layers first by Shift or ⌘-clicking (Ctrl-clicking on a PC) them, and then click the appropriate lock icon(s) in the Layers panel. Hooray for change!

TIP   If you've taken the time to create a layer group (as explained next), you can lock all the layers in it by activating it and then choosing Layer→"Lock All Layers in Group." (You can also find this same menu item in the Layers panel's menu.) Photoshop pops open a dialog box where you can turn on any of the locks listed above; click OK to apply them.

Grouping Layers into Folders

You can rein in a fast-growing Layers panel by tucking layers into folders called *layer groups*. You can expand and collapse layer groups just like the folders on your hard drive, and they'll save you a heck of a lot of scrolling when you're layer hunting, as you can see in Figure 3-21.

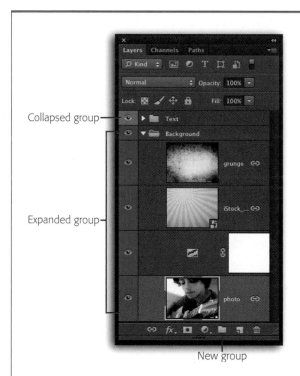

FIGURE 3-21

Layer groups not only help you shorten your Layers panel, but they also let you apply masks to all the layers in the group simultaneously.

Just click a layer group's flippy triangle to expand or collapse that group. Here, the down-pointing flippy triangle next to the Background group's folder shows that the group is expanded, while the Text group is collapsed. (These groups have been color coded to make them easier to spot.)

A handy new feature in CS6 is the ability to collapse or expand all layer groups at the same time by Option-clicking (Alt-clicking on a PC) the flippy triangle to a group's left.

Collapsed group

Expanded group

New group

Say you're creating a poster for a concert, and you've got several layers that comprise the background, some photos of the band, some text, and so on. You can put all the layers associated with the background in a group cleverly named *Background*, the photos in a group called *Photos*, and the Type layers in a group called *Text*. Then you can add some color-coding (blue for background, red for photos, and so on) to make it easy to quickly spot the group you want to work with instead of wasting time scrolling through the Layers panel.

Here are the different ways you can group layers:

- **Create the group first** by clicking the "Create a new group" button at the bottom of the Layers panel (it looks like a tiny folder) or by choosing New Group from the Layers panel's menu. (If you go the latter route, you'll get a dialog box where you can name the group, assign it color, and change its blend mode and opacity if you want.) Photoshop adds the group to the Layers panel; just drag layers onto the group's folder icon in the layer stack to add them to it.

NOTE Straight from the factory, the blend mode of a layer group is set to Pass Through, meaning any Adjustment layers or blend mode changes within the group trickle down and affect any layers underneath it. For more on this blend mode, see the box on page 292.

- **Activate the layers first** and then press ⌘-G (Ctrl+G on a PC) or choose "New Group from Layers" in the Layers panel's menu. Photoshop adds a group named *Group 1* to your Layers panel that includes all the layers you activated; double-click the group's name to rename it.

- **Option-drag (Alt-drag on a PC) layers** onto the "Create a new group" button at the bottom of the Layers panel.

You can do the same things to layer groups that you can to regular layers: duplicate them, hide them, lock them, color code them, and so on. You can also create *nested* groups by dragging and dropping one group into another (see the box below for more info).

POWER USERS' CLINIC

Nesting Layer Groups Deeply

Photoshop lets you nest layer groups up to 10 levels deep, meaning you can put a layer group inside of another layer group that lives inside yet *another* layer group that lives...well, you get the picture. This kind of nesting is helpful if you're a stickler for organization or are working on a complicated file and your Layers panel is a mile long. For example, a photographer might have a layer group named Retouching with another group inside it named Healing, which houses another layer group named Nose, and so on.

This kind of organization works great until you have to share the file with someone using a version of Photoshop earlier than CS5. If you open the file with Photoshop CS3 or CS4, you'll be greeted with a dialog box stating, among other things, that it encountered "unknown data" and that "groups were altered." At this point, the program gives you two choices (you can also click Cancel to close the document, but what fun is that?):

- **Flatten** makes Photoshop preserve the appearance of the original document (provided the document was saved using the Maximum Compatibility option discussed on page 32) but not its layers, which makes further editing impossible.

- **Keep Layers** makes Photoshop *try* to preserve the document's appearance and layers, though this doesn't always work. For example, if you've changed a layer group's blend mode (page 280) or used advanced blending options (page 293), they're toast.

Once you've crossed your fingers and made a choice, Photoshop opens the document (which can take a while). If you choose Keep Layers, you'll see empty layers where the nested layer groups used to be.

To split apart grouped layers, activate the group and then choose Layer→Ungroup Layers, press Shift-⌘-G (Shift+Ctrl+G on a PC), or Control-click (right-click) the group and then choose Ungroup Layers from the shortcut menu. Whichever method you use, Photoshop deletes the group but leaves the layers intact.

To delete a group, activate it and then choose Layer→Delete→Group or Control-click (right-click) the group and then choose Ungroup Layers from the shortcut menu. Either way, Photoshop displays a dialog box asking whether you want to delete the group *and* all the layers inside it, or just the group itself (leaving the layers within it in the Layers panel). (If the group doesn't contain any layers, you don't see this dialog box—Photoshop simply deletes the group.) If you activate a group and then press the Delete key, Photoshop deletes the group and all the layers inside it.

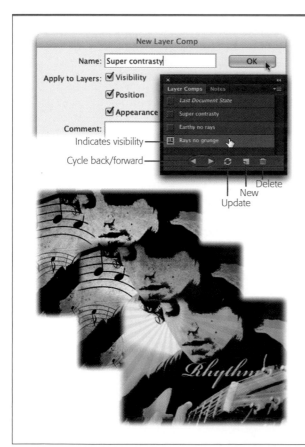

FIGURE 3-22

Like layer groups, layer comps work only if your document has more than one layer.

Top: Give each layer comp a name that describes that version of your design. To summon this panel, choose Window→Layer Comps. Then you can use the arrow buttons circled here to cycle through the various comps.

Bottom: Showing, hiding, and rearranging layers lets you quickly produce several versions of the same design.

Layer Comps: Capturing Different Document Versions

Going back to that hypothetical concert poster from the previous section, you'll probably want to show your client different versions of it so she can pick the one she likes best. Photoshop can help by saving multiple versions of the document as *layer comps*—snapshots of your Layers panel in various states (see Figure 3-22).

It's much better than having to juggle multiple files you could lose track of. Layer comps can record the position and visibility of layers, as well as the blend modes (page 280) and layer styles (page 131) you've applied.

You capture layer comp "snapshots" as you're working. For instance, you could start off with a baseline version and record what it looks like, then make some changes and record that new version, and so on. When you're ready to save your first layer comp, follow these steps:

1. **Choose Window→Layer Comps to summon the Layer Comps panel, and then click the Create New Layer Comp button at the bottom of the panel.**

   The button looks like the New Layer button—a piece of paper with a folded corner.

2. **In the New Layer Comp dialog box, give the snapshot a meaningful name and then tell Photoshop which attributes to save.**

   The dialog box has three checkboxes you can turn on or off:

   - **Visibility** captures the layers' current visibility status (whether they're on or off).

   - **Position** captures the layers' positions within the document (think layer *location*, not layer stacking order).

   - **Appearance** captures any blend modes and layer styles.

   It's a good idea to turn on all three of these settings *just in case* you decide to tweak that stuff later. Type a comment if you'd like, and then click OK.

3. **Back in the Layers panel, rearrange, show, or hide layers; add layer styles; or change blend modes to produce another version of the image.**

   Unfortunately, if you change a layer's color, opacity, or fill, Photoshop can't capture that in a layer comp. But there is a workaround: Duplicate those layers, make the changes, and then show or hide them when you save the next layer comp. (This trick works because Photoshop *can* capture layer visibility when creating comps.)

4. **Click the Create New Layer Comp button at the bottom of the Layer Comps panel to create another layer comp and give it a name.**

   Repeat these steps as many times as you want to save lots of different versions of your document.

When you're ready to stroll through the different versions, click the little forward and back arrows at the bottom of the Layer Comps panel (Figure 3-22). To get back to the way the document looked when you last tweaked it (or when you saved your last layer comp), at the top of the Layer Comps panel, click the empty square to the left of the words "Last Document State."

You can duplicate and delete layer comps just like layers and layer groups. To *edit* a layer comp, activate it in the Layer Comps panel and then change whatever you want in the Layers panel. When you're finished, click the Update button at the bottom of the Layer Comps panel.

If you make certain edits, like cropping or deleting a layer, or changing a layer's color, opacity, or fill—basically, any edit that's beyond the layer-comp feature's tracking capabilities—Photoshop gets cranky and locks you out of your layer comps. You can tell which comps are affected because they'll have little warning triangles to the right of their names (see Figure 3-23). These triangles mean that Photoshop needs you to update the layer comp(s) because it can't keep track of every change you made. (Don't worry, it *doesn't* mean Photoshop lost your changes.) If you didn't delete any layers, then fixing the problem is easy: Just activate the affected layer comp(s) and then click the Update button shown in Figure 3-22. If you *did* delete a layer, then you need to create a new comp.

FIGURE 3-23

If a little warning triangle appears next to your layer comp (circled), you can click it to see this dialog box, which gently chastises you for messing up the layer comp. Click Clear to get rid of the warning triangle and close the dialog box.

If you turn on the "Don't show again" checkbox, Photoshop won't display this message anymore, but you'll still have to update your layer comps when you see the warning triangle.

■ EXPORTING LAYER COMPS

When you're ready to show the client your layer comps, export them by choosing File→Scripts→"Layer Comps to Files." Photoshop creates a separate file for each layer comp in whatever format you choose (you get the same options as when you export layers to files; see Figure 3-18).

Older versions of Photoshop (CS3 and earlier) let you export layer comps as both PDF files *and* Web Photo Gallery (WPG) files right from the Scripts menu. Happily, the PDF feature has *reappeared* in Photoshop CS6: Choose File→Scripts→

"Layer Comps to PDF," and Photoshop displays the dialog box shown in Figure 3-24. Creating a web gallery has been offloaded to Bridge; see page 749 for details.

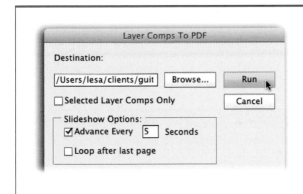

FIGURE 3-24

Click the Browse button to tell Photoshop where you want it to save the file(s). If you want to export only the comps you've activated in the Layer Comps panel (rather than all the document's comps), turn on the Selected Layer Comps Only checkbox.

Unless you turn off the Advance Every setting, the PDF will advance from page to page like a slideshow (if you want each layer comp to remain onscreen for more than 5 seconds, enter a new number into the Advance Every field). To make the slideshow start over automatically, turn on "Loop after last page." When you're finished, click Run button and Photoshop creates the file.

Rasterizing Layers

If you try to paint or run a filter on a Shape or Type layer (covered in Chapters 13 and 14, respectively), Photoshop puts up a fuss: It displays a dialog box letting you know—in no uncertain terms—that you've got to *rasterize* that layer first. Why? Because as you learned back in Chapter 2, vectors aren't made of pixels, and to use pixel-based tools—like the Brush, Eraser, and Clone Stamp—on a vector-based layer, you have to convert it to pixels first. This process is called *rasterizing*.

Beware: There's no going back once you've rasterized a layer. You can't resize former Smart Objects or Shape layers without losing quality, you can't double-click a former Fill layer and change its color, *and* you can't edit a rasterized Type layer. That's why it's a good idea to do your rasterizing on a duplicate layer so you can always go back to the original. Just duplicate the layer by pressing ⌘-J (Ctrl+J on a PC) before you rasterize and then turn off the original layer's visibility so you don't accidentally rasterize the *wrong* layer.

Rasterizing is easy: Just activate a vector-based layer or Smart Object and then choose Layer →Rasterize→Layer. (Choose Layer→Rasterize→All Layers to rasterize *everything*.) Better yet, activate the layers(s), Control-click (right-click) near the layer's name in the Layers panel, and then choose Rasterize Layer from the shortcut menu that appears.

Merging Layers

Layers are great, but sometimes you need to squash 'em together. Yes, this goes against what you've learned in this chapter so far—that you *should* keep everything on its own layer—but in some situations you have no choice but to *merge* or *stamp* layers—or worse, completely *flatten* your file. Here's what those scary-sounding commands mean, along with how and why you might need to use 'em:

- **Merge.** If you've whipped pixels into perfection and know that you'll *never* want to change them, you can merge two or more layers into one (see Figure 3-25). Not only does that reduce the length of your Layers panel, but it also knocks a few pounds off the file's size. Photoshop gives you several ways to merge layers:

  — **Merge down.** To merge two *visible* layers that live next to each other in the Layers panel—and the bottom one is a pixel-based layer—activate the top layer and then choose Layer→Merge Down, choose Merge Down from the Layers panel's menu, or press ⌘-E (Ctrl+E on a PC).

NOTE You can merge any kind of layers, but you need to have a *pixel-based* layer underneath them in the Layers panel to use the merge commands (or else they'll be grayed out). Photoshop then merges everything onto that pixel-based layer.

  — **Merge visible.** To merge just some of your layers, hide the ones you *don't* want to squash, activate a pixel-based layer as your target, and then go to Layer→Merge Visible, choose Merge Visible from the Layers panel's menu, or press Shift-⌘-E (Shift+Ctrl+E).

  — **Merge activated.** Activate the layers you want to merge (either pixel- or vector-based) and then go to Layer→Merge Layers, choose Merge Layers from the Layers panel's menu, or press ⌘-E (Ctrl+E).

  — **Merge linked.** If you've linked layers together (page 106), you can merge them in one fell swoop—though you've got to activate them first by choosing Layer→Select Linked Layers or choosing Select Linked Layers from the Layers panel's menu, and then following the instructions for merging active layers (above).

- **Stamp.** You can think of stamping as a safer version of merging because it combines the active layers on a *new* layer, leaving the original layers intact. This command is great when you need to edit *more* than one layer with tools that affect only one layer at a time (like filters and layer styles). Here are your stamping options:

  — **Stamp active layers.** Activate the layers you want to stamp and then press Option-⌘-E (Alt+Ctrl+E).

  — **Stamp visible.** Turn off the layers you *don't* want to stamp by clicking their visibility eyes, and then press Shift-Option-⌘-E (Shift+Alt+Ctrl+E). You can also hold Option (Alt) as you choose Merge Visible from the Layers panel's menu to make Photoshop merge everything onto a new layer.

TIP An alternative to stamping layers is to use layer groups (page 108) or create a Smart Object from multiple layers, as explained on page 128.

FIGURE 3-25

If you need to edit a multilayer file using tools that affect one layer at a time, you can stamp layers into a merged-layer copy (like the top layer here) to avoid having to flatten the file. If you flatten your document by accident, you can get the layers back using your History panel or by pressing ⌘-Z (Ctrl+Z on a PC). Whew!

- **Flatten.** This command makes your file flatter than a pancake, giving you a locked background that, as you know from the box on page 87, doesn't allow for transparency (any areas that were transparent become white instead). Alas, you have no choice but to flatten a file if you're exporting it to a format that doesn't *support* layers (like JPEG, PNG, and so on—see page 721); just be sure to save the document as a PSD file *first* so you can go back and edit it later. You've got three flattening options:

  — **Flatten image.** To flatten a whole file, go to Layer→Flatten Image or choose Flatten Image from the Layers panel's menu.

WARNING   Danger, Will Robinson! After flattening a file, be sure to choose File→Save As instead of File→Save to avoid saving over your original, layered document.

— **Flatten All Layer Effects.** Instead of flattening a whole file, you can flatten just its layer styles (page 131) so they become one with the layer they're attached to. But be aware that, if you've applied any layer styles to vector-based layers (like Type or Shape layers), those layers will get rasterized in the process. To flatten layer styles, choose File→Scripts→Flatten All Layer Effects.

— **Flatten All Masks.** You can also flatten just layers that you've applied layer masks to (page 116) so the masks are permanently applied by choosing File→Scripts→Flatten All Masks.

Layer Blending

In Photoshop, *blending* refers to the way colors on one layer interact with colors on other layers. Photoshop gives you some pretty powerful layer blending options in the form of layer blend modes, advanced blending, and "blend if" sliders. You can do some amazing stuff with these tools, and since they're used in combining images, you'll learn all about them in Chapter 7 beginning on page 280.

Layer Masks: Digital Masking Tape

Remember the last time you gave your walls a fresh coat of paint? You probably broke out a roll of masking tape and taped up the baseboards and molding so you wouldn't get paint all over them. Sure, you could've have taken the baseboards *off* and put them back on once the paint had dried, but *dadgum* that's a lot of work. Besides, masking tape covers everything just fine. Hiding and protecting is masking tape's special purpose in life and—what luck!—you've got its digital equivalent right in Photoshop: *layer masks*.

A layer mask lets you hide the content of the layer it's attached to, whether it's a pixel-based image layer, Smart Object, Shape layer, Fill layer or—in the case of Adjustment layers—a color or lighting change. Learning to use masks will keep you from having to *erase* parts of an image to produce the effect you want. Once you erase, there's no going back, and if your hand isn't steady enough to erase around detailed areas, you may accidentally erase bits you want to keep. So, for example, instead of *deleting* a background so you can swap it with another one, you can use a layer mask to *hide* it, as shown in Figure 3-26. (You'll find all kinds of other uses for layer masks sprinkled throughout this book.) As long as you save the document as a PSD file, you can go back and edit the mask anytime.

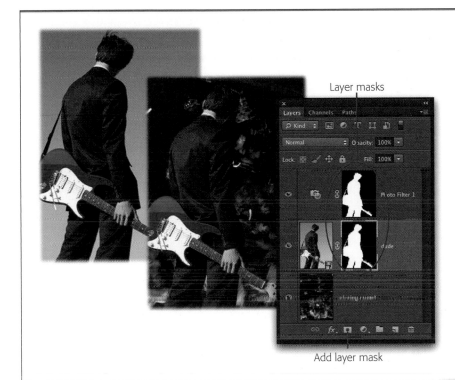

FIGURE 3-26

Left: Wanna be a rock star? No problem: A layer mask can make that happen. Here you can see the original, boring blue background, as well as the new, exciting, clamoring crowd.

Right: If you peek at the Layers panel, you can see that the original background wasn't deleted—it was hidden with a mask instead. (To make the color of the guitarist and the crowd match a bit more, a Photo Filter Adjustment layer—page 354—was added that uses the same mask.)

Layer masks

Add layer mask

Adding Layer Masks

You can add a mask to any layer, though some layers—like Fill, Adjustment, and Shape layers—automatically come with their own masks. As you can see in Figure 3-26, the mask shows up in the Layers panel to the right of the layer thumbnail.

> **NOTE** You can't add a layer mask to a locked Background layer; you first have to double-click the background to make it editable *and then* add a mask.

Layer masks are grayscale creatures, so when you're dealing with them you work only in black, white, and shades of gray, depending on what you want to do. A black mask hides the layer completely, and a white mask reveals it completely. A gray mask falls somewhere in between—it's partially transparent. All this is easy to remember if you memorize the rhyme, "Black conceals and white reveals." Masks can also be pixel- or vector-based. This section covers pixel-based masks; vector-based masks are covered on page 572.

To add a layer mask, activate the layer you want to add it to, choose Layer→Layer Mask, and then pick one of the following:

- **Reveal All.** Creates a solid white mask that shows everything on the layer, so it doesn't change anything in your image. You can also add a white (empty) mask by clicking the Add Layer Mask button at the bottom of the Layers panel (it looks like a circle within a square, as shown in Figure 3-26). If you want to hide just a *little* bit of a layer, Reveal All is the way to go; after you add the mask, just paint the areas you want to hide with a black brush.

- **Hide All.** Creates a solid black mask that conceals everything on the layer. (Option-clicking [Alt-clicking on a PC] the Add Layer Mask button does the same thing.) If you want to hide the majority of the layer, add this kind of mask and then go back with a white brush to reveal specific areas.

- **Reveal Selection.** Choose this option if you've created a selection and want to hide everything but the selection. Photoshop adds a mask where the selected area is white and the background is black. (You'll learn all about selections in Chapter 4.)

- **Hide Selection.** This command adds a mask where the selected area is black and the background is white.

> **TIP** You can also add a pixel- or vector-based layer mask by using the Properties panel (shown on page 123).

- **From Transparency.** This command creates a layer mask from the *transparent* pixels in an image layer (handy if you're working with an image layer that has no background, like a brushstroke). Just activate a partially transparent layer before choosing this command, and Photoshop adds a layer mask that's black in the transparent (empty) areas, gray in the areas that are partially transparent, and white in the areas that contain info. (As of this writing, this command doesn't work with Shape layers or Smart Objects.)

Using Layer Masks

You can use any painting tool you want to add black, white, or gray paint to a layer mask, although the Brush tool is especially handy (Chapter 12 covers all your brush options), and the Gradient tool is great if you want to create a smooth transition from black to white (see the color fade effect on page 88). Selection tools (Chapter 4) also work in masks, and once you create a selection, you can fill it with black, white, or shades of gray by choosing Edit→Fill.

One of the simplest uses for layer masks is to hide bits of text so the text looks like it's behind a person or object in a photo, as shown in Figure 3-27. Here's how to create that effect:

1. **Open a photo and press T to activate the Type tool.**

   Don't worry about double-clicking the Background layer to make it editable; you don't need to touch your original image in this technique.

Corner frame indicates
active mask

FIGURE 3-27

Top: Here you can see that this couple and the text live on different layers. If you add a white (empty) layer mask to the text layer and then paint within the mask with a black brush (circled), you can hide parts of the text, revealing the couple's cute hats. Over in the Layers panel, the corner frame lets you know which part of the document is active: the Type layer or its mask.

Bottom: Magazines use this trick all the time on their covers to make text look like it's behind people.

2. **In the Options bar, pick a font, a size, and a color.**

   For this technique, select a thick font like Impact and set it to a fairly large size, like 70 points (for a high-resolution image, you'll need a bigger size). You'll learn all about formatting text in Chapter 14.

3. **Mouse over to your document, type some text, and then commit it.**

Click where you want the text to begin and start typing. To move the text around, mouse away from the text until your cursor turns into a little arrow; then simply drag the text wherever you'd like. To let Photoshop know you're finished, press Enter—not Return—or click the little checkmark in the Options bar.

4. **Add a layer mask to your Type layer by clicking the circle-within-a-square button at the bottom of the Layers panel.**

Photoshop adds an all-white layer mask to the Type layer, so that everything on that layer is visible. In the Layers panel, you'll now see the mask thumbnail next to the Type layer thumbnail. See the thin border around the corners of the mask thumbnail (labeled in Figure 3-27)? That means it's active and you're about to paint on the mask (good) instead of the photo (bad).

> **TIP** One of the biggest mistakes folks make is not paying attention to which thumbnail they've activated in the Layers panel (it takes a single click to activate either one). The little corner frame always shows which part of the layer is active: the layer mask or the layer itself.

5. **Press B to grab the Brush tool and pick a soft-edged brush set to black.**

After you activate the Brush tool, head up to the left side of the Options bar and open the Brush preset picker (page 38) by clicking the down-pointing triangle next to the little brush preview. Pick a soft-edged brush that's about 60 pixels (or larger if you're working with a high-resolution image). Since you want to *hide* bits of the text, you need to paint with black (remember, black conceals and white reveals). To do that, take a peek at the color chips at the bottom of the Tools panel (page 23) and press D to set 'em to factory-fresh black and white, and then press X until black hops on top. *Now* you're ready to start painting.

6. **Mouse over to your document and paint the parts of the text you want to hide.**

In the example in Figure 3-27, you'd position your cursor over one of the Santa hats and click to start painting (hiding). When you release the mouse button—you don't have to do all your painting with one brushstroke—you'll see black paint on the layer mask in the Layers panel.

7. **If you accidentally hide too much of the text, press X to swap color chips so you're painting with white, and then paint that area back in.**

When you're working with a layer mask, you'll do tons of color-chip swapping (from black to white and vice versa). You'll also use a variety of brush sizes to paint the fine details as well as large areas. To keep from going blind when you're doing detailed work like this, zoom in or out of your document by pressing ⌘ and then the + or – key (Ctrl and then the + or – key on a PC).

TIP You can change your brush cursor's size and hardness by dragging, which is handy when it comes to painting on layer masks. To resize your brush, Control-Option-drag (Alt+right-click+drag on a PC) to the left to decrease brush size or to the right to increase it. The same keyboard shortcut also lets you change brush hardness: Drag up to soften the brush or down to harden it. Inside your brush cursor, you'll see a red preview of what the new brush will look like—if your computer supports OpenGL, that is (see the box on page 64). To change that preview color to something other than red, flip to page 499. And if you're a creature of habit, you can *still* decrease brush size by pressing the left bracket key ([) and increase it by pressing the right bracket key (]).

That wasn't too bad, was it? You just learned *core* Photoshop skills that you'll use over and over. The more you use layer masks, the more natural this stuff will feel.

■ FIXING EXPOSURE WITH MASKS

Masks are especially handy for quickly fixing an over- or underexposed image (one that's too light or too dark). This trick is important to have up your sleeve if you're short on time, or if other lighting fixes (see Chapter 9) aren't working. Here's what you do:

1. **Open an image and add a Levels Adjustment layer to it by clicking the half-black/half-white circle at the bottom of the Layers panel and then choosing Layers.**

   You're not actually going to adjust Levels (page 375); you're merely adding an empty Adjustment layer so you can quickly swap blend modes and then use the mask that tags along with it. Sure, you *could* duplicate your image layer and then add a layer mask, but this method is faster and won't bloat the document's file size. The reason you're using a Levels Adjustment layer is because that kind of layer doesn't *do* anything to your image the second you add it.

2. **Using the pop-up menu at the top of the Layers panel, change the empty Adjustment layer's blend mode from Normal to Multiply.**

   Blend modes control how colors on one layer interact with colors on other layers, which is terrific when it comes to combining images (you'll learn all about blend modes in Chapter 7). For now, you'll focus on two blend modes that you'll use often because they let you quickly darken or lighten an image, respectively: Multiply and Screen (see Figure 3-28). For this example, pick Multiply from the menu at the top of the Layers panel to darken your image dramatically. You'll hide the too-dark bits with the Adjustment layer's mask in the next step.

3. **Press B to grab the Brush tool and set your foreground color chip to black.**

   Check to make sure the Adjustment layer's mask is active (it will be unless you clicked on another layer after adding it). To hide the over-darkened areas, you can paint them with black because—all together now!—black conceals and white reveals. Peek at your color chips, and if black isn't on top, press X. Now you're ready to paint.

4. **With a big soft brush, paint the areas that are too dark.**

   Those keyboard shortcuts for resizing and changing brush hardness come in handy here (see the Tip at the top of this page). Remember, if you mess up and hide too much of the darkened part of the image, simply flip-flop your color chips by pressing X and then reveal the dark part again by painting it with white.

5. **If your image is still a little too dark, lower the empty Adjustment layer's opacity (page 97).**

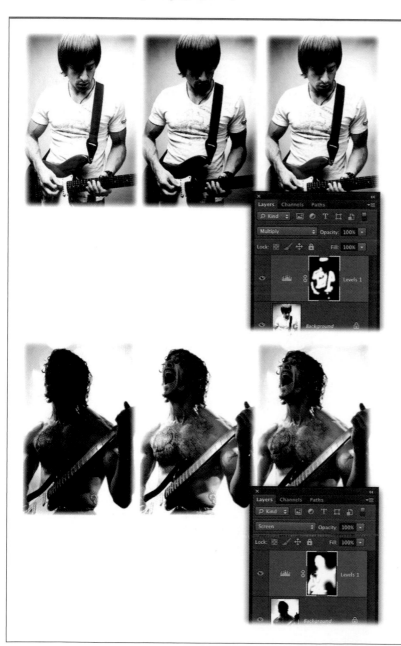

FIGURE 3-28

You can darken or lighten an image by using a brush to fine-tune a layer mask. (Photo-editing veterans call this technique "painting with light.")

Top: This guy's shirt and arms are too light in the original image (left). If you change the Adjustment layer's blend mode to Multiply, his face and guitar are too dark (middle). But if you then hide his face and guitar using the layer mask, he looks much better (right).

Bottom: You can do the same thing to a photo that's too dark. On the left is the super-dark original. The middle image shows what happens when you change the Adjustment layer's blend mode to Screen. You can then use the accompanying layer mask to hide the over-lightened areas (mainly the background and his tattoo) as shown on the right. Now you can see the rocker dude's face (though on second thought, maybe that isn't such a good idea after all!).

ties) when

ent, which
ransparent
w through,
mask com-

blends into
feathering,
s or left to

Refine Mask
ask smaller
this dialog

you can add
ou can also
ake a ma

otedly need to fine-tune it, turn it off or on, and
gram, you had to mouse *all* over the Photoshop
lly, all of your mask tasks are now consolidated
re 3-29).

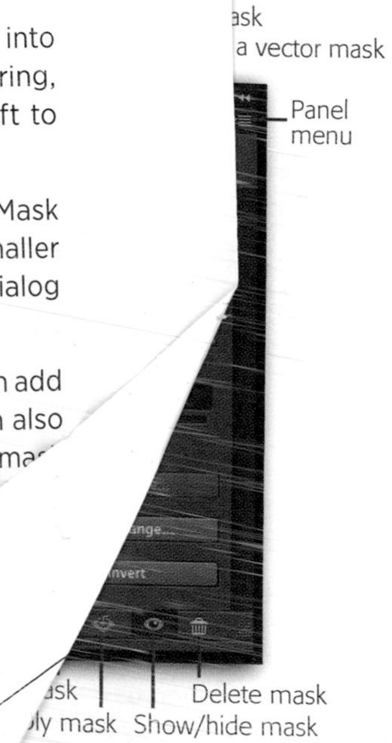

ask
a vector mask

Panel
menu

FIGURE 3-29

*The Properties panel is your one-stop shop for working with layer
masks and Adjustment layers (whether they're pixel- or vector-based).
Heck, you can even add a layer mask right from this panel!*

In Photoshop CS5, these mask options lived in the Masks panel.

ask   Delete mask
ly mask   Show/hide mask

a Layer from Its Mask

es that if you reposition the contents of a
mask to come along for the ride. But that's
. For example, if you use a mask to frame a
vignette instructions on page 146), you may
t's *inside* the mask (the photo) independent
, or vice versa. No problemo—you just need
t.

s panel, there's a tiny chain icon between
ail and the mask's thumbnail (you can see

it in Figure 3-28). To separate the layer from the mask, click
the chain or choose Layer→Layer Mask→Unlink (you'll know
they're separated because the chain disappears). Then press
V to grab the Move tool, click the thumbnail of the piece you
want to move (the layer or the mask), and then drag. Once
you've got everything where you want it, click where the chain
used to be (between the layer and mask thumbnails) or choose
Layer→Layer Mask→Link to relink 'em. Easy, huh?

You'll find the following controls in the Properties panel (Window→Prope[...] a mask is active in the Layers panel:

- **Density.** Photoshop sets the opacity of new layer masks to 100 per[...] means you can't see through them. If you want to make a mask semit[...] so the contents of the layer (like the original background, say) sho[...] drag this slider to the left. Dragging it *all* the way left makes your [...] pletely transparent—in other words, useless.

- **Feather.** This slider lets you soften the edges of the mask so that it [...] the background a little better. (New layer masks don't have any [...] so their edges are sharp.) Drag it right to soften the mask's edge[...] sharpen them.

- **Mask Edge.** When you click this button, Photoshop opens the [...] dialog box, where you can smooth the mask's edges, make the m[...] or larger, add feathering to it, and so on. Page 171 has the details o[...] box (which is also called Refine Edge).

- **Color Range.** This button opens the Color Range dialog box, where [...] to or subtract from the mask based on the colors in your image. Y[...] use this dialog box to help create a selection that you can then m[...] *from*; page 157 has more info.

- **Invert.** This button lets you flip-flop the mask so what *was* mask[...] what *wasn't* masked is (you're gonna use this button a lot).

- **Load Selection from Mask.** Once you've created a layer mask, you [...] button to load it as a selection that you can then use somewhere e[...] Adjustment layer (as in Figure 3-26, right).

- **Apply Mask.** Once you get the mask just right, you can permanently[...] it to the layer by clicking this button. Applying a mask permanen[...] layer and limits the changes you can make later, so don't use this o[...] you're *certain* you won't need to change the mask down the roa[...] this button by accident, use the History panel or the Undo co[...] Ctrl+Z on a PC) to get the mask back or you won't be able to e[...]

- **Disable/Enable Mask.** This visibility eye works just like the [...] panel (page 84): Click it to turn your mask off or on.

- **Delete Mask.** If you decide you don't want the mask, you can [...] by clicking this little trash can at the bottom of the Properties [...]

TIP To copy a mask to another layer, press and hold Option (Alt on a PC), click the ma[...] and then drag it to another layer. (You have to press Option or Alt *before* you click the[...] move it from one layer to the other.) When you start to drag, your cursor turns into a [...] arrowhead and you see a ghosted image of the mask.

The Properties panel's menu (labeled in Figure 3-29) contains these goodies:

- **Mask Options.** When you're editing masks, you've got a few different viewing options. In the masking examples discussed earlier, the mask was edited while the image was viewed in full color. However, as Figure 3-30 shows, you can also work on a mask while you're looking at a grayscale version of the image, or turn the mask into a color overlay. Which one you choose depends on the colors in your image and the area you're trying to select. If you choose the color overlay and Photoshop's standard red isn't doing it for you, use the Layer Mask Display Options dialog box to pick another color that makes it easy to distinguish the mask from the unmasked parts of the image (Figure 3-30, bottom).

FIGURE 3-30

Left: To edit a grayscale version of the mask like this (rather than a full-color one)—a good option if your image has lots of colors—Option-click (Alt-click on a PC) the mask's thumbnail in the Layers panel. You can then copy and paste pixels—including text—right into the layer mask. (Page 623 has a cool example involving snatching texture from a photo and using it to add texture to text.) When you're finished editing the mask, click the layer's thumbnail.

Right: To edit the mask with a red overlay, press the backslash key (\). To change the overlay's color, open the Masks panel's menu and choose Mask Options. In the resulting dialog box (shown here), click the color square and then pick a new color from the resulting Color Picker, Press the backslash key again to see your full-color image.

- **Add Mask To Selection.** If you create a mask and then make a selection (see Chapter 4), you can choose this option to add the area you've masked to the selection. This is an easy way to expand the currently selected area to include the mask in one quick step.

- **Subtract Mask From Selection.** This option deletes the shape of the mask from your selection.

- **Intersect Mask With Selection.** To select only areas where your selection and mask overlap (if you need to add a color or pattern only to those places, for example), choose this option.

■ Using Smart Objects

A *Smart Object* is a container-like layer into which you can plop all kinds of stuff, like Raw files (page 57), vectors (drawings) from programs like Adobe Illustrator (Chapter 13), whole PSD files, and even other layers. Smart Objects are smart because Photoshop remembers the original content and what program created it, which lets you do the following:

- **Transform or resize it without losing quality.** Instead of resizing the *instance* (a copy) of the content that you inserted into your document, Photoshop remembers info about the *original*, resizes that, and then places that information back into your image (without altering the original file). It doesn't matter whether that original lives elsewhere on your hard drive or right there in your Photoshop document (on another layer, say). In the blink of an eye, Photoshop updates your document with the newly resized content *without* making it look blocky (so long as you don't exceed the file's original dimensions—unless it's a vector, of course). You can also use the full range of transform tools (page 259) on Smart Objects.

- **Compress a bunch of layers into a single layer nondestructively.** Unlike merging layers (page 113), converting several layers into a single Smart Object preserves the original layers. This ability is super helpful if you want to edit several layers as if they were one, which is great for masking several layers at once, applying filters to a composite image, applying layer styles (page 131), or using tools that work on only one layer at a time.

FREQUENTLY ASKED QUESTION

Clipping Masks

What the heck is a clipping mask? Is it similar to a layer mask?

Clipping masks and layer masks are similar in that they both hide parts of an image, but that's about all they have in common. Clipping masks are like Photoshop's version of stencils: They let you take one layer's contents (a photo of bluebonnets, say) and shove it through the contents of the layer directly below (for example, text that says "Texas"). The result? The image on the top layer is "clipped" so that you only see the bluebonnets inside the text. (Hop over to page 627 for step-by-step instructions on this technique.)

You can give clipping masks a spin by opening a photo and double-clicking the Background layer to make it editable. Next, add a new layer below it by using one of the methods described on page 82. Press B to grab the Brush tool and then paint a big ol' brushstroke across the new layer (don't worry about what color it is). In the Layers panel, activate the photo layer (which should be on top of your layer stack), and then choose

Layer→Create Clipping Mask or press Option-⌘-G (Alt+Ctrl+G on a PC), and Photoshop makes your photo visible *only* through the brushstroke, regardless of what color the brushstroke is (layer transparency is the only thing that matters).

When you use a clipping mask, you don't get another thumbnail in your Layers panel like you do with a layer mask. Instead, the photo layer's thumbnail scoots to the right and you see a tiny down arrow letting you know that it's clipped to the layer below.

You can clip as many layers together as you want. For example, you can clip three image layers to a layer containing a brushstroke so the photos show *through* it. To release a clipping mask, activate the clipped layer (the top layer—in this example, that's the brushstroke layer), go to Layer→Release Clipping Mask, choose Release Clipping Mask from the Layers panel's menu, or press Option-⌘-G (Alt+Ctrl+G). You should see your entire photo again.

- **Run filters nondestructively.** When you run a filter on a Smart Object, Photoshop automatically adds a layer mask to the Smart Object, plus the filtering happens on *its* own layer (similar to layer styles, page 131) so you can tweak, hide, or undo the filter's effects. See Chapter 15 (page 634) to learn how to run filters on Smart Objects.

- **Update multiple instances of the same content.** If you've placed the same content in several places in your document—like a big version of a logo in one spot and a smaller version of it somewhere else—and you make changes to the original file, Photoshop automatically updates that content wherever it appears in your document.

- **Swap content.** Once you've formatted a Smart Object just right, you can swap its contents for another image, and the new image takes on the original's attributes. This content swapping is powerful magic when it comes to making creative templates that you can use over and over with different images (photographers and designers love this kind of thing). Figure 3-31 has the details.

FIGURE 3-31

You can create some pretty amazing templates using Smart Objects. Just open an Image as a Smart Object (as described later in this section) and then make all the changes you want, like giving it a sepia tint, adding a dark-edge vignette, and sharpening it.

Then, to swap the original photo for another one, activate the Smart Object layer (note the little badge that indicates it's a Smart Object, circled) and then choose Layer→Smart Objects→Replace Contents. Navigate to another photo on your hard drive, click Open, and it'll take on the same characteristics automatically! Thank ya, thank ya very much.

NOTE Smart Objects are especially useful when you're working with Raw files because you can double-click them in Photoshop to open them in Camera Raw (page 57). However, placing multiple Smart Objects in a single document—especially one that contains Raw files—will bloat your file size in a hurry and cause Photoshop to run as fast as molasses (especially if you're using an older computer, or have a slow hard drive or very little memory).

The following sections teach you how to create and manage Smart Objects.

Creating Smart Objects

How you create a Smart Object depends on two things: where the original content lives and which document you want to put it in. Here are your options:

- **To create a new document containing a file that lives on your hard drive, choose File→"Open as Smart Object."** In the resulting Open dialog box, navigate to the file and then click Open to make Photoshop create a new document containing a single Smart Object (without a Background layer). The image you've opened appears at its original size, and you'll see the Smart Object badge on its layer thumbnail (circled in Figure 3-31).

TIP You can Shift-click multiple files in the Open dialog box to open more than one file as a Smart Object. Each file opens as its own document with a single Smart Object layer.

- **To import a file into a document that's currently open, choose File→Place.** You get the same Open dialog box so you can navigate to the file, but this time the file opens as a Smart Object *inside* the current document. Photoshop puts little handles around the object so you can resize it. When you press Return (Enter on a PC) to accept the object, you'll see the Smart Object badge appear on the new layer's thumbnail.

NOTE Photoshop includes a preference setting that makes the program automatically open dragged or placed files as Smart Objects (see page 30). This setting is turned on out of the box, and it's the only way to roll. If you've got a document open, the Smart Object appears on a new layer inside that document; if you don't, it opens as a Smart Object in a new document.

- **Copy and paste an Adobe Illustrator file.** If you copy Illustrator art into your computer's memory, you can paste it into an open Photoshop document using ⌘-V (Ctrl+V on a PC). Photoshop will then ask whether you want to paste it as a Smart Object, pixels, path, or Shape layer (the last three are covered in Chapter 13).

- **In Bridge, choose File→Place→In Photoshop.** If you're using Bridge to peruse your files, this command pops 'em open as Smart Objects in Photoshop (see Chapter 21 for more on Bridge).

- **To turn existing layers into a Smart Object in the current document, activate the layer(s) and then choose "Convert to Smart Object" from the Layers panel's menu.** If you're working with an image that has a bunch of Adjustment layers associated with it (to change stuff like color and lighting), you can use this command to group the whole mess into a single Smart Object. That way, you can apply additional changes to all those layers at *once* with tools that work only on individual layers (like filters and layer styles). Figure 3-32 has the details.

FIGURE 3-32

Top: To convert multiple layers to a Smart Object, activate them in the Layers panel and then choose "Convert to Smart Object" from the panel's menu. (Alternatively, you can choose Layer→Smart Objects→"Convert to Smart Object," or choose Filter→"Convert for Smart Filters." All these commands do the same thing.)

Bottom: Photoshop converts all those layers into a single Smart Object that you can run filters on nondestructively. To edit the Smart Object's contents, choose Edit Contents from the Layers panel's menu and Photoshop opens a new document containing the original layers. When you're finished editing, press ⌘-S (Ctrl+S on a PC) to save your changes and then close the document; Photoshop automatically updates your Smart Object in the original document. How cool is that?

NOTE You can add a mask to Smart Objects just like you can to any other layer. Photoshop automatically *links* the mask to the layer so you can move 'em around together. To unlink them, just click the little chain between their thumbnails in the Layers panel. (See the box on page 123 for more on linked masks.)

Managing Smart Objects

Once you've created a Smart Object, you can duplicate it, edit it, and export its contents. You'll find the following options in both the Layer→Smart Objects submenu and the shortcut menu you get by Ctrl-clicking (right-clicking on a PC) near the layer's name in the Layers panel:

- **New Smart Object via Copy.** When you choose this command, Photoshop makes a duplicate of your Smart Object that's *not linked* to the original, so if you edit the content of the original Smart Object, the duplicate won't change.

This unlinked copy is helpful if you want to create more than one instance of the same Smart Object in a single file and edit them in different ways. You can also run this command by mousing over to the Layers panel and Control-clicking (right-clicking on a PC) near—but not on—the existing Smart Object's name and then choosing "New Smart Object via Copy" from the pop-up menu.

- **Edit Contents.** Choose this option or double-click the Smart Object's thumbnail in the Layers panel if you want to edit the original file in the program that created it (for example, Adobe Illustrator).

- **Export Contents.** This command pulls the contents of the active Smart Object out of the current document and puts them into a new file that's the same format as the original. If the file began life as a Raw file, for example, Photoshop will save the Smart Object contents in Raw format. When you choose this command, Photoshop displays a dialog box where you can name the new file and choose where to save it.

- **Replace Contents.** As you learned back in Figure 3-31, you can use this command to swap the contents of a Smart Object so the new image takes on the appearance of the old one.

- **Stack Mode.** This option, available only in Photoshop Extended, contains a slew of processing options that you can apply to a Smart Object composed of a series of similar images (called an *image stack*) in order to produce a perfect image that's free of noise or other accidental elements that snuck into the shot (like birds flying across the sky, a car passing in front of the subject, and so on).

- **Rasterize.** You can't paint or edit a Smart Object directly like you can its contents. But if you're ready to give up all the goodness that comes with using a Smart Object, choose this option to rasterize it and make it behave like any other layer.

WORKAROUND WORKSHOP

Nested Smart Objects

If you've got a Smart Object that contains several layers and you try to apply a layer style to it (page 131), you'll run into some difficulty. For example, if you apply a drop shadow to a Smart Object full of layers, Photoshop tacks a drop shadow onto *every* layer. So instead of a nice, subtle shadow, you end up with a shadow on top of a shadow on top of a shadow—yuck. The fix is to convert the Smart Object into *another* Smart Object inside the original before you add the layer style.

In the Layers panel, activate the Smart Object you want to convert and then choose Layer→Smart Objects→"Convert to Smart Object." Photoshop creates a new Smart Object within the original one (which is why it's called a *nested* Smart Object).

Now you can apply the layer style to the new Smart Object and the style will look like you expect it to.

TIP To create a duplicate Smart Object that *is* linked to the original, drag the Smart Object onto the "Create a new layer" button at the bottom of the Layers panel, or just activate the Smart Object in the Layers panel and duplicate it by pressing ⌘-J (Ctrl+J on a PC). This is handy if you've repeated a graphical element in your design—if you edit that element in the original Smart Object, Photoshop updates *all* the copies of that Smart Object in your document.

Layer Styles

After all that hard work learning about layers, you're probably ready for some fun. This section is all about *layer styles*: a set of 10 fully adjustable, ready-made special effects for layers that you can apply in all kinds of cool ways. Consider this section your reward for sticking with this chapter till the bitter end.

Layer styles are a lot of fun and, since they appear on their own layers, they're non-destructive *and* they remain editable as long as you save the document as a PSD file. Layer styles are great for adding finishing touches to your designs, and they can really make text and graphical elements pop off the page (see Figure 3-33). They also update automatically as your layer *content* changes.

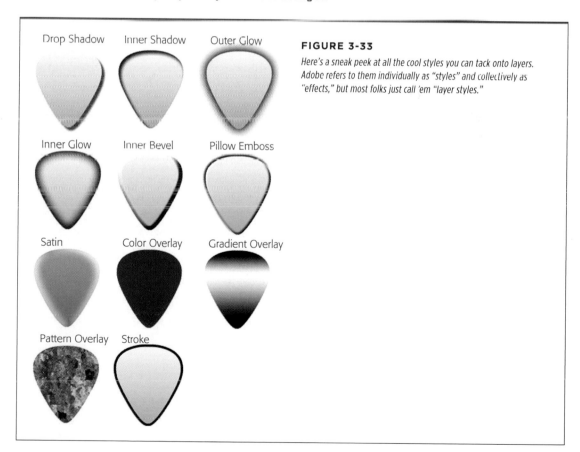

FIGURE 3-33

Here's a sneak peek at all the cool styles you can tack onto layers. Adobe refers to them individually as "styles" and collectively as "effects," but most folks just call 'em "layer styles."

Here's how to add The Lord of All Styles, the drop shadow, to a layer:

1. **Activate the soon-to-be-shadowed layer in the Layers panel.**

   Photoshop limits you to activating a single layer when you're adding a style. That said, CS6 lets you add layers styles to layer groups (page 108).

2. **Click the "Add a layer style" button at the bottom of the Layers panel and choose Drop Shadow (see Figure 3-34, top).**

   The button looks like a tiny cursive *fx* that stands for "layer *effects*" (though this book refers to them as layer styles).

3. **In the Layer Style dialog box that appears, adjust the settings to produce a respectable (soft)—not gaudy (black and 10 feet away from the object)—drop shadow.**

   There are a bazillion options for each style in the Layer Style dialog box, as Figure 3-34 shows (middle), and it's a good idea to experiment with all of 'em so you know how they work.

TIP You can also open the Layer Style dialog box by double-clicking a layer's thumbnail or double-clicking near (but not *on*) the layer's name in the Layers panel.

---

4. **Click OK when you're satisfied with the effect and then marvel at your very first drop shadow.**

   Photoshop closes the Layer Style dialog box and adds a couple of things to the Layers panel: a category named Effects and, beneath it, an item named Drop Shadow. (If you add *more* layer styles, they stack up beneath the word "Effects.") The program also adds a special badge to the right of the image layer's name (it looks like a cursive *fx*).

To edit the style later on, just double-click it in the Layers panel. To move it to another layer, just grab it and drag (you'll see a big *fx* as you drag). You can add as many styles to a layer as you want, all from the Layer Style dialog box. Just turn on the checkboxes for the styles you want (they're all in the Styles column on the left) and then click a style's name to see its options. And remember the Fill setting discussed back on page 97? You can use it to make the *contents* of a layer see-through while the *style* remains 100 percent solid.

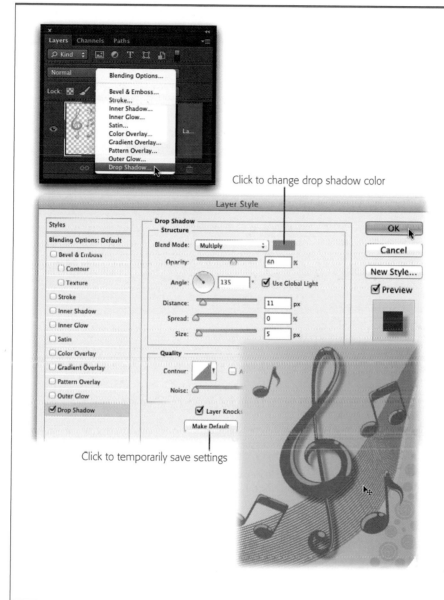

Click to change drop shadow color

Click to temporarily save settings

FIGURE 3-34

When it comes to drop shadows, the classiest ones are rarely black—instead, they pick up a darker color from the image. Just click the color swatch labeled here (middle), and Photoshop summons the Color Picker (page 491). To snatch a color that already lives in the image, mouse over to your image and, when your cursor turns into an eyedropper, click once; your shadow takes on that color.

You'll also likely need to lower the shadow's opacity so it's nice and soft, and use the Spread and Size sliders to make it wider. Don't bother messing with the Angle dial or the Distance slider because you can change those settings visually by heading over to your document and dragging the shadow around—while the Layer Style dialog box is still open—as shown here (bottom).

Once you get the drop shadow just right, click the Make Default button (labeled). The next time you need to add a drop shadow, Photoshop will use those same settings.

Managing Layer Styles

Once you've tacked on a layer style or two, you'll undoubtedly want to apply them to other layers and turn them off or on. Here's how:

- **To copy a style from one layer to another,** head over to the Layers panel and Option-drag (Alt-drag on a PC) the style to the new layer. Your cursor turns into a double black-and-white arrowhead when you drag, and you see a big, ghosted *fx*.

- **To turn a style off,** click the visibility eye to the left of the style's name in the Layers panel.

FREQUENTLY ASKED QUESTION

Hiding Styles with Masks

Help! I have a mask on my layer and Photoshop is showing the styles through the darn mask! How do I hide those pesky styles?

Ah, you seek the elusive style cloak. To summon it, you must boil the stalk of a West Texas tumbleweed, season it with eye of toad, and drink it from the shell of an armadillo three days dead...

Just kidding. To hide styles with a layer mask, you've got to change the layer's blending options. Double-click the word "Effects" in the Layers panel and Photoshop opens the Layer Style dialog box set to display the Blending Options settings.

In the Advanced Blending section in the center of the dialog box (shown here), you'll see a list of checkboxes that includes Layer Mask Hides Effects and Vector Mask Hides Effects. Turn on the appropriate option for the kind of layer you're working with (Vector Mask [page 572] for vector-based layers, and Layer Mask for all other layers), and then click OK. Back in your document, the mask should hide any styles you've applied to that layer. In CS6, a tiny icon that looks like two intersecting squares appears at the far right of the layer in the Layers panel to indicate that its blending options have been changed.

Now, back to that magic potion...

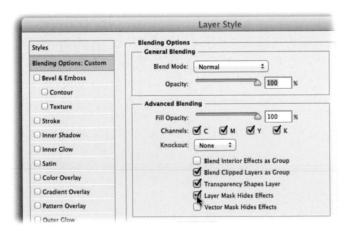

If you Control-click (right-click) a style in the Layers panel, you see a shortcut menu with these options:

- **Disable Layer Effects** turns off *all* the styles on that layer. To turn them back on, open the menu again and choose Enable Layer Effects. (Clicking the visibility eye to the left of Effects in the Layers panel does the same thing.)

- **Copy Layer Style** copies all the styles you've applied to the active layer so you can apply them to other layers. After you choose this command, Shift- or ⌘-click (Ctrl-click on a PC) to activate the layer(s) you want to apply the styles to, and then Control-click (right-click) to open the shortcut menu again and choose Paste Layer Style.

- **Clear Layer Style** deletes the style from the active layers. You can also drag a style to the trash can at the bottom of the Layers panel to remove it from a layer.

- **Global Light** tells Photoshop to use the same lighting angle in every style you add, which is useful when you're applying drop shadows or inner shadows. If you've got more than one drop shadow in your document, turn on this option so the lighting stays consistent.

- **Create Layer** takes the style applied to the selected layer and converts it into a regular image layer, which means you lose the ability to edit the style later. Though it sounds limiting, you can use this option to further customize a layer style into your own personal vision; once it's a regular layer, you can run filters on it, use the painting tools, and so on.

- **Hide All Effects** turns off the styles applied to *every* layer. After you've hidden them, this menu item changes to read "Show Effects" so you can choose it to turn 'em back on.

- **Scale Effects** lets you resize the style itself, independent of the layer's contents, by entering a percentage. This option is useful if you want to fine-tune drop shadows and glows by making them slightly larger or smaller.

Last but not least, there may be a time when you want to rasterize a layer style so it's part of the layer itself (though it's tough to think of a reason why). In CS6, you can do that by Ctrl-clicking (right-clicking on a PC) to the right of the layer thumbnail and then choosing Rasterize Layer Style. When you do, Photoshop *permanently* applies the layer style to the layer.

The Styles Panel

Photoshop comes with all kinds of layer style presets made from some pretty psychedelic style combinations. You'll find a couple of them useful, but most of them are just funky. To get at them, open the Styles panel by clicking its tab in the panel dock on the right side of your screen or by choosing Window→Styles (see Figure 3-35).

Admittedly, the preloaded styles aren't anything to write home about, but if you open the Styles panel menu, you'll see 10 *more* sets you can load: Abstract Styles, Buttons, and so on. To load another set, just choose it from the panel's menu;

Photoshop asks if you'd like to add them to the existing styles or replace the existing ones. If you're a web designer, you may find the Glass Buttons and Web Styles sets useful for that clear, plastic look. Otherwise, you probably won't find much use for many of these styles.

To apply one of these styles, simply select the layer you want to use it on and then click the style's thumbnail. You can tweak the style by double-clicking the style's layer in the Layers panel or by choosing its name from the left-hand list in the Layer Style dialog box. You can also drag and drop a style's thumbnail from the Styles panel onto a layer in the Layers panel, but doing so makes that style replace any styles already added to that layer. To add a saved style on *top* of existing styles, hold down the Shift key as you drag and drop or as you click the style's thumbnail.

Panel menu

Clear style   Delete style
New style

FIGURE 3-35

You'll find all manner of weird and wacky presets in the Styles panel (top). (To make the style thumbnails larger or to view them in a list, open the Styles panel's menu and choose Text Only, Small Thumbnail, Large Thumbnail, Small List, or Large List.) Some of the styles are more useful than others (middle).

You can add your own creations to the mix, too. Just activate the layer your style is applied to and then click the "Create new style" button shown here or choose New Style from the Styles panel's menu.

In the resulting dialog box (bottom), give your style a name, turn on the Include Layer Effects checkbox to make sure you don't lose any of your changes, and—if you've changed any layer blending options—turn on the Include Layer Blending Options checkbox, too. When you click OK, Photoshop saves your style for posterity and adds it to the Styles panel (though it's a good idea to safeguard your presets, as online Appendix B explains).

To bypass this dialog box next time you want to save a style, Option-click (Alt-click on a PC) the New Style button. You'll get a new Style called "Style" that you can rename later, but you don't get to change any other settings.

■ EXPORTING AND LOADING STYLES

If you're really proud of the styles you've created and want to share them with the masses (or at least load 'em onto another computer), here's what to do: From the Styles panel's menu, choose Save Styles, give your style a name, and tell Photoshop where to save it. You can then take the resulting file to another computer, launch Photoshop, and pick one of the following options from the Styles panel's menu:

- **Load Styles** adds the new style to the ones currently in your Styles panel.

- **Replace Styles** zaps the ones you've got in favor of the new one.

- **Reset Styles** returns your styles to the factory settings.

Selections: Choosing What to Edit

Life is all about making choices, and the time you spend in Photoshop is no exception. Perhaps the biggest decision you'll make is which part of an image to edit—after all, your edits don't have to affect the *whole* thing. Using a variety of tools, you can tell Photoshop exactly which portion of the image you want to tinker with, right down to the pixel, if you so desire. This process is called making a *selection*.

As you'll learn in this chapter, Photoshop has a bunch of tools that you can use to create selections based on shape, color, and other attributes. You can also draw selections by hand, although that requires a bit of mouse prowess. True selection wisdom lies in learning which tool to start with, how to use the tools together, and how to fine tune your selections quickly and efficiently. The following pages will help you with all that and then some.

■ Selection Basics

What's so great about selections, anyway? Lots. After you make a selection, you can do all kinds of neat things with it:

- **Fill it with color or pixels from the image's background.** Normally, the Edit→Fill command or a Solid Color Adjustment layer floods an entire layer with color, but by creating a selection first, you can color just that area. You can also use the Fill command in conjunction with a selection to delete a person from your photo as if they were never there (see page 414).

- **Add an outline.** You can add a *stroke* (Photoshop's term for an outline) to any selection. For instance, you can use selections to give a photo a black border or to circle yourself in a group photo (page 186). (In Photoshop CS6 you can also add a stroke to shapes and paths; you'll learn all about that on page 554.)

- **Move it around.** To move part of an image, you need to select it first. You can even move selections from one document to another, as discussed on page 183. For example, a little head swapping is great fun after family reunions and breakups. If you want to stick your ex's head onto a ballerina's body, hop on over to page 184.

- **Resize or transform it.** Need to change the size or shape of the selection before you manipulate the pixels inside it? No problem: Once you've made a selection, you can transform it into whatever size or shape you need (page 178). With this maneuver Photoshop won't reshape any pixels that are in the selected area; it just changes the shape of the selection itself. This trick is handy when you're trying to select part of an image that's in perspective, as shown on page 179.

- **Use it as a mask.** When you create a selection, Photoshop protects the area outside it, so that anything you do to the image affects only the selected area. For example, if you paint with the Eraser tool (page 161) across the edge of a selection, it erases only the area *inside* the selection. Likewise, if you create a selection before adding a layer mask (page 116), Photoshop loads the selected area into the mask automatically, letting you adjust only that part of the image. So selections are crucial when you need to correct color or lighting in just one area (Chapter 9), or change the color of an object (page 329).

This chapter discusses all these options and more. But, first, you need to understand how Photoshop indicates selections.

Meet the Marching Ants

When you create a selection, Photoshop calls up a lively army of animated "marching ants" (shown in Figure 4-1). These tiny soldiers dutifully march around the edge of the selected area, awaiting your command. You can select part of a layer's contents or everything on a single layer. Whenever you have an active selection (that is, whenever you see marching ants), Photoshop has eyes only for that portion of the document—any tool you use (except the Type, Pen, and shape tools) will affect only the area *inside* the selection.

> **NOTE** Selections don't hang around forever—when you click somewhere else on your screen (outside the selection) with a selection tool, the original selection disappears, forcing you to recreate it. To find out how to save a selection so you can use it again later, flip to page 184.

Here are the commands you'll use most often when making selections:

- **Select All.** This command selects the whole document and places marching ants around the perimeter, which is helpful when you want to copy and paste an entire image into another program or create a border around a photo (see page 186). To run this command, go to Select→All or press ⌘-A (Ctrl+A on a PC).

- **Deselect.** To get rid of the marching ants after you've finished working with a selection, choose Select→Deselect or press ⌘-D (Ctrl+D). Alternatively, if you've got one of the selection tools activated in the Tools panel, you can click once outside the selection to get rid of it.

- **Reselect.** To resurrect your last selection, choose Select→Reselect or press Shift-⌘-D (Shift-Ctrl-D). This command reactivates the last selection you made, even if it was five filters and 20 brushstrokes ago (unless you've used the Crop or Type tools since then, which render the Reselect command powerless). Reselecting is helpful if you accidentally deselect a selection that took you a long time to create. (The Undo command [⌘-Z or Ctrl+Z] can also help you in that situation.)

- **Inverse.** This command, which you run by going to Select→Inverse or pressing Shift-⌘-I (Shift-Ctrl-I), flip-flops a selection to select everything that *wasn't* selected before. You'll often find it easier to select what you *don't* want and then inverse the selection to get what you *do* want (the box on page 156 has more on this useful technique).

- **Load a layer as a selection.** When talking to people about Photoshop, you'll often hear the phrase "load as a selection," which is (unavoidable) Photoshop-speak for activating a layer that contains the object you want to work with and then summoning the marching ants so they run around that object; that way, whatever you do next affects *only* that object. To load everything that lives on a single editable layer as a selection, mouse over to the Layers panel and ⌘-click (Ctrl-click) the layer's thumbnail (page 78). Photoshop responds by putting marching ants around everything on that layer. Alternatively, you can Control-click (right-click on a PC) the layer's thumbnail and then choose Select Pixels from the resulting shortcut menu.

FIGURE 4-1

To let you know an area is selected, Photoshop surrounds it with tiny, moving dashes that look like marching ants. Here you can see the ants running around the armadillo.

(FYI, the nine-banded armadillo is the state animal of Texas. Didn't think you'd learn that from this book, did ya?)

Now it's time to discuss the tools you can use to make selections. Photoshop has a ton of 'em, so in the next several pages, you'll find them grouped according to which *kind* of selections they're best at making.

Selecting by Shape

Selections based on shape are probably the easiest ones to make. Whether the object you need to grab is rectangular, elliptical, or rectangular with rounded corners, Photoshop has just the tool for you. You'll use the first couple of tools described in this section often, so think of them as your bread and butter when it comes to making selections.

The Rectangular and Elliptical Marquee Tools

Photoshop's most basic selection tools are the Rectangular and Elliptical Marquees. Anytime you need to make a selection that's squarish or roundish, reach for these little helpers, which live at the top of the Tools panel, as shown in Figure 4-2.

FIGURE 4-2

You'll spend loads of time making selections with the Rectangular and Elliptical Marquee tools. To summon this menu, click the second item from the top of the Tools panel and hold down your mouse button until the menu of additional tools appears.

To make a selection with either marquee tool, just grab the tool by clicking its icon in the Tools panel or by pressing M, and then mouse over to your document. When your cursor turns into a tiny + sign, drag across the area you want to select (you'll see the marching ants appear as soon as you start to drag). Photoshop starts the selection where you clicked and continues it in the direction you drag as long as you hold down the mouse button. When you've got marching ants around the area you want to select, release the mouse button.

You can use a variety of tools and techniques to modify your selection, most of which are controlled by the Options bar (Figure 4-3). For example, you can do the following:

- **Move the selection.** Click anywhere within the selected area and then drag to another part of your document (your cursor turns into a tiny arrow the second you release the mouse button after drawing a selection—as long as your cursor remains inside the selection, that is).

TIP You can move a selection *as* you're drawing it by moving your mouse while pressing the mouse button *and* the space bar. When you've got the selection where you want it, release the space bar—but not your mouse button—and continue drawing the selection.

New selection
Add to selection
Subtract from selection
Intersect with selection

FIGURE 4-3

Using the buttons in the Options bar, you can add to or subtract from a selection, as well as create a selection from two intersecting areas.

Since all selections begin at the point where you first click, you can easily select one of these doors by dragging diagonally from the top-left corner to the bottom right as shown here. You can tell from the tiny + sign next to the crosshairs-shaped cursor that you're in "Add to selection" mode, so this figure now has two selections: the blue door and the red door.

In CS6 you get a handy a handy overlay that displays the width and height info as you drag to create a selection (shown here). If you move a selection, you see X and Y axis info instead that indicates how far you've moved the selection in the document.

Give this selection technique a spin by downloading the practice file, Doors. jpg, from this book's Missing CD page at www.missingmanuals.com/cds.

- **Add to the selection.** When you click the "Add to selection" button in the Options bar (labeled in Figure 4-3) or press and hold the Shift key, Photoshop puts a tiny + sign beneath your cursor to let you know that whatever you drag across next will get added to the current selection. This mode is handy when you need to select areas that don't touch each other, like the doors in Figure 4-3, or if you've selected *most* of what you want but notice that you missed a spot. Instead of starting over, you can switch to this mode and draw around that area as if you were creating a new selection.

- **Subtract from the selection.** Clicking the "Subtract from selection" button (also labeled in Figure 4-3) or pressing and holding the Option key (Alt on a PC) has the opposite effect. A tiny – sign appears beneath your cursor to let you know you're in this mode. Mouse over to your document and draw a box (or oval) around the area you want to *deselect*.

- **Intersect one selection with another.** If you click the "Intersect with selection" button after you draw a selection, Photoshop lets you draw another selection that overlaps the first; the marching ants then surround only the area where the two selections *overlap*. It's a little confusing, but don't worry because you'll rarely use this mode. The keyboard shortcut is Shift-Option (Shift+Alt on a PC). Photoshop puts a tiny multiplication sign (x) beneath your cursor when you're in this mode.

- **Feather the selection.** If you want to soften the edges of your selection so that it blends into the background or another image, use *feathering*. You can enter a value in pixels in this field *before* you create the selection, as it applies to the next selection you make. As you'll learn later in this chapter, feathering a selection lets you gently fade one image into another. See the box on page 145 for more on feathering, including how to feather a selection *after* you create it.

- **Apply anti-aliasing.** Turn on the Anti-alias checkbox to make Photoshop smooth the color transition between the pixels around the edges of your selection and the pixels in the background. Like feathering, anti-aliasing softens the selection's edges slightly so that they blend better, though with anti-aliasing you can't control the *amount* of softening Photoshop applies. It's a good idea to leave this checkbox turned on unless you want your selection to have super crisp—and possibly jagged and blocky—edges.

- **Constrain the selection.** If you want to constrain your selection to a fixed size or aspect ratio (so that the relationship between its width and height stays the same), you can select Fixed Size or Fixed Ratio from the Style pop-up menu and then enter the size you want in the resulting width and height fields. (Be sure to enter a unit of measurement into each field, such as *px* for pixels.) If you leave the Normal option selected, you can draw any size selection you want.

Here's how to select two objects in the same photo, as shown in Figure 4-3:

1. **Click the marquee tool icon in the Tools panel and choose the Rectangular Marquee from the pop-up menu (shown in Figure 4-2).**

   Photoshop remembers which marquee tool you last used, so you'll see that tool's icon in the Tools panel. If that's the one you want to use, just press M to activate it. If not, in the Tools panel, click and hold whichever marquee tool icon is showing until the pop-up menu appears and then choose the tool you want.

TIP To cycle between the Rectangular and Elliptical Marquee tools, press M to activate the marquee toolset and then press Shift-M to activate each one in turn. If that doesn't work, make sure that a gremlin hasn't turned off the preference that makes this trick possible. Choose Photoshop→Preferences→General (Edit→Preferences→General on a PC) and make sure the "Use Shift Key for Tool Switch" checkbox is turned on.

2. **Drag to draw a box around the first object.**

   For example, to select the blue door shown in Figure 4-3, click its top-left corner and drag diagonally toward its bottom-right corner. When you get the whole door in your selection, release the mouse button. Don't worry if you don't get the selection in exactly the right spot; you can move it around in the next step.

3. **Move your selection into place if necessary.**

   If you need to move the selection, just click *inside* the selected area (your cursor turns into a tiny arrow) and drag the selection box where you want it. You can also use the arrows on your keyboard to nudge the selection in one direction or another (you don't need to click it first).

FREQUENTLY ASKED QUESTION

The Softer Side of Selections

How come my selections always have hard edges? Can I make them soft instead?

When you first install Photoshop, any selection you make has a hard edge, but you can apply *feathering* to soften it up. Feathered selections are perfect for blending one image—or a portion of an image—into another, as in the soft oval vignette effect, an oldie but goody shown on page 146. You can also feather a selection when you retouch an image, so the re-touched area fades gently into the surrounding pixels, making it look more realistic. This technique is especially helpful when you're whitening teeth (page 425), fixing animal white-eye (page 445), or swapping heads (page 184).

You can feather a selection in a variety of ways:

After you choose a selection tool from the Tools panel—but *before* you create the selection—hop up to the Options bar and enter a Feather amount in pixels (you can enter whole numbers or decimals, like *0.5*). Feathering by just a few pixels blurs and softens the selection's edges only slightly, whereas increasing the Feather setting creates a wider, more intense blur and a super-soft edge.

After you draw a selection, you can change its Feather setting either by choosing Select→Modify→Feather and then entering

a number of pixels or by Control-clicking (right-clicking on a PC) the selection and then choosing Feather from the resulting shortcut menu.

However, by far the *best* method is to use the Properties panel's Feather slider, which lets you *see* how the feathered edge will look as well as change it later on. To use this method, create a selection and then add a layer mask. Next, open the Properties panel by choosing Window→Properties and, with the mask active in the Layers panel, drag the Feather slider to the right. Photoshop shows you the feathering in your document in real time. If you decide to change the amount of feathering later on, just activate the mask, pop this panel back open, and then tweak the same slider.

You can also use the Refine Edge dialog box to add and view feathering in real time, though this dialog box is best in cases where you need to feather the selection and tweak it in other ways (such as expanding or contracting it). That said, this method doesn't give you the ability to change the feathering amount later. (For more on using the Refine Edge dialog box, see page 171.)

---

4. **Click the "Add to selection" button in the Options bar and then select the second object by drawing a selection around it.**

Photoshop lets you know that you're in "Add to selection" mode by placing a tiny + sign below your cursor. Once you see it, mouse over to the second door and drag diagonally from its top-left corner to its bottom right, as shown in Figure 4-3. Alternatively, you can press and hold the Shift key to put the tool into "Add to selection" mode.

If you need to move this second selection around, do that *before* you release the mouse button or you'll end up moving both selections instead of just one. To move the selection while you're drawing it, hold down your mouse button, press and hold the space bar, and then move your mouse to move the selection. When it's in the right place, release the space bar—but keep holding the mouse button—and continue dragging to draw the selection. This maneuver feels a bit awkward at first, but you'll get used to it with practice.

Congratulations! You've just made your first selection and added to it. Way to go!

TIP To draw a perfectly square or circular selection, press the Shift key as you drag with the Rectangular or Elliptical Marquee tools, respectively. If you want to draw the selection from the center outward (instead of from corner to corner), press and hold the Option key (Alt on a PC) instead. And if you want to draw a perfectly square or circular selection from the center outward, press and hold Shift-Option (Shift+Alt) as you drag with either tool. Be sure to use these tricks only on new selections—if you've already got a selection, the Shift key pops you into "Add to selection" mode.

■ CREATING A SOFT VIGNETTE

The Elliptical Marquee tool works just like the Rectangular Marquee tool except that it draws round or oval selections. It's a great tool for selecting eyes, circling yourself in a group photo (page 186), or creating the ever-popular, oh-so-romantic, soft oval vignette shown in Figure 4-4.

Here's how to create a soft oval vignette:

1. **Open two images and combine them into the same document.**

Simply drag one image from its Layers panel into the other document's window, as shown on page 103.

2. **Reposition the layers so the soon-to-be-vignetted photo is at the top of the Layers panel.**

Over in the Layers panel, make sure that both layers are editable so you can change their stacking order. If you see a tiny padlock to the right of either layer's name, double-click that layer's thumbnail to make it editable. Then drag the layer containing the photo you want to vignette (in Figure 4-4, that's the picture of the armadillo) to the top of the Layers panel.

FIGURE 4-4

By adding a layer mask (page 116) and then feathering a selection you've made with the Elliptical Marquee tool, you can create a quick two-photo collage like this one. Wedding photographers and moms—not to mention armadillo fans—love this kind of thing! By using the Properties panel to do your feather, you gain the ability to change the feather amount later on (provided you save the document as a PSD file).

Once you get the hang of this technique, try creating it using the Ellipse tool set to draw in path mode instead, as described on page 572; it's a little bit quicker and slightly more efficient.

3. **Grab the Elliptical Marquee tool and select the part of the image you want to vignette (here, the armadillo's head).**

   Peek at your Layers panel to make sure the correct image layer is active (the armadillo) and position your mouse near the center of the image. Press and hold the Option key (Alt on a PC), mouse over to the image, and drag to draw an oval-shaped selection from the inside out. When you've got the selection big enough, release the Option (or Alt) key and your mouse button.

4. **Hide the area outside the selection with a layer mask.**

   You *could* simply inverse the selection (page 141) and then press the Delete key (Backspace on a PC) to zap the area outside it, but that'd be mighty reckless. What if you changed your mind? You'd have to undo several steps or start over completely! A less destructive and more flexible approach, which you learned about back on page 116, is to *hide* the area outside the selection with a layer mask. Over in the Layers panel, make sure you have the correct layer active (in this case, the armadillo) and then add a layer mask by clicking the tiny circle-within-a-square icon at the bottom of the panel. Photoshop hides everything outside the selection, letting you see through to the bluebonnet layer below. Beautiful!

5. **Feather the selection's edges by using the Properties panel's Feather slider.**

   With the layer mask active, open the Properties panel by choosing Window→Properties. In the panel, drag the Feather slider to the right and Photoshop softens the selection right there in the document as you watch. (New in CS6, the Feather slider accepts decimal values!)

6. **Choose File→Save As, and then pick Photoshop as the format.**

   Doing so lets you tweak the Feather amount later on by activating the layer mask and then reopening the Properties panel.

That armadillo looks right at home, doesn't he? You'll want to memorize these steps because this method is perhaps the easiest—and most romantic!—way to combine two images into a new and unique piece of art (although you'll learn how to use the vector shape tools to do the same thing starting on page 572).

The Single Row and Column Marquee Tools

The Marquee toolset also contains the Single Row Marquee and Single Column Marquee tools, which can select exactly one row or one column's worth of pixels, spanning either the width or the height of your document. You don't need to drag with your mouse to create a selection with these tools; just click once in your document and the marching ants appear.

You may be wondering, "When would I want to do that?" Not often, it's true, but consider these circumstances:

- **Mocking up a web page design.** If you need to simulate a column or row of space between certain areas in a web page, you can use either tool to create a selection that you fill with the website's background color.

- **Create a repeating background on a web page.** If you're creating an image that you'll use as a repeating background on a web page, select a horizontal row and then instruct your HTML-editing program to repeat or stretch the image as far as you need it. This trick can really decrease the time it takes to download a web page.

- **Stretching an image to fill a space.** If you're designing a web page, for example, you can use these tools to extend an image by a pixel or two. Use either tool to select a row of pixels at the bottom or side of the image, grab the Move tool by pressing V, and then tap the arrow keys on your keyboard while holding the Option key (Alt on a PC) to nudge the selection in the direction you need and duplicate it at the same time. However, a better option is to use Content-Aware Scale (see page 254).

- **Making an image look like it's melting or traveling through space at warp speed.** You can use either tool to create a selection and then stretch it with the Free Transform tool (see Figure 4-5).

NOTE Create your own speeding hen by downloading the practice file, *Hen.jpg*, from this book's Missing CD page at *www.missingmanuals.com/cds*.

FIGURE 4-5

Good luck catching this hen! To achieve this look, start by using the Single Column Marquee to select a column of pixels. Then "jump" the selection onto its own layer by pressing ⌘-J (Ctrl+J on a PC). Next, summon the Free Transform tool by pressing ⌘-T (Ctrl+T), and drag one of the square, white center handles leftward. Last but not least, add a gradient mask (page 278) and then experiment with blend modes until you find one that makes the stretched pixels blend into the image (for more on blend modes, see Chapter 7, page 280).

Unfortunately you can't activate the Single Row and Single Column Marquee tools with a keyboard shortcut; you've got to click their icons in the Tools panel instead.

The Vector Shape Tools

Technically, vector shapes aren't selection tools, but you *can* use them to create selections (turn to page 550 to learn more about vector shapes). Once you get the hang of using them as described in this section, you'll be reaching for 'em all the time.

Perhaps the most useful of this bunch is the Rounded Rectangle tool. If you ever need to select an area that's rectangular but has rounded corners, this is your best bet. For example, if you're creating an ad for a digital camera, you can use this technique in a product shot to replace the image shown on the camera's display screen with a different image. Or, more practically, you can use it to give your photos rounded corners, as shown in Figure 4-6.

Here's how to round the corners of a photo:

1. **Open a photo and double-click the Background layer to make it editable.**

   Because you'll add a mask to the photo layer in step 6, you need to make sure the Background layer is unlocked or Photoshop won't let you add the mask.

2. **Activate the Rounded Rectangle tool in the Tools panel.**

   Near the bottom of the Tools panel lies the Vector Shape toolset. Unless you've previously activated a different tool, you'll see the Rectangle tool's icon. Click the icon and hold down your mouse button until the pop-up menu appears, and then choose the Rounded Rectangle tool.

FIGURE 4-6

If you're tired of boring, straight corners on your images, use the Rounded Rectangle tool to produce smooth corners like the ones shown here. Be sure to put the tool in Path mode first using the pop-up menu near the far left of the Options bar, or else you'll create a Shape layer that you don't really need.

You can use the same technique with the Ellipse tool to create the vignette effect shown in the previous section. To feather the mask after you've added it, activate it, choose Window→Properties, and then drag the Properties panel's Feather slider to the right.

TIP To cycle through all of Photoshop's shape tools, press Shift-U repeatedly.

3. **In the Options bar, set the tool's mode to Path and change the Radius field to 40 pixels (or whatever looks good to you).**

   As you'll learn on page 550, the vector shape tools can operate in various modes. For this technique, you want to use Path mode. Click the pop-up menu near the left end of the Options bar (it's probably set to Shape) and choose Path. Next, change the number in the Radius field, which controls how rounded the image's corners will be: A lower number causes less rounding than a higher number. This field was set to 40 pixels to create the corners shown in Figure 4-6. However, you'll need to use a larger number if you're working with a high-resolution document.

4. **Draw a box around the image.**

   Mouse over to your image and, starting in one corner, drag diagonally to draw a box around the whole image. When you let go of the mouse button, Photoshop creates a thin gray outline that appears atop your image called a *path,* which you'll learn all about in Chapter 13. If you need to move the path while you're drawing it, press and hold the space bar. If you want to move the path *after* you've drawn it, press A to grab the Path Selection tool (it looks like a black arrow and lives below the Type tool in the Tools panel), click the path to activate it, and then drag to move it wherever you want.

5. **Hide the area outside the path by adding a layer mask.**

   In the Layers panel, click the photo layer once to activate it and then add a *vector* layer mask by ⌘-clicking (Ctrl-clicking) the tiny circle-within-a-square icon at the bottom of the Layers panel. (Why a vector mask? Because the path you drew with the shape tool is *vector*-based, not pixel-based. As you learned on page 52, you can resize a vector anytime without losing quality by activating it and then using Free Transform [page 259]. For more on vector masks, skip ahead to page 572.) Once you add the mask, Photoshop hides the photo's boring, square edges.

Who knew that giving your photo rounded corners was so simple?

■ Selecting by Color

In addition to tools for selecting areas by shape, Photoshop has tools that let you select areas by *color*. This option is helpful when you want to select a chunk of an image that's fairly uniform in color, like someone's skin, the sky, or the paint job on a car. Photoshop has lots of tools to choose from, and in this section, you'll learn how to pick the one that best suits your needs.

The Quick Selection Tool

The Quick Selection tool is shockingly easy to use and lets you create complex selections with just a few brushstrokes. As you paint with this tool, your selection expands outward to encompass pixels similar in color to the ones you're brushing *across.* It works insanely well if there's a fair amount of contrast between what you want to select and everything else. This tool lives in the same toolset as the Magic Wand, as you can see in Figure 4-7.

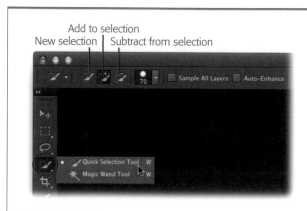

Add to selection

New selection | Subtract from selection

FIGURE 4-7

You can press the W key to activate the Quick Selection tool. (To switch between it and the Magic Wand, press Shift-W.)

When you activate the Quick Selection tool, the Options bar sports buttons that let you create a new selection as well as add to or subtract from the current selection.

To use this wonderfully friendly tool, click anywhere in the area you want to select or *drag* the brush cursor across it, as shown in Figure 4-8. When you do that, Photoshop thinks for a second and then creates a selection based on the color of the pixels you clicked or brushed across. The size of the area Photoshop selects is proportional to the size of the brush you're using: A larger brush creates a larger selection. You adjust the Quick Selection tool's brush size just like any other brush: by choosing a new size from the Brush picker in the Options bar, or by using the left and right bracket keys ([and]) to decrease and increase brush size (respectively). (Chapter 12 covers brushes in detail.) For the best results, use a hard-edged brush to produce well-defined edges (instead of the slightly transparent edges produced by a soft-edged brush) and turn on the Auto-Enhance setting shown in Figure 4-7 and discussed in the box on page 154.

FIGURE 4-8

If the color of the objects you want to select differs greatly from the color of their background, like these chili peppers, use the Quick Selection tool. With this tool active, you can either click the area you want to select or drag your cursor (circled) across the area as if you were painting. As soon as you start painting with this tool, you see a tiny + sign inside the cursor (as shown here) and Photoshop puts the tool in "Add to selection" mode, which lets you add to an existing selection or make multiple selections.

When the Quick Selection tool is active, the Options bar includes these settings (see Figure 4-7):

- **New selection.** When you first grab the Quick Selection tool, it's set to this mode, which creates a brand-new selection when you click or drag (indicated by the tiny + sign that appears inside the cursor, as shown in Figure 4-8).

- **Add to selection.** Once you've clicked or made an initial brushstroke, the Quick Selection tool automatically switches to this mode. Now Photoshop adds any areas you brush over or click to the current selection. If you don't like the selection Photoshop has created and want to start over, press ⌘-Z (Ctrl-Z on a PC) to undo it, or click the Options bar's "New selection" button and then brush across the area again. (The old selection disappears as soon as you start a new one.) To get rid of the marching ants altogether, choose Select→Deselect.

- **Subtract from selection.** If Photoshop selected more than you wanted it to, click the "Subtract from selection" button (a tiny – sign appears in your cursor) and then simply paint across the area you *don't* want selected to make Photoshop exclude it. You can also press and hold the Option key (Alt on a PC) to enter "Subtract from selection" mode.

NOTE To get the most out of the Quick Selection tool, you'll probably need to do a fair amount of adding to and subtracting from your selections. That said, you can change how picky this tool is by adjusting the Magic Wand's *Tolerance* setting (sounds strange, but it's true). Skip ahead to page 155 in the next section to learn how.

- **Brush Size/Hardness.** Use a larger brush to select big areas and a smaller brush to select small or hard-to-reach areas. As explained earlier, you'll get better results with this tool by using a hard-edged brush instead of a soft-edged one.

TIP You can change a brush cursor's size by Control-Option-dragging left or right (Alt+right-click+dragging on a PC); to adjust hardness, drag up or down instead. Alternatively, you can press the left bracket key ([) to decrease brush size or the right bracket key (]) to increase it.

- **Sample All Layers.** This setting is initially turned off, which means Photoshop examines only the pixels on the active layer (the one that's highlighted in the Layers panel). If you turn on this setting, Photoshop examines the whole enchilada—everything in your document—and grabs all similar pixels no matter which layer they're on.

- **Auto-Enhance.** Because the Quick Selection tool makes selections extremely quickly, their edges can end up looking blocky and imperfect. Turn on this checkbox to tell Photoshop to take its time and think more carefully about the selections it makes. This feature gives your selections smoother edges, but if you're working with a really big file, you could do your taxes while it's processing. The box below has tips for using this feature.

The Magic Wand Tool

The Magic Wand lets you select areas of color by clicking rather than dragging. It's in the same toolset as the Quick Selection tool, and you can grab it by pressing Shift-W (it looks like a wizard's wand, as shown back in Figure 4-7). The Magic Wand is great for selecting solid-colored backgrounds or large bodies of similar color, like a cloudless sky, with just a couple of clicks. (The Quick Selection tool is better at selecting objects.)

When you click once with the Magic Wand in the area you want to select, Photoshop magically (hence the name) selects all the pixels on the currently active layer that are both similar in color *and* touching one another (see page 155 to learn how to tweak this behavior). If the color in the area you want to select varies a bit, Photoshop may not select all of it. In that case, you can add to the selection either by pressing and holding the Shift key as you click nearby areas or by modifying the Magic Wand's *tolerance* in the Options bar as described in a sec and shown in Figure 4-9. To subtract from the selection, just press and hold the Option key (Alt on a PC) while you click the area you don't want included.

When you activate the Magic Wand, the Options bar includes these settings:

- **Sample Size.** In CS6, this menu lets you change the way the Magic Wand calculates which pixels to select (in previous versions, you had to switch to the Eyedropper tool to see this menu). From the factory, it's set to Point Sample, which makes the tool look only at the color of the specific pixel you clicked when determining its selection. However, the menu's other options cause it to look at the original pixel *and* average it with the colors of surrounding pixels. For example, you can make the Magic Wand average the pixel you clicked plus the eight surrounding pixels by choosing "3 by 3 Average," or as much as the surrounding 10,200 pixels by choosing "101 by 101 Average." The "3 by 3 Average" setting works well for most images. If you need to select a really big area, you can experiment with one of the higher settings, like "31 by 31 Average."

WORKAROUND WORKSHOP

Smart Auto-Enhancing

The Quick Selection tool's Auto-Enhance feature is pretty cool, but it's a bit of a processing hog. If you have an older computer, you may have better luck using the Refine Edge dialog box to create selections with smooth edges. (See page 171 for more on the Refine Edge command.)

That being said, you don't have to avoid Auto-Enhance altogether. When you're working with a large file (anything over 100 MB),

leave the Auto-Enhance checkbox turned off until you're *almost* finished making the selection. When you've got just one or two brushstrokes left to complete your selection, turn on the checkbox to make Photoshop re-examine the edges of the selection it's already created to see if it needs to extend them. That way, you get the benefit of using Auto-Enhance *and* keep your computer running quickly until the last possible moment.

FIGURE 4-9

With its tolerance set to 32, the Magic Wand did a good job of selecting the sky behind downtown Dallas.

You've got several ways to select the spots it missed, like the area circled at the bottom left: You can add to the selection by pressing the Shift key as you click in that area, increase the Tolerance setting in the Options bar and then click the sky again to create a brand-new selection, or skip to page 156 to learn how to expand the selection with the Grow and Similar commands.

Give this selection technique a shot by downloading the practice file Dallas.jpg from this book's Missing CD page at www.missingmanuals.com/cds.

- **Tolerance.** This setting controls both the Magic Wand's and the Quick Selection tool's sensitivity—how picky each tool is about which pixels it considers similar in color. If you increase this setting, the tool gets less picky (in other words, more tolerant) and selects every pixel that could possibly be described as similar to the one you clicked. If you decrease this setting, the tool gets pickier and selects only pixels that *closely* match the one you clicked.

  Out of the box, the tolerance is set to 32, but it can go all the way up to 255. (If you set it to 0, Photoshop selects only pixels that *exactly* match the one you clicked; if you set it to 255, the program selects every color in the image.) It's usually a good idea to keep the tolerance fairly low (somewhere between 12 and 32); you can always click an area to see what kind of selection you get, increase the tolerance if you need to, and then click that area again (or add to the selection using the Shift key, as described above).

NOTE When you adjust the Magic Wand's tolerance, Photoshop doesn't adjust your *current* selection. You have to click the area *again* to make Photoshop redo its selection.

- **Anti-alias.** Leave this setting turned on to make Photoshop soften the edges of the selection ever so slightly. If you want a super-crisp edge, turn it off.

- **Contiguous.** You'll probably want to leave this checkbox turned on; it makes the Magic Wand select pixels that are adjacent to one another. If you turn it off, Photoshop goes hog wild and selects all similar-colored pixels no matter where they are.

- **Sample all layers.** If your document has multiple layers and you leave this check-box turned off, Photoshop examines only pixels on the active layer and ignores the other layers. If you turn this setting on, Photoshop examines the whole image and selects all pixels that are similar in color, no matter which layer they're on.

NOTE The Magic Wand is rather notorious for making the edges of selections jagged because it concentrates on selecting *whole* pixels, instead of partially transparent ones (this doesn't happen as much with the Quick Selection tool). The fix is to click the Refine Edge button in the Options bar after you make the selection, and then adjust the Smooth slider in the resulting dialog box. Skip ahead to page 171 to learn how.

■ EXPANDING YOUR SELECTION

Sometimes the Magic Wand makes a *nearly* perfect selection, leaving you with precious few pixels to add to it. If this happens, it simply means that the elusive pixels are just a little bit lighter or darker in color than what the Magic Wand's toler-ance setting allows for. You *could* Shift-click the elusive areas to add them to your selection, but the Select menu has a couple of options that can quickly expand the selection for you:

- **Choose Select→Grow** to make Photoshop expand the selection to all similar-colored pixels adjacent to it (see Figure 4-10, top).

- **Choose Select→Similar** to make Photoshop select similar-colored pixels throughout the *whole* image even if they're not touching the original selection (see Figure 4-10, bottom).

NOTE Because both of these commands base their calculations on the Magic Wand's Tolerance setting (page 155), you can adjust their sensitivity by adjusting that setting in the Options bar. You also can run these commands more than once to get the selection you want.

UP TO SPEED

Selecting the Opposite

You'll often find it easier to select what you *don't* want in order to get the selection you *do* want. For example, look back at the photo of the Dallas skyline shown in Figure 4-9. If you want to select the buildings, it's easier to select the sky instead because its color is practically uniform. (It'd take you a lot longer to select the buildings because they're irregularly shaped and vary so much in color.)

No problem. After selecting the sky, you can inverse (flip-flop) your selection to select the buildings instead. Simply choose Select→Inverse or press Shift-⌘-I (Shift+Ctrl+I on a PC). The lesson here is that it pays to spend a few moments studying the area you want to select and the area *around* it. If the color of the surrounding area is uniform, reach for one of the tools described in this section, select that area, and then inverse the selection to save yourself tons of time!

The Color Range Command

The Color Range command is similar to the tools in this section in that it makes selections based on colors, but it's much better at selecting areas that contain lots of details (for example, the flower bunches in Figure 4-11). The Magic Wand tends to select *solid* pixels, whereas Color Range tends to select more *transparent* pixels than solid ones, resulting in softer edges. This fine-tuning lets Color Range produce selections with smoother edges (less blocky and jagged than the ones you get with the Magic Wand) and get in more tightly around areas with lots of details. As a bonus, you also get a handy preview in the Color Range dialog box, showing you which pixels it'll select *before* you commit to the selection (unlike the Grow and Similar commands discussed in the previous section).

FIGURE 4-10

Top: Say you're trying to select the red part of this Texas flag. After clicking once with the Magic Wand (with a Tolerance setting of 32), you still need to select a bit more of the red (left). Since the red pixels are all touching one another, you can run the Grow command a couple of times to make Photoshop expand your selection to include all the red (right).

Bottom: If you want to select the red in these playing cards (what a poker hand!), the Grow command won't help because the red pixels aren't touching one another. In that case, click once with the Magic Wand to select one of the red areas (left) and then use the Similar command to grab the rest of them (right). Read 'em and weep, boys!

TIP In Photoshop CS6, you can use the Color Range command's new Skin Tones option to select people in your images. The box on page 159 has details.

Open the Color Range dialog box by choosing Select→Color Range, either before or after you make a selection. If you haven't yet made a selection, Color Range examines the entire image. If you already have a selection, Photoshop looks only at the pixels within the selected area, which is helpful if you want to isolate a certain area. For example, you could throw a quick selection around the red flower in the center of Figure 4-11 and then use Color Range's subtract-from-selection capabilities (explained in a moment) to carve out just the red petals. By contrast, if you want to use Color Range to help expand your current selection, press and hold the Shift key while you choose Select→Color Range.

Use the Select pop-up menu at the top of the Color Range dialog box to tell Photoshop which colors to include in the selection. The menu is automatically set to Sampled Colors, which lets you mouse over to the image (your cursor turns into a tiny eyedropper as shown in Figure 4-11) and click the color you want to select. If you change the Select menu's setting to Reds, Blues, Greens, or whatever, Color Range will examine your image and grab that range of colors all by itself once you click OK.

If you're trying to select adjacent pixels, turn on the Localized Color Clusters checkbox. When you do, the Range slider becomes active so you can tweak the range of colors Photoshop includes in the selection. Increase this setting and Photoshop includes more colors and makes larger selections; lower it and Photoshop creates a smaller selection because it gets pickier about matching colors.

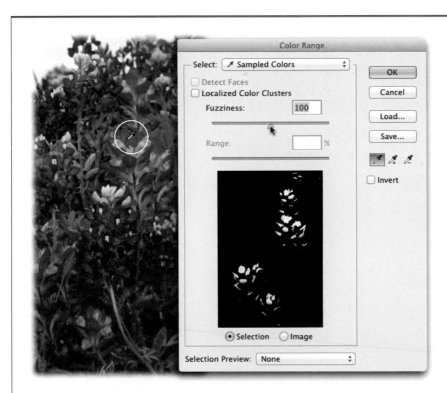

FIGURE 4-11

The Color Range command is handy when you need to select an area with lots of details, like the red and blue petals of these flowers.

The dialog box's preview area shows which parts of the image Photoshop will select when you click OK (they're displayed in white).

You can tweak the point at which Photoshop *partially* selects pixels by adjusting the Fuzziness setting. Its factory setting is 40, but you can set it to anything between 0 and 200. As you move the Fuzziness slider (or type a number in the text box), keep an eye on the dialog box's preview area—the parts of the image that Photoshop will fully include in the selection appear white, and any pixels that are partially selected appear gray (see Figure 4-11).

GEM IN THE ROUGH

Selecting Skin Tones and Faces

New in Photoshop CS6, you can use the Color Range dialog box to help select skin tones. This feature is helpful for making a quick selection of skin tones in order to correct just that part of an image, or to create a layer mask that *protects* skin tones when you're sharpening, blurring, and so on.

To use it, head to the dialog box's Select menu and choose Skin Tones. Photoshop immediately hunts down all the colors in the image that are similar to those found in a wide variety of human skin (though don't expect it to work well on all ethnicities). You can then use the Fuzziness slider to fine-tune the selection; drag it left to include less skin or right to include more.

If you're after faces in particular, turn on the Detect Faces checkbox, and Photoshop looks for faces and includes 'em in your selection. (The Detect Faces checkbox becomes active when you choose Skin Tones from the Select menu; if you choose Sampled Colors instead, you have to turn on the Localized Color Clusters checkbox before you can turn on Detect Faces.) Selections made with Detect Faces turned on include partially transparent pixels around the faces' edges so the changes you make will blend better with surrounding pixels (partially transparent pixels look gray in the preview area).

While this new feature is a grand idea, it works on only a handful of images. If your image includes a face that's turned in profile or if skin-like colors are found elsewhere in the image—think light-colored hair, a nude-colored shirt, and so on—you're better off using the Quick Selection tool (page 151) or a Hue/Saturation adjustment with a targeted color range (page 333).

NOTE As mentioned in the box on page 156, it's sometimes easier to select what you *don't* want in order to get the selection you need. To use the Color Range dialog box to select what you don't want, turn on its Invert checkbox.

Use the eyedroppers on the dialog box's right side to add or subtract colors from your selection; the eyedropper with the tiny + sign adds to the selection, and the one with the − sign subtracts from it. (Use the plain eyedropper to make your initial selection.) When you click one of these eyedroppers, mouse over to your image, and then click the color you want to add or subtract, Photoshop updates the Color Range dialog box's preview to show what the new selection looks like. It sometimes helps to keep the Fuzziness setting fairly low (around 50 or so) while you click repeatedly with the eyedropper.

TIP You can use the radio buttons beneath the Color Range dialog box's preview area to see either the selected area (displayed in white) or the image itself. But there's a better, faster way to switch between the two views: With the Selection radio button turned on, press the ⌘ key (Ctrl on a PC) to temporarily switch to image preview. When you let go of the key, you're back to selection preview.

The Selection Preview pop-up menu at the bottom of the dialog box lets you display a selection preview on the image itself so that, instead of using the dinky preview in the dialog box, you can see the proposed selection right on your image. But you'll probably want to leave this menu set to None because the preview options that Photoshop offers (Grayscale, Black Matte, and so on) get really distracting!

The Background and Magic Erasers

These two tools let you erase parts of an image based on the color under your cursor *without* having to create a selection first. You're probably thinking, "Hey, I want to create a selection, not go around erasing stuff!" And you have a valid point except that, after you've done a little erasing, you can always *load* the erased area (or what's left) as a selection. All you have to do is think ahead and create a duplicate layer before you start erasing, as this section explains.

Say you have an image with a strong contrast between the item you want to select and its background, like a dead tree against the sky. In that case, Photoshop has a couple of tools that can help you erase the sky super fast (see Figure 4-12). Sure, you *could* use the Magic Wand or Quick Selection tool to select the sky and then delete or mask it (page 116), but the Background Eraser lets you erase more carefully around the edges of the tree.

TIP The Eraser tool's keyboard shortcut is the E key. To switch among the various eraser tools, press Shift-E repeatedly.

FIGURE 4-12

You may never see these tools because they're hidden inside the same toolset as the regular Eraser tool. Just click and hold the Eraser tool's icon until this little pop-up menu appears. Pick an eraser based on how you want to use it: You drag with the Background Eraser (as if you were painting, which is great for getting around the edges of an object), whereas you simply click with the Magic Eraser.

■ THE BACKGROUND ERASER

This tool lets you delete an image's background by painting (dragging) across the pixels you want to delete. When you activate the Background Eraser, your cursor turns into a circle with tiny crosshairs in its center. The crosshairs cursor controls which pixels Photoshop deletes, so be extra careful that it *touches only* pixels you want to erase. Up in the Options bar, you can tweak the following settings (see Figure 4-13):

- **Brush Preset picker.** This is where you choose the shape and size of your brush cursor. For best results, stick with a soft-edged brush. Just click the down-pointing triangle next to this menu to grab one.

- **Sampling.** This setting is made up of three buttons whose icons all include eyedroppers. Sampling controls how often Photoshop looks at the color the crosshairs are touching to decide what to erase. If your image's background has a lot of color variation, leave this set to Continuous so Photoshop keeps a constant watch on what color pixels the crosshairs are touching. But if the background's color is fairly uniform, change this setting to Once; Photoshop then checks the color the crosshairs touch just once and resolves to erase only pixels that closely match it. If you're dealing with an image where there's only a small area for you to paint (like a tiny portion of sky showing through a lush tree), change this setting to Background Swatch, which tells Photoshop to erase only colors that are similar to your current background color chip (*how* similar they have to be is controlled by the Tolerance setting described in a sec). To choose the color, click the background color chip at the bottom of the Tools panel (page 23), mouse over to your image, and then click an area that's the color you want to erase.

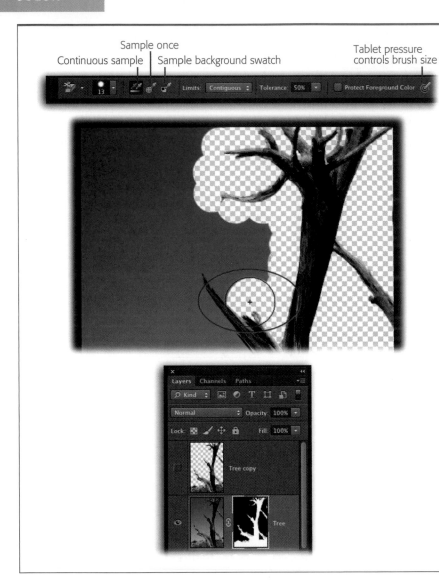

FIGURE 4-13

Even though the Background Eraser is destructive (it erases pixels), you can use it in a nondestructive way by remembering to duplicate the soon-to-be-erased layer first. Then load the erased layer as a selection and use it as a layer mask on the original layer. As you can see here, Photoshop pays attention only to the color you touch with the crosshairs in the center of the cursor; even though the tree's branches are within the brush area (circled), Photoshop deletes only the blue pixels.

If you want to practice erasing this background, you can download DeadTree.jpg from this book's Missing CD page at www.missingmanuals.com/cds.

- **Limits.** When you first launch Photoshop, this field is set to Contiguous, which means the tool erases only pixels adjacent to those you touch with the crosshairs. If you want to erase similar-colored pixels elsewhere in your image (for example, the background behind a really thick tree or a bunch of flowers), change this setting to Discontiguous. Find Edges erases only adjacent pixels, but it does so while preserving the sharpness of the object's edge.

- **Tolerance.** This setting works just like the Magic Wand's Tolerance setting (page 155): A lower number makes the tool pickier about the pixels it erases, and a higher number makes it less picky.

- **Protect Foreground Color.** If you can't seem to get the Tolerance setting high enough and you're *still* erasing some of the area you want to keep, turning on this checkbox can help. When it's on, you can tell Photoshop which area you want to keep (the foreground) by Option-clicking (Alt-clicking on a PC) that area. If the area you want to keep is a different color in different parts of your image, turn this setting off or Option-click (Alt-click) to resample the foreground area.

Here's how to use the Background Eraser to remove the sky behind a dead tree *without* harming the original pixels, as shown in Figure 4-13:

1. **Open a photo and double-click its Background layer to make it editable (page 87), duplicate the Background by pressing ⌘-J (Ctrl+J on a PC), and then hide the original Background layer.**

   Since you'll add a layer mask to the original layer in the last step of this list, you need to unlock the Background to make it editable. And because you'll do your erasing on the duplicate layer, you don't need to see the original layer. Over in the Layers panel, click the little visibility eye to the left of the original layer's thumbnail to turn it off.

2. **Grab the Background Eraser tool and paint away the background.**

   This tool is in the same toolset as the Eraser tool (see Figure 4-12). Once you've activated it, mouse over to your document; your cursor morphs into a circle with tiny crosshairs in the center. Remember that the trick is to let the crosshairs touch *only* the pixels you want to erase (it doesn't matter what the circle part of the cursor touches). If you need to, increase and decrease your brush cursor's size by pressing the left and right bracket keys on your keyboard, respectively.

3. **If the tool is erasing too much or too little of your image, tweak the Tolerance setting in the Options bar.**

   If an area in your image is *almost* the same color as the background, lower the tolerance to make the tool pickier about what it's erasing so that it erases only pixels that closely match the ones you touch with the crosshairs. Likewise, if it's not erasing enough of the background, raise the tolerance to make it zap more pixels.

TIP It's better to erase *small* sections at a time instead of painting around the entire object in one continuous stroke. Press your mouse button to erase some of the area around the object, let go of the button, click again to erase a little more, and so on. That way, if you need to undo your erasing with the History panel or the Undo command (⌘-Z; Ctrl+Z on a PC), you won't have to watch *all* that erasing unravel before your eyes.

4. **Once you get a clean outline around the object, switch to the regular Eraser tool or the Lasso tool (page 166) to get rid of the remaining background.**

   After you erase the hard part—the area around the edges—with the Background Eraser, you can use the regular Eraser tool, set to a large brush, to get rid of the remaining background quickly. Or you can use the Lasso tool to select the remaining areas and then press the Delete key (Backspace on a PC) to get rid of 'em.

5. **Load the erased layer as a selection and turn off its visibility.**

   Over in the Layers panel, ⌘-click (Ctrl-click on a PC) the thumbnail of the layer you did the erasing work on to create a selection around the tree. When you see the marching ants, click the layer's visibility eye to hide it.

6. **Activate the original layer, turn on its visibility, and then add a layer mask to it**.

   In the Layers panel, click once to activate the original layer (the unlocked Background) and then click the area to the left of its thumbnail to make it visible again. While you have marching ants running around the newly erased area, add a layer mask (page 116) to the original layer by clicking the circle-within-a-square icon at the bottom of the Layers panel.

You're basically done at this point, but if you need to do any cleanup work (if the Background Eraser didn't do a perfect job getting around the edges, say), now's the time to edit the layer mask. To do so, click the mask's thumbnail over in the Layers panel. Then press B to grab the Brush tool and set your foreground color chip to black (page 23). Now, when you brush across your image, you'll hide more of the sky. If you need to reveal more of the tree, set your foreground color chip to white, and then paint the area you want to reveal. (See page 116 for a detailed discussion of creating and editing layer masks.) Alternatively, you can use the Refine Edge dialog box to fine-tune your selection *before* adding the mask. Page 171 tells you how.

Sure, duplicating the layer you're erasing adds an extra step, but that way you're not deleting any pixels—you're just hiding them with a layer mask, so you can get 'em back if you want to. How cool is that?

■ THE MAGIC ERASER

This tool works just like the Background Eraser except that, instead of a brush cursor that you paint with, it has a cursor that looks like a cross between the Eraser tool and the Magic Wand. Just as the Magic Wand can select color with a single click, the Magic Eraser can *zap* color with a single click, so it's great for instantly erasing areas of solid color. Since this tool is an eraser, it really will *delete* pixels, so you'll want to duplicate your Background layer before using it.

You can alter the Magic Eraser's behavior by adjusting these Options bar settings:

- **Anti-alias.** Turning this checkbox on makes Photoshop slightly soften the edges of what it erases.

- **Contiguous.** To erase pixels that touch one another, leave this checkbox turned on. To erase similar-colored pixels no matter where they are in your image, turn it off.

- **Sample All Layers.** If you have a multilayer document, turn on this checkbox to make Photoshop look at the pixels on *all* the layers instead of just the active layer.

- **Opacity.** To control how strong the Magic Eraser is, you can enter a new value here. Out of the box, this option is set to 100, which removes 100 percent of the image, but you can enter *50* to make it wipe away 50 percent of the image's color, for example.

Selecting Irregular Areas

As you might imagine, areas that aren't uniform in shape *or* color can be a real bear to select. Luckily, Photoshop has a few tools in its arsenal to help you get the job done as easily as possible. In this section, you'll learn about the three lassos and the Pen tool, as well as a few ways to use these tools together to select hard-to-grab spots.

The Lasso Tools

The lasso toolset contains three freeform tools that let you draw an outline around the area you want to select. If you've got an amazingly steady mouse hand or if you use a graphics tablet (see the box on page 518), you may fall in love with the plain ol' Lasso tool. If you're trying to select an object with a lot of straight edges, the Polygonal Lasso tool will do you proud. And the Magnetic Lasso tries to create a selection *for* you by examining the color of the pixels your cursor is over. The following sections explain all three tools, which share a slot near the top of the Tools panel (see Figure 4-14).

WORKAROUND WORKSHOP

Erasing Every Bit of Background

Now that you know how to use the Background and Magic Erasers, keep in mind that you can't always believe what you see onscreen. Most of the time, you'll use these tools to erase to a transparent (checkerboard) background like the one shown in Figure 4-13. And while it may *appear* that you've erased all the background, you may not have. The checkerboard pattern is notorious for making it hard to see whether you've missed a pixel or two here and there, especially if the background you're trying to delete is white or gray (like clouds).

Fortunately, it's easy to overcome this checkered obstacle. The next time you're ready to use one of these eraser tools, first

create a new Solid Color Adjustment layer and pick a bright color that contrasts with what you're trying to delete and place it at the bottom of the layer stack. That way, you can see whether you've erased everything you wanted to.

Here's how: Click the half-black/half-white circle at the bottom of the Layers panel and choose Solid Color from the pop-up menu. Select a bright color from the resulting Color Picker, and then click OK. Drag the new layer beneath the layer you're erasing, and you're good to go. (See Chapter 3 for more on Fill layers.)

Modes

FIGURE 4-14

So many lassos, so little time! The regular Lasso tool is great for drawing a selection freehand, the Polygonal Lasso is good for drawing selections around shapes that have a lot of straight lines, and the Magnetic Lasso is like an automatic version of the regular Lasso—it tries to make the selection for you.

■ LASSO TOOL

The regular Lasso tool lets you draw a selection completely freeform as if you were drawing with a pencil. To activate this tool, simply click it in the Tools panel (its icon looks like a tiny lasso—no surprise there) or press the L key. Then click in your document and drag to create a selection. Once you stop drawing and release the mouse button, Photoshop automatically completes the selection with a straight line (that is, if you don't complete it yourself by mousing back over your start point) and you see marching ants.

> **TIP** It's nearly impossible to draw a straight line with the Lasso tool, unless you've got the steady hand of a surgeon. But if you press and hold the Option key (Alt on a PC) and then release your mouse button, you'll temporarily switch to the Polygonal Lasso tool so you can draw a straight line (see the next section). When you release the Option (Alt) key, Photoshop completes your selection with a straight line.

The Options bar (shown in Figure 4-14) sports the same settings whether you have the Lasso tool or the Polygonal Lasso tool active. Here's what it offers:

- **Mode.** These four buttons (whose icons look like pieces of paper and are labeled in Figure 4-14) let you choose among the same modes you get for most of the selection tools: New, "Add to selection," "Subtract from selection," and "Intersect with selection." They're discussed in detail back on pages 143–144.

- **Feather.** If you want Photoshop to soften the edges of your selection, enter a pixel value in this field. Otherwise, the selection will have a hard edge. (See the box on page 145 for more on feathering.)

- **Anti-alias.** If you leave this setting turned on, Photoshop slightly blurs the edges of your selection, making them less jagged—page 144 has the details.

■ POLYGONAL LASSO TOOL

If your image has a lot of straight lines in it (like the star in Figure 4-15), the Polygonal Lasso tool is your ticket. Instead of letting you draw a selection that's any shape at all, the Polygonal Lasso draws only *straight* lines. To use it, click once to set the starting point, and move your cursor along the shape of the item you want to select; click again where the angle changes; and then repeat this process until you've outlined the whole shape. It's super simple to use, as Figure 4-15 illustrates. To close your selection, point your cursor at the first point you created. When a tiny circle appears below your cursor (it looks like a degree symbol), click once to close the selection and summon the marching ants.

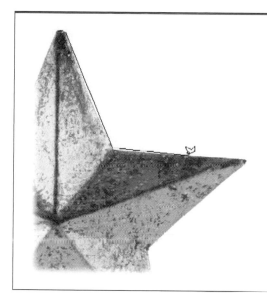

FIGURE 4-15

The Polygonal Lasso tool is perfect for selecting geometric shapes and areas that have a lot of angles. However, if you want to temporarily switch to the regular Lasso tool, press and hold Option (Alt on a PC) to draw freehand.

TIP To bail out of a selection you've started to draw with the Polygonal or Magnetic Lasso tool, just press the Esc key.

■ MAGNETIC LASSO TOOL

This tool has all the power of the other lasso tools, except that it's smart—or at least it tries to be! Click once to set a starting point, and from there the Magnetic Lasso tries to *guess* what you want to select by examining the colors of the pixels your cursor is over (you don't even need to hold your mouse button down). As you move your cursor over the edges you want to select, it sets additional *anchor points* for you (anchor points are fastening points that latch onto the path you're tracing; they look like tiny, see-through squares). To close the selection, put the cursor above your starting point. When a tiny circle appears below the cursor, click once to close the selection and summon the marching ants (or close the selection with a straight line by triple-clicking).

As you might imagine, the Magnetic Lasso tool works best when there's strong contrast between the item you want to select and the area around it (see Figure 4-16). However, if you reach an area that doesn't have much contrast—or a sharp corner—you can give the tool a little nudge by clicking to set a few anchor points of your own. If it goes astray and sets an erroneous anchor point, tap the Delete key (Backspace on a PC) to get rid of the point and then click to set more anchor points until you reach an area of greater contrast where the tool can be trusted to set its own points.

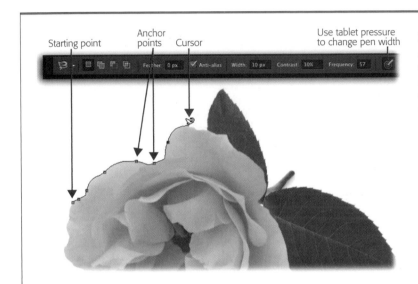

Starting point   Anchor points   Cursor   Use tablet pressure to change pen width

FIGURE 4-16

If you're trying to select an object on a plain, high-contrast background, the Magnetic Lasso works great because it can easily find the edge of the object. For best results, glide your cursor slowly around the edge of the item you want to select (you don't need to hold your mouse button down). To draw a straight line, temporarily switch to the Polygonal Lasso tool by Option-clicking (Alt-clicking on a PC) where you want the line to start and then clicking where you want it to end. Photoshop then switches back to the Magnetic Lasso, and you're free to continue gliding around the rest of the object's edges.

TIP   If you're not crazy about the Magnetic Lasso's cursor (which looks like a triangle and a horseshoe magnet), press the Caps Lock key and it changes to a brush cursor with crosshairs at its center. Press Caps Lock again to switch back to the standard cursor. Alternatively, you can use Photoshop's preferences to change it to a precise cursor; page 499 explains how.

You can get better results with this tool by adjusting its Options bar settings (shown in Figure 4-16). Besides the usual suspects like selection mode, feather, and anti-alias settings (all discussed on page 144), the Magnetic Lasso also lets you adjust the following:

- **Width** determines how close your cursor needs to be to an edge for the Magnetic Lasso to select it. Out of the box, this field is set to 10 pixels, but you can enter a value between 1 and 256. Use a lower number when you're trying to select an area whose edge has a lot of twists and turns and a higher number for an area with fairly smooth edges. For example, to select the yellow rose in Figure 4-16, you'd use a higher setting around the petals and a lower setting around the leaves because they're so jagged.

TIP You can change the Width setting in 1-pixel increments *before* you start drawing with the Magnetic Lasso by pressing the [and] keys. You can also press Shift-[to set the width to 1 and Shift-] to set it to 256.

- **Contrast** controls how much color difference there needs to be between neighboring pixels before the Magnetic Lasso recognizes it as an edge. You can try increasing this percentage when you want to select an edge that isn't well defined, but you might have better luck with a different selection tool. If you're a fan of keyboard shortcuts—and you haven't started drawing a selection—press the comma (,) or period (.) key to decrease or increase this setting in 1 percent increments, respectively; add the Shift key to these keyboard shortcuts to set it to 1 percent or 100 percent, respectively.

- **Frequency** determines how many anchor points the tool lays down. If you're selecting an area with lots of details, you'll need more anchor points than for a smooth area. Setting this field to 0 makes Photoshop add very few points, and 100 makes it have a point party. The factory setting—57—usually works just fine. Before you draw a selection, you can press the semicolon (;) or apostrophe (') key to decrease or increase this setting by 3, respectively; add the Shift key to these keyboard shortcuts to jump between 1 and 100.

- **Use tablet pressure to change pen width**. If you have a pressure-sensitive graphics tablet, turning on this setting—whose button looks like a pen tip with circles around it—lets you override the Width setting by pressing harder or softer on your tablet with the stylus. (The box on page 518 has more about graphics tablets.)

Selecting with the Pen Tool

Another great way to select an irregular object or area is to trace its outline with the Pen tool. Technically, you don't draw a selection with this method; you draw a *path* (page 538), which you can then *load* as a selection or use to create a *vector mask* (page 566). This technique requires quite a bit of skill because the Pen tool isn't your average, everyday, well...*pen*, but it'll produce the smoothest-edged selections this side of the Rio Grande. Head on over to Chapter 13 to read all about it.

Creating Selections with Channels

As you'll learn in Chapter 5, the images you see onscreen are made up of various colors. In Photoshop, each color is stored in its own *channel* (which is kind of like a layer) that you can view and manipulate. If the object or area you're trying to select is one that you can isolate in a channel, you can load that channel as a selection with a click of your mouse. Chapter 5 discusses this incredibly useful technique in detail, starting on page 169.

Using the Selection Tools Together

As wonderful as the aforementioned selection tools are *individually*, they're much more powerful if you use them *together*.

Remember how every tool discussed so far has an "Add to selection" and "Subtract from selection" mode? This means that, no matter which tool you start with, you can add to—or subtract from—the active selection with a completely different tool. Check out Figure 4-17, which gives you a couple of ideas for using the selection tools together. And thanks to the spring-loaded tools feature (see the Tip on page 23), switching between tools is a snap.

FIGURE 4-17

Top: It's worth taking a moment to try to see the shapes that make up the area you want to select. For example, you can select the circular top of this famous Texas building (shown in red) using the Elliptical Marquee, and then switch to the Rectangular Marquee set to "Add to selection" mode to select the area shown in green.

Bottom: Another way to use the selection tools together is to draw a rectangular selection around the object you want to select, and then switch to the Magic Wand to subtract the areas you don't want. Hold down the Option key (Alt on a PC) so you're in "Subtract from selection" mode and then click the areas you don't want included in your selection, like this grayish background. With just a couple of clicks, you can select the prickly pear shown here.

As you can see, there are a gazillion ways to create selections, though any selection you make will likely need tweaking no matter *which* method you use. The next section is all about perfecting selections.

NOTE You can also *paint* selections onto your image by using Quick Mask mode, which is discussed in the next section on page 181.

Modifying Selections

The difference between a pretty-good-around-the-edges selection and a perfect one is what separates Photoshop pros from mere dabblers. As you're about to learn, there are a bunch of ways to modify, reshape, and even *save* selections, all of which are explained in the following pages.

Refining Edges

The best selection modifier in town is the Refine Edge dialog box (Figure 4-18), which is great for selecting the tough stuff like hair and fur. It combines several edge-adjustment tools that used to be scattered throughout Photoshop's menus and includes an extremely useful preview option.

Anytime you have a selection tool active and some marching ants on your screen, you'll see the Refine Edge button sitting pretty up in the Options bar; simply click it to open the dialog box. You can also open it by choosing Select→Refine Edge, pressing Option-⌘-R (Alt+Ctrl+R on a PC), or by clicking the Properties panel's Mask Edge button (see Figure 3-29 on page 123).

The Refine Edge dialog box gives you *seven* different ways to preview your selection. Because the preview appears in the main document window, you'll want to move the Refine Edge dialog box aside so it's not covering your image. Depending on the colors in your image, one of these View modes will let you see the selection better than the rest:

- **Marching Ants.** This view just shows the selection on the image itself. Keyboard shortcut: M.

- **Overlay.** As the name indicates, this view displays your selection overlaid with the Quick Mask (page 181) which, unless you've changed its color, is light red. (To change that color, see the box on page 182.) Because the red overlay is see-through, it's the best choice when your selection will include hair or fur that isn't included in the selection just yet. Keyboard shortcut: V.

TIP You can cycle through the preview modes by pressing the F key repeatedly when you have the Refine Edge dialog box open. To temporarily see your original image, press the X key; press X again to go back to the View mode you were using.

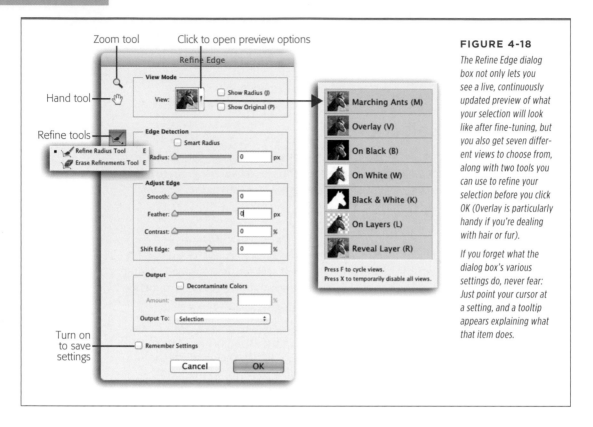

FIGURE 4-18

The Refine Edge dialog box not only lets you see a live, continuously updated preview of what your selection will look like after fine-tuning, but you also get seven different views to choose from, along with two tools you can use to refine your selection before you click OK (Overlay is particularly handy if you're dealing with hair or fur).

If you forget what the dialog box's various settings do, never fear: Just point your cursor at a setting, and a tooltip appears explaining what that item does.

- **On Black.** This view displays the selection on a black background, which is helpful if your image is light colored and doesn't have a lot of black in it. Keyboard shortcut: B.

- **On White.** Choose this view if your image is mostly dark. The stark white background makes it easy to see your selection and the *object* you're selecting while you're fine-tuning it using the dialog box's settings. Keyboard shortcut: W.

- **Black & White.** This view displays your selection as an *alpha channel* (page 201). Photoshop makes your selection white and the mask black; transitions between the two areas are subtle shades of gray. The gray areas let you see how detailed your mask is, so you'll spend a fair amount of time in this mode. Keyboard shortcut: K.

- **On Layers.** To see your selection atop the gray-and-white transparency checkerboard, choose this mode. Keyboard shortcut: L.

- **Reveal Layer.** This mode displays your image *without* a selection. Keyboard shortcut: R.

Once you've chosen a View mode, you can tweak the following settings (and for best results, Adobe suggests you adjust them in this order):

- **Smart Radius.** Turn this checkbox on to make Photoshop look closely at the edges of your selection to determine whether they're hard (like the outline of your subject's body) or soft (like your subject's hair or fur). It's a good idea to turn this setting on each time you open the Refine Edge dialog box. (If you turn on the Remember Settings option at the bottom of the dialog box, Smart Radius will *stay* on until you turn it off.)

- **Radius.** This setting controls the size of the area affected by the settings in this dialog box—in other words, how far beyond the edge of your selection Photoshop looks when it's refining that edge. You can think of this setting as the selection's degree of difficulty. For example, if your selection is really complex, like the horse's mane in Figure 4-19, increase this setting to make Photoshop look beyond the original selection boundary for all the wispy stuff (which also makes the program slightly soften the selection's edge). If your selection is fairly simple, lower this setting so Photoshop analyzes just the selection's boundary, which creates a harder edge. There are no magic numbers for this setting—it varies from image to image—so you'll need to experiment in order to get your selection just right.

- **Refine Radius tool.** Once you've turned on Smart Radius, you can use this tool (shown in Figure 4-18) to paint over the edges of your selection to make Photoshop fine-tune them even more in particular spots (see Figure 4-19, top). This is where the Refine Edge dialog box *really* works its magic: As you drag with this tool's brush cursor, you can extend your selection beyond its original boundaries, creating a more precise selection of extremely fine details. This tool is also intuitive: As you brush across the edges of your selection, it pays attention and tries to *learn* how you want it to behave.

- **Erase Refinements tool.** If Photoshop gets a little overzealous and includes too much of the background in your selection as you drag with the Refine Radius tool, use this tool to drag across the areas you *don't* want to include in the selection.

TIP To temporarily switch between the Refine Radius and Erase Refinements tools while the Refine Edge dialog box is open, press and hold the Option key (Alt on a PC). Alternatively, you can flip-flop between the tools by pressing Shift-E.

- **Smooth.** Increasing this setting makes Photoshop smooth the selection's edges so they're less jagged, but increasing it too much can make you lose details (especially on selections of things like hair). To bring back some details without decreasing this setting, try increasing the Radius and Contrast settings.

- **Feather.** This setting controls how much Photoshop softens the edges of your selection, which is useful when you're combining images, as discussed in the box on page 145.

- **Contrast.** This setting sharpens your selection's edge, even if you softened it by increasing the Radius setting mentioned above. A higher number here creates a sharper edge and can actually reduce the noisy or grainy look that's sometimes caused by a high Radius setting. (If you spend some quality time with Smart Radius and its refinement tools, you probably won't use this slider much, if at all.)

FIGURE 4-19

Top: After creating a rough selection with the Quick Selection tool, you can use the Refine Edge dialog box's Refine Radius tool to brush across areas you want to add to your selection.

Bottom: Within minutes, you can settle this mare onto a new background, as shown here. What horse wouldn't be happier hanging out on a field of bluebonnets?

To try this yourself, trot on over to this book's Missing CD page at www.missingmanuals.com/cds and download the file Horse.zip.

- **Shift Edge.** You can tighten your selection (make it smaller) by dragging this slider to the left, which is a good idea if you're dealing with hair or fur. To expand your selection and grab pixels you missed when you made the initial selection, drag this slider to the right.

- **Decontaminate Colors.** This option helps reduce *edge halos*: leftover colored pixels around the edges of a selection that you see only *after* you put the object on a new background (as shown on page 178). Once you turn this checkbox on, Photoshop tries to replace the color of selected pixels with the color of pixels *nearby* (whether they're selected or not). Drag the Amount slider to the right to change the color of more edge pixels, or to the left to change fewer. To see the color changes for yourself, choose Reveal Layer from the View menu near the top of the dialog box (or just press R).

- **Output To.** This setting lets you tell Photoshop what you'd like it to *do* with your new and improved selection. Here are your options:

  — **Selection** adjusts your original selection, leaving you with marching ants on your original layer just like you started with.

  — **Layer Mask** adds a layer mask to the current layer according to the selection you just made. You'll choose this option most of the time.

  — **New Layer** deletes the background and creates a new layer containing only the selected item, with no marching ants.

  — **New Layer with Layer Mask** adds a new layer complete with layer mask.

  — **New Document** deletes the background and sends only the selected item to a brand-new document.

  — **New Document with Layer Mask** sends the selected item to a new document complete with editable layer mask.

Whew! Those settings probably won't make a whole lot of sense until you start using 'em. To get you off and running, here's how to select a subject with wispy hair, like the horse in Figure 4-19:

1. **Open an image and select the item using the Quick Selection tool.**

   Press W to grab the Quick Selection tool and paint across the object you want to select (Figure 4-19, top left). Don't worry too much about the quality of the selection, because you'll tweak it in a moment.

2. **Open the Refine Edge dialog box.**

   Hop up to the Options bar and click the Refine Edge button.

3. **Choose Overlay as your View mode.**

   To see the horse's mane better—in all its wispy goodness—press V to view it with a red overlay.

4. **Turn on the Smart Radius checkbox and drag the Radius slider to the right.**

   How far you should drag the Radius slider depends on your image. Your goal is to drag the slider as far to the right as you can while still maintaining some hardness in the selection's edges. There's no magic Radius setting that'll work on every selection (a setting of 3.2 was used in Figure 4-19); it varies with every image. You won't see anything change in your image right away when you tweak this setting, though a tiny rotating circle at the bottom left of the dialog box indicates that Photoshop is rethinking the selection.

5. **Use the Refine Radius tool to brush across the soft edges of your selection (Figure 4-19, top right).**

   Press E to grab the Refine Radius tool, or click its icon near the top left of the Refine Edge dialog box (it looks like a tiny brush atop a curved, dotted line).

Then mouse over to your image and brush across the soft areas you want to add to your selection, like the wispy bits of the horse's mane. Try to avoid any areas that are correctly selected (such as the horse's nose), as Photoshop tends to overanalyze them and exclude parts it shouldn't. If you end up adding too much to the selection, press Option (Alt) to switch to the Eraser Refinement tool and then brush across the areas you *don't* want selected.

6. **Turn on the Decontaminate Colors checkbox and adjust the Amount slider.**

   Turn on the checkbox and then drag the slider slightly to the right to shift the color of *partially* selected edge pixels so they more closely match pixels that are *fully* selected. Once again, this value varies from image to image (15 percent was used for Figure 4-19).

7. **From the Output To pop-up menu, chose "New Layer with Mask."**

   Photoshop adds a layer mask to the active layer reflecting your selection, as shown in the Layers panel in Figure 4-19 (bottom).

Exhausted yet? This kind of thing isn't easy, but once you master using Refine Edges, you'll be able to create precise selections of darn near anything!

■ ADDING A CREATIVE EDGE

You can also use the Refine Edge dialog box to add creative edges to photos. For example, grab the Rectangular Marquee tool and draw a box around an image about half an inch inside the document's edges (Figure 4-20, top). Then click the Options bar's Refine Edge button and, in the resulting dialog box, drag the Radius slider to the right for a cool, painterly effect (how *far* you drag it is up to you). Be sure to choose Layer Mask from the dialog box's Output To menu before you click OK to keep from harming your original image.

Fixing Edge Halos

When you're making selections, you may encounter *edge halos* (also called *fringing* or *matting*). An edge halo is a tiny portion of the background that stubbornly remains even after you try to delete it (or hide it with a layer mask, page 116). They usually show up after you replace the original background with something new (see Figure 4-21).

Here are a few ways to fix edge halos:

- **Contract your selection.** Use the Refine Edge dialog box (page 171) or choose Select→Modify→Contract to contract the selection (though the latter method won't give you a preview). Use this technique while you still have marching ants—in other words, before you delete the old background (or, better yet, hide the background with a layer mask [page 116]).

- **Run the Minimum filter on a layer mask.** Once you've hidden an image's background with a layer mask, you can run the Minimum filter on the *mask* to tighten it around the object. Page 671 explains this super-useful trick. This is an *excellent* quick fix to have in your bag of Photoshop tricks.

- **Use the Defringe command.** Run this command after you delete the background (alas, it doesn't work on layer masks or while a selection is active). Choose Layer→Matting→Defringe and then enter a value in pixels. Photoshop analyzes the active layer and changes the color of the pixels around the object's edge to the color of nearby pixels. For example, if you enter *2 px*, it'll replace a 2-pixel rim of color all the way around the object.

- **Remove Black/White Matting.** If Photoshop has blessed you with a halo that's either black or white, you can make the program try to remove it automatically. After you've deleted the background, select the offending layer and then choose Layer→Matting→Remove Black Matte or Remove White Matte. (Like Defringe, this command doesn't work on layer masks or while you have an active selection.)

FIGURE 4-20

Top: The first step to creative edges is to draw a rectangular selection around the focal point of the image.

Bottom: Once you turn on Smart Radius and drag the Radius slider to the right, the edges of the image begin to change. Use the remaining sliders to tweak the look to your liking. As you can see, the Refine Edge dialog box makes short work of giving images an interesting painted edge (here, the image is shown atop a deep red Solid Color Fill layer).

FIGURE 4-21

Here you can see the intrepid cowboy on his original green background (top) and on the new background (bottom). The green pixels stubbornly clinging to his hat are an edge halo.

This aggravatingly tiny rim of color can be your undoing when it comes to creating realistic images because they're a sure sign that the image has done time in Photoshop. Edge halos make a new sky look fake and won't help convince anyone that Elvis actually came to your cookout.

Creating a Border Selection

If you peek at the Select→Modify submenu, you'll find the same options as in the Refine Edge dialog box (but without a preview). There is, however, one addition: Border, which lets you turn a solid selection into a hollow one. Let's say you drew a circular selection with the Elliptical Marquee tool (page 142). You can turn that selection into a ring (handy if you want to make a neon sign or select the outer rim of an object) by choosing Select→Modify→Border. Just enter a pixel width, click OK, and poof! Your formerly solid selection is now as hollow as can be.

Transforming a Selection

Have you ever tried to make a slanted rectangular selection like the one shown in Figure 4-22? If so, you may have found the experience frustrating. Sure, you can try using one of the lasso tools, but it's quicker to *transform* (meaning "reshape") a rectangular selection instead. (Page 259 in Chapter 6 has more on the transform tools.)

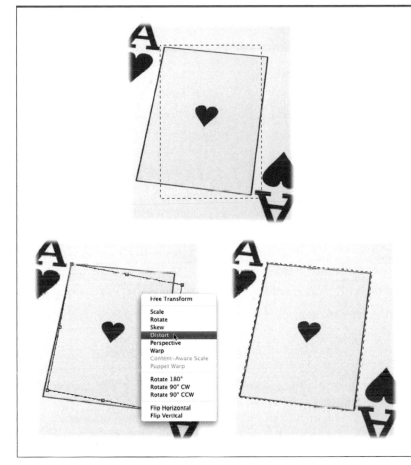

FIGURE 4-22

Top: You can easily select the center part of this playing card with the Rectangular Marquee tool. Once you see the marching ants, choose Select→Transform Selection and rotate the resulting bounding box to get the correct angle.

Bottom Left: Next, Control-click (right-click on a PC) inside the bounding box and choose Distort from the shortcut menu, as shown here. Then drag each corner handle so it's over a corner of the yellow box on the card.

Bottom Right: When you're all finished, press Return (Enter on a PC) to accept the transformation. Or, if you change your mind, press the Esc key to reject it.

NOTE   When you transform a selection (as opposed to part of your image), Photoshop won't mess with any of your image's pixels. Instead, the program simply changes the shape of the *selection*—in other words, the shape of the marching ants.

Once you've made a selection, choose Select→Transform Selection or Control-click (right-click on a PC) inside the selection and, from the shortcut menu that appears, choose Transform Selection. Photoshop puts a rectangular box with little, square resizing handles on its four sides around your selection (this is called a *bounding box*). You can move the selection around by clicking inside the bounding box and dragging in any direction. (If you want to get rid of the bounding box without making any changes, press the Esc key.)

The resizing handles let you do the following:

- **Scale (resize).** Drag any handle to change the size and shape of your selection. Drag diagonally toward the center of the selection to make it smaller or diagonally away to make it bigger.

- **Rotate.** When you position your cursor outside one of the bounding box's corners, the cursor turns into a curved, double-headed arrow. That's your cue that you can drag to rotate the selection (just drag up or down in the direction you want to rotate).

If you need to change the shape of the selection, just Control-click (right-click on a PC) inside the bounding box and you'll see a shortcut menu with the following options (see Figure 4-22, bottom left):

- **Free Transform** lets you apply any of the transformations listed below freely and in one action (instead of having to choose and apply them one at a time). See page 259 for more info.

- **Scale** and **Rotate** work as described in the previous list.

- **Skew** lets you slant the selection by dragging one of the bounding box's side handles.

- **Distort** lets you drag any handle to reshape the selection.

- **Perspective** lets you drag any corner handle to give the selection a one-point perspective—that is, a vanishing point where it seems to disappear into the distance.

- **Warp** makes Photoshop place a grid over your selection that lets you reshape it in any way you want. Drag any *control point* (the two evenly spaced points on all four sides of the selection) or line on the grid to twist the selection however you like, or choose a ready-made preset from the Options bar's Warp pop-up menu.

> **TIP** Using Warp is your ticket to a quick page-curl effect. Trot on over to this book's Missing CD page at *www.missingmanuals.com/cds* to learn how.

- **Content-Aware Scale** can intelligently resize the unimportant background areas of your image while the subject remains unchanged. You'll learn all about it on page 254.

- **Puppet Warp** lets you twist and turn the selection any which way you want, like Silly Putty. It's covered in detail beginning on page 448.

- **Rotate 180°, Rotate 90° CW,** and **Rotate 90° CCW** turn your selection 180 degrees, 90 degrees clockwise, or 90 degrees counterclockwise, respectively.

- **Flip Horizontal** and **Flip Vertical** flip your selection either horizontally (like it's reflected in a mirror) or vertically (like it's reflected in a puddle).

When you're finished transforming the selection, press Return (Enter on a PC) to accept the changes. (If you change your mind and want to reject the changes, press Esc instead.)

Using Quick Mask Mode

If you'd rather fine-tune selections by painting with a brush, no problem; in fact, you can *create* a selection from scratch using this method. Just enter Quick Mask mode and you'll find all of Photoshop's painting tools (even filters!) waiting to help you tweak your selection. This mode gives you the freedom to work on selections with almost any tool.

You can enter Quick Mask mode by pressing the Q key or clicking the circle-within-a-square button at the bottom of the *Tools* panel (not the Layers panel). When you do, Photoshop looks to see whether you have an active selection. If you do, it puts a red overlay over everything *but* the selection. (If you don't have an active selection, you won't see any change, but you can still use the directions in this section to *create* a selection.) This color-coding makes it easy to edit your selection *visually* by painting.

While you're in Quick Mask mode, you can use the Brush tool to do any of the following.

- **Deselect a portion of your selection**—in other words, to add an area to the mask—by setting your foreground color chip to black and then painting across the unwanted area.

- **Extend the area covered by your selection** by painting the spot you want to add with white (you may need to press X to flip-flop your color chips).

- **Create a soft-edged selection or semi-transparent area** by painting with gray. For example, by painting with 50 percent gray (to do that, lower a black brush's opacity in the Options bar to 50 percent), you'll create a selection that's partially see-through. You can create a similar effect by painting with a soft-edged brush.

All the usual tools and document tricks work while you're in Quick Mask mode: You can zoom in or out by pressing ⌘ and the + or – key (Ctrl and + or – on a PC), press and hold the space bar to move around within the document once you're zoomed in, and use any of the selection tools covered in this chapter. You can also fill the entire mask, or your selection, with black or white (see page 185), which is helpful when you have a large area to paint or when you want to paint the entire selection by hand. You can run filters in this mode to create interesting edges (page 661) or use the Gradient tool, set to a black-to-white gradient, to create a fade (page 322).

Once you finish fine-tuning your selection, press the Q key to exit Quick Mask mode and the marching ants come rushing back, as shown in Figure 4-23, so you can see the newly edited selection.

FIGURE 4-23

Top left: To select the area around this badge, start by selecting the white background with the Magic Wand tool.

Top right: When you pop into Quick Mask mode, Photoshop leaves the area you've selected in full color (in this case, white) and puts a red overlay over everything else. Now you can quickly clean up problem areas—like the drop shadow peeking out from beneath the badge—because they're so easy to spot with the red overlay. Use the Brush tool set to paint with black or white, or the Polygonal Lasso tool (and then fill the selection area with black or white).

Bottom: Once you're finished, exit Quick Mask mode by pressing Q, and you see the fine-tuned selection marked by marching ants.

FREQUENTLY ASKED QUESTION

Changing Quick Mask's Color

Why is Quick Mask red? Am I stuck with red? And while we're at it, why does the mask mark unselected *areas? Can I make it mark the* selected *areas instead?*

Whoa, now! Just hold your horses; one question at a time.

First, a bit of history: The Quick Mask's default setting is red because of its real-world counterpart, rubylith plastic, which came in sheets like paper. Back in the days before desktop publishing, this red plastic was cut with X-Acto knives and placed over the parts of images that needed to be hidden. Because the plastic didn't register with the printing presses (it appeared black), those parts of the images didn't appear in the printed publication. It was a neat trick at the time.

Printing technology has come a long way since then—there's no need for X-Acto knives when you've got Photoshop. And since

you're working with modern printers and not old-fashioned printing presses, you're not stuck with using a red mask; you can change Quick Mask's color to anything you want (which is quite helpful when the area you're trying to select has red in it). So if the red overlay isn't working for you, with Quick Mask mode active (press Q), double-click the circle-within-a-square button at the bottom of the Tools panel. In the Quick Mask Options dialog box that opens, click the color swatch and choose any color you like from the resulting Color Picker. You can also make the overlay more or less intense by changing the dialog box's Opacity setting.

And, yes, you can make Quick Mask mark the areas you've selected instead of the unselected areas. Simply open the Quick Mask Options dialog box and, in the Color Indicates section, turn on the Selected Areas option and then click OK.

Moving Selections

If you create a selection that's not in exactly the right spot or you've got several objects of the same shape that you want to alter, you may need to move the selection itself. Or maybe you need to move the pixels *underneath* the selection, or move them onto their own layer. In any of those cases, you've got plenty of options:

- **Moving the selection (the marching ants) within the same layer.** Make sure you have a selection tool active (it doesn't matter which one), and then click inside the selection and drag it to another part of the document. You can also nudge the selection into place with the arrow keys on your keyboard.

TIP To move a selection as you're drawing it, press and hold the space bar while you still have the mouse button pressed. Drag to move the selection, release the space bar, and then continue dragging to draw the selection.

- **Moving the selected object (the actual pixels) within the same document.** Press V to select the Move tool and then drag with your mouse to reposition the object. Just be aware that a big, gaping hole will appear where the object used to be! (If you're on a Background layer, the hole will be filled with your current foreground color.)

NOTE Photoshop CS6 sports a new Content-Aware Move tool that you can use to move a selected object from one place to another. Jump ahead to page 447 for the scoop!

- **Moving the selected object onto its own new layer within the same document.** Press ⌘-J (Ctrl+J on a PC) to "jump" the selected pixels onto their very own layer, just above the current layer. That way, whatever you do to the selected area won't harm the original image. If you don't like your changes, you can throw the extra layer away. Or, if you create an effect that's a little too strong—maybe you overwhitened a set of teeth—you can reduce the layer's opacity (page 97) to lessen the effect. (Flip back to Chapter 3 for more on layers.)

- **Moving the selected object to another document.** Press ⌘-C (Ctrl+C) to copy the selected pixels and then open the other document and press ⌘-V (Ctrl+V) to paste the pixels. The pasted object appears on its very own layer that you can reposition with the Move tool. This technique is essential for performing the classic head swap, shown in Figure 4-24.

- **Moving the selected object to a new document.** Copy the object as described above and then choose File→New. Photoshop opens a new document, sized to match the object you copied; press ⌘-V (Ctrl+V) to paste the object.

FIGURE 4-24

Here's a fun little prank to pull on your family, friends, and exes. Open a photo of someone and select their head using any of the selection tools discussed in this chapter (the Quick Selection tool was used here). Be sure to feather the selection so it doesn't have a hard edge (page 145) and then copy it by pressing ⌘-C (Ctrl+C). Next, open the document that contains the new body and paste your selection into it by pressing ⌘-V (Ctrl+V).

You can then use the Move tool to reposition it onto the new body and, if you need to, use the Clone Stamp tool to hide parts of the original head. Good times!

Saving a Selection

If you'd like Photoshop to remember a selection so you can use it again later, it's happy to oblige. After you create the selection, choose Select→Save Selection. In the resulting dialog box (Figure 4-25), give your selection a meaningful name (like *handsome devil*) and then press OK. When you're finished working with that document, be sure to save it as a PSD file (see page 49).

When you're ready to use the selection again, pop open the document in which it was saved and choose Select→Load Selection. In the resulting dialog box, click the Channel pop-up menu and pick your selection from the list (if you've saved only one selection in this particular document, Photoshop chooses it automatically). Leave the Operation section of the dialog box set to New Selection to bring back the saved selection as a whole (instead of adding to or subtracting from another selection). Press OK and the marching ants reappear, just like you saved them.

Although the radio buttons in the Operation section of the Load Selection dialog box let you add to, subtract from, or intersect other selections with the *saved* selection, it's easier just to load the selection, close the dialog box, and then edit it using the selection tools discussed in this chapter.

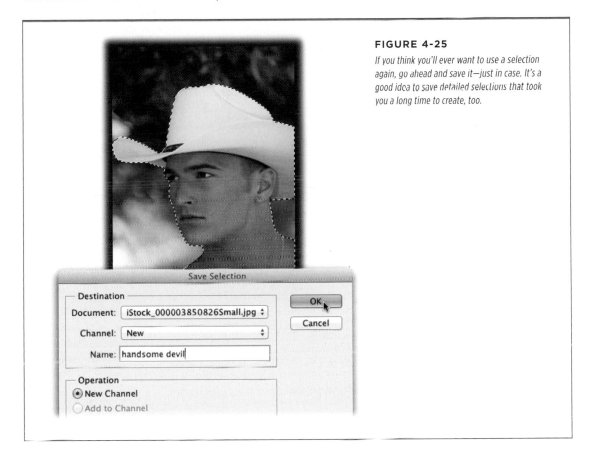

FIGURE 4-25

If you think you'll ever want to use a selection again, go ahead and save it—just in case. It's a good idea to save detailed selections that took you a long time to create, too.

Filling a Selection with Color

Filling selections with color is a great way to create shapes and add colorful photo borders to images. After you've created the selection of your dreams, you can fill it with color in a couple of ways. One option is to choose Edit→Fill and, from the Use pop-up menu, choose Color. Pick something nice from the resulting Color Picker, and then click OK twice to dismiss the dialog boxes. Photoshop fills your selection with the color you picked.

Alternatively, a more flexible way to fill a selection with color is to add a Solid Color Adjustment layer. Once you've made a selection, click the half-black/half-white circle at the bottom of the Layers panel and then choose Solid Color (or choose Layer→New Fill Layer→Solid Color instead). Then grab a color from the resulting Color Picker and click OK. Photoshop dutifully fills the selected area with color, and you see a new Solid Color Fill layer appear in the Layers panel. To change the color of this layer, simply double-click its thumbnail to reopen the Color Picker. (Chapter 3 has more on using Solid Color, Gradient, and Pattern Fill layers.)

> **TIP** You have yet *another* option for filling selections: Content-Aware Fill, which works with the Fill command and the Spot Healing brush. You'll learn all about it in Chapter 10 beginning on page 414.

Stroking (Outlining) a Selection

Sometimes you'll want to give your selection a *stroke* (as in an outline, not the medical condition). While you can stroke selections of any shape, this technique comes in really handy when you use it in conjunction with the Photoshop's vector tools. That's right: In CS6, you can stroke *any* vector shape you create—whether it's with the Pen tool or one of the shape tools—with a variety of line widths and colors, including dashes or dots. This much-anticipated feature is covered in Chapter 13 on page 554.

That said, if you want to add a stroke to a layer, you can do it with layer styles (page 131). For example, when it comes to adding a bit of class to a photo, few effects beat a thin black outline. Whether you're floating the image within text or posting it in your blog, an outline gives the edge a little definition, making the design look nicely finished. If the image lives on its own layer, click the tiny *fx* button at the bottom of the Layers panel and choose Stroke. In the resulting Layer Style dialog box, enter a size for the stroke and then choose a Location from the pop-up menu (if the image is the same size as your Photoshop document, be sure to choose Inside so the stroke appears inside the margins instead of outside 'em). Last but not least, click the colored square to pop open the Color Picker and choose a color for the stroke. Click OK to close the Layer Style dialog box and call it done. To edit the stroke's size or color later on, just double-click the Stroke layer style in the Layers panel and the Layer Style dialog box pops open.

If the object you want to stroke *isn't* isolated on its own layer—say, you want to circle yourself in a photo—use CS6's Ellipse tool instead and then add the stroke using the Options bar's new settings. Page 554 has the full scoop on this glorious feature.

Controlling Color with Channels

At the heart of any Photoshop file lie *channels*—storage containers for all the color information in your image, selections you've saved, masks you've created, and instructions for printing with special inks. Channels sound intimidating at first, and folks have been known to shudder at their mention and avoid them completely. But to really understand Photoshop, it's good to get a grip on channels. Luckily, you don't need a PhD to do that—just a little patience.

This chapter gets a little technical at times, but if you soldier through, you'll be rewarded with wisdom that'll help you perform some amazing pixel wizardry. You'll get a warm, fuzzy, enlightened feeling as you learn to:

- Use channels to make complex selections and masks (page 116).

- Map one image to the contours of another (page 307).

- Create a beautiful black-and-white image from a color version (pages 198 and 317).

- Perform highly targeted color adjustments (see Figure 9-23 on page 397).

- Sharpen your images without introducing noise (page 216).

And that's just the tip of the iceberg. *Everything* you do in Photoshop involves channels (well, save for paths and text, which you'll learn about in Chapters 13 and 14), so it's important to get familiar with them. If you understand *how* Photoshop does what it does, you can make it do even *more* in less time and with less effort. That's called working smarter, not harder—which is why, Grasshopper, you're reading this book.

To understand how channels work, you first need to learn a bit about the two color systems you'll encounter during your Photoshop career: *additive* and *subtractive*. Once you've got that under your belt—and fear not, there's plenty more ahead about how both systems work—you'll dive into the color channels themselves to see what kind of info lives there and how you can use it to manipulate your images. Last but not least, you'll explore an entirely different kind of channel that can help you create the toughest selections this side of the Rio Grande: *alpha channels*. Read on!

How Color Works

The images you see on computer monitors and TVs are made of light; without light, these screens would be completely dark. While your eyes are sensitive to hundreds of wavelengths of light (each associated with a different color), it takes just three—red, green, and blue—to produce all the colors you see onscreen. So to create color, monitors *add* individual pixels of colored light. That's why the onscreen color system is called "additive." Each tiny *pixel* (short for *picture element*) can be red, green, blue, or some combination of the three. All image-capture and input devices—digital cameras, video cameras, and scanners—use the additive color system, as do all digital-image display devices.

> **NOTE** Onscreen images are also called *composite* images because they're made up of a combination of red, green, and blue light (also known as *RGB*).

In the additive color system, areas where red, green, and blue light overlap appear white (see Figure 5-1). Does that sound crazy, or does it ring a bell from high school physics? Think about it this way: If you aim red, green, and blue spotlights at a stage, you see white where all three lights overlap. Interestingly, you also see cyan, magenta, or yellow where just *two* of the three lights overlap (also shown in Figure 5-1). Areas where no light is shining appear jet black.

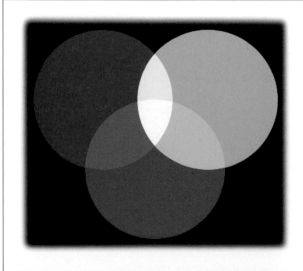

FIGURE 5-1

If you overlap red, green, and blue spotlights, you see white light. This is a prime example of the additive color system, which starts with black and adds light to produce different colors. Notice how cyan, magenta, and yellow appear where just two lights overlap.

You can try this spotlight experiment in Photoshop yourself by creating red, green, and blue circles on separate layers on a black background. Make the circles overlap, switch each layer's blend mode to Lighten and voilà—the other colors appear where the circles overlap.

That's how computer monitors and TVs create onscreen color. Now it's time to talk about printed color, which—brace yourself—works in a totally different way.

Printing presses use what's called a *subtractive* color system, where the colors result from a combination of light that's reflected (which you see) and light that's absorbed (which you don't see). In a printed photo, magazine, or book, the subtractive system operates as kind of a joint venture between the inks used (generally cyan, magenta, yellow, and black, all of which absorb color) and the paper the ink is printed on (a reflective surface). The ink serves as a filter by absorbing some of the light that hits the paper. The paper bounces the rest of the light back at you, so the whiter the paper, the truer the colors will look when they're printed.

In the subtractive system, different-colored inks absorb different-colored light. For example, cyan ink absorbs red light and reflects green and blue light back at you, so you see a mix of green and blue—in other words, cyan. Similarly, magenta ink absorbs green light and reflects red and blue light; in other words, magenta. One last example: A mix of cyan, magenta, and yellow ink absorbs *most* of the primary colors—red, green, and blue—so you see what's left over: dark brown.

> **NOTE** In order to produce true black, grays, and shades of color (colors mixed with black to produce darker colors), the folks who ran printing presses added black as a fourth printing ink. They couldn't abbreviate it with B because they were afraid it'd be confused with blue (as in RGB), so they used K instead—as in "blacK." That's where the abbreviation CMYK comes from.

To summarize: Subtractive color is generated by light hitting an object and bouncing back to your eyes, whereas additive color is generated by different-colored light mixing together *before* you see any of it.

RGB Mode vs. CMYK Mode

Photoshop stores all the color information that gets relayed to your monitor, your printer, and so on, in separate *channels*. The channels' names change depending on which *color mode* (a.k.a. *image mode*) you're using for that particular Photoshop document. As a rule of thumb, you should use RGB mode for images destined for onscreen viewing or inkjet printing, and CMYK mode for images you plan on sending to a commercial printing press.

> **NOTE** These days it's best to ask your printing company which color mode they prefer before you start editing. Some newer digital printing presses use RGB because they can produce a wider range of colors than with CMYK. And some printing companies just prefer to use their *own* software to convert images from RGB to CMYK.

To find out what color mode your image is in, choose Image→Mode; the current mode has a little checkmark to the left of its name. In *RGB mode*, your Photoshop document has a red channel, a green channel, and a blue channel. When you look at each channel individually—you'll learn how in a moment—you actually see a grayscale representation of where and at what strength that particular color appears in your image. ("Why doesn't Photoshop display them in color" you ask? The box on page

192 has the answer.) One of the best things about RGB mode is that it can display an enormous range of colors.

If you're preparing an image for a commercial printing press, they'll probably print it using a mix of cyan, magenta, yellow, and black ink. Enter *CMYK mode*, where your document includes—you guessed it—cyan, magenta, yellow, and black channels. The drawback to working in this mode is that ink reproduces *far fewer* colors than light, so this mode limits the hues at your disposal. But never fear: Even if you need to *end up* in CMYK mode, there's no harm in starting off in RGB. (Chapter 16 explains more than you ever wanted to know about when and how to change color modes.)

As you discovered in Chapter 2 (page 45), Photoshop includes other color modes, such as Grayscale and Lab, which are handy for specific tasks that you'll learn about throughout this book. Nevertheless, you'll spend most of your time editing in RGB mode.

Whew! Now that the really confusing stuff is out of the way, it's time to focus on where in Photoshop you can *see* channels and the different flavors of channels you'll find there.

■ The Channels Panel and You

To peek inside a channel, open the Channels panel (Figure 5-2)—its tab is lurking in the Layers panel group on the right side of your screen. (If you don't see it, choose Window→Channels.) This panel looks and works like the Layers panel, which you learned about in Chapter 3.

When you single-click a channel in the panel, Photoshop highlights it to let you know it's active and temporarily turns off the other channels (see Figure 5-2); anything you do from that point on affects only that channel. This is extremely useful when you want to, say, blur only the red channel in order to soften skin (since skin tones are mostly pink, it makes sense that more of 'em live in the red channel). To activate more than one channel at a time, Shift-click each one (handy for sharpening two channels at once, as shown on page 217).

Photoshop uses several kinds of channels, all of which this chapter covers in detail:

- **Composite channels.** Technically, these aren't really channels; they're combinations of channels and are for your viewing pleasure only. When you're using a mode that contains more than one color channel (like RGB, CMYK, and Lab—all discussed later in this chapter), the composite channel shows all the channels simultaneously, revealing your image in its full-color glory. The name of the composite channel depends on which mode you're in. In RGB mode, for example, the composite channel is named RGB (creative, huh?). But no matter what Photoshop calls it, the composite channel is always at the top of the Channels panel.

NOTE It takes Photoshop longer to run filters on composite channels than on other types of channels because it requires more memory (RAM).

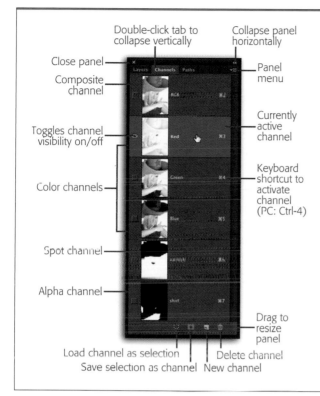

Close panel

Composite channel

Double-click tab to collapse vertically

Toggles channel visibility on/off

Color channels

Spot channel

Alpha channel

Collapse panel horizontally

Panel menu

Currently active channel

Keyboard shortcut to activate channel (PC: Ctrl-4)

Drag to resize panel

Load channel as selection

Save selection as channel New channel

Delete channel

FIGURE 5-2

The Channels panel is your gateway to the color info that makes up your image. The composite channel at the top of the panel (here it's the one labeled RGB) shows what your image looks like with all the channels turned on; click it to turn all the channels back on if you've temporarily turned some off. You can't turn off every channel, though, since at least one has to be visible in order for you to see your image!

The little numbers to the right of each channel are its keyboard shortcut. These shortcuts changed back in CS4, but if you'd like to revert to the old ones, choose Edit → Keyboard Shortcuts and turn on Use Legacy Channel Shortcuts.

- **Color channels.** As explained earlier, if you're working in RGB mode, your color channels are Red, Green, and Blue. In CMYK mode, they're Cyan, Magenta, Yellow, and Black. In Lab mode (page 199), they're Lightness, a, and b. In most other modes, you'll find only a single channel, named after the mode you're in.

- **Alpha channels.** These ever-so-useful channels are grayscale representations of a temporary selection you're in the process of making using Quick Mask mode (page 181), or a selection that you've saved in your Photoshop document (page 184). The latter version comes in handy when you're making tough selections that you may need to tweak later, or when you can't complete the selection before your coffee break. Page 201 explains these channels in detail.

- **Spot channels.** Used only in commercial printing, these channels let you define areas in your image that should be printed with special premixed inks (like Pantone colors), or with a fancy coat of varnish, foil, or metallic ink. For example, if you're designing a holiday card and you want the snow to be sparkly, you can create a spot channel for the glitter so the printer knows where it goes. Page 199 has details on when to use spot channels and how to create them.

At the bottom of the Channels panel, you'll find the following buttons:

- **Load channel as selection.** This button, which looks like a tiny circle made of dots, creates a selection of whatever's in the active channel based on its lightness values (not everything gets selected). This is handy when you're using channels to swap backgrounds (page 206) or create silhouettes (page 212). You can also load a channel as a selection by ⌘-clicking (Ctrl-clicking on a PC) the channel's thumbnail.

- **Save selection as channel.** When you have an active selection in your document, press this button to save it as an alpha channel so you can continue to edit it or use it again later (page 184). Photoshop cleverly names your selections Alpha 1, Alpha 2, Alpha 3, and so on. If you want a more memorable name, simply double-click the channel's name and change it to something like "Tony's toupee" or "Nancy's nose." If you'd rather name your selection before you save it, Option-click (Alt-click on a PC) this button or choosing Select→Save Selection instead.

- **Create new channel.** If you drag an existing channel onto this button (which looks like a tiny piece of paper with an upturned corner), Photoshop duplicates that channel. This is helpful if you need to lighten or darken a channel in order to create a good selection (page 213), as altering the original channel can destroy your image. If you click this button instead, Photoshop creates a new, empty alpha channel that you can use to create a selection from scratch using the red overlay of Quick Mask mode (see Figure 5-8 on page 205).

FREQUENTLY ASKED QUESTION

Why Are Channels Gray?

With all this talk about color, how come Photoshop displays channels in black and white?

Although you *can* make Photoshop display channel info in color, you really don't want to; the colors would be so bright and distracting that it'd be hard to see anything useful. It's much easier to see a particular color's strength (called *luminosity*) when it's represented in shades of gray.

In RGB mode, white areas indicate a color at its full strength, and black areas indicate the color at its weakest. (In CMYK mode, the reverse is true—black indicates full strength and white indicates the weakest concentration.) For example, take a peek at the Red channel in Figure 5-2. The lighter-colored pixels represent high concentrations of red, whereas the darker pixels represent almost no red at all (and the tiny preview in the RGB channel shows that the image really *does* contain a lot of red).

As you can see, just glancing at grayscale channel information shows you quite clearly where a color is at full strength, where it's lacking, and what lies somewhere in between.

That said, if you're determined to see channel info in color, choose Photoshop→Preferences→Interface (Edit→Preferences→Interface on a PC). Turn on the "Show Channels in Color" checkbox in the Options section of the dialog box and then see if you can make heads or tails out of anything.

Actually, there is one situation where you *do* see channels displayed in color—in your document, at least—whether you like it or not: If you activate more than one channel, Photoshop previews your image in just those colors (see the figure on page 217). Why? If the program displayed multiple channels in grayscale, you wouldn't be able to tell *which* shades of gray represented which color.

- **Delete current channel.** Clicking this tiny trash can deletes the currently active channel (you can also drag and drop a channel onto this button to do the same thing). After you've tweaked a duplicate or an alpha channel to create the perfect selection, you can toss it by clicking this button.

Just like every other panel in Photoshop, the Channels panel has a menu tucked into its top-right corner (it looks like a down arrow next to four little lines). This handy menu includes some of the same commands mentioned earlier and a few all its own:

- **New Channel.** This command creates a brand-new alpha channel, just like clicking the "Create new channel" button at the bottom of the panel. The difference is that, by going this route, you get a nifty dialog box where you can name the new channel and tell Photoshop how to display the channel's information (see Figure 5-7 on page 204). However, it's quicker to Option-click (Alt-click) the "Create new channel" button, as described in the previous section.

- **Duplicate Channel.** To create a copy of a channel so you can edit it, choose this command. When you do, Photoshop displays a dialog box so you can name the new channel and choose its destination (the same document or a new one). The destination option is helpful when you're creating a displacement map (page 307) or using channels to make a high-contrast, black-and-white image (page 198).

- **Delete Channels.** This command deletes the current channel or, if you've Shift-clicked to activate more than one channel, all active channels. You have to keep one channel, though, so if you've activated all of 'em, Photoshop grays out this command.

- **New Spot Channel.** This option lets you create a new channel to mark an area that should be printed with a premixed, specialty ink—including varnish, foil, metallic ink, and so on—called a *spot color*. Chapter 16 has more about spot channels beginning on page 695.

- **Merge Spot Channel.** Only commercial printing presses use spot channels, so if you need to print a proof on a regular desktop printer, you first have to run this command to merge your spot channels. See the box on page 710 for details.

- **Channel Options.** This menu item is available only if you've activated an alpha channel. When you're creating or editing an alpha channel, choose Channel Options to change the way Photoshop displays masked and selected areas. Page 204 has the scoop.

- **Split Channels.** If you need to put each channel into its own document, choose this command. Photoshop grabs each channel and copies it into a new, grayscale document (page 45 has info on Grayscale mode). This technique is useful when, for example, you're creating a black-and-white image based on one of its color channels and you need the resulting document to end up in Grayscale mode so it can be printed in a newspaper. (For more on preparing grayscale images for a printing press, see the box on page 319.)

- **Merge Channels.** You might think this command merges more than one channel into a single channel. Negative, good buddy. Instead, it merges the channels of up to four Grayscale documents into a single document, whose resulting color mode depends on how many documents you had open when you began: RGB if you started with three open documents, CMYK if you started with four. You can also have Photoshop merge all the open documents' channels into a Multichannel document (see page 201). This command comes in handy if you've used Split Channels to work on each channel separately and now you want to reunite them in one document.

- **Panel Options.** In the Channels panel, Photoshop automatically displays a thumbnail preview of each channel (see Figure 5-2). If you want to turn off this preview or choose a different thumbnail size, pick this menu item. If you've got a decent-sized monitor (17″ or larger), do your eyes a favor and go for the biggest preview possible.

- **Close and Close Tab Group.** Choose Close to make the Channels panel disappear, or Close Tab Group to get rid of a whole group of related panels (such as Channels, Layers, and Paths). See Chapter 1 for more on panel wrangling.

■ Meet the Color Channels

Understanding what you're seeing in each channel gives you the know-how to create complicated selections and fine-tune your images. In this section, you'll look inside the different color channels, beginning with the most common color mode: RGB.

> **NOTE** This section doesn't cover alpha channels; they're so important, they get their very own section that begins on page 201.

RGB Channels

Unless you're preparing an image that's headed for a commercial printing press (as opposed to the inkjet printer you've probably got at home) and they *require* you to use CMYK, RGB mode is the place to be. After all, your monitor is RGB, as are your digital camera and scanner. But as the box on page 192 explains, Photoshop doesn't display individual channels in red, green, and blue—they're in grayscale so you can easily see where the color is most saturated. Because colors in RGB mode are made from light (page 188), white indicates areas where the color is at full strength, black indicates areas where it's weakest, and shades of gray represent everything in between (see Figure 5-3).

Composite

Red

Green

Blue

FIGURE 5-3

*Most likely, your image
is already in RGB mode,
especially if it came from
a digital camera or a
stock-image company.*

*See how the red, green,
and blue channels
differ in this cute cowgirl
portrait? White areas
indicate where the color
in that channel is most
concentrated, and black
areas indicate where the
color is weakest.*

*Back in earlier versions of
Photoshop, if you wanted
to generate a black-
and-white version of a
color photo, you typically
picked the channel with
the highest contrast and
used that.*

*Now, Photoshop gives you
much better ways to con-
vert from color to shades
of gray such as Black
& White and Gradient
Map Adjustment layers
(described on pages 312
and 316, respectively).*

TIP No matter which color mode you're in, you can cycle through its various channels by pressing ⌘-3, 4, 5, and 6 (Ctrl+3, 4, 5, and 6 on a PC), though you'll only use that last one if you're in CMYK mode—which has four channels instead of three—or if you're trying to activate an alpha channel in RGB mode. To go back to the composite channel so you can see the image in full color, press ⌘-2 (Ctrl+2). When you use these shortcuts, be sure to hold down the ⌘ or Ctrl key; otherwise, typing numbers will change layer or Brush tool opacity instead (see pages 97 and 497, respectively).

Each color channel contains different information:

- **Red.** This channel is typically the lightest of the bunch and shows the greatest difference in color range. In Figure 5-3, this channel is very light because there's a lot of red in the woman's skin, hair, and hat. This channel can be *muy importante* when you're correcting skin tones (page 389). You can also run a blur filter on this channel to instantly soften skin (page 433).

- **Green.** You can think of this channel as "contrast central" because it's usually the highest in, well, contrast. (This makes sense because digital cameras have twice as many green sensors as red or blue ones in order to mimic the human eye, which is most sensitive to green light.) Remember this channel when you're creating an edge mask for sharpening (page 475) or working with displacement maps (page 307).

- **Blue.** Typically the darkest of the group, this channel is super useful when you want to create complex selections in order to isolate an object (page 206). It's also where you'll find problems like *noise* and *grain*. See the box on page 459 to learn how to run the Reduce Noise filter on this channel.

CMYK Channels

Though you'll probably spend most of your time working with RGB images, you may also need to work with images in CMYK mode. Its name, as you learned earlier, stands for the cyan, magenta, yellow, and black inks commercial printing presses use in newspapers, magazines, product packaging, and so on. It has a composite channel at the top of the Channels panel named CMYK. You can pop into this mode by choosing Image→Mode→CMYK Color.

NOTE If you plan to print your image on a regular laser or inkjet printer, you don't need to be in CMYK mode (unless you want to create a quick, high-key effect as described in a moment). Also, this mode limits you to precious few filters (Chapter 15) and color or lighting adjustments (Chapter 9).

A professional printing press separates the four CMYK channels of your image into individual *color separations* (see page 691). Each separation is a perfect copy of the color channel you see in Photoshop, printed in its respective color (cyan, magenta, yellow, or black). When the printing press places these four colors atop each other, they form the full-color image. This technique is known as *four-color process* printing.

Because CMYK channels represent ink rather than light (as explained back on page 189), the grayscale information you see in your Channels panel represents the *opposite* of what it does in RGB mode. In CMYK mode, black indicates color at full strength and white indicates color at its weakest (see Figure 5-4). Does your brain hurt yet?

Cyan

Magenta

Yellow

Black

FIGURE 5-4

Here's the same cowgirl you met back in Figure 5-3, but this time she's in CMYK mode. The yellow channel is really dark because she's got so much yellow in her skin, hat, and hair.

■ CREATING A HIGH-KEY PORTRAIT EFFECT

Even if you're not sending your image to a printing press, you can still have some fun in CMYK mode. For example, you may have noticed that the Black channel in Figure 5-4 looks pretty darned neat. It resembles a popular portrait effect called *high-key* lighting, in which multiple light sources are aimed at the victim, er, subject to create a dazzling image with interesting shadows. Some folks labor long and hard to achieve this look in Photoshop when they could simply resort to a bit of channel theft instead. To create this effect, just extract the Black channel from a CMYK version of the image. Here's how:

1. **If your image is in RGB mode, make a copy of it by choosing Image→Duplicate.**

   Because you're going to change color modes in the next step, it's a good idea to do that on a copy of your image since you lose a bit of color info when you switch from one mode to another. If your image is already in CMYK mode, skip ahead to step 3.

2. **In the duplicate image, choose Image→Mode→CMYK Color.**

   If your document includes more than one layer, Photoshop asks if you want to combine them into one by flattening the image (compressing all layers into one). If those additional layers affect the way your image looks (for example, Adjustment layers), click Flatten. (Flattening a document is typically a scary move, but here you're working with a duplicate of your original document.)

   If you see another dialog box asking about color profiles, just click OK. You'll learn about profiles in Chapter 16. For now, all you need to know is that, since you'll end up back in your original RGB document in step 5, the CMYK profile won't affect anything.

TIP If you're preparing the high-key image for printing in true grayscale, meaning the image itself will be printed with black ink only (think newspapers), then you can skip the following steps and instead choose Split Channels from the Channels panel's menu. Photoshop instantly creates separate documents from each color channel. Simply find the one with "Black" in its name and call it a day. (For more on preparing grayscale images for a printing press, see the box on page 319.)

---

3. **In the duplicate image's Channels panel, activate the Black channel.**

   When you click the Black channel to activate it, Photoshop automatically turns off the other channels' visibility.

4. **Copy the Black channel.**

   Press ⌘-A (Ctrl+A on a PC) to select everything in the Black channel, and then copy it by pressing ⌘-C (Ctrl+C).

5. **Switch back to your original RGB document and paste the Black channel into the Layers panel.**

Click the original RGB image's tab or inside its window. Next, open the Layers panel by clicking its icon in the panel dock or choosing Window→Layers. Then paste the Black channel by pressing ⌘-V (Ctrl+V). (You don't have to create a new layer; Photoshop does that for you.) The beauty of producing this effect inside your original RGB document is editing flexibility. For example, you can lower the layer opacity of the new Black layer for a completely different, yet interesting, partial high-key/partial color effect.

6. **Close the duplicate document because you don't need it anymore.**

That's it! You've now got yourself a beautiful, high-contrast look that took only minutes to achieve.

Spot Channels

In the realm of CMYK printing, there's a special kind of premixed ink called a *spot color*, which requires a special kind of channel that tells the printer where to put that ink. If you're a graphic designer working in prepress (see the Note below), in packaging design, or at an ad agency, you need to know this stuff, and Chapter 16 (page 695) has the details. If you're a photographer or a Web designer, save your brainpower and forget you ever heard about spot channels.

> **NOTE** *Prepress* refers to the process of preparing images and documents—usually in a page-layout program like Adobe InDesign or QuarkXPress—for printing on a commercial press.

Lab Channels

Lab mode separates an image's lightness values (how bright or dark it is) from its color information. This mode gets its name from the channels it includes: Lightness, a, and b. Lab mode isn't used for output like RGB and CMYK modes; instead, it's useful when you want to alter an image's lightness values—when you're sharpening or brightening, for instance—but not its colors. (Likewise, you can adjust the color information without affecting the lightness values to, say, get rid of a color cast.) You can pop into Lab mode by choosing Image→Mode→Lab Color, and if you peek at the Channels panel, you'll see x-rayish images like the ones in Figure 5-5.

Here's what's in each channel:

- **Lightness.** This is where you'll find the details of your image, minus color; it looks like a really good black-and-white version.

- **a.** This channel contains half of the color information: a mixture of magenta (think "red") and green.

- **b.** Here's the other half: a mixture of yellow and blue.

Techniques that involve Lab mode are sprinkled throughout Part 2 of this book.

Lightness

a (red and green)

b (yellow and blue)

FIGURE 5-5

Here's that cowgirl again, now in Lab mode. In the a channel, lighter areas represent greens and darker areas represent magentas (reds). In the b channel, lighter areas represent blues and darker areas represent yellows.

Some folks swear that by splitting the Lightness channel into its own document and then making a few adjustments, you can create a black-and-white image worthy of Ansel Adams. See page 317 for the scoop on how to do that and then judge for yourself!

Multichannel Mode

Unless you're preparing an image for a commercial printing press, you'll never use this mode—although you may switch to it accidentally. If you delete one of the color channels in an RGB, CMYK, or Lab mode document, Photoshop plops you into Multichannel mode without even asking. If that happens, just use the History panel to go back a step or press ⌘-Z (Ctrl+Z on a PC) to undo and bring back the channel you accidentally deleted.

Multichannel mode doesn't have a composite channel; it's strictly for two- or three-color print jobs. So when you enter this mode—by choosing Image→Mode→Multichannel—Photoshop converts any existing color channels to spot channels (page 199).

When you convert an image to Multichannel mode, Photoshop promptly does one of the following (depending on which color mode you were in before):

- **Converts the RGB channels** to cyan, magenta, and yellow spot channels.
- **Converts the CMYK channels** to cyan, magenta, yellow, and black spot channels.
- **Converts the Lab channels** to alpha channels named Alpha 1, Alpha 2, and Alpha 3.
- **Converts the Grayscale channel** to a black spot channel.

These radical channel changes cause drastic color shifts, but you can edit each channel individually—both its contents and its spot color—to create the image you want. When you're finished editing, save the image as a Photoshop (PSD) file by choosing File→Save As and picking Photoshop from the Format pop-up menu.

Single-Channel Modes

The rest of Photoshop's image modes aren't very exciting when it comes to channels: They each have just one. They include Bitmap, Grayscale, Duotone, and Indexed Color mode (the latter is used in GIF files), and they're discussed back on page 45.

■ The Mighty Alpha Channel

Photoshop has one other type of channel: alpha channels. Their job is to store selections so you can use or edit them later.

These channels get their name from a process called *alpha compositing*, which combines a partially transparent image with another image. (Filmmakers use this process to create special effects and fake backdrops.) Information about the shape of the transparent area and the pixels' level of transparency has to be stored somewhere, and that somewhere is an alpha channel.

This is powerful stuff because the same technology lets you save selections. And, as you've learned, making selections can take a *ton* of time. (Heck, you may not have the stamina to finish creating a particularly challenging selection in one sitting!) And since clients change their minds occasionally—"Put the model in front of *this* bush, and change her hair color while you're at it"—the ability to save selections so you can mess with them later is a lifesaver. As long as you save your document as a Photoshop file (page 49), that alpha channel will always be there for you to use. That ought to make you sleep better at night!

> **TIP** You can drag alpha channels between documents as long as both documents have the same pixel dimensions.

Folks sometimes refer to alpha channels as *channel masks* because, once you've made an alpha channel (as explained in the next section), you can use it to help you adjust certain portions of your image—kind of like when you use a layer mask (page 116). In fact, creating a layer mask by loading an alpha channel as a selection is the most common use for alpha channels. That's because, as you'll learn on page 206, you can use channels to make incredibly detailed selections that are tough to get any other way.

> **NOTE** When you're in Quick Mask mode (page 181), you're actually working on a temporary alpha channel. Who knew?

Creating an Alpha Channel

It can be helpful to think of an alpha channel as a grayscale representation of your selection. Unless you change Photoshop's settings, the black parts of the channel are the unselected portion of your image—also referred to as the *protected* or *masked* part—and the white parts are the selection (see page 204 to learn how to reverse these colors). And, just like in a layer mask (page 116), shades of gray represent areas that are only partially selected, which means they're partially transparent.

Photoshop gives you several different ways to create an alpha channel:

- **Create a selection and then choose Select→Save Selection** (see page 184).

- **Create a selection and then click the "Save selection as channel" button at the bottom of the Channels panel.** It looks like a circle within a square (see Figure 5-6).

- **Click the "Create new channel" button at the bottom of the Channels panel** (see Figure 5-2 on page 191). When you do that, Photoshop creates an alpha channel named Alpha 1 and sticks it at the bottom of the Channels panel. The new channel is solid black because it's empty. To create a selection, turn on the composite channel's visibility to summon the red overlay of Quick Mask mode so you can see your image. Then grab the Brush tool (page 497) and paint the area you want to select white (think of this process as painting a hole through the mask so you can see—and therefore select—what's below it).

NOTE Though you can certainly start with an empty alpha channel, it's usually easier to create your selection (or at least a rough version of it) on the full-color image *before* adding the alpha channel. Then you can fine-tune the alpha channel using the methods explained in the box on page 211.

Alpha channel

FIGURE 5-6

In most cases, you'll find it easier to create a selection first (even if it's rough) and then add your alpha channel, as shown here. (That way, you see the full-color image instead of a screen full of black or red.)

To do that, select something in your image and then, once you've got marching ants, click the "Save selection as channel" button (circled). Photoshop adds an alpha channel—which includes your selection—to the bottom of the Channels panel.

- **Choose New Channel from the Channels panel's menu** (see Figure 5-2). When you choose this command, a dialog box opens that lets you name the new channel and tell Photoshop how to display the channel's info.

  Straight from the factory, Photoshop shows selected areas (the parts of your image inside the marching ants) in white and unselected areas in black. Partially selected areas, which have soft edges, appear in shades of gray. If you'd rather see your selections in black and everything else in white, turn on the dialog box's Selected Areas radio button. If you want to edit your alpha channel using Quick Mask mode (as described later in this section), you can change the Quick Mask's color and opacity here. When you've got everything the way you want it, click OK to make Photoshop create your alpha channel.

TIP If you Option-click (Alt-click on a PC) the "Save selection as channel" button instead of just clicking it, you get the same dialog box as if you had chosen New Channel from the Channels panel's menu, which lets you name your sparkling new alpha channel. (You can rename a channel anytime by double-clicking its name.)

Editing Alpha Channels

Once you've got yourself an alpha channel, you can fine-tune it just like a layer mask (page 116) by painting with the Brush tool or using any selection tool. If you use a selection tool, you can choose Edit→Fill and then pick black or white from the Use pop-up menu, depending on whether you want to add to or subtract from your selection (selected areas are white, and everything else is black). If you want to reverse the way Photoshop displays the channel's info—so that your selection appears in black instead of white—just double-click the alpha channel's thumbnail in the Channels panel and, in the resulting Channel Options dialog box, turn on the Selected Areas option. When you do, Photoshop flip-flops your mask's colors, as shown in Figure 5-7.

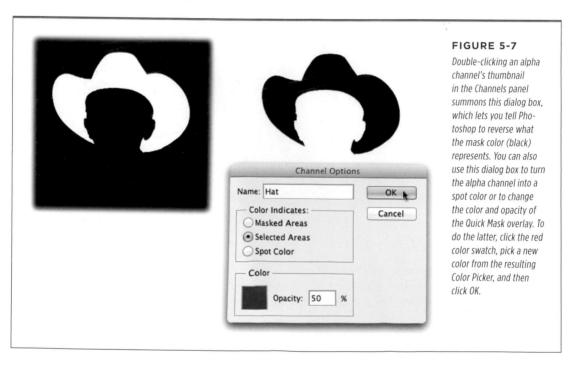

FIGURE 5-7

Double-clicking an alpha channel's thumbnail in the Channels panel summons this dialog box, which lets you tell Photoshop to reverse what the mask color (black) represents. You can also use this dialog box to turn the alpha channel into a spot color or to change the color and opacity of the Quick Mask overlay. To do the latter, click the red color swatch, pick a new color from the resulting Color Picker, and then click OK.

NOTE It doesn't matter whether you use black to mark the masked (protected) or selected (unprotected) areas of your image—it's a personal preference. Just pay careful attention to what the ants are marching 'round when you load an alpha channel as a selection, as *that's* the part of the image you'll modify when you start making changes. And keep in mind that, as you learned in the box on page 156, sometimes it's easier to select what you *don't* want and then use Select→Inverse to flip-flop your selection than to select what you *do* want.

You can also edit your alpha channel using Quick Mask mode (page 181). To do that, in the Channels panel, activate the alpha channel and then click the composite channel's visibility eye, as shown in Figure 5-8. When you do, Photoshop puts Quick Mask mode's signature red overlay atop your image. (If you're editing an alpha channel in an image with a lot of red in it, you won't be able to see diddly through the mask, so change the overlay color as described in Figure 5-7.)

FIGURE 5-8

If you activate an alpha channel and then turn on the composite channel's visibility eye (circled), you can edit or create a selection from scratch in Quick Mask mode. In this example, the Brush tool (the white circle beneath the hat brim) set to paint with black is being used to fine-tune the masked area around the little cowboy's forehead. If you mess up and mask too much—by painting with black across part of the hat, thereby subtracting it from your selection, say—press X to flip-flop your color chips and paint across that area with white to add it back to your selection (just like you would with a layer mask).

You can also run filters on an alpha channel, just like you can with a layer mask. Among the most useful are Gaussian Blur for softening the selection's edge (helpful if you're trying to select a slightly blurred area) and the Minimum filter for tightening your selection (page 671). Chapter 15 shows these filters in action.

Loading an Alpha Channel as a Selection

Once you're finished editing your alpha channel, you can transform it into a selection so you can actually *do* something with it. You can summon the marching ants in several ways:

- ⌘-click (Ctrl-click on a PC) the alpha channel's thumbnail in the Channels panel.

- Click the "Load channel as selection" button at the bottom of the Channels panel (it looks like a tiny dotted circle) while you've got an alpha channel active.

- Drag the alpha channel onto the "Load channel as selection" button (let go of your mouse as soon as Photoshop highlights the button).

Now you can perform all the amazing color and lighting adjustments explained throughout this book, and they'll affect only the area you've selected. Pretty sweet, huh?

Deleting Alpha Channels

When you're finished using an alpha channel (or if you want to start over with a new one), you can get rid of it by dragging it onto the Delete button (the little trash can) at the bottom of the Channels panel. Or just click the trash can while the alpha channel is active and then click Yes when Photoshop asks if you're *sure* you want to throw it away.

> **NOTE** Unless you're a panel neat freak, you don't have to throw out old alpha channels. They don't add all that much to your document's file size because they're black and white (if they contain a lot of gray, they'll add slightly more to the file size, but not enough that it's worth tossing 'em). If you've created a slew of incredibly complex alpha channels, then you might see a bump in file size. Nevertheless, if there's even the slightest chance you'll ever use them again, save your document as a PSD file to keep those hard-earned alpha channels intact.

■ Basic Channel Stunts

Now that you know what channels are all about, it's time to learn some of the cool things you can do with them. This section covers a few of the most practical channel tricks, and you'll find other techniques involving channels throughout this book.

Selecting Objects with Channels

As you learned in Chapter 4, true selection wisdom lies in knowing which tool to start with so you'll have the least fine-tuning to do later. If you have an image with a decent amount of contrast between the object you want to select and its background, you can give channels a spin. All you need to do is create an alpha channel that contains only black-and-white objects, load it as a selection, and then use it to make a layer mask. Here's how to use channels to select all the balloons in Figure 5-9 so you can, for example, swap in a new sky:

1. **Open an image that's in RGB mode and that has a background you want to swap.**

    If your image came from a scanner or digital camera, it's already in RGB mode. To check, choose Image→Mode. If necessary, choose RGB Color to switch modes.

> **NOTE** Want to follow along? Visit this book's Missing CD page at *www.missingmanuals.com/cds* and download the practice file *Balloons.jpg*.

2. **Find the channel where the objects you want to select look the darkest.**

   In the Channels panel, click each channel to find the one where the balloons are the darkest. (You can also cycle through channels by pressing ⌘-3, 4, and 5 [Ctrl+3, 4, 5 on a PC].) Objects will usually be darkest on the blue channel, as is the case here.

FIGURE 5-9

Once you find the channel where the objects appear darkest (typically the blue channel), make a copy of that channel so you don't mess up your original photo with the lightening or darkening you're about to perform.

To copy a channel, simply drag it onto the "Create new channel" button, and Photoshop adds the copy to the bottom of your Channels panel, as shown here.

TIP   In the past, using channels was the only way to create really tough selections around hair and fur. However, in Photoshop CS5, the Refine Edge dialog box improved so much that it's becoming the preferred method. That said, it can be extremely helpful to use Channels to create a selection that you then *fine tune* with the Refine Edge dialog box. Page 171 has more on Refine Edge.

3. **Duplicate the blue channel so you don't destroy your original image.**

   Either Control-click (right-click on a PC) the blue channel in the Channels panel and then pick Duplicate Channel from the shortcut menu, or drag the channel onto the "Create new channel" button. (You can also choose Duplicate Channel from the Channels panel's menu, but dragging is quicker.) Whichever method you use, Photoshop puts the duplicate at the bottom of the Channels panel and cleverly names it "Blue copy."

4. **Adjust the duplicate blue channel's Levels to make the balloons black and the background white.**

   Chapter 9 covers Levels in detail, but this exercise gives you a sneak peek at how useful this type of adjustment can be. Choose Image→Adjustments→Levels or press ⌘-L (Ctrl+L on a PC) to summon the Levels dialog box. To make the balloons darker, drag the shadows slider (Figure 5-10, top) to the right until the balloons turn *almost* black. (As you drag the slider, the background gets darker, too. That's OK—you'll fix the background in the next step.) Don't close the Levels dialog box just yet!

5. **Using the white eyedropper, click the gray background to make it white.**

   The little white eyedropper on the right side of the dialog box lets you tell Photoshop what should be white (pros call this technique "resetting the white point"). Click the eyedropper to activate it (Figure 5-10, bottom), mouse over to your document, and then click a gray part of the background. Keep clicking on different gray areas until the background is completely white (or as close to white as you can get it). When you're finished, click OK to close the Levels dialog box.

FIGURE 5-10

Top: Depending on the amount of contrast in your image, you may have to drag the shadows slider (circled) quite a ways to the right to make the balloons black. But be careful: If you drag it too far to the right, you'll start to lose some of the detail around their edges.

Bottom: Next, click the white eyedropper (circled) and then, over in your image, click the background area until it's as white as it'll get. When your image is pure black and white, as shown here, you're ready to load the channel as a selection. (If you can't seem to make it pure black and white, don't panic; just proceed to step 6.)

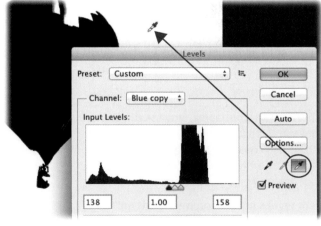

6. **If necessary, touch up the inside of the balloons with black paint and the background with white paint.**

   If adjusting the shadows slider in step 4 didn't make the balloons *completely* black (as in Figure 5-10, top), use the Brush tool to touch them up (otherwise the balloons will be only partially selected). Press B to grab the Brush tool, set your foreground color chip to black (press D to set the color chips to black and white, and then press X until black hops on top), and then mouse over to the balloons and paint them solid black. And, if resetting the white point in step 5 didn't get rid of all the gray in the background—like in the upper-right corner of the balloon image in Figure 5-10, bottom—you can use the Brush tool to paint those areas white. (Alternatively, you can use the Lasso tool to hand draw a selection around an area, choose Edit→Fill, pick Black from the Use pop-up menu, and then click OK.) When you're finished, you should have a pure black-and-white image.

TIP When you're touching up an alpha channel using the Brush tool, be sure to zoom in on your image to make sure you're being precise with your brushstrokes (on a 4 MB image, for example, you need to zoom in to at least 500 percent). You may also need to switch to a hard-edged brush using the Brush preset picker in the Options bar to ensure you don't create too soft an edge around the object you're painting. See page 60 for more on zooming and page 497 for more on changing Brush tool options.

---

7. **In the Channels panel, load the duplicate blue channel as a selection by ⌘-clicking (Ctrl-clicking on a PC) the channel's thumbnail or clicking the "Load channel as selection" button (the dotted circle) at the bottom of the panel.**

   Now that you've got a perfectly black-and-white image (it looks just like a layer mask or alpha channel, doesn't it?), you can load it as a selection. When you do, Photoshop puts marching ants around the *background* of your image, which is the opposite of what you want. No worries! You'll solve that problem in the next step.

8. **Invert the selection to select the balloons instead of the background.**

   Choose Select→Inverse or press Shift-⌘-I (Shift+Ctrl+I on a PC) to flip-flop your selection so the marching ants run around the balloons instead of around the edges of the document.

9. **In the Channels panel, turn on the composite channel and hide the duplicate blue channel.**

   Scroll to the top of the Channels panel and click near the composite channel's name (RGB) to turn it back on so you can see the full-color version of your image again. (This also turns off the visibility of the duplicate blue channel.) You can delete the duplicate blue channel by dragging it to the tiny trash can at the bottom of the Channels panel or leave it hanging around in case you need to edit it later.

10. **Open your Layers panel, make the Background layer editable, and then add a layer mask.**

Click the Layers tab to open the Layers panel or choose Window→Layers. If the Background layer still has a little padlock icon next to it, double-click the icon to make the layer editable. If you like, type a name for the Background layer in the resulting dialog box and then click OK. (If you're working with an image you've edited before, you may have already named your Background layer something other than "Background.") To add a layer mask, click the circle-within-a-square button at the bottom of the Layers panel. Photoshop adds a layer mask that hides the photo's original background (the sky), as shown in Figure 5-11, left. Sweet!

You're all finished! You can now copy and paste a new background into the Layers panel and then drag it to the bottom of the layer stack to put the balloons on a brand new sky (see Figure 5-11). If you need to edit the layer mask (page 116), activate it in the Layers panel and then paint with either black or white according to what you want to do.

FIGURE 5-11

Look, Ma, no selection tools! Whenever you have an image like this one that's got a decent amount of contrast between its subject and its background, using channels is an easy way to create an accurate selection fast.

Touching Up Alpha Channels

When you're editing an alpha channel to make a selection, it's important that you end up with a pure black-and-white channel with very few shades of gray. (The alpha channel shown in Figure 5-10 is almost there but needs a tiny bit of touch-up on the balloons). If there are any gray areas around the edge of the object, those edges will look soft—as if you've feathered them (page 145). If there's any gray in the center of the object, those pixels will be only partially selected (and if there's any white, they won't be selected at all). Adjusting the alpha channel's Levels usually gets your image *close* to pure black and white, but that method can only do so much: You're often left with stray gray pixels here and there, a selection that isn't quite solid black or white, or some stuff in the background that you don't need. Your only choice at that point is to touch up the image by hand.

Sure, this kind of work is tedious, but it goes much faster if you use one of the following methods. Remember that when you're in Channels Land, you've got most (but not all) of Photoshop's tools at your command. With that in mind, here are a few tricks for touching up alpha channels:

- **Fill the background with black or white.** If you've managed to make your object pure black, you can use a selection tool to grab everything else in the channel and make it white. For example, use the Lasso tool to draw a rough selection around your black object and then choose Select→Inverse to select the background instead. Next, choose Edit→Fill, pick white from the Use pop-up menu, and then click OK. Now your background is solid white and your touch-up work is limited to the area right around your object. (If the object you want to select is solid white, use this method to fill the background with black instead.)

- **Fill in the object with black or white.** When the object you want to select isn't *quite* solid black or white, your best bet is to set the Brush tool to either black or white and then paint the object by hand. Or use the Lasso tool to draw a rough selection around that area and then choose Edit→Fill and pick black or white from the Use pop-up

menu. (If the area is square or oval, use the Rectangular or Elliptical Marquee tool to select it instead.) When you click OK, Photoshop fills that area with color. (For more on the selection tools, see Chapter 4.)

- **Get rid of stray gray pixels inside a black object.** If you've cleaned up the rest of your alpha channel but still see a few gray pixels in your black object, use Levels to turn them black. Remember how you used Levels to turn gray pixels white by resetting the white point (step 5 on page 208)? You can use the same technique to turn gray pixels black. Just open the Levels dialog box by pressing ⌘-L (Ctrl+L on a PC), select the *black* eyedropper, mouse over to your image, and then click one of those pesky gray pixels. Photoshop turns all the gray pixels in your document black.

- **Get rid of stray gray pixels next to a black object.** If you end up with a few gray pixels near the object you want to select, use a white brush set to paint in Overlay mode (see page 288) to paint them white. Press B to select the Brush tool and set your foreground color chip to white (page 23). Then hop up to the Options bar and set the Mode menu to Overlay and Opacity to 100%. In this mode, the Brush tool *completely* ignores the color black and turns gray pixels white, letting you brush away gray pixels near black areas without fear of messing up the black. Even if you paint right over the black area, nothing happens to it!

- **Turn gray pixels in delicate edges black.** If you're dealing with hair or fur, some of the wispier edges may end up more gray than black. If that happens, grab the Brush tool and set your foreground color chip to black. Then trot up to the Options bar and change the Mode menu to Soft Light (page 288). Now, when you paint over the hair or fur, Photoshop turns the gray pixels black. However, you may not want to turn those delicate parts *completely* black or they'll have hard edges and won't blend into the background very well. You'll have to experiment to see what looks best.

Creating a Silhouette Effect

Apple made silhouettes famous by using them in its iPod and iTunes advertising campaigns. You can use the channel-selection technique described in the previous section to create the same effect. The only difference is that, instead of adding a layer mask, you'll add a Solid Color Fill layer set to black. That way, the silhouette lives on its own layer, making it easy for you to edit it later, as the Apple-esque images in Figure 5-12 show.

FIGURE 5-12

Using channels to make a selection lets you create a slick silhouette in no time flat. You can even get a clean selection of curly hair (top) and dangling feathers (bottom).

When you're dealing with delicate edges like those around hair, be careful not to drag the Levels dialog box's shadows slider too far to the right or the edges will become really jagged. You'll have a little more touch-up work to do before you're finished, but it's worth it. Here, the Lasso tool was used to select areas that didn't become black by dragging the shadows slider, and then they were filled with black using the Edit→Fill command.

Heck, these two images require less fine-tuning than the balloons back in Figure 5-11!

To create a quick silhouette, follow steps 1–9 in the previous section so you've got a nice selection and you're looking at the full-color image. Then:

1. **Add a new Solid Color Fill layer at the top of your layer stack.**

   When you see marching ants running around your subject, you're ready to create a Solid Color Fill layer. Take a peek at the bottom of the Layers panel and click the Adjustment layer icon (the half-black/half-white circle). Choose Solid Color from the menu to make Photoshop open the Color Picker; pick black, and then click OK. (Sure, you could create a regular ol' image layer and fill it with black, but this way is faster; see page 77 for the full story on Fill layers). Photoshop adds the new layer to the top of your layer stack, creating a silhouette.

2. **Add a new background by creating another Solid Color Fill layer and filling it with a bright color.**

   Create another Solid Color Fill layer as you did in step 1, but this time choose a really bright color, such as lime green, and then click OK.

3. **Drag the bright-colored Fill layer below the silhouette layer in your layer stack.**

   This keeps the new background from covering your silhouette. You can also press ⌘-[(Ctrl+[on a PC) to move a layer down one position, or Shift-⌘-[(Shift+Ctrl+[) to move it to the bottom of the layer stack.

> **NOTE** Try this silhouette technique by visiting this book's Missing CD page at *www.missingmanuals.com/ cds* and downloading the practice file *Indian.jpg*.

Now you're starting to see the power of using channels to help make selections! If you need to edit the silhouette—maybe you want to erase something or do a little touch-up with a black brush—activate the black Solid Color Fill layer's mask and have at it. Likewise, if you want to change the silhouette or background color, simply double-click the appropriate Solid Color Fill layer's *thumbnail* and then pick a new color from the resulting Color Picker (double-clicking the layer itself opens the Layer Style dialog box instead).

Lightening and Darkening Channels

There will be times when you wish a channel were lighter or darker so you'd have an easier time making a selection. Remember back in Chapter 3 when you learned how to quickly lighten and darken photos using blend modes? While there's no blend mode pop-up menu in the Channels panel, you can make your channel lighter or darker with the Apply Image command. Folks mainly use this command to blend two images together (see the third bullet on page 282)—which is why the Apply Image dialog box has a blend mode pop-up menu—but you can also use it to apply a channel to *itself* (as if the channel were duplicated) and change its blend mode at the same time.

To lighten or darken a channel, activate it in the Channels panel and then create a copy of it (see page 207) so you don't destroy your original image. Then choose

Image→Apply Image and, in the resulting dialog box (shown in Figure 5-13), choose either Screen (to lighten) or Multiply (to darken) from the Blending pop-up menu. When you click OK, Photoshop applies the channel to itself using the blend mode you picked. Depending on the image you're working with, your channel will lighten or darken by about 15 to 30 percent. If it needs to be even lighter or darker, simply run the Apply Image command as many times as you need to.

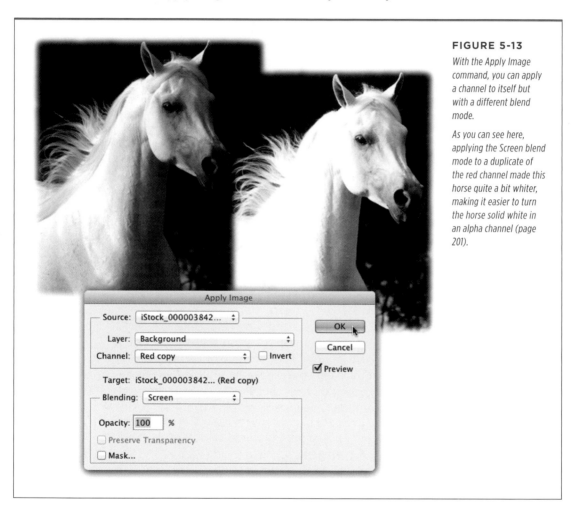

FIGURE 5-13

With the Apply Image command, you can apply a channel to itself but with a different blend mode.

As you can see here, applying the Screen blend mode to a duplicate of the red channel made this horse quite a bit whiter, making it easier to turn the horse solid white in an alpha channel (page 201).

> **TIP** If the Apply Image command isn't lightening or darkening your duplicate channel enough to make a good alpha channel, you can always pump up the contrast by adding a temporary Curves or Levels Adjustment layer (both are covered in Chapter 9). By using an Adjustment layer, the temporary contrast boost happens on its own layer, so you can throw it away after you've created the alpha channel.

Combining Channels

Not all images have enough contrast to let you make a good alpha channel by using just one channel—sometimes you'll have to use *two*. This process takes a bit more time, but the steps are essentially the same.

For example, if you want to select the hat and guitar in Figure 5-14, a quick glance at the Channels panel tells you that the hat is darkest in the red channel, but the guitar has the most contrast in the green channel. So your best bet is to build your selection one channel at a time, using the optimal channel for each part. Duplicate the red channel and adjust it using Levels, the Brush tool, and so on until the hat is solid black. Next, duplicate the green channel and work on the guitar while you erase (or paint over) the parts of that channel you don't need (the hat). When you're finished, you may want to merge them, but, alas, Photoshop won't let you. But you *can* combine them into a brand-new channel using the *Calculations* command.

Choose Image→Calculations to summon the Calculations dialog box (if this command is grayed out, check to make sure you've got only *one* channel active in the Channels panel). From the pop-up menus in the Source 1 and Source 2 sections, pick the channels you want to combine as shown in Figure 5-14. This dialog box also lets you set the blend mode, so if you're working with a black object and a white background as shown in the figure, set the blend mode to Multiply so Photoshop keeps the darkest parts of both channels and gets rid of everything else. (If you're working with a white object and a black background, use the Screen blend mode instead so Photoshop keep the *lightest* parts of both channels.) When everything's set, click OK, and Photoshop creates a new channel based on the two you picked.

FREQUENTLY ASKED QUESTION

Selecting with the Lightest Channel

How come I always have to make objects black and the background white when I'm using channels to create a selection? Can I do it the other way around instead?

Trying to buck the system, are ya? Lucky for you, the answer is yes—you can make the object white and the background black instead, if you prefer. It doesn't matter whether the area you want to select is black or white; all that matters is what the marching ants surround once you load that channel as a selection.

For example, if you're trying to select a light object that lives on a dark background, it's *much* easier to make the object white and the background black. In that case, search for the *lightest* channel (which, in RGB mode, is usually red). Once you find it, duplicate that channel and then use Levels to make it pure black and white (see page 207, step 4). You won't even need to inverse your selection: You'll see marching ants around your object as soon as you load the channel as a selection (page 209, step 7).

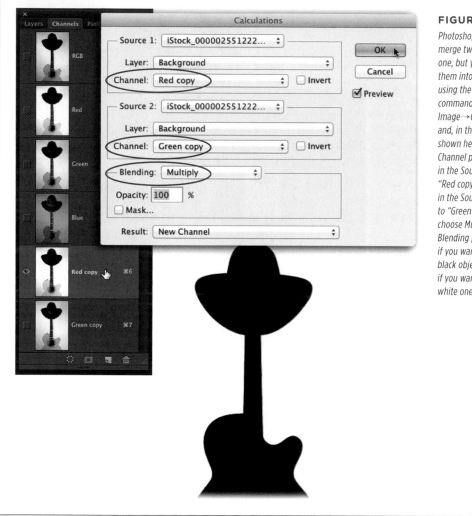

FIGURE 5-14

Photoshop doesn't let you merge two channels into one, but you can combine them into a new channel using the Calculations command: Choose Image→Calculations and, in the dialog box shown here, set the Channel pop-up menu in the Source 1 section to "Red copy" and the menu in the Source 2 section to "Green copy." Then choose Multiply from the Blending pop-up menu if you want to create a black object or Screen if you want to create a white one.

NOTE You can also use the *Channel Mixer* to simulate combining channels to create grayscale images. It doesn't actually combine channels, but it makes your image *look* like it did. The box on page 479 has the details.

Sharpening Individual Channels

As you'll learn in Chapter 11, if you sharpen an image that has a lot of noise in it, you'll sharpen the noise and grain right along with the rest of the image, making it look ten times worse than it did before (see the box on page 459). That's why it's important to get rid of—or, at the very least, reduce—those nasties *before* you sharpen an image.

NOTE What's the difference between noise and grain? They both describe tiny flecks in your image, but, technically speaking, noise occurs in digital images, whereas grain occurs in analog prints, film, and transparencies. In other words, grain becomes noise once you scan the image.

However, let's say you're in RGB mode and you dutifully followed the instructions on page 459 and ran the Reduce Noise filter on your blue channel (which typically has the most noise, though sometimes noise can hide in the red channel, too), and it didn't do squat. What do you do? You can try bringing out some of the details in your image by sharpening *only* the red and green channels, as shown in Figure 5-15.

FIGURE 5-15

If you activate the red and green channels before running a sharpening filter, you restrict the sharpening to just those two channels. This helps you avoid sharpening—and therefore accentuating—noise or other unwanted, ahem, skin textures.

TIP The next time you need to sharpen a portrait of someone who's sensitive about his or her appearance, try sharpening only the red channel to avoid bringing out unwanted details in the person's skin. (As you learned earlier in this chapter, your camera has twice as many green sensors as red or blue, meaning that a lot of the fine details lurk in the green channel.)

Here's how to sharpen an image without making the noise in it any worse than it already is:

1. **Open your image and make a copy of the layer(s) you're going to sharpen.**

   If you're working with a document that has just one layer, activate it in your Layers panel and then duplicate it by pressing ⌘-J (Ctrl+J on a PC). If you like, double-click the layer's name and rename it *Sharpen*.

   If you're working on a multilayer document, Shift-click to activate all the layers and then choose Layer→Smart Objects→Convert to Smart Object. Photoshop combines all the layers into a single Smart Object.

2. **Open the Channels panel and activate both the red and green channels.**

   Click to activate one channel and then Shift-click to activate the other one, so they're both highlighted in the Channels panel. Don't panic if your image turns a weird color like the horse in Figure 5-15; Photoshop is just showing you the image using only those two color channels.

3. **Choose Filter→Sharpen→Unsharp Mask (page 460).**

   When you run a filter while you've got only certain channels active, Photoshop applies the sharpening to just those channels. In this case, it won't apply any sharpening to the blue channel. Click OK to close the Unsharp Mask dialog box.

4. **In the Channels panel, turn on the composite channel (here, that's RGB) to see your new and improved full-color image.**

You're done! If you want to see before and after versions of the image, open the Layers panel and toggle the Sharpen layer's visibility eye—or the Unsharp Mask filter layer, if you used a Smart Object—off and on.

TIP Another, more advanced way to sharpen an image is to use the channel with the highest contrast to create an intricate edge mask, or by using the High Pass filter. You can read all about those techniques—including how to sharpen only certain areas of your image—in Chapter 11.

Cropping, Resizing, and Rotating

ropping and resizing images are among the most basic edits you'll ever make, but they're also among the most important. A bad crop—or no crop—can ruin an image, while a good crop can improve it tenfold by snipping away useless or distracting material. And knowing how to resize an image—by changing either its file size or its overall dimensions—can be crucial when it's time to email an image, print it, or post it on a website. Cropping is pretty straightforward (though the process changed drastically in CS6); resizing, not so much. To resize an image correctly, you first need to understand the relationship between pixels and resolution—and how they affect image quality. (That can of worms gets opened on page 237.) Rotating images, on the other hand, is just plain fun.

In this chapter, you'll learn more than you ever wanted to know about cropping, from general guidelines to the many ways of cropping in both Photoshop and Camera Raw (a powerful photo-correcting application that comes with Photoshop—see Chapter 9). You'll also discover how to resize images *without*—and this is crucial— losing image quality. Perhaps most important, you'll understand once and for all what resolution really is, when it matters, and how to change it without trashing your image. Finally, you'll spend some quality playtime with the various Transform commands.

■ Cropping Images

There's a reason professional photos look so darn good. Besides being shot with fancy cameras and receiving some post-processing fluffing, they're also composed or cropped extremely well (or both). *Cropping* means eliminating distracting elements in an image by cutting away unwanted bits around the edges. Good crops accentuate the subject, drawing the viewer's eye to it; and bad crops are, well, just bad, as you can see in Figure 6-1.

FIGURE 6-1

Left: A poorly cropped image can leave the viewer distracted by extraneous stuff around the edges, like the wall and window reflection here.

Right: A well-cropped image forces the viewer to focus on the subject by eliminating distractions (in this case, the empty space in the background). This crop also gives the subject a little breathing room in the direction she's facing, which is always a good idea (see Figure 6-2 for more examples).

Technically, you can crop *before* you take a photo by moving closer to the subject (called "cropping with your feet") and repositioning the subject within the frame. However, if you don't get the shot right when you're out in the field, Photoshop can fix it after the fact. But before you go grabbing the Crop tool, you need to learn a few guidelines.

The Rule of Thirds

Once you understand the rule of thirds, a compositional guideline cherished by both photography and video pros, you'll spot it in almost every image you see. The idea is to divide every picture into nine equal parts using an imaginary tic-tac-toe grid. If you position the image's horizon on either the top or the bottom line—never the center—and the focal point (the most important part of the image) on one of the spots where the lines intersect, you create a more interesting shot. It's simpler than it sounds—just take a look at Figure 6-2.

> **NOTE** The Crop tool actually *comes with* a rule-of-thirds grid, making this rule easier than ever to grasp and follow!

FIGURE 6-2

Top: Imagine a tic-tac-toe grid atop every image. Notice that the interesting bits of the photos are positioned where the lines intersect. Most digital cameras let you add such a grid to the camera's screen to help you compose shots, though to figure out how to turn it on, you may have to root through the camera's menus or (shudder) dig out the owner's manual.

Bottom: Before you crop, notice the direction the subject is facing. A good crop gives the subject room to move—or, in this case, fly—through the photo. If the image were cropped tightly to the boy's face on the right side, it'd look weird because he'd (theoretically) smack into the edge of the image if he flew away.

Creative Cropping

Along with applying the rule of thirds, pros also crop in unexpected ways, as Figure 6-3 shows. Unconventional cropping is yet another way to add visual interest in order to catch the viewer's eye.

Creative cropping is especially important when you're dealing with super-small images, such as those in a thumbnail gallery or on a website where several images vie for attention. In such tiny images, people can see few, if any, details, and, if the photo contains people, *forget* being able to identify them. Here are some tips for creating truly enticing teensy-weensy images:

- **Recrop the image.** Instead of scaling down the original, focus on a single element in the image. You often don't need to include the *whole* subject for people to figure out what it is (Figure 6-3, middle, is a good example).

- **Sharpen again after resizing.** Even if you sharpened (digitally enhanced the focus of) the original, go ahead and resharpen it post-resizing using one of the techniques covered in Chapter 11.

- **Add a border.** To add a touch of class to that tiny ad or thumbnail, give it an elegant hairline border (page 186) or a rounded edge (page 150).

Now that you've absorbed a few cropping guidelines, you're ready to learn the many ways you can crop in Photoshop, starting with the most common.

FIGURE 6-3

Top: Challenge yourself to think outside the box and crop in unexpected ways. You may not think cropping someone's face in half is a good idea, but here's an example where it works.

Middle: When you're close-cropping, you often don't need to reveal the whole subject. For example, this piece of zebra is more visually interesting than the whole animal, and it's still obvious what it's a photo of.

Bottom: Here's proof that you can't always trust what you see. Cropping can easily alter the perceived meaning of an image. For example, the left-hand photo has been creatively cropped to suit the headline "Sea Muffin Wins by a Mile!" But the original photo on the right reveals another story.

The Crop Tool

Photoshop tools don't get much easier to use than the good ol' Crop tool, though it got a major overhaul in CS6. Press C to grab it from the Tools panel and a crop box automatically surrounds your image. Grab any handle to resize the box, and then click *inside* the box and drag to reposition *your image* underneath it (your cursor turns into a tiny arrow). If you'd rather draw your *own* crop box instead of resizing the one Photoshop put around the image, just click and drag in your image to draw another one (if you've already adjusted the automatic crop box, press Esc to start over). To move the crop box *as* you're drawing it, press and hold the space bar while dragging; when you've got the crop box where you want it, let go of the space bar and continue drawing the box.

Either way, as soon as you let go of your mouse, Photoshop helpfully darkens the outer portion of the image to give you an idea of what's destined for the trash can (this darkened portion is called a *shield*) and places a rule-of-thirds grid over the unshielded portion (Figure 6-4). When you like what you see, press Return (Enter on a PC) or double-click inside the crop box to accept it, and Photoshop deletes the unwanted pixels.

TIP In CS6 you see a crop box around your image *whenever* the Crop tool is active, but that doesn't mean a crop is necessarily in progress; you can switch to any other tool and the crop box disappears. However, if you click, resize, or move the crop box, that means a crop *is* in progress. If you then decide you *don't* want to crop the photo after all, you need to communicate that to Photoshop by pressing the Esc key or clicking the Cancel button in the Options bar (the circle with a slash through it). If you switch to another tool after tweaking the crop box, a message appears asking if you want to crop the image first. Click Don't Crop and continue on your merry way.

FIGURE 6-4

Top: The Crop tool lives near the top of the Tools panel; just click its icon and hold down your mouse button to expand its toolset, as shown here. The Perspective Crop tool is new in CS6 (see page 226).

Right: After you tweak the automatic crop box or draw your own, Photoshop places a rule-of-thirds grid atop your image and gives you an idea of what the end result will look like by darkening the parts that'll be cropped out. You can easily resize and rotate the crop box using the handles circled here (they look like little bars, and their color changes depending on the image colors underneath 'em). New in CS6, a handy info overlay appears near your cursor. If you're dragging a handle to resize the crop box, the overlay includes info about the size of the box (as shown here). If you're repositioning the crop box, you see info indicating how much the crop box has moved, and if you're rotating the box, you see angle of rotation. Handy!

Keep in mind, though, that when you accept a crop, Photoshop *deletes everything in the shielded area permanently*—that is, unless you *uncheck* the Delete Cropped Pixels checkbox in the Options bar (circled in Figure 6-5, top; as of this writing, it's turned on when you install the program). So if you change your mind immediately after wielding the crop ax, press ⌘-Z (Ctrl+Z on a PC) to undo it or step backward in the History panel (page 25). Better yet, if you like the crop but want to make sure you keep a copy of the original, *uncropped* version, go to File→Save As right after you crop the photo and give it a new name.

TIP You can toggle the crop shield off and on by pressing the forward slash key (/); Photoshop CS6 shows you a preview of what your cropped image looks like. You can also change the shield's color and transparency using the Crop Options pop-up menu (the gear icon labeled in Figure 6-5, top).

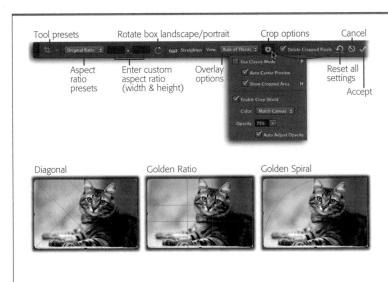

Tool presets   Rotate box landscape/portrait   Crop options   Cancel

Aspect   Enter custom   Overlay   Reset all
ratio   aspect ratio   options   settings
presets   (width & height)   Accept

Diagonal   Golden Ratio   Golden Spiral

FIGURE 6-5

Top: The Crop tool's behavior and Options bar settings changed drastically in CS6. For example, a crop box now automatically appears when the tool is active, and dragging in your image moves the image rather than the crop box. These changes take some getting used to, though if they drive you crazy you can revert to the behavior of the old Crop tool by clicking the gear icon shown here and then turning on Use Classic Mode.

Bottom: CS6 includes a bushel of new overlay options, three of which are shown here, that you can access in the Options bar's View pop-up menu. Once you click the crop box to activate it, you can cycle through the various overlays by pressing the O key repeatedly. To change an overlay's orientation (to, say, make the Golden Spiral appear at the upper left of your image instead of the lower right), press Shift-O repeatedly.

TIP You can now use the Crop tool to straighten images, too. Skip to page 231 to see this new option in action.

If you turn *off* the Delete Cropped Pixels checkbox (labeled "Hide" in earlier versions of the program), Photoshop doesn't vaporize the cropped material; it politely *dangles* it outside the document's margins instead (in other words, it's hidden). That way, even though you don't see it onscreen, it's still part of your document. To resurrect the cropped portion—*even after you've saved and closed the document*—press C to activate the Crop tool again and then immediately press Return (Enter on a PC). Photoshop displays the previously hidden edges of the image and places an active crop box around the previously cropped area. At this point you can resize the crop box, reposition it, and so on.

■ CROPPING TO A SPECIFIC SHAPE, SIZE, AND RESOLUTION

The Crop tool in Photoshop CS6 lets you *constrain* your crop box to the aspect ratio—the relationship between width and height—of your original image (a good idea if you want the cropped image to be the same shape as the original). To do so, choose Original Ratio from the Aspect Ratio presets pop-up menu labeled in Figure 6-5, top, and the crop box restricts itself accordingly (why this menu isn't labeled in the Options bar is anyone's guess). Other options in this menu include common aspect ratios such as 1×1, 4×5, 8.5×11, and so on; give one a click and those aspect ratios appear in the fields to the menu's right. If you don't see the aspect ratios you want, just enter 'em into the fields yourself.

Choosing an aspect ratio from this menu or entering numbers manually changes the *shape* of the image but *doesn't* change its resolution (resolution controls pixel size, as explained on page 237). For example, if you're preparing an image for a 5×7 frame, changing the aspect ratio lets you adjust the photo's *shape* to fit the frame; Photoshop then alters the pixel dimensions accordingly by trimming pixels off the edges of the image to make it match the aspect ratio you picked, but it doesn't mess with the image's resolution. Once the image is the right shape, you can always use the Image Size dialog box to alter resolution manually as described on page 244.

If you *want* to change the size and/or pixel dimensions of the image, just include a unit of measurement in the aspect ratio fields (use *px* for pixels or *in* for inches). That way, Photoshop changes the *dimensions* of the image rather than just its shape. Alternatively, you can choose one of the generic size and resolution combos listed in the Tool presets menu at the left end of the Options bar, or open the Size & Resolution dialog box (described in the first bullet point below). Once you accept the crop by pressing Return (Enter on a PC) or clicking the checkmark in the Options bar, Photoshop picks the best mathematical formula to resize the image for maximum quality (the formula is called *Bicubic Automatic* and you'll learn all about it on page 241). As a result, the image area inside the box perfectly matches the dimensions you entered or picked from the preset menu (you can pop open the Image Size dialog box [page 238] to verify the change).

If you frequently enter the same dimensions into the aspect ratio fields, you can save them as a preset. After you enter them in the Options bar, choose Save Preset from the Aspect Ratio presets pop-up menu and, in the resulting New Crop Preset dialog box, give them a meaningful name and then click OK. Your new preset shows up in the same menu for easy access later on.

Here are the last two items in the Aspect Ratio presets pop-up menu:

- **Size & Resolution.** In previous versions of Photoshop, you'd see a Resolution field in the Options bar whenever the Crop tool was active. Adobe removed it in CS6 so you can't *accidentally* change an image's resolution when cropping it. If you really *do* want to crop and change the resolution of your image at the same time, choose this option to open the dialog box in Figure 6-6.

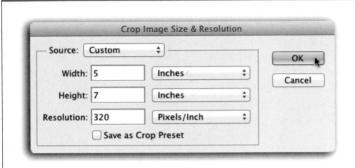

FIGURE 6-6

To change the dimensions and resolution of an image while you're cropping it, type those figures into CS6's new Crop Image Size & Resolution dialog box. (If you think you'll use the same size and resolution combo later, turn on "Save Crop as Preset.") To copy another image's dimensions so you can base a crop on those measurements, open that image, open this dialog box, and then choose Front Image from the Source pop-up menu shown here.

- **Rotate Crop Box.** Choose this option to rotate your crop box to make it landscape (short and wide) or portrait (tall and thin) in orientation. In CS6 the crop box is *supposed* to rotate automatically to fit the aspect ratio of your image, but it doesn't always work. You can also click the Rotate button in the Options bar or, once you've clicked to activate the crop box, simply press the X key to do the same thing.

■ CROPPING WITH PERSPECTIVE

If you shoot an image at an angle and then need to straighten it (like the painting shown in Figure 6-7, top), you can crop the image *and* change its perspective at the same time using CS6's new Perspective Crop tool.

The new Perspective Crop tool lives in the Crop toolset; just click the Crop tool's icon and hold down your mouse button to pop open the toolset and then choose Perspective Crop (or press Shift-C repeatedly to cycle through the Crop tools). To use it, click the four corners of the object you want to straighten, and Photoshop creates a crop box containing a grid overlay atop the object *for* you. (The box doesn't have to be *exactly* aligned with the object, but be sure that it surrounds the whole object.) Next, drag the square corner handles so the lines of the crop box are parallel to (or on top of) the angled lines of the object. When everything's lined up, press Return (Enter on a PC) or double-click inside the box to accept the crop. If the planets are properly aligned, the cropped image looks nice and straight, as shown in Figure 6-7 (bottom).

FIGURE 6-7

As you can see here, cropping to perspective can instantly (and painlessly) straighten objects shot at an angle, such as this painting. This kind of thing works well on inanimate objects, but not so great on living things (unless you like that distorted, fun house-mirror look).

(Painting by iStockphoto/Renee Keith.)

■ ADDING POLAROID-STYLE PHOTO FRAMES

The Crop tool isn't all work and no play; you can use it for fun stuff like creating a Polaroid-style photo frame like the one in Figure 6-8. Besides being a fast way to add a touch of creativity to an image, this kind of frame lets you add a caption to commemorate extra-special moments. Here's how to add a frame to a photo:

NOTE To practice the Polaroid maneuver on your own computer, visit this book's Missing CD page at *www.missingmanuals.com/cds* and download the practice file *Trekkers.jpg*.

1. Open an image and double-click its Background layer to make it editable.

Remember, the Background layer is initially locked for the reasons explained on page 87. To unlock it, give it a quick double-click, and—if you want—type a new name in the resulting dialog box. Alternatively, you can Option-double-click (Alt-double-click on a PC) to bypass the dialog box.

FIGURE 6-8

Top: To create the look of a Polaroid, use the Crop tool to add canvas space around the photo as shown here. Be sure to add a little extra room at the bottom for a caption!

Bottom: When you add a solid white layer and then add even more canvas space, the Polaroid really starts to take shape. Next, add a caption, activate the layers, and then rotate 'em. Finish off the effect by adding a drop shadow large enough to show around all four edges.

Engage!

Playing dress-up with Jack

2. Add canvas space with the Crop tool.

Activate the Crop tool by pressing C and then, while holding down the Option key (Alt on a PC), drag one of the corner crop handles outward about one-quarter inch and then release the key. Holding down Option (Alt) while you drag the corner handles of a crop box forces *all four sides* of the box to expand or shrink simultaneously by the same amount. (Otherwise, you'd have to move each handle one after another.) Press and hold the Shift key to resize the box as a perfect square instead.

Next, drag the bottom-middle crop handle down another one-quarter inch (that's where the caption goes). Finally, press Return (Enter on a PC) to tell Photoshop you want to keep the new canvas space. You should see a checkerboard background around the photo as shown in Figure 6-8, top.

NOTE If you don't make the Background layer editable before you increase the canvas space, the area around the photo ends up the color of your background color chip instead of transparent, so you don't see the checkerboard pattern. If you have this problem, press ⌘-Z (Ctrl+Z on a PC) and start over with step 1.

3. **Create a new layer and drag it below the original photo layer.**

   At the bottom of the Layers panel, click the new layer icon (it looks like a piece of paper with a folded corner). To keep from covering up the whole photo in the next step, drag the new layer's thumbnail *below* the original layer. (Alternatively, you can ⌘-click (Ctrl-click) the new layer icon to make Photoshop add the layer below the currently active layer.)

4. **Fill the new layer with white to form the Polaroid edges.**

   Choose Edit→Fill, pick "white" from the Use pop-up menu, and then click OK. Now you've got a Polaroid-style frame around the photo. (You *have* to use an image layer for this technique rather than a Solid Color Fill layer—see page 77—because the latter automatically resizes to fill your canvas, making the Polaroid effect impossible.)

5. **Increase your canvas space again so you have room to rotate the image and add a drop shadow.**

   Press C to grab the Crop tool again and then add equal space on all four sides by dragging any corner handle while you hold down the Option key (Alt on a PC). Press Return (Enter) to accept the crop.

6. **Add a caption with the Type tool.**

   Press T to activate the Type tool (page 582) and add a caption in the white space at the bottom of the frame. Here's your big chance to use a handwriting typeface! (Bradley Hand was used in Figure 6-8.) When you're done, accept your prose by clicking the checkmark in the Options bar, or just click the Type layer in the Layers panel.

7. **Activate all three layers.**

   When you have everything just right, hop over to the Layers panel and ⌘-click (Ctrl-click) to activate the image layer, Type layer, and white Polaroid-frame layer so you can rotate the whole mess in the next step.

8. **Rotate the image just a bit to give it more character.**

   Summon the Free Transform command by pressing ⌘-T (Ctrl+T on a PC) and then rotate the photo by positioning your cursor just below the bottom-right handle. When the cursor turns into a curved, two-headed arrow, drag slightly up or down. Press Return (Enter) to accept the rotation or Esc to reject it and try again.

9. **Activate the white background layer and add a drop shadow (page 132).**

In the Layers panel, click the white background layer to activate it. Next, click the tiny cursive *fx* at the bottom of the panel and choose Drop Shadow, and then increase the shadow's Size setting quite a bit so it's visible on all four sides of the Polaroid frame. Move the shadow around by adjusting the Angle setting, or by clicking and dragging within your document. Soften the shadow by lowering its opacity in the Layer Style dialog box, and then click OK.

10. **Add a solid white Fill layer to the bottom of your layer stack.**

To make your image look like Figure 6-8 (bottom), you need to add another white background. Choose Layer→New Fill Layer→Solid Color or click the half-black/half-white circle at the bottom of the Layers panel and choose Solid Color. Either way, choose white in the resulting Color Picker and then click OK.

When you're all done, save the document as a PSD in case you need to go back and edit it later. Fun stuff!

Cropping with Selection Tools

You can also crop an image within the boundaries of a selection. This technique is helpful if you've made a selection and then need to trim the image down to roughly that same size. The Rectangular Marquee tool (page 142) works best for this kind of cropping—though *all* the selection tools work—because Photoshop, bless its electronic heart, can crop only in rectangles (though you can remove a background from an object and then save it in a format that understands *transparency*, but that's a discussion for page 721).

After you draw a selection, press C to activate the Crop tool and Photoshop places a crop box atop the image that matches the shape of your selection. Easy peasy!

Trimming Photos Down to Size

If your image has a solid-colored or transparent (checkerboard) background, you may find yourself chipping away at its edges to save space in the image's final destination (a website, a book—whatever). The Trim command is incredibly handy in such situations, especially when you're trying to tightly crop an image that has a drop shadow or reflection. Such embellishments make the image's *true* edges hard to see—and therefore tough to crop—because they fade into the background. So it's easy to, say, accidentally chop a drop shadow in half when you're cropping. Fortunately, you can enlist Photoshop's help in finding the edges of the image and have it do the cropping for you.

To whittle a photo down to its smallest possible size, choose Image→Trim and, in the resulting dialog box (shown in Figure 6-9), use the radio buttons to tell Photoshop whether you want to zap transparent pixels or pixels that match the color at the document's top left or bottom right (the program needs *some* instructions to know what part of the image to trim). Next, choose which sides of the image you want to trim by turning their checkboxes on or off and then clicking OK. Photoshop trims the document down to size with zero squinting—or error—on your part.

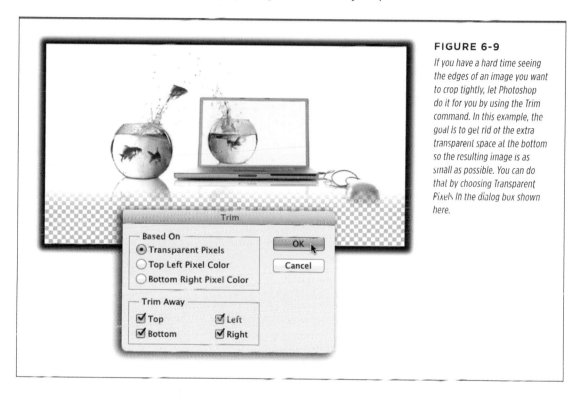

FIGURE 6-9

If you have a hard time seeing the edges of an image you want to crop tightly, let Photoshop do it for you by using the Trim command. In this example, the goal is to get rid of the extra transparent space at the bottom so the resulting image is as small as possible. You can do that by choosing Transparent Pixels in the dialog box shown here.

NOTE The Trim command was used on every screenshot in this book to crop the images as closely as possible. It's a massive timesaver if you work in production!

Cropping and Straightening Photos

In Photoshop CS6, you can use the Crop tool to straighten individual images in a snap. To do so, open an image and then press C to activate the Crop tool. Next, click the Straighten Image icon in the Options bar (it looks like a tiny level), mouse over to your image, and then drag to draw a line across something that should be straight, such as the fridge door in Figure 6-10. When you release your mouse button, Photoshop rotates the image. If you like the results, press Return (Enter on a PC) to accept the crop; if not, press Esc to undo it.

FIGURE 6-10

Photoshop CS6 gives you two ways to straighten images with the Crop tool.

Left: You can click the Straighten icon in the Options bar and then draw a line across an area that should be straight (it doesn't matter whether the line is horizontal or vertical).

Right: Or you can position your cursor just outside the crop box near one of its corner handles, and then click and drag to rotate the image (your cursor turns into a curved double arrow). Photoshop shrinks the crop box to fit the rotated photo so you don't end up with any extra space around its edges.

Straightening one image at a time is all well and fine, but if you've painstakingly scanned a *slew* of photos into a single document, you can save yourself a lot of work by having Photoshop crop, straighten, and split them into separate files *for* you—all with a single menu command. With the page of photos open, choose File→Automate→"Crop and Straighten Photos." Photoshop instantly calculates the angle of the overall image's edge (that is, the edge of the photo bits) against the white background, rotates the images, and then duplicates all the photos into their own perfectly cropped and straightened documents, as shown in Figure 6-11. It's like magic!

NOTE The "Crop and Straighten Photos" command also works on documents that contain just *one* image, provided the picture has white space on all four sides of it. It works on layered files, too. Just activate the layer that contains the image you want to extract, run the command, and Photoshop strips that layer out into its own document and deletes it from the original document. (If the layer contains several images, they'll get stripped out into their own individual documents.)

FIGURE 6-11

It's tough to get a bunch of photos perfectly straight when you're scanning (heck, just putting the lid down moves 'em!). This is a prime opportunity to use the "Crop and Straighten Photos" command. In one fell swoop, the photos (top) get straightened, cropped, and copied into their own individual documents (bottom) right before your eyes.

TIP If you want Photoshop to crop and straighten a *few* photos that all reside on a single layer (but not all of them), draw a selection around each of the photos before you run the command (use any selection tool and hold the Shift key to add to the selection). Photoshop then processes only those photos, provided they (and their individual selection boxes) are next to each other. If they're not, Photoshop crops and straightens everything in between, forcing you to close the unwanted new documents.

Cropping and Straightening in Camera Raw

Camera Raw is an amazing piece of software that photographers use to edit the color and lighting of images; you'll learn loads more about it in Chapter 9. It gets installed with Photoshop, so you don't have to download it or pay for it separately. Using Camera Raw to crop and straighten photos has two big advantages:

- **You can undo the crop or straighten (or both) anytime**—whether the file you're working on is Raw, JPEG, or TIFF. In Chapter 9, you'll learn how to use Camera Raw with all three file formats.

- **If you have several photos that need to be cropped in a similar manner, you can crop them all at once.** Talk about a timesaver!

To open an image in Camera Raw, double-click the image's icon on your hard drive or choose File→"Browse in Bridge." Once Bridge opens, Ctrl-click (right-click on a PC) the image and choose "Open in Camera Raw" from the resulting shortcut menu. (You can also click the image in Bridge to activate it and then press ⌘-R [Ctrl+R on a PC] or use the Mini Bridge panel; see Chapter 21 for more info.) Once the image is open in Camera Raw, follow the instructions in the next section to crop one or more images.

■ CROPPING IMAGES

With one or more images open, click the Crop tool button at the top of the Camera Raw window and hold down your mouse button to reveal a handy menu that includes common aspect ratios, as well as the new "Constrain to Image" options, which maintains the shape of your original, and the Show Overlay option, which places a rule-of-thirds grid atop the image (both are turned on in Figure 6-12). Next, click and drag diagonally downward around the part of the image that you want to keep.

If the aspect ratio you need isn't in the Crop tool's menu, choose Custom and a dialog box appears where you can enter a specific ratio or dimensions in pixels, inches, or centimeters. Click OK and Camera Raw places a crop box atop the image, which you can resize by dragging any of its handles or reposition by dragging within the box itself. Press Return (Enter on a PC) to see what the newly cropped image looks like. If you need to edit or undo the crop, just activate the Crop tool again to make the crop box reappear for your editing pleasure.

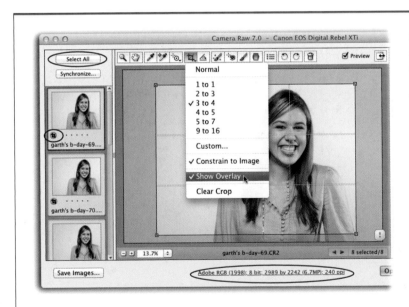

FIGURE 6-12

Open one or more images in Camera Raw and then use the Crop tool to whittle it down to size. Simply drag across the image to draw a box and then press Return (Enter) to accept the crop. If you've opened multiple images (as shown here), you see their thumbnails in the filmstrip on the left side of the Camera Raw window. To crop 'em all at once, click the Select All button in the upper left (circled, top) and then draw the crop box. You'll see the crop, along with a tiny Crop tool icon (circled, left), applied to all active thumbnails. The blue, underlined text below the preview window (circled, bottom) changes to reflect the size of the crop box as you draw.

TIP You can exit the crop box by pressing the Esc or Delete key (Backspace on a PC) while the Crop tool is active or by choosing Clear Crop from the menu shown in Figure 6-12.

When you're finished, click one of the buttons at the bottom right of the Camera Raw window:

- **Save Image(s)** lets you convert, rename, or relocate the file(s)—or any combination of those tasks—so you don't overwrite the original. If you save them in Photoshop format, you can tell Camera Raw to preserve the cropped pixels in case you want to resurrect 'em later (see Figure 6-13 for details).

- **Open Image(s)** applies your changes and opens the photo(s) in Photoshop.

- **Cancel** exits Camera Raw without applying the changes.

- **Done** applies your changes (which you can edit the next time you open the image[s] in Camera Raw) and exits the Camera Raw window.

TIP You can use keyboard shortcuts to change how the Save, Open, Cancel, and Done buttons at the bottom of the Camera Raw window behave: To open a copy of the image in Photoshop without updating the original Raw file, Option-click (Alt-click on a PC) the Open button (it changes to an Open Copy button). To open the image as a Smart Object (page 126), Shift-click the Open button (it changes to Open Object). To skip the Save As dialog box and make Camera Raw use the same location, name, and format you used last time you saved the file, Option-click (Alt-click) the Save Image button. And to change the Camera Raw settings back to what they were originally, Option-click (Alt-click) the Cancel button (it changes to a Reset button).

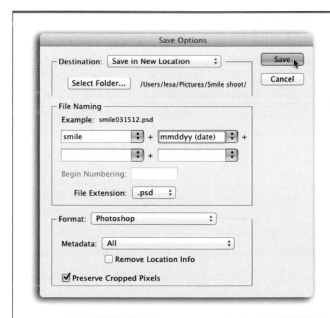

FIGURE 6-13

To see and work with the original, uncropped image in Photoshop, click Camera Raw's Save Images button. Next, in the Save Options dialog box shown here, choose Photoshop from the Format pop-up menu near the bottom of the dialog box, turn on the Preserve Cropped Pixels checkbox, and then click Save.

Next time you open that file in Photoshop, the photo appears on its own layer. If you want to see the hidden, cropped bits, use the Move tool to drag them back into view or choose Image→Reveal All.

■ STRAIGHTENING IMAGES

If you need to straighten a bunch of images at a similar angle, Camera Raw can handle 'em all at once, too. Open the images and then click the Select All button at the top left of the Camera Raw window. Then grab the Straighten tool (circled in Figure 6-14) and draw a line across the horizon—or anything in the image that's supposed to be straight—as shown in Figure 6-14, top.

The image won't straighten immediately—instead, you see what looks like a rotated crop box so you can check the angle. If it's OK, press Return (Enter on a PC) and Camera Raw straightens the photo. If you didn't get it *perfectly* straight, you can have another go by choosing the Straighten tool again or, if you closed the image, by *opening* it in Camera Raw again.

FIGURE 6-14

Unlike in Photoshop, Camera Raw's Straighten tool lets you straighten multiple images simultaneously; just make sure you click the Select All button at the top left of the Camera Raw window first. Next, activate the Straighten tool and draw a line across a part of the image that's supposed to be straight (circled). Just press Return (Enter on a PC) to accept the line, and Camera Raw straightens all the images instantly.

■ Resizing Images

No matter what you've whipped up in Photoshop, there will come a time when you need to change the size of your image. For example, if you want to print it, email it, or post it on a website, you need different-sized versions for each task. Changing an image's size isn't hard—Photoshop gives you oodles of options. The challenge lies in doing it *without* sending the image's quality down the tubes.

Sure, you can let the "Save for Web" dialog box (page 246) or the Print dialog box (page 685) do the resizing for you, but if you're aiming to be a serious pixel-pusher, you'll want *far* more control. That, dear friend, brings you up against the granddaddy of Photoshop principles: image resolution—the measurement that determines the *size* of the pixels in the image, which in turn controls the quality of your prints.

Resolution is arguably one of the toughest digital-image editing concepts to wrap your brain around. Many people grapple with questions like "What the heck is resolution?" "How do I change an image's resolution?" and "What's the minimum resolution I need to print good-looking photos?" In the following pages, you'll learn all the nitty-gritty you need to answer these—and other—questions.

> **NOTE** Resolution doesn't mean a hill of beans unless you're sending the image to a printer. If you're not going to print it, don't worry about resolution—focus on the pixel dimensions instead.

Pixels and Resolution

As you learned in Chapter 2, the smallest element of a raster image is a pixel (short for picture element). When they're small enough and viewed together, these tiny blocks of color form an image (see Figure 6-15).

> **NOTE** Some digital images aren't comprised of pixels—they're made up of *vectors*, a series of points and paths. One of the best things about working with vectors is that none of the size-versus-quality challenges you run into with pixel-based images apply: You can make vectors as big or as small as you like and they'll always look great. To learn more about vectors, trot over to Chapter 13.

FIGURE 6-15

Raster images are comprised of individual blocks of color called pixels. To see them, zoom into the image by pressing ⌘-+ (Ctrl-+ on a PC) repeatedly or use the Zoom tool. (Press ⌘ or Ctrl and the - key to zoom out.)

At 3,200 percent magnification, you can see the individual pixels that make up a tiny section of this sunflower.

Pixels have no predetermined size, which is where *resolution* enters the, uh, picture. Resolution is a measurement that determines how many pixels get packed into a given space, which in turn controls how big or small they are. It's helpful to think of resolution as pixel density—how closely the pixels are packed together. In fact, it's measured in terms of pixels per inch—or *ppi*, as folks typically call it.

> **NOTE** You'll also hear resolution referred to as *dpi*, which stands for "dots per inch." This usage isn't strictly accurate because dpi is technically a measurement used by printers (since they actually print dots). Nevertheless, many folks mistakenly say "dpi" when they mean "ppi."

One helpful way to understand resolution is to relate it to something in the real world. Imagine you're baking cookies (hang in there; it'll make sense in a minute). When you pour brown sugar into a measuring cup, the sugar reaches the one-cup line. But after you pack the granules firmly into the cup, the sugar only reaches the half-cup line. You still have the same number of granules (which are like pixels); they're just smaller because they're packed more tightly together (they have a higher resolution) in the confines of the measuring cup (the Photoshop document). The loosely packed granules you started with are like low resolution, and the firmly packed granules are like high resolution. (Hungry yet?)

Since increasing image resolution—from, say, 72 ppi to 300 ppi—makes the pixels smaller and packs them together more tightly, it results in a printed image that's physically smaller but also smoother and better-looking. Lowering image resolution, on the other hand, enlarges and loosens the pixels, which results in a physically larger image that, as you might suspect, looks like it was made from Legos because the pixels are so big you can see each one.

Printers are capable of much higher resolution than your computer monitor (*thousands* of dots per inch rather than hundreds), plus they're one of the few devices that can modify their output (that is, the print) based on image resolution. In other words, send your inkjet printer a low-res version and a high-res version of the same picture and it'll spit out images that differ vastly in size and quality. The resolution on a computer monitor, on the other hand, is handled by the computer's video driver (the software that controls what appears on the monitor), *not* the resolution specified in the image. That's why an 85 ppi image looks identical to an 850 ppi image onscreen. The bottom line: Printers can take advantage of higher resolutions (scanners can, too, but that's a story for page 57), but monitors can't.

The Mighty Image Size Dialog Box

If you can't trust your monitor to show an image's true resolution, what can you trust? Why, the Image Size dialog box, shown in Figure 6-16, which not only displays the current resolution of any open document, but also lets you *change* it.

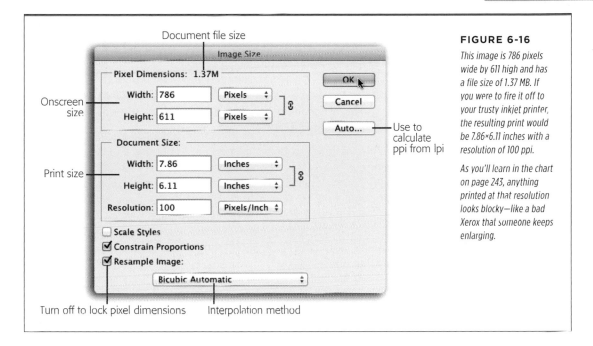

Document file size

Onscreen size

Print size

Turn off to lock pixel dimensions

Interpolation method

Use to calculate ppi from lpi

FIGURE 6-16

This image is 786 pixels wide by 611 high and has a file size of 1.37 MB. If you were to fire it off to your trusty inkjet printer, the resulting print would be 7.86×6.11 inches with a resolution of 100 ppi.

As you'll learn in the chart on page 243, anything printed at that resolution looks blocky—like a bad Xerox that someone keeps enlarging.

To summon this dialog box and check a document's resolution, choose Image→Image Size or press Option-⌘-I (Alt+Ctrl+I on a PC). The dialog box reveals all kinds of info about the image: its file size (how much space it takes up on your hard drive), its pixel (onscreen) dimensions, how big it would be if you printed it, and its resolution. If you're preparing an image to email or post on the Web, you only need to worry about the Pixel Dimensions section of the dialog box. If you're going to print the image, focus your attention on the Document Size portion in the middle instead.

The checkboxes at the bottom of the dialog box control how Photoshop resizes the image if you make changes in this dialog box. Here's what each one does:

- **Scale Styles** determines whether Photoshop resizes any layer styles (page 131) you've applied to the image along with the image itself. It's a good idea to leave this setting turned on; otherwise, that pretty drop shadow you added might end up bigger or smaller than the image itself.

- **Constrain Proportion** locks the aspect ratio of the image (the relationship between its width and height) so it doesn't get squashed or stretched when you resize it. You'll want to leave this setting turned on, too.

- **Resample Image** is your key to changing resolution *without* changing image quality. *Resampling* is the process by which Photoshop responds to your size-change request by either adding or subtracting pixels. The problem, as you'll learn in a moment, is that resampling involves guesswork on Photoshop's part, which can obliterate image quality.

When you first launch Photoshop, the Resample Image setting is turned on, which tells the program to increase or decrease the number of pixels in the image—processes that reduce image quality because Photoshop either invents pixels or picks ones to eliminate, respectively. By turning Resample Image *off,* you protect the image's quality by *locking* the pixel dimensions. If you plan to print the image, turning this setting off lets you fiddle with the resolution for hours without altering the quality because you're just changing pixel *size*, not pixel *quantity*. (Take a peek at page 244 to see this concept in action.)

When the Resample Image checkbox is *on*, you get to choose a resample method from the pop-up menu below it. Why would you want to go this route? Well, sometimes you need Photoshop's help making an image bigger or smaller. For example, if you've got a 200-ppi image that's going to print at 4×6 but you *need* a 5×7 print *and* you want to maintain that 200-ppi resolution, you can turn on this checkbox to make it so. On the flip side, if you've got a honkin' image that's too big to email, you can use resampling to make Photoshop reduce its pixel dimensions (and thus file size) in a way that doesn't destroy image quality.

NOTE There are two kinds of resampling: If you delete pixels, you're *downsampling* (see page 246); if you add them, you're *upsampling* (the box on page 241 has tips for that). When you upsample, Photoshop adds pixels that weren't originally there through a mathematical process called *interpolation*, in which it uses the pixels that *are* there to guess what the new ones should look like.

The options in the menu below the Resample Image checkbox determine which kind of mathematical voodoo Photoshop uses to either add or delete pixels. Since better image quality means more work for Photoshop, the better the image, the more time the program takes to perform the aforementioned voodoo. Here are your choices, listed in order of quality (worst to best) and speed (fastest to slowest):

- **Nearest Neighbor** gives you the lowest image quality. With this method, Photoshop looks at the colors of surrounding pixels and copies them. Nearest Neighbor is known for creating jagged edges, so you'll want to use it only on images with hard edges like illustrations that aren't anti-aliased (see Chapter 13).

- **Bilinear** tells Photoshop to guess at the color of new pixels by averaging the colors of the pixels directly surrounding the ones it's adding. Bilinear produces slightly better results than Nearest Neighbor and is still pretty fast, but you're better off using one of the next four methods instead.

- **Bicubic** makes Photoshop figure out the colors of new pixels by averaging the colors of even *more* pixels surrounding the new one in order to make a better guess. This method takes longer than the previous two but produces smoother transitions in areas where one color fades into another.

- **Bicubic Smoother** is similar to Bicubic in the way it creates new pixels, but this method blurs pixels slightly to blend the new ones into the old ones, making the image smoother and more natural looking. Adobe recommends this method for enlarging images.

- **Bicubic Sharper** is also similar to Bicubic in the way it creates new pixels, but instead of blurring whole pixels to improve blending between the new and old like Bicubic Smoother, it softens only the pixels' *edges*. Adobe recommends this method for downsizing images, though some Photoshop gurus claim that it also produces better *enlargements* than Bicubic Smoother.

- **Bicubic Automatic** is new in CS6, and it tells Photoshop to pick the best method depending upon the content of your image *and* whether you're making the image bigger or smaller. Believe it or not, the Crop tool and Free Transform command use this method, too, though the resizing option in the "Save for Web" dialog box doesn't (weird!).

POWER USERS' CLINIC

Upsampling Without Losing Quality

If you leave the Image Size dialog box's Resample Image checkbox (page 239) turned on and increase an image's resolution, Photoshop adds pixels to your image that weren't originally there. Increasing resolution this way is *usually* a bad idea because faked pixels never look as good as real ones (though this is less of a problem in each new version of the program). However, there may come a time when you've got no choice.

For example, maybe you've snatched an image from the Web that you need to print (like a book cover or a headshot of your group's next speaker) or the image needs to be printed in an *extremely* large format (like a billboard). If you find yourself in such a pickle, you've got a few options. Happily, the first two are free:

Method 1. Open the Image Size dialog box, make sure both the Constrained Proportions and Resample Image checkboxes are turned on, and then choose Bicubic Smoother from the pop-up menu below them. Next, in the dialog box's Document Size section, change either the Width or Height pop-up menu to Percent (the other field changes automatically). Then enter a number into the Width field—such as *200* to double the pixel dimensions—and click OK (the Height field changes to the same number automatically). Photoshop enlarges your im-

age by the percentage you entered. (In older versions of the program, adding pixels 5 to 10 percent at a time *repeatedly* didn't damage image quality quite as much as doing it all at once, though in CS6 you end up with an image that looks slightly mushy because the details get softened.)

Method 2. Some Photoshop pros (Scott Kelby, for example) swear by this method for large-format printing: Open the Image Size dialog box and make sure the Constrain Proportions and Resample Image checkboxes are turned on. In the Document Size section, enter *either* the width or the height of the desired print and the desired resolution. Then choose Bicubic Sharper from the pop-up menu at the bottom of the dialog box and click OK. The pros swear this method gives them terrific results, though it defies the resizing guidelines discussed so far. Give it a shot and see what happens.

Method 3. Buy a third-party plug-in specifically designed to help you upsample, like Perfect Resize (formerly named Genuine Fractals) by onOne Software (*www.ononesoftware. com*) or PhotoZoom Pro by BenVista (*www.benvista.com*). Both plug-ins manage to pull off some serious pixel-adding witchery with truly amazing results. (See Chapter 19 for more on third-party plug-ins.)

If you know your printer's *lpi* (lines per inch—see the box on this page), you can click the Image Size dialog box's Auto button to bring up the Auto Resolution dialog box (see Figure 6-17). Just enter the lpi, pick a quality setting, and let Photoshop calculate the proper resolution for a good print.

FIGURE 6-17

If you know the lpi of your printer, enter it in the Screen field, and Photoshop calculates the resolution (ppi) for you. You've got a choice of three different quality settings: Draft gives you a resolution of 72 ppi, Good multiplies the lpi by 1.5, and Best multiplies it by 2.

■ RESOLUTION GUIDELINES FOR PRINT

Now that you understand what resolution is and how it works, you're probably wondering "How much resolution do I need when I print?" Because different printers work in different ways—inkjets spray, dye-subs fuse, laser printers and professional presses print shapes, and so on—the resolution you need for a beautiful print depends on the *printer*.

It's tempting to practice resolution overkill just to be on the safe side, but doing that makes for larger files that take up more hard drive space and take longer to process, save, *and* print. Instead, rein yourself in and consider the resolution guidelines in Table 6-1.

FREQUENTLY ASKED QUESTION

Understanding LPI

What the heck is lpi? I thought all I had to worry about was ppi!

Laser printers and professional printing presses print a little differently than inkjet and dye-sublimation printers. Inkjets spray dots of color onto paper and simulate shades of gray by using wide or narrow dot dispersal patterns. Dye-subs fuse color dyes—including shades of gray—onto paper through a heating process (they tend to produce higher-quality, water- and smudge-proof prints than inkjets but are more expensive).

Professional printing presses use yet another printing method: If you hold a magnifying glass to a professionally printed newspaper or magazine, you can see that the image is comprised of a gazillion tiny shapes (typically circles, though they can be diamonds or squares, depending on the printer). If the shapes are small enough, you'll never see them with your naked eye

(although some folks have been quite successful enlarging them to galactic proportions and calling it pop art—think Lichtenstein and Warhol).

The setting that determines how many lines of little shapes get printed in an inch of space is called *lines per inch*, or lpi. (It's also referred to as screen frequency, line screen, or halftone screen.) It's important to understand lpi because there may come a day when you're forced to figure the appropriate ppi from lpi (also helpful in scanning; see page 57). When this happens, breathe deeply, smile smugly, and proceed to Table 6-1 on page 243. Or just click the Auto button in the Image Size dialog box and let Photoshop figure out the ppi from lpi *for you* as explained in Figure 6-17.

NOTE When you send files off to a professional print shop, it's always a good idea to ask how much resolution they want. If they don't know, find another printer—fast!

TABLE 6-1. *Resolution guidelines for print*

DEVICE	PAPER	RESOLUTION	USE FOR
Desktop laser printer	Any kind	Resolution should match the printer's dpi (which is listed in the owner's manual). Some folks call this resolution 1:1, which just means ppi matches dpi exactly. For color or grayscale images, ppi should be one-third of the printer's dpi.	Business documents and line art
Inkjet printer	Regular or textured	150–240 ppi	Color and grayscale images, black-and-white documents
Inkjet printer	Glossy or matte photo	240–480 ppi. Use the upper end of this range only for large images (13×19 inches and up).	Color and grayscale images
Dye-sublimation printer	Any kind	Resolution should match the printer's dpi.	Color and grayscale images
Web offset press	Newsprint or uncoated stock	1.5–2 times the lpi, depending on how detailed you want the print to be (use 2 if what you're printing has a slew of sharp edges in it).	Newspaper ads and community papers (like *Auto Trader* and *The Village Voice*)
Commercial printing press	Uncoated or coated stock	2–2.5 times the lpi	Magazines, coffee table books, fancy brochures, business cards, and line art

Resizing Images for Print

Throughout your Photoshop career, you'll need to resize and change the resolution of images so they'll print well. Perhaps the most common situation where you'll have to do this is when you download stock photography or import a snapshot from a digital camera. Unless you change their resolution, images you download from stock-image companies or import onto your hard drive from your camera will be the resolution of the *camera* that took them, which could be 72, 180, or 240 ppi depending on the camera's make, model, and year.

Keep in mind that today's digital cameras can capture *tons* of info: Consumer-level, 10-megapixel cameras produce images packed with around 3648×2048 pixels (width by height), and pro-level, 21-megapixel models capture images in excess of 4080×2720 pixels. That's a veritable smorgasbord of pixels, letting you crop the image and alter resolution however you like.

Resizing images is a snap, but the risk of reducing image quality in the process is high. As you learned in the previous section, the key to preserving quality lies in turning on the Resample Image checkbox, as Figure 6-18 illustrates.

NOTE If you're printing a generic-size image (like 8×10 or 5×7) straight from Photoshop, you can turn on the Print dialog box's "Scale to Fit Media" checkbox to make the program calculate the resolution for you, according to the paper size you pick (though you'll probably end up with resolution overkill). Head on over to page 689 for the details.

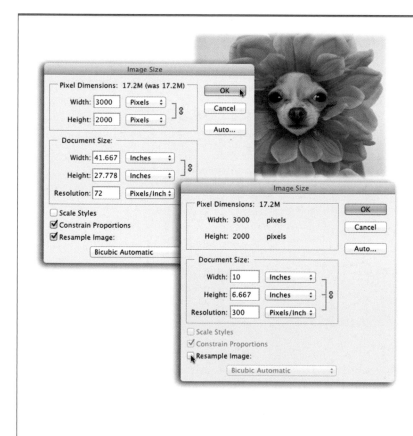

FIGURE 6-18

Say you want to print this image and the largest paper size your printer can use is 8"×10". A peek at the Image Size dialog box reveals that if you tried to print it at its current resolution, you'd need a huge piece of paper—one larger than 41×27 inches! Even worse, at the current resolution of 72 ppi, that massive print would look like it was made from blocks. Fortunately, you can use the settings in this dialog box to change the resolution so the image prints at a more manageable size.

Turning off the Resample Image checkbox locks the image's pixel dimensions and protects its quality. Now you can increase the resolution without worrying how the image will print—it'll get physically smaller, sure, but it won't be blocky and pixelated. Think about it this way: As the resolution goes up, the document's print size goes down because Photoshop makes the pixels smaller. For example, at 300 ppi this image produces a print that's 10×6.667 inches. Compare that to the file's original settings of 72 ppi and 41.667×27.778 inches. Wow!

Here's how to use the Resample Image checkbox to resize an image for printing without sacrificing quality:

1. **Open a photo, and then choose Image→Image Size or press Option-⌘-I (Alt+Ctrl+I on a PC) to open the Image Size dialog box.**

   The image shown in Figure 6-18 (top) weighs in at 3000×2000 pixels at a resolution of 72 ppi. If you want to print it, you need a ridiculously big piece of photo paper (over 41×27 inches). Luckily, those dimensions come way down once you increase the resolution. Remember, increasing resolution makes the pixels smaller, creating a physically smaller image whose quality (that is, resolution) is much higher.

2. **Lock the image's quality by turning off the Resample Image checkbox.**

   As Figure 6-18 (bottom) shows, the pixel dimension text boxes disappear when you turn off the Resample Image option. Now the only info you can change is the document's size and resolution, which affect how tightly the pixels are packed together. You can't change the *number* of pixels contained in the image, which means Photoshop won't add or delete any pixels. See how the gray line on the right side of the Document Size section now connects width, height, and resolution? That line is there to remind you that changing *one* of these fields affects the other two.

3. **Increase the resolution.**

   The value you should enter in the Resolution field depends mostly on which kind of printer you're using; see Table 6-1 for some recommended settings, and then do some tests to see which ones work best for you. For example, if you know your printer does a respectable job printing at 240 ppi, enter that value in the Resolution field, and the document dimensions decrease to 10×6.667 inches (Figure 6-18, bottom). The pixel dimensions and file size, however, remain the same—the image is still 3000×2000 pixels and 17.2 MB; only the resolution changes.

   NOTE Popping open the Image Size dialog box is a handy way to learn what size print you can make with your image's pixel dimensions. If your printer does a decent job at 240 ppi, for example, type that value into the Resolution field and see how big a print that'll create. If it's a funky size, you can always crop the image to a specific, more common shape using the Crop tool (see page 222).

4. **Click OK when you're done.**

   Now you can print the image and it'll look great (though you may need to do a tiny bit of trimming).

Did you notice how much the onscreen image changed when you tweaked the resolution? That's right: Not at all. That's part of the reason resolution is so confusing. The 72 ppi image looks just like the 300 ppi version because the monitor's resolution can't go that high. The lesson here is that, as long as you turn off the

Resample Image checkbox, you can tweak an image's resolution 'til the cows come home without altering its quality. Sure, you'll change the image's printed size, but you won't add or delete any pixels.

Resizing for Email and the Web

Not everyone has a high-speed Internet connection...at least, not yet. Some poor souls are doomed to live with dial-up for the foreseeable future, and even wireless hot-spots don't exactly provide warp-speed connections (especially when a lot of people are using 'em). That's why it's important to decrease the file size of that monster photo from Debra's divorce party *before* emailing it to your pals—if you don't, it might take them forever to download it. The same goes for images you plan to post online: The smaller their file size, the faster they'll load in a web browser. (You'll learn a lot more about posting images online in Chapter 17, but the info in this section will get you started.)

To make an image smaller, you have to decrease its pixel dimensions. This process is called *downsampling*, and you can go about it in a couple of ways. Read on to learn both methods.

> **NOTE** See page 719 if you'd rather resize images destined for the Web visually by entering a percentage instead of pixel dimensions.

■ USING THE "SAVE FOR WEB" DIALOG BOX

If you want to see a preview of the new, smaller image and maybe experiment with different file formats (if you're torn between a JPEG and a PNG, say), use the "Save for Web" dialog box. This method is a great way to reduce file size while monitoring image quality. Here's how to resize a photo for email or use on the Web:

1. **Open a photo and then choose File→"Save for Web."**

    The dialog box shown in Figure 6-19 takes over your screen. It lets you choose from a variety of file formats and quality levels that Photoshop can use to make the image Web- or email-friendly. You can see up to four previews of what the image will look like in various formats before you choose one, which is why the dialog box is so darn big.

2. **In the upper-left part of the dialog box, make sure the 4-Up tab (circled in Figure 6-19) is active and then pick JPEG High from the preset pop-up menu in the top-right corner (also circled).**

    The 4-Up tab is great for monitoring the size and quality difference between the original image and, say, a JPEG at various quality settings (as you learned on page 50, JPEG is the best choice for photos). To keep the photo's quality relatively intact while you reduce its file size, choose JPEG High from the preset pop-up menu (also circled in Figure 6-19, top right). To make the file smaller, Photoshop tosses out some details, but the overall quality doesn't suffer much. But if you choose a quality level of Low (numeric equivalent: 10), Photoshop throws away *significantly* more details and the result is a low-quality image. (See page 50 for more about the JPEG format.)

FIGURE 6-19

The quickest way to resize an image for emailing or posting on the Web is to head straight for the "Save for Web" dialog box. It lets you reduce the image's size and save it in a different format in one fell swoop, complete with up to four previews.

3. **Reduce the Image's size.**

   At the bottom right of the dialog box lies a section labeled Image Size. If you know the dimensions you want, enter the width or height (it's best to make the width 800 pixels or less). If you don't know what size you want and are only concerned with making the *file size* smaller, you can enter a percentage reduction like 25 percent. (That's a good percentage if you're emailing an image captured on a 10-megapixel camera at a high quality setting.)

4. **Choose a resample method.**

   In the dialog box's Image Size section, choose Bicubic Sharper from the Quality pop-up menu (unfortunately, Bicubic Automatic isn't available here). This method (explained on page 241) works particularly well when you're downsampling. Some folks say it even works great for enlargements—see the box on page 241. As you can see in the middle of Figure 6-19, the resulting file is 91.82 KB at a quality setting of 60. That's less than 10 percent of its original size!

5. **Click the Save button at the bottom of the dialog box, and then give the file a new name so you don't overwrite the original.**

TIP It's a good idea to sharpen images after you downsample them because they tend to get blurry from both losing details and getting compressed. (See Chapter 11 for more sharpening methods than you can shake a stick at.)

Resizing Web Images for Print

Unfortunately, there will come a time when you need to print an image snatched from the Web (though make sure you have the proper permissions, as the box below explains). Such images are usually fairly small so they'll load quickly in web browsers, but that also means they contain precious few pixels for you to work with. Most of 'em are 72 ppi—a resolution so low that the individual pixels are big enough to see when you print the images—which means that, unless you like that blocky look, you *have* to increase the resolution before you print them. And, as you learned earlier in this chapter, when you bump up resolution, you wind up with a print the size of a postage stamp. It's a lose-lose situation.

TIP A good rule of thumb is that Web images print decently at about half the size they appear onscreen. So if you start with an image that's about 2×2 inches onscreen, it prints decently at 1×1.

For all those reasons, printing a Web image isn't ideal, but if you have no choice, you've got to make do. In that case, follow these steps to beef up its print quality:

1. **Save the image to your hard drive.**

   Find the image on the Web and Control-click (right-click on a PC) it to summon your web browser's shortcut menu, and then choose Save Image As. Or you can choose Copy Image from the shortcut menu and then paste the image into a new Photoshop document.

2. **Open the image in Photoshop and then choose Image→Image Size.**

   Photoshop displays the now-familiar Image Size dialog box (Figure 6-16).

NOTE FROM THE LAWYERS

Thou Shalt Not Steal

This whole "snatching images from the Web" business opens a copyright can of worms. You're committing image theft if you download an image created by someone else and then use it in another format—except in these situations:

- You've obtained express permission from the photographer or artist (or other copyright holder) who created it.

- The image is clearly designated as being in the public domain.

- The image was published under a Creative Commons license (*www.creativecommons.org*).

- You're grabbing the image purely for personal use.

That said, if you're promoting a book raffle at your computer club and snatch cover art from the publisher's website or if you need a headshot to promote your camera club's speaker and you snag one from her blog, the chances of finding the image police at your front door are slim to none.

3. **At the bottom of the dialog box, turn off the Resample Image checkbox, enter *150* in the Resolution field, and then click OK to close the dialog box.**

A resolution of 150 ppi works OK if you're printing to an inkjet printer. The resulting print may not be frame-worthy, but it'll be identifiable.

4. **Back in the main Photoshop window, save the resulting file as a PSD or TIFF.**

Choose File→Save As, and then choose PSD or TIFF from the Format pop-up menu (see page 677 for more on TIFFs). The photo is now primed and ready for popping into Word, InDesign, or any other word-processing or page-layout program.

If the image is still too small after you follow these steps, visit the box on page 241 for tips on upsampling.

Resizing Images for Presentations

You're probably thinking, "I thought this book was about Photoshop and here you are talking about *presentations*. What gives?" Someday, you may be asked to prepare presentation graphics, and if that happens, the info in this section can save your skin. Luckily, in that situation, you don't have to worry about resolution; since your audience will view the images onscreen, it's the pixel dimensions that matter most.

Some folks claim to be more afraid of public speaking than they are of death. Standing before an expectant audience *can* be unnerving; obviously, you want everything to run smoothly and the graphics to look perfect. Oversize images bloat the presentation's file size and can cause it to run slowly, or worse, crash. On the flip side, small images may look fine on a computer monitor but terribly blocky when projected onto a larger screen.

The solution to both problems is to decide how big the images need to be and resize them *before* you import them into PowerPoint or Keynote. It's OK to resize images a little bit in those programs, but you don't want to put a dozen ginormous, 10 MB photos in your presentation—that's just asking for trouble.

If you want an image to fill a whole slide, find out the pixel dimensions of the projector you'll be using (the slides should be that size, too). If you don't know, find out how big the slides are. Here's how to sniff out (and change) slide dimensions in the two most popular presentation programs:

- **Microsoft PowerPoint 2010.** Head to the Design tab and click Page Setup on the left side of the Ribbon. In the dialog box that appears, look for the Width and Height fields. Now, here's where things get tricky: For some unknown reason, PowerPoint lists slide dimensions in inches instead of pixels. This poses a challenge because, to ensure that the image fills the slide perfectly, you have to convert the inches to pixels. Luckily, Table 6-2 lists the most common conversions. Once you know the slide dimensions, hop on over to page 225 for instructions on how to crop the image so that it fits the slide perfectly.

- **Apple Keynote.** Open the Inspector palette by clicking View→Show Inspector. Then open the Document Inspector by clicking the icon on the far left of the palette (it looks like a piece of paper with a folded corner) and peek at the Slide Size pop-up menu at the bottom of the palette, which lists the slide dimensions in pixels; those are the magic numbers. Back in Photoshop, grab the Crop tool, enter those numbers in the Options bar—leave the resolution blank because the image won't be printed—crop the image, and then save it as a JPEG or PNG (as discussed on page 721).

TIP Most projectors have a resolution of 1024×768 pixels, although high-definition projectors, which are becoming more common, have a resolution of 1280×720 or 1920×1080 pixels. If you've got no clue which kind of projector you'll be using, 1280x720 is a safe bet.

TABLE 6-2. *Slide size conversions*

PIXEL DIMENSIONS	PC SLIDE SIZE	MAC SLIDE SIZE
800×600	8.33×6.25 inches	11.11×8.33 inches
1024×768	10.66×8 inches	14.22×10.66 inches
1280×720	13.33×7.5 inches	17.77×10 inches
1920x1080	20x11.25 inches	26.66x15 inches

NOTE Because the Mac and Windows operating systems handle pixels a little differently (they're slightly bigger in Windows), you have to enter a resolution of 96 ppi when you resize images in Photoshop for use on a Windows machine. If you're designing presentation graphics on a Windows machine for use on a Mac, enter a resolution of 72 ppi instead. And if you're designing graphics on a Mac for use on a Mac, you can leave the Resolution field blank—honest!

Resizing Smart Objects

When designing a document—a poster, a magazine cover, whatever—you'll probably do a fair amount of resizing before you get the layout just right. What if you shrink a photo down only to realize it worked better at its original size? Can you enlarge the image without lessening its quality? Negative, good buddy—unless you opened or placed it as a Smart Object.

As you learned in Chapter 3, Smart Objects are the best thing since sliced bread. They let you apply all kinds of transformations to files, including decreasing and then increasing their size—all without affecting the quality of that image as it appears in your document. Here's how to resize a Smart Object that contains an image:

- **To decrease the size of a Smart Object,** activate the relevant layer in the Layers panel and then choose Edit→Free Transform. Grab any of the resulting square handles and drag diagonally inward to reduce its size (remember to hold down the Shift key as you drag if you want to resize it proportionately). Let Photoshop know you're finished resizing by pressing Return (Enter on a PC).

> **NOTE** If you've used the Place command to import the Smart Object, or if you drag and drop a raster image into an open Photoshop document (see page 30), then resizing handles appear *automatically* when the image opens in your document—on its very own layer, of course.

- **To increase the size of a Smart Object,** make sure you've got that layer activated in the Layers panel and then choose Edit→Free Transform. Drag any of the resulting corner handles diagonally outward (hold down the Shift key if you want to preserve the image's proportions). If you don't enlarge the image beyond its original pixel dimensions, its quality remains pristine (and if you do make it a little bigger, you probably won't notice the difference, as each version of Photoshop gets better at faking pixels). Unfortunately, there's no quick and easy way to *return* the Smart Object to its original size if you forget what it was.

Automated Resizing with the Image Processor

As you'll learn in Chapter 18, you can record a series of steps as a replayable *action* that resizes and saves a batch of images en masse. But Photoshop has a niftier automatic resizing feature built in: the Image Processor. This little *script* (similar to a program within a program) was developed specifically to convert images' file formats and change their size—fast (see Figure 6-20). It can save you tons of time whenever you need to convert files to the JPEG, PDF, or TIFF format (it doesn't convert PNGs or GIFs). Here's how to run the Image Processor script:

1. **Choose File→Scripts→Image Processor.**

   Photoshop opens the aptly named Image Processor dialog box.

2. **In the top section of the dialog box, tell Photoshop which images you want to run the Image Processor on.**

   Your options are to run it on the images you currently have open (Use Open Images) or on a folder of images (Select Folder). You can also include all subfolders (if you choose Select Folder) and open the first image Photoshop changes—just to make sure everything is OK—by turning on the appropriate checkbox(es).

3. **Pick where you want to save the images.**

   You can save the images in the same folder they're currently in or click the radio button next to Select Folder and then pick a new one. If you're sending the files somewhere new, turn on the "Keep folder structure" checkbox to make Photoshop preserve your organization scheme.

4. **Pick the format(s) you want Photoshop to save the files as and, if you want to resize them, enter a new size in pixels.**

   Here's where the real magic lies. You have three options:

   - **Save the files as JPEGs** and choose a quality setting (see page 725); you can also convert the color profile to sRGB (as page 729 describes, this is a good idea).

3. Mouse over to the image and paint the areas you want to protect.

When you start painting, you'll see the red overlay of Quick Mask mode (see Figure 6-23, top). When everything you want to protect is covered with red (like the shrubs, golfers, and flag), press Q to exit Quick Mask mode. You'll see marching ants appear around everything *except* those areas, which you'll fix in the next step.

FIGURE 6-23

Top: The areas you paint in Quick Mask mode turn red, as shown here. This mode is one of the fastest ways to make a selection, and you don't have to be that careful about the area you paint; anything you touch with the brush is protected. Once you exit Quick Mask mode and flip-flop the selection, click the "Save selection as channel" button at the bottom of the Channels panel (circled).

Middle: Once you've activated the Content-Aware Scale tool, you can choose the protective alpha channel from the Protect pop-up menu in the Options bar (circled).

Bottom: Because you protected the tall grass and the man, Photoshop leaves them alone and resizes everything else.

4. Flip-flop your selection by choosing Select→Inverse or pressing Shift-⌘-I (Shift+ Ctrl+I on a PC).

Since Photoshop selected everything *except* the area you painted in the previous step, you need to invert it.

5. **Save the selection as an alpha channel and then deselect.**

    As you learned in Chapter 5, alpha channels are a great way to save selections. Open the Channels panel by choosing Window→Channels. Then save the selection as an alpha channel by clicking the little circle-within-a-square icon at the bottom of the panel (circled in Figure 6-23, top); Photoshop adds a channel called Alpha 1 to the panel. Get rid of the marching ants by choosing Select→Deselect or by pressing ⌘-D (Ctrl+D).

6. **Tell Photoshop you want to resize the image by choosing Edit→Content-Aware Scale or pressing Shift-Option-⌘-C (Shift+Alt+Ctrl+C).**

    Photoshop puts see-through, square resizing handles all around the image; but don't grab them just yet!

7. **From the Options bar's Protect pop-up menu, choose Alpha 1 (Figure 6-23, middle).**

    Choosing the alpha channel you just created tells Photoshop which areas to protect. If the image contains people, you can preserve their skin tones by clicking the little silhouette icon to the right of the Protect menu.

    To make the image smaller or larger by a certain percentage, enter numbers in the W (width) and H (height) fields or the Amount field. (Most of the time, you won't mess with these fields because it's easier to resize the image visually, as you'll do in the next step.)

8. **Mouse over to the image, grab one of the resizing handles, and drag it toward the center of the image.**

    As you can see in Figure 6-23, bottom, the image has been narrowed, but the bushes, golfers and the flag remain unchanged. CAS did a great job of resizing only the unimportant parts of the image.

Is this amazing technology? Yes. Is Adobe still working to improve it? Heck, yes! Even so, it has lots of practical uses. For example, if you have to fit an image into a small space (like wedging a photo into a tiny spot in a magazine article), you can use CAS instead of cropping it. Or if you've created a panorama, you can stretch out the sky a little to fill it back in. Just don't expect CAS to work on images that don't have plain backgrounds like a portrait or other close-up image. Nevertheless, this exciting tool keeps getting better in each new version of Photoshop. And just wait till you see what this feature's cousin, Content-Aware Fill, can do! See page 414 for the lowdown.

> **NOTE** CS6 includes two *new* tools based on this same technology: Content-Aware Move and Content-Aware Patch. They're both covered in detail in Chapter 10.

NOTE You may find yourself wondering, "Why does Photoshop have both a Free Transform command *and* a Transform menu if I can use them to do the exact same things?" Good question! The only real difference between these two options is that choosing an item from the Transform menu locks you into performing that particular task (using the Scale tool, for example), whereas the Free Transform command lets you perform several transformations at the same time (without having to press Return [Enter] between transformations).

You can transform any objects you wish. Vectors, paths, Shape and Type layers, and Smart Objects are especially good candidates for transformation because they can all be resized without harming (pixelating) the image. Don't try to enlarge raster images very much because you have no control over resolution, resampling, or any of the other important stuff mentioned back on page 52. To play it *really* safe, resize images using the Transform commands for only the following reasons:

- **To decrease the size of a selection on a single layer.** Page 178 has more info about transforming a selection without altering any pixels on that layer.

- **To decrease the size of everything on a single layer or multiple layers.** You can activate multiple layers by Shift- or ⌘-clicking (Ctrl-clicking on a PC) them, and then Free Transform can change 'em all simultaneously.

- **To increase the size of a vector, path, portion of a path, Shape layer, Type layer, or Smart Object on one layer or across several layers.**

No matter what you're resizing, simply activate the layer(s) or path(s), or create a selection and then press ⌘-T (Ctrl+T) or choose Edit→Free Transform. Photoshop puts a bounding box around the item, complete with handles that let you apply any or all of the following transformations to the object (they're all illustrated in Figure 6-26):

- **To scale (resize) an object,** grab a corner handle and drag diagonally inward to decrease or outward to increase the size of the object. Press and hold the Shift key while you drag to resize proportionately so the object doesn't get distorted. You can drag one handle at a time or press and hold the Option key (Alt on a PC) to scale from the center outward (meaning that all four sides of the bounding box move simultaneously).

TIP If you summon the Free Transform command to resize something big, the transform handles may end up outside the document's edges (or margins), making them impossible to see, much less grab. To bring them back into view, choose View→"Fit to Screen" or press ⌘-0 (that's the number zero, not the letter O) or Ctrl+0 on a PC.

- **To rotate an image,** put your cursor outside any corner handle. When the cursor turns into a curved, double-headed arrow, drag up or down in the direction you want to turn the image. To rotate in 15-degree increments, press and hold the Shift key while you drag.

- **To skew (slant) an object,** press ⌘-Shift (Ctrl+Shift) and drag one of the side handles; your cursor turns into a double-headed arrow.

- **To distort an image freely,** press ⌘ (Ctrl) while you drag any corner handle.

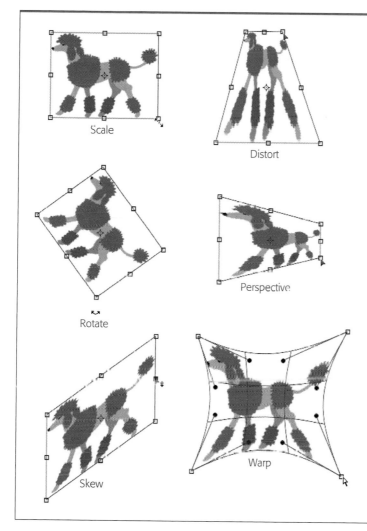

Scale

Distort

FIGURE 6-26

The Transform commands let you scale, rotate, skew, distort, apply perspective, and warp objects in all kinds of interesting ways.

You can apply several transformations in a row if you like; just keep choosing different options from the Transform submenu or use the keyboard shortcuts listed in this section. To undo the last change you made without exiting the bounding box, press ⌘-Z (Ctrl+Z).

Rotate

Perspective

Skew

Warp

- **To alter an object's perspective,** press Shift-Option-⌘ (Shift+Alt+Ctrl) and drag any corner handle (your cursor turns gray). This maneuver gives the object a one-point perspective (in other words, a single vanishing point).

- **To warp an image,** click the "Switch between free transform and warp modes" button in the Options bar (page 262). Photoshop puts a warp mesh over the image so you can reshape it in any way you want. Drag a control point or line on the mesh to warp the image or choose a ready-made preset from the Options bar's Warp pop-up menu. See page 597 for the scoop on warping text. To learn how to warp part of an image, skip ahead to page 448 to read about the Puppet Warp tool.

NOTE The warp mesh grid can help you create the slickest page-curl effect you've ever seen. Head over to this book's Missing CD page at *www.missingmanuals.com/cds* for the scoop!

- **To rotate or flip an image,** Control-click (right-click on a PC) inside the bounding box and choose one of these preset options. Flip is shown on page 259. If you choose one of these little jewels, you won't get a bounding box; Photoshop just rotates or flips the image.

When you're finished with the transformations, press Return (Enter on a PC), double-click inside the bounding box, or click the checkmark icon in the Options bar to accept them.

If you apply a transformation only to realize that it's not quite enough, you can repeat that transformation by choosing Edit→Transform→Again. You don't get a bounding box—Photoshop just reapplies the same transformation. For example, if you rotated the image 90 degrees, Photoshop rotates it another 90 degrees. If you're resizing a raster image, try to transform it only once: The more you transform a pixel-based image, the blurrier and more jagged it can become.

If you want more precise transformations than the ones you get by dragging handles around, you can use the Options bar to enter specific dimensions for scaling, rotating, and skewing, as Figure 6-27 illustrates.

TIP All transformations are based on a tiny *reference point* that appears in the center of a transform box—it looks like a circle with crosshairs. You can drag it around or set your own point by heading up to the Options bar and either clicking one of the reference point locator squares (shown in Figure 6-27) or entering X and Y coordinates.

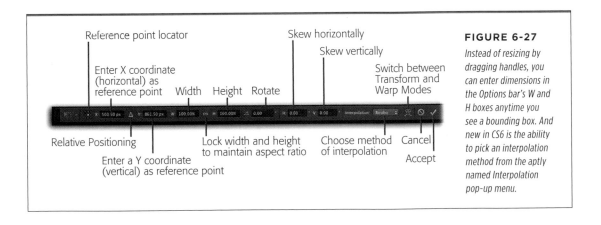

Reference point locator
Enter X coordinate (horizontal) as reference point
Width
Height
Rotate
Skew horizontally
Skew vertically
Switch between Transform and Warp Modes

Relative Positioning
Enter a Y coordinate (vertical) as reference point
Lock width and height to maintain aspect ratio
Choose method of interpolation
Cancel
Accept

FIGURE 6-27

Instead of resizing by dragging handles, you can enter dimensions in the Options bar's W and H boxes anytime you see a bounding box. And new in CS6 is the ability to pick an interpolation method from the aptly named Interpolation pop-up menu.

TIP You can have Photoshop display the Free Transform bounding box around the contents of a layer whenever the Move tool is active *without* having to choose the Free Transform command. To do so, press V to activate the Move tool and then, in the Options bar, turn on the Show Transform Controls checkbox. (The only problem with this tactic is that you might end up resizing something when you don't mean to.)

■ CREATING A REFLECTION

A great little trick you can perform with the Transform command is adding a simple image reflection (see Figure 6-28). Though this technique takes a few steps, it's well worth the effort. Besides adding depth to an otherwise flat photo, a reflection can make an object look like it was shot on another surface, like a table (handy for making product shots without a proper studio setup).

FIGURE 6-28

Here's what the image looks like after you place the reflection on a black background and lower the reflection's opacity slightly to soften the effect. Adds a bit of visual interest, don't you think?

To follow along, visit this book's Missing CD page at www.missingmanuals.com/cds and download the file Leaves.jpg.

handles diagonally inward, as shown in Figure 7-3 (top), to shrink the image proportionally. Next, position your cursor inside the bounding box; the cursor turns into an arrow that lets you drag the photo around inside the frame (Figure 7-3, bottom). When you're done adjusting the image, press Return (Enter).

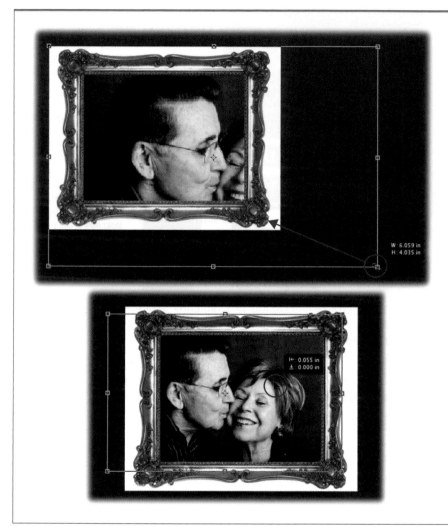

FIGURE 7-3

Top: If the photo is too big for the frame, you can resize it using Free Transform. Just make sure to press and hold Shift as you drag one of the corner handles (circled) so you don't squash or distort the image.

Bottom: Once you get the image sized just right, click and drag within the bounding box to move it around inside the frame. (The cursor is circled here.)

> **TIP** If the Free Transform bounding box hangs off the edges of your document, press ⌘-0 (Ctrl+0) to make Photoshop resize the document window *just* enough so you can see all four corners of the box. This keyboard shortcut is worth memorizing 'cause you'll use it *all* the time.

6. **Lock the pasted photo and the mask together.**

Once you get the photo sized and positioned just right, lock it to the layer mask that Photoshop created in step 4 so everything stays in place. Over in the Layers panel, click the blank space *between* the layer thumbnail and the mask thumbnail. When you do, a little chain icon appears (you can see it in the highlighted layer in Figure 7-2). You're basically finished with this image-combining technique now, but you can add even *more* creativity by rotating the frame, adding a shadow, and giving it a new background. The next few steps explain how.

7. **Hide the white area around the frame with a layer mask.**

The frame shown in Figure 7-2 was originally on a white background. To get rid of the white edges, activate the frame layer in the Layers panel and then double-click it to make it editable. Next, press W to grab the Magic Wand and then click the white area outside the frame to select it. (If you've chosen a frame with all kinds of nooks and crannies around its edges, you can choose Select→Similar to make sure you've got *all* the white areas selected.) Once you've got a good selection, use the Refine Edge dialog box to smooth the selection's edges. Then flip-flop the selection by choosing Select→Inverse to make Photoshop place the marching ants around the frame instead of the white edges. Finally, add a layer mask to the frame layer by clicking the circle-within-a-square button at the bottom of the Layers panel.

8. **Use the Crop tool to make your canvas bigger.**

In order to rotate the frame and add a nice, fluffy drop shadow, you need some extra canvas space. The menu command for increasing canvas size is discussed on page 253, but it's quicker to use the Crop tool: Press C to grab the tool, and then drag to draw a box around your image. Next, Option-drag (Alt-drag on a PC) one of the crop box's corner handles outward to make it bigger on all four sides, and then press Return (Enter). Now you've got all kinds of room to work!

9. **Select the frame and photo layers and rotate them with Free Transform.**

In the Layer's panel, Shift-click to activate both layers and then press ⌘-T (Ctrl+T) to summon Free Transform. Position your cursor outside the bounding box that appears and, when it turns into a curved double arrow, drag upward slightly to rotate the frame and photo. Press Return (Enter) when you've got them at an angle you like.

10. **Add an inner shadow to the photo layer.**

To make the photo look like it's really *inside* the frame, it needs a shadow. First, make sure that only the photo layer is activated in the Layers panel. Next, click the *fx* button at the bottom of the Layers panel and, from the pop-up menu, choose Inner Shadow. Tweak the settings in the resulting Layer Style dialog box to your liking and then click OK.

11. **Add a drop shadow to the frame layer.**

    To add a little depth and make the frame look as if it's really hanging on a wall, activate the frame layer in the Layers panel, click the panel's *fx* button, and choose Drop Shadow. (See page 132 for more on drop shadows.)

12. **Add a Solid Color Fill layer and pick a color.**

    To complete the design, put a new, colored background behind the frame. Choose Layer→New Fill Layer→Solid Color, or click the half black/half white circle at the bottom of the Layers panel and choose Solid Color from the menu that appears. In the resulting Color Picker, choose the color you want for the frame's background and then click OK. (To change this color later on, simply double-click the Fill layer's thumbnail to summon the Color Picker again.)

TIP If you mouse over your image while the Color Picker is open, your cursor turns into a little eyedropper, which lets you click anywhere in the image to choose a color. Snatching a color that's already in the image is a *great* way to pick a background color that matches the image.

---

13. **Drag the Color Fill layer to the bottom of the layer stack.**

    In your document window, the background appears behind the newly framed image.

    Whew! That was a lot of steps, but you're done. Be sure to save the document as a Photoshop (PSD) file in case you want to change the color of the new background. Now go find a place to digitally hang your creation!

Sky Swapping

You can also use the Paste Into technique described in the previous section to replace a bland sky with a more pleasing vista, as shown in Figure 7-4. Using the Paste Into command makes Photoshop add a layer mask *for* you, but it's just as easy to add a mask yourself (either method gets you the same result). Here's how:

1. **Open an image with an area that you want to replace (like the sky) and double-click its Background layer to make it editable (page 87).**

    Photoshop won't let you add a layer mask to the Background layer unless you unlock it (which converts it to a normal layer that supports transparency). If you've worked with this particular image before, your Background layer may already be unlocked or named something else entirely. In that case, onward ho!

2. **Select the sky.**

    Use any of the bazillion selection techniques you learned in Chapter 4. The channels method—discussed on page 169 and used to create the image shown in Figure 7-4—is a good one, as is using the Quick Selection tool with the Refine Edge dialog box (page 171).

3. **Add a layer mask to hide the old sky.**

   Once you've selected the sky, add a layer mask by clicking the circle-within-a-square button at the bottom of the Layers panel.

TIP If the mask hides the *opposite* of what you want it to hide, make sure the mask is active in the Layers panel, and then open the Properties panel by choosing Window→Properties. Click the Invert button in the panel and Photoshop flip-flops the mask.

FIGURE 7-4

Instead of deleting the sky in the original image, you can hide it with a layer mask.

Swapping skies makes this rider's accomplishment a bit more impressive, don't you think?

4. **Open the image with the replacement sky and copy it.**

   Press ⌘-A (Ctrl+A on a PC) to select the whole image, and then press ⌘-C (Ctrl-C) to copy it.

5. **In the other document (the one with the mask), paste the new sky onto its own layer by pressing ⌘-V (Ctrl+V).**

If copying and pasting isn't your thing, arrange your workspace so you can see both open documents (page 66) and then drag the sky layer from the Layers panel into the other document's window (see page 103). You can also drag the document from your desktop into the Photoshop document (page 83) or choose File→Place (page 128).

6. **Position the sky at the bottom of the layer stack.**

    In the Layers panel, drag the new sky to the bottom of the layer stack and you're done.

You just swapped your first sky! If you want to try out other skies, just paste or drag them into the document and position them below the layer with the layer mask. Then hide the first new sky by clicking its visibility eye in the Layers panel.

■ Fading Images Together

So far, you've learned how to combine images with relatively high contrast such as wedging a portrait into a white frame or adding a brand-new sky to an extremely light-colored background. But if your soon-to-be-combined images don't have such stark boundaries, then you're better off using big, soft brushes to do your erasing or, better yet, hiding parts of your image with a layer mask. You can also use the Gradient tool to create a gradual transition from one image to another as if they're faded together. Read on to learn all these methods.

Soft Erasers

Because you can set the Eraser tool to use a brush cursor, you can use a soft brush to erase part of an image so you can see the image on the layer below. Once you've wrangled the two images you want to combine into the same document (each on its own layer), grab the Eraser tool by pressing E and then, in the Options bar, set the Mode pop-up menu to Brush. Next, from the Brush Preset picker, choose a big, soft brush (see Chapter 12 for more on brushes). Then, in the Layers panel, drag the layer you want to partially erase to the top of the layer stack, and then mouse over to your image and simply brush away the parts you want to get rid of. If you mess up or change your mind, undo a step by pressing ⌘-Z (Ctrl+Z on a PC) or use the History panel to go back a few brushstrokes (page 25).

Sure, this technique gets the job done, but keep in mind that it's just as *destructive* as cutting a hole—if you change your mind about how to combine the images, you have to start over. A *better* idea is to do the erasing nondestructively by using a soft-edged brush inside a layer mask. The next section explains how.

Soft Brushes and Layer Masks

A wonderfully practical and flexible way to fade two images together is to paint on a layer mask with a big, fluffy brush. That way you're merely *hiding* part of the image instead of deleting it. For example, say you want to create a striking image for a photography client by blending an image of a baseball player into an image of a baseball, as shown in Figure 7-5. Here's how:

NOTE To create this collage, visit this book's Missing CD page at *www.missingmanuals.com/cds* and download *Player.zip.*

1. **Combine the images into one Photoshop document with each image on a separate layer.**

   If you're following along, name the layer with the boy *player* and the other layer *baseball*.

2. **In the Layers panel, position the player layer at the top of the stack and add a layer mask to it.**

   Drag the player layer to the top of the layer stack. (If you're working with your own imagery, just decide which layer you want to be on top of the collage.) Then, at the bottom of the panel, click the circle-within-a-square button to add a layer mask to it.

FIGURE 7-5

Combining images is a wonderful way to create eye-catching imagery. As you can see in this Layers panel, nary a pixel in the original images was harmed during the making of this collage.

Using a Gradient Map Adjustment layer to hide most of the color in the collage creates a moody and grungy feel.

3. **Press B to grab the Brush tool and pick a big, soft brush.**

   In the Options bar, use the Brush Preset picker to choose a big (500-pixel, say), soft-edged brush.

4. **Set the foreground color chip to black.**

   As you learned in Chapter 3, in the realm of layer masks, painting with black *conceals*, which is exactly what you want to do here. So peek at your color chips at the bottom of the Tools panel and, if they're black and white, press X until black hops on top. If they're any other color, press D to reset them to black and white and *then* press X until black is on top.

5. **Mouse over to your image and paint to hide part of the player layer.**

   If you mess up and hide too much of the boy, press X to flip-flop your color chips (so white is on top) and then paint that area with white to reveal it again. You're basically done at this point, though the next step explains how to create the color effect shown in Figure 7-5.

6. **Add a black-to-white Gradient Map Adjustment layer to the top of your layer stack and lower its opacity to 75 percent.**

   With your color chips set to black and white, press X to flip-flop them so that black is on top. Then click the half-black/half-white circle at the bottom of the Layers panel and choose Gradient Map. Photoshop drains the color from both image layers, though you can lower the Adjustment layer's opacity a bit (to 75 percent or so) to bring back a little of the color. (As you'll learn in Chapter 8, a Gradient Map Adjustment layer creates beautiful high-contrast black-and-white images.)

7. **Save the image as a PSD file so you can go back and tweak it later on.**

   After seeing the final version, you may decide to tweak the Adjustment layer's opacity to achieve the color effect you want. In that case, you can pop open this document, activate the Adjustment layer, and then change its settings without having to start over. Whee!

If you're a pro photographer, this kind of collage is a *fantastic* additional product to offer your clients...for an extra fee, of course!

Gradient Masks

All that soft-brush business aside, the way to create the smoothest fades of all between two images is to use a *gradient*—a soft, gradual transition from one color to another. The steps for combining two images using a gradient are basically the same as the soft-brush method in that you're adding both images to one Photoshop document and then adding a layer mask to the top layer. But instead of painting on the layer mask with a brush, you use a black-to-white gradient for a smooth and seamless fade from one image to the other, as shown in Figure 7-6.

NOTE To follow along, visit this book's Missing CD page at *www.missingmanuals.com/cds* and download the file *Baby.zip*.

Once you've put two images into one document (each on its own layer), take a spin through these steps:

1. **In the Layers panel, drag the image you want on the top of the collage to the top of the layer stack and then add a layer mask to it.**

   In this example, you want the baby on top, so drag it to the top of the Layers panel. Then add a layer mask to it by clicking the circle-within-a-square button at the bottom of the panel. The layer mask thumbnail appears in the Layers panel, but your document doesn't change yet because the mask is empty. (Technically the mask is white, but because "black conceals, white reveals," a white mask fully reveals the layer.)

Gradient picker

FIGURE 7-6

Adding a black-to-white linear gradient to a layer mask is an easy and nondestructive way to softly blend two or more images together. Be sure to experiment with dragging with the Gradient tool different distances and at different angles.

To create the sepia-tint effect shown here, add a Black & White Adjustment layer and then turn on the Tint option in the Properties panel that appears.

(Trot over to page 312 in Chapter 8 for more on using Black & White Adjustment layers).

2. **Press G to grab the Gradient tool and choose a black-to-white, linear gradient.**

   In the Options bar, click the down-pointing triangle to open the Gradient picker (labeled in Figure 7-6, top). Choose the black-to-white gradient from the preset menu that appears (third from left in the top row) and, in the Options bar's row of gradient types, click the linear gradient button (circled in Figure 7-6, top).

3. **Mouse over to your image, click once where you want the fade to begin, drag slightly downward and to the right, and then let go of your mouse.**

   As you drag, Photoshop draws a line that represents the width of the fade: The shorter the line (the distance you drag), the narrower the fade and the harsher the transition (it won't be a hard edge, but it'll be close); the longer the line, the wider the gradient and the softer the fade. As soon as you release your mouse, Photoshop plops the gradient into the layer mask, which effectively fades your images together. If you're not happy with the gradient, just keep clicking and dragging until you get it right; Photoshop updates the mask automatically. To empty the mask and start over, click the mask's thumbnail in the Layers panel, select the whole thing by pressing ⌘-A (Ctrl+A on a PC), and then press Delete (Backspace).

4. **Save your document as a PSD file.**

   This format preserves the layers so you can go back and edit the gradient mask later.

Not bad, eh? Incidentally, this technique is a *great* example of how to use your own imagery along with stock photos. Just think of the possibilities: a wedding photo faded into a bouquet of flowers, piano keys faded into a sheet of music, Captain Kirk faded into a shot of the Starship Enterprise, and so on.

TIP You can also *rotate* a layer to get the image in the right spot for your collage. Just activate the layer you want to twirl and then summon Free Transform by pressing ⌘-T (Ctrl+T on a PC). Next, position your cursor just outside a corner of the bounding box that appears, and when your cursor turns into a double-sided arrow, click and drag in the direction you want to rotate the image. Press Return (Enter) when you're finished.

■ Layer Blend Modes

Perched near the upper-left corner of the Layers panel is an unlabeled pop-up menu of *blend modes,* which control how pixels on different layers interact with one another. (Unless you change it, this menu is set to Normal.) For example, when layers overlap, the top one can either block the bottom one completely, or the layers can blend together in some way (these effects, and many more, are shown in Figure 7-7). You can control exactly *how* they blend together by using blend modes.

TIP To truly understand these modes, try duplicating an image layer and then using your keyboard to cycle through 'em all. Press Shift-plus to go forward through the blend mode menu or Shift-minus to go backward.

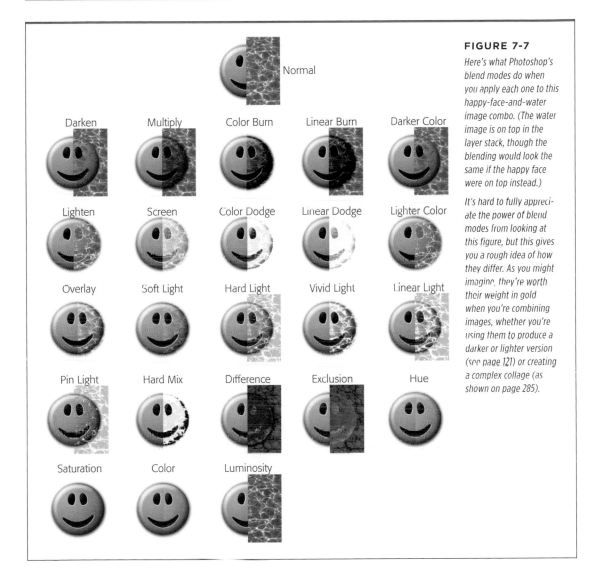

FIGURE 7-7

Here's what Photoshop's blend modes do when you apply each one to this happy-face-and-water image combo. (The water image is on top in the layer stack, though the blending would look the same if the happy face were on top instead.)

It's hard to fully appreciate the power of blend modes from looking at this figure, but this gives you a rough idea of how they differ. As you might imagine, they're worth their weight in gold when you're combining images, whether you're using them to produce a darker or lighter version (see page 121) or creating a complex collage (as shown on page 285).

This section covers how to use *layer* blend modes, but you can find other blend mode menus all over the place in Photoshop:

- In the Layer Style dialog box, where you can add effects like drop shadows, glows, and so on (page 131).

- In some filters' dialog boxes (see Chapter 15).

- In the Fade dialog box, which you can access via Edit→Fade right after you run a filter (see the box on page 464), apply any of the adjustments in the Image→Adjustments menu, and so on.

- In the Options bar when you're using a tool you can paint with, like the Brush, Paint Bucket, Healing Brush, Pencil, Clone Stamp, History Brush, Gradient, Blur, Sharpen, and Smudge tools.

- In the Calculations (page 216) and Apply Image dialog boxes. (To learn how to combine two images using the Apply Image command, which lets you pick the channel Photoshop uses to do the blending, head to this book's Missing CD page at *www.missingmanuals.com/cds*.)

When you're dealing with blend modes, it's helpful to think of the colors on your layers as being made up of three parts:

- **Base.** This is the color you start out with, the one that's already in your image.

- **Blend.** This is the color you're adding to the base color, whether it's in an image on another layer or one you're painting onto another layer with the Brush tool.

- **Result.** This is the color you get after mixing the base with a blend color using a blend mode.

To help you make sense of Photoshop's growing set of blend modes (and you'll need all the help you can get), the blend mode menu is divided into categories based on each mode's *neutral color*—the color that causes *no* change in that particular mode. For example, some modes ignore white, some ignore black, and so on. This info doesn't mean a hill of beans to you just yet, but it'll start to make sense as you learn more about the various modes in the next few pages. Here's a quick tour of the layer blend mode menu.

Normal and Dissolve Blend Modes

These two modes are at the very top of the blend mode menu. Here's what they do:

- **Normal.** When you first use Photoshop, it's set to use this mode, which doesn't actually cause any blending at all; as Figure 7-7 shows, the pixels on the top layer (the water image) totally block what lies below (the happy face). Its keyboard shortcut is Shift-Option-N (Shift+Alt+N on a PC).

> **NOTE** Photoshop includes lots of keyboard shortcuts you can use to change the current layer's blend mode. However, if you're using one of the painting tools listed at the beginning of this section, these shortcuts change the blend mode of that particular *tool* instead of changing the *layer's* blend mode.

- **Dissolve.** This mode turns semi-transparent pixels into a spray of dots (if you don't have any semi-transparent pixels, your image won't change). Dissolve isn't very useful unless you want to make a drop shadow look coarse instead of soft (see Figure 7-8). Keyboard shortcut: Shift-Option-I (Shift+Alt+I).

My brain hurts.

My brain hurts.

FIGURE 7-8

To create the spatter effect shown here, add a drop shadow with layer styles (page 132) and then, in the Layer Style dialog box, change the shadow's blend mode to Dissolve. Photoshop changes the formerly see-through drop shadow into a spray of pixels.

Darken Blend Modes

The modes in this category have the power to darken, or *burn*, your image (see pages 324 and 356 for info on using the Burn tool). Simply put, when you apply these modes, the base and blend colors go to war and the darkest color wins. These modes are incredibly useful when you want to swap a light-colored background for something darker. The neutral color in this category is white, which means that white has no effect on the blend at all, and any white parts of your images disappear.

- **Darken.** In this mode, Photoshop analyzes the base and blend colors and combines the darkest ones to create the result color. Any colors on the top layer that are darker than the colors on the layer below get to stay, and any lighter colors on the bottom layer disappear. Darken mode is helpful for fixing areas in an image that are too light or overexposed, and can be used with the Brush or Clone Stamp tools to fix shiny areas on skin (page 422). Keyboard shortcut: Shift-Option-K (Shift+Alt+K on a PC).

- **Multiply.** In Multiply mode, Photoshop *multiplies* (increases) the base color by the blend color. You can think of this mode like a double coat of ink since the result color will always be darker than the base. Multiply does a lot of cool things, including fixing images that are too light or overexposed (see page 121) or creating an *overprint* effect in which the graphic on the top layer looks like it's been printed on the layer below (like the fake tattoo in Figure 7-9). Keyboard shortcut: Shift-Option-M (Shift+Alt+M).

FIGURE 7-9

By changing the blend mode of the tattoo layer to Multiply, its white background disappears so you can see through the rooster to the skin below. All you need to do now is lower the opacity of the tattoo layer to make it look a little faded and not quite so fresh.

- **Color Burn.** This mode darkens your image by increasing its overall contrast. When you use it on a layer filled with 50 percent gray, it intensifies color on the layers below, which can beautify an ugly sky in a hurry. You can also use it to colorize a grayscale image, though the paint will be really dark and intense (it's better to use Hue mode, discussed on page 343). Keyboard shortcut: Shift-Option-B (Shift+Alt+B).

> **TIP** 50 percent gray is, not surprisingly, the color exactly halfway between pure black and pure white. An easy way to fill a layer with 50 percent gray is to make a new layer, go to Edit→Fill, and then choose 50% Gray from the Use pop-up menu. Those Adobe programmers think of everything!

- **Linear Burn.** In this mode (which is actually a combination of Multiply and Color Burn), Photoshop darkens your image by decreasing its brightness. Linear Burn produces the darkest colors of any Darken blend mode, though with a bit more contrast than the others. It has a tendency to turn dark pixels solid black, which makes it ideal for grungy, textured collages like the one in Figure 7-10. Keyboard shortcut: Shift-Option-A (Shift+Alt+A).

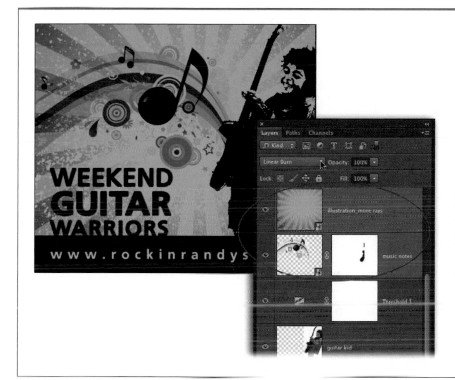

FIGURE 7-10

In this Layers panel, you can see the original image near the bottom and a Threshold Adjustment layer above it. Popping in two pieces of art (circled) and changing their blend modes to Linear Burn created this trendy ad.

Happily, Photoshop CS6 lets you change the blend mode of multiple layers at the same time by activating them and then choosing a new option from the blend mode menu.

- **Darker Color.** This mode compares the base and blend colors and keeps the darkest pixels. No blending going on here—the lighter colors just vanish. It's ideal for removing white backgrounds (a technique sometimes called "knocking out"), as Figure 7-11 illustrates. (Darker Color doesn't have a keyboard shortcut, because this mode didn't come around until Photoshop CS3 when Adobe started running out of keyboard shortcut combos. Same goes for Lighter Color mode [page 287]).

FIGURE 7-11

By placing two images on separate layers, you can use Darker Color mode to zap a white background. Here, the top layer has a fairly light sunburst and the bottom layer has a dark-colored kid on a white background. If you change the blend mode of the sunburst layer to Darker Color, the white background on the layer below disappears.

Since parts of the kid's boot are lighter than the sunburst—meaning the sunburst wins the color war explained on page 283 and covers him up in those spots—you can hide that part of the sunburst with a layer mask to keep him whole.

Lighten Blend Modes

These modes, not surprisingly, do the opposite of the Darken modes: They lighten, or *dodge*, your image (see pages 325 and 356 for info on using the Dodge tool). Black is the neutral color for this group; it disappears in all but one of the following modes:

- **Lighten.** In this mode, the lightest pixels win the color war. Photoshop compares all the colors and keeps the lightest ones from the base and the blend, and then combines them to produce the result color. Everything else is nixed (including black), which makes this mode useful for blending a black background with something lighter (see Figure 7-12). Keyboard shortcut: Shift-Option-G (Shift+Alt+G on a PC).

- **Screen.** In this mode, Photoshop multiplies the *opposite* of the blend and base colors, making everything a lot lighter as though a bottle of bleach was spilled on it. It's great for fixing images that are too dark or underexposed (like when your camera's flash doesn't fire; see page 121). Keyboard shortcut: Shift-Option-S (Shift+Alt+S).

- **Color Dodge.** This mode lightens your image by decreasing its contrast. It has a tendency to turn light pixels solid white, and, unlike the other Lighten modes, it keeps black pixels, so the dark parts of your image don't change. You can use this mode on a light-colored texture to add depth and brightness to a dark background on the layer below, as in Figure 7-13. And by using Color Dodge on a layer filled with 50 percent gray, you can give dark hair instant highlights. Keyboard shortcut: Shift-Option-D (Shift+Alt+D).

FIGURE 7-12

To zap most of the black background of this fireball (the top layer), change its blend mode to Lighten. Now the flames are visible only where they're lighter than the colors in the steel ball.

A layer mask was added to hide a few rogue flames underneath the ball.

- **Linear Dodge (Add).** This mode lightens your image by increasing its brightness. It's a combo of Screen and Color Dodge modes, so it lightens images more than any other blend mode. But since it tends to turn *all* light colors white, it can make an image look unnatural. Keyboard shortcut: Shift-Option-W (Shift+Alt+W).

- **Lighter Color.** With this mode, Photoshop compares the base and blend colors and keeps only the lightest pixels. Unlike Lighten mode, it doesn't combine any colors; it just keeps the lightest ones. (There's no keyboard shortcut for this mode.)

FIGURE 7-13

By adding a layer with a light-colored texture and changing its blend mode to Color Dodge, you can significantly brighten a dark and boring background (the bottom layer).

Just add a layer mask to protect other parts of the image (like the guitar) from the brightening.

Lighting (Contrast) Blend Modes

In contrast to the Lighten and Darken modes, Lighting blend modes do a little darkening *and* a little lightening to increase the contrast of an image. They have a neutral color of 50 percent gray, which doesn't affect the result color; it just disappears.

- **Overlay.** In this mode, if the base color is darker than 50 percent gray, Photoshop multiplies its color value with the base color. If the base color is lighter than 50 percent gray, Photoshop multiplies its color value with the *inverse* of the base color (like it does in Screen mode). You can use this mode to increase contrast or colorize a grayscale image, though it's especially useful for sharpening an image with the High Pass filter (page 467). Keyboard shortcut: Shift-Option-O (Shift+Alt+O on a PC).

- **Soft Light.** As its name suggests, this mode is equivalent to shining a soft light on your image. It makes bright areas brighter (as if they were dodged) and dark areas darker (as if they were burned). If you paint with black in this mode, you'll darken the underlying image; if you paint with white, you'll lighten it. You can use this mode to add texture to an image or to make an image look like it's reflected in metal (see Figure 7-14). Seasoned Photoshop jockeys use Soft Light with the Dodge and Burn tools to retouch portraits nondestructively (see page 436). Keyboard shortcut: Shift-Option-F (Shift+Alt+F).

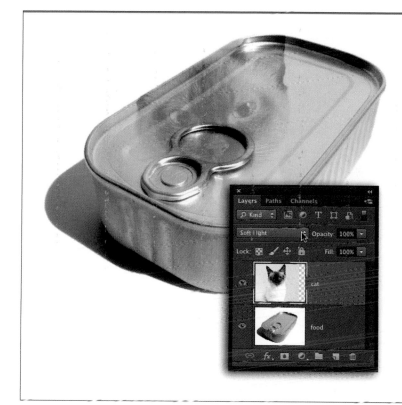

FIGURE 7-14

To create a quick reflection in a metal object, change the top layer's blend mode to Soft Light.

- **Hard Light.** This mode, which is equivalent to shining a harsh light on your image, combines Multiply and Screen modes: If the blend color is lighter than 50 percent gray, the image gets lighter (like Screen mode); if it's darker than 50 percent gray, the image gets darker (like Multiply). If you paint with black or white in this mode, you simply get black or white. If you *really* want to increase the level of detail in an image, use this mode in conjunction with the Emboss filter (page 668). Keyboard shortcut: Shift-Option-H (Shift+Alt+H).

- **Vivid Light.** In this mode, Photoshop applies Color Burn to increase the contrast of colors *darker* than 50 percent gray and Color Dodge to decrease the contrast of colors *lighter* than 50 percent gray. Use Vivid Light to make an image pop or to add texture. Keyboard shortcut: Shift-Option-V (Shift+Alt+V).

- **Linear Light.** This mode combines the Linear Burn and Linear Dodge modes; It uses Linear Burn to decrease the brightness of colors *darker* than 50 percent gray and Linear Dodge to increase the brightness of colors *lighter* than

50 percent gray. Linear Light is great for adding texture to images, as shown in Figure 7-15. Keyboard shortcut: Shift-Option-J (Shift+Alt+J).

FIGURE 7-15

Want to turn a loved one to stone? No problem! Simply use the Quick Selection tool to select the person's skin and then add a layer mask to a layer containing marble or stone (the top layer here). Change the marble layer's blend mode to Linear Light, and you've got an instant statue.

In this example, the opacity of the marble layer was also lowered to 60 percent to reveal some of the skin tone.

- **Pin Light.** This mode combines Lighten and Darken: If the blend color is *lighter* than 50 percent gray, it replaces areas of the base color darker than 50 percent gray with the blend color; pixels lighter than 50 percent gray don't change at all. But if the blend color is *darker* than 50 percent gray, Pin Light replaces lighter areas of the base color with the blend color, and darker areas don't change. You'll rarely use this mode because it can produce odd results (or none at all), but feel free to experiment with it—especially with filters (see Chapter 15). Keyboard shortcut: Shift-Option-Z (Shift+Alt+Z).

- **Hard Mix.** This mode greatly reduces the range of colors in your image (an effect known as *posterizing*), so you end up with large blocks of super-bright colors like red, green, or blue. In this mode, Photoshop analyzes the sum of the RGB values in the blend color and adds them to the base color. For example, if the value of the red, green, or blue channel is 255, Photoshop adds that value to the base; if the value is less than 255, Photoshop doesn't add anything to the base. (See page 46 for more on color values.) You can reduce the effect of this mode to a visually pleasing level by lowering the Fill setting at the top of the Layers panel to about 25 percent, resulting in a nice contrast boost (see Figure 7-16). Keyboard shortcut: Shift-Option-L (Shift+Alt+L).

FIGURE 7-16

In Hard Mix mode, Photoshop changes all the pixels to primary colors (see the figure on page 341), leaving you with solid blocks of bright, high-contrast color. By lowering its Fill opacity to 25 percent, you get a nice color boost like this one. To quickly change the Fill setting to 25 percent, press Shift-2-5. To change Opacity instead, just press the number you want to apply, such as 2-5. And new in CS6 is the ability to set Fill to zero by pressing Shift-0-0 and Opacity to zero by pressing 0-0 respectively. (All of these shortcuts work only if you're not using the Brush, Spot Healing, or Healing Brush tools.)

As you can see here, combining images isn't just about using different images; there's opportunity aplenty to combine different versions of the same image.

Comparative Blend Modes

This category should really be called "psychedelic." Its two modes are similar, and they both produce freaky results that are useful only on Halloween or in grungy collages (discussed earlier in this chapter). However, as you'll soon find out, they can be *temporarily* useful. Black is the neutral color in both modes.

- **Difference.** This mode analyzes the brightness of both the base and the blend colors and subtracts the brightest pixels. If you use white as your blend color, Photoshop inverts (flip-flops) the base color, making the image look like a film negative. If you use black as your blend color, Photoshop doesn't change anything. You wouldn't want to use this mode on an image permanently, but you can use it temporarily to locate the midtones (see the box on page 385 for details). You can also use it to align two layers of the same image (if, say, they were shot at different exposures): Just change the top layer to Difference mode and then use your arrow keys to move the image until both versions line up. Keyboard shortcut: Shift-Option-E (Shift+Alt+E on a PC).

- **Exclusion.** This mode is similar to Difference but results in a little less contrast. Blending with white inverts the base color, and blending with black doesn't do anything. It produces some fairly freaky effects so you won't use it much. That said, you can also use Exclusion to align images by following the steps in the previous bullet point. Keyboard shortcut: Shift-Option-X (Shift+Alt+X).

- **Subtract.** Introduced in CS5, this mode subtracts the blend color from the base color, which significantly darkens your image. It's does practically the same as Linear Burn, though, so there's little reason to use this mode.

- **Divide.** Also introduced in CS5, this mode divides the blend color by the base color, which significantly brightens your image. It's practically the same as Color Dodge, so (you guessed it) there's little, if any, reason to use it.

Hue Blend Modes

All the modes in this category relate to color and luminance (brightness) values (see page 486 for more on brightness). Depending on the colors in your images, Photoshop applies one or two of these values (these modes don't have a neutral color like the other ones). Hue blend modes are extremely practical because you can use them to change, add, or intensify colors.

- **Hue.** This mode keeps the lightness and saturation (color intensity) values of the base color and adds the *hue* (another word for "color") of the blend color. Use this mode to change an object's color without changing how light or dark it is (see page 336). However, Hue mode can't introduce a color that isn't already there to colorize grayscale images, so you have to use another mode for that (like Color, explained later in this list). Keyboard shortcut: Shift-Option-U (Shift+Alt+U on a PC).

- **Saturation.** This mode keeps the luminance and hue of the base color and picks up the saturation of the blend color. If you want to increase an image's color intensity, this mode can help you out (though try using a Vibrance Adjustment layer first, as it usually produces better results). You can also use Saturation to drain color from part of an image by painting that area black; because black has no saturation value, black *desaturates* any colors that intersect with it. Keyboard shortcut: Shift-Option-T (Shift+Alt+T).

UP TO SPEED

Pass Through Mode

When you create a layer group (page 108), Pass Through appears at the top of the blend mode pop-up menu. In this mode, Photoshop makes sure that any blend modes, blending slider settings (page 293), opacity settings, and fill settings you've applied to layers in the group trickle down to layers *below* the group.

For example, let's say you've created a layer group consisting of several image layers set to Linear Burn mode to make a grunge collage. Pass Through mode makes the Linear Burn effect trickle down to any background or text on layers below the group. If you *don't* want the blending to affect the layers below the group, change the group's blend mode to Normal instead.

- **Color.** In this mode, Photoshop keeps the luminance of the base color and picks up the hue and saturation of the blend color, which makes it handy for colorizing grayscale images (see page 343). Keyboard shortcut: Shift-Option-C (Shift+Alt+C).

- **Luminosity.** This mode keeps the base color's hue and saturation and picks up the blend color's luminance. Use Luminosity when you're sharpening an image (see page 458) or using a Curves or Levels Adjustment layer (see Chapter 9). Keyboard shortcut: Shift-Option-Y (Shift+Alt+Y).

Zapping Backgrounds with Blending Sliders

If the subject of your image is radically brighter or darker than its background, you'll want to sit up and pay attention to this section. While blend modes are pretty powerful in their own right (and several of them can pulverize a white or black background instantly), *another* set of blending options in the Layer Style dialog box (page 131) can eat backgrounds for lunch—nondestructively!

Photoshop gives you a few different ways to open the Layer Style dialog box (Figure 7-17). Once you've activated the image layer you want to work with, open the dialog box using one of the following methods:

- **Double-click the layer's thumbnail in the Layers panel.**

- **Click the *fx* button at the bottom of the Layers panel and then choose Blending Options.**

- **Choose Layer→Layer Style→Blending Options.**

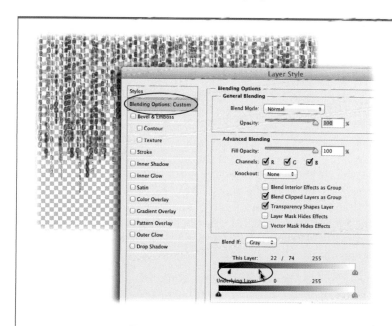

FIGURE 7-17

You can use the Blend If sliders in this dialog box to make short work of removing solid-colored backgrounds. In this image, the black background has been hidden by dragging the shadow slider to the right.

To soften the edges of the bits that remain, you can split the slider in half (as described in a sec) and then drag its left half back to the left, as shown here (circled).

NOTE The Blending sliders won't work on a locked Background layer; you have to double-click the layer first to make it editable.

At the bottom of the Layer Style dialog box lie two pairs of sliders (they look like triangles): one set for the This Layer bar and another for the Underlying Layer bar, shown in Figure 7-17. Each slider lets you make parts of your image transparent based on the brightness value of the pixels. The left-hand sliders represent the shadows (blacks) in the image, and the right-hand ones represent the highlights (whites). To affect the currently active layer, tweak the This Layer slider (you'll learn about the Underlying Layer slider in a moment).

For example, if the background of the active layer is black and the subject (or object in the foreground) is much brighter, you can hide the black part by dragging the shadow slider (the one on the left) right toward the middle of the This Layer bar until the black part is transparent. To hide a white background instead, drag the highlight slider (the one on the right) left toward the middle of the bar until the white part is transparent.

NOTE If you save your document as a PSD file, you can adjust these sliders anytime you want by activating the layer and summoning the Layer Style dialog box.

To soften your subject's edges once you've hidden the background, you can make the edge pixels partially transparent by splitting the shadow or highlights slider in half. To soften the edge pixels after you've hidden a black background, for example, Option-click (Alt-click on a PC) the left half of the shadows slider and drag it slightly back to the left (circled in Figure 7-17). Likewise, if you've hidden a white background, you can Option-click (Alt-click) the right half of the highlights slider and drag it slightly to the right to tell Photoshop to make pixels with that particular brightness value partially transparent.

TIP You can perform this pixel-hiding magic on colors, too. Just pick the channel (see Chapter 5) you want to work with from the Blend If pop-up menu above the bars, and then that particular color appears in the bars instead of black and white.

The Underlying Layer sliders let you control the range of visible colors on layers *below* the active layer. As you drag the sliders, parts of the image on underlying layers appear *through* the pixels on the active layer as if you'd cut a hole through it. If you drag the shadows slider right toward the middle of the Underlying Layer bar, you'll begin to see the darkest parts of the underlying image show through the active layer. If you drag the highlight slider left toward the middle of the bar, you'll start to see the lightest parts of the underlying image.

As you can see in Figure 7-18, the blending sliders can do an amazing job of hiding backgrounds based on color. But if your *subject* contains some of the colors in the background, the blending sliders will zap those areas, too. In that case, you'll have to use a different method to hide the background, like another blend mode or a layer mask (as discussed earlier in this chapter).

FIGURE 7-18

Once you've hidden the black in this Matrix-like background, you can see through to the image on the layer below, which makes for a quickie collage.

Photoshop adds a special badge to the right of the layer's name to let you know its blending options have changed; the badge looks like two intersecting squares and is shown on the matrix layer here.

Auto-Aligning Layers and Photomerge

If you've ever needed to combine a few group shots to get an image where everybody is smiling and their eyes are open, you'll appreciate the Auto-Align Layers command. Sure, you can *manually* align layers, but when you run this command, Photoshop does all the hard work *for you* by examining the active layers and aligning them so identical areas overlap (see Figure 7-19).

NOTE The Auto-Align feature isn't magic; the angle and the distance from the subject in both shots need to be the same for it to work. However, since CS5, this command has taken a peek at the lens-correction profiles specified in the Lens Correction dialog box (page 642), which helps this feature do a better job of aligning layers and creating panoramas (discussed in the next section).

Once you've got your images on different layers in the same document—they need to be exactly the same size—activate at *least* two layers by Shift- or ⌘-clicking them (Ctrl-clicking on a PC) in the Layers panel, and then choose Edit→Auto-Align Layers (this menu item is grayed out unless you have two or more layers activated). In the resulting dialog box, you can choose from these alignment methods:

- **Auto.** If you're not sure which method will work best to align your images, let Photoshop decide. When you choose this option, the program picks either Perspective or Cylindrical, depending on which one it thinks will create the best composition. It usually does a good job aligning images, though you may notice some distortion (as explained in the following bullet points).

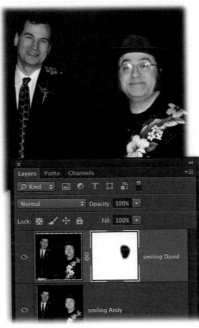

FIGURE 7-19

The Auto-Align Layers command is great for merging a few imperfect shots into one perfect image (or at least one where each subject is smiling). To do that, combine the images into one document and place the non-smiling layer (left) atop the smiling layer (right). Then run the Auto-Align layers command. Finally, add a layer mask to the top layer and then paint the non-smile away with a black brush so your smiling pal shows through!

- **Perspective.** When you choose this method, Photoshop adjusts the four corners of your layers and repositions, stretches, and skews each one so any overlapping areas match in perspective. The final image looks slightly warped—both ends are a little larger than the center of the image, as if they were closer to you. This method can also make one of your layers look like it's coming out of the screen toward you, which can be visually interesting.

> **TIP** Photoshop picks its own *reference layer* (the layer it tries to align all the other layers with) unless you designate one yourself using the Lock All layer lock discussed on page 107.

- **Collage.** This method tells Photoshop to scale, rotate, and reposition the layers to align them with overlapping content without changing their shape. Choose Collage if you don't want your images to get distorted in any way.

- **Cylindrical.** If you're combining several images into a panorama, choose this option. Along with repositioning, stretching, and skewing your layers, Cylindrical helps get rid of any bow-tie lens distortion (where the subject looks like it's being pinched inward) by curving the images slightly (see Figure 7-20, middle).

FIGURE 7-20

Top: If you want to stitch these forest images together, you can use the Auto-Align Layers command or Photomerge to get it done.

Middle: To compensate for bow-tie lens distortion, the Cylindrical alignment method curves your final image slightly (notice that the top and bottom edges of the image aren't straight).

Bottom: The Spherical method gives you a perfectly rectangular panorama.

- **Spherical.** Like Cylindrical, this method repositions, stretches, and skews layers to match up overlapping areas. It also tries to correct barrel distortion (where the subject looks rounded) by making your panorama perfectly rectangular (see Figure 7-20, bottom).

- **Reposition.** If you're aligning a group shot to hide a frown or closed eyes, choose this option. It won't stretch or skew your layers; it'll just reposition them so they line up.

The Auto-Align Layers dialog box also gives you two ways to correct camera lens distortion. Turn on the Vignette Removal checkbox to get rid of darkened or soft edges caused by wide-angle lenses, or the Geometric Distortion checkbox to make Photoshop warp your image slightly to reduce the spherical look caused either by wide-angle lenses or being too close to your subject with a regular lens.

Once you've aligned the images, flip to page 299 to see how you can make Photoshop blend them together seamlessly using the Auto-Blend command.

Building Panoramas with Photomerge

Photoshop has an automatic photo-stitcher called Photomerge that gives you all the same options as the Auto-Align Layers dialog box, but you don't have to combine the images into a single document first—Photoshop does that for you. This is really helpful when you're merging images into a wide shot, though you can't manually arrange your images into a panorama (that feature disappeared back in CS4).

To use Photomerge, choose File→Automate→Photomerge. In the resulting dialog box's Use pop-up menu, tell Photoshop whether you want to use individual files or a whole folder. Then click the Browse button to find the images on your hard drive, or, if you've already opened the documents, click the Add Open Files button. On the left side of the dialog box, you can pick an alignment method or leave it set to Auto and let Photoshop choose for you. If you want Photoshop to use layer masks to help cover up any seams, leave the Blend Images Together checkbox at the bottom of the dialog box turned on (this setting has the same effect as running the Auto-Blend command discussed on page 299). The Vignette Removal and Geometric Distortion checkboxes work the same way here as they do in the Auto-Align Layers dialog box.

When you've got all the settings the way you want them, click OK. Photoshop combines your images into a new document with each image on its own layer, rotated and positioned to fit with all the others. All you need to do is crop the image to get rid of any transparent bits around the edges, or you can recreate that portion of the image by hand using the Clone Stamp tool or, even simpler, the Content-Aware Scale command.

UP TO SPEED

Shooting Panoramas

If you're taking photos specifically to make a big honkin' panorama, here are a few things to think about while you're snapping away:

- **Use a tripod.** A tripod or some other stabilizing surface (like your mate's shoulder) helps you take steadier shots. You don't want your panorama to be blurry, right?

- **Include an overlapping element in each shot.** If you're taking three shots, make sure you include some of what's in the first shot in the second, and some of the second shot in the third. That way you have overlapping bits that Photoshop can use to align the images.

- **Keep the lighting (exposure) consistent.** Though Photomerge is pretty darn good at blending images, you're going to notice if you took one shot in the shade and the other in direct sunlight. For the best results, keep the lighting constant by exposing for the brightest portion of the image manually (even if it means consulting your camera's manual).

- **Make sure the angles are the same.** Photoshop has one heck of a time matching up images shot at different angles, but mismatched shots can make for some interesting creative possibilities.

TIP You'll find cropping and cloning easier if you stamp (page 114) or flatten the layers first (page 115), though, if you pick the latter, be sure to choose File→Save As and give the image another name so you can flatten it without worrying about saving over the original. Also, you can choose Edit→Content-Aware Scale (page 254) to slightly stretch the image to fill in empty pixels so you don't have to crop it quite so much.

Auto-Blending Layers

The Auto-Blend Layers command, which was designed to be used after the Auto-Align Layers command, helps you blend images for a panorama or collage, or combine multiple exposures of the same image to create an extended *depth of field* so more of an object looks like it's in focus. When you use this command, Photoshop creates complex layer masks to blend your images, saving you a lot of hard work.

NOTE You can use the Auto-Blend Layers command only when you're working in RGB or Grayscale mode (see page 45 for more on color modes).

To get the best results, run the Auto-Align Layers command as explained on page 295, and then choose Edit→Auto-Blend Layers. In the resulting dialog box (Figure 7-21, left), choose one of the following blending options:

- **Panorama.** Select this option to have Photoshop search for overlapping areas in your images so it can piece them together into a single image.

- **Stack Images.** If you've fired off several shots of an object with different parts in focus (known as different depths of field) and you want to combine them into a single shot where the *whole* object is in focus, choose this option. Let's say you shot a tiger—with a big zoom lens, of course—that was stretched out lengthwise and facing you. If one image has his head in focus, another has the middle of his body in focus, and a third has his tail in focus, you can choose Stack Images to make Photoshop combine the three images into a single shot with the *whole* cat in focus.

TIP In Photoshop CS6, you can use the new Field, Iris, and Tilt-Shift Blur filters to produce even better and more complex depth of field effects than you can get with Stack Images.

- **Seamless Tones and Colors.** Leave this checkbox turned on to make Photoshop smooth out any noticeable seams and color differences between the images during the blending process.

As mentioned earlier, this command has a ton of potential uses. One visually interesting possibility is to make a collage of two or more action shots to create a stop-motion effect. Figure 7-21 has the details.

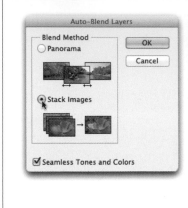

FIGURE 7-21

You can use the Auto-Blend Layers command to create interesting collages like this in mere seconds. The best part is that Photoshop does all the masking for you, as shown in this Layers panel. Woo-hoo!

TIP You can also use the Auto-Blend Layers command to help scan really big images. For example, if the image is too big to fit onto your scanner in one piece, scan different sections of it—being careful to create overlapping areas—and then let Photoshop piece it together for you by first running the Auto-Align Layers command and then running Auto-Blend Layers.

■ Cloning Between Documents

The Clone Stamp tool is great for tricks like banishing shiny spots (page 422) or giving someone a third eye, but it has other uses, too. You can also use it to copy bits and pieces of an image from one open document to another. Using the Clone Source panel—the *clone source* is the object you're copying—you can clone from up to five different sources whether or not they're in the same Photoshop document. Here's how to clone from one open image into another:

1. **Open the source document(s) (the image[s] you're cloning from) and the target document (the image you're cloning to) and arrange your workspace.**

    To choose clone sources in documents other than the current image, open the source documents. Then choose Window→Arrange and pick a setup that lets you see all the open documents, or just click each document's tab to activate it (see page 68 in Chapter 2 for more on working with tabbed documents).

2. **Press S to grab the Clone Stamp tool, and then open the Clone Source panel.**

Choose Window→Clone Source or click the panel's icon in the panel dock. (Full coverage of the Clone Source panel's many options starts on page 302.)

3. **Set the clone source.**

Click the window (or tab) of the image you want to clone from (like the cats in Figure 7-22, top left). Then Option-click (Alt-click on a PC) the area you want to copy to set it as the clone source.

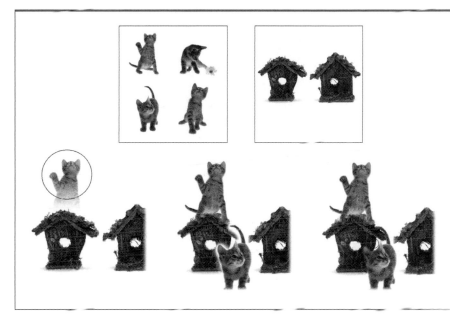

FIGURE 7-22

Top: By cloning the kitties from one image onto the birdhouses in another, you can create a mischievously cute collage.

Bottom: The brush preview is extremely helpful in positioning the cloned art (left). If you mess up and clone in a little too much (middle), grab the History Brush and paint to reveal that part of the original image (right). If you're cloning onto a new layer, you can also use the Eraser tool.

4. **Create a new layer.**

Unless you want to clone the new image on top of your original image (and you don't!), head back to your target document and add a new layer to it by clicking the "Create a new layer" button at the bottom of the Layers panel. That way, if you don't like the result, you can simply toss the new layer instead of having to start over.

5. **Paint to clone the item.**

As shown in Figure 7-22 (bottom left), Photoshop displays a preview of the image you're about to paint *inside* the brush cursor. If you don't want the clone source point to move as your brush cursor moves—because you want to create multiple instances of an object, for example—turn off the Options bar's Aligned checkbox.

TIP To change your brush settings—or keyboard shortcuts. You can alter brush size and hardness by Control-Option-dragging (Alt+right-click+dragging) in horizontal or vertical strokes, respectively.

You need a pretty steady hand when working with the Clone Stamp tool because it's easy to clone too much and cover up parts of your image. You can solve that problem by first selecting an area to restrict your brushstrokes to that part of the image. This technique is handy when you want to fill an area with another image, as shown in Figure 7-23.

FIGURE 7-23

If you select the destination area first (like these silhouettes), you don't have to be as careful with your brushstrokes. As you can see here, the brush cursor (circled) extends well past the edges of these digital business dudes, but Photoshop applies the Matrix-like background only within the selected area.

If you want to get a little fancy and start doing things like pulling source points from *multiple* images and changing the *angle* of your cloned objects, then you need to enlist the help of the Clone Source panel (Figure 7-24).

NOTE In Photoshop CS6, you can use the Frame Offset and Lock Frame options shown in Figure 7-24 to clone content in video or animation frames.

The Clone Source panel includes the following settings:

- **Offset.** Use this section of the panel to move, resize, or rotate the object you're copying (a.k.a. the clone source). If you want to move your clone source, you can change its X and Y coordinates (measured in pixels) here. If you've got the Show Overlay checkbox (explained next) turned on, you see a preview of the source point on your image that moves as you tweak these settings. To clone the object at a different size, enter new percentages in the W and H fields (for width and height). To rotate your clone source—so the cloned item is turned— enter a number of degrees in the field next to the triangle icon. To reset all these options, click the little curved arrow button.

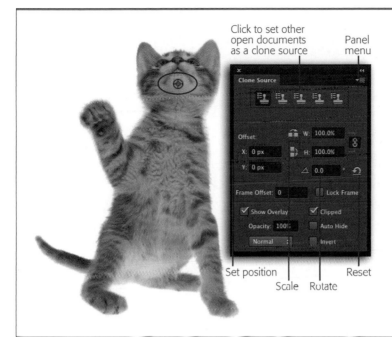

Click to set other
open documents
as a clone source

Panel
menu

Set position

Scale   Rotate

Reset

FIGURE 7-24

Assigning multiple clone sources is handy when you want to clone items between open documents or create a complex scene from different elements. For example, if you're trying to remove a cat that's standing in front of a birdhouse, one clone source can be the cat and another can be the birdhouse.

Once you've activated the Clone Stamp tool, you can use the five source buttons shown here to quickly switch between different source points without having to reset them manually each time. To set a source point, just Option-click (Alt-click on a PC) the area you want to clone, and your cursor turns into a crosshairs icon like the one circled here.

TIP   You can position your cursor above any of the field labels in the Offset section—X, Y, W, and so on—to get the handy scrubby cursor (see the figure on page 331). Then drag left to decrease the setting and right to increase it. You can Shift-drag to change it in larger increments or Option-drag (Alt-drag on a PC) for smaller increments. If you're a fan of keyboard shortcuts, press Option-Shift-[(Alt+Shift+[on a PC) to decrease your clone source's width and height proportionally and Option-Shift-] (Alt+Shift+]) to increase them. To rotate your source, press Option-Shift-< (Alt+Shift+<) to turn it counterclockwise or Option-Shift-> (Alt+Shift+>) to turn it clockwise.

- **Show Overlay.** With this checkbox turned on (it's on automatically), you see a preview of what you're about to paint *inside your brush cursor*. This handy feature shows you exactly what the cloning will look like before you commit to it.

- **Opacity.** Use this field to adjust the opacity of the overlay preview. (To change the opacity of what you're *cloning*—in other words, your actual brushstrokes— change the Opacity setting in the Options bar instead.)

- **Clipped.** This checkbox restricts the preview overlay to the area inside your brush cursor. For Thor's sake, leave this setting turned on. If you don't, Photoshop previews the *entire* clone source image right underneath your cursor, which keeps you from seeing anything *except* the preview.

- **Auto Hide.** If you turn on this checkbox, the overlay preview disappears as soon as you click to start painting. It's a good idea to turn it on so you can see how much you've painted so far.

- **Invert.** Turning on this checkbox makes Photoshop invert the overlay preview so it looks like a film negative, which can be helpful if you're trying to align the cloned area with something that's already in your image.

- **Blend Mode.** Use this pop-up menu to change the blend mode of the overlay preview. Your choices—Normal, Darken, Lighten, and Difference—are explained earlier in this chapter, starting on page 280. (To change the blend mode of the *cloned pixels*, use the Options bar's Mode pop-up menu instead.)

◼ Combining Vectors and Rasters

A fun trend in the design world is to combine vectors with rasters (page 52 explains the difference); in other words, to combine illustrations with photographs, a technique that provides an interesting look and lets you get creative. Because you can load vectors as Smart Objects (page 126), they remain infinitely resizable, letting you experiment with them as backgrounds, artful embellishments, and even ornamental photo frames. As you can see in Figure 7-25, adding vectors to photos is a ton of fun.

FIGURE 7-25

A dash of vector art can spice up any photo. It's as if you're blending real images with imaginary ones.

Even if you can't draw these little goodies yourself, stock-image companies like iStock-photo (www.istockphoto. com) sell affordable vector images so you can still join in the fun. In fact, if you visit www. lesa.in/istockdeal, you can download 10 images for free!

You can add vector art to your images in a couple of ways:

- **Place it.** With a document open, choose File→Place and navigate to the vector file on your hard drive (these files are usually in EPS [Encapsulated PostScript] or AI [Adobe Illustrator] format). This inserts the file as a Smart Object (page 126). Since you'll most likely need to resize the artwork, Photoshop considerately surrounds it with the Free Transform bounding box and resizing handles. Just Shift-drag any corner to make the art bigger or smaller. If you need to rotate it, place your cursor outside the bounding box and then drag in the direction you want to rotate. Press Return (Enter on a PC) when you're finished.

- **Paste it.** If you're working in a vector-based program like Adobe Illustrator, you can copy artwork and then paste it into a Photoshop document by choosing Edit→Paste or pressing ⌘-V (Ctrl+V on a PC). When you do, Photoshop displays the dialog box shown in Figure 7-26 (left), asking *how* you want to paste it. If you choose Smart Object, you can resize the illustration as much as you want without losing quality.

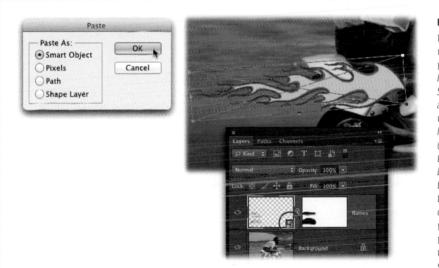

FIGURE 7-26

When you paste a piece of vector art, Photoshop lets you decide how to paste it (left). If you choose Smart Object, the object appears in your document with helpful resizing handles, as shown here (right). It also carries the special Smart Object badge (circled) over in the Layers panel. And if the illustration includes other bits and pieces that you don't want to use, you can simply hide 'em with a layer mask, as shown here.

Framing a photo with an illustration is not only fun, it's also incredibly flexible because you can continually resize the frame without starting over. Here's how:

1. **Open the photo you want to frame and, if necessary, double-click the Background layer to make it editable and give it another name (if you like).**

   If your Background layer isn't locked, or if you've already worked with the photo and renamed this layer, you can skip this step.

2. **Choose File→Place to import the illustration you want to use as the frame.**

Activating the photo layer first ensures that Photoshop puts the Smart Object layer at the top of your layer stack. Navigate to the file on your hard drive and then click the Place button.

3. **Resize the illustration.**

Conveniently, the illustration appears in your document with resizing handles around it, which you'll probably need to use to make it bigger or smaller. Grab a corner handle and drag until the frame is big enough to hold the photo. (To resize all four sides of the illustration at once, press and hold Shift-Option [Shift+Alt] as you drag a corner handle.) Drag inside the bounding box to move it around. When it's just right, press Return (Enter).

4. **Over in the Layers panel, drag the illustration layer below the image layer.**

The maneuver you're performing won't work if the illustration layer is *above* the photo layer.

5. **Clip the photo layer to the illustration layer.**

With the photo layer active, choose Layer→Create Clipping Mask, or press and hold Option (Alt on a PC) while pointing your cursor at the dividing line between the two layers in the Layers panel (when the cursor turns into a square with a down-pointing arrow, click once). Either way, the thumbnail of the photo layer scoots to the right, and a tiny downward-pointing arrow appears to let you know that it's clipped (masked) to the illustration layer directly below it, as shown in Figure 7-27. You should now see the photo peeking through the illustration.

6. **Use the Move tool to position the photo and frame.**

Press V to grab the Move tool and reposition the photo and/or frame layer as necessary.

7. **Add a Fill layer to create a colorful background for your new frame.**

Choose Layer→New Fill Layer→Solid Color, or click the half-black/half-white circle at the bottom of the Layers panel and choose Solid Color from the resulting pop-up menu. Once the Color Picker opens, mouse over to your image and click to grab a color from it (such as the copper color of the mermaid's hair in Figure 7-27). Then click OK to close the Color Picker.

8. **Save your document as a PSD file.**

You're done! To resize the illustration, activate the Smart Object layer and summon Free Transform by pressing ⌘-T (Ctrl+T) and use one of the corner handles to resize the illustration; press Return (Enter) when you're finished. And to give the frame a little depth, you can tack on a drop shadow using layer styles (page 132).

FIGURE 7-27

This detailed illustration makes a gorgeous photo frame. After you place it as a Smart Object and resize it, just clip it to a photo layer (bottom), add a new background color, and you're done!

Mapping One Image onto Another

You can combine two images in an impressive way by wrapping one around the contours of another so the first image follows every nook and cranny of the second. To perform this feat, you need to create a *displacement map*—a grayscale image that Photoshop uses to warp and bend one image to the curvature of another. Applying this technique to photos of friends and family is great fun. For example, you can take a circuit board and wrap it around a body or a face, as shown in Figure 7-28. Here's what you do:

1. **Open the image you want to map another image onto (like a face) and then hunt down the channel with the greatest contrast.**

To make the best possible displacement map, you need the channel with the highest contrast. If you're in RGB mode (and you probably are), you can cycle through the channels by pressing ⌘-3, 4, and 5 (Ctrl+3, 4, and 5 on a PC). Because digital cameras have so many more green sensors than red or blue ones, you'll most likely pick the green channel.

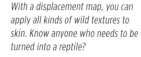

FIGURE 7-28

With a displacement map, you can apply all kinds of wild textures to skin. Know anyone who needs to be turned into a reptile?

NOTE Want to follow along with this tutorial? Visit this book's Missing CD page at *www.missingmanuals. com/cds* and download the practice file *Map.zip*.

2. **Duplicate the high-contrast channel and send it to a new document.**

   Open your Channels panel (page 191) by clicking its icon in the panel dock or choosing Window→Channels. Then, from the Channels panel's menu, choose Duplicate Channel. In the resulting dialog box, choose New from the Destination pop-up menu and name the channel something memorable like *Map*. When you click OK, Photoshop opens a displacement map document that contains the grayscale channel you picked in step 1.

NOTE If the highest-contrast channel in your image isn't very contrasty, the results of this technique will be too subtle to notice. The fix is to *exaggerate* the contrast of the channel in your Map document with a Levels or Curves *adjustment* (not an Adjustment layer). To apply a Levels adjustment to the image layer, press ⌘-L (Ctrl+L); for a Curves adjustment, press ⌘-M (Ctrl+M). For more on those adjustments, skip ahead to Chapter 9.

---

3. **Blur the displacement map slightly.**

   With the map document active, choose Filter→Blur→Gaussian Blur. Enter a value of 1–4 pixels (for low-resolution images, enter 1; for high-resolution ones, enter 4) and then click OK. The goal here is to blur the image just a bit so the map is slightly smooth (page 434 has more on the Gaussian Blur filter).

4. **Save the map and close the file.**

   Choose File→Save As and choose Photoshop from the Format pop-up menu at the bottom of the dialog box. Make sure the Alpha Channel option is turned on and then click Save. Close the file by pressing ⌘-W (Ctrl+W).

5. **Go back to the original document and turn the composite channel back on.**

   When you cycled through the different channels in step 1, Photoshop temporarily turned off the composite channel (the one that shows your image in full color). Go back to the original document (the one you opened in step 1) and turn all the channels back on by pressing ⌘-2 (Ctrl+2 on a PC).

6. **Select the face.**

   In the bottom image in Figure 7-28, it's easy to select the face because it's on a solid background. Grab the Magic Wand by pressing W, click once in the white area, and then Shift-click to select the other white parts until you have everything *except* the face selected. Then, if necessary, invert your selection by pressing Shift-⌘-I (Shift+Ctrl+I on a PC) or choosing Select→Inverse; Photoshop flip-flops your selection so the face is surrounded by marching ants.

7. **Feather the edges of your selection slightly.**

   Click the Options bar's Refine Edge button and feather the selection by 1 pixel. (See page 145 for more on feathering.)

To drive that point home, open a colorful image—or download *Dragon.jpg* from this book's Missing CD page at *www.missingmanuals.com/cds* if you want to follow along—and then choose Image→Adjustments→Desaturate. (*Desaturating* means draining all color from an image.) Photoshop converts your image to black and white all right, but the results are less than inspiring (see Figure 8-1, top). You can also glance through your channels (page 191), pick the one with the highest contrast, and then choose Image→Mode→Grayscale. Photoshop keeps the currently active channel, tosses the rest, and you're left with a black-and-white image. But unless you're using an old, pre-CS version of Photoshop, neither method is much good. As you're about to find out, the program has come a long way when it comes to black-and-white conversions.

FIGURE 8-1

Top: The Desaturate command lets you convert photos to black and white in one step, but as you can see, this method produces a fairly lame dragon.

Bottom: A Black & White Adjustment layer lets you introduce all kinds of contrast, making it a much better option for black-and-white conversions (and for producing a respectably menacing creature).

> **NOTE** To learn how to use Color Mixer Adjustment layers to drain color from an image, head to this book's Missing CD page at *www.missingmanuals.com/cds*.

Black & White Adjustment Layers

Adding a Black & White Adjustment layer is hands down the easiest way to convert a color image to a beautiful black and white in no time flat. The process couldn't be simpler, and, best of all, it's nondestructive. As Chapter 3 explains, when you use

Adjustment layers, Photoshop makes the changes on *another* layer—not on your original image—letting you tweak the opacity, toggle the visibility on or off, and so on. (You'll learn about other kinds of Adjustment layers throughout this book.)

To create a black-and-white image, follow these steps:

1. **Pop open your soon-to-be-colorless image.**

   Since you're using an Adjustment layer, you don't need to bother double-clicking the Background layer to make it editable because you won't be messing with the original image.

> **NOTE** To follow along, head to this book's Missing CD page at *www.missingmanuals.com/cds* and download the practice file *Dragon.jpg*.

2. **Create a Black & White Adjustment layer.**

   Choose Layer→New Adjustment Layer→Black & White; in the resulting New Layer dialog box, give the layer a name, if you'd like, and then click OK. Photoshop turns your image black and white, and opens the Properties panel, which contains several sliders you can use to fine-tune the image's contrast (Figure 8-2).

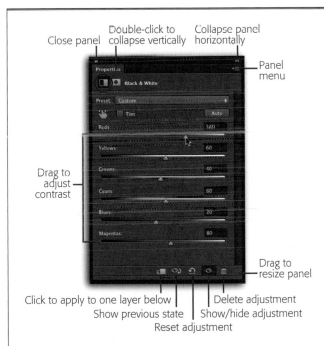

FIGURE 8-2

The Properties panel gives you access to the settings for the particular adjustment you picked—in this case, Black & White—and its presets (one-click, canned settings). If you click the Auto button, Photoshop shows you how it thinks the black-and-white image should look, though you can use the panel's sliders to show Photoshop what you think it should look like!

If your document contains several layers and you want the adjustment to affect only the layer directly below it—rather than all the layers underneath it—click the Clip To Layer button at the panel's bottom left, labeled here. (The Tint checkbox is explained in the next section.)

TIP You can also create a Black & White Adjustment layer by clicking the Black & White icon in the Adjustments panel (choose Window→Adjustments if the panel isn't visible)—it's the same half-black/half-white square that's circled in Figure 8-2. Or you can click the half-black/half-white circle icon at the bottom of the Layers panel and then choose Black & White from the menu that appears. Whew!

3. **Move the Properties panel's various sliders to adjust the contrast of your newly black-and-white image.**

   Even though Photoshop has drained the color from your image, there's always room for improvement. Drag a particular color's slider to the left to turn those areas a darker shade of gray, or to the right to make them lighter gray. The colored bars under each slider give you a clue as to what dragging in each direction does to your image (Figure 8-2). Or, instead of adjusting a bunch of sliders, you can tweak a certain range of colors by dragging on the image itself, as Figure 8-3 shows. Also, the Preset menu at the top of the panel has a slew of useful canned settings—just click each one to see what it looks like applied to your image (in Windows, you can use your keyboard's up and down arrow keys to cycle through the presets).

FIGURE 8-3

To adjust your image visually, click the On-Image Adjustment button circled here (right) and then mouse over to the image; your cursor temporarily turns into an eyedropper (not shown) to let you know you're about to sample a color. Position the cursor atop the area you want to adjust, click and hold your mouse button, and then drag to the left to make that area darker or to the right to make it lighter. The cursor turns into a pointing hand with an arrow on each side (circled, left) to indicate that you can drag from side to side to adjust that range of color. With this method, you skip the "Which slider do I drag?" guessing game.

4. **Save your document as a PSD file so your layers remain intact.**

To change the Black & White Adjustment layer's settings later, just double-click its thumbnail in the Layers panel (it's that familiar half-black/half-white square icon) to reopen the Properties panel. Or, if the Properties panel is open, just click once to activate the layer and you'll see the sliders reappear. If you print the image and then decide it needs more contrast, being able to edit the existing Adjustment layer is a real timesaver.

■ WARP-SPEED COLOR TINTING

You can give a black-and-white image a uniform color tint by using the Tint checkbox lurking near the top of the Properties panel (available only with a Black & White Adjustment layer). When you turn on this checkbox, Photoshop adds a brown tint (called a *sepia tone*) to your whole image, as shown in Figure 8-4 (top). This technique produces what's known as a *fake duotone* (the real ones are explained on page 327).

FIGURE 8-4

Top: After you add a Black & White Adjustment layer to an image, you can give it a sleek color overlay by turning on the Tint checkbox (circled). As you can see, adding a tint dramatically changes the image's mood. But are you stuck with brown, you ask? Heck no. To choose a different color, just click the colored square to the right of the Tint checkbox to summon the Color Picker.

Bottom: Once the Color Picker opens, you can choose a range of color by clicking within the vertical, rainbow-colored bar (circled, right). Let Photoshop know how light or how dark you want the new color to be by clicking inside the large colored area (circled, left). Click OK to close the Color Picker and the new overlay color appears in the Properties panel and atop your image. Pretty slick, huh?

FIGURE 8-11

By adding a layer of solid color, you can create another popular look. Feel free to experiment with other background colors, too!

6. **Create a new layer for the red background.**

   Click the half-black/half-white circle at the bottom of the Layers panel and then choose Solid Color. Photoshop opens the Color Picker, where you can pick a nice, bright red. Click OK to close the Color Picker, and Photoshop adds the new layer to the top of your layer stack. (If the new layer appears somewhere else in your Layers panel, just drag it to the top.)

   > **TIP** To change the color of the Fill layer later on, just double-click the Solid Color layer's thumbnail to summon the Color Picker.

7. **Change the red layer's blend mode to Darken.**

   With the red layer active, use the pop-up menu near the top of the Layers panel to change its blend mode to Darken. As you learned on page 280, blend modes in the darken category tell Photoshop to look at the colors on the active layer and the colors on the layers below and keep the darkest ones. In this case, those colors are black and red, so you end up with the black face on a red background. Pretty neat, huh?

8. **Save your document as a PSD file and rejoice at your creativity.**

The High-Key Effect

Another nifty black-and-white effect is known as *high key*. In the real world, you can create this effect by aiming *tons* of lights at your subject (or, in this case, victim) and shooting a picture. This gives you a high-contrast image—though not quite as high-contrast as the technique explained in the previous section—where the shadows are shades of gray and everything else is almost pure white. Fortunately, you can create this same look in Photoshop without spending a ton on light bulbs. Mosey back to page 198 in Chapter 5 for the scoop.

Delicious Duotones

There are a couple of reasons you may be interested in learning to create duotones: to save on professional printing costs and to create some *seriously* high-end looking black-and-white prints, like the ones in Figure 8-12. (Most black-and-white images displayed in galleries actually contain a bit of color!) To understand what's going on, you first need a quick primer on duotones—they're covered in more detail in Chapter 16—and a *brief* excursion back into some of the color mode nitty-gritty you learned in Chapter 5.

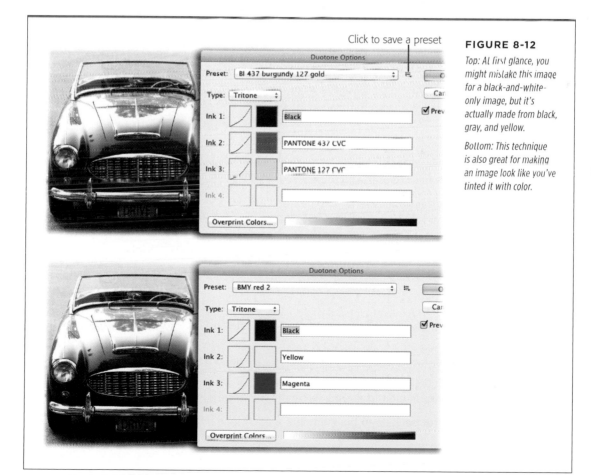

FIGURE 8-12

Top: At first glance, you might mistake this image for a black-and-white-only image, but it's actually made from black, gray, and yellow.

Bottom: This technique is also great for making an image look like you've tinted it with color.

Duotone refers to an image that's made from two colors (black is usually one of them). Photoshop's Duotone mode lets you add special colors to genuine grayscale images. (See the box on page 319 to learn what qualifies as *true* grayscale.) If you add one color to a grayscale image, you get a duotone. If you add another color, you get a *tritone* (grayscale plus two colors), and if you add one more you get a *quadtone* (grayscale plus three colors). For the purposes of this discussion and as far as Photoshop is concerned, the term "duotone" includes tritones and quadtones, too (as confusing as that may sound).

As you learned in Chapter 5, printing presses generally use CMYK ink that prints on four separate plates, which correspond to the four channels in CMYK mode. A duotone or tritone has fewer channels, so it prints on fewer plates—grayscale plus one or two special inks (for duotone and tritone, respectively)—and *that* reduces your printing costs. So if your document is headed for a printing press, making a duotone is an affordable way to produce a striking, one-of-a-kind image. (See page 702 for the scoop on preparing duotone images for print.)

Another reason to love duotones is that, because they're used so much in professional printing, Adobe has spent beaucoup bucks concocting color combinations that produce some of the most amazing images you've ever seen—and you can access them only in Duotone mode. In fact, most (if not all) award-winning black-and-white photos hanging in galleries aren't black and white at all—they're duo-, tri-, and quadtones with subtle color tints that give them extra depth and richness (see Figure 8-12).

Even if your image *isn't* headed for a professional printer, you'll want to get your paws on Photoshop's built-in color combos. You can get at them by popping into—and then back out of—Duotone mode. Here's how:

1. **Convert your image to black and white using one of the methods described in this chapter, and then save it as a PSD file.**

   It doesn't matter which method you use; just don't let Photoshop do the conversion for you because you'll end up with a drab grayscale image like the one you saw back on page 312.

NOTE To practice this technique at home, download *Car.jpg* from this book's Missing CD page at *www.missingmanuals.com/cds*.

---

2. **Change the image's mode to Grayscale and let Photoshop flatten the file.**

   Choose Image→Mode→Grayscale and, when Photoshop asks if you want to flatten or preserve your layers (if you've got more than one), take a deep breath and click Flatten. Then, when it asks if you want to discard the image's color information, steel yourself and click Discard.

3. **Trot back up to the menu bar and choose Image→Mode→Duotone.**

   You have to be in Duotone mode to pick one of those built-in color combos.

4. **At the top of the resulting Duotone Options dialog box, choose the color combination you want.**

Photoshop has *hundreds* of duo-, tri-, and quadtones in the Preset menu. (You could spend a whole evening looking through all the options.) When you choose one of these settings, Photoshop flips the dialog box's Type pop-up menu to the appropriate option.

If you'd rather have a go at mixing colors yourself, choose Duotone, Tritone, or Quadtone from the Type menu and then click the little color squares below the menu to pick your inks (remember, Duotone mode thinks you're sending your file to a professional printing press that uses ink). If you want to save the combination you create, click the button to the right of the Preset menu (labeled in Figure 8-12, top) and give your combo a name to make Photoshop add it to the Preset menu. Click OK when you're finished to close the Duotone Options dialog box. (Page 702 has more on creating custom duotone combos and the printing concerns that go along with them.)

5. **Go back to the color mode from whence you came by choosing Image→ Mode→RGB.**

Because Duotone mode is a special mode meant for printing (not editing), you don't want to hang around there. When you go back to RGB mode, you won't notice anything different—except the awesome new color of your image.

That's it! You've just snatched your first color combo from Duotone mode. It's like bank-robbing for Photoshop jockeys.

Changing Color

Photoshop is the ultimate recolorizing tool because it gives you the power to put a fresh coat of paint on *anything*. You can repaint your car, change the color of your cabinets, and even recolor your hair. You can also create cartoonish pop art (page 345) or reverse the color in your image (page 342). The next few pages describe how to do all that and more.

Hue/Saturation Adjustment Layers

If you're experimenting with color, start by creating a Hue/Saturation Adjustment layer, which offers a friendly set of sliders that let you change either the overall color of an image or a specific range of colors (see page 333). Because you're working with an Adjustment layer, any color changes take place on a separate layer, leaving the original unharmed. And since a layer mask automatically tags along with the Adjustment layer, you can use it to hide the color change from certain parts of the image.

If you select an object or specific area of the image before creating a Hue/Saturation Adjustment layer, you can change the color in just that one spot. Here's how:

1. **Open an image and create a selection using one of the techniques discussed in Chapter 4.**

   For example, if you want to change the color of a car, you could use the Quick Selection tool to select the car. Once it's surrounded by marching ants, you're ready for the next step.

   > **NOTE** To practice the following technique, download *Corvette.jpg* from this book's Missing CD page at *www.missingmanuals.com/cds*.

2. **Create a Hue/Saturation Adjustment layer.**

   To do so, choose Layer→New Adjustment Layer→Hue/Saturation. You can also open the Adjustments panel and click the Hue/Saturation icon (which looks like three vertical stripes above a gradient), or click the half-black/half-white circle at the bottom of the Layers panel and then choose Hue/Saturation. Photoshop opens the Properties panel containing the three sliders shown in Figure 8-13, bottom. (In the Layers panel, notice how Photoshop filled in the Adjustment layer mask based on the area you selected. If you don't make a selection before creating the Adjustment layer, the mask stays empty—meaning the color change affects the whole image.)

3. **To change the color of the selected area, drag the Hue slider to the left or right.**

   Hue is really a graphic geek's way of saying "color" (though technically it refers to pure color, before it has been tinted with white or shaded with black). As you drag the slider, the selected area's color changes. If you watch closely, you'll see one of the rainbow-colored bars near the bottom of the Adjustments panel change, too. The top rainbow bar shows the color in your original image, and the bottom one shows what you're changing that color *to*. (In Figure 8-13, you can see the turquoise of the original Corvette at the far left of the top bar and the purple it's been changed to at the far right of the bar below it.) It's helpful to think of these rainbow-colored bars as flattened-out color wheels; flip ahead to page 485 in Chapter 12 to see a real live color wheel.

   > **NOTE** This color-changing trick works only on colored areas; anything that's black, white, or gray remains completely unchanged.

4. **To adjust the color's intensity, drag the Saturation slider.**

   To decrease the intensity, drag this slider to the left (if you drag it all the way to the left, you'll completely desaturate the image, making it grayscale). To increase the intensity, drag it to the right (if you drag it too far, your colors will become so vivid you'll need sunglasses, and skin tones will become an otherworldly hot pink). To get an idea of what this adjustment does, look closely at the color slider beneath the word "Saturation" in Figure 8-13, bottom, which ranges from gray on the left to a vivid red on the right.

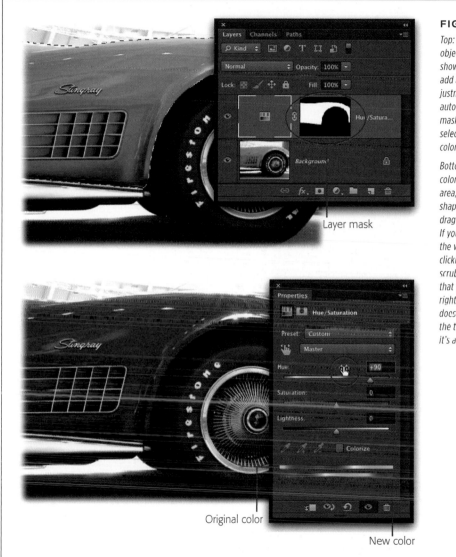

Layer mask

Original color

New color

FIGURE 8-13

Top: If you select an object (like the car body shown here) before you add a Hue/Saturation Adjustment layer, Photoshop automatically fills the mask (circled) with your selection, limiting the color change to that area.

Bottom: To change the colors of the selected area, grab the triangle-shaped Hue slider and drag it in either direction. If you point your cursor at the word "Hue" (without clicking), it turns into a scrubby cursor (circled) that you can drag left or right. The scrubby cursor does the same thing as the triangular sliders, but it's a bit easier to control.

5. **To adjust the color's brightness, drag the Lightness slider.**

   Lightness is what civilians call "brightness"; think of it as the amount of light shining on the selected object. Drag this slider to the left to darken the color or to the right to lighten it.

6. **Save the image as a PSD file.**

If you save the document as a PSD file, you can go back and edit your color changes anytime by double-clicking the Hue/Saturation Adjustment layer's thumbnail in the Layers panel. This is extremely handy if you're recoloring an object for a nitpicky client (even if that client is you!).

There are a few other settings lurking in the Properties panel for Hue/Saturation Adjustment layers that are worth mentioning:

- **Targeted Adjustment tool.** This tool lets you pick a range of colors to adjust and then change the saturation of those colors by clicking directly on the image instead of using the sliders. In the upper left of the Properties panel, give the tool a click—it looks like a pointing hand with a double-headed arrow—and then mouse over to your image (your cursor turns into an eyedropper). Click the color that you want to change, and Photoshop activates the appropriate color channel in the Properties panel's Edit pop-up menu (described later in this list). Then drag left to decrease the saturation (make the color less intense), or right to increase the saturation (make the color more vivid).

> **NOTE** Technically, the Targeted Adjustment tool doesn't have a name. Adobe *used* to call it the Targeted Adjustment tool, but it revoked that moniker in CS6. Since this book has to call the tool *something* (and "the No Name tool" isn't a good option), you'll see the old name in these pages.

- **Preset menu.** This pop-up menu lets you choose from a few canned settings. Once you start tweaking the sliders, this menu changes to the Custom setting, as shown in Figure 8-13, bottom.

- **Edit pop-up menu.** This menu, which doesn't have a label, lets you pick the color channels you want to adjust. When you first use Photoshop, this menu is set to Master, which means you're changing the composite channel and affecting all the colors in your image. If you want to target a specific channel, pick it from this menu, and then any changes you make affect *only* the colors in that channel. For example, say you've got an image with too much red in it (a common problem in people photos). You can choose the red channel from this menu and then drag the Saturation slider to the left to desaturate the reds without affecting the other colors (a great way to zap color casts that you can't get rid of any other way!). If you don't know which channel to pick, use the Targeted Adjustment tool described earlier in this list to click a color in your image and make Photoshop pick the channel *for* you. Once you've selected the color, you can drag the sliders like you normally would.

- **Eyedroppers.** The eyedroppers near the bottom of the panel also let you pick the colors in your image that you want to change. You'll see these guys in action in the next section.

- **Colorize checkbox.** This setting lets you use the Hue slider to add color to an image that doesn't have any, like a black-and-white photo. If you're working with an image that *does* have color, turning on this checkbox will add a color tint much like the kind you can make with a Black & White Adjustment layer (page 312).

■ TARGETING A SPECIFIC RANGE OF COLORS

When you add a Hue/Saturation Adjustment layer, Photoshop assumes you want to change *all* the colors in your image, which is why the Edit pop-up menu just mentioned is set to Master. But if you want Photoshop to change just the reds, yellows, greens, or whatever, then choose the appropriate option from the Edit pop-up menu first. To narrow your focus even *more*, you can use the Targeted Adjustment tool along with the eyedroppers near the bottom of the Properties panel to adjust very specific *ranges* of color.

Let's say you're thinking about repainting your scooter. If the scooter's current paint job isn't super dark to begin with, you can take a photo of it and then do your experimenting in Photoshop rather than at the body shop. Just follow these steps:

1. **Open the image and leave the Background layer locked.**

   If you're experimenting on an image that you've worked with before, this layer may be named something besides Background. If the image is comprised of many layers, activate 'em all and then, in the Layers panel's menu, choose "Convert to Smart Object."

   NOTE If you want to follow along, download *Scooter.jpg* from this book's Missing CD page at *www.missingmanuals.com/cds*.

2. **Add a Hue/Saturation Adjustment layer as described in step 2 of the previous section.**

3. **Use the Targeted Adjustment tool to choose the range of colors you want to change.**

   In the upper left of the Properties panel, click the Targeted Adjustment tool (the hand with the two arrows poking out of it), mouse over to your image, and then click the color you want to change (the red scooter, for example). Photoshop then picks the predominant color channel in the Edit pop-up menu (in Figure 8-14, top, this menu is set to Reds).

   TIP If you duplicate the Adjustment layer by pressing ⌘-J (Ctrl+J on a PC), you can experiment with all kinds of scooter colors before you head to the body shop!

4. **Edit the range of colors you want to adjust using the eyedroppers near the bottom of the Properties panel.**

   Once you click a color in the previous step, Photoshop marks that color range with a small gray bar that appears between the two rainbow-colored bars at the bottom of the Properties panel (circled in red in Figure 8-14, top). To edit that range, use the + and – eyedroppers near the bottom of the panel to add or subtract colors from the targeted range. For example, to expand the range to catch all the scooter's colors, grab the eyedropper with a + sign, mouse over to your image, and then click another part of the scooter (you'll see the gray bar get a little wider). To narrow the range of colors, use the eyedropper with a – sign to subtract the colors you don't want to change.

As usual, Photoshop gives you several ways to do the same thing. You can also edit the color range by dragging the tiny sliders on the gray bar, which, you may have noticed—if your eyesight is really good!—is two different shades of gray. The dark gray part in the middle represents the hues that will change completely when you make a change (to see those hues, just look at the rainbow-colored bars directly above and below the gray one), and the lighter gray parts on either end of the gray bar represent hues that will *partially* change. To narrow the range of colors, drag the little half triangles on the ends inward toward the middle of the gray bar; to widen the range, drag them outward.

> **TIP** If the gray bar representing your targeted color range (technically called the *range indicator*) gets split across the left and right ends of the rainbow bars, press ⌘ (Ctrl on a PC) and drag the pieces to the left or right until it becomes solid again.

5. **Recolor the scooter by tweaking the Hue, Saturation, and Lightness sliders as discussed in the previous section.**

    Photoshop reflects your changes in real time, so you can watch as the scooter changes from green to blue to magenta. Good times!

6. **If necessary, use the Adjustment layer's mask to hide the color change from other parts of your image.**

    When you start moving the Properties panel's sliders, you may notice that your scooter isn't the *only* thing that changes color. If any part of the image is similar in color to the area you're changing, it may change, too; you can also try using the + and – eyedroppers as mentioned earlier, but they may not work if the colors are too similar. In that case, use the Adjustment layer's mask to keep the rest of the image from getting a makeover. Just activate the mask thumbnail in the Layers panel, press B to grab the Brush tool, and set your foreground color chip to black (press X if you need to flip-flop color chips). Then mouse over to your image and paint the parts that you *don't* want to change. If you hide too much, flip-flop your color chips by pressing X and paint that area white.

> **NOTE** To go back and edit the Hue/Saturation Adjustment layer later—assuming you've saved the image as a PSD file—you have to remember to change the Properties panel's Edit pop-up menu first. While Photoshop remembers all the changes you made with the sliders, it can't remember which color channel you used, so it resets the menu to Master each time you double-click the Hue/Saturation Adjustment layer's thumbnail in the Layers panel. Bummer!

FIGURE 8-14

Top: Instead of changing all the colors in your image, you can use the Targeted Adjustment and eyedropper tools to target a certain color range instead. When you click the Targeted Adjustment tool (circled in white), the Edit pop-up menu near the top of the Properties panel changes to reflect the predominant color channel for the part of the image you clicked (in this case, Red), and the color range is indicated by the small gray bar near the bottom of the panel (circled in red).

Bottom: If other parts of your image start changing color as you adjust the panel's sliders—such as this girl's face and skin—just grab the eyedropper with a minus sign and click those areas to make Photoshop leave 'em alone, as shown here. (You can also start over anytime by clicking the Properties panel's Reset button, labeled here.)

Or, instead of moving the sliders, you can use the Targeted Adjustment tool. Once you've activated the tool, click the color in your image that you want to change, keep holding down your mouse button, and then drag left to make that color less intense (desaturate), or drag right to make it more intense (saturate). To change the hue, ⌘-drag (Ctrl-drag on a PC) left or right to move the Hue slider left or right, respectively.

Reset adjustment

You can also use this technique to experiment with hair color before heading to the salon. However, if your subject's skin color is similar to her hair color, you're better off selecting her hair *before* adding the Hue/Saturation Adjustment layer. Happily, the Refine Edge dialog box makes selecting those wily wisps of hair easier than ever. Page 171 has the scoop.

Hue Blend Mode

Another easy way to repaint an object is to put the paint on a separate layer and then change the paint layer's blend mode to Hue. (As you learned in Chapter 7, blend modes control how color on one layer interacts with color on another; page 292 explains how the Hue blend mode works.)

To give this method a spin, open an image and then create a new layer by pressing Shift-⌘-N (Shift+Ctrl+N on a PC). In the resulting New Layer dialog box, type *paint* into the Name field, change the Mode pop-up menu to Hue (it's near the bottom of the list), and then click OK. Next, press B to grab the Brush tool, click your foreground color chip, and then pick a color from the resulting Color Picker and click OK. Then, with the new layer active, start painting over the object as shown in Figure 8-15.

> **NOTE** To try this technique yourself, download *Superbike.jpg* from this book's Missing CD page at *www.missingmanuals.com/cds*.

FIGURE 8-15

The goal here is to repaint this red motorcycle blue. If the area you want to repaint has a lot of black, white, and gray around it (like this bike), you can paint right over those areas and they won't change a bit (note the brush cursor circled here). That's because, in Hue blend mode, the new paint affects only areas that previously contained color.

If you end up changing too much color, temporarily switch to the Eraser tool by pressing and holding the E key (the tool's keyboard shortcut). Or you can prevent the problem by adding a layer mask (page 116) to the paint layer and then hiding the areas you want to leave unchanged by painting them black.

Replacing Color

Remember the Color Range command you learned about in Chapter 4 (page 157)? You can use a similar command—Replace Color—to select one color and swap in another. This command works really well if the color you want to replace is fairly consistent and concentrated in one area, like the car in Figure 8-16. It's also a little easier to choose a paint color from the friendly Color Picker than to mix the color yourself using a bunch of sliders.

Choose Image→Adjustments→Replace Color to summon the Replace Color dialog box shown in Figure 8-16. The Eyedropper tool is already active, so just click in your image to tell Photoshop what color you want to change (you may need to move the dialog box to get a good view of your image), and then that color appears in the Color square in the upper right of the dialog box. In the lower half of the dialog box, click the color square above the word "Result" to choose a new color from the Color Picker. When you click OK, the new color appears in the square. To make further adjustments to the color, you can use the dialog box's Hue, Saturation, and Lightness sliders.

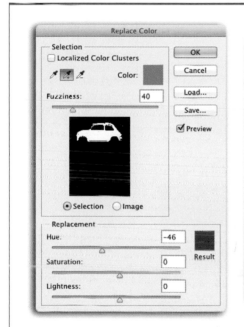

FIGURE 8-16

You can use the eyedropper tools to add to or subtract from the range of colors you want to change (and it's helpful to zoom into your image while doing so by pressing ⌘-+ [Ctrl+plus] repeatedly). Since the Replace Color command isn't available as an Adjustment layer, it affects your original image, so it's a darn good idea to duplicate the image layer before you use this command.

Selective Color Adjustment Layers

Selective Color Adjustment layers are gloriously useful because they let you make a single color in your image brighter or darker—helpful when you need to make whites whiter or blacks blacker. You can also use them to shift one color to another, but that technique can be a bit challenging if you don't know anything about color theory (that is, mixing certain colors together to create other colors).

To add a Selective Color Adjustment layer to an image, choose Layer→New Adjustment Layer→Selective Color. You can also click the Selective Color icon in the Adjustments panel (it looks like a square divided into four triangles), or the half-black/half-white circle at the bottom of the Layers panel, and then choose Selective Color.

Then, from the Colors pop-up menu at the top of the Properties panel, choose the color closest to the one you want to change. For example, to change the color of the bike and the matching leathers shown in Figure 8-17, choose Reds. Next, use the Cyan, Magenta, Yellow, and Black color sliders to change that color to something else. (Don't let it throw you that these sliders represent the CMYK color mode—they work just fine on RGB images.)

FIGURE 8-17

With a well-placed Selective Color Adjustment layer, you can change the red bike and matching leathers to hot pink in seconds. Just point to one of the sliders in the Properties panel until your pointer turns into a handy scrubby cursor like the one shown here (top), and then drag left or right.

The direction you drag each slider determines exactly how the color you've chosen in the Colors menu changes. By dragging a slider to the left, you decrease the percentage of that color. For example, if you choose Reds from the pop-up menu and then drag the yellow slider all the way to the left, you drain all the yellow out of the reds, making them look hot pink (as shown in Figure 8-17). If you drag a slider to the right, you increase the percentage of that color. (How can you know what color you'll end up with after some quality slider-dragging? Through experimentation or by learning to read a color wheel. Flip over to page 485 for a short lesson that'll get you started.)

Matching Colors

The Match Color command makes the colors in one image resemble those in another. It's a *huge* timesaver when you're working with several images in a magazine spread or a book and need to make their colors somewhat consistent (see Figure 8-18). Since this command isn't available as an Adjustment layer, be sure to duplicate your *image layer* first by pressing ⌘-J (Ctrl+J on a PC).

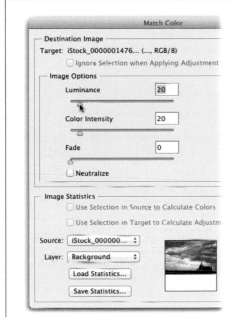

FIGURE 8-18

The Match Color dialog box lets you copy the colors from one image (like the golds in the tiny image on the left here) onto another. The result? The golden-hued bike shown at bottom right. You can use the Luminance (lightness) and Color Intensity (saturation) sliders to make the colors match a little better, and adjust the Fade slider to use more or less of the source document's original color. If your target image has a bit of a color cast, turn on the Neutralize checkbox to make Photoshop try to get rid of it for you.

To get started, open two images in RGB mode: the one whose color you're trying to match (the *source*) and the one whose color you want to change (the *target*). Click within the target document to activate it and then choose Image→Adjustments→Match Color. In the resulting dialog box, Photoshop automatically picks the current document as the target (which is why you activated it first). Next, tell Photoshop the name of the source document by choosing it from the Source pop-up menu in the lower half of the dialog box (you'll see a thumbnail preview of the image at the bottom right).

If the source document has several layers, you can choose the one you want from the Layer pop-up menu or choose Merged to have Photoshop combine those layers into one (handy if you've used several Adjustment layers to create the color you want). If the source document has only one layer, Photoshop chooses it automatically.

To confine your color-matching to specific spots in the source and target images, create selections in each document before you open the Match Color dialog box. If the dialog box detects an active selection, it lets you turn on the "Use Selection in Source to Calculate Colors" and "Use Selection in Target to Calculate Adjustment" checkboxes, both of which can be helpful when you're trying to match colors in two different images—skin tones, for example.

> **TIP** If you've got a source color that you might want to use on other images, save your Match Color settings as a preset: When you get everything just right, click the Save Statistics button at the bottom of the dialog box and then give your preset a name. The next time you want to use those settings, you won't have to open the source image—just open the Match Color dialog box, click the Load Statistics button, and then choose your preset.

Photo Filter Adjustment Layers

Photo Filter Adjustment layers let you gently adjust the colors in an image, as if you'd attached a subtly colored filter to your camera's lens. For example, you can quickly warm an image with golden tones like those in the "after" photo in Figure 8-19 (right). The effect is fairly subtle, making the image look like it's been lightly tinted with a color rather than having its color changed completely.

To get started, click the Photo Filter icon in the Adjustments panel (it looks like a camera with a circle on it). Then, in the Filter pop-up menu that appears in the Properties panel, choose from a list of 20 presets that range from warming and cooling filters to shades of red, violet, and so on. To choose your own color instead, turn on the Color option and click the square color swatch to its right; choose a color from the resulting Color Picker and then click OK. You can use the Properties panel's Density slider to soften or strengthen the effect (just pretend the slider is called "intensity" if "Density" confuses you), and keep the Preserve Luminosity checkbox turned on to prevent Photoshop from lightening or darkening the image.

FIGURE 8-19

A Photo Filter Adjustment layer is really handy when you've combined images whose color doesn't quite match or when you want to add a warming tone to a photo, as shown here.

TIP You can also use a Photo Filter Adjustment layer to reduce a color cast. For example, if your image has a strong blue cast, you can introduce a little orange with a Photo Filter adjustment to neutralize it (orange is opposite blue on the color wheel). If your image has a yellow cast, use purple to even it out. Skip ahead to Chapter 12 to learn more about color wheels (page 485).

Posterizing: Your Ticket to Cartoon Art

You'll use this adjustment once in a blue moon, but if you need to make an image look like a cartoon, a Posterize Adjustment layer is just the thing. Choose Layer→New Adjustment Layer→Posterize, or click the Posterize icon (the one with diagonal stripes) in the Adjustments panel. (You can also click the half-black/half-white circle at the bottom of the Layers panel and then choose Posterize.) When you do, Photoshop analyzes the image's colors and throws out the majority of 'em, leaving you with big ol' blocks of solid color. On some images, posterizing has interesting results, as the examples in Figure 8-20 show. On other images, well, not so much.

FIGURE 8-20

Posterizing doesn't work well on portraits (unless you use a Blur filter to smooth the edges), but on images with relatively solid colors, like those shown at left, the results are pretty neat, as you can see on the right.

Inverting Colors

Graphic designers, this one's for you! If you need to reverse the colors in your image—turning orange to blue, yellow to purple, and so on—you can add an Invert Adjustment layer.

TIP   To find out the reverse (or opposite) of a color, use a color wheel like the one on page 485.

If you're a photographer, you'll use this adjustment even *less* often than Posterize because it turns most images into a negative (which might be useful on Halloween). That said, if you've got an image of a black silhouette that you want to make white, this Adjustment layer can do that in one click (see Figure 8-21). To add an Invert Adjustment layer, choose Layer→New Adjustment Layer→Invert, or open the Adjustments panel and click the half-black/half-white icon with the half-black/half white circle in it. You can also click the half-black/half-white circle at the bottom of the Layers panel and then choose Invert.

FIGURE 8-21

An Invert Adjustment layer turns black into white, blue into orange, and so on. For graphic designers, this is an incredibly useful trick. The images on the left here are the originals. Just for fun, try running various Smart Filters on your image—pick any one of 'em—and then add an Invert Adjustment layer to see what it does.

You can use the included layer mask to hide the adjustment from certain areas of your image to create some pretty wacky—and sometimes wonderfully weird—results!

Adding Color

There will be times when you want to add color that wasn't originally part of an image, and Photoshop gives you lots of ways to do that. The techniques in this section will serve you well whether you're colorizing a black-and-white image or adding color to an empty canvas by hand. Read on!

NOTE In previous versions of Photoshop, you could use a Variations adjustment to add color that wasn't originally part of your image. These days, that adjustment works only in 32-bit mode in Windows. To find out how to use it, visit this book's Missing CD page at *www.missingmanuals.com/cds*.

Colorizing Images

Due to the expense of color film, full-color images didn't become commonplace until the late '60s. So chances are good that you've got some vintage black-and-white photos lying around, just dying to be scanned. Happily, you can use Photoshop to give them a little color (which, by the way, can be a nice side business if you get really good at it). Colorizing a black-and-white (or true grayscale) photo *seems* straightforward—just grab a brush and paint the image. Unfortunately, while that method adds color, it also covers up all the photo's details, as shown in Figure 8-22, left.

FIGURE 8-22

Unless you change the paint layer's blend mode, the paint covers up all the details of this girl's cute dress (left). But once you set the blend mode to Color (right), the details come shining through.

TIP Before you colorize a black-and-white image, choose Image→Mode and make sure the document is set to RGB Color mode. If it's in Grayscale mode, Photoshop won't let you add any color no matter *how* hard you try.

Fortunately, you can use blend modes to add color while keeping an image's details intact. Here's how:

1. **Add a new layer for the paint and change its blend mode to Color.**

Flip back to page 324 and follow steps 1–4 to add a Threshold adjustment to create a high-contrast face. Then, once you've got yourself a Smart Object, follow these steps:

1. **Select all the black areas in the Smart Object you created.**

   Grab the Quick Selection tool (or the Magic Wand), click a black area, and then choose Select→Similar to make Photoshop grab *all* the black bits in the Smart Object (you could select them yourself, but it'd take days).

2. **Jump the selection onto its own layer.**

   To isolate the selected black parts onto their own layer, press ⌘-J (Ctrl+J on a PC). Then double-click the layer's name in the Layers panel and rename it *face*. (Since you're about to add a bazillion layers, it's helpful to give each one a descriptive name.) Then turn the original photo layer's visibility off because you don't need it anymore. Now you're ready to start painting!

3. **Add a new layer below the face layer.**

   ⌘-click (Ctrl-click on a PC) the "Create a new layer" button at the bottom of the Layers panel to create a new layer below the currently active layer (the face layer). Name this new layer *skin*.

4. **Grab the Polygonal Lasso tool and draw a selection around the woman's face and shoulders (see Figure 8-24, top left).**

   Since the Polygonal Lasso tool uses straight lines, it's perfect for creating blocks of color. Just click once where you want the selection to start and then click again each time you need to change angles. Don't worry about being precise; the point is to make it blocky. When you're finished, close your selection by putting your cursor over the starting point. When you see a tiny circle (it looks like a degree symbol) next to the cursor, click once to complete your selection.

5. **Fill your selection with color.**

   Click the foreground color chip at the bottom of the Tools panel, pick a nice peachy color for the woman's skin, and then click OK. Next, fill the selection with color by pressing Option-Delete (Alt+Backspace on a PC) and then get rid of the marching ants by pressing ⌘-D (Ctrl+D) to deselect.

6. **Add another new layer above the skin and the face layers, and name it *lips*.**

   Repeat steps 4 and 5 to give her some hot-pink lipstick. Remember, you want to make the colored areas blocky, so don't be afraid to make your selection go *outside* of her lips.

TIP Instead of changing the color of every single block you make, you can vary color a little by changing the Opacity setting near the top right of the Layers panel (see page 97).

7. **Keep adding new layers and repeating steps 4 and 5 to give her some eye shadow and to add color to the iris of each eye.**

When you're all done, your Layers panel should look something like the one in Figure 8-24, right.

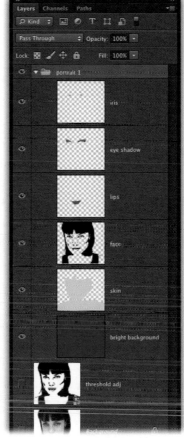

FIGURE 8-24

To make five more versions of this portrait, activate all the layers that make up this version and stuff them into a group by choosing "New Group from Layers" from the Layers panel's menu. This not only helps you keep track of each version, but it also makes creating additional versions easier: Simply duplicate the layer group instead of each individual layer. And because you wisely placed each block of color on its own layer, changing those colors is as simple as loading a layer as a selection by ⌘-clicking (Ctrl-clicking) its thumbnail, and then filling it with a new color. Because your duplicated layers are all sitting on top of one another, you can toggle the visibility of each group off or on while you're changing colors. Once you've created several versions of the portrait, you can enlarge your canvas and then use the Move tool to position the layer groups next to one another to create the artwork shown back in Figure 8-23.

8. **Add a Solid Color Fill layer (page 77), pick a bright color from the resulting Color Picker, and then make this layer your new background.**

   Drag this layer below the skin layer so it becomes the background of the whole piece of art you're building.

Congratulations—you've just finished your first Warhol-style portrait! The really fun thing about this technique is how creative it lets you be (not to mention that you're using almost every skill you've learned in the preceding chapters). Sure, you *could* seek out Warhol's pop-style art online and use the same colors he did, but what fun is that? By using your own vision, you're creating something unique. Also, try experimenting with images of people who have light-colored hair. If the model for this portrait were blonde, you could color her hair, too. The possibilities are endless!

Building a Better Sunrise (or Sunset)

Believe it or not, you can use a Gradient Map Adjustment layer to turn a mediocre sunrise photo into something spectacular. Rather than adding one color to your image like the Tint option in a Black & White Adjustment layer (page 315) or Photo Filter Adjustment layer (page 354), a Gradient Map Adjustment layer lets you add as many colors as you want. Here's how to use one to add a punch of color to a big ol' boring sky:

1. **Add a Gradient Map Adjustment layer and change its blend mode to Color.**

   Option-click (Alt-click on a PC) the half-black/half-white circle at the bottom of the Layers panel and choose Gradient Map. In the resulting dialog box, name the layer *sun* and change the Mode pop-up menu to Color. (That way, the gradient you're about to add will affect only the image's color values and not its lightness values; page 293 has more on this blend mode.) Click OK and Photoshop adds the new layer and opens the Properties panel. Don't worry about what color the gradient is—you'll pick colors in the next step.

2. **In the Properties panel, click to open the gradient preset menu.**

   Click the downward-pointing triangle next to the gradient preview to open the preset menu (labeled in Figure 8-25). In the menu that appears, you can choose a preset gradient (best for newcomers) or make one of your own by performing the next couple of steps (which requires a bit of patience and practice).

   You can load even *more* ready-made gradients by clicking the tiny gear icon at the top right of the preset menu (also labeled in Figure 8-25). In fact, there's a nice orange-to-yellow gradient lurking in the Color Harmonies 2 set that works quite well for this technique. If you go that route, when Photoshop asks if you'd like to replace your current gradients with the new set, click Append. That way, Photoshop adds the new gradients below the factory set. Locate the aforementioned yellow-to-red gradient and click it.

   At this point you're finished, though if you want to build your own gradient, keep on truckin' through the next two steps.

FIGURE 8-25

As you can see, a Gradient Map Adjustment layer set to Color mode took this sky from boring to beautiful by adding a gradual blend of colors. To reverse the gradient's colors—say, to turn a sunset into a sunrise—turn on the Reverse checkbox in the Properties panel (not shown).

If you want to keep any part of your image from being affected, click to activate the Adjustment layer's mask thumbnail, grab the Brush tool, and then paint those areas with black.

Preset menu   Click to load more presets

TIP   For even more fun, load the Photographic Toning gradient set (named for a chemical process used with prints). New in CS6, these presets add an interesting array of sepia and sepia-mixed-with-blue tones to images.

3. **In the Adjustments panel, click the gradient preview to open the Gradient Editor and then tweak the gradient's color stops to create a yellow-to-orange-to-red gradient.**

    In the middle of the Gradient Editor dialog box are little colored squares called *color stops* (Figure 8-26) that you can drag around to control the width of the color fade. When you click a stop, its color appears in the Color field (also called a *color well*) at the bottom of the dialog box. To change the stop's color, click the color well to make Photoshop open the Color Picker so you can choose another color. If you click *between* existing color stops, you'll add a new stop. Once you click a color stop, tiny diamonds appear beneath the gradient that you can drag left and right to determine where one color stops and another one starts.

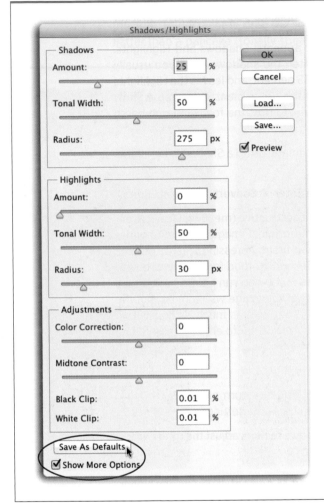

FIGURE 9-5

Turning on Show More Options (circled) gives you a slew of sliders. If your image's shadows are OK but its highlights need darkening, apply the settings shown here in the Shadows section of the dialog box (Amount: 25, Tonal Width: 50, Radius: 275) in the Highlights *section instead. Just be sure to set the Shadows section's Amount slider to 0 percent to turn that section off if you don't need to use it.*

When you're finished, click the Save As Defaults button so you don't have to remember these magic numbers the next time you use this adjustment (though you'll still have to tweak them slightly for each image).

4. **In the Adjustments section at the southern end of the dialog box, adjust the various settings.**

   Here are some guidelines:

   • **Set the Color Correction field to 0.** Doing so keeps Photoshop from shifting the image's colors and introducing funky pinks into skin tones.

   • **Leave the Midtone Contrast setting at 0.** When you use this setting, Photoshop increases the contrast in the image by making dark pixels a little darker and light pixels a little lighter. Since the point of a Shadows/

Highlights adjustment is usually to lighten shadows, increasing this setting would pretty much cancel out what you're trying to accomplish.

NOTE If your image needs more contrast, you can add a Levels or Curves Adjustment layer (as described later in this chapter) and then change its blend mode to Luminosity, which affects only pixel brightness.

- **Leave the Black Clip and White Clip fields set to 0.01 percent.** Leaving these fields alone keeps your light and dark pixels from getting clipped. Clipping is when Photoshop turns a light pixel pure white or a dark pixel pure black, stripping the pixel of all its details. As you might imagine, clipping is more worrisome in highlights than shadows, since highlights usually contain more important details.

5. **Click the Save As Defaults button.**

    Photoshop saves the current settings so you don't have to reset everything the next time you use this adjustment. You'll still have to tweak the settings some because each image is different, but at least you won't have to *memorize* the magic numbers mentioned above.

6. **Click OK to close the Shadows/Highlights dialog box.**

    In the Layers panel, you'll see a new layer called Smart Filters with the Shadows/Highlights adjustment beneath it (Figure 9-6), indicating that Photoshop ran the adjustment as a Smart Filter instead of applying it directly to the Image.

7. **If necessary, hide the adjustment from a portion of your image by painting within the mask that came with the Smart Filter.**

    When you click the Smart Filter mask's thumbnail to activate it, Photoshop puts a tiny white border around it so you can tell it's active. Next, press B to grab the Brush tool, press D to set your color chips to black and white, and then press X until black hops on top. Then mouse over to your image and paint the areas you don't want adjusted. Pretty cool, huh? You can think of this technique as Smart Shadows.

8. **For a quick before-and-after comparison, turn the Shadows/Highlights adjustment's visibility eye off and on.**

As Figure 9-6 shows, this adjustment does a bang-up job of lightening shadows without introducing a funky color cast. To get even *better* results, run the Shadows/Highlights adjustment on the Lightness channel in Lab mode.

Making Colors Pop

To intensify your image's colors, give the next three sliders in Camera Raw's Basic tab a tug:

- **Clarity.** This slider boosts contrast in the midtones, increasing their depth so your image looks clearer. You'd be hard-pressed to find an image that wouldn't benefit from dragging this slider to about +50. In Camera Raw 7, this slider's positive side uses new tone-mapping math, so boosting clarity shouldn't introduce honkin' big *halos* (white areas) around the edges of objects in your image. Yay!

- **Vibrance.** Use this slider to intensify colors without altering skin tones; it has more of an effect on bright colors than on light colors (like some skin tones). If there are people in your image, this is the adjustment to use (see Figure 9-10).

- **Saturation.** Intensifies *all* the colors in an image, including skin tones. So don't use it on people pictures unless you like fluorescent skin.

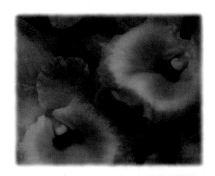

FIGURE 9-10

As you can see here, Camera Raw can greatly improve the color and light in an image. The original, underexposed image is on the top and the end result is on the bottom. That's an impressive result from just dragging a few sliders back and forth!

To reset any slider in Camera Raw back to its original position, simply double-click the slider. To reset the image to its original state, open the Basic panel's menu and choose Camera Raw Defaults.

Camera Raw's Adjustment Brush

The Adjustment Brush lets you selectively tweak certain areas of an image by painting them (see Figure 9-11). When you activate the Adjustment Brush by pressing K, a host of adjustments appears on the right side of the Camera Raw window—in Camera Raw 7, there are *twice* as many as in previous versions. They're the same adjustments you've learned about so far, along with these extras:

- **Sharpness** lets you accentuate areas of high contrast in an image to make them look sharper (you'll learn all about sharpening in Chapter 11). Use this slider to add extra sharpening to important areas like the image's focal point.

> **NOTE** Camera Raw applies a round of sharpening to your *whole* image as soon as you open it. To find out how much or to turn it off (if, say, you plan on sharpening in Photoshop instead), skip ahead to page 480.

- **Noise Reduction,** new in Camera Raw 7, lets you selectively paint away the colored speckles that appear in images shot in extremely low-light conditions, or at a high *ISO* (your camera's light-sensitivity setting).

- **Moiré Reduction** is also new in Camera Raw 7 and helps remove the repeating pattern that sometimes appears in scans of printed images (think dots upon dots but not precisely lined up).

- **Color** lets you paint a colored tint onto an image.

The sliders below the Color setting (you may have to scroll down to see them all) control the Adjustment Brush's cursor, and are explained in Figure 9-11.

To use the Adjustment Brush, choose the type of adjustment(s) you want to make using the sliders on the right, mouse over to your image, and then paint to apply the adjustment(s). Or, paint the area you want to adjust first and *then* tweak the sliders. Either way, a little greenish pin appears to mark the area you adjusted; press V to show or hide the pin. Behind the scenes, Camera Raw creates a mask that hides the rest of your image so you can continue to tweak the adjustment sliders even after you've finished painting. Camera Raw updates the area you painted to reflect those changes.

> **TIP** Click the little + and – signs on either end of an adjustment's slider to strengthen or lessen that adjustment (respectively) by a preset amount (0.5 for Exposure—whose scale ranges in f-stops from −4 to +4—and 25 for most other sliders, which range from −100 to +100).

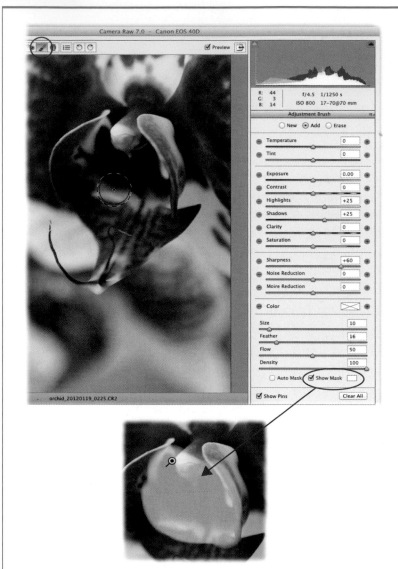

FIGURE 9-11

See the dotted line around the brush cursor in the top image? It indicates the cursor's feather amount, which softens the edge of your adjustment to make it blend in with the rest of the image. The solid line indicates the cursor's brush size, and the crosshairs let you know where you're applying the adjustment. To adjust the feather amount or cursor size, drag the Feather or Size slider, respectively. The Flow slider controls the strength of the adjustment, and the Density slider controls the transparency of your brushstroke (think of it as the brush's opacity).

If you want to see the Adjustment Brush's mask—the white overlay shown in the bottom image here, which indivcates your brushstrokes and, therefore, where the adjustment is visible—turn on Show Mask (circled) or press Y. You can change the color of the mask's overlay by clicking the little white square to the right of the Show Mask checkbox and then choosing a new color from the resulting Color Picker. Turn on the Auto Mask checkbox to limit your adjustment to pixels that are similar in color to the ones you're painting across.

To apply an existing adjustment to more areas in your image, turn on the Add radio button in the upper-right part of the Camera Raw window and then paint across the parts that need adjusting. To add a new adjustment, turn on the New radio button, set the sliders to your liking (set any sliders you don't want applied in the new adjustment to zero), and then paint across that area. If you've added more than one adjustment and you want to add to just one of 'em, click the Add button and Camera Raw displays pins representing the different adjustments you've made; simply click the pin representing the one you want to add to *and then* paint *across* that part of your image.

To *undo* part of an adjustment in your image, turn on the Erase radio button and, if necessary, click the pin that represents the adjustment you want to erase (if, say, you've used the Add button mentioned above to create multiple adjustments), and then paint the area in question or, better yet, simply Option-drag (Alt-drag on a PC) across that area. To completely delete single adjustment, click its pin and then press Delete (Backspace on a PC). To erase *all* the adjustments you've made with the Adjustments Brush, click the Clear All button near the bottom right of the Camera Raw window.

Camera Raw's Graduated Filters

The Graduated Filter tool lets you apply adjustments much like a real graduated filter that screws onto the end of a camera lens. (The filter is a thin piece of glass that fades from gray to white so it darkens overly bright parts of the scene you're shooting.) When you activate this tool by clicking its button at the top of the Camera Raw window (it's circled in Figure 9-12) or pressing G, you get the same set of adjustments as with the Adjustment Brush (except for Erase mode). The difference is that, with the Graduated Filter tool, you apply them by dragging a line to apply a gradient (like Photoshop's Gradient tool), rather than *painting* across the area that needs adjusting with a brush cursor. This adjustment is great for fixing overexposed skies because Photoshop gradually applies it across the full width or height of your image in the direction you drag (and you can drag in any direction you want!).

Behind the scenes, this tool creates a gradient mask, which restricts the adjustment to specific parts of your image. As you click and drag, you can create a gradient at any angle, as shown in Figure 9-12. Even after you've used this tool, you can continue to make adjustments using the sliders on the right side of the window.

NOTE Camera Raw 7 sports several new Graduated Filter adjustments: Temperature, Tint, Highlights, Shadows, Noise, and Moiré Reduction. The previous section explains what these adjustments do.

FIGURE 9-12

You can use the Graduated Filter tool to gradually darken and intensify this image's background. The green-and-white dotted line on the left edge of this image that runs through the green dot represents the start of the mask, and the similar red-and-white dotted line running through the red dot represents the end.

To constrain the adjustment to be perfectly horizontal or vertical, press and hold the Shift key as you drag.

To move the midpoint of the mask (where the adjustment begins to fade), drag the green and red dots. To delete the mask, click the red dot and then press Delete (Backspace on a PC).

More Fun with Camera Raw

As you can see, the Camera Raw plug-in is crazy powerful and each new version is bursting with new features. You can use it to adjust Curves (page 390), softly darken the edges of an image (called *vignetting*; see page 641 to learn how to do it in Photoshop), and much more. Camera Raw deserves a whole book all to itself, and there are plenty of 'em out there. When you're ready to learn more, pick up *Getting Started with Camera Raw, Second Edition* by Ben Long (Peachpit Press, 2009), a great guide for beginners. Or check out *Real World Camera Raw with Adobe Photoshop CS5* (Peachpit Press, 2010) by Jeff Schewe and the late Bruce Fraser. If you'd rather learn by watching a video, check out your author's page at *www.lesa.in/clvideos*.

Using Levels

The adjustments you've seen so far are OK when you're just starting out with Photoshop, and they're darn handy when you're pressed for time. But to become a serious pixel wrangler, you've got to kick it up a notch and learn to use *Levels* and *Curves*. With a single Levels adjustment, you can fix lighting problems, increase contrast, and—in some cases—balance the color in your image. (If you've got *major* color problems, you need to use Curves; skip ahead to page 390 to learn how.) Levels adjustments change the intensity levels—hence the tool's name—of shadows, midtones, and highlights. They're a very visual and intuitive way to improve images. And because they're available as Adjustment layers (yay!), they're nondestructive and won't harm your original image.

In this section, you'll learn how to use Levels adjustments in a few different ways so you can pick the one you like best. But first, you need to get up close and personal with the mighty *histogram*, your secret decoder ring for interpreting problems in your images.

Histograms: Mountains of Information

A histogram (Figure 9-13) is a visual representation—a collection of tiny bar graphs, to be precise—of the info contained in an image. Once you learn how to read it, you'll gain an immensely valuable understanding of why images look the way they do. More importantly, you'll learn how to tweak the histogram itself or (more commonly) make changes with other tools while using the histogram's changing readout to monitor the image's vibrancy. It sounds complicated, but once you watch the histogram in action, you'll see that it's actually pretty straightforward—and tremendously powerful.

Photoshop automatically displays a histogram in the new Properties panel when you create either a Levels or a Curves Adjustment layer. You can also summon one by choosing Window→Histogram to open the Histogram panel shown in Figure 9-13.

The histogram looks like a mountain range, which is a perfectly fine way to think about it (more on that analogy in a moment). Its width represents your image's *tonal range*—the range of colors between the darkest and lightest pixels—on a scale of 0 to 255. Pure black (0) is on the far left, and pure white (255) is on the far right. All told, the histogram measures 256 values. If that number sounds familiar, it should—it's the same 256-value range you learned about back in Chapter 2, which represents the minute gradations between a total absence of light (black) and full-on illumination (white).

> **NOTE** The histogram's width is also referred to as the image's *dynamic range*, which you'll learn more about in the High Dynamic Range (HDR) section later in this chapter (page 398).

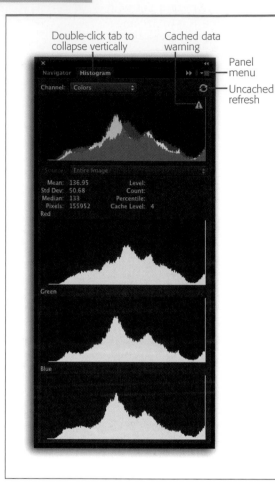

Double-click tab to collapse vertically

Cached data warning

Panel menu

Uncached refresh

FIGURE 9-13

Photoshop gives you three different ways to view the Histogram panel: Compact View (displays histogram only), Expanded View (displays the histogram with stats underneath it), and honkin' big All Channels View (shown here). To switch views, choose a different one from the panel's menu.

In All Channels View, you see your image's composite histogram at the top in color and the individual channel histograms below that in light gray. If the full-color composite histogram is too funky for you, from the Channel pop-up menu at the top of the Histogram panel, choose RGB and the composite histogram turns light gray, too.

The cached data warning triangle (labeled) means that the info displayed in the histogram isn't based on the current version of your image (the cache is part of your computer's memory). You'll see this icon periodically when you're editing large files. Just click the triangle or the Uncached Refresh button to make Photoshop update the histogram.

The histogram's height at any particular spot represents how many pixels are at that particular level of brightness. Using the mountain analogy, a noticeable cluster of tall, wide mountains means that particular brightness range makes up a good chunk of your image. Short or super-skinny mountains mean that particular brightness range doesn't appear much. And a big ol' flat prairie means there are few or no pixels in that range. In other words, the histogram can tell you at a glance whether you've got a good balance of light and dark pixels, whether the shadows or highlights are getting clipped, whether the image is over- or underexposed (see Figure 9-14), and whether it's been adjusted before.

Here are a few tips for understanding the histogram:

- An extremely jagged mountain range means the image's color info is unbalanced. The image may contain a decent amount of some colors but very little of others.

- A narrow mountain range means you've got a narrow tonal range and little difference between the darkest and lightest pixels. The whole image probably looks rather flat and lacks both details and contrast.

- If you see a sharp spike on the left side of the histogram, the image's shadows have probably been clipped (by the camera or scanner). If the spike is at the right side of the histogram, the highlights may have been clipped instead. (See page 361 for more on clipping.)

- If the mountain range is bunched up against the left side (near 0, a.k.a. black) with a vast prairie on the right, the image is underexposed (too dark); see Figure 9-14, left.

- If the mountain range is snug against the right side (near 255, a.k.a. white) with a vast prairie on the left, the image is overexposed (too light); see Figure 9-14, right.

- An image that has a good balance of light and dark colors has a wide mountain range—one that spans the entire width of the histogram—that's fairly tall and somewhat uniform in height. Basically, you want the histogram to look like the older, eroded Appalachians (Figure 9-14, middle) rather than the newer, super-jagged peaks of the Himalayas (Figure 9-14, right).

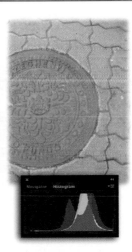

FIGURE 9-14

These histograms—shown here in Compact View— can tell you whether an image is underexposed (left), has a good balance of color (middle), or is overexposed (right).

- If the histogram looks like a comb—with a bunch of gaps between its spikes (see Figure 9-16, right)—the image is either a really lousy scan or was adjusted at some point in the past. (Anytime you shift the brightness values of pixels, you introduce gaps between the histogram's tiny bar graphs.)

All this histogram and correction business is subjective; if your histogram looks terrible but the image looks great to you, that's fine—in the end, your opinion is all that matters.

Thankfully, you can fix a lot of the problems listed above using the correction methods discussed in this chapter. For example, you can balance an image's color to smooth out the height of the histogram's mountains, and expand the image's tonal range and increase its contrast to widen the mountain range. And by keeping the Histogram panel open, you can watch how it changes in real time as you edit images.

If the whole histogram concept is clear as mud, don't fret—it'll make more sense once you start using Levels. In fact, if you've got a little free time, you can use the Dodge and Burn tools to help gain an understanding of the relationship between what you see in an image and how the histogram looks. With the Histogram panel open, use the Dodge and Burn tools on different areas of an image. Use the Dodge tool to lighten dark areas and see how the histogram changes, and then use the Burn tool to darken light areas and see how that affects it. With a little experimentation, you can get a clearer idea of what the histogram is telling you.

> **TIP** Many digital cameras can also show you a histogram, though you may have to root through your owner's manual to learn how to turn it on. Once you get comfy with histograms, you can use them to see whether the shot you're about to take will have good exposure.

The Levels Sliders

Now that you know how to read histograms, you're ready to make a Levels adjustment, which involves using a set of three sliders to reshape and expand the information in your histogram. You can add a Levels Adjustment layer by choosing Layer→New Adjustment Layer→Levels, by clicking the Levels button in the Adjustments panel (it looks like a tiny histogram), or by clicking the half-black/half-white circle at the bottom of the Layers panel and choosing Levels from the resulting list. (You can also summon a Levels adjustment by pressing ⌘-L [Ctrl+L on a PC] or by choosing Image→Adjustments→Levels, though in both cases the adjustment happens on your *original* image instead of on an Adjustment layer. Scary!) Whichever method you use, Photoshop displays a light-gray histogram in the Properties panel, as shown in Figure 9-15.

TIP When you add a Levels Adjustment layer, you'll spot an Auto button near the top right of the resulting Properties panel. In CS6, Adobe changed the math that Photoshop uses when you click this button: Instead of the Enhance Per Channel Contrast method (wherein Photoshop adjusted the red, green, and blue channels individually—so the highlights got a little lighter and the shadows got a little darker whether they needed it or not), it now uses the "Enhance Brightness and Contrast" method, wherein Photoshop analyzes your image and then adjusts the brightness and contrast accordingly. So feel free to go give this button a good, swift click; you'll be surprised at the improved results!

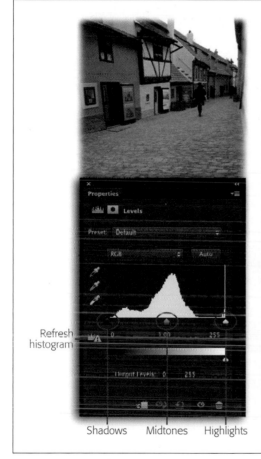
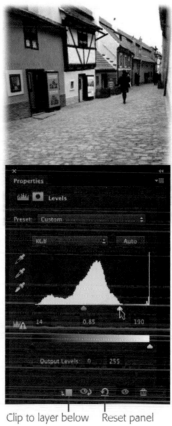

Shadows   Midtones   Highlights   Clip to layer below   Reset panel

Refresh histogram

FIGURE 9-15

The simplest way to use a Levels adjustment is by dragging the Input levels sliders circled here. You'll also find a slew of options in the Preset pop-up menu at the very top of the panel; feel free to give them a spin to see what they do to your image and how they change your histogram.

As you drag each Input Levels slider, press and hold the backslash key (\) to see what your image looked like previously. To apply the adjustment to just one layer below (instead of all layers below), click the "Clip to layer below" button labeled here (right).

As shown in Figure 9-15, the black slider at the far left of the histogram represents the shadows in your image. It starts out at 0, the numeric value for pure black. The white slider on the far right, which represents highlights, starts out at 255—pure white. To give your image the greatest possible tonal range and contrast, move the shadows and highlights sliders so they point to wherever your histogram's values begin to slope upward (at the foot of the mountains, so to speak). In other words, if there's a gap between the shadows slider and the beginning of the histogram's bars, drag that slider to the right. And if there's a gap between the highlights slider and the bars on the right end of the histogram, drag the slider to the left.

When you move the sliders, Photoshop adjusts the tonal values in your image accordingly. For example, if you drag the highlights slider left to 190, Photoshop changes all the pixels in the image that were originally at 190 or higher to 255 (white). (Translation: They get brighter.) Similarly, if you move the shadows slider right to 14, Photoshop darkens all the pixels with a brightness level of 14 or lower to 0 (black). The pixel levels in between 14 and 190 get redistributed, too, boosting the image's overall contrast by increasing its tonal range (widening the histogram's mountain range). Figure 9-15 shows what a difference this can make.

The gray midtones slider in the middle lets you brighten or darken an image by changing the intensity of the middle range of grays (the box on page 391 explains why you're dealing with grays instead of color). Drag it left to lighten your image (or decrease contrast), or right to darken it (or increase contrast), as shown in Figure 9-16. Because this slider focuses on the image's midtones, it won't make the highlights too light or the shadows too dark—unless you go hog wild and drag it *all* the way left or right!

Histogram Statistics

If you choose Expanded View or All Channels View from the Histogram panel's menu, you'll see a bunch of cryptic info below the histogram. The most useful thing there is the Source pop-up menu, which lets you choose whether the histogram represents your whole image, an active layer, or an *adjustment composite*. If your document contains Adjustment layers, that last option displays a histogram that's based on the active Adjustment layer and all the layers below it. (See page 77 for more on Adjustment layers.)

The other stuff below the Source menu is pretty heady, but here's the gist of what each item means:

- **Mean** represents the average intensity value of the pixels in the image.
- **Standard Deviation** (abbreviated "Std. Dev.") shows how widely the image's intensity values vary.
- **Median** is the midpoint of the intensity values.
- **Pixels** tells you how many pixels Photoshop analyzed to generate the histogram.

- **Cache Level** shows the current image cache Photoshop used to make the histogram. When this number is higher than 1, Photoshop is basing the histogram on a representative sampling of pixels in the image rather than on all of them. You can click the Uncached Refresh button (shown in Figure 9-13) to make the program redraw the histogram based on the current version of the image.

If you position your cursor over the histogram, you also see values for the following:

- **Level** displays the intensity level of the area beneath the cursor.
- **Count** shows the total number of pixels that are at the intensity level beneath the cursor.
- **Percentile** indicates the number of pixels at or below the intensity level beneath the cursor, expressed as a percentage of all the pixels in the image.

Math geeks, bless their hearts, love this kind of stuff.

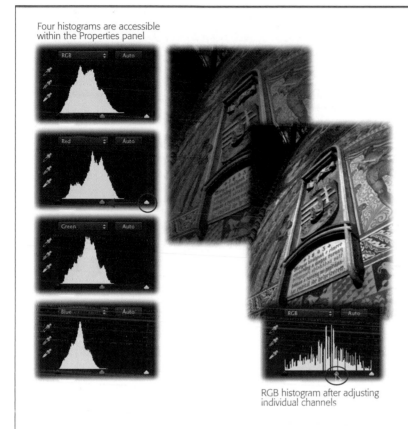

Four histograms are accessible within the Properties panel

RGB histogram after adjusting individual channels

FIGURE 9-16

Left: In the Properties panel, the unlabeled pop-up menu perched above the histogram is the Channel menu, which lets you view and adjust either the composite channel (page 190) or an individual channel. If each channel's histogram differs greatly, it's worth adjusting each one separately; but if their histograms are nearly identical, you can get away with adjusting only the composite channel. Here you see the composite and individual color channel histograms for an RGB image. Since the gaps on the right side vary quite a bit, you should adjust each channel separately.

Right: Here are the before (top) and after (bottom) versions of the image, along with the new composite channel histogram. Notice how the mountain range has become a little flatter and much wider overall; that means the image's tonal range has expanded. And you can tell this image has been adjusted from its original state because the new histogram looks like a comb: lots of vertical lines with gaps in between.

TIP If you hold down the Option key (Alt on a PC) as you drag the shadows or highlights sliders, you can see which parts of your image you're forcing to pure black or white. For example, Option-drag (Alt-drag) the shadows slider to the right, and the image turns completely white. The darkest parts of the image begin to reappear as you drag, first in black and then in other colors. Option-drag (Alt-drag) the highlights slider to the left, and the opposite happens: The image turns completely black, and the lightest parts are the first ones to reappear, first in white and then in color. Option-dragging (Alt-dragging) is a great way to tell whether you're dragging the sliders too far because whatever areas are visible while you drag are the ones that will be pure black or pure white. It's also a great trick for finding the image's lightest highlights and darkest shadows, as the next section explains.

■ OUTPUT LEVELS

The black-and-white bar near the bottom of the Properties panel (shown in Figure 9-15) includes a couple of sliders you can use to control the darkness of black pixels and the lightness of white pixels in your image. Drag the black slider to the right to lighten the pure-black pixels or the white slider to the left to dim the pure-white pixels. These adjustments used to be crucial if you were sending grayscale images to a commercial press because the printing process was notorious for making highlights too light and shadows too dark. Nowadays, if you use good-quality color profiles (page 674), these adjustments aren't such a big deal, but knowing how to change the way your blacks and whites look when they're printed is still useful if you can't trust your printer to properly reproduce shadows and highlights.

The Levels Eyedroppers

Another way to apply a Levels adjustment is to use the eyedroppers on the left side of the histogram in the Properties panel (shown back in Figure 9-15). Instead of dragging the sliders below the histogram, you use the eyedroppers to sample pixels that should be black (the darkest shadows that contain details), white (the lightest highlights that contain details), or neutral gray (midtones), and Photoshop adjusts the sliders for you. The only problem with this method is that it can be darn tough to figure out *which* pixels to sample, though there's a trick you can use to solve this problem, as you'll learn shortly. Open an image, and then follow these steps:

1. **Grab the Eyedropper tool and change the Options bar's Sample Size pop-up menu to "3 by 3 Average."**

    Press I to activate the Eyedropper tool. Because you're about to use eyedroppers in a Levels adjustment to reset black and white points, you need to change the way the tool measures color (the eyedroppers in both Levels and Curves use the main Eyedropper tool's settings). In the Options bar, you'll see that the Sample Size pop-up menu is set to Point Sample, which means the Eyedropper samples exactly *one* pixel when you click with it. By changing the sample size to "3 by 3 Average," you tell Photoshop to average several pixels around the spot where you click, which is much better for color-correcting.

    > **TIP** If you have the Eyedropper or Color Sampler tool (see Appendix C) activated, you can also pick a new sample size by Control-clicking (right-clicking on a PC) anywhere in your image. If you're working with extremely high-resolution files, the pixels are so tiny and so tightly packed that you may want to increase the sample size to, say, 51 × 51 or higher. (See page 237 in Chapter 6 for more on resolution.)

2. **Create a Levels Adjustment layer.**

    Click the half-black/half-white circle at the bottom of the Layers panel and choose Levels from the menu that appears. Photoshop adds an Adjustment layer to your image and opens the Properties panel.

3. **In the Properties panel, click the black eyedropper to the left of the histogram.**

    The left side of the panel sports three eyedroppers. The black one resets the image's black point (shadows), the gray one resets its gray point (midtones), and the white one resets its white point (highlights). Simple enough!

4. **Mouse over to your image and click an area near your focal point that should be black.**

In most cases it's fairly obvious which parts of an image should be black, though sometimes it's hard to tell. If you need help figuring out where the darkest pixels in your image live, make sure the black eyedropper is active, and then hold down the Option key (Alt on a PC) as you drag the shadows slider to the right (see Figure 9-17). At first, your image turns completely white, but as you continue to drag, Photoshop displays neon colors in some areas; the first colored area that appears is the darkest spot in your image. While still holding down the Option (Alt) key, mouse over to your image and then click that spot with the black eyedropper. When you mouse away from the Properties panel, your image goes back to its regular colors, but as soon as the cursor is over your image in the document window, it'll go back to funky neons (if it *doesn't*, you forgot to activate the black eyedropper first).

NOTE If you'd like to play around with the image shown in Figure 9-17, download *Manhole.jpg* from this book's Missing CD page at *www.missingmanuals.com/cds*.

When you click, the colors in your image will probably shift a bit. If you don't like the results, click somewhere else to set a *new* black point, or undo your click by pressing ⌘-Z (Ctrl+Z on a PC).

5. **In the Properties panel, click the white eyedropper and then click an area in your image that should be white.**

The same rules apply when it comes to choosing a new white point as choosing a black one: Try to pick an area that's close to the focal point and not pure white (because a pure white one doesn't have any details). You also don't want to pick a reflection from a light source as your white point because it's not a *true* white. You can use the same Option-drag (Alt-drag on a PC) trick to find the image's lightest highlights, though this time you'll need to click to activate the white eyedropper, and the image turns black rather than white. As you drag the highlight slider to the left, the first area that appears in color is the lightest. While still holding the Option (Alt) key, mouse over to your image and click that spot (your image temporarily changes to full color when you mouse away from the Properties panel, but it reverts to neon once your cursor reaches your image).

6. **Activate the gray eyedropper and then click an area that should be neutral gray.**

Unfortunately, the Option-drag (Alt-drag) trick doesn't work here, but if you're willing to jump through a few hoops, you can track down a neutral gray. (The box on page 385 has the details.) If you don't have time for that, try clicking within gray areas until the image's color looks good to you.

7. **To see before and after versions of your image, turn off the Levels Adjustment layer's visibility.**

In the Layers panel, click the visibility eye to the left of the Levels Adjustment layer to see whether the adjustment made a difference.

FIGURE 9-17

Top: It's tough to spot the darkest and lightest pixels in this image, so try this trick: In the Properties panel, Option-drag (Alt-drag) the shadows slider to the right (see the circle with an arrow on the right here). Your image turns white and the first areas to appear in color are the darkest ones. Mouse over to the image and click the darkest spot (circled at left).

Middle: Likewise, when you Option-drag (Alt-drag) the highlights slider to the left, your image turns black and the first colors to appear are the lightest. Mouse over to the image and click the lightest spot (circled, left).

Bottom: There's no trick for picking a neutral gray, so just click the gray eyedropper and then find a spot in your image that looks gray and give it a click (both are circled here). As you can see, a little Levels adjusting can go a long way toward improving an image's color and contrast!

Correcting by the Numbers

Ever heard the phrase, "Numbers don't lie"? That old adage applies to color correcting in Photoshop, too: Using numbers helps you take the guesswork out of it. Instead of relying on what looks good to your naked—and possibly tired—eye, you can use color values to balance an image's color perfectly.

To see pixels' color values, open the Info panel by choosing Window→Info. Once you do that, you can mouse over your image with any tool and the panel displays a numeric value for the particular pixel your cursor is over (see Figure 9-18). For RGB images, you'll see values for R, G, and B. If you're in CMYK mode, you see C, M, Y, and K values instead; in Lab mode you get L, a, b; and so on. (You also see C, M, Y, and K values in the Info panel when you're in RGB mode, which is useful if you need to keep an eye on the values of one mode while you're working in another.)

WORKAROUND WORKSHOP

Good Gray Hunting

Alas, if you're looking for a neutral gray to click with the gray Levels or Curves eyedropper and nothing in your image is gray, there's no quick trick for finding a good gray. Some images don't even *have* any neutral grays.

One way to look for them is to open the Info panel (Figure 9-18) and activate the Eyedropper tool (see Appendix C). Then, keep an eye on the Info panel's R, G, and B, values as you put your cursor over areas in your image that appear gray. When you find a spot with nearly equal RGB values (like R: 222, G: 222, B: 224, for example), you've found a neutral gray—so click it.

The Info panel method works just fine if you've got a few extra hours to spend mousing around an image checking pixel values. But if you're pressed for time, here's a foolproof way to hunt down neutral grays—if they actually exist in your image. (Photoshop guru Dave Cross—*www.dcross.com*—came up with this technique, and he's graciously given your humble author permission to include it here for your reading enjoyment.) With an image open, follow these steps:

1. Create a new layer by clicking the "Create a new layer" button at the bottom of the Layers panel. Make sure this layer sits *above* the image layer.

2. Fill the new layer with gray by choosing Edit→Fill, picking 50 percent gray from the Use pop-up menu, and then clicking OK.

3. Use the pop-up menu near the top of the Layers panel to switch the gray layer's blend mode from Normal to Difference (page 291). Your photo now looks really funky, but don't panic; this layer won't live long.

4. Create a Threshold Adjustment layer by choosing Layer→New Adjustment Layer→Threshold.

5. In the resulting Properties panel, drag the Threshold slider all the way to the left until the image turns solid white, and then slowly drag the slider back to the right. The first areas that appear black are your neutral grays. As soon as you see a good-sized black spot, stop dragging.

6. Remember that spot or mark it with the Color Sampler tool (see online Appendix C): Press Shift-I repeatedly to activate the tool (it looks like an eyedropper with a tiny circle above it), and then click once in the black spot. A tiny circle with the number 1 next to it appears where you clicked. (Feel free to mark more than one spot if you'd like; the Color Sampler tool lets you place up to four markers.)

7. Delete both the Threshold Adjustment layer and the gray layer (you don't need 'em anymore). Shift-click to activate them both in the Layers panel, and then press Delete (Backspace on a PC).

That's it! With the neutral gray point marked, you don't have to wonder where to click with the gray eyedropper in a Levels or Curves adjustment. To delete the marker once you've set your gray point, grab the Color Sampler tool, mouse over the marker, and then Option-click (Alt-click) it. Your cursor turns into the tiniest, *cutest* pair of scissors you've ever seen.

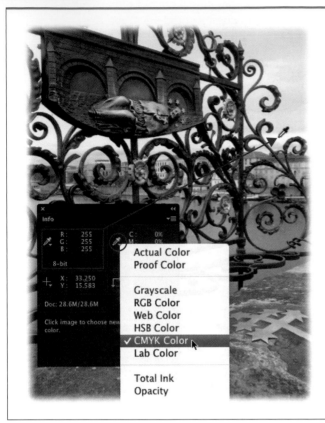

FIGURE 9-18

The Info panel displays various bits of info about your image. The top two sections show before and after color values (once you've made an adjustment). Here you can see that the white cloud is pure white (255,255,255) so this would not be a good spot to click when resetting your white point, as described earlier. If you happen upon a gray area with (nearly) equal RGB values, congratulations—you've found a neutral gray!

Click one of the little eyedroppers (circled) in the panel's top two sections to summon this menu, and then choose the info you want displayed in that section. To change the info displayed in the panel's other sections, choose Panel Options from the Info panel's menu.

In RGB mode (which is where you spend the majority of your time), these values correspond to the 0–255 scale you learned about earlier in this chapter. Depending on the color of the area your cursor is over, the numbers may lean more toward one channel than the others. For example, when it's over a pixel in a sky, the B (blue) value spikes higher than the R or G (red or green) values. When it's over reddish skin, the R value is higher than the B or G values. This info is useful in several situations:

- **You can use it to figure out what's causing a color cast.** For example, if your cursor is over a white cat and the B value is really high, you have a problem in the blue channel. If the G value is off the charts, then that's where the problem is.

- **It can help you find the darkest and lightest pixels when you're making a Levels or Curves adjustment.** If you put your cursor over the area you're considering using to reset the black or white points, you can see if it's really pure black (0, 0, 0) or pure white (255, 255, 255).

TIP If you're mousing around a shadowy area and the Info panel's numeric values keep changing, that means there are details lurking in that spot; if you lighten the image's shadows using the techniques in this section, you may be able to bring 'em out.

- **Monitoring these values can keep you from overadjusting your image and losing details.** For example, since you know that three 0's means pure black and three 255s means pure white, you can take care that pixels in the important parts of your image don't reach those values when you're making an adjustment. You can use the Color Sampler tool, with the Info panel, to monitor the original and adjusted values of up to four sample points by following the steps below.

Here's how to correct an image in RGB mode by the numbers:

1. **Open the Info panel by choosing Window→Info.**

   As you move your cursor over various parts of your image, watch how the Info panel's numbers change to reflect the pixel underneath the cursor.

2. **Grab the Color Sampler tool and make sure the Sample Size is set to "3 by 3 Average."**

   Press I to activate the Eyedropper tool and then press Shift-I until you see the Color Sampler tool (it lives in the same toolset). Take a peek in the Options bar and make sure the Sample Size pop-menu is set to "3 by 3 Average."

3. **Create a Levels Adjustment layer.**

   Click the half-black/half-white circle at the bottom of the Layers panel and choose Levels, or click the Levels button in the Adjustments panel. Technically, you don't *have* to create this layer just yet, but if you've already got a Levels adjustment open, you can use the Option-drag (Alt-drag on a PC) trick (page 384) to help you find the highlights and shadows points in the next two steps—just don't forget to drag the sliders *back* to their original positions when you're done performing the trick!

4. **Mark the darkest shadow and lightest highlight in the image.**

   Following the guidelines explained in the previous section (starting on page 383), locate the darkest shadow that's not pure black (0) and click it once with the Color Sampler tool; Photoshop adds a marker like the ones circled in Figure 9-19. Then find the lightest highlight that's not pure white (255) and mark it, too (you'll see a little 2 next to the marker). Photoshop adds two sections to the Info panel—one for each of the markers you added (they're boxed in Figure 9-19).

FIGURE 9-19

Top: When you place sample-point markers (circled), the Info panel sprouts new sections that correspond to each of the markers. These new sections let you monitor the marked pixels' values before and during an adjustment (in the Info panel, the two values are separated by a slash). As explained in steps 5 and 6, your goal is to make the highlight's color values 245 and the shadow's color values 10. You may not be able to get your numbers to match these exactly because they change as you adjust individual channels, but if the image has a halfway decent exposure, you should be able to get pretty close.

Bottom: As you can see, making adjustments based on the Info panel's data took care of this image's yellow color cast and improved its contrast.

TIP Strictly speaking, you don't have to activate the Color Sampler tool to place sample-point markers. If you're using the Eyedropper tool, you can Shift-click to place a marker, and Option-Shift-click (Alt+Shift-click on a PC) a marker to delete it.

5. **In the Properties panel, use the histogram to adjust each channel's highlight value.**

   Your goal in fixing the highlights is to make all three channels' color values match the *optimal* highlight value, which is about 245 (close to—but not quite—pure white). To balance the channels' highlight values, you have to adjust the highlight in *each* channel. To do that, head over to the Properties panel and pick a channel from the unlabeled pop-up menu near the top of the panel. Then, while watching the numbers in the Info panel (undock it from its panel group if necessary), drag the Properties panel's highlights slider (Figure 9-15) left until it reaches 245, or just type *245* into the text field below the slider. Repeat this step for the other two channels. When all three channels' highlight values are nearly (or exactly) equal, you've got yourself a balanced image (well, in the highlights at least!).

6. **Adjust each channel's shadow value.**

   Use the same process to balance the shadows: Choose each channel from the menu near the top of the Properties panel, and then drag the shadows slider to the right until it reaches 10 (close to but not pure black), or type *10* into the slider's text field.

7. **Adjust the image's midtones, if necessary.**

   You don't always have to adjust midtones, since your image may look just fine the way it is (though you may not realize how much better it *could* look!). In the Properties panel, pick the composite channel (RGB) and then drag the gray slider to the left to lighten the image, or to the right to darken it.

8. **Take a peek at the "before" version of the image by turning off the Levels Adjustment layer's visibility.**

   In the Layers panel, click the layer's visibility eye so you can see what a difference your changes have made.

If you need to go back and make further adjustments, just double-click the Levels Adjustment layer to reopen its Properties panel. As you can see in Figure 9-19, this technique makes a big difference.

TIP   When you're using the Info panel, it can help to rearrange the various panels in your workspace. For example, if you really dig having the Info and Properties panels open—and you will once you get used to using them—you can create a custom workspace so they automatically open and appear wherever you'd like. Flip back to page 21 to find out how.

Color-Correcting Skin

You're not limited to monitoring the Info panel's values of highlights and shadows; you can slap sample points anywhere you want. If you're correcting a people picture, you most certainly want to monitor the values of skin tones. While you won't find any magic target values that work for *every* skin type, here are a few tips that can help you make sure skin tones at least look human, which is (hopefully!) your goal:

- When color-correcting photos of women, try to place sample points on your subjects' necks. Women don't typically put makeup on their necks, so you get a more accurate reading of the woman's *real* skin tone based on her neck than you would on, say, her cheek.

- Skin tones should have red values greater than their green values and green values greater than their blue values. This rule is easy to remember because that's the order of the letters in RGB.

- The difference between the red and green values in skin should be about double the difference between the green and blue values. For example, if the difference between the red and green values is 60, the difference between the green and blue values should be around 30.

- The fairer a person's complexion, the closer the RGB values should be to one another.

- The darker a person's complexion, the lower the blue value in her skin should be.

By following these guidelines, you should end up with nicely balanced skin colors in your images. And if you'd like to use a color swatch as a reference, you can find skin tone color charts lurking on the Web. An oldie but goodie is Bruce Beard's skin tone and hair color chart, available at *www.lesa.in/brucebeard.*

TIP Photoshop CS6 includes a brand-new way to select the skin tones in an image. This new method involves the Color Range command, and you can learn all about it back in Chapter 4 on page 159.

■ Working with Curves

The last stop on the Color Correction Express is Curves, the most powerful—and fear-inducing—adjustment in all of Photoshop. The basic idea is that, by curving a diagonal line on a grid, you change the brightness of the pixels in an image. Instead of the three main adjustment sliders you get with Levels (shadows, highlights, and midtones), Curves gives you up to *16* adjustments. But that's not as scary as it sounds. If you survived the section on Levels (page 375) relatively unscathed, you already know a *ton* about Curves. For example:

- You can use Curves as an Adjustment layer so that it's nondestructive, which means you can also use the included layer mask to restrict the adjustment to certain areas of an image. The Curves grid shows up in the Properties panel, just like Levels.

- A Curves adjustment uses a histogram (page 375) and the same 256 shades of gray you saw in Levels. It also has the same shadows and highlights sliders (though no midtones slider), and it harbors the same trio of eyedroppers for resetting the black, white, and midtone points (page 382). So far so good!

- You can Option-drag (Alt-drag on a PC) the shadows and highlights sliders to find the darkest and lightest areas of your image, like you learned on page 384.

- You can use Curves to correct an image using the Info panel and the Color Sampler tool, and you can type target values into the Properties panel's Input field. To summon the Input field (shown in Figure 9-20), click a point on the curve (you may need to resize the panel—or scroll down in it—to see the field). If you haven't added any points yet (which you'll learn how to do shortly), click either the shadows or highlights slider beneath the grid to activate the corresponding *curve point* at the tip of the diagonal line to summon the Input Field.

TIP In CS6, the Properties panel's Auto button triggers Photoshop to use a new-and-improved mathematical formula to analyze your image and adjust brightness and contrast only where it thinks your image needs it (instead of throughout the whole image). Be sure to take the new math for a spin by giving the Auto button a click!

FREQUENTLY ASKED QUESTION

There Is No Color

What's all this talk about black, white, and gray? I'm trying to fix color!

Consider this concept: There *is* no color in Photoshop, so you can't use the program to *fix* color.

After you clean off the coffee you just splurted onto your screen, take a moment to think about the channel information you learned about in Chapter 5. Remember how Photoshop displays it all in grayscale (page 192)? That's because the information really *is* grayscale in each channel that's captured by your camera or scanner: red, green, and blue. The color you see is actually created by output devices like your monitor, printer, and professional printing presses (which you'll learn more about in Chapter 16); they're the ones responsible for converting the captured grayscale info into colors they can reproduce.

Your computer (and the programs on it like Photoshop), your digital camera, and your scanner are all digital devices; all they really understand are *bits*, which represent either zero or one (see the box on page 46). When you send these bits to an output device, the device assigns color values to that information.

If you can wrap your brain around this mind-bending concept, a few things start to make sense. For example:

- **Why it's so hard to match what you see onscreen with what you print.** When you realize that output devices are responsible for how the grayscale info is translated into

color, you understand why it's such a nightmare getting colors to match across devices that work differently (like LCD and CRT monitors) or that use different inks (like inkjet printers and printing presses). Chapter 16 has more on *color management*, the science behind matching colors.

- **Why color-correction tools like Levels and Curves focus on white, gray, and black values.** Since you're working with grayscale info, it makes sense that, to change a grayscale image, you have to change what Photoshop thinks should be black, neutral gray, or white (or change the intensity or brightness values) to alter the image. Shades of gray are all that matter when you're correcting in Photoshop.

- **Why the histogram measures color intensity (brightness) on a scale from 0 to 255.** A typical RGB image has 256 shades of gray, which correspond to brightness values of 0 percent to 100 percent gray. You see this 0–255 scale in the Info panel when you put your cursor over pixels in an RGB image (page 386). Each pixel has a value ranging from 0–255 for each channel.

All this talk of grayscale can sound pretty abstract since we see in color, not grayscale. But what it boils down to is that your *real* goal in color-correcting images is to get the *grayscale* information right. Once you do, your output device has a much better chance of getting the colors right. Now go refill that coffee cup!

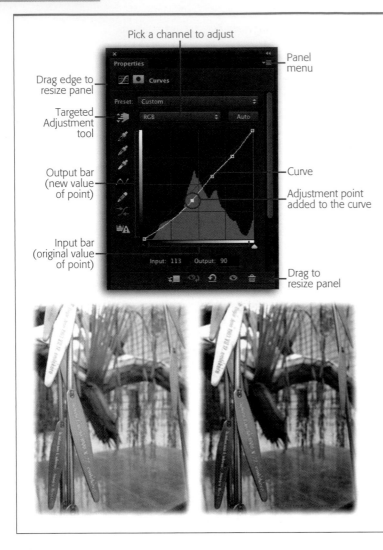

Pick a channel to adjust

Panel menu

Drag edge to resize panel

Targeted Adjustment tool

Output bar (new value of point)

Curve

Adjustment point added to the curve

Input bar (original value of point)

Input: 113   Output: 90

Drag to resize panel

FIGURE 9-20

Top: Photoshop's Curves tool is incredibly flexible—and that's what scares most folks: They don't know when, how, or why to add adjustment points or in which direction to move them. Fear not: You'll learn everything you need to know about this powerful tool in the following pages. Once you add points to the curve—here, they were added by clicking the Auto button—you can use the grayscale bars on the left and bottom of the grid to figure out which direction you need to drag each point. You can follow a point down the grid to see its original brightness value (on the input bar) and follow it to the left to see its new brightness value (on the output bar). After you click a point on the curve, those numeric values also appear in the Input and Output fields below the grid.

Bottom: Clicking the Auto button in CS6 makes Photoshop analyze your image and adjust brightness and contrast all by itself. As you can see here, the new math the program uses makes a big difference and, in some cases, may be all your image needs.

NOTE   In Photoshop CS6, you can make the Curves grid bigger by dragging the left edge of the Properties panel. Yippee!

- You can use the unlabeled pop-up menu near the top of the Properties panel (to the left of the Auto button) to pick individual channels to adjust with Curves, just like with Levels.

- The Presets pop-up menu at the top of the Properties panel has some settings that are quite useful. It's worth taking them for a spin just to see how they affect both the curve and your image.

To create a Curves Adjustment layer, choose Layer→New Adjustment Layer→Curves. You can also click the Curves button in the Adjustments panel (it looks like a grid with an S curve on it), or click the half-black/half-white circle at the bottom of the Layers panel and choose Curves. No matter which route you choose, the Properties panel pops open to reveal a grid with a diagonal line running from the bottom left to the top right (see Figure 9-20).

The diagonal line—which is the actual *curve* even though it starts out straight—represents the original brightness values (tonal range) of your image. To adjust these values, you can place up to 14 points along the diagonal line. (You can't delete the points at either end of the curve, but you can adjust them like any other point.)

NOTE   To try your hand at the Curves adjustments described in this section, download *Lisbon.jpg* (shown in Figure 9-21) from this book's Missing CD page at *www.missingmanuals.com/cds*.

To add a point to the curve, simply click the diagonal line, or make Photoshop add it by clicking the Auto button or activating the Targeted Adjustment tool and then clicking your image (Figure 9-21 explains how that maneuver works). Each point on the line corresponds to a brightness value in the horizontal black-to-white gradient bar below the grid (called the *input bar*). The direction you drag a point determines whether the brightness of pixels in that tonal range increases or decreases. Drag *upward* to *increase* brightness or *downward* to *decrease* it. (Even if nothing else about Curves makes sense, that part certainly does!)

NOTE   Technically, the Targeted Adjustment tool doesn't have a name anymore. Adobe *used* to call it the Targeted Adjustment tool, but it doesn't call it anything in CS6. This book has to call the tool *something*, so you'll see the old name in these pages.

Ben Willmore (*www.digitalmastery.com*) compares Curves adjustment points to a row of dimmer switches, which makes perfect sense if you think about how a dimmer switch works. Just as turning up a dimmer switch gradually turns up the light, raising a point on the curve gradually makes your image brighter and lighter. Likewise, just as lowering a dimmer switch gradually turns down the light, lowering a point on the curve makes your image darker. It's a great analogy because the adjustments you make with Curves are as gradual as using a dimmer switch, though Curves is more *sensitive* than a dimmer switch; you generally don't have to move a point very far to introduce a big change. As you move a point, the diagonal line curves in the direction you drag, and you can see its new brightness level represented on the *output bar* (the vertical gradient bar on the grid's left side), as shown in Figure 9-21, bottom.

TIP Instead of dragging the adjustment points around, you can nudge them with the up and down arrow keys on your keyboard. It's easier to make precise adjustments this way, and it keeps you from accidentally changing contrast (discussed in the next section) by dragging the point left or right. Simply click a point on the curve and then use the up arrow to brighten your image and the down arrow to darken it.

Bar on bottom shows original brightness value of point

Point your cursor at a certain spot and a preview (hollow) point appears on curve

Bar on left shows new brightness value of point

Clicking sets adjustment point on curve; drag down to darken

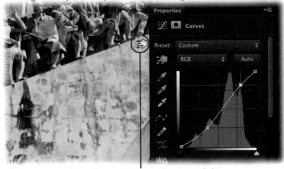

Click to set another adjustment point; drag up to lighten

FIGURE 9-21

Top: Curves is a lot easier to use than it used to be thanks to the Targeted Adjustment tool, which lets you add and move adjustment points by clicking and dragging in your image. Just click the button that looks like a pointing hand (circled, top) to activate this tool and then put your cursor over the area you want to darken (your cursor turns into an eyedropper). A white preview circle appears on the curve (circled, right) that corresponds to the tonal value of the pixels you're hovering above.

Middle: When you're ready to add an adjustment point to the curve, click once in your image and then—while still holding down your mouse button—drag downward to darken those pixels (your cursor turns into a hand with an up-and-down arrow [circled, left]). As you drag, the curve bends in the direction you're dragging, as shown here.

Bottom: Release your mouse button and click in your image to add another point. This time, pick an area you want to lighten and then drag upward, as shown here.

The grid behind the curve is merely a visual aid to help you move points around and determine which part of the tonal range you're affecting. It's set to a 25 percent, quarter-tone grid wherein shadows, midtones, and highlights are split into four parts: The left-hand column represents the darkest shadows, the middle two columns represent the midtones, and the right-hand column represents the lightest highlights. You can change it to a 10 percent grid that displays 10 rows and columns by Option-clicking (Alt-clicking on a PC) the grid in the Properties panel or by opening the Curves Display Options dialog box, shown in Figure 9-22.

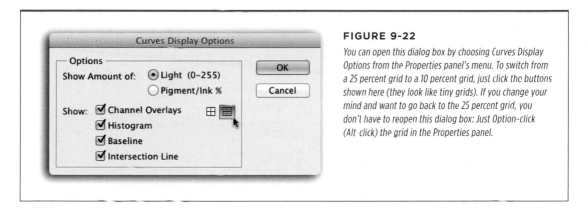

FIGURE 9-22

You can open this dialog box by choosing Curves Display Options from the Properties panel's menu. To switch from a 25 percent grid to a 10 percent grid, just click the buttons shown here (they look like tiny grids). If you change your mind and want to go back to the 25 percent grid, you don't have to reopen this dialog box: Just Option-click (Alt-click) the grid in the Properties panel.

Here's a rundown of the other settings in the Curves Display Options dialog box:

- **Show Amount of.** Unless you change it, the Light radio button is turned on, which means your image's shadows correspond to the bottom-left corner of the Curves grid and its highlights to the top-right corner. You can turn on the "Pigment/Ink %" option instead to show ink percentages on the input and output bars instead of the 0–255 brightness scale. Usually, though, you'll want to leave this set to Light.

- **Show.** This setting has several options that are all turned on to start with:

  - **Channel Overlays** lets you see a separate curve for each channel in your document. If you're new to Curves and find a panel riddled with colorful diagonal lines both distracting and alarming, turn this checkbox off.

  - **Histogram** determines whether Photoshop displays a light-gray version of your image's histogram behind the grid. If you find the histogram distracting, turn this setting off.

  - **Baseline** tells Photoshop to display the original curve as a straight diagonal line, which is a great way to know at a glance, "Dude—that's the original curve!"

  - **Intersection Line** makes Photoshop display horizontal and vertical "helper" lines when you drag a point to help you align it properly (which isn't really necessary if you use arrow keys to nudge points instead of dragging them).

Changing Contrast

The angle of the curve in the Properties panel controls contrast. If you steepen it, you increase the contrast in the image; if you flatten it, you decrease the contrast.

Just select an adjustment point by clicking it and then use the left or right arrow key to nudge it one way or the other.

Another way to increase contrast is to make a subtle S curve, as shown in Figure 9-23 (middle). Here's how: Darken the image's shadows slightly by clicking to add an adjustment point to the lower-left grid intersection and then use the down arrow to nudge it 2-3 notches for a low-resolution image or more for a high-resolution image (you can also use the Targeted Adjustment tool as described earlier). Next, lighten the image's highlights by adding a point to the top-right grid intersection, and then nudge it up the same amount. Finally, adjust the midtones by adding a point to the very center of the grid and then nudge it slightly upward to lighten or downward to darken.

FIGURE 9-23

Top: Here's a flat and rather uninspiring image, though you can use a couple of well-placed Curves Adjustment layers to fix it fast.

Middle: After you adjust the shadows and highlights, you can add a point in the center of the grid (circled) to create a magic contrast-inducing S curve. It doesn't take much of an adjustment to make a major change in an image, so try using the arrow keys to nudge adjustment points up or down.

Bottom: You can add as many Curves Adjustment layers as you want to a document. For example, you can create one to fix shadows, highlights, and midtones, and another to neutralize the suddenly too-blue sky. If you choose the Blue channel from the pop-up menu circled here, you can use the Targeted Adjustment tool to select the super-bright blue and then use your down arrow key to nudge it back down to Earth.

If the effect is a little too strong, just lower the opacity of the Curves Adjustment layer using the pop-up menu at the top of the Layers panel. If you inadvertently intensify a certain color while making a Curves adjustment, just tweak that particular channel: In the Properties panel, choose the appropriate channel from the pop-up menu directly above the grid and then click the panel's Targeted Adjustment button. Then click the color in your image that you want to adjust and press the down arrow key to neutralize it, as shown in Figure 9-23 (bottom).

TIP   Remember, you can also change the blend mode of any Adjustment layer (see page 344). For example, to preserve the color in an image, you can change a Curves Adjustment layer's blend mode to Luminosity so the adjustment affects only the image's lightness values and not its color balance—a great way to avoid color shifts.

Getting good at using Curves simply takes practice. But as long as you use an Adjustment layer, you'll never harm your original image. Heck, if you're feeling really frisky, you can click the pencil icon on the Properties panel's left and then draw your *own* curve by hand. (If you go that route, click the "Smooth the curve values" button just beneath the pencil to smooth the line you drew.) To add points to adjust the curve, click the button just above the pencil called "Edit points to modify the curve." And when you're ready to learn more about Curves, check out Ben Willmore's DVD *Mastering Curves* (*www.lesa.in/benscurves*).

POWER USERS' CLINIC

Keyboard Curves

If you're a fan of keyboard shortcuts and keyboard/mouse combinations, dog-ear this page—or better yet, print a copy of the shortcuts included on this book's Missing CD page at *www.missingmanuals.com/cds*—because there are a slew of 'em that you can use with Curves:

- To cycle through a document's channels (starting with the composite channel), press ⌘-2, 3, 4, 5, 6 (Ctrl+2, 3, 4, 5, 6 on a PC). To cycle through a document's channels in the Properties panel, press Option (or Alt)+2, 3, 4, 5 (and 6, if you're in CMYK mode).

- To show clipped shadows and highlights, Option-drag (Alt-drag) the Properties panel's shadows or highlights sliders, or click the shadows or highlights eyedropper and then press and hold Option (Alt) as you move your cursor over the image.

- To switch between the 25 percent to 10 percent grid (page 395), or vice versa, Option-click (Alt-click) the grid.

- To cycle forward (left to right) through curve points, press =.

- To cycle backward through curve points, press – (that's the minus sign).

- To deselect the selected point(s), press ⌘-D (Ctrl+D).

- To select multiple points, Shift-click them.

- To delete a single point, select it and then press Delete (Backspace), drag it off the grid, or ⌘-click (Ctrl-click) it.

- To nudge the selected point two units in the Properties panel, press one of the arrow keys.

- To nudge the selected point 16 units in the Properties panel, press and hold Shift and then use the arrow keys.

TIP If you create a really useful or incredibly funky Curve, you can save it for use later by choosing Save Curves Preset from the Properties panel's menu. (You can save a favorite Levels adjustment in the same way.) From then on, it'll show up in the Preset pop-up menu at the top of the panel.

■ Creating High Dynamic Range Images

Once you get used to peeking at the histogram (page 375), you'll notice that very few images exploit the full range of brightness values from light to dark. More often than not, you'll have more info on one end of the histogram than the other, meaning the highlights or shadows look really good, but rarely both. That's because digital cameras can collect only so much data in a single shot. If you've got a scene with both light and dark areas—like a black cat on a light background—you have to choose which area to expose for: the cat or the background. To capture more info, you can shoot multiple versions of the same shot at different *exposure values* (called *EV*) by varying your shutter speed, and then combine them later in Photoshop into what's known as a *high dynamic range* (HDR) image.

Back in Photoshop CS5, Adobe put a lot of effort into making it easier for mere mortals to create HDR images. But before you get started, you need to dig out your camera's manual and hunt for a feature called *auto bracketing*, which makes the camera take a series of shots with different exposure settings by varying its shutter speed (better yet, set the exposure differences up yourself manually—see your camera's manual to learn how). Bracketing lets you tell the camera how many shots to take (use a minimum of three, though more is better) and how much of an exposure difference you want between each one (pick one or two if you have the choice). For example, for three shots, you'd have one at normal exposure, one that's one or two EV steps *lighter* than normal, and one that's one or two EV steps *darker* than normal. After you've taken a few series shots with these settings, upload them to your computer (see Chapter 21 to learn how to import images using Bridge).

NOTE As far as file formats and HDR, using Raw files (page 57) is the best approach since they contain more info than JPEGs. Also, be sure to use a tripod so your camera doesn't move between shots!

Here's how to merge several exposures of the same shot into one:

1. **In Photoshop, choose File→Automate→"Merge to HDR Pro."**

   In the resulting dialog box (Figure 9-24) navigate to where the images (or folder) live on your hard drive and then click OK. Photoshop combines the images into one document and auto-aligns them on separate layers. Depending on your computer, this process might take a while. When it's finished, you see the resulting image in the new "Merge to HDR Pro" dialog box (Figure 9-25).

NOTE Want to follow along? Visit this book's Missing CD page at *www.missingmanuals.com/cds* and download the practice file *Mini.zip*.

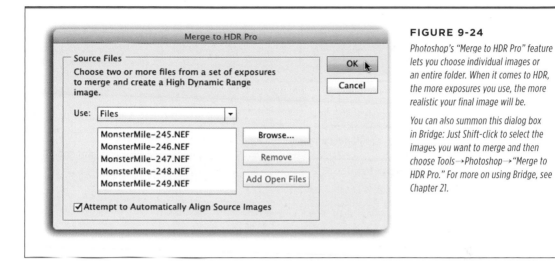

FIGURE 9-24

Photoshop's "Merge to HDR Pro" feature lets you choose individual images or an entire folder. When it comes to HDR, the more exposures you use, the more realistic your final image will be.

You can also summon this dialog box in Bridge: Just Shift-click to select the images you want to merge and then choose Tools→Photoshop→"Merge to HDR Pro." For more on using Bridge, see Chapter 21.

2. **In the full-size "Merge to HDR Pro" dialog box, turn on the "Remove ghosts" checkbox if the subject of your images moved between shots or has a lot of soft edges.**

   Even if you used a tripod, this option is likely to improve the final image. When you turn on this option, Photoshop compares all the images and tries to ignore content that doesn't match throughout the majority of the shots.

3. **From the Mode pop-up menu near the top of the "Merge to HDR Pro" dialog box, choose a final bit depth for your image.**

   Choosing 32-bit makes Photoshop keep all the dynamic range information captured in the original images. However, 32-bit images contain far more info than your monitor can display (plus they take up a ton of your computer's memory), so you'll see only a portion of the images' tonal range. To compress the information into something you can actually use, you need to convert the images to 16- or 8-bit, as explained in the next step. (For more on bit depth, see the box on page 46.) This conversion process is called *tone mapping*: mapping one set of colors to another.

NOTE Just because you *can* do tone-mapping in Photoshop doesn't mean you *should*. Even though the process improved in CS5, you may still find third-party plug-ins—like Photomatix (*www.hdrsoft.com*) or HDR Efex Pro (*www.niksoftware.com*)—faster and easier to use. Both programs work on Macs and PCs and are relatively inexpensive.

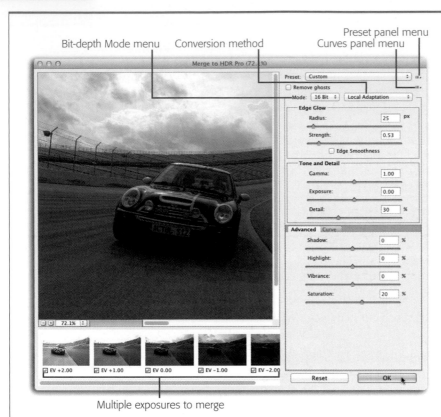

Bit-depth Mode menu   Conversion method

Preset panel menu
Curves panel menu

Multiple exposures to merge

FIGURE 9-25

At the bottom of the "Merge to HDR Pro" dialog box are the five shots that were used to create this image (photos by Karen Nace, www.karennace. com*). Clearly, the sky is much brighter than the car. If you first expose for the car and then shoot the same shot again with your EV a step apart, and then change it again by another step, you eventually have a series of images that span a broader tonal range, even though it's spread out across several images. Be sure to experiment with the canned recipes in the Preset menu shown here. Once you've got your settings just right, save 'em to use later by clicking the Preset panel menu and choosing Save Preset. Using the Curves panel menu, you can load and save Curves presets, too.*

4. **If you picked 8- or 16-bit in the previous step, choose a conversion method from the pop-up menu to the right of the Mode menu.**

   This whole HDR business is purely subjective—there's no right or wrong way to do it—so you'll want to spend some time experimenting with the various settings to figure out what makes the image look good to you:

- **Local Adaptation** gives you a slew of additional options (shown in Figure 9-25) and even lets you apply a Curves adjustment to your image right there in the "Merge to HDR Pro" dialog box. Choose this option if you've mastered Curves and then tweak the settings in the following sections of the dialog box:

  — **Edge Glow** behaves much like the Clarity slider in Camera Raw (page 370). Use the Radius slider to control the size of the hazy glow you see around soft-edge items where there's little or no contrast; drag it left to make the edge glow smaller, or right to make it larger. Use the Strength slider to control the glow's contrast (drag it right to increase contrast, or left to decrease it).

  — **Tone and Detail** has controls much like those in Camera Raw's Basic panel (page 368) with the addition of Gamma, which modifies the overall flatness and brightness of the image.

  — The **Advanced** panel lets you tweak the image's Vibrance and Saturation to alter the intensity of the colors in the image (see page 370), as well as its Shadow and Highlight brightness values.

  — The **Curve** panel (click its tab to display it) lets you make a Curves adjustment. Flip back to page 390 for the scoop on using Curves.

> **NOTE** If you've opened Photoshop in 64-bit mode (see the box on page 4), you'll see an HDR Toning option in the Image→Adjustments menu. If you choose it, Photoshop opens a dialog box with the same options discussed here, but you can apply them to *normal* images—ones that weren't shot with multiple exposures—including TIFFs. If you go this route, expect some rather unusual results!

- **Equalize Histogram** compresses the dynamic range of your HDR image, while trying to maintain contrast (It gives you a peek at what your blended image looks like). This method doesn't work quite as well as the others because it doesn't have as many options, and it tends to make the darkest shadows black.

- **Exposure and Gamma** lets you adjust the image's exposure to make the highlights brighter or the shadows darker, or both. Drag the Exposure slider right to brighten the highlights, and use the Gamma slider to set the comparative brightness difference (across the series of shots) between shadows and highlights (drag it left to darken the shadows or right to brighten them).

- **Highlight Compression** makes the brightest part of the image white, even if it's brighter than white in the 32-bit file. Pick this method if you want to see details in your image's highlights without changing its overall contrast.

5. **Click OK to create the HDR image.**

   Photoshop applies your tone-mapping settings and makes the final HDR image (see Figure 9-26).

Be warned: Once you go HDR, you may not come back. The conversion process takes time, but it can produce amazing (though sometimes unrealistic) images. Once you've recovered from poring over this section, check out *Practical HDRI, Second Edition* by Jack Howard (*Rocky Nook, 2010*) to learn more about HDR photography.

FIGURE 9-26

Top: As you can see, you can produce some colorful and interesting results using the options in the Preset menu (More Saturated was used here).

Bottom: If you choose the Surrealistic High Contrast preset, your image practically screams, "Hey! Look what I made in Photoshop!" But then again, if it looks this good, that can't be a bad thing!

Photos by Karen Nace, www.karennace.com.

■ Making Colors Pop

Once you've corrected an image's color and lighting, you can have some serious fun by boosting or intensifying its colors. You've already learned how to do that in Camera Raw with the Clarity, Vibrance, and Saturation adjustments. In Photoshop, you can adjust two out of those three—sadly, there's no Clarity adjustment...yet!

Intensifying Colors

After you've got an image's colors just right using what you've learned in this chapter, you can boost 'em so they pop right off the page. One of the simplest ways to emphasize colors is with a Vibrance Adjustment layer (see Figure 9-27), which has less of an effect on intense colors (because they're already highly saturated) than on lighter tones—yet it manages to leave skin tones relatively unchanged. You can also use a Vibrance Adjustment layer to tweak an image's saturation (it includes a regular ol' Saturation slider, too), but when you do, Photoshop applies that change evenly to the whole image no matter how intense the colors already are and with no regard for skin tones. So if you've got people in your picture, stay away from the Saturation slider and stick to Vibrance instead...unless you *like* hot-pink skin.

> **TIP** You can also use the Layers panel's Opacity field to lower the Adjustment layer's opacity and, therefore, lessen its effect.

To create a Vibrance Adjustment layer, choose Layer→New Adjustment Layer→Vibrance. You can also click its icon in the Adjustments panel (it looks like a triangle) or click the half-black/half-white circle at the bottom of the Layers panel and choose Vibrance.

> **NOTE** Want to give this technique a spin? Visit this book's Missing CD page at *www.missingmanuals.com/cds* and download the practice file *Sintra.jpg*.

Adjusting Hue/Saturation

If you want to make a specific color pop, you can use a Hue/Saturation Adjustment layer to boost one color channel's contrast. It's a simple and nondestructive way to accentuate a certain range of colors.

To create a Hue/Saturation Adjustment layer, choose Layer→New Adjustment Layer→Hue/Saturation. You can also click its icon in the Adjustments panel (it looks like two horizontal gradient bars) or click the half-black/half-white circle at the bottom of the Layers panel and choose Hue/Saturation. (Whew!) Next, choose the color you want to intensify from the unlabeled pop-up menu near the top of the Properties panel—which is set to Master until you change it—and then drag the Saturation slider to the right. Be careful not to go hog wild or your image's colors will enter the dreaded Neon Realm. You should be fine with a 10–15 percent saturation increase. Good times!

FIGURE 9-27

Unlike a regular saturation adjustment, a big boost of Vibrance (top) won't completely destroy your image, even if it contains skin tones.

However, you can easily hide its effects from part of the image—like the bottom right of this photo—by painting with black in the Vibrance Adjustment layer's mask (bottom).

Adding Lab Pop

Another way to make colors leap out of an image is to creatively blend color channels in Lab mode (page 199). It's incredibly easy and the results can be amazing, as shown in Figure 9-28. With an image open, follow these steps:

1. **Pop into Lab mode by choosing Image→Mode→Lab Color.**

> **NOTE** To follow along, visit *www.missingmanuals.com/cds* and download *Prague.jpg*.

2. **Duplicate the original layer by pressing ⌘-J (Ctrl+J on a PC).**

3. **Choose Image→Apply Image.**

   In the dialog box that appears, choose the layer you just created from (you guessed it) the Layer pop-up menu.

4. **In the Apply Image dialog box, change the Blending pop-up menu to Soft Light.**

   As you learned on page 288, this blend mode makes bright areas brighter and dark areas a little darker; it also helps make colors pop off the page.

5. **In the Channel pop-up menu, pick the channel that makes your image look best.**

   As you choose different channels, take a peek at your image to see how it changes. Remember, this kind of color adjustment is purely subjective; there's no right or wrong channel to pick, and the channel that looks the best to you in this image may not look best in another image. Figure 9-28 shows how the channels can differ.

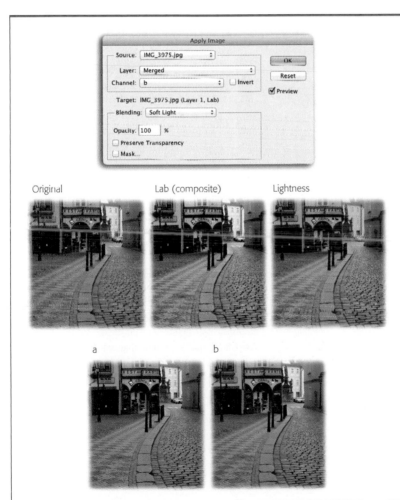

FIGURE 9-28

You can create some super-colorful images using this Lab Pop technique. The hardest part is picking which channel looks best! The Lightness version, for example, has a retro look thanks to its slight orange-greenish tinge.

6. **Lower the channel's opacity (if necessary), and then click OK.**

   If the effect is too intense, lower the channel's opacity by entering a new number in the Opacity field. Click OK to close the Apply Image dialog box.

7. **Switch back to RGB mode.**

   Choose Image→Mode→RGB. If Photoshop asks whether you want to merge layers, say no.

You're done! Put your sunglasses on and smile as you enjoy your image's brilliant new colors. You can toggle the duplicate layer's visibility eye off and on to see before and after views. If you need to tone down the extra color, just lower the duplicate layer's opacity.

POWER USERS' CLINIC

Processing Multiple Files

By now, you've probably realized how time-consuming all this image-correction business can be. That's why it's important to know how to save time by correcting more than one image with a single adjustment. Happily, there are several ways to do that:

- **Open multiple files in Camera Raw.** If you're using Camera Raw, you can adjust several files at once by opening them all at once by selecting them and then Control-clicking (right-clicking) one and choosing "Open in Camera Raw." In the upper left of the window that appears, click the Select All button. From then on, Camera Raw applies anything you do to one image to all the others, too.

- **Drag and drop Adjustment layers.** If you've (wisely) corrected an image using Adjustment layers, you can drag and drop 'em into other open documents (use the Window→Arrange menu to position your documents so you can see 'em both at the same time; page 66 explains how). That way, you can quickly fix a bunch of images from the same shoot that have similar lighting. Even if you have to tweak the adjustment a tiny bit, it's faster than hunting for highlights, shadows, and midtones in each photo.

- **Record repetitive tasks with actions.** While you can't record *every* aspect of color-correcting because it's unique

to each image (or at most applies only to images taken during a single photo shoot), you *can* automate the little things you do over and over—like duplicating the original layer and adding an Adjustment layer—using *actions*. Creating an action that performs those two steps can save you a couple of clicks. You can also automate finishing touches like making colors pop (see the previous section), record an action for the sharpening techniques in Chapter 11, and so on. See Chapter 18 to learn all about actions.

- **Use Adobe Bridge to copy and paste Camera Raw settings.** If you're working on photos from the same shoot that have similar lighting and you don't want to (or can't) open them all at once, you can adjust one and then copy and paste the Camera Raw settings using Bridge. See page 833 for the lowdown.

- **Use Adobe Bridge to rename a bunch of files.** OK, so this one has nothing to do with correcting images, but it can still save you some time! If you like renaming your processed files—before correcting them—and then saving them in a different location than the originals (a wise move), you can have Bridge do that for you for an entire folder of images. Page 830 shows you how.

■ Rescuing the Unfixables

Sadly, even with all the tricks you've learned in this chapter, you can't fix *every* image. If you run into what seems to be a truly unfixable photo and you're desperate to salvage it (if the scene or subject just can't be reshot, say), try one of these techniques:

- Use the Lab Pop technique described on page 404 and use the Lightness channel to create unique, retro-style color.

- Create an overexposed, high-key version (see page 198).

- Convert it to black and white (the whole thing or just part of it). By draining the color from an image, the color problems have no choice but to vanish (Chapter 8, beginning on page 311).

- Add a color tint using a Black & White or Photo Filter Adjustment layer (page 315 or page 340, respectively).

- Turn it into a duotone (page 327).

- Use a Threshold adjustment to create a pure black-and-white image (page 324).

- Use a combination of filters to turn the image into a pencil sketch (page 667).

Changing Reality: Removing and Repositioning

t's no secret that the beautiful models gracing the covers of magazines have been Photoshopped to within an inch of their lives. They've had the digital equivalent of every plastic surgery you can imagine, and then some: skin smoothing, blemish banishing, tummy tucking—they get it all.

This chapter shows you all those tricks and more, but that doesn't mean you should use every technique on every photo. It's easy to get carried away with this kind of stuff, and with great editing skills comes great responsibility. The challenge is to retouch your subjects enough to *enhance* their appearance without making them look fake. For example, if you're tempted to remove a wrinkle completely, soften it instead. If you'd like to hack off 30 pounds, be content with 5 or 10.

All that aside, there's nothing wrong with a little vanity, and it's darn comforting to know you can zap a zit, whiten teeth, and fix red-eye whenever you need to (and you'll never want to let photos of yourself out into the wild until you've spent some quality time with them). When you're finished with this chapter, you'll be able to fix shiny spots, remove unsightly bulges, and enhance eyes with the best of 'em. In other words, you're about to become the most popular picture-fixer-upper in your entire social network.

> **NOTE** For a fascinating profile of one of today's leading Photoshop-using, model-enhancing gurus, check out this *New Yorker* article: *www.lesa.in/nyretouching*.

But these kinds of changes aren't limited to pictures of people; you can also use Photoshop to remove objects from photos, scoot objects from one spot to another, and twist and turn objects any which way you want using the Content-Aware and

Puppet Warp tools. CS6 even includes two brand-new tools for changing reality: Content-Aware Patch and Content-Aware Move.

This chapter explains everything you need to know about turning the photos you have into the photos you want.

■ The Great Healers

Some of the simplest retouching you can do is to remove dark circles and bags under eyes, as well as other blemishes. In the old days, you were stuck with cloning (copying) skin from one area to another, which never *really* looked quite right; texture and tonal (color) differences always made the fix stick out like a sore thumb. These days, Photoshop has a set of tools specifically for retouching skin. Instead of grafting skin by cloning, these tools blend two patches of skin together so the texture and tones actually match (see Figure 10-1).

FIGURE 10-1

Top: Photoshop's magical healing tools, including CS6's new Content-Aware Move tool (discussed later in this chapter on page 447).

Bottom: A lot of moles—and an eyebrow ring—have completely disappeared from this guy's face. With a few clicks here and a few drags there, you can clean up a photo without making it look obviously retouched. Some of the guy's lighter freckles are still hanging around, and the bags under his eyes aren't completely gone; they're just lightened so they're not distracting.

NOTE The first few tools covered in this section—the Spot Healing Brush, Healing Brush, and Patch tools—live in the same toolset. Press J to activate the tool you used last, or press Shift-J repeatedly to cycle through the toolset until you get to the right one.

The Spot Healing Brush

This tool's cursor is a round brush—perfect for fixing round problem areas like pimples, moles, and so on. It's literally a one-click fixer-upper—you don't even have to drag, though you can if you want. When you click a spot with this tool, Photoshop looks at the pixels just *outside* the cursor's edge and blends them with the pixels *inside* the cursor. It's great for retouching people, fixing dust and specks in old photos, and removing anything that's roundish in shape. You can also drag with this tool to remove, say, power lines on a relatively solid background (like a sky) or to fix scratches in old photos. And with the Content-Aware Fill option (explained in a moment), the Spot Healing Brush does an amazing job at zapping unwanted stuff in your images.

To use the Spot Healing Brush, grab it from the Tools panel by pressing J (its icon looks like a Band-Aid with a circle behind it). Then put your cursor over the offending blemish and adjust the cursor's size so it's slightly larger than the area you want to fix (see Figure 10-2).

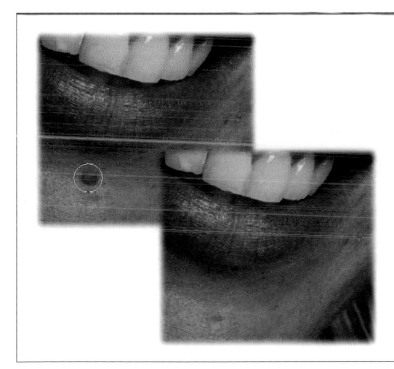

FIGURE 10-2

The key to success with the Spot Healing Brush is to make your cursor a little bit bigger than the area you want to fix.

You can change the cursor's size using the Brush preset picker at the left of the Options bar, the Brush Presets panel (page 501), or the bracket keys on your keyboard: press [to make the cursor smaller, or] to make it bigger. Alternatively, you can also resize it by Control-Option-dragging (Alt+right-click+dragging on a PC) to the left or right.

Using Content-Aware Fill

If you've got plenty of good pixels on either side of the ones you want to delete, the Spot Healing brush's Content-Aware feature works well. However, if you want to be more *precise* with your pixel zapping—say, if the item you want to delete is super close to something you want to keep—create a selection first and then use the Content-Aware version of the Fill command instead. For example, here's how to zap one of the cows in Figure 10-4:

> **TIP** The Fill command's Content-Aware option works best if there's plenty of background on either side of the object you want to remove. So if you plan to use the Fill command for some quality pixel-zapping, it's best to do that *before* you crop your image.

POWER USERS' CLINIC

Fixing Spots in Camera Raw

If you find yourself using the Spot Healing Brush repeatedly to fix a pesky speck that appears in the *exact* same place in every photo you take, there's dust on your camera's sensor. Take the camera to a trustworthy shop and have them clean it, or do it yourself with a bit of bravery and the right tools. But fixing the camera doesn't fix the photos you've already taken with it. Fortunately, you can make Camera Raw zap those spots automatically. Here's how:

1. Open all the problem images in Camera Raw (see page 58).

2. In Camera Raw, press B to grab the Spot Removal brush, click the offending spot, and then drag to resize your cursor. Clicking makes the brush cursor appear (it's a red-and-white circle), and dragging resizes it. If you click once, you create a super tiny brush tip, so it's better to drag until the brush tip is big enough to see. You can also use the Radius slider on the right side of the Camera Raw window to change the brush's size. The goal is to make the brush cursor *slightly* bigger than the spot itself.

3. Set your sample point. When you release the mouse button, Camera Raw displays a green-and-white circle near where you clicked, and the pesky spot should vanish. The green-and-white circle (which is connected to the red-and-white circle by a black-and-white line) marks the

sample point Camera Raw is *using to fix the spot*. Camera Raw usually does a good job of picking a sample point, but if you want to move it to another area that better matches the problem spot, put your cursor inside the green-and-white circle and, when a four-headed arrow appears next to the cursor, drag to move the circle somewhere else. If you need to fix several specks, repeat this step for each one until they're all gone. Now you're ready to apply the fix to the other open images.

4. Activate all the open images and then click the Synchronize button to apply the changes you just made to them, too. In the Camera Raw window's top-left corner, click the Select All button and then click the Synchronize button below it. In the resulting dialog box, choose Spot Removal from the Synchronize pop-up menu.

5. Click OK to close the Synchronize dialog box, and then click the Done button at the bottom of the Camera Raw window to save your changes. If you have hundreds of images open, you probably don't want to click the Open Image button. That'll pop 'em *all* open in Photoshop, which could send both your computer and Photoshop into a deep freeze (eek!).

FIGURE 10-4

Top: There's precious little background space between these two cows, so it's best to create a selection of the cow you want to delete. In order for Photoshop to remove the object completely (instead of leaving a funky outline of what used to be there), you need to include a bit of the background in your selection using the Expand command.

Middle: Once you've created a selection and expanded it, you can use the Fill command set to use Content-Aware to replace the selected pixels with those nearby.

Bottom: As you can see here, it does an amazing job! And by duplicating the image layer first, the original remains unchanged.

Want to follow along? Then trot on over to this book's Missing CD page at www.missingmanuals.com/cds and download Cows.jpg.

1. **Open an image and duplicate the Background layer by pressing ⌘-J (Ctrl+J).**

   Since the Fill command can't sample all layers (bummer!), it won't work on an empty layer. You could use it on a locked Background layer, but that wouldn't protect your original image.

2. **Use the selection tool of your choice to select the cow on the left.**

   Because there's a decent amount of contrast between the cow and the grassy meadow, the Quick Selection tool does a great job. Grab it from the Tools panel by pressing Shift-W until you see its icon. Next, mouse over to the image, and then click and drag to paint a selection onto it. (For more on using this tool, flip back to page 151.)

3. **Expand your selection to include some of the background by choosing Select→Modify→Expand.**

   If you're working with a low-resolution image, try entering a number between 5 and 10 pixels into the Expand Selection dialog box; you'll need to use a higher number on high-resolution images (see page 237 for more on resolution). When you click OK, the selection expands outward.

4. **Choose Edit→Fill and, from the Use pop-up menu, choose Content Aware.**

   As soon as you click OK, Photoshop fills the selection with pixels from the surrounding area.

The voodoo Photoshop uses to fill your selection is random and changes each time you use the command. In other words, if at first you don't succeed, try choosing Edit→Fill again—you'll likely get different results! Until you can actually *wish* an object out of a photo, using the Fill command's Content-Aware option ought to suit you just fine.

The Healing Brush

Like the Spot Healing Brush, this tool also blends two areas of skin together, but you have to tell it *where* to find the skin that looks good (which makes it handy for fixing things that aren't round). This process, called *setting a sample point*, is how you let Photoshop know which portion of skin—or fur, or whatever—you want it to *sample* (blend the offending spot with). To set a point sample, activate the Healing Brush by pressing J (or press Shift-J to cycle through the healing tools) and then Option-click (Alt-click on a PC) an unblemished area of skin. Then mouse over to the bad skin and brush it away. This tool works really well on wrinkles, scratches, and so on, plus you can make the healing happen on its *own* layer, as explained in Figure 10-5. You also get a live preview of the sample point right inside your brush cursor (Figure 10-5, bottom left).

> **TIP** When you set a sample point, try choosing a spot that's as near to the problem spot as possible so the texture and color match better. For example, you wouldn't want to repair skin on Aunt Edna's nose with skin from her neck.

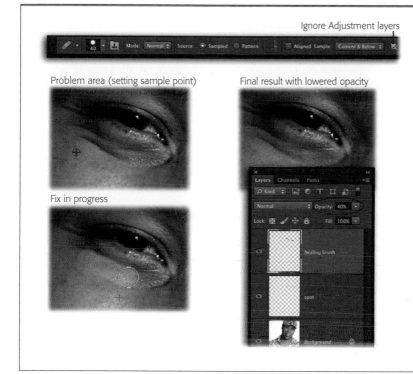

Ignore Adjustment layers

Problem area (setting sample point)

Final result with lowered opacity

Fix in progress

FIGURE 10-5

Top: Set the Options bar's Sample pop-up menu to Current & Below so the healing happens on the new layer that you've created (just be sure to position it above the image layer). If you want the tool to sample from all the layers in the document, choose All Layers from the pop-up menu instead. Like the Spot Healing Brush, this tool also has a tablet-pressure option.

Bottom Left: When you press the Option key (Alt on a PC), your cursor turns into a target; simply click to set a sample point (top). As you start painting over the bad skin, you see a little crosshairs cursor marking your sample point (right) that moves along with your brush.

Bottom right: By healing on another layer, you can lessen the effect of the healing by lowering that layer's opacity. Here it's set to 50 percent.

When you activate the Healing Brush tool, the Options bar includes the following options:

- **Mode.** You get the same set of blend modes for the Healing Brush as you do with the Spot Healing Brush. Both tools work really well in Normal mode, so you probably don't need to change this setting.

- **Source.** You can use a sample (which you choose by Option-clicking [Alt-clicking on a PC]) or a pattern as your source. Photoshop assumes you want to use a sample, but if you turn on the Pattern option, you can choose an option from the Pattern Preset picker pop-up menu to its right. Healing from a pattern is useful if you don't have enough area in your image to heal *from*. For example, if you're using the Healing Brush to remove graffiti from a wall, you can create a pattern from part of the wall texture and save it as a reusable pattern (page 95).

> **TIP** You can also sample from another open document as long as both images are in the same color mode. Just hop over to the other document, Option-click (Alt-click) to set a sample point, and then click back in your original document to do the healing (use the Window→Arrange submenu to position both document windows so you can see them [see page 66]). This technique is handy when you want to snatch texture from one image and apply it to another; the Healing Brush does the heavy lifting of blending the texture with existing pixels.

- **Aligned.** Turn on this checkbox to keep the sample point aligned with your cursor, even if you release your mouse button and move to another area. When this setting is *off*, Photoshop uses the original sample point each time you start to paint even if you move your cursor far away. If your healing requires several brushstrokes, it's helpful to turn this setting on.

- **Sample.** This pop-up menu lets you choose which layers you want to sample from. To make the healing happen on a separate layer, create a new layer above the one you want to fix and then choose Current & Below. To sample from all visible layers, choose All Layers instead; if you do that, you can make Photoshop ignore Adjustment layers by clicking the button to the right of this menu, which is labeled in Figure 10-5, top, and explained next.

- **Ignore Adjustment Layers.** If you added Adjustment layers to alter the color or lighting in the image, you can have Photoshop ignore them by clicking this half-black/half-white circle.

- **Always use Pressure for Size.** If you have a graphics tablets (page 518), clicking this button lets you control the size of the Healing Brush's cursor by applying pressure with your stylus (the pressure-sensitive pen that comes with a graphics tablet). Just like with the Spot Healing brush, pressing harder increases brush size and pressing lighter decreases it.

Here's how to use the Healing Brush:

1. **Add a new layer above the one you want to fix.**

   Click the "Create a new layer" button at the bottom of the Layers panel, and name the new layer something like *Healing*. Make sure that it's above the layer you're fixing and that it's active.

2. **Choose the Healing Brush from the Tools panel.**

   Press J to activate this brush, whose icon is an itty-bitty Band-Aid.

3. **In the Options bar, set the Sample pop-up menu to Current & Below.**

   This setting tells Photoshop, "Create a sample from the current layer and any other layers that lie below it, but make the fixes happen on the layer I'm currently on." This process gives you a ton of flexibility: You can lower the layer's opacity to lessen the strength of the fix, change the layer's blend mode, or toss it in the trash if you decide you don't like it.

4. **Mouse over to your document and set a sample point by Option-clicking (Alt-clicking on a PC).**

   Photoshop has no clue where the good skin is, so you have to tell it. Option-click (Alt-click) an area of good skin that's similar in texture to the bad skin. (It's OK if the good skin is on the opposite cheek from the bad skin, for example, so long as the texture is the same.) Now you're ready to start healing.

5. **Click (or drag across) the area you want to fix.**

Mouse over to the problem area and click it or click and drag to paint it away. You'll see tiny crosshairs marking the sample point as you drag, and a preview of the sample area inside your cursor. If you're fixing a small area, like the bags beneath the guy's eyes in Figure 10-5, you're probably OK with setting just one sample point. If you're fixing a larger area, you may need to set a new sample point every few brushstrokes to match the tone and texture of what you're fixing.

> **TIP** If you accidentally introduce a repeating pattern when using the Healing Brush, it's easy to fix. Just set another sample point and then paint the error away, or switch to the Spot Healing Brush and then click the problem area.

The Patch Tool

The Patch tool may become one of your favorite Photoshop tools because it's so easy to use and does an amazing job. It works like the Healing Brush in that you set a sample point, but it's often better than the Healing Brush for fixing big areas like dark circles or bags beneath tired eyes. It's also handy for removing piercings, tattoos, and with CS6's new Content-Aware option, even entire objects.

To use the Patch tool, grab it from the Tools panel (it lives in the same toolset as the Healing and Spot Healing brushes), mouse over to your image, and then drag to draw an outline around the area you want to fix (marching ants appear when you let go of your mouse). Next, click anywhere inside the selected area and hold down your mouse button as you drag to reposition the selection outline so it's over a *good* patch of skin (see Figure 10-6, top right). (To drag perfectly vertically or horizontally, hold down Shift as you drag.) A live preview of the good skin appears inside the selection as you drag. When you let go of your mouse, Photoshop blends the two areas together.

> **TIP** If you need to adjust the selection while you're drawing it, use the buttons near the left end of the Options bar to add to or subtract from the selection or to create one from two intersecting areas. Better yet, use these keyboard shortcuts: Shift-drag to add to the selection, Option-drag (Alt-drag on a PC) to subtract from it, and Option-Shift-drag (Alt+Shift-drag) to select an intersecting area.

In addition to the "Add to selection," "Subtract from selection," and "Intersect with selection" buttons you're used to from working with the selection tools, the Options bar includes several settings for the Patch tool. The main choice you need to make is what the Patch menu is set to:

- **Normal.** Photoshop is set to use this mode straight from the factory. In this mode, you see the following settings to the right of the Patch menu:

  - **Source.** With this setting, Photoshop takes the texture from the good skin and tries to match it with the color and lighting of the area just outside your original selection. To produce convincing patches, leave this radio button turned on.

— **Destination.** If you'd rather select the good skin first and *then* drag it atop the bad skin, turn on this radio button.

— **Transparent.** Turn on this checkbox if you want to copy an area's texture but not its content. For example, if you're working on a photo of a brick wall, you could use this option to copy the texture of the super grungy bricks onto those that look newer, without duplicating the grungy bricks in their entirety. This setting works best in conjunction with the Use Pattern setting, explained next.

— **Use Pattern.** To apply a pattern to the area you've selected with the Patch tool, click this button and then choose a pattern from the menu next to it. However, you'll rarely use this option because, instead of merely making Photoshop copy and blend pixels from one area to another, it adds the pattern you picked from the pop-up menu to the selected area. That said, it's useful if you're trying to add texture to an area that doesn't have any.

TIP It's a little-known fact that you can actually select the area you want to patch *before* activating the Patch tool. That way, you can use any selection method you want—including using Quick Mask mode (page 181)—instead of drawing the selection freehand (Chapter 4 has the lowdown on creating selections). You can also draw straight lines with the Patch tool by holding down the Option key (Alt on a PC).

• **Content-Aware.** In CS6, the Patch tool sports a new Content-Aware option (Figure 10-7), which greatly improves its ability to remove objects in a realistic way by modifying the pixels *inside* the selected area. When you choose this mode from the Patch menu, you see these settings instead of the ones described above:

— **Adaptation.** This menu lets you determine how much blending Photoshop does inside the selected area, and contains five options ranging from Very Strict to Very Loose. Set the menu to Very Strict for only a slight amount of blending or Very Loose for lots of blending. The other options—Strict, Medium, and Loose—fall somewhere in between. You'll need to experiment with this setting, as the best option varies from image to image depending on what you're trying to remove. You can make a choice from this menu either before or after you use the Patch tool.

— **Sample All Layers.** This option makes Photoshop sample pixel info from *all* layers instead of just the currently active layer. This lets you use the Patch tool on an *empty* layer instead of a duplicate of your image layer, resulting in a slightly smaller file size.

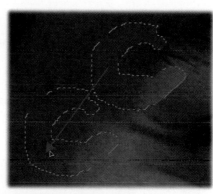

FIGURE 10-6

*If you need to get rid of a
new piercing before the
parents see it, the Patch
tool can get it done fast.*

*Top: First, draw an outline
of the offending area
freehand (left). Once you
see marching ants, click
inside the selection and
drag it to a good patch
of skin and then release
your mouse button
(right).*

*Bottom: Problem solved!
The Patch tool can help
you keep that piercing
secret for a little while
longer. And by doing the
patching on a separate
layer, the original image
remains intact.*

FIGURE 10-7

Top: By setting the Patch tool's pop-up menu to Content-Aware, Photoshop performs a little extra blending to make any lines or patterns inside the selected area match up with its surroundings. This new feature is handy if your image contains a horizon line, buildings, or man-made objects.

Middle: After creating a selection, click and drag it to a new area in your image. Here, the selection was moved to the right and positioned so that the horizon lines remain parallel.

Bottom: As you can see, Photoshop did a remarkable job of removing this little guy from the beach scene. (Hey, even bands of superheroes break up!)

Try this technique yourself by visiting this book's Missing CD page at www.missingmanuals. com/cds and downloading the practice file Heroes.jpg.

■ Zapping Shines and Shadows

Shiny spots (or *hot spots*, as some folks call them) are truly evil. They can ruin a perfectly good photo by making your subject look like a big ol' sweat ball. That's OK if the person just finished a marathon—glistening is expected then—but not if she's sitting for a portrait. Fortunately, the Clone Stamp tool can get rid of shiny spots and unsightly shadows in a hurry. It works by copying pixels from one area of an image to another (see Figure 10-8).

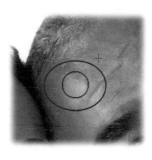

FIGURE 10-8

Top: This photo would be worth framing if the subjects weren't so shiny. To fix it, grab the Clone Stamp tool and set your sample point as close to the shiny area as possible to match tone and texture (right). Be careful not to let the sample point (the crosshairs) go into the shiny area, or you'll replicate the shine.

Bottom: No more shiny spots! The shadows on the subjects' faces and necks have also been lightened. And by setting the Sample pop-up menu to All Layers, you haven't harmed the original image. Toggle the visibility of the layers you just added off and on for a quick before-and-after comparison.

> **TIP** Be careful not to erase *all* the shine and shadows from your images; you want to leave a little bit hanging around so the photos look real. The goal is to remove just enough shine and shadow that viewers aren't *distracted* by 'em.

Here's how to reduce shine and shadows with the Clone Stamp tool:

1. **Open a photo and then add a new layer named *Shine*.**

   Click the "Create a new layer" button at the bottom of the Layers panel, name the layer in the resulting dialog box, and then click OK. Make sure this layer is active and is *above* the image layer you want to fix. By doing your skin-fixing on this layer, you protect the original image and give yourself the option of reducing the strength of the fix by reducing the layer's opacity.

2. **Grab the Clone Stamp tool from the Tools panel.**

   Press S to activate this tool, which looks like a rubber stamp (in fact, it used to be called the Rubber Stamp tool).

3. **In the Options bar, choose a soft-edged brush and set the Opacity to 20–30 percent.**

   Using a soft-edge brush makes the retouching blend better with the surrounding skin. If you leave the tool's opacity at 100 percent, you'll perform a full-on skin graft and the retouching will be painfully obvious. Lowering the opacity lets you fix the area little by little; the more you paint, the more skin gets cloned (or copied).

4. **Set the Sample pop-up menu to All Layers.**

   To make the cloning (copying) happen on its own layer, you have to tell Photoshop to sample other layers. Now you're all set to start cloning.

5. **Create a sample point for the first shiny part.**

   Mouse over to your image and Option-click (Alt-click on a PC) some non-shiny skin. Make sure this sample point is close to the shiny skin so it'll match.

6. **Click and drag across the shiny area to paint away the shine.**

   As you drag, you see little crosshairs representing the sample point. Keep a close eye on it because if it heads into a shiny patch, you'll paint a shine with a shine. If that happens, don't panic; just set another sample point by performing step 5 again. When you've fixed one shiny spot, mouse over to another and repeat steps 5 and 6.

7. **When all the shiny spots are fixed, add another new layer and name it _Shadows_.**

   Not surprisingly, you'll use this layer to fix shadowy areas.

8. **Set a new sample point and paint the shadow away.**

   Option-click (Alt-click) to set a sample point as close to the shadowy area as possible, and then drag across the shadowy area to make it go bye-bye. This technique works _wonders_ for decreasing double chins, deep crevices, and pretty much any problem area that's too dark (even if it's merely underexposed). Repeat this step until you've taken care of all the shadow problems.

9. **Save the document as a PSD file.**

   That way, you can go back and change your fixes later.

Print that baby out and slap it into the nearest frame!

■ Whitening Teeth

If you've ever enjoyed a big cup of coffee or a Texas-sized glass of red wine and then had your picture taken, you'll want to bookmark this page. Stained teeth are even more embarrassing than shiny spots, but they're super easy to fix (see Figure 10-9). You can begin by selecting the teeth—the Quick Selection tool works well—and then feathering the selection, though it's usually easier to apply the lightening to the *entire* image and then hide it with a layer mask instead.

FIGURE 10-9

You can easily whiten teeth with a Hue/Saturation Adjustment layer, as shown here. That way, the fixing happens on its own layer so you don't harm the original image, and you can lower the Adjustment layer's opacity to keep the teeth from looking too white.

Because the teeth are so small, it's easiest to lighten the whole photo and then reveal it only on the teeth using the included layer mask.

Here's how to make those pearly whites, well, white:

1. **Open an image and zoom in so you can see the subject's teeth.**

   Press ⌘ and the + key (Ctrl and the + key on a PC) to zoom in.

2. **Add a Hue/Saturation Adjustment layer.**

Click the half-black/half-white circle at the bottom of the Layers panel and choose Hue/Saturation from the resulting list.

3. **Lower the Adjustment layer's saturation and increase its lightness.**

   In the Properties panel, drag the Saturation slider to the left and the Lightness slider to the right. Keep an eye on your image to make sure you don't make the person's teeth unnaturally white. The whole image lightens as you drag the sliders, but don't worry, you'll fix that in the next step.

4. **Fill the Hue/Saturation Adjustment layer's mask with black.**

   Since you'll reveal this adjustment only on your subject's teeth, it's faster to *fill* the mask with black than to *paint* with black to hide the adjustment from the rest of the image. So activate the mask and then choose Edit→Fill. In the resulting dialog box, choose Black from the Use pop-up menu, and then click OK. (Alternatively, you can press D to set your color chips to black and white, press X until black hops on top, and then press Option-Delete [Alt+Backspace on a PC] to fill the layer mask with your foreground color). Photoshop fills the mask with black, which hides the adjustment from the entire photo (you'll reveal the lightening on the teeth in the next step).

5. **Activate the Brush tool and choose a soft-edged brush set to paint with white.**

   Press B to grab the Brush tool and, in the Options bar, use the Brush picker to choose a soft-edge brush. Then set your foreground color chip to white by pressing X to flip-flop the color chips.

6. **Click and drag to paint across your subject's teeth.**

   As you paint, Photoshop reveals the lightening in that area. If you mess up and reveal too much, just press X to flip-flop your color chips so that black is on top, and then paint across the area you didn't mean to lighten.

7. **Save the document as a PSD file.**

   If you decide to tweak the teeth later, just open the file again, double-click the Hue/Saturation Adjustment layer, and fiddle with the sliders to your heart's content.

This method will whip most teeth into shape, but if you encounter a set with a *serious* yellow cast, there's one extra step you can take: Click the Hue/Saturation Adjustment layer's thumbnail in the Layers panel; then, in the Properties panel, choose Yellows from the unlabeled pop-up menu near the top of the panel and then drag the Saturation slider slightly to the left.

TIP You can use the technique described in the list above to whiten eyes, too, but you don't have to reduce the Adjustment layer's saturation; just increasing the lightness should do the trick. Page 439 explains another way to accentuate eyes, which also works on teeth. (You can't say Photoshop doesn't give you enough options!)

■ Super Slimmers

Photoshop has a slew of tools you can use to do some serious slimming like fixing flabby chins, shrinking paunchy waistlines, and instantly shaving off pounds. Tools of the body-sculpting trade include the Pinch and Liquify filters, the Clone Stamp tool, and more, all explained in this section. Read on!

Fixing Flabby Chins

You can suck the life out of a flabby chin with the Pinch filter. Sure it sounds gross, but it makes a *huge* difference and takes mere seconds.

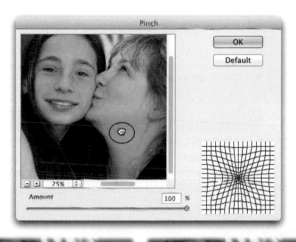

FIGURE 10-10

Top: If you click in the Pinch filter's dialog box preview window and hold down your mouse button, Photoshop shows you the pre-pinched version of the image. You can drag to move the image around (your cursor turns into a little hand, which is circled here). Use the + and – buttons below the preview window to zoom into or out of your image.

Bottom: If you duplicate the image layer by pressing ⌘-J (Ctrl+J) before running the filter, you won't harm the original image. (Alternatively, you can convert the image for Smart Filters, as explained on page 634). A fix like this one will earn you loyal clients for life!

All you have to do is duplicate the image layer and then make a rough selection—the Lasso tool works well—that includes the flab and some of the surrounding details, as shown in Figure 10-10 (bottom left). Next, choose Filter→Distort→Pinch. In the resulting dialog box, enter *100* in the Amount field, and then click OK. If you need to pinch it a little more, press ⌘-F (Ctrl+F on a PC) to run the filter again. Easy, huh?

Liquifying Bulges

Drastic bulges call for drastic action, and the Liquify filter is as drastic as it gets in Photoshop. This filter lets you push, pull, and pucker pixels any which way you want. You can use it to get a waistline under control, add a smile, enlarge lips, and so on (see Figure 10-11). In CS6, this filter uses your graphics card's processing power, so it works much faster than it did in previous versions.

Here's how to do some serious bulge busting:

1. **Pop open a photo and duplicate the image layer.**

   To protect the original pixels, duplicate the image (Background) layer by pressing ⌘-J (Ctrl+J). That way, if you get carried away and create a lumpy mess or an alien, waiflike creature, you can trash this layer and start over. (You can't run Liquify as a Smart Filter, so duplicating the original image layer is the only way to go.)

2. **Choose Filter→Liquify.**

   Photoshop opens the humongous Liquify dialog box, which may take over your whole screen.

3. **Grab the Push Left tool and increase the brush size.**

   The Liquify dialog box has a small toolbar on its left side. Grab the Push Left tool by pressing O (that's the letter O, not the number zero) or clicking its icon in the toolbar—it's selected in Figure 10-11). You can use the Tool Options section on the right side of the dialog box to pick a bigger brush, but it's simpler to press the right bracket key (]) to increase the brush size or the left bracket key ([) to decrease it. You can also Control-Option-drag (Alt+right-click+drag on a PC) to change brush size.

4. **Mouse over to the bulge on the right side of the body and drag upward.**

   If you need to, move your image around in the dialog box's preview area by pressing the space bar while dragging with your mouse. Once you've got a good view of the bulge, position your cursor so the crosshairs touch the background and the edge of the brush touches the bulge where it starts down at the waistband. Then push the bulge back toward the torso by dragging *upward*. If you think that's weird, you're not alone; nobody knows why this process scoots pixels to the left, but it does.

5. **Move to the left side of the body and drag downward.**

Press the space bar and drag to move to the other side of the image. This time, position your cursor at the *top* of the bulge and then drag *down* to nudge the pixels to the right. Again, why this tool works this way is a mystery.

6. **Click OK when you're finished.**

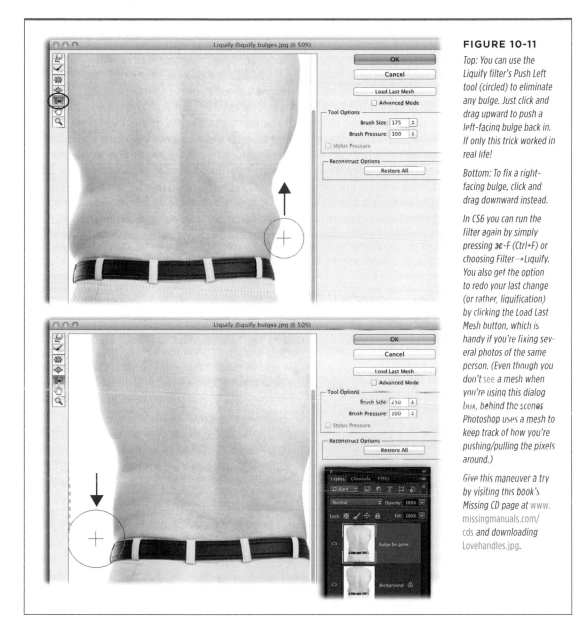

FIGURE 10-11

Top: You can use the Liquify filter's Push Left tool (circled) to eliminate any bulge. Just click and drag upward to push a left-facing bulge back in. If only this trick worked in real life!

Bottom: To fix a right-facing bulge, click and drag downward instead.

In CS6 you can run the filter again by simply pressing ⌘-F (Ctrl+F) or choosing Filter→Liquify. You also get the option to redo your last change (or rather, liquification) by clicking the Load Last Mesh button, which is handy if you're fixing several photos of the same person. (Even though you don't see a mesh when you're using this dialog box, behind the scenes Photoshop uses a mesh to keep track of how you're pushing/pulling the pixels around.)

Give this maneuver a try by visiting this book's Missing CD page at www.missingmanuals.com/cds and downloading Lovehandles.jpg.

TIP To undo a single nudge, press ⌘-Z (Ctrl+Z). To undo *everything* you've done with the Liquify filter *without* closing its dialog box, press Option (Alt) and the dialog box's Cancel button changes to read "Reset"; click it to get the original image back. You can also use the Reconstruct tool discussed below.

You make all the tools in the Liquify dialog box work by holding down your mouse button or by dragging. Here's a rundown of the other tools (Figure 10-12 gives you an idea of what they can do):

- **Forward Warp.** Use this tool to push pixels forward (ahead of your cursor in the direction you're dragging) or Shift-drag with it to push pixels in a straight line. This is another great bulge-buster, and you can also use it to make your subjects smile whether they want to or not. Its keyboard shortcut is W.

Original

Forward warp

FIGURE 10-12

Here's a sampling of what the Liquify tools can do for you (or to you). (The Mirror, Twirl, and Turbulence tools of old weren't very useful, so they didn't make it into CS6.)

Pucker

Bloat

- **Reconstruct.** Think of this one as an undo brush. If you alter pixels with any of the Liquify dialog box's other tools and then change your mind, paint over that area with this tool to restore the pixels to their original state. Keyboard shortcut: R.

- **Pucker.** This tool collapses pixels in on themselves like the Pinch filter (page 427). You can use it to make a tummy or thigh look smaller or shrink a flabby chin, a large nose, and so on. To make it have the opposite effect, press Option (Alt) so that it acts like the Bloat tool. Keyboard shortcut: S.

- **Bloat.** Use this tool to enlarge pixels from the center out. If you're considering collagen injections to fluff up your lips, try this tool first. It's also useful for opening up squinty eyes. Keyboard shortcut: B.

- **Hand.** This Hand tool is the same one that you get by pressing the space bar or clicking the hand icon in the Tools panel. You can use it to move the image around when you're zoomed in. Keyboard shortcut: H.

- **Zoom.** This tool lets you zoom in and out of the document, but it's quicker to press ⌘ (Ctrl on a PC) and the + or – key instead. Keyboard shortcut: Z.

Slimming with the Free Transform

Years ago, Hewlett-Packard came out with a "slimming camera" that promised to make you look five pounds slimmer in every picture. Behind the scenes, the camera's software was squishing the sides of the images inward (reducing their width), making people appear slightly thinner. In Photoshop, you can do the *exact* same thing with the Free Transform tool, as shown in Figure 10-13.

> **NOTE** Follow along by visiting this book's Missing CD page at *www.missingmanuals.com/cds* and downloading the practice file *Belly.jpg*.

Here's how to lose five pounds instantly.

1. **Pop open the soon-to-be-slimmer photo, duplicate the Background layer by pressing ⌘-J (Ctrl+J), and then turn off the original layer's visibility.**

2. **Summon Free Transform.**

   Press ⌘-T (Ctrl+T) and Photoshop puts a bounding box around the whole image. Grab the little square handle in the middle of the right or left edge of the photo (it doesn't matter which), and then drag the handle toward the center of the image while keeping an eye on the Options bar's W field. You want to make the image 5–8 percent narrower (so the W value is 92–95 percent); if you narrow it any more than that, it'll look stretched out. (You can also type a new width into the W field, which is easier but not as much fun.) When you've got the width just right, release the mouse button and press Return (Enter) to accept the transformation.

3. **Trim the image to get rid of the newly transparent area.**

   Choose Image→Trim and in the resulting dialog box, choose Transparent Areas and then click OK. Photoshop deletes the transparent bits, making your retouching impossible to detect.

This simple retouch is absolutely impossible to spot—*if* you keep it between 5 and 8 percent, that is. Anything more than that and your subject will look decidedly smushed.

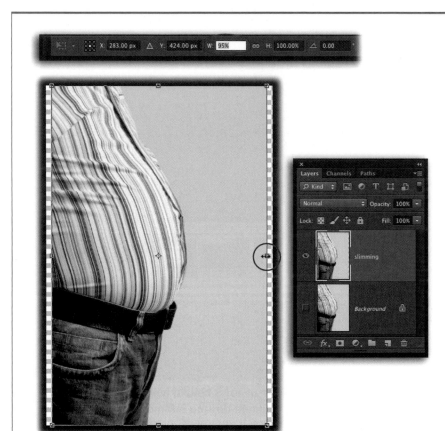

FIGURE 10-13

Top: If you do this kind of retouching while you're working in public, be sure to look over both shoulders first—you don't want to reveal this secret to just anyone! Once you've summoned the Free Transform bounding box, you can simply type 95 into the Width field, circled here.

Bottom: By duplicating the image layer first, you don't mess up your original. Just be sure to turn off its visibility eye so you can see the newer and slightly slimmer version.

■ **SELECTIVE SLIMMING**

Instead of using Free Transform to squish a whole image, you can use it to squish only a certain part. Just create a selection and *then* summon Free Transform by pressing ⌘-T (Ctrl+T). Figure 10-14 has the details.

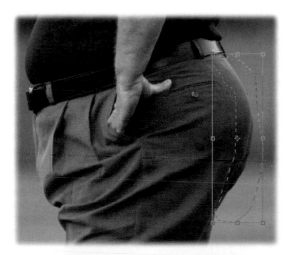

FIGURE 10-14

Top: If you select an area before activating Free Transform, you can use it to shrink just the selected area. (You may need to go back and use the Healing Brush to blend certain areas after you're finished.)

Bottom: This before-and-after shot shows quite a difference, no?

■ Skin Softeners

Skin is the body's largest organ, but not everyone gives it the respect it deserves. Folks sometimes forget to use sunblock, moisturizer, and so on. This section explains how to make skin look like it's *really* well cared for. You'll learn how to make it look soft and glowing, and even how to reduce lines and wrinkles, all without spending tons of money on anti-aging creams.

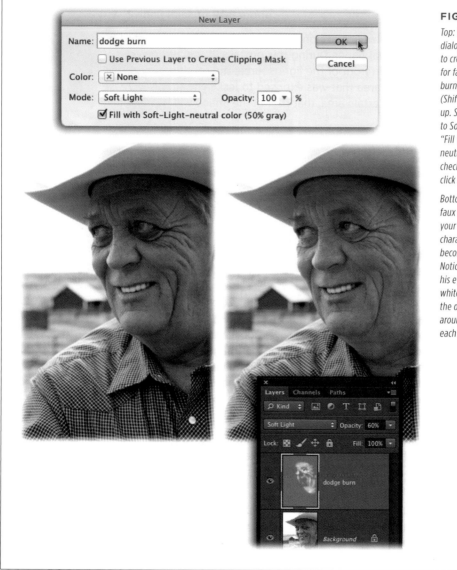

FIGURE 10-17

Top: The New Layer dialog box is a quick way to create a layer to use for faux dodging and burning; press Shift-⌘-N (Shift+Ctrl+N) to call it up. Set the Mode menu to Soft Light, turn on the "Fill with Soft-Light-neutral color (50% gray)" checkbox, and then click OK.

Bottom: When you faux dodge and burn, your subject retains his character but his wrinkles become less distracting. Notice how much brighter his eyes are, too. The whites were dodged and the darker rim of color around the outer edge of each iris was burned.

Here's how to do some faux dodging and burning:

1. **Open an image and, in the Layers panel, Option-click (Alt-click on a PC) the "Create a new layer" button.**

   In the resulting dialog box, name the new layer *Dodge Burn*, choose Soft Light from the Mode pop-up menu, turn on the "Fill with Soft-Light-neutral color

"(50% gray)" checkbox, and then click OK. (Sure, you could create a new layer, use the Edit→Fill command to fill it with gray, and then change its Mode setting, but this way is faster.)

2. **Press B to grab the Brush tool and set its opacity to 10–20 percent.**

   To retouch the image gradually, you need to lower the brush's opacity. Yes, the process takes longer this way, but you can dodge and burn little by little, which is better than doing too much at once.

3. **Set your foreground color chip to white for dodging.**

   Take a peek at the color chips at the bottom of your Tools panel. Press D to set them to black and white, and then press X to flip-flop them so white is on top.

4. **Mouse over to your image and paint across the dark wrinkles.**

   Use a small brush to lighten just the shadowy parts of the wrinkles, or else you'll lighten areas that don't need it. It's helpful to zoom *way* in on the image when you're doing detailed work like this by pressing ⌘ (Ctrl on a PC) and the + key. Photoshop switches to a pixel-grid view when you zoom in more than 500 percent (see page 60).

5. **Swap color chips so black is your foreground color and then paint light areas that you need to burn (darken).**

   If the wrinkles are so deep that they cause highlights, you can darken those a little. In Figure 10-17 the edge of each iris was also darkened to make the man's eyes look brighter.

6. **Lower the Dodge Burn layer's opacity slightly.**

   If you've overdone the changes a bit, you can lower the layer's opacity.

7. **Save the document as a PSD file in case you ever need to go back and alter it.**

TIP For maximum flexibility, you can do your faux dodging on one layer and faux burning on *another* layer. That way, you can lower the opacity of the lightening and darkening layers separately.

■ Show-Stopping Eyes

One of the simplest yet most impressive eye-enhancing techniques is waiting for you over in Chapter 11 (page 471), which explains how to use sharpening to make eyes stand out. Here in this section, you'll learn how to enhance and whiten eyes, fix red-eye a bazillion different ways, and even how to fix your furry friends' eyes.

Enhancing Eyes

A quick and painless way to make eyes stand out and look sultry is to lighten them by changing their blend mode to Screen. This technique enhances the iris *and* brightens

If you end up with a little black outside the pupil, you can use the Eraser tool to fix it because you'll erase to the original layer below. Press E to activate the Eraser and carefully paint away any extra black pixels. Alternatively, you can add a layer mask to the eye layer and then paint with black to hide the excess black.

7. **Save the document as a PSD file and call it a day.**

You won't need to use this technique very often, but at least you know how to do it when you need to!

■ FIXING RED-EYE IN CAMERA RAW

Camera Raw's Red Eye Removal tool looks and works the same as Photoshop's. It's handy to have this option in Camera Raw because, if you're shooting in Raw format and you don't need to do any other editing in Photoshop, you don't have to switch programs just to fix red eyes. After you open the image in Camera Raw (page 58), press E to grab the Red Eye Removal tool. Then simply draw a box around the eyeball, as shown in Figure 10-20, and let go of your mouse button.

FIGURE 10-20

When you're finished using the Red Eye tool in Camera Raw, a black-and-white circle appears around the pupil, letting you know that Raw made the fix. Just switch to another tool to get rid of the box. Click Done to save your changes and close the Camera Raw window.

Fixing Animal White-Eye

OK, *technically* animals aren't people—though to some folks (your author included) they might as well be. Our furry friends also have a version of red-eye; it's called *white-eye*, and it can ruin their photos, too. White-eye is actually more challenging to fix than red-eye because there aren't any pixels in the eye left to work with—the pupils turn white, gold, or green. The Red Eye tool won't work because the pupils aren't red, and the Color Replacement tool won't work because there's no color to replace. The solution is to select the pupil and fill it with black, and then add a couple of well-placed glints (tiny light reflections) to make the new pupils look real (see Figure 10-21).

FIGURE 10-21

Selecting the blown-out pupils (top), adding some black paint, and topping it off with two flicks of a white brush to add a glint transforms this kitty from creepy to cute in minutes.

Here's how to fix your furry friend's eyes:

1. **Open the image and select the colored pupils.**

   Since you're selecting by color, you can use either the Magic Wand or the Quick Selection tool; just click one pupil and then Shift-click the other.

2. **Feather the selection with Refine Edge.**

   Once you've got marching ants around the pupils, click the Refine Edge button in the Options bar. In the resulting dialog box, set the Feather field to 1 pixel and the Smooth field to 1. To make sure you get all the white or gold bits, you might want to expand the selection 10–20 percent or so by dragging the Shift Edge slider to the right. When you're finished tweaking the sliders, click OK.

   NOTE Remember, the settings in the Refine Edge dialog box are sticky—they reflect the last settings you used. So take a second to make sure *all* the sliders are set to zero, save for the ones mentioned here.

3. **Add a new layer named *Pupils*.**

   Click the "Create a new layer" button at the bottom of the Layers panel, name the layer, and make sure it's at the top of the layer stack.

4. **Fill the selection with black.**

   To recreate the lost pupil, press D to set your color chips to black and white and then press X until black is on top. Next, press Option-Delete (Alt+Backspace on a PC) to fill the selection with black. If the color doesn't seem to reach the edges of the selection (which can happen if you feathered or smoothed the edges a little too much in step 2), fill it again by pressing Option-Delete (Alt+Backspace). Once the pupils are filled with color, get rid of the marching ants by pressing ⌘-D (Ctrl+D).

5. **Add another new layer and name it *Glint*.**

   You'll want to soften the glints you're about to create by lowering their opacity, so you need to put them on their own layer.

6. **Grab the Brush tool, set your foreground color to white, and then add the glints.**

   Press X to flip-flop color chips and, with a very small brush (10 pixels or so), click once in the left eye to add a glint to mimic the way light reflects off eyes (every eye has one). Next, click in the *exact* same spot in the right eye to add a sister glint. Then lower the glint layer's opacity to about 75 percent.

7. **Save the document as a PSD file.**

Pat yourself on the back for salvaging such a great shot of your pet.

Other Creative Madness

The retouching techniques you've learned thus far are relatively benign. Save for the Liquify filter, you haven't really done anything *drastic* to your images...until now. In this section, you'll learn how to use Photoshop's new Content-Aware Move tool to make objects (even buildings!) bigger, smaller, taller, or shorter, or to move objects around within in an image. You'll also find out how to reshape pixels using the Puppet Warp command. Read on for some serious image-changing voodoo!

Repositioning and Recomposing with Content-Aware Move

New in CS6, the Content-Aware Move tool lets you change the height and width, as well as position, of a selected object. It uses Photoshop's Content-Aware technology to match up any lines or patterns in your selection so the changes look realistic.

To move an object, pop open an image and create a new, empty layer (this is where you'll do the actual moving of pixels). Then activate the Content-Aware Move tool by choosing it from the Tools panel—it lives in the Healing toolset—or by pressing Shift-J until you see its icon appear (it looks like two arrows overlapping to form an X). In the Options bar, set the Mode menu to Move and turn on Sample All Layers. Then, mouse over to your image and drag to create a selection around an object, like the left-hand soapbox in Figure 10-22, and then drag it elsewhere in the image.

NOTE Follow along by visiting this book's Missing CD page at *www.missingmanuals.com/cds* and downloading the practice file *Racers.jpg*.

The Content-Aware Move tool also lets you change the height and width of an object to, for example, make a building taller, wider, shorter, or thinner. To use it, create a new image layer, activate the Content-Aware Move tool, and then choose Extend from the Options bar's Mode pop-up menu. Then simply select the object you want to change and drag it up to increase its height or left/right to increase its width. As of this writing, this feature works only if you make *very* small changes, and even then you may need to use the Spot Healing Brush or the Clone Stamp tool to make the edit look real.

TIP Just like with the Patch tool, you can also create a selection *before* activating this tool.

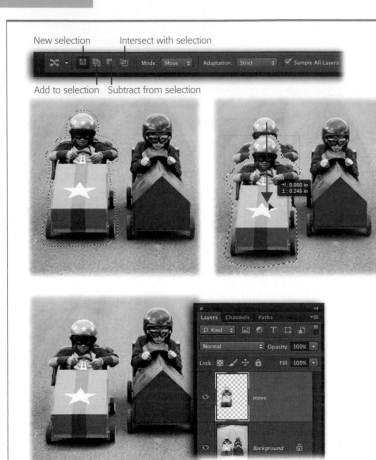

New selection   Intersect with selection

Add to selection   Subtract from selection

FIGURE 10-22

Top: Use the new, add, subtract, and intersect buttons labeled here to alter your selection. The Mode pop-up lets you choose between Move and Extend mode. The Adaptation menu lets you determine how much blending Photoshop does in the selected area, from a lot (Very Loose) to not very much (Very Strict). (These options are explained back on page 420).

Middle: Once you've selected the object, click and drag it to another position in the image. As you drag, you see an overlay that includes position info.

Bottom: If you've got a good-sized chunk of background around the item you're moving and you're not moving it very far, this tool does a good job. That said, you'll probably need to use the Spot Healing Brush set to Content-Aware, or the Clone Stamp tool, to clean up any areas that went astray (both tools were used around the right rear wheel of this now-winning soapbox).

Reshaping Objects with Puppet Warp

The Puppet Warp command made its debut in Photoshop CS5, and most folks are *still* trying to figure out how and when to use it. It lets you distort individual objects in an image while leaving the rest of it unscathed (though it can warp whole images, too, if you like). You can use it to make subtle changes such as repositioning your subject's hair or do more drastic stuff like repositioning an arm, leg, or tail.

To warp an item, you select it and then drop a series of markers (called *pins*) onto the object to let Photoshop know *what* you want to change (to warp a whole image instead, just skip making a selection). Photoshop places a grid-like mesh atop the object that contains handles you can drag to distort it. Once you finish moving the handles, Photoshop tries to adjust the *rest* of the image so it matches, making your alteration look real. While you certainly won't use this command daily, it can come in handy for moving your subject's arm or leg into a more visually pleasing or amusing position, as shown in Figure 10-23.

Pin forward   Pin backward

FIGURE 10-23

Top: Here are the Puppet Warp command's Options bar settings.

Bottom: Once you've prepared your subject or object for use with Puppet Warp as described in the steps on page 450, you can start dropping pins. To move his leg and exaggerate the kick, drop pins onto the parts you want to move (his left foot) as well as the parts you want to remain in place (his left knee, arm, head, and right foot). (The original karate kid is shown on the left.)

If everything seems to go to heck in a handbasket and you want to start over, click the Options bar's Remove All Pins button.

NOTE You can use Puppet Warp on image, Shape, and Type layers (though the latter two need to be rasterized first); Smart Objects (a good choice because you can distort them nondestructively); as well as pixel- and vector-based layer masks.

The Puppet Warp command doesn't work on locked Background layers, so either duplicate that layer or use the command on a Smart Object to protect your original, as described in the steps starting on page 450. Once you choose Edit→Puppet Warp, you see the following settings in the Options bar:

- The **Mode** pop-up menu lets you tell Photoshop how *elastic* (stretchable) you want the mesh to be. Your choices are Rigid (handy for more precise warping of objects you've marked with pins), Normal (the general-purpose mode), and Distort (great for warping an image shot with a wide-angle lens or creating an interesting texture for mapping onto another image [page 307]).

- **Density** controls the spacing of mesh points. Adding more points makes your change more accurate, but it'll take Photoshop longer to process. Fewer points speed up the process, though depending on the object you're warping, it might not look as real.

- **Expansion** lets you expand or contract the outer edge of the mesh by a pixel value. Higher numbers expand the outer edge (even beyond your document's edges), and lower values shrink it. Entering a negative value shrinks the mesh so it's inside your document's edges but also shrinks the image.

- **Show Mesh** turns the mesh on or off. If you turn this setting off, you'll see only the pins you dropped on the image. A better method is to temporarily hide the mesh by pressing ⌘-H (Ctrl+H); use the same keyboard shortcut to turn it back on.

- The **Set Pin Forward/Backward** buttons let you determine how the objects you've warped overlap each other. For example, once you start setting pins, Photoshop treats the pinned areas like layers, which means you can change their stacking order. For example, if you set pins on your subject's hand and elbow and then you drag the pinned hand atop his chest, the hand appears in front of his chest. However, if you then click the Set Pin Backward button once, Photoshop moves the pinned hand *behind* his chest instead. Depending upon how many pins you've set and how you've warped the object(s), you may have to click these buttons several times to arrange the object(s) to your liking.

- **Rotate** lets you turn the item you've dropped pins onto while you're dragging it into a new shape or position. Straight from the factory, this menu is set to Auto, which means the mesh around a pin automatically rotates as you drag the pin. If you want the mesh to rotate a fixed number of degrees instead, click to activate the pin and then press and hold the Option (Alt on a PC) key and Photoshop displays a light gray circle around the pin representing rotation angle; then just click and drag around the circle to rotate the mesh (when you do, this menu changes to Fixed). When you're finished, release the Option/Alt key. Figure 10-24 (top) shows this maneuver in action.

It's next to impossible to grasp how this tool works until you try it. Follow these steps to change the position of your subject's limbs:

> **NOTE** You can go to this book's Missing CD page at *www.missingmanuals.com/cds* and download the practice file *Karate.jpg*.

1. **Open an image, duplicate the Background layer and then turn off the visibility of the original layer.**

   Puppet Warp won't work on a locked Background layer, plus this command is about as destructive as it gets! So press ⌘-J (Ctrl+J on a PC) to duplicate the Background layer and then turn off the visibility of the original.

2. **Create a selection of the object you want to change (like the kid in Figure 10-23, bottom left), jump it onto a new layer named *karate kid*, and then turn off the visibility of that new layer.**

Select the item you want to warp using the techniques you learned back in Chapter 4 (the Quick Selection tool was used here). If necessary, click the Refine Edge button in the Options bar to fine-tune your selection. Once you have the selection just right, press ⌘-Option-J (Ctrl+Alt+J) to put the object on a new layer.

3. **Activate the duplicate Background layer you created in step 1, load a selection of the *karate kid* layer's contents, and then expand the selection to include more of the background.**

To keep from creating another instance of the object you're warping, you have to remove that object from the original image (or rather, the copy you made in step 1), which is easy to do by expanding the selection and then using the Fill command's Content-Aware option. Click to activate the copy of the Background layer and then ⌘-click (Ctrl-click on a PC) the *karate kid* layer's thumbnail to load it as a selection. Next, expand the selection to include a little of the image's background by choosing Select→Modify→Expand. In the resulting dialog box, enter 10 pixels if you're working with a low-resolution image (use a higher number for a high-resolution image) and then click OK. Photoshop expands the selection by the amount your entered.

4. **Use the Fill command's Content-Aware option to delete the object from the image and then deselect.**

Because you expanded the selection to include more of the background in the previous step, Photoshop has an easier time removing the object from the image. Simply choose Edit→Fill and, in the resulting dialog box, make sure the Use menu is set to Content-Aware, and then click OK. (If some of the original item is still visible, create a new, empty layer and then use the Spot Healing Brush, Healing Brush, or Clone Stamp tool to fix it.) When the object is history, press ⌘-D (Ctrl+D) to deselect everything.

5. **Activate the karate kid layer, turn its visibility on, and then Ctrl-click (right-click) near the layer's name and choose "Convert to Smart Object" from the shortcut menu that appears.**

Using Puppet Warp on a Smart Object lets you come back and edit your warping later on, provided you save the document as a PSD file (which of course you will!). Now you're *finally* ready to start warping the object.

6. **Choose Edit→Puppet Warp and then, in the Options bar, turn off the Show Mesh checkbox.**

As soon as you summon Puppet Warp, Photoshop plops a mesh on top of layer's contents (the kid) which keeps you from seeing anything useful. So trot on up to the Options bar and turn off the Show Mesh checkbox.

7. **Click in the image to drop pins on the object you want to move _and_ on the items you want to remain in place.**

You can think of dropping pins as placing control handles that you can then click and drag to move or spin to rotate the object underneath them. Not only do these pins let you tell Photoshop which parts of the image you want to warp or move, but they also anchor areas in place—if you don't drag or spin a pin, the area where you placed it stays perfectly still. To move this little boy's left leg, drop a pin on his left foot and knee. Next, lock the rest of his body in place by dropping pins on his left elbow, head, and right foot. (If you don't, his whole body will rotate as you drag the pin on his left foot.)

> **TIP** If you try to add a pin too close to an existing one, Photoshop displays an error message to let you know. The fix is to either set the Options bar's Density pop-up menu to More Points, or just press ⌘-Z (Ctrl+Z) to remove the pin and then click to place it a little farther away from the others.

8. **Click to activate the pin on his left foot and then drag it slightly up and to the left (as shown in Figure 10-23, bottom right).**

As you drag the pin, the pixels beneath it move, stretch, or contract depending on how far you drag and in what direction. To make the change look realistic, don't drag the pins very far (you don't have to move 'em far to create seriously cartoonish results). Once you start moving pins, you can change the stacking order of the pixels underneath them by using the Pin Depth buttons in the Options bar (labeled back in Figure 10-23, top). For example, if you swing the kid's foot to the _right_ instead of left, his foot moves _behind_ his right leg. Click the "Set pin depth forward" button and Photoshop brings his foot forward in front of his leg.

To _rotate_ the pixels beneath a pin rather than moving them, click to activate the pin (Figure 10-24, top left) and then press and hold Option (Alt) and put your cursor _near_ the pin (but not directly over it); when a circle appears around the pin, drag clockwise or counterclockwise around it to rotate those pixels (you'll see the degree of rotation appear next to your cursor, as shown in Figure 10-24, top right).

> **TIP** If you want to move several pins at once, you can activate more than one pin by Shift-clicking them, or by Ctrl-clicking (right-clicking on a PC) one pin and then choosing Select All Pins from the resulting shortcut menu. To delete a pin, Option (Alt) click it (your cursor turns into a tiny pair of scissors); to delete _multiple_ pins, activate them and then press Delete (Backspace).

9. **When you're finished, press Return (Enter) and then save the document as a PSD file.**

    Photoshop adds a new layer named Puppet Warp beneath the Smart Object's mask (Figure 10-24, bottom) and your pins disappear. Saving the file as a PSD lets you edit the pins anytime you want; simply double-click the Puppet Warp layer in the Layers panel and they reappear.

FIGURE 10-24

Top: To spin the pixels beneath a pin, click to activate the pin (left), and then press and hold Option (Alt) to reveal this handy circle (right); just click and drag around the circle when it appears. Photoshop displays the rotation angle as you drag.

Bottom: Here you can see all the pins needed to expand his cape and move his legs so it appears that he's jumping and kicking at the same time. To edit the pins later, just double-click the Puppet Warp layer in the Layers panel (circled).

Compare this image to the original photo shown back in Figure 10-23 (bottom left) and you'll really appreciate the power of Puppet Warp!

As you might imagine, using Pupped Warp involves a *lot* of trial and error, but isn't that what Photoshop is all about? Just imagine what this command could let you do to photos of your ex! However, a more *practical* use for Puppet Warp is to twist and turn ordinary objects into something extraordinary. For example, you could contort a piece of rope or barbed wire into letters or shapes. The possibilities are limited only by the amount of time you've got to experiment.

The Art of Sharpening

You know the saying "last but not least"? Well, that definitely applies to *sharpening*—a digital attempt to improve an image's focus. Because it's such a destructive process, it's generally the last thing you do before sending images off to the printer. Sharpening is *muy importante* because it brings out details and makes images pop, but it's also one of the least understood processes in Photoshop. In addition to teaching you *how* to sharpen, this chapter also gives you some guidelines about *when* and *how much* to sharpen, so you're not just guessing.

In case you're wondering which of your photos need sharpening, the answer is all of 'em. If your image came from a digital camera or a scanner, it needs sharpening. Why? In their comprehensive book on sharpening, *Real World Image Sharpening, Second Edition* (Peachpit Press, 2009), Jeff Schewe and the late Bruce Fraser explain that images get softened (their pixels lose their hard edges) when cameras and scanners capture light and turn it into pixels. Then, those images get softened even more when they're printed. (Even if you create an image from scratch in Photoshop, the same deterioration occurs if you shrink it.)

While Photoshop is pretty darned good at this sharpening business, it's not magic—it can't take an out-of-focus image and make it *tack sharp* (photographer slang for super-duper sharp, derived from the phrase "sharp as a tack"). (One of the few ways you can produce well-focused photos is to shoot using a tripod [to keep the camera stable] and a remote [so you don't move the camera when you press the shutter button], and use a lens [or camera body] that includes an image stabilizer.) The program doesn't have a magical "make my blurry picture sharp" button, though maybe Photoshop CS25 will. What Photoshop *can* do is take an in-focus image and make it nice and crisp. But before you start sharpening, it's important to understand exactly how the whole process works. Read on.

NOTE You can save a *slightly* blurry image by using the Emboss filter. Flip to page 668 for the scoop.

■ What Is Sharpening?

Sharpening an image is similar to sharpening a kitchen knife. In both instances, you're emphasizing edges. On a knife, it's easy to identify the edge. In a digital image, it's a little more challenging: the edges are the areas where vastly different colored pixels meet (see Figure 11-1).

Unsharpened

Oversharpened

33.33%   Doc: 5.49M/5.49M

FIGURE 11-1

Left: It's easy to spot the edges in this image because its contrast is pretty high, especially between the antlers and the light background.

Right: In this before-and-after closeup of the Chihuahua's antlers—who does that to their pet?—see how the edges are emphasized after some overzealous sharpening (bottom)? The weird white glow around the antlers is the dreaded sharpening halo.

When you sharpen an image—whether in Photoshop, Camera Raw, or a darkroom—you exaggerate the edges in the image by increasing their contrast: Where two colors meet, you make the light pixels a little lighter and the dark pixels a little darker. Though it may sound similar to increasing the overall contrast of the image, it's not. When you run one of Photoshop's sharpen filters, the program analyzes your image and increases the contrast *only* in areas it thinks are edges (and, as you'll learn in a bit, you have some control over what Photoshop considers an edge).

Sharpening is a bit of an art: If you don't sharpen enough (or at all), your image will look unnaturally soft and slightly blurred; if you sharpen too much, you'll get a *sharpening halo*, a nasty white gap between light and dark pixels (Figure 11-1, bottom right). But if you sharpen just the right amount, no one will notice the sharpening—they'll just know that the image looks really good.

One of the downsides to sharpening is that it also emphasizes any kind of *noise*—graininess or color specks—in your image. One way around that problem is to get rid of the noise before you sharpen, or at least have a go at reducing it (see the box on page 459 for tips).

Now that you know what sharpening does, you're ready to give it a whirl in Photoshop. The next few pages focus on basic sharpening techniques; more advanced methods are discussed later in this chapter.

Basic Sharpening

If you've ever peeked inside the Filter menu at the top of Photoshop screen, you've probably noticed a whole set of filters devoted just to sharpening. They include the following:

- **Sharpen, Sharpen Edges, Sharpen More.** When you run any of these filters, you leave the sharpening up to Photoshop (scary!) Each filter analyzes your image, tries to find the edges, and creates a relatively narrow sharpening halo (Figure 11-1, bottom). However, none of these filters gives you any control, which is why you should forget they're even there and stick with the next two filters instead.

- **Smart Sharpen.** When you see three little dots (...) next to a menu item, it means there's a dialog box headed your way—and when it comes to sharpening, that's good! Smart Sharpen lets you control how much sharpening happens in your image's shadows and highlights, and it lets you pick which kind of mathematical voodoo Photoshop uses to do the sharpening. Page 463 discusses this filter in detail.

- **Unsharp Mask.** This filter has been the gold standard sharpening method for years because, until the Smart Sharpen filter came along in Photoshop CS2, it was the only one that gave you dialog box–level control over how it worked. Most folks still prefer this filter because it's easy to use and quick (it runs faster than the Smart Sharpen filter). Page 460 has the lowdown.

NOTE Though it doesn't live inside the Filter→Sharpen submenu, the High Pass filter is gaining popularity as a sharpening tool because it does a nice job and it's a little simpler to use than Unsharp Mask—it has just one setting to tweak instead of three. You can give it a spin on page 467.

No matter which filter you choose, sharpening is a destructive process, so it's a good idea to protect your image by following these guidelines:

- **Resize the image first.** Make sharpening your last step before you print an image or post it on the Web—in other words, after you've resized and retouched it. Because pixel size depends on an image's resolution and sharpening has different effects on different-sized pixels, it's important to sharpen the image after you make it the size you want.

- **Get rid of any noise first.** If you see any funky color specks or grains that shouldn't be in your image, get rid of them *before* you sharpen or they'll look even worse. The box on page 459 tells you how.

- **Sharpen the image on a duplicate layer or run it as a Smart Filter.** Before you run a sharpening filter, activate the image layer and duplicate it by pressing ⌘-J (Ctrl+J on a PC). That way, you can toggle the sharpened layer's visibility on and off to see before and after versions of the image. You can also restrict the sharpening to certain areas by adding a layer mask to the sharpened layer and reducing the sharpened layer's opacity if the effect is too strong (page 468 has tips for sharpening a multilayered file). Better yet, convert your image layer for Smart Filters so Photoshop does the sharpening on its own layer *and* includes a layer mask automatically; page 470 has the details.

- **Change the sharpening layer's blend mode to Luminosity.** Because you're about to make Photoshop lighten and darken a whole lot of pixels, you risk having the colors in your image shift. However, if you change the sharpening layer's blend mode to Luminosity, the sharpening affects only the brightness of the pixels, not their color. (If you use the Smart Filter method described on page 470, change the *filter* layer's blend mode to Luminosity instead.) This little trick does virtually the same thing as changing the color mode to Lab and then sharpening the Lightness channel, but it's a whole lot faster.

- **Sharpen the image a little bit, multiple times.** It's better to apply too little sharpening and run the sharpening filter *again* than to apply too much sharpening all at once. Sharpening an image gradually gives you more control; just use the History panel or press ⌘-Z (Ctrl+Z on a PC) to undo the last sharpening round if you go too far.

In the following pages, you'll learn various ways to sharpen, starting with the most popular method to date: the Unsharp Mask filter.

Keeping the Noise Down

It's best to reduce or get rid of any noise in your image before you sharpen it, or you'll end up sharpening the noise along with the edges. Photoshop gives you a variety of noise-reducing filters that are discussed starting on page 662. All of them work by *reducing* the amount of contrast between different-colored pixels—a process that's the exact opposite of sharpening, which is why removing noise also reduces sharpness!

(Because all filters run on the currently active layer—meaning they affect your original image—be sure to convert your image to a Smart Object [see page 634] before running a noise-reducing filter so the filter runs on its own layer, or run it on a duplicate image layer.)

The aptly named Reduce Noise filter is the best of the bunch because it gives you more control than the others. To use it, choose Filter→Noise→Reduce Noise and, in the resulting dialog box, adjust the following settings:

- **Strength.** If you've got a lot of *grayscale noise*—luminance or brightness noise that looks like grain or splotches—or *color noise* that looks like little specks of color, increase this setting to make Photoshop reduce the noise in each color channel. This setting ranges from 1 to 10 (it's set to 6 unless you change it).

- **Preserve Details.** You can increase this setting to protect the detailed areas of your image, but if you do, Photoshop can't reduce as much grayscale noise. For best results, tweak this setting along with the Strength setting and find a balance between the two.

- **Reduce Color Noise.** If there are colored specks in your image, try increasing this setting so Photoshop zaps even more of 'em.

- **Sharpen Details.** Because every noise-reducing filter blurs your overall image, this option lets you bring back some of the sharpness. However, resist the urge to use it and set it to 0%; it's better to go with one of the other sharpening methods described in this chapter instead.

- **Remove JPEG Artifact.** If you're dealing with an image that's gotten blocky because it was saved as a low-quality JPEG—or because it was saved as a JPEG over and over again—turn on this checkbox and Photoshop tries to reduce that Lego look.

- **Advanced.** This setting lets you tweak each color channel individually (for more on channels, see Chapter 5). If the noise lives in one or two color channels—it's usually notoriously bad in the blue channel—turn on this radio button and adjust each channel's settings individually. (Because Reduce Noise can make your image blurry, it's better to adjust as few channels as possible.)

Once you're finished modifying these settings, click OK to run the filter and then toggle the filter layer's visibility off and on to see how much effect the filter had. (You can preview the effect on your image by pressing P while the filter's dialog box is open.) You can also use the Smart Filter's included layer mask to restrict the noise reduction to certain parts of the image (handy if the noise is only in the shadows, for example).

And if you determine that the filter didn't help one darn bit, run—don't walk!—over to Chapter 19 to find a third-party, noise-reduction plug-in that can. Or, if buying a plug-in isn't in your budget, flip to page 216 to learn how to sharpen individual channels, which lets you bypass the noise-riddled channel altogether.

You may now proceed with sharpening your image.

Sharpening with Unsharp Mask

This filter is many people's favored sharpening method, but its name is confusing—it sounds like it does just the opposite of sharpen. The odd name came from a technique used in darkrooms, which involves using a *blurred* (or "unsharp") version of an image to produce a *sharper* one. In Photoshop, the Unsharp Mask filter studies each pixel, looks at the contrast of nearby pixels, and decides whether they're different enough to be considered an edge (you control how picky the filter is using the Threshold setting, discussed below). If the answer is yes, Photoshop increases the contrast of those pixels by lightening the light pixels and darkening the dark pixels.

FIGURE 11-2

Before the Smart Sharpen filter came along, Unsharp Mask was the only sharpening method in Photoshop that gave you any level of control. Because it's quick and fairly easy to use, it's still the preferred method today.

It's OK if your image looks a little too sharp onscreen. The pixels on your screen are much bigger than the ones your printer prints and, as mentioned earlier, the printing process itself softens the pixels a little, too. So to get a printed image that's nice and crisp, make the onscreen image look a little over sharpened.

To bail out of the Unsharp Mask dialog box without doing anything, click the Cancel button or press Esc.

TIP Anytime you see a preview in a dialog box (like the one in Figure 11-2), you can click the preview and hold your mouse button down to see a before version of the image (in this case, the unsharpened version). You can also drag to move the preview around or click the little + and − buttons below the preview to zoom in or out. You can also use keyboard shortcuts: ⌘-click (Ctrl-click) to zoom in, and Option-click (Alt-click) to zoom out.

Here are the settings you can adjust in the Unsharp Mask dialog box:

- **Amount.** This setting, which controls the sharpening intensity, ranges from 1 percent to 500 percent. The higher the setting, the lighter Photoshop makes the light pixels and the darker it makes the dark pixels. If you set it to 500 percent, Photoshop makes all the light pixels along the edges white and all the dark ones black, giving your image a sharpening halo you can see from outer space. For best results, keep this setting between 50 percent and 150 percent (you can find other magic numbers on page 462).

- **Radius.** This setting controls the width of the sharpening halo by telling Photoshop how many pixels on either side of the edge pixels it should analyze and lighten/darken. When you increase this setting, you may need to reduce the Amount setting to avoid creating a Grand Canyon–sized sharpening halo. For best results, don't set the Radius higher than 4.

- **Threshold.** This setting lets you control how different neighboring pixels have to be from each other before Photoshop considers them an edge. Oddly enough, Threshold works the opposite of how you might expect: Setting it to 0 sharpens *every* pixel in your image! For best results, keep this setting between 3 and 20 (it ranges from 0 to 255).

Here's how to use the Unsharp Mask filter nondestructively using Smart Objects:

1. **Convert your image to a Smart Object.**

   Choose Filter→"Convert for Smart Filters" and Photoshop displays a dialog box letting you know that the image layer will be converted into a Smart Object. Click OK and you'll see a tiny Smart Object badge appear at the bottom right of the image's layer thumbnail.

   TIP If your document contains multiple layers, you can convert 'em all into a single Smart Object. Skip ahead to page 470 to learn how.

   ---

2. **Choose Filter→Sharpen→Unsharp Mask.**

   In the resulting dialog box (Figure 11-2), tweak the settings to your liking. In the next few pages, you'll find some recommended values that you can memorize, but for now, adjust the settings until the image in the preview looks good. Click OK when you're finished to close the dialog box; when you do, a layer named Unsharp Mask appears in your Layers panel (Figure 11-3, left).

3. **Change the filter's blend mode to Luminosity.**

   Double-click the tiny icon to the right of the Unsharp Mask item (labeled in Figure 11-3, left) to view the filter's blending options. In the resulting dialog box, change the Mode pop-up menu to Luminosity and then click OK.

Smart Filter mask   Double-click to open filter blending options

FIGURE 11-3

Left: The Unsharp Mask filter is destructive, but you can run it as a Smart Filter. When you do, you'll see a brand-new item appear in your Layers panel called Unsharp Mask. If necessary, use the Smart Filter's mask (labeled here) to hide the sharpening from areas that don't need it. To adjust the filter's blending options, double-click its icon.

Right: This dialog box lets you change the filter's blend mode and reduce the opacity (strength) of the sharpening.

Sit back and marvel at your new, nondestructive Photoshop sharpening prowess. You can learn more about using Smart Filters (and their masks) in Chapter 15, though you've gotten a nice head start here!

■ **HOW MUCH TO SHARPEN?**

Some images need more sharpening than others. For example, you don't need to sharpen a portrait as much as you do a photo of Times Square because they have different amounts of detail (the Times Square photo has lots of angles and hard lines). If you sharpen the portrait too much, you'll see pores and blemishes with enough details to haunt your next power nap!

Photoshop guru Scott Kelby came up with some especially effective values to use in the Unsharp Mask dialog box and published them in *The Adobe Photoshop CS5 Book for Digital Photographers* (New Riders Press, 2010). With his blessing, here they are:

- **Sharpening soft stuff:** If you're sharpening images of flowers, puppies, babies and other soft, fluffy subjects (stuff that often blends into its background), you don't want to apply much sharpening at all. For extremely soft sharpening, try setting the Amount to 150 percent, the Radius to 1, and the Threshold to 10.

- **Sharpening portraits:** While close-up portraits need a bit more sharpening than the items mentioned above, you don't want to sharpen them as much as something hard like a building with lots of straight lines and angles. To sharpen portraits enough to make their subjects' eyes stand out, try setting the Amount to 75 percent, the Radius to 2, and the Threshold to 3.

- **Sharpening objects, landscapes, and animals:** This stuff tends to be a little harder and contain more details (sharp angles, fur, and so on) than portraits, so it needs a moderate amount of sharpening. Try setting the Amount to 120 percent, the Radius to 1, and the Threshold to 3.

- **Maximum sharpening:** For photos of cars or of buildings (which are chock full of hard lines, angles, and details) or for photos that are a little out of focus, try entering an Amount of 65 percent, a Radius of 4, and a Threshold of 3.

- **Sharpening anything:** For everyday sharpening, regardless of what's in your image, enter an Amount of 85 percent, a Radius of 1, and a Threshold of 4, and then call it a day.

- **Sharpening for the Web:** If you've resized an image so it's small enough to post on the Web (see page 719), it needs more sharpening because downsizing often makes an image appear softer. Set the Amount to 200 percent, the Radius to 0.3, and the Threshold to 0.

> **NOTE** These numbers are merely guidelines—they're not absolute rules. The most important variable is image resolution: Small pixels require *more* sharpening than big ones (and as you know from page 237, the higher the resolution, the smaller the pixels). Be sure to experiment with your own images and printer to see which settings give you the best results.

The Smart Sharpen Filter

The Smart Sharpen filter (Figure 11-4) gives you a lot more options than Unsharp Mask, so it offers a slightly better chance of saving an out-of-focus image. This filter also lets you save your favorite sharpening settings as presets, which is handy. The downside? It's not as easy to use as Unsharp Mask, and it takes longer to run. Like Unsharp Mask, this filter is destructive, so be sure to run it as a Smart Filter (as described in the previous section) or make a copy of the layer you're sharpening first. When you're ready, run this filter by choosing Filter→Sharpen→Smart Sharpen.

FIGURE 11-4

Here's the option-riddled Smart Sharpen dialog box in basic mode. See the tiny disk and trash can icons to the right of the Settings pop-up menu? These let you save or throw away custom settings, respectively.

If you click the disk icon to save your current settings and give 'em a name, Photoshop adds them to the Settings pop-up menu for easy access later. If you want to throw a custom setting away, choose it from the Settings pop-up menu and then click the trash can.

POWER USERS' CLINIC

Fading Filters

You may feel that this chapter is jumping the gun a little by covering sharpening filters because there's a *whole chapter* on filters headed your way (Chapter 15). However, some of the things you can do with filters—like fading a filter you've applied—are too dad-gummed useful to wait until then!

If you run a filter (or an image adjustment, for that matter) and the effect is a little too strong, you have one shot at lowering the filter's opacity to lessen its effect and/or changing its blend mode. However, Photoshop lets you do this only right after you run the filter, so it's super easy to miss your chance. If you didn't duplicate the original layer before running the filter or if you didn't run it as a Smart Filter, this fix is your *only* saving grace.

After you run the filter and before you do or click *anything* else, head up to the Edit menu and choose "Fade [name of the last filter you ran]." In the resulting Fade dialog box, enter a percentage in the Opacity field to let Photoshop know how much you want to fade the filter. For example, if you think the filter is twice as strong as you need, enter *50* to reduce its effect by half. (If you click OK and then change your mind, you can choose Edit→"Fade [name of filter]" again and enter a new number.) The Edit menu's Fade option remains clickable until you run another command or use another tool.

The Fade dialog box also has a Mode pop-up menu that lets you change the filter's blend mode to adjust how the sharpened pixels blend with the original pixels. Changing this setting to Luminosity has the same effect as running the filter on a duplicate layer and setting that layer's blend mode to Luminosity. When you click OK, Photoshop lessens the filter's effect by the percentage you entered.

In the resulting dialog box, you'll be assaulted with options that include Amount and Radius (discussed in the previous section), as well as:

- **Remove.** This menu is where you pick what kind of blur you want Photoshop to remove—or, more accurately, reduce. These are your choices:

    — **Gaussian Blur.** Think of this as the basic mode; it's the one that the Unsharp Mask filter uses.

    — **Lens Blur.** This setting attempts to detect the detail or edges in an image and then make the sharpening halos *smaller.* Pick this setting if your image has a lot of details and/or noise.

    — **Motion Blur.** If your image is blurry because the camera or subject moved, you could use this setting to make Photoshop *try* to fix it, though it doesn't do a very good job. You're better off using the Emboss filter technique, described on page 668.

    Since choosing Gaussian Blur basically makes this filter work like Unsharp Mask (in which case you could just *use* Unsharp Mask instead) and you use Motion Blur only when your picture is blurry, go with Lens Blur for most photos.

- **Angle.** If you choose Motion Blur from the Remove menu, use this dial to set the angle of the blur currently marring your image. For example, if you have a square image and the subject is moving diagonally across the shot from the lower-left corner to the upper-right corner, set this field to 45 degrees.

- **More Accurate.** If you turn on this checkbox, Photoshop thinks long and hard before it does any sharpening. With this setting turned on, you'll get more precise results, but the sharpening won't be as strong. Since turning on this option makes the filter take longer to run, leave it off if you have a slow computer or you're working with a huge file. If, on the other hand, you buy a new computer every time you upgrade your copy of Photoshop, you can turn it on and leave it on.

If you turn on the Advanced radio button near the top of the dialog box, Photoshop adds three tabs to the settings section. Besides the settings just listed, which appear on the Sharpen tab, you get Shadow and Highlight tabs, as shown in Figure 11-5. These two tabs, which contain the same settings, let you control the following:

- **Fade Amount** lets you reduce the sharpening Photoshop applies to your image's highlights or shadows, depending on which tab you're on. So, for example, if you enter *100* in the Sharpen tab's Amount field but want Photoshop to do a bit less sharpening in the shadows, click the Shadow tab and enter a Fade Amount of 25 percent or so. If you want *no* sharpening to happen in the shadows, enter 100 percent. (This setting is similar to the Fade command you learned about in the box on page 464.)

To control how much of the image gets sharpened, you can change the mask channel's contrast with a Levels adjustment: Choose Image→Adjustments→Levels, and then move the gray slider to the left for more sharpening or to the right for less. (Normally you create an Adjustment layer when you use Levels or Curves, but in this case you need to *apply* the adjustment to the mask channel, so a trip up to the Image→Adjustments menu is in order.) Remember, the sharpening won't show in the black areas of the mask channel, only the light gray and white areas. Click OK when you're finished to close the dialog box. (See page 375 for more on using Levels.)

FIGURE 11-12

Left: When you first run the Find Edges filter, your image looks like a pencil sketch, as shown here. (To see the original photo, check out Figure 11-13, left.) The edges in the image are black, which is the opposite of what you want.

Right: After you invert the mask channel, the edges turn white and everything else turns black. Now, when you paste this channel into a layer mask, the sharpening will show through only in the white areas.

5. **Blur the mask channel slightly with the Gaussian Blur filter.**

   To avoid harsh sharpening halos, blur the mask channel a little by choosing Filter→Blur→Gaussian Blur. Enter a radius between 0.5 and 4 to soften the mask's edges (use a lower number for low-resolution images and a higher number for high-resolution ones).

6. **Load the mask channel as a selection, and then turn on the composite channel.**

   Since you're already in the Channels panel, go ahead and load the mask channel as a selection by clicking the tiny dotted circle at the bottom left of the Channels panel; you'll see marching ants appear. (You don't need this selection just yet, but you will in a minute; with an active selection, Photoshop will automatically fill in the layer mask you create in the next step.)

   In order to see your full-color image, turn on the composite channel: Scroll back up to the top of the Channels panel and click near the name of the composite channel—either RGB or CMYK, depending on your document's color mode—to simultaneously turn the composite channel *on* and the mask channel *off*.

7. **Back in the Layers panel, duplicate the layer you want to sharpen (or combine several layers to create a new one, as described on page 469), name it *sharpening*, and add a layer mask to it.**

   Activate the layer you want to sharpen and duplicate it by choose Duplicate Layer from the Layers panel's menu (the usual ⌘-J [Ctrl+J] trick won't work because it'll only duplicate the *selected* parts). In the resulting Duplicate Layer dialog box, type *sharpening* into the As field and then click OK. Next, add a layer mask to the sharpening layer by clicking the circle-within-a-square-icon at the bottom of the Layers panel.

8. **Click the sharpening layer's thumbnail and then choose Filter→Sharpen→Unsharp Mask.**

FREQUENTLY ASKED QUESTION

The Sharpen Tool

What's all this talk about sharpening with filters? Why can't I use the Sharpen tool instead?

Just because Photoshop *has* a certain tool doesn't mean you should use it. While it seems like a no-brainer that the Sharpen tool would be your best bet for sharpening (it's specifically designed for that, right?), you can actually get better results using other methods. That said, since this book covers *all* of Photoshop, here's a quick primer on how that tool works:

The Sharpen tool is part of the blur toolset. When you click its icon (which looks like a triangle) and mouse over to your image, you see a familiar brush cursor. You can then paint areas you want to sharpen and, well, that's it. (You don't get nearly as much control with this tool as you do with the sharpen filters discussed so far in this chapter.) Up in the Options bar, you can adjust the following settings:

- **Brush.** This menu lets you pick brush size and type (big or small, hard or soft).

- **Mode.** In this pop-up menu, you can change the tool's blend mode from Normal to Darken, Lighten, Hue, Saturation, Color, or Luminosity.

- **Strength.** This field is automatically set to 50 percent. But unless you want to over-sharpen your image, lower

this setting to 25 percent or less before you use the Sharpen tool. That way, you apply reasonable amounts of sharpening and can brush over areas repeatedly to apply more.

- **Sample All Layers.** Photoshop assumes you want to sharpen only the active layer. If you want to sharpen *all* the layers in your document (or rather, the ones that you can see through the current layer, if it's partially transparent), turn on this checkbox.

- **Protect Detail.** This option prompts Photoshop to be extra careful about what it sharpens (technically, it triggers a set of sharpening instructions called an *algorithm*). Added in CS5, this setting is a definite improvement, and it could be handy if you need to sharpen a small area quickly without fussing with Smart Filters or a duplicate (or merged) layer. But the extra thinking Photoshop has to do to accomplish this means it'll run like molasses on large images (or slow computers).

As you might imagine, using this tool can be a time-suck of epic proportions because you're sharpening with a brush *by hand*, so it's best to use it only on small areas. And by all means, duplicate your image layer *before* using the Sharpen tool so you're not harming the original.

Head up to the Filter menu and choose Sharpen→Unsharp Mask. In the resulting dialog box, adjust the settings as described on page 461, and then click OK to make Photoshop run the filter.

9. **Change the sharpened layer's blend mode to Luminosity and lower its opacity, if necessary.**

   To avoid weird color shifts that can be caused by sharpening, change the layer's blend mode to Luminosity using the pop-up menu in the Layers panel (Figure 11-13, right). If the sharpening looks too strong, you can also lower the sharpened layer's opacity (you may not need to, but it's sure nice to have the option).

Whew! That was a lot of work, but your image should look light-years better, as shown in Figure 11-13. You can toggle the sharpened layer's visibility off and on to see what a difference the edge sharpening made. Thanks to the edge mask, only the building's details got sharpened, leaving areas like the sky untouched (which all but eliminates sharpening-induced noise).

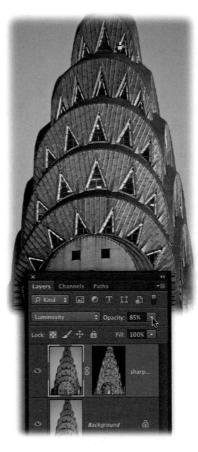

FIGURE 11-13

Left: The original, unsharpened photo of the Chrysler Building in New York City looks pretty soft and lacks detail.

Right: Sharpening the same photo with an edge mask (visible in the Layers panel) confines the sharpening to the image's details.

Sharpening in Camera Raw

Camera Raw's sharpening capabilities have improved greatly in the last few versions of the plug-in, especially in Camera Raw 6—released with Photoshop CS5—where it produced smaller sharpening halos and better noise reduction (which Adobe says works better than the third-party plug-in, Noise Ninja [page 778]). Sharpening in Camera Raw even affects your image's luminosity (lightness or brightness values) and leaves the color alone.

But *should* you use Camera Raw for sharpening? The answer is yes—*if* you're not going to edit the image much in Photoshop. If you *are* going to do a lot of editing in Photoshop, you should make sharpening the very last step (after resizing and retouching) and then use one of the methods described earlier in this chapter instead.

You *don't* want to sharpen in both programs—at least, not the whole image. Sharpening in Camera Raw is a global process, meaning it affects the entire image (though you can wield a little control using Camera Raw's Adjustment Brush, discussed later in this section). It's also a somewhat automatic process: The image gets sharpened the minute you open it in Camera Raw (unless you turn off automatic sharpening as described in the next section). If you let Camera Raw sharpen your image, you'll need to practice local or selective sharpening (page 471) once the image is in Photoshop to avoid over-sharpening it and introducing halos.

POWER USERS' CLINIC

Creating a High-Contrast Edge Mask

If you're trying to create an edge mask (page 475) but your color channels don't have much contrast, you can always create a *new* channel with contrast aplenty. If creating a new channel sounds hard, don't panic; it's easier than you think. There are two ways to go about it:

- **The Calculations adjustment** can combine two channels for you. After strolling through your channels to see which ones have the most contrast (let's say they're the red and green channels), head up to the Image menu and choose Calculations. In the resulting dialog box, tell Photoshop which channels you want to combine by choosing Red from the Channel pop-up menu in the Source 1 section and Green from the Channel pop-up menu in the Source 2 section. From the Blending pop-up menu near the bottom of the dialog box, pick one of the blend modes in the Overlay category like Soft Light (Chapter 7 describes all these blend modes in detail, beginning on page 280). When you click OK, Photoshop creates a brand-new

channel you can tweak into a high-contrast edge mask. *Now* you're ready to proceed with step 2 back on page 475. (Since this channel is totally new, you don't have to duplicate it like you did in step 1 on that page.) To learn more about the Calculations adjustment, flip to page 215.

- **The Channel Mixer** doesn't really create another channel; instead, it lets you create a black-and-white version of your image that you can use as if it *were* a channel. Duplicate your Image layer by pressing ⌘-J (Ctrl+J), and then choose Image→Adjustments→Channel Mixer. In the dialog box that appears, turn on the Monochrome checkbox and then tweak the various sliders. When you get some really good contrast, click OK. Next, start with step 2 on page 475 and run the Find Edges filter in the Layers panel instead of the Channels panel (the steps are exactly the same). For more on using the Channel Mixer, head to this book's Missing CD page at *www.missingmanuals.com/cds*.

Global Sharpening

You can sharpen in Camera Raw by first opening an image and then clicking the tiny Detail icon circled in Figure 11-14. If you don't want any global sharpening, drag the Amount slider to zero (from the factory, it's set to 25). If you *do* want to sharpen the image, mosey on down to the lower-left corner of the Camera Raw dialog box and change the view percentage to 100 so you can see the effect of the changes you'll make to the Detail settings (otherwise it'll look like your sharpening isn't having any effect). Then, tweak the following settings to your liking:

- **Amount.** This setting works just like Unsharp Mask dialog box's Amount slider (page 461); it controls the sharpening's intensity. Setting it to 0 means no sharpening, no how; setting it to 150 means tons of sharpening (way too much). Try setting it to 40 and toggling the Preview checkbox at the top of the Camera Raw window off and on to see if it makes a difference (be sure you're zoomed in to 100 percent, though!).

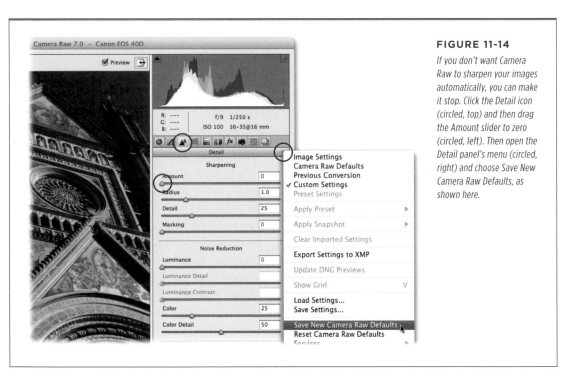

FIGURE 11-14

If you don't want Camera Raw to sharpen your images automatically, you can make it stop. Click the Detail icon (circled, top) and then drag the Amount slider to zero (circled, left). Then open the Detail panel's menu (circled, right) and choose Save New Camera Raw Defaults, as shown here.

- **Radius.** This slider controls the size of the details that Camera Raw sharpens. If you're sharpening a photo with lots of fine details, leave this set to 1. If your photo doesn't have many details, you can pump it up to 1.5, or if you're feeling wild and crazy, *maybe* 2.

- **Detail.** This slider lets you control the level of detail Camera Raw brings out (how much it emphasizes the edges). Crank this setting way up (to 90 or so) if you've got an image with tons of details and textures (like a rocky landscape, a close-up of a tree, or a fancy-schmancy building). This slider ranges from 0 to 100; for most images, keep it around 40 (but be sure to experiment to see what looks good).

- **Masking.** If you increase this setting, Camera Raw reduces the amount of sharpening it applies to areas that aren't edges. It's sort of like using a layer mask on a sharpened layer in Photoshop, except that it's automatic, so you can't really control where the sharpening is hidden. Nevertheless, it's worth experimenting with. If you set Masking to 0, Camera Raw sharpens everything; at 100, it sharpens only edges.

- **Luminance.** This setting controls the amount of grayscale noise (see the box on page 459) that Camera Raw tries to decrease in your image by *smoothing* the pixels (similar to blurring). Make sure you're zoomed in to at least 100 percent and then drag this slider to the right to reduce the grains or splotches in your image. For example, a setting of 25 should provide a reasonable balance of noise reduction and image detail, though you'll need to experiment with your own images.

- **Luminance Detail.** This slider controls the *luminance noise threshold*—how much smoothing Camera Raw performs on grayscale noise in detailed parts of the image. Drag it to the right to preserve more details and apply less noise reduction in those areas. On really noisy images, drag it to the left to produce a smoother image and apply more noise reduction (though low numbers can zap detail, so keep an eye on that). Straight from the factory, it's set to 50.

- **Luminance Contrast.** This setting lets you safeguard the image's contrast. Drag it to the right to preserve contrast and texture, or to the left to throw caution to the wind and produce a smoother, less noisy image. Out of the box, this slider is set to 0.

> **NOTE** The Luminance Detail and Luminance Contrast sliders are *dependent* on the Luminance slider—if it's set to 0, they'll both be grayed out. The fix is to increase the Luminance slider in order to activate the other two.

- **Color.** If your image has a lot of color noise (funky specks of color), which can happen if you shoot in really low light or at a high ISO (your camera's light-sensitivity setting), move this slider to the right to make Camera Raw try to remove the specks. A value of 25 produces a decent amount of speck zapping.

- **Color Detail.** This slider controls the *color noise threshold*. Drag it to the left to remove more color specks, though that may cause color to bleed into other areas. If you've got a lot of thin, detailed color edges in your image, drag the slider to the right for less noise reduction.

TIP To see what's *really* going on with any of Camera Raw's sharpening options, zoom in to 100 percent or more and then hold the Option key (Alt on a PC) as you drag the individual sliders. Your image goes grayscale, letting you see which areas Camera Raw is adjusting (though it's tough to see *anything* when you're tweaking the Radius setting). The most useful setting is Masking—if you hold the Option (Alt) key while you tweak it, you see what looks like an edge mask that shows exactly which parts of your image are being sharpened and which parts are being hidden by the mask.

Local Sharpening

As you learned in Chapter 9, Camera Raw sports an Adjustment Brush that lets you paint slider-based adjustments directly onto an image. Behind the scenes, Camera Raw builds a mask to hide the adjustments from the rest of your image. Great, but how does the Adjustment Brush relate to sharpening, you ask? The Sharpness slider lets you selectively increase or decrease the amount of global sharpening you set in the Detail tab by painting certain areas with the Adjustment Brush. Sure, the global sharpening still affects your whole image, but by using the Adjustment Brush, you can turn the volume of that global sharpening up or down in specific areas, as shown in Figure 11-15. The Sharpness slider ranges from –100 to +100.

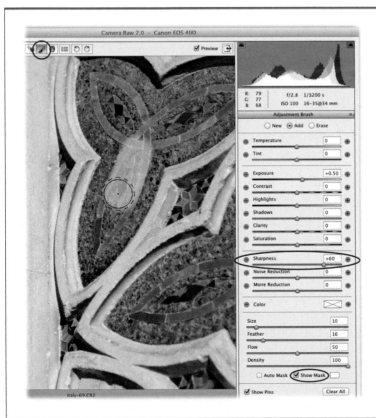

FIGURE 11-15

If you've applied a round of sharpening to your whole image by adjusting the Detail tab's settings, you can apply even more sharpening to specific areas like this beautiful mosaic. Press K to grab the Adjustment Brush, increase the Sharpness slider (circled here), and then paint the mosaic.

To decrease the sharpening in a specific area, drag the Sharpness slider to the left into negative numbers instead. To better see the area you're adjusting, turn on the Show Mask option near the bottom right of the Camera Raw window (circled).

Painting in Photoshop

Many artists who learned to sketch and paint using pencils, oils, and brushes have come to love the creativity that the digital realm affords. The biggest advantage is that there aren't any brushes to clean or paints to mix! And you can't beat the infinitely forgiving Undo command. Most important, as you can see in Figure 12-1, there's no limit to the kind of artwork you can create in Photoshop.

If you're a traditional artist, the techniques covered in this chapter will set you on the path of electronic creativity. You'll learn how to use Photoshop's color tools and built-in brushes to create a painting from start to finish, in full step-by-step detail. And in CS6, the program's brushes behave more realistically than ever before! You'll also discover how to load additional brushes, customize the ones Photoshop provides, and create new brushes of your very own.

If you're a graphic designer or a photographer, there's a ton of info here for you, too. Just think about how much time you spend with brushes when you're working in Photoshop. Whether you're retouching an image with one of the healing brushes, painting on a layer mask to hide an adjustment, or duplicating objects with the Clone Stamp tool—all of those things (and more) involve either the Brush tool itself or a tool that uses a brush cursor. For that reason, learning how to work with and customize brushes is extremely important. Plus you'll learn all kinds of other fun and useful stuff like the basics of color theory, how to use Photoshop's various tools to choose the colors you work with—including the Kuler panel from which you can snatch whole color schemes!—and how to give your photos a painted edge.

Since painting is all about using color, that's where your journey begins.

FIGURE 12-1

This beautiful painting by Deborah Fox of her daughter, Jordan, was created entirely in Photoshop.

You can see more of her artwork at www.deborahfoxart.com.

■ Color Theory: The Basics

Color can evoke emotion, capture attention, and send a message. That's why choosing the *right* color is so important. It may also explain why picking colors that go well together can be an exercise in frustration. Some colors pair up nicely, some don't, and who the heck knows why.

The great thing about using Photoshop is that you don't actually need to know *why* certain colors go together. Instead, thanks to a circular diagram called a *color wheel*, you can easily identify which colors live in sweet visual harmony. A color wheel won't turn you into the next Matisse, but for most mortals it's the tool of choice for deciding which colors to use in a project.

Before you take the color wheel for a spin, you need to understand a few basic color concepts. Consider this section *Color Theory: The Missing Manual*:

- **A color scheme** (or color palette) refers to the group of colors you use in a project or painting. Just take a look at any book cover, magazine ad, or website and you'll see that it's made from a certain set of colors (usually between three and five colors, plus white or black). The designer usually picks a main color (like blue) and then chooses the other colors according to how they look together and the feeling they evoke when they're viewed as a group. There's a whole science behind picking colors based on what they mean to us humans and how they make us feel. For example, hospitals are typically bathed in pale blue or green because researchers have found that those colors have a soothing effect. If this type of thing interests you, pick up a copy of *Color: Messages and Meanings* by Leatrice Eiseman (Hand Press Books, 2006).

- **A color wheel** is a tool that helps you pick colors that look good together. Without diving too deeply into the science of color relationships, let's just say that all colors are related because they're derivatives of one another. The color wheel, which dates back to the 17th century, arranges visible colors on a round diagram according to their relationships. It's based on the three basic colors: yellow, blue, and red—the *primary colors*—from which all other colors spring. By mixing equal amounts of the primary colors, you get a second set of colors called—surprise—*secondary colors*. As you might suspect, mixing equal parts of the secondary colors gives you a third set of colors called *tertiary colors*. Together, all these colors form the color wheel shown in Figure 12-2.

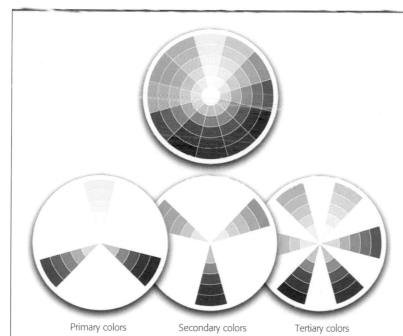

FIGURE 12-2

Top: You can pick up a color wheel at your local art-supply store or order one from the Color Wheel Company (www.colorwheelco.com). It may not look exactly like the one shown here (it might have more colors), but it'll be similar. Once you learn a few rules about which colors go best together (described in the next section), you can easily use a color wheel to pick visually pleasing color schemes.

Bottom: Here's the same color wheel with a few of the color wedges hidden so you can see the primary, secondary, and tertiary colors.

Primary colors   Secondary colors   Tertiary colors

NOTE Photoshop has a built-in color wheel in the Kuler panel, a color scheme generator discussed in detail later in this chapter.

You'll also run into three different terms used to describe color: hue, saturation, and brightness (you've seen 'em here and there throughout this book). Together, they form all the glorious colors the human eye can perceive:

- **Hue** can mean a few different things, but for the purposes of this discussion, think of it as another word for "color," as in red, blue, lime green, or cotton-candy pink. So when you see it in a Photoshop dialog box, just substitute the word *color* in your mind.

- **Saturation** describes a color's strength or intensity. For example, a highly saturated hue has a vivid, intense color. A less saturated hue looks dull and gray. Think "vibrancy" and you'll have this one down pat.

- **Brightness** (or lightness), which is usually measured in terms of percent, determines how light or dark a color appears. You can think of brightness as the amount of light shining on an object, ranging from white (100 percent) to black (0 percent). For example, if you shine an incredibly powerful flashlight on an apple, the apple looks almost white (100 percent lightness). When the flashlight is off, you've got no light, so the apple appears almost black (0 percent lightness).

■ Selecting a Color Scheme

As mentioned earlier, if you're picking a color scheme for your project, you usually begin by choosing a main (or *base*) color. This color can come from a piece of art that you're starting with (like a logo or photo) or it can be a color that you want to build your design around. Once you know the main color, you can use a few simple rules to find other colors that go well with it. In this section, you'll learn how to use a color wheel to pick a color scheme based on four popular *color scheme harmonies* (color combinations proven by color experts to go well together). But don't worry: You'll also learn where to find tools to automate this process in case picking colors *manually* isn't your cup of tea.

NOTE The rule of thirds you learned about back on page 220 applies to colors, too. Imagine splitting the colors in your painting or design into two categories: dominant and accent. You can think of the *dominant* color as the color of the environment in the image (like white in a photo of a field of snow); it sets the mood of your piece. The *accent* color is the color of the focal point (like a brown tree in the field of snow). If you shoot for using 2/3 dominant color and 1/3 accent color, you can't go wrong!

Using a Color Wheel

Let's say you've gotten your hot little hands on a color wheel. Great! Now, what the heck do you do with it? For starters, you need to pick the main color you want the color scheme to revolve around and then find it on the color wheel. Then you can use one of the following color scheme harmonies to help you pick other colors that go well with it (to see what these color schemes look like, skip ahead to Figure 12-4):

- **Monochromatic** schemes use colors from the same wedge of colors on the color wheel.

- **Analogous** schemes use colors from the wedges on both sides of the main color.

- **Complementary** schemes use colors from the wedge directly across from the main color.

- **Split complementary** schemes use colors from the wedges on either side of the main color's complement.

To use a color wheel to pick a color scheme, follow these steps:

1. **Open an image and choose a main color.**

   Every project starts with something, whether it's a photo, a company logo, or a piece of art. Give it a good long stare and decide on a main color to use for the color scheme. Let's say you want to add color to the design shown in Figure 12-3. Since there's quite a bit of blue in the image, you could easily start there and designate one of the blues as your main color.

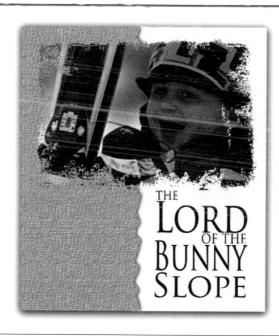

FIGURE 12-3

Instead of racking your brain trying to pick colors for the text and background of this greeting card, it's much easier to start with a color that's already in the design.

In this case, you could start with one of the blues in the photo.

THE
LORD
OF THE
BUNNY
SLOPE

2. **Once you've picked a color, find its general location on the color wheel.**

   If you've got an actual color wheel in your hand, you can do this simply by looking at the wheel.

3. **Locate other colors that go with the main color by using one of the color scheme harmonies described earlier in this section and shown in Figure 12-4.**

If you choose your other colors from the related color wedges, you can be sure they'll look good when you use them together.

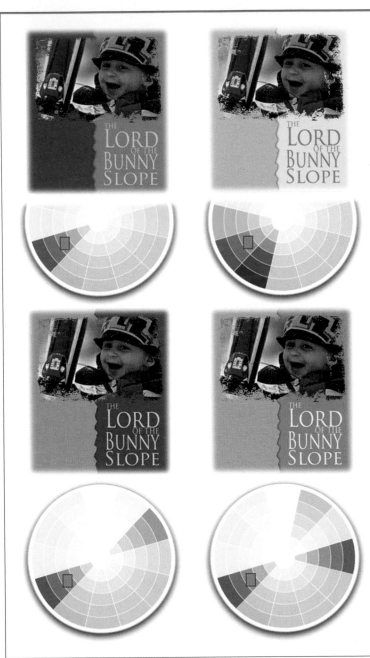

FIGURE 12-4

There are tons of color scheme harmonies out there (you'll need to study up on color theory to learn about 'em all), but you can think of the ones shown here as the Fantastic Four. Here you can see what the design looks like using monochromatic (top left), analogous (top right), complementary (bottom left), and split complementary (bottom right) color schemes.

The red box marks the main color's location on the wheel, and each color wedge used in the color schemes is highlighted (the other wedges are faded out).

(These are only the four most common color scheme harmonies. To learn others, grab a copy of Color Index, Revised Edition *[How, 2010] by Jim Krause.)*

Using the Kuler Panel

Kuler is an amazingly useful, community-driven color scheme generator that debuted back in Photoshop CS4, though before that it was a Web application. If you're not a fan of color wheels, don't have one handy, or just need some fresh new color schemes, you can choose from many *themes*—Kuler's name for color schemes—that folks in the Kuler community have created. To pop open the panel, choose Window→Extensions→Kuler (see Figure 12-5).

> **NOTE** In order for the Kuler panel to download the latest and greatest themes from the Kuler online community, you need to be connected to the Internet.

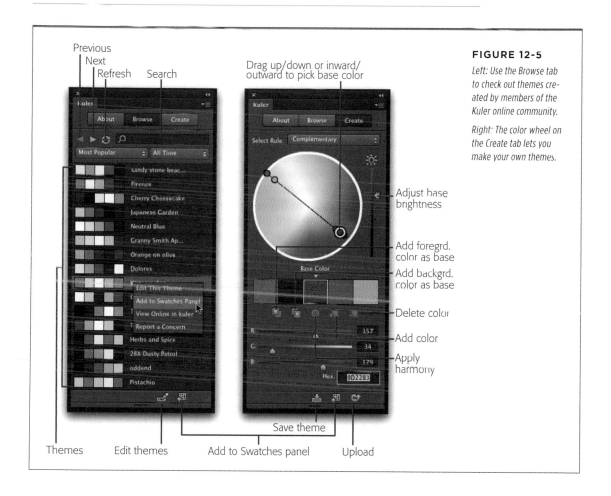

FIGURE 12-5

Left: Use the Browse tab to check out themes created by members of the Kuler online community.

Right: The color wheel on the Create tab lets you make your own themes.

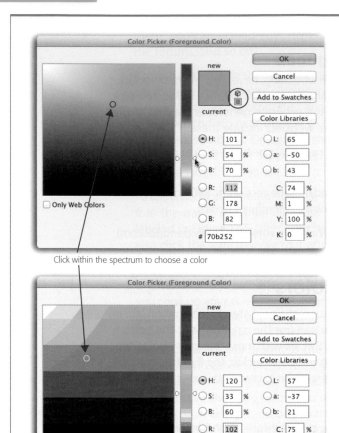

Click within the spectrum to choose a color

FIGURE 12-6

Use the Color Picker to tell Photoshop which color you want to use with a particular tool.

If you see a tiny gray triangle with an exclamation point (shown in Figure 12-8) beside one of the color swatches, it means the color can't be reproduced with CMYK ink (see Chapter 16 for more info on printing images). A little 3D cube beside the swatch (circled) means the color isn't Web safe (the box on page 723 explains what that means and why it's not such a big deal anymore).

Once you get used to working with colors and seeing their numeric values, you may begin to visualize the color from the values alone. But to really understand how colors mix to make other colors, you need to study color theory.

> **NOTE** You can also summon a heads-up version of the Color Picker while you're painting: just ⌘-Ctrl-Option-click (Alt+Shift+right-click on a PC) your image. Flip ahead to page 504 to see it in action!

As you learned back in Chapter 2, each color mode identifies colors with specific numeric values. When you click within the color field on the left side of the dialog box, you'll see the values on the right side change to reflect the currently selected color. If you need to pick a *specific* color, enter its color values in the HSB (hue, saturation, brightness), RGB (red, green, blue), hex number, Lab, or CMYK (cyan, magenta, yellow, black) fields. Or, if you want to use a color that already exists in your Photoshop document, just mouse away from the Color Picker and your cursor turns into an eyedropper. When you click the color you want to snatch, it appears in the color swatch in the Color Picker. Sweet!

> **TIP** Photoshop even lets you mix your own colors by using the Mixer Brush. Skip to page 500 to learn how!

The Eyedropper Tool

When you're developing a color scheme, you may want to start by grabbing colors that are already in your image. The Eyedropper tool is perfect for that job, and it includes a handy Sample Ring that lets you more accurately snatch the *exact* color you're after (as shown in Figure 12-7). Grab the tool by pressing I, mouse over to your image, and then click once to make your foreground color chip match the color your cursor is over. If you want to hunt around for a good color, press your mouse button and drag around your image until you find just the right hue, and then let go of your mouse to choose it. To use the Eyedropper tool to set your *background* color chip, Option-click (Alt-click on a PC) your image instead.

> **TIP** In previous versions of Photoshop, you could use the Eyedropper tool's Sample pop-up menu (in the Options bar) to grab color from all layers or the currently active layer...and that was it. But in CS6, that menu has expanded to include Current & Below (which samples the current layer and any layers below it), "All Layers no Adjustments" (samples all layers except Adjustment layers), and "Current & Below no Adjustments" (samples the current layer and any layers below *except* Adjustment layers).

FIGURE 12-7

The Eyedropper's Sample Ring displays the current foreground color on the bottom and the new color (the one your cursor is pointing at) on the top. To help isolate those colors from the rest of the colors in your image so you can actually see 'em, Photoshop places a neutral gray ring around them. If you're unimpressed by the Sample Ring, you can turn it off by clicking the Show Sampling Ring checkbox in the Options bar (circled).

Author caricature by Richard and Tanya Horie.

New color
Neutral color
Previous color

Loading Color Libraries

Sometimes, you need to be very precise when picking colors. Maybe a client has given you specific colors to match or you're creating a piece of art that needs to mesh with another designer's work. Enter Photoshop's built-in *color libraries*, which feature specialized color collections. Figure 12-8 shows you how to get started with them.

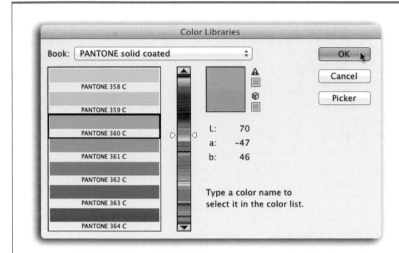

FIGURE 12-8

Click the Color Libraries button on the right side of the Color Picker to open this dialog box (you can also load libraries using the Swatches panel, discussed in the next section). Choose a library from the Book pop-up menu and then use the slider (or your up and down arrow keys) to move through the list. Once you've found the color you want, click it once to make it your foreground color. Then click OK to close the Color Libraries dialog box or click the Picker button to go back to the Color Picker.

The most popular library is the Pantone Matching System (PMS), which lets designers keep colors consistent across projects. Each PMS color has a number corresponding to a very specific ink mixture that lets professional printers reproduce the color with the same results every time. That said, to use *true* PMS colors you have to create a spot channel (see page 697). If you pick a color from a color library without using spot channels, Photoshop picks the nearest RGB or CMYK equivalent (depending on which color mode you're in).

TIP If the Color Libraries dialog box is open and you know the name of the color you want (for example, Pantone 375), you can choose it by entering a shorthand version of its name with your keyboard; simply type the color's number. This feels weird because there's no text field to enter it in, but you must trust in the Force! Type *375*, for example, and you'll see a lovely light-green swatch appear in the dialog box's list.

The Swatches Panel

The built-in color libraries are actually just collections of swatches. If you want to save a certain group of colors that you've created yourself—or snatched from Kuler (page 489)—you can store them in the Swatches panel for easy access (see Figure 12-9). Think of this panel as a holding pen for frequently used colors, each of which you can summon with a quick click. To open the panel, choose Windows→Swatches. To use a swatch as your foreground color, just click it.

> **TIP** Both the Color Picker and Kuler panel have buttons for adding colors to the Swatches panel, too.

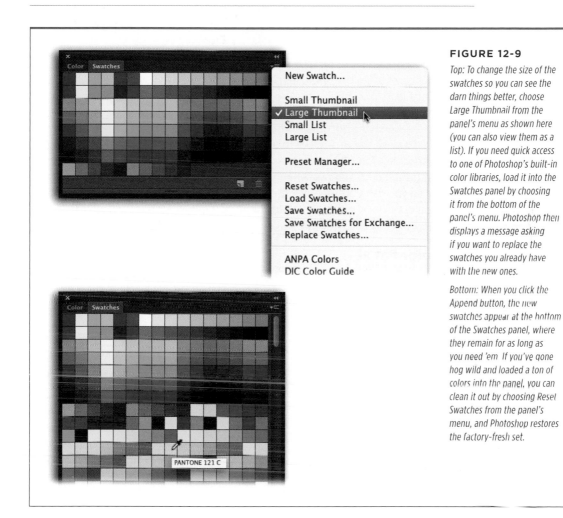

FIGURE 12-9

Top: To change the size of the swatches so you can see the darn things better, choose Large Thumbnail from the panel's menu as shown here (you can also view them as a list). If you need quick access to one of Photoshop's built-in color libraries, load it into the Swatches panel by choosing it from the bottom of the panel's menu. Photoshop then displays a message asking if you want to replace the swatches you already have with the new ones.

Bottom: When you click the Append button, the new swatches appear at the bottom of the Swatches panel, where they remain for as long as you need 'em. If you've gone hog wild and loaded a ton of colors into the panel, you can clean it out by choosing Reset Swatches from the panel's menu, and Photoshop restores the factory-fresh set.

Here's how to manage the Swatches panel like a pro:

- **To add a new swatch that matches your current foreground color,** point your cursor at an empty area of the panel. When the cursor turns into a little paint bucket, click to add the swatch. Photoshop displays a dialog box where you can give the new swatch a meaningful name.

- **Use the Preset Manager to arrange your swatches.** Since Photoshop lets you load additional swatches only at the end of the list, you may want to use the Preset Manager to rearrange them by project, client, and so on. Flip to page 38 for the details.

- **To make a swatch's color your foreground color,** click the swatch.

- **To make a swatch's color your background color,** ⌘-click (Ctrl-click on a PC) the swatch.

- **To delete a swatch,** Option-click (Alt-click) it.

The downside of using the Swatches panel is that there's no way to open a certain set of swatches *in its own panel*—they're always intermingled with the other swatches in the panel. You can keep 'em all together using the Preset Manager, or make your own swatch layer in the document where you're using those colors. Just create a new layer and then use the Brush tool to add little blobs of color to it from your project or color scheme (you can even place these blobs just outside the margins of your design and then crop 'em out when you're ready to save your masterpiece). Lock the layer so you can't accidentally paint on it, and then use the Eyedropper tool to sample colors from it when you need them. You can keep the swatch layer out of the way by turning off its visibility.

The Color Panel

Photoshop has yet *another* place where you can choose colors: the Color panel (Figure 12-10). It's a lot smaller than the Color Picker and, since it's a panel, it won't pop open a dialog box that covers up your image. To open it, choose Window→Color. You'll see the color values of your foreground or background color chip on the right side of the panel (just click the appropriate swatch in the panel to pick it). The sliders let you adjust the color of the current color chip. To pick a new color, click within the spectrum bar at the bottom of the panel (your cursor turns into an eyedropper).

> **TIP** You can capture the hex value of any color after you've chosen it by opening the Color panel's menu and choosing Copy Color's Hex Code. For more on what you can *do* with that info, skip ahead to the box on page 731.

FIGURE 12-10

Though the Color panel stays nicely tucked out of the way in the panel dock, it's much smaller than the Color Picker, making it a little tough to see. If your eyesight is good, you'll probably enjoy using it because it takes up so much less space. It's also customizable; you can use its menu to control what it displays. Here, the sliders are set to RGB, and the spectrum bar at the bottom is set to Grayscale.

■ (Re)Introducing the Brush Tool

You've already used the Brush tool for all kinds of things in previous chapters: editing layer masks, creating selections, colorizing grayscale images, and so on. In this section you'll learn how to *paint* with it, and in CS6 it's a more realistic experience than ever before. But first you need to understand a bit more about how this tool works. Grab the Brush tool by pressing B or by clicking its icon in the Tools panel (see Figure 12-11).

> **TIP** Photoshop CS6 lets you increase brush size to a whopping 5000 pixels!

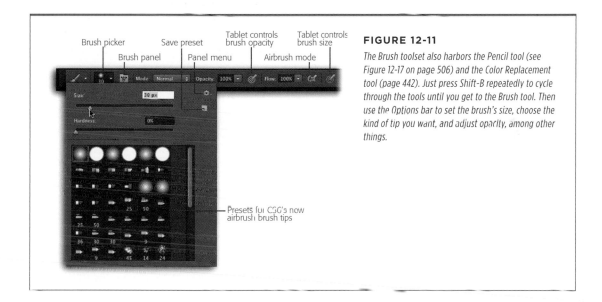

FIGURE 12-11

The Brush toolset also harbors the Pencil tool (see Figure 12-17 on page 506) and the Color Replacement tool (page 442). Just press Shift-B repeatedly to cycle through the tools until you get to the Brush tool. Then use the Options bar to set the brush's size, choose the kind of tip you want, and adjust opacity, among other things.

> **TIP** You can control brush size and hardness with a keyboard shortcut: Control-Option-drag (Alt+right-click+drag on a PC) left or right to change the size, or up or down to change the hardness. New in CS6, you'll see brush diameter, hardness, and opacity info appear next to your cursor. Sweet!

If you peek at the Options bar, you'll see a slew of settings:

- **Tool presets.** Use this pop-up menu at the left end of the Options bar to access brush settings you've previously saved.

- **Brush picker.** Photoshop has a ton of built-in brushes, and this pop-up menu lets you access and manage them, control brush size and edge hardness, *and* save your settings as a preset. Think of it as a mini version of the full-fledged Brush panel (page 516).

- **Brush panel.** This tiny icon gives you one-click access to the Brush panel discussed on page 516 that lets you customize brushes in ways you've never imagined.

- **Mode.** This pop-up menu contains all the blend modes you've seen so far, along with two others: Behind and Clear. Behind mode acts like the pixels you're painting are *behind* the pixels already on that layer (which is essentially the same, though not quite as safe, as painting on a new layer below it)—if there are transparent pixels on that layer, then your brushstrokes are visible (if there aren't, nothing happens). Clear mode mimics the Eraser tool and makes the pixels you paint over transparent.

- **Opacity.** This setting controls how transparent your brushstrokes are; you'll use it a lot since it lets you change the appearance of the paint you're applying. For example, you can start by painting with bright green at 100 percent opacity and then keep lowering the opacity to produce lighter and lighter shades of green.

- **Tablet pressure controls opacity.** If you use a graphics tablet, click this icon to make the opacity vary when you change the amount of pressure you're applying to the tablet. Press harder to increase opacity or more lightly to decrease it.

- **Flow.** To control the flow of paint to the brush (the rate at which the color is applied to your image), use this setting. Set Flow to a low number for less paint and a high number for more paint. When you paint by dragging across an area multiple times, the paint builds up in that spot.

- **Airbrush.** Click this button to make your brush work like an artist's airbrush, which sprays paint onto the canvas with compressed air (see Figure 12-12). Photoshop CS6 includes several new airbrush brush tips, too, that behave *much* more like a professional airbrush system (they're labeled back in Figure 12-11).

- **Tablet pressure controls size.** If you have a graphics tablet, click this icon to control brush size with your stylus.

Once you've adjusted these settings, you can paint with the brush by mousing over to your image and dragging. Your cursor reflects the size and shape of the brush you picked. Most of the time, the cursor is round like in Figure 12-12, top, unless you've chosen one of the textured or more creative brushes discussed later. When you mouse over a dark part of your image, the ring representing your cursor turns white; when you mouse over a light area, it turns black.

TIP To paint a straight horizontal or vertical line (or one that's at a 45-degree angle) with the Brush tool, click once where you want the line to start and then Shift-click where you want it to end. Who knew?

FIGURE 12-12

Top: In Airbrush mode, the Brush tool "sprays" paint onto your canvas with (fictitious) compressed air. If you drag or continue to hold down your mouse button, it keeps applying more paint (left) than in regular mode or with a single click (right). Several of the new airbrush brush tips in CS6 also trigger this spray-paint behavior.

Middle: Here you can see the difference between a soft-edged brush (top), which has very soft, semitransparent pixels around the edge, and a hard-edged brush (bottom).

Bottom: Photoshop's Bristle Tips work like their real-world counterparts, letting you create more natural strokes. If you're using a graphics tablet, pressing down with the stylus makes the bristles splay, just like a real brush (the Round Blunt Medium Stiff brush was used here). You can also use these tips with other tools that employ a brush cursor, such as the Mixer Brush (see the next section), Eraser, and Clone Stamp tools.

Controlling the Brush Cursor's Appearance

Straight from the factory, your brush cursor reflects the size and shape of whatever brush you've chosen, but you can change the cursor using Photoshop's preferences. Choose Photoshop→Preferences→Cursors (Edit→Preferences→Cursors on a PC) to control how Photoshop displays your brush's cursor (Figure 12-13).

Most of the time, you'll want to stick with either the Normal Brush Tip or the Full Size Brush Tip setting because they give you a more natural painting experience (the Normal Brush Tip is slightly smaller than your actual brushstroke). The Precise version of the cursor has crosshairs so small they're nearly *impossible* to see; the Standard option is even less useful because it makes the cursor look like the Brush tool's icon, and neither option gives you any indication of the brush size. The "Show only Crosshair While Painting" option came along in CS5, but again, the crosshairs icon gives you no indication of size, and so darn small you'd probably use it for painting only the tiniest of details when you're zoomed in.

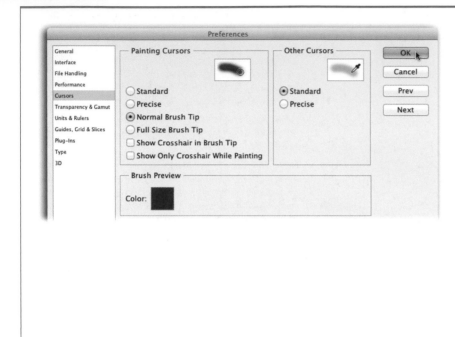

FIGURE 12-13

The Painting Cursors settings control what the Brush tool's cursor looks like, while the Other Cursors settings let you choose between the standard, tool-shaped version or a precise (crosshairs) version for tools like the Eyedropper, Patch, and Eraser tools. To put the crosshairs in the middle of the cursor so you know exactly where it's centered, turn on the "Show Crosshair in Brush Tip" checkbox. The color swatch in the Brush Preview section shows which color you see when you use the drag-to-resize keyboard shortcut (see the Tip on page 153).

TIP If the brush cursor suddenly turns into a microscopic dot inside the crosshairs, check your keyboard to see if Caps Lock is turned on. Pressing Caps Lock lets you switch between the precise cursor (the crosshairs) and the cursor you're currently using, which can be useful when you're zoomed in and painting tiny details. (Turning on Caps Lock is a *fantastic* trick to play on your coworkers; just make sure you 'fess up before they reinstall the program! Other good tricks include setting the Crop tool's width to 1 pixel and then setting the Brush tool's mode to Behind.)

Meet the Mixer Brush

Back in CS5, Photoshop's brush engine—the electronic brains behind its Brush tool—got a major overhaul (the first since CS1) and Adobe also added a brand-new tool: the Mixer Brush. As the name implies, you can use it to mix colors just like you can mix paints in real life, as well as load multiple colors onto its tip for painting.

You can use this tool on a blank canvas or with a photograph to create realistic, "painterly" effects, as shown in Figure 12-14. The Options bar lets you control the "wetness" of the canvas, the amount of paint you're mixing from canvas to brush, and whether Photoshop *cleans* or *refills* the brush after each stroke. (If you're feeling extremely creative, you can paint with a *dirty* brush!)

TIP   Photoshop CS6 includes a new filter that can turn a photo into a painting in no time flat. It's called Oil Paint and you can see it in action on page 643.

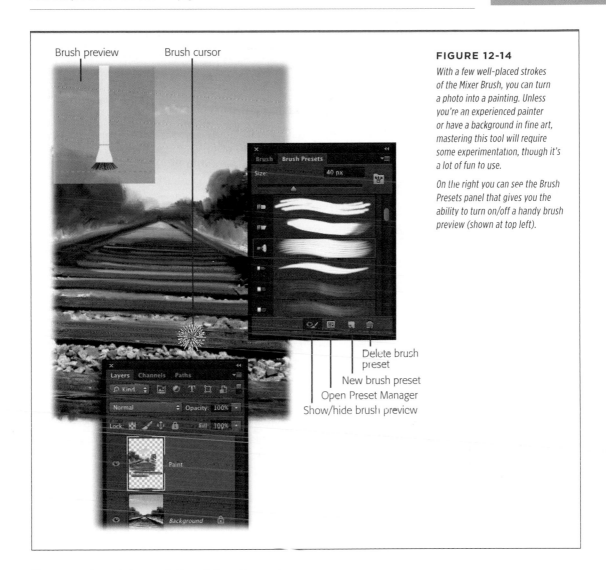

Brush preview   Brush cursor

FIGURE 12-14

With a few well-placed strokes of the Mixer Brush, you can turn a photo into a painting. Unless you're an experienced painter or have a background in fine art, mastering this tool will require some experimentation, though it's a lot of fun to use.

On the right you can see the Brush Presets panel that gives you the ability to turn on/off a handy brush preview (shown at top left).

Delete brush
preset

New brush preset

Open Preset Manager

Show/hide brush preview

To turn a photo into a painting, follow these steps:

1. **Open a photo and add a new layer at the top of the layer stack.**

   Click the "Create a new layer" icon at the bottom of the Layers panel, and then position the new layer above your image layer. (This new layer is where the new paint will go, as shown in Figure 12-14.) If you like, name the new layer something clever, like *Paint*.

NOTE You can follow along by visiting this book's Missing CD page at *www.missingmanuals.com/cds* and downloading the practice file *Railroad.jpg*.

2. **With the Paint layer selected, grab the Mixer Brush by pressing Shift-B repeatedly until you see its icon in the Tools panel.**

   The Mixer Brush lives in the Brush toolset and looks like a brush with a drop of paint above it.

3. **In the Options bar, turn on Sample All Layers.**

   Turning on this checkbox makes Photoshop sample colors from the image layer below, though the paint will appear on the new layer. This keeps you from completely destroying the original image.

4. **Click the Brush panel icon in the Options bar (see Figure 12-15) to open the Brush panel, and then click the Brush Presets button.**

   In the Brush panel, trot up to its top-left corner and click the Brush Presets button (Figure 12-14) to open another panel—within the same panel group—that includes a list of built-in brushes.

5. **In the Brush Presets panel, scroll down the list of brushes until you see the Round Fan and then give it a click to activate it.**

   If your computer can run OpenGL (see the box on page 64), you'll see a preview of the bristle near the top left of your Photoshop window, as Figure 12-14 shows. If not, well—you won't. You can turn this preview off and on using the button at the bottom of the Brush Presets panel (labeled in Figure 12-14).

6. **Adjust the brush's size.**

   You can use the Brush Preset picker in the Options bar, or—better yet—Control-Option-drag (Alt+right-click+drag on a PC) to the right to increase the brush size, or to the left to decrease it. You can also change brush hardness (opacity) with the same shortcut—drag up to make the brush softer or down to make it harder. (If that's one too many keys to remember, you can also decrease/increase brush size by tapping the left/right square bracket keys.)

TIP If you're using a graphics tablet, try assigning the scroll button on your stylus (pen) to resize brushes. (To find out how, you'll need to dig out your graphics tablet's manual.)

7. **From the Brush Combinations menu in the Options bar, choose "Wet, Light Mix."**

   This menu lets you tell Photoshop how you want the brush to behave. After you make a choice from this menu, you can fine-tune it using the Wet, Load, and Mix settings shown in Figure 12-15.

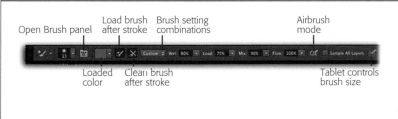

FIGURE 12-15

You see a slew of settings in the Options bar the minute you activate the Mixer Brush. For example, the "Current brush load" preview displays the color loaded on the brush tip, but by clicking the tiny down-pointing triangle to its right, you can load another color, ask Photoshop to clean your brush, or tell it to Load Solid Colors Only instead of grabbing a mix of colors each time you Option-click (Alt-click on a PC). The pop-up menu to the left of the Wet field contains useful setting combinations; choosing one populates all the fields to the menu's right.

8. **Mouse over to your image and start painting.**

   Photoshop begins applying paint to the layer you created in step 1. As you brush across the image, the Mixer Brush samples color from the image and mixes it with the color shown in the color swatch in the Options bar (which comes from your foreground color chip). You can vary your brushstrokes by tweaking the Bristle Tip settings in the Brush panel (page 517), or switch brush tips by picking a new one in the Brush Presets panel.

9. **Change the Options bar's Mix setting to 70 percent and then Option-click (Alt-click) a color in your image to load it onto the brush tip.**

   You can change the Mix setting by double-clicking its field in the Options bar and typing a new percentage, or by clicking its down-pointing triangle and dragging the resulting slider to the right. Option-clicking (Alt–clicking) your image lets you add more colors to your brush tip to create a different painting effect. To switch to a completely different color, summon the *heads-up display* (HUD) Color Picker by Control-Option-⌘-clicking (Shift+Alt-right-clicking on a PC). Figure 12-16 has the scoop.

TIP Be careful not to add too many colors onto the Mixer Brush, as the paint can quickly turn to a yucky muddy-brown. If that happens, turn on the "Clean brush after each stroke" setting in the Options bar.

---

10. **Continue painting until you've covered the whole image with brushstrokes.**

    If you like the results, save the image as a PSD file. If you don't, delete the paint layer by activating it and pressing the Delete key (Backspace on a PC).

Whew! Painting a photo is a lot of work, but it's also lots of fun (if you like paint-ing, that is). And you don't have to start with a photo—you can use a blank canvas instead. In fact, that's what the next section is all about.

> **TIP** Photoshop CS6 includes a new *action* (see Chapter 18) created by painting wizard John Derry that prepares all the layers you'll need for painting automatically. Just pop open a photo and then choose Window→Actions. Scroll down to near the bottom of the list and double-click the Mixer Brush Cloning Paint Setup action to run it. Photoshop instantly creates a slew of layers, complete with proper opacity and blend modes, primed and ready for you to start painting.

FIGURE 12-16

Top: To summon the HUD Color Picker (shown here in Hue Strip mode), Control-Option-⌘-click (Shift+Alt-right-click on a PC) your image. This handy feature lets you swap paint colors while *you're painting. When it's onscreen, you can mouse over to the Hue selector bar on the right to change color range and then press your space bar to pick a range of colors (reds, for example). Next, mouse over to the Lightness and Saturation selector on the left to pick the color you want to paint with (just point at it with your cursor). Release your mouse button and the HUD Color Picker disappears. It takes some getting used to, as any additional clicks—or releasing your mouse button—will close it. Oy!*

Bottom: You can also change the HUD Color Picker to this groovy Hue Wheel by opening Photoshop's Prefer-ences (Photoshop→Preferences→General on a Mac; Edit→Preferences→General on a PC). From the HUD Color Picker menu near the top of the Preferences dialog box, choose Hue Wheel. The Hue Wheel works the same way as the Hue Strip.

And new in Photoshop CS6, you get small, medium, and large choices for both the Hue Strip and Hue Wheel.

Painting from Scratch

Now you're ready for the really good stuff: actually painting in Photoshop. Not only is it fun, but it's a *great* way to get used to the Brush tool.

One thing to remember about painting is that different people use different techniques. Some folks start by drawing a sketch, while others dive right into painting. People even have different ways of creating sketches: Some draw pencil sketches on paper, scan them into their computers, and then paint over them, while others sketch right in Photoshop. And some folks use graphics tablets (which make painting a lot easier and more natural) while others fare quite well with a mouse. The following steps are very basic and explain how most folks paint from scratch, but, in the end, it's all about what works for you, so feel free to adapt these steps to suit your style.

TIP You can rotate the canvas so it's at a more natural angle while you paint. Just grab the Rotate View tool by pressing R, and then click and drag your canvas to spin it. See page 65 for more details.

Turn on some music, think about what you want to draw, and then follow these steps:

1. **Create a new document by pressing ⌘-N (Ctrl+N on a PC), give it a white background, and then save it.**

   Which canvas size and resolution to use depends on what you want to do with your painting. If you've got a new computer with a lot of memory, you may as well make it big enough to print just in case it turns out really well; 3600x5400 pixels at a resolution of 300 ppi is a good choice. If you have a slow computer and/or you're going to post it on the Web or view it only onscreen, make it 1200x1800 at a resolution of 72 ppi instead. It's a good idea to make your document at least 1200 pixels wide or high (it doesn't matter which); that way, you'll have enough pixel info to show details when you zoom in to work on tiny stuff. (If it's less than 1200 pixels in one direction, it'll look really blocky when you zoom in.) And since the steps ahead are a bit long and involved, protect your hard work by saving the document as a PSD file now by choosing File→Save.

NOTE This is also a good time to make sure you're using the right color profile for your document by choosing Edit→Color Settings. The last thing you want is for the colors to shift after you're finished painting! See page 674 to learn which profile to use.

---

2. **Create a new layer and name it *Sketch*.**

   It's usually best to start with a rough sketch, though you certainly don't have to. You can draw the sketch on paper and scan it into Photoshop (see the box on page 507 for the scoop on isolating a sketch onto its own layer) or sketch it with the Brush tool, as explained in the following steps. (If you're starting with a photo, skip ahead to page 666 for tips on quickly creating a pencil sketch from a photo.) To add a layer to the document, click the "Create a new layer" button at the bottom of the Layers panel (see Chapter 3 for more on layers) or press Shift-⌘-N (Shift+Ctrl+N on a PC).

3. **Press B to grab the Brush tool, choose a brush, and pick a color.**

   Hop up to the Options bar and pick a fairly small, round, hard-edged brush using the Brush picker or the Brush Presets panel (Figure 12-14, right). Then set your foreground color chip to a dark gray (the color of pencil lead).

4. **Draw your sketch.**

   With the Sketch layer active, mouse over to your document and draw a rough sketch of what you want to paint, like the one shown in Figure 12-17. Don't worry about fine lines or getting things perfect; you can add details later.

> **TIP** To follow along and practice painting this sketch, download *Angel.psd* from this book's Missing CD page at *www.missingmanuals.com/cds*.

FIGURE 12-17

Here's the original sketch (left) and the more detailed, refined drawing (right). If you set the Refined Drawing layer's blend mode to Multiply, it appears much darker, which helps you paint over it later.

Technically, you could use the Pencil tool to draw your sketch, but the Brush tool is far more flexible and produces nice, soft-edged lines instead of the Pencil tool's hard, jagged edges. The only redeeming feature of the Pencil tool is its Auto Erase option that lets you erase previous strokes by drawing over them again (which is mainly just cool to watch!).

5. **Lower the Sketch layer's opacity to about 40 percent.**

   At the top of the Layers panel, lower the opacity of the sketch until it looks kind of ghostly. You'll create a more detailed drawing in the next step.

6. **Create a new layer named *Refined Drawing* and set its blend mode to Multiply.**

   Press Shift-⌘-N (Shift+Ctrl+N) to add another new layer, name it, and then click OK. Use the pop-up menu at the top of the Layers panel to change this new layer's blend mode to Multiply (Figure 12-17, bottom) to make it appear darker so it's easier to paint over later.

   This new layer helps you fine-tune your sketch—think of this layer as a piece of tracing paper you've placed on top of the original sketch. The Sketch layer underneath acts like a guide to help you draw more precise and intricate details on the Refined Drawing layer.

7. **Using the Brush tool, refine the drawing until you're happy with it.**

   By refining your sketch on another layer, you're protecting the original. If you need to erase some of your brushstrokes, hold the E key to switch temporarily to the Eraser tool. Once you're satisfied with the refined drawing, hide the original sketch layer by clicking its visibility eye.

8. **Create another new layer named *Blue Background* and drag it below the Refined Drawing layer.**

   Adding the background before you paint gives you a strong color foundation on which to build the painting. That way, you can bind the painting together using the background color(s).

9. **Fill the background layer with whatever you want the dominant background color to be.**

   Over in the Tools panel, click the foreground color chip and choose a fairly dark blue from the Color Picker, and then fill the Blue Background layer with that color by pressing Option-Delete (Alt-Backspace on a PC). Alternatively, you can choose Edit→Fill and then pick Other from the Use pop-up menu to open the Color Picker; then click OK twice to fill the layer—once to close the Color Picker and again to close the Fill dialog box.

10. **In the Options bar, grab a large, round, textured brush, lower its opacity to 25 percent, and start painting over the background.**

FREQUENTLY ASKED QUESTION

Isolating a Scanned Sketch

Help! I scanned my sketch, but it's got a white background! How do I get rid of it?

If you go the pencil-and-paper route rather than drawing a sketch in Photoshop, you'll end up with a white background when you bring the scanned image into Photoshop. Luckily, you can get rid of it quickly using channels.

Flip back to page 206 for the scoop on using channels to create a selection. Once you've got marching ants around the sketch, open the Layers panel and create a new layer for the sketch. Fill the selection with the color of your choice by choosing Edit→Fill. Poof! That's all there is to it. Now you've got an inked outline of the sketch, ready for you to fill with paint.

Why add even more paint to the Blue Background layer? To keep the angel from looking flat by adding some texture. Choose a textured brush or one with rough edges (like the speckled spatter brushes). Once you pick a brush, lower its opacity to 25 percent in the Options bar. Then mouse over to your document and start painting over the dominant background color until you get the look you want, varying brushes, brush sizes, color, and opacity as you go (see Figure 12-18, top).

FIGURE 12-18

Top left: A variety of grainy, textured brushes were used at varying sizes and opacities to create this chalky pastel look. To give the background some depth, use darker versions of similar colors for shadows and lighter versions of similar colors for highlights. (A major newbie mistake is to use pure white for highlights and pure black for shadows—doing that just makes paintings look flat. However, experienced painters can get away with using white or black sparingly and lowering their brush opacity, then building the highlight or shadow by repeatedly brushing over the same area.)

Top right: While you'd normally keep the background turned on when you're filling a sketch with color, it's turned off here so you can get a good look at the blocked colors. Though the areas of dark shading may look black, they're really darker versions of the colors they're attached to (here, that's purple and red).

Bottom: Here's how the colors and refined drawing look on top of the background.

TIP To paint with a color that's already in your document, Option-click (Alt-click on a PC) to temporarily turn the brush cursor into an eyedropper. This lets you click a color to make it your foreground color without switching tools. You can also use the HUD Color Picker described back on page 504.

11. **Create a new layer named _Blocked Colors_ and drag it between the Blue Background and Refined Drawing layers (Figure 12-18, bottom).**

   You'll use this layer to add colors to your drawing (also referred to as "blocking with color" or "roughing in" because you'll add more details later).

TIP   If all this color-picking business feels overwhelming, you can always create a painting with black, white, and shades of gray—which, in fact, is a great way to learn!

---

12. **Use a big, round brush with an opacity of 25 percent to colorize the drawing.**

   For this step, pretend you're a kid with a coloring book; you don't have to worry much about staying within the lines. Start with the big stuff first—painting works best when you work from the general (larger areas) to the specific (tiny details). Using a big brush at a low opacity (25 percent) lets you build up color with multiple strokes (see Figure 12-18, top right). For a smooth look, paint with a soft-edge brush. To add more character, use one of the textured or spatter brushes. Use the foreground color chip or any of the other color-picking tools you learned about earlier in this chapter when you need to change colors.

13. **Create a new layer named _Refining and Detailing_ and drag it above the Blocked Colors layer.**

   You'll use this layer to add fine details like lined edges and other embellishments. That being said, if the lined edges on your Refined Drawing layer are good enough (as is the case in the angel painting), you don't need to add more lines, so concentrate on adding other color details to the Refining and Detailing layer instead.

14. **Using a variety of brush sizes, add details to your painting.**

   Use a big, soft brush set to 65 percent opacity for large areas of color and blend them by painting over them again and again, changing colors as necessary. Switch to a small (about 5-pixel), textured brush at 100 percent opacity for finer details (see Figure 12-19, top).

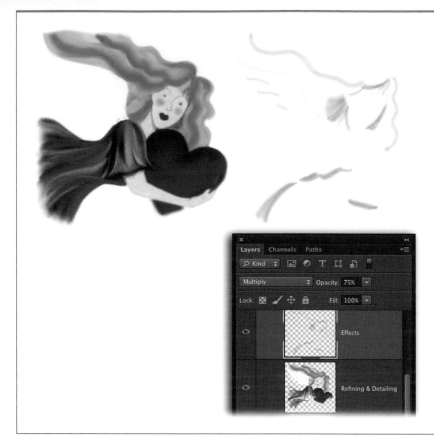

FIGURE 12-19

Left: The painting really starts to take shape when you add details. Brushes from the Dry Media set work really well in this situation (see page 512 for the scoop on loading 'em), though the Rough Round Bristle brush from the Assorted Brush Set at 100 pixels was used here. You'd normally leave the background turned on so you can pick up color from it, but it's turned off here so you can see what the colorized drawing looks like by itself.

Right: For a bit of extra polish, add some blue highlights using a new, separate layer. Remember to experiment with different layer blend modes and opacities to get just the right effect. (Flip back to Chapter 7 for a refresher on blend modes.)

> **TIP** If you're having trouble getting certain colors to blend with others, try the Mixer Brush or the Spot Healing Brush—both can do wonders for blending stubborn areas. Steer clear from the Smudge tool (see Appendix C, online at *www.missingmanuals.com/cds*) because all it does is smear the paint and move it around, creating a truly awful effect.

15. **Create a new layer named *Effects* and drag it to the top of your layer stack.**

    If your painting needs a bit more punch, add some special lighting effects. Figure 12-19 (right) shows blue-tinted shadows around the edges of the angel's face and in her hair. If you change this layer's mode to Multiply, the blue paint acts like a double coat of ink, although lowering the layer's opacity to about 75 percent makes the effect subtle.

16. Add some texture.

To keep the painting from looking too perfect and, well, *digital*, mess it up a bit with additional texture. You can use *anything* to create texture, including grainy, funky-edged brushes or a photo set to Overlay blend mode. Figure 12-20 describes one texture-inducing maneuver—adding, get this, a photo of a piece of tile.

FIGURE 12-20

Texture can give a painting life and keep it from looking plastic because it's too perfect (left). In this example, a photo of a slate tile was added at the top of the layer stack. Changing the photo layer's blend mode to Overlay (page 288) gives the painting a little depth and makes it look more believable (right).

This image, created by Deborah Fox (www.deborahfoxart.com), was recognized for creative excellence in advertising with an ADDY award.

17. Save your painting one last time by pressing ⌘-S (Ctrl+S).

Congratulations for sticking through a *ton* of steps to create your first digital painting from scratch!

As you can see, Photoshop paintings are a lot of work, but they can be very rewarding. Putting every aspect of the painting on a separate layer lets you build the image gradually so you don't destroy the whole thing if you mess up. OK, who needs a nap?

TIP   To learn more about digital painting techniques, pick up a copy of *ImagineFX* magazine (*www.imaginefx.com*) or visit these websites: Computer Graphics Society (*www.cgsociety.org*), Concept Art (*www.conceptart.org*), and Epilogue (*www.epilogue.net*). You'll be glad you did!

FIGURE 12-22

Top: Be sure to use short brushstrokes or you'll create an edge that looks like a repeating pattern of your brush cursor's shape. Just keep brushing back and forth until you get an interesting look (Alternatively, skip ahead to page 520 to learn how to adjust Angle Jitter in the Brush panel.)

Bottom: By using a layer mask to create this effect, the original image remains unharmed, as shown in this Layers panel. If you like this edge effect, you can create something similar by using the Refine Edge dialog box. Flip back to page 177 for more info.

10. **Save your image as a PSD file.**

    If you decide to go back and edit the painted edges, just activate the layer mask, grab the Brush tool, and have a ball.

■ MAKING AN OBJECT SPARKLE

Another fun use for interesting brushes is to make an object look like it's sparkling. Just follow steps 6–7 in the previous list, but instead of loading the Faux Finish Brushes, load the Assorted Brushes. Once the new brushes are in your Brush Preset menu, scroll down the list of brush previews and you'll spot a couple of crosshatch brushes that make a perfect sparkle if you rotate them (see Figure 12-23). Click one of the crosshatches to activate it, click your foreground color chip at the bottom of the Tools panel, and then pick a nice gold from the resulting Color Picker. Over in the Layers panel, create a new layer for each sparkle, so you can rotate 'em individually.

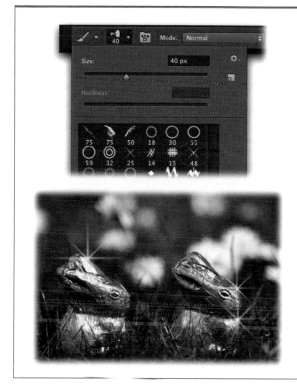

FIGURE 12-23

Top: The Assorted category's crosshatch brushes, like the one circled here, are perfect for making an object look like it's sparkling.

Bottom: The beauty of putting each sparkle on its own layer is that you can move them around, spin 'em, and control their intensity with the layers' opacity settings.

With the first new layer active (it should be at the top of the Layers panel), click once in your image to add a sparkle. Add another new layer and then click again to add another sparkle. Finally, rotate the sparkle using Free Transform by pressing ⌘-T (Ctrl+T); page 259 has the lowdown on Free Transform. Press Return (Enter) when you're finished rotating and then Shift-click both sparkle layers in the Layers panel to activate them. Then press V to grab the Move tool and drag the sparkle into place.

> **TIP** You can press the V key to switch temporarily to the Move tool. When you let go of the key, you switch back to whatever tool you were using before.

Painted photo edges and sparkles are just two of an infinite number of visually interesting effects you can create using the extra brushes that come with Photoshop. Look through the various brush sets and see if some of the unusual shapes inspire you to try another technique!

- **Invert.** Since texture in Photoshop doesn't literally mean that some parts of your image stick up farther than others, the program bases texture on the colors in a pattern. It considers dark areas "lower" than lighter ones, which makes sense because, in the real world, more light reaches the parts of a textured surface that protrude than lower areas, which are darker because they're filled with shadows. Also as in real life, when you paint over a textured part of a document, the lighter (higher) areas get more paint than darker (lower) ones since the hairs on your brush have a hard time reaching down into those low areas. If you turn on this checkbox, Photoshop reverses the high and low points of the texture, so light areas are low points that don't get very much paint and dark areas are the high points that get lots of paint.

- **Scale.** This slider lets you adjust the size of the pattern. Drag it left to make the pattern smaller or right to make it bigger.

- **Brightness** and **Contrast.** These two sliders are new in CS6. They let you tweak the brightness and contrast of the texture within a brushstroke. In previous versions of Photoshop, there was no way to do this; you had to create different *versions* of the texture to produce lighter, darker, or higher-contrast brushstrokes.

- **Texture Each Tip.** This checkbox makes Photoshop apply the texture to each brush mark *within* the stroke, rather than the *whole* stroke, creating a more textured look (and slightly less chance of a painfully obvious repeating pattern). You have to turn this setting on to use the Depth setting discussed later in this list.

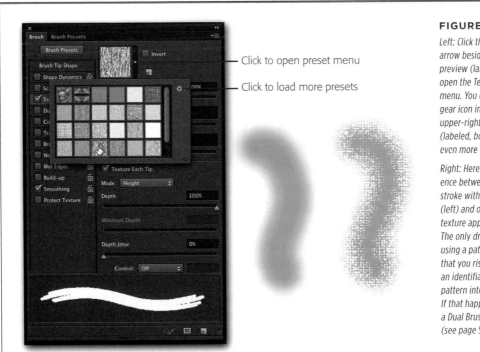

Click to open preset menu

Click to load more presets

FIGURE 12-27

Left: Click the down arrow beside the texture preview (labeled, top) to open the Texture preset menu. You can click the gear icon in the menu's upper-right corner (labeled, bottom) to load even more textures.

Right: Here's the difference between a brushstroke with no texture (left) and one with the texture applied (right). The only drawback to using a pattern texture is that you risk introducing an identifiable repeating pattern into your image. If that happens, try using a Dual Brush tip instead (see page 523).

- **Mode.** Use this pop-up menu to pick the blend mode Photoshop uses to apply the pattern to the brushstroke (see page 280 for more on blend modes).

- **Depth.** This slider controls how deeply the paint "seeps into" the texture by increasing the contrast of the colors in the texture. Changing this to a high percentage means the "low" points of the texture won't get any paint, and entering a low percentage means all the areas get the same amount of paint, which reduces the contrast so much you can't see the texture.

- **Minimum Depth.** This slider lets you set the minimum depth that paint can seep into the texture.

- **Depth Jitter** and **Control.** These settings let you introduce randomness into how the depth varies when the Texture Each Tip checkbox is turned on. Drag this slider left to decrease the amount of depth jitter, or right to increase it. In the Control pop-up menu, you can choose from Off, Fade, Pen Pressure, Pen Tilt, Stylus Wheel, and Rotation (discussed on page 519).

Dual Brush

These options let you combine two brush tips to introduce more texture and randomness into a brushstroke or to give texture to a brush that doesn't have any. Photoshop applies the second brush's texture to the first brush's brushstrokes wherever the two strokes overlap, as shown in Figure 12-28 (brush tips of differing shapes will overlap in different places). To choose two brushes, pick your first brush in the Brush Tip Shape category by clicking one of the presets and then adjusting its options. Then click the Dual Brush category and follow the same process to choose a second brush.

FIGURE 12-28

To introduce texture to a brush that doesn't have any, like the leaf brush shown here (left), head to the Dual Brush category and choose a textured brush tip as your second brush. The image on the right shows what such a combination looks like.

- **Mix Jitter** and **Control.** Also available when you're using the Mixer Brush, these settings let you vary how much paint you're mixing from your canvas onto your brush.

- **Minimum.** Once you make a choice from the Control pop-up menus for the Opacity, Flow, Wetness, and Mix Jitter settings, you can use these sliders to set their minimum values.

FIGURE 12-30

To make your brushstroke's opacity vary randomly, increase the Opacity Jitter setting. Here you see the difference between a brushstroke with no opacity jitter (top) and one with the opacity jitter set to 100 percent (bottom).

Brush Pose

New in Photoshop CS6, you can use this setting to control brush tilt, rotation, and pressure with a graphics tablet or mouse. If you're using a graphics tablet, you can override its input by turning on the Override checkboxes beneath each slider, which can be handy when you need to create exactly the same brushstroke over and over and over again. If you don't have a graphics tablet, this setting lets you make your mouse behave more like a stylus.

Noise

Turn on this checkbox to make Photoshop apply a dose of random, grainy texture to the semi-transparent edges of a soft brush tip (if you're using a dual brush tip, the noise applies to both tips; if you're using a hard-edged brush, nothing happens). You can use this setting to introduce more texture and randomness into brushstrokes you make with soft-edges brushes.

Wet Edges

Turning on this checkbox makes the center of your brushstrokes transparent, so the paint looks like it's building up along the edges of the stroke (similar to painting with watercolors).

Build-up

Turn on this checkbox—called Airbrush in previous versions of Photoshop—to make your brush behave like a real airbrush (the old Airbrush behaved like a can of spray paint, but in CS6 it's more like a professional artist's airbrush rig). This setting has the same effect as clicking the Airbrush button in the Options bar (page 497). Basically, Photoshop adds brush marks as long as you hold down your mouse button, and extends the brush marks past your cursor to create a real-world spray effect.

Smoothing

To make your brushstrokes look smoother than they were when you painted them, turn this checkbox on. It's especially helpful if you don't have a very steady hand, which can make for jagged brushstrokes.

Protect Texture

This checkbox lets you apply the same texture, pattern, and size to all the built-in brush presets that have a texture. So, for example, you could use this option to make it look like you're painting on the same surface with a variety of brushes without actually having to turn on the Texture category for each brush. You can think of this as a global texture option.

Suggested Brush Customizations

With so many settings, it can be confusing to figure out which brushes really need changing. You'll find that the built-in presets are really handy, and with just a few tweaks here and there, they can become indispensable. Figure 12-31 shows a sample of some extremely useful yet simple customizations. If you like what you see, check out Table 12-1 to learn about specific settings.

■ Defining a New Brush

For some seriously creative fun, try making your own brushes. You can make them out of anything—a stroke that you've drawn with another brush, your logo, even an image that you've scanned into your computer to use as texture (like a leaf). Some folks call brushes that you create yourself *sampled brushes* because you *sample* part of a pattern, object, or image to create them; in other words, you have to select the pattern, object, or image you want to base the brush on.

The first step is to create the *paint dab*—a dab of paint in the shape of the brush tip—you want to turn into a custom brush (see Figure 12-32, left). You can create a paint dab in a variety of ways, which range from quick to incredibly involved. The basic premise is to create a new 300x300–pixel document and then use a variety of brushes at various opacity settings to create the dab. You can even add texture to it—the more irregular and messy the dab, the more interesting your brush will be. To turn the dab into a brush that you can use to apply color, you *have* to create it using black and gray paint at 100 percent opacity (that's the Options bar's opacity setting). When you paint with the brush later, the 100 percent black areas will create opaque color and the gray areas will be semitransparent.

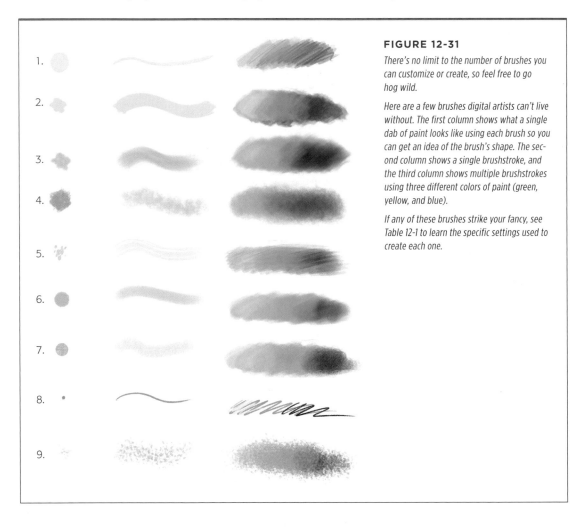

FIGURE 12-31

There's no limit to the number of brushes you can customize or create, so feel free to go hog wild.

Here are a few brushes digital artists can't live without. The first column shows what a single dab of paint looks like using each brush so you can get an idea of the brush's shape. The second column shows a single brushstroke, and the third column shows multiple brushstrokes using three different colors of paint (green, yellow, and blue).

If any of these brushes strike your fancy, see Table 12-1 to learn the specific settings used to create each one.

TABLE 12-1. *Suggested brush customizations*

BRUSH NUMBER IN FIGURE 12-31	DESCRIPTION	OPACITY[1]	SPACING[2]	SHAPE DYNAMICS	OTHER DYNAMICS	USES
1	Round, hard-edged brush	25%	0%	Size Jitter = Pen Pressure	None	Shading, blocking in color, sketching
2, 3	Rough-edged brush	25%	0%	None	With (2) or without (3) Flow Jitter = Pen Pressure	Shading, adding texture, making hair
4	Rough brush (custom)[3]	30%	0%	Angle Jitter = 20%; Control = Off	None	Adding texture, shading
5	Small dot brush (custom)[3]	30%	0%	Size Jitter = Pen Pressure	Opacity Jitter = Pen Pressure	Making hair, shading
6	Round, rough edged brush	100%	20–25%	Size Jitter – Pen Pressure	Opacity Jitter and Flow Jitter = Pen Pressure	Shading, blocking in color
7	Textured round brush	30%	0%	None	Flow Jitter = Pen Pressure	Adding texture, shading
8	Textured round brush	100%	0%	Size Jitter = Pen Pressure	Flow Jitter = Pen Pressure	Sketching, creating line art, adding fine details in small areas
9	Scattered spot brush (custom)[3]	70%	25%	Scatter = 20%; Size Jitter = Pen Pressure	Opacity Jitter and Flow Jitter = Pen Pressure	Adding texture

[1] Adjust this setting in the Options bar.
[2] Set this in the Brush Tip Shape section of the Brush panel—see page 516.
[3] Meaning a custom-made brush you make from scratch as described in the next section.

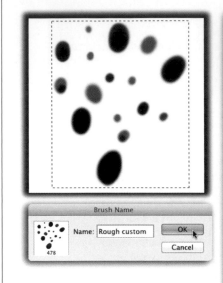

FIGURE 12-32

Left: You can create this paint dab by starting with one of the small, soft-edged brush presets. Set your foreground color chip to black, paint a few dots, and then switch to some shade of gray and paint a few more. Just make sure that the Options bar's Opacity field is set to 100 percent.

Right: If you tweak a few settings in the Brush panel, you can create an extremely useful texture and shading brush.

NOTE To practice making a custom brush using the paint dab shown in Figure 12-32, download *DotsBrush. psd* from the Missing CD page at *www.missingmanuals.com/cds*.

Once you've created a paint dab, follow these steps to turn it into a brush:

1. **Use the Rectangular Marquee tool to select the dab.**

   To define a brush, you have to select the image first. Press M (or Shift-M) to grab the Rectangular Marquee and draw a selection around the dab (Figure 12-32, left).

2. **Choose Edit→Define Brush Preset.**

   In the resulting dialog box (Figure 12-32, left), give your brush a name and then click OK.

3. **Create a new document (it can be any size) and then press B to grab the Brush tool.**

   Press ⌘-N (Ctrl+N on a PC) to open a new document so you can test drive your new brush.

4. **In the Options bar, choose your new brush from the Brush Preset picker in the Options bar and then open the Brush panel.**

Once you've activated your new brush, click the button to the right of the Brush Preset picker (or choose Window→Brush) to open the Brush panel. Alternatively, you can open the Brush panel first: just click the Brush Presets button at the top of the Brush panel (or the Brush Presets tab, if you've already opened that panel) and then choose your new brush from there.

5. **In the Brush panel, click the Brush Tip Shape setting.**

To create a brush similar to number 4 in Figure 12-31, change the size to 100 pixels, the angle to 70 degrees, and the spacing to 1 percent. If you have a graphics tablet, click the Other Dynamics setting and adjust the Opacity Jitter and Flow Jitter options' Control menus to Pen Pressure.

6. **Click the Shape Dynamics category.**

If you have a graphics tablet, set Size Jitter to Pen Pressure and Minimum Diameter to 30 percent. If you don't have a graphics tablet, try entering a Size Jitter of 25 percent instead (you just won't be able to change it by applying more or less pressure with your pen).

7. **Turn on the Smoothing checkbox.**

As explained on page 527, this setting makes your brushstrokes smoother, so they look less jagged.

8. **Save your brush again.**

Click the "Create new brush" button at the bottom right of the Brush panel (it looks like a piece of paper with a folded corner). If you don't save the brush again, you lose the settings you just changed. In the resulting dialog box, give it the same name that you did in step 2.

Not only have you created a brush that's great for adding textures to digital paintings, but you can also use it to create some interesting grunge effects when you're editing photos. The ability to make your own brushes gives you a ton of control when you're applying textures.

> **TIP** If you want to share your new brush with the masses, choose Save Brushes from the Brush Preset panel's menu (the Brush panel's menu doesn't have this option). Give the brush a name and then hop on over to the Adobe Photoshop Marketplace (*www.lesa.in/custompsbrushes*) and upload your file to achieve Photoshop fame!

■ Installing New Brushes

You're not alone when it comes to creating new brushes. Folks love sharing their creations, and once they've made a really cool brush, they're usually happy to share it with the masses. That's why all manner of free brushes are available on the Web.

One of the best resources is the Adobe Studio Exchange website. Going to *www. lesa.in/custompsbrushes* leads you straight to the Brushes category, though you can use the list on the right side of the page to find all manner of actions, custom shapes, gradients, and so on there, too. You can even download a brush set that'll make your image look like it was printed on torn paper as shown in Figure 12-33. Once you've downloaded the brush set to your hard drive, choose Load Brushes from the Brush picker's presets menu in the Options bar (or from the Brush Preset panel's menu) and navigate to where the brush set lives (look for a file whose name ends in ".abr," such as *Paper_Damage.abr*) and then click Load (you can also double-click the .abr file and Photoshop will put it in the right spot). The new brushes appear in the Brush Preset menu, ready for you to use.

The streaks in Figure 12-33 (bottom) were made by setting the foreground and background chips to white and brown (respectively) and then choosing Filter→Render→Cloud, followed by Filter→Blur→Motion Blur. Next, the streak layer's blend mode was changed to Hard Light. With a few clicks of the funky Paper Damage brushes, the photo looks ancient!

FIGURE 12-33

At the Adobe Studio Exchange site (top left), you can download some amazing brushes and share your own creations. After you download and install the Paper Damage brush set (top right), for example, you can use its brushes to age a photo (bottom). You can go straight to this brush set by visiting www.lesa.in/ pspaperdamage.

In the bottom image, each damaging brush-stroke was painted in white on its own layer to control the layer's opacity and protect the original image.

The Art History Brush

Adobe would have you believe that you can use the Art History Brush to turn a photo into a painting, but the darn thing doesn't work very well (as is painfully clear in the figure below). It's similar to the more useful History Brush in that you can choose a snapshot of your image (a previous version saved at a particular time) to work from, which is why it's in the same toolset. That said, take this tool for a spin and decide for yourself whether it deserves a spot in your regular tool rotation. Here's how:

1. **Grab the Art History Brush by pressing Y.** (If pressing Y selected the History Brush, simply press Shift-Y to activate the Art History Brush instead.)

2. **In the History panel, pick a snapshot or history state.** Open the History panel by choosing Window→History and then choose a state by clicking the left column beside the state or snapshot you want to work with.

3. **Pick a small, soft-edged brush from the Options bar's Brush menu.** You can set the tool's blend mode and opacity in the Options bar just like you can with the Brush tool, and use the Control-Option-drag (Alt+right-click+drag on a PC) keyboard shortcut to resize your brush on the fly—drag left to make it smaller or right to make it bigger.

4. **In the Options bar's Style menu, choose Tight Short.** You'll find 10 different painting styles in this pop-up menu, including Tight Short, Loose Medium, Loose Long, and so on. Any option with the word "tight" in its name works a little better than the others because it keeps the brushstrokes close together.

5. **Change the Options bar's Area field to 50 pixels.** This setting controls the area covered by the artsy (and totally destructive) brushstrokes you create as you brush across the image. Enter a large number for more strokes or a smaller number for fewer strokes. If you have any hope of recognizing the object you're painting, keep this number relatively low (less than 40 percent).

6. **Make sure the Tolerance field is set to 0 percent.** A low tolerance lets you paint strokes anywhere you want. A high tolerance limits them to areas that differ from the color in the snapshot or history state you picked in step 2.

7. **Mouse over to your image and paint it.** As you paint, your clear, recognizable photo will be replaced with random, supposedly artistic swaths of paint, transforming it into madness and mayhem. Undo command, anyone?

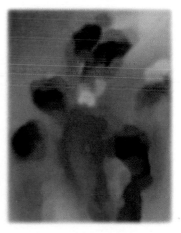

Drawing with the Vector Tools

I f your first thought when someone mentions drawing is, "But I can't even draw a straight line!" don't worry: You *can* draw in Photoshop. To draw a straight line, just grab the Line tool (it's one of the shape tools—see page 550) and drag from one spot to another. Or, as you learned in the previous chapter, grab the Brush tool, click in one spot, and then Shift-click another spot; it's that simple. The program also includes all kinds of built-in shapes like circles, rectangles, and rounded rectangles that are incredibly easy to use.

But what about creating more sophisticated drawings and illustrations? The good news is you don't have to worry about drawing *anything* freehand, whether it's a line or a curvy shape. Instead, the vector drawing tools you'll learn about in this chapter let you create a series of *points*; Photoshop then adds a *path* in between those points to form the outline of the shape. Unlike the things you draw by hand with the Brush tool or a real-world pencil, these vector objects are infinitely tweakable: You can move points and adjust the paths to create any shape you want, letting you make complex yet flexible works of art from scratch, as Figure 13-1 shows.

Now, if you're tempted to bail from this chapter because you're not an artist, hold your horses—you can use the vector drawing tools in a variety of other ways. For example:

- Once you get the hang of these tools, you can use them to add elements to images that don't exist and can't be photographed, like the ornamental shapes and embellishments shown on page 304.

- You can use the drawing tools to create precise selections that you can't make any other way. In fact, the Pen tool is a favorite of seasoned Photoshop jockeys because of its selection prowess (see page 566).

- You can use the shape tools to mask (hide) parts of an image (see page 572). Because those masks are vector based, they're a lot more flexible than the regular ol' layer masks you learned about back on page 116.

Learning to draw with Photoshop's vector tools takes time and patience because they work *very* differently from any other tool you've used so far. But taking the time to master them sets you on the path (pun intended) to becoming a true Photoshop guru.

Before you dive into using the tools themselves, though, you need a quick tour of the different drawing modes you can use. Take a deep breath and read on!

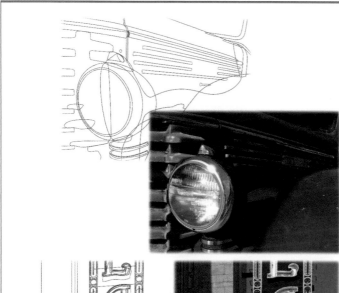

FIGURE 13-1

Top: Here you can see the paths that make up the basic shapes of this digital painting by Bert Monroy called "Red Truck." You read that correctly: It's not a photograph—Bert drew every detail by hand. He created the basic shapes using the Pen tool, and then filled in the details with the Brush tool. Instead of a mouse, he used a Wacom interactive pen display (a monitor you can draw directly on; see www.wacom.com/cintiq*).*

Bottom: This wire-frame drawing (called "Oakland" and also by Bert) is even more complex. If you look closely, you can make out the shapes he created with the Pen tool to make the neon tubes and the sockets that the tubes go into. Now that's something to aspire to!

You can see more of Bert's amazing work at www.bertmonroy.com*.*

■ Photoshop's Drawing Modes

In the real world, the word *drawing* implies that you're sketching lines and shapes by hand. But in Photoshop and in this book, drawing refers to creating objects using Photoshop's vector tools: the Pen tool and the various shape tools. Drawing with these tools is more like drafting (think technical illustrations such as blueprints) because you're creating precise *outlines* of shapes instead of the varying lines of a sketch or painting.

NOTE Here's a way to make sense of the difference between Photoshop's painting tools and its vector drawing tools: If Van Gogh or Michelangelo had used Photoshop, they would have liked the Brush tool because of its similarity to real-world paintbrushes. However, artists like Matisse, Mondrian, and Picasso would have favored the vector drawing tools because their painting styles are more precise and angular and depend on creating smooth, clean geometric shapes and lines.

Photoshop has three different drawing modes, accessible from the Options bar (see Figure 13-2), and you can use 'em to determine exactly what happens when you use the Pen (and shape tools, though they're discussed later on). Here's what each mode does:

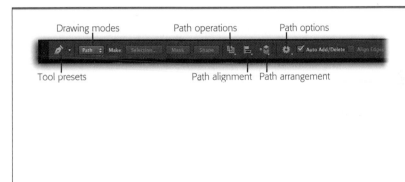

FIGURE 13-2

When you press P to grab the Pen tool in CS6, you see a pop-up menu for different drawing modes near the left end of the Options bar (instead of the buttons in previous versions). The buttons to the right of the Make label let you tell Photoshop what you want to create once you've drawn a shape: a selection (marching ants), a vector mask, or a Shape layer.

- **Shape**. When you're in this mode and you make your first click with any vector drawing tool, Photoshop creates a new Shape layer for you to work on. When you finish drawing the shape, Photoshop automatically fills it with black, though you can use the new Fill and Stroke settings in the Options bar to change fill color as well as add a solid, dashed, or dotted line (skip ahead to page 553 for more on this fabulous new feature). Drawing in this mode is similar to using a pair of scissors to cut shapes out of a piece of construction paper—these shapes can *hide* content on any layers below 'em, where the layers overlap.

  Shape mode works with the Pen tool and the shape tools. It's great for creating geometric shapes filled with color that you can use in designs or overlay onto images (like the embellishments shown on page 304). You can also use this mode to add a symbol or a logo to a product in an image (see page 551). Photoshop comes with a slew of built-in shapes to choose from, but you can also create your own (page 556) and download shapes created by other folks on the Internet. As you learned back in Chapter 4, you can also use the shape tools to create selections. (See page 150, for example, to learn how to round the edges of a photo using the Rounded Rectangle tool.)

- **Path.** As you learned earlier, paths are lines and curves between *points*, which you'll find out more about in the next section. Path mode doesn't create a new Shape layer or fill the path with color; instead, when you're in this mode, Photoshop turns whatever you draw into an empty outline. Use this mode when you want to use the Pen tool to make selections (page 556) or create a clipping path (page 568), or want to create a vector mask that you may need to resize (see page 572). You can also fill paths with color (page 564) and give them a stroke (page 562), but Photoshop doesn't automatically create a new layer when you use the Pen tool or a shape tool in Paths mode; you have to create a new layer first *and then* add the fill or stroke. The paths you create in this mode live in the Paths panel, which you'll learn about on page 548.

- **Pixels.** This mode works only with the shape tools (page 550). Normally when you use one of these tools, Photoshop plops you into Shape mode and fills the vector shape with your foreground color. But in Pixels mode, Photoshop creates a *pixel*-based layer instead (it still fills the shape with your foreground color). This is handy if you need to edit the shape using tools that don't work with vectors, like filters, painting tools, and so on. That said, you could just as easily rasterize a Shape layer (see page 113) and then use those tools. So unless you know *for sure* that you'll never need to change the shape of the object you're drawing, you won't use this mode very often.

The basic drawing process is the same no matter which mode you choose: You pick the Pen tool or one of the shape tools, choose a drawing mode, draw the shape, edit the shape, and then save it for future use. In the following sections you'll learn how to do all that and more.

Now that you have a bird's-eye view of the process, it's time to dig into drawing with the Pen tool.

■ Drawing Paths with the Pen Tool

The Pen tool made its debut in Adobe Illustrator way back in the late '80s and offered people precision and control the likes of which they'd never seen. The only problem was that the tool was (and still is) *darn* hard to use. It was met with all kinds of resistance from the artistic community because it didn't conform to the way folks were used to working with digital graphics (not to mention pens and pencils). Instead of dragging to draw a line, with the Pen tool you create *anchor points* and *control handles*, which are collectively referred to as *vector paths* or *Bézier curves* (named for their inventor). The handles aren't actually part of the line; they're little levers you use to control each line segment's curvature (see Figure 13-3).

As you learned back in Chapter 2, you can edit and resize vectors without losing quality. For example, you can adjust an object's points and paths (see Figure 13-3, bottom) to tweak its shape and then use Free Transform to resize, rotate, distort, warp, or flip the object. When it's just right, you can fill the shape with color (page

564), trace its outline with one of the painting tools (page 562), or use it to create a mask (page 566).

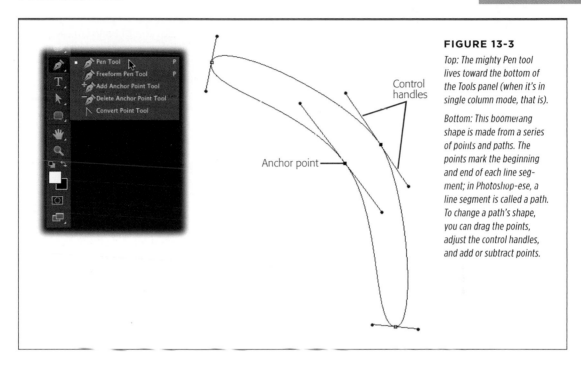

FIGURE 13-3

Top: The mighty Pen tool lives toward the bottom of the Tools panel (when it's in single column mode, that is).

Bottom: This boomerang shape is made from a series of points and paths. The points mark the beginning and end of each line segment; in Photoshop-ese, a line segment is called a path. To change a path's shape, you can drag the points, adjust the control handles, and add or subtract points.

To create a line with the Pen tool, you have to click *twice*: The first click creates the line's starting anchor point, the second click adds the ending anchor point, and Photoshop *automatically* adds the path in between. It's kind of like digital connect-the-dots: Each time you add a new anchor point, a path appears connecting it to the previous point.

You use two different kinds of anchor points to tell Photoshop whether you want a curved or straight path:

- **Smooth.** Use these anchor points when you want the path to curve. If you click to set an anchor point and then drag in any direction—before releasing your mouse button—the Pen tool creates a *control handle* that you can drag to make the next path curve. (The direction you drag is extremely important, as you're about to learn.) When you click to make the second anchor point, Photoshop creates the actual path—a curved line between the two points.

- **Corner.** Use these anchor points when you want to draw a straight line. Simply click *without* dragging to set a point, and you don't get any control handles; instead, the Pen tool creates points connected by straight paths. To draw perfectly horizontal or vertical lines, press and hold the Shift key while you click to set more points. This limits the Pen tool to drawing straight lines at angles that are multiples of 45 degrees (45, 90, and so on), which is great when you want to draw geometric shapes.

Once you have, well, a *handle* on points and handles, you can make any shape you want. In the following pages you'll learn how to create both straight and curved paths.

Drawing Straight Paths

The easiest thing you'll ever do with the Pen tool is create straight paths. To give the tool a spin, create a new document by choosing File→New and then follow these steps:

1. **Press P to grab the Pen tool.**

   The Pen tool lives above the big T in the Tools panel, and its icon looks like a fountain pen nib.

2. **Choose Path mode in the Options bar.**

   From the mode pop-up menu toward the left of the Options bar, choose Path (shown in Figure 13-2) looks like a fountain pen nib in a box with little square corners. You could use Shape mode for this exercise, but in that mode, Photoshop starts filling the path with color as soon as you start drawing it, which gets visually confusing (and these techniques are hard enough as it is!). So to see only the path itself—with no fill color—work in Path mode instead.

3. **Mouse over to your document and click once to create an anchor point.**

   Photoshop puts a tiny black square where you clicked (Figure 13-4, top).

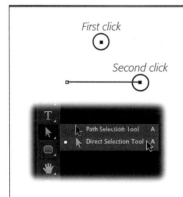

First click

Second click

FIGURE 13-4

Each time you click, Photoshop adds another anchor point, and connects each point with a path that forms your shape. If you want to start a new path instead of adding to an existing one, just tap the Esc key and then click somewhere else in the document.

4. **Move your cursor to the right of the first anchor point and click to create a second anchor point.**

   Photoshop adds a straight line that connects the two points.

5. **Move your cursor down an inch or so, and click to create another anchor point.**

Photoshop continues to connect the points with paths after you create each point. If you want to create a perfectly horizontal or vertical line, press and hold the Shift key as you click to add another anchor point (you can also use this trick to create lines at 45-degree angles).

6. **When you're finished drawing lines, press the Esc key or ⌘-click (Ctrl-click on a PC) elsewhere in the document.**

The anchor points you created disappear, and you see a thin gray line representing the path you just drew.

7. **If you want to move an anchor point to change the angle of the line, grab the Direct Selection tool by pressing Shift-A until a white arrow appears in the Tools panel.**

The Direct Selection tool lives in the toolset just below the big T in the Tools panel (see Figure 13-4, bottom). You'll learn more about this tool when you start editing paths on page 557.

8. **Click to activate and then drag one of the line's anchor points.**

As long as you hold your mouse button down, you can move the point wherever you want. When you get it positioned just right, release the mouse button.

Congratulations! You've just drawn your first path with the Pen tool. Enjoy your success because it gets a *lot* harder from here on out.

Drawing Curved Paths

Drawing curves with the Pen tool is more complicated because you have to use the control handles mentioned on page 539 to tell Photoshop how *big* you want the curve to be and in what *direction* you want it to go. Here's what you do:

1. **With the Pen tool active, click within the document to set an anchor point and then—without letting go of your mouse button—drag to the left or right to make the point's control handles appear.**

The control handles pop out from the point you created, and one of the handles sticks to your cursor. These handles indicate the direction the path will take; if you drag to the right, the path curves right when you add the next anchor point; if you drag left, the path curves left. For this exercise, drag upward and to the right about half an inch, and then release your mouse button (see Figure 13-5, top).

NOTE It's next to *impossible* to get a sense of how the control handles work by reading about 'em. So if you're near a computer, turn it on and fire up Photoshop so you can follow along. Better yet, visit this book's Missing CD page at *www.missingmanuals.com/cds* and download the file *Curve.tif* so you can practice drawing the curves shown in Figure 13-5.

2. **About two inches to the right of the first point, click to add a second point and, while holding your mouse button down, drag the new handle downward and to the right half an inch, and then release your mouse button.**

In step 1, you pulled the first handle upward and the curve obediently bent upward. By dragging this second control handle downward, your next curve heads downward (see Figure 13-5, middle).

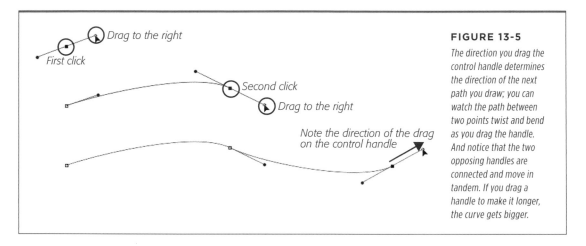

FIGURE 13-5

The direction you drag the control handle determines the direction of the next path you draw; you can watch the path between two points twist and bend as you drag the handle. And notice that the two opposing handles are connected and move in tandem. If you drag a handle to make it longer, the curve gets bigger.

3. **Create a third point by clicking and dragging upward and to the right.**

The path that appears when you click to add this third point curves downward because you pulled the control handle downward in the previous step. Drag the third point's control handle upward and slightly to the right to make the curve shown in Figure 13-5, bottom.

4. **When you're finished, press the Esc key to let Photoshop know you're done drawing the path.**

You can also ⌘-click (Ctrl-click on a PC) elsewhere in the document.

You've just drawn your first curved path! With practice, you'll get the hang of using the control handles to determine the direction and size of the curves. And as you may have guessed, the drawing process gets even more complicated from here.

Converting Anchor Points

As you learned on page 539, there are two kinds of anchor points in Photoshop: smooth and corner. To draw complicated paths, you need to know how to *switch* between these point types so you can create curves within a single path that go the same direction. (Take a peek ahead at Figure 13-7, bottom, to see what this looks like.) To do that, you start by creating a series of curves, and then convert some of the smooth points to corner points.

Here's how:

1. **With the Pen tool active, click and hold with your mouse button to create a point, and then drag the control handle up and away from the anchor point to set the direction of the next curve (Figure 13-6, top left).**

   Release your mouse button when you're ready to set the next anchor point.

   NOTE To practice drawing these paths yourself, visit this book's Missing CD page at *www.missingmanuals.com/cds* and download the file *ComboPath.tif*.

2. **Move your cursor an inch or so to the right, and then click to set a second point to the right of the first and drag downward (Figure 13-6, top right).**

   When the path has the curve you want, release your mouse button.

3. **Move your cursor another inch to the right and then click and drag downward to create a third point (Figure 13-6, middle).**

4. **Hop right another inch and then click and drag downward once again to create a fourth point (Figure 13-6, bottom).**

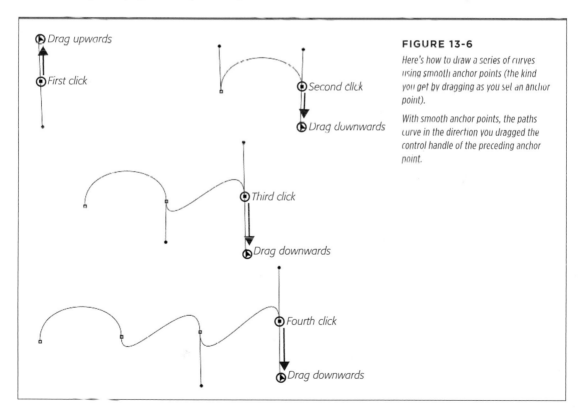

Drag upwards

First click

Second click

Drag downwards

Third click

Drag downwards

Fourth click

Drag downwards

FIGURE 13-6

Here's how to draw a series of curves using smooth anchor points (the kind you get by dragging as you set an anchor point).

With smooth anchor points, the paths curve in the direction you dragged the control handle of the preceding anchor point.

5. **Head over to the Tools panel and grab the Convert Anchor Point tool (Figure 13-3).**

The Convert Anchor Point tool is tucked away inside the Pen toolset (its icon looks like an upside-down V). Just click and hold on the Pen tool to see the rest of the toolset, and then give it a click (for unknown reasons, the Shift-P trick doesn't work for the Insert, Delete, or Convert Anchor Point tools).

6. **Drag the bottom control handle that's attached to the third anchor point (see Figure 13-7, top) up so it's close to the opposite control handle on the same anchor point.**

The Convert Anchor Point tool "breaks" the bottom half of the control handle away from the top half so it can move all by itself. This nifty little maneuver converts the anchor point from a smooth point to a corner point and changes the path from a smooth curve to a sharp angle. Once you break control handles apart, they behave much like the hands of a clock and you can move them independently to adjust the angle and curve of the path.

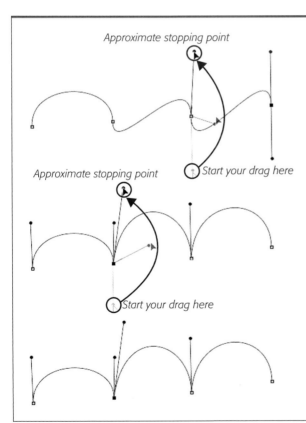

Approximate stopping point

Approximate stopping point

Start your drag here

Start your drag here

FIGURE 13-7

Once you convert smooth anchor points into corner points, you can adjust each control handle separately to create a series of curves that bend in the same direction, as shown here.

If you move both parts of the control handle so they're on top of each other, you see only one handle (like the third anchor point shown at the middle and bottom), just as you see only one hand of a clock at noon, when the hour and minute hands overlap. If that happens, grab the Direct Selection tool and drag one of the handles out of the way so you can see them both.

7. **Use the Direct Selection tool to grab the path's second point from the left.**

Unfortunately, you can't select points with the Convert Anchor Point tool, so to see the second anchor point's control handles, you have to use the Direct Selection tool. You can use Photoshop's spring-loaded tools feature to temporarily grab the Direct Selection tool: Just press and hold A, click the point, and then release the A key. As soon as you select the anchor point, its control handles appear.

> **TIP** Holding down the ⌘ key (Ctrl on a PC) changes the Convert Anchor Point tool to the Direct Selection tool temporarily, saving you a trip to the Tools panel.

8. **Grab the Convert Anchor Point tool (or release the A key), click the bottom control handle that just appeared, and drag it upward next to its partner (see Figure 13-7, middle).**

When you're finished, you should have a series of curves that all bend in the same direction (see Figure 13-7, bottom).

UP TO SPEED

Drawing with a French Curve

This Bezier curve business is darn tough to wrap your brain around. But if you've taken any kind of art class—even if it was as far back as middle school—there's a real-world counterpart that makes the curved paths you draw with the Pen tool a *little* easier to understand.

Drawing with Photoshop's Pen tool is similar to using a brush, pencil, or art knife with a set of *French curves*—plastic stencils that folks use as guides to create flowing, curved lines. French curves have some of the same limitations as the Pen tool. For example, the main challenge when using French curves is picking the stencil that will give you the longest sweep (or arc) possible. You often have to switch stencils or change its position to follow a particular sweep.

With the Pen tool, you can take a similar approach: Try creating the longest possible distance between two points to keep your paths as simple—that is, with as few anchor points—as possible. The more points in a path, the longer Photoshop takes to draw the path, which is especially important when you want to turn the path into a *clipping path* (see page 568) that you can use in a page-layout program like Adobe InDesign or QuarkXPress. Those other programs have to translate and draw the path, so keeping it as simple as possible helps avoid problems.

Path Drawing Tips

Here are some things to keep in mind when you're drawing curved paths with the Pen tool:

- **Exaggerating curves.** If you want to create an exaggerated curve or one that curves back on itself, you need to drag one side of the control handle in the opposite direction from the way you drew the path (see Figure 13-8, left). Also, keep in mind that it's the *length* of the handle that determines the height or depth of the curve. (You lengthen a control handle by dragging it farther in any direction.) Figure 13-8, right, shows the effect of different-length handles on two similar paths.

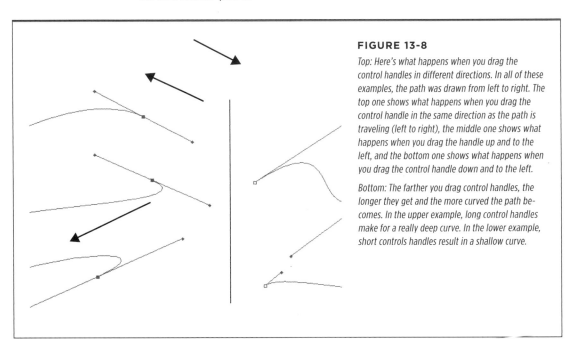

FIGURE 13-8

Top: Here's what happens when you drag the control handles in different directions. In all of these examples, the path was drawn from left to right. The top one shows what happens when you drag the control handle in the same direction as the path is traveling (left to right), the middle one shows what happens when you drag the handle up and to the left, and the bottom one shows what happens when you drag the control handle down and to the left.

Bottom: The farther you drag control handles, the longer they get and the more curved the path becomes. In the upper example, long control handles make for a really deep curve. In the lower example, short controls handles result in a shallow curve.

- **Closing a path.** The paths you've seen so far have all been left open, meaning the starting and ending anchor points aren't connected. If your goal is to draw an arc, you *want* to leave the path open. To make an open path, after you create the last anchor point, just press the Esc key, ⌘-click (Ctrl-click on a PC) somewhere else in the document, or activate another tool from the Tools panel. But if you want to fill the path with color, you need to close it to create a *closed shape*, where the path's two ends are connected. To create a closed path, add the last anchor point and then point your cursor at the path's starting anchor point until a tiny circle that looks like a degree symbol appears next to your cursor. Once you see the tiny circle, click the starting anchor point and Photoshop adds a straight path that joins the two points and closes the shape.

TIP If you Option-click (Alt-click on a PC) to close a path, Photoshop adds *smooth* anchor point handles automatically.

- **Adding control handles.** If you want to add a control handle to an anchor point that doesn't have one—like the starting or ending anchor point of a straight line—grab the Pen tool and Option-click (Alt-click on a PC) the anchor point. You'll see a tiny, upside-down V (called a *caret*) appear next to your cursor. Keep holding the mouse button down and drag outward to create a *new* control handle that you can adjust to any angle you want, as shown in Figure 13-9. (If you Option-click (Alt-click) an anchor point that already has handles, you'll just grab that point's handles instead of creating a new one.)

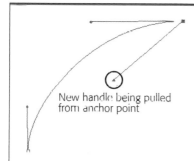

New handle being pulled from anchor point

FIGURE 13-9

If you need to change the direction of a curve, you have to create a control handle, as shown here. When you drag the new control handle away from the path, you get a curve that heads in the direction you're dragging. But if you Option-click (Alt-click on a PC) the control handle and drag toward the path, you'll create a corner point that changes the direction of the curve. This gives you independent control over each of the point's control handles.

TIP You can adjust the length of a path's control handles by ⌘-dragging (Alt-dragging on a PC) the path. This trick changes the depth of the curve as you drag. If the anchor point at the other end of the path segment doesn't have control handles, you'll end up with an angled corner at the far end of the path segment. You can move anchor points that don't have control handles by ⌘-dragging (Ctrl-dragging on a PC). These tricks make it easier to edit paths while you're drawing 'em.

◼ Saving Paths

After all your hard work creating a path, it's a good idea to save it so you can edit it and use it later. Or you might want to use the path with other objects in the image, like when you're using a path as a vector mask, as explained on page 572. Since paths are vector-based, they don't take up much memory and won't increase a file's size much at all, so feel free to save as many paths as you want.

As you're drawing a path, Photoshop stores it in the Paths panel as a temporary *work path* (see Figure 13-10) and displays it in your document as a thin gray line. If you want to hide the gray line—so you don't accidentally edit or move it—just press Return (Enter on a PC). To create multiple paths in a single document, you have to save each path before starting on the next one, or Photoshop adds the subsequent path to the previous one. To work with your paths, open the Paths panel by choosing Window→Paths (see Figure 13-10).

> **NOTE** Miraculously, Photoshop keeps an unsaved work path in your document even if you close the file and don't open it for a year. The catch is you can have only *one* unsaved work path in a document at a time. If you want to add to that work path, simply activate it in the Paths panel and start drawing. Don't forget to select the path in your document, too, because if you start drawing *without* selecting the work path first, the original path goes the way of the dodo bird. To be safe, you're better off saving a path if you think you'll want to reuse it.

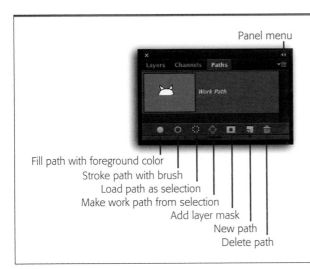

Panel menu

Fill path with foreground color
Stroke path with brush
Load path as selection
Make work path from selection
Add layer mask
New path
Delete path

FIGURE 13-10

The Paths panel works pretty much like any other panel. Photoshop highlights the current path in the panel. If you want to delete a path, activate it and then press Delete (Backspace on a PC) or drag it onto the trash can at the bottom of the panel.

As with layers, you can change your paths' stacking order, double-click to rename them, and so on. Changing the stacking order is a good way to keep related paths together; unfortunately, you can't organize paths into groups like you can with layers.

Photoshop gives you several ways to save a path:

- **Choose Shape mode** (page 536) from the Options bar before you start drawing and Photoshop stores the path on its own layer. Don't forget to name the layer so you can keep track of the different paths you make.

- **Save the path before you draw it** by clicking the "Create new path" button at the bottom of the Paths panel (it looks like a piece of paper with a folded corner). Photoshop names the currently empty placeholder *Path 1*, but you can double-click its name later to change it.

- **Save the path after you draw it** by choosing Save Path from the Paths panel's menu.

- **Save the path as a custom shape** (page 553) that you can access through the Options bar's Custom Shape menu. You can save as many paths as you want (they won't bloat the file's size), so go ahead and have a path-saving party so you can reuse 'em again later.

- **Save the path as a clipping path** (see page 568) that you can use to *isolate* an object (hide its background) in a page-layout program like QuarkXpress or InDesign. If you plan on working with the image in older versions of these programs—which don't understand layered Photoshop documents—this method is your best bet.

Drawing with the Freeform Pen Tool

Lurking in the Pen toolset is the *Freeform Pen* tool, which lets you draw simply by dragging (kind of like how you draw with a real pen) instead of clicking to add points and tugging on control handles. Once you've used it to draw a path, you can edit that path using any of the techniques discussed in this chapter. If you're comfortable working with a graphics tablet (see the box on page 518), the Freeform Pen tool may be the way to go. For precise shapes, however, you're better off sticking with the Pen tool.

When using the Freeform Pen tool, you can turn on the Magnetic checkbox in the Options bar to switch to *Magnetic Pen* mode, which lets you create a path by clicking and then moving your cursor around the edge of the shape you want to select, trace, or mask (like you do with the Magnetic Lasso tool). (When you turn on the Magnetic checkbox, Photoshop puts a tiny horseshoe magnet next to your cursor.) The downside is that this tool sometimes produces more points than you can shake a stick at, which means you have to go back and do some point pruning, as explained in a moment.

To change the Magnetic Pen tool's settings, in the Options bar, click the gear icon to the left of the Magnetic checkbox. The resulting menu lets you change the following settings:

- **Curve Fit** lets you control the error tolerance when Photoshop fits Bezier curves along the path you're making. Straight from the factory it's set to 2 pixels.

- **Width** determines how close to an edge your cursor has to be before Photoshop selects the edge, like the Magic Wand's tolerance setting. You can enter a value from 1 to 256 pixels.

- **Contrast** tells the tool how much contrast there has to be between pixels before it considers an area an edge and plunks down points. You can enter a percentage between 1 and 100; use a higher value for objects that don't have much contrast.

- **Frequency** lets you control how many points the Magnetic Pen tool adds. Enter a value between 0 and 100; the higher the number, the more points it adds.

- **Pen pressure.** If you're using a graphics tablet and pressure-sensitive stylus, turn on this checkbox.

When you're ready to start drawing, click once to set the starting point and then simply trace the outline of the object with your cursor. If the tool starts to go astray and adds points in the wrong spot, just click to add a point of your own. If you want to delete a point the tool created, move your cursor over the point and then press Delete (Backspace on a PC). When you've got an outline around your shape, move your cursor over the starting point (a little circle appears next to your cursor) and then click once. That's it—the point is gone!

■ Drawing with the Shape Tools

Photoshop has a pretty good selection of built-in, vector-based shapes, which are perfect for adding artistic embellishments or using as vector masks (discussed later in this chapter). They include a rectangle, a rounded rectangle (great for making round-edged selections; see page 150), an ellipse, a polygon, a line, and a gazillion custom shapes (page 555). These preset goodies are huge timesavers because they keep you from having to draw something that already exists. And since these preset shapes are made from paths, you can also use the techniques described later in this chapter to morph them into anything you want.

The shape tools work in all three drawing modes (see page 536). This section focuses on the first mode: Shape. Just like any other kind of layer, you can stroke, fill, and add layer styles to Shape layers, as well as load 'em as selections.

Let's say you want to create a starburst shape to draw a viewer's attention to some important text in an ad (Figure 13-11); there's no sense in drawing the starburst from scratch because Photoshop comes with one. And since the shapes are all vector-based, they're resizable, rotatable, and colorable. If you need to make the shape bigger, for example, just activate the Shape layer, press ⌘-T (Ctrl+T) to summon Free Transform, and then use the little handles to make it as big as you want with no fear of quality loss.

Using the Shape Tools

The shape tools couldn't be easier to use: If you can move your mouse diagonally, you can draw a shape. Each shape—rectangle, rounded rectangle, and so on—has its own Options bar settings; Figure 13-12 shows the Line tool's settings (Photoshop considers a line a shape). These settings let you create shapes that are certain sizes or have certain proportions, specify the number of sides in a polygon, indent the sides to make a star, and so on. In CS6, you get a bunch of *new* options that let you change the Shape layer's fill, stroke, stroke style (solid, dashed, or dotted), width and height, and so on.

TIP To draw a symmetrical shape (like a perfect square or circle), press and hold the Shift key as you drag with a shape tool and Photoshop keeps the shape's sides the same size. To draw a shape from the center out, press and hold Option (Alt on a PC) as you drag.

All the shape tools work pretty much the same way, though they have slightly different settings in the Options bar. Here's how to use the Line tool:

1. **Grab the Line tool from the Tools panel.**

   The Line tool lives in the shape toolset near the bottom of the Tools panel (see Figure 13-12, top). If you've never used the shape tools before, the Rectangle tool is probably on top. Click it and hold down your mouse button to choose the Line tool from the resulting menu, or cycle through the various shape tools by pressing Shift-U repeatedly.

FIGURE 13-11

You can save time and energy by using Photoshop's built-in shapes. Unless you tell the program otherwise (page 538), it puts each shape on its own Shape layer (circled). You can resize and rotate the shape using Free Transform (both the Shape and Type layers are active here so they rotate together; in CS6 a handy info overlay appears showing the rotation angle).

You can change the shape's color by double-clicking its layer thumbnail, or gussy it up even more by adding a layer style like the drop shadow shown here (see page 131 for more on layer styles).

The next section explains even more shape-formatting options.

NOTE Don't forget to set the drawing mode to Shape in the Options bar *before* you draw with the Line tool. If you've used any other drawing mode (page 536), the Options bar will still be set to that previous mode.

---

2. **In the Options bar, choose a fill and stroke color, set the stroke width to 5 points, and then choose a solid line from the Stroke options menu.**

In CS6 you can use the Options bar to set the fill and stroke color, as well as the type of line. Just click the Fill menu that's circled in Figure 13-12 (bottom) and pick a color from the resulting panel to create a solid color fill (otherwise the arrowhead you're about to add in the next step will be hollow; if you don't pick a color, Photoshop uses your foreground color). Click the Stroke menu (also circled) and choose the same color as you did for the fill (the Stroke panel is identical to the Fill panel). Enter 5 points in the stroke width field and then click the Stroke Options menu (it's circled, too) and click the solid line preset at the top of the resulting panel.

3. **Add an arrowhead.**

   Click the gear icon that's circled at the far right in Figure 13-12 (bottom) to open the Arrowheads menu and turn on the Start or End checkbox (or both). If you like, specify a size for the arrowhead(s) by entering percentages in the Width and Length fields (the factory setting of 500 percent of the line weight usually works fine). To curve the sides of the arrowhead inward, enter a percentage in the Concavity field.

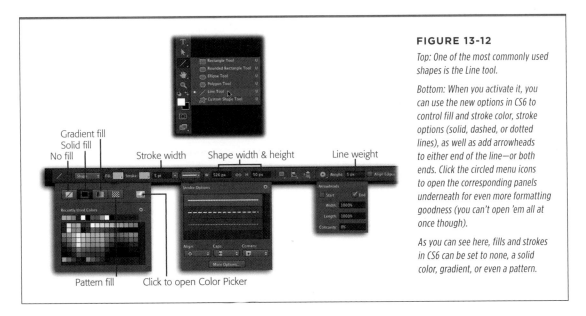

Gradient fill
Solid fill
No fill
Stroke width
Shape width & height
Line weight
Pattern fill
Click to open Color Picker

FIGURE 13-12

Top: One of the most commonly used shapes is the Line tool.

Bottom: When you activate it, you can use the new options in CS6 to control fill and stroke color, stroke options (solid, dashed, or dotted lines), as well as add arrowheads to either end of the line—or both ends. Click the circled menu icons to open the corresponding panels underneath for even more formatting goodness (you can't open 'em all at once though).

As you can see here, fills and strokes in CS6 can be set to none, a solid color, gradient, or even a pattern.

4. **Enter a weight for the line.**

   In the Options bar's Weight field, enter a thickness for the line in pixels.

5. **Mouse over to the document and click where you want the line to start, and then drag and release your mouse button where you want the line to end.**

   Photoshop creates a new Shape layer in the Layers panel that has a large colored box and a mask area. If the line isn't quite at the angle you wanted or it's not long enough, summon Free Transform by pressing ⌘-T (Ctrl+T) and then use the resizing handles to rotate the line or make it longer (be careful, though: The arrowhead might get squished or stretched in the process). Alternatively, you can enter a width and height for the line (or shape if you're using a different tool) in the Options bar's width and height fields (both fields are new in CS6).

6. **Just for fun, change the line's fill color by double-clicking the Shape layer's thumbnail in the Layers panel and choosing a different color from the resulting Color Picker.**

   Click OK when you're finished and the line turns the new color. Changing the color in this way affects the fill, not the stroke.

   NOTE If you don't like how the line turned out, you don't have to start over—just grab the Direct Selection tool (page 540) and click to activate the Shape layer to reveal the Options bar's formatting goodies (though you need to switch to the Line tool to adjust line weight and arrowheads). You can also use the Direct Selection tool to move the line's anchor points until you get the look you want.

For practice, you can try using the Rectangle or Ellipse tool the same way as the Line tool was described above. And remember, once you've created a shape you can modify it in several ways:

- Grab the Direct Selection tool and move the shape's anchor points or alter the points' control handles.

- Use the Pen tool to add or subtract points. You'll learn more about editing paths on page 557.

- Change the shape's color by double-clicking the Shape layer's thumbnail or by clicking to open the Fill panel, shown in Figure 13-12 (bottom).

- Use Free Transform to resize, distort, or rotate the shape.

- Use layer styles to add special effects to the Shape layer.

You can do all kinds of wonderful things with Shape layers, so it's worth taking the time to experiment with all the different shape tools and their various settings.

TIP You can also Shift-click within your document with a shape tool and Photoshop CS6 summons a dialog box where you can enter the shape's dimensions (be sure to enter the unit of measurement, such as *px* for pixels or *in* for inches). Click OK and Photoshop creates the shape *for* you. Alas, this trick doesn't work with the Line or Pen tools.

■ CUSTOMIZING STROKE OPTIONS

There's no end to the different kinds of strokes you can add to shapes and paths in Photoshop CS6. By clicking the More Options button at the bottom of the Stroke options panel (labeled back in Figure 13-12), you get the dialog box shown in Figure 13-13 (right).

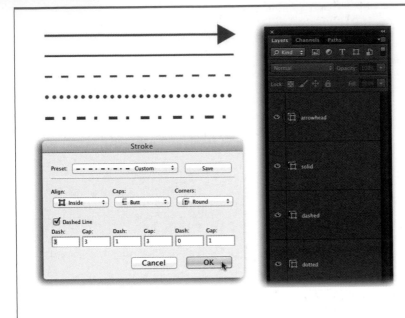

FIGURE 13-13

Left: As you can see, you can create many different line styles in Photoshop CS6 including arrowheads and even dashed and dotted lines. Shape layers in CS6 have a new badge on their layer thumbnails; it looks like a square with clear corner points and is circled here.

Right: Behold, the new Stroke dialog box! Clicking the More Options button at the bottom of the Stroke options panel (visible back in Figure 13-12) opens the Stroke dialog box shown here, which lets you customize exactly how the stroke looks (some of these settings are available in the Stroke options panel, too). For example, a dashed line set to 0 length and a gap setting of 4 was used to create the dotted line you see here at top left.

CS6's new Stroke dialog box lets you customize the stroke in the following ways:

- **Presets.** Use this menu to access Photoshop's stroke presets, which, out of the box, are a solid, dashed, or dotted line. Once you customize a stroke, you can save it as a preset by clicking the Save button to this menu's right. When you do, Photoshop adds the new preset to the menu here, as well as the Stroke options menu in the Options bar. You don't get the opportunity to name your preset; Photoshop shows you a preview of what the line *looks* like instead.

- **Align.** This menu controls the alignment of the stroke itself (not the shape the stroke is attached to). From the factory it's set to Inside, meaning the stroke appears on the inside of the shape you've attached it to. Your other choices are Center and Outside.

- **Caps.** You can use this menu to control the line cap type of the stroke. Your choices are Butt, Round (the factory setting), and Square.

- **Corners.** Use this menu to choose a *join* type for the stroke, which controls the way a straight line changes direction or turns a corner. Your choices are Miter (creates pointed corners), Round (creates rounded corners), and Bevel (creates squared corners that are ever so slightly rounded).

- **Dashed Line, Dash, Gap.** Turn on the Dashed Line checkbox to create a dashed or dotted line. To increase dash length, enter a number in the Dash fields (a dot is really a dash set to 0 length). To increase the space between dashes or dots, enter a number in the Gap field. You can use the other dash and gap fields to vary individual dashes within the *same* stroke.

Once you've formatted a stroke to your liking, you can copy and paste it onto other shapes. Just click the little gear icon at the top right of the Stroke options panel (see Figure 13-12) and choose Copy Stroke Details. Then click to select another shape (or activate a different Shape layer), pop open the Stroke options panel, and choose Paste Stroke Details from its panel menu. This same menu also lets you save your customizations as a preset you can use again later.

Drawing Multiple Shapes on One Layer

Each time you draw with a shape tool in Shape mode (page 537), Photoshop adds a new Shape layer to your document. If you want to keep drawing on the *same* Shape layer instead of creating new ones, use the Options bar's Add, Subtract, Intersect, and Exclude buttons (in CS6, they're nestled in the Path operations menu labeled back in Figure 13-2). Flip ahead to page 560 for details on how these options work. Better yet, press and hold the Shift key to add shapes to the active Shape layer; just release the Shift key once you've clicked to start drawing the shape to keep from constraining it to be perfectly square, elliptical, and so on.

> **TIP** You can move shapes independently of one another even if they live on the same Shape layer. To do that, grab the Path Selection tool from the Tools panel (the black arrow—see page 558), click within your document to select the shape, and then drag it wherever you want. Or instead of dragging, use the arrow keys on your keyboard to nudge it one pixel at a time (add the Shift key to nudge it *10* pixels at a time).

Using Custom Shapes

To find the *really* useful shapes that come with Photoshop, you have to do a bit of foraging. Grab the Custom Shape tool (which looks vaguely like a starfish) from the Tools panel—it's in the same toolset as all the other shape tools (see Figure 13-12, top). Then head up to the Options bar and open the Custom Shape picker by clicking the down-pointing triangle labeled in Figure 13-14.

> **TIP** Technically, you don't have to trot all the way up to the Options bar to access Photoshop's Custom Shapes; just Control-click (right-click on a PC) within your document and the Custom Shape picker menu appears next to your cursor. Who knew?

As soon as the menu opens, click the little gear icon circled in Figure 13-14. In the resulting menu, choose All. A dialog box appears asking if you want to replace the current shapes; click OK. Now you can see a preview of *all* the built-in shapes right there in the Custom Shape picker (why Photoshop doesn't load these shapes automatically is a mystery). You can also use this menu to change the size of the previews or to display them as a text-only list.

Click to open Custom Shape picker

FIGURE 13-14

If you create a shape with the Pen tool, you can save it by choosing Save Shapes from the menu shown here (click the circled gear icon to open it). Give your shape a name and it appears in the list of presets.

You can also do the same thing by creating a shape, activating its layer in the Layers panel, and then choosing Edit→Define Custom Shapes.

You draw with these shapes just as you do with the Line tool (page 550), except that instead of dragging horizontally or vertically, drag *diagonally* to create the shape (though you can also Shift-click within your document to summon a dialog box where you can enter a width and height for the shape). You can also press and hold the Shift key to make the shape perfectly proportional so it looks like the little icon you picked in the Shape picker. You can modify the shape by using the Options bar's Fill and Stroke settings, applying layer styles, or customizing their shapes by using the Direct Selection tool to tweak their anchor points and control handles.

The *real* power of using custom shapes, however, lies in defining your own, which can save you tons of time. For example, if you have a piece of vector art that you need to use over and over, you can save it as a custom shape. Choose File→Place to import the art into Photoshop, and then load it as a selection by ⌘-clicking (Ctrl-clicking on a PC) its layer thumbnail. Next, save it as a path by opening the Paths panel and choosing Make Work Path from the Paths panel's menu. Finally, choose Edit→Define Custom Shape and, in the resulting dialog box, give the new shape a memorable name and then press OK.

From that point on, your custom shape appears in the Options bar's Custom Shapes picker any time you're using the Custom Shape tool. To draw the shape you added, just choose it from the menu and then drag in your document.

■ Editing Paths

All this talk about setting points, dragging handles, and creating shapes can sound a bit intimidating. But it's important to remember that the Pen and shape tools are *very* forgiving—if you don't get the path right the first time, you can always edit it by adding, deleting, and repositioning points and dragging their control handles. The trick lies in knowing *which* tool to use to make the changes you want. This section explains all your options.

Adding, Deleting, and Converting Points

At first, you may have a wee bit of trouble drawing paths that look exactly like you want (surprise!). But don't stress; just add more points, move them around, and adjust the curves until you get the shape you want. You'll need fewer and fewer points as you get more comfortable using the vector drawing tools. And if you've had yourself a point party, you can delete the extra ones.

Adding and deleting points is really easy since the Pen tool figures out what you want to do depending upon what your cursor is pointed at. For example:

- **To add a point,** grab the Add Anchor Point tool (shown on page 539) from the pen toolset (it looks like the Pen tool's icon with a plus sign next to it). When you see a tiny plus sign appear next to the cursor, you can click an existing path to create a new point. You can also just grab the Pen tool, point your cursor at an existing path (but avoid pointing it at anchor points) and the cursor turns into the Add Anchor Point tool automatically. Click anywhere on the path to set new anchor points.

- **To delete a point,** open the pen toolset and grab the Delete Anchor Point tool (it looks like the Pen tool but with a tiny minus sign). Or grab the Pen tool and then place your cursor over an existing point, and a tiny minus sign appears next to the cursor to let you know that the Delete Anchor Point tool (shown on page 539) is active. Either way, click once to get rid of that point.

- **To convert a point from a smooth point to a corner point (or vice versa),** use the Convert Anchor Point tool nested in the pen toolset (see the exercise on page 542). To quickly change to this tool while you're using the Pen tool, press the Option key (Alt on a PC) and place your cursor over an anchor point. (Photoshop puts a tiny, upside-down V next to the cursor to let you know that it's swapped to the Convert Anchor Point tool.) Click to make Photoshop change the anchor point from one type to the other.

> **NOTE** In previous versions of the program, there was a bug involving the Convert Anchor Point tool when it was used to introduce a break in a curved path (dragging the resulting path segment ignored the break). Happily, that problem is fixed in CS6. Now when you use the tool to break a curved path, dragging in the middle of a resulting path segment affects just that segment. If you click on a segment closer to an anchor point, the anchor still moves, but it doesn't straighten out the segment on the other side of it.

- **To add a segment to a path,** put your cursor over the ending anchor point of an open path (shown on page 540) and then click or simply drag to continue drawing. (A tiny forward slash appears next to the cursor.)

- **To join the ends of two open path segments,** grab the Pen tool, click one segment's endpoint and then put your cursor over one of the other segment's endpoints. When a tiny circle with a line on either side of it appears next to the cursor (it looks almost like a chain link), click to connect the two.

Selecting and Moving Paths

Because Photoshop's paths are made from multiple line segments or individual shapes, you can select, move, reshape, copy, or delete parts of a path—or the whole thing—using the Path Selection and Direct Selection tools, which share a toolset near the middle of the Tools panel (their icons look like arrows). To activate 'em, click the arrow icon in the Tools panel or press A (or Shift-A to switch between the two).

> **TIP** You can ⌘-click (Ctrl-click on a PC) outside the shape to deselect a path whenever a shape tool is active.

The Direct Selection tool turns your cursor into a *gray* arrow and lets you select specific points in a path or individual line segments and apply changes only to them, leaving the rest of the path alone (see Figure 13-15, bottom left). The Path Selection tool turns your cursor into a *black* arrow and lets you select a whole path (Figure 13-15, bottom right) so you can do things like move, resize, or rotate the whole thing.

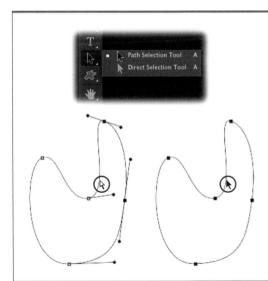

FIGURE 13-15

Top: To move points and paths around, grab 'em with the Direct Selection and Path Selection tools, respectively.

Bottom left: Use the Direct Selection tool to choose specific points. You can tell which points are selected because they turn black (here, two points are selected).

Bottom right: Use the Path Selection tool to select a whole path (notice how all the points are black).

TIP You can make the Direct Selection tool act like the *Path* Selection tool by pressing Option (Alt on a PC). You can also select multiple points by drawing a box around them by dragging with either the Direct Selection or the Path Selection tool.

Once you've selected a path or part of a path, you can do the following:

- **Copy it** by Option-dragging (Alt-dragging on a PC) it to another location. This is handy if you're making a pattern or want to add a bunch of objects to your document. Add the Shift key to copy in a straight line (the copies are all part of the same work path or saved path).

- **Delete a segment** by pressing Delete (Backspace on a PC). If you've got a point selected, you can delete the whole path by pressing Delete (Backspace) twice.

- **Align it** using Photoshop's alignment tools (page 562). Use the Path Selection tool to select two or more paths and Photoshop displays alignment tools in the Options bar.

- **Combine it** with another path by selecting the paths and then clicking the Options bar's Combine button.

- **Resize it.** Turn on the Options bar's Show Bounding Box checkbox and Photoshop adds a bounding box around the path you selected, complete with resizing handles. Or summon Free Transform by pressing ⌘-T (Ctrl+T).

- **Change its intersect mode.** Lurking in CS6's new Path operations menu—it's to the right of the width and height fields when the Path Selection or Direct Selection tools are active—are four options that let you intersect overlapping shapes (closed paths) in a variety of ways. These modes, which are described in the next section, let you combine paths to make new shapes.

- **Change it** (fill it with color or add a stroke to it, for example) without affecting the whole path. As shown in Figure 13-16, by selecting certain segments, you can fill them with color or give them a stroke (you'll learn how on page 564 and page 562, respectively).

FIGURE 13-16

Top: Here's a close-up of the painting shown in Figure 13-1, bottom, with certain paths selected (notice the black anchor points around the selected shapes).

Bottom: By selecting specific paths, you tell Photoshop to apply any changes you make only to those paths. Here, the selected paths were filled with dark blue.

TIP To temporarily hide a path's outline, press Shift-⌘-H (Shift+Ctrl+H on a PC).

Making Paths Intersect

You can use the new Path operations menu in the Options bar to change the *intersect mode* of two or more overlapping paths (Figure 13-17, top). These modes let you combine overlapping shapes in a variety of ways. Here are your options:

- **Combine Shapes.** Use this mode to add one shape to another. The combined shapes merge into one, and Photoshop deletes the paths in the shapes' overlapping areas (Figure 13-17, middle left). Its icon looks like two overlapping squares that blend together in the middle.

- **Subtract Front Shape.** This mode cuts out the area where two shapes overlap (Figure 13-17, bottom left). Its icon looks like a white square overlapping a gray square.

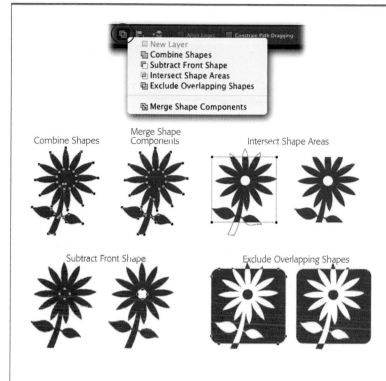

Combine Shapes

Merge Shape Components

Intersect Shape Areas

Subtract Front Shape

Exclude Overlapping Shapes

FIGURE 13-17

Top: In Photoshop CS6, the tools for making paths intersect live in the Path operations menu, shown here.

Middle left: The first piece in this flower was drawn in Shape mode, but the rest of the parts were drawn in Combine Shapes mode so everything stayed on one layer. (Drawing all your shapes on a single layer lets you combine the parts together into a single shape.) Use the Path Selection tool to grab all the shapes in the flower, and then choose Merge Shape Components. Photoshop joins the selected paths together into a single shape.

Bottom left: While you're in Combine Shapes mode, draw a circle in the flower's center. With the new circle selected, choose Subtract Front Shape and Photoshop knocks the center out of the flower.

Middle right: To hide the top and bottom of the flower, grab the Pen tool, and then choose Intersect Shape Areas. Next, grab the Rectangle tool and drag over the flower to hide everything that falls outside the square's edges.

Bottom right: You can hide the whole flower save for its tips by choosing Exclude Overlapping Shapes. Then grab the Rounded Rectangle tool and drag over the flower to hide the parts that overlap the rectangle. (Since the circle in the center of the flower was already hidden, it flips back to its original color.)

> **TIP** Want to see your work without lines and handles? You can hide the shape outlines and handles by pressing Shift-⌘-H (Shift+Ctrl+H on a PC); press the keyboard shortcut again to bring 'em back.

- **Intersect Shape Areas.** Use this mode to get rid of the parts of your shapes that *don't* overlap (Figure 13-17, middle right). Its icon looks like two hollow squares with a dark area where they overlap.

- **Exclude Overlapping Shapes.** This mode hides the areas where shapes overlap (Figure 13-17, bottom right). Its icon looks like two overlapping gray squares that are transparent where they intersect.

■ ALIGNING AND REARRANGING PATHS

Photoshop CS6 also includes a few more helpful settings for arranging paths just the way you want 'em. The following settings live in the Options bar to the right of the Path operations menu and are active any time more than one path or Shape layer is active:

- **Path alignment.** This menu gives you all the same alignment tools that you get with layers (page 100). Once you've selected more than one path, you can choose to align their left edges, horizontal centers, right edges, top edges, vertical centers, bottom edges, as well as distribute their widths and heights. Out of the box, this menu is set to Align To Selection, which aligns the right-most *path* edges. The last option is Align To Canvas which aligns all the paths to the edge of the *canvas* instead.

- **Path arrangement.** You can use this menu to control the stacking order of your paths. Your options are Bring Shape To Front, Bring Shape Forward, Send Shape Backward, and Send Shape To Back.

- **Align Edges.** This checkbox lets you align the edges of a path's stroke (if you've added one) to the pixel grid, ensuring sharper strokes.

- **Constrain Path Dragging.** This option is only available for the Path Selection or Direct Selection tools. You can use this checkbox to adjust a single path contained *within* a shape instead of altering the *entire* shape.

Adding a Stroke to a Path

After you create a path with the Pen tool, you can add a *stroke* (outline) to it using CS6's new Fill setting in the Options bar (page 552); however, you can also stroke a path with Photoshop's painting tools. This is handy when you're trying to draw a long, smooth, flowing line like the one in Figure 13-18 (right). Try drawing that Z freehand using the Brush tool—it's *really* hard to create such a perfect Z shape. But with the Pen tool, you can draw the path first, edit it (if necessary) using the techniques described in the previous sections, and then add the fancy red stroke using your favorite brush (see Chapter 12 for more on brushes).

NOTE When you add color to a path with either a fill or a stroke, the color appears on the current layer. So it's a good idea to take a peek in the Layers panel and make sure you're on the right layer first.

Once you've created a path, open the Layers panel and add a new layer by clicking the "Create a new layer" button at the bottom of the panel. With the new layer active, you can add a stroke to a path in a couple of ways:

- **Choose Stroke Path from the Paths panel's menu.** In the resulting dialog box (Figure 13-18, left), pick the tool you want to use for the stroke. The drawback to this method is that the stroke picks up whatever settings you last applied to that tool (you don't get a chance to change them). For example, if you set the Brush tool to a certain blend mode or lowered its opacity, the stroke uses that blend mode or opacity.

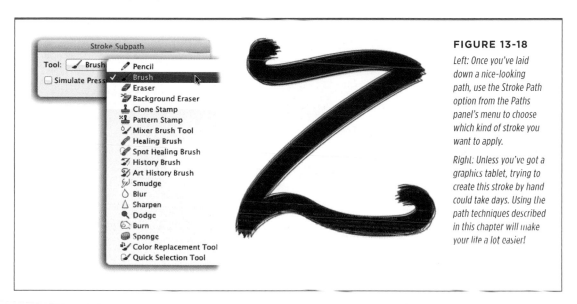

FIGURE 13-18

Left: Once you've laid down a nice-looking path, use the Stroke Path option from the Paths panel's menu to choose which kind of stroke you want to apply.

Right: Unless you've got a graphics tablet, trying to create this stroke by hand could take days. Using the path techniques described in this chapter will make your life a lot easier!

TIP You can open the Stroke Path dialog box by Option-clicking (Alt-clicking on a PC) the Stroke Path button at the bottom of the Paths panel (it looks like a hollow circle), or by Option-dragging (Alt-dragging) the path in the Paths panel onto the Stroke Path button.

- **Activate the tool you want to use to stroke the path.** Adjust its settings in the Options bar and then click the Stroke Path button at the bottom of the Paths panel. This method helps you avoid having to undo the stroke because the tool's settings are all screwy.

Filling a Path

Before you fill a path, take a moment to consider whether it's an open or closed path. As described earlier, the starting and ending anchor points of an open path don't meet. Since you can't really fill a shape that's not closed, if you try to fill an open shape, Photoshop *imagines* a straight line that connects the starting point to the ending point, and then fills all the closed areas created by that imaginary line. This can lead to some rather strange results, as shown in Figure 13-19, top. When you fill a closed path—one where the starting and ending points *do* meet—Photoshop fills the whole shape just like you'd expect (see Figure 13-19, bottom).

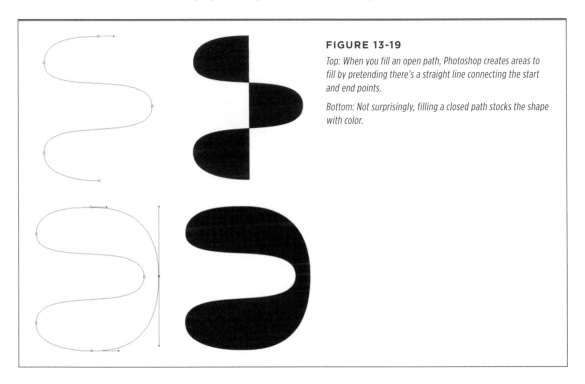

FIGURE 13-19

Top: When you fill an open path, Photoshop creates areas to fill by pretending there's a straight line connecting the start and end points.

Bottom: Not surprisingly, filling a closed path stocks the shape with color.

After you draw a path, choose from the following fill methods:

- **Use CS6's new Fill setting in the Options bar.** When you click this icon, Photoshop opens the Fill panel shown back in Figure 13-12, which lets you fill the path with a solid color, gradient, or pattern. It's discussed earlier in this chapter on page 552.

- **Choose Fill Path from the Paths panel's menu.** Photoshop opens the Fill Path dialog box, where you can choose what you want to fill the shape with (see Figure 13-20). This is handy if you want to use a pattern or a specific blend mode (page 280).

- **Click the "Fill path with foreground color" button** at the bottom left of the Paths panel (it looks like a gray circle) and Photoshop uses your foreground color as the fill color (you don't get a dialog box with this method). Selecting the path in the Paths panel and then dragging it onto this button does the same thing.

- **Option-click (Alt-click on a PC) the "Fill path with foreground color" button** to summon the Fill Path dialog box (Figure 13-20). You can do the same thing by selecting the path in the Paths panel and then Option-dragging (Alt-dragging) it onto this button.

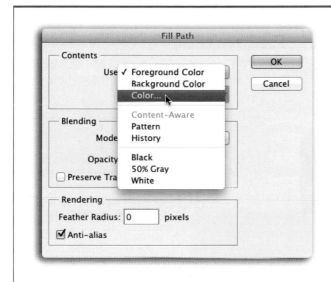

FIGURE 13-20

You can use this dialog box to tell Photoshop exactly what you want to fill the path with and change the fill's blend mode or feather its edges. To open the Color Picker, choose Color from the Use pop-up menu.

The Fill Path dialog box (Figure 13-20) is divided into three sections:

- **Contents.** The Use pop-up menu lets you decide whether to fill the path with your foreground or background color, Content-Aware (see page 414) or a pattern (you can pick a pattern from the Custom Pattern pop-up menu). Choose Color to summon the Color Picker so you can choose any color you want. If you choose History, Photoshop fills the path with the currently active History state or a snapshot of the document in a previously saved state (see page 26).

- **Blending.** Use the Mode pop-up menu to change the fill's blend mode and the Opacity field to change the fill's opacity. Turn on the Preserve Transparency checkbox if you're filling a path on a layer that's partially transparent so Photoshop fills only the part that's *not* transparent.

- **Rendering.** If you want to make the fill's edges soft and slightly transparent, enter a number in the Feather Radius field (this setting works like the Refine Edge dialog box's Feather slider; see page 172). The higher the number, the softer the edge. Leave the Anti-alias checkbox turned on to make Photoshop smooth the fill's edges by adding a slight blur; if you turn it off, the fill's edges will be hard and look blocky in curved areas.

■ Making Selections and Masks with Paths

As you learned in Chapter 4, Photoshop is loaded with selection tools. However, when you're trying to select something *really* detailed, like the column section shown in Figure 13-21, none of the regular selection tools can help. That's because the shape is complex and there's very little contrast between the area being selected and the surrounding pixels.

Luckily, you can use the Pen tool to draw a path that follows the contours of any shape you want to select (Figure 13-21, bottom), no matter how intricate it is. The beauty of this method is that the Pen tool is so forgiving—if you don't get it right the first time, you can edit the path. When you've got the path in place, you can load it as a selection and proceed merrily on your way, doing whatever you want with the selected object.

FIGURE 13-21

The lack of contrast in this image makes it nearly impossible to select just part of the façade (top). But with the Pen tool, you can draw a path around the section you want by hand (bottom).

To load a path as a selection, first create the path with the Pen tool and then choose one of these methods:

- **Click the Make Selection button in the Options bar.** New in CS6, this summons the dialog box shown in Figure 13-22, where you can adjust settings like the selection's feather amount and whether you want Photoshop to apply anti-aliasing. In the Operation section, you can choose to create a new selection, add to or subtract from an existing one, or create a selection from the intersection of this one and an existing one.

- **Choose Make Selection from the Paths panel's menu** and Photoshop opens the Make Selection dialog box.

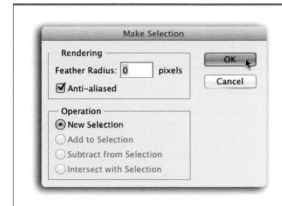

FIGURE 13-22

The Make Selection dialog box lets you feather the selection, apply anti-aliasing to its edges, or combine it with an existing selection (discussed on the next page).

- **Click the "Load path as a selection" button** at the bottom of the Paths panel (it looks like a tiny dotted circle). This method lets you bypass the Make Selection dialog box. Photoshop applies the settings you used the last time you used the Make Selection dialog box (like the feather radius). If you haven't yet used that dialog box, Photoshop sets the feather radius to zero, leaves anti-aliasing turned on, and, if a selection tool is active, creates a brand-new selection.

- **Option-click (Alt-click on a PC) the "Load path as a selection" button** at the bottom of the Paths panel. When you do, Photoshop opens the Make Selection dialog box.

- **Drag the path's thumbnail in the Paths panel onto the "Load path as a selection" button.** This method bypasses the Make Selection dialog box and applies the settings you used last time.

  ⌘-**click (Ctrl-click) the path's thumbnail in the Paths panel.** You won't get a Make Selection dialog box this way, either; the program simply applies the last settings you used.

> **TIP** If you're a fan of keyboard shortcuts, you can load your path as a *new* selection by pressing ⌘-Return (Ctrl-Enter on a PC); add the path to an *existing* selection by pressing Shift-⌘-Return (Shift+Ctrl+Enter); *subtract* the path from an existing selection by pressing Option-⌘-Return (Alt+Ctrl+Enter); or *intersect* the path with an existing selection by pressing Shift-Option-⌘-Return (Shift+Alt+Ctrl+Enter).

At the bottom of the Make Selection dialog box lies a section called Operation (Figure 13-22). If you don't have any active selections, Photoshop assumes you want to make a new selection and doesn't let you choose any of the other options. But if you already have an active selection, you can make the selected path interact with it in different ways:

- **Add to Selection** adds the path's shape and attributes (like feather radius, fill color, stroke thickness, and so on) to the selection.

- **Subtract from Selection** subtracts the path's shape and attributes from the selection.

- **Intersect with Selection** selects only the area where the path and the selection overlap.

Making a Path from a Selection

You can also do the opposite and create a path from an existing selection. This is helpful if you need to alter a selection you made with another tool. For example, you can start out with a selection you created with the Rectangular Marquee tool, turn it into a path, and then tweak it with the Pen tool. Here's how: With an active selection, click the "Make work path from selection" button at the bottom of the Paths panel (it looks like a circle with lines extending from either side). Then, using the path-editing techniques you learned earlier in this chapter, edit away. To transform the path back into a selection, just use one of the options listed in the previous section.

WARNING The paths that Photoshop creates when you turn a selection into a path aren't always terribly sharp. Pixel selections—especially ones you make with the Magic Wand—can create bumpy paths that have too many points. If you select an area that needs to be smoothed, open the Paths panel's menu and choose Make Work Path. In the resulting dialog box, you can adjust the Tolerance setting to smooth out the pixels. The higher the tolerance, the smoother the resulting path will be. But if you set the tolerance too high (anything over 5), you'll start to lose details. (This dialog box does not appear when you click the Make Work Path button at the bottom of the Paths panel.)

Making a Clipping Path

If you want to isolate an object from its background to use it in an older version of a page-layout program like QuarkXPress or Adobe InDesign, you can create a *clipping path* (newer versions of both programs prefer PSD files). A clipping path is like a written description of your selection that those programs can understand even if they can't handle PSD files, layers, and transparency. You still send the whole document to the page layout program, but the clipping path specifies which *portion* of the image to display.

For example, Figure 13-23 shows a cup that's been isolated from its background in Photoshop using a clipping path and then placed on a blue background in a page-layout program. The page-layout program understands the clipping path that travels along with the file, and uses it to hide the cup's original background.

FIGURE 13-23

Top: You can use a clipping path to isolate this cup from its background in a way that older page-layout programs understand.

Bottom: Here's the cup after it was placed on a totally different background in a page-layout program.

Both Adobe InDesign CS4 and later and QuarkXPress 8 can read layered Photoshop files with transparency and recognize paths saved in TIFF files. So if you're using the latest versions of those programs, you don't need to worry about clipping paths. But if you're dealing with an older version, mastering clipping paths can make you the office hero.

To create a clipping path around an image like the cup in Figure 13-23, follow these steps:

1. **Draw a closed path around the cup with the Pen tool.**

   Press P to grab the Pen tool and draw a path around the outside edge of the cup using the techniques discussed earlier in this chapter. (Zoom in nice and close when drawing the path; see Figure 13-24, top.) When you're done, make sure you click the starting point to close the path.

TIP If you're trying to isolate an object from its background, it's a good idea to draw the path about 1 or 2 pixels *inside* the object's edge just to make sure that none of the background sticks around. This way, you're more likely to avoid jagged edges where bits of the background show through the selection.

---

2. **Draw a second path inside the cup's handle.**

   To knock out the area inside the handle, click the Options bar's Path operations menu and choose Exclude Overlapping Shapes so the second path cuts a hole through the first (see Figure 13-24, bottom). Be sure to close this second path by clicking its starting point.

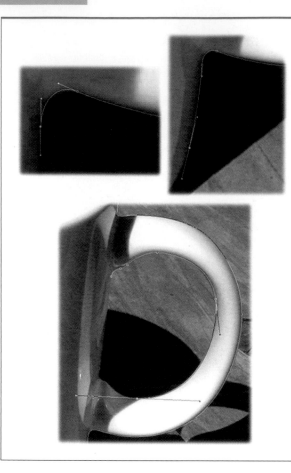

FIGURE 13-24

You can see the path as it travels along the edge of the cup (top left), and continues until the entire cup is surrounded (top right).

To omit the space inside the handle, draw a second path around the inside of the handle (bottom).

3. **Save the paths.**

   Photoshop won't let you make a clipping path until you save the path. Over in the Paths panel, activate the work path (page 547) and drag it onto the "Create new path" button at the bottom of the panel, or choose Save Path from the Paths panel's menu. In the dialog box that appears, give your path a descriptive name like *Cup outline*.

4. **Turn the path into a clipping path.**

   From the Paths panel's menu, choose Clipping Path. In the resulting dialog box (Figure 13-25, top), choose the path's name from the Path pop-up menu. The Flatness field controls how accurately printers will follow the path. A lower number means the printer pays attention to more points on the path (so the print is more accurate), and a higher number means it pays attention to fewer points (so the print is less accurate). Some printers can't handle paths with lots of points, so setting this field to a higher number reduces the path's complexity and helps make things easier on your printer. For now, though, just leave this field blank and click OK. In the Paths panel, the path's name now looks like a hollow outline to let you know that it's a clipping path (Figure 13-25, bottom).

FIGURE 13-25

Top: Pick your path from the pop-up menu at the top of the Clipping Path dialog box.

Bottom: Once Photoshop has converted the path into a clipping path, it displays the path thumbnail's name in (nearly impossible to read) hollow text in the Paths panel.

> **TIP** If you get a call from your printing company complaining that your file caused a printing error, you may need to redo the clipping path and increase the Flatness setting to 4 or 5. This cuts the printer a little slack as far as how precisely it has to follow the clipping path.

5. **Save the document as an EPS or TIFF file.**

    Choose File→Save As and pick EPS or TIFF from the Format pop-up menu. If you're paranoid about print quality, pick EPS to ensure the best results; because this format is based on the same language PostScript printers use, it tends to print a little more crisply.

You've now got yourself a perfectly selected and isolated cup, ready to be beamed up into the nearest page-layout program.

> **TIP** Some stock photography comes with clipping paths, which save you a *ton* of work if you need to place that object on another background. The next time you download a stock image, open it in Photoshop and then take a peek in the Paths panel to see if the file contains a clipping path. If so, you can activate the path's thumbnail and then add a layer mask by clicking the "Add layer mask" button at the bottom of the Paths panel (it looks like a circle inside a square). Sweet!

Using Vector Masks

Photoshop gives you two ways to make *vector masks* with paths: using a path made with a shape tool set to work in Path mode or by using a path drawn with the Pen tool. These masking methods are quick and easy, and you're absolutely gonna love their flexibility (vectors are infinitely resizable and editable, remember?). That said, it's worth noting a few things about using vector masks. First, they work just like the pixel-based masks you learned about in Chapter 3: They can hide any underlying layer content that's *beyond* the shape's edges. Second, because vector masks are made from vector-based paths, they give you much smoother edges than pixel masks. Third, you can feather them nondestructively on the fly by using the Feather slider in the Properties panel. Woo-hoo!

■ MASKING WITH PATHS

You can easily create a vector mask from a path outline made by any shape tool or the Pen tool, as shown in Figure 13-26. A mask created in this way works just like the regular ol' layer masks you learned about back in Chapter 3 and adds a mask thumbnail to the currently active layer, though the mask is filled with gray instead of black. (If the Background layer is locked, you'll need to double-click it before adding the vector mask.) The difference is that, since the mask is vector-based, you can resize it all you want and its edges stay nice and sharp.

FIGURE 13-26

Top: Here's an oval drawn with the Ellipse tool (the Ellipse shape *tool, not the Elliptical Marquee tool).*

Bottom: After placing the Shape layer below the photo, you can clip the two layers together so the photo is only visible through the shape.

Once you've combined two images into the same document, and you've double-clicked to make the Background layer editable, follow these few steps to make a vector mask from a path:

1. **Grab the Elliptical tool by pressing Shift-U repeatedly and, in the Options bar, choose Path mode.**

   You can also use any of the other shape tools, or the Pen tool, set to Path mode.

2. **Draw a path using the method described on page 540 or 541.**

3. **Over in the Layers panel, activate the layer you want to add the mask to and then create the mask by ⌘-clicking (Ctrl-clicking on a PC) the "Add a layer mask" button at the bottom of the panel.**

   Photoshop adds an infinitely resizable vector mask to the layer and pops open the Properties panel.

4. **In the Properties panel, drag the Feather slider to the right to soften the mask's edges.**

   Instantly, Photoshop softens the edges of the mask in real time. To change the Feather amount later, simply click to activate the mask and then open the Properties panel by choosing Window→Properties; then adjust the Feather slider.

5. **Save the document as a PSD file so you can edit it again later if you need to.**

   That's all there is to it! It's a super-fast and super-flexible technique.

If you decide you need to edit the vector mask later on, pop open the document and activate the mask thumbnail in the Layers panel and then use the Path Selection tool to select its anchor points and control handles.

Highlighting Text

Chances are, the text you create won't be perfect right off the bat; it'll need to be massaged, manipulated, and played with (and honestly, that's half the fun). To tweak your text, activate the appropriate Type layer in the Layers panel (it'll be highlighted, as shown in Figure 14-6, left), and then highlight the text you want to change (you'll learn how in a sec). When text is highlighted, you see a black background behind the characters (which are now white), as shown in Figure 14-6, right.

NOTE The color you see when you highlight text is actually a contrasting opposite of the color *underneath* the text (whether it's an image or a solid color). For example, if your text is on a white background, the highlight color is black; if it's on a blue background, the highlight color is orange. Neat, huh?

Click to see just the Type layers

There is no escape;
you have been selected!

There is no escape;
you have been selected!

FIGURE 14-6

Left: To alter text in Photoshop, you've got to activate the Type layer it's on and then highlight the portion you want to change, as shown here. To highlight all the text on a Type layer, simply give its layer thumbnail a quick double-click.

Right: When you highlight text, a colored background appears behind it and Photoshop temporarily makes the text a contrasting color so you can see it, as shown in the upper sentence here. And why does the lower sentence look so blurry? Because it's been loaded as a selection so each letter is surrounded by marching ants.

TIP The background that appears behind text when it's highlighted makes it nearly impossible to see any formatting changes you make. Fortunately, you can toggle this background off and on by pressing ⌘-H (Ctrl+H on a PC)—that is, unless you've reassigned that keyboard shortcut to hide Photoshop on a Mac, as explained in the box on page 13.

Highlighting text is totally different from *loading text as a selection*, which puts marching ants around each character as shown in Figure 14-6, bottom right. To load text as a selection, simply ⌘-click (Ctrl-click on a PC) the Type layer's thumbnail. What's the difference, you ask? Highlighting text lets you edit the characters (to fix a typo, for example), whereas loading text as a selection lets you apply effects to the *shape* of characters, such as adding a stroke (page 620), altering other images in the shape of the characters (page 627), or creating another piece of art out of 'em altogether.

Like most tasks, Photoshop gives you several ways to highlight text (you need to have the Type tool active to use any of them):

- **To highlight a character,** click within the text and, once your cursor turns into a blinking I-beam, drag across the character(s).

- **To highlight a word,** click within the text and then double-click the word.

- **To highlight a whole line**, click within the text and then triple-click anywhere in the line you want to select.

- **To highlight a paragraph,** click within the paragraph and then quadruple-click (that's four quick clicks).

- **To highlight all the text on a single Type layer,** in the Layers panel, double-click the layer's thumbnail or, in your document, click within the text and then click five times really fast.

- **To activate multiple Type layers,** mouse over to the Layers panel and Shift- or ⌘-click (Ctrl-click on a PC) the name—*not* the thumbnail—of each layer you want to activate.

- **To activate all the Type layers in a document,** mosey over to the Layers panel and choose Kind from the pop-up menu at the top left, and then click the button with a T on it (labeled in Figure 14-6, left). Photoshop instantly hides everything but the Type layers in that document. To activate all of 'em, choose Select→All Layers. (This layer-filtering feature is new in CS6 and replaces the Select→Similar Layers command.)

TIP When you've got a single Type layer activated and the Type tool is *also* active (but no text is highlighted and you haven't clicked *within* the text), you can Control-click (right-click on a PC) anywhere in your document to summon a shortcut menu with all kinds of useful options for working with text. These include Check Spelling (page 599), Find and Replace Text (page 597), Rasterize (page 588), Create Work Path or "Convert to Shape" (page 630), and more. (You get a similar menu when you've highlighted some text, but it offers fewer options.)

Resizing Text

Photoshop lets you create everything from nano-sized text that you'd need an electron microscope to read to ginormous letters fit for the side of a building. You can resize text by highlighting it using any of the methods described earlier, and then altering the point size in either the Options bar or Character panel. But where's the fun in that?

Unless you know the *exact* size your text needs to be, you're better off resizing it visually, either while typing or afterward. To resize visually, activate a Type layer in the Layers panel and then click within the line of text (or the text box) so you see an I-beam cursor blinking within the text (if you're typing, you should already see this cursor). Next, press and hold ⌘ (Ctrl on a PC) to make Photoshop display resizing handles around the text (the handles around a *text box* resize the box itself). While keeping the ⌘ (Ctrl) key down, press and hold the Shift key, and then drag any handle to resize the text, as shown in Figure 14-7, left (adding the Shift key makes Photoshop resize the text proportionately so it doesn't get squished or squashed). The point size displayed in both the Options bar and Character panel changes as you drag.

WORD TO THE WISE

Beware of Rasterizing Text

Most of the text you create in Photoshop—whether it's horizontal, upside down, inside a shape, or what have you—begins life as *vector* text. (The exception is text you create with the Type Mask tool; see page 590.) With vector type, each character is made up of curves and lines, rather than pixels. (See the box on page 52 for a detailed discussion of raster vs. vector files.)

This is great news because it means the text is editable and fully *scalable*, so you can make it bigger or smaller without worrying that it'll be blurry when printed. However, some cool effects require you to rasterize the text (convert it to pixels), like running filters (though there is a workaround—see page 627), distorting, and applying perspective, to name a few. If you try to do any of these things to a Type layer, you'll be met with an error message asking your permission to rasterize.

The bad news is that some things in Photoshop *automatically* rasterize text so that it becomes completely un-vectored, un-editable, and pretty much un-resizable. (You can shrink raster text without much quality loss, but making it bigger will give you disastrously jagged results.) Photoshop automatically rasterizes text—without asking for permission—when you do any of the following:

- Merge a Type layer with one or more other layers (page 113).

- Flatten a file (page 115).
- Save a file in any format *other* than PSD, EPS, PDF, or DCS.
- Send a file to a non-PostScript (inkjet) printer (Chapter 16).

If you save a file in EPS or DCS format, Photoshop preserves the text by converting it to vector outlines, which is pretty much the same thing as converting it to a shape (page 630). You won't be able to edit the text anymore, but it'll look nice and crisp when printed. Watch out, though: If you open *either* of these file types again in Photoshop, the program automatically rasterizes the text. However, you can preserve the text by importing the file into your document as a Smart Object (page 128) instead; to do that, choose File→Place. (This method doesn't let you edit the text, though.) If you save the file as a PDF, you can turn on the Preserve Photoshop Editing Capabilities option in the Save Adobe PDF dialog box to keep the text editable.

All that being said, if you truly wish to rasterize text, it's a good idea to duplicate the Type layer first (by pressing ⌘-J or Ctrl+J) just in case you want to edit it later. Once you've duplicated the layer, you can rasterize either the copy or the original by choosing Type→Rasterize Type Layer, or by Control-clicking (right-clicking) the Type layer and choosing Rasterize Type.

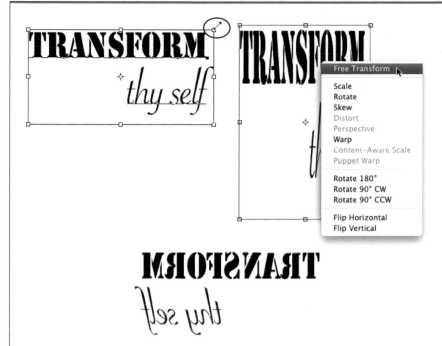

FIGURE 14-7

Top left: To resize text visually while typing, press ⌘ (Ctrl) and then drag one of the resizing handles circled here (just be sure to press and hold the Shift key, too, so the text doesn't get squished).

Top right: You can also resize text using Free Transform. After you summon it by pressing ⌘-T (Ctrl+T on a PC), Control-clicking (right-clicking) in the transform box brings up this shortcut menu, which offers a slew of text-altering options.

Bottom: If you've ever wanted text to flow backward, Free Transform can make it so. Just open the shortcut menu described above, and then choose Flip Horizontal (Flip Vertical gives you upside-down text).

TIP If you're a keyboard shortcut fan, you can increase the font size of highlighted text in 2 point increments by pressing Shift-⌘-> (Shift+Ctrl+> on a PC), and decrease it by pressing Shift-⌘-< (Shift+Ctrl+<). To increase or decrease in *10-point* increments, add the Option key (Alt on a PC) to those key combinations. This is a great keyboard shortcut to memorize if you want to format text quickly.

You can also use Free Transform to resize text. With a Type layer active—not the *text* itself, just the layer it's on—summon the Free Transform tool by pressing ⌘-T (Ctrl+T on a PC). A resizing box (complete with little white handles) appears around the text. Simply drag one of these handles in any direction to resize the text. (You won't see the point size change as you drag because that happens only when the Type tool is active.) Again, hold the Shift key to resize the text proportionately. For more options, Control-click (right-click) in the transform box for a handy shortcut menu (see Figure 14-7, right).

Creating a Hollow Text Selection

Sometimes you don't really need letters *themselves* to create the effect you're after, you just need a *selection* of them—in other words, their outline. Enter the Type Mask tool, which is hidden in the type toolset (shown on page 583). Instead of creating a Type layer, this wonderful tool creates an empty text *selection*, which you can use on other layers, like one that contains an image.

Type Warnings

Sometimes when I open a document, I see a little triangle on the Type layer in the Layers panel. What the heck does that mean?

One day you're bound to open a Photoshop document only to be met with a *type warning*. They come in two flavors and show up in the Layers panel as a tiny yellow or gray triangle on the Type layer's thumbnail:

- **A yellow warning symbol** means you're missing a font. You'll see this icon if you open a document that uses a font that's not installed on your machine (you'll also likely see an error message *before* the document actually opens that lets you either cancel opening the document or proceed). If you don't need to edit the text, you've got nothing to worry about—just do what you need to do and then save the file. If you *do* edit the text, Photoshop will substitute *another* font for the missing one the moment you double-click the Type layer, and this substitution is permanent, even if you send the file back to its creator who *has* the original font. So if it's important to keep the original

font, you'll have to close the document, quit Photoshop (unless you're running font-management software—see the box on page 581), install or activate the font, relaunch Photoshop, and then reopen the document.

- **A gray warning symbol** means that the document you've opened was created in a different version of Photoshop and that the text *may* get reflowed if you edit it (but that doesn't necessarily mean it *will* get reflowed). Because each new version of Photoshop contains new type features, text created in an earlier version might get spaced or hyphenated differently in the new version.

Happily, Photoshop CS6 lets you take action on *both* kinds of warnings swiftly and easily. To replace missing fonts with something else so you can edit the text, choose Type→Replace All Missing Fonts, and Photoshop opens a dialog box kindly asking which font you'd like to use as the replacement. To update all the text in a document created by a previous version of the program, choose Type→Update All Text Layers instead.

When you use the Type Mask tool, it'll look like you're creating normal text, but once you're finished typing, marching ants will surround the edges of the characters, creating a hollow selection in the shape of that text, and Photoshop won't create a new Type layer. Think of a type mask as one of those plastic stencils you used as a kid to draw perfectly formed letters and numbers—the letters are hollow so you can see through them to the layer below.

NOTE Sure, you could just use the regular type tools to create text and then load it as a selection by ⌘-clicking (Ctrl-clicking on a PC) the Type layer's thumbnail. But the Type Mask tool *creates the selection for you*, sparing you that extra step.

The Type Mask tool opens a boatload of graphic design possibilities because it lets you affect other graphical elements (meaning other layers) through the shape of the text, as shown in Figure 14-8. Like the regular Type tool, the Type Mask tool comes in two flavors: one for creating horizontal text and one for creating vertical text. They both merely create a selection of whatever you type without creating a new layer. You can then treat the text selection as you would any other selection: move it around, use it to create a layer mask (page 181), wear it as a hat (kidding), save it to use later (see page 184), or turn it into an editable path (page 568).

One of the many neat effects you can create with the Type Mask tool is a text-shaped photo fade; a unique look that can make an eye-catching magazine ad, for example. Here's how:

1. **Open a photo and grab the Horizontal Type Mask tool.**

   To activate the tool, click the big T in the Tools panel and then click the Horizontal Type Mask tool in the flyout menu (you can also press Shift-T repeatedly to cycle through all the tools in the type toolset). You don't need to bother duplicating the background layer, because this technique is 100% nondestructive, meaning the original pixels will remain untouched.

2. **Choose a font from the font family menu.**

   Be sure to choose a thick font so the selection area will be fairly big (thin or script fonts won't work). Arial Black and Impact are good ones to use for this technique.

3. **Click anywhere in the document and then type your text.**

   You'll notice that the text appears hollow (you can see through it to the photo, as shown in Figure 14-8, top), while the background takes on the red cast of Quick Mask mode (page 181), though you can't use other tools or filters like you *normally* can in Quick Mask mode.

FIGURE 14-8

Top: When the Type Mask tool is active, clicking in a document causes a red overlay or mask to appear (see page 181 for more on this particular mask). As you type, the letters are revealed through the mask. The text remains editable (and resizable) until you accept the mask by clicking the Options bar's checkmark button or pressing Enter on your computer's numeric keypad.

Middle: Once you accept the mask, you'll see a selection of the text appear, indicated by the little army of marching ants surrounding the characters, as shown here (in real life, they actually move).

Bottom: After you inverse (flip-flop) the selection, the area behind the text gets selected, letting you change the background of your design in the shape of the text. Here, the text selection was used in conjunction with an adjustment layer on a photo of pizza.

As you can see, all manner of graphic design goodness is possible with this technique.

4. **Format the text to your liking.**

If you don't like the font, change it by highlighting the text (page 568) and choosing something else from the font family menu. You can reposition the text by moving your cursor away from it about a half inch and then dragging with the resulting arrow cursor. You can also move the text by pressing ⌘ (Ctrl on a PC), clicking inside the resulting box, and then dragging it or nudging it with your keyboard's arrow keys. Drag any of the square handles to resize the text (remember to hold the Shift key to resize it proportionately).

5. **Convert the mask to a selection.**

When the text looks just right, click the checkmark in the Options bar to accept the mask, or just press the Enter key on your numeric keypad (*not* Return). This creates a selection of the text (so you see marching ants) and gets rid of the red overlay, as shown in Figure 14-8, middle.

NOTE If you decide to edit or reformat the text after accepting the mask, you have to start over. Just grab the Type Mask tool and retype the text (you don't have to deselect first).

6. **Inverse the selection.**

In order to fade the area of the photo around the letters, you need to flip-flop the selection. Choose Select ›Inverse to select everything *except* the letters. Now you can adjust the photo's background while leaving the letter area alone.

7. **Create a Hue/Saturation Adjustment layer and use it to desaturate and lighten the part of the photo in the selection area.**

Over in the Layers panel, click the half-black/half-white circle and choose Hue/Saturation from the resulting menu. (Using an Adjustment layer lets you do the desaturating and lightening on a separate layer, instead of on the original image.) In the Properties panel that opens, drain most of the photo's color by lowering the saturation to –65. Next, drag the Lightness slider to +60 to lighten the photo, making the text more legible.

NOTE Since you had an active selection before creating the Adjustment layer, Photoshop plopped the selection into the Adjustment layer's mask for you so that only the selected area was affected by the changes you made. See page 77 for more on Adjustment layers and their masks.

You're done! Figure 14-8 (bottom) shows the final result: clear, photo-filled text with a faded background.

Creating Text on a Path

Photoshop lets you bend text to your every whim, and one of the coolest tricks is to make text march around a shape. The key is to use the Type tool on a preexisting path (either open or closed—see page 546) that was drawn with the Pen tool or created with a vector shape such as one made by the Rectangle, Rounded Rectangle, Ellipse, Polygon, or Custom Shape tool (Figure 14-9). (See Chapter 13 for a detailed discussion of paths and shape tools.) When you attach text to a path, both the text and the path remain editable, so you can reformat the text or reshape the path anytime.

> **TIP** Heck, you can even turn text *into* a path (think outline) or shape—a nifty trick that lets you rotate individual letters and create cool intersecting effects. Head on over to page 630 for the details.

Here's how to attach text to a custom shape:

1. **Create a path.**

   Using either the Pen tool or one of the vector-shape tools mentioned above, create a path for the text to follow. Figure 14-9 shows a snail drawn with the Custom Shape tool (see page 555 to learn how to load other built-in shapes).

> **NOTE** The direction you draw the shape (or path) determines the direction the text flows. For example, draw the shape from left to right and the text will flow normally; draw it from right to left and the text will appear backward and upside down.

2. **Attach text to the path.**

   Grab the Horizontal Type tool (click the big T in the Tools panel) and then point your cursor just above the path or the shape's edge. You'll see a wavy line appear across the I-beam cursor (see Figure 14-9, top). This is the Type tool's way of telling you that it recognizes the path you're about to attach the text to. Click once and then start typing.

3. **Align or reposition the text on the path.**

   You can use any of the alignment buttons in the Options bar or Character panel to align the text on the path.

> **TIP** You may need to adjust tracking (page 606) over in the Character panel to keep letters from colliding in tight spaces.

You can also slide the text back and forth along the path, or flip it from the top of the path to the bottom, using the Path Selection tool—just click the black arrow below the Type tool in the Tools panel to activate it (see page 558 for more on this tool). Put your I-beam cursor over the starting point of the text (which is marked with an x—see Figure 14-9, middle). When a tiny, right-facing arrow appears next to the cursor, drag to the left or right to move the text. (The little arrow points to the left if you put your cursor over the end of the text, which is marked with a black dot.) To flip the text to the opposite side of the path—in this example, that means putting it inside the snail shell rather than on top—drag your cursor below the path (toward the bottom of the shape).

What's really happening here is that Photoshop is adjusting the start and end points of the text. You can move the start point by clicking the path with the left-arrowed cursor. Likewise, you can move the end point by putting your cursor at the end of the text and then clicking with the right-arrowed cursor. (If the text is center aligned, you'll likely see a double-arrowed cursor.)

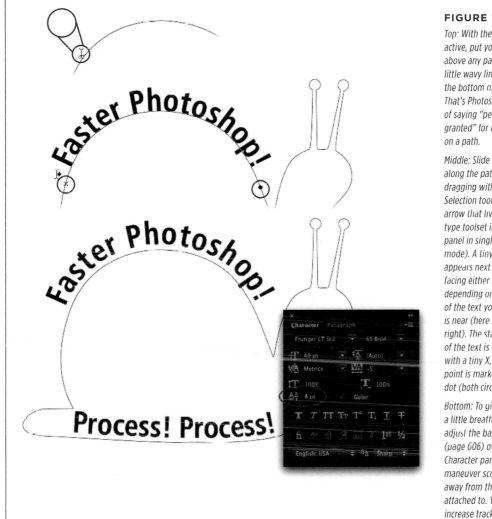

FIGURE 14-9

Top: With the Type tool active, put your cursor above any path and a little wavy line appears at the bottom of the cursor. That's Photoshop's way of saying "permission granted" for creating type on a path.

Middle: Slide the type along the path by dragging with the Path Selection tool (the black arrow that lives below the type toolset in the Tools panel in single-column mode). A tiny black arrow appears next to the cursor facing either left or right, depending on which end of the text your cursor is near (here it's facing right). The starting point of the text is marked with a tiny X, and the end point is marked with a dot (both circled).

Bottom: To give your text a little breathing room, adjust the baseline shift (page 606) over in the Character panel. This maneuver scoots the text away from the path it's attached to. You can also increase tracking if the letters start crashing into one another.

NOTE   If your text disappears, that means the space between the start and end points is too small to house the text. In that case, adjust one of the points or reformat the text to make it fit.

You can format type on a path like any other text. Just switch back to the Type tool and then highlight it using one of the techniques described on page 586. (To highlight all the text on a layer and activate the Type tool at the same time, give the Type layer a quick double-click in the Layers panel.)

Filling a Shape with Text

Placing text inside a shape is even simpler than placing it on an object's edge, and it's a fun little exercise in type design. First, create a closed shape with the Pen tool or one of the shape tools as discussed above, and then grab the Horizontal Type tool. Put your cursor inside the shape and, when it turns into an I-beam surrounded by tiny dots (shown in Figure 14-10, top), just click and type your text. Easy, huh?

FIGURE 4-10

Top: Once your cursor is surrounded by tiny dots, click inside the object and start typing to add your text.

Bottom: Using a centered alignment helps push the text away from the object's edges.

When
moving
to a new
home, always
put the cat in
through a window
instead of the
door. That way it
won't leave.
-Author Unknown

When you're finished typing, you can format the text using any of the options discussed on page 599 and beyond. Centered alignment (page 612) is especially useful for this technique, because it pushes the text away from the edges of the object (see Figure 14-10, bottom). Or, you can give the text a little more space using the Indent Left Margin and Indent Right Margin controls over in the Paragraph panel (page 612).

Warping Text

Another way to create text that follows a shape is to use the Create Warped Text command. Be forewarned, though, that this option distorts the *shape* of the letters (so they might not be very legible when you're done), whereas type on a path alters only the baseline and orientation (direction) of the text.

The Create Warped Text button appears in the Options bar whenever a type tool is active (it looks like a T with a curved line under it). If you're using any other tool, choose Type→Warp Text to access its dialog box (Figure 14-11). Unlike placing type on a path or inside an object, to warp text, you have to create the text first and *then* click the Warp button (or choose the menu command). Next, pick one of the 15 canned settings in the Warp Text dialog box's Style pop-up menu, and then customize the style by tweaking the Bend, Horizontal, and Vertical Distortion sliders (you may have to move the dialog box aside so you can see how the text is changing.)

If you don't like the result, just press Option (Alt on a PC) and the Warp Text dialog box's Cancel button changes to Reset. Click it to snuff out any changes you've made so far (or click Cancel to exit the dialog box completely). Once you've got your text looking good, click OK.

As long as you don't rasterize the Type layer and turn it into pixels (see the box on page 588), you can change the warp settings at any time. Just activate the Type layer and then choose Type→Warp Text to see the warp settings you used previously.

Using Find and Replace

No matter what kind of text you work with, at some point you might need to exchange a word, phrase, or character for something else. It's usually easy enough to make such fixes manually, but if there's a fair amount of text in your document, reach for the Find and Replace command instead.

For example, suppose you're working on a full-page ad for a sports-drink company and they've just changed the name of their flagship product from Dr. Bob's Thirst Remedy to Quenchtastic 4000. In that situation, you can save yourself lots of time by using the Find and Replace feature. Photoshop will seek out the offending word or phrase and replace it with whatever you want.

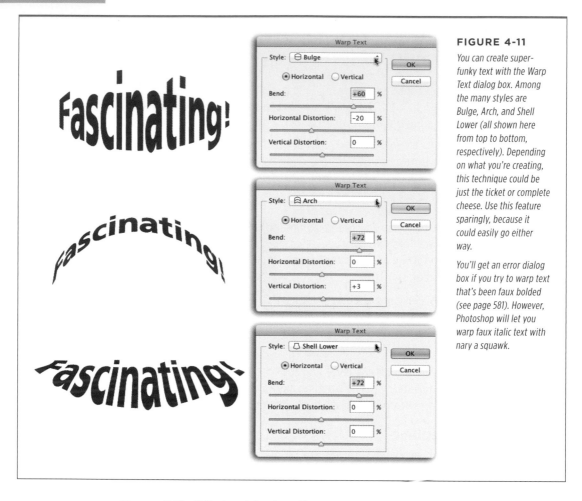

FIGURE 4-11

*You can create super-
funky text with the Warp
Text dialog box. Among
the many styles are
Bulge, Arch, and Shell
Lower (all shown here
from top to bottom,
respectively). Depending
on what you're creating,
this technique could be
just the ticket or complete
cheese. Use this feature
sparingly, because it
could easily go either
way.*

*You'll get an error dialog
box if you try to warp text
that's been faux bolded
(see page 581). However,
Photoshop will let you
warp faux italic text with
nary a squawk.*

Choose Edit→"Find and Replace Text" to summon the dialog box shown in Figure
14-12 (you don't even need to have the Type tool or a Type layer active). Enter the
offending word or phrase in the Find What field and its replacement in the Change
To field. Use the checkboxes to tell Photoshop whether you want it to search through
all the Type layers in your document; look only for instances that match the case
(capitalization) of what you've typed; search from a specific point in a Type layer
forward (this one's only available if you have the Type tool active and the cursor
blinking at a point within the text); look for whole words only; ignore accent marks;
or any combination of these options.

FIGURE 4-12

Hopefully you'll never set enough text in Photoshop to need the Find and Replace Text feature, but it can come in handy in a pinch. New in Photoshop CS6 is the option to ignore accents, handy when you're working with languages other than English.

Formatting Text

Now that you've learned all about the different *kinds* of Photoshop text, it's time to dig in to how to format it. Photoshop CS6 lets you control text to within an inch of its life. Beyond the basics of font, size, and color, you can adjust the softness of the letters' edges, the space between each letter, the space between lines of text, and so on.

The most commonly used settings live in the Options bar, while the more advanced typographic goodies are nestled snugly inside the Character and Paragraph panels. But no matter where the settings live, if they control text, you'll learn about them in the following pages. Read on!

WORD TO THE WISE

Thou Shalt Spell Check

Few mistakes are as embarrassing (or avoidable) for a graphic artist as a misspelled word. Most software comes with a built-in spellchecker, and Photoshop is no exception, so there's little excuse for typos (on the other hand, *wordos*—real words in the wrong place—are another story). And let's face it: The people who create copy can rarely spot their own mistakes, either because they've been staring at it for too long or because they're rushing to meet a deadline. In those situations, using a spellchecker is essential.

To check spelling in Photoshop, choose Edit→Check Spelling.

Photoshop scours your document's Type layers and, in the resulting dialog box, alerts you to words it considers suspect. It dutifully offers a list of suggestions that you can ignore or accept, changing just one instance or all of them. If it encounters an unknown word that is oft used and correctly spelled, just click the Add button and Photoshop assimilates the word into its dictionary.

Whether you're typing five words or five paragraphs, take time to run the spellchecker—you'll be glad you did.

NOTE The brand-new Type menu is home to several options that used to be buried in the Layer menu or deep inside Photoshop's Type preferences.

Formatting with the Options Bar

When you have the Type tool active, the Options bar (Figure 14-13) offers basic text-tweakers such as font family, style, size, anti-aliasing (see page 601), alignment, and color. (The Character panel, discussed on page 602, offers all these settings and more.)

NOTE Remember, any changes you make in the Options bar *remain* until you change them back. So if you suddenly find that your text isn't behaving like you expect, chances are there's a setting in the Options bar that needs changing.

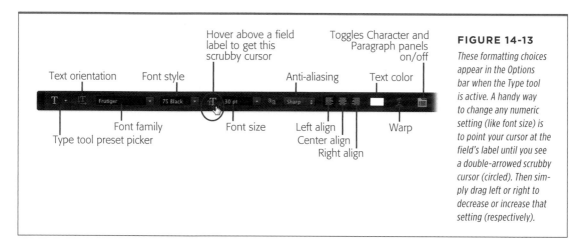

FIGURE 14-13

These formatting choices appear in the Options bar when the Type tool is active. A handy way to change any numeric setting (like font size) is to point your cursor at the field's label until you see a double-arrowed scrubby cursor (circled). Then simply drag left or right to decrease or increase that setting (respectively).

You can apply formatting either before or after you create text:

- **Before you type.** If you know exactly what font, style, and size you want to use before you start hammering out text, applying formatting beforehand is the way to go. Press T to grab the Type tool and then head up to the Options bar or the Character panel to pick your settings.

- **After you type.** This is the more common method, since it's easier to see how formatting choices affect *existing* text than try to imagine how it might look. With the Type tool active, highlight the text you want to format using one of the methods described on page 586, and then use the Options bar or Character panel to change the formatting however you wish.

From left to right, the Options bar gives you control over the following:

- **Type Tool Preset picker.** Out of the box, this setting performs the fairly useless service of letting you quickly summon horizontal 24-point type in the Myriad font. Thankfully, with just a little bit of work, you can create your own presets—a fantastic idea if you use the same formatting over and over again.

Start by formatting some text exactly the way you want it and then make sure its Type layer is active (you don't have to highlight the text itself). Next, click the triangle next to the Tool Preset picker, and then click the gear icon and choose New Tool Preset from the pop-up list. Enter a meaningful name in the resulting box, and then click OK. Photoshop memorizes how you formatted the text so it can apply that formatting automatically the next time around. Just grab the Type tool, pick your style from the Tool Preset picker, and then click in your document and start typing.

TIP In Photoshop CS6 you can create *character* and *paragraph styles:* detailed text formatting recipes that you can apply on the fly. See the box on page 613 for details.

- **Text orientation.** There's no need to decide whether you want horizontal (left to right) or vertical (top to bottom) text before you type: Clicking this little button will flip the whole Type layer on the fly. You don't even have to select any text first.

- **Font family.** This menu lists every font that's active on your machine and includes a preview of what each one looks like. (If you want to turn off this preview, page 582 tells you how.)

- **Font style.** Here's where you can choose a native style (page 581) for the font you selected, such as light, bold, or condensed.

- **Font size.** Enter a point size for the text in this field, or put your cursor over the field's label and then use the scrubby cursor shown in Figure 14-13 to change the size. Though text size is typically stated in points, you can change the unit of measurement to pixels or millimeters by choosing Photoshop→Preferences→Units & Rulers (Edit→Preferences→Units & Rulers on a PC).

TIP If you need to create *super* large text, Photoshop will put up a fight. When you type a number greater than 1296 into the Font size field, you'll see an error message asking you to enter a number between 1 and 1296. This is an odd little quirk of Photoshop's, but if you're sneaky, you can work around this limitation by resizing your text with the Free Transform command (page 259): Enter *1296* into the size field and then choose Edit→Transform ›Scale. Drag the resulting resizing handles outward to make the text really honkin' big, and then press Return (Enter on a PC) to accept the transformation.

- **Anti-aliasing.** Anti-aliasing was mentioned way back in Chapter 4 as a method for smoothing the edges of a selection (page 144). Similarly, this option smooths text by blurring its edges ever so slightly, helping you avoid the dreaded jagged edges so common when printing to a low-resolution inkjet printer or posting on the Web.

    Your choices here are None, Sharp, Crisp, Strong, and Smooth. Each setting has a different effect on various text sizes, so you might have to do a little experimenting. Use None on extremely small text to make it clean and sharp (especially if it's destined for the Web), and Strong or Smooth for larger text to keep it from looking jagged when it's printed (especially if it's headed for an older inkjet printer).

- **Alignment.** These three buttons make text flush left, centered, or flush right (respectively) within a single line of text or a text box. Unless you specifically apply a different alignment, Photoshop automatically left-aligns text. To align a single line of text on a Type layer that contains several paragraphs, press T to activate the Type tool, click anywhere within the line or paragraph, and then click one of these buttons. To center everything on a Type layer, double-click the Type layer's thumbnail in the Layers panel, and then click an alignment button.

TIP You can also use keyboard shortcuts to align text. To left align, highlight some text and press Shift-⌘-L (Shift+Ctrl+L on a PC). For center alignment, press Shift-⌘-C (Shift+Ctrl+C), and for right alignment, press Shift-⌘-R (Shift+Ctrl+R).

- **Text color.** You can set text's color by selecting the text and then clicking this little colored swatch in the Options bar, which shows the current text color. (There's a similar button in the Character panel that does the same thing.) You can also set text color before you type by clicking the foreground or background color chip. To recolor some text to your foreground color, highlight the text using one of the methods described on page 586, and then press Option-Delete (Alt+Backspace on a PC). To use the background color instead, press ⌘-Delete (Ctrl+Backspace) instead.

NOTE When choosing a text color, resist the urge to go hog wild. Bear in mind that black text on a white background is easy to read, as is dark-colored text on a light background. The key is contrast—it's really hard to read text that's similar in color to its background. However, if you're adding text to a *dark* background, you risk the danger of introducing *too* much contrast. For example, a single line of pure white text on a black background is quite legible, but a large block of white text on a black background—especially on the Web—is eye-numbing. In that situation, you'd be better off using light-gray text instead so the contrast won't be quite so high.

- **Create warped text.** You can use this option to curve and distort text in all manner of exciting ways, as explained on page 597. This button is easy to spot: Its icon is a capital T perched atop a curved line.
- **Character and Paragraph panels.** Click this button to pop open the Character and Paragraph panels for even more text formatting goodness, as explained in the next two sections. (Click it again to hide the panels.)

The Character Panel

If you've ever clicked the Options bar's rightmost button when the Type tool is active (see Figure 14-13), then the Character and Paragraph panel icons are probably lurking near the right side of your screen in the panel dock (see page 17 for more on this dock)—they look like a capital A and a paragraph symbol, respectively. If you don't see 'em, choose Type→Panels→Character Panel (or Type→Panels→Paragraph Panel) and Photoshop adds 'em both to the dock for you (you can also open both panels by using the Window menu). It assumes that if you're using one, you'll soon be using the other, which is a pretty safe bet.

The Character panel, shown in Figure 14-14, has enough formatting options to please the most discerning typesetter. It includes all the settings found in the Options bar when you're using the Type tool, plus it lets you control the space in and around individual characters, where they sit on a line, the height of the line, and more. It now also holds the key to unlocking the amazing OpenType features discussed on page 611. Mastering this panel can help you turn ordinary text into a work of art.

NOTE Like the Options bar, any changes you make in the Character panel remain in effect until you change them back. So if you play with leading (explained below) on Monday and then add text to a brand-new document on Tuesday, the leading may look a bit off. Either use the leading pop-up menu to change it back to Auto or go to the Character panel's menu (see Figure 14-14) and choose Reset Character, which reverts *all* the Character panel's settings back to normal.

Close panel
Double-click tab collapse vertically
Collapse panel horizontally
Panel menu
Font family
Built-in styles
Size
Leading
Kerning
Tracking
Vertical scale
Horizontal scale
Baseline shift
Text color
Faux styles
OpenType options
Anti-aliasing
Character set language
Character
Paragraph
Frutiger
75 Black
30 pt
(Auto)
Metrics
0
100%
100%
0 pt
Color:
English: USA
Sharp

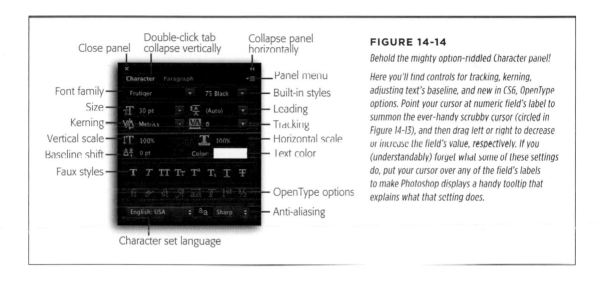

FIGURE 14-14

Behold the mighty option-riddled Character panel!

Here you'll find controls for tracking, kerning, adjusting text's baseline, and new in CS6, OpenType options. Point your cursor at numeric field's label to summon the ever-handy scrubby cursor (circled in Figure 14-13), and then drag left or right to decrease or increase the field's value, respectively. If you (understandably) forget what some of these settings do, put your cursor over any of the field's labels to make Photoshop displays a handy tooltip that explains what that setting does.

A LESSON IN LEADING

If you've ever added extra carriage returns between lines of text to create space or wondered how designers make lines of text appear all squashed together, you've encountered *leading* (rhymes with "bedding"). Leading controls the amount of blank space between lines of text. The term originated back in the days when type was set by hand onto printing presses, and strips of lead in various thicknesses were used to create space between lines. Learning to control leading is a useful design skill, and Photoshop gives you complete control over it, as shown in Figure 14-15.

I never think of the future, it comes soon enough.

I never think of the future, it comes soon enough.

I never think of the future, it comes soon enough.

FIGURE 14-15

Attention Goldilocks: The leading on the left is too little, the leading on the right is too much, but the leading in the middle—set to Auto—is just right (for this situation, anyway; auto leading isn't perfect for every project). As you can see, leading can make a design statement.

Leading is measured in points just like text, though it *includes* the point size of the text itself. Leading that's equal to the point size of text is called *solid leading*, which creates lines of text that almost touch (resulting in spacing that's somewhere between what's shown in the left and middle of Figure 14-15). Unless you change it, Photoshop's leading is set to Auto, which is approximately 120 percent of the text's point size (see Figure 14-15, middle). For example, 10-point type has an auto leading of 12 points.

The Character panel's leading control is labeled with two A's stacked on top of each other. You can adjust the leading of several lines of text at once or one line at a time. To adjust the leading of all the lines of text that are on the same layer, double-click the offending Type layer in the Layers panel so all its text is highlighted, and then choose a point size from the leading pop-up menu, or type directly into the text field. (Better yet, point your cursor above the field's label and then use the handy scrubby cursor.) To adjust the leading of a *single* line of text on a Type layer that contains many lines, highlight the line of text first and then change its leading.

> **TIP** You can also use keyboard shortcuts to change leading: Highlight the text and then press and hold Option (Alt on a PC) and tap the up or down arrow keys to change the leading in increments of 2 points; add ⌘ (Ctrl) to change it in increments of 10 points. To set leading back to Auto, press Shift-Option-⌘-A (Shift+Alt+Ctrl+A). This shortcut works on vertical text, too!

■ LEARNING TO KERN

Kerning means adjusting the amount of space between pairs of letters. Poorly kerned (or unkerned) text looks funky and can be distracting to the reader, as you can see in Figure 14-16, top. A lack of kerning is one of the *biggest* clues that text has been set nonprofessionally (nothing exposes a typographical novice faster!). Admittedly, the problem is more noticeable with less expensive—or free—fonts (think Frolicking

Ferrets), scripts, and decoratives (*especially* fonts that mimic handwriting, like the one in the figure).

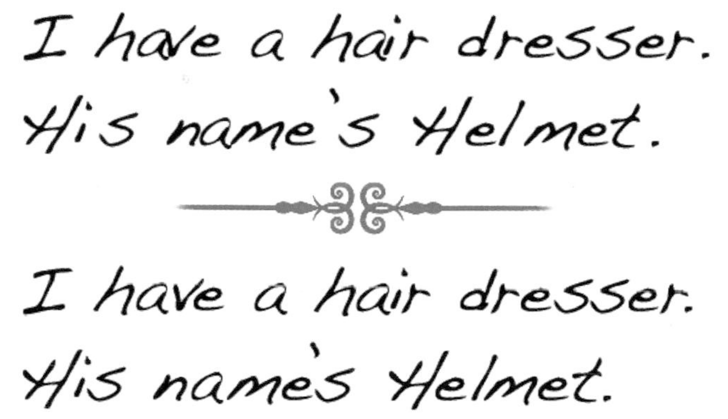

FIGURE 14-16

Top: Here's some text borrowed from a BMW motorcycle ad in a pitiful, unkerned state. Notice how several of the letters appear too close together? The punctuation is even worse—it's practically in a different Zip code.

Bottom: After a little kerning, the text looks normal instead of helter-skelter, so readers can focus on what the copy says instead of the weird spacing.

Get it? My hairstylist is my motorcycle helmet? Oh, nevermind.

Over in the Character panel, the kerning button is marked by the letters VA and a left-pointing arrow. The numbers in the kerning pop-up menu range from positive to negative; positive values increase space, and negative values decrease space. Kerning values are measured in 1/1000 *em*. An em is a relative measurement that's based on the point size of the text. For example, if the text size is 12-point, 1 em equals 12 points. Since you can create text of various sizes, this measurement ensures that your kerning is always based on the size you're currently working with.

NOTE Though Photoshop tries to kern text automatically, it's best to do it manually as described here. The box on page 608 has more on auto vs. manual kerning.

Because the amount of space each letter needs on either side differs according to which letter comes next—an *A* can tuck in closer to a *V* than it can to an *M*, for example—you'll want to kern each space individually. Press T to grab the Type tool and position the cursor in the first problem area you spot. To widen the space, pick a positive value from the kerning pop-up menu, drag the scrubby cursor gently to the right, or type a value into the kerning field. To narrow the space, pick a negative value or drag the scrubby cursor to the left.

TIP There's a keyboard shortcut for changing kerning, but you need to place your cursor *between* the letters you want to adjust first. Press and hold Option (Alt on a PC) while tapping the left or right arrow key to change the kerning in increments of 20. Add the ⌘ key (Ctrl) to change it in increments of 100.

■ TRACK IT OUT

To change the spacing between *all* letters in a word by the same amount, you need to adjust *tracking*. This adjustment is great when you're trying to make text fit into a small area. Also, vast amounts of tracking, as shown in the word "conference" in Figure 14-17, can be a useful design trick. Like kerning, tracking is measured in 1/1000 em. To make an adjustment, first select the word(s) you want to track and then trot over to the Character panel and look for the setting marked with the VA with a double-headed arrow beneath it. Pick a value from the pop-up menu, enter one manually, or use the scrubby cursor you get by putting your cursor over the VA.

FIGURE 14-17

Tracking is a great way to make a word fit into a small space, or fill a big space. In this example, the word "conference" has been tracked out to stretch from the G in "digital" to the last A in "camera." Because the large amount of space between the letters is uniform and obviously deliberate, it becomes a useful design element. (This is also one of the few ways all-caps text looks good—the extra space makes it easier to read.)

TIP As you might suspect, there's a keyboard shortcut for this one too. To adjust tracking in increments of 20, highlight some text and then press and hold Option (Alt on a PC) while tapping the left or right arrow key. Add the ⌘ key (Ctrl) to change tracking in increments of 100.

■ DOIN' THE BASELINE SHIFT

Text's *baseline* is the invisible line on which its letters sit. Changing this line can make a character appear higher or lower than other characters on the same line (see Figure 14-18). This is called *baseline shift*, and you can think of it as an exaggerated super- or subscript control (as in degree and trademark symbols). Remember the section on page 593 about text on a path? Baseline shift was used to scoot the text above the path in that example. It's also helpful when you want to create fractions, use initial caps (shown in Figure 14-18), or manually adjust characters in a decorative font.

FIGURE 14-18

Notice how the big, fancy D is lower than the rest of the word "domestic"? That's because its baseline shift has been decreased to –30 points.

To adjust the baseline of a character, word, or phrase, highlight the text you want to tweak and then head to the Character panel (if you don't highlight anything, the adjustment gets applied to the next thing you type). Use the baseline shift setting (it's marked with a big A, a little A, and an up arrow) to move the text up or down by picking a positive or negative value (respectively) from the pop-up menu, entering a value manually, or using the scrubby cursor.

> **TIP** Once you've highlighted some text, press Shift-Option (Shift+Alt on a PC) while tapping either the up or down arrow on your keyboard to shift the baseline in increments of 2 points. Add the ⌘ key (Ctrl) to shift it in increments of 10 points.

■ OTHER CHARACTER OPTIONS

The Character panel is chock-full of other formatting controls. Just remember that, to apply any of the formatting discussed in this section, you first have to highlight some text.

As shown in Figure 14-14, the Character panel has a whole row of buttons that let you apply faux styles, like bold and italic (meaning they're not built into the font, but faked by Photoshop instead). Feel free to use faux styles if you're creating a piece for online use or at-home printing, but it's best to stay away from the faux stuff if the project is bound for a professional printer, as they can cause unexpected results. Problems include jagged text (due to rasterization); characters that refuse to print (which will cause Photoshop to substitute another font); or a PostScript error, which can halt printing altogether.

Among the other styles offered by the Character panel for your formatting pleasure are underline (which places a line under the text), and strikethrough (which places a line *through* the text).

> **TIP** The keyboard shortcut for faux-bolding text (after it's highlighted) is Shift-⌘-B (Shift+Ctrl+B on a PC), for faux-italicizing, it's Shift-⌘-I (Shift+Ctrl+I), for underlining it's Shift-⌘-U (Shift+Ctrl+U), and for adding a strikethrough, it's Shift-⌘-/ (Shift+Ctrl+/). Whew!

The other options in the Character panel:

- **Vertical and Horizontal Scale.** These two settings (which stretch or shrink text vertically or horizontally) have the power to squish, cram, and spread type to within an inch of its life, rendering it utterly unreadable and unrecognizable, so use these options at your own risk. If you're trying to save space, a better solution is to adjust kerning or tracking (or both). If you're trying to fill space, increase the type size or tracking instead.

> **TIP** If you've played around with your text's scale, you can instantly get it back to normal with the flick of a keyboard shortcut. Reset the vertical scale to 100 percent by highlighting the text and then pressing Shift-Option-⌘-X (Shift+Alt+Ctrl+X on a PC), or reset the horizontal scale to 100 percent by pressing Shift-⌘-X (Shift+Ctrl+X).

- **All Caps/Small Caps.** To switch lowercase text to uppercase, just highlight the text and then click the All Caps button (marked with TT). But keep in mind that, unless you're creating a small amount of text and perhaps tracking it out as shown in Figure 14-17, using all caps is a bad idea. It makes text extremely hard to read because the words all take on the same blocky shape. Besides, they tend to insinuate screaming (LIKE THIS), and that's not very reader friendly.

UP TO SPEED

Auto vs. Manual Kerning

Ever helpful, Photoshop tries to kern text for you. Perched at the top of the kerning pop-up menu in the Character panel are two auto-kerning methods: Metrics and Optical.

Metrics kerning is the most common method. It tells Photoshop to adjust the space between letters according to their *kern pairs*—the amount of spacing between pairs of letters (like *Tr, To, Ta*, and so on) that the designer specified when creating the font. Photoshop applies metrics kerning automatically anytime you create or import text (unless you've changed this menu's setting).

However, some fonts contain little or no info about kern pairs, but you won't know that until you start typing. So, if the kerning looks really bad, Adobe recommends that you manually switch to optical kerning, where Photoshop adjusts the space according to characters' shapes instead. Optical kerning is also helpful when you use more than one font (or font size) in a single word.

Using automatic kerning is fine for large blocks of text—imagine hand-kerning this book!—but for standalone text, the best method is to kern it manually as described on page 604. It takes more time, but the results are *well* worth it.

The Small Caps button (marked with a big T and a smaller T) isn't much better, as it simply creates a smaller version of hard-to-read all caps. The keyboard shortcut for all caps is Shift-⌘-K (Shift+Ctrl+K on a PC); for small caps, it's Shift-⌘-H (Shift+Ctrl+H).

- **Superscript and Subscript.** These buttons cause the baseline and point size of the selected character(s) to change. (If you don't have any text highlighted, the next character you type will be superscript or subscript.) Superscript increases the baseline shift so the character sits above other text in the same line (great for trademark symbols such as ™ and →), while subscript decreases the baseline shift so the character sits below other text (perfect for footnotes and scientific or mathematical text).

TIP The keyboard shortcut for superscript (which you can use after highlighting text) is Shift-⌘-plus (Shift+Ctrl+plus on a PC). For subscript, press Shift-Option-⌘-plus (Shift+Alt+Ctrl+plus).

- **Language.** The language pop-up menu at the bottom of the Character panel won't translate text for you; it merely means that Photoshop will adjust its spell checking and hyphenation to suit the selected language. The 40 or so choices include everything from Bulgarian to Ukrainian. (The box on page 599 has info on spell checking.)

NOTE Speaking of other languages, Photoshop CS6 supports Asian as well as Middle Eastern and North African characters. To turn 'em on, choose Type→Language Options→East Asian Features. In that same submenu, you can also change the leading to "Top-to-Top Leading" or "Bottom-to-Bottom Leading". To switch to Middle Eastern/North African text, choose Photoshop→Preferences→Type (Edit→Preferences→Type on a PC) and turn on Middle Eastern; then you can choose Type→Language Options→Middle Eastern Features).

- **Anti-Aliasing.** The Character panel's anti-aliasing control (in the lower-right corner of the panel) works just like the anti-aliasing control on the Options bar (page 600), and slightly blurs the edges of text so they don't look jagged.

The following goodies used to live in the Character panel's *menu* but now have their own buttons in the panel. They're reserved for OpenType fonts only—they're grayed out if you're using a PostScript or TrueType font. As discussed on page 579, OpenType format lets font designers include alternative character designs and all manner of glyphs. Some have alternate *ligatures* (two or more characters that have been combined into one for better flow—like an *fi* or *fl* combo), fancy flourishes (see Figure 14-19), a whole set of ornaments, and more. These embellishments are perfect for creating fancy initial caps, formatting numbers, and for adding a bit of typographic pizzazz:

- **Standard Ligatures** are alternate character designs for certain letter combinations that tend to touch—like *fi, fl, ff, ffi,* and *ffl.*

TIP To apply these special OpenType features to existing text, you have to highlight the text using one of the methods described on page 586 *and then* click the formatting button. If you don't have any text highlighted, Photoshop will apply the feature to the *next* character you type.

FIGURE 14-19

The top line of text here is in standard Adios Script Pro, a truly gorgeous OpenType font. The middle line was created using Contextual Alternates, which summons different letter designs depending upon where the letter falls within a word. The last line was created using the extra-flourishy Swash option.

Keep in mind that some OpenType fonts have extras and some don't; if one of the Open-Type buttons near the bottom of the Character panel is grayed out, it means the feature doesn't exist in that particular font.

- **Contextual Alternates** substitutes certain letterforms for others that join together more fluidly. This option is common in script fonts because it makes the letters look like cursive handwriting.

- **Discretionary Ligatures** are replacements for letter pairs like *ct, st*, and *ft*. They tend to have a bit more flourish than their standard ligature counterparts.

- **Swash** substitutes a standard character for one with an exaggerated stroke (think calligraphy).

- **Stylistic Alternates** are characters that have extra bits of decoration here and there, as shown at the bottom of Figure 14-19. They're for your visual pleasure only (and, of course, that of the font designer).

- **Titling Alternates** calls to action a special set of all-caps characters designed to be used at large sizes, for things like titles (hence the name).

- **Ordinals** decreases the size of letters appearing next to numbers and increases their baseline shift so they look like this: 2nd, 3rd, 4th, and so on.

- **Fractions** converts a number-slash-number combination (like this: 1/2) into a real fraction (like this: ½).

But wait—that's not all! The Character panel has *even more* settings hidden in its menu, which lives in the panel's upper-right corner (it's labeled in Figure 14-14):

- **Change Text Orientation.** This menu item lets you switch horizontally aligned text to vertical, and vice versa. Just select the Type layer you want to change, not the text itself, and then choose this option.

- **Standard Vertical Roman Alignment.** This is a fun one, though it works only on vertical type. Instead of the letters flowing from top to bottom, perched atop one another, they'll flow from left to right as if they were turned on their sides. (Picture the word "Vertical" back in Figure 14-4 [page 583] laid down on its side.) Another way to create this effect is to use the Free Transform tool to spin the text around 90 degrees.

- **OpenType.** As you just learned, the majority of Photoshop's OpenType formatting goodies now have their own buttons near the bottom of the Character panel. They also live in the panel menu's OpenType submenu, along with a couple of extra options (though not all OpenType fonts include these options):

  — **Oldstyle** prompts Photoshop to use smaller numerals than normal; some even sit below the baseline) so they blend more smoothly into the flow of text. Use this option when you want numbers to appear more elegant, but not when you need them to line up in a stack, as in an annual report.

  — **Ornaments** are symbols or pictographs. Typically this option is available only for symbol-based fonts (like Wingdings). When you choose this option, Photoshop replaces the original symbols with an alternate set.

- **Fractional Widths.** This setting rounds character widths to the nearest *part* of a pixel instead of a whole pixel. This setting is automatically turned on because it usually tightens text spacing, making it more visually pleasing (like kerning, discussed on page 604). However, Adobe recommends turning this option *off* if you're working with anything smaller than 20-point text because the tighter spacing can make it hard to read. When this setting is off, Photoshop uses whole-pixel spacing, which gives characters a bit more breathing room and keeps them from running into one another.

> **NOTE** You can't apply the Fractional Widths setting to individual characters—it's an all or nothing, everything-on-the-Type-layer-is-affected kind of thing. To use whole-pixel increments for the entire document, choose System Layout (explained next) from the Character panel's menu.

- **System Layout.** This option reverts text to the way your particular operating system displays it—similar to what you might see in TextEdit on a Mac or in WordPad on a PC. It switches character widths to whole pixels (as discussed in the previous bullet) and turns off anti-aliasing (page 601). This can be a good option to use when designing text for the Web, because the extra space and letter sharpness makes super small text a little easier to read. That said, the improved text rendering in CS6 should work well enough (see the box on page 583).

- **No Break.** When it comes to hyphenation, some words are meant to be broken and some aren't (as shown in Figure 14-20). To prevent such typographical gaffes, select the word(s) you want to keep together and then choose No Break from the Character panel's menu. This forces Photoshop to reflow the text so the word doesn't end up sliced in two. For more on hyphenation, see page 614.

In MotoGP, Rossi is a leg-end. Angry wife is jailed for mans-laughter.

FIGURE 14-20

This is what happens when good hyphenation goes bad. The fix is to highlight the offending word and then choose No Break from the Character panel's menu.

- **Reset Character.** If you've gone a bit overboard with formatting and want to return some text to its original glory, select it and then choose Reset Character from the Character panel's menu. (If you don't have any text highlighted, the newly restored character settings will affect the next thing you type.)

The Paragraph Panel

The Paragraph panel, shown in Figure 14-21, doesn't have anywhere *near* the number of options as the Character panel, though that doesn't make it any less important. Paragraph formatting controls alignment, hyphenation, justification, indentation, and spacing. Read on for a full discussion of each.

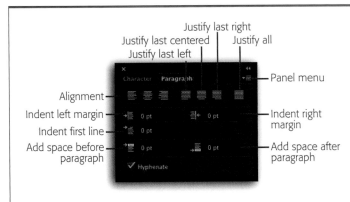

FIGURE 14-21

You can apply the Paragraph panel's formatting options to one or more paragraphs of text. If you don't highlight any text before adjusting these settings, Photoshop changes all the text on the active Type layer. But if the Type layer contains two lines of text separated by a carriage return, you can highlight one line and left-align it, and then highlight the other and right-align it.

■ ALIGNING TEXT

Alignment gives readers' eyes a hard edge to follow as they read through text, with the edge itself forming an invisible line that connects items on a page. The basic alignment types are left, center, and right, and picking the correct one for your document can make it look stronger, cleaner, and more dramatic. So which alignment should you choose? It depends on what you're going for. Here are a few guidelines:

- **Use left alignment for big blocks of text.** Newspapers, books, and magazines (which should not be created in Photoshop, mind you) usually stick with left alignment because it's the easiest to read. Unless you tell it otherwise, Photoshop will left-align everything.

- **Use centered alignment for formal situations.** There's a reason the copy in every graduation and wedding announcement you've ever seen is centered—it conveys a feeling of formality and elegance. So unless you live on Pennsylvania Avenue, resist the urge to center the copy on your next yard sale flyer.

GEM IN THE ROUGH

Character and Paragraph Styles

New in Photoshop CS6, character and paragraph styles give you the option of saving your hand-crafted text formatting to use on *other* text later on. Think of these new features as quick text recipes you can use anytime you want—a nice way to ensure consistent formatting across several documents.

To use character styles, format some text exactly the way you want using any of the Character panel options mentioned in the previous pages. When you get it just right, choose Type→Panels→Character Styles Panel. In the Character Styles panel, choose New Character Style from the panel's menu and then double-click the style and give it a meaningful name like *callout*. The next time you want to apply the exact same formatting, activate the Type layer in the Layers panel, highlight the text using one of the techniques described on page 586, and then pop open the Character Style panel and apply the style by clicking it in the list.

Paragraph styles work the same way, but they let you save both character *and* paragraph formatting. They're useful when you're formatting text like headlines, subheads, and body copy where things like spacing, alignment, indentation, and so on, come into play. (You'll learn all about paragraph formatting in the next section.) To open it, choose Type→Panels→Paragraph Styles Panel. It works the exactly the same way as the Character Styles panel.

If you apply additional formatting to an existing style, a tiny + appears next to its name in the relevant panel. To get rid of the extra formatting and revert back to the original style, click the Clear Override button at the bottom of the panel (it looks like a curved arrow). Or, to add the extra formatting to the style, click the checkmark. To edit or rename a style, simply double-click its name in the panel and then rename it in the dialog box that opens, which contains the myriad options available in both the Character and Paragraph panels. If you copy text that has a style applied to it and then paste it in another Photoshop document, the style comes along for the ride.

While Adobe considers these new styles great timesavers (and they may be in small doses), it's doubtful you'll create enough Photoshop text to use them very often. And if you do, that's a darn good indicator that you should be using a page-layout program such as InDesign or QuarkXPress instead.

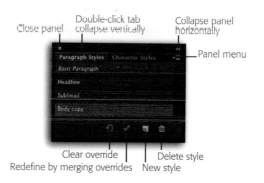

Close panel | Double-click tab collapse vertically | Collapse panel horizontally | Panel menu

Clear override | Delete style
Redefine by merging overrides | New style

- **Use right alignment for small blocks of text or numbers.** Right alignment can make text stand out because it's unusual and therefore draws attention. But it's harder to read than left alignment, meaning you'll want to save it for relatively small chunks of text (so don't right align your next novel). However, it's great for lists of numbers because it makes the decimals points (or commas) line up.

> **TIP** With vertical type, these options align the text based on a vertical line instead of a horizontal one. So instead of left, center, or right alignment, your options are top, center, or bottom.

You can align text on a single layer (or even a single line on a layer) or across multiple Type layers:

- **Aligning text on a single Type layer or on multiple Type layers.** Feel free to use different alignments on lines of text that live on the same Type layer, so long as there's a carriage return after each line. First, activate the Type tool and the Type layer you want to work on. To align a single line of text, click anywhere within that line and then click the appropriate alignment button in the Options bar or the Paragraph panel. To align *all* the text on that layer, highlight it using one of the methods described on page 586, and then click an alignment button.

  To align the text on several Type layers, activate the layers by Shift- or ⌘-clicking (Ctrl-clicking on a PC) to the right of their thumbnails and then click an alignment button. (You can also use Photoshop CS6's new layer-filtering feature to find all the Type layers, as described on page 80.)

- **Aligning Type layers themselves.** To align the left edge of text across several layers, you use a whole different set of alignment tools. Activate the offending layers as described in the previous bullet point, and then press V to grab the Move tool and poof!—a whole slew of alignment options appear in the Options bar. Click the one you want to apply, and the active layers dutifully jump to the left, right, or center. These incredibly useful alignment options are covered more fully on page 100.

■ HYPHENATION AND JUSTIFICATION

Known to page-layout pros as H&J, these controls work together to spread paragraph text so that both the left and right edges are perfectly straight, or *justified*. (The text in most magazines, newspapers, and books—including this one—is justified.) They also determine how the words are sliced and diced (*hyphenated*) in order to make them fit within a text box or to make the margins perfectly straight.

> **NOTE** Hyphenation and justification work only on paragraph text, not point text. Page 584 explains the difference between these two.

Photoshop's hyphenation feature is automatically turned on, but you can turn it off by clicking the checkbox at the bottom of the Paragraph panel, or by selecting the text and then pressing Shift-Option-⌘-H (Shift+Alt+Ctrl+H on a PC). However, you have to turn justification on manually by picking one of the following options (just click the appropriate button near the top of the Paragraph panel):

- **Justify last left.** This setting spreads text so that the left and right edges are perfectly straight, with the last line of the paragraph left aligned (meaning it doesn't reach across to the right margin), like the text in this book. The keyboard shortcut for this kind of justification is to select your text and then press Shift-⌘-J (Shift+Ctrl+J on a PC).

> **TIP** Justification is affected by which *composition method* you've chosen. See the box on page 617 for more info on this.

- **Justify last centered.** This is the same as the previous setting, but with the last line center aligned instead.

- **Justify last right.** Same again, but with the last line right aligned.

> **NOTE** When working with vertical text, your justification options are Justify last top, centered, and bottom.

- **Justify all.** With this setting turned on, the left and right edges of text are perfectly straight, but the last line is spread out to span the entire width of the paragraph. The results usually don't look very good (the last line tends to be really sprawled out), but once in a while some rebellious designer manages to pull it off, as shown in Figure 14-22.

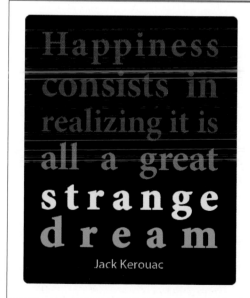

FIGURE 14-22

To truly tax your text, use blocked justification. This forces all the lines of text to line up vertically, even the last one.

It's really hard to make blocked text look good, though the folks at Quotable-Cards.com managed it quite nicely in this magnet design.

It's unlikely you'll ever need to adjust the H&J options, and if you do, that's a sign you should be creating your text in another program (see the box on page 577). Nevertheless, you *can* customize hyphenation and justification via the Paragraph panel's menu. Figure 14-23 has the scoop on adjusting these settings.

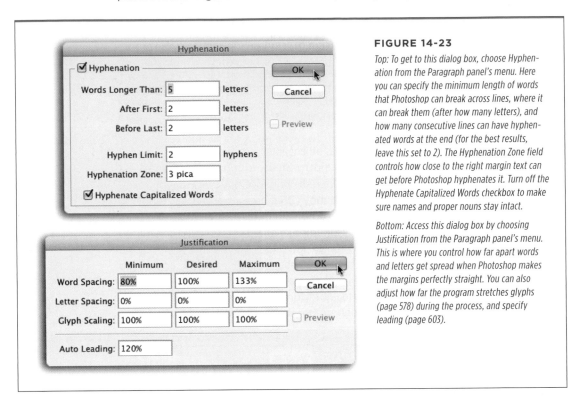

FIGURE 14-23

Top: To get to this dialog box, choose Hyphenation from the Paragraph panel's menu. Here you can specify the minimum length of words that Photoshop can break across lines, where it can break them (after how many letters), and how many consecutive lines can have hyphenated words at the end (for the best results, leave this set to 2). The Hyphenation Zone field controls how close to the right margin text can get before Photoshop hyphenates it. Turn off the Hyphenate Capitalized Words checkbox to make sure names and proper nouns stay intact.

Bottom: Access this dialog box by choosing Justification from the Paragraph panel's menu. This is where you control how far apart words and letters get spread when Photoshop makes the margins perfectly straight. You can also adjust how far the program stretches glyphs (page 578) during the process, and specify leading (page 603).

> **TIP** To prevent Photoshop from hyphenating a word or phrase, use the No Break option over in the Character panel's menu, as described on page 611.

■ INDENTING TEXT

It should be clear by now that Photoshop is no word processor, so don't go rooting around expecting any serious margin controls. However, you do have *some* say in how much space Photoshop puts between the text and the left or right edge of a single line (for point text) or the boundaries of a text box (for paragraph text). You can find the following options in the middle of the Paragraph panel (shown back in Figure 14-21):

- **Indent Left Margin and Indent Right Margin.** These settings scoot a line of text to the left or right, respectively, by the number of points you enter.

- **Indent First Line.** This option indents only the first line of the paragraph. If you need to create a *hanging indent*—where all lines of a paragraph are indented *except* the first—you can do that here. To do so, enter a positive number (like 10) for the left indent and a negative number (like –10) for the first-line indent.

- **Roman Hanging Punctuation.** This totally awesome feature is actually tucked away in the Paragraph panel's menu. You can use it to make the punctuation sit *outside* the text margin, while the letters themselves remain perfectly aligned, as shown in Figure 14-24. (You don't need to highlight any text before applying this setting.)

"To enjoy the flavor of life **take big bites**."

Robert Heinlein

FIGURE 14-24

The Roman Hanging Punctuation setting moves punctuation (in this case, the initial quotation mark) outside the margin, leaving the text perfectly aligned.

Graphic designers love this option!

POWER USERS' CLINIC

Photoshop's Composition Methods

"Great artists steal," or at least that's what Picasso and Steve Jobs supposedly said, and the folks at Adobe clearly agree: Deep within the Paragraph panel's menu you'll find a couple of options snatched unabashedly from InDesign, Adobe's page-layout program.

Displaying text is a complicated matter. To determine how it displays paragraph text, Photoshop takes into consideration word spacing, letter spacing, glyph spacing, *and* any hyphenation options you've set. With that information, it uses a complex formula to determine how lines of text are spaced (and broken, if necessary) in order to fit them within the text box you created. This is called *composition*, and you have two composition methods to choose from:

- Use **Single-Line Composer** if you're dealing with just one line of text, or if you want to handcraft the spacing between letters and lines with kerning or by inserting manual line breaks (carriage returns). With this method, Photoshop composes each line individually, no matter how many lines the paragraph contains.

- Go with **Every-Line Composer** if you've got more than one line of text. (Photoshop uses this method automatically unless you tell it otherwise.) Choosing this method tells Photoshop to compose the paragraph as a whole. The program tries to arrange lines in such a way that it avoids nasty line breaks. This method generally creates more visually pleasing text, in part because it makes Photoshop avoid hyphenation whenever possible.

■ **SPACE BEFORE AND AFTER**

Take a peek at the headers and subheads in this book. Notice how there's more space above them than below? This kind of spacing makes it easy for you to tell—even at a glance—that the paragraph following the header is related to it. That's because the spacing itself is a visual clue: Information that *is* related should appear closer together than information that's *not* related. (In design circles, this is known as the rule of *proximity*.) Proper spacing makes it a lot easier for people to read or scan a document quickly and understand how it's organized.

To adjust the spacing in your document, you could take the easy way out and add a few extra carriage returns, though chances are good that you'll introduce too much—or too little—space. Instead, use the Paragraph panel's Space Before and Space After options, which let you control spacing right down to the point. To do that, activate a Type layer and grab the Type tool by pressing T. Then click anywhere in the offending line (don't highlight it, just click it), and then head to the Paragraph panel and enter an amount (in points) into the Space Before or Space After field, or both (you can also use the scrubby cursor).

■ Special Text Effects

You can spice up Photoshop text in a variety of ways by adding fades, strokes, drop shadows, textures, and more. You can even take a photo and place it *inside* of text. The great thing is that you can perform all these techniques without rasterizing the text, so it remains fully and gloriously editable. Read on to learn all kinds of neat ways to add a little something special to your text.

> **TIP** Perhaps the easiest special effect of all is creating partially opaque or *ghosted* text. All you have to do is lower the Type layer's opacity in the Layers panel, as explained on page 97. That's it!

Faded Text

It's easy to make text look like it fades into an image, as shown in Figure 14-25. This technique is useful when you're creating a photo-centric advertisement or postcard announcement, or want to showcase a collection of photos on your website. Here's what you do:

1. **Open a photo and add some text.**

   Press T to grab the Type tool and type a single word. Be sure to pick a thick font such as Helvetica Bold or Black, Arial Black (used here), or Impact from the Options bar or Character panel.

Instead of straining your brain to choose a color for the text, you can snatch one from the photo instead; that way, it'll match. Simply highlight the text and then click the color square in the Options bar (or the Character panel) to open the Color Picker. Next, mouse away from the dialog box and, when your cursor turns into an eyedropper, click a spot in your image to grab that color; the text changes color instantly. Click OK to close the Color Picker and you're done!

FIGURE 14-25

Text that looks like it fades into an image is eye catching. The best thing about this technique is that the text remains fully editable so you can experiment with formatting to get just the right effect.

2. **Add a layer mask to the Type layer.**

   This mask will let you make the text look like it fades into your photo. With the Type layer active, click the circle-within-a-square icon at the bottom of the Layers panel to add the mask.

3. **Use the Gradient tool to fill the mask with a black-to-white, linear gradient.**

   Press G to grab the Gradient tool and, near the left end of the Options bar, click the down-pointing triangle to the right of the gradient preview to open the Gradient picker. From the resulting preset menu, choose the black-to-white gradient (it's the third one in the first row). Then take a peek at the little Gradient Type buttons to the right of the Gradient picker and make sure the first one is active so you're creating a linear gradient. Next, mouse over to your image and, with the mask active, click and drag from the bottom of the text to the top of the text (or a little past it). When you let go of your mouse, Photoshop automatically fills the mask with the gradient, hiding your text in such a way that it looks like it fades into the photo.

4. **If necessary, use the Move tool to reposition the text.**

That's it! Save the file as a Photoshop document and the text will remain editable until the end of time (well, until the end of *Photoshop,* at least!).

Stroked Text

One of the easiest ways to enhance text is to give it an outline, making it really stand out. Photoshop calls this outline a *stroke*, and it's simple to add one using the Layer Styles menu you learned about back on page 131. The following steps explain how to add a plain black stroke, as shown at the top of Figure 14-26.

FIGURE 14-26

Here are a few ways of stroking text with a layer style. No matter what kind of stroke you create, you can edit it by double-clicking the newly added stroke style layer in the Layers panel.

Top: A classic thick, black, outside stroke.

Middle: By changing the stroke Fill Type to Gradient and selecting Shape Burst from the gradient Style pop-up menu, you can introduce more than one color into the stroke. This gradient stroke was made with the Silver preset from the Metal set (see page 348 for more on loading gradients).

Bottom: By using the Gradient Editor (page 622) to create a custom solid gradient, you can make multistroked text, as explained in the next section.

1. **Add some text and commit it.**

   Press T to grab the Type tool and type a word. Be sure to choose a fairly weighty font like Futura bold or Cooper (the latter was used in Figure 14-26); if the letterforms are too thin, the stroke can overpower them. Then, when you're finished editing the text, tell Photoshop you're done by pressing Enter on your numeric keypad or by clicking the checkmark button in the Options bar (this is technically called *committing* text).

   TIP You might be tempted to choose Edit→Stroke instead of following the steps below. Don't. To use the Edit menu's Stroke command, you have to rasterize the text first (in fact, the Stroke menu item will be grayed out if you've activated a Type layer, since it's vector-based). Using layer styles is a much more flexible way to outline text, because your text remains editable.

2. **From the Layer Style menu at the bottom of the Layers panel (the fx button), choose Stroke.**

   Photoshop pops open the Layer Style dialog box and displays the many options for adding a stroke.

3. **Enter a stroke width.**

In the Size field, enter a pixel width (or drag the slider). Use a lower number for a thin stroke and a larger number for something more substantial (in Figure 14-26, top, the size was set to 8).

4. **Make sure the Position menu is set to Outside.**

Using Outside works well for text because it tells Photoshop to put the stroke on the *outside* of the character (as opposed to the inside, where it takes up more space, or straddling the character's edge, as is the case with a Center position). Leave the blend mode set to Normal and the opacity at 100 percent.

5. **From the Fill Type pop-up menu, choose Color.**

Photoshop assumes you want to fill the stroke with color (as opposed to a gradient, as explained in the next section) and it automatically chooses black. To create a standard black stroke, as shown at the top of Figure 14-26, leave this setting alone. To pick something else, click the little color swatch and then choose something from the resulting Color Picker.

6. **When you're finished, click OK to close the Layer Style dialog box and admire your newly stroked text.**

You can edit the new stroke anytime by double-clicking the stroke style in the Layers panel.

TIP To produce *hollow* text, apply a Stroke layer style and then lower the Type layer's Fill setting to 0% using the field near the top of the Layers panel. The stroke will still be visible, but everything *inside* it will vanish.

■ THE RARE MULTI STROKED TEXT EFFECT

If you *really* want to make text stand out—like in a comic book situation—try giving it more than one stroke, like the "Shazam" at the bottom of Figure 14-26. This technique is rewarding, but it requires a few more steps than the plain ol' single-stroked method in the previous section. Begin with steps 1 and 2 for creating stroked text, and then proceed as follows:

1. **In the Layer Style dialog box, set the Fill Type field to Gradient and the Style menu to Shape Burst, as shown in Figure 14-27, top.**

Using a gradient lets you add a multicolored stroke to the text, though you'll need to do some gradient editing first. Choosing Shape Burst as the gradient style makes the gradient stroke appear on the *outside* of the text only. You don't *have* to select a gradient style before editing the gradient; doing so just lets you see what you're creating.

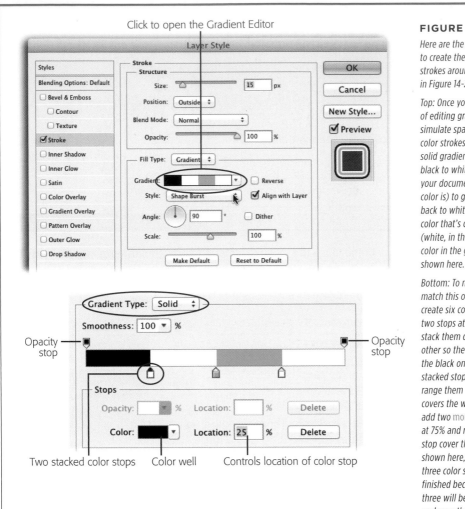

Click to open the Gradient Editor

FIGURE 14-27

Here are the settings that were to create the multicolored strokes around "Shazam" back in Figure 14-26.

Top: Once you get the hang of editing gradients, you can simulate space between the color strokes by creating a solid gradient that goes from black to white (or whatever your document's background color is) to green and then back to white. Note that the color that's closest to the text (white, in this case) is the last color in the gradient preview shown here.

Bottom: To make your gradient match this one, you'll need to create six color stops. Place two stops at the 25% mark and stack them directly atop each other so the white stop covers the black one. Next, add two stacked stops at 50% and arrange them so the green stop covers the white one. Then add two more stacked stops at 75% and make the white stop cover the green one. As shown here, you'll see only three color stops when you're finished because the other three will be hidden directly underneath 'em.

2. **Open the Gradient Editor and choose a new a gradient.**

   To open the Gradient Editor shown in Figure 14-27, bottom, click the rectangular gradient preview. In the resulting dialog box, click once to use one of the handy preset swatches (see page 348 for more on loading and editing gradients).

   If you want to get really creative, proceed to the next step. If not, skip to step 4.

3. **Choose Solid as the Gradient Type and edit the color stops.**

   To edit one of the gradient's colors, double-click one of the tiny color stops (circled in Figure 14-27) to summon the Color Picker. Move the color stops around by dragging them or by entering a number in the Location field. You can create the illusion of space between the strokes by including white in the gradient, as shown in Figure 14-27.

4. **When the preview looks good, click OK in the Gradient Editor, and then click OK again to close the Layer Style dialog box.**

Pretty nifty, eh? Once again, if you want to edit the stroke, just double-click the stroke style layer in the Layers panel.

NOTE To learn how to create text that looks like it's made out of shiny metal, head to this book's Missing CD page at *www.missingmanuals.com/cds*.

Texturizing Text

Design trends come and go, but the distressed, tattered look has been popular for a long time. You can spot it everywhere: movie posters, magazine ads, and book and album covers. Admittedly, it looks pretty darn good when applied to text. After all, text doesn't always have to look new, does it?

As with most effects, Photoshop gives you all kinds of ways to create a textured look. You can swipe the texture from a photo, run a filter (or several) on the text, or hide portions of the text using a layer mask and then paint it back with an artistic brush. Depending on your situation, one of these methods will work better for you than the rest (or at least be faster). They're all covered in the following pages.

■ TEXTURE FROM A PHOTO

You can come up with some unique effects by grabbing texture from a photo and applying it to text through a layer mask. And the great thing about this technique is that it's completely nondestructive: The Type layer remains editable. Start with an extremely busy photo—one with lots of hard lines and angles, like a picture of wood, leaves, or an interesting piece of architecture. In the steps below, you'll use the Threshold adjustment (page 324) to morph that photo into a high-contrast texture primed for plopping into the nearest layer mask, as shown in Figure 14-28.

NOTE Want to follow along? Visit this book's Missing CD page at *www.missingmanuals.com/cds* and download the practice file *Wood.jpg*.

FIGURE 14-28

Top: You can create a texture from any photo using a Threshold adjustment; the more lines the photo contains, the better. Areas in shadow will become black and the highlights become white. For this technique to work, you need to apply the adjustment to your image instead of using an Adjustment layer (just be careful not to save over your original file with this adjusted version).

Bottom: Here's what the wood texture looks like after it's been copied into a Type layer's layer mask. Imagine the possibilities!

Here's how to texturize text using a photo:

1. **Add some hefty text to your document.**

   Use a thick font (like Impact), and set its font size to something high (try 107 point). This will ensure you have plenty of surface area to texturize.

2. **Open a photo and then convert it to a high-contrast, black-and-white image using a Threshold adjustment.**

   Choose Image→Adjustments→Threshold. Drag the slider in the Threshold dialog box almost all the way to the left to make the highlights in the image completely white, and the shadows black. The black areas will become the texture, so bear in mind that too much texture (black) will render the text unreadable. Click OK when it looks good.

3. **Copy the new and contrast-riddled image.**

   Choose Select→All to surround your image with marching ants, and then copy the selection by pressing ⌘-C (Ctrl+C).

4. **Switch back to your text document, add a layer mask to the Type layer, and then open the mask.**

   Give the Type layer a layer mask by clicking the circle-within-a-square icon at the bottom of the Layers panel (see page 116 for more on layer masks). Next, open the mask by Option-clicking (Alt-clicking on a PC) its thumbnail in the Layers panel. Your document should go completely white because the mask is empty.

5. **Paste the texture into the mask and, if necessary, reposition the text, mask, or both with the Move tool.**

   Once you're in the layer mask, press ⌘-V (Ctrl+V on a PC) to paste the new texture into the mask. Feel free to move it around with the Move tool.

6. **Exit the layer mask to reveal the newly textured text.**

   Exit the layer mask by clicking the Type layer's thumbnail to the left of the layer mask, and marvel at your creativity.

> **NOTE**   Photoshop assumes that if you want to move a layer mask, you'll want to move whatever it's attached to as well, though this may not always be the case. For example, if you want to move the text independently of the mask, or vice versa, you have to unlink them first. Just click the little chain icon that lives between the type and layer mask thumbnails in the Layers panel, and the chain vanishes. Next, activate the Move tool and then click the thumbnail of whatever you want to reposition—either the image or its mask—and drag it into place. To lock them back together, click between their thumbnails in the Layers panel and the chain icon reappears.

■ TEXTURE FROM A BRUSH

Another way to texturize text is by painting on a layer mask with the Brush tool. Photoshop has some amazingly funky-shaped brushes, so you might as well make good use of them! With this method, you can be a little more particular about exactly where the texture goes since you paint it by hand, as shown in Figure 14-29.

Add some big, thick text to your document, and then do the following:

1. **Add a layer mask to the Type layer.**

   Activate the Type layer and add a layer mask to it by clicking the circle-within-a-square icon at the bottom of the Layers panel. This mask will let you *hide* bits of the text instead of deleting it.

2. **Grab the Brush tool and choose one of its more artistic manifestations, like Spatter or Chalk.**

   Press B to activate the Brush tool and then open the Brush Preset picker in the Options bar. Scroll through the brush previews and pick one of the more irregular, splotchy brushes. Photoshop CS6 has a ton of super-cool brushes built right in; page 512 explains how to load 'em.)

FIGURE 14-29

By using some of Photoshop's more creative brushes, you can paint a unique texture onto text using a layer mask (circled here). The cursor even takes on the shape of the brush, as you can see on the left side (it looks like a bunch of black squiggles).

As with most text effects, you'll want to start out with a weighty font so you can actually see the texture you've so painstakingly applied (Poplar Std at 134 and 236 points was used here).

3. **Increase the brush size to 100 pixels or so.**

   Making the brush fairly big will help you see its edges more clearly when you paint, so you'll know exactly what kind of texture you're painting where. While the Brush tool is active, you can press the right bracket key (]) repeatedly to increase brush size, or the left bracket key ([) to decrease it. This is an important keyboard shortcut to memorize, because this particular technique looks better if you vary the brush size quite a bit. (There are other, more complicated shortcuts for resizing brushes, but this one has been around forever...plus it's easy to remember!)

4. **Make sure your foreground color chip is set to black and the mask is active, and then mouse over to your document and start clicking on the text to apply the texture (clicking works better than dragging).**

As you've learned, painting with black within a layer mask conceals (hides) whatever is on that layer, while painting with white reveals. To hide portions of the text in the shape of the brush, you need to paint with black, so take a peek at the color chips at the bottom of the Tools panel and make sure black is on top. If it's not, press D to set the color chips to the factory setting of black and white, and press X to flip-flop the chips until black is on top.

If you hide too much of the text, press X to swap color chips so that white is on top, and then click to paint that area back in. (You'll do a lot of swapping color chips when editing masks, as explained in step 7 on page 120.)

The best part of this technique is that, by using a layer mask, you haven't harmed the text. If you don't like the effect, just delete the layer mask and you're back where you started.

■ TEXTURE FROM FILTERS

Running a filter on text is one of the fastest ways to give it extra character. Like the previous two techniques, this method involves using a layer mask, though this time you need to create a selection of the text *before* adding the mask.

Add some chunky text to your document and, in the Layers panel, ⌘-click (Ctrl-click on a PC) the Type layer's thumbnail to load the text as a selection. Once you see marching ants, add a layer mask to the Type layer as described in step 1 in the previous section. Then head to the Filter menu and choose Distort→Ripple. In the resulting dialog box, tweak the filter's settings so that the text's edges look fairly tattered in the handy preview window. Figure 14-30 shows the results of changing the Ripple Size to 8 and Ripple Magnitude to 4, and then running the filter three times. Press OK to dismiss the Filter dialog box and admire your newly distressed text.

> **TIP** To rerun the last filter you used, just press ⌘-F (Ctrl+F on a PC), and Photoshop will use the exact same settings you used last time (don't expect a dialog box, though). This trick works until you quit Photoshop.

Placing a Photo Inside Text

Ever wonder how designers place an image inside text? It takes *years* of practice. (Just kidding!) They do it by creating a *clipping mask* (see the box on page 126), which takes about 5 seconds. All you need is a photo, a Type layer, and the secret layer stacking order. To create the effect shown in Figure 14-31, follow these steps:

1. **Open a photo and make it editable.**

   Double-click the Background layer in the Layers panel to make it editable, and give the layer a new name if you'd like; then click OK.

2. **Create some text.**

   Press T to grab the Type tool and add some text to your document. It doesn't matter what color the text is (as long as you're able to see it while you're typing); what matters is that you pick a really big, thick font. Figure 14-31 was made using Impact—a display font—at 95 points. Short words work better than longer ones (they're easier to read), and you may want to use all caps so more of the photo shows through.

FIGURE 14-30

Top: By loading the text as a selection before adding the layer mask, the mask takes on the shape of the letters, giving you a safe place to run the filter (otherwise, you'd have to rasterize the Type layer before running it).

Bottom: As you can see in this Layers panel, the Type layer remains unscathed after applying this technique, so you can still change the text's color or size. To change the color, double-click the Type layer and then click the color swatch in either the Options bar or Character panel, as described on page 600. Page 588 explains how to resize text.

Other filters that work well with this technique include the Artistic and Distort sets, along with Torn Edges, all found in the Filter Gallery.

3. **Over in the Layers panel, drag the Type layer *below* the image layer.**

   If the Type layer is *above* the photo layer, this technique won't work.

4. **Clip the photo layer to the Type layer.**

   With the photo layer active, choose Layer→Create Clipping Mask, or press and hold Option (Alt on a PC) while pointing your cursor at the dividing line between the two layers in the Layers panel (when the cursor turns into a square with a down-pointing arrow, click once). The thumbnail of the photo layer scoots to the right and a tiny downward-pointing arrow appears to let you know that it's clipped (masked) to the Type layer directly below it. You should now see the photo peeking through the text.

5. **Add a new Fill layer at the bottom of the layer stack.**

Rather than stare into the checkerboard of a transparent document, add a colorful background (in Figure 14-31, the background is sage green). Choose Layer→New Fill Layer→Solid Color and the Color Picker opens. Choose a color, click OK to close the dialog box, and then drag the new Fill layer to the bottom of your layer stack. To make sure the background goes well with the photo, double-click the Fill layer's thumbnail to reopen the Color Picker, mouse over to your image and click within the photo to snatch a color, and then click OK.

FIGURE 14-31

Placing a photo inside text is one of the easiest Photoshop text tricks, though it looks complicated. Be sure to pick a nice, thick font like Impact (used here) so you can see a good chunk of the photo through the letters.

For even more fun, use layer styles to add a stroke and drop shadow to the Type layer, as shown here.

6. **Use the Move tool to reposition either the photo or the text (see the box on page 123 to learn how to move the layer independently of its mask, or vice versa).**

You're basically done at this point, but feel free to play around with text formatting, layer styles, different fonts, or just sit back and admire your handiwork.

> **TIP** Another neat Photoshop trick is to place text *behind* an object. This technique, in all its step-by-step glory, is detailed on page 118.

Converting Text to a Shape

Last but certainly not least, Photoshop lets you do all kinds of cool things with text that's been converted into a vector shape (for more on shapes, see Chapter 13). Though you can't edit the converted text, what used to be the Type layer turns into a resizable, distortable piece of art or editable path that you can do all kinds of interesting things to.

To convert text into a path or shape, just activate the Type layer in the Layers panel and then choose Type→"Convert to Shape." That's it! This miraculous transformation lets you do any of the following:

- **Edit the letterforms.** Want to add an extra flourish here or a swoosh there? Create a work path from the text and then use the Path Selection tool to twist and pull the letters any which way you like.

- **Apply distort and perspective with Free Transform.** You may have noticed that the Free Transform tool's Distort and Perspective options are grayed out when a Type layer is active, but they're ready for action on a Shape layer. If you've ever wanted to create text that fades into the distance in proper perspective, here's your chance.

- **Rotate individual letters.** Instead of creating each letter on its own layer and rotating them individually, you can convert the word into a vector shape layer first, and then use the Path Selection tool to grab one letter at a time and rotate them with Free Transform, as shown in Figure 14-32. Graphic designers *love* doing this kind of thing.

- **Creating intersecting or intertwining text.** Once you've converted text to a vector shape layer, you have the full arsenal of drawing tools at your disposal, including the ever-useful Exclude Overlapping Shape Areas button, whose effect is shown in Figure 14-32. (For more on using Photoshop's drawing tools, see Chapter 13.)

- **Scale to infinity—and beyond!** Because the letter shapes are vectors, you don't have to worry about jagged edges. So after you've performed one of the techniques in this list, feel free to resize the text using Free Transform without fear of losing quality.

- **Enjoy stress-free printing.** That's right: You can send the file off to a professional printer (or to an inkjet printer, for that matter) without a care in the world. By converting text to a shape, you don't have to worry about including the original fonts or about how the text will print.

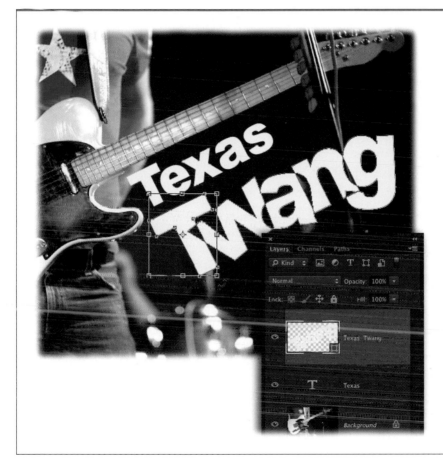

FIGURE 14-32

This effect was created by converting the text (Arial Black) into a shape and then spinning each letter individually using Free Transform. Don't forget to press Return—Enter on a PC—when you're done rotating each letter.

For added fun, you can use the Path Selection tool to move each letter so they overlap just a touch. Next, use the same tool to select all the letters and then click the Path Operations icon in the Options bar (it looks like two overlapping squares) and choose Exclude Overlapping Shape Areas. This makes the color disappear from the overlapping areas, letting the image show through. To tweak the text's color, double-click the Shape layer's thumbnail to open the Color Picker.

■ More Typographic Resources

This book is by no means the be-all and end-all on typography and fonts. To learn more about finding, identifying, and buying fonts, crack open a nice bottle of wine and check out some of the following resources:

- *www.DesignToolsMonthly.com*. The executive summary for graphic designers, this 12-page publication has been around for over 20 years and it's chock-full of design tips and features a slew of fonts each month. (You can even download a free sample issue.)

- *The Non-Designer's Type Book, Second Edition*, by Robin Williams (Peachpit Press, 2005). This book is an easy read and well worth the time; you'll learn more than you ever wanted to know about typography.

- *Fonts & Encodings* by Yannis Haralambous (O'Reilly, 2007) is a priceless resource. If you've ever wondered how our current font situation came to be, or how and why fonts work the way they do, you'll enjoy this tome.

- *www.Helveticafilm.com*. Visit this site for a feature-length film about typography and graphic design made in celebration of the Helvetica font's 50th birthday in 2007. It's fascinating!

- *www.fonts.com*. Hands down the Internet's number one resource for all things font related.

- *www.myfonts.com*. Another great site, which features a font-identification service called WhatTheFont. Just send them an image of some text and they'll tell you the closest matching font. How cool is that?

- *www.fontsite.com*. To get professional fonts at a fraction of their usual price, this is the place to go.

- *www.macworld.com/channels/create.html*. Jay Nelson, founder and publisher of DesignToolsMonthly.com, writes a column for *Macworld* magazine wherein he discusses all manner of font features and type-related news. Just visit this URL and type *Jay Nelson* into the search field near the top of the page to find 'em.

The Wide World of Filters

Photoshop's filters let you create a *multitude* of special effects that you can apply to images or use to conjure interesting backgrounds. You can run filters on image layers, masks, channels, Smart Objects, Shape layers, and even Type layers (provided you convert them into Smart Objects or rasterize 'em first). The list of special effects you can create by applying filters once, twice, or even 10 times is a mile long. There are a bunch of the little critters too, each with its own special brand of pixel wrangling. While Photoshop CS6's Filter menu *appears* to have fewer items than in previous versions—the result of a filter reorganization that you'll either love or loathe—it also includes several *new* filters sure to delight designers and photographers alike.

You've already seen a few filters in action, like the ones for sharpening, blurring, adding texture to text, mapping one image to the contours of another, and so on. But that's just a tiny sliver of what's available. In this chapter, you'll be *immersed* in the realm of filters and discover how you can use 'em to do all kinds of fun and useful stuff. But before you start plowing through the Filter menu, you need to know how to use filters in ways that won't harm your original images. That means learning to use Smart Filters. Onward, ho!

> **TIP** To rerun the last filter you used with the same settings, press ⌘-F (Ctrl+F on a PC). (To summon the filter's dialog box so you can adjust its settings before running it, press Option-⌘-F [Alt+Ctrl+F] instead). You can also click the Filter menu, where the last filter shows up as the first item in the list.

■ The Joy of Smart Filters

Filters, by their very nature, are destructive—they move, mangle, distress, and distort pixels like you wouldn't believe, and they *always* run on the currently active layer (or active selection). Before Photoshop CS3, the only way to protect your image—and retain *any* level of editing flexibility—was to *duplicate* the image layer first and then run the filter on the copy. That way, you could lessen the filter's effect by reducing the duplicate layer's opacity or hide the filter from parts of the image using a layer mask. However, as you know from Chapter 3, duplicating layers can bloat your Layers panel, and then there's the *extra* step of adding a layer mask. Yuck.

Then along came Photoshop CS3 with its nifty *Smart Filters*. If you convert a layer into a Smart Object (page 128) first, you can make the filter run on its *own* layer, complete with blend mode and opacity controls. It even comes with a layer mask.

Smart Filters are the best thing since sliced bread, but unfortunately a few filters—Liquify, Vanishing Point, and Lens Blur, as well as CS6's new Field, Iris, and Tilt-Shift blurs—will run only on regular *image* layers (ones that haven't been converted to Smart Objects). To use one of those filters, just do things the old-fashioned way: Duplicate your image layer and then run the filter on the copy. Smart Filters are also picky about which color mode your image is in; for instance, not all of 'em work in CMYK or Lab mode, but since you spend most of your time in RGB mode, anyway, that isn't a huge deal.

> **TIP** If you can't use a Smart Filter and you forgot to duplicate your image layer before running a filter, you can lessen the filter's strength and change its blend mode by choosing Edit→Fade—but you have to run this command before you do *anything* else, or it won't be available. Flip back to the box on page 464 for the skinny on using the Fade command.

When Smart Filters *are* an option, they're the only way to roll, and using them couldn't be easier: All you have to do is open an image, activate the layer you want to work on, and choose Filter→"Convert for Smart Filters." You'll get a friendly message letting you know that Photoshop is about to turn the active layer into a Smart Object, to which you should reply with a resounding OK. (You'll probably want to turn on the "Don't show again" checkbox to keep Photoshop from displaying this message in the future.)

Over in the Layers panel, the image layer now carries the special Smart Object badge at the bottom right of its thumbnail, and the next filter you run will appear *beneath* the Smart Object as if it were a layer of its own (see Figure 15-1). You can run as many filters as you want; they'll just continue to stack up in the Layers panel, much like layer styles. If you need to rearrange their stacking order—say, to keep one from covering up the effect of another—just drag 'em up or down in the Layers panel. To collapse the layer, temporarily hiding any filters you've run and shortening the Layers panel, click the triangle at the far right of the Smart object; click it again to expand the layer (it's labeled in Figure 15-1).

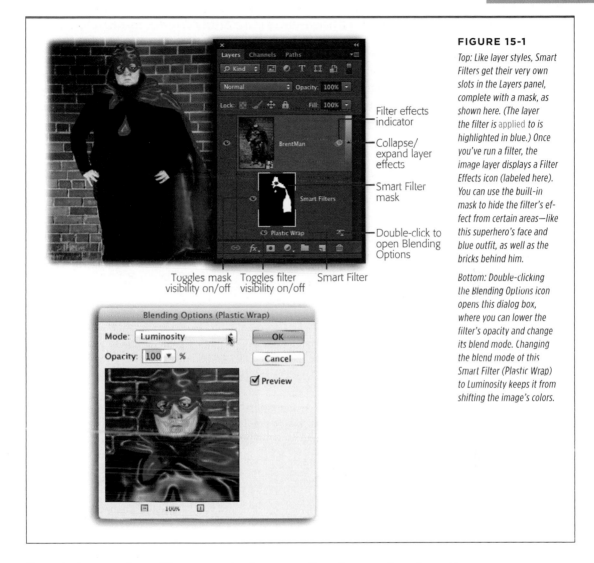

FIGURE 15-1

Top: Like layer styles, Smart Filters get their very own slots in the Layers panel, complete with a mask, as shown here. (The layer the filter is applied to is highlighted in blue.) Once you've run a filter, the image layer displays a Filter Effects icon (labeled here). You can use the built-in mask to hide the filter's effect from certain areas—like this superhero's face and blue outfit, as well as the bricks behind him.

Bottom: Double-clicking the Blending Options icon opens this dialog box, where you can lower the filter's opacity and change its blend mode. Changing the blend mode of this Smart Filter (Plastic Wrap) to Luminosity keeps it from shifting the image's colors.

To apply the same Smart Filters to another layer, copy them from one layer to another by Option-dragging (Alt-dragging on a PC) the Smart Filter layer; you see a ghosted image of the Filter Effects icon beneath your cursor as you drag.

NOTE You can delete a garden-variety layer by activating it and then pressing Delete (Backspace on a PC), but that doesn't work for Smart Filters (or layer styles, for that matter). You have to Ctrl-click (right-click on a PC) the Smart Filter and then choose Delete Smart Filter from the resulting shortcut menu. Alternatively, you can drag the filter layer to the trash or activate the layer, click the trash can icon, and then click OK in the resulting "Are you sure?" dialog box.

■ A Filters Tour

With so many filters to choose from, it can be tough to get a handle on what they all do. That's why several filters—those in the Artistic, Brush Strokes, Distort, Sketch, Stylize, and Texture categories—summon a large dialog box called the Filter Gallery (Figure 15-2) when you choose them from the Filter menu. It has a nice big preview of your image on the left (you can zoom in or out by clicking the + and – buttons below it), a list of *all* the filters in these categories (with cute little preview thumbnails) in the middle, and the specific settings associated with each filter on the right. Sweet!

NOTE Several filters automatically open the Filter Gallery, and while you *can* open it manually by choosing Filter→Filter Gallery, *don't*. If you do, any filter you run gets the generic name of *Filter Gallery* in the Layers panel. To make Photoshop name the filter properly, choose its name from the Filter menu and let *it* open the Filter Gallery instead. For more on this filter-naming conundrum, see the box on page 637.

Once the Filter Gallery opens, you can test drive a filter by clicking its name and then tweaking its settings; Photoshop updates your image preview accordingly. You can even run additional filters *while* you're in the Filter Gallery by clicking the "New effect layer" button at the bottom right (Photoshop includes each filter in the list above this button). You can also delete individual filters you've added by clicking the tiny trash can icon.

NOTE Not *all* of Photoshop's filters are listed in the Filter Gallery, so don't let that throw you; you can choose the others straight from the Filter menu. If the Filter has three dots after its name in the Filter menu, it summons a dialog box that lets you tweak various settings; if it doesn't have dots, the sucker just *runs*.

Throughout this chapter, you'll learn how to use at least one filter in each filter category (they're listed in the order they appear in the *long* version of the Filter menu—see the box on page 637 to learn how to repopulate it). You can think of this as a Filter's Greatest Hits Tour, as a *complete* listing of an example of every filter would swell this book to *War and Peace* proportions. So grab your favorite beverage, sit back, and read on to discover the wide world of filters.

Adaptive Wide Angle

This new filter fixes distortion problems commonly found in photos shot with a wide-angle or fish-eye lens, as well as panoramas. For example, some lenses distort images so that tall buildings appear to *bend* toward a vanishing point in the sky (called *pincushion distortion*, where lines bend inward), or make people, objects, and horizon lines look bowed, as shown in Figure 15-3 (called *barrel distortion*, where lines bend outward). And sometimes the problem isn't the lens but your sense of balance—maybe you accidentally tilted the camera vertically or horizontally, making a lake or ocean look like it's running downhill instead of staying level (called *perspective distortion*).

Photoshop's new Adaptive Wide Angle filter can fix all of these problems quickly and easily, and you don't have to spend a ton of time tweaking settings to use it.

If Photoshop can figure out which lens you used to take the shot (it probably can if you're using fairly recent equipment), all you have to do is draw a line across the part of the image that needs fixing and Photoshop takes care of the rest.

NOTE You can give this new filter a try by downloading the practice file *Horseshoe.jpg* from this book's Missing CD page at *www.missingmanuals.com/cds*.

FIGURE 15-2

The Filter Gallery makes it easy to zip through most filters to get a quick idea of what they do. (Heck, with the right music and snacks, filter browsing can make for an entertaining evening!)

Here you can see what the Film Grain filter looks like on a superhero wannabe.

Choose preview zoom percentage
Zoom in/out of preview
Create new effect layer
Delete effect layer

WORKAROUND WORKSHOP

Repopulating the Filter Menu

In Photoshop CS6, Adobe pruned the Filter menu by removing some categories that also live in the Filter Gallery. While this makes for a *much* shorter Filter menu, it also makes keeping track of *which* filters you've run in a document a bit of a challenge. For example, if you choose Filter→Filter Gallery and then run any filter on a Smart Object, instead of listing the specific name of the filter in the Layers panel (Plastic Wrap, say), Photoshop just lists its name as "Filter Gallery." This is the exact *opposite* of helpful.

Since you can't double-click a Smart Filter's name in the Layers panel to rename it, the only solution is to make

Photoshop list *all* its filters in the Filter menu by changing its Plug-Ins preferences (technically, filters are plug-ins). To do that, choose Photoshop→Preferences→Plug-Ins (Edit→Preferences→Plug-Ins on a PC), turn on the "Show all Filter Gallery groups and names" checkbox, and then click OK. After that, the Filter menu will be longer and you'll see accurate filter names in the Layers panel. This chapter describes filters in the order they appear in the *long* version of the Filter menu, so go ahead and turn this option on.

Apparently to take one step forward you sometimes have to take *two* steps back.

NOTE You can use this filter on Smart Objects *and* when you're recording actions, which is handy if you've got several photos distorted in the same way. (See Chapter 18 for more on actions).

To use it, open an image and duplicate your image layer or choose Filter→"Convert for Smart Filters." Then choose Filter→Adaptive Wide Angle and Photoshop opens the giant Adaptive Wide Angle dialog box and tries to find a lens profile—a detailed set of info about common lenses—for your camera (it knows what kind of equipment you used because of the image's *metadata*). If it locates one, it sets the Correction pop-up menu on the right side of the window to Auto. (The chances of Photoshop finding your lens profile are good because its database is updated constantly; if it *can't* find one, the next paragraph explains what to do.) Next, mouse over to the area that needs fixing and click once to mark the point where the distortion begins. (For example, in Figure 15-3, top, the horizon is bowed, so you'll want to click the horizon's far left edge.) Then move your cursor to the *end* of the distortion and click again to set an end point (the horizon's far right edge, in this example). The thin blue line that appears between the points is called a *constraint*. As soon as you click to set the end point, Photoshop adjusts the image according to the curvature of the constraint (Figure 15-3, bottom). Click OK to apply the changes to your image and close the dialog box.

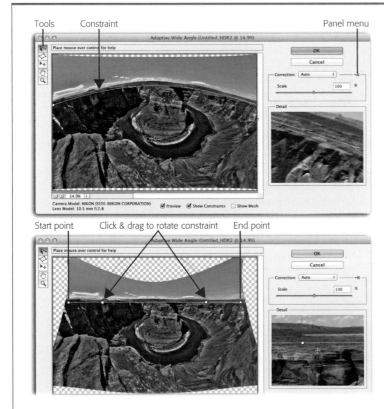

Tools   Constraint   Panel menu

Start point   Click & drag to rotate constraint   End point

FIGURE 15-3

Top: Wide-angle and fish-eye lenses are great for exaggerating the depth and relative size of an object or scene, though you usually end up with some straight areas that look curved, as in this photo of Horseshoe Bend by Karen Nace (www. karennace.com).

Bottom: If Photoshop can find your lens profile, it can fix an image like this in just two quick clicks. If you've clicked to set a start point and then decide to delete it, just press the Esc key. If you've already created a constraint and you press Esc, Photoshop asks if you're sure you want to close the dialog box without saving your changes.

Click the Don't Save button to close the dialog box without applying any changes, click Cancel to return to the Adaptive Wide Angle dialog box for more editing, or click Save to close the dialog box and apply your changes.

If Photoshop *can't* find a lens profile, pick the type of lens you used from the Adaptive Wide Angle dialog box's Correction pop-up menu. Your choices are Fisheye, Perspective, and Full Spherical (think 360-degree panoramas). Photoshop then analyzes the metadata embedded in the image and tries to figure out the image's *focal length* (which determines the angle of view and how much the subject is magnified in relation to your camera's location) and *crop factor* (the level of magnification of your digital camera's sensor in relation to a 35 mm full-frame sensor). If it can't, Focal Length and Crop Factor sliders appear on the right side of the dialog box so you can adjust them manually.

Straight from the factory, the Adaptive Wide Angle filter produces irregularly shaped images that are smaller than the original and that are scaled to fit the area where you placed constraints (see Figure 15-3, bottom). To change the image's size to, say, end up with a larger image so there's less transparency to fill in or crop out, drag the Scale slider to the right or enter a percentage in the Scale field (drag the slider left to make the image smaller).

In the upper-left corner of the Adaptive Wide Angle dialog box, you'll find the following tools:

- **Constraint tool.** Photoshop activates this tool automatically when you first open the Adaptive Wide Angle dialog box. Use this tool to set as many constraints as you need to in order to correct your image. For example, click where the distortion begins and then mouse over to where the distortion ends and click again, and Photoshop adjusts the distortion along the constraint to straighten your image. To create a new constraint with a start point near or atop an existing one, press and hold ⌘ (Ctrl on a PC) while you click. To create a horizontal or vertical constraint, press and hold the Shift key after you set a start point (when you go past 45-degrees, the resulting line is yellow for horizontal or magenta for vertical). To delete a constraint, click one of its points and press Delete (Backspace on a PC), or Option-click (Alt-click) the point itself. To move a constraint, point your cursor at the start or end point (it turns into little crosshairs) and then drag it to a new location. Keyboard shortcut: C.

> **TIP** To change the color of the constraints or mesh, choose Preferences from the Adaptive Wide Angle dialog box's panel menu and then click the colored swatches in the resulting dialog box.

- **Polygon Constraint tool.** Use this tool to create a polygonal constraint instead of a straight or curved one (useful when fixing 360-degree panoramas). Click once to set a start point, and keep adding additional points as needed. To close the polygon, click the start point. Keyboard shortcut: Y.

TIP To save a constraint so you can use it again later (if you've got more photos from the same shoot that need fixing, say), choose Save Constraint from the Adaptive Wide Angle dialog box's panel menu and then give the constraint a meaningful name in the resulting Save dialog box (Photoshop gives it the file extension .wac). You can also import a constraint (perhaps one you created on another machine or one made by a colleague) by choosing Load Constraint from the same menu. In the resulting Load Constraints dialog box, navigate to where the .wac file lives on your hard drive and then click Open.

- **Move tool.** If you increase the Scale setting, part of your image will extend past the edges of the preview area so they won't get fixed. If that happens, you can use this tool to click and drag the important bits of your image back into the preview area so Photoshop can fix them. Keyboard shortcut: M.

- **Hand tool.** This tool lets you move around within the image after you've zoomed in using the Zoom tool (discussed next). Just drag within the preview area to view another part of the image. Keyboard shortcut: H.

- **Zoom tool.** This tool lets you change your view of the image (it's completely unrelated to image scale, discussed earlier). Simply click the image to zoom in on it, or click and drag to draw a box around part of your image to zoom in on just that area; then Option-click (Alt-click on a PC) to zoom back out. You can also use the Zoom controls at the bottom left of the dialog box to do the same thing (they're shown in Figure 15-3, top), or press ⌘ (Ctrl on a PC) and the + or - key. Once you zoom in past 100 percent, you can press and hold the X key to temporarily double the zoom percentage. Keyboard shortcut: Z.

These additional options are at the bottom of the dialog box:

- **Preview.** This checkbox is on from the factory, so you see a preview of the results using your current settings and constraints in real time. To see your original image instead, simply turn it off. Keyboard shortcut: P.

- **Show Constraints.** This setting is turned on automatically whenever the Constraint tool is active. Turn it off to temporarily hide the constraints so you can better see your image.

- **Show Mesh.** This checkbox places a green mesh atop your image preview and shows you exactly how your image will be warped, twisted, and turned in order for it to be fixed according to the constraints you've set.

Lens Correction

Back in Photoshop CS5, the Lens Correction filter got a *major* overhaul. Not only can you use this filter to fix all kinds of weirdness that can be caused by camera lenses (see the box on page 642), but you can also use it to *add* a dark-edge vignette effect that can beautifully frame a portrait (see Figure 15-4). Here's how:

1. **Pop open a portrait and choose Filter→"Convert for Smart Filters."**

   Alternatively you can open the image as a Smart Object by choosing File→"Open as Smart Object."

2. **Choose Filter→Lens Correction.**

   Photoshop opens the petite (ha!) Lens Correction dialog box.

FIGURE 15-4

Even a little thing like softly darkening an image's edges can make a huge difference, especially in portraits. Notice how the dark edges draw your eyes to the pint-sized superhero.

This technique is also handy to use with a sepia tone (page 315) to produce an aged photo look.

3. **Click the Custom tab and adjust the Vignette amount.**

Near the top right of the dialog box are two tabs: Auto Correction and Custom. Click the Custom tab and then, toward the middle of the tab, grab the Vignette section's Amount slider and drag it all the way left; Photoshop softly darkens the edges of the image. Then, to widen the darkening, drag the Midpoint slider left to about 30, as shown in Figure 15-4.

4. **Click OK and then save the document as a PSD file so you can edit it again later.**

See how fast that was? If, after admiring your handiwork, you decide the effect is a little too dark, mouse over to the Layers panel, double-click the icon to the right of the words "Lens Correction" to open the Blending Options dialog box, and then lower the Opacity setting slightly. In most cases, though, full strength looks just fine. If the edge vignette affects part of your subject's face, you can always use the Smart Filter mask to hide it from that area (see page 634).

UP TO SPEED

Fixing Lens Distortion

No matter what kind of image-editing voodoo you've got up your sleeve, you can't hide the quality of your camera's lens. Some potential problems include a darkening in the corners of images called *vignetting*, or a weird color fringe along an object's edges called *chromatic aberration*. Luckily, the Lens Correction filter can fix these problems (that is, if your image is 8- or 16-bit and in RGB or Grayscale mode only).

Choose Filter→Lens Correction and Photoshop updates its database of lens profiles and opens the Lens Correction dialog box with the Auto Correction tab activated. This tab is where you tell Photoshop what kind of problem you have. If Photoshop figures out what camera and lens you used, just turn on the checkbox for the kind of problem your image has: Geometric Distortion (a deformation of the image in a uniform manner), Chromatic Aberration, or Vignette. If it can't find your camera and lens, then these checkboxes boxes are grayed out.

In that case, use the tab's Search Criteria section to tell Photoshop what equipment you used to capture the image. Pick your camera's make, model (this one doesn't have to match exactly), and lens model from the pop-up menus. If Photoshop finds a matching profile, it appears in the Lens Profiles section below. To see all the profiles for a specific brand, choose it from the Camera Make pop-up menu, and then set the other two menus to All. If Photoshop doesn't find a match, click the Search Online button at the bottom of the tab. You can also click the Lens Profiles section's panel menu and then choose Browse Adobe Lens Profile Creator Online, which also lets you create custom profiles. To snag an online profile so you can use it when you don't have an Internet connection, choose Save Online Profile Locally from the panel menu.

Once you find the right (or close-enough) lens profile, give it a click and then use the checkboxes toward the top of the tab to let Photoshop know what kind of problems your image has (you can turn on multiple checkboxes). Photoshop uses the info in the lens profile to fix the problem the moment you click a checkbox. To learn how to create your own lens profile, visit *www.lesa.in/createlensprofile*.

If fixing the image will cause it to expand or shrink beyond its original size, leave the Auto Scale Image checkbox turned on and then use the Edge pop-up menu to tell Photoshop what to do with any resulting blank edges: It can fill the empty spots with transparency or black or white pixels, or enlarge the image to fill the edges (choose Edge Extension).

Liquify

The amazingly powerful Liquify filter lets you push, pull, stretch, bloat, and pinch pixels manually. It's mainly good for reshaping facial features or entire bodies in order to change reality, and that's why it's covered in Chapter 10 beginning on page 428.

Oil Paint

If you've ever wanted to turn a photo into a painting, you can use the new Oil Paint filter to create a fairly realistic piece of art incredibly fast. (This filter used to be part of the optional Pixel Bender plug-in, but now it's built right in to CS6's Filter menu.) This filter is fun to use and it does a surprisingly good job of making your photo look painted *without* you having to make a single brushstroke.

Once you've duplicated the image layer or converted the original layer for Smart Filters, choose Filter→Oil Paint and the dialog box in Figure 15-5 appears. The sliders in the Brush section let you adjust the stylization, cleanliness, and scale of your brushstrokes, along with the level of detail in the brush's bristles (a higher number increases bristle stiffness for deeper-looking brushstrokes). The sliders in the Lighting section let you adjust the direction of the light and control how shiny the reflections are. Each change you make is instantly reflected in the large preview area on the left.

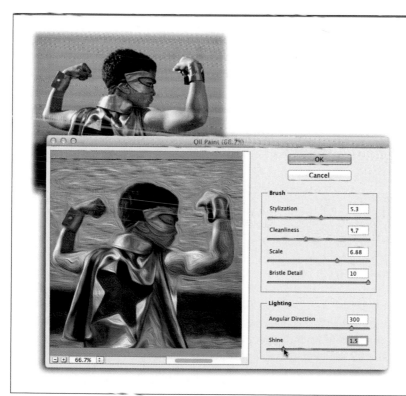

FIGURE 15-5

To quickly create a painting from this photo, reach for the new Oil Paint filter. If you run it on a Smart Object and then save the document as a PSD file, you can tweak the filter's settings anytime by simply double-clicking the Oil Paint filter in the Layers panel to reopen the dialog box shown here. Sweet!

Try this technique for yourself by downloading the file Superkid.jpg *from this book's Missing CD page at www.missingmanuals.com/cds.*

When you're finished, click OK and then save the document as a PSD file so you can go back and edit the filter's settings later. This is serious editing flexibility that you just can't get in the real world. Be sure to give this filter a spin on inanimate objects like flowers, rocks, and landscapes, too; you'll be amazed at the results.

Vanishing Point

During your illustrious Photoshop career, there will be times when you need to edit an object so it appears in proper perspective (meaning it seems to get smaller as it disappears into the distance). Here are a few situations where you'll likely run into perspective problems:

- If you need to affix a graphic or text to any surface that's not flat, like an image of a book cover, a cereal box, or a DVD case that's positioned at an angle to the camera.

- If you need to clone an object that's on a wall or on top of a table.

- If you want to make a building or other structure look taller than it really is.

This kind of editing is a real challenge because Photoshop sees everything as flat, with no perspective at all. The fix is to use the Vanishing Point filter to draw *perspective planes*—a mesh grid that automatically conforms your edits to the perspective of the planes you create—*before* you start painting or cloning. After you draw the grid in the Vanishing Point dialog box (Figure 15-6, top), you can do your editing on the grid inside the dialog box, too. While you're there, you can create a selection, copy and paste an image or text, or use the Clone Stamp or Brush tool, all in perfect perspective.

Here's how to paste one image on top of another in proper perspective:

1. **Select and copy the object you want to paste (for example, the cartoon superhero in Figure 15-6, bottom).**

   Open the image, select the object using one of the techniques in Chapter 4, and then press ⌘-C (Ctrl+C) to copy it. (If you've added a layer mask to the image to make its background transparent, you need to apply the mask *before you copy it*. Since this maneuver deletes the mask, duplicate that layer first by pressing ⌘-J (Ctrl+J) to keep the mask intact in case you need to edit it later. Then, on the duplicate layer, Control-click [right-click on a PC] the mask thumbnail and choose Apply Mask.)

2. **Open the image you want to add the copied image *to* and create a new layer.**

   You can't run Vanishing Point as a Smart Filter, so it runs on the currently active layer. To run this filter nondestructively, you either have to duplicate the image layer or add a *new* layer, depending on what you want to do.

   For example, if you're going to use the Brush or Clone Stamp tool, duplicate the image layer by pressing ⌘-J (Ctrl+J) so you don't harm the original. If, on the other hand, you're pasting another object *into* this document—as in this exercise—you need to create a new layer for the pasted object to land on (because the pasting happens *inside* the filter's dialog box, and not in the Photoshop document), so click the "Create a new layer" button at the bottom of the Layers panel (in Figure 15-7, this new layer is named "perspective hero"). Since the new layer is transparent, you can see through it to the layer below—the original image layer—that you'll use as a guide when you draw your perspective plane in step 4.

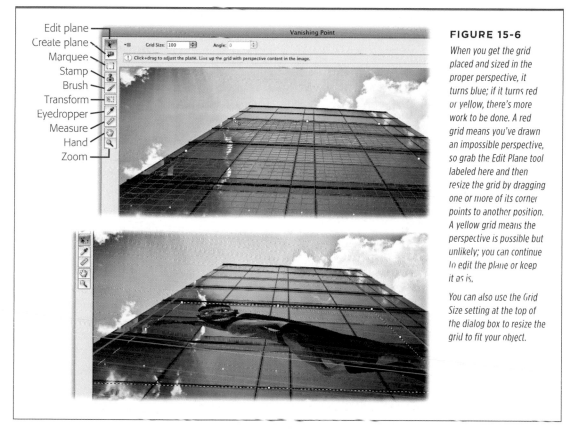

Edit plane
Create plane
Marquee
Stamp
Brush
Transform
Eyedropper
Measure
Hand
Zoom

FIGURE 15-6

When you get the grid placed and sized in the proper perspective, it turns blue; if it turns red or yellow, there's more work to be done. A red grid means you've drawn an impossible perspective, so grab the Edit Plane tool labeled here and then resize the grid by dragging one or more of its corner points to another position. A yellow grid means the perspective is possible but unlikely; you can continue to edit the plane or keep it as is.

You can also use the Grid Size setting at the top of the dialog box to resize the grid to fit your object.

3. **Choose Filter→Vanishing Point or press Option-⌘-V (Alt+Ctrl+V).**

   Photoshop opens the *huge* Vanishing Point filter dialog box.

4. **Use the Create Plane tool to draw your perspective plane.**

   Happily, Photoshop automatically activates the Create Plane tool when you open the Vanishing Point dialog box. Just click once in the image to set the first corner point of your plane (in this example, the building). Next, mouse over to the next corner point and click it, and then mouse to the third corner point and click it; when you do, Photoshop places a blue grid over the area as shown in Figure 15-6 (top). If you have trouble seeing where to click to add corner points, zoom into your image by holding the X key.

5. **Use the Edit Plane tool to position and tweak the grid.**

Once you've drawn the grid, Photoshop automatically activates the Edit Plane tool so you can resize the grid and/or reposition corner points by dragging the white square handles that appear. To extend the bottom of the grid to make it larger, grab the white square handle at the bottom center of the grid and drag it downward. To move the *whole* grid, click inside it and then drag it to another position.

> **TIP** If you need to draw more than one perspective plane in your image (if you have two similar buildings to work on, say), you can copy a plane to another area by Option-dragging (Alt-dragging on a PC) it. If you're working with an object that has more than one side and you need to make the grid wrap around it (like a book cover and its spine), you can ⌘-drag (Ctrl-drag) one of the grid points (it doesn't matter which one) to tear off another plane that you can position at an angle.

6. **Paste the object you copied back in step 1 and drag it on top of the plane.**

Press ⌘-V (Ctrl+V) to paste the object into the Vanishing Point dialog box. At first, the object appears flat (not in perspective) and is surrounded by marching ants, but when you click and drag it on top of the plane, it twists and distorts to conform to the perspective you've drawn. (If you're working with an image that includes a layer mask and you forgot to *apply* it back in step 1, the pasted object won't be transparent. If that happens, press the Esc key to close the Vanishing Point dialog box and, unfortunately, start over.)

7. **If you need to resize the object you just pasted, press T to summon a resizable bounding box.**

Photoshop puts a bounding box around the object. To resize it proportionately, hold the Shift key as you drag one of the box's corner handles. (If the object is bigger than the plane, you can't *see* the handles because they're beyond the edges of the grid. In that case, click the object and drag it in one direction or another until you can see one of the handles, and then drag the handle inward to make the object smaller.) If you need to move the pasted image, click inside it and then drag it to another position. When you're finished, click OK to close the dialog box and Photoshop adds the image onto the new layer you created in step 2.

> **TIP** Interestingly, you're allowed to perform *multiple* undos when you're in the Vanishing Point dialog box—just keep pressing ⌘-Z (Ctrl+Z) and Photoshop keeps undoing the last thing you did. To *redo* the last thing you did, press Shift-Z instead.

8. **In the Layers panel, change the blend mode of the pasted image layer to Soft Light.**

This blend mode makes the superhero's colors blend better with the colors in the building, as shown in Figure 15-7.

FIGURE 15-7

As you learned back on page 288, the Soft Light blend mode is great for creating reflections.

At the top of the Layers panel, you see two layers with their visibility turned off. Since the hero image had a white background, a layer mask was used to hide it; however, the Vanishing Point dialog box doesn't understand masks, so you have to apply it to the image (here that layer is named "hero mask applied"). By duplicating the layer with the mask (here that layer is named "hero mask") before you apply it, you keep the mask intact in case you need to edit it later. Turning off the visibility of those extra layers keeps them from getting in your way.

Here's what the other tools on the left side of the Vanishing Point dialog box are for:

- The **Marquee tool** (keyboard shortcut: M) lets you draw a selection (in perspective) to duplicate an area inside the plane; for example, if you want to make a building taller, you can use this tool to select and then duplicate the top few floors. Or you can use the Marquee tool to restrict the effect of the Stamp and Brush tools (discussed later in this list) to a specific area of your image. You can use the options at the top of the dialog box to feather the selection so its edges are soft or change the opacity of the object inside your selection (handy if you're moving an object from one area in an image to another).

> **TIP** To select the entire plane, simply double-click the grid with the Marquee tool.

If you're copying the selection to another area, use the Heal pop-up menu to determine how the selection blends with the area you're dragging it to. Your options are Off (no blending), Luminance (Photoshop blends the selected pixels

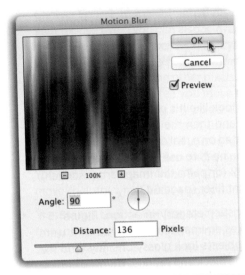

FIGURE 15-8

Applying a Motion Blur to this super family makes it look like they're taking flight. To keep their heads in focus, a stroke of the Brush tool (set to paint with black) was added to the Smart Filter mask.

To try this yourself, download the file Superfamily.jpg from this book's Missing CD page at www.missingmanuals.com/cds.

■ FIXING COLOR FRINGE

You can also use Photoshop's blur filters to eliminate *color fringe*—that slight blue or purple haze loitering around the edges of near-black objects (Figure 15-9, bottom left). The color-fringe problem is especially common when you shoot something really dark on a light background (like black numbers on a white clock face). The image may look OK at a glance, but a closer inspection often reveals some serious bluish or purplish fringing (also called *artifacts*) around the dark objects.

TIP You can also remove color fringe with the Lens Correction Filter. See the box on page 642 to learn how.

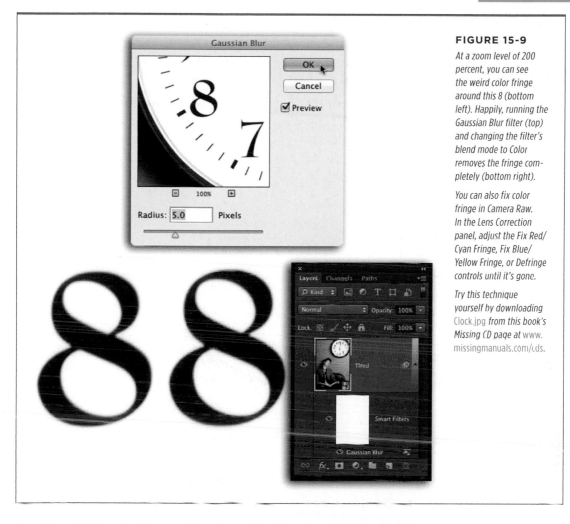

FIGURE 15-9

At a zoom level of 200 percent, you can see the weird color fringe around this 8 (bottom left). Happily, running the Gaussian Blur filter (top) and changing the filter's blend mode to Color removes the fringe completely (bottom right).

You can also fix color fringe in Camera Raw. In the Lens Correction panel, adjust the Fix Red/Cyan Fringe, Fix Blue/Yellow Fringe, or Defringe controls until it's gone.

Try this technique yourself by downloading Clock.jpg from this book's Missing CD page at www.missingmanuals.com/cds.

Here's how to fix color fringe with a dose of the Gaussian Blur filter:

1. **Open the problem image and activate the layer you want to work with.**

2. **Choose Filter→"Convert to Smart Filters."**

3. **Choose Filter→Blur→Gaussian Blur and then adjust the filter's settings.**

   In the resulting dialog box, enter a Radius of 5 to 7 pixels (this setting controls how much blurring Photoshop applies to the image) and then click OK. Depending on the image's pixel dimensions, you may need to experiment with this value; increase it for larger images and reduce it for smaller ones.

4. **Change the filter's blend mode to Color and Opacity to 96 percent.**

In the Layers panel, double-click the Blending Options icon next to the Gaussian Blur layer and then change the Mode pop-up menu to Color. (As you learned on page 293, the Color blend mode affects only hue, and since your goal is to blur the *colored* pixels—as opposed to the black ones—this mode works perfectly.) Then adjust the Opacity setting to 96 percent to keep the blur from being noticeable.

5. **Click OK when you're finished and then save the document as a PSD file.**

A quick zoom-in reveals that the pesky color fringe has left the building, as shown in Figure 15-9. Saving the document in PSD format ensures that you can edit the image again later if you need to.

■ FIELD BLUR

One of the handiest new features in Photoshop CS6 is the Field Blur filter. It's perfect for creating beautifully blurred backgrounds *after* you've taken a photo (images like this are said to have a *shallow depth of field*). It's a million times easier to use than the Lens Blur filter, and you don't have to select anything before you run it (though you can if you want). Instead, you create the blur by dragging over the image itself, as shown in Figure 15-10.

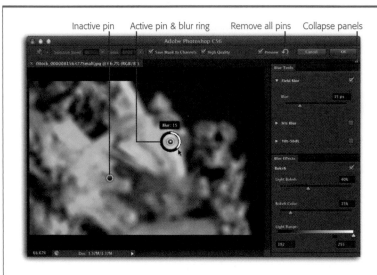

FIGURE 15-10

You can add pins to control exactly which parts of the image are in focus and which parts are blurry. When you add two pins, Photoshop essentially uses a linear gradient mask (page 278) to fade the blur between them. If you add three or more pins, Photoshop constrains the blur so that it affects the vicinity around each pin and extends to about half the distance to the next neighboring pin.

To temporarily hide the blur ring and pins, press and hold the H key.

Try this technique yourself by heading to this book's Missing CD page at www.missingmanuals.com/cds and downloading the practice file Kryptonite.jpg.

Here's how to make an image look like it was shot with a shallow depth of field:

1. **Open an image and duplicate the image layer.**

The new blur filters don't work on Smart Objects, so duplicate the image layer to safeguard your original image. Simply activate the layer and then press ⌘-J (Ctrl+J) to duplicate it. Then double-click its name in the Layers panel and rename it *blur*. If your image is made up of multiple layers, double-click the Background layer (if you have one) to make it editable, and then Shift- or ⌘-/Ctrl-click to activate all the layers that make up the image. Then press and hold the Option (Alt) key and choose Merge Layers from the Layers panel's menu to create a *stamped* layer (page 114) on which you can safely run the filter.

2. **Choose Filter→Blur→Field Blur and adjust the filter's strength.**

   Your Photoshop window changes to include a big image preview on the left and a set of collapsable controls on the right (Figure 15-10). In the image preview, you see a single *pin* (it looks like a dot inside a circle) with a black-and-white *blur ring* around it. The pin controls which part of the image is blurred—one pin makes the whole image blurry—and the blur ring lets you adjust the blur's strength; you see the ring anytime a pin is active (Photoshop activates the initial pin automatically when you run the filter). To *increase* the blur, drag the black part of the ring clockwise (so there's more white than black; solid white is 100 percent blur strength); to *decrease* the blur, drag the black part counter-clockwise (so there's more black than white; solid black is a blur strength of 0 pixels). As you drag, a handy overlay appears showing the blur's strength from 0 to 500 pixels. Alternatively, you can drag the Blur slider on the right side of the window.

3. **Click the image's focal point to add another pin, and then reduce its blur strength to 0 pixels.**

   As you mouse around your image, your cursor looks like a pushpin with a tiny plus sign next to it, indicating that clicking will add a pin. To keep part of your image in focus (like, say, your subject's face), click to add another pin. If you don't get the pin in quite the right spot, just drag it somewhere else. Then use the blur ring (or Blur slider) to reduce the blur's strength to 0 pixels so there's no blurring in that spot.

TIP To delete a pin, click it and then press Delete (Backspace on a PC). To zap *all* the pins in one fell swoop, click the Options bar's "Remove all pins" button (labeled in Figure 15-10).

---

4. **Adjust the settings in the Blur Effects panel to your liking.**

   In the Blur Effects panel on the right side of the window is a group of settings labeled *Bokeh*, which is a Japanese term used to describe the aesthetic quali-ties of out-of-focus highlights (also known as *specular* highlights). Use the Light Bokeh slider to increase the brightness of the out-of-focus areas to make them sparkle (see Figure 15-11, bottom). The Bokeh Color slider changes the highlights from natural color (0 percent) to colorful (100 percent), and the Light Range slider lets you pick *which* lightness values are impacted by the Bokeh settings; just drag the black and white triangular sliders to set a range of colors (a fairly small range of the lighter highlights usually works well). To make Photoshop display a more accurate preview of your changes to the Bokeh settings, turn on the High Quality checkbox in the Options bar.

FIGURE 15-11

As you can see in this before (top) and after example (bottom), the new Field Blur filter can produce nice results. By adjusting the Bokeh settings, you can really make the highlights in these crystals sparkle! It takes some experimenting to get the filter's pins placed correctly and the blur strength just right, but the controls are easy to use.

To bail out of using the Field Blur without applying it to the image, click the Options bar's Cancel button or tap the Esc key on your keyboard.

5. **In the Options bar, turn on the "Save Mask to Channels" checkbox.**

   Once you start adding pins, Photoshop creates a temporary mask that shows/hides the blur as you've specified by placing pins (you don't see or have access to the mask). Turning on the "Save Mask to Channels" option makes Photoshop save the temporary blur mask as an alpha channel (page 201). This is handy when you want to adjust your image or add another effect to it using the exact same mask as you did for blurring (say, to add a bit of noise or grain to make the image look less perfect).

6. **Click OK in the Options bar to apply the filter.**

   As soon as you click OK (or press Return/Enter), the program applies the blur to the currently active layer and switches you back to the regular Photoshop window.

■ IRIS BLUR

For even *more* control over the shape and size of the blur Photoshop applies, use the new Iris Blur filter. You get the same large preview and panels that you do with Field Blur, and the same kind of on-image controls (though more of 'em). To use it, open an image, duplicate the image layer, and then choose Filter→Blur→Iris Blur. (If you're already *in* the Field Blur filter's window, simply head over to the Blur Tools panel on the right side of your screen and click the checkbox next to Field Blur to turn it off, and then click the checkbox next to Iris Blur to turn it on. Click the flippy triangle to its left to expand its options.)

Photoshop places a pin in the center of your image inside an elliptical-shaped blur with a white outline. To move the blur, just drag anywhere inside the blur's outline. To change the blur's strength, use the blur ring as described in the previous section or adjust the Blur slider in the Blur Tools panel. In the Options bar, the Focus setting lets you determine how blurry the area inside the outline is (from the factory, it's set to 100 percent, which means no blur). Figure 15-12 explains how to use the filter's various controls to customize the blur's size and shape.

Active pin with
blur ring   Roundness handle   Feather handles   Size & rotation handles

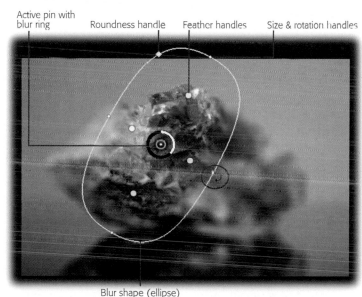

Blur shape (ellipse)

FIGURE 15-12

The Iris Blur filter includes four size handles (they look like tiny dots on the blur outline) that you can drag to change the blur's size. If you position your cursor just outside the blur outline near one of these handles, your cursor turns into a curved, double-sided arrow (circled here) that you can use to rotate the blur.

To adjust the shape of the blur, drag the roundness handle to make the outline rounder or more square. To adjust the feather of the blur's edges, drag one of the four circles inside the blur outline; drag it toward the pin to increase the feather amount or away from the pin to decrease it.

Before

After (with Bokeh applied)

TIP When you drag one feather handle, they *all* move. If you want to move 'em independently of one another, Option-drag (Alt-drag on a PC) instead.

■ TILT-SHIFT

Also new in CS6 is the Tilt-Shift filter, which you can use to mimic a popular tilt lens called Lensbaby (*www.lensbaby.com*), a bendable lens—if you can imagine—that lets you control which part of the picture is in focus. It's a great way to draw the viewer's eye to your subject, but at $150 or more, it's not quite an impulse buy. Fortunately, the Tilt-Shift filter doesn't cost extra. Adding a tilt-shift blur to a bird's-eye view of a cityscape makes the city look miniature. You won't want to use this kind of effect on *every* image, but it can certainly enhance some, especially those with distracting backgrounds.

The Tilt-Shift filter works just like Field and Iris Blur, though you get (you guessed it) even *more* controls. Give this new filter a spin by duplicating your image layer first and then choosing Filter→Blur→Tilt-Shift (or, if you've already got Field Blur or Iris Blur open, just click the checkbox next to Tilt-Shift in the Blur Tools panel to turn it on and click the other filter's checkboxes to turn them off, and then click the flippy triangle next to Tilt-Shift to reveal its options). Either way, Photoshop places an active pin and blur ring in the middle of the image and surrounds 'em with a series of solid and dashed lines that you can use to adjust the size of the in-focus and blurry areas (see Figure 15-13). The Options bar's Focus setting controls how in focus the non-blurry area is; you'll probably want to leave it set to 100 percent for no blur.

NOTE Give the Tilt-Shift Blur filter a spin by downloading *Dubai.jpg* from this book's Missing CD page at *www.missingmanuals.com/cds*.

■ LENS BLUR

The Lens Blur filter is another super useful one. It's been around for several versions of Photoshop, and you can use it to produce effects similar to the ones you get with CS6's new blur filters, though Lens Blur is harder to use. But because it lets you create a blur mask (in the form of an alpha channel) by hand, this filter gives you maximum control and lets you produce extremely accurate and photo-realistic blurring. And in CS6, the Lens Blur filter is faster than ever because it takes advantage of multi-core processors (provided your computer *has* more than one). Here's how to use it:

1. **Open an image and the Channels panel.**

   To tell Photoshop which part of the image to blur and which part should stay in focus, you need to create a selection that the Lens Blur filter can use. An easy way to do that is by adding an alpha channel (page 202), which you'll do in the next step. To get started, open the Channels panel by clicking its tab in the Layers panel's group or by choosing Window→Channels.

2. **Create a new alpha channel.**

Click the New Channel icon at the bottom of the Channels panel. Then, at the top of the panel, click the visibility eye next to the RGB channel (a.k.a. the composite channel). Your entire image takes on the Quick Mask mode's red overlay, which lets you create your selection. Don't worry: The red overlay is temporary—your image won't end up pink.

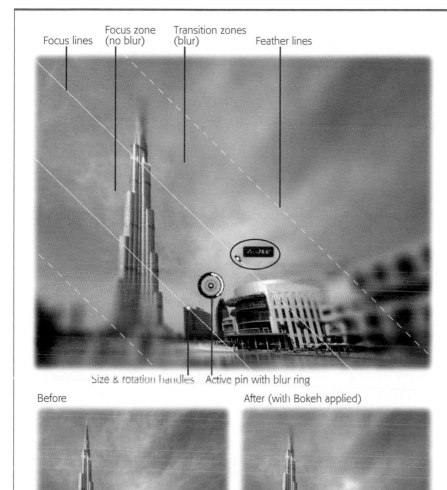

Focus lines · Focus zone (no blur) · Transition zones (blur) · Feather lines

Size & rotation handles · Active pin with blur ring

Before

After (with Bokeh applied)

FIGURE 15-13

The various lines that appear when you summon the Tilt-Shift filter control different things. The area between the two solid lines is in focus (though you can change that by adjusting the Options bar's Focus setting). The area between a solid line and a dashed line is partially blurred, and the area beyond the dashed lines is completely blurred. Drag anywhere on any of these lines to adjust an area's size by dragging up or down. To rotate the blur, point your cursor at one of the two resizing handles and then drag. When you do, Photoshop displays the rotation's angle (circled).

The Distortion slider in the Blur Tools panel on the right side of the window lets you change the shape of the lower blur zone (or, if you've rotated the blur as shown here, the blur zone on the left). Turn on the Symmetric Distortion checkbox to make Photoshop adjust the blur zones on both sides.

TIP For serious fun, try applying several of CS6's new blur filters to the *same* image. While you're applying one of the new filters, you can turn on the others using the checkboxes next to their names in the Blur Tools panel on the right side of your screen.

3. **Grab the Brush tool and set your foreground color chip to white.**

Your goal here is to edit the mask so that the area you want to keep in focus doesn't have any red on it (the red areas will become blurry once you finish this technique). Make sure your color chips are set to black and white (press D if they're not), and press X until white is on top.

4. **Choose a big, soft brush and lower its opacity to 50 percent.**

Hop up to the Options bar and, from the Brush Preset picker, choose a soft brush (one with fuzzy edges) that's fairly big (around 200 pixels). To create a subtle transition from in-focus pixels to blurry ones, lower the brush's opacity to 50 percent (and, while you're up there, make sure Flow is set to 100 percent).

TIP You can also resize the brush by Option-Ctrl-dragging (Alt-right-click-dragging on a PC) left to make it smaller or right to make it bigger. To adjust the brush's hardness, use the same keyboard shortcut but drag vertically instead. New in CS6, brush size, hardness, and opacity info appear next to your cursor as you drag.

5. **Paint across the areas you want to keep in focus.**

In Figure 15-14, top, for example, paint over the boy's face. As you paint, the photo starts to show through just a little, but since you lowered the brush's opacity, you need to keep painting over an area to achieve 100 percent focus. Remember: Anything that's red will be blurry when you're done, and the rest of the image will remain sharp. To create a perfectly sharp area, lower your brush size and paint over that area until all the red is gone. If you mess up and bring back too much of the photo, press X to flip-flop the color chips and paint that area with black to make it red (blurry) again.

6. **Turn off the alpha channel's visibility eye and activate the RGB channel.**

There's no need to leave the alpha channel turned on, so go ahead and hide it by clicking its visibility eye in the Channels panel. Next, click the RGB channel so you can see the full-color version of your image again.

7. **Open the Layers panel and duplicate the original layer.**

Since Lens Blur isn't available as a Smart Filter, the only way to protect your original image is to copy the layer and then run the filter on the copy. Click the image layer to activate it, and then duplicate it by pressing ⌘-J (Ctrl+J).

8. **With the duplicate layer active, choose Filter→Blur→Lens Blur.**

Don't worry that the parts of the image that you want to be blurry are in focus and vice versa; you'll fix that in step 10.

9. **In the Lens Blur dialog box, change the Depth Map section's Source setting to Alpha 1.**

Tell the filter about the alpha channel you created by selecting it from the Depth Map section's Source pop-up menu. Unless you gave it a different name, the channel goes by Alpha 1.

Alpha channel

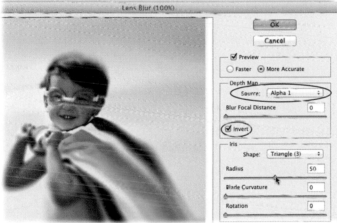

FIGURE 15-14

Top: Since you used an alpha channel to create this effect, you can change the results. If you don't like how the image looks, just toss the duplicate image layer, pop open the Channels panel, grab the Brush tool, and edit the alpha channel. Then repeat steps 6–12 to run the filter again. Nice, eh?

Bottom: When you first run the Lens Blur filter, it does the exact opposite of what you want—it blurs what's supposed to be sharp, and vice versa. To fix that, just turn on the Invert checkbox, circled here.

10. **Turn on the Invert setting.**

    Turning on the Invert checkbox flip-flops the blurry and sharp areas, as shown in Figure 15-14 (bottom).

11. **Adjust the Shape pop-up menu and Radius slider until you get the blur just right.**

    The Shape pop-up menu lets you change the blur's shape, and the Radius slider lets you determine just *how* blurry the background is. Be sure to release your mouse button so Photoshop can generate a new preview.

TIP To make the image look less perfect, you can add a little noise to the blurry bits. At the bottom right of the Lens Blur dialog box, adjust the Noise Amount slider and turn on both the Gaussian radio button and the Monochromatic checkbox.

12. **Click OK when you're finished, and save the document as a PSD file.**

Brush Strokes

There are a slew of filters in this category and, like the Artistic set, they're geared toward creating traditional fine-art effects. If you want to add interesting edge treatments to your images, these filters work especially well when used with layer masks (see Figure 15-15). Among the most useful for these kinds of edge effects are Spatter and Sprayed Strokes (Filter→Brush Strokes→Spatter or Sprayed Strokes).

NOTE If you don't see this category in the Filter menu, flip to the box on page 637 to learn how to adjust your preferences so that it appears.

When you're ready to spice up the edges of an image, take this technique for a spin:

1. **Open a photo and double-click the Background layer to make it editable.**

   Since you'll run the filter on a layer mask, you don't need to use Smart Filters.

NOTE To give this technique a spin, trot on over to this book's Missing CD page at *www.missingmanuals. com/cds* and download *Superchick.jpg*.

2. **Grab the Rectangular Marquee tool and draw a box where you want the new edges to be.**

   For best results, draw the box at least a quarter of an inch in from the edges of your photo as shown in Figure 15-15, left. The filter will run outside this selection, on the edges of the image.

3. **Add a layer mask.**

   At the bottom of the Layers panel, click the circle-within-a-square icon to add a layer mask to the part of the image where you'll apply the filter.

4. **With the layer mask active, choose Filter→Brush Strokes→Spatter.**

   In the resulting Filter Gallery dialog box, increase the Spray Radius to 20 and the Smoothness to 8. (These numbers are purely subjective, so adjust them until they look good to you.)

5. **Click OK to make Photoshop run the filter.**

   If you want to soften the new edges just a bit, you can run an additional filter: Choose Filter→Blur→Gaussian Blur, adjust the blur radius until you get the look you want, and then click OK.

FIGURE 15-15

By drawing a selection around the image (left) and then adding a layer mask (right), you can run the filter on the mask, which makes for some really nice edge effects—without harming the original image. Tack on a well-placed inner shadow for an even more interesting look!

A few other filters that work well for this technique are Glass, Ocean Ripple, Twirl (all found under Filter→Distort), and Torn Edges (Filter→Sketch→Torn Edges).

You can also use the Refine Edge dialog box to give your photo interesting edges. Flip back to page 176 for the scoop.

Because the layer mask hides the edges of the image, you'll see the checkerboard transparency pattern there. To create a new background, add a colored layer *beneath* the image layer by choosing Layer→New Fill Layer→Solid Color, and then dragging it below the image layer. Pick a color from the resulting Color Picker, click OK, and Photoshop adds the new layer. As a final touch, add an inner shadow or a drop shadow to the image by clicking the *fx* at the bottom of the Layers panel. (For more on layer styles, see page 131.)

TIP To reposition either the photo or the frame, you have to unlink the layer from the mask by heading to the Layers panel and clicking the little chain icon between the layer and mask thumbnails. Then click the thumbnail of the layer or mask and reposition it with the Move tool. To link them together again, just click between the two thumbnails and the chain icon reappears.

Distort

The filters in this category, not surprisingly, distort and reshape images. It includes all kinds of goodies like the Displace filter, which lets you apply one image to the contours of another (page 307); the Pinch filter, which is great for shrinking double chins (page 427); and the Glass, Ocean Ripple, and Twirl filters, which work well as edge effects, as you learned in the previous section. (The Lens Correction filter used to be in this category, but Adobe repositioned it back in CS5, so it's covered on page 641.)

Noise

These filters let you add or remove *noise* (graininess or color speckles). If you're working on an extremely noisy image or restoring an old photo, these filters can come in really handy. For example, if you've scanned an old photo that has scratches in it, run the Dust & Scratches filter to make Photoshop scour the image for irregular pixels and blur them to smooth 'em out. Of the filters in this category, you'll likely use the Reduce Noise filter most often; it helps lessen noise in the dark areas of images shot in low light (a good idea before sharpening). The box on page 459 has the scoop.

Sometimes, you may need to *add* noise to an image, as odd as that sounds. For example, if you're working with a portrait that's been corrected to within an inch of its life and it looks *too* perfect (as if it were airbrushed), run the Add Noise filter to introduce some random speckles and make the image look more realistic.

Pixelate

You probably won't use these filters often, but once in a while they're useful for applying funky blurs and textures to images. For example, the Crystallize filter makes an image look like it's behind a textured shower door. And if you're aiming for the newspaper image look (think lots of tiny, visible dots) try the Halftone filter.

Render

These filters can generate cloud patterns, introduce lens flare, and add lighting to images. Two in particular—Clouds and Difference Clouds—are great for creating all kinds of backgrounds, such as the splotchy-colored ones you see in studio portraits. These filters mix your foreground and background colors into what look like soft, fluffy clouds. The more times you apply each filter, the more clouds you get (Difference Clouds gives you clouds with higher contrast). If you run the Motion Blur filter after the Cloud filter, you can create some terrific streaks to make an image look old (see page 532).

> **TIP** A little-known fact about the Lens Flare filter, which lives in this category, is that Option-clicking (Alt-clicking on a PC) in the dialog box's preview lets you reposition the flare and/or enter precise coordinates for it. Who knew?

Another useful filter in this category is Lighting Effects, which in CS6 was *completely* redesigned so it's easier to use and works in 64-bit mode (page 4). This filter, which works only on RGB images, gives you a window with a big preview on the left and a Properties panel on the right (Figure 15-16) where you choose among three kinds of light sources: Point (shines in all directions like a light bulb), Spot (shines in a beam like a flashlight), and Infinite (shines from a distance and is slightly diffused, like sunlight through a cloud).

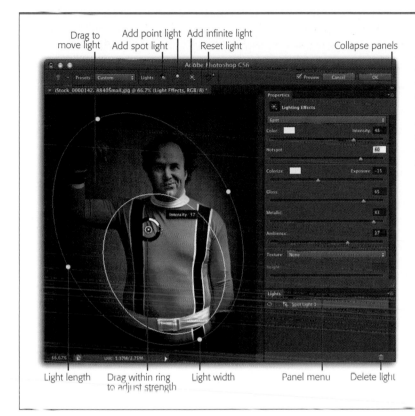

Drag to move light · Add spot light · Add point light · Add infinite light · Reset light · Collapse panels

Light length · Drag within ring to adjust strength · Light width · Panel menu · Delete light

FIGURE 15-16

If you didn't get your subject lit right in the studio, there's a good chance you can fix it here. Click the little light icons in the Options bar (labeled) to add additional light sources. To delete a light, grab its icon in the Lights panel and drag it onto the trash can icon at the bottom right.

Once you choose a kind of light from the unlabeled pop-up menu near the top of the Properties panel, you can adjust its strength with the Intensity field or the slider below it (drag it left to weaken the light or right to strengthen it). To change the light's color, click the colored box to the left of the Intensity field and choose a new color from the resulting Color Picker. For example, instead of adding a stark white light to a portrait, you could change it to light peach or yellow to give the subject a slight warm glow. If you've chosen Spot, you can also adjust the angle of its *hot spot* (the brightest point of light) with the Hotspot slider; drag it left to make the light small and narrow or right to make it tall and wide (Figure 15-16 shows a fairly wide hot spot).

You can find some excellent presets for the Lighting Effects filter in the Options bar's Presets pop-up menu. Once you choose one, you can pick a different type of light (Point, Spot, or Infinite) as mentioned earlier, as well as the following:

- **Exposure.** You can control the total amount of available light with this setting. Drag the slider left to decrease the amount of light or right to increase it. To change the color of the exposure (or color of light), click the colored box to the left of this field and choose another color from the resulting Color Picker.

- **Gloss.** This setting controls how reflective the surface in the image is. For example, if you shine light onto a plain old piece of paper, it doesn't reflect very much. But if you shine light onto a *glossy* piece of paper, the reflection is much greater. Drag this slider left for less reflection or right for more.

- **Metallic.** This setting lets you change the surface the light is reflecting off of. For example, a plastic surface reflects the light's color, while a metallic surface reflects your subject's color. Drag the slider left to make the surface more plastic or right to make it more metallic (anything in between reflects both your light's color and your subject's color).

- **Ambience.** This setting lets you tone down the light source you've been painstakingly creating by mixing in more light from *another* source (as if the sun were also shining in the room or you turned on an overhead light). Drag this slider left to remove the additional light source or right to mix in more light from it.

- **Texture.** You may need to scroll down in the Properties panel to see this pop-up menu, which lets you tell Photoshop to shine the light through your image's red, green, or blue channel information to give your lighting some depth (referred to as a *bump map*). Once you've made a choice in the menu, use the Height slider below it to intensify the effect by dragging it right, or decrease the effect by dragging it left.

TIP To save a light source as a preset so you can use it again later, click the panel menu (labeled in Figure 15-16) and then choose Save Lights Preset. Give your custom light source a memorable name, and then click OK to add it to the Option bar's Presets pop-up menu.

Sharpen

The filters in this category let you exaggerate areas of high contrast in an image (called *edges*) to make them appear sharper. Since resizing and editing an image can make its pixels a little soft, it's a good idea to sharpen each and every image you open in Photoshop. Sharpening is incredibly important and it has the power to make or break an image. That's why you'll find full coverage of these filters in Chapter 11.

Sketch

If you want to add a bit of texture to an image, reach for this category. It includes a variety of filter-driven pens, crayons, paper, and so on that give images a hand-drawn look. The Graphic Pen filter is perfect for adding realistic snow, as shown in Figure 15-17.

NOTE If your Filter menu doesn't include the Sketch category, the box on page 637 tells you how to make it show up.

Here's how to use the Graphic Pen filter to add some realistic-looking flurries:

1. **Open a snowless photo and add a new layer filled with black.**

   As you learned back in Chapter 7, blend modes have various neutral colors that disappear when a particular blend mode is used. If you run the Graphic Pen filter on a solid black layer, you can use a blend mode to make the black disappear, leaving just the streaks made by the filter (which look like snow). To add the black layer, click the "Create a new layer" icon at the bottom of the Layers panel. To fill it with black, choose Edit→Fill, pick Black from the Use pop-up menu, and then click OK. (If this new layer isn't at the top of the layer stack, drag it up so it is.)

2. **With the black layer active, choose Filter→"Convert for Smart Filters."**

   To make the Graphic Pen filter run on this layer, you have to convert it for Smart Filters first.

3. **In the Layers panel, change the black layer's blend mode to Screen (see Figure 15-17, right).**

   As you learned on page 286, the Screen blend mode lightens the underlying photo and completely ignores black, so the snow-like streaks you create in the next step will lighten the photo and the black will disappear.

FIGURE 15-17

Meet the Graphic Pen filter, which generates random streaks in the direction and length you choose, so it's perfect for making fake snow.

To create a visually pleasing snowfall that doesn't completely bury your subject, lower the filter's Stroke Length setting to around 5 and increase the Light/Dark Balance setting to about 90. (If the Stroke Length is too high and the Light/Dark Balance is too low, your subject will look like he's stuck in a blizzard of sleet.)

4. **Choose Filter→Sketch→Graphic Pen.**

Photoshop opens the Filter Gallery dialog box set to the Graphic Pen filter.

5. **On the right side of the dialog box, change the Stroke Direction pop-up menu to Vertical.**

This setting makes the snow fall straight down.

6. **Set the Stroke Length to 5 and the Light/Dark Balance to 90.**

Think of Stroke Length as flake size; lowering it to around 5 creates fairly small flakes. And think of Light/Dark Balance as the amount of snowfall: Set it to 60 for a blizzard or to a higher number (like 90) for light snow (on your own image, you may have to experiment with different settings). When you're done, click OK to close the Filter Gallery dialog box.

7. **Choose Filter→Blur→Gaussian Blur and, in the resulting dialog box, enter a Radius of 1.5.**

This filter softens the snowflakes so they don't have hard edges.

8. **Click OK when you're finished, and save the document as a PSD file.**

The beauty of creating artificial snow using a Smart Filter is that you can control the snow's opacity—if the effect is too strong, just trot over to the Layers panel and double-click the icon to the right of the Graphic Pen Smart Filter and then, in the Blending Options dialog box, lower the Opacity setting. If the snow looks terrible, you can trash the filter and start over. It's lots of fun to add snow to *completely* inappropriate photos, too!

Stylize

This category is also artistic, but its filters let you create looks with more contrast than you can with the Artistic filters. One filter in this category (Emboss, discussed later in this section) can save out-of-focus images. Several of the filters found here enhance the edges in images, and Find Edges does such a good job that you can use it to create a pencil-sketch effect. It's a great technique to have in your bag of tricks because it can single-handedly save an image with color problems that can't be fixed with any of the techniques you learned back in Chapter 9. As a bonus, you create an image with a totally different look and feel from the original, as shown in Figure 15-18. Here's how to use Find Edges to convert a photo into a pencil sketch:

1. **Pop open a photo and add a Black & White Adjustment layer.**

The first step toward a pencil sketch is to get rid of the image's color, which you can do easily with a Black & White Adjustment layer. Click the half-black/half-white circle at the bottom of the Layers panel and choose Black & White. In the Properties panel that appears, adjust the various sliders until you're happy with the image's contrast.

2. **Activate the image layer and choose Filter→"Convert for Smart Filters."**

   To make the filter run on its own layer, you have to convert the image for Smart Filters first. In addition to protecting your original image, Smart Filters let you change the filter's blend mode and opacity (which you'll do in a couple of steps).

3. **Choose Filter→Stylize→Find Edges.**

   You won't get a dialog box with this filter; it just runs. Don't panic when your image turns into a freaky-looking outline; you'll reduce the filter's strength in a second.

FIGURE 15-18

As you can see, the Find Edges filter can help you completely change a photo's feel, and it can do wonders to rescue an image with lousy color.

The lighter color of the pencil sketch brings out tons of details that you couldn't see before because the original photo was so dark and saturated

4. **In the Blending Options dialog box, change the Mode to Hard Mix and lower the Opacity to about 85 percent.**

   In the Layers panel, double-click the little icon to the right of the Find Edges filter to open the Blending Options dialog box. As you change the dialog box's settings, keep an eye on how your image looks (you may need to move the dialog box out of the way). As you learned in Chapter 7, the blend modes in the Lighting category increase an image's contrast, which is great when you're trying to create a pencil sketch. You may need to experiment with other Lighting blend modes for this technique because some will work better than others depending on the colors in your image. The best Opacity setting also varies according to how much contrast the original image has, though a setting between 75 and 85 percent usually works well. Click OK to close the Blending Options dialog box. Your image should start resembling a pencil sketch at this point, though you'll want to soften it by blurring it slightly.

5. **Choose Filter→Blur→Gaussian Blur and, in the resulting dialog box, enter a Radius of 2.**

   A Radius of 2 usually works well, but, again, you'll have to experiment with this setting. Click OK to close the Gaussian Blur dialog box.

6. **Open the Gaussian Blur layer's Blending Options dialog box, change the blend mode to Lighten, and then click OK.**

   In the Layers panel, double-click the icon to the right of the Gaussian Blur layer to open the dialog box, and then change the Mode setting. When you choose Lighten, the Gaussian Blur filter blurs only the light pixels in the image, preserving the darker pixels' details (the edges you accentuated with the Find Edges filter).

You're finished, but if the sketch is too dark, try placing it atop a white background and then lowering its opacity. Click the half-black/half-white circle at the bottom of the Layers panel, choose Solid Color, and then pick white from the resulting Color Picker. If the original image layer is a locked Background layer, double-click it to make it editable (Photoshop won't let you place any layers beneath it if it's locked). Drag the white layer *below* the original image layer, and then activate the original image layer and lower its opacity to about 85 percent. That oughta soften your sketch right up!

> **TIP** To create a watercolor look, activate the Black & White Adjustment layer and then lower its opacity slightly to let some of the original color show through. If you do this, you'll definitely need to add a white Solid Color Fill layer below the image layer, as described in the previous paragraph.

■ EMBOSS

Although no magic fixer-upper can make an out-of-focus image look like it's in focus, the Emboss filter comes close. Technically it's not really *fixing* the image and making it sharp, it's merely bringing out the edges that are already there, making the image *look* sharper (see Figure 15-19). Here's how to use it:

1. **Open the out-of-focus image and choose Filter→"Convert for Smart Filters."**

2. **Choose Filter→Stylize→Emboss.**

   In the resulting dialog box, leave the Angle, Height, and Amount settings as they are. Your image will be mostly gray, and the edges of your subject will be brightly colored (see Figure 15-19, top), but that's exactly what you want, so click OK to close the Emboss dialog box. In the next step, you'll change the blend mode to make the gray parts disappear.

3. **Open the Emboss filter's Blending Options dialog box and change the Mode to Hard Light.**

4. **Over in the Layers panel, double-click the tiny icon to the right of the Emboss layer.** As you learned on page 288, the blend modes in the Lighting category add contrast to images *and* ignore gray. Since the Emboss filter turned your image gray and gave it brightly colored edges, changing the blend mode to Hard Light makes the gray vanish, leaving only the edges visible so they stand out more and appear sharper than before. Who knew?

5. **Click OK to close the Blending Options dialog box, and save your document as a PSD file.**

That's all there is to it—well, aside from grinning triumphantly because you fixed the image.

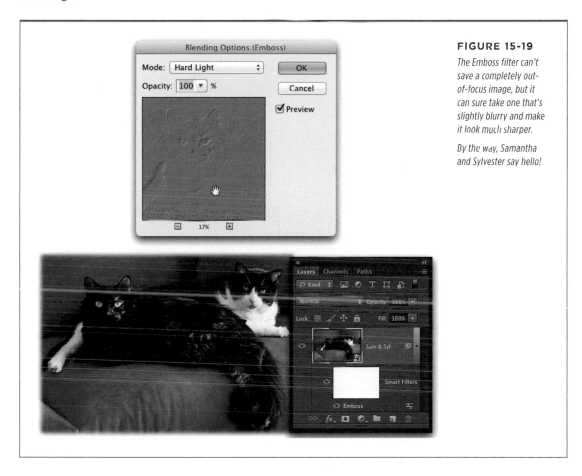

FIGURE 15-19

The Emboss filter can't save a completely out-of-focus image, but it can sure take one that's slightly blurry and make it look much sharper.

By the way, Samantha and Sylvester say hello!

Texture

As you'd expect, the filters in this category add texture to images, which can help add depth and visual interest, as shown in Figure 15-20. For example, to spice up an image's background, you can add a texture to just that area by selecting it and then running one of these filters.

NOTE Out of the box, the Texture category isn't included in the Filter menu. Happily, there's an easy fix—hop back to the box on page 637 to learn what to do.

FIGURE 15-20

If you select the dark-green rays in this background with the Quick Selection tool before *running the Craquelure filter (Filter→Texture→Craquelure), the filter's effect is visible in just those areas.*

As you can see here, Photoshop filled in the Smart Filter mask for you. Remember from Chapter 3 that, when you're dealing with layer masks, black conceals and white reveals (see page 116 for a refresher on layer masks).

The technique is super simple: Just open an image and choose Filter→"Convert for Smart Filters." Then select the area behind your subject using any of the techniques in Chapter 4. Next, choose Filter→Texture and pick one of the six options: Craquelure, Grain, Mosaic Tiles, Patchwork, Stained Glass, or Texturizer. (The Texturizer filter actually lets you load your *own* images and use them as a texture; see page 623 for an example of how you can snatch texture from a photo and use it on text.) Adjust their various sliders in the Filter Gallery dialog box and then click OK.

Video

As the name suggests, the two filters in this category deal strictly with individual frames extracted from videos. De-Interlace smooths moving images and NTSC Colors restricts the image's color palette to colors that TVs can display. For more on working with video in Photoshop, head to Chapter 20.

Other

Since these filters don't really fit into any *other* category, they get their own. Custom, for example, lets you design your own filters to manipulate images' brightness. As you learned on page 467, you can use the High Pass filter to sharpen images. Maximum and Minimum have more practical uses—you can use 'em to enlarge or shrink a layer mask. For example, if you select an object, add a layer mask, and then place it atop *another* image, you may find some stray pixels around the object's edges from the original background. To eliminate those strays, use the Minimum filter to shrink the mask itself (Figure 15-21, bottom right).

The last filter in this category is Offset, which you can use to shift a selected object horizontally or vertically a precise amount in pixels. Since *moving* a selection creates a hole in its original location, you get to tell Photoshop what to do with the empty spot. Your choices are "Set to Transparent," Repeat Edge Pixels, and Wrap Around.

Phc

G etting
challen
your m
learned in the
mation—it's th
volume of mor
can be a *night*

Thankfully, the
begin with. Unf
and color profi
The main conce
chapter (an ene
able high-qualit

■ The Ch

WYSIWYG (pror
get." For image-e
what's onscreen.
monitors versus

A monitor's surfa
you learned in Ch
light-emitting do
light, and cyan, n

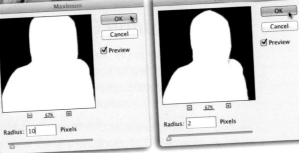

FIGURE 15-21

Top: Here's the original image before the background was hidden by the layer mask.

Bottom Left: If you run the Maximum filter on the layer mask, Photoshop expands it. Notice how a wee bit of the original background is visible around the hero.

Bottom Right: The Minimum filter does the exact opposite—it shrinks the layer mask—a great way to snip away leftover edge pixels.

You can give these filters a try by downloading the file Spanish.zip from this book's Missing CD page at www.missingmanuals.com/cds.

2. **Open the Image Size dialog box, turn off the Resample Image checkbox, and then resize the image.**

   Choose Image→Image Size or press Option-⌘-I (Alt+Ctrl+I on a PC) and then turn off the Resample Image option at the bottom of the dialog box. Then change the document's width and height if you need to. For example, the image in Figure 16-2 started at 9″x9″, but is now 5″x5″. This change caused the resolution to balloon from 348 ppi to 691 ppi, but you'll lower that number to a more reasonable level in the next step (see page 242 for a discussion of resolution overkill).

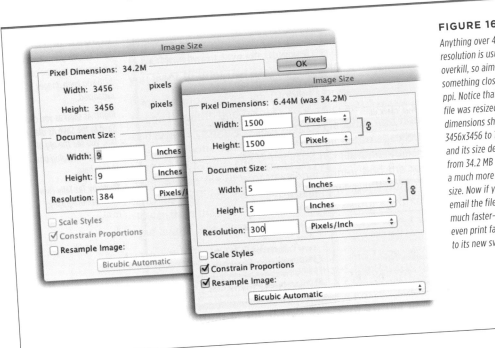

FIGURE 16-2

Anything over 450 ppi resolution is usually overkill, so aim for something closer to 300 ppi. Notice that when this file was resized, its pixel dimensions shrank from 3456x3456 to 1500x1500 and its size decreased from 34.2 MB to 6.44 MB, a much more manageable size. Now if you need to email the file, it'll transfer much faster—heck, it'll even print faster thanks to its new svelte size.

3. **At the bottom of the Image Size dialog box, turn the Resample Image checkbox back on and then lower the resolution to 300 ppi.**

   The Resample Image checkbox has to be on for you to change the resolution. Once you turn it on, enter *300* in the Resolution field.

4. **Choose "Bicubic Sharper (best for reduction)" from the resample method pop-up menu at the bottom of the dialog box.**

   Choosing Bicubic Sharper makes Photoshop reduce the softening (blurring) that results from making the image smaller. Alternatively, you can leave this menu set to Bicubic Automatic so Photoshop picks the best method *for* you. (See page 239 for more about resampling.) Click OK to close the Image Size dialog box.

TIP You may want to apply a round of sharpening after you resize and resample an image to help maintain its sharpness (an amount between 50 percent and 75 percent should do the trick). See Chapter 11 for some serious sharpening enlightenment.

5. **Summon the Save As dialog box by choosing File→Save As or pressing ⌘-S (Ctrl+S on a PC).**

   Since you're working on a copy that you haven't saved yet, you need to tell Photoshop where to save it and in what format.

6. **In the Format pop-up menu, choose Photoshop PDF and then turn off the Layers and Alpha Channels checkboxes, if they're on.**

   Turning off these checkboxes forces Photoshop to create a single-layer PDF for printing.

7. **Name your file and tell Photoshop where to save it, and then click Save.**

   When you do, Photoshop alerts you that, "The settings you choose in the Save Adobe PDF dialog can override your current settings in the Save As dialog box." Click OK and the Save Adobe PDF dialog box appears.

8. **On the left side of the Save Adobe PDF dialog box, choose General and make sure the Compatibility pop-up menu on the right side is set to Acrobat 5 (PDF 1.4) as shown in Figure 16-3, top.**

   If you think you'll want to edit this PDF in Photoshop later, make sure the Preserve Photoshop Editing Capabilities checkbox is turned on (though you're better off editing the PSD you made the PDF from instead).

9. **Click the Compression category on the left and, from the first pop-up menu in Options section of the dialog box, choose Do Not Downsample, and then set the Compression pop-up menu to None (see Figure 16-3, bottom).**

   These options let you retain all the original pixel info so you can create a high-quality print. However, if you want to reduce the file's size without losing too much image quality, choose Zip and "8 bit," or JPEG and Maximum, from the Compression and Image Quality pop-up menus (respectively). A maximum-quality JPEG is a great choice when you're sending an image to a print company that lets you upload files to its website.

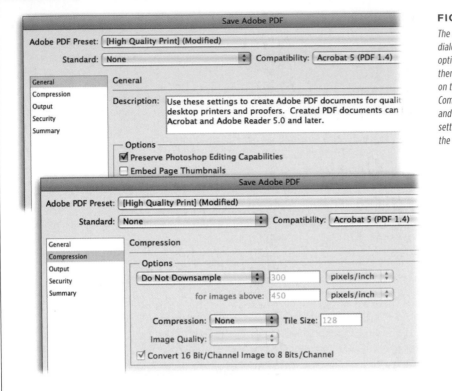

FIGURE 16-3

*The Save Adobe PDF
dialog box has a slew of
options. To go through
them, choose a category
on the left (General,
Compression, and so on)
and then adjust the
settings that appear on
the right.*

10. **Click the Output category and then pick No Conversion from the Color Conversion pop-up menu.**

    This option makes Photoshop retain all the image's color info.

11. **Optionally, save these settings as a preset so you can use them again later.**

    Before you click the Save PDF button, think about whether you'll ever want to use these settings again. If the answer is yes (and it probably is), click the Save Preset button in the lower-left corner of the dialog box (Figure 16-4). Give your preset a descriptive name like *Print Image PDF*, and then click Save.

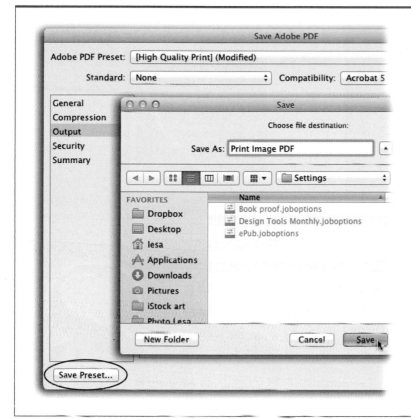

FIGURE 16-4

If you save your settings as a preset, you can access them via the Adobe PDF Preset pop-up menu at the top of the Save Adobe PDF dialog box. Photoshop lets you save as many presets as you want, which can be a huge timesaver.

You can also choose one of the built-in PDF presets listed in the Standard pop-up menu, shown here; when you make a choice from this menu, Photoshop sets all the other options for you. Ask your printer which standard they'd like for you to use.

12. **Click the Save PDF button.**

You can place your newly created PDF file in an Adobe InDesign document or send it to somebody via email or FTP site. Unlike TIFF and EPS files, which usually need to be encased in a protective .zip archive (a compressed document container—see the Tip on page 677), PDF files are Internet compatible and safe.

■ Printing on an Inkjet Printer

If you're a photographer, you probably use an inkjet printer—most likely an *expand-ed-gamut* one that uses six to eight inks, rather than the standard four (they're technically dyes, but most folks call 'em inks). The most common combination of expanded-gamut ink includes the four standard *process colors*—cyan, magenta, yellow and black (CMYK)—plus light cyan and light magenta. You may also have a choice of black inks, like glossy or photo black, matte black, light black, and even light *light* black (seriously!).

> **NOTE** Inkjet printers are more common than dye-sublimation or color laser printers, so they're the focus of this section, but you can use printer and paper profiles as explained in this section no matter what kind of printer you use.

Nearly all expanded-gamut inkjet printers can convert RGB images to CMYK (plus any additional inks they may have). For the brightest and most saturated colors, let the printer convert the colors for you (see step 8 below). (But if you've already converted your RGB image to CMYK, don't panic—all of these printers can print regular, four-color CMYK files, too.) For the most accurate results, manage the

---

FREQUENTLY ASKED QUESTION

Why Not Print JPEGs?

Hey, what do you have against JPEGs? It seems like a decent enough file format.

You may be wondering why you shouldn't save and print images in JPEG format. That's a legitimate question because, after all, JPEG is the format used by most digital cameras. There's certainly nothing wrong with printing a first generation JPEG (the one from your camera); the problem occurs once you start editing, resaving, and then printing *subsequent* JPEGs.

When you save images as JPEGs, Photoshop automatically shrinks 'em using a process known as *lossy compression*, which reduces the amount of info in the image (mainly in areas of fine detail), lowering the image's quality. The amount of compression, and the resulting loss of info and quality, varies from one JPEG to another (you can set the level of compression yourself, as discussed on page 723). If you have no choice but to use JPEG—because you're sending the image to an online lab for printing, like your local camera store or *www.mpix.com*, for example—use the highest quality and lowest compression settings to preserve as much quality as possible.

However, when you *resave* a JPEG without changing its format

to something else like PSD or TIFF, you apply yet *another* round of compression, and *that's* when everything goes to heck in a hand basket. Here's what you should do instead:

- Save any JPEGs you receive in PSD format when you first open them for editing in Photoshop, and then create a JPEG *from* the PSD if you need to (say, for posting on the Web or emailing). To speed up this file conversion, you can use Photoshop actions (Chapter 18) and/or the Image Processor script (page 251) to quickly convert several images from one format to another.

- If your images are going to be edited extensively, set your digital camera to capture images in an uncompressed format like TIFF or Raw to prevent any initial compression and resulting loss of info and quality. As you learned on page 365, Raw is the most flexible format, so choose that option if possible (most cameras can save images in Raw format; consult your owner's manual to see whether yours can).

Now you can relax knowing you're not *re*-compressing already compressed files. Whew!

conversion *yourself* in the Photoshop Print Settings dialog box. Here's how to do it when printing a high-quality image on an expanded-gamut printer:

1. **Prepare your image for printing by cropping, editing, and resizing it.**

   Make sure you've cropped, color-corrected (Chapter 9), and resized the image and set its resolution to between 200 ppi and 450 ppi (Chapter 6). If you don't crop the image to the exact dimensions you want, your printer may crop it for you (it's *far* better to do it yourself). It's also a good idea to double-check the Image Size dialog box to confirm that the document's dimensions and resolution are correct (open it by pressing Option-⌘-I or Alt+Ctrl+I on a PC).

2. **Choose File→Print or press ⌘-P (Ctrl+P) to summon the Photoshop Print Settings dialog box, shown in Figure 16-5 (top).**

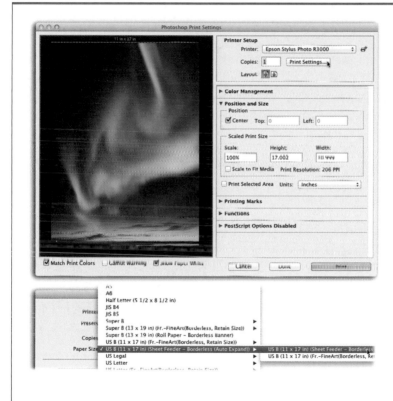

FIGURE 16-5

Top: Adobe redesigned and simplified its Print dialog box in CS6; it has a big preview area on the left and sports multiple sections on the right that are brimming with options. Click a section's name to collapse or expand it and use the scroll bar on the right to move down through the sections. (You can make the dialog box bigger by dragging any edge or its lower-right corner.) Click the Print Settings button near the top for more printer-specific options like paper and quality. If you're on a Mac and your printer offers a utility for nozzle cleaning and the like, you can summon it by clicking the icon to this menu's right that looks like a tiny printer.

Bottom: If your printer can print to the edges of the paper (called a full-bleed or borderless print), head to the Paper Size pop-up menu in your printer's dialog box (the one that opens when you click Print Settings at the top of the Photoshop Print Settings dialog box) and choose an option that includes the word "borderless." Otherwise, your printer will slap a white border around the image.

3. **In the Printer pop-up menu at the top of the dialog box, pick your printer.**

   If your printer isn't listed, visit the manufacturer's website and download the latest driver for your printer (see page 675).

NOTE When you make changes in the Photoshop Print Settings dialog box and then click the Done or Print button, Photoshop saves those settings—in the document, as well as in its own *program* preferences—the moment you save the document. (If you *don't* save the document, your print settings fly out the window [unless you saved them as a preset]). This lets you print the same document with the same print settings quickly by choosing File→Print One Copy. In fact, *any* document you print will automatically use those same print settings unless you change them (at which point, Photoshop will use those *new* settings the next time you print, provided you saved the document after changing them). To start fresh with all *new* print settings, press and hold down the space bar when choosing File→Print; this can help you troubleshoot printing weirdness. (In CS6, the print settings in your operating system aren't affected by the print settings you choose in Photoshop.)

4. **Click the Print Settings button at the top of the dialog box.**

   Most folks miss this critical step. The dialog box that opens when you click Print Settings belongs to your *printer*, not Photoshop, so the settings you see might be slightly different than what's described in steps 5 and 6 (which were written using an Epson model). In other words, you may have to hunt around a bit to find settings similar to the ones discussed here.

5. **In your printer's dialog box, from the Paper Size pop-up menu, choose your paper's dimensions.**

   If you're printing borderless, be sure to choose a borderless version of the paper dimension you picked (see Figure 16-5, bottom). If you *don't* pick an option that includes the word "borderless," your image will print with a pesky white border around it. (If you don't see an option that includes "borderless," that means your printer can't create borderless prints).

TIP If your printer driver isn't the latest version, it may have trouble communicating with Photoshop and you may not be able to print to the edges of the paper or change paper size. Trot on over to the manufacturer's website to make sure you have the current driver, and then you should be good to go.

6. **In your printer's dialog box, choose Print Settings (circled in Figure 16-6).**

   The wording of your printer's dialog box may vary slightly, or you may not have this option at all. Instead, you may see some or all of the following settings:

   - **Media Type.** Choose the paper you're printing on, like Ultra Premium Photo Paper Luster.

   - **Print Mode.** Your printer controls this menu, which chooses the appropriate mode for the Media Type you picked, so you don't need to adjust this setting.

   - **Color Mode.** This setting is controlled by the Color Management section of Photoshop's Print dialog box. If you choose Photoshop Manages Colors (see page 688), this setting is turned off. That said, it's important to make *sure* it's turned off so your printer doesn't try to adjust the document's color, too.

   - **Output Resolution.** You can think of this as a quality setting. Your printer automatically adjusts this setting based on the Media Type you chose earlier so, once again, you don't need to change this setting.

- **High Speed.** This option lets your printer's *print head* (the bit that applies the ink to the paper) print while it's moving in *both* directions instead of just one. If you turn it off, your image will print more slowly, but it might look a little better. (If you like, fire off a couple of test prints—one with this setting turned on and one with it off—and then look closely to see if you can spot any differences.)

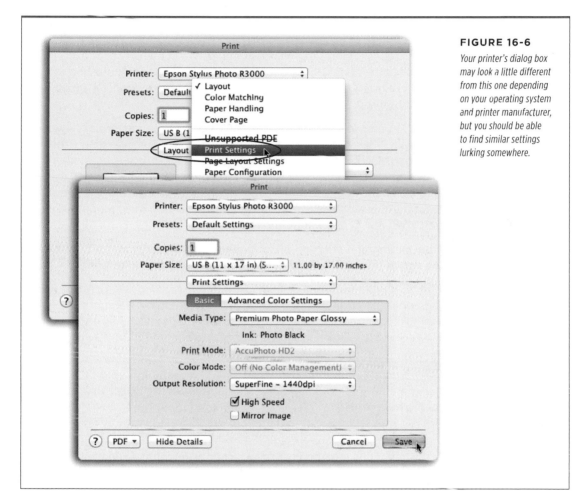

FIGURE 16-6

Your printer's dialog box may look a little different from this one depending on your operating system and printer manufacturer, but you should be able to find similar settings lurking somewhere.

7. **Click Save (or OK, or the equivalent button) to close your printer's dialog box and return to the Photoshop Print Settings dialog box.**

   Back in Photoshop's dialog box, check the paper's orientation to make sure it's what you want; you can select portrait or landscape by clicking the Layout buttons (see Figure 16-5, top). Also, in the preview area on the left side of the dialog box, make sure your image fills the whole thing. If you wisely cropped the image to your exact print dimensions, it should fill the preview area perfectly.

8. **In the Color Management section's Color Handling menu (see Figure 16-7), choose Photoshop Manages Colors.**

Color management is the process of making the colors produced by the devices you work with—your digital camera, monitor, and printer—match as closely as possible by referencing specific color profiles.

This menu controls whether Photoshop or your printer driver converts the image's colors from RGB to CMYK-Plus. For the brightest and most vibrant colors, choose Printer Manages Color and then skip to step 10. For more accurate results, choose Photoshop Manages Colors. It's certainly worth experimenting with both options, though you'll likely find that letting Photoshop manage colors will give you higher quality and more consistent results *if* you're using paper-specific profiles.

When you choose Photoshop Manages Colors, the program displays a warning that reads, "Remember to disable the printer's color management in the print settings dialog box." Most printers are configured to apply *some* kind of color management to your image, which can conflict with the color management you're trying to apply through Photoshop (usually with unsavory results). Photoshop CS6 automatically turns color management *off* in your printer's dialog box when you choose Photoshop Manages Colors.

9. **From the Printer Profile pop-up menu in the Color Management section, choose the option that matches the paper and print settings you're using.**

Click the Printer Profile menu and scroll through the long list of profiles (which gets longer each time you install new profiles) to find the appropriate one. For example, if you're using an Epson SPR3000 printer, look under E or S, and then pick the profile that matches your paper, such as Epson SPR300 Premium Glossy.

NOTE If you're letting Photoshop manage color (see step 8), Photoshop communicates with your printer and picks the best printer profile *all by itself*. It does it by reading the printer's JobOptimalDestinationColorProfile tag (don't ask). But don't jump for joy just yet: As of this writing, hardly any printer manufacturers included this info, though boy howdy it'll be cool when they do! (And at that point, you can skip step 9 entirely.)

---

10. **In the Rendering Intent pop-up menu, choose Perceptual and then make sure the Black Point Compensation checkbox is turned on.**

These options help maintain the color relationships in your image, and preserve contrast by making sure that the black shadows in your original RGB image are also black in the final print.

11. **In the "Position and Size" section, make sure the Center checkbox is turned on (see Figure 16-5, top).**

If you *didn't* crop your image before starting this process, this setting will make your image print from the center outward—as much of it as will fit on the paper size you picked—instead of aligning the upper-left corner of the image with the upper-left corner of the paper.

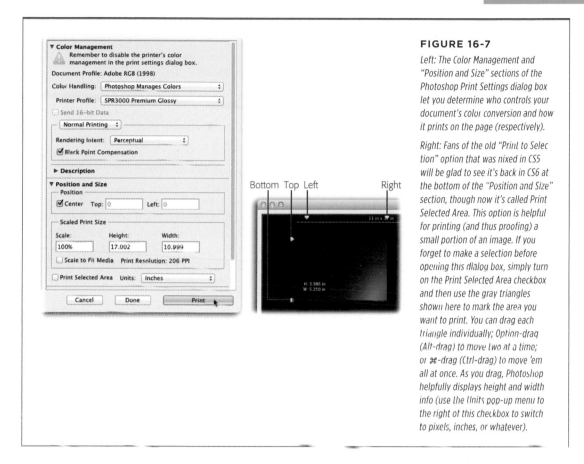

FIGURE 16-7

Left: The Color Management and "Position and Size" sections of the Photoshop Print Settings dialog box let you determine who controls your document's color conversion and how it prints on the page (respectively).

Right: Fans of the old "Print to Selection" option that was nixed in CS5 will be glad to see it's back in CS6 at the bottom of the "Position and Size" section, though now it's called Print Selected Area. This option is helpful for printing (and thus proofing) a small portion of an image. If you forget to make a selection before opening this dialog box, simply turn on the Print Selected Area checkbox and then use the gray triangles shown here to mark the area you want to print. You can drag each triangle individually; Option-drag (Alt-drag) to move two at a time; or ⌘-drag (Ctrl-drag) to move 'em all at once. As you drag, Photoshop helpfully displays height and width info (use the Units pop-up menu to the right of this checkbox to switch to pixels, inches, or whatever).

12. In the Scaled Print Size area, make sure the Scale option is set to 100%.

You can use this setting, along with the Position setting mentioned in the previous step, to control which part of your image prints if you didn't crop it first. However, just because you *can* scale (resize) your image while it's being printed doesn't mean you *should*. Besides preventing you from sharpening the image after you make it smaller, scaling it via the Print dialog box makes it take longer to print (and Photoshop doesn't perform any image resampling [see page 239 for more on resampling]). If you don't care about such things, you can turn on "Scale to Fit Media" and Photoshop adjusts the Scale, Height, and Width settings in this section to make the image fit the paper size you picked earlier.

TIP   New in CS6, you can drag within the preview area of the Photoshop Print Settings dialog box to scale and position your image on the page. Your cursor turns into a four-sided arrow when you mouse over the preview, and Photoshop displays height and width info as you drag: Just drag the corners or edges of the image to resize it. However, these adjustments cancel out any changes you've made in the "Position and Size" section.

13. **If you're using paper that's bigger than your image, take a peek at the options in the Printing Marks and Functions sections.**

These sections let you turn on different kinds of marks that can help you trim the image once it's printed, as well as control background and border colors (handy for making your print look like it has a matte behind it).

In the Printing Marks section, turn on Corner Crop Marks to make Photoshop place a small horizontal and vertical line just outside of each corner of the image. If you plan to fold the image in half (say, if you're creating a greeting card), turn on Center Crop Marks. Professional printers use registration marks for printing separations (page 705), but you can leave them turned off. The Description option instructs Photoshop to print the info you've entered into the Description field in the File Info dialog box (page 745) below the image, though you can also use the Edit button to its right to add a description here. The Labels option prints the document's name above the image.

The Functions section lets professional print shops—like those that use offset presses, discussed in the next section—do things like flip the image on the film (Emulsion Down) and reverse its colors (Negative); this film is then used to make plates for the printing press. Professional printing aside, you can click the Background button to summon the Color Picker and Photoshop prints the color of your choice around the outside of the image like a matte. Use the Border button to add an outline around the image. The Bleed button lets you tell Photoshop how far to move the corner crop marks *into* your image so there's a little sliver of the image hanging outside the trim lines. (That way you don't end up with a white strip around the edge of your image if your trim job isn't perfect.)

NOTE   In the off chance that you're using a printer that understands the PostScript language (some laser printers and image-setters do), you can use the PostScript Options section of the Photoshop Print Settings dialog box to control things like halftone line frequency, angle, and other options available for your particular printer. If this section is labeled PostScript Options Disabled, your printer doesn't speak PostScript! (Don't confuse a PostScript *printer* with a PostScript *font*; while they share the same language, they're not the same thing. In fact, Photoshop rasterizes fonts the second you click the Print button, so the printer doesn't have to understand PostScript to draw the characters.)

14. **If you picked Photoshop Manages Colors in step 8, take a peek below the preview area and make sure the Match Print Colors and Show Paper White settings are turned on so you can view an onscreen proof (also called a *soft proof*).**

Photoshop displays a simulation of what your printed image will look like (see page 706 for more on proofing). Adobe improved Photoshop's soft-proofing accuracy back in CS4, so the preview should give you a good sense of what the print will look like—assuming you've calibrated your monitor (page 675), of course.

15. **Turn on the Gamut Warning checkbox to make Photoshop highlight any out-of-gamut pixels in gray.**

You can ask Photoshop to show you a proof of any colors in your image that are *out of gamut* (meaning they're unprintable) for the printer and paper you've picked. When using an expanded-gamut printer, you'll encounter far fewer out-of-gamut colors than you would with a standard CMYK printing press. If the gray areas aren't important parts of your image, then don't worry about this warning (though the printed color in those spots won't match the color you see onscreen). If the gray areas are important, use the techniques discussed in Chapter 9 to adjust the image's colors, which usually means desaturating those spots slightly. Alternatively, try printing on different paper or, if possible, using a different printer.

16. **Glance over your choices in the Photoshop Print Settings dialog box one last time and, if they look OK, click the Print button.**

After *all* that hard work, you see the fruit of your labors in the form of a gloriously accurate, high-quality print. Yippee!

TIP You can save time by recording your print settings in an *action* (see Chapter 18). Bear in mind, though, that the program will memorize *everything* in the Photoshop Print Settings dialog box, including print size and positioning. So if you typically print both landscape and portrait images, you need to record two actions, one for each orientation.

◼ Printing on a Commercial Offset Press

If you prepare artwork for stuff that's printed using a commercial offset printing press (magazines, product packaging, newspapers, and so on), you've got *loads* more to worry about than if you're sending an image to an inkjet printer. Unlike printing to an inkjet printer, where your images get converted from RGB to CMYK during the printing process, a commercial offset press usually requires you to convert the image to CMYK *before* it's printed. This section explains the very specific steps you need to follow to preserve an image's color when you convert it to CMYK. But before you dive too deeply into color-mode conversion, you need to understand a bit more about how offset presses work.

Commercial offset presses are huge, noisy, ink-filled metal beasts. An inkjet printer sprays ink from a print head directly onto a page, whereas an offset press transfers, or *offsets*, ink from an image on a plate onto a rubber blanket and *then* onto a page. As you learned back in Chapter 5, they split an image's four CMYK channels into individual color separations, which are loaded onto big cylinders aligned so that all four colors are printed, one on top of another, to form the final image. If these cylinders aren't aligned properly, you'll see faint traces of one or more colors peeking outside the edges of the image, making it look blurry (this blurriness is called being "out of registration").

Instead of the dyes used by inkjet printers, commercial offset presses use two types of ink: *process* and *spot*. Process inks include cyan, magenta, yellow, and black (CMYK), and they're printed as overlapping patterns of halftone dots (Figure 16-8, left) that can economically reproduce the wide range of colors found in *continuous-tone images* like photos (Figure 16-8, right).

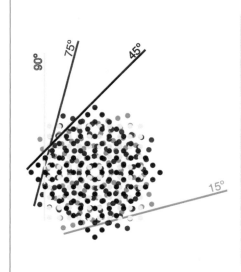 

FIGURE 16-8

Left: If you look closely at an image printed on a press, you can see the dots it's made from. (The next time you pick up a magazine or newspaper, stick it right up to your nose and you'll see 'em.) To keep the dots from printing on top of each other, they're printed at specific angles according to ink color.

Right: Images that contain a wide range of smooth colors are called continuous-tone images, like this beautiful photo by iStockphoto/Arild Heitmann.

Spot inks, on the other hand, are used to match very *specific* color requirements (like a color in a corporate logo, such as the official UPS brown), and they're printed using *additional* plates on the press. More spot colors mean more plates and therefore more separations, which translates into higher printing costs. Since it's easy to get hit with unexpected costs when you're sending out a print job, make *darn* sure you know exactly how many colors it'll take to print the image (most print jobs involving color photos use only the four process colors). You'll learn all about spot colors later in this chapter.

Finally, unlike sending an image straight from Photoshop to your inkjet printer, you'll *rarely* (if ever) send a single image to an offset press. Instead, you'll send the image over to a page-layout program like Adobe InDesign or QuarkXPress and put it in a document that contains other images, along with text (referred to as *copy*), and *that's* what you send to the printing company. So you need to make sure the image has the right print dimensions and resolution (discussed on page 667), and that it's in the right color mode *before* you place it in InDesign. The following pages explain how to do that as painlessly as possible.

Converting RGB Images to CMYK Using Built-In Profiles

First and foremost, you need to know who's handling the conversion from RGB to CMYK mode. Historically, printing companies have requested (or required!) you to convert images yourself, but this is *slowly* changing, particularly with the increased use of digital presses (see page 708).

If you have no idea whether you're supposed to convert the RGB image to CMYK yourself or if you want to know whether the printing company has a custom profile you can use for the conversion, *pick up the phone*. Communication is crucial in situations like this, because if your print job hits the press at 2:00 a.m., it'll be *your* phone that rings if there's a problem. This is definitely a call you're better off making than receiving.

If you have to convert the image yourself, it's important to choose the proper printer and paper profiles. You can do that in a couple of ways, but the following steps will lead you down a simple and foolproof path:

1. **Open your RGB image and duplicate it.**

   Choose Image→Duplicate to create a copy of the image to *guarantee* that you won't accidentally save over your original.

2. **Name the new file and save it as a TIFF file.**

   Choose File→Save or press ⌘-S (Ctrl+S on a PC) and then give it a name. (It's a good idea to include the file's color mode in the name so you can see at a glance which mode it's in.) Choose TIFF from the Format pop-up menu at the bottom of the Save dialog box and then click Save. In the TIFF Options dialog box that appears, choose None in the Image Compression section and leave the Pixel Order section set to Interleaved. In the Byte Order section, turn on the IBM PC radio button. Leave the "Discard Layers and Save a Copy" option turned on (it's grayed out if your image has just one layer), and then click OK.

3. **Choose Edit→"Convert to Profile."**

   In the Conversion Options section of the dialog box that appears (see Figure 16-9), set the Engine menu to Adobe (ACE) and the Intent menu to Perceptual. Also, make sure Use Black Point Compensation is turned on.

4. **From the Profile pop-up menu (Figure 16-9), choose a profile that reflects the type of ink, press, and paper your printing company will use to print the image.**

   You can think of this menu as a printer profile menu. If you can't find a custom profile (see the next section), hunt for the best match for your current print job. If the image is being printed in North America on a sheetfed printing press using coated paper stock, for example, you can pick the tried-and-true "U.S.

Sheetfed Coated v2" profile. A newer commercial sheetfed profile that also might work is "Coated GRACoL 2006." But before you guess, *ask* your printing company what profile to use.

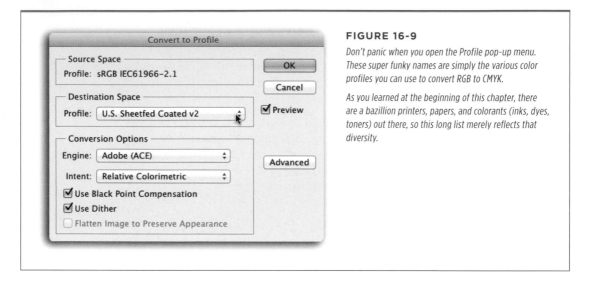

FIGURE 16-9

Don't panic when you open the Profile pop-up menu. These super funky names are simply the various color profiles you can use to convert RGB to CMYK.

As you learned at the beginning of this chapter, there are a bazillion printers, papers, and colorants (inks, dyes, toners) out there, so this long list merely reflects that diversity.

5. **Click OK to complete the color-conversion process, and then save the image.**

   Press ⌘-S (Ctrl+S) to save the image in the new color mode.

After you save your new CMYK image, you're ready to place it in a page-layout document.

Custom RGB to CMYK Profile Conversions

If your printing company has painstakingly created its own custom color profile, you're much better off using it than one of Photoshop's built-in ones. The process is similar to the one just described, but you need to *install* the custom profile (as explained on page 675) before you can use it. Once you've downloaded it, follow these steps to put it to use:

1. **Find where color profiles are stored on your hard drive.**

   Figuring out where to store the profile is the biggest challenge, since different operating systems *and* different versions of Photoshop store profiles in different places:

   • On a Mac running OS X 10.5 or later, color profiles live in *Macintosh HD→Library→Application Support→Adobe→Color→Profiles*.

   • On a Windows 7 computer, head to *C:→Windows→System32→Spool→Drivers→Color*. (If you don't see the Windows folder, you'll need to turn on hidden folders by going to Control Panel→"Appearance and Personalization"→Folder Options; in the dialog box that appears, click the

View tab and then turn on the "Show hidden files, folders, and drives" radio button, and then click OK.)

If you have trouble finding the right folder or just want to double-check that you've found the right spot, call your printing company and ask them where to store profiles on your particular operating system.

NOTE If your computer uses Windows, you can use the Color Management Control Panel to add and remove profiles. Go to Start→Control Panel→Color Management.

2. **Copy the custom profile to the Profiles folder (the Color folder on a PC).**

   Printing companies that have embraced color management have CMYK color profiles for a *variety* of paper stocks, so be sure you load the one for the paper you're printing on by dragging the file into the folder.

3. **Open your image, duplicate it, and save it as a TIFF file.**

   To duplicate the image, choose Image→Duplicate and then choose File→Save or press ⌘-S (Ctrl+S on a PC) and give the copy a name. Pick TIFF from the Format pop-up menu at the bottom of the Save dialog box and then click Save. In the TIFF Options dialog box that appears, choose None in the Image Compression section and leave the Pixel Order section set to Interleaved. In the Byte Order section, turn on the IBM PC radio button. Leave the "Discard Layers and Save a Copy" option turned on, and then click OK.

4. **Choose Edit→"Convert to Profile" and, in the resulting dialog box, choose the new profile from the Profile pop-up menu.**

   If you don't see the right profile in the list, try restarting Photoshop. Press ⌘-Q (Ctrl+Q) to quit, and then double-click the image file to relaunch the program.

5. **Change the Conversion Options settings, if necessary.**

   Ask the printing company if you need to adjust any settings in the Conversion Options section of the "Convert to Profile" dialog box.

6. **Click OK and then press ⌘-S (Ctrl+S) to save the image.**

You've just completed your first custom CMYK conversion.

Using Spot Color

As mentioned earlier, commercial printing presses sometimes use special premixed, custom inks called *spot colors*. If you're a graphic designer working in *prepress* (the department that preps files for printing), the info that lies ahead is really important. If you're a photographer or Web designer, save your brainpower and skip this part. Really.

Photoshop wizard Ben Willmore (*www.DigitalMastery.com*) has come up with a great analogy to explain spot colors. Remember the box of crayons you used as a kid? A small box had eight basic colors, like blue, orange, and yellow. And then there was the big box of 64—with a sharpener on the back!—that had special colors like cornflower, melon, and thistle. No matter how hard you tried, you couldn't reproduce those special colors with a box of eight crayons. In Photoshop, you can think of the box of eight crayons as CMYK color mode and those special colors as spot colors.

NOTE   The most popular brand of spot-color ink is Pantone (*www.pantone.com*). You'll also hear Pantone colors called *PMS* colors, which stands for "Pantone Matching System."

Because of the impurity and variety of CMYK inks, they can't produce all the colors you see in RGB mode (just like you can't reproduce, say, cornflower with those original eight crayons). If you're tooling around in the Color Picker and choose a color that *can't* be produced in CMYK, Photoshop places a little gray triangle next to it (see Figure 16-10). This triangle is known as an *out-of-gamut warning* (gamut, as you learned earlier, means the full range of colors). If you click the triangle (or the tiny color swatch below it), Photoshop will change that color to the closest possible match that *can* be printed with CMYK inks.

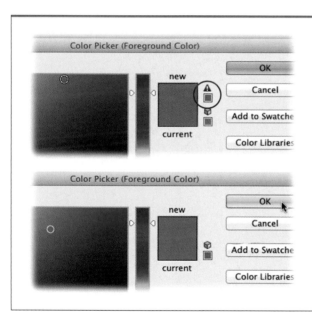

FIGURE 16-10

Top: If you pick a color that can't be produced with CMYK inks, a little warning triangle appears next to the color swatch. Click the triangle or the tiny square of color below it to make Photoshop pick the next best color.

Bottom: In most cases, you can't see much difference between the original color and the new one, but if you check your cursor's location in the color field, you can see that Photoshop has moved it slightly.

In some cases, the closest color match is good enough, but spot-color ink comes in handy in certain situations, like when you need:

- **To reduce printing costs.** As you learned earlier, the more colors you use, the more cylinders and separations the printer needs and the more the job will cost. But if you print an image using black and just one or two spot colors, you can actually *reduce* your printing costs because you'll use only two or three separations instead of four. This technique is common with line art (illustrations or outline drawings like those in a coloring book), though you can also use it for photos.

- **To ensure color accuracy.** If your paycheck depends on color accuracy, you *have* to use spot colors. For example, if UPS hires you to design a flyer for their company party, you need *your* version of brown to match their *official* brown. Unless you use a spot color (which is consistent because it's premixed), your brown will be printed using a mix of CMYK inks and may end up looking, say, maroon.

- **To use specialty inks.** To add a bit of pizzazz to a printed image, you can use specialty inks like metallics or a varnish that looks glossy when it's printed. You can also add a vibrant spot color to a particular area to make that part stand out. However, if you use specialty inks on a CMYK document, you're *adding* color separations to the job, which increases the cost.

Before you can use a spot color, you have to create a special channel for it called a *spot channel*. Each spot color you use needs its very own spot channel. (See Chapter 5 for more on channels.)

Let's say you're preparing the cover photo for the next issue of *Cutting Horse* magazine, and, to reduce printing costs, the magazine has decided to use a grayscale image with one spot color for visual interest. (That way, they're paying for two separations instead of four.) Your mission is to make the horse's bridle Pantone Red. No problemo! Just make a selection of the bridle and then create a spot channel for the special ink (see Figure 16-11).

> **NOTE** To follow along, download the practice image *Bridle.jpg* from this book's Missing CD page over at *www.missingmanuals.com/cds*.

Here's how to add a spot channel:

1. **Select the area you want to colorize and, if necessary, convert the image to grayscale.**

   If you're lucky enough to start with the full-color version of the photo, you can easily select the horse's bridle by using the Quick Selection tool. Then see page 311 for the scoop on converting a color image to black and white and page 318 for changing the image's color mode to Grayscale.

2. **From the Channels panel's menu (see Figure 16-11, top), choose New Spot Channel.**

   You can also add a spot channel by ⌘-clicking (Ctrl-clicking on a PC) the New Channel icon at the bottom of the Channels panel. Either way, Photoshop opens a dialog box where you can name the new channel and pick its color.

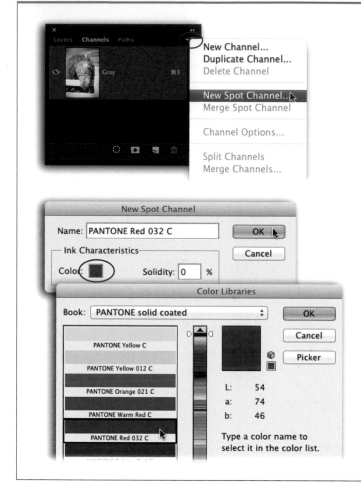

FIGURE 16-11

Top: Once you've selected the area you need to colorize, add a new spot channel by choosing New Spot Channel from the Channels panel's menu (circled, top).

Bottom: Click the little color swatch (circled) in the New Spot Channel dialog box to open the Color Picker. There, click the Color Libraries button to see the oh-so-helpful list of Pantone presets shown here. Photoshop will automatically add the ink you choose here to your selection.

3. **In the New Spot Channel dialog box, click the color swatch to open the Color Picker, and then choose an ink color.**

   To see a list of Pantone presets, click the Color Libraries button. In the Color Libraries dialog box (see Figure 16-11, bottom), choose a color library from the Book pop-up menu. (For example, if you're preparing a photo for a magazine that prints on glossy paper, pick "PANTONE solid coated"; if you don't know which one to choose, ask your print shop.)

   Next, pick a spot color. If you know the number or name of the ink you want (like *150* or *red*), type the number or name and Photoshop will flip to that color in the list. You can also drag the triangles along the vertical scroll bar to find the one you want, or use the arrow keys to move through the list of ink swatches. When you find the right color, click its swatch to choose it, and then click OK to close the Color Libraries dialog box.

NOTE By picking a color from the Color Library, you don't have to worry about naming your new spot channel—Photoshop names it automatically.

4. **Back in the New Spot Channel dialog box, leave Solidity set to 0% and click OK to close the dialog box.**

   You can think of solidity as ink opacity, though it affects only the onscreen image and not the printed version. Depending on the image you're working with, increasing the ink's opacity so it appears solid and not see-through may be helpful (it's a personal preference).

   When you click OK, you'll see a new spot channel appear in the Channels panel (see Figure 16-12).

FIGURE 16-12

Here's the final cover shot for your magazine. As you can see, there are just two channels in the Channels panel (and thus this image can be printed with just two separations).

If you send this grayscale Photoshop document straight to InDesign, that program adds a color swatch for the spot color and makes sure that the new color prints on top of the black ink (a technique called overprinting).

■ EDITING SPOT CHANNELS

Once you've created a spot channel, you can change its ink color by double-clicking it in the Channels panel. You can also add or remove color from the spot channel by painting with the Brush tool, or by using any selection tool and filling the selection with color as described on page 185.

Since Photoshop shows channel information in grayscale, you can edit a spot channel just like a layer mask (page 118)—by painting with black, white, or shades of gray:

- **To add color at 100 percent opacity**, grab the Brush tool by pressing B and set your foreground color chip to black. Then mouse over to the image and paint where you want to add color.

- **To remove color at 100 percent opacity**, set your foreground color chip to white before you paint.

- **To add or remove color at any other opacity**, set your foreground color chip to a shade of gray before you paint.

■ SAVING A DOCUMENT WITH SPOT CHANNELS

To keep spot channels intact, you need to save the document in a format that understands them: DCS, PSD, or PDF. So which one do you pick? It depends on what you're going to do with the file.

If you're the hired Photoshop gun and you'll be handing the file off to someone else for further fluffing, save it as a PSD file, get your motor runnin', and head out on the highway (insert guitar riff here). If you're importing the image into InDesign or QuarkXPress 6.5 or later, you'll also want to save it as a PSD file.

If you're using the image in QuarkXPress 6 or earlier, you need to save it as a DCS 2.0 or a PDF file (see page 701). DCS (short for Desktop Color Separation) is a special format that pre-separates the image's color channels into plates for a printing press. To save a document as a DCS file, make sure it's in either Grayscale or CMYK color mode, and then choose File→Save As and pick Photoshop DCS 2.0 from the Format pop-up menu. When you click Save, you'll see the DCS 2.0 Format dialog box (Figure 16-13) where you can fine-tune the following settings:

- **Preview.** This menu controls which kind of image preview you see in Quark-XPress. Your choices include "TIFF (1 bit/pixel)" and "TIFF (8 bits/pixel)." Choose the latter if you want a nice, 256-color preview. If you don't need to see the image preview in QuarkXPress (because, say, you're building a catalog with hundreds of images and that many previews would slow down your vintage computer), choose None. (The box on page 46 explains what "8 bits" means.)

FIGURE 16-13

DCS 2.0 is one of three formats you can use to save spot channels intact. While most page-layout programs can read DCS files, you'll find that using a PDF is easier, as discussed on the next page.

- **DCS.** Leave this menu set to "Single File DCS, No Composite" so Photoshop doesn't generate all kinds of files that only the printing press peeps know what to do with.

- **Encoding.** This menu controls how Photoshop *encodes* (represents and stores) the print information in the file. If you're on a Mac, choose Binary. If you're on a Windows computer, choose ASCII or (for a more compact file) ASCII85.

> **NOTE** *ASCII* stands for "American Standard Code for Information Interchange." ASCII was developed as a way to convert binary (computer) information into text, and ASCII85 is the newest version. (This stuff is *great* bar-bet trivia.)

Leave the checkboxes at the bottom of the dialog box (Include Halftone Screen, Include Transfer Function, Include Vector Data, and Image Interpolation) turned off and then click OK. You're now ready to import the DCS file into QuarkXPress 6 or earlier. Party on!

■ SAVING SPOT COLORS IN PDF FORMAT

DCS 2.0 has long been the standard format for saving documents with spot colors, but PDF format yields a smaller and more flexible file. To see for yourself, follow these steps:

1. **Open an image with a spot color and then choose File→Save As.**

2. **In the Save As dialog box, pick Photoshop PDF from the Format pop-up menu.**

   If your document has layers, turn off the Layers checkbox to flatten the image.

3. **Turn on the Spot Colors checkbox.**

   This step ensures that Photoshop includes your spot colors in the PDF, along with process colors (CMYK).

4. **Rename the image to indicate that it harbors a spot color and then save it.**

   For example, call it "Autumn Art_CMYK_Spot" and then click Save. Photoshop warns you that the PDF settings you're about to make cancel out the settings in the Save As dialog box. Simply click OK and Photoshop opens the Save Adobe PDF dialog box.

5. **At the top of the Save Adobe PDF dialog box (shown back in Figure 16-3), choose Acrobat 5 (PDF 1.4) from the Compatibility pop-up menu.**

   This setting lets you specify the PDF version. As of this writing, version 1.4 is the safest and most widely accepted choice.

6. **Click Compression on the left side of the dialog box and adjust the settings so your images don't get compressed.**

   From the first pop-up menu in the Options section, choose Do Not Downsample. Then, from the Compression pop-up menu, pick None.

7. **Click Output on the left side of the dialog box and then make sure the Color Conversion pop-up menu is set to No Conversion.**

8. **Click Save PDF.**

That's it. You're now free to send the PDF file to the page-layout program of your choice.

If you save the settings you entered as a preset (see page 682), this method is much faster than saving a file in DCS 2.0 format. However, be sure to ask your printing company if it accepts PDFs with spot colors. Although almost everyone can take PDFs these days (and most places prefer them), some companies using older equipment may not, so be sure to ask—change is hard, you know!

Printing Duotone (Multitonal) Images

One advantage of using a commercial printer is that you can print duotones and other multitonal images by adding *additional* ink to grayscale images (see the box on page 706). You can add Pantone inks, additional gray inks, or even process inks—great news if you want to add an overall color tint to a grayscale image, add some tonal depth and richness, or both. These techniques let you create some amazingly beautiful effects, as discussed back in Chapter 8. However, it's really easy to add *too* much ink, which can make the image way too dark once it's printed. If that happens, you lose details in the shadows and the image's contrast goes down the tubes.

TIP New in Photoshop CS6 is a set of 38 gradient presets called *Photographic Toning*. When you use them with a Gradient Map Adjustment layer, you get the look of a multitonal image *without* having to use Duotone mode. See page 317 for more info.

To produce a truly amazing duotone or multitone image, you need to start with a good quality grayscale image—one that has high contrast and isn't overly dark. Once you've settled on an image and converted it to black and white (Chapter 8) and then switched it to Grayscale mode (page 319), follow these steps:

1. **Duplicate the image.**

   Choose Image→Duplicate and then give the copy a name. Consider incorporating the word "duotone" into the name, as in "Cowgirl_Duotone."

2. **Choose Image→Mode→Duotone.**

   If this option is grayed out, you're not in Grayscale mode. In that case, choose Grayscale mode first and then switch to Duotone. When the Duotone Options dialog box opens, it shows that the image is a monotone made from nothing but black ink.

3. Click the Curve icon to the left of the black ink (see Figure 16-14).

Clicking this icon opens the Duotone Curve dialog box, where you can peek at how the ink will be applied in your image. For this particular ink, you have a straight 45-degree curve from the highlight to shadow areas, and it's being applied at 100 percent. Click OK to close the Duotone Curve dialog box.

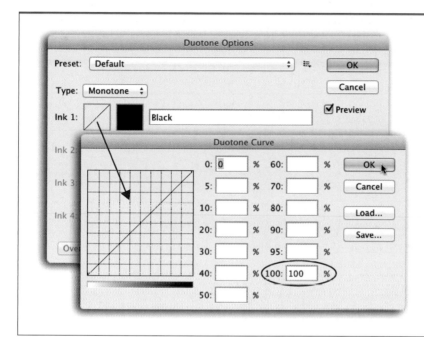

FIGURE 16-14

Duotone Curves are just like the Curves you learned about back in Chapter 9, except that here they let you know how much ink will be applied to the image's shadows, midtones, and highlights. The percentages (circled) tell you how much ink is being added.

4. In the Duotone Options dialog box, choose Duotone from the Type pop-up menu.

This menu gives you a choice of various kinds of multitonal images. When you choose Duotone, Photoshop activates two inks in the dialog box (choosing Tritone activate three inks, and so on). However—and this is key—both inks have straight, 45-degree highlight-to-shadow curve lines, which means they print with the same amount of ink in the same color range. That's *not* good! Why? Because if you were to click the Ink 2 color swatch and choose a new color, you'd add too much of that ink for the image to print decently unless you edited the Duotone Curve, which is tricky to do. So instead, use one of the many presets as described in the next step.

5. Click the Preset pop-up menu and choose one of the gazillion Duotone presets.

Feel free to experiment with the wide variety of choices in the Preset menu. Some items, like the true duotones, come in anywhere from one to four variations, which represent substitutions for the second ink ranging from stronger to weaker. (In other words, presets with 1's in their names add the most color, and ones with 4's in their names add the least). These are excellent starting points for your creations. There's nothing wrong with tweaking the Duotone Curves to fine-tune your results (see Figure 16-15), but you'll want to print some tests to make sure you're not adding too much ink.

Testing duotones is tough because you *can't* proof them unless they're made from process colors (in which case they're really quadtones). If you select a preset with inks not available on your printer, you won't get an accurate proof. The best you can do is contact your printing company and see if they'll print you a test on the paper they'll use for the final image. (If you don't need the proof right away, they may be able to hold onto it and slide it in with another job that uses a similar ink-and-paper combo.)

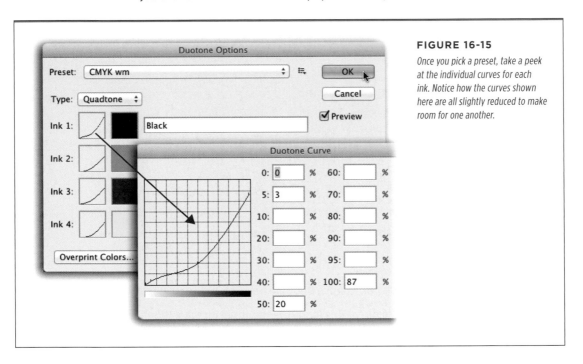

FIGURE 16-15

Once you pick a preset, take a peek at the individual curves for each ink. Notice how the curves shown here are all slightly reduced to make room for one another.

6. **Save the document in EPS or PDF format.**

Here's yet another opportunity to chat with your printing company! Give 'em a ring and ask whether they prefer EPS or PDF format for duotones or multitones. If they say EPS, ask them which settings to use. Then choose File→Save As and pick Photoshop EPS from the Format pop-up menu. In the EPS Options dialog box (Figure 16-16, bottom), choose an 8-bit option from the Preview pop-up menu and pick Binary from the Encoding pop-up menu. Unless your printing company told you otherwise, leave the rest of the options turned off and then click OK.

FIGURE 16-16

As you can see, the difference between a grayscale image (top) and the quadtone preset "CMYK wm" (middle) can be impressive. (Photo by iStockphoto/Andrew Rich.)

To save a duotone as a PDF file instead, you can use the same settings you used to save a spot-color image in the previous section (page 701).

TIP If you're working with a CMYK image and want to add a warm tone to it (like the one shown in Figure 16-16, middle), try switching the document's color mode to Duotone. Then, in the Duotone Options dialog box, choose Quadtone from the Type menu and "CMYK wm" from the Preset menu.

Printing Color Separations

To avoid running into unexpected printing costs, it's a good idea to print separations (called *seps* around the water cooler) before sending your image to a print shop. That way, you can make sure an extra color hasn't snuck its way into your document—especially if you've toyed with some spot colors that you're not going to use. However, you probably won't use Photoshop to print separations—in most cases, you'll place an RGB or CMYK image in a page-layout program along with text and other images, and then use *that* program to print the separations. But if you ever *do* need to print separations from Photoshop, visit this book's Missing CD page at *www.missingmanuals.com/cds* for step-by-step instructions.

Proofing Images Onscreen

When you're sending images out for printing, it'd be nice to peek into the future and *see* what they'll look like. Happily, Photoshop can create an onscreen proof simulation known as a *soft proof*, a straightforward process that involves the color profiles you learned about in the previous sections. Here's what you do:

1. **Calibrate your monitor using the tools described earlier (page 675).**

   If your monitor isn't calibrated, soft-proofing is a *galactic* waste of time.

2. **Open an RGB image you intend to print.**

   You can soft-proof either RGB or CMYK images, but it's especially cool to proof an RGB image and see what it will print like in CMYK without having to color-convert it first.

3. **Choose Window→Arrange→"New Window for [name of image file]" to open a second window containing a copy of your image.**

   Then position the two windows so they're side by side by choosing Window→Arrange→2-up Vertical.

UP TO SPEED

Duotones Explained

The term *duotone* generally refers to a grayscale image that has had additional inks added to it. Technically, if you add one ink, it's a duotone; adding two inks make it a tritone; and adding three inks make it a quadtone. The correct *general* term that describes all these variations is "multitonal images." But most folks use the term "duotone" to describe all these alternatives, which can get confusing.

So why add other inks to grayscale images to begin with? A couple of reasons: Some folks use duotones to add color to an image inexpensively (as you learned earlier, reducing the number of colors in an image can mean a cheaper print job). However, duotone (or multitone) aficionados will tell you the additional inks add tonal range and depth to an image—and they're right! In fact, you can add a second gray ink to enhance tonality without adding any color at all.

The two keys to creating quality duotones are:

- Start with a high-quality grayscale image with a good tonal range and lots of contrast. (See Chapter 8 for more black-and-white conversion methods than you can shake a stick at.)

- Substitute the second ink for part of the original black ink, rather than just adding it to the black (see page 703). This prevents the image from becoming too dark and flat because it's drowning in ink.

With a bit of practice, you'll gain confidence in creating duotones and enjoy doing it. However, it's always a good idea to plan extra time in your production schedule to print some tests. Since you can't trust your monitor or proof non-process duotones (see page 704), a test print is worth its weight in gold.

---

4. **Click the right-hand window to activate it and then choose View→Proof Setup→Custom.**

5. **In the resulting Customize Proof Condition dialog box, make sure the Preview checkbox is turned on (Figure 16-17, top).**

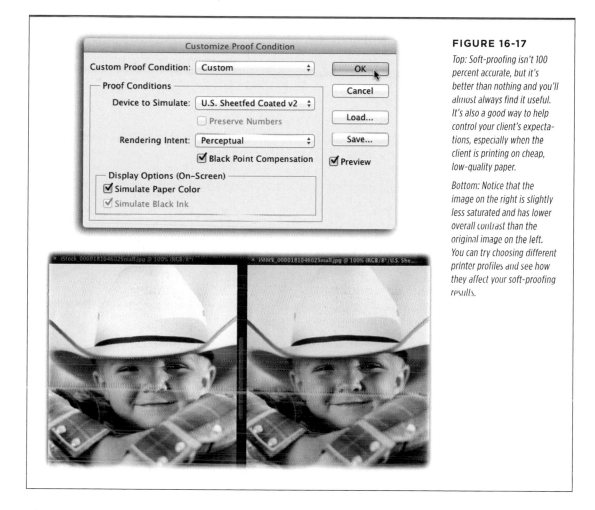

FIGURE 16-17

Top: Soft-proofing isn't 100 percent accurate, but it's better than nothing and you'll almost always find it useful. It's also a good way to help control your client's expectations, especially when the client is printing on cheap, low-quality paper.

Bottom: Notice that the image on the right is slightly less saturated and has lower overall contrast than the original image on the left. You can try choosing different printer profiles and see how they affect your soft-proofing results.

6. **From the "Device to Simulate" menu, choose the profile for your final printer.**

   If the image is headed to a printing press, for example, pick your old profile friend, U.S. Sheetfed Coated v2.

7. **Choose Perceptual from the Rendering Intent menu and make sure the Black Point Compensation checkbox is turned on.**

   The Perceptual option takes into account how humans see color. The Black Point Compensation option helps preserve the contrast of your original.

8. **In the Display Options (On-Screen) section, turn on the Simulate Paper Color checkbox.**

   You can watch your onscreen proof change if you turn this option on and off.

9. **Click OK and then sit back and examine the differences between the two windows.**

You can perform soft-proofing for other printers, too, like your inkjet printer or a digital press (page 710). All you need to achieve good results is a calibrated monitor, an accurate printer, and a paper-specific profile.

Printing Proofs

If you're working in a prepress environment—and especially if you're *not* printing on a digital press—you're often proofing on a different printer than the one that will print the final document. For example, you might print a proof using an inkjet, but the final image will print on a commercial offset printing press. In that situation, you can make the proof printer print a *simulation* of what will happen on the printing press.

Simulating an image involves reining in the proof printer's large color gamut to include only the colors that the printing press can reproduce. You can prepare a simulation in Photoshop using profiles and the proofing feature you learned about in the previous section. Here's how to do it:

1. **Pop open an image and then choose File→Print.**

2. **At the top of the Photoshop Print Settings dialog box, pick your proofing printer from the Printer pop-up menu.**

3. **In the Color Management section, choose Photoshop Manages Colors from the Color Handling menu.**

> **NOTE** If you leave the Color Handling menu set to Printer Manages Color—which you might do if your color-conversion tool is a special *RIP* (page 711) set up for proofing—then Photoshop has zero effect on your color; all the color conversion occurs at the RIP. In that case, you can't soft-proof your image using the Photoshop Print Settings dialog box as discussed here, but you *can* still use the soft-proofing tools discussed in the previous section.

4. **Click the Print Settings button and make *sure* your printer's color management is turned off.**

   In the resulting dialog box, pick your paper size and then verify that the printer's color settings are turned off (they should be) to keep the printer driver from interfering with the color management voodoo you've got going on in Photoshop. See step 8 on page 688 for help finding this setting.

5. **Click Save or OK to return to the Photoshop Print Settings dialog box.**

6. **From the Printer Profile menu, choose the setting that matches the printer, paper, and quality you'll use to print the proof.**

7. **In the next pop-up menu down (it doesn't have a label), choose Hard Proofing.**

This setting lets Photoshop know you intend to simulate a proof on one printer as if it were *another* printer (see Figure 16-18).

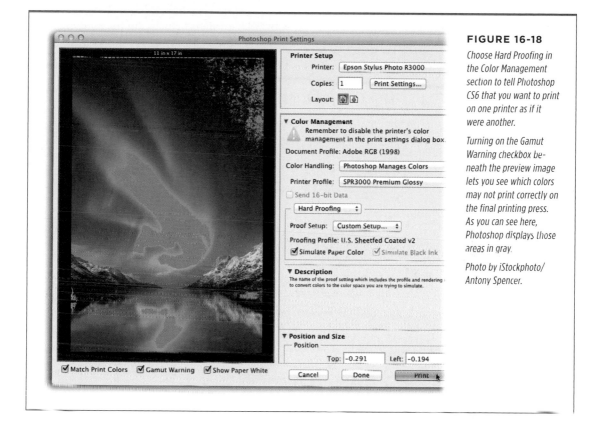

FIGURE 16-18

Choose Hard Proofing in the Color Management section to tell Photoshop CS6 that you want to print on one printer as if it were another.

Turning on the Gamut Warning checkbox beneath the preview image lets you see which colors may not print correctly on the final printing press. As you can see here, Photoshop displays those areas in gray.

Photo by iStockphoto/ Antony Spencer.

8. **From the Proof Setup menu, pick either Working CMYK or Current Custom Setup.**

Straight from the factory, this menu is set to Working CMYK, but be sure to pick Current Custom Setup if you've set up a custom soft-proofing profile as described in the previous section.

9. **Turn on Simulate Paper Color to get the best simulation.**

10. **Beneath the preview area on the left side of the dialog box, turn on all three checkboxes: Match Print Colors, Gamut Warning, and Show Paper White.**

These options let you see an onscreen view of your image that indicates which, if any, colors might not print on the final printer because they're out of gamut (Figure 16-18). If the gray areas aren't important parts of the image, then don't worry about this warning (though the printed color in those spots won't match the color you see onscreen). If the gray areas *are* important, use the techniques described in Chapter 9 to adjust the image's colors (you'll likely want to desaturate those spots slightly). For the fun of it, test the Gamut Warning results using both coated and uncoated paper to see how the paper affects the printed image.

11. **Click Print and wait eagerly to see what your proof looks like.**

Isn't it amazing what you can do with color profiles? Quick, go tell everyone you know how cool this stuff is—and watch their eyes glaze over.

■ Printing on a Digital Press

It used to be the case (and sometimes still is) that, when you prepared a document for a commercial printer, you would convert the images to the CMYK color mode *before* you inserted them in a page-layout document and certainly before you fired them off to the printing company. However, that process is changing because an increasing number of print shops now use *digital presses*.

Digital presses work just like laser printers or copiers; they use electrostatic charges to transfer images from cylinders to the print surface. Like commercial offset presses, digital presses are primarily CMYK printers, but they use powdered toners instead of inks (which is why they can't print spot colors). Some digital presses, like the Kodak NexPress, actually do offer toner spot-color printing, but they're limited to very specific colors like red, green, or blue. And rather than being used for special objects like logos, these additional spot colors typically expand the gamut of the CMYK toners, much like light cyan and light magenta do in inkjet printers.

Because of these quirks, you have to perform some special steps if your project is headed for a digital printer. The following sections explain how to prepare various types of images for a run on a digital press.

WORKAROUND WORKSHOP

Printing Spot-Channel Proofs

Since spot channels are used only by commercial printing presses, getting them to print on your *own* printer for proofing can be...exciting. The solution is to pop into RGB mode temporarily and merge the spot channels. Here's how:

To safeguard your original document, save it and then create a copy by choosing Image→Duplicate. Next, choose Image→Mode→RGB Color and then, in the Channels panel, Shift-click to activate each spot channel in the document. Then open the Channels panel's menu and choose Merge Spot Channels.

When Photoshop asks if it's OK to flatten the layers, click OK. Each spot channel is instantly swallowed up by the closest matching RGB equivalent.

At this point, you can fire it off to your printer without a fuss. The colors won't be *exact*, but you'll get a decent approximation of what the image will look like when you finish editing it. After you print the temporary RGB document, you can toss it and continue editing the original.

Printing RGB Images on a Digital Press

Digital presses handle images much the same way that expanded-gamut inkjet printers do (page 684), so feel free to send 'em an RGB file. Because the RGB to CMYK-Plus conversion occurs at the printing press's processing *RIP* (see the box below), you're dealing with RGB images the whole time instead of converting them to CMYK. That's great news because, as you learned at the beginning of this (exhausting!) chapter, RGB mode provides you with the widest range of printable colors. So if your image is already in RGB mode, you're good to go.

Printing CMYK Images on a Digital Press

If your images are already in CMYK mode, it's OK to leave them that way. Most digital presses recognize CMYK values and print them well enough. That said, you might want to confirm with your printing company that the press will use your current CMYK values rather than converting the image to another color mode and then back to CMYK on the press. (This type of color-shuffling can lead to unpredictable—and usually terrible—results.) Also, keep in mind that your CMYK images will be darker and more saturated if they're printed on a digital press than if they're printed on a conventional, ink-based printing press.

Printing Spot Colors on a Digital Press

Toner-based digital presses are becoming more common, so it's important to know which kind of digital press your document will end up on. If it's destined for one that uses gamut-expanding digital spot toners, leave it in RGB mode to take full advantage of the press's expanded color gamut.

Since digital presses don't print conventional spot color inks, if you send a file that contains any spot colors to a digital printing company, those colors will get converted into CMYK or CMYK-Plus colors (depending on the toners the press uses) before they're printed. The printing press automatically performs this conversion using a built-in spot-to-process *color lookup table* (also called a *color LUT*). Just be sure to use the name provided by Photoshop when you created the spot channel. (For example, PANTONE 810 C is a proper color name, but "Logo spot color" is *not*.) That's because the printer's RIP needs to identify the spot color properly in order to produce the best simulation of it.

FREQUENTLY ASKED QUESTION

Meet the RIP

I thought RIP meant "rest in peace." What the heck does it have to do with printing?

Quite a lot, actually—and it has nothing to do with funerals.

The acronym RIP refers to a device known as a Raster Image Processor. It's a term you'll often hear tossed around at com-

mercial printing companies (also called *service bureaus*). RIPs convert raster images, vectors, text, and transparency info in page-layout documents into print-ready formats for specific printers, image-setters, sign-cutters, and other output devices. You can think of RIPs as super sophisticated printer drivers.

■ Printing Multiple Images

Sometimes it's handy to print multiple images at one time. For example, you can combine images into a single document that prints across several pages—so you don't have to wade through the Print Settings dialog box 10 times—or gather several images onto a *single* page for comparison and/or client approval. Photoshop used to include three handy features that let you quickly and easily organize, format, and print multiple images: PDF Presentation, Picture Package, and Contact Sheet. They were wildly useful and folks squealed when Adobe removed them in CS4. Happily, two of 'em made their way *back* into Photoshop CS6: PDF Presentation and Contact Sheet II.

TIP No matter which option you choose—PDF Presentation or Contact Sheet II—you can simplify things by gathering the images you want to use into a single folder *first*. That way, you can choose that folder instead of rooting through your hard drive for files scattered here and there.

PDF Presentation

To create a multipage PDF that contains one image per page, or a PDF that advances automatically like a slideshow, choose File→Automate→PDF Presentation. In the resulting dialog box (Figure 16-19) pick the images you want to include (by clicking Browse), what color background you want 'em displayed on (white, black, or gray), and which tidbits of info you want printed with them (such as file name, description, and so on).

When you get your settings just right, click Save and you'll see the Save dialog box. Choose where you'd like to put the new PDF, name it, and then click Save. Up pops the Save Adobe PDF dialog box you saw back on page 682. Click Save PDF and Photoshop CS6 does all the heavy lifting of combining those images into a single PDF faster than you could ever do it yourself.

Contact Sheet II

The Contact Sheet II plug-in works in the exact same way as it did in previous versions of Photoshop, so if you've used it before, it'll feel familiar. Contact Sheet II lets you choose multiple images and then have Photoshop shrink them to fit onto a single page (and if they won't fit on one page, Photoshop adds more pages). This kind of thing is incredibly handy when you need to compare and evaluate images for use in a project, or send images to a client so *she* can pick the one she likes best.

To create a contact sheet, choose File→Automate→Contact Sheet II. In the Source Images section at the top of the resulting dialog box (Figure 16-20, top), click Choose and then locate the images you want to include (or pick Open Documents if you've already got 'em open). In the Document section, enter the paper size you want use (for example, to print on U.S. letter-size paper, enter 8.5 in the Width field and 11 in the Height field). Leave the Resolution set to 300 for a nice, high-quality print, and then use the Thumbnails section to tell Photoshop how many columns and rows you want (these settings determine the *size* of the thumbnails). If you want each image's file name to appear beneath its thumbnail, leave the checkbox below "Use Filename as Caption" turned on, and then choose a font and size for the file names from the pop-up menus to the right of the checkbox. Click OK and Photoshop creates a sheet of beautiful miniatures like the one in Figure 16-20, bottom.

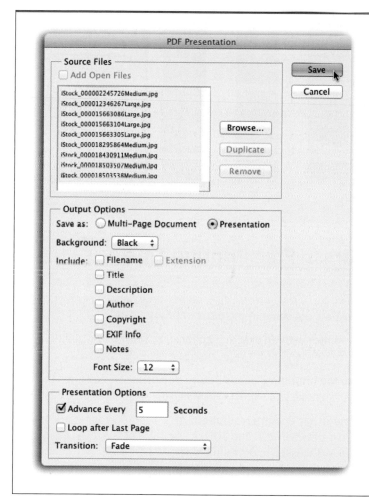

FIGURE 16-19

Choosing Presentation in the Output Options section (instead of Multi-Page Document) turns your images into a self-running PDF slideshow.

The Presentation Options at the bottom of this dialog box let you control how long each image stays onscreen, whether the slideshow starts again after it finishes, and what kind of transition you'd like between slides, if any (Fade is a good choice).

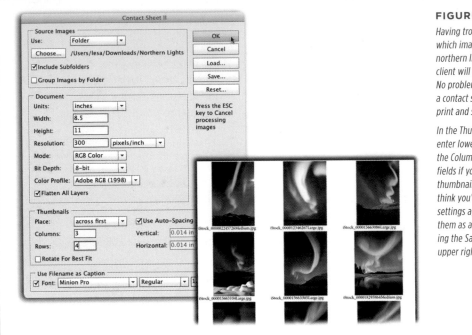

FIGURE 16-20

Having trouble deciding which image of the northern lights your client will like the best? No problem, just create a contact sheet you can print and send to her.

In the Thumbnails section, enter lower numbers in the Columns and Rows fields if you want larger thumbnail images. If you think you'll use the same settings again later, save them as a preset by clicking the Save button in the upper right.

Recap: Stress-Free Printing Tips

Congratulations! You've just waded through a ton of dense information. Some of it you'll remember and some of it you won't, but, no matter what, it's here whenever you need it. To recap, here are some of the most important tips:

- **Calibrate your monitor with an external calibration tool.** This is the only way you can accurately view and proof your images onscreen.

- **Resize images to the print dimensions before you print.** This ensures that the image will print at the size you expect. Besides, smaller images print faster.

- **Make sure the image has enough resolution.** After resizing your image, check that its resolution is between 200 and 300 ppi so it will produce a high-quality print. (Resolution is discussed in detail in on page 237.)

- **Sharpen the image if you've made it substantially smaller.** Anytime you change the number of pixels in an image, it gets softened (blurred) just a bit. A final round of sharpening (see Chapter 11) can help you get some focus back.

- **Save editable PSD files.** Saving your Photoshop document in its native format lets you go back and edit its layers, alpha channels, and so on. When you're creating a version for printing (described in the next bullet), duplicate the file or use File→Save As to make a copy so you don't overwrite the original.

- **Create a flattened version for printing.** Though this step isn't essential, flattening layers and removing alpha channels makes documents less complex, resulting in a smaller files that print faster and more reliably.

- **Proof, convert, and print with printer- and paper-specific profiles.** Now that you've seen how powerful profiles can be, take the time to download and use them (or make your own). Using proper profiles lets you proof, change color modes, and print your images with the most reliable, most predictable, and highest-quality results.

- **Know your target color mode.** Be sure to choose the correct color mode for your image, whether it's RGB for expanded-gamut printers like inkjets and digital presses or CMYK for commercial printing presses.

- **Choose a high-quality file format.** Use compression-free, print-compatible file formats like TIFF, PDF, and EPS for saving, sending, and printing your images.

- **Use real names for spot colors.** When you're printing spot colors, use the names listed in Photoshop's Color Libraries instead of custom names. This increases the chance that the colors will be recognized by other programs like InDesign, or by RIPs that may have to convert them to process colors during printing.

- **Use duotone or multitone presets.** When you're creating duotones or multitonal images, be sure to use Photoshop's presets rather than adding additional colors yourself (at least as a starting point). The presets ensure that your original black ink and any additional inks are properly controlled by Duotone Curves, which reduce the amount of ink used during printing. This keeps the image from losing details and contrast because it's dripping with ink.

- **Communicate with your printing company.** Find out at the beginning of your project *exactly* which file format and settings the company wants. Knowing this info ahead of time can help keep your project from going past its deadline and over its budget.

Photoshop and the Web

Preparing graphics for a website is a journey into the unknown: You've got no idea what kind of monitor folks will use to view your images, how fast (or slow) their Internet connections are, or which web browsers they use. It's a proposition riddled with variables that you have zero control over; all you can do is prepare your graphics well and hope for the best.

The main challenge in preparing images for the Web in Photoshop boils down to finding a balance between image quality and file size. Premium-quality, minimally compressed JPEGs look stunning under almost any conditions—but if your site visitor has a pokey dial-up connection, she might decide to click elsewhere rather than wait for the darn thing to download. On the other hand, if you try to satisfy the slowest common denominator by making ultra-lightweight images, you'll deprive those with broadband (high-speed) connections from seeing the impressive details you've lovingly created.

Luckily, there are several tricks for keeping file sizes down *and* retaining quality. That's what this chapter is all about. You'll learn which size and file format to use when creating images destined for the Web. You'll also discover how to make animations; craft *favicons* (those tiny graphics you see in web browsers' address bars); mock up web pages; and publish professional-looking online photo galleries.

NOTE For a tutorial on creating your own custom Twitter page using Photoshop, visit this book's Missing CD page at *www.missingmanuals.com/cds*.

■ Creating Web- and Email-Friendly Images

Whether you're designing an image destined for life on the Web or creating an email-friendly version of a digital photo, you need to follow three very specific steps to create a high-quality image that people can download quickly:

1. **Adjust the image's dimensions.**

    First, you need to decide how big the image should be. In some cases, someone else may give you the size (like when you're hired to make a web banner or an ad). Other times, you choose the size (like when you email a digital photo, send a sample design to a client, or post an image in an online discussion forum). Once you know the size you need, grab the Crop tool and enter those dimensions into the Width and Height fields on the left side of the Options bar—just be sure to include the unit of measurement, such as "800 px." (For more on resizing with the Crop tool, see Chapter 6).

2. **Decide which file format you want to use.**

    The most common choices are JPEG, PNG, and GIF. See page 721 for the pros and cons of each web-friendly format.

> **NOTE** As you learned in Chapter 2, you should always save your master file as a PSD file (Photoshop document) so you can open, edit, and resave it as often as you want without losing quality. (Each time you save a JPEG as *another* JPEG, Photoshop recompresses it, degrading the image's quality.) The PSD format also retains any layers you created during the editing process.

3. **Save and compress the file.**

    When you're finally ready to create the version that's going to live online, you can squeeze it down to the smallest size possible using the "Save for Web" dialog box, which you'll learn all about beginning on page 723.

If you follow each of these steps, you'll end up with images that match the dimensions you want, look great, and download quickly. The following pages explain how to do all those things.

Resizing an Image

As you learned in Chapter 6, resolution matters when you *print*, but it doesn't mean a hill of beans when you're preparing images for the Web, presentation software, or an email. In the online realm, it's the *pixel dimensions* that matter instead. If you reduce the image's pixel dimensions before posting or emailing it, you won't force unsuspecting folks to download an image that's so big it takes over their whole screen, and you'll end up with a smaller file, which means it'll download faster.

> **NOTE** If you're emailing an image to someone who needs to print it, send him a full-size version in one of the print-friendly formats discussed on page 677. Just be sure to compress the image into a .zip file before you send it so it transfers as fast as possible (see the Tip on page 667).

If you're a designer, someone may give you the pixel dimensions for your project so you can create a new document at that size to start with. But if you're emailing a digital photo or a sample design, or posting an image to an online forum, *you* pick the size. In that case, here are a few all-purpose width-by-height pixel dimension guidelines:

- **800x600 (or 600x800).** Use this size if you're sending a design or photo sample to a client and she doesn't need to print the image. This size image is almost big enough to fill a web browser window (unless your viewer has a 30-inch screen, that is), so she won't have to scroll much to see the whole thing.

- **640x480 (or 480x640).** Use these dimensions if you're emailing a photo or posting it to an online forum. These dimensions produce an image big enough to see well and a file size of less than 1 megabyte (so it transfers nice and fast).

- **320x240 (or 240x320).** These dimensions work well if you're emailing multiple photos or posting to an online forum that contains *a lot* of images. If your recipient has a slow Internet connection, she'll appreciate the smaller file size. And if you crop it wisely these dimensions produce a photo that's big enough for your subject to be identifiable.

- **100x133 (or 133x100).** If you're creating headshots for the company web page—a great way to humanize your firm—this size makes for a nice, small portrait. If you're building a catalog page with a ton of product thumbnails (small preview pictures), this size won't bog down the page. (Linking the thumbnails to full-sized versions lets visitors view enlargements if they want to.)

Once you pick a size, flip back to Chapter 6 for step-by-step instructions on how to resize images using the Crop tool or the Image Size dialog box.

■ RESIZING WEB IMAGES VISUALLY

Sometimes, it's easier just to choose the size you want for your resized image by *looking* at it. For example, you can use the Zoom tool to decrease the size of your image until it looks good onscreen, and then enter *that* zoom percentage in the Image Size dialog box. Here's how:

1. **Open the image you want to resize and zoom in or out until it looks like it's the right size on your screen.**

   Press Z to grab the Zoom tool and click within your image to zoom in, or Option-click (Alt-click on a PC) to zoom out. To use keyboard shortcuts instead, press ⌘ (Ctrl on a PC) and the + or – key to zoom in or out (respectively).

2. **Make a note of the zoom percentage.**

   You can find this percentage in several places: in the document's tab at the top of the screen, in its title bar if you're using floating windows (page 66), and in the status bar at the bottom left of the document window; the last two are circled in Figure 17-1, top.

3. **Open the Image Size dialog box by choosing Image→Image Size or pressing Option-⌘-I (Alt+Ctrl+I on a PC).**

   At the bottom of the resulting dialog box (Figure 17-1, bottom), make sure the Resample Image checkbox is turned *on*.

4. **Set the Width and Height pop-up menus to Percent.**

   If the Constrain Proportions checkbox at the bottom of the dialog box is turned on, Photoshop automatically changes the second menu when you change the first.

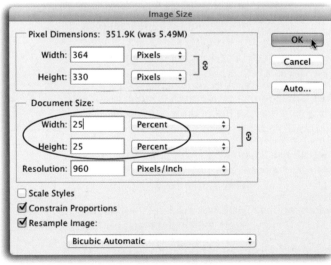

FIGURE 17-1

Top: After you use the Zoom tool to resize your image onscreen, make a note of the zoom percentage shown in the title bar or status bar (both circled).

Bottom: Then pop open the Image Size dialog box and enter the percentage in the Document Size section.

5. **Enter the zoom percentage into the Width or Height field.**

   Again, if the Constrain Proportions checkbox is turned on, you only have to enter the percentage in one field.

6. **Make sure the Resample Image pop-up menu at the bottom of the dialog box is set to Bicubic Automatic.**

   Happily, in Photoshop CS6, the Image Size dialog box chooses the best resampling method *for* you, so you shouldn't have to adjust it. (If you're using an earlier version of the program, choose Bicubic Sharper instead; when you make an image smaller, you lose some details because the pixels become softer, but with this particular method, you get a little sharpening that helps make up for it).

7. **Click OK when you're finished to close the Image Size dialog box.**

Now you can upload the image to the Web (or fire it off in an email) knowing you did your part to be a respectful web citizen. Your mom would be proud.

TIP   To *really* make up for the tiny amount of image softening that occurs when you make it smaller, give it another round of sharpening (see Chapter 11).

Choosing the Best File Format

Once you've resized an image, you need to save it in a format that's not only compatible with both the Web and email, but also reduces it to the smallest possible file size. As you learned back in Chapter 2, those formats include JPEG, PNG, GIF, and WBMP (see Figure 17-2). The one you should pick depends on how many colors are in the image and whether or not it has any transparent (empty) areas:

- **Use JPEG for photos.** This format supports millions of colors, although, as you learned in the box on page 684, it's a *lossy* format, meaning it throws away fine details in order to create a smaller file. However, you can choose the level of compression in the "Save for Web" dialog box (page 246) by setting the amount of compression using the Quality pop-up menu (it ranges from Low to Maximum) or by entering a number from 0 to 100 in the Quality field (0 is the most compression and lowest quality; 100 is the least compression and highest quality).

TIP   No matter which file format you choose, be sure to crop the image as close to the artwork's edges as possible before you save it. That way, you shave off extra pixels you don't need. The Image→Trim command is especially handy for this particular job. In fact, that very command was used on every figure in this book!

- **Use GIF for images with solid blocks of color.** If you're dealing with line art (black and white with no shades of gray) or images made from areas of solid color (logos, comic strips, and so on), GIF is the way to go (see Figure 17-2). It supports fewer colors than JPEGs, so it doesn't work very well on photos. GIFs can be lossy or not; it's up to you. If you want to make 'em lossy, use the "Save for Web" dialog box's 0–100 scale (it works just the *opposite* of JPEGs: 0 is lossless and 100 is full-on lossy). To make the files smaller without resorting to lossy compression, you can limit the number of colors included in the image to anywhere between 2 and 256 (fewer colors equal a smaller file).

FIGURE 17-2

Once you learn each format's strengths and weaknesses, it's easy to decide which one to use when.

Here are prime examples for two of the best Web formats: Use JPEG for photos (top left) and GIF for solid blocks of colors (bottom left) and line art (right).

- **Use GIF or PNG for images with transparent backgrounds.** Use one of these formats when you want a graphic (a logo, say) to blend seamlessly into the background of a web page. If you've painstakingly deleted the background in your image, JPEG won't work since Photoshop *automatically* sticks a solid background behind any empty spaces in that kind of file. Only GIF and PNG lets you retain transparent regions.

The newer PNG-8 format is *lossless* (meaning it doesn't throw away any details) and can create a higher-quality file at smaller file sizes than GIF. The PNG-24 format supports 256 levels of transparency so it produces the highest-quality transparent image of all—making it perfect for images containing transparency *and* a drop shadow—though the file size is substantially larger than a PNG-8 or GIF. The drawback to PNGs is that some older web browsers—Internet Explorer 6 in particular—don't display transparent PNGs properly and stick a white background behind them. PNG is still a relatively new kid on the file-format block, so hopefully this problem won't be around forever. If you know your Web audience will view your site on outdated browsers, then stick with GIF. But if you think they'll have the latest and greatest browsers, go with PNG.

- **Use PNG for super high-quality files.** If quality is more important than download speed, save your image as a PNG. For example, if you're a photographer trying to sell your images, use PNG-8 for the enlarged versions in your portfolio so potential clients can see every last detail in the images. (Resist the urge to use PNG-24 unless you need the extra transparency detail mentioned above, as this format can create files that are *twice* as big as PNG-8.)

- **Use GIF for animations.** If you want to combine several images into an automatic slideshow, save it as an animated GIF. These are handy when you have too much ad copy to fit in a small space on a website; an animated GIF can cycle through the content automatically. You'll learn how to create animated GIFs starting on page 731.

- **Use WBMP (Wireless Bitmap) for black-and-white images headed for mobile devices.** If you're designing black-and-white images for handheld devices (cellphones, smart phones, and so on), choose WBMP. This format supports only black and white pixels and gives you crisp text and logos that are readable on those itty-bitty screens.

Saving and Compressing Files

The "Save for Web" dialog box can save an image *and* compress the heck out of it at the same time. It also gives you four big preview windows—one for your original image and three for other file type and compression levels of the same image—so you can monitor the image's quality while you're trying to squeeze it into a smaller file size (see Figure 17-3).

FREQUENTLY ASKED QUESTION

A Farewell to Web-Safe Colors

Do I still have to use web-safe colors in my graphics? That feels so 1990.

Negative, good buddy. Computer monitors have come a long way over the years, and they can now display a much wider range of colors than they used to. Heck, today's iPods display more colors than the monitors of the early '90s! For that reason, there's no need to stick with the boring, 256-color web-safe palette.

However, if you're convinced that the majority of your audience is afflicted with prehistoric monitors—ones that can display only 256 colors—you can find the web-safe color palette in the Color Picker by turning on the Only Web Colors checkbox at the bottom left of the dialog box. You can also convert other colors

to their web-safe equivalents by using the Color Table section of the "Save for Web" dialog box (see page 726).

These days, it's more important to make sure you have decent contrast in your images than to worry about web-safe colors. Sure, you can upload them and check their contrast on as many monitors or devices as you can get your hands on, but you can't possibly see how they look on *every monitor* (although the "Save for Web" dialog box can help with that). The cold, hard fact is that your images will look darker on some monitors and lighter on others—that's just the way it is. But as long as there's a decent amount of contrast between the darkest and lightest colors, your images will still look good.

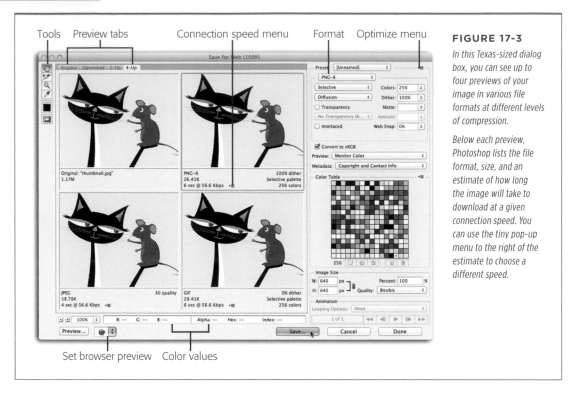

Tools Preview tabs Connection speed menu Format Optimize menu

FIGURE 17-3

In this Texas-sized dialog box, you can see up to four previews of your image in various file formats at different levels of compression.

Below each preview, Photoshop lists the file format, size, and an estimate of how long the image will take to download at a given connection speed. You can use the tiny pop-up menu to the right of the estimate to choose a different speed.

Set browser preview Color values

You saw this dialog box in action when you resized a JPEG back in Chapter 6 (page 246). To explore even *more* of its settings, follow these steps:

1. **With an image open, choose File→"Save for Web" and then, in the resulting dialog box, click the 4-Up tab.**

   At the top of the dialog box, you'll notice four tabs that let you view the original image and up to three other versions so you can see what it looks like when you change its settings. The most useful tabs are 2-Up and 4-Up. Pick 2-Up if you already know the format you want to use and 4-Up if you want to make more comparisons. Optimize gives you no comparison at all and shows only the resized image, not your original.

2. **Click the preview window to the right of the original and, at the top right of the dialog box, choose a file format from the Preset pop-up menu.**

   The Preset menu contains a list of frequently used file format/compression level combinations for the formats previously mentioned (all of which are discussed later in this section). Photoshop changes the various quality and color settings on the right side of the dialog box for you and displays the file size and estimated download time below the preview. (You can change the connection speed

Photoshop uses to calculate the download time by clicking the tiny icon to the right of the listed speed as shown in Figure 17-3.) If you don't want to go the preset route, pick the format from the unlabeled pop-up menu *underneath* the Preset menu and then adjust the quality/color settings manually, as discussed in the next step.

TIP   If you've been experimenting with different file formats in your preview windows, you can have Photoshop return them all to the *same* format automatically. Click to activate the preview window with the file type you want (say, JPEG) and then choose Repopulate Views from the "Save for Web" dialog box's Optimize menu (see Figure 17-3). Photoshop looks at the active preview window's file format and then loads up the *other* windows with previews of the same format at different compression or color settings.

---

3. **In the panel on the right side of the "Save for Web" dialog box, adjust the quality and color settings for the format you picked.**

   Each item in the Preset menu has its own entourage of settings related to quality and color. Different settings appear in the upper-right part of the dialog box depending on the format you chose in the previous step. Here's the lowdown on what they all mean:

   • **JPEG.** This format is the one you'll probably use most often. When you choose one of the Preset menu's JPEG options, you see the following settings:

     — **Quality.** Right below the Format menu is an unlabeled pop-up menu that lets you set the image's compression level. This menu includes five settings that range from Low (highest compression, smallest file size) to Maximum (least compression, largest file size). You can fine-tune the image's quality by using the numeric Quality field to its right (0 is the highest compression/smallest file size, and 100 is the least compression/largest file size). The preset menu also changes if you happen to choose a format and quality level combination that matches one of the presets.

     — **Progressive.** Normally, an image has to download completely before it appears in a web browser, but if you turn on this checkbox, the image loads a little bit at a time (row by row), sort of like a waterfall effect. If your audience is still on dial-up, turn it on.

     — **Optimized.** Turning on this checkbox creates a slightly smaller, though somewhat less compatible file. Leave it off if your audience is likely to use older browsers.

     — **Embed Color Profile.** If you want the image's color profile to tag along with the file, turn on this checkbox. In the off chance that the viewer's monitor can actually *read* the profile correctly (some can't), the colors will look more accurate. If the monitor can't read the profile, you've added a little file size for nothing (which is why you should probably leave this checkbox off).

— **Blur.** Use this field to add a slight Gaussian Blur to the image (page 434) to reduce its file size a little. For a decent-quality image, you can get away with a setting of 0.1 to 0.5 pixels, but anything higher looks terrible.

— **Matte.** This color swatch lets you pick a color to use in place of any transparent (or partially transparent) pixels in your image. Since JPEG doesn't support transparency, those pixels will turn white unless you pick another color here. (Transparency options are discussed on the next page.)

- **GIF and PNG.** You get similar options for both these formats:

   — **Colors.** This pop-up menu is the most crucial setting. It controls the number of colors the image contains (shown in the Color Table a little lower in the dialog box). If you reduce the number of colors in the image, you greatly reduce its file size; the downside is that Photoshop substitutes the closest match for any missing colors, which can produce some weird-looking images. Both GIF and PNG-8 let you choose anywhere between 2 and 256 colors. You don't see this menu if you're using PNG-24, though, as that format gives you 16.8 *million* colors and you can't delete a single one of 'em.

   — **Color reduction method.** This unlabeled pop-up menu lives below the Format menu (see Figure 17-3). If you've reduced the number of colors as described in the previous bullet, this menu lets you pick the method Photoshop uses when it tosses them out. From the factory, it's set to Selective, which makes Photoshop keep colors that your eyes are most sensitive to, although it favors colors in large areas (like a sky) and those that are safe for the Web. Selective usually produces the most visually pleasing palette, so feel free to leave this menu alone. But in case you're interested, here's what the other options do: The Perceptual method is similar to Selective but ignores large areas of color, and Adaptive creates a palette from the most dominant colors in the image (like greens and blues in landscape images and peachy colors in portraits). Restrictive uses only the web-safe palette (see the box on page 723), and Custom lets you modify the color palette yourself (eek!) using the Color Table section of the dialog box. Choose "Black – White," Grayscale, Mac OS, or Windows to use those respective color palettes.

   — **Dither method and amount.** If your image contains colors that the viewer's monitor can't display, you can fake 'em with a process called *dithering*. Use the pop-up menu to the left of the word "Dither" to choose a dither method (or to turn dithering on or off), and the numeric field to its right to set the amount. A high dither amount (percentage) produces more accurate colors; the tradeoff is larger file size (try a setting between 80 and 90 percent). If you're desperate to make the file smaller, lower the dither amount. As far as how dithering does what it does, Diffusion simulates missing colors with a random pattern that's not too noticeable, so it's usually the best choice. Pattern simulates missing colors with a square pattern (which can sometimes create a weird color seam), and Noise uses a random pattern that doesn't spread across nearby pixels (so you won't get a weird seam). If you choose No Dither, Photoshop won't fake any colors. As of this writing, only a tiny number of web users' monitors are still limited to 256 colors, so you can leave dither turned off (you'll end up with a smaller file size by doing so).

— **Transparency and Matte.** If you've deleted the image's background, turn on the Transparency checkbox. If you want to change partially transparent pixels (those around the edges; see Figure 17-4) to a certain color, click the Matte swatch and then pick a color from the resulting Color Picker. You can also choose a matte color from within your image by choosing Eyedropper Color from the Matte pop-up menu. Then grab the Eyedropper tool at the far left of the dialog box—*not* the one in Photoshop's main Tools panel—and click in the image; whatever color you clicked shows up on the left side of the dialog box in the square color swatch beneath the Eyedropper tool. Use the pop-up menu below the Transparency option to turn dithering on or off for any partially transparent pixels around the matte color, and use the numeric field to its right to set that dither amount. You'll typically leave transparency dithering off.

NOTE The Refine Edge dialog box got a major overhaul back in Photoshop CS5. If you've masked (hidden) your background using the Color Decontamination feature, this whole Matte color business is less of an issue. Skip back to page 171 for the scoop on using Refine Edge.

— **Interlaced, Web Snap, Lossy.** Turn on the Interlaced checkbox to make your image appear a little at a time in your visitor's web browser. If you want to convert the image's colors to the web-safe color palette (see the box on page 723), use the Web Snap slider (the higher the number, the more web-safe colors you get). The Lossy slider (which is available only for GIF format, not PNG) lets you lower the image's quality to make the file smaller. You'll typically leave these settings turned off or set to 0, but feel free to experiment with them if you're feeling frisky.

• **WBMP.** If you've made a black-and-white image that's destined for a cellphone or other handheld device with an itsy-bitsy screen, choose this format from the unlabeled pop-up menu below the Preset menu. Since you're dealing only with black and white pixels, you just need to decide whether to turn on dithering (to fake colors the viewer's screen can't display) and, if so, the amount. For the best results, choose Diffusion dithering and then shoot for the lowest percentage possible that lets you maintain some detail in the image.

TIP If you're saving a graphic that has to weigh in at a certain size (like a Web banner ad), you can choose "Optimize to File Size" from the Optimize menu (labeled in Figure 17-3). In the resulting dialog box, enter the target size and pick a Start With option. Choose Current Settings to make Photoshop use the settings in the "Save for Web" dialog box. If you want Photoshop to pick a format, choose Auto Select GIF/JPEG. If you're dealing with an image that contains slices, you can choose to optimize the current slice, each slice, or all of 'em. When you click OK, Photoshop tries to make the image as close to your target size as possible. You may still have some tweaking to do afterward, but the program does most of the work for you.

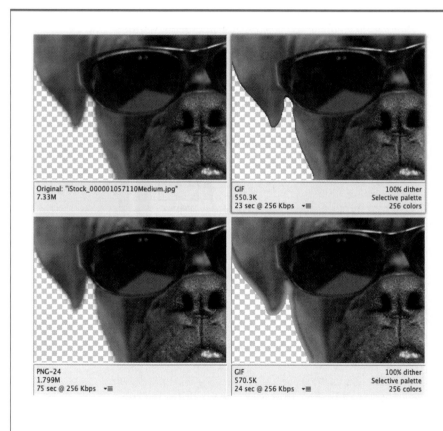

FIGURE 17-4

The edges of a transparent image with a drop shadow look much better as a PNG-24 (bottom left) than a GIF (top right) because the PNG-24 can display so many more colors. But, as the file sizes beneath each preview show, the PNG-24 is also larger and takes longer to download. If file size is more important than download speed, use the Matte menu to change the shadow's partially transparent pixels to the color of your destination background (here that's blue, shown at bottom right). This trick makes the shadow look nice and soft again because Photoshop mixes the matte color with the shadow. It also keeps you from seeing edge halos—leftover pixels from the image's original background.

4. **Make sure the "Convert to sRGB" checkbox is turned on.**

   With this option turned on, Photoshop converts the image to sRGB, a color space designed to mimic the characteristics of a Windows monitor. Since the majority of monitors are attached to Windows computers, that's what you want.

5. **Use the Preview pop-up menu to see what the image looks like on a Mac or Windows computer with no color management or with the document's current color profile.**

   This setting doesn't change your image; it just lets you see it through the eyes of someone with a different monitor. From the factory, this menu is set to Monitor Color, so you see the image exactly as your monitor sees it. Choose Legacy Macintosh (No Color Management) to check what it looks like on a Mac, and Internet Standard RGB (No Color Management) to check what it looks like in Windows. (Windows monitors make images look darker than Macs due to a difference in *gamma* value. So if you're designing images for the Web on a Mac, it's worth choosing Windows to see how dark they'll look.) If the image has a color profile attached to it, choose Use Document Profile to make the preview match.

6. **Set the Metadata pop-up menu to "Copyright and Contact Info."**

   This pop-up menu lets you include the information Photoshop captured from your camera (metadata) or the copyright and contact info you stored using the File Info dialog box (located in the File menu). As you might suspect, including data in your document increases its file size a hair, but it's a good idea to include it anyhow so your image carries info with it about where it came from; otherwise it can appear *orphaned* (visit Wikipedia.com and search for "orphan works" for more on this topic).

7. **Use the Color Table to edit the colors in your image, if necessary.**

   This chart of color swatches lets you change or delete colors in your image. If your viewers are certain to have super old monitors, use the tiny menu near the table's upper right to shift the colors in a GIF or PNG-8 image to web-safe colors. If you need to make your file even smaller, you can delete colors by clicking the swatch you want to zap and then clicking the little trash can icon below the Color Table (shown in Figure 17-3); the number at the bottom left of the table tells you how many colors the image includes. To make a certain color transparent, choose the swatch and then click the transparency button below the table (it looks like a white-and-gray checkerboard). To shift a color to its closest web-safe equivalent, click the little cube. To prevent a color from being tossed, click the tiny lock.

8. When you're finished, click Save.

Photoshop opens the Save dialog box so you can pick a name and storage space for the new file.

TIP If you decide you've got some image editing left to do but you want Photoshop to remember your current settings, click Done instead.

The left side of the "Save for Web" dialog box contains these tools:

- **Hand.** This tool lets you move the image around within the preview windows just like the regular Hand tool. You can also press the space bar (or H) to activate it and then move your mouse to see another part of the image.

- **Slice Select.** If you've mocked up a web page and sliced it accordingly (see page 737), use this tool to choose slices you want to save in specific formats. Keyboard shortcut: C.

- **Zoom.** You can use this tool to zoom in and out of your image just like the regular Zoom tool, though it's faster to press ⌘-plus or – (Ctrl+plus or minus on a PC). Alternatively, in the field at the bottom left of the dialog box, you can enter a zoom percentage or choose a preset from the pop-up menu. You can also Control-click (right-click) within the preview window and choose a zoom percentage from the shortcut menu. Keyboard shortcut: Z.

- **Eyedropper.** Use this tool to snatch colors from the image in the dialog box's preview area, which is helpful when you're creating a matte color for a transparent background as discussed on page 726. Keyboard shortcut: I.

- **Eyedropper Color.** This color swatch shows the Eyedropper's current color.

- **Toggle Slices Visibility.** To see the slices in your image, click this button. (Slicing is discussed starting on page 737.) Keyboard shortcut: Q.

And finally, here's what the buttons at the bottom of the dialog box do:

- **Preview.** To see what the image looks like in a web browser, click this button. Photoshop automatically uses the main browser on your computer, but you can choose a different browser by choosing Other from the pop-up menu to the Preview button's right. In the Preview In Other Browser dialog box, navigate to where that browser lives on your hard drive and then click Open. The next time you click the Preview button, Photoshop uses the browser you just picked.

- **Save, Cancel, Done.** Once you have the settings just right, click the Save button to save the image and give it a name. If you want to bail and do nothing, click the Cancel button. Clicking Done makes Photoshop remember the current settings and close the dialog box. Holding Option (Alt on a PC) changes the last two buttons to Reset and Remember, respectively. Click Reset to revert all the settings in this dialog box to the last ones you saved (in other words, what they were the last time you clicked the Save button). Clicking Remember makes Photoshop uses your current settings the next time you open the "Save for Web" dialog box (whether you click Save or not).

Animating a GIF

You may think that creating an animation is a complicated process, but it's really not. In Photoshop, all you do is create a slideshow that plays automatically. You can control which images the program uses, the amount of time it displays each one, whether it *loops* the slideshow (automatically starts over), and so on. This kind of control is really handy when you're making website ads. For example, if you're designing a 140×140 pixel ad for your costume shop, you need to include a logo, a few costume

---

POWER USERS' CLINIC

Matching and Snatching Colors on the Web

If you're designing an image destined for an existing web page, you may find yourself in a color-matching conundrum. If you need to match the color scheme or colors in a company logo, you can do that by finding out the colors' *hexadecimal* values.

Hex numbers, as they're affectionately called, are six-digit, alphanumeric programming codes for color values. The first two digits represent red, the next two represent green, and the last two represent blue (since your image will appear only onscreen, RGB values are the only ones that matter). You can find a color's hex number in several different ways:

- Grab the Eyedropper tool by pressing I and then click a color in an open Photoshop document to load it as your foreground color. Next, choose Window→Color to open the Color panel and then, from the panel's menu, choose Copy Color's Hex Code. You can also choose "Copy Color as HTML" from the same menu; it does the same thing except that it adds the HTML tag "Color" to what's copied to your computer's Clipboard.

- Using the Eyedropper tool, click a color in an open Photoshop document and then click the foreground chip to open the Color Picker. The color's hex number appears at the bottom of the dialog box in the field labeled #.

- Choose Window→Info and, from the panel's menu, choose Panel Options. In the dialog box that appears,

from the Mode menu, choose Web Color and then click OK. After that, when you mouse over a color in your Photoshop document, its hex number appears in the Info panel no matter which tool is currently active.

- Using the Eyedropper tool, Control-click (right-click on a PC) any color in an open Photoshop document. From the resulting shortcut menu, choose Copy Color's Hex Code.

- Snatch color from *anywhere* on your screen, whether it's on your desktop or in a web browser. In Photoshop, click the foreground color chip to open the Color Picker, mouse over to your document, and then click and hold your mouse button down *while you're in the Photoshop window* and keep it held down as you mouse *outside* Photoshop. Point to the color you want to snatch, *and then* release your mouse button. As long as you first click *within* Photoshop, your cursor remains an eyedropper no matter where you drag it. (You can do the same thing with the Eyedropper tool or by pressing and holding Option [Alt] while using the Brush tool.)

Once you've captured the hex number, you can enter in the field marked # at the bottom of the Color Picker dialog box, or use it in your favorite HTML editor when you're building the web page (just choose Edit→Paste).

- **Rearrange frames.** To change the frames' order, simply drag them into place (easy peasy!).

- **Delete frames.** Just like most panels in Photoshop, this one has its own little trash can icon. To zap a frame, activate it and then click the trash can or drag it onto the trash can. To delete more than one frame, activate them first by Shift- or ⌘-clicking (Ctrl-clicking) them and then click the trash can. In the resulting "Are you sure?" dialog box, click Yes. Alternatively, choose Delete Frame from the Timeline panel's menu.

- **Tween frames.** At first, there isn't any transition between your frames; the animation works just like a regular slideshow, with one frame abruptly giving way to the next. To make the frames fade in and out, you can add *tweening* (short for "in-betweening"). Just tell Photoshop *which* frames to tween, along with how many frames of fading you want, and it adds the new frames for you. When you play the animation, the frames blend softly into one another. Figure 17-6 has the details.

FIGURE 17-6

Top: To fade the first frame (shown in Figure 17-5) into the second, activate the first one and then click the Tween button (circled, bottom). In the Tween dialog box, choose Next Frame from the Tween With pop-up menu, enter 5 in the "Frames to Add" box, and then click OK.

Bottom: Here, Photoshop has added five additional frames (numbered 2–6) that gradually change opacity. When you play the animation, it'll look like the text and Chihuahua photos fade together. For a more gradual fade, enter 10 in the "Frames to Add" box.

NOTE Once you start adding tweened frames, you may need to speed up the whole animation's frame duration so it doesn't take forever to play!

You can create all kinds of special effects using tweening, though you'll need to play around with it to learn what you can do. It's all about setting up a layer for each frame, creating the frames, and then adjusting what you want to happen *between* each frame. For example, if you move the contents of a layer in one frame, you can use tweening to make it look like the object is moving. You can also turn layer styles on or off, add solid-colored frames to make the animation look like it fades into that color, and so on. The creative possibilities are endless!

Saving Your Animation

When you've got the animation just right, you need to do just a couple of things before you post it on the Web. Save it as a Photoshop (PSD) document so you can go back and edit it later, and then do the following:

- **Optimize it.** Choose Optimize Animation from the Timeline panel's menu to create a slightly smaller file, which makes the animation download faster and run more smoothly. The resulting Optimize Animation dialog box has two settings:

  - **Bounding Box** crops each changed frame to the part that's different from the previous frame. This is like running the Trim command on each frame, so that each one is cropped closely to the content.

  - **Redundant Pixel Removal** makes unchanged pixels transparent in subsequent frames, making the file a little smaller.

  Both settings are turned on straight from the factory, but Photoshop doesn't *apply* them until you choose Optimize Animation and then click OK.

- **Save it as an animated GIF.** Last but not least, choose File→"Save for Web" and, in the upper right of the resulting dialog box, choose GIF from the unlabeled format pop-up menu (below the Preset menu). When you do, Photoshop activates the Animation section at the bottom right of the dialog box, giving you one last chance to change the Looping Options and preview your handiwork. When you've finished, click Save and exclaim with gusto, "I'm an animator!"

◼ Designing a Website Favicon

You know those tiny little icons on the left edge of your web browser's address bar (see Figure 17-7). They're called *favicons* (short for "favorites icons"), and they're great for adding a bit o' branding to web pages. They show up not only in web browsers, but also in news feeds (clickable headlines from your favorite websites that you can access through a newsreader program or your browser). Creating them in Photoshop is a snap, and you'll be designing them like a pro after you read this section.

The first step is to spend some quality time looking at other sites' favicons. Your goal is to brand your website with a graphic that's exactly 16x16 pixels—no more, no less. It's tough to design anything that small that's recognizable, but it *can* be done. For example, you might use a portion of your logo rather than the whole thing or your company's initials rather than its full name.

FIGURE 17-7

Here are three different favicons for various websites (circled).

Designing favicons is a good way to test your design skills, since you're limited to 16 pixels square!

Next, you need to download a plug-in that lets Photoshop save the file in the Windows Icon (ICO) file format. The free plug-in ICO Format is a good option: *www.telegraphics.com.au/sw*. Just quit Photoshop and follow the instructions on page 772 to install this plug-in. When you relaunch Photoshop, you should see ICO appear in Save As dialog box's Format pop-up menu. Now you're ready to create your teeny-weeny work of art. Here's how:

1. **Create a new document that's 64x64 pixels with a resolution of 72.**

   Choose File→New or press ⌘-N (Ctrl+N on a PC) to start a new document. Your favicon will *ultimately* be 16x16 pixels, but that's too small a size to work with initially. To save yourself some eyestrain, start out with a 64x64-pixel canvas; you'll reduce its size later.

2. **Create or place your artwork in the new document.**

   If you designed a logo using Adobe Illustrator, choose File→Place to open it as a Smart Object. If you're creating it in Photoshop, be sure to turn off anti-aliasing so the edges are nice and crisp (this is especially important when creating tiny text for the Web, as discussed on page 601).

3. **If you need to, resize the artwork to fit the canvas.**

   If you placed your artwork as a Smart Object, Photoshop automatically surrounds it with resizing handles. If you went another route, you can resize it by pressing ⌘-T (Ctrl+T on a PC) to summon Free Transform and then dragging one of the corner handles. When you're happy with the size, press Return (Enter) to let Photoshop know you're done.

4. **Resize the document.**

   When your design is finished, choose Image→Image Size. Make sure the Constrain Proportions checkbox at the bottom of the dialog box is turned on. In the Pixel Dimensions section, set the Width or Height field to 16 pixels (Photoshop automatically changes the other field to 16), and then click OK.

5. **Sharpen the image if you need to.**

   If your design looks a bit blurry, run a sharpening filter on it (see Chapter 11).

6. **Save the file in the ICO format and name it *favicon*.**

   Choose File→Save As and pick Windows Icon (ICO) from the Format pop-up menu at the bottom of the dialog box and then click Save.

That's it! You've created your very first favicon. If a client asked you to create the favicon and send it to her, email the *favicon.ico* file so she can add it to her website. If you created it for your own site, you're ready to upload the file to the root level of your website, where your index (home) page lives. (If you have no idea what that last sentence means, check out *Creating a Web Site: The Missing Manual*, Third Edition.)

Be aware that not *all* web browsers support favicons, and some even want you to bury a link to the favicon in the code of each page. If you want to take that extra step, you can insert the following code somewhere within the <head> section of your web pages:

```
<link rel="SHORTCUT ICON" href="/favicon.ico">
```

If you've got a big website, adding that line of code can be time consuming, so you may want to use the "Find and Replace" command found in most HTML editors, which lets you search for a piece of code that appears in every page, like the closing </title> tag. For example, you could search for *</title>* and Replace it with *</title><link rel="SHORTCUT ICON" href="/favicon.ico">*.

◼ Creating Web Page Mockups and Image Maps

As you've learned throughout this book, Photoshop is an amazingly powerful image editor, which means it's great for designing web pages. In fact, Photoshop has a tool that'll let you *slice* your design into web-friendly pieces that, when clicked, lead to whatever web address you want to link them to. Photoshop churns out the proper code that you can then paste into your own web page using your favorite HTML editor.

But does all that mean you *should* use Photoshop to build a website? Heck, no. Remember how back in Chapter 14 you learned that, even though Photoshop has a powerful text tool, you shouldn't use it to create a book? The same principle applies here. While you *could* use it to build real web pages, you shouldn't; you're much better off using a program designed for the job, like Adobe Dreamweaver. That said, the Slice tool comes in really handy in a few situations:

- **Building a website prototype.** If you've designed a website for a client in Photoshop and want to give him an idea of how the site will look and behave, you can use the Slice tool to get that done fast. If you slice up your design and assign different hyperlinks to navigation bars, you can give the client a good idea of how the navigation in the final website will *feel*.

- **Making an image map.** The Slice tool lets you add hyperlinks to certain portions of a single image.

- **Making an image-heavy page load a bit faster.** Chopping images into pieces makes them load a little at a time instead of in one big piece. However, this is becoming less of a problem as more people get faster Internet connections.

> **TIP** An alternative to slicing images yourself is to buy a plug-in called SiteGrinder, which can build a fully functional website from a layered Photoshop document. See page 784 for details or visit *www.medialab.com*.

Slicing an Existing Image

Once you've created an image or design that you want to chop up, you can use the Slice tool to draw the pieces by hand or make *Photoshop* create slices from individual layers by choosing Layer→New Layer Based Slices. You can also make Photoshop slice an images according to the guides you've drawn (discussed later in this section). Here's how to slice and dice a web page mockup:

1. **Turn on Photoshop's Rulers and draw guides around the areas you want to slice.**

   Instead of drawing each slice yourself, make Photoshop do the hard work by dragging a few well-placed guides around each slice you want to create. Turn on Rulers by pressing ⌘-R (Ctrl+R on a PC) and then click within the horizontal ruler and drag downward to create a horizontal guide. Do the same thing in the vertical ruler to create vertical guides until you've placed a guide around every slice you want to make, as shown in Figure 17-8.

2. **Press C to grab the Slice tool.**

   The Slice tool, which looks like a tiny X-Acto knife, hides in the crop toolset (it's circled in Figure 17-8).

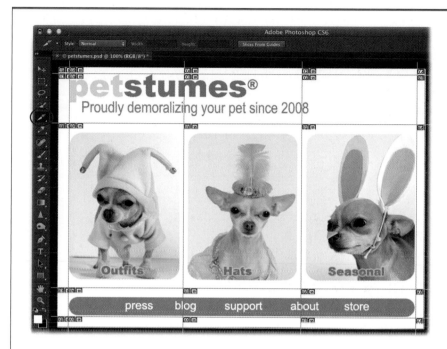

FIGURE 17-8

Here, Photoshop created individual slices from the guides. A bounding box and a tiny number appear at the top left corner of each slice; Photoshop numbers each slice, beginning at the document's top left and working down to the bottom right. If you draw the slices yourself (to create what are called user slices*), the number appears in a blue box. If you make Photoshop draw the slices for you (to create* auto slices*), the number appears in a gray box instead (not shown).*

3. **Trot up to the Options bar and click the Slices From Guides button.**

   In less than a second, Photoshop draws slices around the areas you specified, following the guides you placed in the first step. If you opted out of drawing guides first, you can slice areas yourself by clicking where you want the slice to begin and then dragging diagonally to the right. (To draw a perfectly square slice, hold Shift as you drag.) When you let go of your mouse button, Photoshop puts a blue bounding box around the slice. This kind of slice is called a *user slice*. To account for the rest of your image (the areas you haven't yet sliced), Photoshop draws other slices (called *auto slices*) automatically and marks them with a gray bounding box. Auto slices are discussed in the next section.

   TIP If you've drawn a slice that's perfectly suited for another graphic, you can duplicate it by Option-dragging (Alt-dragging on a PC) the slice onto another image.

Modifying Slices

Once you create a slice, you may need to move or change it. If so, select it using the Slice Select tool. (Press Shift-C to activate the tool or, if the Slice tool is active, you can grab the Slice Select tool temporarily by pressing ⌘ [Ctrl on a PC]; when you let go of that key, Photoshop switches back to the regular Slice tool.) To select a slice, just click it. Its bounding box turns brown and little resizing handles (squares) appear in the center of each side, as shown in Figure 17-9.

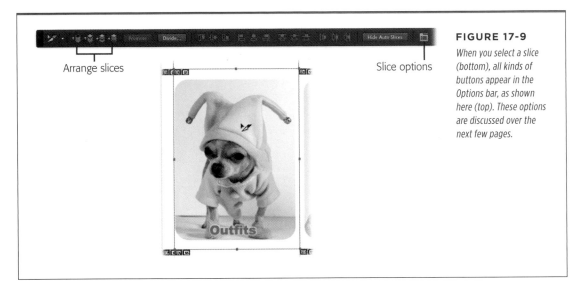

Arrange slices

Slice options

FIGURE 17-9

When you select a slice (bottom), all kinds of buttons appear in the Options bar, as shown here (top). These options are discussed over the next few pages.

Now you're ready to:

- **Resize the slice.** Once you select a slice, you can drag any of its corner or center handles (they look like tiny solid squares) to make it bigger or smaller.

- **Move the slice.** Click within the slice and then drag it to another location. To make it so you can drag the slice only horizontally or vertically, hold the Shift key as you drag.

> **TIP** To make your slices to snap to guides, other slices, or objects, choose View→Snap To. (Unless you've previously turned it off, this option is already turned on.)

- **Promote slices.** You can change a layer or an auto slice into a user slice by clicking the Option bar's Promote button (Figure 17-9, top). This is useful because you can't edit auto slices. For example, if you placed guides and let Photoshop make the slices for you, as described in the previous section, you can't move or resize any of those slices until you promote them to user slices (as shown in Figure 17-10). Similarly, layer-based slices are tied to the pixel content of that layer. Before you can change the slice itself or the layer's contents, you have to promote it to a user slice.

FIGURE 17-10

Notice that the auto slices around the document's edges are tagged with gray icons while the user slices are tagged with blue ones. Promoting auto slices to user slices lets you do things like divide them, as was done in the pink navigation bar shown here.

- **Arrange slices.** Because the Slice tool draws only rectangles, you have to overlap slices to make other shapes. To do that, you may need to fiddle with their stacking order by first selecting a slice with the Slice Select tool and then clicking the arrange buttons labeled in Figure 17-9, top.

- **Align slices.** Photoshop lets you align slices just like you can align layers (page 101). Using the Slice Select tool, Shift-click to select more than one slice and then click the appropriate alignment button in the Options bar.

TIP To change the color of the slice lines, choose Photoshop→Preferences→"Guides, Grid & Slices" (Edit→Preferences→"Guides, Grid & Slices" on a PC). In the Slices section at the bottom of the dialog box, use the pop-up menu to select a new color. You can turn off the Show Slice Numbers checkbox here, too.

- **Divide slices.** If you need to slice a slice (oy!), select it with the Slice Select tool and click the Options bar's Divide button. In the resulting Divide Slice dialog box, turn on either the Divide Horizontally Into or the Divide Vertically Into checkbox, enter the number of slices you want to create, and then click OK.

- **Combine slices.** Select two or more slices by Shift-clicking with the Slice Select tool. Then Control-click (right-click on a PC) and choose Combine Slices from the resulting shortcut menu. This technique is helpful when Photoshop creates too many auto-slices and you want to combine 'em so they'll load as one image.

- **Copy and paste slices.** You can copy and paste a slice by selecting it and then pressing ⌘-C (Ctrl+C). Next, open the target document and press ⌘-V (Ctrl+V). The slice and graphics from the associated layers appear in your new document, but they're all on one layer (which means you can't edit them individually—you have to do that in your original document).

- **Give it a URL.** To transport visitors to a particular web address when they click a slice, select the slice and then click the Slice Options button shown in Figure 17-9 or double-click the slice itself. In the resulting Slice Options dialog box, enter the *full* web address into the URL field (for example, *http://www.petstumes. com*). (The next section also discusses Slice Options.)

- **Delete it.** To delete a slice, select it with the Slice Select tool and then press Delete (Backspace on a PC).

- **Hide.** If you find all those slice borders and numbers distracting, you can hide them temporarily by pressing ⌘-H (Ctrl+H on a PC)—unless you've reassigned that keyboard shortcut to hide Photoshop on your Mac, as described in the box on page 37.

- **Lock.** To lock your unlocked slices so they can't be changed, choose View→Lock Slices (you can't lock individual slices).

- **Clear.** To zap all your slices, choose View→Clear Slices.

To forget you ever heard of slices, hire a web designer (kidding!).

■ SLICE OPTIONS

Once you've drawn slices and put them in the right spots, you can start controlling how they behave in your web browser by setting Slice Options (see Figure 17-11). The Slice Options dialog box lets you control the following:

- **Slice Type.** Most of your slices consist of an image, although they can also be solid blocks of color or plain text. If you want to create an empty space that you can fill with HTML color or HTML text later, choose No Image from this pop-up menu and a "Text Displayed in Cell" field appears that lets you enter text that'll be—you guessed it—displayed in that cell (the empty space).

- **Name.** Photoshop automatically gives slices generic names that include the document name and a number. To use a name that's more descriptive (and useful), enter it here.

- **URL.** One of the big benefits of slicing images is that you can make part of the image act as a *hyperlink* that takes visitors to another web page. Enter the full web address here to make that happen. Photoshop doesn't actually embed this info into your image; instead, it stores the info in a separate HTML file that you can copy and paste into your *own* web page.

NOTE Assigning a hyperlink to part of your image is called *creating an image map*. Now if you hear image maps mentioned at the water cooler, you'll be in the know!

- **Target.** This field determines where the hyperlink opens. For example, to make the hyperlink open the URL in another browser window, enter _blank_ into this field (complete with underscore). If you want the page to load within the same window, leave this field blank.

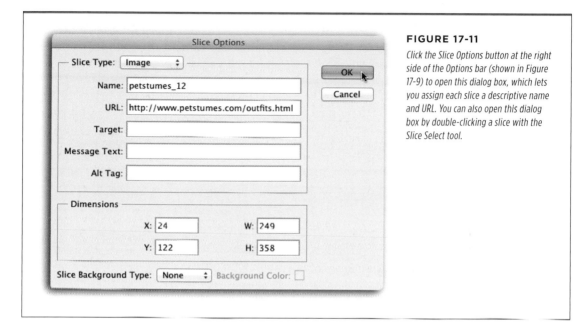

FIGURE 17-11

Click the Slice Options button at the right side of the Options bar (shown in Figure 17-9) to open this dialog box, which lets you assign each slice a descriptive name and URL. You can also open this dialog box by double-clicking a slice with the Slice Select tool.

- **Message Text.** Almost every web browser has a status bar at the bottom of the window that let folks know what's going on in the background. For example, when you type a URL into your browser's address bar and press Return (Enter on a PC), you'll see some kind of "loading" message. If you want to include messages in the status bar (like a love note to your visitors: "Dude—thanks for clicking!"), enter text in this field. But since few folks ever look down that far, your efforts may be in vain.

- **Alt Tag.** Because some folks surf the web with graphics turned off (to make sites load faster), you can use this field to give your image an alternate text description. Visually impaired people using *web readers*—special software that speaks the contents of web pages—will hear this text read to them. The text also pops up as a balloon or tooltip when visitors point to it with their cursors.

- **Dimensions.** This info lets you know the width and height of your slice, along with its X and Y coordinates.

- **Slice Background Type.** If you chose "No Image" in the Slice Type menu, or if part of the image is transparent, you can use this pop-up menu to give the selected cell a color. Your choices include None, Matte (page 726), White, Black, and Other (which summons the almighty Color Picker).

Saving Slices

Once you've set all the options for your slices, it's time to save them to use on the Web (finally!). Use the File→"Save for Web" dialog box to set all those file-type, compression, and other options discussed earlier in this chapter. (If you use File→Save As, all your slice options will fly right out the window.)

On the left side of the "Save for Web" dialog box, click the Slice Select tool to grab each slice so you can apply different format and compression settings to each one (though if you're building a website prototype, choosing one file format for the whole thing works just fine). When you're finished, click Save and tell Photoshop where you want to store the files. If you've assigned URLs to the slices, be sure to choose "HTML and Images" from the Format pop-up menu at the bottom of the Save Optimized As dialog box, as shown in Figure 17-12. (Then make sure to change the Format menu back to Images the next time you use the Save Optimized As dialog box.)

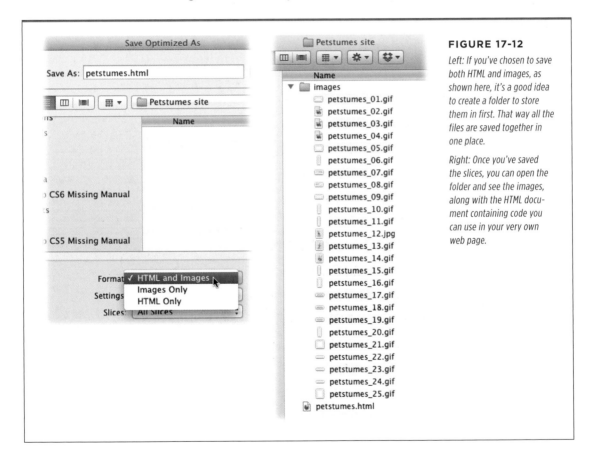

FIGURE 17-12

Left: If you've chosen to save both HTML and images, as shown here, it's a good idea to create a folder to store them in first. That way all the files are saved together in one place.

Right: Once you've saved the slices, you can open the folder and see the images, along with the HTML document containing code you can use in your very own web page.

Protecting Your Images Online

Being able to share images with the world via the Web is a glorious thing, but, in doing so, you risk having your images stolen (gasp!). It's frighteningly easy for thieves to snatch photos from your website to sell or use as their own, so it's important to take a few extra steps to protect them. You can deter evildoers in several different ways, including posting smaller versions of your images (640x480 pixels, for example), using photo galleries such as *www.smugmug.com* that prevent folks from Control-clicking (right-clicking on a PC) to copy images to their hard drives, embedding copyright info, adding watermarks, or using Zoomify (see the box on page 749). Keep reading for the scoop on each option.

Embedding Copyright Info

One of the first steps you can take toward protecting your work is to embed copyright and contact info into the image file by choosing File→File Info (see Figure 17-13). Sadly, this won't keep folks from stealing your image (heck, they won't even see it unless they choose File→File Info themselves), but they *might* think twice about taking it if they do find a name attached to it. Alternatively, you can declare that the image is in the public domain, granting anyone and everyone a license to use it.

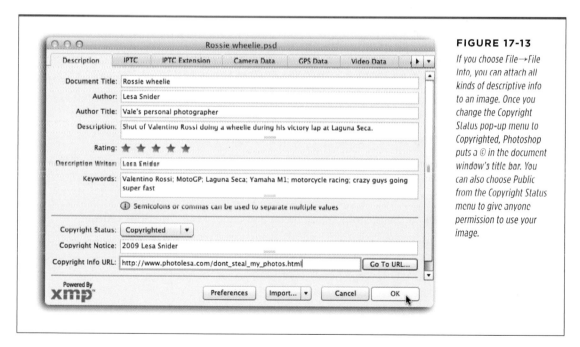

FIGURE 17-13

If you choose File→File Info, you can attach all kinds of descriptive info to an image. Once you change the Copyright Status pop-up menu to Copyrighted, Photoshop puts a © in the document window's title bar. You can also choose Public from the Copyright Status menu to give anyone permission to use your image.

TIP The File Info dialog box in Photoshop CS6 gives you more info than ever before. It sports a new GPS Data tab that you can use to view any location information that was stored when you took the shot (assuming you have a GPS-enabled camera or memory card). And the Camera Data panel now includes more info about the moment of capture, such as the date and time, the lens you used, the metering mode, and the color space.

Watermarking Images

One of the best ways to protect images online is to add a *watermark* to them—a recognizable image or pattern that you either place atop the images (as shown in Figure 17-14, bottom) or embed into them invisibly. A watermark is a great deterrent because would-be thieves will have one *heck* of a time trying to get rid of it. You can add watermarks in Photoshop in a couple of ways:

- **Use custom shapes to add an opaque copyright symbol or logo.** The simplest way to watermark an image is to stick a big ol' copyright symbol (or your logo) on top of it. This process is called *visual watermarking*. If you make the logo partially see-through, folks can still see the image but won't, presumably, steal it because of the huge graphic stamped on top of it.

- **Use the Digimarc filter.** This paid service creates a nearly invisible watermark by adding noise to your image (called *digital watermarking*). It's not cheap, but you also get other features like image linking and tracking, online backups, and visual watermarking. The cost depends on the number of images you use it on and the type of service you pick. A basic account runs $50 per year for 1,000 images; a pro account (which includes an online image-tracking service) is $100 for 2,000 images; and so on. You can learn all about it by visiting *www. digimarc.com*.

Since you've already plunked down good money on both Photoshop *and* this book, here's how to watermark images for *free* using the Custom Shape tool:

1. **Open an image and grab the Custom Shape tool.**

   You can find this tool in the shape toolset, or grab it by pressing Shift-U repeatedly (the tool's icon looks like a rounded star).

2. **Set your foreground color chip to light gray.**

   Setting the foreground color now means you won't need to change the watermark's color later. At the bottom of the Tools panel, click the foreground color chip, pick a light gray from the resulting Color Picker, and then click OK.

3. **Open the Custom Shape menu and choose the copyright symbol.**

   In the right half of the Options bar, click the downward-pointing arrow to the right of the word "Shape" to open the menu of custom shape presets (see Figure 17-14, top). Scroll down until you see the copyright symbol (©), and then click it once to activate it.

4. **Draw the shape on top of your image.**

   Mouse over to your image, click once where you want the shape to begin, and then Shift-drag diagonally to draw the shape. (Holding Shift keeps the symbol perfectly square instead of squished.) When you let go of the mouse, Photoshop adds a layer named Shape 1 to your document. If you want to resize the shape, summon Free Transform by pressing ⌘-T (Ctrl+T).

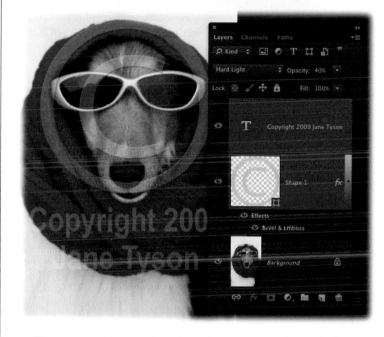

FIGURE 17-14

Top: The Custom Shape tool makes creating your own watermark a snap.

Bottom: If you change the blend mode to Hard Light and lower the opacity to about 50 percent, you can create a nice, professional-looking watermark that doesn't completely obscure your image.

New in Photoshop CS6 is the ability to change the blend modes of multiple layers at once. Yippee!

5. **Add a Bevel & Emboss layer style.**

   To give your watermark a little depth, tack on a layer style. Click the tiny *fx* at the bottom of the Layers panel and choose Bevel & Emboss from the pop-up menu. Feel free to fiddle with the settings (though they're probably fine the way they are), and then click OK to close the Layer Style dialog box.

   TIP The shape's gray outline can make it darn difficult to see a preview of the layer style you're about to apply. Luckily, you can hide the outline by pressing ⌘-H (Ctrl+H). This trick works with paths, too!

6. **Grab the Type tool and type your name below the copyright symbol.**

   Press T to fetch the Type tool, mouse over to your image, and then click where you want the text to start (Photoshop adds a Type layer to your document). You can type whatever you want, but it's a good idea to include "Copyright," followed by the current year and your name or studio name. To change the font and text size, double-click the Type layer in the Layers panel and tweak the Options bar's settings (Arial Black is a good choice). Flip back to Chapter 14 for more on formatting text.

7. **Copy the Shape layer's style to the Type layer to make the text look similar to the copyright symbol.**

   You can copy a layer style from one layer to another by Option-dragging (Alt-dragging on a PC) the layer effect to the new layer (your cursor turns into a double-headed arrow, and you'll see a little *fx* icon behind it when you drag). In this example, Option-click (Alt-click) the layer named Bevel & Emboss, and then drag it to the new layer and release your mouse button. If you don't press Option (Alt) *before* you start to drag, you'll *move* the layer style instead; if that happens, just press ⌘-Z or Ctrl+Z to undo and then try again.

8. **Change the Shape and Type layers' blend modes to Hard Light.**

   Doing this makes your watermark see-through. Remember that in Photoshop CS6, you can change the blend mode of multiple layers at the same time. Just Shift-click to activate both the Shape and Type layers, and then change their blend modes to Hard Light using the pop-up menu at the top of the panel.

9. **Lower the Shape and Type layers' opacity to 40 percent.**

   While you've got the Shape and Type layers active, lower their opacity to 40 percent using the Opacity slider at the top of the Layers panel. This keeps the watermark from overpowering your image.

10. **Save the file and upload it to the Web.**

    Now you can enjoy peace of mind knowing that it'd take someone *weeks* to clone away your watermark.

Protecting your images takes a bit of effort, but it's well worth it. In fact, watermarking is *exactly* the type of thing you should record as an action. Just follow the instructions in Chapter 18 for creating a new action (page 759) and then repeat the steps in this list. You can even include the bit about embedding copyright info in your file (page 745). Once you create the action, you can run it on a whole folder of files to save yourself tons of time!

NOTE You can also use the Image Processer script (page 251) to resize images, run a watermarking action on them, and add copyright info to them all at the same time!

◼ Building Online Photo Galleries

Once you've massaged and tweaked your images to perfection, why not have Photoshop prepare a web-ready photo gallery, complete with thumbnails and enlargements, like the one shown in Figure 17-15? Actually, *Bridge* does all the work using the Adobe Output Module, but that doesn't make it any less cool.

NOTE   In previous versions of Photoshop, you could create a gallery by choosing File→Automate→Web Photo Gallery, but back in CS4, Adobe offloaded that feature to Bridge.

POWER USERS' CLINIC

Zoomify Your Enlargements

It can be dangerous to post a full-sized image on the Web—you're practically giving thieves permission to steal it. But if you're a photographer and you want folks to see all the intricate details of your work, you can protect your images by using a Photoshop feature called Zoomify.

Instead of posting an image as one high-quality piece, Zoomify chops it into pieces and displays it in a Flash-based window with controls that visitors can use to zoom in on and move around within the image. (People who view the image need to have Flash installed on their computers, but if they don't, their browser should prompt them to get it.) That way, instead of seeing the whole thing at full size, they see only one piece at a time, so they can't grab it by taking a screenshot or downloading the whole image. And the new version of Zoomify exports to Flash *and* HTML5, which gives your image's admirers a few more viewing options. To see Zoomify in action, visit *www.bertmonroy.com/timessquare/timessquare.html*.

To use Zoomify, follow these steps:

1. Adjust the image's size using the techniques discussed in Chapter 6. (This step is optional; if you want to upload a full-size image from your camera, feel free, although Zoomify won't work on Raw files).

2. Choose File→Export→Zoomify.

3. In the Zoomify Export dialog box, use the Output Location section to name the file and tell Photoshop where to save it.

4. In the Image Tile Options section, choose an image quality.

Use the Quality text box, pop-up menu, or slider to set the quality of the individual pieces. (Behind the scenes, Zoomify chops your image into a bunch of pieces—called *tiles*—that it reassembles on the fly when your visitor looks at a given area.) Leave the Optimize Tables checkbox turned on so Photoshop optimizes the compression tables for each tile.

5. Enter a width and height (in pixels) for the Zoomify window to determine how large it is in your visitor's web browser.

6. Click OK, and Zoomify creates a block of code that you can paste into your web page. If you left the Open In Web Browser checkbox turned on, Photoshop opens your browser to show you what your Zoomify window looks like.

Now, just open the HTML document that Zoomify made, copy and paste the code into your web page, and then upload the page and image pieces that Zoomify created to your server. After that, folks who look at your image online can see all its exquisite details but can't swipe it and claim it as their own.

Here's how to create a web gallery using Bridge:

1. **Place the images in a single folder.**

   It's a lot easier to grab all the images you want to create a web gallery from if you stick 'em in a folder first.

2. **Fire up Adobe Bridge.**

   You'll learn tons about Bridge in Chapter 21. For now, launch it by choosing File→"Browse in Bridge" or by pressing Shift-⌘-O (Shift+Ctrl+O on a PC).

3. **On the left side of the Bridge window, use the Folders panel to navigate to your images.**

   The images appear in the Content panel in the middle of the Bridge window.

4. **In the Content panel, arrange your images in the order you want them to appear in the gallery.**

   A vertical orange line appears as you drag an image around. When the image is in the right place, just let go of your mouse button.

5. **Activate the images you want to include in your gallery.**

   If you've taken the time to place your images in a single folder as described in step 1, press ⌘-A (Ctrl+A on a PC) to activate 'em all. If you've changed your mind about including some of the images, ⌘-click (Ctrl-click) to pick just the ones you want in the gallery.

6. **At the top left of the Bridge window, click the Output button (which looks like a piece of paper with a folded corner) and choose "Output to Web or PDF" as shown in Figure 17-16, top.**

   On the right side of the Bridge window, the Output panel opens.

7. **Click the Web Gallery button at the top right of the Output panel.**

   Because Bridge can create either a PDF or a web gallery, you have to tell it which one you want.

8. **In the Output panel's Template pop-up menu, choose HTML Gallery.**

   Each version of Photoshop offers more templates to choose from. For a basic photo gallery, the HTML Gallery template is tough to beat (Figure 17-15 shows it in action).

9. **In the panel's Site Info section, add a title, caption, and description.**

   You can add all sorts of other stuff, too, if you want, including your name, email address, and copyright info. These extra tidbits appear at the top and bottom of your web page (see Figure 17-15).

FIGURE 17-16

Top: Bridge has both an Output menu (circled) and Output workspace that let you create a web gallery or PDF page.

Bottom: When you click the Web Gallery at the top of the Output panel, Bridge adds all kinds of options to the panel so you can customize your gallery. Once you've got the settings just right, click the tiny icon labeled here to save those settings as a preset style you can use later.

Save settings as style

10. **Scroll down to the Output panel's Color Palette section and edit the background, text, and link colors.**

    Bridge has all kinds of settings that let you customize how your web gallery looks. To change one of the gallery's colors, just click one of the little color swatches and choose something else from the Color Picker.

11. **In the Appearance section, set the photo size, quality, and number of columns and rows.**

    Unless you change these settings, your gallery will have three rows and columns, and the previews will be medium sized. (If it needs to, Bridge automatically builds more pages to accommodate all your images.)

12. **Back near the top of the Output panel, click the "Preview in Browser" button to get a sneak peek at your web gallery.**

    This button lets you take a peek at your gallery in a real web browser. Depending on the number of images in the gallery, this process may take a few seconds.

13. **Head back to Bridge and, if you want to make changes to your gallery, scroll to the appropriate Output panel section and tweak the settings.**

    If necessary, preview your changes by clicking the "Preview in Browser" button again.

14. **When everything looks good, scroll down to the Create Gallery section of the Output panel to tell Bridge whether to save the gallery to your hard drive or upload it to the Web.**

    At the bottom of the Output panel, you can give your gallery a name and save it to your hard drive or upload it to your web server. If you upload it, you'll need to enter your website's *FTP* (file transfer protocol) settings, along with your login and password.

15. **Click Save (if the gallery is headed for your hard drive) or Upload (if it's bound for the Web).**

Creating web galleries using Bridge is incredibly painless and, in Photoshop CS6, faster than ever. And if you take the time to create a preset, as described in Figure 17-16, you won't have to fiddle with all the Output panel's settings the next time around. Sweet!

Working Smarter with Actions

S ure it's fun to spend hours playing and working in Photoshop, but once you've used the program for a while, you'll start to notice that you repeat the same steps over and over on most of your images. At first, the repetition probably won't bother you—it's actually good while you're learning—but when a deadline approaches and the boss is eyeing you impatiently, you need a way to speed things up.

Luckily, Photoshop includes all manner of automated helpers (some of which you've already learned about), including these:

- The Image Processor script, which resizes images *and* converts them to different file formats (page 251).

- The Contact Sheet II script (page 712).

- Automated photo stitching with Photomerge (page 295).

- Automated lens correction that fixes distortion problems caused by your camera's lens and/or sensor (page 641).

- Automated layer aligning and blending with the Auto-Align and Auto-Blend Layers commands (Chapter 7, beginning on page 295).

- Adobe Bridge, which can create web galleries and rename lots of files at once (Chapter 21).

Some of the best timesavers of all, however, are *actions*—all-purpose, amazingly customizable systems for automating mundane tasks like adding or duplicating layers, running filters with specific settings, and so on. You can use actions to record nearly every keystroke and menu choice you make and then play them back on another image or a whole *folder* of images. Because Photoshop doesn't need to press keys or move and click a mouse when it's running actions, it can blast through them at warp speed. And for the first time ever, Photoshop CS6 lets you record Brush and Pen tool strokes so you can replay, and thereby recreate, a painting or drawing from start to finish. Just imagine how much time you'll save!

This chapter explains how to use the actions that come with Photoshop and how to create, edit, and save your own. You'll also learn how to create drag-and-drop actions called *droplets*—icons you can drop files on to trigger an action—as well as how to find and load actions made by other folks. By the time you're finished reading, you'll be working 10 times smarter and not one bit harder.

The Actions Panel

You record, play, and edit keystrokes using the Actions panel (Figure 18-1). Choose Window→Actions to display the panel in the panel dock on the right side of your screen (its icon is a triangular "play" symbol).

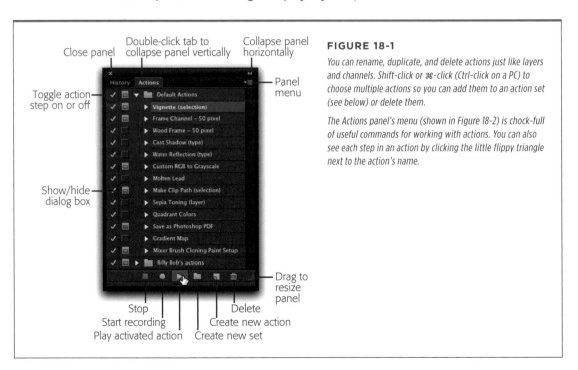

FIGURE 18-1

You can rename, duplicate, and delete actions just like layers and channels. Shift-click or ⌘-click (Ctrl-click on a PC) to choose multiple actions so you can add them to an action set (see below) or delete them.

The Actions panel's menu (shown in Figure 18-2) is chock-full of useful commands for working with actions. You can also see each step in an action by clicking the little flippy triangle next to the action's name.

The panel's controls are pretty straightforward. The Stop, Record, and Play buttons do what you'd expect: They stop, record, and play actions. The "Create new set" button at the bottom of the panel (it looks like a folder) lets you store actions in a set just like you can store layers in a group. You can create a brand-new action by clicking the "Create new action" button, and duplicate an action by dragging it onto that same button or Option-dragging (Alt-dragging on a PC) it up or down in the panel. Duplicating an action comes in handy when you want to run the same filter more than once within an action, or when you want to edit a copy of an action to make it do something slightly different (which is faster than rerecording the action from scratch).

The Actions panel has three unlabeled columns that let you do the following:

- **Turn steps on or off.** The leftmost column lets you turn individual steps in an action on or off via a checkmark next to each step, which is useful if you've made a fairly complex action and only want to run, say, half of it. For example, if you record an action that creates a Smart Object out of all visible layers (page 128), sharpens your image (Chapter 11), and then saves it as a TIFF file, you can turn off the "save" step and stop at sharpening instead. To turn off a step, click the flippy triangle next to the action's name to expand it and then click the checkmark to the left of that particular step. To turn off *all* the steps in an action or all the actions in a set, click the checkmark to the left of the action or set's name. To turn off all the steps *except* one, Option-click (Alt-click on a PC) the checkmark next to the step you want to leave on.

> **TIP** In the Actions panel, a *gray* checkmark next to an action's name means Photoshop will run all the steps in that action; a *red* checkmark means that it'll skip some steps (the ones you've turned off). This handy visual clue lets you keep actions *collapsed* in the panel but still see that you've turned some steps off.

- **Show/hide dialog boxes.** The next column is for showing or hiding dialog boxes associated with the action's steps. When you create an action, you can design it so that, at a certain point, it stops and opens a dialog box that prompts you to enter settings such as feather amount, filter values, and so on. If the action needs your input, you see a light gray icon in the column next to the action's name (it's supposed to look like a tiny dialog box); if the action doesn't need your input, the column displays a dark gray square. If you'd rather not be bothered by dialog boxes, you can hide them by clicking the dialog-box icon, and Photoshop will use the settings you entered when you originally recorded the action. Keeping dialog boxes turned on is handy when you're using Photoshop's built-in actions because entering different values changes the actions' effects on your image. For example, you can increase the feather setting in the Vignette action from the factory setting of 5 pixels to a higher number to create a softer edge.

> **TIP** If the tiny dialog-box icon to the left of an action's name has a dash in the middle of it, that means only some of the steps in that action need your input. If the icon doesn't include a dash, then *all* the steps in that action need your input.

- **Expand or collapse an action.** The third column in the Actions panel lists each action's name and keyboard shortcut (if you've assigned one). To see the individual steps within an action, expand the action by clicking the little flippy triangle to the left of its name—handy when you want to turn off individual steps (as explained earlier) or explore the inner workings of a built-in action (great for learning how to make your own).

> **TIP** To expand or collapse all the actions in a set or all the steps in an action, Option-click (Alt-click on a PC) the action or step's flippy triangle.

Straight from the factory, Photoshop displays your actions as a list (see Figure 18-1), though you can also display them as clickable buttons (see Figure 18-2). Just open the Actions panel's menu and choose Button Mode. Now, instead of triggering an action by choosing it in the panel and then clicking the Play button, you can just click the button with the action's name on it. Unless you're creating or editing actions, this is the way to roll.

FIGURE 18-2

One drawback to using Button mode is that it doesn't let you edit actions or create new ones. You also can't turn individual steps in an action on or off. Darn!

◼ Using Actions

Photoshop comes loaded with dozens of built-in actions, though only a smidgen appear in the main part of the Actions panel. Nine additional sets of built-in actions are tucked away in the panel's menu (shown in Figure 18-2): Commands, Frames, Image Effects, LAB - Black & White Technique (see page 199 for more on Lab mode), Production, Star Trails, Text Effects, Textures, and Video Actions. To load one of these sets, simply choose it from the menu and Photoshop adds it to the panel's main list.

NOTE New among Photoshop CS6's built-in actions is the Mixer Brush Cloning Paint Setup by Photoshop painting pioneer John Derry (*www.pixlart.blogspot.com*). Give it a swift double-click, and Photoshop adds a slew of well-organized layers to the current document that you can then use to turn a photo into a painting. For more on this action, see the Tip on page 504.

Each set includes several actions that you can use as is or edit to your own personal taste. For example, if you think the Spatter Frame action (part of the Frames set) is a little lame with its 15-pixel spray radius, you can bump it up to 25 pixels instead. (Editing actions is discussed later in this chapter.) You can also duplicate that particular step to make the Spatter filter run twice!

TIP An easy way to duplicate an action that you want to edit is to Option-drag (Alt-drag on a PC) it to a different set.

To use one of Photoshop's built-in actions, follow these steps:

1. **Open an image.**

   With most actions, you simply need to open an image and then you're ready to invoke the action's magic. You don't even have to unlock the Background layer because Photoshop duplicates it for you.

2. **If necessary, tell Photoshop which part of the image you want to work with by creating a selection.**

   Occasionally, you need to create a selection before you run some of the built-in actions (like the ones with "selection" in parentheses after their names, such as "Vignette (selection)" [see Figure 18-3]).

3. **Choose the action you want to run.**

   In the Actions panel, click an action to activate it. If you're in Button mode (page 756), simply clicking an action's name triggers that action, so you're done. If you're not in Button mode, continue with the next step.

4. **Click the Play button.**

   Click the little Play button at the bottom of the Actions panel to run the action. Before you can blink, Photoshop is finished and dusting off its hands. If the program displays a dialog box that requires your input, the action pauses while you enter settings. Once you click OK, it continues on its merry way.

   > **TIP** To run just *one* step of an action, double-click that step in the Actions panel or single-click the step and then ⌘-click (Ctrl-click on a PC) the panel's Play button. (Remember, you have to click the flippy triangle next to the action's name to see the individual steps.)

FIGURE 18-3

Top: Photoshop's built-in actions include "Vignette (selection)." Before you can use it, you have to create a selection.

Bottom: Another useful built-in action adds a sepia (brown) tone to your image. In both cases, the action created all the layers you see here, except for the original Background layer (which shows you what the original images looked like).

Creating Actions

When you're trying to decide on an action to record, start by thinking of any repetitive tasks you often perform. For example, back in Chapter 4 you learned that a simple one-pixel black border adds a classy touch to an image headed for a website, newspaper, or newsletter (page 186). If you add those borders regularly, that process is an excellent candidate for an action.

TIP Before you record an action, it's a good idea to create a new *set* (group) for it to live in. There's no limit to how many sets you can make or how many actions you can add to each set. If you forget to make a set before you record an action, you can drag and drop the action into a set later. You can also copy actions between sets by Option-dragging (Alt-dragging) them.

Here's how to create an action that adds a black border around an image:

1. **Open an image.**

   To record the steps, you have to perform them, so you need an open image to play with.

2. **Open the Actions panel and create a new set.**

   Choose Window→Actions, and then click the folder icon at the bottom of the panel. In the resulting dialog box, enter a descriptive name for your new action set (see Figure 18-4, top) and then click OK.

3. **Click the panel's "Create new action" button.**

   The button looks like a piece of paper with a folded corner (just like the "Create new layer" and "Create new channel" buttons). In the resulting dialog box, give the action a short but meaningful name, like *Black border* (Figure 18-4, bottom) You can also assign it a keyboard shortcut and a color (you see these colors only in Button mode [page 756], but they're still handy). When everything looks good, click the Record button to close the dialog box and start recording your action.

NOTE You can edit these settings after recording the action by choosing the action in the Actions panel and then picking Action Options from the panel's menu, or by double-clicking to the *right* of the action's set or name.

Here's how to run an action on more than one file:

1. **Open all the files or place them in a single folder.**

   Photoshop's Batch command works on all open files or a whole folder (unless you're using Bridge, as noted in step 3 below). So depending on how many files you want to work on, you'll probably want to stick 'em in a folder first.

2. **Choose File→Automate→Batch.**

   In the resulting dialog box (Figure 18-5), choose the action you want to run from the Actions menu.

3. **Select the files or folders you want to process.**

   Use the Source pop-up menu to tell Photoshop whether to run the action on all open files or on a folder. If you pick Folder, click the Choose button and navigate to the folder containing your images. You can also choose Import to snatch files parked in your scanner or on an attached digital camera or memory card.

   If you've selected a few files and/or folders in Adobe Bridge, you can run the action on them by choosing Tools→Photoshop→Batch in the Bridge window (see Chapter 21 for more on using Bridge). Likewise, if you've selected files in Photoshop's Mini Bridge panel, Control-click (right-click) one of the thumbnails and choose Photoshop→Batch from the shortcut menu that appears.

WORKAROUND WORKSHOP

Different Files, Different Results

When you're recording actions, it's important to realize that not only is Photoshop recording every step *exactly* as you perform it, but it's also memorizing info about your document. It remembers stuff like file size, color mode, layer names, and even what color your foreground color chip is set to.

For that reason, if you try to run an action on a file that's in a different color mode or is a different size than the document you used to record it, you may encounter errors. For example, if you create an action that applies a 20-pixel feather to a selection in a 320x240-pixel image and then run it on a 3888x2492-pixel image, you won't get the same results. (In fact, you'll barely see the feather, if at all.) Since the pixel dimensions of those two images differ so much, you have to create two separate actions: One for the smaller pixel-size file and one with a higher feather amount for the larger pixel-size file. Alternatively, turn on the dialog box option discussed on page 755 so you can enter a feather amount each time you run the action.

Also, when you use certain tools while you're recording an action, Photoshop remembers the tool's position within the image by snagging coordinates from your vertical and horizontal rulers. Among these are the Marquee, Slice, Gradient, Magic Wand, Lasso, Shape, Path, Eyedropper, and Notes tools. So if you run an action involving these tools on files of varying pixel dimensions, you'll run into problems. For example, if you record an action that includes drawing an Elliptical Marquee in the center of a document and then run that action on a document with vastly different pixel dimensions, the document's center won't be in the same place. The fix is to change the unit of measurement for your rulers to *percentages* (page 35) before you record the action. That way, Photoshop records your cursor's location as a *relative* position instead of an absolute position.

4. **Adjust other settings, if needed.**

Turn on the "Override Action 'Open' Commands" checkbox if there's a step in your action that opens a file. That way, Photoshop opens the files you've selected in the Source menu instead of hunting for the file name recorded in the action. However, leave this checkbox off if you recorded the action to open a *specific* file that's necessary for the action to work properly, like when you're using Match Color to snatch the color from one image and apply it to others.

If you've chosen Folder as your source and the folder you want to work with contains *other* folders of images that you want Photoshop to process, turn on the Include All Subfolders checkbox.

If you want to bypass any options associated with the Open dialog box, turn on the Suppress File Open Options Dialogs checkbox. Doing so hides the options in Photoshop's Open dialog box so you can open a group of images without seeing the Open dialog box for each one (handy if you batch process Camera Raw images from your digital camera).

Finally, turn on the Suppress Color Profile Warnings checkbox if you want Photoshop to always use its own color profile (page 674) without asking if that's OK.

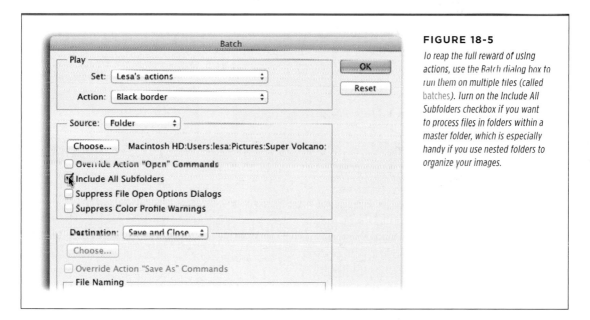

FIGURE 18-5

To reap the full reward of using actions, use the Batch dialog box to run them on multiple files (called batches). Turn on the Include All Subfolders checkbox if you want to process files in folders within a master folder, which is especially handy if you use nested folders to organize your images.

5. **Tell Photoshop where you want to save the processed files.**

From the Destination pop-up menu, choose None to have Photoshop leave your files open *without* saving them (not a good idea if you're running the action on hundreds of files!). Pick "Save and Close" to overwrite the originals and close the files. To preserve the originals, choose Folder and then click the Choose button to tell Photoshop where it should save the new files.

If you've got any Save As steps in your action, turn on the "Override Action 'Save As' Commands" checkbox to make Photoshop use the settings you've specified in this dialog box. If you don't turn on this checkbox, Photoshop saves your images *twice*: once where you specified in your original action and a second time in the location you set in the Batch dialog box.

6. **If you want to rename the resulting files, enter a naming scheme in the File Naming section.**

   You can name the new files anything you want. Choose Document Name from the first pop-up menu to have Photoshop keep the original file name, or enter something else in the name field. You can also rename files with the current date (in several formats), using an alphabetical code or numeric serial number, and so on. Keep the second field in each row set to "extension" so you don't encounter any problems with incompatible file formats down the road.

7. **Turn on the appropriate Compatibility checkbox(es) based on where the files are headed.**

   If you know your images will be opened or stored on a computer that runs a different operating system than yours, then turn on the checkboxes for each system your file is likely to end up on (Photoshop automatically turns on the checkbox for the operating system you're using). For example, if you're using a Mac and your images are destined for a Unix-based web server or a Windows-based file server, check Mac and Unix or Windows. (It's OK to turn on all three compatibility checkboxes.)

TROUBLESHOOTING MOMENT

Action Errors

Using actions is typically a trial-and-error operation—it can be challenging to get them just right. If Photoshop encounters *any* condition that varies from what you recorded, it slings an error dialog box at you and comes to a full stop.

One of the most common errors is Layer Unavailable, because most folks don't realize that Photoshop captures *layer names* when you record an action. For instance, if you start an action by double-clicking the Background layer to make it editable, Photoshop searches for a layer named Background when you run that action. If it doesn't find one, you'll be greeted with an error dialog box that says, "The object 'layer Background' is unavailable." At that point, you can either continue running

the action (by clicking Continue) or stop right there (by clicking Stop). If you choose to proceed and Photoshop *can* finish the remaining steps, it will. If it can't, you get (surprise!) another error dialog box expressing Photoshop's regret.

Admittedly, having to click Continue once in a while is no biggie, but it brings your action to a screeching halt. To cut down on this type of error, use keyboard shortcuts to activate layers instead of clicking them in the Layers panel. That way, Photoshop records the *shortcuts* instead of specific layer names. (The box on page 85 has a honkin' big list of shortcuts for activating and moving layers.)

---

8. **Choose an error-handling method from the Errors pop-up menu.**

This is where you tell Photoshop what to do if it encounters a problem while it's running the action. Your options are "Stop for Errors" and "Log Errors to File." If you choose the latter, Photoshop writes down all the errors in a text file and continues to process your images; click the Save As button below this pop-up menu to tell the program where to save that text file.

9. **Click OK to run the action.**

Sit back and smile smugly as Photoshop does all the work for you (and cross your fingers that you don't get any errors!).

■ Managing Actions

If you don't get your action quite right the first time (which is perfectly normal), you can go back and edit it, though it's usually easier to just start over from scratch. That said, the Actions panel's menu has a few commands that can help you whip misbehaving actions into shape:

- **Record Again.** When you choose this option, Photoshop runs through all the steps in the action and opens all the dialog boxes associated with them so you can adjust their settings, and then updates the action accordingly.

- **Insert Menu Item.** For some unknown reason, you can't record any items in the View and Window menus when you're creating an action, but you can *insert* them—or any other menu item—using this command, either while you record the action or after. Simply select the step above where you want the menu item to go, or, if you want to insert the menu item at the end of the action, select the action's name. Then choose Insert Menu Item from the Actions panel's menu and, in the resulting dialog box, select the item and then click OK. If the menu item pops open a dialog box, Photoshop won't record any settings, so you'll have to enter them when you run the action.

> **TIP** There's no way for you or anyone else running an action to turn off a dialog box that you've added using the Insert Menu Item command (though you can turn off *other* action dialog boxes—see page 755), so it's a good way to *force* whomever is running the action to enter a particular menu's settings. You can use this command to insert any menu item you want, even ones like a feather radius that you can record in an action.

- **Insert Stop.** Use this command to pause the action so you can do something that you can't record, like change the Brush tool's tip and size (CS6 can capture strokes made with the Brush or Pen tools, but it can't capture the tool's *settings*). To add a stop after a particular step, select the step in the Actions panel and then choose Insert Stop (see Figure 18-6). Photoshop includes a dialog box that says what to do next, like "Change the Brush tip to Charcoal Pencil." When you're running an action and come across a stop, after you've done what you need to do, click the Play button in the Actions panel to run the rest of the action's steps.

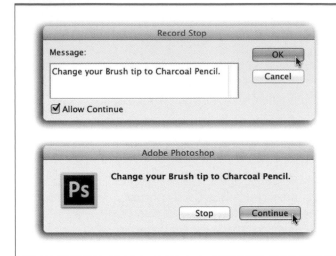

FIGURE 18-6

Top: When you insert a stop, you get to include instructions for the person running the action; you can type whatever you want. The message appears when that person triggers the action's stop point. If you want to let folks continue with the action after they've preformed the step described by the message, turn on the Allow Continue checkbox.

Bottom: Here's what you see when you run the action and hit the stop point. Since there's no Continue button, your only choice is to click Stop. After you've performed the part that couldn't be recorded, click the Actions panel's Play button to finish the action.

- **Insert Path.** Photoshop CS6 can record the act of drawing a path (as explained in the last bullet in this list), though it can't record Pen tool *settings*, so you can use this command to insert a path you've *already* drawn. Just open the Paths panel (page 547), pick the one you want, and then choose this command.

- **Action Options.** This command opens the Action Options dialog box so you can edit the action's name, keyboard shortcut, and color (this maneuver works on custom actions as well as built-in ones). You can also open this dialog box by Option-double-clicking (Alt-double-clicking on a PC) the action, or rename an action by double-clicking its name in the Actions panel.

- **Playback Options.** If you can't figure out where an action has gone haywire, you can make Photoshop play the action more slowly by selecting this command. In the resulting dialog box, you can choose Accelerated (normal speed), "Step by Step" (Photoshop completes each step and refreshes the screen before going to the next step), or "Pause For _ seconds" (Photoshop pauses between each step for the number of seconds you specify).

- **Allow Tool Recording.** New in CS6, this option tells Photoshop to capture strokes you make with the brush tools and paths you draw with the Pen or shape tools (though it doesn't capture the tool's *settings*). Be sure to turn it on *before* you begin recording the painting of your next masterpiece, and you'll be able to replay, and thus recreate, the painting anytime you want.

Editing Actions

You can add, delete, or tweak actions' steps, and scoot them around within the Actions panel (just like Layers). To rearrange your Actions panel, just drag an action to a new position in the panel; when you see a thick black line where you want the action to go, release your mouse button. This lets you keep certain actions together so they're easier to spot (handy when you're in Button mode [page 756]). You can also drag and drop steps *within* an action to rearrange them. To change an action's settings (such as the feather amount), just double-click the relevant step while an image is open, enter a new amount in the resulting dialog box, and then click OK.

> **NOTE** Clicking OK actually *runs* the command associated with the dialog box (feathering a selection, for example), but you can undo it by pressing ⌘-Z (Ctrl+Z on a PC). Photoshop still remembers the new settings you entered and will use them the next time you run that action.

You can also add steps to an action—just choose the step that comes *before* the one you want to add and then click the Record button. Perform the new step(s) and then click the Stop button. Photoshop adds the new steps below the one you chose.

To get rid of a step, action, or set of actions, just choose what you want to delete and then drag it onto the trash can icon at the bottom of the Actions panel. (To bypass the "Are you sure?" dialog box Photoshop displays when you use that method, choose the items and then Option-click [Alt-click on a PC] the trash can button to delete them.) To do a *thorough* spring cleaning of the Actions panel, choose Clear All Actions from the Actions panel's menu and, when Photoshop asks if you *really* want to delete everything (including Photoshop's built-in Default Actions set), take a deep breath and click OK.

> **TIP** To get the Default Actions set back after using the Clear All Actions command, just choose Reset Actions from the Actions panel's menu. Whew!

◾ Creating Droplets

Droplets are actions that you trigger by dragging and dropping files onto special icons, so they're great for running actions on images without actually opening them (such as changing file format, image size, converting an image to black and white, or applying an overall color boost). As self-contained mini-applications, they can live outside Photoshop on your desktop, as *aliases* (pointer or shortcut files) in your Dock (or taskbar on a PC), or on someone else's computer.

It's easy to create a droplet from an action; just follow these steps:

1. **Trot over to the Actions panel and choose an existing action.**

   You can't put the cart before the horse! To make a droplet, you've got to record the action first.

2. **Choose File→Automate→Create Droplet.**

   The resulting dialog box looks like the Batch dialog box shown in Figure 18-5 (page 763). Click the Choose button at the top to tell Photoshop where to save your droplet, and then set the other options according to the advice on pages 762–765.

3. **Click OK when you're finished.**

   Your droplet (which looks like the one shown in Figure 18-7, top) magically appears wherever you specified.

FIGURE 18-7

Top: Your droplet looks like a big, fat, blue arrow.

Bottom: To use a droplet, simply drag and drop a file or folder onto its icon, and Photoshop performs the action on the file(s). (If Photoshop isn't currently running, it launches automatically.)

If you're using a Mac, you need Snow Leopard (OS X 10.6) or higher to use Droplets in 64-bit mode. If you're using an earlier version of OS X, you can always launch Photoshop in 32-bit mode instead (the box on page 4 tells you how).

FREQUENTLY ASKED QUESTION

Sharing Droplets

I want to send my extra-special Mac droplet to a Windows computer. Is that legal?

Sure! It's within your Photoshop User Bill of Rights to share droplets between computers with different operating systems; however, the droplet won't work unless you know these secrets:

- Save the droplet with an *.exe* extension, which tells a Windows computer that it's an *executable file*—in other words, a program you can run (this extension isn't necessary on Macs).

- If you created the droplet on a Windows computer and want to move it to a Mac, drag it onto the Photoshop CS6 icon on the Mac to make Photoshop update it so it works on Macs, too.

- File name references aren't understood between operating systems, so if your action includes an Open or Save As step that references a specific file, the action pauses and demands the file from the poor soul who's using the droplet. If that happens to you, use the error dialog box to find the file Photoshop is asking for so the droplet can resume its work.

■ Sharing Actions

When it comes to actions, folks love to share—there are tons of actions floating around on the Web. Most are free (though you'll probably have to register with the website you're downloading from), but you have to pay for the more useful and creative ones. Sharing actions is pretty easy; the only requirement is that you save your actions as a set (see below) before uploading them to a website.

Loading Actions

Downloading and analyzing actions made by other folks is a fantastic way to learn what's possible. That said, actions that are short and sweet—ones that expand your canvas, add a new layer and fill it with white, and so on—can be even more useful than more complex actions because you'll use 'em more often.

One of the best places to find useful actions is the Adobe Photoshop Marketplace (*www.tinyurl.com/psmarketplace*). Others include Action Central (*www.atncentral.com*), PanosFX (*www.panosfx.com*), and ActionFx (*www.actionfx.com*). (These sites are also great resources for brushes, textures, and so on.) Most of these sites arrange their goodies by category, so you'll probably have to choose Actions from a menu.

Here's how to load somebody else's action onto your computer:

1. **Download the action or action set.**

   What you're actually downloading is an ATN file (if the set is compressed, you'll end up with a Zip file that you need to double-click to expand). Save it somewhere you'll remember (like on your desktop or in your Downloads folder).

2. **Drag and drop the action into an empty Photoshop window (no documents open), as shown in Figure 18-8.**

   You can also load a new action by choosing Load Action from the Actions panel's menu, by double-clicking the ATN file, or by right-clicking the ATN file and choosing Open With→Adobe Photoshop CS6. No matter which method you use, the new action appears in your Actions panel.

3. **Choose the action and give it a whirl.**

   Test drive your new action by opening an image, clicking the action's name in the Actions panel, and then clicking the Play button. That's the only way to find out whether it's lovely or lame.

Saving Actions as a Set

Photoshop temporarily stores the actions you create or load in a special spot on your hard drive. If you reinstall or upgrade the program, there's a chance your actions will get zapped in the process (though CS6's new Migrate Presets option helps a lot; just choose Edit→Presets→Migrate Presets [page 39]). If you've grown fond of your actions, you can save them *outside* the Photoshop application folder for easy backup.

When you find a setting you like, click OK to make Dfine create a copy of the currently active layer and apply the noise reduction to the duplicate instead of the original.

FIGURE 19-2

Dfine's handy split-screen view lets you see how much noise the plug-in will remove from the image before you commit to the change. Here, the original is on the left side of the vertical red line and the result on the right.

Thanks to Nik Software's amazing *control points* technology, Dfine lets you reduce noise in certain areas of an image without adding a mask. It also figures out which kind of camera you used to take the photo and then applies the right amount of noise reduction for your particular model (which makes sense because your camera is what introduced noise in the first place). You can buy Dfine for $100, but it's cheaper if you buy it along with other Nik products, such as Sharpener Pro, Color Efex Pro, or Viveza (*www.niksoftware.com*).

NOTE One nice thing about Nik Software's plug-ins is that they all have the same appearance and controls, so once you learn how to use one, you can easily use 'em all.

Noise Ninja

Long considered the king of noise-reduction software (though Noiseware has become extremely popular, too), photographers and newspapers have used this plug-in for years. It helps reduce noise (speckled imperfections) and grain (textured imperfections) while preserving details. It can tackle 16-bit images (see the box on page 46), handle batch processing, and work as a Smart Filter (page 634). It'll set you back about $80 (*www.picturecode.com*).

Making Selections and Masking

As you've learned in previous chapters, selecting stuff like hair and fur is really hard. Sure, there are some tricks that make it simpler, but a plug-in specifically designed for that task can make your life a heck of a lot easier and save you tons of time. That said, you'll need a bit of patience when you start working with masking plug-ins, because they're not for the faint of heart. With practice, though, you can use them to create selections you just can't make any other way.

NOTE Adobe put a lot of work into improving the Refine Edge command back in Photoshop CS5. So before you plunk down cold hard cash on a masking plug-in, make sure you're up to speed on the enhancements discussed starting on page 171.

Fluid Mask

Fluid Mask is a powerful plug-in that helps you mask around complex areas like hair and fur. As soon as you open Fluid Mask, it analyzes your image and marks what it thinks are edges with blue lines (see Figure 19-3) so you can decide which edges keep and which ones to zap. Then it creates a cutout of the image you can send back to Photoshop to use as a mask. You can also save your project and return to it later—a nice touch. Fluid Mask costs about $150 (*www.vertustech.com*).

FIGURE 19-3

These blue lines mark the edges that Fluid Mask found in this image. You can use the plug-in's tools (on the left) to mark edges you want to keep and ones you want to throw away.

Perfect Mask

Perfect Mask (previously called Mask Pro) helps you pick the precise colors you want to keep or remove as you build image masks. It gives you two eyedroppers to work with: Use one to select colors you want to keep and the other to select colors you want to throw away. Then you can use its Magic Brush to paint away the background while the plug-in helps you along by referring to the Keep and Drop color palettes you made. It can also extract partial color from a pixel, leaving you with a partially transparent pixel—important when you're selecting hair or fur (the edges are so soft that they have to be partially see-through to blend in with a new background). You can also view the image in mask mode, which helps you see what the selection looks like because it's displayed in shades of gray (just like a layer or channel mask). Perfect Mask can work with 16-bit images and works as a Smart Filter, though you have to turn the layer into a Smart Object first (page 128); otherwise, the plug-in deletes the selected pixels as soon as you apply it. It costs around $100, though it's cheaper if you buy it as part of a bundle (*www.ononesoftware.com*).

> **TIP** When you install an onOne Software plug-in like Perfect Mask, it shows up in the File→Automate menu.

■ Color Correction and Enhancement

The plug-ins in this category can spruce up or fix the color in your images and produce a startling array of special effects while they're at it. Read on for the scoop!

Viveza

As you've learned in previous chapters, before you adjust the color of a specific part of an image, you need to select that area first. Not so with Viveza. Since this plug-in made its debut in 2008, it has revolutionized selective color and light adjustments. By marking the areas you want to change with *control points* (the small gray circles shown in Figure 19-4), you can adjust the saturation, brightness, and contrast of those areas at warp speed. And Viveza performs its magic on a duplicate layer, so you don't have to worry about destroying your original image. It's available from *www.niksoftware.com* and costs around $100.

> **TIP** Hot off the plug-in presses is an offering from *iStockphoto.com* that lets you access their royalty-free stock image and illustration database via a panel right here inside of Photoshop. To get it, visit *www.lesa.in.istockpsplugin*. Once you install it, you can access it by choosing Window→Extensions→iStockphoto.

Color Efex Pro

If you could buy just one plug-in, Color Efex Pro would be a darn good choice. Using
the same control points as other Nik Software plug-ins, this one lets you selectively
apply up to 55 enhancement filters to your images—all nondestructively. You can
use them to enhance images in creative ways, as well as to fix color casts, smooth
skin, and so on (see Figure 19-5). Drop as many control points as you want and use
them to set the effect's opacity in certain areas of the image, or click the Brush button to paint the effect where you want it. The price ranges from $100 for 26 filters
to $300 for all 55, and it's available from *www.niksoftware.com*.

FIGURE 19-5

Top: This split-screen preview shows you before and after versions of an image. This particular filter, called Bleach Bypass, creates a high-contrast grunge look.

Bottom: The Glamour Glow filter gives the original image (left) a seriously dreamy look (right). But because Color Efex Pro applies the effect on another layer, you can always lower the filter layer's opacity to blend it with the original in order to produce a more realistic result.

Perfect Portrait

With the click of a single button, this plug-in scans your image for faces and facial features so it can whiten eyes and teeth, define lips, soften wrinkles, and reduce shines and blemishes. It can also zap color casts based on the ethnicity of each face in the image. And age- and gender-specific presets give you a head start for a slew of common problems. A handy set of sliders let you adjust each and every improvement, and tools let you paint away stray hairs, blemishes, and wrinkles. When you find a combination of settings that works, you can save it as your own preset for use on other photos. You get to choose whether to apply these amazing fixes as a Smart or as an additional image layer. Perfect Portrait is available for $100 from *www.ononesoftware.com*.

PhotoTune

This plug-in lets you correct color and skin tones more easily than you thought possible. The color-correction part works like an eye exam, asking you which of two images you like better (Figure 19-6). Through a series of six steps based on the choices you make, it resets your black and white points (page 208), applies curves for brightness and contrast, and so on. Since it's incredibly simple, this plug-in is great for newbies or those who (rightly!) fear the Curves dialog box. If you're more advanced (or brave), you can skip to the Fine Tune panel and adjust the settings manually. You can also take a snapshot of your image and compare it with other versions that use different settings.

FIGURE 19-6

PhotoTune asks you to pick the better of two images in a series of six steps. It's by far the easiest way to color-correct images.

The skin-correction feature (Figure 19-7) is designed to produce accurate skin color based on a point you click with the plug-in's eyedropper. PhotoTune also presents you with a row of color swatches similar to that particular skin tone; just click the one that looks best to you. It then zaps any color cast from the skin and removes the same cast from the rest of the photo. You can take a snapshot of your image and compare it with other versions produced with different settings, as well as save your settings and apply them to similar images later. PhotoTune is happy to work using Smart Filters, though you have to convert your image layer to a Smart Object first. PhotoTune costs $100, and it's available from *www.ononesoftware.com*.

FIGURE 19-7

After you click a midtone point on your subject's skin, you can pick from a row of color swatches developed by the folks at onOne Software. They took countless photos of people and assembled their skin tones into a massive database of over 400,000 different skin types. That's a lot of skin!

PhotoTools

This plug-in includes more than 300 photographic effects developed by the onOne team, as well as Photoshop guru Jack Davis and wedding photographer Kevin Kubota. PhotoTools helps you create beautiful portraits and vignettes, combine multiple effects into a layer mask, and more. You can export several versions of an image with different color profiles (page 674), which is handy if the result is headed to a printer or the Web. You can also apply a *watermark* (a partially transparent graphic) to your files to help protect them from copyright violators when you post them on the Web. This plug-in does its thing on its own brand-new layer so it's nondestructive, and it can also batch-process images. It's available from *www.ononesoftware.com* for $100.

■ Miscellaneous Plug-Ins

Most of the plug-ins in this section relate to specific tasks like creating black-and-white images, making enlargements, merging HDR images, building websites, creating actions, and so on.

Silver Efex Pro

This plug-in isn't a black-and-white converter; it's a virtual black-and-white *darkroom* that helps you create stunning black-and-white images (Figure 19-8) from color ones (though you can also use it to improve images that are already black and white). It has more than 30 black-and-white presets and also lets you create your own. You can make global adjustments using the plug-in's sliders or drop control points to tweak the brightness, contrast, and structure (level of detail) in only specific areas of your image. These control points let you quickly sharpen certain parts of the image, like eyes, patterned clothing, and so on. You can also add a color filter just as if you'd put a filter on your camera lens. Silver Efex Pro lets you choose from over 20 different film types to simulate the look and grain of real film, add tints, or burn the edges of your image. It works as a Smart Filter and costs about $200 (*www.niksoftware.com*).

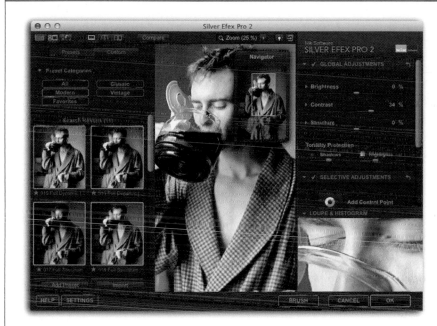

FIGURE 19-8

Silver Efex Pro, currently the most powerful black-and-white plug-In on the market, includes a gazillion gorgeous presets that you can fine-tune. It even helps you create the look of black-and-white images captured on real film. If you want to add a little grain to your image, you can pick from several different options that look like real film grain.

Perfect Resize

Previously known as Genuine Fractals, this plug-in will save your bacon if you need to enlarge an image. It lets you create printable versions of even low-resolution images (like those made for the Web or captured with a low-quality setting on your digital camera). It can blow images up to over 1,000 percent to make honkin' big panoramas, enlarge still frames from old videos to create higher-quality versions, and so on. It can scale any Photoshop document—even if it's brimming with Smart Objects (page 126), paths (Chapter 13), or Type layers (Chapter 14)—without losing resolution or harming the image's quality. Just pick the pixels, dimensions (if you know them), enter a percentage for the enlargement, or enter the print size and resolution you want (page 237). If the image's proportions don't match those of the paper size you pick, Perfect Resize offers you a cropping grid. It also batch-processes images. The pro version costs $200, and the standard version—without CMYK, Adobe Lightroom, or Apple Aperture support—runs $100 (*www.ononesoftware.com*).

HDR Efex Pro

High Dynamic Range photography is all the rage these days, and while Photoshop lets you merge multiple exposures of the same image (page 398), this plug-in makes the process super simple. HDR Efex Pro offers an easy-to-use workspace, mathematical formulas to take your images from great to galactic in a flash, the ability to fine-tune the resulting image with precise adjustments, as well as a slew of incredible presets. This plug-in is $100 and is available from *www.niksoftware.com*.

Eye Candy

This ever-popular set of special effects plug-ins now comes in one big honkin' set. It includes 30 filters that create everything from metal; glass; gel; and natural phenomena like fire, ice, and smoke; to textures like lizard, fur, and stone. The Eye Candy plug-in set runs $250 and is available from *www.alienskin.com*.

SiteGrinder

If you've designed a website in Photoshop and shudder at the thought of slicing it up and turning it into actual code, this plug-in will do that for you in just two steps. SiteGrinder builds a web page based on *CSS* (Cascading Style Sheets) and HTML5 straight from Photoshop so you never have to *see* (much less tweak) any code. You can also make photo galleries, Flash slideshows, CSS3-based menus, and other amazing stuff without losing the design you've painstakingly crafted in Photoshop. The magic lies in naming your layers and layer groups things like "button," "rollover," "pop-up," and so on, so the plug-in can figure out how each part of your web page should work. The basic program is $250, though add-ons for commerce, remote content-management, and the ability to generate WordPress themes start at $150 each (*www.medialab.com*).

Dashboard Pro

Need help with Photoshop actions? Look no further. Longtime pro photographer Kevin Kubota created Dashboard Pro ($80), a collection of over 250 actions that are organized so you can easily find them (categories include black-and-white, color, creative enhancements, romantic, edgy, and so on). You can also assign keywords to your own actions and then search by keyword, name, or category. You can mark favorites for quick recall, and write a searchable description for any action. Kubota also offers dozens of action packs—including a collection of borders, textures, and artistic styles based on popular photographers (*www.kubotaimagetools.com/dashboard.html*).

Photoshop and Video

Everybody's shooting video these days, whether it's with a video camera, a point-and-shoot camera, or a fancy digital SLR. Photoshop has been able to edit videos since CS3, though only in the more expensive Extended version. In CS6, Adobe moved the video editing features into the more affordable standard version of Photoshop. This is great news, especially since you already know how to use Photoshop, so you don't have to learn another program just to edit videos.

While you *can* create an extensive video project in Photoshop, other tools are much better suited for that, such as Adobe Premiere Pro, Apple's Final Cut Pro, Sony's Vegas Pro, and Avid's Media Composer. Instead, you'll want to use Photoshop for creating video projects that contain only a handful of clips, or for cleaning up clips for use in other programs.

Here's what you can do with video in Photoshop CS6:

- Trim the beginnings and ends of clips.

- Create a sequence of clips, and add transitions between them.

- Use the program's tools to clean up unwanted objects or blemishes, frame by frame.

- Adjust a clip's colors, brightness, and sharpness.

- Use the program's filters to give a clip an entirely new look.

- Add text, photos, and other graphics (like logos).

- Add and control audio tracks.

Videos as Smart Objects

You can also import a video clip into an existing document by choosing File→Place. Doing so adds the video to your document as a Smart Object (page 126), meaning it's primed and ready for applying filters nondestructively, plus Photoshop automatically gives the layer the same name as the video clip's filename. Once you place the clip, Photoshop puts a bounding box around it so you can resize it if you need to (just press Return or Enter to accept it).

In fact, using Smart Objects is the only way to apply a filter to a *whole* video clip (otherwise Photoshop only applies the filter to a *single* frame; you'll learn more about that on page 814). You can convert a video layer into a Smart Object anytime by Ctrl-clicking (right-clicking on a PC) near the layer's name in the Layers panel and choosing "Convert to Smart Object," or by activating the layer and then choosing Filter→"Convert for Smart Filters."

Using Smart Objects is also handy if you want the clip to be smaller onscreen than the others (for a picture-in-picture effect), or to apply a Motion effect to it, such as rotating, zooming, or panning across the clip.

Meet the Timeline Panel

Once you've got a few clipsTimeline panel imported into your document, you can use the Timeline panel (Figure 20-2, top) to do all kinds of things to your clips such as play, rewind, or fast forward through them; rearrange them; hide or show them; edit them; and skip to a specific spot within a clip. Before diving into all that, here's an overview of the basics of using the Timeline panel.

The first thing you'll want to do is to play your project. When you first import a clip, Photoshop positions the *playhead* (labeled in Figure 20-2, top) at the beginning of the clip; it looks like a blue triangle with three dots on it, and a thin red line extending down through all your tracks. The playhead moves across the track as it plays to indicate which part of the track you're viewing. You can move the playhead manually by dragging the blue triangle, or control its position by using the first four buttons at the top left of the Timeline panel (labeled in Figure 20-2, top):

- Click the **First** button to move the playhead to the first frame of your project (in other words, the very beginning).

- Click the **Previous** button to position the playhead one frame to the *left* of the playhead's current position.

- Click the **Play** button to, well, play your project and the playhead moves rightward through your tracks. As soon as you click this button, the icon on it changes to a Pause symbol (two vertical lines); click it to halt playback. (You can do the same thing by tapping your space bar once to play and again to pause.) As your project plays, the *timecode* at the bottom of the panel lets you know exactly where you are in the video. Photoshop also displays the *frame rate* (the speed at which the individual frames are played back) to the right of the timecode.

NOTE Even new machines can struggle with playing back lots of video tracks and effects, especially if they're high definition. If the frame rate turns *red* during playback, you aren't seeing all the frames (and Photoshop kindly tells you how many you *are* seeing, instead of the intended frame rate).

- Click the **Next** button to position the playhead one frame to the *right* of the playhead's current position.

To rearrange your clips to change the order in which they play, just click a clip and drag it left or right; when you drag, your cursor turns into a closed fist and you see a ghosted image of the clip. When you get it in the right spot, release your mouse button. That said, it's often easier to drag clips up or down in the Layers panel instead, as explained in the following Tip.

TIP In the Layers panel, layers that are *lower* in the layer stack within a video group appear *earlier* in the Timeline panel, and layers that are *higher* in the layer stack appear *later* in the Timeline panel. (In other words, the bottom-to-top order of Video layers in the Layers panel is the same as the left-to-right order of video clips in the Timeline panel.) So dragging a Video layer down or up in the Layers panel also moves the clip left or right in the Timeline panel, respectively.

■ Editing Video

Very few, if any, video clips begin and end at the perfect moments. That's why it's important to know how to edit video in Photoshop. In this section, you'll learn how to do that as well as add transitions, text, other images, and even audio. Read on!

Changing Clip Length

Fortunately, Photoshop makes it easy to trim a clip—just drag its endpoints in the Timeline panel. As you shorten one clip, the others slide over to keep the video seamless, as shown in Figure 20-3.

FIGURE 20-3

Trimming a clip is as easy as dragging its start point or end point. When you get your cursor in the right spot for dragging, it turns into a bracket with a double-sided arrow (circled); then just click and drag. Photoshop also opens a preview window that shows exactly which frame you're trimming the video down to. Handy, eh?

You can also adjust the length of a clip by clicking the triangle in the upper-right corner of the clip in the Timeline panel. When you do, Photoshop opens a panel containing Video and Audio buttons (Figure 20-4, top).

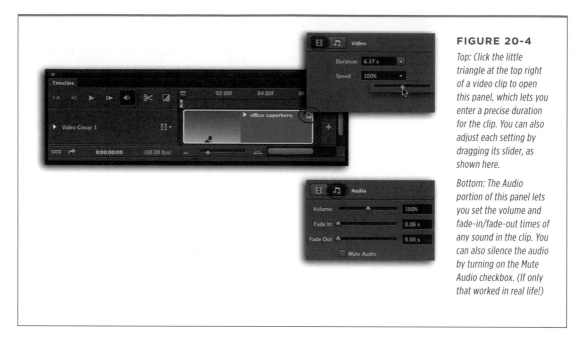

FIGURE 20-4

Top: Click the little triangle at the top right of a video clip to open this panel, which lets you enter a precise duration for the clip. You can also adjust each setting by dragging its slider, as shown here.

Bottom: The Audio portion of this panel lets you set the volume and fade-in/fade-out times of any sound in the clip. You can also silence the audio by turning on the Mute Audio checkbox. (If only that worked in real life!)

NOTE If a Video layer has been converted into a Smart Object (page 790) or if you opened the clip as a Smart Object, clicking the triangle in the clip's top right opens the Motion panel instead (such as Pan, Zoom, Rotate, etc.). This panel is discussed later in this chapter on page 806.

The Video portion of the panel includes the following controls:

- **Duration.** Sets the length of the clip by trimming frames from the end.

- **Speed.** Sets the playback speed of the clip, from 25% to 400%.

NOTE If you increase the speed, Photoshop may shorten the clip's duration. Likewise, if you decrease the speed, Photoshop may lengthen the clip's duration. Consider yourself warned!

When you click the Audio button, you get these options instead:

- **Volume.** Sets the clip's sound level from 0% to 200% of its original volume.

- **Fade In/Fade Out.** Controls the time at which the clip's sound fades in or out.

- **Mute Audio.** Turn on this checkbox to hear nothing but the sound of silence.

When you're finished tweaking the panel's settings, press Return (Enter on a PC) to accept your changes and then click anywhere on the Timeline panel or within your document to close the panel. If you change your mind about editing the clip, press the Esc key instead to dismiss the panel and cancel your changes.

Adding Transitions

If your video project contains more than one clip (and it probably will), you can add a *transition* that connects two clips by fading them into each other. You can also add transitions at the beginning and end of your project. Photoshop CS6 offers the following transition styles for your video-viewing pleasure:

- **Fade.** Fades the clip to transparent (empty) pixels.

- **Cross Fade.** Fades the first clip out as the second clip fades in.

- **Fade With Black.** Fades the clip to solid black.

- **Fade With White.** Fades the clip to solid white.

- **Fade With Color.** Fades the clip to the solid color of your choice. (Choose the color before you add the transition by clicking the color chip that appears in the Transition panel when you pick this style, or after you add the transition by Ctrl-clicking [right-clicking] its icon in the Timeline panel.)

To add a transition to a clip, click the aptly named Transition button on the Timeline panel (circled in Figure 20-5). In the resulting panel (Figure 20-5, top), drag a transition style and drop it onto the beginning or end of your clip, or *between* two clips, as shown in Figure 20-5 (bottom). When you drop the transition, an icon appears on the clip where you placed it. If you drop the transition between two clips, the icon appears at the end of the first clip and the beginning of the second.

FIGURE 20-5

Choose a transition style and duration from the Transitions panel (top) and then drag it onto the beginning or end of the clip you want to add it to (middle). (Here the panel has been separated from the Timeline panel so you can see the transition icon.)

If the transition connects two clips, you can drag either end of it to adjust its length asymmetrically to create a longer fade out and shorter fade in, or vice versa (middle and bottom). As you drag, a handy info overlay appears showing the duration of the transition (bottom).

You can control the duration of the transition either by using the slider in the Transition panel *before* dragging the transition onto the Timeline panel, or by dragging the edge of its icon *after* you've dropped it on the Timeline panel. You can also Ctrl-click (right-click on a PC) the transition's icon in the Timeline panel to make Photoshop display another panel that lets you change the transition's style and duration (Figure 20-6).

TIP To adjust a transition's length symmetrically, Option-drag (Alt-drag on a PC) one end of it. This lengthens or shortens the transition equally on both ends.

FIGURE 20-6

Ctrl-click (right-click) a transition's icon to display this handy panel. To delete the transition, click the trash can icon at the bottom-right of this panel. You can also delete a transition by clicking to activate it in the Timeline panel and then pressing the Delete key (Backspace on a PC).

Splitting and Removing Sections from Video Clips

Another kind of edit you'll likely need to make is to *split* a long clip into multiple pieces, or to chop a section out of the middle of a clip. The first maneuver is super easy but the second takes a little more effort.

To split a video clip into multiple pieces, click the clip in the Timeline panel to activate it, and then position the playhead where you want the split to occur. When it's in the right spot, click the "Split at Playhead" icon (the scissors) at the top of the Timeline panel, as shown in Figure 20-7.

> **TIP** You can also split a clip by positioning the playhead in the right spot and then Ctrl-clicking (right-clicking) the clip itself and choosing Split Clip from the resulting shortcut menu.

Removing a section from the *middle* of a clip is a little more complicated and there are a couple of ways you can do it. If all you want to do is to delete a section of a clip, simply split it at two points, click to activate the middle section, and then press Delete (Backspace on a PC). Photoshop scoots the clip segment on the right side over to the left so the clips play one right after the other.

Another way to remove part of a clip is to define a *work area*, which lets you tell Photoshop which section of the clip you want to work with. To do that, first you have to drag the Video layer out of its video group in the Layers panel (just drag it above or below the video group) and then you define the work area (explained in a sec). Once you do that, the next change you make applies only to that area, whether it's deleting that section from the clip or exporting that section to preview what it will look like.

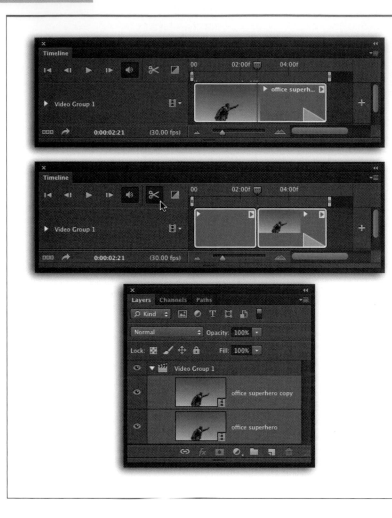

FIGURE 20-7

When you split a video clip, Photoshop cuts it wherever the playhead is and a new Video layer appears within the video group at the top of the layer stack. Photoshop cleverly names the new layer "[original Video layer name] copy" as shown here.

To define the work area, you use the work area sliders that live in the Timeline panel directly below the time ruler (they look like little light gray bars and are labeled in Figure 20-8, top). Click and drag the sliders so that they're on either end of the portion of the clip you want to work with. Alternatively, you can position the playhead where you want the work area to start and then, from the Timeline panel's menu, choose Work Area→"Set Start at Playhead." Then set the end of the work area by repositioning the playhead and, from the same menu, choosing Work Area→"Set End at Playhead."

Once you've defined the work area, you can delete that section of the clip by using the Timeline panel's menu. If you want to leave a hole the length of the section you're removing, choose Work Area→Lift Work Area. This divides the original clip into *two* clips, leaving a gap the length of the section you zapped (Figure 20-8, middle). If you instead want the original clip to play uninterrupted where the axed section used to be, choose Work Area→Extract Work Area. This also *divides* the original clip into two, but the second clip plays immediately after the first one, as if the missing section never existed (Figure 20-8, bottom).

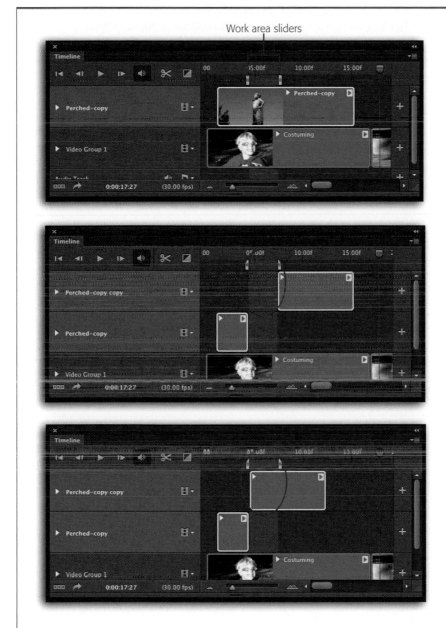

Work area sliders

FIGURE 20-8

Top: After liberating the Perched video clip from its video group, you can position the work area sliders around the section you want to remove.

Middle: Lifting a section of a clip leaves a gap between the two remaining parts of the original clip (circled).

Bottom: Extracting the section instead leaves the two remaining parts with no gap between them (circled).

Adding Text, Logos, and Still Images

One of the more common video-editing tasks is to add text, still images, logos and other vector graphics to a video project. These are all great ways to add brand identity to a project, navigation elements to a video disc or kiosk, or to add visually interesting bits and pieces that you can animate.

Adding such things to your video in Photoshop is super easy. You can drag and drop 'em directly from Bridge or your computer's desktop; copy and paste them from another Photoshop document, drag and drop a layer from another Photoshop document; or create them from scratch in your current document. Whichever method you use, the new goodies appear on their very own layer, either above the currently active layer or, if no layers are active, at the top of the layer stack.

Adding text to video works just like any other text: simply press T to activate the Type tool, click within the document where you want the text to appear, and then start pecking away (be sure to commit the text by clicking the checkmark near the right end of the Options bar or by clicking any other layer or clip in the Timeline panel). Photoshop creates a new Type layer that you can format and reposition in the Layers panel however you'd like. (For more on formatting text, see Chapter 14.)

> **TIP** Once you've added text, you can animate it. The next section explains how.

To add a still image—be it a photo, vector, or whatever—it's easiest to choose File→Place, navigate to where the file lives on your hard drive, and then click Place. Photoshop surrounds the item with a bounding box that you can use to resize or rotate it (to move the item, just click and drag within the bounding box). When you're finished, press Return (Enter on a PC) to accept the transformation.

> **TIP** When you're preparing still images for viewing on a TV (on a DVD, say) make sure the size of those images is 720 x 534 square pixels or 720 x 480 non-square pixels. Also, the color gamut on a TV isn't the same as it is on your monitor. For the best reproduction, try adding a Levels Adjustment layer and then, in the Properties panel, entering *16* into the Output field at the panel's bottom left and *235* into the Output field on the right (see page 381 for more on these fields). Doing so should pull any colors that are too bright back into the TV color gamut.

Adding and Controlling Audio

In Photoshop CS6, you can add audio files to your video project as either a separate track or as part of the Audio Track that automatically appears at the bottom of the Timeline panel. The advantage of using the Audio Track is that doing so lets you control the volume of *each* clip, as well as how it fades in and out. (If you add an audio clip to a video track, Photoshop treats it like a video and you have far less control over it.) To add an audio file to this track, mouse over to the Timeline panel and click the icon to the right of the words "Audio Track" that looks like musical notes (circled in Figure 20-9, top). From the pop-up menu that appears, choose Add Audio, and then navigate to where the audio file lives on your hard drive. When you click Open, Photoshop plops the file into the Audio Track.

NOTE Happily, Photoshop understands most common audio file formats, including AIF, WAV, MP3 and AAC (but not FLAC). Basically, if iTunes can play it, Photoshop can import it. And if Photoshop *refuses* to import it, then it may be protected by a digital rights management (DRM) system (for example, an M4P file).

UP TO SPEED

Timeline Tricks

To master the Timeline panel, you'll need a few tricks up your sleeve. Here are some of the most useful ones to memorize:

- **Switch units.** Out of the box, the Timeline panel's unit of measurement is *time,* and it displays this info both in the time ruler at the top of the panel and in the timecode at the bottom (both are labeled back in Figure 20-2, top). To see frame numbers instead, Option-click (Alt-click on a PC) the timecode. To change the units back to time, simply Option/Alt-click it again.

- **Show or hide track properties.** To expand a track to see any layer properties that you can animate such as the position of an image or Type layer, its opacity, and so on (adding and animating layer properties is discussed on page 801), click the triangle to the left of the track's name. When you do, Photoshop expands the panel to show each property of that layer.

- **Show or hide clips.** To show only some of the clips in a document, first designate the ones you want to display by Shift- or ⌘-/Ctrl-clicking to activate them in the Timeline panel and then choosing Show→Set Favorite Clips from the Timeline panel's menu. To specify which clips are displayed, choose Show→All Clips or Show→Favorite Clips Only (also from the Timeline panel's menu).

- **Create a new video group from multiple clips.** If you have multiple clips in your Timeline panel that are related and you didn't import them into a video group, you can click and drag a clip from one video track onto another and Photoshop combines them into a new video group (just double-click the group's name to change it).

When it comes to moving the playhead, you can use the playback control buttons or drag the playhead to move it manually. You can also move the playhead by doing any of the following:

- Click anywhere on the time ruler to reposition the playhead at that point.

- Point your cursor at the timecode and, when the cursor turns into a double-sided arrow, click and drag left to move the playhead left, or right to move it, well, right.

- Double-click the timecode and, in the resulting Set Current Time dialog box, enter a time or frame number and then click OK.

- Head to the Timeline panel's menu and choose Go To→Time, and Photoshop displays a dialog box that lets you enter a specific time. (The other options in the Go To submenu are Next Frame, Previous Frame, First Frame, Last Frame, "Start of Work Area," and "End of Work Area.")

Just like a video clip, you can adjust the start and end points of an audio clip to trim off its beginning or end. You can also drag the entire clip left or right to control when it begins to play. If you click the triangle at the end of the audio clip in the Timeline panel, you summon a panel that lets you set the time it fades in and out, as well as its volume, as shown in Figure 20-9 (bottom).

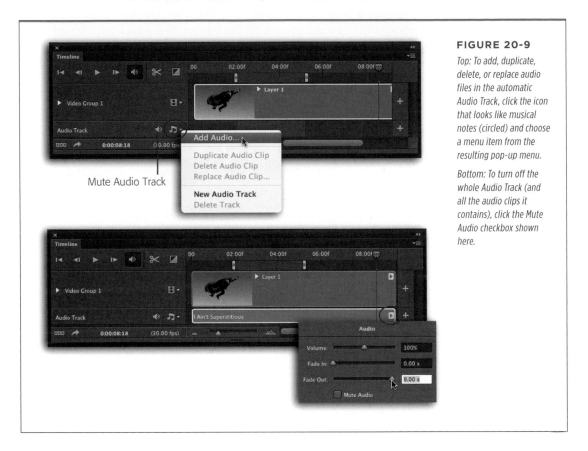

FIGURE 20-9

Top: To add, duplicate, delete, or replace audio files in the automatic Audio Track, click the icon that looks like musical notes (circled) and choose a menu item from the resulting pop-up menu.

Bottom: To turn off the whole Audio Track (and all the audio clips it contains), click the Mute Audio checkbox shown here.

NOTE Unlike all other tracks in the Timeline panel, Audio Tracks *don't* appear in the Layers panel, and you can't change their names.

To create a more complex and *layered* audio effect in which audio clips overlap each other, you can add *additional* Audio Tracks and place audio clips in them. To do so, click the musical-note icon circled in Figure 20-9 (top) and then, from the resulting pop-up menu, choose New Audio Track.

WARNING *Don't* drag an audio file from Bridge, Mini Bridge, or your computer's desktop into your Photoshop document. If you do, it appears as a new *video* track in the Timeline panel (and as a new layer in the Layers panel). This method gives you absolutely no control over the audio: you can't adjust its fade-in and fade-out times, or control its volume.

■ Animating Objects and Effects

In Photoshop, the term "animation" refers to anything that changes over time. For example, an object can change position, or an *adjustment* you apply to a layer can change its opacity over time or even the area to which it's applied. Layer styles can also change over time. This section shows you how to include all those changes, and more, in your video projects.

Creating and Deleting Keyframes

The key concept (ha!) to grasp about animations is that everything happens around a *keyframe*: the moment in an animation when something changes. This could be the direction of an object's movement, the properties of a filter or image adjustment, or whatever. To create an animation in Photoshop, you create multiple keyframes and then Photoshop creates the appropriate frames to go in between them (these in-between frames are called *tween* frames). For example, to create a bouncing ball animation, you'd place the ball on the ground in one keyframe, then you'd move it to the sky in another keyframe, and then you'd place it on the ground again in yet another keyframe; Photoshop then adds all the frames in between to make it look like it's moving.

UP TO SPEED

A Word on Text in Videos

When it comes to adding text to videos, less is more. And aside from formatting it correctly as you learned back in Chapter 14—by using kerning, leading, and so on—there are a couple more things to consider, such as:

Color. The most common color for text in video is white (though an extremely light gray is a better choice because it's slightly lower in contrast). The second most common color is black. Both colors are quite legible, even atop a moving background. Feel free to choose other colors to complement the ones in your project, though be sure to pick a very light or very dark shade. If you're working with a corporate client, they may have an official corporate color that you can specify using the Pantone Matching System, so your project is more likely to appear similar to their other projects. (See page 494 to for more on Pantone colors.)

Readability. Your computer monitor has a much finer resolution than most TVs (meaning the pixels are bigger on a TV), and you're physically closer to the screen than your audience will be. For those reasons, what you're seeing isn't what your audience will see. To ensure that your text is readable, put Photoshop into full-screen mode (press the F key repeatedly to cycle through the different views). Next, zoom in so the project fills your whole screen (press ⌘-+ or Ctrl-+), and then step back at least 10 feet and see if you can easily read the text.

Last but not least, be sure to *preview* your text on the intended output device (if possible) after you export the video (page 815), as the encoding process—the way Photoshop converts the project into a specific file format—can cause unexpected results.

To create a keyframe, drag the playhead to the spot in the video where you want the keyframe to be. Then set your object's location, layer opacity, and/or layer style exactly the way you want it; once you've got it just right, click the flippy triangle to the left of the track's name in the Timeline panel and Photoshop displays several properties of the layer beneath the track's name (see Figure 20-10). Next, click the stopwatch icon to the left of a property to display the controls labeled in Figure 20-10, and then click the diamond that appears to the left of the stopwatch (between the Previous and Next triangles). When you do, Photoshop creates a new keyframe and adds a yellow diamond where the playhead is, as shown in Figure 20-10.

TIP If you press and hold the Shift key as you drag the playhead, it snaps to the next keyframe. However, if you're working with a long project, an easy way to move the playhead to the previous or next keyframe is to click the Previous or Next Keyframe triangles labeled in Figure 20-10.

FIGURE 20-10

Click the tiny stopwatch icon to activate a layer property and Photoshop adds a yellow diamond to the property's left, as well as beneath the playhead (both are circled here). This diamond is called a keyframe indicator.

WARNING Be careful with the stopwatch—one click and Photoshop will delete all your keyframes from that property for that track!

Once you start adding keyframes, it's easy to add too many. To delete one, position the playhead above the keyframe you want to delete and then click the yellow diamond between the Previous and Next triangles (or Ctrl-click [right-click] the keyframe and choose Delete from the resulting pop-up menu). To remove *all* keyframes for a property on that layer, click the stopwatch icon next to its name.

NOTE Once you've clicked the stopwatch icon and activated keyframes, anytime you make a change to a property (by changing opacity from 100% to 50%, say), Photoshop *automatically* adds a keyframe for you.

Editing and Copying Keyframes

Once you've created keyframes, you can easily move 'em around by dragging them left or right or by copying them from one place to another. The quickest way to edit or copy a keyframe is to Ctrl-click (right-click on a PC) its yellow diamond in the Timeline panel. When you do, Photoshop displays a shortcut menu that lets you delete, copy, or paste that keyframe (of course, you can't paste a keyframe until you've copied one first). You can also use these commands on multiple keyframes by choosing Select All from the same pop-up menu, or by clicking and dragging *around* them in the Timeline panel; you won't see a selection marquee but if the keyframes turn yellow, then you've selected 'em. (Once you're finished making changes, reopen the menu and choose Deselect All.) You'll also find these options in the Timeline panel's menu whenever one or more keyframes are active (meaning they're yellow).

Pasting a copied keyframe(s) to another location is a three-step process. First, copy the keyframe(s) as described above, and then move the playhead to the new spot where you want the keyframe(s) to appear. Click the diamond between the Previous and Next Keyframe navigation triangles and Photoshop adds a keyframe to that position. Next, Ctrl-click (right-click) the new keyframe (the yellow diamond that appeared beneath the playhead), and then choose Paste from the shortcut menu that appears. Whew!

NOTE Don't try to use keyboard shortcuts such as ⌘-C/Ctrl-C to copy, paste, or cut (delete) keyframes. If you do, Photoshop applies the commands to the *entire* Video layer instead of individual keyframes!

Choosing an Interpolation Method

The most common use for keyframes is to indicate points in time where something changes, and then let Photoshop *interpolate* (make up) the frames in between. This process is called Linear Interpolation. When you have one or more keyframes activated, both the Timeline panel's menu and the shortcut menu you get by Ctrl-clicking (right-clicking) a keyframe offer another choice: Hold Interpolation. This option tells Photoshop *not* to change the frames *between* the keyframes instead, the program leaves the property the way it's set at the first keyframe and simply makes an abrupt change at the *new* keyframe.

Most often, you'll leave the interpolation method set to Linear Interpolation, but there are creative uses for Hold Interpolation, such as when you really *want* to introduce an abrupt and shocking change in your video.

NOTE If you have a lot of keyframes and tracks, your project can begin to slow down and stutter when you preview it. One way to avoid this is to choose Allow Frame Skipping from the Timeline panel's menu. This tells Photoshop that it's okay to *skip* frames when you click the Play button in the Timeline panel, making the preview run more smoothly. (Photoshop still *creates* all the frames correctly when you export the final video file.) One way to tell whether Photoshop is skipping frames is to look for a tiny, light blue line just beneath the time ruler: if it's a solid line, you're seeing all the frames; it's broken, you're not.

Animating Text

When you add a Type layer to a document that contains video, it appears as a Type layer in the Layers panel *and* as a *text clip* in the Timeline panel. If a video track or video group is active when you add the text, then the text clip appears at the far right of that track; if not, then the text clip appears on its own track. Once you add some text, you can animate it with keyframes just like you can any other clip, though you get an additional layer property called Text Warp (see page 597 for the scoop on warping text.) When you create a Type layer, any Text Warp you've applied appears on the Text Warp property in the Timeline panel, as shown in Figure 20-11.

Starting text position keyframe   Ending text position keyframe

Starting text warp keyframe   Ending text warp keyframe

FIGURE 20-11

Top: In this example, a Type layer was distorted using the Wave Text warp, and a keyframe was added. The text was then moved to another location in the clip, a Flag warp was applied to it, and then a second keyframe was added later in the clip.

Bottom: The yellow diamond marks the keyframe that controls the ending text warp. The gray diamond to its left (at the beginning of the clip) marks the keyframe where the first text warp was applied. The diamonds on the Transform property timeline indicate the beginning and ending locations of the text.

You can also animate text by using the five presets available in the Motion panel; to open it, click the little triangle at the far right of the text clip in the Timeline panel, or Ctrl-click (right-click) the text clip itself. The presets in the Motion panel are a great way to quickly get your text moving, as they animate the text *for* you, beginning at the start point of the text clip and ending when the text clip does. Each preset offers different controls that you can tweak (they all include a "Resize to Fill Canvas" checkbox, which fills your frame with the text, regardless of its original size).

- **Pan & Zoom.** *Panning* refers to the act of moving the text across the frame; the Pan dial controls the *direction* of this movement. The Zoom pop-up menu lets you choose whether the text grows (Zoom In) or shrinks (Zoom Out) during the panning.

- **Pan.** Use the Pan dial to adjust the direction of the movement.

- **Zoom.** The Zoom From setting controls where the zoom starts—click the upper-left square to make the text grow or shrink from its upper-left corner, click the center square to make it grow or shrink from its center, and so on. The Zoom pop-up menu lets you choose whether Photoshop zooms in or out.

- **Rotate.** Use the Rotate pop-up menu to control whether the text rotates clockwise or counterclockwise.

- **Rotate & Zoom.** This preset lets you choose which direction the text rotates and whether Photoshop zooms in our out.

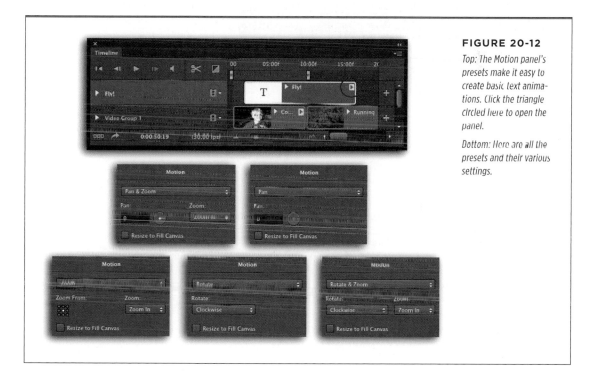

FIGURE 20-12

Top: The Motion panel's presets make it easy to create basic text animations. Click the triangle circled here to open the panel.

Dottom: Here are all the presets and their various settings.

TIP When you choose a preset from the Motion panel, Photoshop creates the appropriate keyframes (the diamonds that appear in the Timeline panel will be red) and applies the right Transform property settings *for* you.

Animating Masks

When you add a layer mask to a layer, it becomes a property that you can animate in the Timeline panel, as shown in Figure 20-13. (See page 116 for the scoop on creating layer masks.) This allows a background image or video to poke *through* the mask. You can animate the mask's position and control whether it's turned on or off, but that's it.

FIGURE 20-13

When a layer has a mask attached to it, you can animate the mask's position over time, and turn the mask on and off. However, you can't animate the mask's opacity.

Rotoscoping and Onion Skins

Rotoscoping is the process of creating new animations from scratch: You create a new video frame, put something on it, duplicate the frame, change its content a tiny bit, and repeat the process until you have a video (you need about 30 frames per second). If you have the patience, you can theoretically create a masterpiece this way.

Photoshop CS6 gives you a tool for rotoscoping called *onion skins*, but you're much better off using a program like Adobe After Effects instead because the process in Photoshop is too tedious to bear. Nevertheless, onion skins let you see a ghosted image of a certain number of frames before and after the one you're working on (you tell it how many frames to display), which helps guide the edits you're making.

To use onion skins, turn 'em on by choosing Enable Onion Skins from the Timeline panel's menu and then set the frame options by choosing Onion Skin Settings from the same menu. When you do, Photoshop displays the dialog box shown in Figure 20-14.

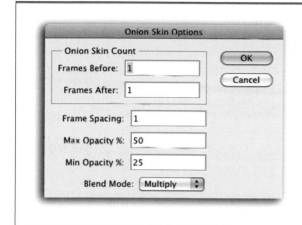

FIGURE 20-14

The Onion Skin Options dialog box lets you control how many ghosted frames you see before and after the current frame, as well as spacing, opacity, and blend mode of those frames. You can change these settings anytime (to see more frames or fewer, say).

The Onion Skin Options dialog box gives you these options:

- **Frames Before/After.** Sets the number of frames that will show through the current frame. You can display up to eight frames before and eight frames after.

- **Frame Spacing.** Often, consecutive frames don't change much, so it's helpful to skip some. This setting lets you show only every other frame, every third frame, or whatever. Setting this field to 1 means Photoshop shows all the frames, setting it to 2 means Photoshop only shows every other frame, and so on.

- **Max/Min Opacity %.** When viewing more than one frame before and after the current frame, you may want to see the closer frames at a higher opacity than those that are farther away. Max Opacity sets the opacity of the closest frame, while Min Opacity sets the opacity of the farthest frame. The frames in the middle range between the two opacities.

- **Blending Mode.** Just like with layers, you can assign a blend mode to the onion skins. Why? Because some videos are easier to see as onion skins when you use a different blend mode. Your four blending options are Normal, Multiply, Screen, and Difference.

◼ Global Lighting

When you add a layer style that includes embossing, a shadow, or other depth-related effects to a Video layer, you can set its lighting angle. And if you apply layer styles to *multiple* layers in a video project, you probably want *all* the light to appear to be coming from the same angle. To ensure consistent lighting, you can add a Global Lighting track by heading to the Timeline panel's menu and choosing Show→Global Light Track. The Global Lighting track overrides any *other* lighting angles that may have been set in individual layers. (To change the angle of the light over time, you can add *multiple* Global Lighting keyframes that have different lighting angles.)

To set a Global Lighting angle and apply it to the Timeline panel:

1. **From the Timeline panel's menu, choose Show→Global Light Track.**

   Photoshop adds the Global Lighting track to the top of your track stack in the Timeline panel.

2. **Create a new layer by clicking the New Layer icon at the bottom of the Layers panel.**

3. **Add a layer style by clicking the *fx* icon at the bottom of the Layers panel.**

   Pick Bevel & Emboss, Inner Shadow, or Drop Shadow, as those are the layer styles that offer a Use Global Light option. When you make a choice from this menu, Photoshop opens the Layer Style dialog box.

4. **In the Layer Style dialog box, set the lighting angle and turn on the Use Global Light checkbox.**

   Use the Angle dial to set the angle you want for the first portion of your project (you can also type a number into the field to its right), click the Use Global Light checkbox, and then click OK to close the dialog box.

5. **In the Timeline panel, move the playhead to the *beginning* of your project and then add a keyframe.**

   To position the playhead at the beginning, just click the First Frame button (labeled back in Figure 20-2, top) or drag the playhead all the way left. To add the keyframe, click the diamond in the Global Lighting track. When you do, the keyframe automatically adopts the Global Light angle you set in the Layer Style dialog box.

6. **If you want the lighting angle to be the same for your entire project, you're done. If you want to change the angle anywhere in the project, move the playhead to that point and continue to the next step.**

7. **Change the lighting angle of the layer style you added in step 2.**

   Back in the Layers panel, double-click the name of the effect you applied to the layer you created in step 1. In the resulting Layer Style dialog box, change the angle settings, and then click OK.

8. **Set a new keyframe where your playhead is.**

   Click the diamond in the Global Lighting track to set a new keyframe, and it adopts the new lighting angle you set in the layer style, and *keeps* this setting through the end of your project, or until you create a new Global Lighting keyframe.

FIGURE 20-15

The Global Lighting track lets you add keyframes to control the lighting angle in all the video clips that have a layer style applied to them. Here, one lighting angle was used at the start of the project, and then it changes to a new angle partway through the second video clip.

Adding Comments

Just like Photoshop lets you use the Note tool to add a hidden comment to a Photoshop document (see Appendix C), you can use the Comments track to add a hidden comment at a specific time in your *video* (handy if there are multiple people working on your project and you need to explain an edit or mark a certain spot for additional editing). First, turn on the Comments Track (Figure 20-16) by going to the Timeline panel's menu and choosing Show→Comments Track.

Comments track

Active comment

FIGURE 20-16

Once you add a comment, it appears as a tiny yellow square in the Comments track beneath the time ruler. If you double-click it, Photoshop opens a dialog box that displays your note (and lets you edit the comment). When you're finished editing or reading it, click OK to close the dialog box.

To add your first comment where the playhead is, click the stopwatch to the left of the word Comments and Photoshop displays the Edit Timeline Comment dialog box where you can enter some text. Once you click OK, a yellow square appears at that point on the Comments track. To add more comments, position your playhead and then click the yellow diamond near the left end of the Comments track.

To edit an existing comment, double-click its icon in the Timeline panel and Photoshop displays a dialog box containing your note. You can also copy, paste, edit or delete a comment by Ctrl-clicking (right-clicking on a PC) its icon (the yellow square) in the Timeline panel to reveal a shortcut menu.

To export all the comments in a video project, click the Timeline panel's menu and choose Comments→Export As HTML or Comments→Export As Text. Either way, Photoshop creates a document containing your comments along with their frame numbers and timecodes (this is a great way to see all the comments in a project).

■ Adding Fill and Adjustment Layers

Just like still images, video clips often look better after you adjust their brightness, contrast, and so on. However, *unlike* still images, the lighting in a video clip often changes over time. Fortunately, the Timeline panel lets you control the *duration* of Fill and Adjustment layers on video clips (you'll learn how in a moment).

You add Fill or Adjustment layers to a Video layer exactly the same way you add them to any other layer—activate the layer in the Layers panel and then click the half-black/half-white circle icon at the bottom of the panel. From the resulting menu, choose the kind of Fill or Adjustment layer you want to add, and then adjust the settings that appear in the Properties panel. (For more on Fill and Adjustment layers, see page 77.)

When you add an Adjustment layer, Photoshop automatically *clips* it to the active Video layer, so you don't have to worry about it affecting other Video layers (Fill layers don't get clipped to the active Video layer). If you *want* the Adjustment layer to affect all the Video layers underneath it, click the "Clip to layer" icon at the bottom of the Properties panel (it's circled in Figure 20-17).

FIGURE 20-17

Top: The down-pointing arrow above the Video layer thumbnail indicates that the Adjustment layer is clipped (attached to) the Video layer. (Unfortunately, Fill layers can't be clipped to the layers below them.)

Bottom: The "Clip to layer" icon at the bottom of the Properties panel controls whether the Adjustment layer affects all the layers below it, or only one. Just give it a click to reverse its behavior.

Adding a Color Tint

You can change the mood of a video by adding a color tint like, say, a sepia tone, which is easy to do with a Black & White Adjustment layer. Just click the half-black/half-white circle at the bottom of the Layers panel and choose Black & White. Then, in the Properties panel, turn on the Tint checkbox. Photoshop adds a nice brown tone to your video, though you can change that color by clicking the color swatch next to the word "Tint" in the Properties panel, and then choosing another color from the resulting Color Picker.

FIGURE 20-18

The Properties panel's Tint checkbox makes it a snap to add a nice sepia tone to your project, giving it a vintage feel.

Changing Fill and Adjustment Layers' Duration

What if you want one Fill or Adjustment layer to affect part of a clip, and then you want *another* Fill or Adjustment layer to affect the rest? No problem—just make sure the Video layer isn't part of a video group (if it is, simply drag it out of the group in either the Layers panel). Next, add the Fill or Adjustment layer and it appears in the Timeline panel on its own track above the video track. Then change the layer's *duration* in the Timeline panel by dragging its start and end points, just like you would with any clip or transition, as shown in Figure 20-19.

FIGURE 20-19

The end point of this Levels Adjustment layer has been dragged to match the duration of the video clip below it.

If you want to add *several* Fill or Adjustment layers to a single Video layer, the process is nearly the same. Simply shorten the first Adjustment layer and then move the second one so it's positioned next to the first, as Figure 20-20 illustrates.

FIGURE 20-20

After adding two Levels Adjustment layers and clipping them to the Running Video layer, they show up as separate layers in the Timeline panel. Their beginning and end points have been dragged to affect only a portion of the Running Video layer.

NOTE You can also restrict the effects of a Fill or Adjustment layer to one Video layer by converting the Video layer to a Smart Object first. Just Ctrl-click (right-click on a PC) near the name of the Video layer in the Layers panel and then choose "Convert to Smart Object." Then double-click the Smart Object's layer thumbnail to display it in a new (temporary) document window. Add your Fill or Adjustment layers to it, and then choose File→Save (*not* File→Save As). Photoshop automatically updates the Video layer in your main document. Sweet!

■ Adding Layer Styles

You can apply any of Photoshop's layer styles to a Video layer by clicking the *fx* button at the bottom of the Layers panel or by choosing Layer→Layer Style (see page 131 for more on layer styles). For example, if you've placed a small video clip on top of larger one (for a picture-in-picture effect), you can make the small clip appear to *float* on top of the larger one by adding a drop shadow to the smaller clip's layer. Another useful layer style is Inner Shadow, which can create a darkened-edge vignette effect (see Figure 20-21).

FIGURE 20-21

To add a darkened-edge vignette effect to a video clip, apply an Inner Shadow layer style. Any layer styles you add apply to the entire length of the video clip.

As you can see here, they can make quite a difference!

Using Smart Filters with Video

The good news is that you can run Photoshop's filters on video clips. The bad news is that if you run a filter on a regular Video layer, it only affects *the current frame* of that video. To make the filter affect *all* the frames in the clip, convert the clip to a Smart Object *first* by opening it as a Smart Object or by activating the Video layer in the Layers panel and then choosing Filter→"Convert for Smart Filters;" *then* run the filter. Alas, you can't adjust the duration of the Smart Filter—it affects the *entire* Video layer. (For more on Smart Objects, flip back to page 126.)

◼ Cloning and Healing

You can use Photoshop's cloning and healing tools on video clips, but it's *incredibly* tedious—you have to edit each frame individually (yawn!). Unfortunately, there's no magic technique that lets you follow an object through a whole scene to fix it in one go. So pour yourself a nice beverage, settle into your chair, tweak one frame, and then use the navigation buttons in the Timeline panel to go to the next frame and repeat the process. And repeat. And repeat again.

NOTE When using the Clone Stamp tool to fix multiple frames of a video, consider turning on the Lock Frame option in the Clone Source panel (page 300). This makes Photoshop keep your source in the same frame you sampled, instead of moving it on to the next frame as you clone onto a new frame. If your video clip is fairly stable, this will give you a clean source to clone from. However, if the video is unstable, it may work better to set the Clone Source panel's Frame Offset field to 1 or 2 so that the source is more similar to your target frame.

◼ Exporting Videos

Once you're satisfied with your project, you can export it to a new video file (this process is called *rendering*). Choose File→Export→Render Video or click the Render Video button at the bottom left of the Timeline panel (it looks like a curved arrow). In the resulting Render Video dialog box, set the options as described below and then click the Render button (see Figure 20-22).

The Render Video dialog box gives you these options:

- **Name.** Use this field to name the video file you're about to export.

- **Select Folder.** Click this button to tell Photoshop where to save the exported file.

- **Create New Subfolder.** If you turn this checkbox on, Photoshop creates a new subfolder *inside* the folder you specified in the Select Folder option and puts your video file in it. Enter a name for the subfolder in the text field next to this checkbox.

- **Export Encoder.** This unlabeled menu includes two options: Adobe Media Encoder and Photoshop Image Sequence. What you choose here determines the *other* settings you see in this section of the dialog box.

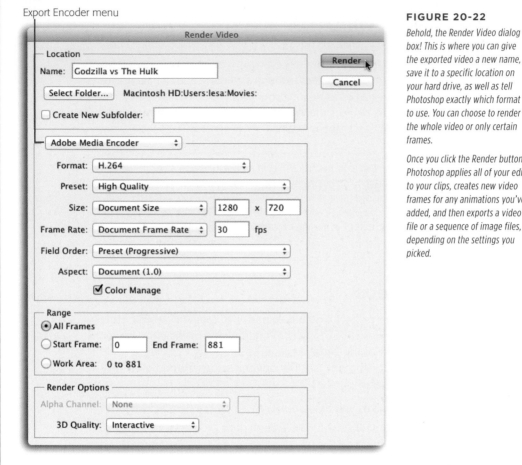

Export Encoder menu

If you choose **Adobe Media Encoder**, Photoshop renders your project as a video file and you see these settings:

— **Format.** DPX (Digital Picture Exchange) is commonly used in the TV and movie industries. H.264 is used for consumer gadgets such as TVs, handheld devices, and iOS devices, as well as websites like YouTube.com and Vimeo.com. QuickTime format is used by desktop video programs.

— **Preset.** This menu includes a number of useful options. When you choose a preset, the controls below this menu reflect the settings appropriate for that preset, though you can change any of those settings manually.

- **Size.** Choose a video frame size appropriate for your intended viewing device. This menu includes sizes for common uses such as North American (NTSC) and PAL TVs, high-definition video systems, and professional film-editing systems. You can also enter a custom size.

- **Frame Rate.** Determines how many frames are included in each second of video. Choose from common rates or enter a custom one.

- **Field Order.** While computers display video in a progressive series of complete frames, TVs slice each frame into two interlaced fields, each containing half of the image. This option lets you choose whether the exported video should have complete frames (Progressive) or interlaced frames that start with the Upper or Lower Frame first. Choose Progressive if you're creating a video folks will watch on their computers, or one of the other options if they'll watch it on a TV.

- **Aspect.** This determines the video's aspect ratio—the frame's ratio of width to height.

- **Color Manage.** Turning on this checkbox tells Photoshop to pay attention to any color-management information that's included in your project. You'll probably want to leave this checked to take advantage of color profiles included in any images you've included.

If you choose **Photoshop Image Sequence**, Photoshop renders your project as a sequence of images instead of a single video file, and you get these options:

- **Format.** Choose a format for your rendered frames. Some formats let you set various options by clicking the Settings button, including compression, transparency, metadata, and so forth. (If the Settings button is grayed out, the format you chose doesn't include any additional options.)

- **Starting # and Digits.** Since Photoshop renders each frame as a separate file, each file needs a unique name. Photoshop names each file beginning with what you entered into the Name field at the top of the dialog box, and tacks on a sequence of numbers to the end of it. The Starting # field lets you specify the number it starts with, while the Digits field lets you tell Photoshop how many numerals to add to the end of the filename. The "Ex:" item to the right of these fields shows you a preview of how your filenames will look.

- **Size** and **Frame Rate.** These settings are the same as the ones described earlier in this list.

- **Range**. Lets you to specify whether Photoshop renders all the frames in your project, a range of frames you specify, or only the currently active work area.

- **Alpha Channel.** This setting lets you specify how Photoshop should combine alpha channels with the video so that transparency can be preserved when you place your video on top of *other* videos or images. Your options are:

  — **None.** Photoshop doesn't include Alpha channels in the rendered video.

  — **Straight - Unmatted.** Photoshop uses the alpha channel to generate transparency when it's rendering.

  — **Premultiplied with Black/White/Color.** These three options make Photoshop place the transparency in the alpha channel over a black background (common in video that will be displayed on TVs), a white background, or a background color (which you choose by clicking the color box to the right of this setting), respectively.

- **3D Quality.** If your project includes 3D objects, this setting controls how Photoshop renders their surfaces. Interactive is suitable for video games and other on-screen uses; Ray Traced Draft results in a low-quality version, but renders quickly; and Ray Traced Final is very high quality but takes a long time to render.

Using Your Project in Other Video Editors

To go beyond Photoshop's editing capabilities, you can import your video project into another video-editing program. To do that, simply save your Photoshop document and then open it in the other video editor. If you're handing the project off to another member of your team, be sure to include all the fonts, audio files and video files that you used in your project. (Your Photoshop document merely *references* those files—it doesn't actually include the source files—so the other video editors will need 'em, too.)

■ Additional Video Resources

This chapter is by no means a comprehensive guide to video editing. When you're ready to learn more, here are a couple of resources worth checking out:

- *www.RodHarlan.com.* Author and video-editing expert Rod Harlan has a website chock full of links to tutorials, tips, and tricks.

- *www.RichardHarringtonBlog.com.* Another author and video-editing pro, Richard Harrington has an informative blog that's worth visiting. Also, keep your eyes peeled for an updated version of his popular book, *Photoshop for Video, Fourth Edition* (Peachpit Press, 2010).

Using Adobe Bridge

As digital images pile up on your hard drive, the ability to sift through them quickly and efficiently becomes more and more important. Enter Adobe Bridge, an image-browsing and organization program that's been shipping with Photoshop for years. Browsing through images in Bridge used to be a painfully slow process, and the program wasn't very intuitive. But in recent versions, Bridge got a speed boost, a makeover, and a Review mode (shown on page 825) that photographers really love. You can also use its Export panel (page 832) to convert a slew of Raw files to JPEGs and then save them. The "Output to PDF" option lets you add watermarks to images (page 746), and you can also use Bridge to create incredibly beautiful web galleries at warp speed. And it just keeps getter better: Bridge CS6 is a 64-bit program just like Photoshop, so you should feel a speed boost when you're perusing and processing files (see page 4 for more on 64-bit).

> **NOTE** You can also access Bridge *inside* Photoshop using the Mini Bridge panel. Choose Window→ Extensions→Mini Bridge, and it appears at the bottom of your screen. Flip to page 836 for a sneak peek.

In the following pages, you'll learn the basics of browsing, importing, and rating images in Bridge. By the end of this chapter, you'll be able to find your favorite photos and plop them into a web gallery in no time.

Browsing through Photos

If you're working in Photoshop CS6, you can open Bridge by choosing File→"Browse in Bridge." If Photoshop *isn't* running, you can double-click the Bridge icon in the Adobe Bridge application folder (on a PC, go to Start→All Programs→Adobe Bridge CS6 (64bit). Either way, you see the window shown in Figure 21-1.

> **NOTE** If you open Bridge and it looks different from Figure 21-1, try clicking the word Essentials near the top of the Bridge window. That will switch you over to the workspace shown here.

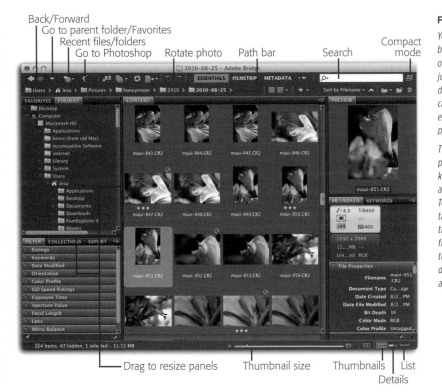

FIGURE 21-1

You can use Bridge to browse all *the images on your hard drive, not just the ones you've downloaded from your camera using Bridge, as explained on the next page.*

The program's various panels harbor different kinds of info, and they're all movable and resizable: To move one, drag its tab; to resize one, drag the bar that divides it from other panels; and to combine two panels, drag one panel's tab into another panel.

The Bridge window displays a variety of info about your images in collapsible panels—just double-click a tab to collapse or expand a panel or group of panels. You can use the Folders panel on the left to navigate to a specific spot on your hard drive to view the images stored there. When you click a folder in this panel, Bridge displays its contents as thumbnails in the Content panel in the middle of the window (use the slider at the bottom right of the Bridge window to control how big these thumbnails are). Click an image in the Content panel to see a larger version of it in the Preview panel on the right.

TIP To see a larger preview of an image whose thumbnail is displayed in Bridge, click the file to activate it and then tap the space bar; Bridge displays the image in all its full screen glory. Press the space bar again to go back to the Bridge window.

At the top of the Bridge window are controls that help you find the files you want (shown in Figure 21-1):

- **Forward and back arrows.** Click these buttons to move through the folders you've recently viewed. For example, if you went to your Pictures folder and then opened the Maui folder inside it, click the back arrow to return to the Pictures folder. (These buttons don't activate files, just folders.)

TIP For quick access to certain folders, add them to Bridge's Favorites panel: Select a folder in the Folders or Content panel, Control-click (right-click) it, and then choose "Add to Favorites" from the resulting menu. (You can also choose File→"Add to Favorites" (or simply drag a folder from the Content panel into the Favorites panel). From then on, you'll have one-click access to that folder in the Favorites panel.

- **Go to parent folder→Favorites.** Like the back-arrow button, this button lets you move up a folder level. For example, if you're perusing the Midnight Madness folder that lives inside your Photoshop World folder, you can click this button to reveal a menu that lets you quickly pop back to the Photoshop World folder (which is called the *parent* folder because it's one level above the Midnight Madness folder in your computer's file-organization family tree). You can also use this button to access folders that you've added to the Favorites panel.

- **Go to recent files/folders.** Click this button to see a menu that lists all the files and folders you've recently viewed in Adobe programs, which includes a list of files and folders categorized by the program that made them. When you choose an item from this menu, Bridge displays a preview of the item along with its location on your hard drive.

- **Path bar.** This outrageously useful bar is a clickable, virtual trail of breadcrumbs that helps you keep track of where you are on your hard drive. It shows which folder you're in, so if you want to jump to a different spot in the trail, simply click the name of another folder in this bar. Since the Path bar shows you how you arrived at the folder you're in, you always know exactly where you are (and the clickable links offer a fast track backward). If you don't see this bar—or if it's mysteriously disappeared, as it sometimes does—choose Window→Path Bar.

- **Search field.** If you know the name of the file you're looking for but don't remember where it lives, type its name (or the first few letters of it) into this field and then press Return (Enter on a PC). Bridge scours the current folder and shows you a list of files that best match what you typed. Click the magnifying glass for a list of recent searches.

TIP If you don't have a big monitor but want to keep Bridge open—so you can drag and drop images from it into Photoshop, say—click the "Switch to Compact Mode" button in Bridge's upper-right corner, and the Bridge window shrinks down to a more manageable size. Click this button again to expand the window back to normal size. Better yet, pop open the Mini Bridge panel, as described on page 836.

POWER USERS' CLINIC

Customizing the Bridge Window

You can customize the Bridge workspace just like you can in Photoshop, or use one of its built-in layouts. Near the top of the Bridge window is a row of workspace buttons that arrange the program's panels in a variety of ways (see Figure 21-1). Here's what each one does:

- **Essentials** is the arrangement you see when you first open Bridge: The Favorites and Folders panels are on the left, the Content panel is in the middle, and the Preview panel is on the right. It's a handy workspace for sifting through files.

- **Filmstrip** is great for looking at photos you've imported. The Favorites and Folders panels are still on the left, but the Content panel is down at the bottom of the window as a wide, thin strip, and the Preview panel takes center stage. Photographers like this workspace because it gives them a nice big preview area.

- **Metadata** shows you all kinds of info about your images. There's no big Preview panel in this workspace; the Content panel takes precedence, displaying a list that includes the date each file was created, its size, type, and so on. The Favorites panel is on the left along with the Metadata panel, which includes stats about the active file like its dimensions, resolution, and so on.

- **Output** sticks the Folders panel on the left, the Preview panel in the middle, and the Output panel on the right. The Output panel lets you create PDFs and web galleries, as explained later in this chapter.

If these workspaces don't float your boat, you can make your own. Once you've moved and resized the panels just the way you like, click the tiny down-pointing triangle to the right of the Output button and choose New Workspace. Give it a meaningful name in the resulting dialog box, and then click Save. Your custom workspace appears as a button at the top of the Bridge window. If you want to get rid of it, click the triangle again, choose Delete Workspace, select the offending workspace in the resulting dialog box, and then click Delete.

You can also customize the color theme in Bridge CS6, just like you can in Photoshop (page 31). Simply choose Bridge→Preferences (Edit→Preferences on a PC) and then click the General category in the left-hand list. You'll see various color squares appear on the right that you can click to change the color scheme, as shown here. You can also use the sliders underneath 'em to tweak the program's overall brightness, change the Image Backdrop (the background color your images are displayed on), and the Accent Color (the highlight color Bridge puts around an image's thumbnail when you click to activate it).

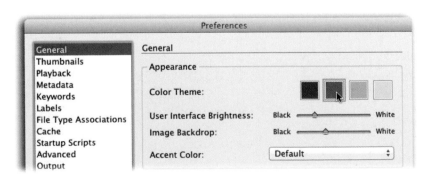

■ Importing and Managing Photos

Bridge makes importing images a snap, and it can perform all kinds of wonderful housekeeping chores for you. For example, it can automatically rename photos and add keywords, descriptions, and copyright info to each file. You can also have it back up your files (either to an external hard drive you've plugged in or to another spot on your internal hard drive) as part of the import process.

To import images, make sure your card reader is attached to your computer (see the box on page 826), and then choose File→"Get Photos from Camera" or click the tiny camera icon at the top left of the Bridge window. Either way, Bridge opens the Adobe Photo Downloader in *standard mode*, which isn't very impressive; its most redeeming feature is the Advanced Dialog button at the bottom left. Click it to switch to *Advanced mode*, shown in Figure 21-2. (If this is the first time you've downloaded photos with Bridge, you'll see the dialog box mentioned in the Tip on page 824.)

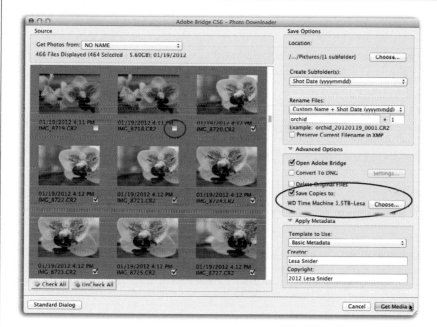

FIGURE 21-2

Importing images with Bridge is a huge timesaver. Plus, if you've got an external hard drive plugged into your computer, you can turn on the "Save Copies to" checkbox (circled) and sleep better knowing you have extra copies of your photos stored somewhere other than your main computer.

For more tips on importing images, flip to the box on the next page.

At the top of this extremely useful dialog box, tell Bridge where to save your precious images by clicking the Choose button (the Browse button on a PC). The Downloader also lets you pick which images to import (turn on the appropriate checkboxes like the one circled in Figure 21-2), give the images meaningful names, *and* instruct Bridge to back them up (by turning on the "Save Copies to" checkbox). Once you've got these options just right, click Get Media and then sit back and relax.

TIP The first time you choose File→"Get Photos from Camera" or click the camera icon on a Mac, Bridge asks if you want it to *automatically* open each time you attach a card reader to your computer (or plug in your camera's USB cable). If you want to always use Bridge to import photos, click Yes. This saves you a couple of clicks each time you import images, because Bridge automatically launches and opens the Photo Downloader dialog box. If you've already hightailed it past this dialog box, you can access it in Bridge's preferences. Choose Bridge→Preferences→General and turn on the "When a Camera is Connected, Launch Adobe Photo Downloader" setting.

In Windows 7, you need to choose your memory card from the Source menu at the top of the Photo Downloader dialog box each time you import photos. Alternatively, you can go to Start→Control Panel→AutoPlay and, from the Pictures pop-up menu, choose Download Images Using Adobe Bridge CS6 and then click Save. That way, each time your computer detects a memory card, the Photo Downloader dialog box automatically opens and picks your memory card in its Source menu.

UP TO SPEED

Tips for Importing Photos

Here are a few pointers for importing photos from a digital camera quickly and safely that will also help you find the little boogers on your hard drive later:

- **Always use a card reader.** The slowest way to import photos is by using the USB cable that came with the camera. It's sweet that the camera manufacturer included it, but those cables are super cheap. The USB cable's low quality also makes using it dangerous—the cheaper the cable, the greater the chance that something will go wrong. Fortunately, you can avoid this risk by getting a *card reader*, which imports photos much faster and more reliably. You simply take the memory card out of your camera, stick it in the card reader, and then connect the reader to your computer. Card readers are inexpensive (you can get a SanDisk ImageMate 12-in-1 for around $20, for example) and most models can read several different kinds of memory cards (that's what the "12-in-1" part means), which is a nice bonus if you have more than one brand of camera. Also, if you're on a Mac, take care that you don't yank a memory card out of the card reader until you've properly ejected or unmounted it from your computer by choosing File→Eject in the Finder.

- **Erase memory cards only in your camera.** Most photo importing/organizing software offers to erase photos from your memory card after it imports them onto your computer. Resist the urge to say yes, and instead stick the memory card back into your camera, and then use the *camera's* menus to reformat the card to erase the images. This protects you from losing files if there's some kind of crash or stall while they're being imported, which can corrupt the photos (and, if the software has already erased them from the memory card, you can't reimport them). Also, many folks believe that reformatting memory cards rather than erasing them helps reduce the risk of cards getting corrupted and losing your photos. To learn how to reformat your memory card, dig out the manual that came with your camera.

- **Give photos meaningful names.** Instead of sticking with the completely useless names your camera assigns to photos, give them meaningful names when you import them. Programs like Bridge can automatically number the files for you and tack on a name like *Photoshop World*. You've got to admit that the name *Photoshop World 08_1. jpg* is a lot more descriptive than *DCS_00102.jpg*.

- **Use several small memory cards instead of one big one.** No matter how well you care for them, memory cards—like any storage device—can fail and lose all the precious images stored on 'em. For that reason, consider carrying four 2 GB cards instead of a single 8 GB card; that way, you'll lose fewer photos if one of the cards goes south. When buying memory cards, do a little research to find a good brand. The cheapest cards can be unreliable and are usually slow. The faster the card, the faster your camera can take photos (and the faster your computer can import them!). Checking reviews on Amazon.com is always a good idea.

Review Mode

After you import images, you can use Bridge's Review mode to view them in a giant, floating carousel (see Figure 21-3). It's a quick and easy way to check out your
images, mark the ones you don't like, and apply star ratings to the ones you do.

Left/Right   Reject   Loupe   Create Collection   Exit

FIGURE 21-3

*In Review mode, press
⌘-1, 2, 3, 4, or 5 (Ctrl+1,
2, 3, 4, or 5 on a PC) to
give an image a rating of
1 to 5 stars, or click the
down arrow button in
the window's lower left
to reject an image (mark
it as one you don't like).
Once you've rejected im-
ages, you can filter them
out and delete 'em in one
fell swoop, as the next
section explains.*

*To take a closer look at
part of an image, either
click the Loupe button in
the window's bottom-
right corner or just click
the image.*

> **NOTE** You can also mark images as rejected in the main Bridge window. Simply activate the image's
> thumbnail and then press Option-Delete (Alt+Backspace on a PC).

To use Review mode, activate a folder in the Folders panel or choose multiple images (more than four) in the Content panel by ⌘-clicking (Ctrl-clicking on a PC) or
Shift-clicking them. Then either press ⌘-B (Ctrl+B on a PC) or click the Refine button
at the top of the Bridge window (it looks like a stack of paper) and choose Review
Mode. Either way, Bridge takes over your screen and displays the images on a dark
gray background. The left and right arrow buttons at the bottom left the window let
you quickly flip through images (you can also use the arrow keys on your keyboard).
You can also click any image in the background to bring it to the front, or drag an
image off the bottom of your screen—or click the down arrow button at the bottom
of the window—to remove it from Review mode (it doesn't get deleted, just removed
from view). To exit Review mode and return to the Bridge window, click the X in the
bottom-right corner of the window or press Esc.

TIP   To rotate an image in Review mode, click the image to activate it, and then press the left or right bracket key to rotate the image clockwise or counterclockwise, respectively. (To rotate images in regular view, add the ⌘ [Ctrl] key.) To see a list of all the keyboard shortcuts you can use while you're in Review mode, press H.

Sorting and Filtering Images

Bridge gives you a lot of flexibility when it comes to viewing your images. For example, you can use the Sort menu at the top of the Bridge window to arrange them by name, date modified, size, and so on (see Figure 21-4). You can also sort them manually (handy for creating web galleries): In the Content panel, drag them into any order you want. Sorting is also a quick way to toss the images you've rejected (page 825). To do that, head to the "Filter items by rating" menu (it looks like a star), choose Show Rejected Items Only, and then choose File→"Move to Trash."

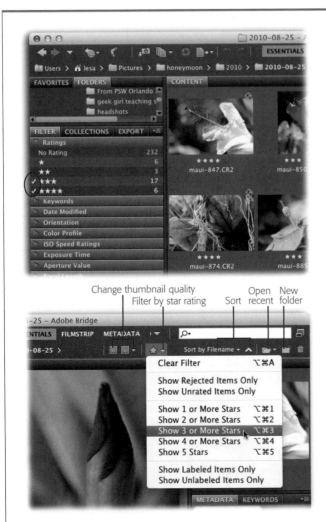

FIGURE 21-4

Top: The Filter panel (Window→Filter Panel) lets you limit the images Bridge displays. For example, if you've rated your images, you can filter your collection by clicking the panel's stars (circled). In this example, Bridge is displaying only 3- and 4-star images; just click the star rating you want to see and a little checkmark appears. To view all your images again, click to the left of No Rating.

To filter your images using other criteria like the date they were created or their orientation, click a category in the Filter panel to expand that section and then click to the left of an item to turn on that particular filter. For example, click Orientation and then click to place a checkmark next to Landscape or Portrait.

If you've filtered your images but now want to see 'em all, press Opt-⌘-A (Alt+Ctrl+A on a PC) to clear all filters.

Bottom: The star menu at the top of the Bridge window also lets you filter images. The Sort menu to its right controls the order in which Bridge displays the thumbnails. If Bridge is taking a long time to display images as you scroll or after you filter them or perform a search, you can use the square icons labeled here to lower the thumbnails' quality, which makes Bridge draw them a little faster.

The Filter panel lets you weed out images by displaying only those that match certain criteria, like a specific star rating (see Figure 21-4, top). (This panel should be lurking near the bottom left of the Bridge window, but if you don't see it, choose Window→Filter Panel.) If you didn't use Review mode to rate your images after you imported them (page 825), you might want to rate them now so you can quickly view the best ones. Rating and sorting is handy if you're a stock photographer: You can give future submissions a 5-star rating and then find them quickly using the 5-star filter.

If you applied keywords when you imported the files, you can use those keywords to filter your images. To see a list of keywords applied to the files in the folder you're viewing, head over to the Filter panel (in most workspaces, it's at the bottom left of the Bridge window) and click the word "Keywords." (If you don't see the Filter panel, just open the Keywords panel instead by choosing Window→Keywords Panel). Click a keyword (it turns bold and a checkmark appears to its left) to make the Content panel display only images containing that particular keyword. Nice!

Grouping Images into Collections

Another way to organize images is to put them into folders called *collections*. Bridge lets you create two types of collections:

- **User-defined collections** are ones you make by dragging and dropping images into a special folder. To create this kind of collection, click the Collections panel at the bottom-left part of the Bridge window or choose Window→Collections Panel (if the panel is already open, this command closes it, so you may have to choose it *twice* to spot the panel!). Select the images you want to include, click the New Collection button (labeled in Figure 21-5, top), and Bridge asks if you want to include the selected files in the new collection. Click Yes and Bridge adds it to the Collection panel and highlights its name so you can enter something meaningful (other than New Collection). To add more images, use the Folders or Favorites panel to find the ones you want to include and then drag them onto the collection's brown envelope icon. To remove an image from the collection, make sure you're actually viewing the collection (it'll be highlighted in the Collections panel), and then in the Content panel Control-click (right-click) the image and choose Remove From Collection from the resulting shortcut menu.

> **TIP** You can create a user-defined collection while you're in Review mode by clicking the Create Collection button shown back in Figure 21-3.

Bridge creates **Smart Collections** based on criteria you set in the dialog box shown in Figure 21-5 (bottom right). Just click the New Smart Collection button at the bottom of the Collections panel and then enter your criteria. Click save when you're finished, and Bridge finds all the images that match your requirements. (If you've told Bridge to look through your whole hard drive, this may take a while!) If a new image meets your criteria in the future, Bridge automatically adds it to the collection. Smart Collections have blue envelope icons.

Renaming Multiple Files

If you forgot to rename your photos when you imported them or if you'd like to rename other files on your hard drive, you don't have to change their names one at a time—that'd take *weeks*. Happily, Bridge can rename entire folders of images for you using a simple process called *batch renaming*. To get started, press Shift-⌘-R (Shift+Ctrl+R on a PC) or head to the Refine menu at the top of the Bridge window (it looks like a stack of paper) and choose Batch Rename.

In the Destination Folder section of the resulting dialog box—which was updated in CS5 to make it easier to use—tell Bridge whether you want to rename the images without moving them, or move or copy them to a different folder. The New Filenames section includes several options for customizing the files' names. Click one of the fields on the left side of this section to see the following options in a drop-down menu:

- **Text.** Choose this option to replace the file name with something more meaningful. For example, if you shot a series of photos at Photoshop World, you could cleverly use "PSW" for your file name—short and sweet!

- **New Extension** adds whatever you enter in this field to the *end* of the images' names, replacing the original extension. Beware, though: Changing or adding a new extension to a file's name doesn't change the file's format, so your computer may not know what kind of file it is in order to open it if, for example, you add a .tif extension to the end of a .jpg file.

- **Current Filename** tells Bridge to keeps the file name that's already assigned to each image and add your other custom name changes to it (such as changing it to upper or lower case).

- **Preserved Filename** tells Bridge to keep the original metadata file name—the cryptic one assigned by your camera that tags along with your image—as part of the new file name.

- **Sequence Number** adds a unique number to each image's name. You pick the starting number, and Bridge counts up by one for each file it renames.

- **Sequence Letter** works just like Sequence Number, but it adds a unique *letter* to each file name instead.

- **Date Time** adds a date and time stamp to each file's name.

- **Metadata** lets you include metadata in each file's name. You can choose from several pieces of info that your camera embedded in your image files.

- **Folder Name** includes the name of the folder the images are in as part of the new file name.

- **String Substitution** lets you find an element in the old file name (a piece of text, for example) and replace it with something else.

You can add and remove items from the New Filenames section by clicking the + or − button to the right of each one. Be sure to remove items you don't plan on using so Bridge doesn't include info you don't want.

In the Options section, turn on the "Preserve current filename in XMP Metadata" checkbox to leave the current file name that's stored in the file's metadata alone (in case you ever need to go back to it). And if there's a chance your renamed images will end up on different computer platforms, be sure to turn the Compatibility checkboxes for the appropriate operating systems. For example, if you use a Mac but your client uses PCs and Unix computers, turn on the Windows and Unix checkboxes.

At the bottom of the dialog box, Bridge displays an example of what your files *are* named and what they *will* be named. (If you think you'll use these settings again in the future, save 'em as a Preset by clicking the Save button in the Presets section at the top of the Batch Rename dialog box.) If everything looks good, take a deep breath, click Rename, and Bridge makes your changes in the blink of an eye.

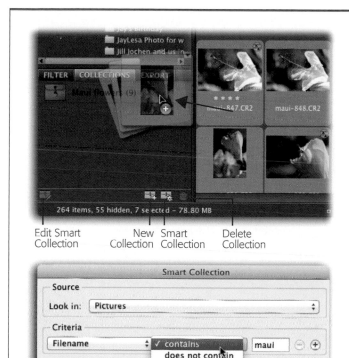

Edit Smart   New Smart   Delete
Collection   Collection Collection Collection

FIGURE 21-5

Top: Once you create a user-defined collection, you can drag several photos into it at once, as shown here. (You can tell this is a user-defined collection because its envelope is brown.)

Bottom: To create a Smart Collection, you use this dialog box to tell Bridge which photos to fetch. Use the "Look in" pop-up menu to tell the program where to look and then set criteria using the pop-up menus below it. To add more criteria, click the + button.

Once you've made the Smart Collection, you can go back and tweak your criteria by clicking the Edit Smart Collection button (labeled in the top image here).

Grouping Images into Stacks

If you typically use your camera in burst mode (meaning it captures three or more images in rapid succession each time you press the shutter button), you can group those images into *stacks*. This is a great way to organize similar images and simplify what you see in Bridge's Content panel. For example, instead of scrolling past *several* versions of the same image, you see a single stack of 'em instead, as shown in Figure 21-6.

> **TIP** To speed up Bridge's playback of an image stack, choose Stacks→Frame Rate, and then choose a larger value in the list.

To create a stack, select the images by Shift- or ⌘-clicking (Ctrl-clicking) them and then choose Stacks→"Group as Stack" or press ⌘-G (Ctrl+G on a PC). You can then expand the stack by choosing Stacks→Open Stack, and Bridge displays the images as individual thumbnails (to close the stack, choose Stacks→Close Stack). If you ever want to free the images from a stack, click the stack to activate it and then choose Stack→"Ungroup from Stack" or press Shift-⌘-G (Shift+Ctrl+G). To change the image at the top of a stack, just expand the stack, click the image you want to appear at the top, and then choose Stacks→"Promote to Top of Stack."

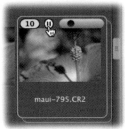

FIGURE 21-6

Top: Photoshop automatically creates image stacks when you stitch photos together into a panorama (page 295) or a High Dynamic Range image (page 398), though you can create 'em manually, too. Bridge even lets you know how many images are in a stack by displaying a number at the top left corner of each one, as shown here.

Bottom: To see all the images in a stack, put your cursor over the stack and you'll see a little Play button appear (you may need to increase the thumbnail size to see it; it looks like a right-pointing triangle, though it turns into a Pause button—as shown here—when you click it.) Give the button a click and Bridge slowly displays the images in the world's tiniest slideshow.

Opening Images in Camera Raw

One of the many benefits of organizing and browsing your images in Bridge is that it gives you easy access to the Camera Raw plug-in (page 363). In fact, Bridge offers several ways to open images in Camera Raw:

- Double-click a Raw file.

- Activate an image in the Content panel and then press ⌘-R (Ctrl+R on a PC). This method lets you open Raw files, JPEGs, and TIFFs in Camera Raw.

- Activate an image in the Content panel and then choose File→"Open in Camera Raw."

- Control-click (right-click) the image in the Content panel and then choose "Open in Camera Raw" from the shortcut menu that appears.

- Activate an image in the Content panel and then click the iris icon at the top of the window.

Once you've edited an image in Camera Raw, a microscopic icon appears next to the image's preview in Bridge's Content panel that represents the edit you made (see Figure 21-7). If you've got several images that need the same edits, you can copy the changes you made and apply them to others right in Bridge. Just Control-click (right-click on a PC) the image in the Content panel and then choose Develop Settings→Copy Settings. Then activate the images you want to apply the edits to, Control-click (right-click) one of them, choose Develop Settings→Paste Settings, and Bridge applies those same edits to the active images. Now that's working smarter instead of harder!

FIGURE 21-7

When you edit an image in Camera Raw and then click Done in the Camera Raw window, tiny icons representing the edits you made appear next to the image in Bridge. The icons circled here indicate that this image was cropped and its exposure was changed. Control-clicking (right-clicking) an image in Bridge's Content panel brings up this shortcut menu that includes all kinds of timesaving choices.

■ Showing Off Your Work

Bridge gives you several ways to display your work, including a nifty slideshow generator and an Output panel that lets you create PDFs and Web galleries. You can even use Bridge's Export panel to automate the process of uploading photos to popular websites (such as Facebook, Flickr, and Photoshop.com), as well as creating JPEG versions of Raw files. Read on!

Making a Slideshow

If you need to show your work to a client or family member, you can quickly filter for your top-rated images (flip back to Figure 21-4) and then have Bridge play them as a full-screen slideshow. Here's how:

- **To start an instant slideshow,** select a folder or several images by Shift- or ⌘-clicking (Ctrl-clicking) them, and then choose View→Slideshow or press ⌘-L (Ctrl+L). That's it! Your photos immediately appear onscreen, one after the other (each one stays onscreen for 5 seconds). To exit the slideshow, press Esc.

- **To customize the slideshow's settings first,** choose View→Slideshow Options or press Shift-⌘-L (Shift+Ctrl+L). In the resulting dialog box, you can make the slideshow repeat, control how many seconds each image stays onscreen, resize the slideshow window to fit your monitor, and add transitions between slides (see Figure 21-8). The only thing you *can't* do is add music—though you can always open iTunes and play music in the background.

The Export Panel

If you like displaying your images on social-networking and photo-sharing websites such as Facebook, Flickr, and Photoshop.com, Bridge's Export panel can help you out. It's also handy for converting a slew of images to JPEGs. The export process takes a few steps, but once you get things set up properly, it goes quite quickly.

Open the Export panel by clicking its tab at the bottom left of the Bridge window (if you don't see it, choose Window→Export Panel). This panel now includes icons for uploading photos to Facebook, Flickr, and Photoshop.com. If that's what you want to do, double-click the appropriate icon (for example, Flickr). The first time you do this, you'll then need to double-click the Flickr icon and enter your account info in the resulting dialog box. This same dialog box also lets you choose which album to put the images into, as well as *if* and *how* you want 'em resized. Click the Save button, and Bridge displays a status bar showing you the upload's progress.

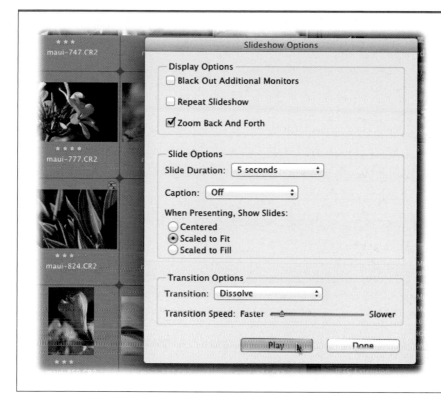

FIGURE 21-8

By adding a transition and making sure the Zoom Back And Forth checkbox is turned on (which makes Bridge zoom in and then back out of each image), you can create a pretty slick slideshow in no time flat.

To make a slideshow you can export, use the PDF option explained in the next section or the PDF Presentation option covered on page 712.

If you want to create JPEGs from Raw files, click the Export panel's "Save to Hard Drive" icon and then click the + at the bottom of the panel to add a new preset (set of instructions). In the resulting dialog box's Destination tab (Figure 21-9, top), pick the folder where you want the exported images to land. Then click the Image Options tab and let Bridge know whether you'd like it to make the images smaller and/or reduce their quality (both great for images you want to post on the Web; not so much if you plan to send the JPEGs to a stock-image site). At the bottom of the dialog box, enter a meaningful name for the preset, click Save, and Bridge adds a new hard drive icon with that name to the Export panel, as shown in Figure 21-9 (bottom).

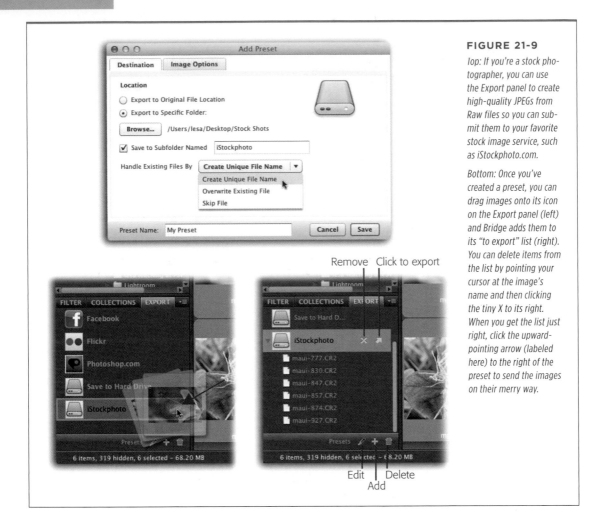

FIGURE 21-9

*Top: If you're a stock pho-
tographer, you can use
the Export panel to create
high-quality JPEGs from
Raw files so you can sub-
mit them to your favorite
stock image service, such
as iStockphoto.com.*

*Bottom: Once you've
created a preset, you can
drag images onto its icon
on the Export panel (left)
and Bridge adds them to
its "to export" list (right).
You can delete items from
the list by pointing your
cursor at the image's
name and then clicking
the tiny X to its right.
When you get the list just
right, click the upward-
pointing arrow (labeled
here) to the right of the
preset to send the images
on their merry way.*

Exporting Images as PDFs

PDFs are really handy because you can open them on any kind of computer without
having to buy any software. Bridge has a few templates you can use to create PDFs,
and a slew of settings for customizing exactly how they look. You can even add watermarks to individual images in your PDFs, instead one watermark per PDF page.

To get started, select the image(s) you want to export and then choose "Output to
Web or PDF" from the Output menu at the top of the Bridge window (it looks like
a piece of paper with a down-pointing arrow and is labeled in Figure 21-10). The
Output panel opens on the right side of the Bridge window.

At the top of the Output panel, make sure the PDF button is active (if not, click it), and then choose an option from the Template pop-up menu. To see a preview of the template you picked, click the Refresh Preview button. The Output Preview tab appears in the center of the Bridge window (circled in Figure 21-10). Each new version of Bridge offers more templates to choose from, though you can always customize them using the Output panel's various settings (use the scroll bar on the panel's right side to see all the settings—there are a ton of 'em). To make your PDF to run as a slideshow, be sure the Playback options near the bottom of the panel are turned on. When everything looks good, click the Save button at the very bottom of the panel and Bridge exports your file as a PDF.

> **TIP** New in Photoshop CS6 is the option to create contact sheets by choosing File→Automate→Contact Sheet II (see page 712 for step-by-step details). That said, you can also create a contact sheet in Bridge (and you'll get *more* options than you do in Photoshop, like the ability to add watermarks) by choosing Tools→Photoshop→Contact Sheet II. Or, if you're already in Bridge's Output workspace, choose one of the Contact Sheet options from the Output panel's Template pop-up menu.

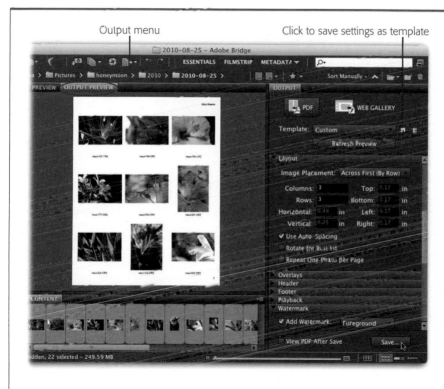

Output menu   Click to save settings as template

FIGURE 21-10

The Template menu includes precious few options, though you can add your own. To see what your PDF will look like, click the Refresh Preview button (circled); the preview appears in the Output Preview tab. And as you make changes to the Output panel's gazillion settings, you have to keep clicking the Refresh Preview button to make Bridge update the Output Preview tab.

Happily, you can save your custom settings by clicking the icon labeled here, which is a welcome option after you've worked hard to create a PDF template or web gallery style that meets your needs.

> **NOTE** Page 112 covers exporting layer comp files as PDFs back in Photoshop.

Making a Web Gallery

You can also use Bridge to make a quick online gallery of your images. Heck, it'll even upload the images for you! Flip back to page 750 for the scoop.

Using Mini Bridge

You can open a smaller version of Bridge—cleverly named Mini Bridge (Figure 21-11)—as a panel *within* Photoshop by choosing Window→Extensions→Mini Bridge in Photoshop. It looks and works like big Bridge, but you get the added bonus of not having to switch program windows to find and open images.

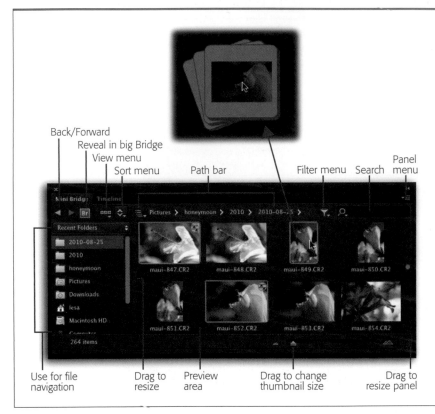

Back/Forward
Reveal in big Bridge
View menu
Sort menu
Path bar
Filter menu   Search   Panel menu

Use for file navigation
Drag to resize
Preview area
Drag to change thumbnail size
Drag to resize panel

FIGURE 21-11

The Mini Bridge panel gives you easy access to images right inside Photoshop. Adobe has simplified the panel's controls, and it now appears at the bottom of your screen instead of on the right. Just like any other panel, you can grab its tab and drag it anywhere else on your screen to make it free-floating (like the version shown here). Use the pop-up menu and list of folders on the panel's left to navigate to images, and then drag and drop 'em from the Mini Bridge panel right into your Photoshop window (or document), as shown here. As soon as you release your mouse button, Photoshop opens each image in its very own tabbed document (if you already have an image open, it'll place the images as new layers within the document).

> **NOTE**   If you undock the Mini Bridge panel and then accidentally close it, don't panic. You can always reopen it by choosing Window→Extensions→Mini Bridge, or by choosing File- ▸"Browse in Mini Bridge." Whew!

When you first open Mini Bridge, it checks to see if big Bridge is running. Why? Because the Mini Bridge panel works only when Photoshop *and* big Bridge are open on your machine. If big Bridge isn't running, you'll see a message inside the Mini Bridge panel that says, "Bridge must be running to browse files" and a Launch Bridge button underneath it. Just click the button and Photoshop sends a message to big Bridge to get its tail in gear. Once Bridge launches, you'll see a pop-up menu and a list of folders on the left side of the Mini Bridge panel that you can use to navigate to your images (labeled in Figure 21-11). Double-click a folder in the list, and any images inside it appear as thumbnails on the right.

In CS6, the Mini Bridge panel is initially docked to the bottom of your screen, and while it's down there a *single row* of image thumbnails is all you get. To change the size of the thumbnails, you have to resize the panel itself: Just grab the top of the panel (to the right of its tab) and drag downward to make 'em smaller or upward to make 'em bigger. To see *more* than a single row of thumbnails, undock the panel by dragging its tab elsewhere on your screen and then use the controls shown in to change the panel and thumbnail sizes.

> **TIP** Mini Bridge displays only *image thumbnails* in its content area, not folders. To navigate to another folder, you have to use the navigation list on the panel's left, its Path bar, or its Search field.

Here's what the various buttons labeled in Figure 21-11 let you do:

- Click the **Reveal in Bridge** button to open the active image(s) in big Bridge, where you can do things like create collections (page 827) and use commands that run on multiple files such as Batch Rename (page 828), "Load Files into Photoshop Layers" (page 59), "Merge to HDR Pro" (page 398), and Photomerge (page 295). You can also summon these options by Control-clicking (right-clicking) a thumbnail (see Figure 21-12).

- The **View menu** lets you refresh (update) the Mini Bridge panel's contents, as well as show and hide rejected files (page 825). You can also choose Select All, Deselect All, or Invert Selection (so what was selected isn't, and what *wasn't* selected is). This menu also lets you start a slideshow containing the selected images, enter Review mode (page 825), and control what info is displayed beneath each thumbnail, such as file name, ratings, file size, and so on.

> **TIP** Tap the space bar to see a full-size preview of any image you select in the Mini Bridge panel. (Tap again to go back to Photoshop.)

- The **Sort menu** lets you determine in what order the thumbnails are shown: by file name, type, date created, and so on (page 826).

- Use the **Filter menu** to make Mini Bridge display files that have a certain star rating, label, and so on (page 826).

You can also Control-click (right-click) a thumbnail—or several—to summon a menu that gives you quick access to handy commands such as "Reveal in Bridge," Slideshow, Review Mode, "Open with," and the ever-useful Photoshop menu (see Figure 21-12).

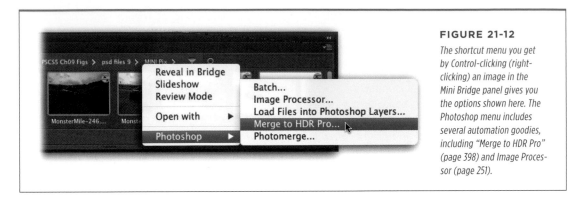

FIGURE 21-12

The shortcut menu you get by Control-clicking (right-clicking) an image in the Mini Bridge panel gives you the options shown here. The Photoshop menu includes several automation goodies, including "Merge to HDR Pro" (page 398) and Image Processor (page 251).

Index

Z

WHERE IDEAS
TAKE FLIGHT.

Get a choice of 5 images from a collection of
50 and 20% off purchases over $50 USD
with coupon code: C55M15

www.iStockphoto.com/CS6photolesa

iStock has the perfect photo, illustration,
video and audio files for any idea.
So go ahead, aim high!

Have it your way.